CANADA

Lake of
the Woods

Lake Superior

Duluth

MICHIGAN

Lake Huron

ST. Lawrence River

MAINE

BAY OF FUNDY

Mount Washington
(6,288 ft/1,917 m)
Augusta

Burlington
Lake
Champlain
Montpelier
VT.
N.H.
Portland

ADIRONDACK
MOUNTAINS
Concord
Manchester

Lake Ontario
Rochester
Albany
Worcester
Boston
Cape Cod

MINNESOTA
St. Paul
Minneapolis

WISCONSIN

Lake Michigan

Green Bay

Grand
Rapids
Lansing

Lake
St. Clair

Detroit

Lake Erie

Buffalo
NEW
YORK
Hudson River

MASS.
Providence
R.I.
Hartford
CONN.
Bridgeport

IOWA

Madison
Milwaukee
Rockford
Chicago
Gary
Fort
Wayne
Toledo
Cleveland

Akron
Pittsburgh
Susquehanna River
PENNSYLVANIA

Harrisburg
Trenton
Jersey City
New York
Long Island
Newark
NEW JERSEY

Cedar
Rapids
Davenport

Des Moines River

Mississippi River

Peoria

CENTRAL

OHIO

Philadelphia
Wilmington
Dover
DELAWARE

MARYLAND

Illinois River

PLAINS

Springfield
ILLINOIS
Indianapolis
INDIANA
Cincinnati
Ohio River

Columbus
WEST
VIRGINIA
Charleston

ALLEGHENY MOUNTAINS
Baltimore
Washington
D.C.
Annapolis

Missouri River

St. Louis
Wabash River
Louisville
Frankfort
Lexington
Huntington
Roanoke

VIRGINIA
James River
Richmond
Delmarva
Peninsula
CHESAPEAKE BAY

Jefferson City

MISSOURI

OZARK PLATEAU

KENTUCKY

APPALACHIAN MOUNTAINS
BLUE RIDGE MOUNTAINS
Mount Mitchell
(6,684 ft/2,030 m)
Greensboro
Raleigh
NORTH CAROLINA
Newport News
Norfolk
Roanoke River
Cape Hatteras

ATLANTIC
OCEAN

ARKANSAS

Fort Smith

Little Rock

Pine Bluff

Knoxville
Nashville
Tennessee River

Charlotte
PIEDMONT
Greenville
COASTAL
SOUTH
CAROLINA
Columbia
Charleston
Savannah River
PLAIN

Memphis

TENNESSEE

Birmingham
Atlanta

MISSISSIPPI
Jackson
Meridian
ALABAMA
Columbus
GEORGIA
ATLANTIC
Savannah

Shreveport
LOUISIANA

Montgomery
Alabama River

Tombigbee River

PLAIN
Biloxi
Mobile
Jacksonville

Baton Rouge
New Orleans

Tallahassee
FLORIDA

Mississippi Delta
Florida River
Orlando
Cape Canaveral

GULF OF
MEXICO

Tampa
Florida Peninsula
St. Petersburg
Lake
Okeechobee
Miami

Florida Keys

CUBA

Tropic of Cancer

Legend	
—·—·—	International boundaries
—··—··—	State boundaries
⊛	National capital
★	State capital
•	Cities
▲	Mountain peaks

0   100   200   300
Miles

0   100   200   300   400
Kilometers

ATLANTIC OCEAN

PUERTO RICO
(U.S.)

San Juan
Ponce

CARIBBEAN SEA

0   100 Miles
0   100 Kilometers

The American Nation

The
American
Nation

A History of the United States

SEVENTH
EDITION

JOHN A. GARRATY
Gouverneur Morris Professor of History
Columbia University

with

ROBERT A. McCAUGHEY
Professor and Dean of the Faculty
Barnard College, Columbia University

HarperCollins*Publishers*

Sponsoring Editors: Lauren Silverman/Bruce Borland
Development Editor: Kathleen Dolan
Project Editor: Karen Trost
Design Supervisor: Dorothy Bungert
Text and Cover Design: Delgado Design, Inc.
Cover Illustration: View of Baltimore from Federal Hill, 1840—Fitz Hugh Lane. Shelburne Museum, Shelburne, Vermont.
Photo Research: Cheryl Mannes and Suzanne Volkman Skloot
Production: Willie Lane
Compositor: Arcata Graphics/Kingsport
Printer and Binder: R.R. Donnelley & Sons Company
Cover Printer: New England Book Components, Inc.

The American Nation: A History of the United States, Seventh Edition

The author makes grateful acknowledgment to:

New Directions Publishing Corporation for permission to quote from "Hugh Selwyn Mauberley" by Ezra Pound. From Ezra Pound, *Personae.* Copyright 1926 by Ezra Pound. Reprinted by permission of New Directions Publishing Corporation. U.S. and Canadian rights.

Liveright Publishing Corporation for permission to quote from "the first president to be loved by his . . ." by e. e. cummings. Reprinted from *ViVa,* poems by E. E. Cummings, edited by George James Firmage, by permission of Liveright Publishing Corporation. Copyright 1931, 1959 by E. E. Cummings. Copyright © 1979, 1973 by the Trustees for the E. E. Cummings Trust. Copyright © 1979, 1973 by George James Firmage.

Library of Congress Cataloging-in-Publication Data

Garraty, John Arthur, 1920–
  The American nation : a history of the United States / John A. Garraty with Robert A. McCaughey. — 7th ed.
    p.   cm.
  Includes bibliographical references and index.
  ISBN 0-06-042312-9 (student edition)
  ISBN 0-06-500035-8 (teacher edition)
  1. United States—History.   I. McCaughey, Robert A.   II. Title.
E178.1.G24   1991
973—dc20   90-38203
                                                            CIP

94 95 96 9 8 7 6

For Kathy, Jack, and Sarah

Contents in Brief

Contents

VERGER'S DRAWINGS OF AMERICAN FOOT SOLDIERS, YORKTOWN CAMPAIGN, 1781. LEFT TO RIGHT: BLACK LIGHT INFANTRYMAN OF THE FIRST RHODE ISLAND REGIMENT, MUSKETEER OF THE SECOND CANADIAN REGIMENT, RIFLEMAN, AND GUNNER OF THE CONTINENTAL ARTILLERY
(see p. xxi)

III America in the British Empire   70

IV The American Revolution   106

V Nationalism Triumphant 136

VI Jeffersonian Democracy 166

XV   The Coming of the Civil War   386

XVI   The War to Save the Union   414

XVII   Reconstruction and the South   448

XVIII   In the Wake of War   478

American Lives: Emma Goldman   *638*

XXIV   Progressivism: The Age of Reform   640

XXV   Woodrow Wilson and the Great War   678

XXIX   War and Peace   796

XXX   The American Century   820

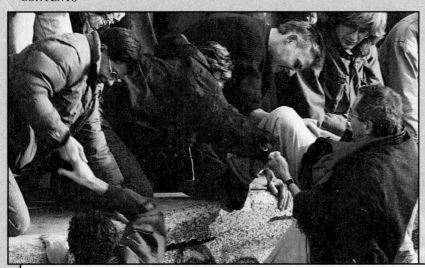

XXXIII   Our Times   914

Maps

Graphs

Preface

This is the seventh edition of *The American Nation,* the sixth time I have revised it, and the process remains for me both challenging and endlessly fascinating. Historians try to explain what happened in the past and of course "what happened" does not change. But what is important to point out about the past is that it changes constantly as more information about past events comes to light and as current events raise new questions about the events and people of earlier times. Year by year hundreds of new books and articles are published about various aspects of American history; when those dealing with any particular subject have been digested and synthesized and combined with already existing knowledge, a new, "up-to-date" description of that topic results. This process keeps authors like me who write American history textbooks very busy.

Goals of This Revision

The work of revising a survey of all American history takes many forms. First there are the small alterations involved in incorporating new details and examples, and in clarifying obscurities that have previously escaped notice. Then there is the matter of bringing the narrative as close to the present as possible, something that is relatively easy to do, but difficult to do well. Nearly always revision also involves changes in emphasis—some subjects need to be condensed or eliminated; others require more space either because more has been discovered about them or because recent developments make them seem more significant. Finally, and most important, are the larger changes made necessary because historians, responding to contemporary interests, to noteworthy work being done by colleagues and other specialists, and to the questions and interests of their students, have produced persuasive new interpretations and even opened up entirely new subjects. Dealing with this work, in turn, requires more of the simpler kinds of revisions just mentioned.

This revision of *The American Nation* contains many examples of all these types of change; in sum, I believe it is the most thorough and broad-ranging restructuring and re-thinking of the six such revisions that I have made.

Organizational Changes

To improve the flow of topics, I have shifted many sections to different chapters, for example, moving the discussion of the Great Awakening and the colonial Enlightenment to the chapter on the events leading to the Revolution, where these inter-colonial, "national" topics seem more properly to belong. I have also consolidated the material on the Federalist era and on the Jefferson administrations into separate chapters, and I have divided the previously combined account of the political and economic events of the Monroe and John Quincy Adams period.

Similarly, several chapters covering the period 1877–1896 have been completely reorganized, and the chapter on World War I has been expanded to include an account of the Red Scare and other events of the immediate postwar period. The three chapters dealing with the 1920s and 1930s in the sixth edition have been drastically restructured; that period now is covered in four chapters. I have also made changes only slightly less extensive in the chapters on the post–World War II period.

New Coverage and Features

As to new topics and significantly expanded coverage of old ones, readers will notice that there is much more information about society in the colonial south and about southern political and religious institutions; on the activities of women during the American Revolution and other social changes of the period; on the Whiskey Rebellion and the opening of the Ohio country after the Revolution; on changes in early 19th-century family life; on the westward movement, the Second Great Awakening, the Know-Nothing movement; and on plantation life, particularly the lives of southern women, slave and free.

In Chapter XX, "American Society in the Industrial Age," there is much new information about middle-class life, about the daily activities of farmers, about the family lives and social attitudes of wage earners of both sexes, about social and economic mobility in the 1870s and 1880s, and about the development of spectator sports and other leisure activities. Chapter XXVI treats these and other aspects of social history before and after World War I in much greater detail than in earlier editions. There is also expanded and more up-to-date coverage of radicalism, the effects of the Great Depression on the unemployed, the treatment of minorities during World War II and the contributions of women in that conflict, the "Baby Boom" generation that followed the war, the counterculture of the 1960s, the modern women's movement, and many other subjects.

I have paid a good deal of attention also to the "Suggestions for Further Reading" that follow each chapter. I have eliminated many older titles that, although valuable, are out of print, and I have substituted more recent and in most instances equally worthwhile volumes that are readily available, often in paperback. This edition also contains a new feature, American Lives, designed to give students a better understanding of how ordinary people lived and thought in various times and places. It consists of accounts of the life-styles of "ordinary" people whom we know a great deal about only because they had children who became famous, and of the childhoods and youths of men and women who were later to become important figures. Most of the material comes from biographies, autobiographies, and other personal writings. There are seven of these features, some treating more than one person in a comparative manner.

Approach

In making all these changes and others less important, I have not, I trust, altered my basic approach to American history, which is to deal with the subject in narrative fashion and to use the political history of the nation as the frame or skeleton on which social, economic, and cultural developments depend. The American nation (the United States) is, after all, a political institution.

The people of the United States, in their infinite variety, also remain central to my account. The theory that a few great individuals, cut from larger cloth than the general run of human beings, have shaped the course of past events oversimplifies history. But the past becomes more comprehensible when attention is paid to how the major figures on the historical stage have reacted to events and to one another. Since generalizations require concrete illustration if they are to be grasped fully, readers will find many anecdotes and quotations on the following pages, along with the facts and dates and statistics every good history must contain. This illustrative material is interesting, and most of it is entertaining, but I believe it is instructive as well.

I also believe that one need not be an uncritical admirer of the American nation and its people to recognize that the history of the United States deserves to be treated with dignity and respect. Individually and as a society, we have rarely lived up perfectly to the principles enunciated in the Declaration of Independence and the Constitution, but recent events in Eastern Europe demonstrate how cherished these "American" values are by people who have been deprived of them. American values are not well served by patriotic hoopla or by slighting or excusing dark and discreditable aspects of the American past. The English radical Oliver Cromwell is said to have told an artist who was painting his picture to portray him "warts and all." Cromwell wanted to be remembered as he was, confident that, on balance, history would judge him fairly. This is another principle on which *The American Nation* continues to be based.

Acknowledgments

I wish to thank the many friends, colleagues, and students who, over the years, have given me the benefit of their advice and encouragement in keeping this book up to date. In particular I am grateful to the following reviewers for their comments and suggestions regarding the revision: Robert M. Barrow, Georgia Southern University; Sidney R. Bland, James Madison University; Paul C. Bowers, The Ohio State University; Dean R. Esslinger, Towson State University; George E. Frakes, Santa Barbara City College; David A. Johnson, Portland State University; George M. Lubick, Northern Arizona University; Thomas C. Mackey, Kansas State University; Michael S. Mayer, University of Montana; Howard N. Rabinowitz, University of New Mexico; G. S. Rowe, University of Northern Colorado; Herbert Shapiro, University of Cincinnati; Harry F. Snapp, University of North Texas; Ken L. Weath-

erbie, Del Mar College; and Herbert H. Wubben, Oregon State University.

John A. Garraty
Gouverneur Morris Professor of History
Columbia University

SUPPLEMENTS

An extensive package of supplements has been developed to accompany the seventh edition of *The American Nation*. To order supplements, contact your HarperCollins representative.

- The *Instructor's Resource Manual*, written by Michael Mayer of the University of Montana, has been designed to aid both the novice and the experienced instructor in teaching the American History course. Each chapter of the *Instructor's Resource Manual* includes a concise chapter overview, a list of points for student mastery, lecture supplements, and questions for class discussion. A special feature of each chapter is a set of excerpted documents with accompanying questions for student analysis. The *Instructor's Resource Manual* also includes essays on teaching American History through films and maps, and a full-length class activity on teaching essay writing using the rhetoric of the Declaration of Independence.

- The *Test Bank*, prepared by Larry Peterson of North Dakota State University, contains over 2000 test items, including multiple-choice, true/false, and essay questions, and map exercises. The questions are referenced by topic, cognitive type (factual, applied, or interpretive), difficulty level, and relevant text page.

  In addition to the printed format, the *Test Bank* is available on *TestMaster*, HarperCollins's computerized testing system. Available for IBM, Apple, and Macintosh computers, this powerful software allows the instructor to scramble and edit questions from the *Test Bank* and add original questions.

- The two-volume *Student Study Guide*, co-authored by Kenneth Weatherbie of Del Mar College and Billy Hathorn of Laredo State University, is designed to provide students

with a comprehensive review of text material, and to encourage application and critical analysis of the material. Each chapter contains a chapter overview, learning objectives, important glossary terms, identification, map, and critical thinking exercises, and multiple-choice and essay questions. In addition, an essay on writing about history is provided.

- *SuperShell*, HarperCollins's computerized tutorial, is an interactive program that provides sophisticated diagnostic feedback including an end-of-session reading assignment based on the student's performance, and tracking of the student's performance from session to session. In addition to review questions in a variety of formats, *SuperShell* contains comprehensive chapter outlines keyed to the headings and subheadings in the text. A "Flash Card" program helps students learn important terms and concepts. *SuperShell* is available for IBM computers only.

- *Mapping American History*, created by Gerald Danzer of the University of Illinois at Chicago, features numerous varied map exercises and activities for students. In addition to increasing basic locational literacy, these exercises provide students with opportunities for map interpretation and analysis, as well as an appreciation of cartographic materials as historical documents. Each copy of *The American Nation* purchased from HarperCollins entitles the instructor to a free copy of this student map workbook.

- *Discovering American History Through Maps and Views*, also prepared by Gerald Danzer, provides 140 four-color transparencies of images selected from key primary sources. Assembled in a three-ring binder, the collection begins with an essay on teaching history using maps, and contains detailed commentary on each transparency. The program consists of cartographic materials, various photos and views including urban plans, building diagrams, and works of art, and is free to adopters of the text.

■ *American Historical Geography: A Computerized Atlas,* prepared by William Hambin of Brigham Young University, offers map exercises pertaining to the rise of the Americas, the Revolutionary War, the Civil War, transportation systems, and elections. Free upon adoption of the textbook, the program is available for Macintosh computers only.

■ *Historical Viewpoints: Notable Articles from* American Heritage, *Sixth Edition,* edited by John Garraty, is a collection of interesting and substantive articles that have appeared in *American Heritage.* Available in a two-volume format, the sixth edition contains many new selections.

■ *Visual Archives of American History,* a new laser disk, provides over 500 photos and 29 minutes of film coverage of major events in American history. Each photo or film clip may be instantly accessed, making this collection ideal for classroom use.

■ *The Winner's Circle* is a collection of recent prize-winning films and videos relating to American History. Available for loan at no charge to adopters of the text.

■ *Grades,* HarperCollins's easy-to-use classroom management software, records quiz and exam scores for up to 200 students.

To help instructors make effective use of this comprehensive supplement package, HarperCollins offers *The Integrator,* a cross-reference and index to all print, software, and media supplements available with *The American Nation. The Integrator* also includes teaching techniques for multimedia presentations.

I

Europe Discovers America

In the beginning, all the world was America.

JOHN LOCKE

The first human beings to set foot on the continents of North and South America were the ancestors of the modern Indians. These people entered the North American continent tens of thousands of years ago during the Ice Age, when a land bridge connected their home in northeastern Asia with Alaska. Hunters and herders, they were simply moving from camp to camp in search of game and green grass. No doubt the first humans in other parts of the world found their way in the same manner and at about the same time to what are now Egypt, Iran, India, China, Australia, and for that matter England, France, and the rest of Europe. Almost certainly the settlers of the Americas were unaware that they were entering "new" territory. So we must look elsewhere (and much later in time) for the "discoverer" of America as we use that word.

Probably the first European to reach America was a Norseman, Leif Eriksson. He ventured before the day of the compass into the void of the North Atlantic and, around the year 1000, reached the shores of Labrador. Yet Eriksson's discovery passed practically unnoticed for centuries, and to most modern inhabitants of the New World he lives only in legend.

Amerigo Vespucci, a clever Italian with an eye for publicity, visited the northern coast of South America in 1499. He wrote an account of his experiences that was widely circulated. In 1507, after reading a distorted copy of Vespucci's tale, a German geographer, Martin Waldseemüller, concluded that the author was the discoverer of the New World and suggested that it be named America in his honor. Today millions call themselves Americans, but few know much about Amerigo Vespucci.

Another Italian mariner, Cristoforo Colombo, brave, persistent, an inspired sailor but a fumbling administrator, spent a decade cruising in the Caribbean Sea under the mistaken impression that he was next door to China. He killed some of the people he encountered, established a few rickety settlements, ventured no nearer to North America than Cuba, and died poor, embittered, and frustrated, hotly denying that he had found anything more than a new route to the Orient. Today, whether he be known as Colombo, Colón, or Columbus, he is honored in the Old World and the New as the discoverer of the Western Hemisphere.

Why Columbus rather than Eriksson, the real European pioneer, or Vespucci, whose name has become immortal? The answer is that Eriksson came on the scene too soon and Vespucci too late. Europe in the year 1000 was not yet ready to find a new world, and by 1499 it had already found one. Amerigo Vespucci gave his name to the region, but the adventures of Christopher Columbus inspired the European invasion and development of the whole area between Hudson Bay and the Strait of Magellan.

Columbus and the Discovery of America

About two o'clock on the morning of October 12, 1492, a sailor named Roderigo de Triana, clinging in a gale to the mast of the ship *Pinta*, saw a gleam of white on the moonlit horizon and shouted: *"Tierra! Tierra!"* The land he had spied was an island in the West Indies called Guanahaní by its inhab-

In this engraving by Theodore de Bry, Columbus is about to depart from Palos; Ferdinand and Isabella, at right, bid him farewell.

itants, a place distinguished by neither beauty nor size. Nevertheless, when Triana's master, Christopher Columbus, went ashore bearing the flag of Spanish Castile, he named it San Salvador, or Holy Savior. Columbus selected this imposing name for the island out of gratitude and wonder at having found it—he had sailed with three frail vessels more than 3,000 miles for 33 days without sight of land. The name was appropriate, too, from history's far larger viewpoint. Neither Columbus nor any of his men suspected it, but the discovery of San Salvador was probably the most important event in the history of western civilization since the birth of Christ.

San Salvador was the gateway to two continents. Columbus did not know it, and he refused to learn the truth, but his voyage threw open to exploitation by the peoples of western Europe more than a quarter of all the land in the world, a region of more than 16 million square miles, an area lushly endowed with every imaginable resource. He made possible a mass movement from Europe (and later from Africa and to a lesser extent from other regions) into the New World. Gathering force rapidly, this movement did not slacken until the 20th century, and it still has not ceased; something on the order of 70 million persons have been involved in the migration.

Columbus was an intelligent as well as dedicated and skillful mariner. He failed to grasp the significance of his accomplishment because he had no idea that he was on the edge of two huge continents previously unknown to Europeans. He was seeking a way to China and Japan and the Indies, the amazing countries described by the Venetian Marco Polo in the late 13th century.

Having read carefully Marco Polo's account of his adventures in the service of Kublai Khan, Columbus had decided that these rich lands could be reached by sailing directly west from Europe. The idea was not original, but while others merely talked about it (in the jawbreaking phrase of one scholar, experts had been slow to consider "the cosmographical implications of the earth's sphericity"), Columbus pursued it with brilliant persistence.

If one could sail to Asia directly, the trading possibilities and the resulting profits would be limitless. Oriental products were highly valued all over Europe. Spices such as pepper, cinnamon, ginger, nutmeg, and cloves were of first importance, their role being not so much to titillate the palate as to disguise the taste of spoiled meats in regions that had little ice. Europeans also prized such tropical foods as rice, figs, and oranges, as well as perfumes (often used as a substitute for soap), silk and cotton, rugs, textiles such as muslin and damask, dyestuffs, fine steel products, precious stones, and various drugs.

These products flowed into western Europe by way of the Italian city-states. By the 11th century, Venice had established a thriving trade with Constantinople, shipping large quantities of European foodstuffs to the metropolis on the Bosporus. The Venetians also supplied young Slavs, captured or purchased along the nearby Dalmatian coast, to the markets of Egypt and Syria (the word *slave* originally meant "Slav").

The Venetians brought back oriental products from these voyages, and the effect was like that of tossing a stone into a pond. Europeans bestirred themselves, searching for more goods to offer in exchange. They possessed surpluses of grain and food, but these bulky products were expensive to transport over long distances. However, in Flanders, in the Low Countries, woolen cloth of high quality was being manufactured. Other areas were producing furs and lumber. Demand led to increased output; thus the flow of commerce stimulated manufacturing, which in turn spurred the growth of towns. As towns became larger and more numerous, the market for food expanded, and surrounding rural areas increased their agricultural output.

Urban growth also created a demand for more clothmakers. The resulting labor shortage in both town and country produced important changes in the structure of medieval society. The manorial system, based on serfdom, soon began to change. As their labor became more valuable, serfs won the right to pay off their traditional obligations in money rather than in service and to leave the manors and move to the towns or to newly opened farmland. The lords themselves often instituted this change, for they wished to increase agricultural output by draining swamps and clearing forests, and they willingly granted freedom to serfs who would move to the new lands. They also needed money rather than the services of serfs to buy the expensive oriental luxuries being dangled before their eyes by traders.

The Crusades further accelerated the tempo of this new activity. Genuine religious motives seem to have inspired these mighty efforts, protracted over two centuries from 1095 to about 1290, to drive the Muslims from the Holy Land. Once the cru-

sading armies had won a foothold in Asia Minor, the commerce of Venice and of other Italian cities increased still more, and their merchant fleets expanded. The business of transporting and supplying the European armies was itself profitable and when Crusaders returned home, they brought with them more oriental products and a taste for these things that persisted after the goods themselves had been consumed.

The volume of this trade kept the fleets of the thriving Italian cities busy, but it was not impressive by modern standards. In the 1920s the Belgian historian Henri Pirenne estimated that the entire tonnage of the 13th-century Venetian fleet would scarcely fill a single freighter, the cargo of which, in turn, would scarcely serve as ballast for a modern supertanker. Nor did the increase in trade cause universal prosperity or even a steady economic expansion in western Europe. In fact, the period of the 14th and early 15th centuries seems to have been marked by depression and economic decline in the West.

This decline resulted principally from the terrible losses occasioned by the plague known as the Black Death, which ravaged Europe in the mid-14th century. Part of the difficulty, however, stemmed from the steady drain of precious metals to the Orient (because of the unfavorable balance of East-West trade) and the high cost of oriental goods. It was easy to blame this on the greed of the Italians, who monopolized East-West trade. Certainly the Venetians have never possessed a reputation for altruism nor the Pisans for being poor businessmen. However, even if the Italians had labored only for the joy of serving their fellow human beings or if other merchants had been able to break the Italian monopoly, the cost of Eastern products would have remained high. To transport spices from the Indies, silk from China, or rugs, cloth, and steel from the Middle East was extremely costly. The combined sea-land routes were long and complicated—across strange seas, through deserts, over high mountain passes—with pirates or highwaymen a constant threat. Every petty tyrant through whose domain the caravans passed levied taxes, a quasi-legal form of robbery. Few merchants operated on a continental scale; typically, goods passed from hand to hand and were loaded and unloaded many times between Eastern producer and Western consumer, with each middleman exacting as large a profit as

Europeans of the 15th century hungered for goods from abroad. In the north, their wants were often supplied by ships of the Hanseatic League, an association of over 70 cities along the Baltic and North seas. These vessels exchanged northern products—wool, furs, fish, and metallic ores—for luxuries imported into southern Europe from Asia. In this miniature painting, Hanseatic merchants prepare shipments for their branch offices.

he could. In the end the western European consumer had to pay for all this.

But during the 15th century, Europe recovered from the human and economic losses of the plague years. By the 1450s strong rulers were consolidating countless small fiefs into what were to become the nations of today. They established uniform laws, maintained internal order, and, in effect, focused the resources and energies of their subjects in ways that led to the exploration of the world and the founding of European settlements in distant lands.

Merchants profited from this concentration of political and economic power, but overland trade with the East remained expensive and arduous. If oriental produce could be carried to Europe by water, the trip would be both cheaper and more comfortable. The goods would have to be loaded and unloaded only once. A small number of sailors could provide all the necessary labor, and the free wind would supply the power to move the cargo to its destination. By the 15th century, this idea was beginning to be transformed into action.

The great figure in the transformation was Prince Henry the Navigator, third son of John I, king of Portugal. After distinguishing himself in 1415 in the capture of Ceuta, on the African side of the Strait of Gibraltar, the prince became interested in navigation and exploration. Sailing a vessel out of sight of land was still, in Henry's day, more an art than a science and was extremely hazardous. Ships were small and clumsy. Primitive compasses and instruments for reckoning latitude existed, but under shipboard conditions they were inaccurate. Navigators could determine longitude only by keeping track of direction and estimating speed; even the most skilled could place little faith in their estimates.

Henry attempted to improve and codify navigational knowledge. To his court at Sagres, hard by Cape St. Vincent, the extreme southwestern point of Europe, he brought geographers, astronomers, and mapmakers, along with Arab and Jewish mathematicians. He built an observatory and supervised the preparation of tables measuring the declination of the sun and other navigational data. Searching for a new route to the Orient, Henry's captains sailed westward to the Madeiras and the Canaries and south along the coast of Africa, seeking a way around that continent. In 1445 Dinis Dias reached Cape Verde, site of present-day Dakar.

Henry was interested in trade, but he cared more for the advancement of knowledge, for the glory of Portugal, and for spreading Christianity. When his explorers developed a profitable business in slaves, he tried to stop it. Nevertheless, the movement he began had, like the Crusades, important commercial overtones. Probably half of the Portuguese voyages were undertaken by private merchants. Without the gold, ivory, and other African goods, which brought great prosperity to Portugal, the explorers would probably not have been so bold or persistent. Yet, like Henry, they were idealists, by and large. The Age of Discovery was in a sense the last Crusade; its leaders displayed mixed religious and material motives along with a love of adventure. In any case,

ICELAND

Hudson 1610

ENGLAND

Cabot 1497

Cartier 1534

FRANCE

*ATLANTIC
OCEAN*

PORTUGAL   SPAIN   ITALY

MEDITERRANEAN SEA

NORTH AMERICA

Verrazano 1524

*GULF OF
MEXICO*

Columbus 1492

AFRICA

Dias 1487

Vespucci 1499

SOUTH AMERICA

SPAIN
PORTUGAL

*STRAIT OF
MAGELLAN*

Demarcation Line 1494

Hudson 1609

Magellan
1519

Drake 1579

Drake 1580

Da Gama
1497

Magellan 1521

Magellan 1522

	Portugal
	Spain
	England
	France

	Portugal		Spain		England		Netherlands

VOYAGES OF DISCOVERY, 1487–1610

the Portuguese realized that if they could find a way around Africa, they might well sail directly to India and the Spice Islands.* The profits from such a voyage would surely be spectacular.

For 20 years after Henry's death in 1460, the Portuguese concentrated on exploiting his discoveries. In the 1480s King John II undertook systematic new explorations focused on reaching India. Gradually his caravels probed southward along the sweltering coast—to the equator, to the region of Angola, and beyond.

Into this bustling, expectant little country in the corner of Europe came Christopher Columbus in 1476. Columbus was a weaver's son from Genoa, born in 1451. He had taken to the sea early, ranging widely in the Mediterranean. His arrival in Portugal was unplanned, since it resulted from the loss of his ship in a battle off the coast. For a time he became a chartmaker in Lisbon. He married a local woman. Then he was again at sea. He cruised northward, perhaps as far as Iceland, south to the equator, westward in the Atlantic to the Azores. Had his interest lain in that direction, he might well have been the first person to reach Asia by way of Africa, for in 1488, in Lisbon, he met and talked with Bartholomeu Dias, just returned from his voyage around the southern tip of Africa, which had demonstrated that the way lay clear for a voyage to the Indies. But by this time Columbus had committed himself to the westward route. When King John II refused to finance him, he turned to the Spanish court, where, after many disappointments, he finally persuaded Queen Isabella to equip his expedition. In August 1492 he set out from the port of Palos with his tiny fleet, the *Santa Maria,* the *Pinta,* and the *Niña.* A little more than two months later, after a stopover in the Canary Islands to repair the *Pinta's* rudder, his lookout sighted land.

Columbus's success was due in large part to his single-minded conviction that the Indies could be reached by sailing westward for a relatively short distance and that a profitable trade would develop over this route. He had persuaded Isabella to grant him, in addition to the title Admiral of the Ocean Sea, political control over all the lands he might discover and 10 percent of the profits of the trade that would follow in the wake of his expedition. Now

the combination of zeal and tenacity that had got him across the Atlantic cost him dearly. He refused to accept the plain evidence that this was an entirely new world. All about were strange plants, known neither to Europe nor to Asia. The copper-colored people who paddled out to inspect his fleet could no more follow the Arabic widely understood in the East than they could Spanish. Yet Columbus, consulting his charts, convinced himself that he had reached the Indies. That is why he called the natives Indians.

Searching for treasure, he pushed on to Cuba. When he heard the native word *Cubanocan,* meaning "middle of Cuba," he mistook it for *El Gran Can* (Marco Polo's "Grand Khan") and sent emissaries on a fruitless search through the jungle for the khan's palace. He finally returned to Spain relatively empty-handed but certain that he had explored the edge of Asia. Three later voyages failed to shake his conviction.

Columbus died in 1506. By that time other captains had taken up the work, most of them more willing than he to accept the New World on its own terms. As early as 1493, Pope Alexander VI had divided the non-Christian world between Spain and Portugal. The next year, in the Treaty of Tordesillas, these powers negotiated an agreement about exploiting the new discoveries. In effect, Portugal continued to concentrate on Africa, leaving the New World, except for what eventually became Brazil, to the Spanish. Thereafter, from their base on Hispaniola (Santo Domingo), founded by Columbus, the Spaniards quickly fanned out through the Caribbean and then over large parts of the two continents that bordered it.

In 1513 Juan Ponce de León made the first Spanish landing on the mainland of North America, exploring the east coast of Florida. In the same year Vasco Núñez de Balboa crossed the isthmus of Panama and discovered the Pacific Ocean. In 1519 Hernán Cortés landed an army in Mexico and overran the empire of the Aztecs, rich in gold and silver. That same year Ferdinand Magellan set out on an epic three-year voyage around the world. By discovering the strait that bears his name, at the southern tip of South America, he gave the Spanish a clear idea of the size of the continent. In the 1530s Francisco Pizarro subdued the Inca empire in Peru, providing the Spaniards with still more treasure, drawn chiefly from the silver mines of Potosí. In 1536 Buenos Aires was founded by Pedro de Men-

---

* In the geography of the 15th century, the Spice Islands were part of "the Indies," a vague region that encompassed the southeastern rim of Asia from India to what is now Indonesia.

SPANISH EXPLORATIONS, 1502–1605

doza. Within another decade Francisco Vásquez de Coronado had marched as far north as Kansas and west to the Grand Canyon, and Hernando de Soto had discovered the Mississippi River. Fifty years after Columbus's first landfall, Spain was master of a huge American empire.

What explains this mighty surge of exploration and conquest? Greed for gold and power, a sense of adventure, the desire to Christianize the Indians—mixed motives propelled the conquistadores onward. Some saw the New World as a reincarnation of the Garden of Eden, a land of infinite promise. Ponce de León and many others actually expected to find the Fountain of Youth in America. Their vision, at once so selfish and so exalted, reveals the central paradox of New World history. This immense land brought out both the best and the worst in human beings. Virgin America—like all virgins—

inspired conflicting feelings in men's hearts. They worshiped it for its purity and promise, yet they could not resist the opportunity to take advantage of its innocence.

The Indian and the European

The conquistadores were brave and imaginative men, well worthy of their fame. It must not, however, be forgotten that they wrenched their empire from innocent hands; in an important sense, the settlement of the New World, which the historian Francis Jennings has called "the invasion of America," ranks among the most flagrant examples of unprovoked aggression in human history. When Columbus landed on San Salvador, he planted a cross, "as a sign," he explained to Ferdinand and

Isabella, "that your Highnesses held this land as your own." Of the Lucayans, the native inhabitants of San Salvador, Columbus wrote:

> The people of this island . . . are artless and generous with what they have, to such a degree as no one would believe. . . . If it be asked for, they never say no, but rather invite the person to accept it, and show as much lovingness as though they would give their hearts.

The Indians of San Salvador behaved this way because the Spaniards seemed the very gods. "All believe that power and goodness dwell in the sky," Columbus reported, "and they are firmly convinced that I have come from the sky." The products of Europe fascinated them. For a bit of sheet copper an inch square, they would part with a bushel of corn, while knives, hatchets, and even fishhooks made of metal were beyond price to a people whose own technology was still in the Stone Age.

But the Spaniards would not settle for the better of the bargain. Columbus also remarked of the Lucayans: "These people are very unskilled in arms . . . with fifty men they could all be subjected and made to do all that one wished." He and his compatriots tricked and cheated the Indians at every turn. Before entering a new area, Spanish generals customarily read a *Requerimiento* (requirement) to the inhabitants. This long-winded document recited a Spanish version of the history of the human race from the Creation to the division of the non-Christian world by Pope Alexander VI and then called upon the Indians to recognize the sovereignty of the reigning Spanish monarch. ("If you do so . . . we shall receive you in all love and charity.") If this demand was rejected, the Spanish promised: "We shall powerfully enter into your country, and . . . shall take you, your wives, and your children, and shall make slaves of them. . . . The death and losses which shall accrue from this are your fault." This arrogant harangue was read in Spanish and often out of earshot of the Indians. When they responded by fighting, the Spaniards decimated them, drove them from their lands, and held the broken survivors in contempt. As Bartolomé de las Casas, a priest among them, said, the conquistadores behaved "like the most cruel Tygres, Wolves, and Lions, enrag'd with a sharp and tedious hunger."

Wherever they went, the Europeans mistreated the people they encountered. When the Portuguese reached Africa, they carried off thousands into slav-

ery. The Dutch behaved shamefully in the East Indies, as did the French in their colonial posessions—although in North America, at least, the French record was better than most.

English settlers described the Indians as being "of a tractable, free, and loving nature, without guile or treachery," yet in most instances they exploited and all but exterminated them. "Why should you take by force from us that which you can obtain by love?" one puzzled chief asked an early Virginia colonist, according to the latter's own account. The first settlers of New England dealt fairly with the local inhabitants. They made honest, if somewhat misguided, efforts to Christianize and educate them and to respect their rights. But within a few years their relations with the Indians deteriorated, and in King Philip's War (1675–1676), proportionately the bloodiest in American history, they destroyed the tribes as independent powers.

Native American Civilizations

Of course, the victims of the Europeans' cruelty were not innocent "noble savages." Being human, Indians suffered from all the human failings in one form or another. During thousands of years they had occupied the hemisphere from Alaska to Tierra del Fuego. By 1500 there were somewhere between 50 and 60 million of them, 1 or 2 million living in what is now the United States. (Exactly how many is impossible to discover. As the anthropologist Bruce Trigger has written, "It is notoriously difficult to determine the size of aboriginal American populations.")

In the course of many centuries the Indians' cultures had evolved in different ways. Climate, soil conditions, wars, and other factors, including pure chance, shaped their ways of life profoundly, just as these forces shaped the civilizations that had developed over the ages in Asia, Africa, and Europe. More than 1,000 languages were spoken in North and South America at the time of Columbus, some as different from one another as English is from Russian or Chinese.

Even in the relatively limited area that the first Spanish explorers visited, the native cultures displayed an extraordinary variety. If the Lucayans who greeted Columbus were a naive people, their institutions relatively primitive, the civilizations of

A page from a codex (illustrated manuscript) shows Cortés's troops with their native allies advancing on Tenochtitlán, now Mexico City. The four major attacking divisions surround Montezuma's capital as dismembered Aztecs are trampled underfoot.

the Incas of Peru and the Aztecs of Mexico were in many respects as highly developed as any in Europe or Asia. The Incas built roads as enduring as those of the Romans. Montezuma, the Aztec emperor, lived in a great palace surrounded by courtiers and servants in a city as large as Madrid, the home of Cortés's master, Charles V, and far more impressive architecturally.

In the immense land north of Mexico no such imposing civilizations existed, but there, too, the number of different patterns of life was enormous. About 200 languages were spoken. Some groups were nomads who traveled in small bands and lived by hunting and fishing. Others lived settled lives based on a combination of hunting and agriculture. It is therefore difficult to generalize, and the problem of describing the lives and attitudes of these original Americans is made more difficult still by the absence of written records before the arrival of the Europeans and the fact that most of the accounts written by European explorers and settlers are biased and incomplete.

Certain traits the Indians had in common, and many of these the Europeans shared. Cruelty and

war, slavery and plunder existed in the New World long before Columbus. When the good Father Las Casas wrote that Indians were "without evil and without guile," he was as far off the mark as the Spaniard who claimed that they indulged in "every kind of intemperance and wicked lust." Indian men were by current standards chauvinists, as indeed were most Europeans of that day. Hunting and fishing—which, again like many Europeans, the Indians regarded as sports as well as sources of food—were usually male occupations, as was warfare. In agricultural communities, men and women shared other tasks; in general, the men did the heavy work of clearing land and building shelters; the women did the planting, cultivating, and harvesting. When Indians observed European men planting seeds and weeding their fields, they scoffed at them for being effeminate.

Most of the terrible decimation that was everywhere the Indians' fate was caused by European diseases such as smallpox and measles. The population of Mexico was at least 20 million when Cortés invaded the country and only 2 million a century later. European germs killed far more of the in-

The watercolor paintings of John White, one of the earliest English settlers, provide a glimpse of the Indians through European eyes. Here White depicts "their sitting at meat"—"deer's flesh, or of some other beast, and fish."

habitants than European gunpowder and steel. The Arawak population of Hispaniola fell from perhaps 8 million when Columbus first touched there to a few hundred 50 years later.

The Europeans could not be blamed for these deaths. They did not understand the diseases any better than the Indians did. The fact remains that in conflicts between Indians and whites, far more often than not, the whites were the main cause of the trouble.

Most Europeans had what the historian David B. Quinn described as "almost complete confidence in the rectitude of whatever they did." They simply assumed that non-Europeans were inferior beings. This was their fundamental misconception. Apparently their prejudices were not always of racial origin; some early colonists seemed to have considered Indians members of the white race whose skin had been darkened by exposure to the elements. The term *red man* did not become current until the 18th century.

The relativity of cultural values escaped all but a handful of the Europeans. If some of the natives were naive in thinking that the invaders, with their huge ships and their potent fire sticks, were gods, these "gods" were equally naive in their thinking. Since the Indians did not worship the Christian God and indeed worshiped a large number of other gods, the Europeans dismissed them as contemptible hea-

thens. Some insisted that the Indians were servants of Satan. "Probably the devil decoyed these miserable savages hither," one English colonist explained.

In fact, most Indians were deeply religious people. But their religious values were so different from those of the Europeans that many of the latter believed that even if the Indians were not minions of Satan, they were unworthy of becoming Christians. Others, such as the Spanish friars, did try to convert the Indians, and with considerable success; but as late as 1569, when Spain introduced the Inquisition into its colonies, the natives were exempted from its control on the ground that they were incapable of rational judgment and thus not responsible for their "heretical" religious beliefs.

Most Indians lived in close harmony with their surroundings. They adjusted to and took advantage of existing ecologies (for example, by trapping fur-bearing animals in winter and netting fish during spring spawning runs), whereas the Europeans sought to change ecologies to their advantage (as by plowing fields and building fences). Indians who depended on hunting and fishing lived nomadic lives and therefore had small use for personal property that was not easily portable. They had little interest in amassing wealth, as individuals or as tribes. Even the Aztecs, with their treasures of gold and silver, valued the metals for their durability and the beautiful things that could be made with them rather than as objects of commerce.

This lack of concern for material things led Europeans to conclude that the native people of America were childlike creatures, not to be treated as equals. Indians "do but run over the grass, as do also foxes and wild beasts," an Englishman wrote in 1622, "so it is lawful now to take a land, which none useth, and make use of it." The first part of this statement contained a grain of truth, though of course the second did not follow from it logically.

Other troubles grew out of similar misunderstandings. English colonists assumed that Indian chiefs ruled with the same authority as their own kings. When Indians, whose loyalties were shaped by complex kinship relations more than by identification with any one leader, sometimes failed to honor commitments made by their chiefs, the English accused them of treachery.

The Europeans' inability to grasp the communal nature of land tenure among Indians also led to innumerable quarrels. Traditional tribal boundaries were neither spelled out in deeds or treaties nor marked by fences or any other sign of occupation. Often corn grown by a number of families was stored in a common bin and drawn upon by all as needed. Such practices were alien to the European mind. Indians put more emphasis on who was using land than on who first obtained or "owned" it. Among some agricultural tribes, if a farmer failed to cultivate a plot of land, another could take over no matter how long the first had previously used it.

The Indians, writes William Cronon in his fascinating book *Changes in the Land: Indians, Colonists, and the Ecology of New England*, "moved from habitat to habitat to find maximum abundance through minimal work, and so reduce their impact on the land." English colonists, Cronon goes on to say, "believed in and required permanent settlements." And he concludes: "English fixity sought to replace Indian mobility; here was the central conflict in the ways Indians and colonists interacted with their environments."

The Spanish Decline

While Spain waxed fat on the wealth of the Americas, the other nations of western Europe did little. In 1497 and 1498 King Henry VII of England sent

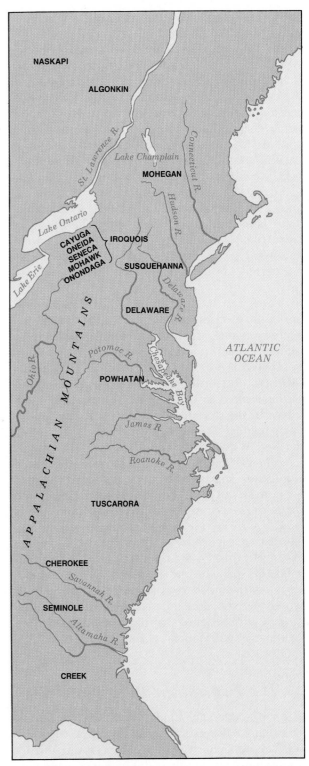

PRIMARY EAST COAST INDIAN TRIBES IN THE 1600s

John Cabot to the New World. Cabot visited New-foundland and the northeastern coast of the continent. His explorations formed the basis for later British claims in North America, but they were not followed up for many decades. In 1524 Giovanni da Verrazano made a similar voyage for France, coasting the continent from Carolina to Nova Scotia. Some ten years later the Frenchman Jacques Cartier explored the St. Lawrence River as far inland as present-day Montreal. During the 16th century, fishermen from France, Spain, Portugal, and England began harvesting the limitless supplies of cod and other fish in the cold waters off Newfoundland. They landed at many points along the mainland coast from Nova Scotia to Labrador to collect water and wood and to dry their catches, but they made no permanent settlements until the next century.

There were many reasons for this delay, the most important probably the fact that Spain had achieved a large measure of internal tranquillity by the 16th century, while France and England were still torn by serious religious and political conflicts. The Spanish also profited from having seized areas in America best suited to producing quick returns. Reinforced by the treasure of the Aztecs and the Incas, Spain seemed too mighty to be challenged in either the New World or the Old.

Under King Philip II Spanish strength seemed at its peak, especially after Philip added Portugal to his domain in 1580. But beneath the pomp and splendor (so well captured by such painters as Velázquez and El Greco), the great empire was in trouble. The corruption of the Spanish court had much to do with this. So did the ever-increasing dependence of Spain on the gold and silver of its colonies, which tended to undermine the local Spanish economy. Even more important was the disruption of the Catholic church throughout Europe by the Protestant Reformation.

The Protestant Reformation

The spiritual lethargy and bureaucratic corruption besetting the Roman Catholic church in the early 16th century made it a fit target for reform. A thriving business in the sale of indulgences, payments that were supposed to win for departed loved ones forgiveness for their earthly sins, was a public scandal. The luxurious life-style of the popes and the papal court in Rome was another. Probably more important were the political possibilities let loose by the challenge of Martin Luther, John Calvin, and other reformers to Rome's spiritual authority. German princes seized upon Luther's campaign against the sale of indulgences to stop all payments to Rome and to confiscate church property within their domains. Swiss cities like Geneva, where Calvin took up residence in 1536, joined the Protestant revolt for spiritual reasons but also to establish their political independence from Catholic kings. Francis I of France remained a Catholic, but he took advantage of Rome's troubles to secure control over the clergy of his kingdom.

The decision of Henry VIII of England to break with Rome was at bottom a political one. The refusal of Pope Clement VII to agree to an annulment of Henry's marriage of 20 years to Catherine of Aragon, the daughter of Ferdinand and Isabella, provided the occasion. Catherine had given birth to six children, but all were girls, and only Mary survived childhood; Henry was without a male heir. By repudiating the pope's spiritual authority and (with the support of Parliament) declaring himself head of the English church in 1533, Henry freed himself to divorce Catherine and to marry whomever—and however often—he saw fit. By the time of his death, five wives and 13 years later, England had become a Protestant nation and the dominant character of the future English colonies in America had also been determined.

The growing political and religious conflict had economic overtones. In some lands the business classes tended to support Protestant leaders, in part because the new sects, stressing simplicity, made fewer financial demands on the faithful than the Catholics did. And as the commercial classes rose to positions of influence, England, France, and the United Provinces of the Netherlands experienced a flowering of trade and industry. The Dutch built the largest merchant fleet in the world. Dutch traders captured most of the Far Eastern business once monopolized by the Portuguese, and they infiltrated Spain's Caribbean stronghold. A number of English merchant companies, soon to play a vital role as colonizers, sprang up in the second half of the 16th century. These joint-stock companies, ancestors of the modern corporation, enabled groups of investors to pool their capital and limit their individual responsibilities to the sums actually invested—a very important protection in such risky enterprises. The Muscovy Company, the Levant Company, and the East India Company were the most important of these ventures.

English Beginnings in America

English merchants took part in many kinds of international activity. The Muscovy Company spent large sums searching for a passage to China around Scandinavia and dispatched six overland expeditions in an effort to reach the Orient by way of Russia and Persia. In the 1570s Martin Frobisher made three voyages across the Atlantic, hoping to discover a northwest passage to the Orient or new gold-bearing lands.

Such projects, particularly in North America, received concealed support from Queen Elizabeth I, who invested heavily in Frobisher's expeditions. England was still too weak to challenge Spain openly, but Elizabeth hoped to break the Spanish overseas monopoly just the same. She encouraged her boldest sea dogs to plunder Spanish merchant ships on the high seas. When Captain Francis Drake was about to set sail on his fabulous round-the-world voyage in 1577, the queen said to him: "Drake . . . I would gladly be revenged on the King of Spain for divers injuries that I have received." Drake, who hated the Spaniards because of a treacherous attack they had once made on the fleet of his kinsman and former chief, Sir John Hawkins, took her at her word. He sailed through the Strait of Magellan and terrorized the west coast of South America, capturing the Spanish treasure ship *Cacafuego*, heavily laden with Peruvian silver. After exploring the coast of California, which he claimed for England, Drake crossed the Pacific and went on to circumnavigate the globe, returning home in triumph in 1580. Although Elizabeth took pains to deny it to the Spanish ambassador, Drake's voyage was officially sponsored. Elizabeth being the principal shareholder in the venture, most of the ill-gotten Spanish bullion went into the Royal Treasury rather than Drake's pocket. He had to settle for a knighthood.

When schemes to place settlers in the New World began to mature at about this time, the queen again became involved. The first English effort was led by Sir Humphrey Gilbert, an Oxford-educated sol-

Sir Francis Drake, one of the boldest sea captains to serve Queen Elizabeth I, sailed around the world from 1577 to 1580 and gratified his sovereign by plundering the Spanish-held west coast of South America.

dier and courtier with a lifelong interest in far-off places. Gilbert owned a share of the Muscovy Company; as early as 1566 he was trying to get a royal grant for an expedition in search of a northeast passage to the Orient. But soon his interests concentrated on the northwest route. He read widely in navigational and geographic lore and in 1576 wrote the persuasive *Discourse . . . to Prove a Passage by the North West to Cathaia.*

Little is known about Gilbert's first attempt except that it occurred in 1578 and 1579; in 1583 he set sail again with five ships and more than 200 settlers. He landed them on Newfoundland, then evidently decided to seek a more congenial site farther south. However, no colony was established, and on his way back to England, his ship went down in a storm off the Azores.

Gilbert's half brother, Sir Walter Raleigh, took up the work. Handsome, ambitious, and impulsive, Raleigh was a great favorite of Elizabeth. He sent a number of expeditions to explore the east coast of North America, a land he named Virginia in honor of his unmarried sovereign. In 1585 he settled about 100 men on Roanoke Island, off the North Carolina coast, but these settlers returned home the next year. In 1587 Raleigh sent another group to Roanoke, including a number of women and children. Unfortunately, the supply ships sent to the colony in 1588 failed to arrive; when help did get there in 1590, not a soul could be found. The fate of this "lost colony" has never been determined.

One reason for the delay in getting aid to the Roanoke colonists was the attack of the Spanish Armada on England in 1588. Angered by English raids on his shipping and by the assistance Elizabeth was giving to the rebels in the Spanish Netherlands, King Philip II had decided to invade England. His great fleet of some 130 ships bore huge crosses on the sails as if on another crusade. The Armada carried 30,000 men and 2,400 guns, the largest naval force ever assembled up to that time. However, the English fleet badly mauled this Armada, and a series of storms completed its destruction. Thereafter, although the war continued and Spanish sea power remained formidable, Spain could no longer block English penetration of the New World.

Experience had shown that the cost of planting settlements in a wilderness 3,000 miles from England was more than any individual purse could bear. (Raleigh lost about £40,000 in his overseas ventures; early in the game he began to advocate government support of colonization.) As early as 1584 Richard Hakluyt, England's foremost authority on the Americas and a talented propagandist for colonization, made a convincing case for royal aid. In his *Discourse on Western Planting*, Hakluyt stressed the military advantages of building "two or three strong fortes" along the Atlantic coast of North America. Ships operating from such bases would make life uncomfortable for "King Phillipe" by intercepting his treasure fleets—a matter, Hakluyt added coolly, "that toucheth him indeede to the quicke." Colonies in America would also enrich the mother country by expanding the market for English woolens, bringing in valuable tax revenues, and by providing employment for the swarms of "lustie youthes that be turned to no profitable use" at home. From the great American forests would come the timber and naval stores needed to build

a bigger navy and merchant marine.

Queen Elizabeth read Hakluyt's essay, but she was too cautious and too devious to act boldly on his suggestions. Only after her death in 1603 did full-scale efforts to found English colonies in America begin, and even then the organizing force came from merchant capitalists, not from the Crown. This was unfortunate, because the search for quick profits dominated the thinking of these enterprisers. Larger national ends (while not neglected, because the Crown was always involved) were subordinated. Yet if private investors had not taken the lead, no colony would have been established at this time.

The Settlement of Virginia

In September 1605 two groups of English merchants petitioned the new king, James I, for a license to colonize Virginia, as the whole area claimed by England was then named. This was granted the following April, and two joint-stock companies were organized, one controlled by London merchants, the other by a group from the area around Plymouth and Bristol.* Both were under the control of the Royal Council for Virginia.

This first charter revealed the commercial motivation of both king and company in the plainest terms. Although it spoke of spreading Christianity and bringing "the Infidels and Savages, living in those Parts, to human Civility," it stressed the right "to dig, mine, and search for all Manner of Mines of Gold, Silver, and Copper."

The London Company dispatched about 100 settlers aboard the *Susan Constant*, the *Discovery*, and the *Godspeed*. This little band reached the Chesapeake Bay area in May 1607 and founded Jamestown. From the start everything seemed to go wrong. The immigrants established themselves in what was practically a malarial swamp simply because it appeared easily defensible against Indian attack. They failed to get a crop in the ground because of the lateness of the season and were soon almost without food. The settlers lacked the skills

---

* The London Company was to colonize south Virginia, while the Plymouth Company, the Plymouth-Bristol group of merchants, was granted northern Virginia.

A 16th-century engraving by John White shows English ships off the coast of Virginia. Wrecked vessels lie along the barrier islands near Hatteras ("Hatorasck"). On Roanoke Island and the mainland beyond it are palisaded Indian villages and warriors armed with bows and arrows.

that pioneers need. More than a third were "gentlemen" unused to manual labor, and the gentlemen's servants, almost equally unequipped for the task of colony building. The rest were hired laborers obliged to work for the company for seven years. During the first winter more than half the settlers died.

All the land belonged to the company, and aside from the gentlemen and their retainers, most of the settlers were only hired laborers who had contracted to work for it for seven years. This was unfortunate. The situation demanded people skilled in agriculture, and such a labor force was available. In England times were bad. The growth of the textile industry had led to an increased demand for wool, and great landowners were dismissing laborers and tenant farmers and shifting from labor-intensive agriculture to sheep raising. Inflation, caused by a shortage of goods to supply the needs of a growing population and by the influx of large amounts of American silver into Europe, worsened the plight of the dispossessed. Many landless farmers were eager to migrate if offered a decent opportunity to obtain land and make new lives for themselves.

The merchant directors of the London Company, knowing little or nothing about Virginia, failed to provide the colony with effective guidance. They set up a council of settlers, but they kept all

real power in their own hands. Instead of stressing farming and public improvements, they directed the energies of the colonists into such futile labors as searching for gold (the first supply ship devoted precious space to two goldsmiths and two "refiners"), glassblowing, silk raising, winemaking, and exploring the local rivers in hopes of finding a water route to the Pacific and the riches of China.

One colonist, Captain John Smith, tried to stop some of this foolishness. Smith had come to Virginia after a fantastic career as a soldier of fortune in eastern Europe, where he had fought many battles, been enslaved by a Turkish pasha, and triumphed in a variety of adventures, military and amorous. He quickly realized that building houses and raising food were essential to survival, and he soon became an expert forager and Indian trader. Smith was as eager as any 17th-century European to take advantage of the Indians, and he had few compunctions about the methods employed in doing so. But he recognized both the limits of the colonists' power and the vast differences between Indian customs and values and his own. It was necessary, he insisted, to dominate the "proud Savages" yet to avoid bloodshed.

Smith pleaded with company officials in London to send over more people accustomed to working with their hands, such as farmers, fishermen, carpenters, masons, and "diggers up of trees," and fewer gentlemen and "Tuftaffety humorists."* "A plaine soldier who can use a pickaxe and a spade is better than five knights," he said.

Whether Smith was actually rescued from death at the hands of the Indians by the princess Pocahontas is not certain, but there is little doubt that without his direction, the colony would have perished in the early days.

Lacking intelligent leaders—Smith only stayed in Virginia two years—and facing appalling hardships, the Jamestown colonists failed to develop a sufficient sense of common purpose. Each year they died in wholesale lots. The causes of death were disease, starvation (there was even a case of cannibalism among the desperate survivors), Indian attack, and, above all, ignorance and folly. Between 1606 and 1622 the London Company invested more than £160,000 in Virginia and sent over about 6,000 settlers. Yet no dividends were ever earned, and of the 6,000, fewer than 2,000 were still alive in 1622. In 1625 the population was down to about 1,300. The only profits were those taken by certain shrewd investors who had organized a joint-stock company to transport women to Virginia "to be made wives" by the colonists.

One major problem, the mishandling of the local Indians, was largely the colonists' doing. It is likely that the settlement would not have survived if the Powhatan Indians had not given the colonists food in the first hard winters, taught them the ways of the forest, introduced them to valuable new crops such as corn and yams, and showed them how to clear dense timber by girdling the trees and burning them down after they were dead. The settlers accepted Indian aid, then took whatever else they wanted by force. They "conciliated the Powhatan people while they were of use," one historian has written, "and pressed them remorselessly, facelessly, mechanically, as innocent of conscious ill will as a turning wheel, when they became of less value than their land."

The Indians did not submit meekly to such treatment. They proved brave, skillful, and ferocious fighters, once they understood that their very existence was at stake. The burden of Indian fighting

might easily have been more than the frail settlement could bear.

What saved the Virginians was not the brushing aside of the Indians but the gradual realization that they must produce their own food—cattle raising was especially important—and cultivate tobacco, which flourished there and could be sold profitably in England. Once the settlers discovered tobacco, no amount of company pressure could keep them at wasteful tasks like looking for gold. The "restraint of plantinge Tobacco," one company official commented, "is a thinge so distastefull to them that they will with no patience indure to heare of it."

John Rolfe, who is also famous for marrying Pocahontas, introduced West Indian tobacco—much milder than the local "weed" and thus more valuable—in 1612. With money earned from the sale of tobacco, the colonists could buy the manufactured articles they could not produce in a raw new country; this freed them from dependence on outside subsidies. It did not mean profit for the London Company, however, for by the time tobacco caught on, the surviving original colonists had served their seven years and were no longer hired hands. To attract more settlers, the company had permitted first tenancy and then outright ownership of farms. Thus the profits of tobacco went largely to the planters, not to the "adventurers" who had organized the colony.

A revised charter in 1612 extended the London Company's control over its affairs in Virginia. Despite serious intracompany rivalry between groups headed by Sir Thomas Smythe and Sir Edwin Sandys, a somewhat more intelligent direction of Virginia's affairs resulted. First the merchants appointed a single resident governor and gave him sufficient authority to control the settlers. Then they made it much easier for settlers to obtain land of their own. In 1619 a rudimentary form of self-government was instituted: A House of Burgesses, consisting of delegates chosen in each district, met at Jamestown to advise the governor. The company was not bound by the actions of the burgesses, but from this seed sprang the system of representative government that became the American pattern.

These reforms, however, came too late to save the fortunes of the London Company. In 1619 the Sandys faction won control and started an extensive development program, but in 1622 a bloody Indian attack took the lives of 347 colonists. Morale sank,

---

* Smith was referring to the gold tassels worn by titled students at Oxford and Cambridge at that time.

and James I, who disliked Sandys, decided that the colony was being badly managed. In 1624 the charter was revoked and Virginia became a royal colony, subject to direct control by the government in London. As a financial proposition the company was a fiasco; the shareholders lost every penny they had invested. Nonetheless, by 1624 Virginia was firmly established and beginning to prosper.

The sociologist Sigmund Diamond has offered an interesting theoretical explanation of how and why the Virginia colony changed from a mere commercial organization to a real society. In the beginning, he asserts, there was no cement binding the colonists into a community; either employees or bosses, they were all oriented toward company headquarters in London. To attract more settlers and motivate them to work, the company had to grant them special privileges and status, such as political power and the right to own land, which had the effect of making them more dependent on one another. By destroying the reliance of the colonists on the company, these actions undermined company control over the colonists. "It was the company's fate to have created a country and to have destroyed itself in the process," Diamond explains.

A 1641 English cartoon comments on the religious turmoil of the period. The Roman Catholic, "The Papist," at lower right joins in a game of "abusing" the Bible along with three Protestant sects opposed to the Church of England.

The English Puritans

Although the prospect of a better material life brought most English settlers to America, for some, economic opportunity was not the only reason they abandoned what their contemporary, William Shakespeare, called "dear mother England." A profound unease with England's spiritual state—and therefore with their own while they remained there—explains why many colonists embarked on their "errand into the wilderness."

The Church of England became once and for all the official Church during the long reign of Elizabeth I (1558–1603). Like her father, Elizabeth took more interest in politics than in religion. She took her religion seriously, but so long as England had its own church, with her at its head, she was content.

This middle way satisfied most, but not all, of Elizabeth's subjects. Steadfast Catholics could not accept it. Some left England; the rest practiced their faith in private. At the other extreme, more radical Protestants, including a large percentage of England's university-trained clergy, insisted that Eliz-

abeth had not gone far enough. Her church was still too much like the Church of Rome, they claimed. They objected to the richly decorated vestments worn by the clergy and to the use of candles, incense, and music in church services. They insisted that emphasis should be put on reading the Bible and analyzing the meaning of the Scriptures in order to encourage ordinary worshipers to understand their faith. Since they wanted to "purify" the Church of England, these critics were called Puritans. At first the name was a pejorative assigned to them by their opponents. Later it became a badge of honor.

Puritans objected to the way Elizabeth's bishops interpreted the Protestant doctrine of predestination. Their reading of the Book of Genesis convinced them that all human beings had been damned by Adam's original sin and that what one did on earth had no effect on a person's fate after death. To believe otherwise was to limit God's power, which was precisely what the Catholic church did in stressing its ability to forgive sins by granting indulgences. The bishops agreed that God had already decided whether or not a person was saved, but they implied that an individual's efforts to lead a good life might somehow cause God to change His mind. They did not insist that good works and faith in God could win a person admission to Heaven—that doctrine was called Arminianism. But they encouraged people to hope that good works were something more than ends in themselves.

Some Puritans—later called Congregationalists—favored a completely decentralized arrangement, with the members of each church and their chosen minister beholden only to one another. Others, called Presbyterians, favored some organization above the local level, but one with power moving up from the local churches, not down from the top as in the Church of England.

Puritans were also of two minds as to whether reform could be accomplished within the Church of England. During Elizabeth's reign most hoped that it could. After King James I succeeded her in 1603, however, their fears that the royal court might be backsliding into its old "popish" ways mounted. James was married to a Catholic, and the fact that he favored toleration for Catholics gave further substance to the rumor that he was himself a secret member of that church. This rumor proved to be false, but in his 22-year reign (1603–1625) James did little to advance the Protestant cause. His one contribution—which had a significance far beyond what he or anyone else anticipated—was to authorize a new translation of the Bible. The King James Version (1611) was both a monumental scholarly achievement and a literary masterpiece of the first order.

"Of Plymouth Plantation"

In 1606, worried about the future of their faith, members of the church in Scrooby, Nottinghamshire, "separated" from the Church of England, declaring it corrupt beyond salvage. In 17th-century England, Separatists had to go either underground or into exile. Since only the latter option would permit them to practice their religious faith openly, exile it was. In 1608 some 125 of the group left England for the Low Countries. They settled in the town of Leyden. In 1619, however, disheartened by the difficulties they had encountered in making a living, disappointed by the failure of others in England to join them, and distressed because their children were being "subjected to the great licentiousness" of the Dutch, these "Pilgrims" decided to move again—to seek "a place where they might have liberty and live comfortably."

Negotiations with Sir Edwin Sandys of the Virginia Company raised the possibility of America. Although unsympathetic to their religious views, Sandys appreciated the Pilgrims' inherent worth and supported their request to establish a settlement near the mouth of the Hudson River, on the northern boundary of the Virginia Company's grant. Since the Pilgrims were short of money, they formed a joint-stock company with other prospective emigrants and some optimistic investors who agreed to pay the expenses of the group in return for half the profits of the venture. In September 1620, about 100 strong—only 35 of them Pilgrims from Leyden—they set out from Plymouth, England, on the ship *Mayflower*.

Had the *Mayflower* reached its intended destination, the Pilgrims might have been soon forgotten. Instead their ship touched America slightly to the north, on Cape Cod Bay. Unwilling to remain longer at the mercy of storm-tossed December seas, they decided to settle where they were. Since they were outside the jurisdiction of the London Company, some members of the group claimed to be free of all governmental control. Therefore, before going ashore, the Pilgrims drew up the Mayflower Compact. "We whose names are underwritten," the Compact ran,

> do by these Presents, solemnly and mutually in the presence of God and one another covenant and combine ourselves under into a civil Body Politick . . . and by Virtue hereof do enact . . . such just and equal laws . . . as shall be thought most meet and convenient for the general Good of the Colony.

This early in American history, the idea was advanced that a society should be based on a set of rules chosen by its members, an idea carried further in the Declaration of Indpendence. The Pilgrims chose William Bradford as their first governor. In this simple manner, ordinary people created a government that they hoped would enable them to cope with the unknown wilderness before them.

The story of the first 30 years of the Pilgrims' colony has been preserved in *Of Plymouth Plantation,* written by Bradford. Having landed on the bleak Massachusetts shore at a place they named Plymouth, the Pilgrims had to endure a winter of desperate hunger. About half of them died. But by great good luck there was an Indian in the area, named Squanto, who spoke English! Squanto had been kidnapped in 1615 by an English sea captain, Thomas Hunt, who took him to Spain and sold him as a slave. Squanto soon escaped, however, and somehow made his way to England, where he fell in with people involved in colonization and exploring. He spent some time in Newfoundland in 1617 and 1618, returned to England, and in 1619 made another voyage to America as a pilot. This time he remained. It is easy to understand why the Pilgrims believed that Squanto was "a special instrument sent of God for their good." In addition to serving as an interpreter, he showed them the best places to fish, as well as what to plant and how to cultivate it. In general, he provided them with all kinds of advice and support in an unfamiliar world. They, in turn, worked hard, got their crops in the ground in good time, and after a bountiful harvest the following November, treated themselves and their Indian neighbors to a Thanksgiving feast.

But if the Pilgrims had quickly secured themselves a safe place in the wilderness, what followed was hardly all cranberries and drumsticks. Bradford's flock grew neither rich nor numerous on the thin New England soil. In 1650 there were still fewer than 1,000 settlers, most of them living beyond the reach of the original church. Among these were a few who tried to take advantage of the freedom from social control afforded by the wilderness. In 1628 a group led by one Thomas Morton, "Lord of Misrule" of the outlying community of Mount Wollaston, which he renamed Merrymount, declared its liberation from all restraints by setting up a maypole. They then invited neighboring Indian women to join them, provided drinks all around, and began (as the disapproving Bradford described the doings) "dancing and frisking together like so many fairies." Troops were dispatched to break up the carousing and take Morton into custody, after which he was packed off to England.

Morton was not a Pilgrim; his antics do not jeopardize the Pilgrims' place in American history. That place is one of honor. Theirs were victories won not with sword and gunpowder like those of Cortés or with bulldozer and dynamite like those of modern pioneers, but with simple courage and practical piety.

A Puritan Commonwealth

The Pilgrims were not the first English colonists to inhabit the northern regions. The Plymouth Company had settled a group on the Kennebec River in 1607. These colonists gave up after a few months, but fishermen and traders continued to visit the area, which was christened New England by Captain John Smith after an expedition there in 1614.

In 1620 the Plymouth Company was reorganized as the Council for New England, which had among its principal stockholders Sir Ferdinando Gorges and his friend John Mason, former governor of an English settlement on Newfoundland. Their particular domain included a considerable part of what is now Maine and New Hampshire. More interested in real estate deals than in colonizing, the council disposed of a number of tracts in the area north of Cape Cod. The most significant of these grants was a small one made to a group of Puritans from Dorchester, who in 1629 founded the Massachusetts Bay Company and obtained a royal grant to the area between the Charles and Merrimack rivers. The Massachusetts Bay Company was organized like any other commercial venture, but the Puritans, acting with single-minded determination, made it a way of obtaining religious refuge in America.

Unlike the Separatists in Plymouth, most Puritans had managed to satisfy both Crown and conscience while James I was king. The England of his son Charles I, who succeeded to the throne in 1625, posed a more serious challenge. Whereas James had been content to keep Puritans at bay, Charles and his favorite Anglican cleric, William Laud, intended to bring them to heel. With the king's support, Laud proceeded to embellish even further the already elaborate Anglican ritual and to tighten the central control that the Puritans found so distasteful. He removed ministers with Puritan leanings from their pulpits and threatened church elders who harbored such ministers with imprisonment.

No longer able to remain within the Anglican fold in good conscience and now facing prison if they tried to worship in the way they thought right, the Puritans decided to migrate to America in force.

Noah did view
The old World & new

Young *Obadias*,
David, *Jolias*,
All were pious.

Peter deny'd
His Lord, and cry'd.

Queen *Esther* sues,
And saves the *Jews*.

Young pious *Ruth*,
Left all for Truth.

Young *Samuel* dear
The Lord did fear.

A page from this New England primer reflects the pervasive influence of religion on every aspect of Puritan life, from politics to the education of the young.

In the summer of 1630 nearly 1,000 of them set out from England, carrying the charter of the Massachusetts Bay Company with them. By the fall they had founded Boston and several other towns. The Puritan commonwealth was under way.

Massachusetts settlers suffered fewer hardships in the early years than had the early Jamestown and Plymouth colonists. Luck played a part in this, but so did the careful planning that went into the transplantation. They also benefited from a constant influx of new recruits, who came with families and worldly possessions in tow. Continuing bad times and the persecution of Puritans at home led to the Great Migration of the 1630s. Many thousands

more poured into new English colonies in the West Indies, but by 1640 well over 10,000 had arrived in Massachusetts. These industrious, well-educated, and fairly prosperous colonists swiftly created a complex and distinct civilization on the edge of what one of the pessimists among them called "a hideous and desolate wilderness, full of wild beasts and wild men."

The directors of the Massachusetts Bay Company believed their enterprise to be divinely inspired. Before leaving England, they elected John Winthrop, a 29-year-old attorney, as governor of the colony. Throughout his 20 years of almost continuous service as governor, Winthrop spoke for the solid and sensible core of the Puritans and their high-minded experiment. His lay sermon, "A Modelle of Christian Charity," delivered in mid-Atlantic on the deck of the ship *Arbella* in 1630, made clear his sense of the momentousness of that experiment:

> Wee must Consider that wee shall be as a Citty upon a Hill, the eies of all people are upon us; soe that if wee shall deale falsely with our god in this worke wee have undertaken and soe cause him to withdrawe his present help from us, wee shall be made a story and a by-word through the world, wee shall open the mouthes of enemies to speake evill of the wayes of god and all professours for Gods sake.

The founders also established an elected legislature, the General Court. Their system was not democratic in the modern sense because the right to vote and hold office was limited to church members, but this did not mean that the government was run by clergymen or that it did not reflect the popular will. Clergymen were influential, but since they were not allowed to hold public office, their authority was indirect and based on the respect of the parishioners, not on law or force. At least until the mid-1640s, most families contained at least one adult male church member. Since these "freemen" soon secured the right to choose the governor and elect the representatives ("deputies") to the General Court, a kind of practical democracy existed.

The Puritans had a clear sense of what their churches should be like. After getting permission from the General Court, a group of colonists who wished to form a new church could select a minister and conduct their spiritual affairs as they saw fit.

Membership, however, was restricted to those who could present satisfactory evidence of their having experienced "saving grace," such as by a compelling recounting of some extraordinary emotional experience or some mystical sign of intimate contact with God. This meant that full membership in the churches of early Massachusetts was reserved for "visible saints." During the 1630s, however, the need for harmony in the community was so important that few applicants were denied membership. Having removed oneself from England was considered in most cases sufficient proof of spiritual purity.

Troublemakers

As Winthrop had more than one occasion to lament, most of the colony's early troublemakers came not from those of doubtful spiritual condition but from its certified saints. The "godly and zealous" Roger Williams was a prime example. The Pilgrim leader William Bradford described Williams as possessed of "many precious parts, but very unsettled in judgment." Even by Plymouth's standards, Williams was an extreme separatist. He was ready to bring down upon New England the wrath of Charles I rather than accept the charters signed by him or his father, even if these documents provided the only legal basis for the governments of the Plymouth and Massachusetts Bay colonies.

Williams had arrived in Massachusetts in 1631. Following a short stay in Plymouth, he joined the church in Salem, which elected him minister in 1635. Well before then, however, his opposition to the alliance of church and civil government turned both ministers and magistrates against him. Part of his contrariness stemmed from his religious libertarianism. Magistrates should have no voice in spiritual matters, he insisted—"forced religion stinks in God's nostrils." He also offended property owners (which meant nearly everyone) by advancing the radical idea that it was "a Nationale sinne" for anyone, including the king, to take possession of any American land without buying it from the Indians.

As long as Williams enjoyed the support of his Salem church, there was little the magistrates could do to silence him. But his refusal to heed those who counseled moderation—"all truths are not seasonable at all times," Governor Winthrop reminded him—swiftly eroded that support. In the fall of 1635, economic pressure put on Salem by the General Court turned his congregation against him. The General Court then ordered him to quit the colony.

Williams left Massachusetts in January 1636, traveling south to the head of Narragansett Bay. There he worked out mutually acceptable arrangements with the local Indians and founded the town of Providence. In 1644, after obtaining a charter from Parliament, he established the colony of Rhode Island and Providence Plantations. All religions were tolerated, and church and state were rigidly separated. Whatever Williams's temperamental excesses, he was more than ready to practice what he preached when given the opportunity.

Anne Hutchinson, who arrived in Boston in 1631, was another "visible saint" who, in the judgment of the Puritan establishment, went too far. Hutchinson was not to be taken lightly. According to Governor Winthrop, her husband William was "a man of mild temper and weak parts, wholly guided by his wife." (He was not too weak to father Anne's 15 children.) Duties as a midwife brought her into the homes of other Boston women, with whom she discussed and more than occasionally criticized the sermons of their minister, John Wilson. Where Wilson and virtually all the ministers in the Bay Colony except her favorite, John Cotton, went wrong, she contended, was in emphasizing the obligation of the saved to lead morally pure lives in order to be models for the unregenerate. By taking the Puritan view that there was no necessary relationship between moral conduct and salvation to its extreme limits, she concluded that those possessed of saving grace were exempt from the rules of good behavior and even from the laws of the commonwealth. As her detractors pointed out, this was the conclusion some of the earliest German Protestants had reached, for which they were judged guilty of the heresy of antinomianism ("belief against the law") and burned at the stake.

In 1636 the General Court charged Hutchinson with defaming the clergy and brought her to trial. When her accusers quoted the Bible ("Honor thy father and thy mother") to make their case, she coolly announced that even the Ten Commandments must yield to one's own insights if these were directly inspired by God. When pressed for details, she acknowledged that she was a regular recipient of divine insights, communicated, as they were to Abraham, "by the voice of His own spirit in my soul." The General Court, upon hearing this claim, banished her.

Hutchinson, together with her large family and a group of supporters, left Massachusetts in the spring of 1637 for Rhode Island, thereby adding to the reputation of that colony as the "sink" of New England. After her husband died in 1642, she and six of her children moved to the Dutch colony of New Netherland, where, the following year, she and all but her youngest daughter were killed by Indians.

The banishments of Roger Williams, whom some historians have called the first American democrat, and Anne Hutchinson, who, if not a feminist in the modern sense, refused to defer to her male "betters," did not endear the Massachusetts Puritans to posterity. In both cases, outspoken individualists seem to have been done in by frightened politicians and self-serving ministers. Yet Williams and Hutchinson posed genuine threats to the Puritan community. Massachusetts was truly a social experiment. Could it accommodate such uncooperative spirits and remain intact? When forced to choose between the peace of the commonwealth and sending dissenters packing, Winthrop, the magistrates, and the ministers did not hesitate.

Other New England Colonies

From the successful Massachusetts Bay Colony, settlement radiated outward, propelled by an expanding population and Puritan intolerance. In 1629 Sir Ferdinando Gorges and John Mason divided their holdings, Gorges taking the Maine section (enlarged in 1639) and Mason getting New Hampshire, but neither succeeded in making much of his claim. Massachusetts bought title to Maine for a pittance (£1,250) in 1677 and New Hampshire became a royal colony in 1680.

Meanwhile, beginning in 1635, a number of Massachusetts congregations had pushed southwestward into the fertile valley of the Connecticut River. A group headed by the Reverend Thomas Hooker founded Hartford in 1636. Hooker was influential in the drafting of the Fundamental Orders, a sort of constitution creating a government for the valley towns, in 1639. The Fundamental Orders resembled the Massachusetts system, except that they did not limit voting to church members. Other groups of Puritans came directly from England to settle towns in and around New Haven in the 1630s. These were incorporated into Connecticut shortly after the Hooker colony obtained a royal charter in 1662.

French and Dutch Settlements

While the English were settling Virginia and New England, other Europeans were challenging Spain's monopoly in the New World. French explorers had pushed up the St. Lawrence River as far as the site of Montreal in the 1530s, and beginning in 1603, Samuel de Champlain made several voyages to the region. In 1608 he founded Quebec, and he had penetrated as far inland as Lake Huron before the Pilgrims left Leyden. The French also planted colonies on Guadeloupe, Martinique, and other islands in the West Indies after 1625.

Through their West India Company, the Dutch also established themselves in the Caribbean. On the mainland they founded New Netherland in the Hudson Valley, basing their claim to the region on the explorations of Henry Hudson in 1609. As early as 1624 there was a Dutch outpost, Fort Orange, on the site of present-day Albany. Two year later New Amsterdam was located at the mouth of the Hudson River, and Manhattan Island was purchased from the Indians by Peter Minuit, the director general of the West India Company, for trading goods worth about 60 guilders. The Dutch traded with the Indians for furs and plundered Spanish colonial commerce enthusiastically. Through the Charter of Privileges of Patroons, which authorized large grants of land to individuals who would bring more than 50 settlers, they tried to encourage large-scale agriculture. Only one such estate—Rensselaerswyck, on the Hudson south of Fort Orange, owned by the rich Amsterdam merchant Kiliaen Van Rensselaer—was successful. Peter Minuit was removed from his post in New Amsterdam in 1631, but he organized a group of Swedish settlers several years later and founded the colony of New Sweden on the lower reaches of the Delaware River. New Sweden was in constant conflict with the Dutch, who finally overran it in 1655.

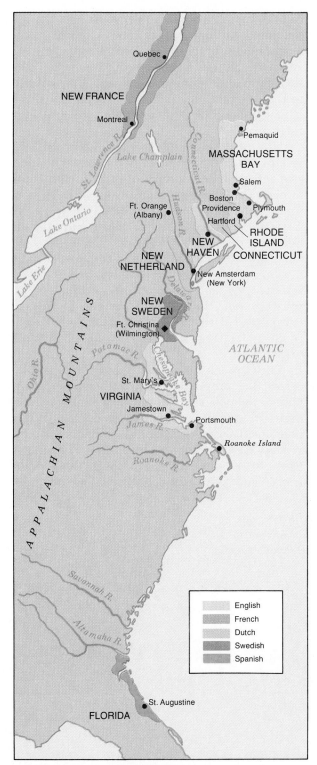

**NORTH AMERICAN COLONIES
TO 1650**

English
French
Dutch
Swedish
Spanish

Maryland and the Carolinas

The Virginia and New England colonies were essentially corporate ventures. Most of the other English colonies in America were founded by individuals or by a handful of partners who obtained charters from the ruling sovereign. It was becoming easier to establish settlements because experience had taught the English a great deal about the colonization process. Settlers knew better what to bring with them and what to do after they arrived. Moreover, the psychological barrier was much less formidable. Like a modern athlete seeking to run a mile in less than four minutes, colonizers knew after about 1630 that what they were attempting could be accomplished. And conditions in Europe in the mid-17th century encouraged thousands to migrate. Both in England and on the Continent the economic future seemed unpromising, and political and religious persecution erupted in one country after another, each time supplying America with waves of refugees.

Numbers of influential Englishmen were eager to try their luck as colonizers. The grants they received made them "proprietors" of great estates which were, at least in theory, their personal property. By granting land to settlers in return for a small annual rent, they hoped to obtain a steadily increasing income while holding a valuable speculative interest in all undeveloped land. At the same time, their political power, guaranteed by charter, would become increasingly important as their colonies expanded. In practice, however, the realities of life in America limited their freedom of action and their profits.

One of the first of the proprietary colonies was Maryland, granted by Charles I to George Calvert, Lord Baltimore. Calvert had a deep interest in America, being a member of both the London Company and the Council for New England. He hoped to profit financially from Maryland, but since he was a Catholic, he also intended the colony to be a haven for his coreligionists.

Calvert died shortly before Charles approved his charter, so the grant went to his son Cecilius. The first settlers arrived in 1634, founding St. Mary's, just north of the Potomac. The presence of the now well established Virginia colony nearby greatly aided the Marylanders; they had little difficulty in getting started and in developing an economy based, like Virginia's, on tobacco. However, an acrimonious dispute raged for some years between the two colonies over their common boundary. Despite the emptiness of the American wilderness, settlers could squabble over a few acres as bitterly as any European peasants.

The Maryland charter was similar to that of the old county palatine of Durham in the north of England, whose bishop-overlords had held almost regal authority. Lord Baltimore had the right to establish feudal manors, hold people in serfdom, make laws, and set up his own courts. He soon discovered, however, that to attract settlers he had to allow them to own their farms and that to maintain any political influence at all he had to give the settlers considerable say in local affairs. Other wise concessions marked his handling of the religious question. He would have preferred an exclusively Catholic colony, but there existed from the beginning a large Protestant majority. Baltimore dealt with this problem by agreeing to the Toleration Act (1649), which guaranteed freedom of religion to anyone "professing to believe in Jesus Christ." Even so, religious conflicts occurred repeatedly in the early years. However, because the Calverts adjusted their pretensions to American realities, they made a fortune out of Maryland and maintained an influence in the colony until the Revolution.

During the period of the English Civil War and Oliver Cromwell's Protectorate, no important new colonial enterprises were undertaken. With the restoration of the monarchy in 1660 came a new wave of settlement, for the government wished to expand and strengthen its hold on North America. To do so, it granted generous terms to settlers: easy access to land, religious toleration, and political rights—all far more extensive than those available in England.

Most of the earlier colonies were organized by groups of merchants; those of the Restoration period reflected the concerns of great English landowners. The first new venture involved a huge grant south of Virginia to eight proprietors with large interests in colonial affairs. The proprietors did not intend to recruit large numbers of European settlers. Instead they depended on the "excess" population of New England, Virginia, and the West Indies. They (and the Crown) hoped for a diversified economy, the charter granting tax concessions to exporters of wine, silk, oil, olives, and other exotic products. The region was called Carolina in honor of Charles I.

The Carolina charter, like that of Maryland, accorded the proprietors wide authority. With the help of the political philosopher John Locke, they drafted a grandiose plan of government called the Fundamental Constitutions, which authorized a hereditary nobility and provided for huge paper land grants to a hierarchy headed by the proprietors and lesser "landgraves" and "caciques." The human ef-

The earliest known painting of Charles Town, South Carolina (Charleston after 1783), shows the harbor in the 1730s. As the most important seaport in the southern colonies, the city carried on a busy export trade in rice, indigo, and deerskins.

fort to support the feudal society was to be supplied by peasants (whom the Fundamental Constitutions called "leet-men").

This pretentious system proved unworkable. The landgraves and caciques got grants, but they could not find leet-men willing to toil on their domains. Probably the purpose of all this feudal nonsense was promotional; the proprietor hoped to convince investors that they could make fortunes in Carolina rivaling those of English lords. Life actually followed a more mundane pattern similar to what was going on in Virginia and Maryland, with property relatively easy to obtain.

The first settlers arrived in 1670, most of them from the sugar plantations of Barbados, where slave labor was driving out small independent farmers. Charles Town (now Charleston) was founded in 1680. Another center of population sprang up in the Albemarle district, just south of Virginia, settled largely by individuals from that colony. Two quite different societies evolved. The Charleston colony, with an economy based on a thriving trade in furs and on the export of foodstuffs to the West Indies, was prosperous and cosmopolitan. The Albemarle settlement, where the soil was less fertile, was poorer and more primitive. Eventually, in 1712, the two were formally separated, becoming North and South Carolina.

The Middle Colonies

Gradually it became clear that the English would dominate the entire coast between the St. Lawrence Valley and Florida. After 1660 only the Dutch challenged their monopoly. The two nations, once allies against Spain, had fallen out because of the fierce competition of their textile manufacturers and merchants. England's efforts to bar Dutch merchant vessels from its colonial trade also brought the two countries into conflict in America. Charles II precipitated a showdown by granting his brother James, duke of York, the entire area between Connecticut and Maryland. This was tantamount to declaring war. In 1664 English forces captured New Amsterdam without a fight—there were only 1,500 people in the town—and soon the rest of the Dutch settlements capitulated. New Amsterdam became New York. The duke did not interfere much with the way of life of the Dutch settlers, and they were quickly reconciled to English rule.

In 1664, even before the capture of New Amsterdam, the duke of York gave New Jersey, the region between the Hudson and Delaware rivers, to John Lord Berkeley and Sir George Carteret. To attract settlers, these proprietors offered land on easy terms and established freedom of religion and a democratic local government. A considerable number of Puritans from New England and Long Island moved to the new province.

In 1674 Berkeley sold his interest in New Jersey to two Quakers. Originally a sect emotional to the point of fanaticism, by the 1670s the Quakers had come to stress the doctrine of the Inner Light—the direct, mystical experience of religious truth, which they believed possible for all persons. They were at once humble and fiercely proud, pacifistic yet unwilling to bow before any person or to surrender their right to worship as they pleased. They distrusted the intellect in religious matters, and though ardent proselytizers of their own beliefs, they tolerated those of others cheerfully. When faced with opposition, they resorted to passive resistance, a tactic that embroiled them in grave difficulties in England and in most of the American colonies.

The acquisition of New Jersey (when Sir George Carteret died in 1680, they purchased the rest of the colony) gave the Quakers a place where they could practice their religion in peace. The proprietors, in keeping with their principles, drafted an extremely liberal constitution for the colony, the Concessions and Agreements of 1677, which created an autonomous legislature and guaranteed settlers freedom of conscience, the right of trial by jury, and other civil rights. The main Quaker effort at colonization came in the region immediately west of New Jersey, a fertile area belonging to William Penn, the son of a wealthy English admiral. Penn had early rejected a life of ease and had become a Quaker missionary. As a result, he was twice jailed. Yet he possessed qualities that enabled him to hold the respect and friendship of people who found his religious ideas abhorrent. From his father, Penn had inherited a claim to £16,000 that the admiral had lent Charles II. The king, reluctant to part with that much cash, paid off the debt in 1681 by giving Penn the region north of Maryland and west of the Delaware River, insisting only that it be named Pennsylvania, in honor of the admiral. The duke of York then added Delaware, the region between Maryland and Delaware Bay, to Penn's holdings.

William Penn considered his colony a "Holy Experiment." He treated the Indians fairly, buying title to their lands and trying to protect them in their dealings with settlers and traders. Anyone who believed in "one Almighty and Eternal God" was entitled to freedom of worship. Penn's political ideas were paternalistic rather than democratic; the assembly he established could only approve or reject laws proposed by the governor and council. But individual rights were as well protected in Pennsylvania as in New Jersey.

Altruism, however, did not prevent Penn from taking excellent care of his own interests. He sold land to settlers large and small on easy terms but reserved huge tracts for himself and attached quit-rents (see page 34) to the land he disposed of. He promoted Pennsylvania tirelessly, writing glowing, although perfectly honest, descriptions of the colony that were circulated widely in England and, in translation, on the Continent. These attracted many settlers, including large numbers of Germans—the Pennsylvania "Dutch" (a corruption of *Deutsch*, meaning "German").

William Penn was neither a doctrinaire nor an ivory-tower philosopher. He came to Pennsylvania himself when trouble developed between settlers and his representatives and agreed to adjustments in his first Frame of Government when he realized that local conditions demonstrated the need for change. His combination of toughness, liberality, and good salesmanship helped the colony to prosper. Of course, the presence of well-settled colonies on all sides and the richness of the soil had much to do with this happy state of affairs. By 1685 there were almost 9,000 settlers in Pennsylvania, and by 1700 twice that number, a heartening contrast to the early history of Virginia and Plymouth. Pennsylvania produced wheat, corn, rye, and other crops in abundance and found a ready market for its surpluses on the sugar plantations of the West Indies.

William Penn met with a group of Delaware Indians in the fall of 1683 to arrange the terms of a land transfer in eastern Pennsylvania. Good will between Indians and settlers lasted for about 50 years, until the latter began forcing the Indians westward. This re-creation of Penn's famous treaty is an engraving based on a painting by Benjamin West.

This 1651 engraving, the first known view of Manhattan Island, shows the new fort of New Amsterdam in the 1620s. Indians bring beaver pelts in their canoes to sell to the Dutch.

Indians and Europeans as "Americanizers"

Interaction with the native peoples was characteristic of life in all the English colonies. *Interaction* is the key word. The so-called Columbian Exchange between Indian and European was a two-way street. The Indians taught the colonists a great deal about how to live in the American forest: the names of plants and animals (hickory, pecan, raccoon, skunk, moose); what to eat in their new home and how to catch or grow it; what to wear (leather leggings and especially moccasins); how best to get from one place to another; how to fight; and in some respects how to think.

The colonists learned from the Indians how best to use many wild plants and animals for food and clothing, but they would probably have discovered most of these if the continent had been devoid of human life when they arrived. Corn, however, the staple of the diet of agricultural tribes, was something the Indians had domesticated. Its contribution to the success of English colonization was enormous.

The colonists also took advantage of that marvel of Indian technology, the birchbark canoe. An early explorer, Martin Pring, brought one back to England in 1603; it was 17 feet long and 4 feet wide and capable, according to Pring, of carrying nine full-grown men. Yet it weighed "not at the most above sixtie pounds," a thing, Pring added, "almost incredible in regard to the largenesse and capacitie thereof."

For their part, the Indians adopted European technology eagerly. All metal objects were indeed of great usefulness to them, though the products and tools that metals replaced were neither crude nor inefficient in most cases. (To say that a gun is a more deadly weapon than a bow and arrow is a more accurate statement about modern guns than about a 17th-century firelock. A bowman could get off six times as many shots in a given time as a soldier armed with a firelock and would probably hit the target more frequently.)

Indians took on many of the colonists' attitudes along with their tools, clothing, weapons, alcohol, and ornaments. Some tribes used the products of European technology to tyrannize tribes in more remote areas. During wars Indians fought almost as often with colonists against other Indians as with other Indians against colonists.

The fur trade illustrates the pervasiveness of Indian-colonist interaction. It was in some ways a perfect business arrangement. Both groups profited greatly. The colonists got "valuable" furs for "cheap" European products, while the Indians got "priceless" tools, knives, and other trade goods in exchange for "cheap" beaver pelts and deerskins. The market for furs caused the Indians to become more efficient hunters and trappers and even to absorb some of the colonists' ideas about private property and capitalist accumulation. Hunting parties became larger. Farming tribes shifted their villages in order to be nearer trade routes and waterways. In some cases, tribal organization was altered:

Small groups combined into confederations in order to control more territory when their hunting reduced the supplies of furs nearer home. Early in the 17th century, Huron Indians in the Great Lakes region, who had probably never seen a Frenchman, owned French products obtained from eastern tribes in exchange for Huron corn. All in all, as one historian puts it, "the fur trade set off a chain reaction . . . within the Indian world." In *The European and the Indian,* James Axtell makes an important point about the relative impact of the two cultures on each other. Although the colonists learned much from the Indians and adopted certain elements of Indian culture and technology eagerly, their objective was not to be like the Indians, whom they considered the epitome of savagery and barbarism. That they feared they might become "Indianized," Axtell notes, is clear from the adage "It is very easy to make an Indian out of a white man,

but you cannot make a white man out of an Indian." Yet this very fear, the colonial rejection of Indian ways, caused what Axtell calls "reactive changes" that are at the heart of what made them Americans rather than transplanted Europeans. The constant conflicts with Indians forced the colonists to band together and in time gave them a sense of having shared a common history. And later, when they broke away from Great Britain, they used the image of the Indian to symbolize the freedom and independence they sought for themselves.

In sum, during the 200-odd years that followed Columbus's first landfall in the Caribbean, a complex development had taken place in the Americas, one that profoundly affected the civilizations of the people who preceded Columbus and those who followed him. We shall now turn to a more detailed look at how this happened in the part of that vast region on which our own civilization has evolved.

Milestones

Exploration

c. 1000	Leif Eriksson reaches Newfoundland
1445–1488	Portuguese captains explore the west coast of Africa
1492	First voyage of Christopher Columbus
1497	John Cabot explores the east coast of North America
1498	Vasco da Gama sails around Africa to India
1513	Ponce de León explores Florida
1519–1521	Hernán Cortés conquers Mexico
1519–1522	Ferdinand Magellan's crew circumnavigates the globe
1539–1542	Hernando de Soto explores the lower Mississippi River valley
1540–1542	Francisco Vásquez de Coronado explores the Southwest
1579	Francis Drake explores the coast of California
1609	Henry Hudson discovers the Hudson River

Settlement

c. 50,000 B.C.	First humans reach North America from Asia
1493	La Navidad, Hispaniola, founded by Columbus
1494	Treaty of Tordesillas divides the New World between Spain and Portugal
1576	St. Augustine, Florida, settled
1587	"Lost colony" of Roanoke Island founded
1607	Jamestown settled
1620	Plymouth settled; Mayflower Compact signed
1624	New Amsterdam settled
1630	Massachusetts Bay Colony established
1634	Maryland settled
1636	Rhode Island founded
1639	Connecticut founded
1664	New Amsterdam conquered by the English
1670	Charles Town (Charleston) settled
1681	Philadelphia settled

SUPPLEMENTARY READING

Titles marked with an asterisk have been published in paperback.

On the explorers and the world they opened up, see D. B. Quinn, **North America from Earliest Discovery to First Settlements*** (1977), S. E. Morison, **The European Discovery of America** (1971–1974), and C. O. Sauer, **Sixteenth-Century North America*** (1971). Morison's biography of Columbus, **Admiral of the Ocean Sea** (1942), is a model of sound scholarship and good writing.

Accounts of the English background of colonization can be found in A. L. Rowse, **The Elizabethans and America*** (1959), and Carl Bridenbaugh, **Vexed and Troubled Englishmen*** (1968). J. H. Elliott, **The Old World and the New*** (1970), analyzes the impact of the discovery of America on Europe.

On French and Spanish colonization, see W. J. Eccles, **France in America*** (1972), and Charles Gibson, **Spain in America*** (1966). On the interactions of European and Indian civilizations, consult James Axtell, **The European and the Indian** (1981), Karen Kupperman, **Settling with the Indian** (1980), and William Cronon, **Changes in the Land** (1981). W. E. Washburn, **The Indian in America** (1975), contains a good discussion of the culture and history of North American Indian groups. Francis Jennings, **The Invasion of America*** (1975), is extremely critical of white dealings with the Indians. A. T. Vaughan, **New England Frontier*** (1965), argues that New Englanders treated the Indians fairly.

W. F. Craven, **The Colonies in Transition*** (1968), is a first-rate study of late 17th- and early 18th-century English colonization. On the southern colonies, W. F. Craven, **The Southern Colonies in the Seventeenth Century*** (1949), is also excellent, as is, on Virginia, E. S. Morgan, **American Slavery, American Freedom** (1975). For Maryland, consult G. T. Main, **Tobacco Colony** (1982), and A. C. Land, **Colonial Maryland** (1981).

D. R. Rutman, **Winthrop's Boston** (1965), is good on Massachusetts Bay. For the middle colonies, see Michael Kammen, **Colonial New York** (1975), and G. B. Nash, **Quakers and Politics** (1968). For Carolina, consult A. R. Ekirch, **Poor Carolina** (1981).

No student should miss at least dipping into the works of Francis Parkman on the French in America. His **Pioneers of France in the New World** (1855) covers the early period. William Bradford's classic **Of Plymouth Plantation** is also well worth sampling.

Biographies worth noting include A. T. Vaughan, **American Genesis: Captain John Smith*** (1975), and E. S. Morgan, **The Puritan Dilemma: The Story of John Winthrop*** (1958).

American Society in the Making

The great Increase of Offspring in particular Families is not always owing to greater Fecundity of Nature, but sometimes to Examples of Industry in the Heads, and industrious Education; by which the Children are enabled to provide better for themselves, and their marrying earlier is encouraged from the Prospect of good Subsistence.

BENJAMIN FRANKLIN, *1751*

The colonies were settled chiefly by English people at first, with a leavening of Germans, Scots, Scotch-Irish, Dutch, French, Swedes, Finns, a scattering of other nationalities, a handful of Sephardic Jews, and a gradually increasing number of black African slaves. The cultures these people brought with them varied according to the nationality, social status, intelligence, and taste of the individual. The newcomers never lost this heritage entirely, but they—and certainly their descendants—became quite different from

their relatives who remained in the Old World. They became what we call Americans.

But not right away.

What Is an American?

The subtle but profound changes that occurred when Europeans moved to the New World were hardly self-willed. Most of the settlers came, it is true, hoping for a more bountiful existence, and sometimes also for nonmaterialistic reasons, such as the opportunity to practice their religions in ways barred to them at home. For some whose alternative was prison or execution, there was really no choice. Still, even the most rebellious or alienated seldom intended to develop an entirely new civilization; rather, they wished to reconstruct the old on terms more favorable to themselves. Nor did a single "American" type result from the careful selection of particular kinds of Europeans as colonizers. Settlers came from every walk of life and in rough proportion to their numbers in Europe (if we exclude the very highest social strata). Certainly there was no systematic selection of the finest grain to provide seed for cultivating the wilderness.

Why then did America become something more than another Europe? Why was New England not merely a new England, Virginia not simply an English province west of Ireland? If not just another "poor European immigrant" away from home, a French settler, Hector St. John de Crèvecoeur, wondered in 1762, "What then is the American, this new man?" And how did this American come to be?

The fact of physical separation provides an important part of the answer. America was isolated from Europe by 3,000 miles of ocean. The Atlantic served as an umbilical cord but also as a barrier. The crossing took anywhere from a few weeks to several months, depending on wind and weather. No one undertook an ocean voyage lightly in colonial times, and few who made the westward crossing ever thought seriously of returning. The modern mind can scarcely grasp the awful isolation that enveloped the settler. One had to face forward (westward) and construct a new life or perish—if not of hunger, then of loneliness.

More than physical separation went into the process by which the people Crèvecoeur called this "promiscuous breed" fashioned for themselves a new national identity and the outlines of a distinctive civilization. Unlike separation from Europe, some factors affected some settlers differently than others. Factors as material as the landscape encountered, as quantifiable as population patterns, as elusive as chance and calculation all shaped colonial social arrangements. Their cumulative impact did not at first produce anything like a uniform society throughout the 2,000-mile-long and 50-mile-wide corridor that contained England's American colonies. Two quite different societies developed, one at each end of the corridor. A third society in the middle shared elements of both. The Americans who evolved in these regional societies were in many ways as different from each other as all were from their European cousins. The process by which these identities merged into an American nation remained incomplete. It was—and is—ongoing.

The Southern Colonies: A Hustling People

The southern parts of English North America comprised three regions: the Chesapeake Bay, consisting of "tidewater" Virginia and Maryland; the "low country" of the Carolinas (and eventually Georgia); and the "back country," a vast territory that extended from the fall line in the foothills of the Appalachians where falls and rapids put an end to navigation on the tidal rivers to the farthest point of western settlement. Not until well into the 18th century would the emergence of common features—export-oriented agricultural economies, a labor force in which black slaves figured prominently, the absence of towns of any size—prompt people to think of "the South" as a single region.

The Chesapeake: "Seasoning Time"

When the English philosopher Thomas Hobbes wrote in 1651 that human life tended to be "nasty, brutish, and short," he might well have had in mind the royal colony of Virginia. Although the colony grew from about 1,300 to nearly 5,000 in the decade after the Crown took it over in 1624, the death rate remained appalling. Since more than 9,000 immi-

grants had entered the colony, nearly half the population died during that decade.

The climate helped make the Chesapeake area a death trap. "Hot and moist" is how Robert Beverly described the weather in *The History and Present State of Virginia* (1705), the dampness "occasioned by the abundance of low grounds, marshes, creeks, and rivers." Europeans found that these conditions took getting used to. Almost without exception, newcomers underwent "seasoning," a period of illness that in its mildest form consisted of "two or three fits of a feaver and ague." If they survived this period, and a great many did not, settlers still ran the seasonal risk of contracting a particularly virulent strain of malaria, which, though seldom fatal in itself, could so debilitate its victims that they often died of dysentery and other ailments.

Long after food shortages and Indian warfare had ceased to be serious problems, life in the Chesapeake remained precarious. Well into the 1700s a white male of 20 in Middlesex County could look forward to about 25 more years of life. Across Chesapeake Bay, in Charles County, Maryland, the average life expectancy was even lower. "Grandparents," writes David Freeman Hawke in this connection, "were all but nonexistent."

Because of the persistent shortage of women in the Chesapeake region (men outnumbered women by three to two even in the early 1700s), widows easily found new husbands. Many men spent their entire lives alone or in the company of other men. Others married Indian women and became part of Indian society.

All Cheasapeake settlers felt the psychological effects of their precarious and frustrating existence. Random mayhem and calculated violence posed a continuous threat to life and limb. Social arrangements were rude at best and often as "brutish" as Hobbes had claimed, even allowing for the difficulties involved in carving out a community in the wilderness. "Success," writes Gloria T. Main in *Tobacco Colony: Life in Early Maryland,* "was primarily the product of good timing and good health." If a white man got started when tobacco prices were high and survived the seasoning period, he could "begin to amass the necessary capital with which to acquire land, a wife, and then a servant. . . . By rigorously saving and reinvesting his cash income, he could secure his own enterprise and help his children launch theirs."

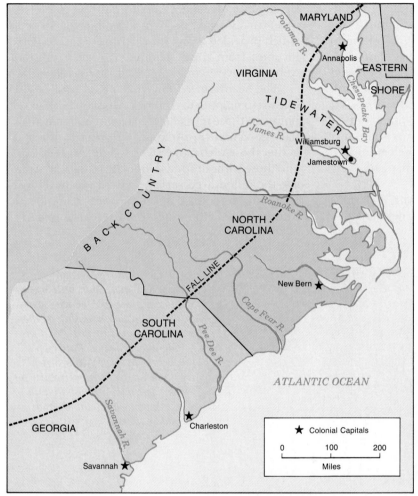

THE SOUTHERN COLONIES

The Lure of Land

Agriculture was the bulwark of life for the Chesapeake settlers and the rest of the colonial south; the tragic experiences of the Jamestown settlement revealed this quickly enough. Jamestown also suggested that a colony could not succeed unless its inhabitants were allowed to own their own land. The first colonists, it will be recalled, were employees of the London Company who had agreed to work for seven years in return for a share of the profits. When their contracts expired, there were few profits. To satisfy these settlers and to attract new capital, the company declared a "dividend" of

land, its only asset. The surviving colonists each received 100 acres. Thereafter, as prospects continued poor, the company relied more and more on grants of land to attract both capital and labor. A number of wealthy Englishmen were given immense tracts, some running to several hundred thousand acres. Lesser persons willing to settle in Virginia received more modest grants. Whether dangled before a great tycoon, a country squire, or a poor farmer, the offer of land had the effect of encouraging immigration to the colony. This was a much-desired end, for without the labor to develop it, the land was worthless.

Soon what was known as the headright system

became entrenched in both Virginia and Maryland. Behind the system lay the eminently sound principle that land should be parceled out according to the availability of labor to cultivate it. For each "head" entering the colony, the government issued a "right" to take any 50 acres of unoccupied land. To "seat" a claim and receive title to the property, the holder of the headright had to mark out its boundaries, plant a crop, and construct some sort of habitation. This system was adopted in all the southern colonies and in Pennsylvania and New Jersey.

The first headrights were issued with no strings attached, but generally the grantor demanded a small annual payment called a quitrent. A quitrent was actually a tax, perhaps a shilling for 50 acres, which provided a way for the proprietors to derive incomes from their colonies. However, quitrents were usually resented and difficult to collect.

The headright system encouraged landless Europeans to migrate to America. More often than not, however, those most eager to come could not afford passage across the Atlantic. In order to bring together those with money who sought land and labor and those without funds who wanted to go to America, the indentured servant system was developed. Indenture resembled apprenticeship. In return for transportation, the indentured servants agreed to

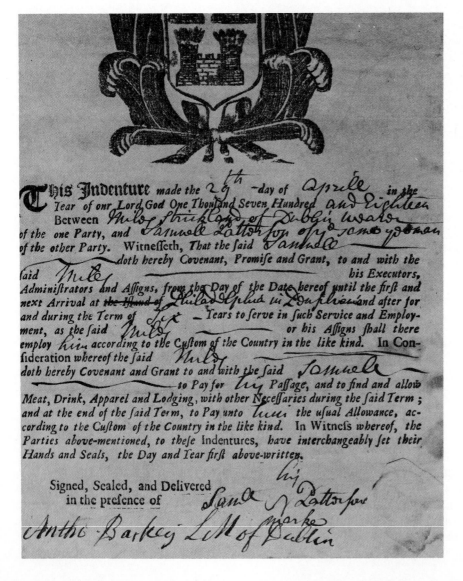

The indentured servant system allowed those with little money to emigrate to America, sometimes on the same ship as their new master. In this 1718 indenture, Samuel Patterson agrees to serve Miles Strickland for six years in return for his passage to Pennsylvania as well as food, clothing, and other necessary effects.

work for a stated period, usually about five years. During that time they were subject to strict control by the master and received no compensation beyond their keep. Indentured women were forbidden to marry, and if they became pregnant (as many did in a land where men outnumbered women by seven to one), the time lost from work that resulted was added to their terms of service. Servants lacked any incentive to work hard, whereas masters tended to "abuse their servantes . . . with intollerable oppression." In this clash of wills the advantage lay with the master; servants lacked full political and civil rights, and masters could administer physical punishment and otherwise abuse them. An indenture, however, was a contract binding on both parties; servants could and did sue when planters failed to fulfill their parts of the bargain, and surviving court records suggest that they fared reasonably well when they did so.

Servants who completed their years of labor became free. Usually the ex-servant was entitled to an "outfit" (a suit of clothes, some farm tools, seed, and perhaps a gun). Custom varied from colony to colony and according to the bargain struck by the two parties when the indenture was signed. In the Carolinas and in Pennsylvania, for example, servants received small grants of land from the colony when their service was completed.

The headrights issued when indentured servants entered the colonies went to whoever paid their passage, not to the servants. Thus the system gave a double reward to capital—land and labor for the price of the labor alone. Since well over half of the white settlers of the southern colonies came as indentured servants, the effect on the structure of southern society was enormous.

Most servants eventually became landowners, but with the passage of time their lot became harder. The best land belonged to the large planters, and low tobacco prices and high local taxes combined to keep many ex-servants in dire poverty. Some were forced to become "squatters" on land along the fringes of settlement that no one had yet claimed. Squatting often led to trouble; eventually someone was sure to turn up with a legal title to the squatter's homestead. Squatters then demanded what they called squatters' rights, the privilege of buying the land from the legal owner without paying for the improvements they had made on it. This led to arguments and lawsuits and sometimes to violence.

By the 1670s conflicts between Virginians who owned choice land and ex-servants on the outer edge of settlement brought the colony to the brink of class warfare. The costs of meeting the region's ever-growing need for labor with indentured servants were becoming prohibitive. Some other solution was needed.

The Resort to Slavery

The first African blacks brought to English North America arrived on a Dutch ship and were sold at Jamestown in 1619. Early records are vague and incomplete, so it is not possible to say whether these Africans were treated as slaves or freed after a period of years like indentured servants. What is certain is that by about 1640 *some* blacks were slaves (a few, with equal certainty, were free) and that by the 1660s local statutes had firmly established the institution in Virginia and Maryland.

Whether slavery produced race prejudice in America or prejudice slavery is a hotly debated, important, and difficult-to-answer question. Most 17th-century Europeans were prejudiced against Africans; the usual reasons that led them to look down on "heathens" with customs other than their own were in the case of Africans greatly reinforced by their blackness, which the English equated with dirt, the devil, danger, and death. "Black is the Colour of Night, Frightful, Dark and Horrid," a popular disquisition of 1704 proclaimed.

Yet the English knew that the Portuguese and Spaniards had enslaved blacks—*negro* is Spanish for "black." Since the English adopted the word as a name for Africans, their treatment of Africans in the New World may also have derived from the Spanish, which suggests that they treated the first blacks in their colonies as slaves from the start.

Probably the Africans' blackness lay at the root of the tragedy. Winthrop D. Jordan, whose research has added enormously to our understanding of the question, has stressed the process by which prejudice and existing enslavement interacted as both cause and effect, bringing about the total debasement of the African. With specific reference to the Chesapeake region, Jordan writes

> The concept of Negro slavery was neither borrowed from foreigners, nor extracted from books, nor invented out of whole cloth, nor extrapolated for servitude, nor generated by English reaction to Negroes

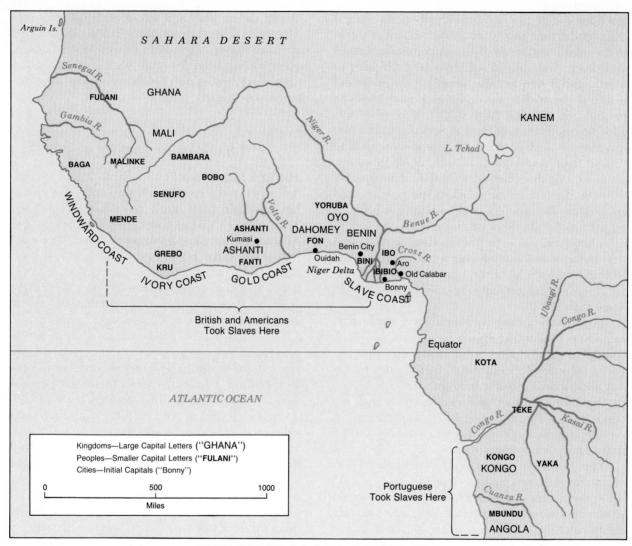

THE WEST COAST OF AFRICA

as such, nor necessitated by the exigencies of the New World. Not any one of these made the Negro a slave, *but all.*

Slavery soon spread throughout the colonies. As early as 1626 there were 11 slaves in New Netherland, and when the English conquered that colony in 1664 there were 700 slaves in a population of about 8,000. The Massachusetts Body of Liberties of 1641—strange title—provided that "there shall never be any bond-slavery . . . amongst us; unlesse it be lawful captives taken in just warrs [i.e., Indians]

and such strangers as willingly sell themselves, or *are solde* to us." However, relatively few blacks were imported until late in the 17th century, even in the southern colonies. In 1650 there were only 300 blacks in Virginia and as late as 1670 no more than 2,000.

White servants were much more highly prized. The African, after all, was utterly alien to both the European and the American ways of life. In a country starved for capital, the cost of slaves—roughly five times that of servants—was another disadvantage. In 1664 the governor of Maryland informed

"Their Darling Tobacco"

TO BE SOLD on board the Ship *Bance-Island*, on tuesday the 6th of *May* next, at *Ashley-Ferry*; a choice cargo of about 250 fine healthy NEGROES, just arrived from the Windward & Rice Coast. — The utmost care has already been taken, and shall be continued, to keep them free from the least danger of being infected with the SMALL-POX, no boat having been on board, and all other communication with people from *Charles-Town* prevented.

Austin, Laurens, & Appleby.

N. B. Full one Half of the above Negroes have had the SMALL-POX in their own Country.

Announcements for the sale of newly imported slaves were plentiful in colonial newspapers—notice the claim that these captives are free from smallpox, an important selling point.

Lord Baltimore that local planters would use more "neigros" "if our purses would endure it."

For these reasons, so long as white servants could be had in sufficient numbers, there were few slaves in the Chesapeake and those that were there generally worked alongside white servants and shared roughly the same food, clothing, and quarters.

In the 1670s the flow of new servants slackened, the result of improving economic conditions in England and the competition of other colonies for servants. At the same time, the formation of the Royal African Company (1672) made slaves more readily available. Then in 1689 a war in Europe cut off a principal market for tobacco, causing the price to fall and thus making migration to the colonies less attractive. The indenture system began to give way to slavery as the "permanent" solution to the region's chronic need for labor. An additional inducement causing planters and politicians to switch was the recognition that, unlike white servants, black slaves (and their offspring) would be forever barred from competing with whites for land or political power.

Labor and land made agriculture possible, but it was necessary to find a market for American crops in the Old World if the colonists were to enjoy anything but the crudest sort of existence. They could not begin to manufacture all the articles they required; to obtain from England such items as plows and muskets and books and chinaware, they had to have cash crops, what their English creditors called "merchantable commodities." Here, at least, fortune favored the Chesapeake.

The founders of Virginia tried to produce all sorts of things that were needed in the old country: grapes and silk in particular, indigo, cotton, oranges, olives, sugar, and many other plants. But it was tobacco, unwanted, even strongly opposed at first, that became for farmers on both sides of Chesapeake Bay "their darling."

Tobacco was unknown in Europe until Spanish explorers brought it back from the West Indies. It was not common in England until the time of Sir Walter Raleigh. Then it quickly proved irresistible to thousands of devotees.

At first the London Company discouraged its colonists from growing tobacco. Since it clearly contained some habit-forming drug, many people opposed its use. King James I wrote a pamphlet attacking the weed, in which, among other things, he anticipated the findings of modern cancer researchers by saying that smoking was a "vile and stinking" habit "dangerous to the Lungs." But English smokers and partakers of snuff ignored their king, and the Virginians ignored their company. By 1617 a pound of tobacco was worth more than 5 shillings in London. Company and Crown then changed their tune, granting the colonists a monopoly and encouraging them in every way.

Unlike wheat, which required expensive plows and oxen to clear the land and prepare the soil, tobacco plants could be set on semicleared land and cultivated with a simple hoe. Tobacco required lots of human labor, but a single laborer working 2 or 3 acres could produce as much as 1,200 pounds of cured tobacco, which, in a good year, yielded a profit of more than 200 percent. This being the case, production in America leaped from 2,500 pounds in 1616 to nearly 30 million pounds in the late 17th century, or roughly 400 pounds of tobacco for every man, woman, and child in the Chesapeake colonies.

The tidewater region was blessed with many navigable rivers, and the planters spread along their banks, giving the Chesapeake a shabby, helter-skelter character of rough habitations and growing tobacco, mostly planted in stump-littered fields, surrounded by fallow land and thickets interspersed with dense forest. There were no towns and almost no roads. English ships made their way up the rivers from farm to farm, gathering the tobacco at each planter's wharf. The vessels also served as general stores of a sort where planters could exchange tobacco for everything from cloth, shoes, tools, salt, and nails to such exotic items as tea, coffee, chocolate, and spices.

However, the tremendous expansion of the supply of tobacco caused the price to plummet in the last decades of the 17th century. This did not stop the expansion of the tobacco colonies, but it did alter the structure of their society. Small farmers found it more difficult to make a decent living. At the same time, men with capital and individuals with political influence were engrossing large tracts of land. If well managed, a big plantation gave its owner important competitive advantages over the small farmer. Tobacco was notorious for the speed with which it exhausted the fertility of the soil. Growers with a lot of land could shift frequently to new fields within their holdings, allowing the old fields to lie fallow and thus maintain high yields, but the only option that small farmers had when their land gave out was to sell it for whatever it would bring, pack up, and move to unsettled land on the frontier. To do that in the 1670s was to risk trouble with properly indignant Indians. It might also violate colonial laws designed to slow westward migration and limit tobacco production—not that either was about to stop settlement.

Bacon's Rebellion

Chesapeake settlers showed little respect for constituted authority, partly because most people lived on isolated plantations and partly because the government in London was usually ignorant of their needs and relatively powerless to control them. The first Virginians often ignored directives of the London Company, and early Marylanders regularly disputed the right of the Calverts' agents to direct the affairs of the proprietorship. The most serious challenge took place in Virginia in 1676. Planters in the outlying counties had many reasons for disliking the officials in Jamestown who ran the colony. The royal governor, Sir William Berkeley, and his "Green Spring" faction (the organization took its name from the governor's plantation, where the leaders customarily met) had ruled Virginia for more than 30 years. Outsiders resented the way Berkeley and his henchmen used their offices to line their pockets. They also resented their social pretensions, for Green Springers made no effort to conceal their opinion, which had considerable basis in fact, that western planters were a crude and vulgar lot.

Early in 1676 planters on the western edge of settlement, always looking for excuses to grab land by doing away with the Indians who owned it, asked Berkeley to authorize an expedition against Indians who had been attacking nearby plantations. Berkeley refused. The planters then took matters into their own hands. Their leader, Nathaniel Bacon, was (and remains today) a controversial figure. His foes described him as extremely ambitious and possessed "of a most imperious and dangerous hidden Pride of heart." But even his sharpest critics conceded that he was "of an inviting aspect and powerful elocution" and well qualified "to lead a giddy and unthinking multitude."

When Berkeley refused to authorize him to attack the Indians, Bacon promptly showed himself only too willing to lead that multitude not only against Indians but even against the governor. Without permission, he raised an army of 500 men, described by the Berkeley faction as "rabble of the basest sort." Berkeley then declared him a traitor.

Several months of monumental confusion followed. Bacon murdered some peaceful Indians, marched on Jamestown and forced Berkeley to legitimize his authority, then headed west again to kill more Indians. In September he returned to Jamestown and burned it to the ground. Berkeley fled across Chesapeake Bay to the Eastern Shore. The Baconites plundered the estates of some of the Green Spring faction. But a few weeks after the destruction of Jamestown, Bacon came down with a "violent flux"—probably a bad case of dysentery—and he died. Soon thereafter an English naval squadron arrived with enough soldiers to restore order. Bacon's Rebellion was over.

On the surface, the uprising changed nothing. No sudden shift in political power occurred. Indeed, Bacon had not sought to change either the political

Sir William Berkeley looks every inch the autocrat in this portrait, a copy of one painted by Sir Peter Lely. After Bacon's death, the governor took his revenge and had 23 rebels hanged. Said King Charles II: "The old fool has killed more people in that naked country than I have done for the murder of my father."

system or the social and economic structure of the colony. But if the rebellion did not change anything specifically, nothing was ever again quite the same after it ended. With seeming impartiality, the Baconites had warred against Indians and against other planters. In retrospect, we might wonder which was the real enemy of anyone interested in growing tobacco. Surely Baconite and Green Springer had no differences that could not be compromised. And their common interest extended beyond the question of how to deal with Indians. "For men bent on the maximum exploitation of labor," the historian Edmund S. Morgan has written, "the implication should have been clear."

There is every reason to think that it was clear. In the quarter century following Bacon's Rebellion, the Chesapeake region, for the reasons just explained, became committed to black slavery. Large differences in the wealth and life-styles of growers

of tobacco resulted. The few who succeeded in accumulating 20 or more slaves and enough land to keep them occupied grew richer. The majority either grew poorer or at best had to struggle to hold their own.

More important, Bacon's Rebellion sealed an implicit contract between the inhabitants of the "great houses" and those who lived in more modest lodgings: Southern whites might differ greatly in wealth and influence, but they stood as one and forever behind the principle that blacks must have neither. This was the basis—the price—of the harmony and prosperity achieved by those who survived "seasoning" in the Chesapeake colonies.

The Carolinas: "More Like a Negro Country"

The English and, in increasing proportions after 1700, the Scotch-Irish settlers of the tidewater parts of the Carolinas turned to agriculture as enthusiastically as their Chesapeake neighbors had. In substantial sections of what became North Carolina, tobacco flourished. In South Carolina, after two decades in which furs and cereals were the chief products, Madagascar rice was introduced in the low-lying coastal areas in 1696. It quickly proved its worth as a cash crop. By 1700 almost 100,000 pounds were being exported annually; by the eve of the Revolution, rice exports from South Carolina and Georgia exceeded 65 million pounds a year.

Rice culture required water for flooding the fields. At first freshwater swamps were adapted to the crop, but by the middle of the 18th century the chief rice fields lay along the tidal rivers and inlets. Dikes and floodgates allowed fresh water to flow across the fields with the rising tide; when the tide fell, the gates closed automatically to keep the water in. The process was reversed when it was necessary to drain the land. Then the water ran out as the tide ebbed, and the pressure of the next flood pushed the gates shut.

In the 1740s another cash crop, indigo, was introduced in South Carolina by Eliza Lucas. Indigo did not compete with rice for either land or labor. It prospered on high ground and needed care in seasons when the slaves were not busy in the rice paddies. The British were delighted to have a new source of indigo because the blue dye was important in their woolens industry. Parliament quickly placed a bounty on it to stimulate production.

The production of tobacco, rice, and indigo, along with furs and forest products such as tar and resin, meant that the southern colonies had no difficulty in obtaining manufactured articles from abroad. Planters dealt with agents in England and Scotland, called factors, who managed the sale of their crops, filled their orders for manufactures, and supplied them with credit. This was a great convenience but not necessarily an advantage, for it prevented the development of a diversified economy. Throughout the colonial era, while small-scale manufacturing developed rapidly in the north, it was stillborn in the south.

Reliance on European middlemen also retarded the development of urban life. Until the rise of Baltimore in the 1750s, Charleston was the only city of importance in the south, but it never rivaled Boston, New York, or Philadelphia, despite its rich export trade and fine harbor.

On the South Carolina rice plantations, slave labor predominated from the beginning, for free workers would not submit to the backbreaking and unhealthy regimen. The first quarter of the 18th century saw an enormous influx of Africans into all the southern colonies. By 1730 roughly three out of every ten people south of Pennsylvania were black, and in South Carolina the blacks were in the majority. "Carolina," remarked a newcomer in 1737, "looks more like a negro country than like a country settled by white people."

Given the existing race prejudice and the degrading impact of slavery, this demographic change had an enormous impact on life wherever blacks were concentrated. In each colony, regulations governing the behavior of blacks, both free and slave, increased in severity as the density of the black population increased. The South Carolina Negro Act of 1740 denied slaves "freedom of movement, freedom of assembly, freedom to raise (their own) food, to earn money, to learn to read English." The blacks had no civil rights under any of these codes, and punishments were sickeningly severe. Whipping was common for minor offenses, death by hanging or by being burned alive for serious crimes. Blacks were sometimes castrated for sexual offenses—even for lewd talk about white women—or for repeated attempts to escape.

That blacks resented slavery goes without saying, but since slavery did not mean the same thing to all of them, their reactions to it varied. Throughout the 18th century a constant stream of new slaves was arriving from Africa. These "outlandish" blacks tended to respond differently than American-born slaves. Among the latter, field hands experienced a different kind of slavery than household servants, and slave artisans faced still another set of circumstances. In short, the slaves' places in society influenced their behavior.

The master race sought to acculturate the slaves in order to make them more efficient workers. A slave who could understand English was easier to order about; one who could handle farm tools or wait on table was more useful than one who could not; a carpenter or a mason was more valuable still. But acculturation increased the slave's independence and mobility, and this posed problems. Field hands seldom tried to escape; they expressed their dissatisfactions by pilferage and petty sabotage, by laziness, or by feigning stupidity. Most runaways were artisans who hoped to "pass" as free in a nearby town. It was one of the many paradoxes of slavery that the more valuable a slave became, the harder that slave was to control.

Yet few runaway slaves became rebels. Indeed, organized slave rebellions were rare, and though individual assaults by blacks on whites were common enough, personal violence was also common among whites, then and throughout American history. But the masters had sound reasons for fearing their slaves; the particular viciousness of the system lay in the fact that oppression bred resentment, which in turn produced still greater oppression.

What is superficially astonishing is that the whites—absolute masters of their human property—grossly exaggerated the danger of slave revolts. They pictured the black as a kind of malevolent ogre, powerful, bestial, and lascivious, a caldron of animal emotions that had to be restrained at any cost. Probably the characteristics they attributed to the blacks were really projections of their own passions. The most striking illustration of this process was the universal white fear of the "mongrelization" of the race: If blacks were free, they would breed with whites. Yet in practice the interbreeding, which indeed took place, was almost exclusively the result of white men using their power as masters to have sexual relations with female slaves.

Thus the "peculiar institution" was fastened upon America with economic, social, and psychic

An idealized view of slave life shows the black family when work for the master is finished, catching their own fish, harvesting fruits from their own garden plot. In reality most slaves had time to pursue such tasks only at the end of an exhausting day in the master's fields.

barbs. Ignorance and self-interest, lust for gold and for the flesh, primitive prejudices and complex social and legal ties all combined to convince the whites that black slavery was not so much a good thing as a fact of life. A few isolated reformers, mostly Quakers, attacked the institution on the religious ground that all human beings are equal before God: "Christ dyed for all, both *Turks, Barbarians, Tartarians,* and *Ethyopians.*" Yet a few Quakers owned slaves, and even the majority who did not usually succumbed to color prejudice. Blackness was a defect, but it was no justification for enslavement, they argued. And they attracted little attention anywhere—none in areas where slavery was important.

Home and Family in the Colonial South

Life for all but the most affluent planters was by modern standards crude and uncomfortable. Houses were mostly one- and two-room affairs. Professor Gloria L. Main describes them as "small, dark, crowded . . . crudely built of green wood, unpainted and unadorned," and another colonial historian, David Freeman Hawke, employs the word *hovel.* Furniture and utensils were sparse and crudely made. Chairs were rare; if a family possessed one it was reserved for the head of the house (hence *chairman,* the man in the chair). People sat, slept, and ate on benches and planks. The typical dining table (the term itself was not in use) was made of two boards nailed together and covered, if at all, with a "board cloth." Toilets and plumbing of any kind were unknown; even chamber pots were beyond the reach of poorer families.

Work clothes—and few ordinary people possessed anything else—were equally crude, and since soap was expensive, they were rarely washed and therefore foul-smelling and often infested with vermin. Food was plentiful but nearly always prepared without art. Corn, served as bread, hominy, pancakes, and in various other forms, was the chief staple. But there was plenty of beef and pork (as well as a profusion of game), usually boiled in a pot along with various vegetables over an open fire.

Women (even indentured ones) rarely worked in the fields, but every aspect of household maintenance was their responsibility, including tending to farm animals, making butter and cheese, pickling and preserving, spinning and sewing, and, of course, caring for the children, which often involved orphans and stepchildren because of the fragility of life in the region. For exceptional women, the labor shortage created opportunities to develop their talents. Some managed large plantations; Eliza Lucas ran three in South Carolina for her absent father while still in her teens, and after the death of her husband, Charles Pinckney, she successfully managed his large properties.

Because of the high death rate, second and third marriages were common. Despite the likelihood that a widow would soon remarry, studies of wills reveal that most southern men took special pains to provide for their wives and expressed confidence in their ability to manage the inheritance effectively. The effects of the deaths of so many parents on children are hard to gauge but apparently were not often psychologically damaging, no doubt because they were so common and because someone could always be found to take in and care for an orphan.

Southern children were not usually subjected to the strict discipline that children in New England were (see page 48), but the difference was relative. Formal schooling for ordinary youngsters was nonexistent; the isolated rural character of society made the maintenance of schools prohibitively expensive. Whatever most children learned, they got from their parents or other relatives. A large percentage of

A southern plantation of the "middling" sort was this Virginia property, Rippon Lodge. The steeply pitched roofs and tall chimneys show English influence. Like almost all colonial homes, no matter how grand, this one lacked screens or nets to keep out the numerous flies and mosquitoes.

southerners were illiterate. As in other regions, children were put to some kind of useful work at an early age.

More well-to-do, "middling" planters had different, more comfortable life-styles, but they still lived in relatively crowded quarters, having perhaps three rooms to house a family of four or five and a couple of servants. To sleep between sheets in a soft bed under blankets and quilts was luxury indeed in that world. Food in greater variety and abundance was another indication of a higher standard of living, but cooking methods remained for such families rudimentary.

Until the early 18th century only a handful achieved real affluence. (The richest by far was Robert "King" Carter of Lancaster County, Virginia, who at the time of his death in 1732 owned 1,000 slaves and 300,000 acres.) That fortunate few, masters of several plantations and many slaves, lived in solid, two-story houses of six or more rooms, fur-

nished with English and other imported carpets, chairs, tables, wardrobes, chests, china, and silver. When the occasion warranted, the men wore fine broadcloth, the women the latest (or more likely the next-to-latest, for this was a provincial society) fashions. Some even sent their children abroad for schooling. The founding of the College of William and Mary in Williamsburg, Virginia, in 1696 was an effort to provide the region with its own institution of higher learning. However, staffing problems and insufficient funding kept William and Mary from offering much more than a grammar school education for decades.

These large planters also controlled politics; they held the commissions in the militia, the county judgeships, and the seats in the colonial legislatures. The control that these "leading families" exercised over their neighbors was not entirely unearned, and it was not, of course, total. They were, in general, responsible leaders, and ordinary planters deferred to them in most instances as a matter of course. Custom required that they throw open their houses and serve copious amounts of punch and rum to ordinary voters when election time rolled around. Such gatherings served to acknowledge the representative nature of the system.

Their scattered existence meant that no matter what their station, southern families led relatively isolated lives. Churches, which might be expected to serve as centers of community life, were few and far between. By the middle of the 18th century, the Anglican church was the official religion, its ministers supported by public funds. The Virginia assembly had made attendance at Anglican services compulsory in 1619. In Maryland, Lord Baltimore's Toleration Act did not survive the invasion of the colony by militant Puritans. It was repealed in 1654, reenacted in 1657, then repealed again in 1692 when the Anglican church was established. But for all its legal standing, the Anglican church was not a very powerful force in the south. Most of the ministers the bishop of London sent to America were second-rate men unable to obtain a decent living at home. If they had intellectual or spiritual ambitions when they arrived, their rural circumstances provided little opportunity to develop them. Most people, regardless of their particular faith, had few opportunities to attend formal services. One result was that marriages tended to become civil rather than religious ceremonies.

Social events of any kind, such as the aforementioned politicking, were great occasions. Births, marriages, and especially funerals called for much feasting; if there were neither heirs nor debts to satisfy, which was not unusual in the early days, it was possible to consume the entire contents of a modest estate in celebrating the deceased's passing. (At one Maryland funeral the guests were provided with 55 gallons of an alcoholic concoction composed of brandy, cider, and sugar.)

Other forms of entertainment and relaxation included hunting and fishing, cockfights, and horse racing. Horses were widely owned, used for getting from place to place rather than as draft animals, since tobacco was transported by water and cultivated with hoes, not plows.

However, southern planters, even the most successful, were hardworking, conserving types, not idle grandees concerned chiefly with conspicuous display. The vast, undeveloped country encouraged them to produce and then invest their savings in more production. William Byrd II (1674–1744), one of the richest men in Virginia, habitually rose before dawn. Besides his tobacco fields, he operated a sawmill and a gristmill, prospected for iron and coal, and engaged in the Indian trade. Of another wealthy planter, Robert Beverly, a visitor wrote: "Though rich, he has nothing in or about his house but what is necessary. . . . He lives upon the product of his land."

Georgia and the Back Country

West of the fall line of the rivers that irrigated tidewater Chesapeake and Carolina lay the back country, or "back parts." This region included the Great Valley of Virginia, the Piedmont, and what became the final English colony to be founded in North America, Georgia.

The circumstances of the founding of Georgia were most unusual. A group of London philanthropists concerned over the plight of honest persons imprisoned for debt conceived of settling these unfortunates in the New World, where they might make a fresh start. (Here is striking evidence that Europeans were still beguiled by the prospect of regenerating their society in the New World. All told, about 50,000 British convicts were "transported" to America in the colonial period, partly to get rid of "undesirables" but partly for humane reasons.) They petitioned for a grant south of the Carolinas, and the government, eager to create a buffer between South Carolina and the hostile Spanish in Florida, readily granted a charter (1732) to a group of "trustees" who were to manage the colony without profit to themselves for a period of 21 years.

In 1733 the leader of the trustees, James Oglethorpe, founded Savannah. Oglethorpe was a complicated person, vain, high-handed, and straitlaced, yet hardworking and idealistic. He hoped to people the colony with sober and industrious yeoman farmers. Land grants were limited to 50 acres and made nontransferable. To ensure sobriety, rum and other "Spirits and Strong Waters" were banned. To guarantee that the colonists would have to work hard, the entry of "any Black . . . Negroe" was prohibited. The Indian trade was to be strictly regulated in the interest of fair dealing.

Oglethorpe intended that silk, wine, and olive oil be the main products—none of which, unfortunately, could be profitably produced in Georgia.

His noble intentions came to naught. The settlers swiftly found ways to circumvent all restrictions. Rum flowed, slaves were imported, and large landholdings were amassed. Georgia developed an economy much like South Carolina's. In 1752 the trustees, disillusioned, abandoned their responsibilities. Georgia then became a royal colony.

It was only about this time that settlers in any numbers penetrated the rest of the southern back country. So long as cheap land remained available closer to the coast and Indians along the frontier remained a threat, only the most daring and footloose hunters or fur traders lived far inland. But once settlement began, it began with a rush. Chief among those making the trek were Scotch-Irish and German immigrants. By 1770 the back country contained about 250,000 settlers, 10 percent of the population of the colonies.

This internal migration did not proceed altogether peacefully. In 1771 a pitched battle was fought in North Carolina between frontiersmen calling themselves Regulators and 1,200 troops dispatched by the Carolina assembly, which was dominated by low-country interests. The Regulators were protesting their lack of representation in the assembly. They were crushed and their leaders executed. This was neither the last nor the bloodiest sectional conflict in American history.

Salem was an early settlement in the Piedmont region of North Carolina, founded in the 1760s by Moravians. It boasted brick dwellings more substantial than the usual frontier cabins. Early in the 20th century Salem was united with nearby Winston to form the city of Winston-Salem.

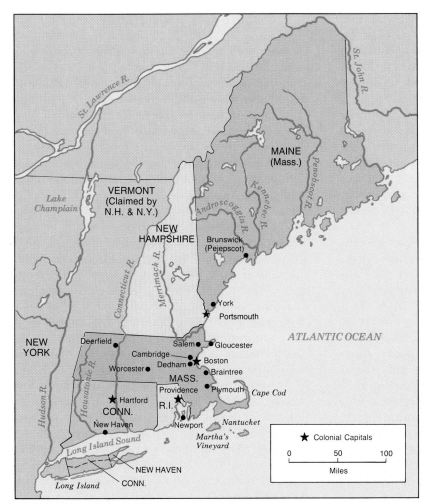

COLONIAL NEW ENGLAND

Colonial New England: A Covenanted People

If survival in the Chesapeake required junking many European notions about social arrangements and submitting to the dictates of the wilderness, was this also true in Massachusetts and Connecticut? Ultimately it probably was, but in the early going, Puritan ideas certainly fought the New England reality to a draw.

Boston is located slightly more than 5° latitude north of Jamestown and almost 10° north of Charleston. Like other early New England towns and unlike these southern ones, Boston had a dependable water supply. The surrounding patchwork of forest, pond, dunes, and tide marsh was much more open than the malaria-infested terrain of the tidewater and low-country south. These differences alone made New England a much healthier habitat for settlers. "Seasoning" proceeded so imperceptibly as almost to escape notice. One consequence was that New Englanders escaped the "agues and fevers" that beset settlers to the south, leaving them free to attend to their spiritual, economic, and social well-being.

The Stamp of Puritanism: Family Bonds

New England's Puritans were set apart from other English settlers by how much—and how long—they lived out of their baggage. The supplies the first arrivals brought with them eased their adjustment, as did the wherewithal of later, equally heavily laden arrivals. The Puritans' baggage, however, included besides pots and pans, saws and shovels, a plan for the proper ordering of society.

At the center of the plan was a covenant, or agreement, to ensure the upright behavior of all who took up residence. They sought to provide what John Winthrop described to the passengers on the *Arbella* as the two imperatives of human existence: "that every man might have need of other, and from hence they might be all knitt more nearly together in the Bond of brotherly affection."

The first and most important covenant governing Puritan behavior was that binding family members. The family's authority was backed by the Fifth Commandment: "Honor thy father and thy mother, that thy days may be long upon the land." In a properly ordered Puritan family, as elsewhere in the colonies, authority flowed downward. Sociologists describe such a family as nuclear and patriarchal; each household contained one family, and in it, the father was boss. His principal responsibilities consisted of providing for the physical welfare of all members of the household, including any servants, and making sure that they behaved properly, in private and in public. Economic dealings between the family and other parties were also transacted by him, even when the property involved had been owned by his wife prior to their marriage.

The Reverend John Cotton's outline of a woman's responsibilities clearly establishes her subordinate position: She should keep house, educate the children, and improve "what is got by the industry of the man." Cotton, please recall, had been Anne Hutchinson's favorite minister! The poet Anne Bradstreet reduced the functions of a Puritan woman to two: "loving Mother and obedient Wife." Colonial New England, and the southern colonies as well, did have their female blacksmiths, silversmiths, shipwrights, gunsmiths, and butchers as well as shopkeepers and teachers. Such early examples of domestic "liberation," however, were mostly widows and the wives of incapacitated husbands. Even so, most widows, especially young ones, quickly remarried. According to the historian Laurel Thatcher Ulrich, colonial women generally, and New England women in particular, "were by definition basically domestic."

Women and Children

Dealings with neighbors and relatives and involvement in church activities marked the outer limits of the social range of most Puritan women. Care of the children was a full-time occupation when broods of 12 or 14 were more common than those of 1 or 2. Fewer children died in New England than in the Chesapeake or in Europe, though few families escaped a miscarriage or a child's death along the way. Childbearing and motherhood, therefore, likely extended over two decades of a woman's life. Meanwhile, she also functioned as the chief operating officer of the household. Cooking, baking, sewing, and supervising servants, as well as mastering such arcane knowledge as the chemistry needed to make cheese from milk, bacon from pork, and beer from malt, all fell to her. These jobs were physically demanding, though not so debilitating as to prevent large numbers of New England wives from seeing one or more husbands off to the hereafter.

As Puritan social standards required husbands to rule over wives, so parents ruled over children. As in the South, the virtue most insistently impressed upon New England children was obedience. Refusal to submit to parental direction was disturbing in itself and for what it implied about the child's eternal condition. Cotton Mather's advice, "Better whipt, than damned," graced many a New England rod taken up by a parent in anger, from there to be rapidly transferred to the afterparts of misbehaving offspring.

Besides the generous use of corporal punishment, chores kept children out of mischief. By age 6 or 7, girls were set to sewing and helping with housework and boys put to work outdoors. When a few years older, a child might be sent to live with another family to take up the duties of a servant or apprentice. Discussing a later period, the historian Mary P. Ryan writes: "Parents conceived of their children as their own flesh, blood, and labor supply." Only when well into adulthood would children emerge from under parental control.

Such practices, particularly when set beside portraits of early New England families, which depict toddlers as somber-faced miniature adults wearing clothes indistinguishable from those of their parents, convey the impression that Puritans hustled their young through childhood with as little love as possible. New Englanders harbored no illusions.

New England children like David, Joanna, and Abigail Mason (painted by an unknown artist about 1670) were expected to emulate adults in their chores and their appearance. Nevertheless, indications are that they were cherished by their parents in a way closer to modern family love than what their European contemporaries experienced.

"Innocent vipers" is how one minister described children, having 14 of his own to submit as evidence. Anne Bradstreet, mother of eight, characterized one as harboring "a perverse will, a love of what's forbid / a serpent's sting in pleasing face lay hid."

Yet for all their acceptance of the Calvinist doctrine of infant damnation, Puritan parents were not indifferent to the fate of their children. "I do hope," Cotton Mather confessed at the burial of one of the eight children he lost before the age of 2, "that when my children are gone they are not lost; but carried unto the Heavenly Feast with Abraham." Even the dour Michael Wigglesworth assigned children who died in infancy "the easiest room in hell."

Population growth reinforced Puritan ideas about the family. With the end of the Great Migration in the early 1640s, immigration virtually ceased. Thereafter growth was entirely due to the region's extraordinarily high birthrate (50 births for every 1,000 population, more than three times the rate today) and strikingly low mortality rate (about 20 per 1,000). This resulted in a population much more evenly distributed by age and sex than that in the south. The fact that most New England women married in their early twenties rather than their late teens suggests that the demand for women matched the supply. Demographic realities joined with Puritan expectations to create a society of nuclear families distinct to the region.

Visible Saints and Others

When it came to religion, Puritans believed that church membership ought not to be a presumptive right, as in Catholic countries or in Anglican England, but the joint decision of a would-be member and those already in the church.

Obvious sinners and people ignorant of Christian doctrine were rejected out of hand. But what of "outwardly just" applicants who lacked compelling evidence that they had experienced God's saving grace? In the late 1630s, with the Great Migration in full swing and new arrivals clamoring for admission to the churches, such "merit-mongers" were excluded, thereby limiting church membership to the community's "visible saints." A decade later, the Great Migration over and applications down, some of the saints began to have second thoughts.

By the early 1650s fewer than half of all New England adults were church members, and so exacting had the examination for membership become, particularly in churches where the minister and elders outdid each other in the ferocity of their questioning, that most young people refused to submit themselves to such scrutiny. How these growing numbers of nonmembers could be compelled to attend church services was a problem ministers could not long defer. Meanwhile, the magistrates found it harder to defend the policy of not letting taxpayers vote because they were not church members. But what really forced reconsideration of the membership policy was the concerns of nonmember parents about the souls of their children, who could not be baptized.

At first the churches permitted baptism of the children of church members. Later, some biblical purists (including a Harvard president fired for insisting as much) came out against infant baptism altogether. But most early Puritans approved of the practice, which allowed them the hope that a child who died after receiving baptism might at least be spared Hell's hottest precincts. Since most of the first generation were church members, nearly all the second-generation New Englanders were baptized, whether they became church members or not. The problem began with the third generation, the offspring of parents who had been baptized but who did not become church members. By the mid-1650s it was clear that if nothing were done, soon a majority of the people would be living in a state of original sin. If that happened, how could Puritan values, and for that matter the churches themselves, remain the dominant force in New England life?

Fortunately, a way out was at hand. In 1657 an assembly of Massachusetts and Connecticut ministers recommended a form of intermediate church membership that would permit the baptism of people who were not visible saints. Five years later, some 80 ministers and laymen met at Boston's First Church to hammer out what came to be called the Half-Way Covenant. It provided limited (halfway) membership for any applicant not known to be a sinner who was willing to accept the provisions of the church covenant. They and their children could be baptized, but the sacrament of communion and a voice in church decision making were reserved for full members.

The General Court of Massachusetts promptly endorsed the recommendations of the Half-Way Synod and urged all the churches of the commonwealth to adopt them. Two years later it quietly extended the right to vote to halfway church members.

Opponents of the Half-Way Covenant argued that it reflected a slackening of religious fervor. Michael Wigglesworth gave poetic voice to these views in "God's Controversy with New England" and "The Day of Doom," both written in 1662.

Perry Miller, an authority on Puritan New England, argued that the early 1660s marked the beginning of the decline, or "declension," of the Puritan experiment. Some loss of religious intensity there may have been, but the rise in church memberships, the continuing prestige accorded ministers, and the lessening of intrachurch squabbling in the decades after the Half-Way Covenant was adopted suggest that the secularization of New England society had a long way to go.

Democracies Without Democrats

Like the southern colonies, the governments of Massachusetts, Connecticut, Rhode Island, and New Hampshire derived their authority from charters granted by the Crown or Parliament. Except for rare fits of meddling London bureaucrats, they were largely left to their own devices where purely local interests were concerned. This typically involved maintaining order by regulating how people behaved.

According to Puritan theory, government was both a civil covenant, entered into by all who came within its jurisdiction, and the principal mechanism for policing the institutions on which the maintenance of the social order depended. When the Massachusetts and Connecticut general courts passed laws requiring church attendance, levying taxes for the support of the clergy, and banning Quakers from practicing their faith, they were acting as a "shield of the churches." When they provided the death penalty both for adultery and for blaspheming a parent, they were defending the integrity of families, the "nurseries of the commonwealth." When they set the price a laborer might charge for his services or even the amount of gold braid that servants might wear on their jackets, they believed they were enforcing the Puritan principle that people must accept their assigned stations in life.

Most of these laws went unnoticed in England. Those upholding the privileged position of the Congregational church, however, came under sharp attack from English Anglicans, Presbyterians, and Quakers. When the Massachusetts General Court condemned to death four stubborn Quakers who returned after being expelled from the colony, a royal order of 1662 forbade further executions.

Laws like these have prompted historians and Americans generally to characterize New England colonial legislation as socially repressive and personally invasive. Yet many of the laws remained in force through the colonial period without arousing much local opposition. Others, particularly those upholding religious discrimination or restricting economic activity, were repealed at the insistence of Parliament.

A healthy respect for the backsliding ways of humanity obliged New Englanders not to depend too much on provincial governments, whose jurisdiction extended over several thousand square miles. Almost of necessity, the primary responsibility for maintaining "Good Order and Peace" fell to the more than 500 towns of the region. These differed greatly in size and development. By the early 18th century the largest—Boston, Newport, and Portsmouth—were well along toward becoming urban centers. This was before "frontier" towns like Amherst, Kent, and Hanover had even been founded. Nonetheless, town life gave New England the distinctiveness it has still not wholly lost.

Dedham: A Typical Town

Dedham, Massachusetts, whose early history has been meticulously reconstructed by Kenneth Lockridge, illustrates how this worked. In 1634 the heads of 30 households in Watertown, already feeling crowded in that then two-year-old village, petitioned the General Court for a grant of land to establish a new town. A year later they became the proprietors of a 200-square-mile tract west of Watertown on the condition that they all move there, "gather" a church, and organize a town government. These "proprietors" then drew up a town covenant, which committed all who signed it to conduct themselves "according to that most perfect rule, the foundation wherof is everlasting love." Other clauses bound them to keep out the "contrary minded," to submit personal differences to the judgment of the town, and to conduct their business so as to create a "loving and comfortable society in our said town."

The covenant provided that town business be decided at semiannual town meetings, at which all male adults who had subscribed to the covenant could vote. At these meetings a representative to the General Court was to be elected and seven selectmen chosen to run the town between town meetings. In addition, matters relating to town lands were to be decided, taxes to pay the minister's salary set, and provisions for poor and incompetent people made.

The next century brought many changes to Dedham. Yet when the town's 1,200 residents celebrated its centenary in 1736, they were governing themselves much as their great-grandparents had. Looking back, they could only be struck by the continuities that shaped their lives.

But was colonial New England democratic? To be democratic, a government must at least offer those subject to its authority a voice in its operations. With the possible exception of the 1670s and 1680s, when a stiff property-holding requirement (£80 of taxable estate) was in effect in Massachusetts and Connecticut, most adult male New Englanders could vote. Compared with England or with the southern colonies, where blacks had no political rights, the New England governments were democratic.

Relatively few voters, however, bothered to participate in elections because most offices went uncontested. Furthermore, the men elected to office consistently came from the wealthiest and most established levels of the community. In Dedham, 5 percent of the adult males filled 60 percent of the town's positions. Even in Rhode Island, widely regarded as almost too democratic, Providence and Newport voters usually elected their wealthiest and longest-settled townsmen. Important families, such as the Otises of Barnstable, the Quincys of Braintree, and the Wolcotts of Windsor, had members serving as moderator of the town meeting or deputy to the General Court so often as to make these offices almost hereditary.

Ordinary voters tended to choose their "betters," and those they selected took the responsibilities of public office seriously. Together they created what one voter called "a speaking aristocracy in the face of a silent democracy."

The Dominion of New England

The most serious threat to these arrangements occurred in the 1680s. Following the execution of Charles I in 1649, England was ruled by one man, the Lord Protector, Oliver Cromwell. Cromwell's death in 1658 led to the restoration of the Stuart monarchy in the person of Charles II (1660–1685). During his reign and the abbreviated one of his brother, James II (1685–1688), the government sought to bring the colonies under effective royal control.

Massachusetts seemed in particular need of supervision. Accordingly, in 1684 its charter was annulled, and the colony, along with all those north of Pennsylvania, became part of the Dominion of New England, governed by Edmund Andros.

Andros arrived in Boston in late 1686 with orders to make the northern colonies, Massachusetts most of all, behave in ways consistent with their status as colonies. Specifically, he set out to abolish popular assemblies, to change the land-grant system so as to provide the king with quitrents, and to enforce religious toleration, particularly of Anglicans. The historian Stephen Saunders Webb has characterized the Dominion as designed to bring about the political and cultural "Anglicization" of New England. Andros, a professional soldier and administrator, scoffed at people who resisted his authority. "Knoweing no other government then their owne," he said, they "think it best, and are wedded to . . . it."

Fortunately for New Englanders so wedded, the Dominion fell victim two years later to yet another political turnabout in England, the Glorious Revolution. In 1688 Parliament decided it had had enough of the Catholic-leaning Stuarts and sent James II packing. In his place it installed a more resolutely Protestant Dutchman, William of Orange, and his wife, James's daughter Mary. When news of these events reached Boston in the spring of 1689, a force of more than 1,000 colonists led by a contingent of ministers seized Andros and lodged him in jail. Two years later Massachusetts was made a royal colony that also included Plymouth and Maine. As in all such colonies, the governor was appointed by the king. The new General Court was elected by property owners; church membership was no longer required for voting.

Crisis in Salem Village

Many New England towns resembled "peaceable kingdoms." But in some, tensions developed between generations when they ran out of land sufficient to support the grandchildren of the founders. Others allowed petty disputes to divide townspeople into rival camps. Still others seemed doomed to serious discord. Among these, Salem Village provides a singular example.

In 1666, families living in the rural outback of the thriving town of Salem petitioned the General Court for the right to establish their own church. Politically and economically, this was a questionable move and the Salem selectmen, fearing the loss of taxes, vigorously objected. But in 1672 the General Court authorized the establishment of a separate

parish. In so doing the court put the 600-odd inhabitants of the village politically on their own as well.

Over the next 15 years three preachers came and went before, in 1689, one Samuel Parris became minister. He had spent 20 years in the Caribbean as a merchant and had taken up preaching only three years before coming to Salem Village. Accompanying him were his wife; a daughter, Betty; a niece, Abigail; and the family's West Indian slave, Tituba, who told fortunes and practiced magic on the side.

Parris proved as incapable of bringing peace to the feuding factions of Salem Village as his predecessors had. In January 1692 the church voted to dismiss him.

At this point Betty and Abigail, now 9 and 11, along with Ann Putnam, the 12-year-old daughter of their father's principal supporter, started "uttering foolish, ridiculous speeches which neither they themselves nor any others could make sense of." A doctor diagnosed the girls' ravings as the work of the "Evil Hand" and declared them bewitched.

But who had done the bewitching? The first persons accused were three women whose unsavory reputations and frightening appearances made them likely candidates. Sarah Good, a pauper with a nasty tongue, Sarah Osborne, a bedridden widow, and the slave Tituba, who had brought suspicion on herself by volunteering to bake a "witch cake," made of rye meal and the girls' urine. The cake should be fed to a dog, Tituba said. If the girls were truly afflicted, the dog would show signs of bewitchment!

The three women were brought before the local deputies to the General Court to determine whether they should be formally charged. As each was questioned, the girls went into contortions; "their arms, necks and backs turned this way and that way . . . their mouths stopped, their throats choked, their limbs wracked and tormented." Tituba, likely impressed by the powers ascribed to her, promptly confessed to being a witch. Sarah Good and Sarah Osborne each claimed to be innocent, although Sarah Good expressed doubts about Sarah Osborne. All three were sent to jail on suspicion of witchcraft.

These proceedings triggered new accusations. By the end of April, 24 more people had been charged with practicing witchcraft, among them several prominent residents of the town of Salem.

These scenes from an English treatise on witches, devils, and other supernatural beings reflect common beliefs about what such creatures might do. Belief in witchcraft was widespread in Europe and America in the 17th century, but no other episode in the colonies matched the Salem crisis in severity. All convictions were eventually reversed—the last ones in 1957.

Officials in neighboring Andover, lacking their own "bewitched," called in the girls to help with their investigations. By May the hunt had extended to Maine and Boston and up the social ladder to some of the colony's most prominent citizens, including Lady Mary Phips, whose husband, William, had just been appointed governor.

By June, when Governor Phips convened a spe-cial court consisting of members of his council, more than 150 persons (Lady Phips no longer among them) stood formally charged with practicing witch-craft. In the next four months the court found grounds for convicting 28 persons, most of them women. Five "confessed" and were spared; the rest were condemned to death. One woman won a re-prieve because she was pregnant. Two others es-caped. But 19 persons were hanged. The husband of a convicted witch refused to enter a plea when charged with being a "wizard." He was executed by having stones piled on him until he suffocated.

Because anyone who spoke in defense of the accused was in danger of being charged with witch-craft, hostile testimony dominated the proceedings. Even so, some brave souls did challenge both the procedures and the findings of the court. Finally, at the urging of the leading ministers of the com-monwealth, Governor Phips adjourned the court and forbade any further executions.

No one involved in these gruesome proceedings escaped with reputation intact, but those whose rep-utations suffered most were the ministers. Among the clergy, only Increase Mather deserves any credit. He persuaded Phips to halt the executions, arguing that "it were better that ten witches should escape, than that one innocent person should be con-demned."

The behavior of his son Cotton defies apology. It was not that Cotton Mather accepted the existence of witches—at the time everyone did, which suggests that Tituba was not the only person in Salem who practiced witchcraft—or even that Mather took such pride in being the resident expert on demonology. It was rather his vindictiveness. He insisted re-peatedly that only the most "vigorous prosecution" could rid the commonwealth of its demonic afflic-tions. He even stood at the foot of the gallows bul-lying hesitant hangmen into doing "their duty."

"To Advance Learning"

Along with the farmers and artisans who settled in New England with their families during the Great Migration came nearly 150 university-trained col-onists. Nearly all had studied divinity. Most of the older ones had started out as Anglican ministers. The younger ones despaired of securing pulpits in the England of King Charles and Bishop Laud. For both generations, New England held the promise of religious freedom and professional fulfillment.

These men became the first ministers in Massachusetts and Connecticut. In the late 1630s, churches were being founded at a rate of more than 15 a year. A brisk "seller's market" existed for would-be ministers. Larger churches began stockpiling candidates by hiring newly arrived Cambridge and Oxford graduates as assistants or teachers in anticipation of the retirement of their senior ministers. But what to do when as a 1643 promotional pamphlet, *New Englands First Fruits,* put it, "our present ministers shall lie in the dust"? More than any other factor, fear of leaving "an illiterate Ministry to the Churches" turned New Englanders early and resolutely to finding a way to "advance learning and perpetuate it to Posterity."

In 1636 the Massachusetts General Court appropriated £400 to found "a schoole or colledge." Two years later, just as the first freshmen gathered in Cambridge, John Harvard left the college £800 and his library. After a shaky start, during which students conducted a hunger strike against a sadistic and larcenous headmaster, Harvard settled into an annual pattern of admitting a dozen or so 14-year-old boys, stuffing their heads with four years of theology, logic, and mathematics, and then sending them out into the wider world of New England.

Immediately below Harvard on the educational ladder came the grammar schools, where boys spent seven years learning Latin and Greek "so far as they may be fitted for the Universitie." Boston founded the first, the Boston Latin School, in 1636. Massachusetts and Connecticut soon passed education acts that required all towns of any size to establish such schools. New Englanders hoped, as the preamble to the Massachusetts law of 1647 stated, to thwart "that old deluder, Satan," whose "chief object was to keep men from the knowledge of the Scriptures."

Not every New England town required to maintain a school actually did so. Towns that did often paid their teachers poorly. Only the most dedicated or otherwise unemployable Harvard graduates took up teaching as a career. Some parents kept their children at their chores rather than at school. Yet the cumulative effect of the Puritan community's educational institutions, the family and the church as well as the school, was impressive. Historians estimate that a majority of men in 17th-century New England could read and write and by the middle of the 18th century, the region was approaching universal male literacy. In Europe only Scotland and Sweden had achieved this happy state so early. Literacy among women also improved steadily, despite the almost total neglect of formal education for girls.

Spreading literacy created a thriving market for the printed word. Many of the first settlers brought impressive libraries with them, and large numbers of English books were imported throughout the colonial period. The first printing press in the English colonies was founded in Cambridge in 1638, and by 1700 Boston's many presses were producing a veritable avalanche of printed matter.

Most of these publications were reprints of sermons. Ministers required only the smallest encouragement from their congregations to send off last Sunday's remarks to the local printer. But if ministers exercised a near-monopoly of the printed word, they did not limit their output entirely to religious topics. They also produced modest amounts of history, poetry, reports of scientific investigations, and treatises on political theory.

By the early 18th century the intellectual life of New England had taken on a character different from and potentially at odds with the ideas of the first Puritans. In the 1690s Harvard acquired a reputation for encouraging religious toleration. According to orthodox Puritans, its graduates were unfit for the ministry and its professors were no longer interested in training young men for the clergy. In 1701 several Connecticut ministers, most of them Harvard graduates, founded a new "collegiate school" designed to uphold the Puritan values that Harvard seemed ready to abandon. The new college was named after its first English benefactor, Elihu Yale. It fulfilled its founders' hopes by sending more than half of its early graduates into the ministry. Nonetheless, as became all too clear at commencement ceremonies in 1722 when its president and six tutors announced themselves Anglicans, Yale quickly acquired purposes well beyond those assigned it by its creators.

The assumption that the clergy had the last word on learned matters, still operative at the time of the witchcraft episode, came under direct challenge in 1721. When a smallpox epidemic swept through Boston that summer, Cotton Mather, at the time the most prestigious clergyman in New England, recommended that the citizenry be inoculated. He

MAMVSSE
WUNNEETUPANATAMWE
UP-BIBLUM GOD
NANEESWE
NUKKONE TESTAMENT
KAH WONK
WUSKU TESTAMENT.

Ne quoſhkinnumuk naſhpe Wuttinneumoh *CHRIST*
noh aſooweſit
JOHN ELIOT·

CAMBRIDGE:
Printeuoop naſhpe *Samuel Green* kah *Marmaduke Johnſon.*
1 6 6 3.

The Bible, translated into the Algonkian language of the Massachuset Indians, was the first book printed in the English colonies. Its translator, John Eliot, was known as the "Apostle to the Indians" for his missionary labors.

favored a method described in the *Transactions of the Royal Society* in England, of which, he informed the community, he was a member. But instead of accepting Mather's authority, his heretofore silent critics seized on his support of the then radical idea of inoculation to challenge both his motives and his professional credentials. They filled the unsigned contributor columns of New England's first newspaper, the *Boston Gazette,* and the *New England Courant,* which opened in the midst of the inoculation controversy, with their views.

The *Courant* was published by James Franklin, a printer just back from London, where he had been impressed by the commercial possibilities of jour-

nalistic satire. He was soon joined in the enterprise by his 16-year-old brother, Benjamin. The younger Franklin's "Silence Dogood" essays were particularly infuriating to members of the Boston intellectual establishment. Franklin described Harvard as an institution where rich and lazy "blockheads . . . learn little more than how to carry themselves handsomely . . . and from whence they return, after Abundance of Trouble, as Blockheads as ever, only more proud and conceited."

James Franklin was jailed in 1722 for criticizing the General Court, and shortly thereafter the *New England Courant* went out of business. Meanwhile, Ben had left Boston for Philadelphia, where, as everyone knows, fame and fortune awaited him.

The Serpent Prosperity

Prior experience (and the need to eat) turned the first New Englanders to farming. They grew barley (used to make beer), rye, oats, green vegetables, and native crops such as potatoes, pumpkins, and, most important, Indian corn, or maize. Corn was easy to cultivate, and its yield per acre under rough frontier conditions exceeded that of other grains. It proved versatile and tasty when prepared in a variety of ways and also made excellent fodder for livestock. In the form of corn liquor, it was easy to store, to transport, and, in a pinch, to imbibe.

The colonists also had plenty of meat. They grazed cattle, sheep, and hogs on the common pastures or in the surrounding woodlands. Deer, along with turkey and other game birds, abounded. The Atlantic provided fish, especially cod, which was easily preserved by salting. In short, New Englanders ate an extremely nutritious diet. Abundant surpluses of firewood kept the winter cold from their doors. The combination contributed significantly to their good health and longevity.

The trouble was that virtually everything that New England farmers grew could be grown in Europe. The shortness of the growing season, the rocky and often hilly terrain, and careless methods of cultivation, which exhausted the soil, meant that farmers did not produce large surpluses. Thus while New Englanders could feed themselves without difficulty, they had relatively little to spare and no place to sell it.

The earliest Puritans accepted this economic

marginality. The more pious positively welcomed it as insurance against "the serpent prosperity," which might otherwise deflect their spiritual mission into commercial opportunism. No prominent English merchants joined the Great Migration, though many were devoted Puritans and some had invested in the Massachusetts Bay Company. Settlers who turned to business upon arrival attracted suspicion, if not open hostility. Laws against usury (lending money at excessive rates) and profiteering in scarce commodities were in effect from the first days of settlement. In 1639 and again in 1643, Robert Keayne, a prosperous Boston merchant, was fined £200 by the General Court and admonished by his church for "taking above six-pence in the shilling profit; in some above eight-pence; and in some small things, above two for one." Keayne paid the fines and made "penitential acknowledgment" to his church, all the while convinced that "my goods and prices were cheap pennyworths."

Winthrop and the other early leaders resisted the argument of people like Keayne that business was a calling no less socially useful than the ministry or public office. Differences in wealth should be modest and should favor those to whom the community looked for leadership. In the Puritan scheme of things, since Governor Winthrop was a far more valuable member of the community than Robert Keayne, he should stand higher than Keayne in all rankings, wealth included. But Winthrop died in 1649 broke and in debt, whereas Keayne died three years later in sufficient prosperity (despite those stiff fines) to leave the town of Boston and Harvard College impressive benefactions. The gap between the Puritan ideal and the emerging reality was becoming embarrassingly clear.

A Merchant's World

Winthrop's generation had tried to minimize dependence on European-manufactured goods such as iron tools, glass, and cloth by producing their own. When their efforts failed, they next pinned their hopes on establishing direct trade links with European suppliers by offering the skins of beaver and such other fur-bearing animals as otter, muskrat, and mink. Several towns in the Connecticut Valley and New Hampshire became collection centers for these furs. Unfortunately, the beavers soon caught wind of what was going on and took off for

points west and north. By the end of the 1650s the New Englanders were back where they had started. As one English merchant wrote, as trading partners "they have noe returns."

The colonists then turned to indirect trading schemes, in which merchants like Robert Keayne played a central role and from which they ultimately derived stature as well as wealth. The anticommercial bias of the early Puritans did not, however, vanish as quickly as the elusive beaver had. At the beginning of the 18th century a Boston minister could still tell his congregation this story with every confidence that they shared his belief that his colleague got the better of the Maine fisherman: Once, some years after Keayne's death, a minister in Maine was reminding his flock that "the main end of planting this wilderness" was religion. A prominent member of the congregation could not contain his disagreement. "Sir," he cried out, "you are mistaken. You think you are preaching to the people of the Bay; our main end was to catch fish."

Actually, fish, caught offshore on grounds that extended from Cape Cod to Newfoundland, provided merchants with their opening into the world of transatlantic commerce. In 1643 five New England vessels set out with their holds packed with fish, which they sold in Spain and the Canary Islands; they took payment in sherry and madeira, for which a market existed in England. One of these ships also had the dubious distinction of initiating New England into the business of trafficking in human beings when her captain took payment in African slaves, whom he subsequently sold in the West Indies.

This was the start of the famous "triangular trade," for once New England merchants discovered that access to English markets was no less feasible or less profitable for being indirect, they were in business for keeps. Only occasionally was the pattern truly triangular; more often, intermediate legs gave it a polygonal character. So long as their ships ended up with something that could be exchanged for English goods needed at home, it did not matter what they started out with or how many things they bought and sold along the way.

So maritime trade and the people who engaged in it became the driving force of the New England economy, important all out of proportion to the number of persons directly involved. Because those engaged congregated in Portsmouth, Salem, Boston, Newport, and New Haven, these towns soon differed greatly from towns in the interior. They were larger and growing faster, and fewer of their inhabitants were engaged in farming.

The largest and most thriving town was Boston, which by 1720 had become the commercial hub of the region. It had a population of more than 10,000; in the entire British Empire, only London and Bristol were larger. More than one-quarter of Boston's male adults either had invested in shipbuilding or were directly employed in maritime commerce. Ship captains and merchants held most of the public offices.

Beneath this emergent mercantile elite lived a stratum of artisans and small shopkeepers, and be-neath these a substantial population of mariners, laborers, and "unattached" people with little or no property and still less political voice. By 1720 street crime had become a serious problem, as had prostitution (of which the town fathers first took public notice in the 1670s, when at least a dozen women plied the trade in Boston). The public relief rolls during this period frequently exceeded 200 souls, while dozens of criminals languished in the town jail.

All in all, as Boston approached the centennial of its founding, it bore little resemblance to what the first Puritans had in mind when they planted their "Citty upon a Hill." But neither was it like any

This map summarizes the chief routes of colonial trade in the 1700s. An instance of the so-called triangular slave trade is shown in black for clarity. Most southern exports went to England, but a lack of suitable English markets led the northern and middle colonies to seek outlets for their products in the West Indies and southern Europe.

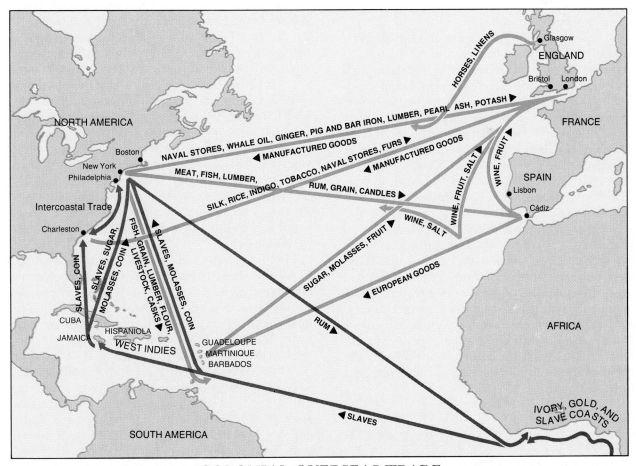

COLONIAL OVERSEAS TRADE

European city of the time. It stood there on Massachusetts Bay, midway between its Puritan origins and its American future.

The Middle Colonies: A Rising People

New York, New Jersey, Pennsylvania, and Delaware owe their collective name, the Middle Colonies, to geography. Sandwiched between New England and the Chesapeake region, they often receive only passing notice in accounts of colonial America. The lack of a distinctive institution, such as slavery or the town meeting, explains part of this neglect.

Actually, both institutions existed there. Black slaves made up about 10 percent of the population; indeed, one New York county in the 1740s had proportionally more blacks than large sections of Virginia. And eastern Long Island was settled by people from Connecticut who brought the town meeting system with them.

Like colonists elsewhere, most of the inhabitants became farmers. But where northern farmers concentrated on producing crops for local consumption and southerners for export, they did both. In addition to raising foodstuffs and keeping livestock, they grew wheat, which the thin soil and shorter growing season of New England did not permit but for which there existed an expanding market in the densely settled Caribbean sugar islands.

Unlike New England settlers, who clustered together in agricultural villages, families in the Hudson Valley of New York and in southeastern Pennsylvania lived on the land they cultivated, often as spatially dispersed as the tobacco planters of the Chesapeake. In contrast with Virginia and Maryland, however, substantial numbers congregated in the seaport centers of New York City and Philadelphia. They also settled interior towns like Albany, an important center of the fur trade on the upper Hudson, and Germantown, an "urban village" northwest of Philadelphia where many people were engaged in trades like weaving and tailoring and flour milling.

"This Promiscuous Breed"

The New Yorkers and Pennsylvanians also possessed traits that later would be seen as distinctly "American." Their ethnic and religious heterogeneity is a case in point. Traveling through Pennsylvania in 1744, the Swedish botanist Peter Kalm encountered "a very mixed company of different nations and religions." In addition to "Scots, English, Dutch, Germans, and Irish," he reported, "there were Roman Catholics, Presbyterians, Quakers, Methodists, Seventh day men, Moravians, Anabaptists, and one Jew."

The English population of New York City was smaller than the Dutch for decades. Scandinavian and Dutch settlers outnumbered the English in New Jersey and Delaware even after the English took over these colonies. William Penn's first success in attracting colonists was with German Quakers and other persecuted religious sects, among them Mennonites and Moravians from the Rhine Valley. The first substantial influx of immigrants into New York after it became a royal colony consisted of French Huguenots.

Early in the 18th century, hordes of Scotch-Irish settlers from Northern Ireland and Scotland descended on Pennsylvania. These colonists spoke English but felt little loyalty to the English government, which had treated them badly back home, and less to the Anglican church, since most of them were Presbyterians. Large numbers of them followed the valleys of the Appalachians south into the back country of Virginia and the Carolinas.

Why so few English? Here again, timing provides the best answer. The English economy was booming. There seemed to be work for all. Migration from England to the North American colonies, though never drying up, slowed to a trickle. The result was colonies in which English settlers were in the minority.

The intermingling of ethnic groups gave rise to many prejudices. Benjamin Franklin, although generally complimentary toward Pennsylvania's hardworking Germans, thought them clannish to a fault. The already cited Hector St. John de Crèvecoeur, while marveling at the adaptive qualities of "this promiscuous breed," complained that "the Irish . . . love to drink and to quarrel; they are litigious, and soon take to the gun, which is the ruin of everything." Yet by and large the various types managed to get along with each other successfully enough. Crèvecoeur attended a wedding in Pennsylvania where the groom's grandparents were English and Dutch and one of his uncles had married a Frenchwoman. The groom and his three brothers,

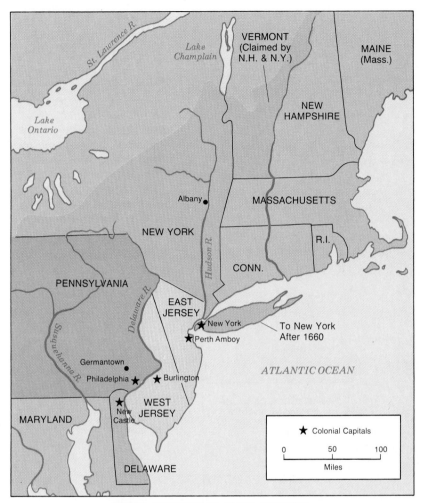

THE MIDDLE COLONIES

Crèvecoeur added with some amazement, "now have four wives of different nations."

"The Best Poor Man's Country"

Ethnic differences seldom caused conflict in the Middle Colonies because they seldom limited opportunity. The promise of prosperity (promotional pamphlets proclaimed Pennsylvania "the best poor man's country in the world") had attracted all in the first place, and achieving prosperity was relatively easy, even for those who came with only a willingness to work. From its founding, Pennsylvania granted upward of 500 acres of land to families upon arrival, provided that they would pay the pro-

prietor an annual quitrent. Similar arrangements existed in New Jersey and Delaware. Soon travelers were being struck by the "pleasing uniformity of decent competence."

New York was something of an exception to this favorable economic situation. When the English took over New York, they extended the Dutch patroon system by creating 30 manorial estates covering 2 million–odd acres. But ordinary New Yorkers never lacked ways of becoming landowners. A hundred acres along the Hudson River could be bought in 1730 for what an unskilled laborer could earn in three months. Even tenants on the manorial estates could obtain long-term leases that had most of the advantages of ownership but did not require the investment of any capital. "One may think one-

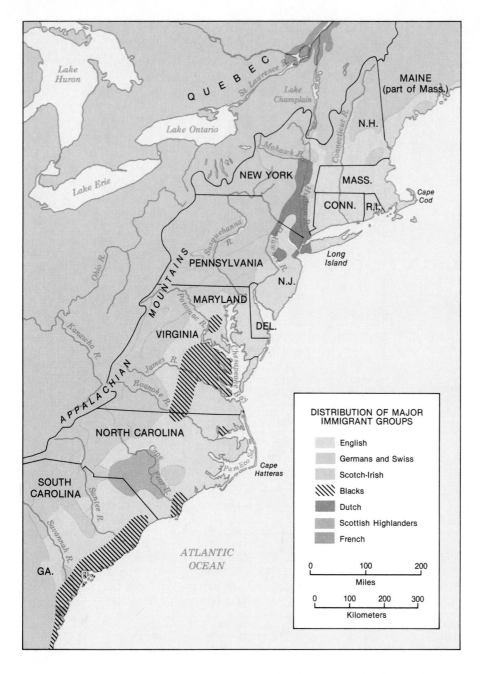

ETHNIC GROUPS IN EASTERN NORTH AMERICA, 1750

From early settlement, the future United States was a multiethnic society. For the first time, national and religious groups were mixed. In a frontier environment there was no room for intergroup bickering; the different groups had to learn to get along and work together.

DISTRIBUTION OF MAJOR IMMIGRANT GROUPS

- English
- Germans and Swiss
- Scotch-Irish
- Blacks
- Dutch
- Scottish Highlanders
- French

self to be a great lord," one frustrated "lord" of a New York manor wrote a colleague, "but it does not amount to much, as you well know."

Mixed farming offered the most commonly trod path to prosperity, but not the only one. Inland communities offered comfortable livelihoods for artisans. Farmers always needed barrels, candles, rope, horseshoes and nails, and dozens of other articles in everyday use. Countless opportunities awaited the ambitious settler in the shops, yards,

and offices of New York and Philadelphia. Unlike Boston, New York and Philadelphia profited from navigable rivers that penetrated deep into the back country. Although founded half a century after New York and Boston, Philadelphia grew more rapidly than either. In the 1750s, when its population reached 15,000, it passed Boston to become the largest city in English America.

Most Philadelphians who stuck to their business, particularly if it happened to be maritime commerce, did well for themselves. John Bringhurst, a merchant, began his career as a clerk. At his death in 1751 he left an estate of several thousand pounds. According to the historian Gary Nash, the city's "leather-apron" artisans often accumulated estates of more than £400, a substantial sum at the time. By contrast, in Boston after 1710, economic stagnation made it much more difficult for a skilled artisan to rise in the world.

The Politics of Diversity

"Cannot more friendly and private courses be taken to set matters right in an infant province?" an exasperated William Penn asked the people of Pennsylvania in 1704. "For the love of God, me, and the poor country, be not so governmentish." However well intentioned Penn's advice, however justified his annoyance, the Pennsylvanians ignored him. Instead, they and their fellows throughout the region constructed a political culture that diverged sharply from the patterns of New England and the south both in contentiousness and in the sophistication required of local politicians.

Superficially, the governments of these colonies closely resembled those of earlier settlements. All had popularly elected representative assemblies and most male adults could vote. In Pennsylvania, where Penn had insisted that there be no religious test and where 50 acres constituted a freehold, something close to universal manhood suffrage existed. In New York even non-property-holding white male residents voted in local elections, and rural tenants with lifetime leases enjoyed full voting rights.

In Pennsylvania and most of New York, representatives were elected by counties. In this they resembled Virginia and Maryland. But unlike the southerners, voters did not tend to defer in politics to the landed gentry. In New York in 1689, during the political vacuum following the abdication of King James II, Jacob Leisler, a disgruntled merchant and militia captain, seized control of the government. "Leisler's Rebellion" did not amount to much. He held power for less than two years before he was overthrown and sent to the gallows. Yet for two decades New York politics continued to be a struggle between the Leislerians, and other self-conscious "outs" who shared Leisler's dislike of English rule, and anti-Leislerians, who had in common only that they had opposed his takeover. Each group sought the support of a succession of ineffective

governors, and the one that failed to get it invariably proceeded to make that poor man's tenure as miserable as possible. (Governor Edward Cornbury [1702–1708] had an especially difficult time asserting the royal authority after being spotted on the streets of New York wearing a dress.)

In the early 1730s conflict broke out over a claim for back salary by Governor William Cosby. When Lewis Morris, who was also chief justice of the supreme court, opposed Cosby's claim, the governor replaced him. Morris and his assembly allies responded by establishing the *New York Weekly Journal*. To edit the paper they hired an itinerant German printer, John Peter Zenger.

Governor Cosby might have tolerated the *Weekly Journal*'s front-page lectures on the right of the people to criticize their rulers had the back pages not contained advertisements referring to his supporters as spaniels and to him as a monkey. After submitting to two months of "open and implacable malice against me," he shut down the paper, arrested Zenger, and charged him with seditious libel.

What began as a squalid salary dispute became one of the most celebrated tests of freedom of the press in the history of journalism. At the trial, Zenger's attorney, James Hamilton, argued that the truth of his client's criticisms of Cosby constituted a proper defense against seditious libel. This reasoning (though contrary to English law at the time) persuaded the jury to acquit Zenger.

Politics in Pennsylvania turned on conflict between two interest groups. One clustered around the proprietor, the other around the assembly, which was controlled by a coalition of Quaker representatives from Philadelphia and the German-speaking Pennsylvania Dutch.

Neither the proprietary party nor the Quaker party qualifies as a political party in the modern sense of being organized and maintained for the purpose of winning elections. Nor can either be categorized as standing for "democratic" or "aristocratic" interests. But their existence guaranteed that the political leaders had to take popular opinion into account. Moreover, having once appealed to public opinion, they had to be prepared to defer to it. Success turned as much on knowing how to follow as on knowing how to lead.

The 1763 uprising of the "Paxton Boys" of western Pennsylvania put this policy to a full test. The uprising was triggered by eastern indifference to Indian attacks on the frontier—an indifference

Pennsylvania welcomed newcomers of ethnically diverse backgrounds, most of whom prospered. This view of Philadelphia dates from the 1730s, when the city was a half-century old. Engraved "prospects" like this one were widely circulated to attract new settlers.

made possible by the fact that the east outnumbered the west in the assembly, 26 to 10. Fuming because they could obtain no help from Philadelphia against the Indians, a group of Scotch-Irish from Lancaster County fell upon a village of peaceful Conestoga Indians and murdered them in cold blood. Then these Paxton Boys marched on the capital, several hundred strong.

Fortunately, a delegation of burghers, headed by Benjamin Franklin, talked them out of attacking the town by acknowledging the legitimacy of their grievances about representation and by promising to vote a bounty on Indian scalps! It was just such fancy footwork that established Franklin, the leader of the assembly party, as Pennsylvania's consummate politician. "Tell me, Mr. Franklin," a testy member of the proprietary party asked, "how is it that you are always with the majority?" Soon thereafter, the assembly sent Franklin to London to defend local interests against the British authorities, a situation in which he would definitely not be "with the majority."

Milestones

1609–1611	"Seasoning time" in Jamestown
1612	Tobacco cultivation introduced in Virginia
1619	First Africans sold in Virginia
1630–1640	"Great Migration" of Puritans to America
1636	Boston Latin School and Harvard College founded
1657	Half-Way Covenant
1676	Bacon's Rebellion
1684–1688	Dominion of New England
1689	Leisler's Rebellion
1692	Salem witchcraft trials
1693	College of William and Mary founded
1696	Rice cultivation introduced in South Carolina
1733	Georgia settled

SUPPLEMENTARY READING

Titles marked with an asterisk have been published in paperback.

Among general interpretations of colonial society, D. J. Boorstin, **The Americans: The Colonial Experience*** (1958), and H. M. Jones, **O Strange New World*** (1964), remain stimulating. D. F. Hawke, **The Colonial Experience** (1966), provides a good survey of colonial history generally, while Richard Hofstadter, **America at 1750*** (1971), offers a compelling social portrait of the colonies at mid-century. S. S. Webb, **1676: The End of American Independence** (1984), is similarly pointed in time and comprehensive in regional coverage.

J. A. Henretta, **The Evolution of American Society*** (1973), R. V. Wells, **The Population of the British Colonies in America Before 1776** (1975), and G. B. Nash, **The Urban Crucible*** (1979), present the results of recent demographic research on the period. Among older interpretations, David Potter's **People of Plenty*** (1954), which stresses economic abundance as a shaping influence on American development, remains illuminating.

On economic conditions, E. J. Perkins, **The Economy of Colonial America** (1980), is an up-to-date survey, while Stuart Bruchey, **The Roots of American Economic Growth** (1965), explores the dynamics of American economic development. On the institution of slavery generally, see Herbert Klein, **The Middle Passage** (1978), D. B. Davis, **The Problem of Slavery in Western Culture** (1966), and W. D. Jordan, **White over Black: American Attitudes Toward the Negro*** (1968). A. E. Smith, **Colonists in Bondage*** (1971), is a good study of indentured servitude, but see also W. D. Galenson, **White Servitude in Colonial America** (1981); A. B. Ekirch, **Bound for America** (1987), which deals with convict labor; and R. B. Morris, **Government and Labor in Early America** (1946).

On life in the colonial south, see T. W. Tate and David Ammerman (eds.), **The Chesapeake in the Seventeenth Century** (1979), D. B. and A. H. Rutman, **A Place in Time** (1984), P. H. Wood, **Black Majority: Negroes in Colonial South Carolina** (1974), and T. H. Breen and Stephen Innes, **"Myne Owne Ground": Race and Freedom on Virginia's Eastern Shore*** (1980).

Family and community life are surveyed in D. F. Hawke, **Everyday Life in Early America** (1988), C. N.

Degler, **At Odds** (1980), and E. S. Morgan, **The Puritan Family*** (1966). See also John Demos, **A Little Commonwealth*** (1970), R. L. Bushman, **From Puritan to Yankee*** (1967), K. A. Lockridge, **A New England Town*** (1970), and Philip Greven, **Four Generations*** (1970). The places of women and children are effectively presented in L. T. Ulrich, **Good Wives: Image and Reality in the Lives of Women in Northern New England** (1982), and Philip Greven, **The Protestant Temperament: Patterns of Child-rearing, Religious Experience, and the Self in Early America** (1980).

For the evolution of the New England landscape and ideas about it, see William Cronon, **Changes in the Land*** (1983).

The works of Perry Miller remain the starting point for any serious study of the cultural life of colonial New England. Among them, **Errand into the Wilderness*** (1956) provides a good introduction. More recent studies, most of which seek to modify Miller's judgments, include E. S. Morgan, **Visible Saints*** (1963), and R. G. Pope, **The Half-Way Covenant** (1969).

On the interplay of religion and social thought, see Stephen Foster, **Their Solitary Way** (1971), T. H. Breen, **The Character of the Good Ruler** (1970), and E. S. Morgan's biography of John Winthrop, **The Puritan Dilemma*** (1958). The disturbances in Salem Village are discussed in Paul Boyer and Stephen Nissenbaum, **Salem Possessed*** (1974), while the subject is considered generally in John Demos, **Entertaining Satan: Witchcraft and the Culture of Early New England*** (1982).

Educational and intellectual developments are treated in Bernard Bailyn, **Education in the Forming of American Society*** (1960), and L. A. Cremin, **American Education: The Colonial Experience*** (1970).

On the Middle Colonies, see R. C. Ritchie, **The Duke's Province** (1977), Patricia Bonomi, **A Factious People: Politics and Society in Colonial New York** (1971), and G. B. Nash, **Quakers and Politics** (1968). The best brief biographical account of the region's leading citizen is V. W. Crane, **Benjamin Franklin and a Rising People*** (1954).

Patterns of Development

Before Europeans like the Van Bergens settled on the land, the Indians had their own types of dwellings, all attuned to the climate of the area in which they lived. John White's watercolor shows the houses of Pomeiock, in the Virginia tidewater region; they are made of poles covered with bark and woven mats. Shade and fresh air could be controlled by adjusting these coverings.

This panorama of the Van Bergen farm in New York's Catskill Mountains was painted by an unknown artist about 1735. The picture graced the farm's living-room mantel. It gives a clear sense of the family's self-sufficiency, with their house, outbuildings, servants, and domestic animals, and of their general prosperity.

Climate, wealth, family size, and many other influences shaped the patterns of life that developed in the colonies. The three sections—north, middle, south—were distinct entities throughout the period, and this was true despite the fact that in each region the people came from diverse social and economic backgrounds and encountered widely different experiences after they arrived.

At the same time, the colonists became increasingly American (as distinct from European or African) as the generations passed. By the middle of the 18th century they were beginning to notice the uniqueness of some aspects of their civilization, and this was certainly a stage in their transition from dependence on Great Britain (psychological as well as material) to independence.

But if the sectional differences were ultimately less significant than the trends common to all the colonies, they were nonetheless important. In all three sections farming was the principal occupation, but in New England and the Middle Colonies the growing towns were exerting political and cultural influence out of proportion to their populations. In most families, fathers ruled the roost; children, while cherished, were expected to obey orders and work hard. However, growing up on a New England farm was a far different experience from growing up on a southern plantation. Foreigners were always struck by the general prosperity of the people compared to conditions in Europe, but the gap between the circumstances of a well-to-do eastern merchant and a frontier farmer was large, and widening.

The Virginia plantation "Greenway," later owned by President John Tyler, is typical of southern plantations, with its large but unostentatious main house and its numerous outbuildings. Far different were the slave cabins of a South Carolina plantation, which provided only the minimum shelter needed in a warm climate.

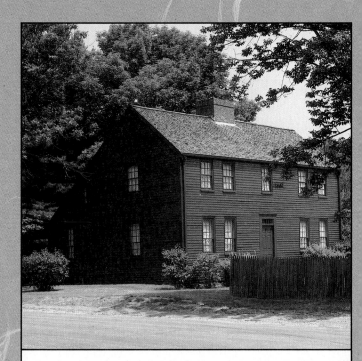

New England houses—this parsonage in Newington, New Hampshire, is typical—tended to be built as a single "salt-box" in order to conserve heat during the long, hard winters. As families grew and prospered, rooms were added, hugging the original structure.

BY THE HONORABLE
RICHARD PENN, Esq.

Lieutenant Governor and Commander in Chief of the Province of PENNSYLVANIA, and Counties of
NEW-CASTLE, KENT, and SUSSEX, on DELAWARE.

To any PROTESTANT MINISTER.

Rich.ᵈ Penn

WHEREAS Application hath been made unto me by

to be joined together in HOLY MATRIMONY, and there appearing no lawful Let or Impe-
diment, by Reason of *Pre-Contract*, *Consanguinity*, *Affinity*, or any just Cause whatsoever, to
hinder the said Marriage; These are therefore to licence and authorise you to join the said

in the HOLY BANDS OF MATRIMONY, and them to pronounce MAN and WIFE.

GIVEN *under my Hand and Seal at Arms, at* Philadelphia, *the*   *Day of*
in the Year of our LORD *One Thousand Seven Hundred and Seventy*

*Then, as now, couples had to ob-
tain a marriage certificate from
the civil authorities before having
a religious ceremony. This pre-
printed version issued in the
name of Richard Penn (William
Penn's son) is addressed to any
Protestant minister, and is good
for the province of Pennsylvania
and the counties of Delaware.*

*A charming primitive painting of
a toddler napping in a red high
chair gives an idyllic picture of
colonial childhood.*

This group portrait of the New England Cheneys shows what is apparently three generations of the family. Genealogies indicate that Dr. Samuel Cheney's first wife had seven children. Since his second wife (in the white cap) had none, the youngest children are presumably her stepgrandchildren.

Two contrasting views of prosperous families of the late 1700s, one from New England and one from the South.

This handsome painting of Alexander Spotswood Payne and his younger brother John Robert Dandridge Payne, with their black nurse and their dog, provides a glimpse of youth in an upper-class Virginia family.

American Lives:
Benjamin Franklin and John Adams

Benjamin Franklin was born in Boston in 1706, the next-to-last of the 13 children of Josiah Franklin, a candle and soap maker, and Abiah Franklin. Although early on he exhibited a "Thirst for Knowledge" and a "Bookish Inclination," he was taken out of school when he was ten in order to help his father. He disliked that trade, and after two years he was apprenticed to his half-brother, James, a printer. Besides learning to be a compositor and type maker, Ben was soon writing articles for his brother's newspaper, the *New England Courant*, at first anonymously, since being so young, he did not think his brother would consider anything he produced worth printing.

To improve his style, Ben practiced writing by the hour. He would read over a passage he admired in a book or article, making notes (he called them "short hints") on its contents. He would put the notes aside for a few days and then use them to try to reconstruct the passage. By comparing the result with the original, he learned to correct awkward phrases and imprecise passages in his work. Another somewhat more difficult technique was to turn the passages into verse, and later turn the verse back into prose in the same manner.

Ben's articles in the *Courant* attracted much notice, but his brother resented his success. The two were constantly at odds. Finally, without telling his parents, Ben left Boston by ship for New York. Not finding work there he moved on to Philadelphia, where he arrived in October 1723, knowing not a soul and with only "a Dutch Dollar and about a shilling in Copper" in his pocket.

Being an exceptionally skilled printer, he soon found work in the shop of Samuel Kleimer. Through the trade he met many "Lovers of Reading" and other people with intellectual interests like his own, including some of what he called "the leading men of the Province." One of these was the governor, Sir William Keith, who offered to set him up in his own business; Keith sent him off to England to buy the necessary press, type, and other equipment, and promised to provide a letter of credit to cover the cost.

However, when Ben arrived in England, there was no letter of credit, for Sir William was better at making promises than at keeping them. Undismayed, he practiced his trade in London for two years before returning to Philadelphia in 1726. Four years later he was sole owner of the *Pennsylvania Gazette*. In 1732 he began publishing his *Poor Richard's Almanack*, the instant success of which assured his prosperity.

John Adams of Braintree, Massachusetts, was of old Puritan stock; the first Adams came to Massachusetts in 1638. John was a bright boy and his parents were determined that he get a good education, but while the family was eminently respectable (his father was a selectman and a deacon of the church) the Adamses were farmers, comfortably off but by no means wealthy. They sent John to the local public school. He did not do well there, however, primarily because the teacher, one Joseph Cleverly, was "the most indolent Man I ever knew." Bored, John spent much time sailing toy boats, flying kites, swimming, skating, and playing marbles and other games with his friends. Finally he persuaded his father to send him to a private school run by a neighbor, whereupon his work improved spectacularly—within a year he was ready to apply to Harvard College.

Doing so was far less complicated, although not necessarily easier, than getting into any college today. After a brief interview with President Edward Holyoke, he was taken by one of Harvard's four tutors, Joseph Mayhew, into another room, given a Latin dictionary, paper and pen, and a passage of English prose, and was told to translate the passage into Latin. After Mayhew read the translation and found it satisfactory, he admitted John to Harvard on the spot.

The Harvard curriculum consisted chiefly of Latin, Greek, logic, mathematics, and theology; the teaching, which involved an enormous amount of memorization, was uninspiring. But John enjoyed his college years. He was what can best be described as a stern self-disciplinarian. "I was of an amorous disposition," he wrote in a famous passage in his *Autobiography,* "and very early from ten or eleven Years of Age, was very fond of the Society of females. . . . This disposition . . . engaged me too much until I was married." But he added, "my natural temperament was always overawed by my Principles and Sense of decorum."

After graduating Adams decided to study law and, not wanting to be a further financial drain on his parents, he took a job teaching in the town of Worcester. Once established there, he approached James Putnam, Worcester's lone lawyer, who agreed to take him into his home; for the sum allowed by the town for his room and board and "an hundred dollars when I should find it convenient," Putnam supervised his legal training. This took two years, and consisted of reading "all the most essential Law Books" and discussing them with Putnam.

When he finished his studies he was invited to practice in Worcester, but he decided to return to Braintree. "I panted for want of Breezes from the Sea," he explained. Back home he presented himself to Jeremiah Gridley, a leader of the Boston bar, who asked him a few questions about his reading and pronounced him qualified to practice law in Massachusetts.

Franklin and Adams were exceptional people, intelligent, energetic, and ambitious. But their early lives throw light on much that was typical of colonial society. That both were omnivorous readers might be explained by their high intelligence, but their experiences suggest that love of books and learning was characteristic of the times. Franklin tells of visiting New York while traveling from Boston to Philadelphia by ship and being invited to the residence of William Burnet, the governor of the province. Burnet had heard from the captain of the ship that a young man on his vessel had a great many books. "The Governor treated me with great Civility, show'd me his Library, which was a very large one, and we had a good deal of conversation about Books and Authors," Franklin recalled in his autobiography.

Adams's account of his life in Worcester is full of the titles of books and his conversations about them with James Putnam, which ranged over history, philosophy, and theology. Jeremiah Gridley also owned a substantial library, access to which he generously provided the young lawyer.

Their lives also illustrate the openness of 18th-century society. Franklin was an exceptionally outgoing person, and he excelled, as the historian Carl Becker once wrote, "in the fine art of inducing others to appropriate as their own the ideas or the projects which he wished to have prevail." He was open-minded and tolerant, of himself as well as others. Adams was quite different. He tended to take a dim view of most people. He noted, for example, that Jeremiah Gridley was more a buyer of books than a reader. He was also extremely straitlaced. Unlike Franklin, who had two illegitimate children, he was able to assure his descendants that he had never wandered from the straight and narrow, before or after his marriage to Abigail Smith. But he too entered easily into the upper ranks of New England society. While an obscure young schoolmaster in Worcester, he was invited to meet General Jeffrey Amherst, who spent a few days there in 1758 while en route from Boston to Albany at the head of 4,000 Redcoats during the French and Indian war. On another occasion Adams volunteered to deliver an urgent call for militiamen to the governor of Rhode Island. He found the governor riding with a single aide on the road between Providence and Newport, handed him the dispatch, and watched him open and read it and then dash off to Providence to raise the troops.

The American colonies were large geographically; however, their inhabitants lived in small, but remarkably open and interesting, worlds.

Harvard College, by Paul Revere

III

America in the British Empire

A VIEW OF PART OF THE TOWN OF BOSTON IN NEW ENGLAND AND BRITTISH SHIPS OF WAR LANDING THEIR TROOPS! 1768

North America was once indeed a great strength to this nation. . . . We found her a sound, an active, a vigorous member of the empire. I hope, by wise management, she will again be so. But one of our capital present misfortunes is her discontent and disobedience.

EDMUND BURKE, *1769*

S ince the colonies were founded piecemeal by persons with varying motives and backgrounds, common traditions and loyalties developed slowly. For the same reason, the British government was slow to think of its American possessions as a unit or to deal with them in any centralized way. They were the king's possessions. No authority challenged his right to dispose of one section of his American domain to this group of merchants under such-and-such terms and another to that personal friend or creditor under a different arrangement. The specific form of each colony's government and the degree of local independence permitted depended on how this was done.

The British Colonial System

There was a pattern basic to all colonial governments and a general framework of imperial control for all the king's overseas plantations. English political and legal institutions (the common law, private property, more or less representative legislative assemblies, systems of local administration) took hold everywhere in British America. While the colonists and the home authorities often had different motives in establishing new settlements, they were seldom conflicting motives. Colonists might leave home with grievances, bent on securing certain rights denied them in England, but prosperity, political and economic expansion, and the reproduction of Old World civilization were aims common to ruler and ruled.

In the earliest days of any settlement, the need to rely on home authorities was so obvious that few questioned England's sovereignty. Thereafter, as the fledglings grew strong enough to think of using their own wings, distance and British political inefficiency combined to allow them a great deal of freedom. Although royal representatives in America tried to direct policy, the Crown generally yielded the initiative in local matters to the colonies while reserving the right to veto actions it deemed to be against the national interest. External affairs were controlled entirely in London.

Each colony had a governor. By the 18th century he was an appointed official, except in Rhode Island and Connecticut. Governors were chosen by the king in the case of the royal colonies and by the proprietors of Maryland, Delaware, and Pennsylvania. The governors' powers were much like those of the king in Great Britain. They executed the local laws, appointed many minor officials, summoned and dismissed the colonial assemblies, and proposed legislation to them. They possessed the right to veto colonial laws, but in most colonies, again like the king, they were financially dependent on their "subjects."

Each colony also had a legislature. Except in Pennsylvania, these assemblies consisted of two houses. The lower house, chosen by qualified voters, had general legislative powers, including control of the purse. In the royal colonies, members of the upper house, or council, were appointed by the king except in Massachusetts, where they were elected by the General Court. The councils served primarily

Typical of colonial governors was Lewis Morris, a wealthy landowner with extensive holdings in the Middle Colonies. He was named New Jersey's first governor when the colony became politically independent from New York in 1738. Honest but overbearing, Morris quarreled constantly with the state assembly over taxation, the militia, and land titles.

as advisers to the governors, but they also had some judicial and legislative powers. Judges were appointed by the king and served at his pleasure. Yet both councilors and judges were normally selected from among the leaders of the local communities; London had neither the time nor the will to investigate their political beliefs. The system therefore tended to strengthen the influence of the entrenched colonials.

Although the power of the lower houses was severely restricted in theory, they dominated the government in nearly every colony. Financial power (including the right to set the governor's salary) gave them some importance, and the fact that the assemblies usually had the backing of public opinion was significant.

Most colonial legislators were practical men. Knowing their own interests, they pursued them

steadily, without much regard for political theories or the desires of the royal authorities. In the words of one Virginia governor, they were "Expedient Mongers in the highest Degree." They extended their influence by slow accretion. Governors came and went, but the lawmakers remained, accumulating experience, building on precedent, widening decade by decade their control over colonial affairs.

The official representatives of the Crown, whatever their powers, whatever their intentions, were prisoners of their surroundings. A royal governor lived thousands of miles fromh London, alone in a colonial world. To defend the British position at every turn when one had to make one's life amid a vigorous and strong-willed people who usually had solid practical arguments to buttress their side if it clashed with the Crown's was no easy task. In their dealings with the assemblies they were often bound by rigid and impractical royal instructions that restricted their ability to maneuver. They had few jobs and favors to offer in their efforts to influence the legislators. Judges might interpret the law according to English precedents, but in local matters colonial juries had the final say. And juries were seldom awed by precedents that clashed with their own conceptions of justice.

Within the British government, the king's Privy Council had the responsibility for formulating colonial policy. It did so on an ad hoc basis, treating each situation as it arose and seldom generalizing. Everything was decentralized, managed by departments that had been created long before the colonies were founded: The Treasury had charge of financial matters, the Army and the Admiralty of military and naval affairs, and so on. The Privy Council could and did disallow (annul) specific colonial laws, but it did not proclaim constitutional principles to which all colonial legislatures must conform. It acted as a court of last appeal in colonial disputes and handled each case individually. One day the council might issue a set of instructions to the governor of Virginia, the next a different set to the governor of South Carolina. No one person or committee thought broadly about the administration of the overseas empire.

Parliamentary legislation applied to the colonies, yet there was little distinctively *American* legislation. For example, Parliament passed laws regulating the trade of the entire British Empire, and until late in the colonial period it directed its attention specifically to North American conditions only on rare occasions.

At times the British authorities, uneasy about their lack of control over the colonies, attempted to create a more effective system. Whenever possible, the original, broadly worded charters were revoked. To transform proprietary and corporate colonies into royal colonies (whose chief officials were appointed by the king) seems to have been London's official policy by the late 17th century. The Privy Council appointed a number of subcommittees to advise it on colonial affairs at this time. The most important was the Lords of Trade. In the 1680s when James II brought New York, New Jersey, and all of New England under one administration, the Dominion of New England, he apparently planned to unify the southern colonies in a similar manner. The colonists deeply resented James's actions, and after the Glorious Revolution and the collapse of the Dominion of New England, no further important efforts at unification were attempted. Instead, the tendency was in the other direction. Delaware partially separated from Pennsylvania in 1704, and the two Carolinas formally split in 1712.

In 1696 the new Board of Trade took over the functions of the Lords of Trade and expanded them considerably. It nominated colonial governors and other high officials. It reviewed all the laws passed by the colonial legislatures, recommending the disallowance of those that seemed to conflict with imperial policy. The efficiency, assiduousness, and wisdom of the Board of Trade fluctuated over the years, but the Privy Council and the Crown nearly always accepted its recommendations.

Colonists naturally disliked having their laws disallowed, but London exercised this power with considerable restraint; only about 5 percent of the laws reviewed were rejected. Furthermore, the board served as an important intermediary for colonists seeking to influence king and Parliament. All the colonies in the 18th century maintained agents in London to present the colonial point of view before board members. The most famous colonial agent was Benjamin Franklin, who represented Pennsylvania, Georgia, New Jersey, and Massachusetts at various times during his long career. In general, however, colonial agents were seldom able to exert much influence on British policy.

The British never developed an effective centralized government for the American colonies. By and large, their American "subjects" ran their own affairs. This fact more than any other explains our present federal system and the wide areas in which the state governments are sovereign and independent.

Mercantilism

The Board of Trade, as its name implies, was concerned with commerce as well as colonial administration. According to prevailing European opinion, colonies were important chiefly for economic reasons. The 17th century being a period of hard times and considerable unemployment, some authorities saw the colonies as excellent dumping grounds for surplus people. If only two idlers in each parish were shipped overseas, one clergyman calculated in 1624, England would be rid of 16,000 undesirables. But most 17th-century economic thinkers envisaged colonies more as potential sources of raw materials. To obtain these, they developed a number of loosely related policies that later economists called mercantilism. The most important raw materials in the eyes of mercantilists were gold and silver, since these metals, being universally valued and relatively rare, could be exchanged at any time for anything the owner desired or, being durable and compact, stored indefinitely for future use. For these reasons, how much gold and silver ("treasure," according to mercantilists) a nation possessed was considered the best barometer of its prosperity and power.

Since gold and silver could not be mined in significant amounts in western Europe, every early colonist dreamed of finding "El Dorado." The Spanish were the winners in this search; from the mines of Mexico and South America a treasure in gold and silver poured into the Iberian peninsula. Failing to control the precious metals at the source, the other powers tried to obtain them by guile and warfare (witness the exploits of Francis Drake).

In the mid-17th century another method, less hazardous and in the long run far more profitable, called itself to the attention of the statesmen of western Europe. If a country could make itself as nearly self-sufficient as possible and at the same time keep all its citizens busy producing items marketable in other lands, it could sell more abroad than it imported. This state of affairs was known as "having

The value of sugar from the West Indies far outweighed the value of imports to Britain from the mainland American colonies. Refining the sugar before shipping, as shown in the engraving, resulted in far higher import duties.

a favorable balance of trade." The expression is misleading; in reality, trade, which involves an exchange, *always* balances unless some party simply gives its goods away, a practice not recommended by mercantilists. A country with a favorable balance in effect made up the difference by "importing" money in the form of gold and silver. Nevertheless, mercantilism came to mean concentrating on producing for export and limiting imports of ordinary goods and services in every way possible. Colonies that did not have deposits of precious metals were well worth having if they supplied raw materials that would otherwise have to be purchased from foreign sources or if their people bought substantial amounts of the manufactured goods produced in the mother country.

Of the English colonies in the New World, those in tropical and subtropical climes were valued for their raw materials. The more northerly ones were important as markets, but because they were small in the 17th century, in English eyes they took second place. In 1680 the sugar imported from the single West Indian island of Barbados was worth more than the goods sent to England by all the mainland colonies.

If the possession of gold and silver signified wealth, trade was the route that led to riches, and merchants were the captains who would pilot the ship of state to prosperity. "Trade is the Wealth of the World," Daniel Defoe wrote in 1728. One must, of course, have something to sell, so internal production must be stimulated. Parliament encouraged the British people to concentrate on manufacturing by placing tariffs on foreign manufactured goods and subsidizing British-made textiles, iron, and other products.

The Navigation Acts

The nurture of commerce was fundamental. Toward this end Parliament enacted the Navigation Acts. These laws, put into effect over a period of more than half a century, were designed to bring money into the Royal Treasury, to develop the imperial merchant fleet, to channel the flow of colonial raw materials into England, and to keep foreign goods and vessels out of colonial ports (since the employment of foreign ships in the carrying trade was as much an import as the consumption of foreign wheat or wool).

The system originated in the 1650s in response to the stiff commercial competition offered by the Dutch, whose sailors roamed the world's oceans in search of business. Before 1650 a large share of the produce of the English colonies in America reached Europe in Dutch vessels; the first slaves in Virginia, it will be recalled, arrived on a Dutch ship and were doubtless paid for in tobacco that was later burned in the clay pipes of the burghers of Amsterdam and Rotterdam.

Dismayed by this trend, Parliament in 1650 and 1651 barred foreign ships from the English colonies (except when specially licensed) and prohibited the importation into England of goods that were not carried in English ships or those of the country where the goods had been originally produced. All foreign vessels were excluded from the English coastal trade. Although phrased in general terms, this legislation struck primarily at the Dutch, and in 1652 the English provoked the first of three wars with the Dutch Republic that were only extensions of the policy laid down in the first Navigation Acts.

The laws of 1650 and 1651 were not rigidly enforced because England did not have enough ships to supply its overseas possessions. The colonies protested vigorously and then ignored the regulations. Nevertheless, the English persisted. New laws were passed, and as the merchant marine expanded (tonnage doubled between 1660 and 1688) and the Royal Navy gradually reduced Dutch power in the New World, enforcement became fairly effective.

The Navigation Act of 1660 reserved the entire trade of the colonies to English ships and required that the captain and three-quarters of his crew be English. (Colonists, of course, were English, and their ships were treated on the same terms as those sailing out of London or Liverpool.) The act also provided that certain colonial "enumerated articles"—sugar, tobacco, cotton, ginger, and dyes like indigo and fustic—could not be "shipped, carried, conveyed or transported" outside the empire. Three years later Parliament required that with trifling exceptions, all European products destined for the colonies be brought to England before being shipped across the Atlantic. Since trade between England and the colonies was reserved to English vessels, this meant that the goods would have to be unloaded and reloaded in England.

Legislation in 1673 and 1696 was concerned with enforcing these laws: It dealt with the posting of bonds, the registration of vessels, and the appointment of customs officials. Early in the 18th century the list of enumerated articles was expanded to include rice, molasses, naval stores, furs, and copper.

The English looked on the empire broadly; they envisioned the colonies as part of an economic unit, not as servile dependencies to be exploited for England's selfish benefit. The growing of tobacco in England was prohibited, and valuable bounties were paid to colonial producers of indigo and naval stores. A planned economy, England specializing in manufacturing and the colonies in the production of raw materials, was the grand design. By and large the system suited the realities of life in an underdeveloped country that was rich in raw materials and suffering from a chronic labor shortage.

Much has been made by some historians of the restrictions that the British placed on colonial manufacturing. The Wool Act of 1699 prohibited the export (but not the manufacture for local sale) of colonial woolen cloth. A similar law regarding hats was passed in 1732, and in 1750 the Iron Act outlawed the construction of new rolling and slitting mills in America. No other restrictions on manufacturing were imposed.

At most the Wool Act stifled a potential American industry; the law was directed chiefly at Irish woolens rather than American. The hat industry cannot be considered a major one. Iron, however, was important; by 1775 the industry was thriving in Virginia, Maryland, New Jersey, and Pennsylvania, and America was turning out one-seventh of the world supply. Yet the Iron Act was designed to steer the American iron industry in a certain direction, not to destroy it. Eager for iron to feed English mills, Parliament eliminated all duties on colonial pig and bar iron entering England, a great stimulus to the basic industry.

The Effects of Mercantilism

All this legislation reflected, more than it molded, the imperial economy. It made England the colonies' main customer and chief supplier of manufactures, but that would have happened in any case, and it remained the case after the Revolution, when the Navigation Acts no longer applied to America. The chronic colonial shortage of hard money was superficially caused by the flow of specie to England to meet the "unfavorable" balance that resulted from this trade, and this, too, reflected natural conditions. The rapidly growing colonial economy consumed far more manufactured products than it could pay for out of current production. To be "in debt" to England really meant that the English were investing capital in America, a state of affairs that benefited borrower and lender alike.

Important colonial products for which no market existed in England (such as fish, wheat, and corn) were never enumerated and moved freely and directly to foreign ports. Most colonial manufacturing was untouched by English law. Shipbuilding benefited from the Navigation Acts, since many English merchants bought vessels built in the colonies. Between 1769 and 1771, Massachusetts, New Hampshire, and Rhode Island yards constructed perhaps 250 ships of 100 to 400 tons for transatlantic commerce and twice that many sloops and schooners for fishermen and coastal traders. The manufacture of rum for local consumption and for the slave trade

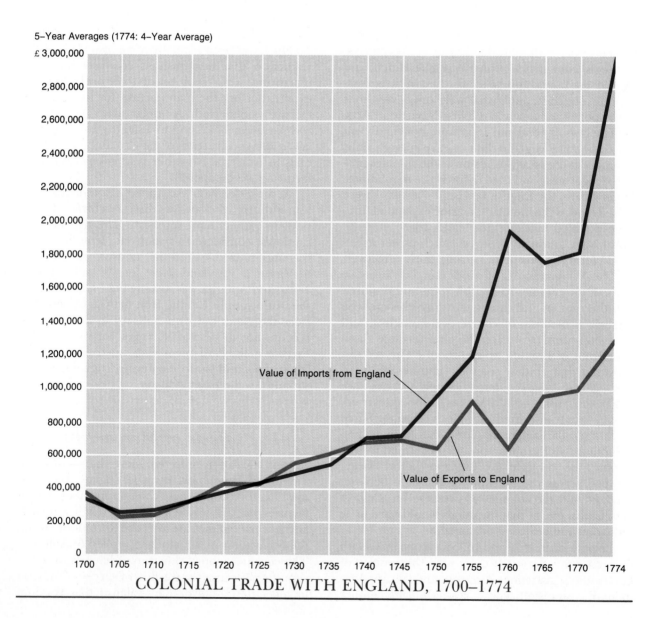

COLONIAL TRADE WITH ENGLAND, 1700–1774

was significant; so were barrelmaking, flour milling, shoemaking, and dozens of other crafts that operated without restriction.

Two forces that worked in opposite directions must be considered before arriving at any judgment about English mercantilism. Although the theory presupposed a general imperial interest above that of both colony and mother country, when conflicts of interest arose, the latter nearly always predominated. Whenever Parliament or the Board of Trade resolved an Anglo-American disagreement, the colonists tended to lose out.

The requirement that foreign goods destined for the colonies must first be unloaded in England increased the cost of certain goods to Americans for the benefit of English merchants and dockworkers. The enumeration of tobacco and other colonial products meant that English merchants could profit by reexporting surpluses to the Continent; by 1700 this reexport trade amounted to 30 percent of the value of all England's exports.

Complementary interests conspired to keep conflicts at a minimum, but in the long run, as the American economy became more complex, the colonies would have been seriously hampered and much more trouble would have occurred had the system continued to operate.

However, the restrictions of English mercantilism were greatly lessened by inefficiency. The king and his ministers handed out government posts to win political favor or to repay political debts, regardless of the recipient's ability to perform the duties of the office.

Transported to remote America, this bumbling and cynical system scarcely functioned at all when local opinion resisted it. Smuggling became a respected profession, bribery of English officials standard practice. Despite a supposedly prohibitive duty of sixpence a gallon imposed by the Molasses Act of 1733, molasses from the French West Indies continued to be imported. The duty was seldom collected. A customs officer in Salem offered to pass French molasses for 10 percent of the legal tax, and in New Jersey the collectors "entered into a composition with the Merchants and took a Dollar a Hogshead or some such small matter."

Mercantilistic policies hurt some colonists such as the tobacco planters, who grew far more than British consumers could smoke. But the policies helped others, and most people proved adept at getting around the aspects of the system that threatened them. In any case, the colonies enjoyed almost continuous prosperity, as even so dedicated a foe of mercantilistic restrictions as Adam Smith admitted.

By the same token, England profited greatly from its overseas possessions. With all its inefficiencies, mercantilism worked. Prime Minister Sir Robert Walpole's famous policy of "salutary neglect," which involved looking the other way when Americans violated the Navigation Acts, was partly a bowing to the inevitable, partly the result of complacency. English manufactures were better and cheaper than those of other nations. This fact, together with ties of language and a common heritage, predisposed Americans toward doing business in England. All else followed naturally; the mercantilistic laws merely steered the American economy in a direction it had already taken.

The Great Awakening

Although a majority of the settlers were of English, Scottish, or Scotch-Irish descent, and their interests generally coincided with those of their cousins in the mother country, people in the colonies were beginning to recognize their common interests and character. Their interests and loyalties were still predominantly local, but by 1750 the word *American*, used to describe something characteristic of all the British possessions in North America, had entered the language. Events in one part of America were beginning to have direct effects on other regions. One of the first of these developments was the so-called Great Awakening.

By the early 18th century, religious fervor had slackened in all the colonies. Prosperity turned many colonists away from their forebears' preoccupation with the rewards of the next world to the more tangible ones of this world. John Winthrop invested his faith in God and his own efforts in the task of creating a spiritual community; his grandsons invested in Connecticut real estate.

The proliferation of religious denominations made it impracticable to enforce laws requiring regular religious observances. Even in South Carolina, the colony that came closest to having an "Anglican establishment," only a minority of persons were churchgoers. Settlers in frontier districts lived beyond the reach of church or clergy. The result was a large and growing number of "persons careless of all religion."

This state of affairs came to an abrupt end with the Great Awakening of the 1740s. The Awakening began in the Middle Colonies as the result of religious developments that originated in Europe. In the late 1720s two newly arrived ministers, Theodore Frelinghuysen, a Calvinist from Westphalia, and William Tennent, an Irish-born Presbyterian, sought to instill in their sleepy Pennsylvania and New Jersey congregations the evangelical zeal and spiritual enthusiasm they had witnessed among the Pietists in Germany and the Methodist followers of John Wesley in England. Their example inspired other clergymen, including Tennent's two sons.

A more significant surge of religious enthusiasm followed the arrival in 1738 in Georgia of the Reverend George Whitefield, a young Oxford-trained Anglican minister. Whitefield was a marvelous pulpit orator and no mean actor. He played on the feelings of his audience the way a conductor directs a symphony orchestra.

He undertook a series of fund-raising tours throughout the colonies. The most successful began in Philadelphia in 1739. Benjamin Franklin, not a very religious person and not easily moved by emotional appeals, heard one of these sermons. "I silently resolved he should get nothing from me," he later recalled.

> I had in my Pocket a Handful of Copper Money, three or four silver Dollars, and five Pistoles in Gold. As he proceeded I began to soften and concluded to give the Coppers. Another Stroke of his Oratory . . . determin'd me to give the Silver; and he finish'd so admirably that I empty'd my Pocket wholly into the Collector's Dish.

Whitefield's visit changed the "manners of our inhabitants,' Franklin added.

Wherever Whitefield went he filled the churches. If no local clergyman offered his pulpit, he attracted thousands to meetings out-of-doors. During a three-day visit to Boston, 19,000 people (more than the population of the town) thronged to hear him.

His oratorical brilliance aside, Whitefield succeeded in releasing an epidemic of religious emotionalism because his message was so well suited to American ears. By preaching a theology that one critic said was "scaled down to the comprehension of twelve-year-olds," he spared his audiences the rigors of hard thought. Though he usually began by chastising his listeners as sinners, "half animals and half devils," he invariably took care to leave them with the hope that eternal salvation could be theirs. While not denying the doctrine of predestination, he preached a God responsive to good intentions. He disregarded sectarian differences and encouraged his listeners to do the same. "God help us to forget party names and become Christians in deed and truth," he prayed.

Whitefield attracted some supporters among ministers with established congregations, but many more from among younger "itinerants," as preachers who lacked permanent pulpits were called. A visit from him or one of his followers inevitably prompted comparisons between this new, emotionally charged style and the more restrained "plaine style" favored by the typical settled minister. Parishioners who had heard a revivalist preacher listened the next Sunday to the droning of their regular minister with what one of Whitefield's imitators claimed was the fear that their souls were at risk because they had been "living under the ministry of dead men."

Of course, not everyone found the Whitefield style edifying. When those who did not spoke up, churches sometimes split into factions. Those who supported the incumbent minister were called, among Congregationalists, "Old Lights," and among Presbyterians, "Old Sides," while those who favored revivalism were known as "New Lights" and "New Sides."

These splits often ran along class lines. The richer, better-educated, and more influential members of the church tended to stay with the traditional arrangements.

The strains these divisions put on communities already struggling to maintain a sense of civic unity produced what the historian Richard Bushman has called a "psychological earthquake." Persons chafing under the restraints of Puritan authoritarianism and made guilt-ridden by their rebellious feelings now found release. For some the release was more than spiritual; Timothy Cutler, a conservative Anglican clergyman, complained that as a result of the

Phyllis Wheatley, one of America's first black poets, was a 17-year-old slave when she wrote this testimony to George Whitefield: "Thou didst, in strains of eloquence refin'd, / Inflame the soul, and captivate the mind."

Awakening, "our presses are forever teeming with books and our women with bastards." Whether or not Cutler was correct, the Great Awakening helped some people to rid themselves of the idea that disobedience to authority guaranteed damnation. Anything that God justified, human law could not condemn.

Other institutions besides the churches were affected by the Great Awakening. In 1741 the president of Yale College criticized the theology of itinerant ministers. One of these promptly retorted that a Yale faculty member had no more divine grace than a chair! Other revivalists called on the New Light churches of Connecticut to withdraw their support from Yale and endow a college of their own. The result was the College of New Jersey (now Princeton), founded in 1746 by New Side Presbyterians. Three other educational by-products of the Great Awakening followed: the College of Rhode Island (Brown), founded by Baptists in 1765; Queen's College (Rutgers), founded by Dutch Reformers in 1766; and Dartmouth, founded by New Light Congregationalists in 1769. These institutions promptly set about to refute the charge that the evangelical temperament was hostile to learning.

The Rise and Fall of Jonathan Edwards

Jonathan Edwards, the most famous native-born revivalist of the Great Awakening, was living proof that it need not be. Edwards, though deeply pious, was passionately devoted to intellectual pursuits. But in 1725, four years after graduating from Yale, he was offered the position of assistant at his grandfather Solomon Stoddard's church in Northampton, Massachusetts. He accepted, and when Stoddard died two years later, Edwards became pastor.

During his six decades in Northampton, Stoddard had so dominated the ministers of the Connecticut Valley that some referred to him as "pope." His prominence came in part from the "open enrollment" admission policy he adopted for his own church. Evidence of saving grace was neither required nor expected of members; mere good behavior sufficed. As a result, the grandson inherited a congregation whose members were possessed of an "inordinate engagedness after this world." How ready they were to meet their Maker in the next was another question.

Edwards set out to change this. When a 5-year-old girl begged her mother to take her to church so that she could "hear Mr. Edwards preach," he knew he was on the right track.

For all his learning and intellectual brilliance, Edwards did not stick at dramatizing what unconverted listeners had to look forward to. The heat of Hell's consuming fires and the stench of brimstone became palpable at his rendering. In his most famous sermon, "Sinners in the Hands of an Angry God," delivered at Enfield, Connecticut, in 1741, he pulled out all the stops, depicting a "dreadfully provoked" God holding the unconverted over the pit of Hell, "much as one holds a spider, or some loathsome insect." Later, on the off chance that his listeners did not recognize themselves among the "insects" in God's hand, he declared that "this is the dismal case of every soul in this congregation that has not been born again, however moral and strict, sober and religious, they may otherwise be." A great moaning reverberated through the church. People cried out, "What must I do to be saved?"

Unfortunately for some church members, Edwards's warnings about the state of their souls caused much anxiety. One disconsolate member, Joseph Hawley, slit his throat. Edwards took the suicide calmly. "Satan seems to be in a great rage," he declared. But for some of Edwards's most prominent parishioners, Hawley's death aroused doubts. They began to miss the easy, Arminian ways of Solomon Stoddard.

Rather than soften his message, Edwards persisted, and in 1749 his parishioners voted unanimously to dismiss him. He became a missionary to some Indians in Stockbridge, Massachusetts. In 1759 he was appointed president of Princeton, but he died of smallpox before he could take office.

By the early 1750s, a reaction had set in against religious "enthusiasm" in all its forms. Except in the religion-starved south, where traveling New Side Presbyterians and Baptists continued their evangelizing efforts, the Great Awakening had run its course. Whitefield's last tour of the colonies in 1754 attracted little notice.

Although it caused divisions, the Great Awakening also fostered religious toleration. If one group claimed the right to worship in its own way, how could it deny to other Protestant churches equal freedom? The Awakening was also the first truly national event in American history. It marks the time when the previously distinct histories of the colonies began to intersect. Powerful links were being forged. As early as 1691 there was a rudimentary intercolonial postal system. In 1754, not long after the Awakening, the farsighted Benjamin Franklin advanced his Albany Plan for a colonial union to deal with common problems, such as defense against Indian attacks on the frontier. Thirteen once-isolated colonies, expanding to the north and south as well as westward, were merging.

The Enlightenment in America

The Great Awakening pointed ahead to an America marked by religious pluralism; by the 1740s many colonists were rejecting not only the stern Calvinism of Edwards but even the easy Arminianism of Samuel Stoddard in favor of a far less forbidding theology, one more in keeping with the ideas of the European Enlightenment.

The Enlightenment had an enormous impact in America. The founders of the colonies were contemporaries of the astronomer Galileo Galilei (1564–1642), the philosopher-mathematician René Descartes (1596–1650), and Sir Isaac Newton (1642–1727), the genius who revealed to the world the workings of gravity and other laws of motion. American society developed amid the excitement generated by these great discoverers, who provided both a new understanding of the natural world and a mode of thought that implied that impersonal, scientific laws governed the behavior of all matter, animate and inanimate. Earth and the heavens, human beings and the lower animals—all seemed parts of an immense, intricate machine. God had set it all in motion and remained the master technician (the divine watchmaker) overseeing it but had fewer and fewer occasions to interfere with its immutable operation.

If human reasoning powers and direct observation of natural phenomena, rather than God's revelations, provided the key to knowledge, it followed that knowledge of the laws of nature, by enabling people to understand the workings of the universe, would enable them to control their earthly destinies and to have at least a voice in their eternal destinies.

Most creative thinkers of the European Enlightenment realized that human beings were not entirely rational and that a complete understanding of the physical world was beyond their grasp. They

Benjamin Franklin is most often depicted as he looked in later life, with his own thinning hair rather than the wig which was de rigueur for an 18th-century man of good family. In this 1767 portrait, a younger Franklin follows the fashion.

did, however, believe that human beings were becoming more rational and would be able, by using their rational powers, to discover the laws governing the physical world. Their faith in these ideas produced the so-called Age of Reason. And while their confidence in human rationality now seems naive and the "laws" they formulated no longer appear so mechanically perfect (the universe is far less orderly than they imagined), they added immensely to knowledge.

Many churchgoing colonists, especially better-educated ones, accepted the assumptions of the Age of Reason wholeheartedly. Some repudiated the doctrine of original sin and asserted the benevolence of God. Others came to doubt the divinity of Christ and eventually declared themselves Unitarians. Still others, among them Benjamin Franklin, embraced Deism, a faith that revered God for the marvels of His universe rather than for His power over humankind.

The impact of Enlightenment ideas went far beyond religion. The writings of John Locke and other political theorists found a receptive audience. So did the work of the Scottish philosophers Francis

Hutcheson and David Hume and the French *philosophes* Montesquieu and Voltaire. Ideas generated in Europe often reached America with startling speed. *Cato's Letters,* a series of essays attacking political and religious corruption, written in the 1720s by the Englishmen John Trenchard and Thomas Gordon, appeared only months later in America, where they were quoted in newspapers from Massachusetts to Georgia. No colonial political controversy really heated up in America until all involved had published pamphlets citing a half dozen European authorities. Radical ideas that in Europe were discussed only by an intellectual elite became almost commonplace in the colonies.

As the topics of learned discourse expanded, ministers lost their monopoly on intellectual life. By the 1750s only a minority of Harvard and Yale graduates were becoming ministers. The College of Philadelphia (later the University of Pennsylvania), founded in 1751, and King's College (later Columbia), founded in New York in 1754, were two of the growing ranks of American colleges that were never primarily training grounds for clergymen.

Lawyers, who first appeared in any number in colonial towns in the 1740s, swiftly asserted their intellectual authority in public affairs. Physicians and the handful of professors of natural history declared themselves better able to make sense of the new scientific discoveries than clergymen. Yet because fields of knowledge were far less specialized than in modern times, self-educated amateurs could also make useful contributions.

The most famous instances of popular participation occurred in Philadelphia. It was there, in 1727, that 21-year-old Benjamin Franklin founded the Junto, a club at which he and other young artisans gathered on Friday evenings to discuss "any point of morals, politics, or natural philosophy." In 1743 Franklin established an expanded version of the Junto, the American Philosophical Society, which he hoped would "cultivate the finer arts and improve the common stock of knowledge."

Colonial Scientific Achievements

America produced no Galileo or Newton, but colonists contributed significantly to the collection of scientific knowledge. The unexplored continent provided a laboratory for the study of natural phenomena. The Philadelphia Quaker, John Bartram, a "down right plain Country Man," ranged from Florida to the Great Lakes during the middle years of the 18th century, gathering and classifying hundreds of plants. Bartram also studied Indians closely, speculating about their origins and collecting information about their culture. Cadwallader Colden, lieutenant governor of New York from 1761 to 1776, made important contributions to the systematic study of American flora and fauna.

Astronomy was another science to which 18th-century Americans were able to contribute by virtue of their distance from Europe. In 1761 Professor John Winthrop of Harvard, a descendant of the first governor of the Massachusetts Bay Colony, led a scientific expedition to Newfoundland, the only place in British North America from which the transit of the planet Venus could be observed. Winthrop's observations enabled him to calculate the distance of the sun from the earth with an error of only 2 percent. Another transit of Venus passed directly over several colonies in 1769. It attracted the attention of amateur astronomers from Massachusetts to Maryland. The most accurate observations were made by David Rittenhouse of Phil-

The first orrery (model of the solar system) constructed in America was built by David Rittenhouse in 1767 as a teaching tool. This is a modern restoration.

adelphia. Thomas Jefferson later described Rittenhouse somewhat hyperbolically as "second to no astronomer living." Rittenhouse's other claim to scientific eminence was his construction of the first orrery (a mechanical model of the solar system) in America.

Jefferson was on firmer ground when he said of Benjamin Franklin that "no one of the present age has made more important discoveries." One of Franklin's biographers called him a "harmonious human multitude." His studies of electricity, which he capped in 1752 with his famous kite experiment, established him as a scientist of international stature. He also invented the lightning rod, the iron Franklin stove (a far more efficient way to heat a room than an open fireplace), bifocal spectacles, and several other ingenious devices. In addition, he served 14 years (1751–1764) in the Pennsylvania assembly. He founded a circulating library, helped get the first hospital in Philadelphia built, and was an organizer of a volunteer fire company. In his spare time he taught himself Latin, French, Spanish, and Italian.

Franklin wrote so much about the virtues of hard work and thrift that some historians have described him as stuffy and straitlaced. Nothing could be further from the truth. He recognized the social value of conventional behavior, but he was no slave to convention. He fathered two illegitimate children and wrote satirical essays on such subjects as the advantage of having affairs with older and plain-looking women (who were, he claimed, more likely to appreciate the attention). And he had the perfect temperament, being open-minded and imaginative as well as shrewd and judicious—an unbeatable combination.

Franklin's international fame notwithstanding, the theoretical contributions of American thinkers and scientists were modest. No colony produced a Voltaire, a Gibbon, a Rousseau. Most were practical rather than speculative types, tinkerers rather than constructors of grand designs. As one observer noted, they were easily diverted "by Business or Inclination from profound Study, and prying into the Depth of Things." Thomas Jefferson, for example, made no theoretical discovery of importance, but his range was almost without limit: linguist, bibliophile, political scientist, architect, inventor, scientific farmer, and, above all, apostle of reason. "Fix reason firmly in her seat," he wrote, "and call to her tribunal every fact, every opinion."

Involvement at even the most marginal level in

the intellectual affairs of Europe gave influential New Englanders, middle colonists, and southerners a chance to get to know one another. Although their role in what Jefferson called "the Republic of Letters" was still minor, by mid-century their influence on the intellectual climate of the colonies was growing. That climate was one of eager curiosity, flexibility of outlook, and confidence.

Other People's Wars

The British colonies were part of a great empire that was part of a still larger world. Seemingly isolated in their remote communities, scattered like a broken string of beads between the wide Atlantic and the trackless Appalachian forests, Americans were constantly affected by outside events both in the Old World and in the New. Under the spell of mercantilistic logic, the western European nations competed fiercely for markets and colonial materials. War—hot and cold, declared and undeclared—was almost a permanent condition of 17th- and 18th-century life, and when the powers clashed, they fought wherever they could get at one another, in America, in Europe, and elsewhere.

Although the American colonies were minor pieces in the game and were sometimes casually exchanged or sacrificed by the masterminds in London, Paris, and Madrid in pursuit of some supposedly more important objective, the colonists quickly generated their own international animosities. North America, a huge and, compared to densely populated Europe, almost empty stage, evidently did not provide enough room for French, Dutch, Spanish, and English companies to perform. Frenchmen and Spaniards clashed savagely in Florida in the 16th century. Before the landing of the Pilgrims, Samuel Argall of Virginia was sacking French settlements in Maine and carrying off Jesuit priests into captivity at Jamestown. Instead of fostering tranquillity and generosity, the abundance of America seemed to make the settlers belligerent and greedy.

The North Atlantic fisheries quickly became a source of trouble between Canadian and New England colonists, despite the fact that the waters of the Grand Banks teemed with cod and other fish. To dry and salt their catch, the fishermen needed land bases, and French and English Americans struggled constantly over the harbors of Maine, Nova Scotia, and Newfoundland.

Even more troublesome was the fur trade. The yield of the forest was easily exhausted by indiscriminate slaughter, and traders contended bitterly to control valuable hunting grounds. The French in Canada conducted their fur trading through tribes such as the Algonquins and the Hurons. This brought them into conflict with the Five Nations, the powerful Iroquois confederation of central New York.

As early as 1609 the Five Nations were at war with the French and their Indian allies. For decades this struggle flared sporadically, the Iroquois more than holding their own both as fighters and as traders. They combined, according to one terrified Frenchman, the stealth and craftiness of the fox, the ferocity and courage of the lion, and the speed of a bird in flight. The Iroquois brought quantities of beaver pelts to the Dutch at Albany, some obtained by their own trappers, others taken by ambushing the fur-laden canoes of their enemies. They preyed on and ultimately destroyed the Hurons in the land north of Lake Ontario and dickered with Indian trappers in far-off Michigan. When the English took over the New Amsterdam colony, they eagerly adopted the Iroquois as allies, buying their furs and supplying them with trading goods and guns.

By the last decade of the 17th century it had become clear that the Dutch lacked the strength to maintain a big empire and that Spain was declining fast. The future, especially in North America, belonged to England and France. In the wars of the next 125 years, European alliances shifted dramatically, yet the English and what the Boston lawyer John Adams called "the turbulent Gallicks" were always on opposite sides.

In the first three of these conflicts, colonists played only minor parts. The fighting in America consisted chiefly of sneak attacks on isolated outposts. In King William's War (1689–1697), the American phase of the War of the League of Augsburg, French forces raided Schenectady in New York and frontier settlements in New England. English colonists retaliated by capturing Port Royal, Nova Scotia, only to lose that outpost in a counterattack in 1691. The Peace of Ryswick in 1697 restored all captured territory in America to the original owners.

The next struggle was the War of the Spanish

English ties with the Iroquois aided the colonists both economically and politically. Here, Sir William Johnson supervises a treaty session with tribal leaders. Johnson, a rich fur trader, was sympathetic to the Indians (he married a Mohawk woman) but drove a hard bargain when negotiating with them to add to his own vast estates.

Succession (1702–1713), fought to prevent the union of Spain and France under the Bourbons. The Americans named this conflict Queen Anne's War. French-inspired Abenaki Indians razed Deerfield, Massachusetts. A party of Carolinians burned St. Augustine in Spanish Florida. The New Englanders retook Port Royal. However, in Europe the forces of England, Holland, and Austria, led by the duke of Marlborough, won a series of decisive victories. In the Treaty of Utrecht in 1713, France yielded Nova Scotia, Newfoundland, and the Hudson Bay region to Great Britain.

If the colonies were mere pawns in these wars, the people of New England (and of Canada) paid heavily in them. Many frontier settlers were killed in the raids. Hundreds of townspeople died during the campaigns in Nova Scotia. Massachusetts taxes went up sharply, and the colony issued large amounts of paper currency to pay its bills, causing an inflation that ate into the living standards of wage earners.

The American phase of the third Anglo-French conflict, the War of the Austrian Succession (1740–1748), was called King George's War. The usual Indian raids were launched in both directions across the lonely forests that separated the St. Lawrence settlements from the New York and New England frontier. A New England force captured the strategic fortress of Louisbourg on Cape Breton Island, guarding the entrance to the Gulf of St. Lawrence.

The Treaty of Aix-la-Chapelle in 1748, however, required the return of Louisbourg, much to the chagrin of the New Englanders.

As this incident suggests, the colonial wars generated a certain amount of trouble between England and the colonies; matters that seemed unimportant in London might loom large in American eyes, and vice versa. But the conflicts were seldom serious. The wars did, however, increase the bad feelings between settlers north and south of the St. Lawrence. Every Indian raid was attributed to French provocateurs, although more often than not the English colonists themselves were responsible for the Indian troubles. Conflicting land claims further aggravated the situation. Massachusetts, Connecticut, and Virginia possessed overlapping claims to the Ohio Valley, and Pennsylvania and New York also had pretensions in the region. Yet the French, ranging broadly across the midcontinent, insisted that the Ohio country was exclusively theirs.

The Great War for the Empire

In this beautiful, almost untouched land, a handful of individuals determined the future of the continent. Over the years the French had established a chain of forts and trading posts running from Mackinac Island in northern Michigan to Kaskaskia on the Mississippi and Vincennes on the Wabash and from Niagara in the east to the Bourbon River, near Lake Winnipeg, in the west. By the 1740s, however, Pennsylvania fur traders, led by George Croghan, a rugged Irishman, were setting up posts north of the Ohio River and dickering with Miami and Huron Indians who ordinarily sold their furs to the French. In 1748 Croghan built a fort at Pickawillany, deep in the Miami country, in what is now western Ohio. That same year agents of a group of Virginia land speculators who had recently organized what they called the Ohio Company reached this area.

With trifling exceptions, an insulating band of wilderness had always separated the French and English in America. Now the two powers came into contact. The immediate result was a showdown battle for control of North America, the "great war for the empire." Thoroughly alarmed by the presence of the English on land they had long considered their own, the French struck hard. Attacking suddenly in 1752, they wiped out Croghan's post at Pickawillany and drove his traders back into Pennsylvania. Then they built a string of barrier forts south from Lake Erie along the Pennsylvania line: Fort Presque Isle, Fort Le Boeuf, Fort Venango.

The Pennsylvania authorities chose to ignore this action, but Lieutenant Governor Robert Dinwiddie of Virginia (who was an investor in the Ohio Company) dispatched a 21-year-old surveyor named George Washington to warn the French that they were trespassing on Virginia territory.

Washington, a gangling, inarticulate, and intensely ambitious young planter, made his way northwest in the fall of 1753 and delivered Dinwiddie's message to the commandant at Fort Le Boeuf. It made no impression. "[The French] told me," Washington reported, "that it was their absolute Design to take Possession of the Ohio, and by G—— they would do it." Governor Dinwiddie thereupon promoted Washington to lieutenant colonel and sent him back in the spring of 1754 with 150 men to seize a strategic junction south of the new French forts, where the Allegheny and Monongahela rivers join to form the Ohio.

Eager but inexperienced in battle, young Washington botched his assignment. As his force labored painfully through the tangled mountain country southeast of the fork of the Ohio, he received word that the French had already occupied the position and were constructing a powerful post, Fort Duquesne. Outnumbered by perhaps four to one, Washington foolishly pushed on. He surprised and routed a French reconnaissance party, but this brought upon him the main body of enemy troops.

Hastily he threw up a defensive position, aptly named Fort Necessity, but the ground was ill chosen; the French easily surrounded the fort, and Washington had to surrender. After tricking the young officer, who could not read French, into signing an admission that he had "assassinated" the leader of the reconnaissance party, his captors, with the gateway to the Ohio country firmly in their hands, permitted him and his men to march off. Nevertheless, Washington returned to Virginia a hero, for although still undeclared, this was war, and he had struck the first blow against the hated French.

In the resulting conflict, which they called the French and Indian War, the English colonists outnumbered the French by about 1.5 million to 90,000. But the English were divided and disorganized, the

French disciplined and united. The French controlled the disputed territory, and most of the Indians took their side. As a colonial official wrote, together they made formidable forest fighters, "sometimes in our Front, sometimes in our Rear, and often on all sides of us, Hussar Fashion, taking the Advantage of every Tree and Bush." With the ignorance and arrogance typical of 18th-century colonial administration, the British mismanaged the war and failed to make effective use of local resources. For several years they stumbled from one defeat to another.

General Edward Braddock, a competent but uninspired soldier, was dispatched to Virginia to take command. In June 1755 he marched against Fort Duquesne with 1,400 Redcoats and a smaller number of colonials, only to be ambushed and decisively defeated by a much smaller force of French and Indians. Braddock died bravely in battle, and only 500 of his men, led by Colonel Washington, who was serving as his aide-de-camp, made their way back to Virginia.

Elsewhere Anglo-American arms fared little better in the early years of the war. Expeditions against

A key phase of Pitt's American strategy involved capturing the French strongpoints guarding the approaches to Canada: Louisbourg, protecting the St. Lawrence; Fort Ticonderoga and Crown Point, on Lake Champlain; and Fort Duquesne, in the Ohio country. Colonial forces played a significant role in this strategy, with John Forbes seizing Fort Duquesne, John Bradstreet winning control of Lake Ontario, and William Johnson taking Fort Niagara.

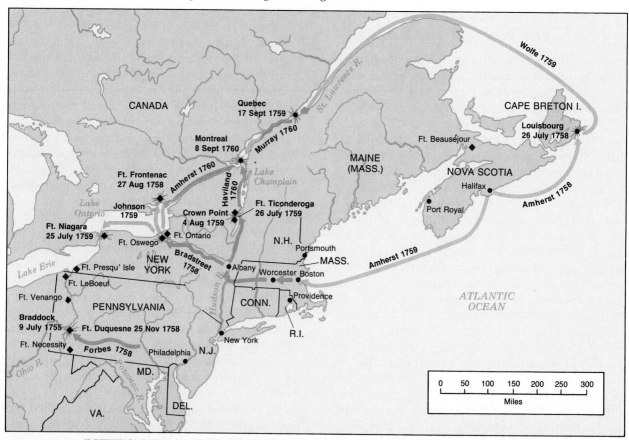

PITT'S STRATEGY, FRENCH AND INDIAN WAR, 1758–1760

Wolfe and Amherst recaptured the French fortress of Louisbourg in July 1758. This watercolor is the work of Thomas Davies, an English artillery officer. Louisbourg is at center, under attack from Amherst's siege lines at right and Admiral Boscawen's British fleet lying offshore. French ships are aflame in the harbor.

Fort Niagara, key to all French defenses in the west, and Crown Point, gateway to Montreal, bogged down. Meanwhile Indians, armed by the French, bathed the frontier in blood. Venting the frustration caused by 150 years of white advance, they attacked defenseless outposts with unrestrained brutality. They poured molten lead into their victims' wounds, ripped off the fingernails of captives, even drank the blood of those who endured their tortures stoically.* The most feared of the "French" Indians were the Delawares, a once-peaceful Pennsylvania tribe that had been harried from their homelands by the English and the Iroquois. General Braddock paid his Indian allies only £5 each for French scalps but offered £200 for the hair of Shinngass, the Delaware chieftain.

In 1756 the conflict spread to Europe to become the Seven Years' War. Prussia sided with Great Brit-ain, Austria with the French. On the world stage, too, things went badly for the British. Finally, in 1757, as defeat succeeded defeat, King George II was forced to allow William Pitt, whom he detested, to take over leadership of the war effort. Pitt, grandson of "Diamond" Pitt, a *nouveau riche* East India merchant, was an unstable man who spent much of his life on the verge of madness, but he was a brilliant strategist and capable of inspiring the nation in its hour of trial.

Pitt recognized, as few contemporaries did, the potential value of North America. Instead of relying on the tightfisted and shortsighted colonial assemblies for men and money, he poured regiment after regiment of British regulars and the full resources of the British treasury into the contest, mortgaging the future recklessly to secure the prize. Grasping the importance of sea power in fighting a war on the other side of the Atlantic, he used the British navy to bottle up the enemy fleet and hamper French communications with Canada. He possessed a keen eye for military genius, and when he discovered it, he ignored seniority and the outraged

---

* The anthropologist Bruce Trigger writes: "If the prisoner had been a brave man, his heart was cooked and eaten by the young [Huron] warriors, who believed that they would acquire his courage in this manner. . . . It was an act of religious significance."

feelings of mediocre generals and promoted talented young officers to top commands. (His greatest find was James Wolfe, whom he made a brigadier at 31.)

In the winter of 1758, as Pitt's grand strategy matured, Fort Duquesne fell. It was appropriately renamed Fort Pitt, the present Pittsburgh. The following summer Fort Niagara was overrun. General Jeffrey Amherst took Crown Point, and Wolfe sailed up the St. Lawrence to Quebec. There General Louis Joseph de Montcalm had prepared formidable defenses, but after months of probing and planning, Wolfe found and exploited a chink in the city's armor and captured it. Both he and Montcalm died in the battle. In 1760 Montreal fell and the French abandoned all Canada to the British.

Spain attempted to stem the British advance but failed utterly. A Far Eastern fleet captured Manila in 1762, and another British force took Cuba. The French sugar islands in the West Indies were also captured, while in India, British troops reduced the French posts one by one.

The Peace of Paris

Peace was restored in 1763 by the Treaty of Paris. Its terms were moderate considering the extent of the British triumph. France abandoned all claim to North America except for two small islands near Newfoundland; Great Britain took over Canada and the eastern half of the Mississippi Valley. Although the British considered the French sugar islands, Guadeloupe and Martinique, more economically valuable than the cold Canadian wilderness, they kept Canada for military and strategic reasons and returned the islands to France, along with some of the captured French bases in India and Africa. Spain got back both the Philippine Islands and Cuba but in exchange ceded East and West Florida to Great Britain. In a separate treaty, Spain also got New Orleans and the huge area of North America west of the Mississippi River. France and Spain thus remained important colonial powers.

"Half the continent," the historian Francis Parkman wrote, "had changed hands at the scratch of a pen." From the point of view of the English colonists in America, the victory was overwhelming. All threat to their frontiers seemed to have been swept away. Surely, they believed in the first happy

moments of victory, their peaceful and prosperous expansion was assured for countless generations.

No honest American could deny that the victory had been won chiefly by British troops and with British gold. Colonial militiamen fought well in defense of their homes or when some highly prized objective seemed ripe for the plucking; they lacked discipline and determination when required to fight far from home and under commanders they did not know. As one American official admitted, it was difficult to get New Englanders to enlist "unless assurances can be given that they shall not march to the southward of certain limits."

Colonials were delighted that scarlet-clad British regulars had borne the brunt of the fighting and happier still that the Crown had shouldered most of the financial burden of the long struggle. The local assemblies contributed to the cost, but except for Massachusetts and Virginia, their outlays were trivial compared with the £82 million poured into the worldwide conflict by the British.

Little wonder that the great victory produced a burst of praise for king and mother country throughout America. Parades, cannonading, fireworks, banquets, the pealing of church bells— these were the order of the day in every colonial town. Ezra Stiles, later president of Yale, extolled "the illustrious House of Hanover," whose new head, the young George III, had inherited the throne in 1760. "Nothing," said Thomas Pownall, wartime governor of Massachusetts and a student of colonial administration, "can eradicate from [the colonists'] hearts their natural, almost mechanical affection to Great Britain."

Putting the Empire Right

In London peace proved a time for reassessment; that the empire of 1763 was not the same as the empire of 1754 was obvious. The new, far larger dominion would be much more expensive to maintain. Pitt had spent a huge sum winning and securing it, much of it borrowed money. Great Britain's national debt had doubled between 1754 and 1763. Now this debt must be serviced and repaid, and the strain that this would place on the economy was clear to all. Furthermore, the day-to-day cost of administering an empire that extended from Hudson Bay to India was far larger than what the already burdened British taxpayer could be expected to bear. Before the great war for the empire, Britain's North American possessions were administered for about £70,000 a year; after 1763 the cost was five times as much.

The American empire had also grown far more complex. A system of administration that treated it as a string of separate plantations struggling to exist on the edge of the forest would no longer suffice. The war had been fought for control of the Ohio Valley. Now that the prize had been secured, ten thousand hands were eager to make off with it. The urge to expand was, despite the continent's enormous empty spaces, an old American drive. As early as the 1670s, eastern stay-at-homes were lamenting the "insatiable desire after Land" that made people willing to "live like Heathen, only that so they might have Elbow-room enough in the world." Frontier warfare had frustrated this urge for seven long years. How best could it be satisfied now that peace had come?

Conflicting colonial claims, based on charters drafted by men who thought the Pacific lay over the next hill, threatened to make the great valley a battleground once more. The Indians remained unpacified. Rival land companies contested for charters, while fur traders strove to hold back the wave of settlement that must inevitably destroy the world of the beaver and the deer. One Englishman who traveled through America at this time predicted that if the colonists were left to their own devices, "there would soon be civil war from one end of the continent to the other."

Apparently only Great Britain could deal with these problems and rivalries, for when Franklin had proposed a rudimentary form of colonial union— the Albany Plan of 1754—it was rejected by almost everyone. Unfortunately, the British government did not rise to the challenge. Perhaps this was to be expected. A handful of aristocrats (fewer than 150 peers were active in government affairs) dominated British politics, and they were more concerned with local offices and personal advantage than with large questions of policy. An American who spent some time in London in 1764 trying to obtain approval for a plan for the development of the west reported: "The people hear Spend thire time in Nothing but abuseing one Another and Striveing who shall be in power with a view to Serve themselves and Thire friends." King George III was not a tyrant, as once

was commonly believed, but he was an inept politician and the victim of frequent bouts of illness.

Even the best-educated English leaders were nearly all monumentally ignorant of American conditions. The British imperial system lacked effective channels of communication. Information about American attitudes came from royal officials in the colonies and others with special interests to protect or advance, or from the colonial agents and merchants in London, whose information was often out-of-date.

Serene in their ignorance, most English leaders insisted that colonials were uncouth and generally inferior beings. During the French and Indian War, General Wolfe characterized colonial troops as "the dirtiest, most contemptible cowardly dogs you can conceive," and another English officer compared the ordinary run to "broken innkeepers, horse jockeys and Indian traders."

Any officer with a royal commission outranked all officers of the colonial militia, regardless of title. Young Colonel Washington, for example, had to travel all the way from Virginia to the headquarters of the commander in chief in Boston to establish his precedence over one Captain John Dagworthy, a Maryland officer who had formerly held a royal commission and who did not propose to let a mere colonial colonel outrank him.

Many English people resented the colonists because they were rapidly becoming rich and powerful. Shortly after the war, John Adams predicted that within a century America would be wealthier and more populous than Great Britain.* If the English did not say much about this possibility, they too considered it from time to time—without Adams's relish.

Tightening Imperial Controls

The attempt of the inefficient British government to deal with the intricate colonial problems that resulted from the great war for the empire led to the American Revolution—a rebellion that was costly but produced excellent results for the colonists, for Great Britain, for the rest of the empire, and eventually for the entire world. Trouble began when the

---

* As early as 1751, Franklin predicted that in a century "the greatest number of Englishmen will be on this Side of the Water."

British decided after the war to intervene more actively in American affairs. Theoretically, the colonies were entirely subordinate to Crown and Parliament, yet except for the disastrous attempt to centralize control of the colonies in the 1680s, they had been allowed a remarkable degree of freedom to manage their own affairs. Of course, they had come to expect this as their right.

Parliament had never attempted to raise a revenue in America. "Compelling the colonies to pay money without their consent would be rather like raising contributions in an enemy's country than taxing Englishmen for their own benefit," Benjamin Franklin wrote. Sir Robert Walpole, initiator of the policy of salutary neglect, recognized the colonial viewpoint. He responded to a suggestion that Parliament tax the colonies by saying: "I will leave that for some of my successors, who may have more courage than I have." Nevertheless, the *legality* of parliamentary taxation, or of other parliamentary

intervention in colonial affairs, had not been seriously contested. During King George's War and again during the French and Indian War, many British officials in America suggested that Parliament tax the colonies.

Nothing was done until 1759, when British victories had made ultimate triumph sure. Then a general tightening of imperial regulations began. Royal control over colonial courts was strengthened. In Massachusetts the use of general search warrants (writs of assistance) was authorized in 1761. These writs enabled customs officers searching for smuggled goods to enter homes and warehouses without evidence or specific court orders. Nearly all Americans resented the invasions of privacy that the writs caused. A Boston lawyer, James Otis, argued in a case involving 63 merchants that the writs were "against the Constitution" and therefore void. Otis lost the case but by boldly suggesting that Parliament's authority over the colonies was not absolute, he became a colonial hero.

After the signing of the peace treaty in 1763, events pushed the British authorities to still more vigorous activity in America. Freed of the restraint posed by French competition, Englishman and colonist increased their pressure on the Indians. Fur traders now cheated them outrageously, while callous military men hoped to exterminate them like vermin. One British officer expressed the wish that they could be hunted down with dogs.

Led by an Ottawa chief named Pontiac, the tribes made one last effort to drive the whites back across the mountains. What the whites called Pontiac's "rebellion" caused much havoc, but it failed. By 1764 most of the western tribes had accepted the peace terms offered by a royal commissioner, Sir William Johnson, one of the few whites who understood and sympathized with them. The British government then placed 15 regiments, some 6,000 soldiers, in posts along the entire arc of the frontier, as much to protect the Indians from the settlers as the settlers from the Indians. It proclaimed a new western policy: No settlers were to cross the Appalachian divide. Only licensed traders might do business with the Indians beyond that line. The purchase of Indian land was forbidden. In compensation, three new colonies—Quebec, East Florida, and West Florida—were created, but they were not permitted to set up local assemblies.

(Russians)

Great Lakes

ATLANTIC OCEAN

GULF OF MEXICO

CARIBBEAN SEA

English

French

Spanish

EUROPEAN CLAIMS IN ALL OF NORTH AMERICA, 1763

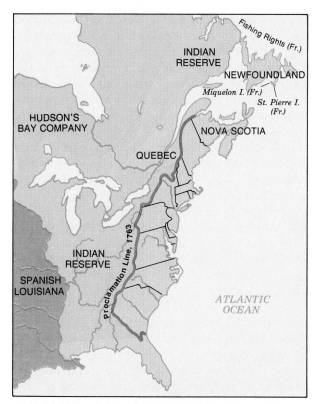

EASTERN NORTH AMERICA, 1763

George III's Proclamation of 1763 in effect reserved for the Indians the vast area across the Appalachians (except for the new royal colonies of Quebec, East Florida, and West Florida) as far west as Spanish Louisiana and as far north as the Hudson's Bay Company preserve.

This Proclamation of 1763 excited much indignation in America. The frustration of dozens of schemes for land development in the Ohio Valley angered many influential colonists. Colonel Washington referred to the proclamation contemptuously as "a temporary expedient to quiet the minds of Indians," and he continued to stake out claims to western lands.

Originally the British had intended the proclamation to be temporary. With the passage of time, however, checking westward expansion seemed a good way to save money, prevent trouble with the Indians, and keep the colonies tied closely to the mother country. The proclamation line, the Board of Trade declared, was "necessary for the preser-

vation of the colonies in due subordination."* Naturally, this attitude caused resentment in America. To close off the west temporarily in order to pacify the Indians made some sense; to keep it closed was like trying to contain a tidal wave.

The Sugar Act

Americans disliked the new western policy but realized that the problems were knotty and that no simple solution existed. Their protests were somewhat muted. Great Britain's effort to raise money in America to help support the increased cost of colonial administration caused far more vehement complaints. George Grenville, who became prime minister in 1763, was a fairly able man, although long-winded and rather narrow in outlook. His reputation as a financial expert was based chiefly on his eagerness to reduce government spending. Under his leadership Parliament passed, in April 1764, the so-called Sugar Act. This law placed tariffs on sugar, coffee, wines, and other things imported into America in substantial amounts. Taxes on European products imported by way of Great Britain were doubled, and the enumerated articles list was extended to include iron, raw silk, and potash. The sixpence-per-gallon tax on foreign molasses, imposed in 1733 and designed to be prohibitively high, was reduced to threepence, at which level the foreign product could compete with molasses from the British West Indies.

At the same time, measures aimed at enforcing all the trade laws were put into effect. (A threepenny molasses duty would not produce much revenue if it were as easy to avoid as the old levy had been.) Anyone accused of violating the Sugar Act was to be tried before British naval officers in vice-admiralty courts. Grenville was determined to end smuggling, corruption, and inefficiency. Soon the customs service was collecting each year 15 times as much in duties as it had before the war.

The Sugar Act and the decision of the government in London to restrict the printing of paper

---

* The British were particularly concerned about preserving the colonies as markets for their manufactures. They feared that the spread of population beyond the mountains would stimulate local manufacturing because the high cost of land transportation would make British goods prohibitively expensive.

money in the colonies disturbed Americans deeply. Throughout the 18th century, local assemblies had issued paper currency in anticipation of tax payments to finance emergencies such as wars. The act of 1764 did not entirely ban the use of colonial paper money. But the colonists saw the law as an attack on the power of their assemblies. The law also came at a bad time. During the war the seaports prospered and shipbuilding boomed. Merchants earned fat profits supplying the British forces with food and other goods. British soldiers and sailors, 40,000 of them, spent most of their wages in the colonies.

When the fighting shifted to the Caribbean after the fall of Canada, most of this spending stopped. The soldiers "are gone to drink [rum] in a warmer Region, the place of its production," a New York merchant mourned. A depression increased the impact of the new laws. Hard-hit merchants and artisans found British policy alarming.

Far more alarming was the nature of the Sugar Act and the manner of its passage. The Navigation Act duties had been intended to regulate commerce, and the sums collected had not cut deeply into profits. Indeed, the Navigation Acts might well be considered an instrument of imperial foreign policy, an area of government that everyone willingly conceded to London. Yet few Americans were willing to concede that Parliament had the right to tax them. As *Englishmen* they believed that no one should be deprived arbitrarily of property and that, as James Otis put it in his stirring pamphlet *The Rights of the British Colonies Asserted and Proved*, written during the controversy over writs of assistance, everyone should be "free from all taxes but what he consents to in person, or by his representative." John Locke had made clear in his *Second Treatise on Government* (1690) that property ought never be taken from people without their consent, not because material values transcend all others but because human liberty can never be secure when arbitrary power of any kind exists. "If our Trade may be taxed why not our Lands?" the Boston town meeting asked when news of the Sugar Act reached America. "Why not the produce of our Lands and every Thing we possess or make use of?"

"Essential Rights and Liberties"

To most people in Great Britain, the colonial protest against taxation without representation seemed a hypocritical quibble, and it is probably true that in 1764 many of the protesters had not thought the argument through. The distinction between tax laws and other types of legislation was artificial, the British reasoned. Either Parliament was sovereign in America or it was not, and only a fool or a traitor would argue that it was not. If the colonists were loyal subjects of George III, as they claimed, they should bear cheerfully their fair share of the cost of governing his widespread dominions. As to representation, the colonies *were* represented in Parliament; every member of that body stood for the interests of the entire empire. If Americans had no say in the election of members of Commons, neither did most English subjects.

This concept of "virtual" representation accurately described the British system. But it made no sense in America, where from the time of the first settlements members of the colonial assemblies had represented the people of the districts in which they stood for office. The confusion between virtual and actual (geographically based) representation revealed the extent to which colonial and British political practices had diverged over the years.

The British were correct in concluding that selfish motives influenced colonial objections to the Sugar Act. The colonists denounced taxation without representation, but an offer of a reasonable number of seats in Parliament would not have satisfied them. They would probably have complained about paying taxes to support imperial administration even if imposed by their own assemblies. American abundance and the simplicity of colonial life had enabled them to prosper without assuming any considerable tax burden. Now their maturing society was beginning to require communal rather than individual solutions to the problems of existence. Not many of them were prepared to face up to this hard truth.

Over the course of colonial history, Americans had taken a narrow view of imperial concerns. They had avoided complying with the Navigation Acts whenever they could profit by doing so. Colonial militiamen had compiled a sorry record when asked to fight for Britain or even for the inhabitants of colonies other than their own. True, most Americans professed loyalty to the Crown, but not many would voluntarily open their purses except to benefit themselves. In short, they were provincials, in attitude and in fact.

But the colonists were opposed in principle to

taxation without representation. They failed, however, to agree on a common plan of resistance. Many of the assemblies drafted protests, but these varied in force as well as in form. Merchant groups that tried to organize boycotts of products subject to the new taxes met with indifferent success. Then in 1765 Parliament provided the flux necessary for welding colonial opinion by passing the Stamp Act.

The Stamp Act: The Pot Set to Boiling

The Stamp Act placed stiff excise taxes on all kinds of printed matter—newspapers, legal documents, licenses, even playing cards. Stamp duties were intended to be relatively painless to pay and cheap to collect; in England similar taxes brought in about £100,000 annually. Grenville hoped that the Stamp Act would produce £60,000 a year in America, and the law provided that all revenue should be applied to "defraying the necessary expenses of defending, protecting, and securing" the colonies.

Hardly a farthing was collected. As the Boston clergyman Jonathan Mayhew explained, "Almost every British American . . . considered it as an infraction of their rights, or their dearly purchased privileges." The Sugar Act had been related to Parliament's uncontested power to control colonial trade, but the Stamp Act was a direct tax. When Parliament ignored the politely phrased petitions of the colonial assemblies, more vigorous protests quickly followed.

Virginia took the lead. In late May 1765 Patrick Henry, fresh from his triumph in the "Parson's Cause" controversy, in which he had opposed the right of the British Privy Council to void a law passed by the House of Burgesses, introduced resolutions asserting redundantly that the Burgesses possessed "the only and sole and exclusive right and power to lay taxes" on Virginians and suggesting that Parliament had no legal authority to tax the colonies at all. Henry spoke for what the royal governor called the "Young, hot and Giddy Members" of the legislature (most of whom, incidentally, had absented themselves from the meeting). The more extreme of Henry's resolutions failed of enactment, but the debate they occasioned attracted wide and favorable attention. On June 6 the Massachusetts assembly proposed an intercolonial Stamp Act Con-

gress, which, when it met in New York City in October, passed another series of resolutions of protest. The Stamp Act and other recent acts of Parliament were "burthensome and grievous," the delegates declared. "It is unquestionably essential to the freedom of a people . . . that no taxes be imposed on them but with their own consent."

During the summer, irregular organizations known as the Sons of Liberty began to agitate against the act. Far more than anyone realized, this marked the start of the revolution. For the first time, extralegal organized resistance was taking place, distinct from protest and argument conducted by constituted organs of government like the House of Burgesses and the Massachusetts General Court.

Although led by men of character and position, the "Liberty Boys" frequently resorted to violence to achieve their aims. In Boston they staged vicious riots, looting and vandalizing the houses of the stamp master and his brother-in-law, Lieutenant Governor Thomas Hutchinson. In Connecticut stamp master Jared Ingersoll, a man of great courage and dignity, faced an angry mob demanding his resignation. When threatened with death if he refused, he coolly replied that he was prepared to die "perhaps as well now as another Time." Probably his life was not really in danger, but the size and determination of the crowd convinced him that resistance was useless, and he capitulated.

The stamps were printed in England and shipped to stamp masters (all Americans) in the colonies well in advance of November 1, 1765, the date the law was to go into effect. The New York stamp master had resigned, but the stamps were stored in the city under military guard. Radicals distributed placards reading, "The first Man that either distributes or makes use of Stampt Paper let him take care of his House, Person, and Effects. We dare." When Major Thomas James, the British officer who had charge of the stamps, promised that "the stamps would be crammed down New Yorkers' throats," a mob responded by breaking into his house, drinking all his wine, and smashing his furniture and china, reducing the place to a shambles.

In some colonies the stamps were snatched by mobs and put to the torch amid rejoicing. Elsewhere they were locked up in secret by British officials or held on shipboard. For a time no business requiring stamped paper was transacted; then, gradually, people began to defy the law by issuing and accepting unstamped documents. Threatened by mob action

Outrage at the Stamp Act was demonstrated all over the colonies in incidents like this, where the effigy of a New Hampshire stamp master is ridiculed by the townspeople.

should they resist, British officials stood by helplessly. The law was a dead letter.

The looting associated with this crisis alarmed many colonists, including some prominent opponents of the Stamp Act. "When the pot is set to boil," the lawyer John Adams remarked sadly, "the scum rises to the top." Another Bostonian called the vandalizing of Thomas Hutchinson's house a "flagrant instance of to what a pitch of infatuation an incensed populace can rise." Such people worried that the protests might be aimed at the wealthy and powerful in America as well as at British tyranny. This does not mean that they disapproved of crowd protests, or even the destruction of property during such protests, as distinct from stealing. Many such people took part in the rioting. "State-quakes," John Adams also said, this time complacently, were comparable to earthquakes and other kinds of natural violence.

Rioters or Rebels?

That many of the poor resented the colonial elite goes without saying, as does the fact that in many instances the rioting got out of hand and took on a social as well as a political character. Times were hard, and the colonial elite, including most of the leading critics of British policy, had little compassion for the poor, who they feared could be corrupted

by anyone who offered them a square meal or a glass of rum. Once aroused, laborers and artisans may well have directed their energies toward righting what they considered local wrongs.

Yet the mass of the people, being owners of property and capable of influencing political decisions, were not social revolutionaries. They might envy and resent the wealth and power of the great landowners and merchants, but there is no evidence that they wished to overthrow the established order.

The British were not surprised that Americans disliked the Stamp Act. They had not anticipated, however, that Americans would react so violently and so unanimously. Americans did so for many reasons. Business continued poor in 1765, and at a time when 3 shillings was a day's wage for an urban laborer, the stamp tax was 2 shillings for an advertisement in a newspaper, 5 shillings for a will, and 20 shillings for a license to sell liquor. The taxes would hurt the business of lawyers, merchants, newspaper editors, and tavernkeepers. Even clergymen dealt with papers requiring stamps. The protests of such influential and articulate people had a powerful impact on public opinion.

The greatest cause of concern to the colonists was Great Britain's flat rejection of the principle of no taxation without representation. This alarmed them for two closely related reasons. First of all, as *Americans* they objected to being taxed by a legislative body they had not been involved in choosing. To buy a stamp was to surrender all claim to self-government. Second, as *British subjects* they valued what they called "the rights of Englishmen." They saw the Stamp Act as only the worst in a series of arbitrary invasions of these rights.

Already Parliament had passed yet another measure, the Quartering Act, requiring local legislatures to house and feed new British troops sent to the colonies. A standing army was universally deemed to be a threat to liberty. Why were Redcoats necessary in Boston and New York where there was no foreign enemy for thousands of miles in any direction? Soldiers were particularly unwelcome in hard times because, being miserably underpaid, they took any odd jobs they could get in their off hours, thus competing with unemployed colonists.

Reluctantly, many Americans were beginning to fear that the London authorities had organized a conspiracy to subvert the liberties of all British subjects.

Taxation or Tyranny?

In the 18th century the English were universally recognized as the freest people in the world. In Mozart's opera *The Abduction from the Seraglio* (1782), when the Turk Osmin tells the kidnapped Blonde that she is his slave, a "gift" from his master, she replies contemptuously: "A slave! I am an English-woman, born to freedom." Americans, like their English cousins, attributed their freedom to what they called their balanced government. In Britain power appeared to be shared by the Crown, the House of Lords (representing the aristocracy), and the House of Commons (representing the rest of the realm). The governors, councils, and assemblies seemed to play analogous roles in the colonies.

In reality this balance of separate forces never existed, either in Britain or in America. The apparent harmony of society was in both instances the product of a lack of seriously divisive issues, not of dynamic tension between rival forces. But the new laws seemed to Americans to threaten the balance, and this idea was reinforced by their observations of the corruption of English elections. Benjamin Franklin, being at the time a colonial agent in London, knew British politics well. He complained that the entire country was "at market" and "might be bought . . . by the Devil himself" for about £12

A decorated teapot—made in England!—symbolizes both American rejoicing over repeal of the Stamp Act and the resumption of colonial trade with the mother country.

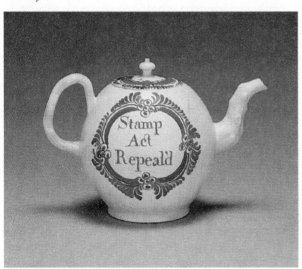

million. A clique seeking unlimited power was trying to destroy balanced government in Britain and in America, or so many colonists thought.

There was no such conspiracy; yet to the question. "Were American rights actually in danger?" no certain answer can be given. Grenville and his successors were English politicians, not tyrants. They looked down on bumptious colonials but surely had no wish to destroy either them or their prosperity. The British attitude was like that of a parent making a recalcitrant youngster swallow a bitter medicine: Protests were understandable, but in the patient's own interest they must be ignored.

At the same time, British leaders believed that the time had come to assert royal authority and centralize imperial power at the expense of colonial autonomy. The need to maintain a substantial British army in America to control the western Indians tempted the government to use some of the troops to control white Americans as well. This attitude probably had as much to do with the coming of the revolution as any specific act of Parliament because it flew in the face of the reality that the colonies had progressed beyond the childhood stage. They were no longer entirely dependent on the mother country. Indeed, an increasing number of important colonists believed that America would soon become what Franklin called "a great country, populous and mighty . . . able to shake off any shackles that may be imposed on her."

This view of America's future place in the world did not necessarily mean breaking away from the British Empire. However, it surely meant dealing with Great Britain on terms approaching equality. But psychologically British leaders were not ready to deal with Americans as equals or to consider American interests on a par with their own. In the long run, American liberty would be destroyed if this attitude was not changed.

Besides refusing to use stamps, Americans responded to the Stamp Act by boycotting British goods. Nearly 1,000 merchants signed nonimportation agreements. These struck British merchants hard in their pocketbooks, and they in turn began to bring pressure on Parliament for repeal. After a hot debate—Grenville, whose ministry had fallen over another issue, advocated using the army to enforce the act—the hated law was repealed in March 1766. In America there was jubilation at the news. The ban on British goods was lifted, and the colonists congratulated themselves on having stood fast in defense of principle.

The Declaratory Act

The great controversy over the constitutional relationship of colony to mother country was only beginning. The same day that it repealed the Stamp Act, Parliament passed the Declaratory Act, which stated that the colonies were "subordinate" and that Parliament could enact any law it wished "to bind the colonies and people of America."

To most Americans this bald statement of parliamentary authority seemed unconstitutional, a flagrant violation of their understanding of how the British imperial system was supposed to work. Actually, the Declaratory Act highlighted the degree to which British and American views of the system had drifted apart. The English and the colonials were using the same words but giving them different meanings. Their conflicting definitions of the word *representation* was a case in point. Another involved the word *constitution*, the term that James Otis had used in his attack on writs of assistance. To the British the constitution was the totality of laws, customs, and institutions that had developed over time and under which the nation functioned. In America, partly because governments were based on specific charters, the word meant a written document or contract spelling out, and thus limiting, the powers of government. If in England Parliament passed an "unconstitutional" law, the result might be rebellion, but that the law existed none would deny. "If the parliament will positively enact a thing to be done which is unreasonable," the great 18th-century English legal authority Sir William Blackstone wrote, "I know of no power that can control it." In America people were beginning to think that an unconstitutional law simply had no force.

Even more basic were the differing meanings that English and Americans were giving to the word *sovereignty*. As Bernard Bailyn has explained in *The Ideological Origins of the American Revolution*, 18th-century English political thinkers believed that sovereignty (ultimate political power) could not be divided. Government and law being based ultimately on force, some "final, unqualified, indivisible" authority had to exist if social order was to be preserved. The Glorious Revolution in England had

settled the question of where sovereignty resided: in Parliament. The Declaratory Act, so obnoxious to Americans, seemed to the English the mere explication of the obvious. That colonial governments had passed local laws the English did not deny, but they had done so at the sufferance of the sovereign legislative power, Parliament.

Given these ideas and the long tradition out of which they had sprung, one can sympathize with the British failure to follow the colonists' reasoning (which had not yet evolved into a specific proposal for constitutional reform). But most responsible British officials refused even to listen to the American argument.

The Townshend Duties

Despite the repeal of the Stamp Act, the British did not abandon the policy of taxing the colonies. If direct taxes were inexpedient, indirect ones like the Sugar Act certainly were not. To persuade Parliament to repeal the Stamp Act, some Americans (most notably Benjamin Franklin) had claimed that the colonists objected only to direct taxes. To draw such a distinction as a matter of principle was absurd, and in fact few colonists had done so. British leaders saw the absurdity but easily convinced themselves that Americans were making the distinction.

Therefore, in June 1767, the chancellor of the exchequer, Charles Townshend, introduced a series of levies on glass, lead, paints, paper, and tea imported into the colonies. Townshend was a charming man experienced in colonial administration, but he was something of a playboy (his nickname was Champagne Charlie), and he lacked both integrity and common sense. He liked to think of Americans as ungrateful children; he once said he would rather see the colonies turned into "Primitive Desarts" than treat them as equals. Townshend thought it "perfect nonsense" to draw a distinction between direct and indirect taxation, yet in his arrogance he believed that the colonists were stupid enough to do so.

By this time the colonists were thoroughly on guard, and they responded quickly to the Townshend levies with a new boycott of British goods. In addition, they made elaborate efforts to stimulate colonial manufacturing. By the end of 1769, imports from the mother country had been almost halved. Meanwhile, administrative measures enacted along with the Townshend duties were creating more ill will. The Board of Customs Commissioners, with headquarters in Boston, took charge of enforcing the trade laws, and new vice-admiralty courts were set up at Halifax, Boston, Philadelphia, and Charleston to handle violations. These courts operated without juries, and the new commissioners proved to be a gang of rapacious racketeers who systematically attempted to obtain judgments against honest merchants in order to collect the huge forfeitures—one-third of the value of ship and cargo—that were their share of all seizures.

The struggle forced Americans to do some deep thinking about both American and imperial political affairs. The colonies' common interests and growing economic and social interrelationships probably made some kind of union inevitable. Trouble with England speeded the process. In 1765 the Stamp Act Congress (another extralegal organization and thus a further step in the direction of revolution) had brought the delegates of nine colonies to New York. Now, in 1768, the Massachusetts General Court took the next step. It sent the legislatures of the other colonies a "circular letter" expressing the "humble opinion" that the Townshend Acts "imposing Duties on the People . . . with the sole & express purpose of raising a Revenue are Infringements of their natural & constitutional Rights."

The question of the limits of British power in America was much debated, and this too was no doubt inevitable, again because of change and growth. Even in the late 17th century the assumptions that led Parliament to pass the Declaratory Act would have been unrealistic. In 1766 they were absurd.

After the passage of the Townshend Acts, John Dickinson, a Philadelphia lawyer, published "Letters from a Farmer in Pennsylvania to the Inhabitants of the British Colonies." Dickinson considered himself a loyal British subject trying to find a solution to colonial troubles. "Let us behave like dutiful children, who have received unmerited blows from a beloved parent," he wrote. Nevertheless, he stated plainly that Parliament had no right to tax the colonies, though it might collect incidental revenues in the process of regulating commerce.

Some Americans were much more radical than Dickinson. Samuel Adams of Boston, a genuine revolutionary agitator, believed by 1768 that Parliament had no right at all to legislate for the colonies.

If few were ready to go that far, fewer still accepted the reasoning behind the Declaratory Act.

The British ignored American thinking. The Massachusetts Circular Letter had been framed in moderate language and clearly reflected the convictions of most of the people in the Bay Colony, yet when news of it reached England, the secretary of state for the colonies, Lord Hillsborough, ordered the governor to dissolve the legislature. Two regiments of British troops were transferred from the frontier to Boston, part of the aforementioned policy of bringing the army closer to the centers of colonial unrest.

In Copley's flattering portrait painted in 1771, Samuel Adams points to the Massachusetts charter as if reminding Great Britain of the colonists' rights.

The Boston Massacre

These acts convinced more Americans that the British were conspiring to destroy their liberties. Resentment was particularly strong in Boston, where the postwar depression had come on top of two decades of economic stagnation. Crowding 4,000 tough British soldiers into a town of 16,000 people, many of them as capable of taking care of themselves when challenged as any Redcoat, was a formula for disorder.

How many scuffles and minor riots took place in waterfront taverns and darkened alleys that winter is lost to history. But on March 5, 1770, real trouble erupted. Late that afternoon a crowd of idlers began tossing snowballs at a company of Redcoats guarding the Custom House. Some of these missiles had been carefully wrapped around suitably sized rocks. Gradually the crowd increased in size and its mood grew meaner. The soldiers panicked and began firing their muskets. When the smoke cleared, five Bostonians lay dead and dying on the bloody ground.

This so-called Boston Massacre infuriated the populace. The violence played into the hands of radicals like Samuel Adams. But just as at the time of the Stamp Act riots, cooler heads prevailed. Announcing that he was "defending the rights of man and unconquerable truth," John Adams volunteered his services to make sure that the soldiers got a fair trial. Most were acquitted; the rest were treated leniently by the standards of the day. In Great Britain confrontation also gave way to adjustment. In April 1770 all the Townshend duties except the threepenny tax on tea were repealed. The tea tax was maintained as a matter of principle. "A peppercorn in acknowledgment of the right was of more value than millions without it," one British peer declared smugly—a glib fallacy.

At this point the nonimportation movement collapsed; although the boycott on tea was continued, many merchants imported British tea and paid the tax too. "Drank green tea," one patriot wrote in describing an afternoon at the merchant John Hancock's. "From Holland, I hope, but don't know."

A kind of postmassacre truce settled over Boston and the rest of British America. During the next two years no serious crisis erupted. Imports of British goods were nearly 50 percent higher than before the nonimportation agreement. So long as the British continued to be conciliatory, the colonists seemed satisfied with their place in the empire.

Paul Revere's engraving of the Boston Massacre was potent propaganda fully exploited by the Boston radicals. Many copies were made. His view of a deliberately ordered, concerted volley fired into a group of innocent citizens bore slight resemblance to fact. At the trial of the British soldiers, the jury was warned against "the prints exhibited in our houses" that added "wings to fancy." Two soldiers were punished mildly, the rest acquitted.

The Pot Spills Over

In 1772 this informal truce ended and new troubles broke out. The first was plainly the fault of the colonists involved. Early in June the British patrol boat *Gaspee* ran aground in Narragansett Bay, south of Providence, while pursuing a suspected smuggler. The *Gaspee*'s commander, Lieutenant Dudingston, had antagonized everyone in the area by his officiousness and zeal; that night a gang of local people boarded the helpless *Gaspee* and put it to the torch. This action was clearly criminal, but when the British attempted to bring the culprits to justice, no one would testify against them. The British, frustrated and angry, were strengthened in their conviction that the colonists were utterly lawless.

Then Thomas Hutchinson, now governor of Massachusetts, announced that henceforth the Crown rather than the local legislature would pay his salary. Since control over the salaries of royal officials gave the legislature a powerful hold on them, this development was disturbing. Groups of radicals formed "committees of correspondence" and stepped up communications with one another, planning joint action in case of trouble. This was another monumental step along the road to revolution; an organized colonywide resistance movement, lacking in any "legitimate" authority but ready to consult and act in the name of the public interest, was taking shape.

The Tea Act Crisis

In the spring of 1773 an entirely unrelated event precipitated the final crisis. The British East India Company held a monopoly of all trade between India and the rest of the empire. This monopoly had yielded fabulous returns, but decades of corruption and inefficiency together with heavy military expenses in recent years had weakened the company until it was almost bankrupt.

Among the assets of this venerable institution were some 17 million pounds of tea stored in English warehouses. The decline of the American market, a result first of the boycott and then of the smuggling of cheaper Dutch tea, partly accounted for the glut. Normally, East India Company tea was sold to English wholesalers. They in turn sold it to American wholesalers, who distributed it to local merchants for sale to the consumer. A substantial British tax was levied on the tea as well as the threepenny Townshend duty. Now Lord North, the new prime minister, decided to remit the British tax and to allow the company to sell directly in America through its own agents. The savings would permit a sharp reduction of the retail price and at the same time yield a nice profit to the company. The Townshend tax was retained, however, to preserve (as Lord North said when the East India Company directors suggested its repeal) the principle of Parliament's right to tax the colonies.

The company then shipped 1,700 chests of tea to colonial ports. Though the idea of high-quality tea offered at bargain prices was tempting, after a little thought nearly everyone in America appreciated the dangers involved in buying it. If Parliament could grant the East India Company a monopoly of the tea trade, it could parcel out all or any part of American commerce to whomever it pleased. More important, the act appeared utterly diabolical, a dastardly trick to trap them into paying the tea tax. The plot seemed obvious: The real price of Lord North's tea was American submission to parliamentary taxation.

Public indignation was so great in New York and Philadelphia that when the tea ships arrived, the authorities ordered them back to England without attempting to unload. The tea could only be landed "under the Protection of the Point of the Bayonet and Muzzle of the Cannon," the governor of New York reported. "Even then," he added, "I do not see how the Sales or Consumption could be effected."

The situation in Boston was different. The tea ship *Dartmouth* arrived on November 27. The radicals, marshaled by Sam Adams, were determined to prevent it from landing its cargo; Governor Hutchinson (who had managed to have two of his sons appointed to receive and sell the tea) was equally determined to collect the tax and enforce the law. For days the town seethed. Crowds milled in the streets, harangued by Adams and his friends, while the *Dartmouth* and two later arrivals swung with the tides on their moorings. Then, on the night of December 16, as Hutchinson was preparing to seize the tea for nonpayment of the duty, a band of colonists disguised as Indians rowed out to the ships and dumped the hated tea chests in the harbor.

The destruction of the tea was a serious crime, and it was obvious that a solid majority of the people of Boston approved of it. The painted "Patriots" who jettisoned the chests were a veritable cross section of society, and a huge crowd gathered at wharfside and cheered them on. The British burned with indignation when news of the "Tea Party" reached London. People talked (fortunately it was only talk) of flattening Boston with heavy artillery. Nearly everyone, even such a self-described British friend of the colonists as Edmund Burke, agreed that the colonists must be taught a lesson. George III himself said, "We must master them or totally leave them to themselves." What particularly infuriated the

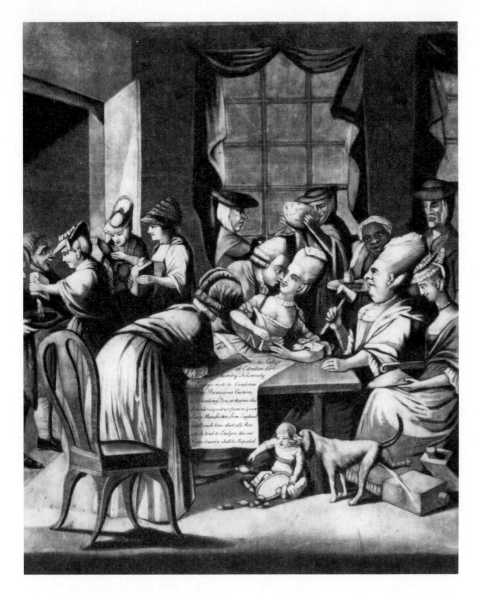

This English caricature of 1775 mocks the protest of the "Patriotic Ladies at Edenton in North Carolina." While women in the background empty their tea canisters, others (amidst some distractions) sign a pledge "not to Conform to that Pernicious Custom of Drinking Tea."

British was the certain knowledge that no American jury would render a judgment against the criminals; the memory of the *Gaspee* affair was fresh in everyone's mind in England, as undoubtedly it was in the minds of those Bostonians who, wearing the thinnest of disguises, brazenly destroyed the tea.

From Resistance to Revolution

Parliament responded in the spring of 1774 by passing the Coercive Acts. The Boston Port Act closed the harbor of Boston to all commerce until its citizens paid for the tea. The Administration of Justice Act provided for the transfer of cases to courts outside Massachusetts when the governor felt that an impartial trial could not be had within the colony. The Massachusetts Government Act revised the colony's charter drastically, strengthening the power of the governor, weakening that of the local town meetings, making the council appointive rather than elective, and changing the method by which juries were selected. These were unwise laws—they cost Great Britain an empire. All of them, and especially the Port Act, were unjust laws as well. Parliament was punishing the entire community for the crimes of individuals. Even more significant, they marked a drastic change in British policy, from legislation and strict administration to treating colonial protesters as criminals, from attempts at persuasion and conciliation to coercion and punishment.

The Americans renamed the Coercive Acts (together with a new, more extensive Quartering Act and the Quebec Act, an unrelated measure that attached the area north of the Ohio River to Canada and gave the region an authoritarian centralized government) the Intolerable Acts. That the British answer to the crisis was coercion the Americans found unendurable. Although neither the British nor the colonists yet realized it, the American Revolution had begun.

Step by step, in the course of a single decade, a group of separate political bodies, inhabited by people who (if we put aside the slaves, who were outside the political system) were loyal subjects of Great Britain, had been forced by the logic of events—by new British policies and by a growing awareness of their common interests—to take political power into their own hands and to band together to exercise that power effectively. This did not yet mean that their purpose was independence. Nearly every colonist was willing to see Great Britain continue to control, or at least regulate, such things as foreign relations, commercial policy, and other matters of general American interest. Parliament, however—and in the last analysis George III and most Britons—insisted that their authority over the colonies was unlimited. Behind their stubbornness lay the arrogant psychology of the European: "Colonists are inferior. . . . We own you."

Lord North directed the Coercive Acts at Massachusetts alone because he assumed that the other colonies, profiting from the discomfiture of Massachusetts, would not intervene and because of the British tendency to think of the colonies as separate units connected only through London. His strategy failed because his assumption was incorrect: The colonies began at once to act in concert.

Extralegal political acts now became a matter of course. In June 1774 Massachusetts called for a meeting of delegates from all the colonies to consider common action. This First Continental Congress met at Philadelphia in September; only Geor-

As the colonists saw it, the flames of rebellion in America, here portrayed as a helpless woman, were fanned by the so-called Intolerable Acts. In this colonial cartoon, well-meaning colonists struggle unsuccessfully to quench the fire.

gia failed to send delegates. Many points of view were represented, but even the so-called conservative proposal, introduced by Joseph Galloway of Pennsylvania, called for a thorough overhaul of the empire. Galloway suggested an *American* government, consisting of a president general appointed by the king and a grand council chosen by the colonial assemblies, that would manage intercolonial affairs and possess a veto over parliamentary acts affecting the colonies.

This was not what the majority wanted. If taxation without representation was tyranny, so was all legislation. Therefore, Parliament had no right to legislate in any way for the colonies. John Adams, while prepared to *allow* Parliament to regulate colonial trade, now believed that Parliament had no inherent right to control it. "The foundation . . . of all free government," he declared, "is a right in the people to participate in their legislative council." Americans "are entitled to a free and exclusive power of legislation in their several provincial legislatures."

Propelled by the reasoning of Adams and others, the Congress passed a declaration of grievances and resolves that amounted to a complete condemnation of Britain's actions since 1763. A Massachusetts proposal that the people take up arms to defend their rights was endorsed. The delegates also organized a "continental association" to boycott British goods and to stop all exports to the empire. To enforce this boycott, committees were appointed locally "to observe the conduct of all persons touching this association" and to expose violators to public scorn.

If the Continental Congress reflected the views of the majority—there is no reason to suspect that it did not—it is clear that the Americans had decided that drastic changes must be made. It was not merely a question of mutual defense against the threat of British power, not only (in Franklin's aphorism) a matter of hanging together lest they hang separately. A nation was being born.

Looking back many years later, one of the delegates to the First Continental Congress made just these points. He was John Adams, and he said: "The revolution was complete, in the minds of the people, and the Union of the colonies, before the war commenced."

The First Continental Congress met for almost two months in the fall of 1774. The man in the raised chair at left is probably Peyton Randolph of Virginia, president of the assembly and much admired for his calm and moderation.

Milestones

1650–1696	Navigation Acts enacted by Parliament
1689–1697	King William's War (War of the League of Augsburg)
1699–1750	Parliament enacts laws regulating colonial manufacturing
1702–1713	Queen Anne's War (War of the Spanish Succession)
1733	Molasses Act
1738–1742	Height of the Great Awakening
1740–1748	King George's War (War of the Austrian Succession)
1743	Franklin founds the American Philosophical Society
1752	Franklin discovers the nature of lightning
1754	Albany Congress
1754–1763	French and Indian War (Seven Years' War)
1760	George III becomes king of England
1763	Proclamation of 1763
1764	Sugar Act
1765	Stamp Act, leading to the Stamp Act Congress
1766	Repeal of the Stamp Act and passage of the Declaratory Act
1767	Townshend Duties, leading to the Massachusetts Circular Letter
1770	Boston Massacre
1772	Burning of the *Gaspee*
1773	Tea Act, leading to the Boston Tea Party
1774	Coercive Acts, leading to the First Continental Congress

SUPPLEMENTARY READING

Titles marked with an asterisk have been published in paperback.

The fullest analysis of the British imperial system can be found in the early volumes of L. H. Gipson, **The British Empire Before the American Revolution** (1936–1968). See also J. A. Henretta, **The Evolution of American Society** (1973), and Michael Kammen, **Empire and Interest** (1974). J. P. Greene, **The Quest for Power*** (1963), describes how the colonists extended their control of political affairs.

The best study of mercantilism is still Eli Heckscher, **Mercantilism** (1935). The colonial wars are described in H. H. Peckham, **The Colonial Wars*** (1963), but see also Fred Anderson, **A People's Army: Massachusetts Soldiers and Society in the Seven Years' War** (1984). Francis Jennings, **Empire of Fortune** (1988), is a revisionist's interpretation of the war, critical of all the whites involved in the conflict. On the problems posed for the British by the acquisition of French Canada, see J. M. Sosin, **Whitehall and the Wilderness** (1961).

On the causes of the Revolution, see Pauline Maier, **From Resistance to Revolution** (1972), E. S. Morgan, **The Birth of the Republic*** (1956), and Edward Countryman, **The American Revolution** (1985). Two works by Bernard Bailyn, **The Ideological Origins of the American Revolution*** (1967) and **The Origins of American Politics*** (1968), brilliantly analyze the political thinking and political structure of 18th-century America. G. B. Nash, **The Urban Crucible*** (1979), contains valuable data on political, social, and economic conditions in the largest towns, which Nash calls "crucibles of revolutionary agitation." See also Pauline Maier, **The Old Revolutionaries** (1980), and A. F. Young (ed.), **The American Revolution*** (1976).

American Lives:

George Washington

The northern neck of Virginia. The [color] line shows the route taken by sixteen-year-old Washington on the surveying expedition to Lord Fairfax's western holdings.

George Washington was born in 1732 on the tobacco plantation of his parents, Augustine and Mary Ball Washington, in the region between the Potomac and Rappahannock rivers known as the Northern Neck of Virginia. The Washingtons were members of the gentry, but not one of the great landed families. They owned some 10,000 acres and about 50 slaves. George was the first child, but Augustine Washington had three others by his first wife, who had died a few years earlier.

When George was six the family moved to Ferry Farm, a plantation further upstream on high land bordering the Rappahannock. The house was substantial but far from luxurious. It consisted of a central hall that served as a dining room, a master bedroom with its own fireplace, four other bedrooms, a kitchen, and a combination dairy and laundry room. Twenty of the Washingtons' slaves lived and worked at Ferry Farm, the rest at various other properties. A lane ran down to the Rappahannock ferry, which gave the place its name. On the other bank of the river was Fredericksburg, a town not much older than George, where there were some tobacco warehouses, the county courthouse, a prison, and St. George's Anglican church. Round about were other plantations owned by people with names like Spotswood, Taliaferro, and Mercer.

Little is known about George Washington's education except that it was supervised by tutors, perhaps fortified by some time at a school in Fredericksburg. He displayed small interest in literature (certainly nothing comparable to Franklin's and Adams's avid pursuit of reading matter). But early on he developed skill in mathematics and through that in surveying, a valuable tool in a country populated by well-to-do planters eager to engross new lands on the frontier.

In 1743 Augustine Washington died of what was diagnosed as "gout of the stomach." The bulk of his estate went to George's half-brother Lawrence, who had recently returned to Virginia after serving under Admiral Edward Vernon in the Caribbean during a conflict with Spain known as the War of Jenkins' Ear. George inherited Ferry Farm, ten slaves, and some house lots in Fredericksburg. Over the next few years, however, he lived with various relatives, including Lawrence, who had recently married Anne Fairfax; Anne was a relative of Lord Thomas Fairfax, an Englishman who had claims to more than 5 million acres in the wild upper reaches of the Northern Neck.

Growing up at Lawrence's plantation, Mount Vernon (named after the Admiral), set the course that determined George's future. He became a familiar at the Fairfax seat, Belvoir, and there got a taste of the life of the colonial elite. He grew tall and powerful; like his father he eventually topped six feet and weighed close to 200 pounds. He sedulously strove to develop the social graces, which did not come naturally to him—when he was 13 a tutor made him copy out one hundred "Rules of Civility" from an etiquette book of the period. They covered such gaffes as picking one's teeth with a fork and killing fleas in public. But he learned to dance, play cards and billiards, and ride with the hounds; above all, he mastered self-discipline and devotion to duty. Like so many others of his generation he admired the heroes of the Roman Republic, in his case particularly Cato the Younger, famous for his honesty and commitment to public service.

When George was 16 the great Lord Fairfax allowed him and his own young kinsman, George William Fairfax, to accompany a surveying party sent to locate some of the vast Fairfax holdings west of the Shenandoah valley. It was an unforgettable month-long adventure on horseback, over the "worst road ever trod by man or beast," fording rivers, and sleeping under "one threadbare blanket with double its weight of vermin, such as lice, fleas, etc." Sometimes they camped in the woods, pitching tents and cooking on an open fire. "Our spits were forked sticks," George recorded, "our plate was a large chip; and for dishes we had none." At one point they came upon a party of 30 Indians, returning from a conflict of some sort, chagrined at having taken only a single scalp. As they proceeded, pioneers emerged from the woods to gape at the mysterious activities of the surveyors. One day the party came upon a group of German settlers. "They seemed to be as ignorant a set of people as the Indians," George wrote in his diary. "When spoken to they speak all Dutch."

He returned to Mount Vernon a seasoned frontiersman and an experienced surveyor, eager to invest in western lands. The next year he was again surveying for Lord Fairfax, this time on his own and for a doubloon a day, which he saved in order to buy land for himself. Then, in 1752, Lawrence Washington died. George, at age 20, inherited Mount Vernon.

Young Washington's experiences and his reactions to them have much to tell us about southern life in the 18th century. More than a century and a quarter after the settlement of Jamestown, life remained extremely precarious. George's great-grandfather had died at age 46, his grandfather at 38. His aunt Mildred Washington buried two husbands and married a third well before her 40th birthday. In a hot and humid region plagued by clouds of mosquitoes and the various "vermin" George experienced on the frontier, where sanitary facilities were often rudimentary and medical knowledge abysmal, malaria, typhoid, smallpox, and such unfathomable lethal mysteries as the "gout of the stomach" that carried off Augustine Washington were of epidemic proportions. The Virginians appear to have lived uncomplainingly with the constant threat of extinction, certainly without doing anything about it.

Washington's youth coincided with the influx of more than 30,000 slaves into Virginia, the greatest in all history, between his birth and his 30th birthday; nearly all came directly from Africa. Neither he nor most of the whites he knew had much to say about them or the institution, although their prosperity depended entirely upon both. In later life Washington treated his slaves decently by the standards of his time and place. But in his youth (and probably always) he did not question his right to own them.

In one way Washington's early experiences resembled those of Franklin and Adams. All three, ardent revolutionaries in the 1770s, expressed not the slightest resentment of British rule as late as the early 1760s.

A View of Mount Vernon

IV

The American Revolution

*By referring the matter from argument to arms, a new era for politics
is struck; a new method of thinking hath arisen.*

THOMAS PAINE, Common Sense, *1776*

T he actions of the First Continental Congress led the British authorities to force a showdown with their bumptious colonial offspring. "The New England governments are in a state of rebellion," George III announced. "Blows must decide whether they are to be subject to this country or independent." Already General Thomas Gage, veteran of Braddock's ill-fated expedition against Fort Duquesne and now commander in chief of all British forces in North America, had been appointed governor of Massachusetts. Some 4,000 Redcoats were concentrated in Boston, camped on the town common once peacefully reserved for the citizens' cows. Parliament echoed with demands for a show of strength in America. General James Grant announced that with 1,000 men he "would undertake to go from one end of America to the other, and geld all the males, partly by force and partly by a little coaxing." Some opposed the idea of crushing the colonists, and others believed that it could not be easily managed, but they were a small minority. The House of Commons listened to Edmund Burke's magnificent speech on conciliating the colonies and then voted 270 to 78 against him.

"The Shot Heard Round the World"

The London government decided to use troops against Massachusetts in January 1775, but the order did not reach General Gage until April. In the interim both sides were active. Parliament voted new troop levies and declared Massachusetts to be in a state of rebellion. The Massachusetts Patriots, as they were now calling themselves, formed an extralegal provincial assembly, reorganized the militia, and began training "Minute Men" and other fighters. Soon companies armed with anything that would shoot were drilling on town commons throughout Massachusetts and in other colonies too.

When Gage received his orders on April 14, he acted swiftly. The Patriots had been accumulating arms at Concord, some 20 miles west of Boston. On the night of April 18, Gage dispatched 700 crack troops to seize these supplies. The Patriots were forewarned. Paul Revere set out on his famous ride to alert the countryside and warn John Hancock and Sam Adams, leaders of the provincial assembly, whose arrests had been ordered.

When the Redcoats reached Lexington early the next morning, they found the common occupied by about 70 Minute Men. After an argument, the Americans began to withdraw. Then someone fired a shot. There was a flurry of gunfire and the Minute Men fled, leaving eight of their number dead. The British then marched on to Concord, where they destroyed whatever supplies the Patriots had been unable to carry off.

But militiamen were pouring into the area from all sides. A hot skirmish at Concord's North Bridge forced the Redcoats to yield that position. Becoming alarmed, they began to march back to Boston. Soon they were being subjected to a withering fire from American irregulars along their line of march. A strange battle developed on a "field" 16 miles long and only a few hundred yards wide. Gage was obliged to send out an additional 1,500 soldiers, and total disaster was avoided only by deploying skirmishers to root out snipers hiding in barns and farmhouses along the road to Boston. When the first day of the Revolutionary War ended, the British had sustained 273 casualties, the Americans fewer than 100.

For a brief moment of history tiny Massachusetts stood alone at arms against an empire that had humbled France and Spain. Yet Massachusetts assumed the offensive! The provincial government organized an expedition that captured Fort Ticonderoga and Crown Point, on Lake Champlain. The other colonies rallied quickly to the cause, sending reinforcements to Cambridge.

The Second Continental Congress

On May 10, the day Ticonderoga fell, the Second Continental Congress met in Philadelphia. It was a distinguished group, more radical than the First Congress. Besides John and Sam Adams, Patrick Henry and Richard Henry Lee of Virginia, and Christopher Gadsden of South Carolina, all holdovers from the First Congress, there was Thomas Jefferson, a lanky, sandy-haired young planter from Virginia. Jefferson had recently published "A Summary View of the Rights of British America," an essay criticizing the institution of monarchy and warning George III that "kings are the servants, not the proprietors of the people." The Virginia convention had also sent George Washington, who knew more than any other colonist about commanding men and who wore his buff-and-blue colonel's uniform, a not-too-subtle indication of his willingness to place this knowledge at the disposal of the Congress. The renowned Benjamin Franklin was a delegate, moving rapidly to the radical position.

In this engraving by Amos Doolittle, made from a sketch by Ralph Earle, British forces at the North Bridge in Concord fight a rear-guard action. A line of riflemen holds off the Massachusetts militia on the left, while the mass of the Redcoats retreats toward Boston.

The Boston merchant John Hancock was chosen president of the Congress, which, like the first, had no legal authority. Yet the delegates had to make agonizing decisions under the pressure of rapidly unfolding military events, with the future of every American depending on their actions. Delicate negotiations and honeyed words might yet persuade king and Parliament to change their ways, but precipitate, bold effort was essential to save Massachusetts.

In this predicament the Congress naturally dealt first with the military crisis. It organized the forces gathering around Boston into the so-called Continental Army and appointed George Washington commander in chief. After Washington and his staff left for Massachusetts on June 23, the Congress turned to the task of requisitioning men and supplies.

The Battle of Bunker Hill

Meanwhile, in Massachusetts, the first major battle of the war had been fought. The British position on the peninsula of Boston was impregnable to direct assault, but high ground north and south, at Charlestown and Dorchester Heights, could be used to pound the city with artillery. When the Patriots seized Bunker Hill and Breed's Hill at Charlestown and set up defenses on the latter, Gage determined at once to drive them off. This was accomplished on June 17. Twice the Redcoats marched in close ranks, bayonets fixed, up Breed's Hill, each time being driven back after suffering heavy losses. Stubbornly they came again, and this time they carried the redoubt, for the defenders had run out of ammunition.

The British then cleared the Charlestown peninsula, but the victory was really the Americans', for they had proved themselves against professional soldiers and had exacted a terrible toll. More than 1,000 Redcoats had fallen in a couple of hours, out of a force of some 2,500, while the Patriots had lost only 400 men, most of them cut down by British bayonets after the hill was taken. "The day ended in glory," a British officer wrote, "but the loss was uncommon in officers for the number engaged."

The Battle of Bunker Hill, as it was called for no good reason, greatly reduced whatever hope remained for a negotiated settlement. The spilling of so much blood left each side determined to force

THE BATTLE OF BUNKER HILL, 1775

Most of the so-called Battle of Bunker Hill actually took place on Breed's Hill nearby. This area today is all part of the city of Boston.

the other's submission. The British recalled General Gage, replacing him with General Sir William Howe, a respected veteran of the French and Indian War, and George III formally proclaimed the colonies to be "in open rebellion." The Continental Congress dispatched one last plea to the king (the Olive Branch Petition), but this was a sop to the moderates. Immediately thereafter it adopted the

Declaration of the Causes and Necessity of Taking Up Arms, which condemned everything the British had done since 1763. Americans were "a people attacked by unprovoked enemies"; the time had come to choose between "submission" to "tyranny" and "resistance by force." The Congress then ordered an attack on Canada and created committees to seek foreign aid and to buy munitions abroad. It authorized the outfitting of a navy under Commodore Esek Hopkins of Rhode Island.

The Great Declaration

The Congress (and the bulk of the people) still hung back from a break with the Crown. To declare for independence would be to burn the last bridge, to become traitors in the eyes of the mother country. Aside from the word's ugly associations, everyone knew what happened to traitors when their efforts failed. It was sobering to think of casting off everything that being English meant: love of king, the traditions of a great nation, pride in the power of a mighty empire. "Where shall we find another Britain?" John Dickinson had asked at the time of the Townshend Acts crisis. "Torn from the body to which we are united by religion, liberty, laws, affections, relation, language and commerce, we must bleed at every vein."

Then, too, rebellion might end in horrors worse than submission to British tyranny. The disturbances following the Stamp Act and the Tea Act had revealed an alarming fact about American society. The organizers of the protests, mostly persons of wealth and status, had thought in terms of "ordered resistance." They countenanced violence only as a means of forcing the British authorities to pay attention to their complaints. But protest meetings and mob actions had brought thousands of ordinary citizens into the struggle for local self-government. Some of the upper-class leaders among the Patriots, while eager to have their support, were concerned about what they would make of actual independence. In addition, not all the property that had been destroyed belonged to Loyalists and British officials. Too much exalted talk about "rights" and "liberties" might well give the poor (to say nothing of the slaves) an exaggerated impression of their importance. Finally, in a world where every country had some kind of monarch, could common people

really govern themselves? The most ardent defender of American rights might well hesitate after considering all the implications of independence.

Yet independence was probably inevitable by the end of 1775. The belief that George III had been misled by evil or stupid advisers on both sides of the Atlantic became progressively more difficult to sustain. Mistrust of Parliament—indeed, of the whole of British society—grew apace.

Two events in January 1776 pushed the colonies a long step toward a final break. First came the news that the British were sending hired Hessian soldiers to fight against them. Colonists associated mercenaries with looting and rape and feared that the German-speaking Hessians would run amok among them. Such callousness on the part of Britain made reconciliation seem out of the question.

The second decisive event was the publication of *Common Sense*. This tract was written by Thomas Paine, a onetime English corsetmaker and civil servant turned pamphleteer, a man who had been in America scarcely a year. *Common Sense* called boldly for complete independence. It attacked not only George III but the idea of monarchy itself. Paine applied the uncomplicated logic of the zealot to the recent history of America. Where the colonists had been humbly petitioning George III and swallowing their resentment when he ignored them, Paine called George a "Royal Brute" and "the hardened sullen-tempered Pharaoh of England." Many Americans had wanted to control their own affairs but feared the instability of untried republican government. To them Paine said: "We have it in our power to begin the world again." "A government of our own is our natural right," he insisted. "O! ye that love mankind! Ye that dare oppose not only tyranny but the tyrant, stand forth!"

Virtually everyone in the colonies must have read *Common Sense* or heard it explained and discussed. About 150,000 copies were sold in the critical period between January and July. Not every Patriot was impressed by Paine's arguments. John Adams dismissed *Common Sense* as "a tolerable summary of arguments which I had been repeating again and again in Congress for nine months." But no one disputed the impact of Paine's pamphlet on public opinion.

The tone of the debate changed sharply as Paine's slashing attack took effect. In March the Congress unleashed privateers against British commerce; in April it opened American ports to foreign shipping; in May it urged the extralegal provincial conventions that had been set up by the Patriots to frame constitutions and establish state governments.

On June 7 Richard Henry Lee of Virginia introduced a resolution of the Virginia Convention:

RESOLVED: That these United Colonies are, and of right ought to be, free and independent States, that they are absolved from all allegiance to the British Crown, and that all political connection between them and the State of Great Britain is, and ought to be, totally dissolved.

This momentous resolution was not passed until July 2; the Congress first appointed a committee consisting of Thomas Jefferson, Benjamin Franklin, John Adams, Roger Sherman, and Robert Livingston to frame a suitable justification of independence. Livingston, a member of one of the great New York landowning families, was put on the committee in an effort to push New York toward independence. Sherman, a self-educated Connecticut lawyer and merchant, was a conservative who opposed parliamentary control over colonial affairs. Franklin, the best known of all Americans and an experienced writer, was a natural choice; so was John Adams, whose devotion to the cause of independence combined with his solid conservative qualities made him perhaps the typical man of the Revolution.

Thomas Jefferson was probably placed on the committee because politics required that a Virginian be included and because of his literary skill and

A detail from John Trumbull's Declaration of Independence *portrays the five-man drafting committee presenting its handiwork to the Congress: from left, Massachusetts's John Adams, Connecticut's Roger Sherman, New York's Robert Livingston, Virginia's Thomas Jefferson, and Pennsylvania's Benjamin Franklin. Trumbull's skillful composition "ranks" the contributors, with Jefferson dominating.*

general intelligence. Aside from writing "A Summary View of the Rights of British America," he had done little to attract notice. At 33 he was the youngest member of the Continental Congress and was only marginally interested in its deliberations. He had been slow to take his seat in the fall of 1775, and he had gone home to Virginia before Christmas. He put off returning several times and arrived in Philadelphia only on May 14. Had he delayed another month, someone else would have written the Declaration of Independence.

The committee asked Jefferson to prepare a draft. The result, with a few amendments made by Franklin and Adams and somewhat toned down by the whole Congress, was officially adopted by the delegates on July 4, 1776, two days after the decisive break with Great Britain had been voted.

Jefferson's Declaration of Independence consisted of two parts. The first was by way of introduction: It justified the abstract right of any people to revolt and described the theory on which the Americans based their creation of a new, republican government. The second, much longer section was a list of the "injuries and usurpations" of George III, a bill of indictment explaining why the colonists felt driven to exercise the rights outlined in the first part of the document. Here Jefferson stressed the monarch's interference with the functioning of representative government in America, his harsh administration of colonial affairs, his restrictions on civil rights, and his maintenance of troops in the colonies without their consent.

Jefferson sought to marshal every possible evidence of British perfidy and he made George III, rather than Parliament, the villain because the king was the personification of the nation against which the Americans were rebelling. He held George responsible for Parliament's efforts to tax the colonies and restrict their trade, for many actions by subordinates that George had never deliberately authorized, and for some things that never happened. He even blamed the king for the existence of slavery in the colonies, a charge the Congress cut from the document not entirely because of its concern for accuracy. The long bill of particulars reads more like a lawyer's brief than a careful analysis, but it was intended to convince the world that the Americans had good reasons for exercising their right to form a government of their own.

Jefferson's general statement of the right of rev-

olution has inspired oppressed peoples all over the world for more than 200 years:

> We hold these truths to be self-evident, that all men are created equal, that they are endowed by their Creator with certain unalienable Rights, that among these are Life, Liberty and the pursuit of Happiness. That to secure these rights, Governments are instituted among Men, deriving their just powers from the consent of the governed, That whenever any Form of Government becomes destructive of these ends, it is the Right of the People to alter or to abolish it, and to institute new Government. . . .

The Declaration was intended to influence foreign opinion, but it had little immediate effect outside Great Britain, and there it only made people angry and determined to subdue the rebels. A substantial number of European military men offered their services to the new nation, and a few of these might be called idealists, but most were adventurers and soldiers of fortune, thinking mostly of their own advantage. Why, then, has the Declaration had so much influence on modern history? Not because the thought was original with Jefferson. As John Adams later pointed out—Adams viewed his great contemporary with a mixture of affection, respect, and jealousy—the basic idea was commonplace among 18th-century liberals. "I did not consider it any part of my charge to invent new ideas," Jefferson explained, "but to place before mankind the common sense of the subject, in terms so plain and firm as to command their assent. . . . It was intended to be an expression of the American mind."

Revolution was not new, but the spectacle of a people solemnly explaining and justifying their right, in an orderly manner, to throw off their oppressors and establish a new system on their own authority was almost without precedent. Soon the French would be drawing on this example in their revolution, and rebels everywhere have since done likewise. And if Jefferson did not create the concept, he gave it a nearly perfect form.

1776: The Balance of Forces

A formal declaration of independence merely cleared the way for tackling the problems of founding a new nation. Lacking both traditions and authority based in law, the Congress had to create political institutions and a new national spirit, all in the midst of war.

Always the military situation took precedence, for a single disastrous setback might make everything else meaningless. At the start the Americans had what we might call the home-court advantage. They already possessed their lands (except for the few square miles occupied by British troops). Although thousands of colonists fought for George III, the British soon learned that to put down the American rebellion they would have to bring in men and supplies from bases on the other side of the Atlantic. This was a most formidable task.

Certain long-run factors also operated in America's favor. Whereas nearly everyone in Great Britain wanted to crack down on Boston after the Tea Party, many boggled at engaging in a full-scale war against all the colonies. Aside from a reluctance to spill so much blood, there was the question of expense. Finally, the idea of dispatching the cream of the British army to America while powerful enemies on the Continent still smarted from past defeats seemed risky. For all these reasons the British ap-

proached gingerly the task of subduing the rebellion. When Washington fortified Dorchester Heights overlooking Boston, General Howe withdrew his troops to Halifax rather than risk another Bunker Hill.

For a time the initiative remained with the Americans. An expedition under General Richard Montgomery had captured Montreal in November 1775, and another small force under Benedict Arnold advanced to the gates of Quebec after a grueling march across the wilderness from Maine. Montgomery and Arnold attempted to storm the Quebec defenses on December 31, 1775, but were repulsed with heavy losses. Even so, the British troops in Canada could not drive the remnants of the American army—perhaps 500 men in all—out of the province until reinforcements arrived in the spring.

Awareness of Britain's problems undoubtedly spurred the Continental Congress to the bold actions of the spring of 1776. However, on July 2, 1776, the same day that Congress voted for independence, General Howe was back on American soil, landing in force on Staten Island in New York harbor in preparation for an assault on the city.

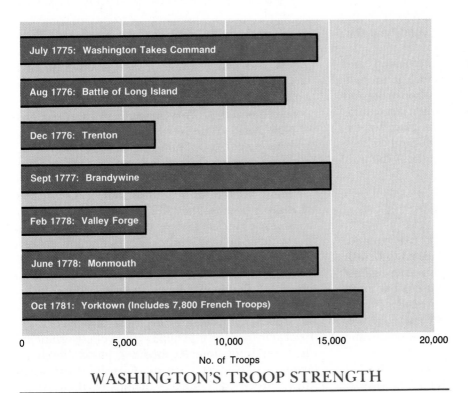

The troop count shown here includes militias as well as regular Continental Army forces. Washington's troop strength varied greatly from month to month and year to year, and at times militias accounted for more than one-third of the total.

WASHINGTON'S TROOP STRENGTH

Soon Howe had at hand 32,000 well-equipped troops and a powerful fleet commanded by his brother, Richard, Lord Howe. If the British controlled New York City and the Hudson River, they could, as Washington realized, "stop intercourse between the northern and southern Colonies, upon which depends the Safety of America."

Suddenly the full strength of the empire seemed to have descended on the Americans. Superior British resources (a population of 9 million to the colonies' 2.5 million, large stocks of war materials and the industrial capacity to boost them further, mastery of the seas, a well-trained and experienced army, a highly centralized and, when necessary, ruthless government) were now all too evident.

The demonstration of British might in New York harbor accentuated American military and economic weaknesses: Both money and the tools of war were continually in short supply in a predominantly agricultural country. Many of Washington's soldiers were armed with weapons no more lethal than spears and tomahawks. Few had proper uniforms. Even the most patriotic resisted conforming to the conventions of military discipline; the men hated drilling and all parade-ground formality. And all these problems were complicated by the fact that Washington had literally to create an army organization out of whole cloth at the same time that he was fighting a war.

Supply problems were handled inefficiently and often corruptly. Few officers knew much about such mundane but vital matters as how to construct and maintain proper sanitary facilities when large numbers of soldiers were camped at one place for extended periods of time. What was inelegantly known as "the itch" afflicted soldiers throughout the war.

Loyalists

Behind the lines, the country was far from united. Whereas nearly all colonists had objected to British policies, many still hesitated to take up arms against the mother country. Even Massachusetts harbored many Loyalists, or Tories, as they were called; about 1,000 Americans left Boston with General Howe, abandoning their homes rather than submit to the rebel army.

No one knows exactly how the colonists divided on the question of independence. John Adams's off-the-cuff estimate was that a third of the people were ardent Patriots, another third loyal to Great Britain, and the rest neutral or tending to favor whichever side seemed to be winning. This guess is probably as useful as any, though in keeping with Adams's character he may have understated the number who agreed with him and overstated those opposed to his position. Most historians think that about a fifth of the people were Loyalists and about two-fifths Patriots, but there are few hard figures to go by. What is certain is that large elements, perhaps a majority of the people, were more or less indifferent to the conflict or, in Tom Paine's famous phrase, were summer soldiers and sunshine patriots—they supported the Revolution when all was going well and lost their enthusiasm in difficult hours.

The divisions cut across geographic, social, and economic lines. Edward Countryman makes this clear in *A People in Revolution:*

> The positions that people took grew out of the lives they had led and out of what people who counted in those lives were doing. . . . They became rebels or Tories or they tried to stay out of it by reference to the whole set of material, cultural, geographical, economic, and political complexities that had been their world.

A high proportion of those holding royal appointments and many Anglican clergymen remained loyal to King George, as did numbers of merchants with close connections in Britain. There were important pockets of Tory strength in rural sections of New York, in the North Carolina back country, and among persons of non-English origin and other minority groups who tended to count on London for protection against the local majority.

Many became Tories simply out of distaste for change or because they were pessimistic about the condition of society and the possibility of improving it. "What is the whole history of human life," wrote the Tory clergyman and schoolmaster Jonathan Boucher of Virginia, "but a series of disappointments?" Still others believed that the actions of the British, however unfair and misguided, did not justify rebellion. Knowing that they possessed a remarkably free and equitable system of government, they could not stomach shedding blood merely to avoid paying more taxes or to escape from what they considered minor restrictions on their activities. "The Annals of no Country can produce an Instance of so virulent a Rebellion . . . originating from such trivial Causes," one Loyalist complained.

The Tories lacked organization. While Patriot leaders worked closely together, many of the Tory "leaders" did not even know one another. They had no central committee to lay plans or coordinate their efforts. When the revolutionaries took over a colony, some Tories fled; others sought the protection of the British army; others took up arms; others accommodated themselves silently to the new regime.

If the differences separating Patriot from Loyalist are unclear, feelings were nonetheless bitter. Individual Loyalists were often set upon by mobs, tarred and feathered, and otherwise abused. Some were thrown into jail for no legitimate reason; others were exiled, their property confiscated. Battles between Tory units and the Continental Army were often exceptionally bloody. "Neighbor was against

The events in and around New York, so nearly disastrous to Washington and his army, are detailed in this map.

NEW YORK—NEW JERSEY CAMPAIGNS, 1776–1777

neighbor, father against son and son against father," one Connecticut Tory reported. "He that would not thrust his own blade through his brother's heart was called an infamous villain."

Early Defeats

General Howe's campaign against New York brought to light another American weakness: the lack of military experience. Washington, expecting Howe to attack New York, had moved south to meet the threat immediately after Howe had abandoned Boston. But both he and his men failed badly in this first major test. Late in August, Howe crossed from Staten Island to Brooklyn. In the Battle of Long Island he easily outflanked and defeated Washington's army. Had he acted decisively, he could probably have ended the war on the spot, but Howe could not make up his mind whether to be a peacemaker or a conqueror. This hesitation in consolidating his gains permitted Washington to withdraw his troops to Manhattan Island.

Howe could still have trapped Washington simply by using his fleet to land troops on the northern end of Manhattan; instead he attacked New York City directly, leaving the Americans an escape route to the north. Again Patriot troops proved no match for British regulars. Though Washington threw his hat to the ground in a rage and threatened to shoot cowardly Connecticut soldiers as they fled the battlefield, he could not stop the rout and had to fall back on Harlem Heights in upper Manhattan. Yet once more Howe failed to pursue his advantage promptly.

Still Washington refused to see the peril in remaining on an island while the enemy commanded the surrounding waters. Only when Howe shifted a powerful force to Westchester, directly threatening his rear, did Washington move north to the mainland. Finally, after several narrow escapes, he crossed the Hudson River and marched south to New Jersey, where the British could not use their naval superiority against him.

The battles in and around New York City seemed to presage an easy British triumph. Yet somehow Washington salvaged a moral victory from these ignominious defeats. He learned rapidly; seldom thereafter did he place his troops in such vulnerable positions. And his men, in spite of repeated failure, had become an army. In November and December 1776 they retreated across New Jersey and into Pennsylvania. General Howe then abandoned the campaign, going into winter quarters in New York but posting garrisons at Trenton, Princeton, and other strategic points.

The troops at Trenton were hated Hessian mercenaries, and Washington decided to attack them. He crossed the ice-clogged Delaware River with 2,400 men on Christmas night during a wild storm. The little army then marched 9 miles to Trenton, arriving at daybreak in the midst of a sleet storm. The Hessians were taken completely by surprise. Those who could fled in disorder; the rest—900 of them—surrendered.

The Hessians were first-class professional soldiers, probably the most competent troops in Europe at that time. The victory gave a boost to American morale. A few days later Washington outmaneuvered General Cornwallis, who had rushed to Trenton with reinforcements, and won another battle at Princeton. These engagements had little strategic importance, since both armies then went into winter quarters. Without them, however, there might not have been an army to resume the war in the spring.

Saratoga and the French Alliance

When spring reached New Jersey in April 1777, Washington had fewer than 5,000 men under arms. Great plans—far too many and too complicated, as it turned out—were afoot in the British camp. The strategy called for General John Burgoyne to lead a large army from Canada down Lake Champlain toward Albany while a smaller force under Lieutenant Colonel Barry St. Leger pushed eastward toward Albany from Fort Oswego on Lake Ontario. General Howe was to lead a third force north up the Hudson. Patriot resistance would be smashed between these three armies and the New England states isolated from the rest.

As a venture in coordinated military tactics, the British campaign of 1777 was a fiasco. General Howe had spent the winter in New York wining and dining his officers and prominent local Loyalists and having a torrid affair with the wife of the officer

Britain's difficulties in the Revolutionary War are derided in an etching entitled "Poor old England endeavoring to reclaim his wicked American Children." In spite of their leashes, the colonists shoot pellets, shout, and otherwise show their disrespect for their peg-legged master in this English cartoon of 1777.

in charge of prisoners of war. Now he managed, in the words of his biographer, Ira Gruber, "to ignore his responsibilities toward the British army advancing south from Canada." (Sir William, Gruber notes, "had never inspired subordinates with a single-minded devotion to business.")

General "Gentleman Johnny" Burgoyne, a charming if somewhat bombastic character, part politician, part poet, part gambler, part ladies' man, yet also a brave soldier, had begun his march from Canada in mid-June. By early July his army, which consisted of 500 Indians, 650 Loyalists, and 6,000 regulars, had captured Fort Ticonderoga, at the southern end of Lake Champlain. He quickly pushed beyond Lake George but then bogged down. Burdened by a huge baggage train that included 138 pieces of generally useless artillery, more than 30 carts laden with his personal wardrobe and supply of champagne, and his mistress, he could advance at but a snail's pace through the dense woods north of Saratoga.* Patriot militia

---

* Many soldiers, enlisted men as well as officers, were accompanied by their wives or other women on campaigns. More than 2,000 accompanied the Burgoyne expedition. At one point Washington complained of "the multitude of women . . . especially those who are pregnant, or have children [that] clog upon every movement." Actually, women in 18th-century armies worked hard, doing most of the cooking, washing, and other housekeeping tasks.

impeded his way by felling trees across the forest trails.

St. Leger was also slow in carrying out his part of the grand design. He did not leave Fort Oswego until July 26, and when he stopped to besiege a Patriot force at Fort Stanwix, General Benedict Arnold had time to march west with 1,000 men from the army resisting Burgoyne and drive him back to Oswego.

Meanwhile, with magnificent disregard for the agreed-on plan, Howe wasted time trying to trap Washington into exposing his army in New Jersey. This enabled Washington to send some of his best troops to buttress the militia units opposing Burgoyne. Then, just when St. Leger was setting out for Albany, Howe took the bulk of his army off by sea to attack Philadelphia, leaving only a small force commanded by General Sir Henry Clinton to aid Burgoyne.

When Washington moved south to oppose Howe, the Britisher taught him a series of lessons in tactics, defeating him at the Battle of Brandywine, then feinting him out of position and moving unopposed into Philadelphia. But by that time it was late September, and disaster was about to befall General Burgoyne.

The American forces under Philip Schuyler and later under Horatio Gates and Benedict Arnold had erected formidable defenses immediately south of Saratoga near the town of Stillwater. Burgoyne struck at this position twice and was thrown back both times with heavy losses. Each day more local militia swelled the American forces. Soon Burgoyne was under siege, his troops pinned down by withering fire from every direction, unable even to bury their dead. The only hope was General Clinton, who had finally started up the Hudson from New York. Clinton got as far as Kingston, about 80 miles below Saratoga, but on October 16 he decided to return to New York for reinforcements. The next day, at Saratoga, Burgoyne surrendered. Some 5,700 British prisoners were marched off to Virginia.

This overwhelming triumph changed the course and character of the war. France would probably have entered the war in any case; the country had never reconciled itself to its losses in the Seven Years' War and had been building a navy capable of taking on the British for years. Helping the Americans was simply another way of weakening their British enemy. As early as May 1776 the Comte de Vergennes,

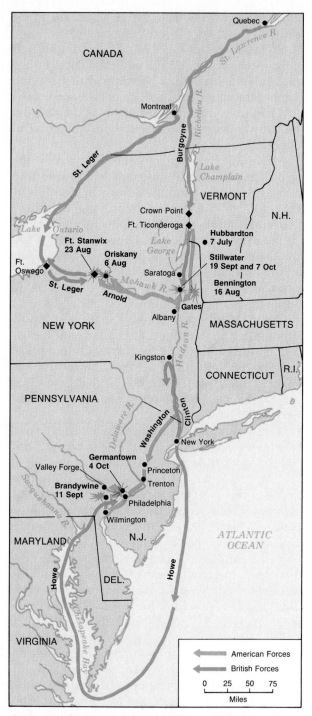

**SARATOGA AND PHILADELPHIA
CAMPAIGNS, 1777**

France's foreign minister, had persuaded Louis XVI to authorize the expenditure of 1 million livres for munitions for America, and more was added the next year. Spain also contributed to the cause. Soon vital supplies were being funneled secretly to the rebels. When news of the victory at Saratoga reached Paris, the time seemed ripe, and Louis XVI recognized the United States. Then Vergennes and three American commissioners in Paris, Benjamin Franklin, Arthur Lee, and Silas Deane, drafted a commercial treaty and a formal treaty of alliance. The two nations agreed to make "common cause and aid each other mutually" should war "break out" between France and Great Britain. Meanwhile, France guaranteed "the sovereignty and independence absolute and unlimited" of the United States.

When the news of Saratoga reached England, Lord North realized that a Franco-American alliance was almost inevitable. To forestall it, he was ready to give in on all the issues that had agitated the colonies before 1775. Both the Coercive Acts and the Tea Act would be repealed; Parliament would pledge never to tax the colonies.

Instead of implementing this proposal promptly, Parliament delayed until March 1778. Royal peace commissioners did not reach Philadelphia until June, a month after Congress had ratified the French treaty. The British proposals were icily rejected, and while the peace commissioners were still in Philadelphia, war broke out between France and Great Britain.

The American Revolution, however, if no longer being lost, had yet to be won. After the loss of Philadelphia, Washington had settled his army for the winter at Valley Forge, 20 miles to the northwest. The army's supply system collapsed. Often the men had nothing to eat but "fire cake," a mixture of ground grain and water molded on a stick or in a pan and baked in a campfire. According to the Marquis de Lafayette, one of many Europeans who volunteered to fight on the American side, "the unfortunate soldiers . . . had neither coats, nor hats, nor shirts, nor shoes; their feet and legs froze till they grew black, and it was often necessary to amputate them."

To make matters worse, there was grumbling in Congress over Washington's failure to win victories and talk of replacing him as commander in chief with Horatio Gates, the "hero" of Saratoga. (In fact, Gates was an indifferent soldier, lacking in decisiveness and unable to instill confidence in his subordinates. "Historical accounts of the Saratoga campaign have given abundant reasons for the American victory other than the military skill of Horatio Gates," one of his biographers has confessed.)

As the winter dragged on, the Continental Army melted away. So many officers resigned that Washington was heard to say that he was afraid of "being left Alone with the Soldiers only." Since enlisted men could not legally resign, they deserted by the hundreds. Yet the army survived. Gradually the soldiers who remained became a tough, professional fighting force. Their spirit has been described by the historian Charles Royster as a "mixture of patriotism, resentment, and fatalism."

The War Moves South

Spring brought a revival of American hopes in the form of more supplies, new recruits, and, above all, word of the French alliance. In May the British replaced General Howe as commander with General Clinton, who decided to transfer his base back to New York. While Clinton was moving across New Jersey, Washington attacked him at Monmouth Court House. The fight was inconclusive, but the Americans held the field when the day ended and were able to claim a victory.

Thereafter British strategy changed. Fighting in the northern states degenerated into skirmishes and other small-unit clashes. Instead, relying on sea power and the supposed presence of many Tories in the south, the British concentrated their efforts in South Carolina and Georgia. Savannah fell to them late in 1778, and most of the settled parts of Georgia were overrun during 1779. In 1780 Clinton led a massive expedition against Charleston. When the city surrendered in May, more than 3,000 soldiers were captured, the most overwhelming American defeat of the war. Leaving General Cornwallis and some 8,000 men to carry on the campaign, Clinton then sailed back to New York.

The Tories in South Carolina and Georgia came closer to meeting British expectations than in any other region, but the callous behavior of the British troops persuaded large numbers of hesitating citizens to join the Patriot cause. Guerrilla bands led by men like Francis Marion, the "Swamp Fox," and

Thomas Sumter—after whom Fort Sumter, famous in the Civil War, was named—provided a nucleus of resistance in areas that had supposedly been subdued.

In June 1780 Congress placed the highly regarded Horatio Gates in charge of a southern army

In an era when communications were slow and erratic at best, the coordination between the American and French land and naval forces that sealed up Cornwallis in Yorktown was nothing short of remarkable.

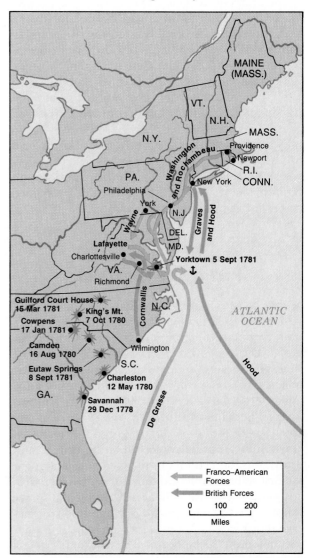

YORKTOWN AND THE WAR IN THE SOUTH, 1778–1781

consisting of the irregular militia units and a hard core of Continentals transferred from Washington's command. Gates encountered Cornwallis at Camden, South Carolina. Foolishly, he entrusted a key sector of his line to untrained militiamen, who panicked when the British charged with fixed bayonets. Gates suffered heavy losses and had to fall back. Congress then recalled him, sensibly permitting Washington to replace him with General Nathanael Greene, a first-rate officer.

A band of militiamen had trapped a contingent of Tories at King's Mountain and forced its surrender. Greene, avoiding a major engagement with Cornwallis's superior numbers, divided his troops and staged a series of raids on scattered points. In January 1781, at the Battle of Cowpens in northwestern South Carolina, General Daniel Morgan inflicted a costly defeat on Colonel Banastre Tarleton, one of Cornwallis's best officers. Cornwallis pursued Morgan hotly, but the American rejoined Greene and at Guilford Court House they again inflicted heavy losses on the British. Then Cornwallis withdrew to Wilmington, North Carolina, where he could rely on the fleet for support and reinforcements. Greene's Patriots quickly regained control of the Carolina back country.

Victory at Yorktown

Seeing no future in the Carolinas and unwilling to vegetate at Wilmington, Cornwallis marched north into Virginia, where he joined forces with troops under Benedict Arnold. (Disaffected by what he considered unjust criticism of his generalship, Arnold had sold out to the British in 1780. He intended to betray the bastion of West Point on the Hudson River. The scheme was foiled when incriminating papers were found on the person of a British spy, Major John André. Arnold fled to the British, and André was hanged.) As in the Carolina campaign, the British had numerical superiority at first but lost it rapidly when local militia and Continental forces concentrated against them. Cornwallis soon discovered that Virginia Tories were of little help in such a situation. "When a Storm threatens, our friends disappear," he grumbled.

General Clinton ordered Cornwallis to take up a defensive position at Yorktown, where he could be supplied by sea. Cornwallis objected; Yorktown, he said, was "an unhealthy swamp" where his army would be "liable to become a prey to a Foreign enemy with a temporary superiority at sea." But Clinton insisted.

It was a terrible mistake. The British navy in American waters far outnumbered American and French vessels, but the Atlantic is wide, and in those days communication was slow. The French had a fleet in the West Indies under Admiral François De Grasse and another squadron at Newport, Rhode Island, where a French army was stationed. In the summer of 1781 Washington, De Grasse, and the Comte de Rochambeau, commander of French land forces, designed and carried out with an efficiency unparalleled in 18th-century warfare a complex plan to bottle up Cornwallis.

The British navy in the West Indies and at New York might have forestalled this scheme had it moved promptly and in force. But Admiral Sir George Rodney sent only part of his Indies fleet. As a result, De Grasse, after a battle with a British fleet commanded by Admiral Thomas Graves, won control of the Chesapeake and cut Cornwallis off from the sea.

The next move was up to Washington, and this was his finest hour as a commander. He desperately wanted to attack the British base at New York, but at the urging of Rochambeau he agreed instead to strike at Yorktown. After tricking Clinton into thinking he was heading for New York, he pushed boldly south. In early September he reached Yorktown and joined up with an army commanded by Lafayette and troops from De Grasse's fleet. He soon had nearly 17,000 French and American veterans in position.

Cornwallis was helpless. He held out until October 17 and then asked for terms. Two days later more than 7,000 British soldiers marched out of their lines and laid down their arms. Then the jubilant Lafayette ordered his military band to play "Yankee Doodle."

The Peace of Paris

The British gave up trying to suppress the rebellion after Yorktown, but the event that confirmed the existence of the United States as an independent

Major John André was caught by American militiamen while trying to make his way south to New York City after a meeting with Benedict Arnold. If, as instructed by General Clinton, he had worn his uniform instead of changing into civilian clothes, he would have been treated as an officer. But as a spy, he could not escape the spy's fate of death by hanging.

nation was the signing of a peace treaty with Great Britain. Yorktown had been only one of a string of defeats suffered by British armies in the Mediterranean, the West Indies, Africa, and Asia. The national debt had doubled again since 1775. In March 1782 Lord North resigned after Parliament renounced all further efforts to coerce the colonies. At once the new ministry of Lord Rockingham prepared to negotiate a peace settlement with America.

The problem of peacemaking was complicated. The United States and France had pledged not to make a separate peace. Spain, at war with Great Britain since 1779, was allied with France but not with America. Although eager to profit at British expense, the Spanish hoped to limit American expansion beyond the Appalachians, for they had ambitions of their own in the eastern half of the Mississippi Valley. France, while ready enough to see America independent, did not want the new country to become *too* powerful; in a conflict of interest between America and Spain, France tended to support Spain.

The Continental Congress appointed John Adams, Benjamin Franklin, John Jay, Thomas Jefferson, and Henry Laurens as a commission to conduct peace talks. Franklin and Jay did most of the actual negotiating. Congress, grateful for French aid during the Revolution, had instructed the commissioners to rely on the advice of the Comte de Vergennes. In Paris, however, the commissioners soon discovered that Vergennes was not the perfect friend of America that Congress believed him to be. He was, after all, a French official, and France had other interests far more important than concern for its American ally. Vergennes "means to keep his hand under our chin to prevent us from drowning," Adams complained, "but not to lift our head out of the water."

Franklin, perhaps because as a famous scientist and sage he was wined and dined by the cream of Paris and petted and fussed over by some of the city's most beautiful women, did not press the American point of view as forcefully as he might have. But this was because he took the long view, which was to achieve a true reconciliation with the British, not simply to drive the hardest bargain possible. John Jay was somewhat more tough-minded. But on basic issues all the Americans were in agreement. They hinted to the British representative, Richard Oswald, that they would consider a separate peace if it were a generous one and suggested that Great Britain would be far better off with America, a nation that favored free trade, in control of the trans-Appalachian region than with a mercantilist power like Spain.

The British government reacted favorably, authorizing Oswald "to treat with the Commissioners appointed by the Colonys, under the title of Thirteen United States." Soon the Americans were deep in negotiations with Oswald. They told Vergennes what they were doing but did not discuss details.

Oswald was cooperative, and the Americans drove a hard bargain. One scrap of conversation reveals the tenor of the talks.

OSWALD: We can never be such damned sots as to disturb you.

ADAMS: Thank you. . . . But nations don't feel as you and I do, and your nation, when it gets a little refreshed from the fatigues of the war, and when men and money become plentiful, and allies at hand, will not feel as it does now.

OSWALD: We can never be such damned sots as to think of differing again with you.

ADAMS: Why, in truth I have never been able to comprehend the reason why you ever thought of differing with us.

By the end of November 1782, a preliminary treaty had been signed. "His Britannic Majesty," Article 1 began, "acknowledges the said United States . . . to be free, sovereign and independent States." Other terms were equally in line with American hopes and objectives. The boundaries of the nation were set at the Great Lakes, the Mississippi River, and 31° north latitude (roughly the northern boundary of Florida). Britain recognized the right of Americans to take fish on the Grand Banks off Newfoundland and, far more important, to dry and cure their catch on unsettled beaches in Labrador and Nova Scotia. The British agreed to withdraw their troops from American soil "with all convenient speed." Where the touchy problem of Tory property seized during the Revolution was concerned, the Americans agreed only that the Congress would "earnestly recommend" that the states "provide for the restitution of all estates, rights and properties which have been confiscated." They promised to prevent further property confiscation and prosecutions of Tories—certainly a wise as well as a humane policy—and they agreed not to impede the collection of debts owed to British subjects. Vergennes was flabbergasted by the success of the Americans. "The English buy the peace more than they make it," he wrote. "Their concessions . . . exceed all that I should have thought possible."

" 'Tis lost!" cries John Bull as America flies away in the hands of the devil. Spain, France, and Holland chide the Briton for his negligence.

The American commissioners obtained these favorable terms because they were shrewd diplomats and because of the rivalries that existed among the great European powers. In the last analysis, Britain preferred to have a weak nation of English-speaking people in command of the Mississippi Valley rather than France or Spain.

From their experience at the peace talks, the American leaders learned the importance of playing one power against another without committing themselves completely to any. This policy demanded constant contact with European affairs and skill at adjusting policies to changes in the European balance of power. It enabled the United States, a young and relatively feeble country, to grow and prosper.

Forming a National Government

Independence was won on the battlefield and at the Paris Peace Conference, but it could not have been achieved without the work of the Continental Congress and the new state governments. The delegates recognized that the Congress was essentially a legislative body rather than a complete government and from the start they struggled to create a workable central authority. But their effort was handicapped by much confusion and bickering, and early military defeats sapped their energy and morale. In July 1776 John Dickinson prepared a draft national constitution, but it could not command much support. The larger states objected to equal representation of all the states, and the states with large western land claims refused to cede them to the central government. It was not until November 1777 that the Articles of Confederation were submitted to the states for ratification.

It was necessary to obtain the approval of all the states before the Articles could go into effect. All but Maryland acted fairly promptly, but that state did not ratify the document until 1781. Maryland held out in order to force a change that would authorize Congress to determine the western limits of states with land claims beyond the Appalachians. There were many good reasons why this should be done. The state claims to the west were overlapping, vaguely defined, and in some instances preposter-

ous. To have permitted a few states to monopolize the west would have unbalanced the Union from the start.

Many people in the "landed" states recognized the justice of Maryland's suggestion, yet Maryland had a more selfish motive. Land speculators in the state had obtained from the Indians rights to large tracts in the Ohio Valley claimed by Virginia. Under Virginia, the Maryland titles would be worthless, but under a national administration they might be made to stand up.

Virginia resented its neighbor's efforts to grasp these valuable lands by indirection, but with the British about to advance into the state, Virginia agreed to surrender its claim to all land west and north of the Ohio River. It thwarted the Maryland speculators by insisting that all titles based on Indian purchases be declared void. Maryland then had no recourse but to ratify the Articles.

The Articles merely provided a legal basis for authority that the Continental Congress had already been exercising. Each state, regardless of size, was to have but one vote; the union it created was only a "league of friendship." Article 2 defined the limit of national power: "Each state retains its sovereignty, freedom, and independence, and every Power, jurisdiction, and right, which is not by this confederation expressly delegated to the United States, in Congress assembled." Time would prove this an inadequate arrangement, chiefly because the central government lacked the authority to impose taxes and had no way of enforcing the powers it did have. As the historian David Ramsay explained in 1789, "No coercive power was given to the general government, nor was it invested with any legislative power over individuals."

Financing the War

In practice, Congress and the states carried on the war cooperatively. General officers were appointed by Congress, lesser ones locally. The Continental Army, the backbone of Washington's force, was supported by Congress. The states raised militia chiefly for short-term service. Militiamen fought well at times but often proved unreliable, especially when asked to fight at any great distance from their homes. Washington continually fretted about their "dirty mercenary spirit" and their "intractable" na-

The Continental Army's lack of financial support is demonstrated in requisitions like this one, issued by General Washington the day after his troops limped into Valley Forge.

ture, yet he could not have won the war without them.

The fact that Congress's requisitions of money often went unhonored by the states does not mean that the states failed to contribute heavily to the war effort. Altogether they spent about $5.8 million in hard money, and they met Congress's demands for beef, corn, rum, fodder, and other military supplies. In addition, Congress raised large sums by borrowing. Americans bought bonds worth between $7 and $8 million during the war. Foreign governments lent another $8 million, most of this furnished by France. Congress also issued more than $240 million in paper money, the states over $200 million more. This currency fell rapidly in value, resulting in an inflation that caused hardship and grumbling. The people, in effect, paid much of the cost of the war through the depreciation of their savings, but it is hard to see how else the war could have been financed, given the prejudice of the populace against paying taxes to fight a war against British taxation.

At about the time the Articles of Confederation were ratified, Congress established Departments of Foreign Affairs, War, and Finance, with individual heads responsible to it. The most important of the new department heads was the superintendent of finance, Robert Morris, a Philadelphia merchant. When Morris took office, the Continental dollar was worthless, the system of supplying the army chaotic, the credit of the government exhausted. He set up an efficient method of obtaining food and uniforms for the army, persuaded Congress to charter a national Bank of North America, and aided by the slackening of military activity after Yorktown got the country back on a hard money basis. New foreign loans were obtained, partly because Morris's efficiency and industry inspired confidence.

State Governments

However crucial the role of Congress, in an important sense the real revolution occurred when the individual colonies broke their ties with Great Britain. Using their colonial charters as a basis, the states began framing new constitutions even before the Declaration of Independence. By early 1777 all but Connecticut and Rhode Island, which continued under their colonial charters well into the 19th century, had taken this decisive step.

On the surface the new governments were not drastically different from those they replaced. The most significant change was the removal of outside control, which had the effect of making the governments more responsive to public opinion. Gone were the times when a governor could be appointed and maintained in office by orders from London. The new constitutions varied in detail, but all provided for an elected legislature, an executive, and a system of courts. In general the powers of the governor and of judges were limited, the theory being that elected rulers no less than those appointed by kings were subject to the temptations of authority, that, as one Patriot put it, all men are "tyrants enough at heart." The typical governor had no voice in legislation and little in appointments. Pennsylvania went so far as to eliminate the office of governor, replacing it with an elected council of 12.

Power was concentrated in the legislature, which the people had come to count on to defend their interests. In addition to the lawmaking authority exercised by the colonial assemblies, the state constitutions gave the legislatures the power to declare war, conduct foreign relations, control the courts, and perform many other essentially executive functions. While continuing to require that voters be property owners or taxpayers, the constitution makers remained suspicious even of the legislature.

The British concept of virtual representation they rejected out of hand. They saw legislators as representatives, that is, agents reflecting the interests of the voters of a particular district rather than superior persons chosen to decide public issues according to their own best judgment. Gordon S. Wood, whose book *The Creation of the American Republic* throws much light on the political thinking of the period, describes the concept as "acutely actual representation." Where political power was involved, the common American principle was every man for himself. The constitutions contained bills of rights (such as the one George Mason wrote for Virginia) protecting the people's civil liberties against all branches of the government. In Britain such guarantees checked only the Crown; the Americans invoked them against their elected representatives as well.

The state governments combined the best of the British system, including its respect for status, fairness, and due process, with the uniquely American stress on individualism and a healthy dislike of too much authority. The idea of drafting written frames of government—contracts between the people and their representatives that carefully spelled out the powers and duties of the latter—grew out of the experience of the colonists after 1763, when the vagueness of the unwritten British constitution had caused so much controversy, and from the compact principle described in the Declaration of Independence. It represented one of the most important innovations of the Revolutionary era: a peaceful method for altering the political system. In the midst of violence, the states changed their frames of government in an orderly, legal manner—a truly remarkable achievement that became a beacon of hope to reformers all over the world. The states' example, the Reverend Simeon Howard of Massachusetts predicted, "will encourage the friends and rouse a spirit of liberty through other nations."

Social Reform

Back in 1909 the historian Carl Becker wrote that the American Revolution was not merely a fight for "home rule," that is, for independence from Great Britain. It was also, Becker insisted, a fight to determine "who should rule at home." It is certainly true that there were many riots and numerous other indications of social conflict in America during the Revolutionary era, especially in the cities. The destruction of property by mobs during the Stamp Act crisis is only the best-known case where well-to-do people had cause to fear that popular resentment was not entirely directed at the British.

Many states seized the occasion of constitution making to introduce important political and social reforms. In Pennsylvania, Virginia, North Carolina, and other states the seats in the legislature were reapportioned in order to give the western districts their fair share. Primogeniture, entail (the right of an owner of property to prevent heirs from ever disposing of it), and quitrents were abolished wherever they had existed. Steps toward greater freedom of religion were taken, especially in states where the Anglican church had enjoyed a privileged position. In Virginia the movement to separate church and state was given the force of law by Jefferson's Statute of Religious Liberty, enacted in 1786. "Our civil rights have no dependence on our religious opinions, any more than our opinions in physics or geometry," the statute declared. "Truth is great and will prevail if left to herself." Therefore, "No man shall be compelled to frequent or support any religious worship, place, or ministry . . . nor shall otherwise suffer on account of his religious opinions or belief."

Most states continued to support religion; Massachusetts did not end public support of Congregational churches until the 1830s. But after the Revolution the states usually distributed the money roughly in accordance with the numerical strength of the various Protestant denominations.

Many states moved tentatively against slavery. In attacking British policy after 1763, colonists had frequently claimed that Parliament was trying to make slaves of them. No less a personage than George Washington wrote in 1774: "We must assert our rights, or submit to every imposition, that can be heaped upon us, till custom and use shall make us tame and abject slaves." However exaggerated

The Continental Army brought together men from all over the colonies and from a wide range of backgrounds. Their variety is suggested in this watercolor by a French officer who served in America during the Revolution. From left to right are a black infantryman with a light rifle, a musketman, a soldier carrying a heavy rifle, and an artilleryman.

the language, such reasoning led to denunciations of slavery, often vague but significant in their effects on public opinion. The fact that practically every important thinker of the European Enlightenment had criticized slavery on moral and economic grounds (Montesquieu, Voltaire, Diderot, and Rousseau in France, David Hume, Samuel Johnson, and Adam Smith in England, to name the most important) also had an impact on educated opinion. Then, too, the forthright statements in the Declaration of Independence about liberty and equality seemed impossible to reconcile with slaveholding. "How is it," asked Dr. Johnson, who opposed independence vehemently, "that we hear the loudest yelps for liberty among the drivers of negroes?"

The war opened direct paths to freedom for some slaves. In November 1775 Lord Dunmore, the royal governor of Virginia, proclaimed that all slaves "able and willing to bear arms" for the British would be liberated. In fact, the British treated slaves as captured property, seizing them by the thousands in their campaigns in the south. The fate of these blacks is obscure. Some ended up in the West Indies, still slaves. Others were evacuated to Canada and liberated, and some of them settled the British colony of Sierra Leone in West Africa, founded in 1787. Probably many more escaped from bondage

by running away during the confusion accompanying the British campaigns in the south.

About 5,000 blacks served in the Patriot army and navy. Most black soldiers were assigned noncombat duties, but there were some black soldiers in every major battle from Lexington to Yorktown.

Beginning with Pennsylvania in 1780, the northern states all did away with slavery. In most cases slaves born after a certain date were to become free upon reaching maturity. Since New York did not pass a gradual emancipation law until 1799 and New Jersey not until 1804, there were numbers of slaves in the so-called free states well into the 19th century—more than 3,500 as late as 1830. But the institution was on its way toward extinction. All the states prohibited the importation of slaves from abroad, and except for Georgia and South Carolina, the southern states passed laws removing restrictions on the right of individual owners to free their slaves. The greatest success of voluntary emancipation came in Virginia, where between 1782 and 1790, as many as 10,000 blacks were freed.

These advances encouraged foes of slavery to hope that the institution would soon disappear. But slavery died only where it was not economically important. Except for owners whose slaves were "carried off" by the British, only in Massachusetts, where the state supreme court ruled slavery unconstitutional in 1783, were owners deprived of existing slaves against their will.

Despite the continuing subordination of blacks, there is no question that the Revolution permanently changed the tone of American society. In the way they dressed, in their manner of speech, and in the way they dealt with one another in public places, Americans paid at least lip service to the idea of equality.

After the publication of *Common Sense* and the Declaration of Independence, with their excoriations of that "Royal Brute," King George III, it became fashionable to denounce the granting of titles of nobility, all "aristocrats," and any privilege based on birth. In 1783 a group of army officers founded a fraternal organization, the Society of Cincinnati. Although the revered George Washington was its president, many citizens found the mere existence of a club restricted to officers alarming; the fact that membership was to be hereditary, passing on the death of a member to his oldest son, caused a furor.

Nevertheless, little of the social and economic upheaval usually associated with revolutions occurred, before, during, or after 1776. At least part of the urban violence of the period (just how large a part is difficult to determine at this distance) had no social objective. America had its share of criminals, mischievous youths eager to flex their muscles, and other people unable to resist the temptation to break the law when it could be done without much risk of punishment. Certainly there was no wholesale proscription of any class, faith, or profession.

The property of Tories was frequently seized by the state governments, but almost never with the idea of redistributing wealth or providing the poor with land. While some large Tory estates were broken up and sold to small farmers, others passed intact to wealthy individuals or to groups of speculators. The war disrupted many traditional business relationships. Some merchants were unable to cope with the changes; others adapted well and grew rich. But the changes occurred without regard for the political beliefs or social values of either those who profited or those who lost.

That the new governments were liberal but moderate reflected the spirit of the times, a spirit typified by Thomas Jefferson, who had great faith in the democratic process yet owned a large estate and

many slaves and had never suggested a drastic social revolution. More individuals of middling wealth were elected to the legislatures than in colonial times because the Revolution stimulated popular interest in politics and because republican forms subtly undermined the tendency of farmers and artisans to defer automatically to great planters and merchants.

Nevertheless, relatively high property qualifications for officeholding remained the general rule. Few "ordinary" people wanted radical changes. If they were becoming more skeptical about their "betters," they continued to look down their noses at unskilled laborers, servants, and others lower on the social ladder. There were three classes in Philadelphia society, a writer in the *Pennsylvania Packet* noted in 1781:

> The first class consists of commercial projectors . . . speculators, riotous livers, and a kind of loungers. . . . The second class are a set of honest sober men, who mind their business. . . . The third class are thieves, pick-pockets, low-cheats and dirty sots.

During the war, conflicts erupted over economic issues involving land and taxation, yet no single class or interest triumphed in all the states or in the national government. In Pennsylvania, where the western radical element was strong, the constitution was extremely democratic; in Maryland and South Carolina the conservatives maintained control handily. Throughout the country, many great landowners were ardent Patriots, but others became Tories—and so did many small farmers.

In some instances the state legislatures wrote the new constitutions. In others the legislatures ordered special elections to choose delegates to conventions empowered to draft the charters. The convention method was a further important product of the Revolutionary era, an additional illustration of the idea that constitutions are contracts between the people and their leaders. Massachusetts even required that its new constitution be ratified by the people after it was drafted.

Finally, the new governments became more responsive to public opinion, no matter what the particular shape of their political institutions. This was true principally because *Common Sense,* the Declaration of Independence, and the experience of participating in a revolution had made people conscious of their rights in a republic and of their power to enforce those rights. Conservatives swiftly discovered that state constitutions designed to insulate legislators and officials from popular pressures were ineffective when the populace felt strongly about any issue.

Effects of the Revolution on Women

In the late 18th century there was a worldwide trend, barely perceptible at the time, toward increasing the legal rights of women. This movement was strengthened in America by the events leading up to the break with Great Britain and still more by the Declaration of Independence. When Americans began to think and talk about the rights of the individual and the evils of arbitrary rule, subtle effects on relations between the sexes followed. For example, it became somewhat easier for women to obtain divorces. In colonial times divorces were rel-

atively rare, but easier for men to obtain than women. After the Revolution the difference did not disappear, but it became considerably smaller. In Massachusetts, before the 1770s no woman is known to have obtained a divorce on the ground of her husband's adultery. Thereafter, successful suits by wives against errant husbands were not unusual. In 1791 a South Carolina judge went so far as to say that the law protecting "the absolute dominion" of husbands was "the offspring of a rude and barbarous age." The "progress of civilization," he continued, "has tended to ameliorate the condition of women, and to allow even to wives, something like personal identity."

As the tone of this "liberal" opinion indicates, the change in male attitudes that took place in America because of the Revolution was small. When John Adams's wife Abigail warned him in 1776 that if he and his fellow rebels did not "remember the ladies" when reforming society, the women would "foment a Rebellion" of their own, he treated her

Abigail Adams, in asking her husband John to "remember the ladies" when reforming society, was not advocating political rights for women. Rather, she wanted fairer treatment for women within the family. "Do not put such unlimited power into the hands of the husbands," she wrote him. "Remember all men would be tyrants if they could."

remarks as a joke. He believed that voting (and as he wrote on another occasion, writing history) was "not the Province of the ladies."

However, the war effort increased the influence of women in several ways. With so many men in uniform, women took over the management of countless farms, shops, and businesses, and they became involved in the handling of other day-to-day matters that men had normally conducted. Their experiences made both them and in many cases their fathers and husbands more aware of their ability to take on all sorts of chores previously considered exclusively masculine in character. At the same time, women wanted to contribute to the winning of independence, and their efforts to do so made them conscious of their importance. Furthermore, the rhetoric of the Revolution, with its stress on liberty and equality, affected women in the same way that it caused many whites of both sexes to question the morality of slavery.

Attitudes toward the education of women also changed because of the Revolution. According to the best estimates, at least half the white women in America could not read or write as late as the 1780s. But as the historian Linda K. Kerber writes, "The republican experiment demanded a well-educated citizenry." In a land of opportunity like the United States, women seemed particularly important because of their role in training the young. "You distribute 'mental nourishment' along with physical," one orator told the women of America in 1795. "The reformation of the world is in your power. . . . The solidity and stability of your country rest with you." The idea of female education began to catch on. Schools for girls were founded, and the level of female literacy gradually rose.

Growth of a National Spirit

American independence and control of a wide and rich domain were the most obvious results of the Revolution. Changes in the structure of society, as we have seen, were relatively minor. Economic developments, such as the growth of new trade connections and the expansion of manufacturing in an effort to replace British goods, were of only modest significance. By far the most important social and economic changes involved the Tories and were thus by-products of the political revolution rather than a determined reorganization of a people's way of life.

There was another important result of the Revolution: the growth of American nationalism. Most modern revolutions have been *caused* by nationalism and have *resulted* in independence. In the case of the American Revolution, the desire to be free antedated any intense national feeling. The colonies entered into a political union not because they felt an overwhelming desire to bring all Americans under one rule but because unity offered the only hope of winning a war against Great Britain. That they remained united after throwing off British rule reflects the degree to which nationalism had developed during the conflict.

By the middle of the 18th century the colonists had begun to think of themselves as a separate society distinct from Europe and even from Britain. Benjamin Franklin described himself not as a British subject but as "an American subject of the King," and in 1750 a Boston newspaper could urge its readers to drink "American" beer in order to free themselves from being "beholden to Foreigners" for their alcoholic beverages. Little political nationalism existed before the Revolution, however. Local ties remained predominant. A few might say, with Patrick Henry in 1774, "The distinctions between Virginians, Pennsylvanians, New Yorkers, and New Englanders are no more. I am not a Virginian, but an American." But Henry was being carried away by his own oratory; he was actually of two minds on the subject of national versus local loyalty. People who really put America first were rare indeed before the final break with Great Britain.

The new nationalism arose from a number of sources and expressed itself in different ways. Common sacrifices in war certainly played a part; the soldiers of the Continental Army fought in the summer heat of the Carolinas for the same cause that had led them to brave the ice floes of the Delaware in order to surprise the Hessians. Such men lost interest in state boundary lines; they became Americans.

John Marshall of Fauquier County, Virginia, for example, was a 20-year-old militiaman in 1775. The next year he joined the Continental Army. He served in Pennsylvania, New Jersey, and New York and endured the winter of 1777–1778 at Valley Forge. "I found myself associated with brave men from different states who were risking life and everything valuable in a common cause," he later wrote. "I was confirmed in the habit of considering America as my country and Congress as my government."

Andrew Jackson, child of the Carolina frontier, was only 9 when the Revolution broke out. One brother was killed in battle; another died as a result of untreated wounds. Young Andrew took up arms and was captured by the Redcoats. A British officer ordered Jackson to black his boots and when the boy refused, struck him across the face with the flat of his sword. Jackson bore the scar to his grave–and became an ardent nationalist on the spot. He and Marshall had very different ideas and came to be bitter enemies in later life. Nevertheless, they were both American nationalists—and for the same reason.

Civilians as well as soldiers reacted in this way. A Carolina farmer whose home and barn were protected against British looters by men who spoke with the harsh nasal twang of New England adopted a broader outlook toward politics. When the news came that thousands of Redcoats had stacked their arms in defeat after Yorktown, few people cared what state or section had made the victory possible—it was an American triumph.

The war caused many people to move from place to place. Soldiers traveled as the tide of war fluctuated; so too—far more than in earlier times—did prominent leaders. Members of Congress from every state had to travel to Philadelphia; in the process they saw much of the country and the people who inhabited it. Listening to their fellows and serving with them on committees almost inevitably broadened these men, most of them highly influential in their local communities.

With its 13 stars and 13 stripes representing the states, the American flag symbolized national unity and reflected the common feeling that such a symbol was necessary. Yet the flag had separate stars and stripes; local interests and local loyalties remained extremely strong, and these could be divisive when conflicts of interest arose.

Certain practical problems that demanded common solutions also drew the states together. No one seriously considered having 13 postal systems or 13 sets of diplomatic representatives abroad. Every new diplomatic appointment, every treaty of friendship or commerce signed, committed all to a common policy and thus bound them more closely together. And economic developments had a unifying effect. Cutting off English goods encouraged manufacturing, making America more self-sufficient and stimulating both interstate trade and national pride.

The Great Land Ordinances

The western lands, which had divided the states in the beginning, became a force for unity once they had been ceded to the national government. Everyone realized what a priceless asset they were, and all now understood that no one state could determine the future of the west.

The politicians argued hotly about how these lands should be developed. Some advocated selling the land in township units in the traditional New England manner to groups or companies; others favored letting individual pioneers stake out farms in the helter-skelter manner common in the colonial south. The decision was a compromise. The Land Ordinance of 1785 provided for surveying western territories into 6-mile-square townships before sale. Every other township was to be further subdivided into 36 sections of 640 acres (1 square mile) each. The land was sold at auction at a minimum price of $1 an acre. The law favored speculative land-development companies, for even the 640-acre units were far too large and expensive for the typical frontier family. But the fact that the land was to be surveyed and sold by the central government was a nationalizing force. Congress set aside the sixteenth section of every township for the maintenance of schools, another farsighted decision.

Still more significant was the Northwest Ordinance of 1787, which established governments for the west. As early as 1775, settlers in frontier districts were petitioning Congress to allow them to enter the Union as independent states, and in 1780 Congress had resolved that all lands ceded to the nation by the existing states should be "formed into distinct republican States" with "the same rights of sovereignty, freedom and independence" as the original 13. In 1784 a committee headed by Thomas Jefferson worked out a plan for doing this, and in 1787 it was enacted into law. The area bounded by the Ohio, the Mississippi, and the Great Lakes was to be carved into not less than three or more than five

New York and Virginia gave up their claims to the vast area that became the Northwest Territory, and thus set a precedent for trans-Appalachian land policy. By 1802 the various state claims had been ceded to the national government. The original Northwest Territory (the Old Northwest) was bounded by the Ohio River, the Mississippi, and the Great Lakes.

THE UNITED STATES
UNDER THE ARTICLES OF CONFEDERATION, 1787

territories. Until the adult male population of the entire area reached 5,000, it was to be ruled by a governor and three judges, all appointed by Congress. When 5,000 men of voting age had settled in the territory, the ordinance authorized them to elect a legislature and send a nonvoting delegate to Congress. Finally, when 60,000 persons had settled in any one of the political subdivisions, it was to become a state. It could draft a constitution and operate in any way it wished, save that the government had to be "republican" and that slavery was prohibited.

Seldom has a legislative body acted more wisely. That the western districts must become states everyone conceded from the start. The people had had their fill of colonialism under British rule, and the rebellious temper of frontier settlers made it impossible even to consider maintaining the west in a dependent status. (When North Carolina ceded its trans-Appalachian lands to the United States in 1784, the settlers there, uncertain how they would fare under federal rule, hastily organized an extra-legal state of Franklin, and it was not until 1789 that the national government obtained control.) But it would have been unfair to turn the territories over to the first comers, who would have been unable to manage such large domains and would surely have taken advantage of their priority to dictate to later arrivals. A period of tutelage was necessary, a period when the "mother country" must guide and nourish its growing offspring.

Thus the intermediate territorial governments corresponded almost exactly to the governments of British royal colonies. The appointed governors could veto acts of the assemblies and could "convene, prorogue, and dissolve" them at their discretion. The territorial delegates to Congress were not unlike colonial agents. Yet it was vital that this intermediate stage end and that its end be determined in advance so that no argument could develop over when the territory was ready for statehood.

The system worked well and was applied to nearly all the regions absorbed by the nation as it advanced westward. Together with the Ordinance of 1785, which branded its checkerboard pattern on the physical shape of the west, this law gave the growing country a unity essential to the growth of a national spirit.

National Heroes

The Revolution further fostered nationalism by giving the people their first commonly revered heroes. Benjamin Franklin was widely known before the break with Great Britain through his experiments

"The chief human symbol of a common Americanism." George Washington attained heroic status perhaps as much for his modesty as for his devotion to the new nation.

with electricity, his immensely successful *Poor Richard's Almanack,* and his invention of the Franklin stove. His staunch support of the Patriot cause, his work in the Continental Congress, and his diplomatic successes in France, where he was extravagantly admired, added to his fame. Franklin demonstrated, to Europeans and to Americans themselves, that not all Americans need be ignorant rustics.

Washington, however, was "the chief human symbol of a common Americanism." Stern, cold, a man of few words, the great Virginian did not seem a likely candidate for hero worship. "My countenance never yet revealed my feelings," he himself admitted. Yet he had qualities that made people name babies after him and call him "the Father of His Country" long before the war was won: his personal sacrifices in the cause of independence, his integrity, and above all, perhaps, his obvious desire to retire to his Mount Vernon estate (for many Americans feared any powerful leader and worried lest Washington seek to become a dictator).

As a general, Washington was not a brilliant strategist like Napoleon. Neither was he a tactician of the quality of Caesar or Robert E. Lee. His lack of genius made his achievements all the more impressive. He held his forces together in adversity, avoiding both useless slaughter and catastrophic defeat. People of all sections, from every walk of life, looked on Washington as the embodiment of American virtues: a man of deeds rather than words; a man of substance accustomed to luxury yet capable of enduring great hardships stoically and as much at home in the wilderness as an Indian; a bold Patriot, quick to take arms against British tyranny, yet eminently respectable. The Revolution might have been won without Washington, but it is unlikely that the free United States would have become so easily a true nation had he not been at its call.

A National Culture

Breaking away from Great Britain accentuated certain trends toward social and intellectual independence and strengthened the national desire to create an American culture. The Anglican church in America had to form a new organization once the connection with the Crown was severed; in 1786 it became the Protestant Episcopal church. The Dutch and German Reformed churches also became independent of their European connections. Roman Catholics in America had been under the administration of the vicar apostolic of England; after the Revolution, Father John Carroll of Baltimore assumed these duties, and in 1789 he became the first American Roman Catholic bishop.

The impact of post-Revolutionary nationalism on American education was best reflected in the immense success of the textbooks of Noah Webster, later famous for his American dictionary. Webster was an ardent patriot. "We ought not to consider ourselves as inhabitants of a particular state only," he wrote in 1785, "but as *Americans.*" Webster's famous *Spelling Book* appeared in 1783 when he was a young schoolteacher in Goshen, New York. It emphasized American forms and usage and contained a patriotic preface urging Americans to pay proper respect to their own literature. Webster's *Reader,* published shortly thereafter, included selections from the speeches of Revolutionary leaders, who, according to the compiler, were the equals of Cicero and Demosthenes as orators. Some 15 million copies of the *Speller* were sold in the next five decades, several times that number by 1900. The *Reader* was also a continuing best-seller.

Webster's work was not the only sign of nationalism in education. In 1787 John M'Culloch published the first American history textbook. The colleges saw a great outburst of patriotic spirit. King's College (founded in 1754) received a new name, Columbia, in 1784. Everywhere it was recognized that the republic required educated and cultivated leaders.

Nationalism affected the arts and sciences in the years after the Revolution. Jedidiah Morse's popular *American Geography* (1789) was a paean in praise of the "astonishing" progress of the country, all the result of the "natural genius of Americans." The American Academy of Arts and Sciences, founded at Boston during the Revolution, was created "to advance the interest, honor, dignity and happiness of a free, independent and virtuous people."

American painters and writers of the period usually chose extremely patriotic themes. John Trumbull helped capture Dorchester Heights and force the evacuation of Boston, took part in the defense of northern New York against Burgoyne, and fought in Pennsylvania and Rhode Island. When he took up painting, he went to London to study, but he produced such pictures as *The Battle of Bunker's Hill*, *The Surrender of Lord Cornwallis at Yorktown*, and *The Declaration of Independence*. Trumbull referred to these and similar efforts as his "national work." Joel Barlow intended his *Vision of Columbus*, written between 1779 and 1787, to prove that America was "the noblest and most elevated part of the earth." Royall Tyler's play *The Contrast*, which was produced in New York in 1787, compared American virtue (the hero was called Colonel Manly) with British vice and contained such chauvinistic lines as these:

> *Why should our thoughts to distant countries roam*
> *When each refinement may be found at home?*

In a more subtle way, American nationalism revealed itself in the fondness of the Revolutionary generation for ancient Greek and Roman architecture, which they saw as expressing democratic and republican values. Jefferson, for example, built his home at Monticello in classical style and modeled the Virginia Capitol on the Roman *Maison Carré* in Nimes, France.

The United States in the 1780s was far from the powerful centralized nation it has since become. Probably most citizens still gave their first loyalty to their own states. In certain important respects the confederation was pitifully ineffectual. However, people were increasingly aware of their common interests and increasingly proud of their common heritage. The motto of the new nation, *E pluribus unum*—"From many, one"—perfectly describes a process that was rapidly taking place in the years after Yorktown.

Milestones

1774	Thomas Jefferson, "A Summary View of the Rights of British America"
	General Thomas Gage, commander in chief of the British army in America, named governor of Massachusetts
1775	Battles of Lexington and Concord
	Second Continental Congress names George Washington commander in chief of the Continental Army
	Battle of Bunker Hill; Gage replaced as British commander by General Sir William Howe
1776	Tom Paine, *Common Sense*
	Washington occupies Boston
	Declaration of Independence
	Battle of Long Island
	Washington evacuates New York City
	Battle of Trenton
1777	Battle of Saratoga, leading to alliance with France
	Battle of Germantown; British occupy Philadelphia
1777–1778	Continental Army winters at Valley Forge
1778	British capture Savannah
1780	British capture Charleston
1781	Articles of Confederation ratified
	General Cornwallis surrenders at Yorktown
1783	Peace of Paris; Great Britain recognizes the independence of the United States
1785	Land Ordinance of 1785

SUPPLEMENTARY READING

Titles marked with an asterisk have been published in paperback.

Good brief surveys of the Revolutionary years are Edward Countryman, **The American Revolution** (1985), and E. S. Morgan, **The Birth of the Republic*** (1956). Robert Middlekauf, **The Glorious Cause** (1982), is more detailed. Don Higgenbotham, **The War of American Independence*** (1971), provides an up-to-date account of the military aspects of the Revolution, and Charles Royster, **A Revolutionary People at War** (1979), describes the attitudes of soldiers and civilians toward the army. See also Robert A. Gross, **The Minutemen and Their World** (1976). On Washington's role, see J. R. Alden, **George Washington** (1984), and Marcus Cunliffe, **George Washington: Man and Monument*** (1958).

On the Continental Congress and the Articles of Confederation, see J. T. Main, **The Sovereign States** (1973), J. N. Rakove, **The Beginnings of National Politics** (1979), and R. B. Morris, **The Forging of the Union** (1987). Eric Foner, **Tom Paine and Revolutionary America*** (1976), is an excellent brief biography. The classic analysis of the Declaration of Independence is C. L. Becker, **The Declaration of Independence*** (1922).

The early history of the state governments is covered in Elisha P. Douglas, **Rebels and Democrats*** (1955). Edward Countryman, **A People in Revolution** (1982), deals with conditions in New York. The development of political ideas is admirably described and analyzed in G. S. Wood, **The Creation of the American Republic*** (1969), and in D. J. Boorstin, **The Genius of American Politics*** (1953). The financial problems of this period are covered in E. J. Ferguson, **The Power of the Purse*** (1968).

The classic account of the social and economic effects of the Revolution is J. F. Jameson, **The American Rev-**olution Considered as a Social Movement*** (1926). R. E. Brown takes issue with Jameson's view in **Middle Class Democracy and the Revolution in Massachusetts** (1955), as does R. P. McCormick in **Experiment in Independence: New Jersey in the Critical Period** (1950). J. T. Main, **The Social Structure of Revolutionary America*** (1965), provides a general picture against which to evaluate the views of Jameson and his critics. On the Tories, see W. H. Nelson, **The American Tory*** (1962), M. B. Norton, **The British-Americans** (1972), and R. M. Calhoun, **The Loyalists in Revolutionary America** (1973). The effects of the Revolution on slavery are treated in W. D. Jordan, **White over Black*** (1968), Arthur Zilversmit, **The First Emancipation*** (1967), and Benjamin Quarles, **The Negro in the American Revolution*** (1961). See also Ira Berlin and Ronald Holfman (eds.), **Slavery and Freedom in the Age of the American Revolution** (1983). L. K. Kerber, **Women of the Republic** (1980), and M. B. Norton, **Liberty's Daughters** (1980), discuss the effects of the Revolution on women.

On the diplomacy of the Revolution, see J. R. Dull, **A Diplomatic History of the American Revolution** (1985). The fullest account of the peace treaty is R. B. Morris, **The Peacemakers*** (1965).

On the emergence of American nationalism and cultural history generally, see R. B. Nye, **The Cultural Life of the New Nation*** (1960). R. L. Merritt, **Symbols of American Community** (1966), concludes from a study of colonial newspapers that a sense of national identity was well developed before 1763. P. C. Nagel, **One Nation Indivisible** (1964), discusses the various views of the nature of the Union advanced in this period.

V

Nationalism Triumphant

You and I have been sent into life at a time when the greatest lawgivers of antiquity would have wished to live. How few of the human race have ever enjoyed an opportunity of making an election of government . . . for themselves or their children! When, before the present epoch, had three millions of people full of power and a fair opportunity to form and establish the wisest and happiest government that human wisdom can contrive?

JOHN ADAMS *to George Wythe*

A t first, only a relative handful of Americans resented the constraints imposed by the confederation on the power of the central government. Once the war was over, however, the need for unity seemed less pressing, and sectional conflicts reasserted themselves. Modern research has modified the thesis, advanced by John Fiske in *The Critical Period of American History* (1888), that the national government was demoralized and inadequate. If, as Washington said, it moved "on crutches . . . tottering at every step," it did move nevertheless. The negotiation of a successful peace treaty ending the Revolutionary War, the humane and farsighted federal land policies, and even the establishment of a federal bureaucracy to manage routine affairs were remarkable achieve-ments, all carried out under the Articles of Confederation. Yet the country's evolution placed demands on the national government that its creators had not anticipated.

Border Problems

The government had to struggle to win actual control over the territory granted the United States in the treaty ending the Revolution. Both Great Britain and Spain stood in the way of this objective. The British had promised to withdraw all their troops from American soil promptly, and so they did—within the settled portions of the 13 states. Beyond the frontier, however, they had established a string of seven military posts, running from the northern end of Lake Champlain through Niagara and Detroit to the tip of the Michigan peninsula. These, despite the Treaty of Paris, they refused to surrender. Pressing against America's exposed frontier like hot coals, the posts seared national pride. They threatened to set off another Indian war, for the British intrigued constantly to stir up the tribes. The great prize was the rich fur trade of the region, which the British still controlled.

The British justified holding on to these positions by citing the failure of the Americans to live up to some terms of the peace treaty. The United States had agreed not to impede British creditors seeking to collect prewar debts and to "earnestly recommend" that the states restore confiscated Tory property. The national government complied with both requirements (which only called for words on Congress's part), but the states did not cooperate. Many passed laws making it impossible for British creditors to collect debts, and most of the property of Tory émigrés was not returned.

Yet those violations of the peace terms had little to do with the continued presence of the British. They would not have evacuated the posts at this time even if every farthing of the debt had been paid and every acre of confiscated land had been restored. Americans found the presence of British troops galling. When the French had pushed a line of forts into the Ohio country in the 1750s, it had seemed to most colonists a matter of local concern, to be dealt with by Virginia or Pennsylvania. Three decades later the inability to eject the British seemed a national disgrace.

The Mississippi teems with commerce in this watercolor, based on a sketch made about 1790 by Christophe Colomb. Two flatboats (on the right) and a keelboat are in the improbably narrow river; in the center left foreground Colomb sits on a log, sketching his father-in-law's plantation house on the other side of the river.

Then there was the question of the Spanish in the southwest. Spain had been a cobelligerent, not an ally, in the war with Great Britain. In the peace negotiations it had won back Florida and the Gulf Coast region east of New Orleans. Spanish troops had captured Natchez during the war, and although the post lay north of the boundary, Spain refused to turn it over to the United States. Far more serious, the Spaniards had closed the lower Mississippi River to American commerce. Because of the prohibitive cost of moving bulky farm produce over the mountains, settlers beyond the Appalachians depended on the Mississippi and its network of tributaries to get their corn, tobacco, and other products to eastern and European markets. If Spain closed the river, or even if it denied them the right to "deposit" goods at New Orleans while awaiting oceangoing transportation, westerners could not sell their surpluses. Frontier settlers fumed when Congress failed to win concessions from Spain.

A stronger central government might have dealt with these foreign problems more effectively, but it could not have eliminated them. United or decentralized, until the country grew more powerful, or until the Europeans began to fight among themselves, the United States was bound to suffer at their hands.

Foreign Trade

The fact that the Revolution freed American trade from the restrictions of British mercantilism proved a mixed blessing in the short run. The commercial benefits that Tom Paine had described in *Common Sense* did not materialize. Americans could now trade directly with the European powers, and commercial treaties were negotiated with a number of them. Beginning in 1784, when the 360-ton *Empress of China* reached Canton with a cargo of furs and cotton to be exchanged for silks, tea, and spices, a valuable Far Eastern trade sprang up where none had existed before. But exclusion from Britain's imperial trade union brought losses of a much larger magnitude.

Immediately after the Revolution a controversy broke out in Great Britain over fitting the former colonies into the mercantilistic system. Some people, influenced by Adam Smith's *The Wealth of Nations*, published in 1776, argued that any restriction on the buying and selling of goods was wasteful; if people could trade freely, all parties would benefit. Others, while remaining mercantilists, realized how important the American trade was for British prosperity and argued that special treatment should be afforded the former colonists. Unfortunately, a proud empire recently humbled in war could hardly be expected to exercise such forbearance. Persuaded in part by the reasoning of Lord Sheffield's pamphlet *Observations on the Commerce of the American States* that Britain could get all the American commerce it wished without making concessions, Parliament voted to try building up exports to America while holding imports to a minimum, all according to the best tenets of mercantilism.

The British attitude hurt American interests severely. In the southern states rice and tobacco growers were afflicted by a labor shortage in the 1780s because of the wartime British seizure of so many slaves, and the termination of royal bounties hit North Carolina producers of naval stores and South Carolina indigo planters hard. In addition, a new British duty on rice reduced the export of that product by almost 50 percent.

The British struck at the northern states, barring American cured meat, fish, and dairy products from the British West Indies and permitting other American products to enter the islands only in British ships. American fishermen lost the lucrative West Indian market, merchants, a host of profitable opportunities. The value of trade with the West Indies fell steeply, idling many American ships. More than 1,000 American sailors lost their jobs. Shipbuilding slumped because of these facts and because British merchants stopped ordering American-made vessels.

At the same time, British merchants, eager to regain markets closed to them during the Revolution, poured low-priced manufactured goods of all kinds into the United States. Americans, long deprived of British products, rushed to take advantage of the bargains. Soon imports of British goods were approaching the levels of the early 1770s, while exports to the empire reached no more than half their earlier volume.

The influx of British goods aggravated the situation just when the economy was suffering a certain dislocation as a result of the ending of the war. From 1784 to 1786 the country went through a period of bad times. The inability of Congress to find money to pay the nation's debts undermined public confidence. Veterans who had still not been paid, private individuals, and foreign governments that had lent the government money during the Revolution were clamoring for their due. In some regions crop failures compounded the difficulties.

Dinner plate made in China for export, painted with an American vessel named Friendship. *American trade with China, which began after the Revolution, was a profitable three-stage affair. Merchants first sailed around South America to the Northwest coast, where they exchanged manufactured products for furs. Then they voyaged to China and sold the pelts for silks and other luxury goods.*

The depression made the states stingier than ever about supplying the requisitions of Congress; at the same time, many of them levied heavy property taxes in order to pay off their own war debts. Everywhere people were hard pressed for cash. "As Money has ever been considered the root of all evils," one Massachusetts man commented sourly, "may we not presage happy times, as this source is almost done away?"

An obvious way of dealing with these problems would have been to place tariffs on British goods in order to limit imports or force the British to open the West Indies to all American goods, but the Confederation lacked the authority to do this. When individual states erected tariff barriers, British merchants easily got around them by bringing their goods in through states that did not. That the central government lacked the power to control commerce disturbed merchants, other businessmen, and the ever-increasing number of national-minded citizens in every walk of life.

Thus a movement developed to give the Confederation the power to tax imports, and in 1781 Congress sought authority to levy a 5 percent tariff duty. This would enable Congress to pay off some of its obligations and also put pressure on the British to relax their restrictions on American trade with the West Indies. Every state but Rhode Island agreed, but the measure required the unanimous consent of the states and therefore failed.

Defeat of the "impost" pointed up the need for revising the Articles of Confederation, for here was a case where nearly all of the states were ready to increase the power of the national government yet they were unable to do so. Although many individuals in every region were worried about creating a centralized monster that might gobble up the sovereignty of the states, the practical needs of the times convinced many others that this risk must be taken.

The Specter of Inflation

The depression and the unfavorable balance of trade led to increased pressures in the states for the printing of paper money and the passage of laws designed to make life easier for debtors. Before the Revolution the colonists had grappled with the chronic shortage of hard money resulting from their unfavorable balance of trade in many ways: declaring various staple products such as furs, tobacco, and even Indian wampum to be legal tender, deliberately overvaluing foreign coins to discourage their export, making it illegal to ship coins abroad, and printing paper currency. In response to wartime needs, both the Continental Congress and the states issued large amounts of paper money during the Revolution, with inflationary results (the Continental dollar became utterly worthless by 1781, and Virginia eventually called in its paper at 1,000 to 1).

After the war some states set out to restore their credit by imposing heavy taxes and severely restricting new issues of money. Combined with the postwar depression and the increase in imports, this policy had a powerful deflationary effect on prices and wages. Soon debtors, especially farmers, were crying for relief, both in the form of stay laws designed to make it difficult to collect debts (these laws were popular because of the anti-British feeling of the times) and through the printing of more paper money.

More than half the states yielded to this pressure in 1785 and 1786. Issues in South Carolina, New York, and Pennsylvania were conservatively handled and succeeded, but in some states the money depreciated rapidly. The most disastrous experience was that of Rhode Island, where the government attempted to legislate public confidence in £100,000 of paper. Any landowner could borrow a share of this money from the state for 14 years, using real estate as security. Creditors feared that the loans would never be repaid, but the legislature passed a law fining persons who refused to accept it £100. When creditors fled the state to avoid being confronted, the legislature authorized debtors to discharge their obligations by turning the necessary currency over to a judge. A conservative poet described Rhode Island as a "realm of rogues, renown'd for fraud and guile" where "bankrupts their creditors with rage pursue."

Of course these measures further weakened public confidence; when the state tried to use paper money to meet its obligations to the federal government, Congress refused to accept it. Indeed, no one accepted the currency freely. The Rhode Island supreme court, in *Trevett* v. *Weeden*, declared that it was unconstitutional to fine a creditor for refusing it, and soon there was a reaction. The element of compulsion was withdrawn, and the paper depreciated rapidly.

Daniel Shays's "Little Rebellion"

Although the Rhode Island case was atypical, it alarmed conservatives. Then, close on its heels, came a disturbing outbreak of violence in Massachusetts. The Massachusetts legislature was determined to pay off the state debt and maintain a sound currency. Taxes amounting to almost £1.9 million were levied between 1780 and 1786, the burden falling most heavily on those of moderate income. The historian Merrill Jensen estimated that the average Massachusetts farmer paid about a third of every year's income in taxes. Bad times and deflation led to many foreclosures, and the prisons were crowded with honest debtors. "Our Property is torn from us," one town complained, "our Gaols filled & still our Debts are not discharged."

In the summer of 1786 mobs in the western communities began to stop foreclosures by forcibly preventing the courts from holding their sessions. Under the leadership of Daniel Shays, veteran of Bunker Hill, Ticonderoga, and Saratoga, the "rebels" marched on Springfield and prevented the state supreme court from meeting. When the state government sent troops against them, they attacked the Springfield arsenal. They were routed, and the uprising then collapsed. Shays fled to Vermont.

As Thomas Jefferson observed at safe remove from the trouble in Paris, where he was serving as minister to France, Shays's uprising was only "a *little* rebellion" and as such "a medicine necessary for the sound health of government." But Shays and his followers were genuinely exasperated by the refusal of the government even to try to provide relief for their troubles. By taking up arms they forced the authorities to heed them: At its next session the legislature made some concessions to their demands. But the Rhode Island excesses and the uprising in Massachusetts illustrated the clash between local and national interests. Newspapers in all the states followed the bizarre spectacle of debtors in Rhode Island pursuing their creditors with fistfuls of worthless paper money. The revolt of Daniel Shays worried planters in far-off Virginia and the Carolinas almost as much as it did the merchants of Boston. Most well-to-do Americans considered the uprising "liberty run mad." "What, gracious God, is man! that there should be such inconsistency and perfidiousness in his conduct?" the usually unexcitable George Washington asked when news of the riots reached Virginia. "We are fast verging to anarchy and confusion!" During the crisis, private persons had had to subscribe funds to put the rebels down, and when Massachusetts had appealed to Congress for help, there was little Congress could legally do. The lessons seemed plain: Liberty must not become an excuse for license; greater authority must be vested in the central government.

The Road to Philadelphia

If most people wanted to increase the power of Congress, they were also afraid to shift the balance too far lest they destroy the sovereignty of the states and the rights of individuals. The machinery for change established in the Articles of Confederation, which required the unanimous consent of the states for all amendments, posed a particularly delicate problem. Experience had shown it unworkable, yet to bypass it would be revolutionary and therefore dangerous.

The first fumbling step toward reform was taken in March 1785, when representatives of Virginia and Maryland, meeting at the home of George Washington to settle a dispute over the improvement of navigation on the Potomac River, suggested a conference of all the states to discuss common problems of commerce. In January 1786 the Virginia legislature sent out a formal call for such a gathering, to be held in September at Annapolis. However, the Annapolis convention disappointed advocates of reform; delegates from only five states appeared; even Maryland, supposedly the host state, did not send a representative. Being so few, the group did not feel it worthwhile to propose changes.

Among the delegates was a young New York lawyer named Alexander Hamilton, a brilliant, imaginative, and daring man who was convinced that only drastic centralization would save the nation from disintegration. Hamilton described himself as a "nationalist." While the war still raged, he contrasted the virtues of "a great Federal Republic" with the existing system of "petty states with the appearance only of union, jarring, jealous, and perverse." Instead of giving up, he proposed calling another convention to meet at Philadelphia to deal generally with constitutional reform. Delegates should be empowered to work out a broad plan for correcting "such defects as may be discovered to exist" in the Articles of Confederation.

The Annapolis group approved Hamilton's suggestion, and Congress reluctantly endorsed it. This time all the states but Rhode Island sent delegates. On May 25, 1787, the convention opened its proceedings at the State House in Philadelphia and unanimously elected George Washington its president. When it adjourned four months later, it had drafted the Constitution.

The Great Convention

As the decades have passed and the Constitution has grown more and more tradition-encrusted without losing any of its flexibility, each generation has

James Madison was a key figure at the Great Convention of 1787. He not only influenced the shaping of the Constitution but also kept the most complete record of the proceedings. "Every Person," wrote one delegate of him, "seems to acknowledge his greatness."

tried to explain how a people so young and inexperienced, so free-swinging and unruly, could have produced it. At the time of the hundredth anniversary of its signing, the British statesman William E. Gladstone called it "the most wonderful work ever struck off at a given time by the brain of man." One reason for its durability was the ability of those who drafted it. The Founding Fathers were remarkable men. Though he later had reason to quarrel with certain aspects of their handiwork, Jefferson, who was on a foreign assignment and did not attend the convention, called them "demigods." A presumably more impartial French diplomat said that "even in Europe," he had never seen "an assembly more respectable for the talents, knowledge, disinterestedness, and patriotism."

Collectively, the delegates possessed a rare combination of talents. Most of them had had considerable experience in politics and the many lawyers among them were skilled in negotiation. Furthermore, the times made them acutely aware of their opportunities. It was "a time when the greatest lawgivers of antiquity would have wished to live," an opportunity to "establish the wisest and happiest government that human wisdom can contrive," John Adams wrote. "We . . . decide for ever the fate of republican government," James Madison said during the deliberations.

If these remarks overstated the importance of their deliberations, they nonetheless represented the opinion of most of those present. They were boldly optimistic about their country. "We are laying the foundation of a great empire," Madison predicted. At the same time, the delegates recognized the difficulties they faced. The ancient Roman republic was their model, and all knew that it had been overthrown by tyrants and eventually overrun by barbarians.

Fortunately, they were nearly all of one mind on basic questions. That there should be a federal system, with both independent state governments and a national government with limited powers to handle matters of common interest, was accepted by all but one or two of them. Republican government, drawing its authority from the people and remaining responsible to them, was a universal assumption. A measure of democracy followed inevitably from this principle, for even the most aristocratic delegates agreed that ordinary citizens should share in the process of selecting those who were to make and execute the laws.

All agreed that no group within society, no matter how numerous, should have unrestricted authority. They regarded political power much as we today view nuclear energy: a force with tremendous potential value for humanity but one easily misused and therefore dangerous to unleash. People meant well and had limitless possibilities, the constitution makers believed, but they were selfish by nature and could not be counted on to respect the interests of others. The ordinary people—small farmers, artisans, taxpayers—should have a say in government in order to be able to protect themselves against those who would exploit their weakness, and the majority must somehow be prevented from plundering the rich, for property must be secure or no government could be stable. No single state or section must be allowed to predominate, nor should

THE SETTLEMENT

the legislature be supreme over the executive or the courts. Power, in short, must be divided, and the segments must be balanced one against the other.

Although the level of education among them was high and a number might fairly be described as learned, the delegates' approach was pragmatic rather than theoretical. This was perhaps their most useful asset, for their task called for reconciling clashing interests. It could never have been accomplished without compromise and an acute sense of what was possible (as distinct from what was ideally best).

At the outset the delegates decided to keep the proceedings secret. That way no one was tempted to play to the gallery or seek some personal political advantage at the expense of the common good. Next they agreed to go beyond their instructions to revise the Articles of Confederation and draft an entirely new frame of government. This was a bold decision, but it was in no way irresponsible because nothing the convention might recommend was binding on anyone, and it was absolutely essential because under the Articles a single state could have prevented the adoption of any change. Alexander Hamilton captured the mood of the gathering when he said: "We can only propose and recommend—the power of ratifying or rejecting is still in the States. . . . We ought not to sacrifice the public Good to narrow Scruples."

The Settlement

The delegates voted on May 30 that "a national Government ought to be established" and then set to work hammering out a specific plan. Two big questions had to be answered. The first, "What powers should this national government be granted?" occasioned relatively little discussion. The right to levy taxes and to regulate interstate and foreign commerce was assigned to the central government almost without debate. So was the power to raise and maintain an army and a navy and to summon the militia of the states to enforce national laws and suppress insurrections. With equal absence of argument, the states were deprived of their rights to issue money, to make treaties, and to tax either imports or exports without the permission of Congress. Thus in summary fashion was brought about

a massive shift of power, a shift made necessary by the problems that had brought the delegates to Philadelphia and made practicable by the new nationalism of the 1780s.

The second major question, "Who shall control the national government?" proved more difficult to answer in a manner satisfactory to all. Led by Virginia, the larger states pushed for representation in the national legislature based on population. The smaller states wished to maintain the existing system of equal representation for each state regardless of population. The large states rallied behind the Virginia Plan, drafted by James Madison and presented to the convention by Edmund Randolph, governor of the state. The small states supported the New Jersey Plan, prepared by William Paterson, a former attorney general of that state. The question was important; equal state representation would have been undemocratic, yet a proportional system would have effectively destroyed the influence of all the states as states. But the delegates saw it in terms of combinations of large or small states, and this was unrealistic: When the states combined, they did so on geographic, economic, or social grounds that seldom had anything to do with size. Nevertheless, the debate was long and heated, and for a time it threatened to disrupt the convention.

Day after day in the stifling heat of high summer, the weary delegates struggled to find a suitable compromise. Madison and a few others had to use every weapon in their arsenal of argument to hold the group together. (All told, during the 88 sessions of the convention, a total of 569 votes was taken.) July 2 was perhaps the most fateful day of the whole proceedings. "We are at full stop," said Roger Sherman of Connecticut, who, it will be recalled, had been one of the drafters of the Declaration of Independence. "If we do not concede on both sides," a North Carolina delegate warned, "our business must soon be at an end."

But the delegates did "concede on both sides," and the debates went on. Again on July 17 collapse threatened as the representatives of the larger states caucused to consider walking out of the convention. Fortunately, they did not walk out, and finally the delegates adopted what is known as the Great Compromise. In the lower branch of the new legislature, the House of Representatives, places were to be assigned according to population and filled by pop-

On Friday, May 25, 1787, 29 delegates from 9 of the 13 states assembled in Philadelphia to deal with constitutional reform. New Hampshire, Connecticut, and Maryland were not yet there; Rhode Island never did appear. On Monday, September 17, of that same year, 39 of the 42 delegates still in attendance signed the final document. They had met in 88 sessions and taken 569 votes in all.

What backgrounds did these men have? What do we know about them? Here are . . .

FACTS ON THE

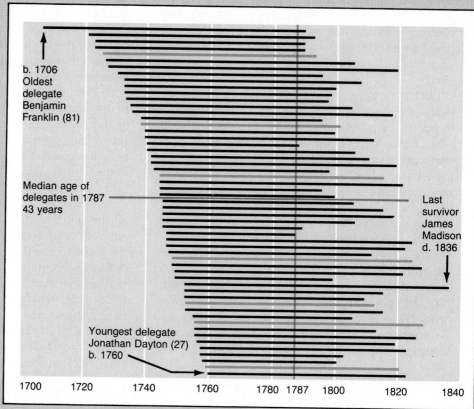

b. 1706
Oldest
delegate
Benjamin
Franklin (81)

Median age of
delegates in 1787
43 years

Last
survivor
James
Madison
d. 1836

Youngest delegate
Jonathan Dayton (27)
b. 1760

The median age of the U.S.
population in 1790 was 16.

The mean age of death in 1800
was about 56.

1700   1720   1740   1760   1780 1787 1800   1820   1840

How Old Were They?

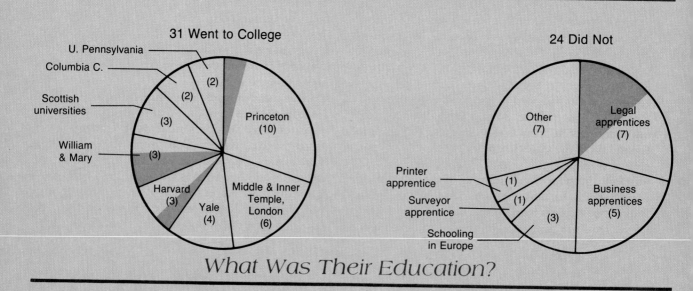

31 Went to College

U. Pennsylvania
Columbia C.
Scottish
universities
William
& Mary
Harvard
(3)
Yale
(4)
Princeton
(10)
Middle & Inner
Temple,
London
(6)
(2)
(2)
(3)
(3)

24 Did Not

Printer
apprentice
Surveyor
apprentice
Schooling
in Europe
Other
(7)
Legal
apprentices
(7)
Business
apprentices
(5)
(1)
(1)
(3)

What Was Their Education?

FRAMERS

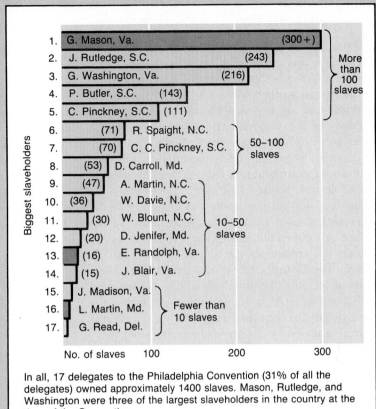

How Many Were Slaveholders?

	Biggest slaveholders	
1.	G. Mason, Va.	(300+)
2.	J. Rutledge, S.C.	(243)
3.	G. Washington, Va.	(216)
4.	P. Butler, S.C.	(143)
5.	C. Pinckney, S.C.	(111)

More than 100 slaves

6.	(71) R. Spaight, N.C.
7.	(70) C. C. Pinckney, S.C.
8.	(53) D. Carroll, Md.

50–100 slaves

9.	(47) A. Martin, N.C.
10.	(36) W. Davie, N.C.
11.	(30) W. Blount, N.C.
12.	(20) D. Jenifer, Md.
13.	(16) E. Randolph, Va.
14.	(15) J. Blair, Va.

10–50 slaves

15.	J. Madison, Va.
16.	L. Martin, Md.
17.	G. Read, Del.

Fewer than 10 slaves

No. of slaves   100   200   300

In all, 17 delegates to the Philadelphia Convention (31% of all the delegates) owned approximately 1400 slaves. Mason, Rutledge, and Washington were three of the largest slaveholders in the country at the time of the Convention.

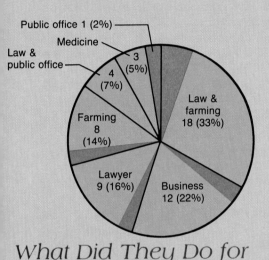

- Public office 1 (2%)
- Medicine 3 (5%)
- Law & public office 4 (7%)
- Farming 8 (14%)
- Lawyer 9 (16%)
- Business 12 (22%)
- Law & farming 18 (33%)

What Did They Do for a Living?

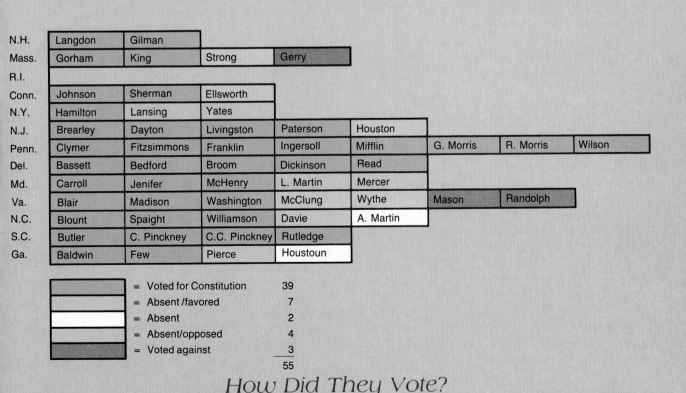

N.H.	Langdon	Gilman					
Mass.	Gorham	King	Strong	Gerry			
R.I.							
Conn.	Johnson	Sherman	Ellsworth				
N.Y.	Hamilton	Lansing	Yates				
N.J.	Brearley	Dayton	Livingston	Paterson	Houston		
Penn.	Clymer	Fitzsimmons	Franklin	Ingersoll	Mifflin	G. Morris	R. Morris	Wilson
Del.	Bassett	Bedford	Broom	Dickinson	Read		
Md.	Carroll	Jenifer	McHenry	L. Martin	Mercer		
Va.	Blair	Madison	Washington	McClung	Wythe	Mason	Randolph
N.C.	Blount	Spaight	Williamson	Davie	A. Martin		
S.C.	Butler	C. Pinckney	C.C. Pinckney	Rutledge			
Ga.	Baldwin	Few	Pierce	Houstoun			

= Voted for Constitution	39
= Absent /favored	7
= Absent	2
= Absent/opposed	4
= Voted against	3
	55

How Did They Vote?

ular vote. In the upper house, the Senate, each state was to have two members, elected by its legislature.

Then a complicated struggle took place between northern and southern delegates, occasioned by the institution of slavery and the differing economic interests of the regions. About one American in seven in the 1780s was a slave. Northerners contended that slaves should be counted in deciding each state's share of direct federal taxes. Southerners, of course, wanted to exclude slaves from the count. Yet southerners wished to include slaves in determining each district's representation in the House of Representatives, though they had no intention of permitting the slaves to vote. In the Three-fifths Compromise it was agreed that "three-fifths of all other Persons" should be counted for both purposes. (As it turned out, the compromise was a victory for the southerners, for no direct taxes were ever levied by Congress before the Civil War.) Settlement of the knotty issue of the African slave trade was postponed by a clause making it illegal for Congress to outlaw the trade before 1808.

Questions involving the regulation of less controversial commerce also caused sectional disagreement. Southerners disliked export taxes because their staple products were largely sold abroad. In return for a clause prohibiting such taxes, they dropped their demand that all laws regulating foreign commerce be approved by two-thirds of both houses of Congress. Many other differences of opinion were resolved by the give-and-take of practical compromise. As the historian David M. Potter once said, the Constitution was "an exchange of promises" whereby different interests gained large advantages by making large concessions.

The final document, signed on September 17, established a legislature of two houses: an executive, consisting of a president with wide powers and a vice-president whose only function was to preside over the Senate, and a national judiciary consisting of a supreme court and such "inferior courts" as Congress might decide to create. The lower, popularly elected branch of Congress was supposed to represent especially the mass of ordinary citizens. It was given the sole right to introduce bills for raising revenue. The 26-member Senate was looked on by many as a sort of advisory council similar to the upper houses of the colonial legislatures. Its consent was required before any treaty could go into effect and for major presidential appointments.

The Founding Fathers also intended the Senate to represent in Congress the interests not only of the separate states but of what Hamilton called "the rich and the well-born" as contrasted with "the great mass of the people."

The creation of a powerful president was the most drastic departure from past experience, and it is doubtful that the Founding Fathers would have gone so far had everyone not counted on Washington, a man universally esteemed for character, wisdom, and impartiality, to be the first to occupy the office. Besides giving him general responsibility for executing the laws, the Constitution made the president commander in chief of the armed forces of the nation and general supervisor of its foreign relations. He was to appoint federal judges and other officials, and he might veto any law of Congress, although his veto could be overridden by a two-thirds majority of both houses. Though not specifically ordered to submit a program of legislation to Congress, he was to deliver periodic reports on the "State of the Union" and recommend "such Measures as he shall judge necessary and expedient." Most modern presidents have interpreted this requirement as authorizing them to submit detailed legislative proposals and to use the full power and prestige of the office to get Congress to enact them.

Looking beyond Washington, whose choice was sure to come about under any system, the Constitution established a cumbersome method of electing presidents. Each state was to choose "electors" equal in number to its representation in Congress. The electors, meeting separately in their own states, were to vote for two persons for president. Supposedly the procedure would prevent anyone less universally admired than Washington from getting a majority in the "electoral college," in which case the House of Representatives would choose the president from among the leading candidates, each state having but one vote. However, the swift rise of national political parties prevented the expected fragmentation of the electors' votes, and only two elections have ever gone to the House for settlement.

The national court system was set up to adjudicate disputes under the laws and treaties of the United States. No such system had existed under the Articles, a major weakness. Although the Constitution did not specifically authorize the courts to declare laws void when they conflicted with the Constitution, the courts soon exercised this right of "ju-

The room in Independence Hall where the Constitutional Convention was held has been scrupulously restored.

dicial review" in cases involving both state and federal laws.

That the Constitution reflected the commonly held beliefs of its framers is everywhere evident in the document. It greatly expanded the powers of the central government yet did not seriously threaten the independence of the states. Foes of centralization, at the time and ever since, have predicted the imminent disappearance of the states as sovereign bodies. But despite a steady trend toward centralization, probably inevitable as American society has grown ever more complex, the states remain powerful political organizations that are sovereign in many areas of government.

The Founders believed that since the new powers of government might easily be misused, each should be held within safe limits by some countervailing force. The Constitution is full of ingenious devices ("checks and balances") whereby one power controls and limits another without reducing it to impotence. "Let Congress legislate, let others execute, let others judge," John Jay suggested. This separation of legislative, executive, and judicial functions is the fundamental example of the principle. Other examples are the president's veto; Congress's power of impeachment, cleverly divided between House and Senate; the Senate's power over treaties and appointments; judicial review; and the balance between Congress's right to declare war and the president's control of the armed forces.

Ratifying the Constitution

Influenced by the widespread approval of the decision of Massachusetts to submit its state constitution of 1780 to the voters for ratification, the framers of the Constitution provided (Article 7) that their handiwork be ratified by special state conventions. This procedure gave the Constitution what Madison called "the highest source of authority"—the endorsement of the people, expressed through representatives chosen specifically to judge it. The framers may also have been motivated by a desire to bypass the state legislatures, where many members might resent the reductions being made in state authority. This was not of central importance because the legislatures could have blocked ratification by refusing to call conventions. Only Rhode Island did so, and since the Constitution was to take effect when nine states had approved it, Rhode Island's recalcitrance did no vital harm.

Such a complex and controversial document as the Constitution naturally excited argument throughout the country. Its advocates called themselves Federalists, thereby avoiding the more accurate but politically unattractive label of Centralizers. Their opponents thus became the Antifederalists.

It is difficult to generalize about the members of these groups. The Federalists tended to be substantial individuals, members of the professions, well-to-do, active in commercial affairs, and somewhat alarmed by the changes wrought by the Revolution. They were more interested, perhaps, in orderly and efficient government than in safeguarding the maximum freedom of individual choice.

The Antifederalists were more often small farmers, debtors, and persons to whom free choice was more important than power and who resented people who sought and held power. "Lawyers and men of learning and money men . . . expect to be the managers of the Const[itution], and get all the power and all the money into their own hands," a Massachusetts Antifederalist complained. "Then they will swallow up all us little folks . . . just as the whale swallowed up *Jonah*." But many rich and worldly citizens opposed the Constitution, and many poor and obscure persons were for it. It seems likely that most did not support or oppose the new system for narrowly selfish reasons. The historian David Ramsay, who lived at the time when these groups were forming, was probably correct when he wrote that "the great body of independent men who saw the necessity of an energetic government" swung the balance in favor of the Constitution.

Whether the Antifederalists were more democratic than the Federalists is an interesting question. The loudest in support of local autonomy do not necessarily believe in equal rights for all the locals. Many Antifederalist leaders, including Richard Henry Lee, the man who had introduced the resolution that resulted in the Declaration of Independence, had reservations about democracy. Yet even Hamilton, no admirer of democracy, believed that ordinary citizens should have some say about their government. In general, practice still stood well ahead of theory when it came to popular participation in politics.

Various Antifederalists criticized many of the specific grants of authority in the new Constitution, some concocting farfetched arguments to show what disasters might ensue should it be put into effect. The routine clause (Article 1, Section 4) giving Congress the power to regulate "the times, places, and manner of holding elections" threatened to "destroy representation entirely," a North Carolina Antifederalist claimed. The chief force behind the opposition was a vague fear that the new system would destroy the independence of the states.

It is important to keep in mind that the country was large and sparsely settled, that communication was primitive, and that the central government did not influence the lives of most people to any great degree. Many persons, including some who had been in the forefront of the struggle for independence, believed that a centralized republican system would not work in a country so large and with so many varied interests as the United States. Patrick Henry considered the Constitution "horribly frightful." It "squints toward monarchy," he added. That Congress could pass all laws "necessary and proper" to carry out the functions assigned it and legislate for the "general welfare" of the country seemed alarmingly all-inclusive. The first sentence of the Constitution, beginning "We the people of the United States" rather than "We the states," convinced many that the document represented centralization run wild. Another old revolutionary who expressed doubts was Samuel Adams, who remarked: "As I enter the Building I stumble at the Threshold."

Many members of the Convention were well-to-do and stood to profit from the establishment of a sound and conservative government that would honor its obligations, foster economic development, and preserve a stable society. Since the Constitution was designed to do all these things, it has been suggested that the Founders were not true patriots but selfish men out to protect their own interests. Charles A. Beard advanced this thesis in 1913 in *An Economic Interpretation of the Constitution*, arguing that most members of the Convention owned large amounts of depreciated government securities that were bound to rise in price if the Constitution was approved. The thesis does not stand up under close examination. The Founders wanted to advance their own interests as every normal human being does. Most of them, however, had no special involvement in securities, being far more concerned with land. The closest thing to a general spirit at Philadelphia was a public spirit.

Very little of the opposition to the Constitution grew out of economic issues. Most people wanted the national debt paid off; nearly everyone opposed an unstable currency; most favored uniform trade policies; most were ready to give the new government a chance if they could be convinced that it would not destroy the states. When backers agreed to add amendments guaranteeing the civil liberties of the people against challenge by the national government and reserving all unmentioned power to the states, much of the opposition disappeared. Sam Adams ended up voting for the Constitution in the Massachusetts convention after the additions had been promised.

No one knows exactly how public opinion divided on the question of ratification. The Federalists were usually able to create an impression of strength far beyond their numbers and to overwhelm doubters with the mass of their arguments. They excelled in political organization and in persuasiveness. James Madison, for example, demolished the thesis that a centralized republican government could not function efficiently in a large country. In rule by the majority lay protection against the "cabals" of special interest groups. "Extend the sphere," Madison argued, "and you take in a greater variety of parties and interests; you make it less probable that a majority of the whole will have a common motive to invade the rights of other citizens." Moreover, the management of national affairs would surely attract leaders of greater ability and sounder character to public service than the handling of petty local concerns ever could in a decentralized system.

The Constitution met with remarkably little opposition in most of the state ratifying conventions, considering the importance of the changes it instituted. Delaware acted first, ratifying unanimously on December 7, 1787. Pennsylvania followed a few days later, voting for the document by a two-to-one majority. New Jersey approved unanimously on December 18; so did Georgia on January 2, 1788. A week later Connecticut fell in line, 128 to 40.

The Massachusetts convention provided the first close contest. Early in February, after extensive debate, the delegates ratified by a vote of 187 to 168. In April, Maryland accepted the Constitution by nearly six to one, and in May, South Carolina approved, 149 to 73. New Hampshire came along on June 21, voting 57 to 47 for the Constitution. This was the ninth state, making the Constitution legally operative.

Before the news from New Hampshire had spread throughout the country, the Virginia convention debated the issue. Virginia, the largest state and the home of so many prestigious figures, was absolutely essential if the Constitution was to succeed. With unquestioned Patriots like Richard Henry Lee and Patrick Henry opposed, the result was not easy to predict. But when the vote came on June 25, Virginia ratified, 89 to 79. Aside from Rhode Island, this left only New York and North Carolina outside the Union.

New York politics presented a complex and baffling picture. Resistance to independence had been

New York's approval of the Constitution on July 26, 1788, inspired this cartoon in the Massachusetts Centinel. *Hopes were high that North Carolina would "rise" to ratify, but prospects in Rhode Island were not as bright—and, as expected, Rhode Island did not ratify the Constitution.*

strong there in 1776 and remained a problem all through the war. Although New York was the third largest state, with a population rapidly approaching 340,000, it sided with the small states at Philadelphia, and two of its three delegates (Hamilton was the exception) walked out of the convention and took the lead in opposing ratification. A handful of great landowning and mercantile families dominated politics, but they were divided into shifting factions. In general, New York City favored ratification, and the rural areas were against it.

The Antifederalists, well organized and competently led in New York by Governor George Clinton, won 46 of the 65 seats at the ratifying convention. The New York Federalists had one great asset in the fact that so many states had already ratified and another in the person of Alexander Hamilton. Although contemptuous of the *weakness* of the Constitution, Hamilton supported it with all his energies as being incomparably stronger than the old government. Working with Madison and John Jay, he produced the *Federalist Papers,* a brilliant series of essays explaining and defending the new system. These were published in the local press and later in book form. Although generations of judges and lawyers have treated them almost as parts of the Constitution, their impact on contemporary public opinion was probably slight. Open-minded members of the convention were undoubtedly influenced, but few delegates were open-minded.

Hamilton became virtually a one-man army in defense of the Constitution, plying hesitating delegates with dinners and drinks, facing obstinate ones with the threat that New York City would secede from the state if the Constitution were rejected. Once New Hampshire and Virginia had ratified, opposition in New York became a good deal less intransigent. In the end, by promising to support a call for a second national convention to consider amendments, the Federalists carried the day, 30 to 27. With New York in the fold, the new government was free to get under way. North Carolina finally ratified in November 1789, Rhode Island the following May.

Washington as President

Elections took place in the states during January and February 1789, and by early April enough con-

gressmen had gathered in New York, the temporary national capital, to commence operation. The ballots of the presidential electors were officially counted in the Senate on April 6, Washington being the unanimous choice. John Adams, with 34 electoral votes, won the vice-presidency. On April 30 Washington took the oath of office at Federal Hall.

Washington made a firm, dignified, conscientious, but cautious president. His acute sense of responsibility led him to face the task "with feelings not unlike those of a culprit who is going to the place of his execution." Each presidential action must of necessity establish a precedent. "The eyes of Argus are upon me," he complained, "and no slip will pass unnoticed." Hoping to make the presidency appear respectable in the eyes of the world, he saw to it that his carriage was drawn by six cream-colored horses, and when he rode (he was a magnificent horseman), it was upon a great white charger, with the saddle of leopardskin and the cloth edged in gold. Twenty-one servants (seven of them slaves) attended his needs at the presidential mansion on Broadway.

Washington meticulously avoided treading on the toes of Congress, for he took seriously the principle of the separation of powers. Never would he speak for or against a candidate for Congress, nor did he think that the president should push or even propose legislation. When he knew a controversial question was to be discussed in Congress, he avoided the subject in his annual message. The veto, he believed, should be employed only when the president considered a bill unconstitutional.

Although the Constitution said nothing about a presidential cabinet, Washington established the system of calling his department heads together for general advice, a practice that was followed by his successors. In selecting these department heads and other important administrators, he favored no particular faction. He insisted only that appointees be competent and "of known attachment to the Government we have chosen." He picked Hamilton as secretary of the treasury, Jefferson as secretary of state, General Henry Knox of Massachusetts as secretary of war, and Edmund Randolph as attorney general. He called on them for advice according to the logic of his particular needs and frequently without regard for their own specialties. Thus he sometimes consulted Jefferson about financial matters and Hamilton about foreign affairs. This system

WASHINGTON'S TRIUMPHAL ENTRY INTO NEW YORK 1783

A spirited tapestry of the period depicts Washington's entry into New York City after the Revolution. When elections were held for the new government, there was little doubt in anyone's mind that he should be its first president, but Washington had little desire for the post. "My movements to the chair of government," he wrote, "will be accompanied by feelings not unlike those of a culprit who is going to the place of his execution."

caused resentment and confusion, especially when rival factions began to coalesce around Hamilton and Jefferson.

Despite his respect for the opinions of others, Washington was a strong chief executive. As Hamilton put it, he "consulted much, pondered much, resolved slowly, resolved surely." His stress on the dignity of his office suited the needs of a new country whose people tended to be perhaps too informal. It was indeed important that the first president be particularly concerned about establishing precedents. His scrupulous care lest he overstep the bounds of presidential power helped erase the prejudices of those who feared that republican government must inevitably succumb to dictatorship and tyranny. When each step is an experiment, when foreign dangers loom at the end of every errant path, it is surely wise to go slowly. And no one should forget that Washington's devotion to duty did not always come easily. Occasionally he exploded. Thomas Jefferson has left us a graphic account of

the president at a Cabinet meeting, in a rage because of some unfair criticism, swearing that "by god he had rather be on his farm than to be made emperor of the world."

Congress Under Way

By September 1789 Congress had created the State, Treasury, and War departments and passed the Judiciary Act establishing 13 federal district courts and three circuit courts of appeal. The number of Supreme Court justices was set at six, and Washington named John Jay chief justice.

True to Federalist promises—for a large majority in both houses was friendly to the Constitution—Congress prepared a list of a dozen amendments (ten were ratified) guaranteeing what Congressman James Madison, who drafted the amendments, called the "great rights of mankind." These amendments, known as the Bill of Rights, provided that

Congress should make no law infringing freedom of speech, the press, or religion. The right of trial by jury was reaffirmed, the right to bear arms guaranteed. No one was to be subject to "unreasonable" searches or seizures or compelled to testify against oneself in a criminal case. No one was to "be deprived of life, liberty, or property, without due process of law."

The Bill of Rights was unique; the English Bill of Rights of 1689 was much narrower and, as an act of Parliament, subject to parliamentary repeal at any time. The Tenth Amendment—strictly speaking not a part of the Bill of Rights—was designed to mollify those who feared that the states would be destroyed by the new government. It provided that powers not delegated to the United States or denied specifically to the states by the Constitution were to reside either in the states or in the people.

As experts pointed out, the amendments were not logically necessary because the federal government had no authority to act in such matters to begin with. But many people had wanted to be reassured. Experience has proved repeatedly that whatever the logic of the situation, the protection afforded individuals by the Bill of Rights has been anything but unnecessary.

The Bill of Rights did much to convince doubters that the new government would not become too powerful. More complex was the task of proving that it was powerful enough to deal with national problems that the Confederation had not been able to solve: the threat to the west posed by the British, Spaniards, and Indians; the disruption of the pattern of American foreign commerce resulting from independence; and the collapse of the financial structure of the country.

Hamilton and Financial Reform

One of the first acts of Congress in 1789 was to employ its new power to tax. The simplest means of raising money seemed to be that first attempted by the British after 1763, a tariff on foreign imports. Congress levied a 5 percent duty on all foreign products entering the United States, applying higher rates to certain products, such as hemp, glass, and nails, as a measure of protection for American pro-

ducers. The Tariff Act of 1789 also placed heavy tonnage duties on all foreign shipping, a mercantilistic measure designed to stimulate the American merchant marine.

Raising money for current expenses was a small and relatively simple aspect of the financial problem Washington's administration faced. The nation's debt was large, its credit shaky, its economic future uncertain. In October 1789 Congress set on the slender shoulders of Secretary of the Treasury Hamilton the task of straightening out the fiscal mess and stimulating the country's economic development.

Hamilton, at 34, had already proved himself a remarkable man. Born in the British West Indies, the illegitimate son of a shiftless Scot who was little better than a beachcomber, and raised by his mother's family, he came to New York in 1773 to attend King's College. When the Revolution broke out, he joined the army. At 22 he was a staff colonel, aide-de-camp to Washington. Later, at Yorktown, he led a line regiment, displaying a bravery approaching foolhardiness. He married the daughter of Philip Schuyler, a wealthy and influential New Yorker, and after the Revolution he practiced law in that state.

Hamilton was a bundle of contradictions. Witty, charming, possessed of a mind like a sharp knife, he was sometimes the soul of practicality, sometimes an incurable romantic. No more hardheaded realist ever lived, yet he was quick to resent any slight to his honor, even—tragically—ready to fight a duel despite his abhorrence of the custom of dueling. A self-made man, he admired aristocracy and disparaged the abilities of the common run of humankind, who, he said, "seldom judge or determine right." Although granting that Americans must be allowed to govern themselves, he was as apprehensive of the "turbulence" of the masses as a small boy passing a graveyard in the dark. "No popular government was ever without its Catilines and its Caesars," he warned—a typical example of that generation's concern about the fate of the Roman republic.

The country, Hamilton insisted, needed strong national government. "I acknowledge," he wrote in one of the *Federalist Papers*, "my aversion to every project that is calculated to disarm the government of a single weapon, which in any possible contingency might be usefully employed for the general defense and security." That government should be "a great Federal Republic," not "a number of petty

"To confess my weakness," Hamilton wrote when he was only 14, "my ambition is prevalent." This pastel drawing by James Sharples was made about 1796.

states, with the appearance only of union, jarring, jealous, perverse, without any determined direction." He wished to reduce the states to mere administrative units, like English counties.

As secretary of the treasury, Hamilton proved to be a farsighted economic planner. The United States, a "Hercules in the cradle," needed capital to develop its untapped material and human resources. To persuade investors to commit their funds in America, the country would have to convince them that it would meet every obligation in full. His *Report on the Public Credit* outlined the means for accomplishing this objective. The United States owed more than $11 million to foreigners and over $40 million to its own citizens. Hamilton suggested that this debt be funded at par, which meant calling in all outstanding securities and issuing new bonds of the same face value in their stead, and establishing an untouchable sinking fund to assure payment of interest and principal. Further, the remaining state debts should be assumed by the United States on the same terms.

While most members of Congress agreed, albeit somewhat grudgingly, that the debt should be funded at par, many believed that at least part of the new issue should go to the original holders of the old securities: the soldiers, farmers, and merchants who had been forced to accept them in lieu of cash for goods and services rendered the Confederation during the Revolution. Many of these people had sold their securities at a fraction of their face value to speculators; under Hamilton's proposal, the speculators would make a killing. To the argument for divided payment, Hamilton answered coldly: "[The speculator] paid what the commodity was worth in the market, and took the risks. . . . He . . . ought to reap the benefit of his hazard."

Hamilton was essentially correct, and in the end Congress had to go along. After all, the speculators had not caused the securities to fall in value; indeed, as a group they had favored sound money and a strong government. The best way to restore the nation's credit was to convince investors that the government would honor all obligations in full. What infuriated his contemporaries and still attracts the scorn of many historians was Hamilton's motive. He deliberately intended his plan to give a special advantage to the rich. The government would be strong, he thought, only if well-to-do Americans enthusiastically supported it. What better way to win them over than to make it worth their while financially to do so?

In part, opposition to the funding plan was sectional, for citizens of the northern states held more than four-fifths of the national debt. The scheme for assuming the state debts aggravated the controversy, since most of the southern states had already paid off much of their Revolutionary War obligations. For months Congress was deadlocked. Finally, in July 1790, Hamilton worked out a compromise with congressman James Madison and Secretary of State Jefferson. The two Virginians swung a few southern votes, and Hamilton induced some of his followers to support the southern plan for locating the permanent capital of the Union on the Potomac River.

Jefferson later claimed that Hamilton had hoodwinked him. Having only recently returned from Europe, he said, "I was really a stranger to the whole subject." Hamilton had persuaded him to "rally around" by the false tale that "our Union" was threatened with dissolution. This was nonsense; Jefferson agreed to the compromise because he expected that Virginia and the rest of the south would profit from having the capital so near at hand.

The assumption bill passed, and the entire funding plan was a great success. Soon the United States had the highest possible credit rating in the world's financial centers. Foreign capital poured into the country.

Hamilton next proposed that Congress charter a national bank. Such an institution would provide safe storage for government funds and serve as an agent for the government in the collection, movement, and expenditure of tax money. Most important, it would issue bank notes, thereby providing a vitally needed medium of exchange for the specie-starved economy. This Bank of the United States was to be partly owned by the government, but 80 percent of the $10 million stock issue was to be sold to private individuals.

The country had much to gain from such a bank, but again—Hamilton's cleverness was never more in evidence—the well-to-do commercial classes would gain still more. Government balances in the bank belonging to all the people would earn dividends for a handful of rich investors. Manufacturers and other capitalists would profit from the bank's credit facilities. Public funds would be invested in the bank, but control would remain in private hands, since the government would appoint only 5 of the 25 directors. Nevertheless, the bill creating the bank passed both houses of Congress with relative ease in February 1791.

President Washington, however, hesitated to sign it, for the bill's constitutionality had been questioned during the debate in Congress. Nowhere did the Constitution specifically authorize Congress to charter corporations or engage in the banking business. As was his wont when in doubt, Washington called on Jefferson and Hamilton for advice.

Hamilton defended the legality of the bank by enunciating the doctrine of "implied powers." If a logical connection existed between the purpose of the bill and powers clearly stated in the Constitution, he wrote, the bill was constitutional.

> If the *end* be clearly comprehended within any of the specified powers, and if the measure have an obvious relation to that *end* . . . it may safely be deemed to come within the compass of the national authority. . . . A bank has a natural relation to the power of collecting taxes, to that of regulating trade, to that of providing for the common defence.

Jefferson disagreed. Congress could only do what the Constitution specifically authorized, he said. The "elastic clause" granting it the right to pass "all Laws which shall be necessary and proper" to carry out the specified powers must be interpreted literally or Congress would "take possession of a boundless field of power, no longer susceptible to any definition." Because a bank was obviously not necessary, it was not authorized.

Although not entirely convinced, Washington accepted Hamilton's reasoning and signed the bill. He could just as easily have followed Jefferson, for the Constitution is not clear. If one stresses *proper* in the "necessary and proper" clause, one ends up a Hamiltonian; if one stresses *necessary*, then Jefferson's view is correct. Historically (and this is the important point), politicians have nearly always adopted the "loose" Hamiltonian "implied powers" interpretation when they favored a measure and the "strict" Jeffersonian one when they do not. Jefferson disliked the bank; therefore, he claimed that it was unconstitutional. Had he approved, he doubtless would have taken a different tack.

In 1819 the Supreme Court officially sanctioned Hamilton's construction of the "necessary and proper" clause (see pages 250–252), and in general that interpretation has prevailed. Because the majority tends naturally toward an argument that increases its freedom of action, the pressure for this view has been continual and formidable. The Bank of the United States succeeded from the start. When its stock went on sale, investors snapped up every share in a matter of hours. People eagerly accepted its bank notes at face value. Business ventures of all kinds found it easier to raise new capital. Soon state-chartered banks entered the field. There were only three state banks in 1791; by 1801 the number was 32.

Hamilton had not finished. In December 1791 he submitted his *Report on Manufactures,* a bold call for economic planning. The pre-Revolutionary nonimportation agreements and wartime shortages had stimulated interest in manufacturing. Already a number of joint-stock companies had been founded to manufacture textiles, and an elaborate argument for economic diversification had been worked out by American economists such as Tench Coxe and Mathew Carey. Hamilton was familiar with these developments. In his *Report* he called for government tariffs, subsidies, and awards to encourage American manufacturing. He hoped to change an essentially agricultural nation into one with a complex, self-sufficient economy. Once again, business and commercial interests in particular would benefit. They would be protected against foreign competition and otherwise subsidized, whereas the general taxpayer, particularly the farmer, would pay the bill in the form of higher taxes and higher prices on manufactured goods. Hamilton argued that in the long run every interest would profit, and he was undoubtedly sincere, being too much the nationalist to favor one section at the expense of another. A majority in Congress, however, balked at so broad a scheme. Hamilton's *Report* was pigeonholed, though many of the specific tariffs he recommended were enacted into law in 1792.

Nevertheless, the secretary of the treasury had managed to transform the financial structure of the country and to prepare the ground for an economic revolution. The constitutional reforms of 1787 had made this possible, and Hamilton turned possibility into reality.

The Ohio Country: A Dark and Bloody Ground

The western issues and those related to international trade proved more difficult than the bank matter because other nations were involved. The British showed no disposition to evacuate their posts on American soil simply because the American people had decided to strengthen their central government, nor did the western Indians suddenly agree to abandon their hunting grounds to the white invaders.

Trouble came swiftly when white settlers moved onto the land north of the Ohio River in large numbers. The Indians, determined to hold this country at all costs, struck hard at the invaders. In 1790 the Miami chief Little Turtle, a gifted strategist, inflicted a double defeat on troops commanded by General Josiah Harmar. The next year Little Turtle and his men defeated the forces of General Arthur St. Clair still more convincingly. Both Harmar and St. Clair resigned from the army, their careers ruined.

By early 1792 the Indians had driven the whites

into "beachheads" at Marietta and Cincinnati on the Ohio. Resentment of the federal government in the western counties of every state from New York to the Carolinas mounted, the people feeling that it was ignoring their interests. They were convinced that the British were inciting the Indians to attack them, yet the supposedly powerful national government seemed unable to force Great Britain to surrender its forts in the west.

Still worse, the westerners believed, was the way the government was taxing them. In 1791, as part of his plan to take over the debts of the states, Hamilton had persuaded Congress to adopt an excise tax of 8 cents a gallon on American-made whiskey. Excise taxes were particularly disliked by most Americans. A duty on imported products was collected from merchants and passed on to consumers as part of the price, and it was by its nature imposed only on foreign-made products. People who did not want to pay it usually could find a domestic alternative. But the collection of excise taxes on American goods required hordes of tax collectors, armed with the power to snoop into everyone's affairs. Westerners, who were heavy drinkers and who turned much of their grain into spirits in order to cope with the high cost of transportation, were especially angered by the tax on whiskey.

Knowing that the tax would be unpopular, Hamilton promised that the distillers would "be secured from every species of injury by the misconduct of the officers to be employed" in collecting it. But he was determined to enforce the law. To western complaints, he coolly suggested that farmers drank too much to begin with. If they found the tax oppressive, they should cut down on their consumption. Of course this did nothing to reduce western opposition to the tax. Resistance was especially intense in western Pennsylvania. When treasury agents tried to collect it there, they were forcibly prevented from doing so.

The New Revolution: France

Momentous events in Europe were also affecting the situation. In 1793 war broke out between France, which was in the midst of its great revolution, and Great Britain and most of the rest of Europe.

With France fighting Great Britain and Spain, there arose the question of America's obligations under the Alliance of 1778. That treaty required the United States to defend the French West Indies "forever against all other powers." What if the British attacked Martinique; must America then go to war? Morally the United States was so obligated, but no responsible American statesman urged such a policy. With the British in Canada and Spanish forces to the west and south, the nation would be in serious danger if it entered the war. Instead, in April 1793, Washington issued a proclamation of neutrality committing the United States to be "friendly and impartial" toward both sides in the war.

Meanwhile, the French had sent a special representative, Edmond Charles Genet, to the United States to seek support. The French Revolution had excited much enthusiasm in the United States, for it seemed to indicate that American democratic ideas were already engulfing the world. The increasing radicalism in France tended to dampen some of the enthusiasm, yet when "Citizen" Genet landed at Charleston, South Carolina, the majority of Americans probably wished the revolutionaries

well. As Genet, a charming, ebullient young man, made his way northward to present his credentials, cheering crowds welcomed him in every town. Quickly concluding that the proclamation of neutrality was "a harmless little pleasantry designed to throw dust in the eyes of the British," he began, in plain violation of American law, to license American vessels to operate as privateers against British shipping and to grant French military commissions to a number of Americans in order to mount expeditions against Spanish and British possessions in North America.

Washington received Genet coolly and soon thereafter demanded that he stop his illegal activities. Genet, whose capacity for self-deception was monumental, appealed to public opinion over the president's head and continued to commission privateers. Washington then requested his recall. The incident ended on a ludicrous note. When Genet left France, he had been in the forefront of the Revolution. But events there had marched swiftly leftward, and the new leaders in Paris considered him a dangerous reactionary. His replacement arrived in America with an order for his arrest. To return might well mean the guillotine, so Genet

Frontier farmers were extremely resentful of the federal excise tax on the whiskey they made. According to this contemporary broadside, "The Distillers and Farmers pay all due deference and respect to Congress, will not refuse to contribute amply for support of Government. But resolve not to be harassed by that opprobrious character (in all free governments) Viz, an Exciseman."

asked the government that was expelling him for political asylum! Washington agreed, for he was not a vindictive man. A few months later the bold revolutionary married the daughter of the governor of New York and settled down to become a farmer on Long Island.

The Genet affair was incidental to a far graver problem. Although the European war increased the foreign demand for American products, it also led to attacks on American shipping by both France and Great Britain. Each power captured American vessels headed for the other's ports whenever it could. In 1793 and 1794 about 600 United States ships were seized.

The British attacks caused far more damage, both physically and psychologically, because the British fleet was much larger than France's, and France at least professed to be America's friend and to favor freedom of trade for neutrals. In addition, the British issued secret orders late in 1793 turning their navy loose on neutral ships headed for the French West Indies. Pouncing without warning, British warships captured about 250 American vessels and sent them off as prizes to British ports. The merchant marine, one American diplomat declared angrily, was being "kicked, cuffed, and plundered all over the Ocean."

The attacks roused a storm in America, reviving hatreds that had been smoldering since the Revolution. The continuing presence of British troops in the northwest (in 1794 the British began to build a new fort in the Ohio country) and the restrictions imposed on American trade with the British West Indies raised tempers still further. To try to avoid a war—for he wisely believed that the United States should not become embroiled in the Anglo-French conflict—Washington sent Chief Justice John Jay to London to seek a settlement with the British.

Federalists and Republicans: The Rise of Political Parties

The furor over the violations of neutral rights focused attention on a new development, the formation of political parties. Why national political parties emerged after the ratification of a Constitution that made no provision for such organizations is a question that has long intrigued historians.

Probably the main reason was the obvious one: By creating a strong central government, the Constitution produced national issues and a focus for national discussion and settlement of these issues. Furthermore, by failing to create machinery for nominating candidates for federal offices, the Constitution left a vacuum, which informal party organizations filled. That the universally admired Washington headed the government was a force limiting partisanship, but his principal advisers, Hamilton and Jefferson, were in sharp disagreement, and they soon became the leaders around which parties coalesced.

In the spring of 1791 Jefferson and James Madison began to sound out other politicians about forming an organization. Jefferson also appointed the poet Philip Freneau to a minor State Department post, and Freneau then began publishing a newspaper, the *National Gazette*, to disseminate the views of what became known as the Republican party. The *Gazette* was soon describing Jefferson as a "Colossus of Liberty" and flailing away editorially at Hamilton's policies. Hamilton hit back promptly, organizing his own followers in the Federalist party, the organ of which was John Fenno's *Gazette of the United States*.

The personal nature of early American political controversies goes far toward explaining why the party battles of the era were so bitter. So does the continuing anxiety that plagued partisans of both persuasions about the supposed frailty of a republican government. The United States was still very much an experiment; leaders who sincerely proclaimed their own devotion to its welfare suspected that their opponents wanted to undermine its institutions. Federalists feared that the Jeffersonians sought a dictatorship based on mob rule, Republicans that the Hamiltonians hid "under the mask of Federalism hearts devoted to monarchy."

At the start, Hamilton had the ear of the president, and his allies controlled a majority in Congress. Jefferson, who disliked controversy, avoided a direct confrontation as long as he could. He went along with Hamilton's funding plan and traded the assumption of state debts for a capital on the Potomac. However, when Hamilton proposed the Bank of the United States, he dug in his heels. It seemed designed to benefit the northeastern commercial classes at the expense of southern and western farmers. He sensed a dastardly plot to milk the

The Federalists often attacked Jefferson for his pro-French attitudes. A dog-eared cartoon, ca. 1790, shows Washington in the national chariot leading troops against an invasion of bloodthirsty French "Cannibals" at the left. The figures trying to halt the chariot are, from left, Albert Gallatin, Citizen Genet (holding the spoke of the wheel), and Jefferson.

producing masses for the benefit of a few capitalists.

The growing controversy over the French Revolution and the resulting war between France and Great Britain widened the split between the parties. After the radicals in France executed Louis XVI and instituted the Reign of Terror, American conservatives were horrified. The Jeffersonians, however, continued to defend the Revolution. Slave owners could be heard singing the praises of *liberté, égalité, fraternité,* and great southern landlords, whose French counterparts were losing their estates—some their heads—were extolling "the glorious successes of our Gallic brethren." In the same way the Federalists began to idealize the British, whom they considered the embodiment of the forces that were resisting French radicalism.

This created an explosive situation. Enthusiasm for a foreign country might tempt Americans, all unwittingly, to betray their own. Hamilton came to believe that Jefferson was so prejudiced in favor of France as to be unable to conduct foreign affairs rationally, and Jefferson could say contemptuously: "Hamilton is panick struck, if we refuse our breech to every kick which Great Britain may choose to give it."

In fact, Jefferson never lost his sense of perspective. When the Anglo-French war erupted, he recommended neutrality. In the Genet affair, although originally sympathetic to the young envoy,

Jefferson ended by characterizing him as "hotheaded, all imagination, no judgment, passionate, disrespectful and even indecent." He cordially approved Washington's decision to send Genet packing. Hamilton perhaps went a little too far in his friendliness to Great Britain, but the real danger was that some of Hamilton's and Jefferson's excitable followers might become so committed as to forget the true interests of the United States.

1794: Crisis and Resolution

During the summer of 1794 several superficially unrelated events brought the partisan conflicts of the period to a peak. For the better part of two years the government had been unable to collect Hamilton's whiskey tax in the west. In Pennsylvania, mobs had burned the homes of revenue agents, and several men had been killed. Late in July, 7,000 "rebels" converged on Pittsburgh, threatening to burn the town to the ground. They were turned away by the sight of federal artillery and the liberal dispensation of whiskey by the frightened inhabitants, but as the historian Thomas P. Slaughter has pointed out, this was "the largest example of armed resistance to a law between the ratification of the Constitution and the Civil War."

Early in August, President Washington determined "to go to every length that the Constitution and laws would permit" to enforce the law. He mustered an enormous army of nearly 13,000 militiamen and marched westward. This had the desired effect; when the troops arrived, rebels were nowhere to be seen; the expected Whiskey Rebellion simply did not happen. Good sense had triumphed. Moderates in the region (not everyone, after all, was a distiller) agreed that even unpopular laws should be obeyed.

More important, perhaps, than President Washington's army in pacifying the Pennsylvania frontier was another event that occurred while that army was being mobilized. This was the Battle of Fallen Timbers in Ohio near present-day Toledo, where the troops of Major General Anthony Wayne decisively defeated the Indians. Wayne's victory opened the way for the settlement of the region. (After the effort to avoid the excise collapsed, some 2,000 of the whiskey rebels simply pulled up stakes and headed for Ohio.)

Jay's Treaty

More important still was the outcome of President Washington's decision to send John Jay to England to seek a treaty settling the conflicts that were vexing the relations of the two nations. On the one hand, the British genuinely wanted to reach an accommodation with the United States—as one minister quipped, the Americans "are so much in debt to this country that we scarcely dare to quarrel with them." They also feared that the two new republics, France and the United States, would draw together in a battle against Europe's monarchies. On the other hand, they were riding the crest of a wave of important victories in the war in Europe and were not disposed to make concessions to the Americans simply to avoid trouble.

The treaty that Jay brought home contained one major concession: The British agreed to evacuate the posts in the west. They also promised to compensate American shipowners for seizures in the West Indies and to open up their colonies in Asia to American ships. They conceded nothing, however, to American demands that the rights of neutrals on the high seas be respected; in effect, Jay submitted to the so-called Rule of 1756, a British regulation stating that neutrals could not trade in wartime with ports normally closed to them by mercantilistic restrictions in time of peace. A provision opening the British West Indies to American commerce was so hedged with qualifications limiting the size of American vessels and the type of goods allowed that the United States refused to accept it.

Jay also assented to an arrangement that prevented the United States from imposing discriminatory duties on British goods, an idea that a number of congressmen had proposed as a means of forcing Great Britain to treat American commerce more gently. He committed the United States government to paying pre-Revolutionary debts still owed to British merchants, a slap in the face to many states whose courts had been impeding their collection. Yet nothing was said about the British paying for the slaves they had abducted during the fighting in the south.

Although Jay might have driven a harder bargain, this was a valuable treaty for the United States. But it was also a humiliating one. Most of what the United States gained already legally belonged to it and the treaty sacrificed principles of tremendous importance to a nation dependent on foreign trade. When the terms became known, they raised a storm of popular protest. It seemed possible that President Washington would repudiate the treaty or, if he did not, that the Senate would refuse to ratify it.

1795: All's Well That Ends Well

Washington did not repudiate the Jay Treaty, and his decision was one of the wisest—and luckiest—of his career. The treaty marked a long step toward the regularization of Anglo-American relations, which in the long run was essential for both the economic and political security of the nation. And the evacuation of the British forts in the northwest was of enormous immediate benefit.

Still another benefit was totally unplanned. Unexpectedly, the Jay treaty enabled the United States to solve its problems in the southwest. Spain, desiring to withdraw from the European war against France and fearing a subsequent British attack on its American possessions, interpreted the Jay Treaty as a prelude to a wider Anglo-American entente. The king's chief minister, Manuel de Godoy, known as "the Prince of Peace," offered the American envoy, Thomas Pinckney, a treaty that granted the United States the free navigation of the Mississippi River and the right of deposit at New Orleans that western Americans so urgently needed. This Treaty of San Lorenzo, popularly known as Pinckney's Treaty, also settled the disputed boundary between Spanish Florida and the United States on terms favorable to the Americans.

The Senate ratified the Jay Treaty in June. Pinckney signed the Treaty of San Lorenzo in October. These agreements put an end, at least

temporarily, to European pressures in the trans-Appalachian region. Between the signings, in August 1795, as an aftermath of the Battle of Fallen Timbers, 12 tribes signed the Treaty of Greenville. The Indians surrendered huge sections of their lands, thus ending a struggle that had consumed a major portion of the government's revenues for years.

After the events of 1794 and 1795, settlers poured into the west as water bursts through a broken dike. Kentucky had become a state in 1792; in 1796 Tennessee was admitted. Two years later, Mis-

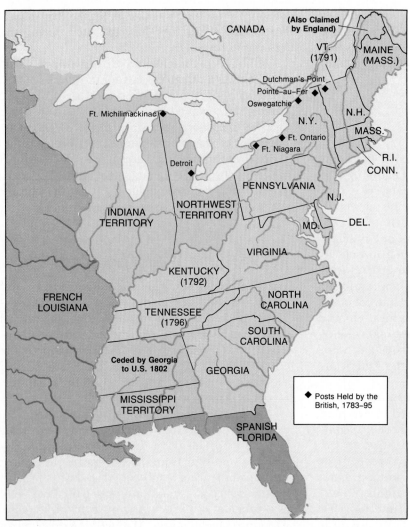

The United States on the eve of the Louisiana Purchase. In 1804 Georgia's cession became part of the Mississippi Territory. The seven British western forts were evacuated as a result of Jay's Treaty (1795).

THE UNITED STATES, 1787–1802

sissippi Territory was organized, and at the end of the century, Indiana Territory. The great westward flood reached full tide.

Washington's Farewell

However, settlement of western problems did not put an end to partisan strife. Even the sainted Washington was neither immune to attack nor entirely above the battle. On questions of finance and foreign policy he usually sided with Hamilton and thus increasingly incurred the anger of the Jeffersonians. But he was, after all, a Virginian. Only the most rabid partisan could think him a tool of northern commercial interests. He remained as he intended himself to be, a symbol of national unity. But he was determined to put away the cares of office at the end of his second term. In September 1796 he announced his retirement in a "farewell address" to the nation.

Washington found the acrimonious rivalry between Federalists and Republicans most disturbing. Hamilton advocated national unity, yet he seemed prepared to smash any individual or faction that disagreed with his vision of the country's future. Jefferson had risked his neck for independence, but he opposed the economic development needed to make America strong enough to defend that independence. Washington was less brilliant than either Hamilton or Jefferson but wiser. He appreciated how important it was that the new nation remain at peace—with the rest of the world and with itself. In his farewell he deplored the "baneful effects of the spirit of party" that led honest people to use unscrupulous means to win a mean advantage over fellow Americans. He tried to show how the north benefited from the prosperity of the south, the south from that of the north, and the east and west also, in reciprocal fashion.

Washington urged the people to avoid both "inveterate antipathies" and "passionate attachments" to any foreign nation. Nothing had alarmed him more than the sight of Americans dividing into "French" and "English" factions. Furthermore, France had repeatedly interfered in American domestic affairs. "Against the insidious wiles of foreign influence," Washington now warned, "the jealousy of a free people ought to be constantly awake." America should develop its foreign trade but steer clear of foreign political connections as far as possible. "Permanent alliances" should be avoided, although "temporary alliances for extraordinary purposes" might sometimes be useful.

The Election of 1796

Washington's farewell address was destined to have a long and important influence on American thinking, but its immediate impact was small. He had intended it to cool political passions. Instead, in the words of one Federalist congressman, people took it as "a signal, like dropping a hat, for the party racers to start." By the time the 1796 presidential campaign had ended, many Federalists and Republicans were refusing to speak to one another.

Jefferson was the only Republican candidate seriously considered in 1796. The logical Federalist was Hamilton, but, as was to happen so often in American history with powerful leaders, he was not considered "available" because his controversial policies had made him many enemies. Gathering in caucus, the Federalists in Congress nominated Vice-President John Adams for the top office and Thomas Pinckney of South Carolina, negotiator of the popular Spanish treaty, for vice-president. In the election the Federalists were victorious.

Hamilton, hoping to run the new administration from the wings, preferred Pinckney, a relatively weak character, to the tough-minded Adams. He arranged for some of the Federalist electors from South Carolina to vote only for Pinckney. Catching wind of this, a number of New England electors retaliated by cutting Pinckney. As a result, Adams won in the electoral college, 71 to 68, over Jefferson, who had the solid support of the Republican electors. Pinckney got only 59 electoral votes. Thus Jefferson became vice-president.

The unexpected result seemed to presage a decline in partisanship. Adams actually preferred the Virginian to Pinckney for the vice-presidency, while Jefferson said that if Adams would "relinquish his bias to an English constitution," he might make a fine chief executive. The two had in common a distaste for Hamilton—a powerful bond.

However, the closeness of the election indicated a trend toward the Republicans, who were making constant and effective use of the canard that the Federalists were "monocrats" (monarchists) determined to destroy American liberty. Without Washington to lead them, the Federalist politicians were already quarreling among themselves; honest, able, hardworking John Adams was too caustic and too scathingly frank to unite them. Everything seemed to indicate a Republican victory at the next election.

The XYZ Affair

At this point occurred one of the most remarkable reversals of public feeling in American history. French attacks on American shipping, begun out of irritation at the Jay Treaty and in order to influence the election, continued after Adams took office. Hoping to stop them, Adams appointed three commissioners (Charles Pinckney, United States minister to France and elder brother of Thomas*; John Marshall, a Virginia Federalist; and Elbridge Gerry of Massachusetts, who was not closely identified with either party) to try to negotiate a settlement.

Their mission was a fiasco. Talleyrand, the French foreign minister, sent three agents (later spoken of as X, Y, and Z) to demand a huge bribe as the price of making a deal. The Americans refused, more because they suspected Talleyrand's good faith than because of any distaste for bribery. "No, no, not a sixpence," Pinckney told the agents. The talks broke up, and in April 1798 President Adams released the commissioners' reports.

They caused a sensation. Americans' sense of national honor, perhaps overly tender because the country was so young and insecure, was outraged. Pinckney's laconic refusal to pay a bribe was translated into the grandiose phrase "Millions for defense, but not one cent for tribute!" and broadcast throughout the land. John Adams, never a man with mass appeal, suddenly found himself a national hero. Federalist hotheads burned for a fight. Congress unilaterally abrogated the French Alliance, created a Navy Department, and appropriated enough money to build 40-odd warships and triple the size of the army. Washington came out of retirement to lead the forces, with Hamilton, now a general, as second in command. On the seas American privateers began to attack French shipping.

A recruiting poster of 1798 appealed for volunteers to defend the nation "against the hostile designs of foreign enemies," the "enemies" being the French.

Adams did not much like the French, and he could be extremely stubborn. A declaration of war would have been immensely popular. But perhaps—it is not an entirely illogical surmise about John Adams, who later in life described himself with some relish as "obnoxious, suspected, and unpopular"—the president did not want to be popular. He was also a realist. Instead of calling for war, he contented himself with approving the buildup of the armed forces.

The Republicans, however, committed to friendship with France, did not appreciate Adams's moderation. Though angered by the XYZ Affair, they tried, one Federalist complained, "to clog the wheels of government" by opposing the military appropriations. Their newspapers referred to Adams derisively as "His Rotundity," a term that particularly annoyed the somewhat plump president. Benjamin Bache, editor of the *Philadelphia Aurora*, described him as "blind, bald, toothless, querulous," which was three-quarters true but irrelevant. John Daly Burk of the *New York Time Piece* called him a "mock Monarch" surrounded by a "court composed of tories and speculators," which of course was a flat lie.

---

* The Pinckney brothers were children of Eliza Pinckney, the woman responsible for the introduction of indigo cultivation in America.

Many Federalists expected the Republicans to side with France if war broke out. Hysterical and near panic, they easily persuaded themselves that the danger of subversion was acute. The French Revolution and the resulting war were churning European society to the depths, stirring the hopes of liberals and striking fear in the hearts of conservatives. Refugees of both persuasions were flocking to the United States. Suddenly the presence of these foreigners seemed threatening to "native" Americans.

The Alien and Sedition Acts

Conservative Federalists saw in this situation a chance to smash the opposition. In June and July 1798 they pushed through Congress a series of repressive measures known as the Alien and Sedition Acts. The least offensive of these laws, the Naturalization Act, increased the period a foreigner had to reside in the United States before being eligible for citizenship from 5 to 14 years. The Alien Enemies Act gave the president the power to arrest or expel aliens in time of "declared war," but since the quasi-war with France was never declared, this measure had no practical importance. The Alien Act authorized the president to expel all aliens whom he thought "dangerous to the peace and safety of the United States." (Adams never invoked this law, but a number of aliens left the country out of fear that he might.)

Finally, there was the Sedition Act. Its first section, making it a crime "to impede the operation of any law" or to attempt to instigate a riot or insurrection, was reasonable enough; but the act also made it illegal to publish, or even to utter, any "false, scandalous and malicious" criticism of high government officials. Although milder than British sedition laws, this proviso rested, as James Madison said, on "the exploded doctrine" that government officials "are the masters and not the servants of the people."

As the election of 1800 approached, the Federalists made a systematic attempt to silence the leading Republican newspapers. Twenty-five persons were prosecuted and ten convicted, all in patently unfair trials. In typical cases, the editor Thomas Cooper, an English-born radical, later president of the University of South Carolina, was sentenced to six months in jail and fined $400; the editor Charles Holt got three months and a $200 fine; and the editor James Callender got nine months and a $200 fine.

The Kentucky and Virginia Resolves

Although Thomas Jefferson did not object to state sedition laws, he believed that the Alien and Sedition Acts violated the First Amendment's guarantees of freedom of speech and the press and were an invasion of the rights of the states. He and Madison decided to draw up resolutions arguing that the laws were unconstitutional. Madison's draft was presented to the Virginia legislature and Jefferson's to the legislature of Kentucky. Jefferson argued that since the Constitution was a compact made by sovereign states, each state had "an equal right to judge for itself" when the compact had been violated. Thus a state could declare a law of Congress unconstitutional. Madison's Virginia Resolves took an only slightly less forthright position.

Neither Kentucky nor Virginia tried to implement these resolves or to prevent the enforcement of the Alien and Sedition Acts. Jefferson and Madison were protesting Federalist high-handedness and firing the opening salvo of Jefferson's campaign for the presidency, not advancing a new constitutional theory of extreme states' rights. "Keep away all show of force," Jefferson advised his supporters.

This was sound advice, for events were again playing into the hands of the Republicans. Talleyrand had never wanted war with the United States. When he discovered how vehemently the Americans had reacted to his little attempt to replenish his personal fortune, he let Adams know that new negotiators would be properly received.

President Adams quickly grasped the importance of the French change of heart. Other leading Federalists, however, had lost their heads. By shouting about the French danger, they had roused the country against radicalism, and they did not intend to surrender this advantage tamely. Hamilton in particular wanted war at almost any price—if not against France, then against Spain. He saw himself at the head of the new American army sweeping first across Louisiana and the Floridas, then on to the south. "We ought to squint at South America," he suggested. "Tempting objects will be without our grasp."

One of the most flattering likenesses of John Adams is this portrait by John Trumbull done in 1793. Public criticism of Adams ran high throughout his term of office.

But the Puritan John Adams was a specialist at resisting temptation. At this critical point his intelligence, his moderate political philosophy, and his stubborn integrity stood him in good stead. He would neither go to war merely to destroy the political opposition in America nor follow "the fools who were intriguing to plunge us into an alliance with England . . . and wild expeditions to South America." Instead he submitted to the Senate the name of a new minister plenipotentiary to France, and when the Federalists tried to block the appointment, he threatened to resign. That would have made Jefferson president! So the furious Federalists had to give in, though they forced Adams to send three men instead of one.

Napoleon had taken over France by the time the Americans arrived, and he drove a harder bargain than Talleyrand would have. But in the end he signed an agreement, the Convention of 1800, abrogating the Franco-American treaties of 1778. Nothing was said about the damage done to American shipping by the French, but the war scare was over.

Milestones

1781	States fail to approve Congress's "impost" (tariff)
1783	British order in council bans trade with the West Indies
1786	Rhode Island supreme court upholds the state legal tender act (*Trevett* v. *Weeden*)
	Shays's Rebellion in Massachusetts
	Annapolis Convention
1787	Philadelphia Constitutional Convention
1787–1788	All states but North Carolina and Rhode Island ratify the Constitution
1789	Washington inaugurated as president
	Storming of Paris Bastille begins French Revolution
1790	Alexander Hamilton, *Report on the Public Credit*
1791	Hamilton, *Report on Manufactures*
	First ten amendments (Bill of Rights) ratified
	Republican and Federalist political parties organized
	Philip Freneau's *National Gazette* and John Fenno's *Gazette of the United States* founded
1793	King Louis XVI of France executed
	Washington's Declaration of Neutrality
1794	Jay's Treaty ratified
	Battle of Fallen Timbers
1795	Whiskey Rebellion in Pennsylvania
1796	Washington's farewell address
	John Adams elected president
1798	XYZ Affair
	Congress passes the Alien and Sedition Acts
	Madison's Virginia Resolves
1798–1799	Jefferson's Kentucky Resolves

SUPPLEMENTARY READING

Titles marked with an asterisk have been published in paperback.

On the "critical period," the drafting of the Constitution, and the early history of the new nation, see R. B. Morris, **The Forging of the Union*** (1987), and J. T. Main, **Political Parties Before the Constitution** (1973). On economic development, see E. J. Ferguson, **The Power of the Purse*** (1968), R. A. East, **Business Enterprise in the American Revolutionary Era** (1938), and C. P. Nettels, **The Emergence of a National Economy*** (1962), which puts this subject in the broader perspective of the period 1775–1815. A lively treatment of Shays's Rebellion is M. L. Starkey, **A Little Rebellion** (1955); D. P. Szatmary, **Shays's Rebellion** (1980), is a more recent study.

The political thinking of the period is discussed lucidly in G. S. Wood, **The Creation of the American Republic*** (1969), and Richard Buel, Jr., **Securing the Revolution*** (1972). A good general account of the convention is Clinton Rossiter, **1787: The Grand Convention*** (1966). The best treatment of Alexander Hamilton's connection with the Constitution and of his political views generally is Clinton Rossiter, **Alexander Hamilton and the Constitution** (1964). Irving Brant, **James Madison: Father of the Constitution** (1950), provides the fullest account of Madison's role.

C. A. Beard, **An Economic Interpretation of the Constitution*** (1913), caused a veritable revolution in the thinking of historians about the motives of the Founders, but later works have caused a major reaction away from the Beardian interpretation; see especially R. E. Brown, **Charles Beard and the Constitution*** (1956), and a more detailed critique, Forrest McDonald, **We the People*** (1958). R. A. Rutland, **The Ordeal of the Constitution** (1966), and J. T. Main, **The Antifederalists*** (1961), are helpful in understanding opposition to the Constitution, while the **Federalist Papers*** of Hamilton, Madison, and Jay, available in many editions, are essential for the arguments of the supporters of the new government. On the Bill of Rights, consult Bernard Schwartz, **The Great Rights of Mankind** (1977).

On the organization of the federal government and the history of the Washington administration, see L. D. White, **The Federalists** (1948), an administrative history, and J. C. Miller, **The Federalist Era*** (1960), a more general history of the period. Washington's presidency is treated in detail in the later volumes of D. S. Freeman, **George Washington** (1948–1957). Joseph Charles, **Origins of the American Party System*** (1961), is thought-provoking, and the early chapters of W. N. Chambers, **Political Parties in a New Nation*** (1963), are also useful.

Good biographies of Hamilton include Broadus Mitchell, **Alexander Hamilton*** (1976), J. E. Cooke, **Alexander Hamilton** (1982), and J. C. Miller, **Alexander Hamilton: A Portrait in Paradox*** (1959). On foreign affairs during the Washington administration, see Alexander De Conde, **Entangling Alliance: Politics and Diplomacy Under George Washington** (1958); Harry Ammon, **The Genet Mission** (1973); two volumes by S. F. Bemis, **Jay's Treaty*** (1923) and **Pinckney's Treaty*** (1926); Alexander De Conde, **The Quasi-War*** (1966); and William Stinchcombe, **The XYZ Affair** (1980).

On the Adams administration, consult S. G. Kurtz, **The Presidency of John Adams** (1957). On the Alien and Sedition Acts, see J. M. Smith, **Freedom's Fetters*** (1956), and L. W. Levy, **Freedom of Speech and Press in Early American History*** (1963).

VI

Jeffersonian Democracy

Nor is it true that Jefferson is zealot enough to do anything in pursuance of his principles, which will contravene his popularity or his interest. He is as likely as any man I know to temporize; to calculate what will be likely to promote his own reputation and advantage. . . . He is too much in earnest with his democracy.

ALEXANDER HAMILTON, *1801*

O nce the furor over war and subversion subsided, public attention focused on the presidential contest between Adams and Jefferson. Because of his stand for peace, Adams personally escaped the brunt of popular indignation against the Federalist party. His solid qualities had a strong appeal to conservatives, and fear that the Republicans would introduce radical "French" social reforms did not disappear when the danger of war with France ended. Many nationalist-minded voters worried lest the strong government established by the Federalists be weakened by the Republicans in the name of states' rights. The economic progress stimulated by Hamilton's financial reforms also seemed threatened. But when the electors' votes were counted in February 1801, the Republicans were discovered to have won narrowly, 73 to 65.

But which Republican was to be president? The Constitution did not distinguish between presidential and vice-presidential candidates; it provided only that each elector vote for two candidates, the one with the most votes becoming president and the runner-up vice-president. The development of national political parties made this system impractical. The vice-presidential candidate of the Republicans was Aaron Burr of New York, a former

senator and a rival of Hamilton in law and politics. But Republican party solidarity had been perfect; Jefferson and Burr received 73 votes each. Because of the tie, the Constitution required that the House of Representatives (voting by states) choose between them.

In the House the Republicans could control only 8 of the 16 state delegations. On the first ballot Jefferson got these 8 votes, one short of election,

The upper percentage figures show the percent of the electoral vote received by the candidate, and the lower figures the actual electoral votes for that candidate. Before the Twelfth Amendment of 1804, the Electoral College voted for two presidential candidates; the runner-up became vice-president.

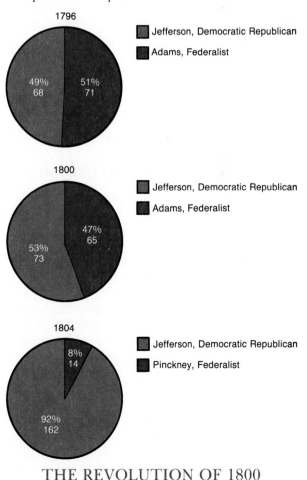

1796

- Jefferson, Democratic Republican
- Adams, Federalist

49% 68 | 51% 71

1800

- Jefferson, Democratic Republican
- Adams, Federalist

53% 73 | 47% 65

1804

- Jefferson, Democratic Republican
- Pinckney, Federalist

8% 14 | 92% 162

THE REVOLUTION OF 1800

while 6 states voted for Burr. Two state delegations, being evenly split, lost their votes. Through 35 ballots the deadlock persisted; the Federalist congressmen, fearful of Jefferson's supposed radicalism, voted solidly for Burr.

Pressures were exerted on both candidates to make deals to win additional support. Officially, at least, both refused. Burr put on a great show of remaining above the battle. (Had he been an honorable man, he would have withdrawn, since the voters had clearly intended him for the second spot.) Whether Jefferson made any promises is uncertain; there is some evidence that to break the deadlock he assured the Federalists that he would preserve Hamilton's financial system and continue the Washington-Adams foreign policy.

In the end, Alexander Hamilton decided who would be the next president. He detested Burr and threw his weight to Jefferson, exerting his considerable influence on Federalist congressmen. Finally, on February 17, 1801, Jefferson was elected. Burr became vice-president.

To make sure that this deadlock would never be repeated, the Twelfth Amendment was drafted, providing for separate balloting in the electoral college for president and vice-president. This change was ratified in 1804, shortly before the next election.

The Federalist Contribution

On March 4, 1801, in the raw new national capital on the Potomac River named in honor of the Father of His Country, Thomas Jefferson took the presidential oath and delivered his inaugural address. The new president believed that a revolution as important as that heralded by his immortal Declaration of Independence had occurred, and for once most of his political enemies agreed with him.

Certainly an era had ended. In the years between the Peace of Paris and Jay's Treaty, the Federalists had practically monopolized the political good sense of the nation. In the perspective of history they were "right" in strengthening the federal government, in establishing a sound fiscal system, in trying to diversify the economy, in seeking an accommodation with Great Britain, and in refusing to be carried away with enthusiasm for France despite the bright dreams inspired by the French Revolution.

The Federalists had displayed remarkable self-control and moderation at least until 1798. They were nationalists who did not try to destroy local patriotism, aristocrats willing to live with the spirit of democracy. The Constitution is their monument, with its wise compromises, its balance of forces, its restraints, and its practical concessions to local prejudices.

But the Federalists were unable to face up to defeat. When they saw the Republicans gathering strength by developing clever new techniques of party organization and propaganda, mouthing slogans about liberty, attacking "monocrats," glorifying both the past with its satisfying simplicity and the future with its promise of a glorious day when all men would be free, equal, and brothers, they panicked. Abandoning the sober wisdom of their great period, they fought to save themselves at any cost. The effort turned defeat into rout. The Re-

This anti-Jefferson cartoon shows the newly elected president kneeling before the altar of Gallic Despotism, whereon he is burning the writings of prominent Enlightenment philosophers. The American eagle appears to be wresting the Constitution from Jefferson's grasp.

THE PROVIDENTIAL DETECTION

publican victory, close in the electoral college, approached landslide proportions in the congressional elections, where popular feeling expressed itself directly.

Jefferson erred, however, in calling this triumph a revolution. The real upheaval had been attempted in 1798; it was Federalist-inspired, and it failed. In 1800 the voters expressed a preference for the old over the new; that is, for individual freedom and limited national power. And Jefferson, despite Federalist fears that he would destroy the Constitution and establish a radical social order, presided instead over a regime that confirmed the great achievements of the Federalist era.

What was most significant about the election of 1800 was that it was *not* a revolution. After a bitter contest, the Jeffersonians took power and proceeded to change the policy of the government. They did so peacefully. Thus American republican government passed a crucial test: Control of its machinery had changed hands in a democratic and orderly way. And only less significant, the new party system had demonstrated its usefulness. The Jeffersonians had organized popular dissatisfaction with Federalist policies, formulated a platform of reform, chosen leaders to put their plans into effect, and elected those leaders to office.

Thomas Jefferson: Political Theorist

Jefferson hardly seemed cut out for politics. Although in some ways a typical, pleasure-loving southern planter, he had in him something of the Spartan. He grew tobacco but did not smoke, and he partook only sparingly of meat and alcohol. Unlike most planters he never hunted or gambled, though he was a fine horseman and enjoyed dancing, music, and other social diversions. His practical interests ranged enormously—from architecture and geology to natural history and scientific farming—yet he displayed little interest in managing men. Controversy dismayed him, and he tended to avoid it by assigning to some thicker-skinned associate the task of attacking his enemies. Nevertheless, he wanted to have a say in shaping the future of the country, and once engaged, he fought stubbornly and at times deviously to get and hold power.

Like Hamilton, Jefferson thought human beings basically selfish. "Lions and tigers are mere lambs compared with men," he once said. Although he claimed to have some doubts about the subject, he suspected that blacks were "inferior to whites in the endowments both of body and mind." (Hamilton, who also owned slaves, stated flatly of blacks: "Their natural faculties are as good as ours.") The historian Winthrop Jordan, who has made a careful study of white attitudes during this period, claims that Jefferson's opinion, however tenuous, was "the strongest suggestion of inferiority expressed by any native American of the time."

Yet like a good child of the Enlightenment, Jefferson believed that "no definite limits can be assigned to the improvability of the human race" and that unless people were free to follow the dictates of reason, the march of civilization would grind quickly to a halt. "To preserve the freedom of the human mind," he wrote, "every spirit should be ready to devote itself to martyrdom." Democracy seemed to him not so much an ideal as a practical necessity. If people could not govern themselves, how could they be expected to govern their fellows? He had no patience with Hamilton's fondness for magnifying the virtues of the rich and the well-born. He believed that "genius" was a rare quality but one "which nature has shown as liberally among poor as rich." When a very old man he wrote: "The mass of mankind has not been born with saddles on their backs, nor a favored few booted and spurred, ready to ride them legitimately, by the grace of God."

Jefferson believed *all* government a necessary evil at best, for by its nature it restricted the freedom of the individual. For this reason, he wanted the United States to remain a society of small independent farmers.* Such a nation did not need much political organization.

Jefferson's main objection to Hamilton was that Hamilton wanted to commercialize and centralize the country. This Jefferson feared, for it would mean the growth of cities, which would complicate society and hence require more regulation. "When we get piled upon one another in large cities, as in

---

* To Jefferson, agriculture was both the most fundamental and the noblest of callings. "The greatest service which can be rendered to any country is to add a useful plant to its culture," he once said.

VENERATE THE PLOUGH

Jefferson's reverence for farming as a way of life was shared by many Americans of his time. In this etching from a periodical of the period, the plowman is followed by an allegorical figure of America, hallowed with 13 stars and carrying a sheaf of grain.

Europe," he wrote Madison in 1787, "we shall become corrupt as in Europe, and go to eating one another as they do there." Twenty years later he warned a nephew to avoid "populous cities" because, he said, in such places young men acquire "habits and partialities which do not contribute to the happiness of their afterlife." Like Hamilton, he believed that city workers were easy prey for demagogues. "I consider the class of artificers as the panderers of vice, and the instruments by which the liberties of a country are usually overturned," he said. "Those who labor in the earth," he also said, "are the chosen people of God, if ever He had a chosen people."

Jefferson objected to what he considered Hamilton's pro-British orientation. Despite his support of the Revolution, Hamilton admired English society and the orderliness of the British government, and he modeled much of his financial program on the British example. To the author of the Declaration of Independence, these attitudes passed all understanding. Jefferson thought English society immoral and decadent, the British system of gov-

ernment fundamentally corrupt. Toward France, the two took opposite positions. Jefferson was in Paris when the French Revolution broke out; he was delighted to see another blow struck at tyranny. Leading French liberals consulted him at every turn. Later, as secretary of state, he excused the excesses of the French upheaval far more than most Americans. To Hamilton, the violence and social disruption caused by the French Revolution were anathema.

Jefferson as President

The novelty of the new administration lay in its style and its moderation. Both were apparent in Jefferson's inaugural address. The new president's opening remarks showed that he was neither a demagogue nor a firebrand. "The task is above my talents," he said modestly, "and . . . I approach it with . . . anxious and awful presentiments." The people had spoken, and their voice must be heeded, but the rights of dissenters must be respected. "All . . . will bear in mind this sacred principle," he said, "that though the will of the majority is in all cases to prevail, that will to be rightful must be reasonable; that the minority possess their equal rights, which equal law must protect, and to violate would be oppression."

Jefferson spoke at some length about specific policies. He declared himself against "entangling alliances" and for economy in government, and he promised to pay off the national debt, preserve the government's credit, and stimulate both agriculture and its "handmaid," commerce. His main stress was on the cooling of partisan passions. "Every difference of opinion is not a difference of principle. We have called by different names brethren of the same principle. We are all Republicans—we are all Federalists." And he promised the country "a wise and frugal Government, which shall restrain men from injuring one another" and "leave them otherwise free to regulate their own pursuits."

Jefferson quickly demonstrated the sincerity of his remarks. He saw to it that the Whiskey Tax and other Federalist excises were repealed, and he made sharp cuts in military and naval expenditures to keep the budget in balance. The national debt was reduced from $83 million to $57 million during his eight years in office. The Naturalization Act of 1798 was repealed, and the old five-year residence requirement for citizenship restored. The Sedition Act and the Alien Act expired of their own accord in 1801 and 1802.

The changes were not drastic. Jefferson made no effort to tear down the fiscal structure that Hamilton had erected. "We can pay off his debt," the new president confessed, "but we cannot get rid of his financial system." Nor did the author of the Kentucky Resolves try to alter the balance of federal-state power.

Yet there was a different tone to the new regime. Jefferson had no desire to surround himself with pomp and ceremony; the excessive formality and punctilio of the Washington and Adams administrations had been distasteful to him. From the moment of his election, he played down the ceremonial aspects of the presidency. He asked that he be notified of his election by mail rather than by a committee, and he would have preferred to have taken the oath at Charlottesville, near Monticello, his home, rather than at Washington. After the inauguration, he returned to his boardinghouse on foot and took dinner in his usual seat at the common table.

In the White House he often wore a frayed coat and carpet slippers, even to receive the representatives of foreign powers when they arrived, resplendent with silk ribbons and a sense of their own importance, to present their credentials. At social affairs he paid little heed to the status and seniority of his guests. When dinner was announced, he offered his arm to whichever lady he was talking to at the moment and placed her at his right; other guests were free to sit wherever they found an empty chair. During business hours congressmen, friends, foreign officials, and plain citizens coming to call took their turn in the order of their arrival. "The principle of society with us," Jefferson explained, "is the equal rights of all. . . . Nobody shall be above you, nor you above anybody, *pell-mell* is our law."

"Pell-mell" was also good politics, and Jefferson turned out to be a superb politician. He gave dozens of small stag dinner parties for congressmen, serving the food personally from a dumbwaiter connected with the White House kitchen. The guests, carefully chosen to make congenial groups, were seated at a round table to encourage general conversation, and the food and wine were first-class.

Jefferson appears more relaxed and approachable in this drawing by the French expatriate Charles Saint-Mémin than he does in more formal portraits.

These were ostensibly social occasions—shoptalk was avoided—yet they paid large political dividends. Jefferson learned to know every congressman personally, Democratic Republican and Federalist alike, and not only their political views but their strengths, their quirks, their flaws as well. And he worked his personal magic on them, displaying the breadth of his knowledge, his charm and wit, his lack of pomposity. "You see, we are alone, and *our walls have no ears*," he would say, and while the wine flowed and the guests sampled delicacies prepared by Jefferson's French chef, the president manufactured political capital. "You drink as you please and converse at your ease," one guest reported.

Jefferson made effective use of his close supporters in Congress, and of Cabinet members as well, in persuading Congress to go along with his proposals. His state papers were models of sweet reason, minimizing conflicts, stressing areas where all honest people must agree. After all, as he indicated in his inaugural address, nearly all Americans did believe in having both a federal government and a republican system. No great principle divided them into irreconcilable camps. Jefferson set out to bring them all into *his* camp, and he succeeded so well in four years that when he ran for reelection against Charles Pinckney, he got 162 of the 176 electoral votes cast. Eventually even John Quincy Adams, son of the second president, became a Jeffersonian.

At the same time, Jefferson was anything but nonpartisan in the sense that Washington had been. His Cabinet consisted exclusively of men of his own party. He exerted almost continuous pressure on Congress to make sure that his legislative program was enacted into law. He did not remove many Federalist officeholders, and at one point he remarked ruefully that government officials seldom died and never resigned. But when he could, he used his power of appointment to reward his friends and punish his enemies.

Attacking the Judiciary

Although notably open-minded and tolerant, Jefferson had a few stubborn prejudices. One was against kings, another against the British system of government. A third was against judges, or rather, against entrenched judicial power. While recognizing that judges must have a degree of independence, he feared what he called their "habit of going out of the question before them, to throw an anchor ahead, and grapple further hold for future advances of power." The biased behavior of Federalist judges during the trials under the Sedition Act had enormously increased this distrust, and it burst all bounds when the Federalist majority of the dying Congress rammed through the Judiciary Act of 1801.

The Judiciary Act created six new circuit courts, presided over by 16 new federal judges and a small army of attorneys, marshals, and clerks. The expanding country needed the judges, but with the enthusiastic cooperation of President Adams, the Federalists made shameless use of the opportunity to fill all the new positions with conservative members of their own party. The new appointees were dubbed "midnight justices" because Adams had stayed up till midnight on March 3, his last day as president, feverishly signing their commissions.

The Republicans retaliated as soon as the new Congress met by repealing the Judiciary Act of 1801, but upon taking office Jefferson had discovered that in the confusion of Adams's last hours, the commissions of a number of justices of the peace for the new District of Columbia had not been distributed. While these were small fry indeed, Jefferson was so angry that he ordered the commissions held up even though they had been signed by Adams.

One of the appointees, William Marbury, then petitioned the Supreme Court for a writ of mandamus (Latin for "we order") directing the new secretary of state, James Madison, to give him his commission.

The case of *Marbury* v. *Madison* placed Chief Justice John Marshall in an embarrassing position. Marbury had a strong claim: If Marshall refused to issue a mandamus, everyone would say he dared not stand up to Jefferson, and the prestige of the Court would suffer. If he issued the writ, however, he would place the Court in direct conflict with the executive. Jefferson particularly disliked Marshall. He would probably tell Madison to ignore the order, and in the prevailing state of public opinion nothing could be done about it. This would be a still more staggering blow to the judiciary. What should the chief justice do?

Marshall had studied law only briefly and had no previous judicial experience, but in this crisis he first displayed the genius that was to mark him as a great judge. By right Marbury should have his commission, he announced. However, the Court could not require Madison to give it to him. Marbury's request for a mandamus had been based on an ambiguous clause in the Judiciary Act of 1789. That clause was unconstitutional, Marshall declared, and therefore void. Congress could not legally give the Supreme Court the right to issue writs of mandamus in such circumstances.

With the skill and foresight of a chess grand master, Marshall turned what had looked like a trap into a triumph. By sacrificing the pawn, Marbury, he established the power of the Supreme Court to invalidate federal laws that conflicted with the Constitution. Jefferson could not check him because Marshall had *refused* power instead of throwing an anchor ahead, as Jefferson had feared. Yet he had certainly grappled a "further hold for future advances of power," and the president could do nothing to stop him.

The Marbury case made Jefferson more determined to strike at the Federalist-dominated courts. He decided to press for the impeachment of some of the more partisan judges. First he had the House of Representatives bring charges against District Judge John Pickering. Pickering was clearly insane—he had frequently delivered profane and drunken harangues from the bench—and the Senate quickly voted to remove him. Then Jefferson went after a much larger fish, Samuel Chase, associate justice of the Supreme Court.

Chase had been prominent for decades, an early leader of the Sons of Liberty, a signer of the Declaration of Independence, active in the affairs of the Continental Congress. Washington had named him to the Supreme Court in 1796, and he had delivered a number of important opinions. But his handling of cases under the Sedition Act had been outrageously high-handed. Defense lawyers had become so exasperated as to throw down their briefs in disgust at some of his prejudiced rulings. However, the trial demonstrated that Chase's actions had not constituted the "high crimes and misdemeanors" required by the Constitution to remove a judge. Even Jefferson became disenchanted with the efforts of some of his more extreme followers and accepted Chase's acquittal with equanimity.

The Barbary Pirates

Aside from these perhaps salutary setbacks, Jefferson's first term was a parade of triumphs. Although

Although the war against the Barbary pirates did not result in a decisive victory for the United States, its gunboats did give a good account of themselves in encounters with pirate ships. Here, in a raid on the harbor at Tripoli, an American sailor threatens a scimitar-wielding Arab.

he cut back the army and navy sharply in order to save money, he temporarily escaped the consequences of leaving the country undefended because of the lull in the European war signalized by the Treaty of Amiens between Great Britain and France in March 1802. Despite the fact that he had only seven frigates in commission, he even managed to fight a small naval war with the Barbary pirates without damage to American interests or prestige.

The North African Arab states of Morocco, Algiers, Tunis, and Tripoli had for decades made a business of piracy, seizing vessels all over the Mediterranean and holding crews and passengers for ransom. The European powers found it simpler to pay them annual protection money than to crush them. Under Washington and Adams, the United States joined in the payment of this tribute; while large, the sums were less than the increased costs of insurance for shippers when the protection was not purchased.

Such pusillanimity ran against Jefferson's grain. "When this idea comes across my mind, my faculties are absolutely suspended between indignation and impatience," he said. When the pasha of Tripoli tried to raise the charges, he balked. Tripoli then declared war in May 1801, and Jefferson dispatched a squadron to the Mediterranean.

In the words of one historian, the action was "halfhearted and ill-starred." The pirates were not overwhelmed, and a major American warship, the frigate *Philadelphia,* had to be destroyed after running aground off the Tripolitanian coast. The payment of tribute continued until 1815. Just the same, America, though far removed from the pirate bases, was the only maritime nation that tried to resist the blackmail. Although the war failed to achieve Jefferson's purpose of ending the payments, the pasha agreed to a new treaty more favorable to the United States, and American sailors, led by Commodore Edward Preble, won valuable experience and a large portion of fame. The greatest hero was Lieutenant Stephen Decatur, who captured two pirate ships, led ten men in a daring raid on another in which he took on a gigantic sailor in a wild battle of cutlass against boarding pike,* and snatched the stricken *Philadelphia* from the pirates by sneaking aboard and setting it afire.

---

* Decatur killed the pirate by drawing a small pistol from his pocket as his opponent was about to skewer him.

The Louisiana Purchase

The major achievements of Jefferson's first term had to do with the American west, and of these the greatest by far was the acquisition of the huge area between the Mississippi River and the Rocky Mountains. In a sense the purchase of this region, called Louisiana, was fortuitous, an accidental by-product of European political adjustments and the whim of Napoleon Bonaparte. Certainly Jefferson had not planned it, for in his inaugural address he had expressed the opinion that the country already had all the land it would need "for a thousand generations." It was nonetheless the perfectly logical— one might almost say inevitable—result of a long series of events in the history of the Mississippi Valley.

Along with every other American who had even a superficial interest in the west, Jefferson understood that the United States must have access to the mouth of the Mississippi and the city of New Orleans or eventually lose everything beyond the Appalachians. "There is on the globe one single spot, the possessor of which is our natural and habitual enemy," he was soon to write. "It is New Orleans." Thus when he learned shortly after his inauguration that Spain had given Louisiana back to France, he was immediately on his guard. Control of Louisiana by Spain, a "feeble" country with "pacific dispositions," could be tolerated; control by a resurgent France dominated by Napoleon, the greatest military genius of the age, was entirely different. Did Napoleon have designs on Canada? Did he perhaps mean to resume the old Spanish and British game of encouraging the Indians to harry the American frontier? And what now would be the status of Pinckney's precious treaty?

Deeply worried, the president instructed his minister to France, Robert R. Livingston, to seek assurances that American rights in New Orleans would be respected and to negotiate the purchase of West Florida in case that region had also been turned over to France.

Jefferson's concern was well founded; France was indeed planning new imperial ventures in North America. Immediately after settling its difficulties with the United States through the Convention of 1800, France signed the secret Treaty of San Ildefonso with Spain, which returned Louisiana to France. Napoleon hoped to use this region as a

breadbasket for the French West Indian sugar plantations, just as colonies like Pennsylvania and Massachusetts had fed the British sugar islands before
the Revolution.

However, the most important French island,
Saint Domingue (Hispaniola), at the time occupied
entirely by the nation of Haiti, had slipped from
French control. During the French Revolution, the
slaves of the island had revolted. In 1793 they were
granted personal freedom, but they fought on under the leadership of the "Black Napoleon," a self-
taught genius named Toussaint Louverture, and by
1801 the island was entirely in their hands. The
original Napoleon, taking advantage of the slackening of war in Europe, dispatched an army of
20,000 men under General Charles Leclerc to reconquer it.

When Jefferson learned of the Leclerc expedition, he had no trouble divining its relationship to
Louisiana. His uneasiness became outright alarm.
In April 1802 he again urged Minister Livingston
to attempt the purchase of New Orleans and Florida
or, as an alternative, to buy a tract of land near the
mouth of the Mississippi where a new port could
be constructed. Of necessity, the mild-mannered,
idealistic president now became an aggressive realist. If the right of deposit could not be preserved
through negotiation, it must be purchased with gun-
powder, even if that meant acting in conjuction with
the despised British. "The day that France takes
possession of New Orleans," he warned, "we must
marry ourselves to the British fleet and nation."

In October 1802 the Spanish, who had not yet
actually turned Louisiana over to France, heightened the tension by suddenly revoking the right of
deposit at New Orleans. We now know that the
French had no hand in this action, but it was beyond
reason to expect Jefferson or the American people
to believe it at the time. With the west clamoring
for relief, Jefferson appointed his friend and disciple James Monroe minister plenipotentiary and
sent him to Paris with instructions to offer up to
$10 million for New Orleans and Florida. If France
refused, he and Livingston should open negotiations for a "closer connection" with the British.

The tension broke before Monroe even reached
France. General Leclerc's Saint Domingue expedition ended in disaster. Although Toussaint surrendered, Haitian resistance continued. Yellow fever raged through the French army; Leclerc himself

fell before the fever, which wiped out practically his
entire force.

When news of this calamity reached Napoleon
early in 1803, he began to have second thoughts
about reviving French imperialism in the New
World. Without Saint Domingue, the wilderness of
Louisiana seemed of little value. Napoleon was preparing a new campaign in Europe. He could no
longer spare troops to recapture a rebellious West
Indian island or to hold Louisiana against a possible
British attack, and he needed money.

For some weeks the commander of the most
powerful army in the world mulled the question
without consulting anyone. Then, with characteristic suddenness, he made up his mind. On April
10 he ordered Foreign Minister Talleyrand to offer
not merely New Orleans but all of Louisiana to the
Americans. The next day Talleyrand summoned
Livingston to his office on the Rue du Bac and
dropped this bombshell. Livingston was almost
struck speechless but quickly recovered his com-
posure. When Talleyrand asked what the United
States would give for the province, he suggested the
French equivalent of about $5 million. Talleyrand
pronounced the sum "too low" and urged Livingston to think about the subject for a day or two.

Livingston faced a situation that no modern diplomat would ever have to confront. His instructions
said nothing about buying an area almost as large
as the entire United States, and there was no time
to write home for new instructions. The offer staggered the imagination. Luckily, Monroe arrived the
next day to share the responsibility. The two Americans consulted, dickered with the French, and finally agreed—they could scarcely have done otherwise—to accept the proposal. Early in May they
signed a treaty. For 60 million francs—about $15
million—the United States was to have all of
Louisiana.

No one knew exactly how large the region was
or what it contained. When Livingston asked Talleyrand about the boundaries of the purchase, he
replied: "I can give you no direction. You have made
a noble bargain for yourselves, and I suppose you
will make the most of it." Never, as the historian
Henry Adams wrote, "did the United States government get so much for so little."

Napoleon's unexpected concession caused consternation in America, though there was never real
doubt that the treaty would be ratified. Jefferson

Robert Livingston was appointed Jefferson's minister to France in 1801. When he signed the treaty for the purchase of Louisiana, he commented: "From this day, the United States take their place among the powers of the first rank."

did not believe that the government had the power under the Constitution to add new territory or to grant American citizenship to the 50,000 residents of Louisiana by executive act, as the treaty required. He even drafted a constitutional amendment: "The province of Louisiana is incorporated with the United States and made part thereof," but his advisers convinced him that it would be dangerous to delay approval of the treaty until an amendment could be acted on by three-fourths of the states. Jefferson then suggested that the Senate ratify the treaty and submit an amendment afterward "confirming an act which the nation had not previously authorized." This idea was so obviously illogical that he quickly dropped it. Finally, he came to believe "that the less we say about constitutional difficulties

the better." Since what he called "the good sense of our country" clearly wanted Louisiana, he decided to "acquiesce with satisfaction" while Congress overlooked the "metaphysical subtleties" of the problem and ratified the treaty.

Some of the more partisan Federalists, who had been eager to fight Spain for New Orleans, attacked Jefferson for undermining the Constitution. One such critic described Louisiana contemptuously as a "Gallo-Hispano-Indian" collection of "savages and adventurers." Even Hamilton expressed hesitation about absorbing "this new, immense, unbounded world," though he had dreamed of seizing still larger domains himself. In the end Hamilton's nationalism reasserted itself, and he urged ratification of the treaty, as did such other important Federalists as John Adams and John Marshall. And in a way the Louisiana Purchase was as much Hamilton's doing as Jefferson's. Napoleon accepted payment in United States bonds, which he promptly sold to European investors. If Hamilton had not established the nation's credit so soundly, such a large issue could never have been so easily disposed of.

It was ironic—and a man as perceptive as Hamilton must surely have recognized the irony—that the acquisition of Louisiana assured Jefferson's reelection and further contributed to the downfall of Federalism. The purchase was popular even in the New England bastions of that party. While the negotiations were progressing in Paris, Jefferson had written of partisan political affairs: "If we can settle happily the difficulties of the Mississippi, I think we may promise ourselves smooth seas during our time." These words turned out to be no more accurate than most political predictions, but the Louisiana Purchase drove another spike into Federalism's coffin.

Federalism Discredited

The west and south were solid for Jefferson, and the north was rapidly succumbing to his charm. The addition of new western states would soon further reduce New England's power in national affairs. So complete did the Republican triumph seem that a handful of die-hard Federalists in New England began to think of secession. Led by former secretary of state Timothy Pickering, a sour, implacable conservative, a group known as the Essex Junto organized in 1804 a scheme to break away from the Union and establish a "northern confederacy."

Even within the dwindling Federalist ranks the Junto had little support. Nevertheless, Pickering and his friends pushed ahead, drafting a plan whereby, having captured political control of New York, they would take the entire northeast out of the Union. Since they could not begin to win New York for anyone in their own ranks, they hit on the idea of supporting Vice-President Aaron Burr, who was running against the "regular" Republican candidate for governor of New York. Although Burr did not promise to bring New York into their confederacy if elected, he encouraged them enough to win their backing. The foolishness of the plot was revealed in the April elections: Burr was overwhelmed by the regular Republican. The Junto's scheme collapsed.

The incident, however, had a tragic aftermath. Hamilton had campaigned against Burr, whom he considered "an embryo Caesar." When he continued after the election to cast aspersions on Burr's character (not a very difficult assignment, since Burr, despite being a grandson of the preacher Jonathan Edwards, frequently violated both the political and sexual mores of the day), Burr challenged him to a duel. It was well known that Hamilton opposed dueling in principle, his own son having been slain in such an encounter, and he certainly had no need to prove his courage. But he believed that his honor was at stake. The two met with pistols on July 11, 1804, at Weehawken, New Jersey, across the Hudson from New York City. Hamilton made no effort to hit the challenger, but Burr took careful aim. Hamilton fell, mortally wounded. Thus a great, if enigmatic, man was cut off in his prime. His work, in a sense, had been completed, and his philosophy of government was being everywhere rejected, yet the nation's loss was large.

Lewis and Clark

While the disgruntled Federalists dreamed of secession, Jefferson was planning the exploration of Louisiana and the region beyond. Early in 1803 he got $2,500 from Congress and obtained the permission of the French to send his exploring party across Louisiana. To command the expedition he appointed his private secretary, Meriwether Lewis, a young Virginian who had seen considerable service with the army in the west and who possessed, according to Jefferson, "a great mass of accurate information on all the subjects of nature." Lewis chose as his companion officer William Clark, another soldier (he had served with General Anthony Wayne at the Battle of Fallen Timbers) who had much experience in negotiating with Indians.

Jefferson, whose interest in the west was scientific as well as political, issued minute instructions to Lewis:

> Other objects worthy of notice will be, the soil and face of the country . . . the remains and accounts of any animals which may be deemed or are extinct; the mineral productions of every kind, climate, as characterized by the thermometer, by the proportion of rainy, cloudy, and clear days, by lightning, hail, snow, ice, by the access and recess of frost, by the winds prevailing at different seasons, the dates at which particular plants put forth or lose their flower or leaf, times of appearance of particular birds, reptiles or insects. . . .

Scientific matters were inextricably intertwined with practical ones, such as the fur trade, for in his nature studies Jefferson concentrated on "useful" plants and animals. He was haunted by imperialistic visions of an expanding America that were not unlike those of Hamilton. After the consummation of the Louisiana Purchase, he instructed Lewis to try to establish official relations with the Indians in the Spanish territories beyond. Lewis should assure the tribes that "they will find in us faithful friends and protectors," Jefferson said. That the expedition would be moving across Spanish territory need not concern the travelers because of "the expiring state of Spain's interests there."

Lewis and Clark gathered a group of 48 experienced men near St. Louis during the winter of 1803–1804. In the spring they set forth, pushing slowly up the Missouri River in a 55-foot keelboat and two dugout canoes called pirogues. By late fall they had reached what is now North Dakota, where they built a small station, Fort Mandan, and spent the winter. In April 1805, having shipped back to the president more than 30 boxes of plants, minerals, animal skins and bones, and Indian artifacts,

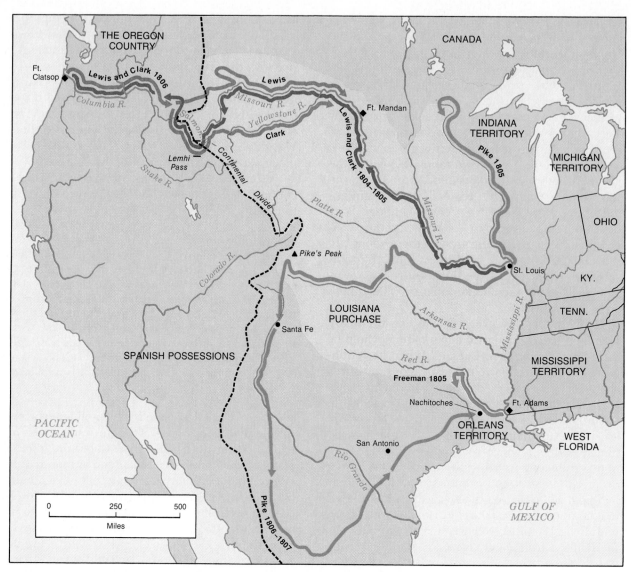

EXPLORING THE LOUISIANA PURCHASE

The explorations of Lewis and Clark, as well as those of Freeman and Pike, are traced in the map. The yellow shading shows the Louisiana Purchase as delineated by its "natural" boundaries. On their return journey, Lewis and Clark divided their party to explore more thoroughly the area around the upper Missouri and Yellowstone rivers.

they struck out again toward the mountains, accompanied by a Shoshone woman, Sacajawea, and her French-Canadian husband, Toussaint Charbonneau, who acted as interpreters and guides. They passed the Great Falls of the Missouri and then clambered over the Continental Divide at Lemhi Pass, in southwestern Montana. Soon thereafter the going became easier, and they descended to the Pacific by way of the Clearwater and Columbia rivers, reaching their destination in November.

Lewis and Clark kept careful journals, with drawings, detailing every aspect of their expedition. In the Northwest they encountered the Chinook Indians, who admired a sloping forehead. The sketch above shows such an Indian in profile. Below is an infant in a cradle especially constructed to achieve this effect.

They had hoped to return by ship, but during the long, damp winter not a single vessel appeared. In the spring of 1806 they headed back by land, reaching St. Louis on September 23.

The country greeted the news of their return with delight. Besides locating several passes across the Rockies, Lewis and Clark had established friendly relations with a great many Indian tribes to whom they presented gifts, medals, American flags, and a sales talk designed to promote peace and the fur trade. They brought back a wealth of data about the country and its resources. The journals kept by members of the group were published and, along with their accurate maps, became major sources for scientists, students, and future explorers. To Jefferson's great personal satisfaction, Lewis provided him with many specimens of the local wildlife, including two grizzly bear cubs, which he kept for a time in a stone pit in the White House lawn.

The success of Lewis and Clark did not open the gates of Louisiana very wide. Other explorers sent out by Jefferson accomplished far less. Thomas Freeman, an Irish-born surveyor, led a small party up the Red River but ran into a powerful Spanish force near the present junction of Arkansas, Oklahoma, and Texas and was forced to retreat. Between 1805 and 1807 Lieutenant Zebulon Pike explored the upper Mississippi Valley and the Colorado region. (He discovered but failed to scale the peak south of Denver that bears his name.) Pike eventually made his way to Santa Fe and the upper reaches of the Rio Grande, but he was not nearly so careful and acute an observer as Lewis and Clark were and consequently brought back much less information. By 1808 fur traders based at St. Louis were beginning to invade the Rockies, and by 1812 there were 75,000 people in the southern section of the new territory, which was admitted to the Union that year as the state of Louisiana. The northern region lay almost untouched until much later.

Jeffersonian Democracy

With the purchase of Louisiana, Jefferson completed the construction of the political institution known as the Republican party and the philosophy of government known as Jeffersonian democracy. From what sort of materials had he built his juggernaut? In part his success was a matter of personality; in the march of American democracy he stood halfway, temperamentally, between Washington and Andrew Jackson, perfectly in tune with the thinking of his times. The colonial American had practiced democracy without really believing in it; hence, for example, the maintenance of property qualifications for voting in regions where nearly everyone owned property. Stimulated by the libertarian ideas of the Revolution, Americans were rapidly adjusting their beliefs to conform with their practices. However, it took Jefferson, a man of large estates, possessed of the general prejudice in favor of the old-fashioned citizen rooted in the soil, yet deeply committed to majority rule, to oversee the transition.

Jefferson's marvelous talents as a writer help to explain his success. He expounded his ideas in language that few people could resist. He had a remarkable facility for discovering practical arguments to justify his beliefs—as when he suggested that by letting everyone vote, elections would be made more honest because with large numbers going to the polls, bribery would become prohibitively expensive.

Jefferson prepared the country for democracy by proving that a democrat could establish and maintain a stable regime. The Federalist tyranny of 1798 was compounded of selfishness and stupidity, but it was also based in part on honest fears that an egalitarian regime would not protect the fabric of society from hotheads and crackpots. The impact of the French Revolution on conservative thinking in the mid-1790s cannot be overestimated. America had fought a seven-year revolution without executing a single Tory, yet during the few months that the Terror ravaged France, nearly 17,000 persons were officially put to death for political "crimes" and many thousands more were killed in civil disturbances. Worse, in the opinion of many, the French extremists had attempted to destroy Christianity, substituting for it a "cult of reason." They confiscated property, imposed price controls, and abolished slavery in the French colonies. Little wonder that many Americans feared that the Jeffersonians, lovers of France and of *liberté, égalite, fraternité*, would try to remodel American society in a similar way.

Jefferson calmed these fears. "Pell-mell" might scandalize the British and Spanish ministers and a few other mossbacks, but it was scarcely revolutionary. The most partisan Federalist was hard put to see a Robespierre in the amiable president scratching out state papers at his desk or chatting with a Kentucky congressman at a "republican" dinner party. Furthermore, Jefferson accepted Federalist ideas on public finance, even learning to live with Hamilton's bank. As a good democrat, he drew a nice distinction between his own opinions and the wishes of the majority, which he felt must always take priority. Even in his first inaugural he admitted that manufacturing and commerce were, along with agriculture, the "pillars of our prosperity," and while believing that these activities would thrive best when "left most free to individual enterprise," he accepted the principle that the government should protect them when necessary from "casual embarrassments." Eventually he gave his backing to modest proposals for spending federal money on roads, canals, and other projects that, according to his political philosophy, ought to have been left to the states and private individuals.

During his term the country grew and prospered, the commercial classes sharing in the bounty along with the farmers so close to Jefferson's heart. Blithely he set out to win the support of all who could vote. "It is material to the safety of Republicanism," he wrote in 1803, "to detach the mercantile interests from its enemies and incorporate them into the body of its friends."

Thus Jefferson undermined the Federalists all along the line. They had said that the country must pay a stiff price for prosperity and orderly government, and they demanded prompt payment in full, both in cash (taxes) and in the form of limitations on human liberty. Under Jefferson these much-desired goals had been achieved cheaply and without sacrificing freedom. A land whose riches could only be guessed at had been obtained without firing a shot and without burdening the people with new taxes. "What farmer, what mechanic, what laborer, ever sees a tax gatherer in the United States?" the president could ask in 1805, without a single Federalist rising to challenge him. Order without discipline, security without a large military establishment, prosperity without regulatory legislation, freedom without license—truly the Sage of Monticello appeared to have led his fellow Americans into a golden age.

Flies in the President's Ointment

Republican virtue seemed to have triumphed, both at home and abroad. "With nations as with individuals," Jefferson proclaimed as he took the oath of office at the start of his second term, "our interests soundly calculated, will ever be found inseparable from our moral duties." And he added more smugly still: "Fellow citizens, you best know whether we have done well or ill." Such smugness and complacency are luxuries that politicians can seldom afford. Jefferson, beginning his second term with pride in the past and confidence in the future and with the mass support of the nation, soon found himself in trouble at home and abroad.

In part his difficulties arose from the extent of the Republican victory. In 1805 the Federalists had no useful ideas, no intelligent leadership, no effective numbers. They held only a quarter of the seats in Congress. As often happens in such situations, lack of opposition weakened party discipline and encouraged factionalism among the Republicans.

At the same time, Napoleon's renewed aggressiveness in Europe, to which the sale of Louisiana had been a prelude, produced a tangle of new problems for the neutral United States. Jefferson could not solve these problems merely by being "just" and "moral," as he had suggested in his second inaugural address. At the end of his second term he was suffering from rheumatism and recurrent headaches that were no doubt of psychosomatic origin, and he wrote feelingly to a friend: "Never did a prisoner, released from his chains, feel such relief as I shall on shaking off the shackles of power."

Jefferson's domestic troubles were not of critical importance, but they were vexing. To a considerable extent they resulted from the elements in his makeup that explain his success: his facility in ad-

John Randolph of Roanoke (as he signed his name to avoid being mistaken for his cousin "Possum" John) was painted in 1805, when he was 32, by Gilbert Stuart.

justing his principles to practical conditions, his readiness to take over the best of Federalism. Some of his disciples were less ready than he to surrender principle to expediency.

The most prominent of the Republican critics was John Randolph of Roanoke, congressman from Virginia. Randolph was unique. Although he had wit, charm, and imagination, he was also intellectually rigid, and when he thought some principle at stake, he was a vitriolic and unyielding obstructionist. Randolph made a fetish of preserving states' rights against invasion by the central government. "Asking one of the States to surrender part of her sovereignty is like asking a lady to surrender part of her chastity," he remarked in one of his typical epigrams.

Randolph first clashed with Jefferson in 1804, over an attempted settlement of the so-called Yazoo land frauds. In 1795 the Georgia legislature had sold a huge area to four land companies for less than 2 cents an acre. When it was revealed that many of the legislators had been corrupted, the next legislature canceled the grants, but not before the original grantees had unloaded large tracts on various third parties. These innocents turned to the federal government for relief when the grants were canceled. Jefferson favored a bill giving 5 million acres to these interests, but Randolph would have none of this. Rising in righteous wrath, he denounced in his shrill soprano all those who would countenance such fraud. The compromise bill was defeated. The controversy then entered the courts, and in 1810 Chief Justice Marshall held in *Fletcher* v. *Peck* that in rescinding the grant, Georgia had committed an unconstitutional breach of contract. Before Marshall's ruling, however, the federal grant was finally approved by Congress. Had it not been, *Fletcher* v. *Peck* would have provided the "victims" of the Yazoo frauds with an area considerably larger than the state of Mississippi! Randolph only rarely mustered more than a handful of supporters in Congress, but his stabbing, nerve-shattering assaults grievously disturbed the president's peace of mind.

The Burr Conspiracy

Another Republican who caused trouble for Jefferson was Aaron Burr, and again the president was partly to blame for the difficulty. After their contest for the presidency in 1801, Jefferson pursued Burr vindictively, depriving him of federal patronage in New York and replacing him as the 1804 Republican vice-presidential candidate with Governor George Clinton, Burr's chief rival in the state.

While still vice-president, Burr began to flirt with treason. He approached Anthony Merry, the British minister in Washington, and offered to "effect a separation of the Western part of the United States." His price was £110,000 and the support of a British fleet off the mouth of the Mississippi. The British did not fall in with his scheme, but he went ahead nonetheless. Exactly what he had in mind has long been in dispute. Certainly he dreamed of acquiring a western empire for himself; whether he intended to wrest it from the United States or from Spanish territories beyond Louisiana is unclear. He joined forces with General James Wilkinson, whom Jefferson had appointed governor of Louisiana Territory, and who, it will be recalled, had been involved in secessionist movements in the west and who was secretly in the pay of Spain.

The opening of the Ohio and Mississippi valleys had not totally satisfied land-hungry westerners. In 1806 Burr and Wilkinson had no difficulty raising a small force at a place called Blennerhassett Island, in the Ohio River. Some six dozen men began to move downriver toward New Orleans under Burr's command. Whether the objective was New Orleans or some part of Mexico, the scheme was clearly illegal. For some reason, however—possibly because he was incapable of loyalty to anyone*—Wilkinson betrayed Burr to Jefferson at the last moment. Burr tried to escape to Spanish Florida but was captured in February 1807, brought to Richmond, Virginia, under guard, and charged with high treason.

Any president will deal summarily with traitors, but Jefferson's attitude during Burr's trial reveals the depth of his hatred. He "made himself a party to the prosecution," personally sending evidence to the United States attorney who was handling the case and offering blanket pardons to associates of Burr who would agree to turn state's evidence. In stark contrast, Chief Justice Marshall, presiding at

---

* John Randolph said of him: "Wilkinson is the only man that I ever saw who was from the bark to the very core a villain."

Aaron Burr was sketched in 1805 by Charles Saint-Mémin, who was well-known for his profile portraits. (See the Jefferson portrait on page 171.)

the trial in his capacity as judge of the circuit court, repeatedly showed favoritism to the prisoner.

In this contest between two great men at their worst, Jefferson as a vindictive executive and Marshall as a prejudiced judge, the victory went to the judge. Organizing "a military assemblage," Marshall declared in his charge to the jury, "was not a levying of war." To "advise or procure treason" was not in itself treason. Unless two independent witnesses testified to an overt act of treason as thus defined, the accused should be declared innocent in the light of this charge. The jury, deliberating only 25 minutes, found Burr not guilty.

Throughout the trial, Burr never lost his self-possession. He seemed to view the proceedings with amiable cynicism. Then, since he was wanted either for murder or for treason in six states, he went into exile in Europe. Some years later he returned to New York, where he spent an unregenerate old age, fathering two illegitimate children in his seventies and being divorced by his second wife on grounds of adultery at 80.

The Burr affair was a blow to Jefferson's prestige; it left him more embittered against Marshall and the federal judiciary, and it added nothing to his reputation as a statesman.

Napoleon and the British

Jefferson's difficulties with Burr may be traced at least in part to the purchase of Louisiana, which, empty and unknown, excited the cupidity of men like Burr and Wilkinson. But problems infinitely more serious were also related to Louisiana.

Napoleon had jettisoned Louisiana to clear the decks before resuming the battle for control of Europe. This war had the effect of stimulating the American economy, for the warring powers needed American goods and American vessels. Shipbuilding boomed; foreign trade, which had quintupled since 1793, nearly doubled again between 1803 and 1805. By the summer of 1807, however, the situation had changed: A most unusual stalemate had developed in the war.

In October 1805 Britain's Horatio Nelson demolished the combined Spanish and French fleets in the Battle of Trafalgar, off the coast of Spain. Napoleon, now at the summit of his powers, quickly redressed the balance, smashing army after army thrown against him by Great Britain's continental allies. By 1807 he was master of Europe, while the British controlled the seas around the Continent. Neither nation could strike directly at the other.

They therefore resorted to commercial warfare, striving to disrupt each other's economy. Napoleon struck first with his Berlin Decree (November 1806), which made "all commerce and correspondence" with Great Britain illegal. The British retaliated with a series of edicts called orders in council, blockading most continental ports and barring from them all foreign vessels unless they first stopped at a British port and paid customs duties. Napoleon then issued his Milan Decree (December 1807), declaring any vessel that submitted to the British rules "to have become English property" and thus subject to seizure.

The blockades and counterblockades seemed designed to stop commerce completely, yet this was not the case. Napoleon's "Continental System" was supposed to make Europe self-sufficient and isolate Great Britain, yet he was willing to sell European products to the British (if the price was right); his chief objective was to deprive them of their continental markets. The British were ready to sell anything on the Continent, and to allow others to do so too, provided they first paid a toll. The Continental System was, in John Quincy Adams's pithy phrase, "little more than extortion wearing the mask of prohibition," and British policy was equally immoral—a kind of piracy practiced with impunity because the Royal Navy controlled the seas.

When war first broke out between Britain and France in 1792, the colonial trade of both sides had fallen largely into American hands because the danger of capture drove many belligerent merchant vessels from the seas. This commerce had engaged Americans in some devious practices. Under the Rule of War of 1756, it will be recalled, the British denied to neutrals the right to engage in trade during time of war from which they were barred by mercantilistic regulations in time of peace. If an American ship carried sugar from the French colony of Martinique to France, for example, the British claimed the right to capture it because such traffic was normally confined to French bottoms by French law.

To avoid this risk, American merchants brought the sugar first to the United States, a legal peacetime voyage under French mercantilism. Then they reshipped it to France as American sugar. Since the United States was a neutral nation and sugar was not contraband of war, the Americans expected the British to let their ships pass with impunity. Continental products likewise reached the French West Indies by way of United States ports, and the American government encouraged the traffic in both directions by refunding customs duties on foreign products reshipped within a year. Between 1803 and 1806 the annual value of foreign products reexported from the United States jumped from $13 million to $60 million! In 1806 the United States exported 47 million pounds of coffee—none, of course, of local origin. An example of this type of trade is offered by Samuel Eliot Morison in his *Maritime History of Massachusetts:*

The brig *Eliza Hardy* of Plymouth enters her home port from Bordeaux, on May 20, 1806, with a cargo of claret wine. Part of it is immediately re-exported to Martinique in the schooner *Pilgrim*, which also carries a consignment of brandy that came from Alicante in the brig *Commerce* and another of gin that came from Rotterdam in the barque *Hannah* of Plymouth. The rest of the *Eliza Hardy*'s claret is taken to Philadelphia by coasters, and thence re-exported in seven different vessels to Havana, Santiago de Cuba, St. Thomas, and Batavia.

This underhanded commerce irritated the British. In the cases of the *Essex* and the *William* (1805–1806), a British judge, Sir William Grant, decreed that American ships could no longer rely on "mere voluntary *ceremonies*" to circumvent the Rule of 1756. Thus just when Britain and France were cracking down on direct trade by neutrals, Britain determined to halt the American reexport trade, thereby gravely threating American prosperity.

The Impressment Controversy

More dismaying were the cruel indignities being visited on American seamen by the British practice of impressment. Under British law, any able-bodied subject could be drafted for service in the Royal Navy in an emergency. Normally, when the commander of a warship found himself shorthanded, he put into a British port and sent a "press gang" ashore to round up the necessary men in harborside pubs. When far from home waters, he might hail any passing British merchant ship and commandeer the necessary men, though this practice was understandably unpopular in British maritime circles. He might also stop a *neutral* merchant vessel on the high seas and remove any British subject. Since the United States owned by far the largest merchant fleet among the neutrals, its vessels bore the brunt of this practice.

Impressment had been a cause of Anglo-American conflict for many years; American pride suffered every time a vessel carrying the flag was forced to back topsails and heave to at the command of a British man-of-war. Still more galling was the contemptuous behavior of British officers when they boarded American ships. In 1796 an American captain named Figsby was stopped twice by British warships while carrying a cargo of poultry and other livestock to Guadeloupe. First a privateer, the *Sea Nymph,* impressed two of his crew, confiscated most of his chickens, "abused" him, and stole his ship's flag. Two days later H.M.S. *Unicorn* took another of Figsby's men, the rest of his poultry, four sheep, and three hogs.

Many British captains made little effort to be sure they were impressing British subjects; any likely-looking lad might be taken when the need was great. Furthermore, there were legal questions in dispute. When did an English immigrant become an American? When he was naturalized, the United States claimed. Never, the British retorted; "once an Englishman, always an Englishman."

America's lax immigration laws compounded the problem. A foreigner could become a citizen with ridiculous ease; those too impatient to wait the required five years could purchase false naturalization papers for as little as a dollar. Because working conditions in the American merchant marine were superior to those of the British, at least 10,000 British-born tars were serving on American ships. Some became American citizens legally; others obtained false papers; some admitted to being British subjects; some were deserters from the Royal Navy. From the British point of view, all were liable to impressment.

The Jefferson administration conceded the right of the British to impress their own subjects from American merchant ships. When naturalized Americans were impressed, however, the administration was irritated, and when native-born Americans were taken, it became incensed. Impressment, Secretary of State Madison said in 1807, was "anomalous in principle, . . . grievous in practice, and . . . abominable in abuse." Between 1803 and 1812 at least 5,000 sailors were snatched from the decks of United States vessels and forced to serve in the Royal Navy. Most of them—estimates run as high as three out of every four—were Americans.

The British did not claim the right to impress native-born Americans, and when it could be proved that boarding officers had done so, the men in question were released by higher authority. During the course of the controversy, the British authorities freed 3,800 impressed Americans, which suggests that many more were seized. However, the British refused to abandon impressment. "The Pretension advanced by Mr. Madison that the American Flag

THE IMPRESSMENT OF AN

American Sailor Boy,

SUNG ON BOARD THE BRITISH PRISON SHIP CROWN PRINCE, THE FOURTH OF JULY, 1814
BY A NUMBER OF THE AMERICAN PRISONERS.

THE youthful sailor mounts the bark,
  And bids each weeping friend adieu :
Fair blows the gale, the canvass swells :
  Slow sinks the uplands from his view.

Three mornings, from his ocean bed,
  Resplendent beams the God of day :
The fourth, high looming in the mist,
  A war-ship's floating banners play.

Her yawl is launch'd ; light o'er the deep,
  Too kind, she wafts a ruffian band :
Her blue track lengthens to the bark,
  And soon on deck the miscreants stand.

Around they throw the baleful glance :
  Suspense holds mute the anxious crew—
Who is their prey ? poor sailor boy !
  The baleful glance is fix'd on you.

Nay, why that useless scrip unfold ?
  They damn'd the "lying yankee scrawl,"
Torn from thine hand, it strews the wave—
  They force thee trembling to the yawl.

Sick was thine heart as from the deck,
  The hand of friendship wav'd farewell ;
Mad was thy brain, as far behind,
  In the grey mist thy vessel fell.

One hope, yet, to thy bosom clung,
  The captain mercy might impart ;

Vain was that hope, which bade thee look,
  For mercy in a Pirate's heart.

What woes can man on man inflict,
  When malice joins with uncheck'd power ;
Such woes, unpitied and unknown,
  For many a month the sailor bore !

Oft gem'd his eye the bursting tear,
  As mem'ry linger'd on past joy ;
As oft they flung the cruel jeer,
  And damn'd the "chicken liver'd boy."

When sick at heart, with "hope defer'd,"
  Kind sleep his wasting form embrac'd,
Some ready minion ply'd the lash,
  And the lov'd dream of freedom chas'd.

Fast to an end his miseries drew :
  The deadly hectic flush'd his cheek :
On his pale brow the cold dew hung,
  He sigh'd, and sunk upon the deck !

The sailor's woes drew forth no sigh ;
No hand would close the sailor's eye :
Remorseless, his pale corse they gave,
Unshrouded to the friendly wave.

And as he sunk beneath the tide,
  A hellish shout arose ;
Exultingly the demons cried,
  "So fare all Albion's Rebel Foes !"

The pathetic story of an "American Sailor Boy" is told in this broadside. Impressed into the British navy, he was pitilessly mistreated by his shipmates; in death "his pale corse they gave,/ Unshrouded to the friendly wave."

should protect every Individual sailing under it," one British foreign secretary explained, "is too extravagant to require any serious Refutation."

The combination of impressment, British interference with the reexport trade, and the general harassment of neutral commerce instituted by both Great Britain and France would have perplexed the most informed and hardheaded of leaders, and in dealing with these problems Jefferson was neither informed nor hardheaded. He believed it much wiser to stand up for one's rights than to compromise, yet he hated the very thought of war. Perhaps, being a southerner, he was less sensitive than he might have been to the needs of New England commercial interests. While the American merchant fleet passed 600,000 tons and continued to grow at an annual rate of over 10 percent, Jefferson kept only a skeleton navy on active service, despite the fact that the great powers were fighting a worldwide, no-holds-barred war. Instead of building a navy that other nations would have to respect, he relied on a tiny fleet of frigates and a swarm of gunboats that

The Ograbme ("embargo" spelled backwards), a unique snapping turtle created by cartoonist Alexander Anderson, effectively frustrates an American tobacco smuggler.

were useless against the Royal Navy—"a macabre monument," in the words of one historian, "to his hasty, ill-digested ideas" about defense.*

The Embargo Act

The frailty of Jefferson's policy became obvious once the warring powers began to attack neutral shipping in earnest. Between 1803 and 1807 the British seized over 500 American ships, Napoleon over 200 more. The United States could do nothing.

The ultimate in frustration came on June 22, 1807, off Norfolk, Virginia. The American 46-gun frigate *Chesapeake* had just left port for patrol duty in the Mediterranean. Among its crew were a British sailor who had deserted from H.M.S. *Halifax* and three Americans who had been illegally impressed by the captain of H.M.S. *Melampus* and had later escaped. The *Chesapeake* was barely out of sight of land when H.M.S. *Leopard* (56 guns) approached and signaled it to heave to. Thinking that *Leopard* wanted to make some routine communication, Cap-

tain James Barron did so. A British officer came aboard and demanded that the four "deserters" be handed over to him. Barron refused, whereupon as soon as the officer was back on board, *Leopard* opened fire on the unsuspecting American ship, killing three sailors. Barron had to surrender. The "deserters" were seized, and then the crippled *Chesapeake* was allowed to limp back to port.

The attack was in violation of international law, for no nation claimed the right to impress sailors from warships. The British government admitted this, though it delayed making restitution for years. The American press clamored for war, but the country had nothing to fight with. Jefferson contented himself with ordering British warships out of American territorial waters. However, he was determined to put a stop to the indignities being heaped on the flag by Great Britain and France. The result was the Embargo Act.

The Embargo Act prohibited all exports. American vessels could not clear for any foreign port, and foreign vessels could do so only if empty. Importing was not forbidden, but few foreign ships would come to the United States if they had to return without a cargo. Although the law was sure to injure the American economy, Jefferson hoped that it would work in two ways to benefit the nation. By keeping U.S. merchant ships off the seas, it would

---

* The gunboats had performed effectively against the Barbary pirates, but Jefferson was enamored of them mainly because they were cheap. A gunboat cost about $10,000 to build, a frigate well over $300,000.

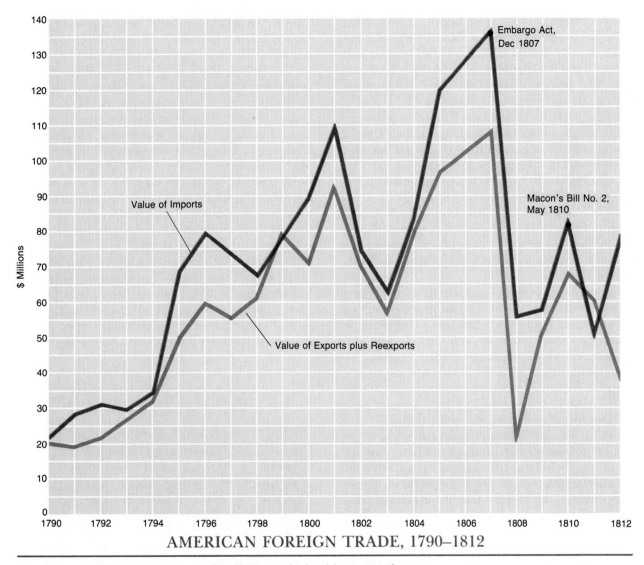

$ Millions

Value of Imports

Value of Exports plus Reexports

Embargo Act,
Dec 1807

Macon's Bill No. 2,
May 1810

AMERICAN FOREIGN TRADE, 1790–1812

*The embargo's effects are shown graphically here. The brief foreign trade spurt
in 1810 was due to congressional passage of Macon's Bill No. 2. The space
between the upper (import) line and the lower (export) line indicates a persistent
foreign-trade deficit.*

end all chance of injury to them and to the national honor. By cutting off American goods and markets, it would put great economic pressure on Britain and France to moderate policies toward American shipping. The fact that boycotts had repeatedly wrested concessions from the British during the crises preceding the Revolution was certainly in Jefferson's mind when he devised the embargo.

Seldom has a law been so bitterly resented and resisted by a large segment of the public. It de-

manded of the maritime interests far greater sacrifices than they could reasonably be expected to make. Massachusetts-owned ships alone were earning over $15 million a year in freight charges by 1807, and Bay State merchants were making far larger gains from the buying and selling of goods. Foreign commerce was the most expansive force in the economy, the chief reason for the nation's prosperity.

Losses through seizure were exasperating, but

they could be insured against. Impressment excited universal indignation, but it hit chiefly at the defenseless, the disreputable, and the obscure and never caused a labor shortage in the merchant marine. The profits of commerce were still tremendous. A Massachusetts senator estimated that if only one vessel in three escaped the blockade, the owner came out ahead. As John Randolph remarked in a typical sally, the administration was trying "to cure the corns by cutting off the toes."

The Embargo Act had catastrophic effects. Exports fell from $108 million in 1807 to $22 million in 1808, imports from $138 million to less than $57 million. Prices of farm products and manufactured goods reacted violently; seamen were thrown out of work; merchants found their businesses disrupted.

How many Americans violated the law is difficult to determine, but they were ingenious at discovering ways to do so. The most obvious way was to smuggle goods back and forth between Canada and the northeastern states. As James Madison recalled in later years, the political boundary lost all significance. People on both sides made the region "a world of itself," treating the Embargo Act as though the laws of Congress did not apply to them.

As for ocean commerce, American ships made hastily for blue water before the machinery of enforcement could be put into operation, not to return until the law was repealed. Shipping between American ports had not been outlawed, and coasting vessels were allowed to put into foreign ports when in distress. Suddenly, mysterious storms began to drive experienced skippers leagues off their courses, some as far as Europe. The brig *Commerce*, en route from Massachusetts to New Orleans, was "forced" by a shortage of water to make for Havana. Having replenished its casks, the brig exchanged its cargo for sugar.

The law permitted merchants with property abroad to send ships to fetch it. About 800 ships went off on such errands. Lawbreakers were difficult to punish. In the seaport towns, juries were no more willing to convict anyone of violating the Embargo Act than their fathers had been to convict those charged with violating the Townshend Acts. A mob at Gloucester, Massachusetts, destroyed a revenue cutter in the same spirit that Rhode Islanders exhibited in 1772 when they burned the

Gaspee. Surely the embargo was a mistake. The United States ought either to have suffered the indignities heaped on its vessels for the sake of profits or, by constructing a powerful navy, made it dangerous for the belligerents to treat its merchant ships so roughly. Jefferson was too proud to choose the former alternative, too parsimonious to choose the latter. Instead he applied harsher and harsher regulations in a futile effort to accomplish his purpose. Militiamen patrolled the Canadian border; revenuers searched out smuggled goods without proper warrants. The illegal trade continued, and in his last months as president Jefferson simply gave up. Even then he would not admit that the embargo was a fiasco and urge its repeal. Only in Jefferson's last week in office did a leaderless Congress finally abolish it, substituting the Nonintercourse Act, which forbade trade only with Great Britain and France and authorized the president to end the boycott against either power by proclamation when and if it stopped violating the rights of Americans.

Milestones

1800	Jefferson elected president (the "Revolution of 1800")
1801	Judiciary Act of 1801 allows President Adams to appoint many Federalist judges before leaving office
1801–1805	War with the Barbary pirates
1803	Supreme Court declares part of Judiciary Act of 1793 unconstitutional (*Marbury* v. *Madison*)
	Louisiana Territory purchased from France
1804	Alexander Hamilton killed by Aaron Burr in a duel
1804–1806	Lewis and Clark expedition
1806	Burr conspiracy
1806–1807	Napoleon's Berlin and Milan decrees
1807	H.M.S *Leopard* attacks U.S.S *Chesapeake*
	Embargo Act

SUPPLEMENTARY READING

Titles marked with an asterisk have been published in paperback.

No student interested in Jefferson's political and social philosophy should miss sampling his writings. A useful compilation is Adrienne Koch and William Peden, **The Life and Selected Writings of Thomas Jefferson** (1944). Lance Banning, **The Jeffersonian Persuasion** (1978), is valuable, as are Joyce Appleby, **Capitalism and a New Social Order** (1984), and M. D. Peterson, **Thomas Jefferson and the New Nation*** (1970).

For a general treatment of the Jeffersonian era, consult Marshall Smelser, **The Democratic Republic*** (1968). On the parties of the era, see N. E. Cunningham, Jr., **The Jeffersonian Republicans in Power*** (1963), and D. H. Fischer, **The Revolution of American Conservatism: The Federalist Party in the Era of Jeffersonian Democracy*** (1965); on the structure of Jefferson's administration, see L. D. White, **The Jeffersonians*** (1951); and on Jefferson's management of the administration and of Congress, read J. S. Young, **The Washington Community*** (1966), a fascinating book.

Jefferson's battle with the judges can be followed in R. E. Ellis, **The Jeffersonian Crisis*** (1971). On *Marbury v. Madison,* see J. A. Garraty (ed.), **Quarrels That Have Shaped the Constitution*** (1964), and D. O. Dewey's more detailed **Marshall Versus Jefferson*** (1970).

On the Louisiana Purchase, see Alexander De Conde, **The Affair of Louisiana** (1976), Harry Ammon, **James Monroe** (1971), and George Dangerfield, **Chancellor Robert R. Livingston** (1960).

Jefferson's interest in the west is discussed in E. T. Martin, **Thomas Jefferson: Scientist*** (1952). An excellent general treatment of western exploration is contained in R. A. Billington, **Westward Expansion** (1967). On Lewis and Clark, see P. R. Cutright, **Lewis and Clark: Pioneering Naturalists** (1976), Richard Dillon, **Meriwether Lewis** (1965), and J. O. Steffen, **William Clark** (1977).

On the Burr Conspiracy, see T. P. Abernethy, **The Burr Conspiracy** (1954), and F. F. Bierbe, **Shout Treason: The Trial of Aaron Burr** (1959).

The best account of the neutral rights question is Bradford Perkins, **Prologue to War*** (1961).

The magnificent portrait of Jefferson at left, painted by Gilbert Stuart in 1805, is the official image of Jefferson that is currently reproduced on postage stamps. It is known as the Edgehill portrait, and it hung at Monticello for many years. The bust at right was made by the French sculptor Houdon when Jefferson was in France in 1789. It deliberately copies the look of the portrait busts so popular during the republican era of ancient Rome.

Monticello, designed in nearly every detail by Jefferson himself, was his home from 1772, the year he married the young widow Martha Skelton Wales, until his death in 1826.

Jefferson, a musician as well as a statesman and scientist, owned a number of instruments, including a harpsichord. The music stand to the right of the harpsichord allows four players to sit in a circle around it, while two more can stand and read their music from the upper tier.

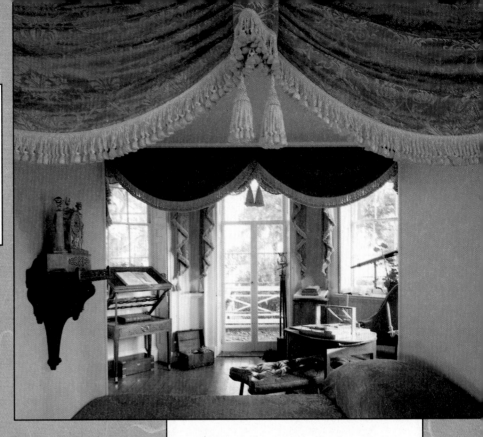

Jefferson's bed was conveniently set in an alcove, so that he could get in and out of it on either side. A clock is handy on the wall at the foot of the bed. In the background, his surveying equipment stands beside the glass door, and his telescope is aimed out the window. The table has a revolving surface, like a lazy Susan.

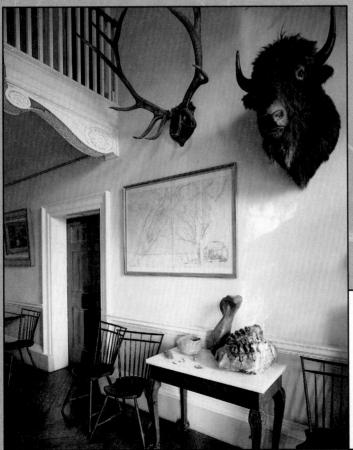

The cluttered entry hall at Monticello greeted visitors in the years after the Lewis and Clark expedition with western mementos: the antlers of a deer and a stuffed bison's head, as well as a tableful of bones, rocks, and other natural history objects. One visitor commented, "There is no private gentleman in the world in possession of so complete a scientific, useful and ornamental collection."

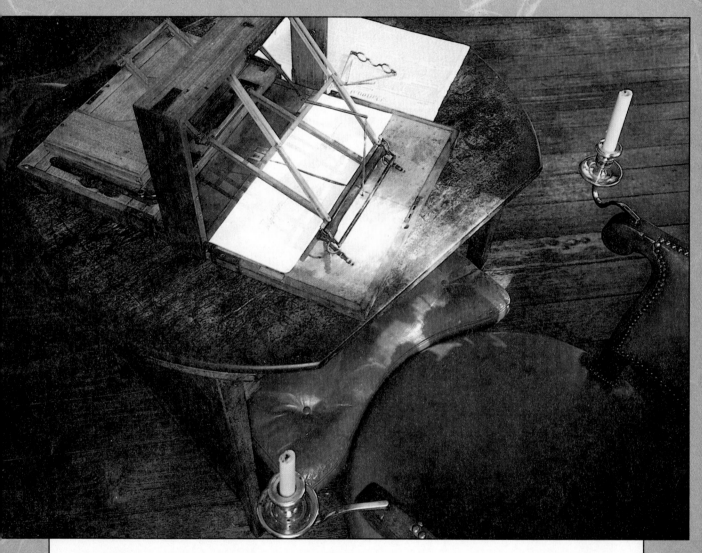

Supremely practical, Jefferson devised a way to make more than one copy of a letter or document at a time. This apparatus, called a polygraph, holds a second pen, which moves over a second piece of paper as the writer composes on the first piece. Jefferson had three polygraphs.

Isaac Jefferson was born in 1775; this daguerreotype was taken about 1845. He was a Monticello slave who worked as a blacksmith and made nails for the plantation. His stories are the source of many details of Jefferson's domestic life.

A Roll of the proper slaves of Thomas Jefferson. Jan. 14. 1774.

Monticello.

Monticello.

* Goliah.
* Hercules.
+ Jupiter. 1743.
* Gill.
* Fanny
+ Ned. 1760.
  Suckey 1765.
  Frankey. 1767.
  Gill. 1769.
* Quash
* Nell.
* Bella. 1757.
* Charles. 1760.
  Jenny. 1768.
* Betty
– Juno
* Toby junr. 1753.
– Luna. 1758.
* Cate. about 1747.
  Hannah 1770.
  Rachael. 1773.

+ George
+ Ursula.
  George.
  Bagwell.
  Archy. 1773
+ Frank 1757.
+ Bett. 1759
+ Scilla. 1762.

* denotes a labourer in the ground.
+ denotes a titheable person following some other occupation
– denotes a person discharged from labor on acct of age or infirmity.

A household as large as Monticello could not have been maintained without the help of many servants, and like other wealthy southerners Jefferson was a slave owner. Twenty-nine slaves are listed on the roll at right dated January 14, 1774. The persons not otherwise designated by a footnote were children under 10.

VII

America Escapes from Europe

WE OWE ALLEGIANCE TO NO CROWN.

Our policy in regard to Europe . . . remains the same, which is, not to interfere in the internal concerns of any of its powers, . . . to leave the parties to themselves, in the hope that other powers will insure the same course.

MONROE DOCTRINE, *1823*

I t is a measure of Jefferson's popularity and of the political ineptitude of the Federalists that the Republicans won the election of 1808 handily despite the embargo. James Madison got 122 of the 173 electoral votes for the presidency, and the party carried both houses of Congress, although by reduced majorities.

Madison in Power

Madison was a small, neat, rather precise person, narrower in his interests than Jefferson but in many ways a deeper thinker. He was more conscientious in the performance of his duties and more consistent in adhering to his principles. Ideologically, however, they were as close as two active and intelligent people could be. Madison had no better solution to offer for the problem of the hour than Jefferson had had. The Nonintercourse Act proved difficult to enforce—once an American ship left port, there was no way to prevent the skipper from steering for England or France—and it exerted little economic pressure on the British, who continued to seize American vessels.

Late in 1809, at the urging of Secretary of the Treasury Albert Gallatin, who was concerned because the government was operating at a deficit, Representative Nathaniel Macon of North Carolina introduced a bill permitting American ships to go anywhere but closing United States ports to the ships of Britain and France. After protracted bickering in Congress, this measure was replaced by another, known as Macon's Bill No. 2, which removed all restrictions on commerce with France and Britain, though French and British warships were still barred from American waters. It authorized the president to reapply the principle of nonintercourse to either of the major powers if the other should "cease to violate the neutral commerce of the United States." This bill became law in May 1810.

The volume of United States commerce with the British Isles swiftly zoomed to preembargo levels. Trade with France remained much more limited because of the British fleet. Napoleon therefore announced that the Berlin and Milan decrees would be revoked in November on the understanding that Great Britain would abandon its own restrictive policies. Treating this ambiguous proposal as a statement of French policy (which it decidedly was not), Madison reapplied the nonintercourse policy to Great Britain. Napoleon, having thus tricked Madison into closing American ports to British ships and goods, continued to seize American ships and cargoes whenever it suited him to do so.

The British grimly refused to modify the orders in council unless it could be shown that the French had actually repealed the Berlin and Milan decrees—and this despite mounting complaints from their own businessmen that the new American nonimportation policy was cutting off a major market for their manufactures. Yet Madison could not afford either to admit that Napoleon had deceived him or to reverse American policy still another time. Reluctantly he came to the conclusion that unless Britain repealed the orders, the United States must declare war.

Tecumseh and the Prophet

There were other reasons for fighting besides British violations of neutral rights. The Indians were again making trouble, and western farmers believed that the British in Canada were egging them on. This had been true in the past but was no longer the case in 1811 and 1812. American domination of the southern Great Lakes region was no longer in question. Canadian officials had no desire to force a showdown between the Indians and the Americans, for that could have but one result. Aware of their own vulnerability, the Canadians wanted to preserve Indian strength in case war should break out between Great Britain and the United States.

American political leaders tended to believe that Indians should be encouraged to become farmers and to copy the "civilized" ways of whites. However, no government had been able to control the frontiersmen, who by bribery, trickery, and force were driving the tribes back year after year from the rich lands of the Ohio Valley. General William Henry Harrison, governor of Indiana Territory, a tough, relentless soldier, kept constant pressure on them. He wrested land from one tribe by promising it aid against a traditional enemy, from another as a penalty for having murdered a white man, from others by corrupting a few chiefs. Harrison justified his sordid behavior by citing the end in view—that "one of the fairest portions of the globe" be secured as "the seat of civilization, of science, and of true religion." The "wretched savages" should not be allowed to stand in the path of this worthy objective. As early as 1805 it was clear that unless something drastic was done, Harrison's aggressiveness, together with the corroding effects of white civilization, would soon obliterate the tribes.

At this point the Shawnee chief Tecumseh made a bold and imaginative effort to reverse the trend by binding all the tribes east of the Mississippi into a great confederation. Traveling from the Wisconsin country to the Floridas, he persuaded tribe after tribe to join him. "Let the white race perish," Tecumseh declared. "They seize your land; they corrupt your women. . . . Back whence they came, upon a trail of blood, they must be driven!"

To Tecumseh's political movement his brother Tenskwatawa, known as the Prophet, added the force of a moral crusade. Instead of aping white customs, the Prophet said, Indians must give up white ways, white clothes, and white liquor and reinvigorate their own culture. Ceding lands to the whites must stop because the Great Spirit intended that the land be used in common by all.

The Prophet, also called "The Open Door," lent religious fervor to his brother Tecumseh's antiwhite doctrine.

The Prophet was a fanatic who saw visions and claimed to be able to control the movement of heavenly bodies. Tecumseh, however, possessed true genius. A powerful orator and a great organizer, he had deep insight into the needs of his people. Harrison himself said of Tecumseh: "He is one of those uncommon geniuses which spring up occasionally to produce revolutions and overturn the established order of things." The two brothers made a formidable team. By 1811 thousands of Indians were organizing to drive the whites off their lands. Alarms swept through the west.

With about 1,000 soldiers, General Harrison marched boldly against the brothers' camp at Prophetstown, where Tippecanoe Creek joins the Wabash, in Indiana. Tecumseh was away recruiting men, and the Prophet recklessly ordered an assault on Harrison's camp outside the village on November 7, 1811. When the white soldiers held their ground despite the Prophet's magic, the Indians lost confidence and fell back. Harrison then destroyed Prophetstown.

While the Battle of Tippecanoe was pretty much

a draw, it disillusioned the Indians and shattered their confederation. Frontier warfare continued, but in the disorganized manner of former times. Like all such fighting, it was brutal and bloody.

Unwilling as usual to admit that their own excesses were the chief cause of the trouble, the settlers directed their resentment at the British in Canada. "This combination headed by the Shawanese prophet is a British scheme," a resolution adopted by the citizens of Vincennes, Indiana, proclaimed. As a result, the cry for war with Great Britain rang out all along the frontier.

Depression and Land Hunger

Some westerners pressed for war because they were suffering an agricultural depression. The prices they received for their wheat, tobacco, and other products in the markets of New Orleans were falling, and they attributed the decline to the loss of foreign markets and the depredations of the British. American commercial restrictions had more to do with the western depression than the British, and in any case the slow and cumbersome transportation and distribution system that western farmers were saddled with was the major cause of their difficulties. But the farmers were no more inclined to accept these explanations than they were to absolve the British from responsibility for the Indian difficulties. If only the seas were free, they reasoned, costs would go down, prices would rise, and prosperity would return.

To some extent western expansionism also heightened the war fever. The west contained immense tracts of virgin land, but westerners wanted more. Canada would surely fall to American arms in the event of war, the frontiersmen believed. So, apparently, would Florida, for Spain was now Britain's ally. Florida in itself provided no cause for a war, for it was sure to fall into American hands before long. In 1810 Madison had snapped up the extreme western section without eliciting any effective response from Spain.

So it was primarily because of Canada, nearby and presumably vulnerable, that westerners wanted war. It is also likely that President Madison saw an attack on Canada as a way to force the British to respect neutral rights. If Napoleon's Continental System cut Great Britain off from trade with northern Europe, Canada would be its only source of lumber and naval stores. Between 1808 and 1812 Canadian exports of lumber to Britain soared. Still more important in Madison's mind, if the United States conquered Canada, Britain's hope of obtaining food in Canada for its West Indian sugar islands would be shattered. Then it would have to end its hateful assaults and restrictions on American merchant ships or the islands' economy would collapse.

But westerners, and many easterners too, were more patriots than imperialists or merchants in 1811 and 1812. When their leaders in Congress, known as the "War Hawks," called for war against Great Britain, they did so because they saw no other way to defend the national honor and force repeal of the orders in council. The choice seemed to lie between war and surrender of true independence. As Madison put it, to bow to British policy would be to "recolonize" American foreign commerce.

Resistance to War

There were, however, large numbers of people who thought that a war against Great Britain would be a national calamity. Some Federalists would have resisted anything the administration proposed; Congressman Josiah Quincy of Massachusetts declared that he "could not be kicked" into the war, which he considered a cowardly, futile, and unconstitutional business designed primarily to ensure Madison's reelection. (Quincy saw no inconsistency between this opinion and his conviction that Madison was a pacifist.) According to Quincy, the War Hawks were "backwoodsmen" willing to wage a "cruel, wanton, senseless and wicked" war in order to swallow up Canada.

But other people based their objections on economics and a healthy realism. Powerful interests in the eastern maritime states were dead set against fighting, for the same reasons that had led them to resist the Embargo Act. No shipowner could view with equanimity the idea of taking on the largest navy in the world. Such persons complained sincerely enough about impressment and the orders in council, but war seemed to them worse by far. Self-interest led them to urge patience.

Such a policy would have been wise, for Great

Britain did not represent a real threat to the United States. British naval officers were high-handed, officials in London complacent, British diplomats in Washington second-rate and obtuse. Yet language, culture, and strong economic ties bound the two countries. Napoleon, in contrast, represented a tremendous potential danger. He had offhandedly turned over Louisiana, but even Jefferson, the chief beneficiary of his largess, hated everything he stood for. Jefferson called Napoleon "an unprincipled tyrant who is deluging the continent of Europe with blood."

No one understood the Napoleonic danger to America more clearly than the British; part of the stubbornness and arrogance of their maritime policy grew out of their conviction that Napoleon was a threat to all free nations. The *Times* of London declared: "The Alps and the Apennines of America are the British Navy. If ever that should be removed, a short time will suffice to establish the headquarters of a [French] Duke-Marshal at Washington." Yet by going to war with Britain, the United States was aiding Napoleon.

What made the situation even more unfortunate was the fact that by 1812 conditions had changed in England in a way that made a softening of British maritime policy likely. A depression caused chiefly by the increasing effectiveness of Napoleon's Continental System was plaguing the country. Manufacturers, blaming the slump on the loss of American markets, were urging repeal of the orders in council. Gradually, though with exasperating slowness, the government prepared to yield. On June 23, after a change of ministries, the new foreign secretary, Lord Castlereagh, suspended the orders. Five days earlier, alas, the United States had declared war.

The War of 1812

The illogic of the War Hawks in pressing for a fight was exceeded only by their ineffectiveness in planning and managing the struggle. By what possible strategy could the ostensible objective of the war be achieved? To construct a navy capable of challenging the British fleet would have been the work of many years and a more expensive proposition than the War Hawks were willing to consider. So hopeless

was that prospect that Congress failed to undertake any new construction in the first year of the conflict. Several hundred merchant ships lashed a few cannon to their decks and sailed off as privateers to attack British commerce. The navy's seven modern frigates, built during the war scare after the XYZ Affair, put to sea. But these forces could make no pretense of disputing Britain's mastery of the Atlantic.

For a brief moment the American frigates held center stage, for they were faster, tougher, larger, and more powerfully armed than their British counterparts. Barely two months after the declaration of war, Captain Isaac Hull in U.S.S. *Constitution* chanced upon H.M.S. *Guerrière* in mid-Atlantic, outmaneuvered the *Guerrière* brilliantly, brought down its mizzenmast with his first volley, and then gunned it into submission, a hopeless wreck. In October U.S.S. *United States*, captained by Stephen Decatur, hero of the war against the Barbary pirates, caught H.M.S. *Macedonian* off the Madeiras, pounded it unmercifully at long range, and forced the Britisher to surrender. The *Macedonian* was taken into New London as a prize; more than a third of the 300-man crew were casualties, while American losses were but a dozen. Then, in December, the *Constitution,* now under Captain William Bainbridge, took on the British frigate *Java* off Brazil. "Old Ironsides" shot away the *Java*'s mainmast and reduced it to a hulk too battered for salvage.

These victories had little influence on the outcome of the war. The Royal Navy had 34 frigates, 7 more powerful ships of the line, and dozens of smaller vessels. As soon as these forces could concentrate against them, the American frigates were immobilized, forced to spend the war gathering barnacles at their moorings while powerful British squadrons ranged offshore. The privateering merchantmen were more effective because they were so numerous; they captured more than 1,300 British vessels during the war. The best of them—vessels like *America* and *True-Blooded Yankee*—were redesigned, given more sail to increase their speed, and formidably armed. *America* captured 26 prizes valued at more than $1 million. *True-Blooded Yankee* took 27 and destroyed 7 more in a Scottish harbor.

Great Britain's one weak spot seemed to be Canada. The colony had but half a million inhabitants to oppose 7.5 million Americans. Only 2,257 British

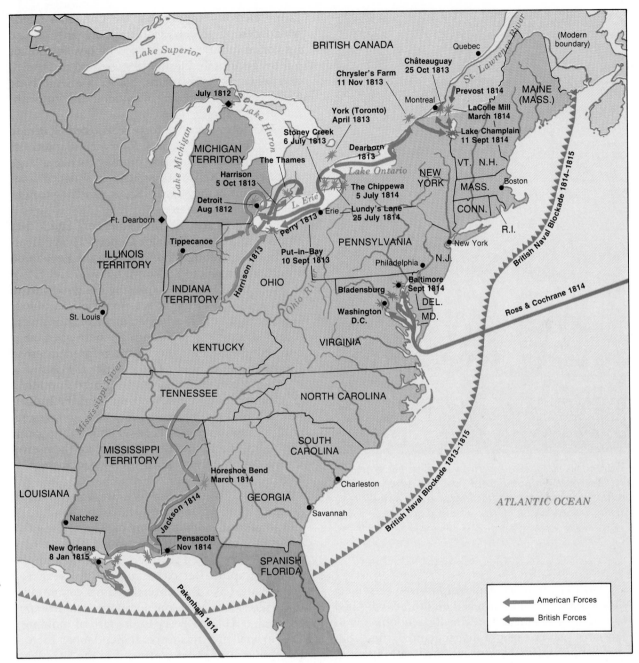

THE WAR OF 1812

regulars guarded the long border from Montreal to Detroit. The Canadian militia was feeble, and many of its members, being American-born, sympathized with the "invaders." According to the War Hawk congressman Henry Clay of Kentucky, the west was one solid horde of ferocious frontiersmen, armed to the teeth and thirsting for Canadian blood. Yet such talk was mostly brag and bluster; when Congress authorized increasing the army by 25,000 men, Kentucky produced 400 enlistments.

With a few exceptions, American forces in the War of 1812 were ill trained and led, and poor strategy resulted in several disgraceful defeats. Here, a resplendently dressed militia officer consults a map.

American military leadership proved extremely disappointing. Madison relied on officers who had served with distinction in the Revolution, but in most cases, as one biographer suggested, their abilities "appeared to have evaporated with age and long disuse." Instead of a concentrated strike against Canada's St. Lawrence River lifeline, which would have isolated Upper Canada, the generals planned a complicated three-pronged attack. It was a total failure. In July 1812 General William Hull, veteran of the battles of Trenton, Saratoga, and Monmouth and now governor of Michigan Territory, marched forth with 2,200 men against the Canadian positions

facing Detroit. Hoping that the Canadian militia would desert, he delayed his assault, only to find his communications threatened by hostile Indians led by Tecumseh. Hastily he retreated to Detroit, and when the Canadians, under General Isaac Brock, pursued him, he surrendered the fort without firing a shot!

In October another force attempted to invade Canada from Fort Niagara. After an initial success, it was crushed by superior numbers, while a large contingent of New York militiamen watched from the east bank of the Niagara River, unwilling to fight outside their own state.

The third arm of the American attack was equally unsuccessful. Major General Henry Dearborn, who had fought honorably in the Revolution from Bunker Hill to Yorktown but who had grown so fat that he needed a specially designed cart to get from place to place, set out from Plattsburg, New York, at the head of an army of militiamen. Their objective was Montreal, but when they reached the border, the troops refused to cross. Dearborn meekly marched them back to Plattsburg.

Meanwhile, the British had captured Fort Michilimackinac in northern Michigan, and the Indians had taken Fort Dearborn (now Chicago), massacring 85 captives. Instead of sweeping triumphantly through Canada, the Americans found themselves trying desperately to keep the Canadians out of Ohio.

Stirred by these disasters, westerners rallied somewhat in 1813. General Harrison, the victor of Tippecanoe, headed an army of Kentuckians in a series of inconclusive battles against British troops and Indians led by Tecumseh. He found it impossible to recapture Detroit because a British squadron controlling Lake Erie threatened his communications. President Madison therefore assigned Captain Oliver Hazard Perry to the task of building a fleet to challenge this force. In September 1813, at Put-in-Bay near the western end of the lake, Perry destroyed the British vessels in a bloody battle in which 85 of the 103 men on Perry's flagship were casualties. "We have met the enemy and they are ours," he reported modestly. About a quarter of Perry's 400 men were blacks, which led him to remark that "the color of a man's skin" was no more an indication of his worth than "the cut and trimmings" of his coat.

In the midst of the battle of Lake Erie, Perry had to abandon his flagship, the Lawrence, *which had been shot to pieces by enemy fire. (Over three-fourths of the ship's crew were killed or wounded.) He was rowed to the* Niagara, *from which he directed the rest of the engagement.*

With the Americans in control of Lake Erie, Detroit became untenable for the British, and when they fell back, Harrison gave chase and defeated them at the Thames River, some 60 miles northeast of Detroit. Although little more than a skirmish, this battle had large repercussions. Tecumseh was among the dead (an eccentric American colonel, Richard Mentor Johnson, was to base a long and successful political career, culminating in his election as vice-president of the United States in 1836,* on his claim of having personally done in the great chief), and without him the Indians lost heart. But American attempts to win control of Lake Ontario and to invade Canada in the Niagara region were again thrown back. Late in 1813 the British captured Fort Niagara and burned the town of Buffalo. The conquest of Canada was as far from realization as ever.

The British fleet had intensified its blockade of American ports, extending its operations to New England waters previously spared to encourage the antiwar sentiments of local maritime interests. All along the coast, patrolling cruisers, contemptuous of Jefferson's puny gunboats, captured small craft, raided shore points to commandeer provisions, and collected ransom from port towns by threatening to bombard them. One captain even sent a detail ashore to dig potatoes for his ship's mess.

Britain on the Offensive

Until 1814 the British put relatively little effort into the American war, being concerned primarily with the struggle against Napoleon. However, in 1812 Napoleon had invaded Russia and been thrown back; thereafter, one by one, his European satellites rose against him. Gradually he relinquished his conquests; the Allies marched into France, Paris fell, and in April 1814 the emperor abdicated. Then the British, free to strike hard at the United States, dispatched some 14,000 veterans to Canada.

By the spring of 1814 British strategists had de-

* Of Johnson, a biographer writes: "His career as vice-president was inconspicuous. . . . As a politician, though not lacking in sagacity, he was lacking in purpose."

vised a master plan for crushing the United States. One army, 11,000 strong, was to march from Montreal, tracing the route that General Burgoyne had followed to disaster in the Revolution. A smaller amphibious force was to make a feint at the Chesapeake Bay area, destroying coastal towns and threatening Washington and Baltimore. A third army was to assemble at Jamaica and sail to attack New Orleans and bottle up the west.

It is necessary, in considering the War of 1812, to remind oneself repeatedly that in the course of the conflict many brave young men lost their lives. Without this sobering reflection, it would be easy to dismiss the conflict as a great farce compounded of stupidity, incompetence, and brag. The British, despite their years of experience against Napoleon, were scarcely more effective than the Americans when they assumed the offensive. They achieved significant success only in the diversionary attack in Chesapeake Bay.

While the main British army was assembling in Canada, 4,000 veterans under General Robert Ross sailed from Bermuda for the Chesapeake. After making a rendezvous with a fleet commanded by Vice-Admiral Sir Alexander Cochrane and Rear Admiral Sir George Cockburn, which had been terrorizing the coast, they landed in Maryland at the mouth of the Patuxent River, southeast of Washington. A squadron of gunboats "protecting" the capital promptly withdrew upstream; when the British pursued, their commander ordered them blown up to keep them from being captured.

The British troops marched rapidly toward Washington. At Bladensburg, on the outskirts of the city, they came upon an army twice their number, commanded by General William H. Winder, a Baltimore lawyer who had already been captured and released by the British in the Canadian fighting. While President Madison and other officials watched, the British charged—and Winder's army turned tail almost without firing a shot. The British swarmed into the capital and put most public buildings to the torch. Before personally setting fire to the White House, Admiral Cockburn took one of the president's hats and a cushion from Dolley Madison's chair as souvenirs and, finding the table set for dinner, derisively drank a toast to "Jemmy's health," adding, an observer coyly recalled, "pleasantries too vulgar for me to repeat."

Harrison's troops charging British artillerists and Indians at the Battle of the Thames. The death of Tecumseh in the battle was a shattering blow to the Indians of the Northwest.

"The Star-Spangled Banner"

This was the sum of the British success. When they attempted to take Baltimore, they were stopped by a formidable line of defenses devised by General Samuel Smith, a militia officer. General Ross fell in the attack. The fleet then moved up the Patapsco River and pounded Fort McHenry with its cannon, raining 1,800 shells on it in a 25-hour bombardment on September 13 and 14. While this attack was in progress, an American civilian, Francis Scott Key, who had been temporarily detained on one of the British ships, watched anxiously through the night. Key had boarded the vessel before the attack in an effort to obtain the release of an American doctor who had been taken into custody in Washington. As twilight faded, Key had seen the Stars and Stripes flying proudly over the battered fort. During the night the glare of rockets and bursting of bombs gave proof that the defenders were holding out. Then, by the first light of the new day, Key saw again the flag, still waving over Fort McHenry.

Drawing an old letter from his pocket, he dashed off the words to "The Star Spangled Banner," which, when set to music, was to become the national anthem of the United States.

To Key that dawn seemed a turning point in the war. He was roughly correct, for in those last weeks of the summer of 1814 the struggle began to move toward resolution. Unable to crack the defenses of Baltimore, the British withdrew to their ships; shortly after, they sailed to Jamaica to join the forces preparing to attack New Orleans.

The destruction of Washington had been a profound shock. Thousands came forward to enlist in the army. The new determination and spirit were strengthened by news from the northern front, where General Sir George Prevost had been leading the main British invasion force south from Montreal. At Plattsburg, on the western shore of Lake Champlain, his 1,000 Redcoats came up against a well-designed defense line manned by 3,300 Americans under General Alexander Macomb. Prevost called up his supporting fleet of four ships and a dozen gunboats. An American fleet of roughly similar strength under Captain Thomas Macdonough, a youthful officer who had served with Decatur against the Barbary pirates, came forward to oppose the British. On September 11, in a brutal battle at point-blank range, Macdonough destroyed the British ships and drove off the gunboats. With the Americans now threatening his flank, Prevost lost heart. Despite his overwhelming numerical superiority, he retreated to Canada.

The Treaty of Ghent

The war might as well have ended with the battles of Plattsburg, Washington, and Baltimore, for later military developments had no effect on the outcome. Earlier in 1814 both sides had agreed to discuss peace terms. Commissioners were appointed and negotiations begun during the summer at Ghent, in Belgium. The American delegation consisted of former secretary of the treasury Albert Gallatin; Speaker Henry Clay of the House of Representatives; James A. Bayard, a former senator; and two veteran diplomats, Jonathan Russell, minister to Sweden, and John Quincy Adams, minister to Russia. Adams was chairman. The British com-

missioners were lesser men by far, partly because they could refer important questions to the Foreign Office in nearby London for decision and partly because Britain's top-flight diplomats were engaged in settling the future of Europe at the Congress of Vienna.

The talks at Ghent were drawn out and frustrating. The British were in no hurry to sign a treaty, believing that their three-pronged offensive in 1814 would swing the balance in their favor. They demanded at first that the United States abandon practically all the Northwest Territory to the Indians and cede other points along the northern border to Canada. As to impressment and neutral rights, they would make no concessions at all. The Americans would yield no territory, for public opinion at home would have been outraged if they had. Old John Adams, for example, told President Madison at this time, "I would continue this war forever rather than surrender an acre."

Fortunately, the British came to realize that by pressing this point they would only spur the Americans to fight on. News of the defeat at Plattsburg modified their ambitions, and when the duke of Wellington advised that from a military point of view they had no case for territorial concessions so long as the United States controlled the Great Lakes, they agreed to settle for status quo antebellum, which is what the Americans sought. The other issues, everyone suddenly realized, had simply evaporated. The mighty war triggered by the French Revolution seemed finally over. The seas were free to all ships, and the Royal Navy no longer had need to snatch sailors from the vessels of the United States or of any other power. On Christmas Eve 1814 the treaty, which merely ended the state of hostilities, was signed. Although, like other members of his family, he was not noted for tact, John Quincy Adams rose to the spirit of the occasion. "I hope," he said, "it will be the last treaty of peace between Great Britain and the United States." And so it was.

The Hartford Convention

Before news of the treaty could cross the Atlantic, two events took place that had important effects yet would not have occurred had the news reached America more rapidly. The first was the Hartford

Convention, a meeting of New England Federalists held in December 1814 and January 1815 to protest the war and to plan for a convention of the states to revise the Constitution.

Sentiment in New England had opposed the war from the beginning. The governor of Massachusetts titled his annual address in 1813 "On the Present Unhappy War," and the General Court went on record calling the conflict "impolitic, improper, and unjust." The Federalist party had been quick to employ the discontent to revive its fortunes. Federalist-controlled state administrations refused to provide militia to aid in the fight and discouraged individuals and banks from lending money to the hard-pressed national government. Trade with the enemy flourished as long as the British fleet did not crack down on New England ports, and goods flowed across the Canadian line in at least as great a volume as during Jefferson's embargo.

Their attitude toward the war made the Federalists even more unpopular with the rest of the country, and this in turn encouraged extremists to talk of seceding from the Union. After Massachusetts summoned the meeting of the Hartford Convention, the fear was widespread that the delegates would propose a New England confederacy, thereby striking at the Union in a moment of great trial.

Luckily for the country, moderate Federalists controlled the convention. They approved a statement that in case of "deliberate, dangerous and palpable infractions of the Constitution" a state has the right "to interpose its authority" to protect itself. This concept, similar to that expressed in the Kentucky and Virginia resolutions by the Republicans when they were in the minority, was accompanied by a list of proposed constitutional amendments designed to make the national government conform more closely to the New England ideal. These would have (1) repealed the Three-fifths Compromise on representation and direct taxes, which favored the slaveholding states, (2) required a two-thirds vote of Congress for the admission of new states and for declaring war, (3) reduced Congress's power to restrict trade by measures such as embargoes, (4) limited presidents to a single term, and (5) made it illegal for naturalized citizens to hold national office.

Nothing formally proposed at Hartford was treasonable, but the proceedings were kept secret, and rumors of impending secession were rife. In this atmosphere came the news from Ghent of an honorable peace. The Federalists had been denouncing the war and predicting a British triumph; now they were discredited.

The Battle of New Orleans

Still more discrediting to Federalists was the second event that would not have happened had communications been more rapid: the Battle of New Orleans. During the fall of 1814 the British had gathered an army at Negril Bay in Jamaica, commanded by Major General Sir Edward Pakenham, brother-in-law of the duke of Wellington. Late in November an armada of 60 ships set out for New Orleans with 11,000 soldiers. Instead of sailing directly up from the mouth of the Mississippi as the Americans expected, Pakenham approached the city by way of Lake Borgne, to the east. Proceeding through a maze of swamps and bayous, he advanced close to the city's gates before being detected. Early on the afternoon of December 23, three mud-spattered local planters burst into the headquarters of General Andrew Jackson, commanding the defenses of New Orleans, with the news.

For once in this war of error and incompetence the United States had the right man in the right place at the right time. After his Revolutionary War experiences, Jackson had studied law, then moved west, settling in Nashville, Tennessee. He served briefly in both houses of Congress and was active in Tennessee affairs. Jackson was a hard man and fierce-tempered, frequently involved in brawls and duels, but he was an honest man and, by western standards, a good public servant. When the war broke out, he was named major general of volunteers. Almost alone among nonprofessional troops during the conflict, his men won impressive victories, crushing the Creek Indians in a series of battles in Alabama.

Jackson's success was due to his toughness and determination, a determination that his biographer Robert Remini describes as "virtually demonic," and "sheer, total, concentrated." Discipline based on fear, respect, and their awareness of his genuine concern for their well-being made his individualistic frontier militiamen into an army. His men called

Jackson Old Hickory; the Indians called him Sharp Knife.

Following these victories, Jackson was assigned the job of defending the Gulf Coast against the expected British strike. Although he had misjudged Pakenham's destination, he was ready when the news of the British arrival reached him. "By the Eternal," he vowed, "they shall not sleep on our soil." "Gentlemen," he told his staff officers, "the British are below; we must fight them tonight."

While the British rested and waited reinforcements, planning to take the city the next morning, Jackson rushed up men and guns. At 7:30 P.M. on December 23 he struck hard, taking the British by surprise. But Pakenham's veterans rallied quickly, and the battle was inconclusive. With Redcoats

Although needless militarily, the American victory at New Orleans stimulated nationalism and made Andrew Jackson a hero overnight. This imaginative view of the battle was printed on a handkerchief.

pouring in from the fleet, Jackson fell back to a point 5 miles below New Orleans and dug in.

He chose his position wisely. On his right was the Mississippi, on his left an impenetrable swamp, to the front an open field. On the day before Christmas (while the commissioners in Ghent were signing the peace treaty), Jackson's army, which included a segregated unit of free black militiamen, erected an earthen parapet about 10 yards behind a dry canal bed. Here the Americans would make their stand.

For two weeks Pakenham probed the American line. Jackson strengthened his defenses daily. At night, patrols of silent Tennesseans slipped out with knife and tomahawk to stalk British sentries. They called this grim business "going hunting." On January 8, 1815, Pakenham ordered an all-out frontal assault. The American position was formidable, but his men had defeated Napoleon. At dawn, through the lowland mists, the Redcoats moved forward with fixed bayonets. Pakenham assumed that the undisciplined Americans—about 4,500 strong—would run at the sight of bare steel.

The Americans did not run. Perhaps they feared the wrath of their commander more than enemy bayonets. Artillery raked the advancing British, and when the range closed to about 150 yards, the riflemen opened up. Jackson had formed his men in three ranks behind the parapet. One rank fired, then stepped down as another took its place. By the time the third had loosed its volley, the first had reloaded and was ready to fire again. Nothing could stand against this rain of lead. General Pakenham was wounded twice, then killed by a shell fragment while calling up his last reserves. During the battle a single brave British officer reached the top of the parapet. When retreat was finally sounded, the British had suffered almost 2,100 casualties, including nearly 300 killed. Thirteen Americans lost their lives, and 58 more were wounded or missing.

Fruits of "Victory"

Word of Jackson's magnificent triumph reached Washington almost simultaneously with the good news from Ghent. People found it easy to confuse the chronology and consider the war a victory won on the battlefield below New Orleans instead of the

standoff it had been. Jackson became the "Hero of New Orleans"; his proud fellow citizens rated his military abilities superior to those of the duke of Wellington, the conqueror of Napoleon. The nation rejoiced. One sour Republican complained that the Federalists of Massachusetts had fired off more powder and wounded more men celebrating the victory than they had during the whole course of the conflict. The Senate ratified the peace treaty unanimously, and the frustrations and failures of the past few years were forgotten. Moreover, American success in holding off Great Britain despite internal frictions went a long way toward convincing European nations that both the United States and its republican form of government were here to stay. The powers might accept these truths with less pleasure than the Americans, but accept them they did.

The nation had suffered relatively few casualties and little economic loss, except to the shipping interests. The Indians were the main losers in the contest. When Jackson defeated the Creeks, for example, he forced them to cede 23 million acres to the United States.

The war completed the destruction of the Federalist party. The success of the Jeffersonians' political techniques had inspired younger Federalists in many parts of the country to adopt the rhetoric of democracy and, more important, to perfect local organizations. In 1812 the party made significant gains in the northeast, electing numbers of congressmen and winning many state and local offices. They did not run a candidate for president, but their support enabled the dissident New York Republican De Witt Clinton to obtain 89 electoral votes to Madison's 128.

Their private correspondence reveals that these Federalists were no more enchanted by the virtues of mass democracy than their elders, but by mouthing democratic slogans they revived the party in many districts. Now the results of the war undermined their efforts. They had not supported the war effort; they had argued that the British could not be defeated; they had dealt clandestinely with the enemy; they had even threatened to break up the Union. So long as the issue remained in doubt, these policies won considerable support, but New Orleans made the party an object of ridicule and scorn. It soon disappeared even in New England, swamped beneath a wave of patriotism that flooded the land.

The chief reason for the happy results of the war had little to do with American events. After 1815 Europe settled down to what was to be a century of relative peace. With peace came an end to serious foreign threats to America and a revival of commerce. European emigration to the United States, long held back by the troubled times, spurted ahead, providing the expanding country with its most valuable asset—strong, willing hands to do the work of developing the land. The mood of Jefferson's first term, when democracy had reigned amid peace and plenty, returned with a rush. And the nation, having had its fill of international complications, turned in on itself as Jefferson had wished. The politicians, ever sensitive to public attitudes, had learned what seemed at the time a valuable lesson. Foreign affairs were a potent cause of domestic conflict. The volatile character of sectional politics was thus another reason why America should escape from involvement in European affairs.

Anglo-American Rapprochement

There remained a few matters to straighten out with Great Britain, Spain, and Europe generally. Since no territory had changed hands at Ghent, neither signatory had reason to harbor a grudge. There was no sudden flowering of Anglo-American friendship. British conservatives continued, in the words of the historian George Dangerfield, to view the United States as "little more than a grimy republican thumbprint" on the pages of history, and the device of "twisting the British lion's tail" remained an important tool in the workchest of many an American politician for the rest of the century. Yet for years no serious trouble marred Anglo-American relations. The war had taught the British to respect Americans, if not to love them.

In this atmosphere the two countries worked out peaceful solutions to a number of old problems. American trade was becoming ever more important to the British, that of the sugar islands less so. In July 1815 they therefore signed a commercial convention ending discriminatory duties and making other adjustments favorable to trade. Boundary dif-

ficulties also moved toward resolution. At Ghent the diplomats had created several joint commissions to settle the disputed boundary between the United States and Canada. Many years were to pass before the line was finally drawn, but establishing the principle of defining the border by negotiation was important. In time, a line extending over 3,000 miles was agreed to without the firing of a single shot.

Immediately after the war the British reinforced their garrisons in Canada and began to rebuild their shattered Great Lakes fleet. The United States took similar steps. But both nations found the cost of rearming more than they cared to bear. When the United States suggested demilitarizing the lakes, the British agreed. The Rush-Bagot Agreement of 1817 limited each country to one 100-ton vessel armed with a single 18-pounder on Lake Champlain and another on Lake Ontario. They were to have two each for all the other Great Lakes.

Gradually, as an outgrowth of this decision, the entire border was demilitarized, a remarkable achievement. In the convention of 1818 the two countries agreed to the 49th parallel as the northern boundary of Louisiana Territory between Lake of the Woods and the Rockies and also to the joint control of the Oregon country for ten years. The question of the rights of Americans in the Labrador and Newfoundland fisheries, which had been much disputed during the Ghent negotiations, was settled amicably.

The Transcontinental Treaty

The acquisition of Spanish Florida and the settlement of the western boundary of Louisiana were also accomplished as an aftermath of the War of 1812, but in a far different spirit. Spain's control of the Floridas was feeble. West Florida had passed into American hands by 1813, and frontiersmen in Georgia were eyeing East Florida greedily. Indians struck frequently into American territory from Florida, then fled to sanctuary across the line. American slaves who escaped across the border could not be recovered. In 1818 James Monroe, who had been elected president in 1816, ordered General Andrew Jackson to clear raiding Seminole Indians from American soil and to pursue them into Florida if necessary. Seizing on these instructions, Jackson marched into Florida and easily captured two Spanish forts.

Although Jackson eventually withdrew from Florida, the impotence of the Spanish government made it obvious even in Madrid that if nothing were done, the United States would soon fill the power vacuum by seizing the territory. The Spanish also feared for the future of their tottering Latin American empire, especially the northern provinces of Mexico, which stood in the path of American westward expansion. Spain and the United States had never determined where Louisiana Territory ended and Spanish Mexico began. In return for American acceptance of a boundary as far east of the Rio Grande as possible, Spain was ready to surrender Florida.

For these reasons the Spanish minister in Washington, Luis de Onís, undertook in December 1817 to negotiate a treaty with John Quincy Adams, Monroe's secretary of state. Adams pressed the minister mercilessly on the question of the western boundary, driving a bargain that would have done credit to the most tightfisted of his Yankee ancestors. Onís opened their talks by proposing a line in the middle of what is now Louisiana, and when Adams countered by demanding a boundary running through present-day Texas, Onís professed to be shocked. Abstract right, not power, should determine the settlement, he said. "Truth is of all times, and reason and justice are founded upon immutable principles." To this Adams replied: "That truth is of all times and that reason and justice are founded upon

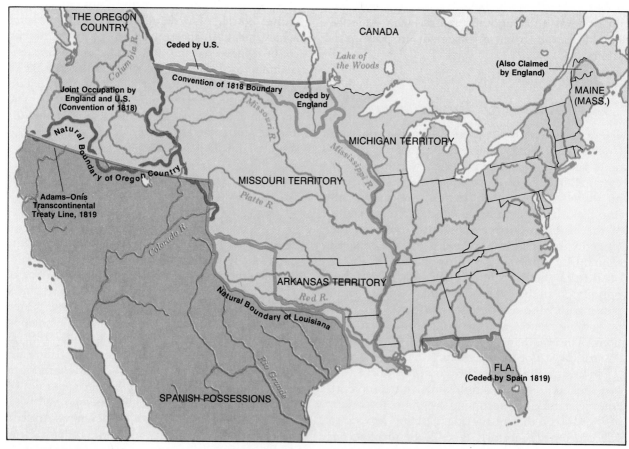

THE UNITED STATES, 1819

immutable principles has never been contested by the United States, but neither truth, reason, nor justice consists in stubbornness of assertion, nor in the multiplied repetition of error."

In the end Onís could only yield. He saved Texas for his monarch but accepted a boundary to Louisiana Territory that followed the Sabine, Red, and Arkansas rivers to the Continental Divide and the 42nd parallel to the Pacific, thus abandoning Spain's claim to a huge area beyond the Rockies that had no connection at all with the Louisiana Purchase. Adams even compelled him to agree that when the boundary followed rivers, United States territory was to extend to the farthest bank, not merely to midstream. The United States obtained Florida in return for a mere $5 million, paid not to Spain but to Americans who held claims against the Spanish government.

This "Transcontinental Treaty" was signed in 1819, though ratification was delayed until 1821. Most Americans at the time thought the acquisition of Florida the most important part of the treaty, but Adams, whose vision of America's future was truly continental, knew better. "The acquisition of a definite line of boundary to the [Pacific] forms a great epoch in our history," he recorded in his diary.

The Monroe Doctrine

Concern with defining the boundaries of the United States did not reflect a desire to limit expansion; rather, the feeling was that there should be no more quibbling and quarreling with foreign powers that might distract the people from the great task of national development. The classic enunciation of this point of view, the completion of America's withdrawal from Europe, was the Monroe Doctrine.

Two separate strands met in this pronouncement. The first led from Moscow to Alaska and down the Pacific Coast to the Oregon country. Beginning with the explorations of Vitus Bering in 1741, the Russians had maintained an interest in fishing and fur trading along the northwest coast of North America. In 1821 the czar extended his claim south to the 51st parallel and forbade the ships of other powers to enter coastal waters north of that point. This announcement was disturbing.

The second strand ran from the courts of the European monarchs to Latin America. Between 1817 and 1822 practically all of the region from the Rio Grande to the Strait of Magellan had won its independence. Spain, former master of nearly all the area except Brazil, was too weak to win it back by force, but Austria, Prussia, France, and Russia decided at the Congress of Verona in 1822 to try to regain the area for Spain in the interests of "legitimacy." There was talk of sending a large French army to South America. This possibility also caused grave concern in Washington.

To the Russian threat, Monroe and Secretary of State Adams responded with a terse warning: "The American continents are no longer subjects for any new European colonial establishments." This statement did not impress the Russians, but they had no intention of colonizing the region. In 1824 they signed a treaty with the United States abandoning all claims below the present southern limit of Alaska (54° 40′ north latitude) and removing their restrictions on foreign shipping.

The Latin American problem was more complex. The United States was not alone in its alarm at the prospect of a revival of French or Spanish power in that region. Great Britain, having profited greatly from the breakup of the mercantilistic Spanish empire by developing a thriving commerce with the new republics, had no intention of permitting a restoration of the old order. But the British monarchy preferred not to recognize the new revolutionary South American republics, for England itself was only beginning to recover from a period of social upheaval as violent as any in its history. Bad times and high food prices had combined to cause riots, conspiracies, and angry demands for parliamentary reform.

In 1823 the British foreign minister, George Canning, suggested to the American minister in London that the United States and Britain issue a joint statement opposing any French interference in South America, pledging that they themselves would never annex any part of Spain's old empire, and saying nothing about recognition of the new republics. This proposal of joint action with the British was flattering to the United States but scarcely in its best interests. The United States had already recognized the new republics, and it had no desire to help Great Britain retain its South American trade. As Secretary Adams pointed out, to agree to the proposal would be to abandon the possibility of someday adding Cuba or any other part of Latin America to the United States. America should act independently, Adams urged. "It would be more candid, as well as more dignified, to avow our principles explicitly . . . than to come in as a cockboat in the wake of the British man-of-war."

Monroe heartily endorsed Adams's argument and decided to include a statement of American policy in his annual message to Congress in December 1823. "The American continents," he wrote,

"by the free and independent condition which they have assumed and maintain, are henceforth not to be considered as subjects for future colonization by any European powers." Europe's political system was "essentially different" from that developing in the New World, and the two should not be mixed. The United States would not interfere with existing European colonies in North or South America and would avoid involvement in strictly European affairs, but any attempt to extend European control to countries in the hemisphere that had already won

The thirty years from 1790 to 1820 saw a sizable increase in population. The growth was especially great in the decade from 1810 to 1820, with a 33.1 percent increase in national population. Some of the largest increases were in what was earlier called the Old Northwest; the population of the area making up Illinois, Indiana, and Michigan territories, for example, grew from 31,000 to more than 200,000 during that decade.

POPULATION DENSITY, 1790

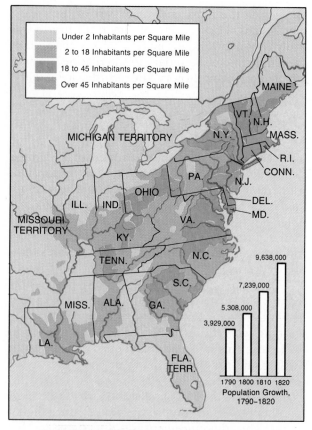

POPULATION DENSITY, 1820

their independence would be considered, Monroe warned, "the manifestation of an unfriendly disposition toward the United States" and consequently a threat to the nation's "peace and safety."

This policy statement—it was not dignified with the title Monroe Doctrine until decades later—attracted little notice in Europe or Latin America and not much more at home. Obviously, the United States, whose own capital had been overrun by a mere raiding party less than a decade before, could not police the entire Western Hemisphere. European statesmen dismissed Monroe's message as "arrogant" and "blustering," worthy only of "the most profound contempt." Latin Americans, while appreciating the intent behind it, knew better than to count on American aid in case of attack.

Nevertheless, the principles laid down by President Monroe so perfectly expressed the wishes of the people of the United States that when the country grew powerful enough to enforce them, there was little need to alter or embellish his pronouncement. However understood at the time, the doctrine may be seen as the final stage in the evolution of American independence.

From this perspective, the famous Declaration of 1776 merely began a process of separation and self-determination. The peace treaty ending the Revolutionary War was a further step, and Washington's neutrality proclamation of 1793 was another, demonstrating as it did the capacity of the United States to determine its own best interests despite the treaty of alliance with France. The removal of British troops from the northwest forts, achieved by the Jay Treaty, marked the next stage. Then the Louisiana Purchase made a further advance toward true independence by assuring that the Mississippi River could not be closed to the commerce so vital to the development of the western territories. The standoff War of 1812 ended any lingering British hope of regaining control of America, and the Transcontinental Treaty pushed the last European power from the path of westward expansion. Monroe's doctrine was a kind of public announcement that the sovereign United States had completed its independence and wanted nothing better than to be left alone to concentrate on its own development. Better yet if Europe could be made to allow the entire hemisphere to follow its own path.

The Era of Good Feelings

The person who gave his name to the so-called doctrine was an unusually lucky man. James Monroe lived a long life in good health and saw close up most of the great events in the history of the young republic. At the age of 18 he shed his blood for liberty at the glorious Battle of Trenton. He was twice governor of Virginia, a United States senator, and a Cabinet member. He was at various times the nation's representative in Paris, Madrid, and London. Elected president in 1816, his good fortune continued. The world was finally at peace, the country united and prosperous. A person of good feeling who would keep a steady hand on the helm and hold to the present course seemed called for, and Monroe possessed exactly the qualities that the times required. "He is a man whose soul might be turned wrongside outwards, without discovering a blemish," Jefferson said, and John Quincy Adams, a harsh critic of most public figures, praised Monroe's courtesy, sincerity, and sound judgment.

Courtesy and purity of soul do not always suffice to make a good president. In more troubled times Monroe might well have brought disaster, for he was neither a person of outstanding intellect nor a forceful leader. He blazed few paths, built no personal machine. Speaking of his policies and beliefs, the historian Ernest R. May concluded: "None was unique to Monroe." May added that Monroe had "less than total confidence in his opinions." The Monroe Doctrine, by far the most significant achievement of his administration, was as much the work of Secretary of State Adams as his own. No one ever claimed that Monroe was much better than second-rate, yet when his first term ended, he was reelected without organized opposition.

Monroe seemed to epitomize the resolution of the conflicts that had divided the country between the end of the Revolution and the Peace of Ghent. In his long career he was always a nationalist—his biographer Harry Ammon has subtitled the story of Monroe's life "The Quest for National Identity."

By 1817 the divisive issues of earlier days had vanished. Monroe dramatized their disappearance by beginning his first term with a goodwill tour of New England, heartland of the opposition. The tour was a triumph. Everywhere the president was greeted with tremendous enthusiasm. After he visited Boston, once the headquarters and now the graveyard of Federalism, a Federalist newspaper, the *Columbian Centinel*, gave the age its name. Pointing out that the celebrations attending Monroe's visit had brought together in friendly intercourse many persons "whom party politics had long severed," it dubbed the times the Era of Good Feelings.

It has often been said that the harmony of Monroe's administrations was superficial, that beneath the calm lay potentially disruptive issues that had not yet begun to influence national politics. The dramatic change from the unanimity of Monroe's second election to the fragmentation of four years later, when four candidates divided the vote and the House of Representatives had to choose the president, supports the point.

Nevertheless, the people of the period had good reasons for thinking it extraordinarily harmonious. Peace, prosperity, liberty, and progress—all flourished in 1817 in the United States. The heirs of Jefferson had accepted, with a mixture of resignation and enthusiasm, most of the economic policies advocated by the Hamiltonians. In 1816 Madison put his signature to a bill creating a new national bank almost exactly in the image of Hamilton's, which had expired before the War of 1812, and to a protective tariff that, if less comprehensive than the kind Hamilton had wanted, marked an important concession to rising manufacturing interests. Monroe accepted the principle of federal aid for transportation projects, approving a bill authorizing Congress to invest $300,000 in the Chesapeake and Delaware Canal Company.

The Jeffersonian balance between individual liberty and responsible government, having survived both bad management and war, had justified itself to the opposition. The new unity was symbolized by the restored friendship of Jefferson and John Adams. In 1801 Adams had slipped sulkily out of Washington without waiting to attend his successor's inauguration, but after ten years of stony silence, the two old collaborators, abetted by Dr. Benjamin Rush, effected a reconciliation. Although they continued to disagree vigorously about matters of philosophy and government, the bitterness between them disappeared entirely. By Monroe's day, Jefferson was writing long letters to "my dear friend," ranging over such subjects as theology, the proper reading of the classics, and agricultural improvements and was receiving equally warm and voluminous replies. "Whether you or I were right," Adams wrote amiably to Jefferson, "Posterity must judge."

When political divisions appeared again, as they soon did, it was not because the old balance had been shaky. Few of the new controversies challenged Republican principles or revived old issues. Instead, these controversies were children of the present and the future, products of the continuing growth of the country.

Milestones

1808 James Madison elected president
1809 Nonintercourse Act
1810 Macon's Bill No. 2
1811 Battle of Tippecanoe
1812 Congress declares war on Great Britain
Naval victories of U.S.S. *Constitution* and U.S.S. *United States*
1813 Battle of Lake Erie
Battle of the Thames, death of Tecumseh
1814 British burn Washington, D.C.

Francis Scott Key writes "The Star Spangled Banner" during the bombardment of Fort McHenry by the British
Hartford Convention
Treaty of Ghent officially ends the War of 1812
1815 Battle of New Orleans
1817 Rush-Bagot Agreement with Great Britain
1819 Transcontinental Treaty with Spain
1823 Monroe Doctrine

SUPPLEMENTARY READING

Titles marked with an asterisk have been published in paperback.

Madison's administration can be followed in Irving Brant, **James Madison: The President** (1956), and Ralph Ketcham, **James Madison** (1971). J. W. Pratt first played up the role of the west in triggering the War of 1812 in his **Expansionists of 1812** (1925). The best modern account of the causes and course of the war is J. C. A. Stagg, **Mr. Madison's War** (1983); a good brief treatment is H. L. Coles, **The War of 1812*** (1965). Irving Brant, **James Madison: Commander in Chief** (1961), vigorously defends Madison's handling of the war. Jackson's part in the conflict is described in R. V. Remini, **Andrew Jackson and the Course of American Empire** (1977).

On the Treaty of Ghent, see F. L. Engelman, **The Peace of Christmas Eve** (1962). Bradford Perkins, **Castlereagh and Adams** (1964), and George Dangerfield, **The Era of Good Feelings*** (1952), also discuss the settlement intelligently. On the decline of the Federalist party and the Hartford Convention, consult D. H. Fischer, **The Revolution of American Conservatism** (1965), and J. M. Banner, **To the Hartford Convention** (1981).

On the postwar diplomatic settlements and the Era of Good Feelings, see E. R. May, **The Making of the Monroe Doctrine** (1975), Perkins's **Castlereagh and Adams,** S. F. Bemis, **John Quincy Adams** (1949), Dangerfield's **Era of Good Feelings,** and Harry Ammon, **James Monroe: The Quest for National Identity** (1971).

VIII

The Cords of Union

Our confederacy comprehends within its vast limits, great diversity of interests; agricultural, planting, farming, commercial, navigating, fishing, manufacturing. . . . Some of these are peculiar to particular sections of the country. But all these great interests are confided to the protection of one government—to the fate of one ship; and a most gallant ship it is, with a noble crew.

HENRY CLAY, *1824*

N ational unity speeded national expansion, yet expansion, paradoxically, endangered national unity. For as the country grew, new differences appeared within its sections even as the ties binding the parts became stronger and more numerous. Growth in the 30 years after the ratification of the Constitution had been phenomenal even for a country that took growth for granted. The area of the United States doubled, but very little of the Louisiana Purchase had been settled by 1820. More significant, the population of the nation had more than doubled, from 4 million to 9.6 million. The pace of westward movement had also quickened; by 1820 more than 2.2 million people had settled in the Mississippi Valley, and the moving edge of the frontier ran in a long, irregular curve from Michigan to Arkansas.

Perhaps the most remarkable feature of this growth was that nearly all of it resulted from natural increase. Only about 250,000 immigrants entered the United States between 1790 and 1820, for the turbulent conditions in Europe during the wars had slowed the flow of humanity across the Atlantic to a trickle.

Sectional Issues: Tariff Policy

The War of 1812 and the depression that struck the country in 1819 shaped many of the controversies that agitated political life during the Era of Good Feelings. The tariff question was affected by both. Before the War of 1812 the level of duties averaged about 12.5 percent of the value of dutiable products, but to meet the added expenses occasioned by the conflict, Congress doubled all tariffs. In 1816, when the revenue was no longer needed, a new act kept duties close to wartime levels. Infant industries that had grown up during the years of embargo, nonintercourse, and war were able to exert considerable pressure, for they could show that imports had rocketed from $12 million in 1814 to $113 million in 1815 and were still rising. The act especially favored textiles because the British were dumping cloth in America at bargain prices in their attempt to regain lost markets. The depression added to the strength of the protectionists. Unemployed workers and many farmers became convinced that prosperity would return only if American industry were shielded against foreign competition.

There was backing for high duties in every section. Except for New England, where the shipping interests favored free trade and where the booming mills of the Boston Associates were not seriously injured by foreign competition, the North favored protection. A few southerners hoped that textile mills would spring up in their region; more supported protection on the grounds that national self-sufficiency was necessary in case of war. In the West small manufacturers in the towns added their support, and so did farmers, who were counting on workers in the new eastern factories to consume much of their wheat and corn and hogs. But with the passage of time the South rejected protection almost completely. Industry failed to develop, and since southerners exported most of their cotton and tobacco, they soon concluded that besides increasing the cost of nearly everything they bought, high duties on imports would limit the foreign market for southern staples by inhibiting international exchange. As this fact became clear, the West tended to divide on the tariff question: The Northwest and much of Kentucky, which had a special interest in protecting its considerable hemp production, fa-

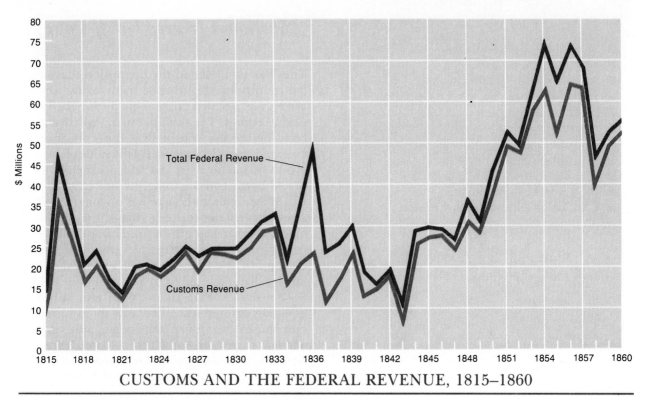

CUSTOMS AND THE FEDERAL REVENUE, 1815–1860

In some years—1841, for example—the amounts received from customs duties supplied nearly all the federal revenues, so it is no surprise that the tariff was a major political and sectional issue in the years between the War of 1812 and the Civil War. The jump in federal revenues in the mid-1830s, over and above the usual customs duties, was caused largely by increased public land sales (see chart on page 271).

vored high duties; the Southwest, where cotton was the major crop, favored low duties.

Sectional Issues: Banks

National banking policy was another important political issue affected by the war and the depression. Presidents Jefferson and Madison had managed to live with the Bank of the United States despite its dubious constitutionality, but its charter was not renewed when it expired in 1811. Aside from the constitutional question, the major opposition to recharter came from state banks eager to take over the business of the Bank for themselves. The fact

that English investors owned most of the Bank's stock (the government had sold 2,200 shares to the British banking house of Baring Brothers in 1802) was also used as an argument against recharter.

The war played havoc with American banking. Many more state banks were created after 1811, and most extended credit recklessly. When the British raid on Washington and Baltimore in 1814 sent panicky depositors scurrying to convert their deposits into gold or silver, the overextended financiers could not oblige them. All banks outside New England suspended specie payments; that is, they stopped exchanging their bank notes for hard money on demand. Paper money immediately fell in value; a paper dollar was soon worth only 85 cents in coin in Philadelphia, less in Baltimore. Government business also suffered from the absence of a national bank. In October 1814 Secretary of the Treasury Alexander J. Dallas submitted a plan for a second Bank of the United States, and after considerable wrangling over its precise form, the institution was authorized in April 1816.

The new Bank was much larger than its predecessor, being capitalized at $35 million. However, unlike Hamilton's creation, it was badly managed at the start. Its first president, William Jones, a former secretary of the navy, was as inept as he was easygoing. He displayed, according to the historian George Dangerfield, "a kindheartedness which, in his new position, was tantamount to corruption." All kinds of chicanery went on under Jones's nose. According to the charter, no shareholder could have more than 30 votes, regardless of the number of shares owned, yet one director who owned 1,172 shares registered each in a different name, with himself as "attorney" for all, and successfully cast 1,172 votes at meetings. More important, Jones allowed his institution to join in the irresponsible creation of credit. By the summer of 1818 the Bank's 18 branches had issued notes in excess of ten times their specie reserves, far more than was prudent, considering the Bank's responsibilities. When depression struck the country in 1819, the Bank of the United States was as hard pressed as many of the state banks. Jones resigned.

The new president, Langdon Cheves of South Carolina, was as rigid as Jones had been permissive. During the bad times, when easy credit was needed, he pursued a policy of stern curtailment. The Bank thus regained a sound position at the expense of hardship to borrowers. "The Bank was saved," the contemporary economist William Gouge wrote somewhat hyperbolically, "and the people were ruined." Just at the time when John Marshall was establishing its constitutionality, it reached a low point in public favor. Irresponsible state banks resented it, as did the advocates of hard money.

Regional lines were less sharply drawn on the Bank issue than on the tariff. Northern congressmen voted against the Bank 53 to 44 in 1816—many of them because they objected to the particular proposal, not because they were against any national bank. Those from other sections favored it, 58 to 30. The collapse occasioned by the Panic of 1819 produced further opposition to the institution in the West.

Sectional Issues: Land Policy

Land policy also caused sectional controversy. No one wished to eliminate the system of survey and sale, but there was continuous pressure to reduce the price of public land and the minimum unit offered for sale. The Land Act of 1800 set $2 an acre as the minimum price and 320 acres (a half section) as the smallest unit. Buyers could pay for the land in four annual installments, which meant that one needed only $160 to take possession of a good-sized farm. In 1804 the minimum was cut to 160 acres, which could be had for about $80 down, roughly a quarter of what the average artisan could earn in a year.

Since banks were pursuing an easy-credit policy, land sales boomed. The outbreak of the War of 1812 caused a temporary slump, but by 1814 sales had reached an all-time high and were increasing rapidly. Postwar prices of agricultural products were excellent, for the seas were now free and European agriculture had not yet recovered from the ravages of the Napoleonic wars. In 1818 the government sold nearly 3.5 million acres. Thereafter, continuing expansion and the rapid shrinkage of the foreign market as European farmers resumed production led to disaster. Prices fell, the panic struck, and western debtors were forced to the wall by the hundreds.

Sectional attitudes toward the public lands were fairly straightforward. The West wanted cheap land; the North and South tended to regard the national domain as an asset that should be converted into as much cash as possible. Northern manufacturers feared that cheap land in the West would drain off surplus labor and force wages up, while southern planters were concerned about the competition that would develop when the virgin lands of the Southwest were put to the plow to make cotton. The West, however, was ready to fight to the last line of defense over land policy, while the other regions would usually compromise on the issue to gain support for their own vital interests. Sectional alignments on the question of internal improvements were almost identical, but this issue, soon to become very important, had not greatly agitated national affairs before 1820. The only significant federal internal improvement project undertaken before that date was the National Road.

Sectional Issues: Slavery

The most divisive sectional issue was slavery. After the compromises affecting the "peculiar institution" made at the Constitutional Convention, it caused remarkably little conflict in national politics before 1819. Although the importation of blacks rose in the 1790s, Congress abolished the African slave trade in 1808 without major incident. As the nation expanded, free and slave states were added to the Union in equal numbers, Ohio, Indiana, and Illinois being balanced by Louisiana, Mississippi, and Alabama. In 1819 there were 22 states, 11 slave and 11 free. The expansion of slavery occasioned by the cotton boom led southerners to support it more aggressively, which tended to irritate many northerners, but most persons considered slavery mainly a local issue. To the extent that it was a national question, the North opposed it and the South defended it ardently. The West leaned toward the southern point of view, for in addition to the southwestern slave states, the Northwest was sympathetic, partly because much of its produce was sold on southern plantations and partly because at least half of its early settlers came from Virginia, Kentucky, and other slave states.

Northern Leaders

By 1824 the giants of the Revolutionary generation had completed their work. Washington, Hamilton, Franklin, Samuel Adams, Patrick Henry, and most of their peers were dead. John Adams (88), Thomas Jefferson (81), and James Madison (73) were passing their declining years quietly on their ancestral acres, full of memories and sage advice but no longer active in national affairs. In every section new leaders had come forward, men shaped by the past but chiefly concerned with the present. Quite suddenly, between the war and the panic, they had inherited power. They would shape the future of the United States.

John Quincy Adams was the best-known political leader of the North in the early 1820s. Just completing his brilliant work as secretary of state under Monroe, he had behind him a record of public service dating to the Confederation period. At 11 he was giving English lessons to the French minister to the Continental Congress and his secretary. ("He shows us no mercy and makes us no compliments," the minister remarked.) While in his teens he served as secretary of legation in Russia and Great Britain. Later he was American minister to the Netherlands and to Prussia and a Federalist United States senator from Massachusetts. Then he gradually switched to the Republican point of view, supporting the Louisiana Purchase and even the Embargo Act. His work at Ghent on the peace commission and as Madison's secretary of state has already been mentioned.

Adams was farsighted, imaginative, hardworking, and extremely intelligent, but he was inept in personal relations. He had all the virtues and most of the defects of the Puritan, being suspicious both of others and of himself. He suffered in two ways from being his father's child: As the son of a president, he was under severe pressure to live up to the Adams name, and his father expected a great deal of him. When the boy was only 7, John Adams wrote his wife: "Train [the children] to virtue. Habituate them to industry, activity, and spirit. Make them consider vice as shameful and unmanly. Fire them with ambition to be useful. . . . Fix their ambition upon great and solid objects, and their contempt upon little, frivolous and useless ones."

Such training made John Quincy an indefatigable worker. Even in winter he normally rose at 5 A.M., and he could never convince himself that most of his associates were not lazy dolts. He was tense, compulsive, conscience-ridden. He set a standard no one could meet and consequently was continually dissatisfied with himself. As one of his grandsons remarked, "He was disappointed because he was not supernatural." Toward enemies he was merciless and overwhelming, toward friends inspiring but demanding.

Like his father, John Quincy Adams was a strong nationalist. While New England was still antiprotectionist, he was at least open-minded on the subject of high tariffs. He supported the second Bank of the United States, and unlike most easterners, he believed that the federal government should spend freely on roads and canals in the West. To slavery he was, like most New Englanders, personally opposed. As Monroe's second term drew toward its close, Adams seemed one of the most likely candidates to succeed him, and at this period his ambition to be president was his great failing. He said he would like to be elected because it would please his father, but he did not deny that being president would please him too. His ambition led him to make certain compromises with his principles, which in turn plagued his oversensitive conscience and had a corrosive effect on his peace of mind.

Daniel Webster was recognized as one of the coming leaders of New England. Born in New Hampshire in 1782, he graduated from Dartmouth College in 1801, and by the time of the War of 1812 he had made a local reputation as a lawyer and orator. After serving two terms in Congress during the conflict, he moved to Boston to concentrate on his legal practice. He soon became one of the leading constitutional lawyers of the country. In 1823 he was again elected to Congress.

Webster owed much of his reputation to his formidable presence and his oratorical skill. Dark, large-headed, craggy of brow, with deep-set, brooding eyes and a firm mouth, he projected a remarkable appearance of heroic power and moral strength. His thunderous voice, his resourceful vocabulary, his manner—all backed by the mastery of every oratorical trick—made him unique. "He . . . is never averse, whilst traversing the thorny paths of political disputation," one contemporary admirer recorded, "to scatter the flowers of rhetorical elegance around him."

Webster had a first-rate mind, powerful and logical. His faults were largely those of temperament. He was too fond of good food and fine broadcloth, of alcohol and adulation. Hard work over an extended period of time was beyond him; generally he bestirred himself only with great effort and then usually to advance his own cause. Webster could have been a lighthouse in the night, guiding his fellow citizens to safe harbor. More often he was a weather vane, shifting to accommodate the strongest breeze. The good opinion of "the best people" meant so much to him that he rarely used his gifts to shape and guide that opinion in the national interest.

Unlike the independent-minded Adams, Web-

ster nearly always reflected the beliefs of the dominant business interests of New England. His opposition to the embargo and the War of 1812 got him into Congress, where he faithfully supported the views of New England merchants. He opposed the high tariff of 1816 because the merchants favored free trade, and he voted against establishing the Bank chiefly on partisan grounds. (His view changed when the Bank hired him as its lawyer.) He was against cheap land and federal construction of internal improvements. His opposition to slavery accorded with the opinion of most of his constituents, but on this question he stood more solidly for principle. Basically he was a nationalist (as was seen in his arguments before the Supreme Court), yet he sometimes allowed political expediency and the prejudices of New England to obscure his feelings. Ahead of him lay fame and considerable construc-

Eyes like "anthracite furnaces," the English historian Thomas Carlyle remarked of Daniel Webster; this is the "Black Dan" portrait by Francis Alexander.

His ready wit and cheerful disposition made Martin Van Buren immensely likable in spite of the intensity of his political ambitions.

tive service but also bitter frustration. And one hour of greatness.

New York's man of the future was a little sandy-haired politico named Martin Van Buren. The Red Fox, as he was called, was one of the most talented politicians ever to play a part in American affairs. He was clever and hardworking, but his mind and his energy were always devoted to some political purpose. From 1812 to 1820 he served in the state legislature; in 1820 he was elected United States senator.

Van Buren had great charm and immense tact. By nature affable, he never allowed partisanship to mar his personal relationships with other leaders. The historian Richard Hofstadter once described him as the type of politician whose influence "comes in large part out of his taste for political association, his liking for people, and his sportsmanlike ability to experience political conflict without taking it as

ground for personal rancor." The members of his political machine, known as the Albany Regency, were almost fanatically loyal to him, and even his enemies could seldom dislike him as a person.

Somehow Van Buren could reconcile deviousness with honesty. He "rowed to his objective with muffled oars," as Randolph of Roanoke said, yet he was neither crooked nor venal. Politics for him was like a game or a complex puzzle: The object was victory, but one must play by the rules or lose all sense of achievement. Only a fool will cheat at solitaire, and despite his gregariousness, Van Buren was at heart a solitary operator.

His positions on the issues of the 1820s are hard to determine because he never took a position if he could avoid doing so. In part this was his politician's desire to straddle every fence; it also reflected his quixotic belief that issues were means rather than ends in the world of politics. He opposed rechartering the first Bank yet was not conspicuous among those who fought the second. He did not oppose internal improvements. No one could say with assurance what he thought about the tariff, and since slavery did not arouse much interest in New York, it is safe to suppose that at this time he had no opinion at all about the institution. Any intelligent observer in the 1820s would have predicted that "the Little Magician" would go far, for he was obviously a master of his craft. How far, and in what direction, no one could have guessed.

Southern Leaders

The most prominent southern leader was William H. Crawford, Monroe's secretary of the treasury. Born in 1772 in the shadow of Virginia's Blue Ridge, he was taken to the Deep South while still a lad, settling finally in Georgia. A giant of a man, ruddy-faced and strong jawed, he became a leader of the conservative faction in the state, speaking for the large planters against the interests of the yeomen farmers. Following service in the legislature, he was elected to the Senate in 1807. Later he put in a tour of duty as minister to France, and in 1816 he was appointed secretary of the treasury.

Crawford was direct and friendly, a marvelous storyteller, and one of the few persons in Washington who could teach the fledgling senator Martin

The striking portrait of John C. Calhoun was painted sometime between 1818 and 1825, probably by Charles Bird King. The handsome Calhoun was in his thirties.

Van Buren anything about politics. Van Buren supported him enthusiastically in the contest for the 1824 presidential nomination. (So, although not publicly, did Jefferson and Madison.) Crawford was one of the first politicians to try to build a national machine. "Crawford's Act" of 1820, limiting the term of minor federal appointees to four years, was passed, as the name suggests, largely through his efforts, for he realized before nearly anyone else that a handful of petty offices, properly distributed, could win the allegiance of thousands of voters.

Crawford had something interesting to say on most of the important issues of the times. Although predisposed toward the states' rights position, he favored recharter of the Bank and was willing to go along with a moderately protective tariff. During the depression that began in 1819 he devised an excellent relief plan for farmers who were unable to meet installment payments due on land purchased from the government. He suggested a highly original scheme for a flexible paper currency not convertible into hard money.

Crawford was controversial. Many of his contemporaries considered him no more than a cynical spoilsman, though his administration of the treasury was first-rate. Yet he had many friends. His ambition was vast, his power great. Fate, however, was about to strike Crawford a crippling blow.

John C. Calhoun, the other outstanding southern leader, was born in South Carolina in 1782 and graduated from Yale in 1804. He studied law at Tapping Reeve's remarkable law school in Litchfield, Connecticut, which in half a century turned out 15 future United States senators, 10 governors, 2 Supreme Court justices, and a number of other men prominent in public affairs. Calhoun served in the South Carolina legislature and, beginning in 1811, in Congress. A prominent War Hawk, he took a strong nationalist position on all the issues of the day. In 1817 Monroe made him secretary of war.

Although devoted to the South and its institutions, Calhoun took the broadest possible view of political affairs. "Our true system is . . . to support such measures and such men, without regard to sections, as are best calculated to advance the general interest," he said in 1820. John Quincy Adams, seldom charitable in his private opinions of colleagues (he called Crawford "a worm" and Henry Clay a "gamester" with an "undigested system of ethics"), praised Calhoun's "quick understanding" and "enlarged philosophic views" and considered him "above all sectional and factional prejudices."

Calhoun was intelligent, bookish, and given to the study of abstractions. Basically a gentle person, he was cold and restrained in most of his relationships. He had no hobbies and was utterly humorless. Legend has it that he once tried to write a poem but after putting down the word *Whereas* gave it up as beyond his powers. Some obscure failing made it impossible for him to grasp the essence of the human condition. An English observer once said that Calhoun had "an imperfect acquaintance with human nature." Yet he burned to lead his fellows. Few contemporaries could maintain themselves in debate against his powerful intelligence, yet that mind—so sharp, so penetrating—was the blind bondsman of his ambition.

This portrait of Henry Clay was completed in 1824, when he was Speaker of the House. An unidentified artist painted it after a portrait by John Neagle.

Western Leaders

The outstanding western leader of the 1820s was Henry Clay of Kentucky, one of the most charming and colorful of American statesmen. Tall, lean, gray-eyed, Clay was the kind of person who made men cheer and women swoon. On the platform he ranked with Webster; behind the political scenes he was the peer of Van Buren. In every environment he was warm and open—what a modern political scientist might call a charismatic personality. Clay loved to drink, swear, tell tales, and play poker. It was characteristic that at one sitting he won $40,000 from a friend and then cheerfully told him that a note for $500 would wipe out the obligation. He was a reasonable man, skilled at arranging political compromises, but he possessed a reckless streak: Like so many westerners, his sense of honor was

exaggerated. Twice in his career he called men out for having insulted him. Fortunately, all concerned were poor shots.

After some years in the Kentucky legislature, Clay was elected to Congress in 1810. He led the War Hawks in 1811 and 1812 and was Speaker of the House from 1811 to 1820 and from 1823 to 1825.

Clay was intellectually the inferior of Adams and Calhoun, even of Webster. But he had a perfect temperament for politics. He loved power and understood that in the United States it had to be shared to be exercised. His great gift was in seeing national needs from a broad perspective and fashioning a program that could inspire ordinary citizens with something of his vision.

In the early 1820s he was just developing his "American System." In return for eastern support of a policy of federal aid in the construction of roads and canals, the West would back the protective tariff. He justified this deal on the widest national grounds. By stimulating manufacturing, it would increase the demand for western raw materials, while western prosperity would lead to greater consumption of eastern manufactured goods.

Washington did not describe the interdependence of the sections better in his farewell address than Clay did, repeatedly, in Congress and on the stump. And like Washington, Clay was conservative. He opposed the national bank in 1811 on constitutional grounds but supported the one in 1816 and thereafter, saying, with typical candor and shrewdness, that "the force of circumstance and the lights of experience" had convinced him that he had previously misread the Constitution. His view of slavery, as his biographer Glyndon Van Deusen wrote, was "a combination of theoretical dislike and practical tolerance." He would have preferred to ignore the subject. Nevertheless, slavery repeatedly played a crucial role in Clay's career.

The West had other spokesmen in the 1820s. Thomas Hart Benton, elected to the Senate by the new state of Missouri, was an expansionist and a hard-money man of the uncompromising sort, suspicious of paper currency and therefore of all banks. He championed the small western farmer, favoring free homesteads for pioneers and an extensive federal internal improvements program. Poor workers should cast aside their tools and head west, he believed. Opposed in principle to high tariffs, he tended to vote for them "with repugnance and misgiving" to obtain protection for Missouri's lead and furs.

For 30 years Benton advocated his ideas in the Senate in bluff, colorful language. "Nobody oposes Benton but a few blackjack prairie lawyers," he would roar. "Benton and democracy are one and the same, sir; synonymous terms, sir; synonymous terms, sir." A bighearted man, though vain and pompous, he remained essentially a sectional rather than a national figure.

Another western leader was General William Henry Harrison. Although he sat in the Ohio legislature and in both houses of Congress between 1816 and 1828, Harrison was primarily a soldier. During the Panic of 1819 he took an anti-Bank and pro-high-tariff stand, but he did not identify himself closely with any policy other than the extermination of the Indians. He had little to do with the newly developing political alignments of the 1820s.

Much like Harrison was Andrew Jackson, the "Hero of New Orleans," whose popularity greatly exceeded Harrison's. He had many friends, shrewd in the ways of politics, who were working devotedly, if not entirely unselfishly, to make him president. No one knew his views on most questions, but few cared. His chief assets as a presidential candidate were his military reputation and his forceful personality, but both, and especially the latter, were equally likely to get him into political hot water.

The Missouri Compromise

The sectional concerns of the 1820s repeatedly influenced politics. The depression of 1819–1822 increased tensions by making people feel more strongly about the issues of the day. For example, manufacturers who wanted high tariffs in 1816 were more vehemently in favor of protection in 1820 when their business fell off. Even when economic conditions improved, geographic alignments on key issues tended to solidify.

One of the first and most critical of the sectional questions concerned the admission of Missouri as a slave state. When Louisiana entered the Union in 1812, the rest of the Louisiana Purchase was organized as Missouri Territory. Building on a nucleus of Spanish and French inhabitants, the region west and north of St. Louis grew rapidly, and in 1817 the Missourians petitioned for statehood. A large percentage of the settlers—the population exceeded 60,000 by 1818—were southerners who had moved into the valleys of the Arkansas and Missouri rivers. Since many of them owned slaves, Missouri would become a slave state.

The admission of new states had always been a routine matter, in keeping with the admirable pattern established by the Northwest Ordinance. But during the debate on the Missouri Enabling Act in February 1819, Congressman James Tallmadge of New York introduced an amendment prohibiting "the further introduction of slavery" and providing that all slaves born in Missouri after the territory became a state should be freed at age 25.

While Tallmadge was merely seeking to apply in the territory the pattern of race relations that had developed in the states immediately east of Missouri, his amendment represented, at least in spirit, something of a revolution. The Northwest Ordinance had prohibited slavery in the land between the Mississippi and the Ohio, but that area had only a handful of slaveowners in 1787 and little prospect of attracting more. Elsewhere, no effort to restrict the movement of slaves into new territory had been attempted. If one assumed (as whites always had) that the slaves themselves should have no say in the matter, it appeared democratic to let the settlers of Missouri decide the slavery question for themselves. Nevertheless, the Tallmadge amendment passed the House, the vote following sectional lines closely. The Senate, however, resoundingly rejected it. The less populous southern part of Missouri was then organized separately as Arkansas Territory, and an attempt to bar slavery there was stifled. The Missouri Enabling Act failed to pass before Congress adjourned.

When the next Congress met in December 1819, the Missouri issue came up at once. The vote on Tallmadge's amendment had shown that the rapidly growing North controlled the House of Representatives. It was vital, southerners felt, to preserve a balance in the Senate. Yet northerners objected to the fact that Missouri extended hundreds of miles north of the Ohio River, which they considered slavery's natural boundary. Angry debate raged in Congress for months.

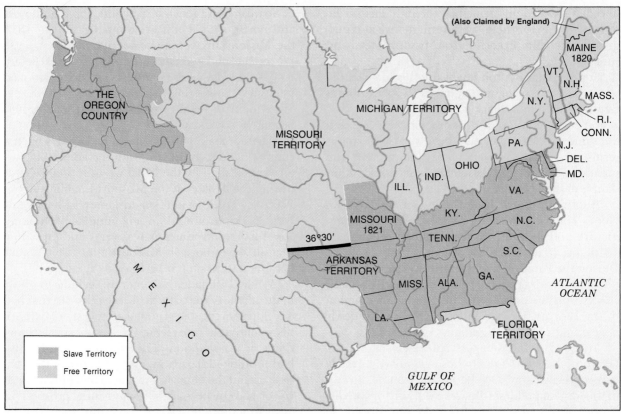

THE MISSOURI COMPROMISE, 1820–1821

*This was the lineup of the slave and free states resulting from the Missouri Com-
promise. The Compromise was repealed by the Kansas-Nebraska Act (1854) and
declared unconstitutional in the Dred Scott Case (1857).*

The debate did not turn on the morality of slavery or the rights of blacks. Northerners objected to
adding new slave states because under the Three-
fifths Compromise these states would be over-
represented in Congress (60 percent of their slaves
would be counted in determining the size of the
states' delegations in the House of Representatives)
and because they did not relish competing with slave
labor. Since the question was political influence
rather than the rights and wrongs of slavery, a compromise was worked out in 1820. Missouri entered
the Union as a slave state and Maine, having been
separated from Massachusetts, was admitted as a
free state to preserve the balance in the Senate.

To prevent further conflict, Congress adopted
a proposal of Senator Jesse B. Thomas of Illinois,
which "forever prohibited" slavery in all other parts
of the Louisiana Purchase north of 36°30′ north
latitude, the westward extension of Missouri's southern boundary. Although this division would keep
slavery out of most of the territory, southerners
accepted it cheerfully. The land south of the line,
the present states of Arkansas and Oklahoma,
seemed ideally suited for the expanded plantation
economy, and most persons considered the treeless
northern regions little better than a desert. One
northern senator, decrying the division, contemptuously described the land north and west of Mis-

souri, today one of the world's richest agricultural regions, as "a prairie without food or water."

The Missouri Compromise did not end the crisis. When Missouri submitted its constitution for approval by Congress (the final step in the admission process), the document, besides authorizing slavery and prohibiting the emancipation of any slave without the consent of the owner, required the state legislature to pass a law barring free blacks and mulattos from entering the state "under any pretext whatever." This provision plainly violated Article 4, Section 2 of the United States Constitution: "The Citizens of each State shall be entitled to all Privileges and Immunities of Citizens in the several States." It did not, however, represent any more of a break with established racial patterns, north or south, than the Tallmadge amendment; many states east of Missouri barred free blacks without regard for the Constitution.

Nevertheless, northern congressmen hypocritically refused to accept the Missouri constitution. Once more the debate raged. Again, since few northerners cared to defend the rights of blacks, the issue was compromised. In March 1821 Henry Clay found a face-saving formula: Out of respect for the "supreme law of the land," Congress accepted the Missouri constitution with the demurrer that no law passed in conformity to it should be construed as contravening Article 4, Section 2. Of course this was pure cant.

Every thinking person recognized the political dynamite inherent in the Missouri controversy. The sectional lineup had been terrifyingly compact. What meant the Union if so trivial a matter as one new state could so divide the people? Moreover, despite the timidity and hypocrisy of the North, everyone realized that the rights and wrongs of slavery lay at the heart of the conflict. "We have the

A comment by David Claypoole Johnston on the 1824 presidential "foot-race" has Adams leading by a head, trailed by Crawford and Jackson. Clay (far right, hand on head), well behind, pulls up in dismay. The many figures and the dreadful puns ("How is Clay now?" "Oh dirt cheap" and "Hurra for our son Jack" "Hurra for our Jack-son") are typical of cartoons of the era.

wolf by the ears, and we can neither safely hold him, nor safely let him go," Jefferson wrote a month after Missouri became a state. The dispute, he said, "like a fire bell in the night, awakened and filled me with terror." Jefferson knew that the compromise had not quenched the flames ignited by the Missouri debates. "This is a reprieve only," he said. John Quincy Adams called it the "title page to a great tragic volume." Yet one could still hope that the fire bell was only a false alarm, that Adams's tragic volume would remain unread.

The Election of 1824

Other controversies that aroused strong feelings did not seem to divide the country so deeply. The question of federal internal improvements caused endless debate that split the country on geographic lines. In 1816 the nationalist-minded Calhoun had pressed a plan to set up a $1.5 million fund for roads and canals. Congress approved this despite strong opposition in New England and a divided South. In 1822 a bill providing money for the upkeep of the National Road caused another sectional split. Both measures were vetoed, but in 1824 Monroe approved a differently worded internal improvement act. Such proposals excited intense reactions. John Randolph, opposing the 1824 bill with his usual ferocity, threatened to employ "every . . . means short of actual insurrection" to defeat it. Yet no one—not even Randolph, it will be noted—threatened the Union on this issue.

The tariff continued to divide the country. When a new, still higher tariff was enacted in 1824, the slave states voted almost unanimously against it, the North and Northwest voted in favor, and New England remained of two minds. Webster (after conducting a poll of business leaders before deciding how to vote) made a powerful speech against the act, but the measure passed without creating a major storm.

These divisions were not severely disruptive, in part because the major politicians, competing for the presidency, did not dare risk alienating any section by taking too extreme a position. Calhoun, for example, had changed his mind about protective tariffs by 1824, but he avoided declaring himself because of his presidential ambitions. Another reason was that the old party system had broken down; the Federalists had disappeared as a national party, and the Jeffersonians, lacking an organized opposition, had become less aggressive and more troubled by factional disputes.

The presidential fight was therefore waged on personal grounds, though the heat generated by the contest began the process of reenergizing party politics. The candidates, in addition to Calhoun, were Jackson, Crawford, Adams, and Clay. The maneuvering among them was complex, the infighting savage. In March 1824 Calhoun, who was young enough to wait for the White House, withdrew and declared for the vice-presidency, which he won easily. Crawford, who had the support of many congressional leaders, seemed the likely winner, but he suffered a series of paralytic strokes that gravely injured his chances.

Despite the bitterness of the contest, it attracted relatively little public interest; barely a quarter of those eligible took the trouble to vote. In the electoral college Jackson led with 99; Adams had 84, Crawford 41, and Clay 37. Since no one had a majority, the contest was thrown into the House of Representatives, which, under the Constitution, had to choose from among the three leaders, each state delegation having one vote. By employing his great influence in the House, Clay swung the balance. Not wishing to advance the fortunes of a rival westerner like Jackson and feeling, with reason, that Crawford's health made him unavailable, Clay gave his support to Adams, who was thereupon elected.

J. Q. Adams as President

Adams, who took a Hamiltonian view of the future of the country, hoped to use the national authority to foster all sorts of useful projects. He asked Congress for a federal program of internal improvements so vast that even Clay boggled when he realized its scope. He came out for aid to manufacturing and agriculture, for a national university, and even for a government astronomical observatory. For a nationalist of unchallengeable Jeffersonian origins like Clay or Calhoun to have pressed for so extensive a program would have been politically risky. For the son of John Adams to do so was disastrous; every doubter remembered his

Asher B. Durand's portrait of an uncompromising John Quincy Adams dates from 1835, when the former president was a congressman from Massachusetts.

Federalist background and decided that he was trying to overturn the glorious "Revolution of 1800."

Adams proved to be his own worst enemy, for he was as inept a politician as ever lived. Although capable on occasion of turning a phrase—in his first annual message to Congress he described astronomical observatories as "light-houses of the skies"—his general style of public utterance was bumbling and cumbersome. Knowing that many citizens considered things like observatories impractical extravagances, he urged Congress not to be "palsied by the will of our constituents." To persuade Americans, who were almost pathological on the subject of monarchy, to support his road-building program, he cited with approval the work being done abroad by "the nations of Europe and . . . their rulers," which revived fears that all Adamses were royalists at heart. He was insensitive

to the ebb and flow of public feeling; even when he wanted to move with the tide, he seldom managed to dramatize and publicize his stand effectively. There was wide support in the country for a federal bankruptcy law, but instead of describing himself in plain language as a friend of poor debtors, Adams called for the "amelioration" of the "often oppressive codes relating to insolvency" and buried the recommendation at the tail end of a dull state paper.

One of Adams's worst political failings was his refusal to use his power of appointment to win support. "I will not dismiss . . . able and faithful political opponents to provide for my own partisans," he said. The attitude was traditional at the time, but Adams carried it to extremes—in four years he removed only 12 men from office. Nevertheless, by appointing Henry Clay secretary of state, he laid himself open to the charge that he had won the presidency by a "corrupt bargain." Thus despite his politically suicidal attitude toward federal jobs, he was subject to the annoyance of a congressional investigation of his appointments, out of which came no less than six bills designed "to reduce the patronage of the executive."

Calhoun's "Exposition and Protest"

The tariff question added to the president's troubles. High duties, increasingly more repulsive to the export-conscious South, attracted more and more favor in the North and the West. Besides manufacturers, lead miners in Missouri, hemp raisers in Kentucky, woolgrowers in New York, and many other interests demanded protection against foreign competition. The absence of party discipline provided an ideal climate for logrolling in Congress. Legislators found themselves under pressure from their constituents to raise the duties on products of local importance; to satisfy these demands, they traded votes with other congressmen similarly situated. In this way massive support for protection was generated.

In 1828 a new tariff was hammered into shape by the House Committee on Manufactures. Northern and western agricultural interests were in command; they wrote into the bill extremely high duties on raw wool, hemp, flax, fur, and liquor. New England manufacturers protested vociferously, for although their products were protected, the proposed law would increase the cost of their raw materials. This gave southerners, now hopelessly in the minority on the tariff question, a chance to block the bill. When the New Englanders proposed amendments lowering the duties on raw materials, the southerners voted nay, hoping to force them to reject the measure on the final vote. This desperate strategy failed. New England had by this time committed its future to manufacturing, a change signalized by the somersault of Webster, who, ever responsive to local pressures, now voted for protection. After winning some minor concessions in the Senate, largely through the intervention of Van Buren, enough New Englanders accepted the so called Tariff of Abominations to assure its passage.

Vice-President Calhoun, who had watched the debate from the vantage point of his post as president of the Senate, now came to a great turning point in his career. He had thrown in his lot with Jackson, whose running mate he was to be in the coming election, and had been assured that the Jacksonians would oppose the bill. Yet northern Jacksonians had been responsible for drafting and passing it. The new tariff would impoverish the South, he believed. He warned Jackson that relief must soon be provided or the Union would be shaken to its foundations. Then he returned to his South Carolina plantation and wrote an essay, the "South Carolina Exposition and Protest," repudiating the nationalist philosophy he had previously championed.

The South Carolina legislature released this document to the country in December 1828, along with eight resolutions denouncing the protective tariff as unfair and unconstitutional. The theorist Calhoun, however, was not content with outlining the case against the tariff. His "Exposition" provided an ingenious defense of the right of the people of a state to reject a law of Congress. Starting with John Locke's revered concept of government as a contractual relationship, he argued that since the states had created the Union, logic dictated that they be the final arbiters of the meaning of the Constitution that was its framework. If a special state convention, representing the sovereignty of the people, decided that an act of Congress violated the Constitution, it could interpose its authority and "nullify" the law within its boundaries. Calhoun did not seek to implement this theory in 1828, for he hoped that the next administration would lower the tariff and make nullification unnecessary.

Milestones

1804	Size of minimum purchase reduced to 160 acres by Land Act
1808	Further importation of slaves outlawed by Congress
1816	Second Bank of the United States chartered by Congress
	Protection for manufactured goods provided by Tariff Act
1819	Beginning of Panic of 1819
1820	Federal officeholders limited to 4-year terms by Crawford's Act
1820–1821	Missouri Compromise
1820–1824	American System developed by Henry Clay
1824	J. Q. Adams elected president by House of Representatives
1828	Calhoun's "South Carolina Exposition and Protest"
	Congress passes Tariff of Abominations

SUPPLEMENTARY READING

Titles marked with an asterisk have been published in paperback.

On the economic issues of this period, see F. W. Taussig, **Tariff History of the United States*** (1923), Bray Hammond, **Banks and Politics in America from the Revolution to the Civil War*** (1957), and R. M. Robbins, **Our Landed Heritage*** (1942).

M. D. Peterson, **The Great Triumvirate** (1987), is an interesting study of Clay, Calhoun, and Webster. Other biographies of statesmen of the period include S. F. Bemis, **John Quincy Adams** (1949–1956), M. G. Baxter, **One and Indispensable: Daniel Webster and the Union** (1984), John Nivens, **Martin Van Buren** (1983), R. V. Remini, **Andrew Jackson and the Course of American Empire** (1977), and C. C. Mooney, **William H. Crawford** (1974). The fullest study of Calhoun's early career is C. M. Wiltse, **John C. Calhoun: Nationalist** (1949), but see also R. N. Current, **John C. Calhoun*** (1963). The best brief biography of Clay is **Clement Eaton, Henry Clay and the Art of American Politics*** (1957). On the Missouri Compromise, see Glover Moore, **The Missouri Controversy*** (1953).

Toward a National Economy

Nothing can exceed their activity and perseverance in all kinds of speculation, handicraft, and enterprise which promise a profitable pecuniary result.

FRANCES TROLLOPE, Domestic Manners of the Americans, *1832*

Politicians might attribute the growth of the country and the preservation of the Union to their own patriotism and ingenuity, but without the economic and technological developments of the period, neither of these much-to-be-desired objectives could have been attained. The country was still overwhelmingly agricultural in 1820, but the nation was on the brink of a major economic readjustment. Certain obscure seeds planted in the early years of the republic had taken root. Almost unnoticed, new ways of producing goods and making a living were beginning to take hold. The industrial revolution was coming to America with a rush.

America's Industrial Revolution

The growth of industry required certain technological advances and the development of a new type of business organization. Both elements existed in Europe by the time of the War for Independence, but only after the ratification of the Constitution did they cross the Atlantic. In 1790 a young English-born genius named Samuel Slater, employed by the Rhode Island merchant firm of Almy & Brown, began to spin cotton thread by machine in the first effective factory in the United States. In 1800 a youthful graduate of Yale College, Eli Whitney, having contracted to make 10,000 rifles for the government, succeeded in manufacturing them by such precise methods that the parts were interchangeable, a major step toward the perfection of the assembly-line system of production. Three years later Oliver Evans, a Philadelphia inventor, had come close to achieving automation in flour milling. A worker poured wheat down a chute at one end of the plant and a second worker headed the barrels of superfine flour which emerged at the other end. The intervening steps of weighing, cleaning, grinding, and packing were all performed by machines.

Other important technological advances included John Fitch's construction and operation of the world's first regularly scheduled steamboat in 1790 and Eli Whitney's invention of the cotton gin in 1793. The steamboat and the gin affected American history almost as much as the factory system and mass production. The former, when employed on western waters, cut the cost of transportation dramatically and brought the West into the national economy. The latter made possible the widespread cultivation of cotton, which transformed the South and fed the world's cotton factories for decades.

Innovations in the way businesses were organized and financed accompanied technological developments. The most spectacular step was the sudden flowering of American banking. Here the establishment of the First Bank of the United States was of key importance. Aside from aiding government financial operations, the Bank provided an important source of credit for private business. Its success led to the founding of many state-chartered banks. When the great Bank was created in 1791, there were only three banks in the entire country. By 1800 there were 29, located in all the major towns. Bank credit, in the historian Bray Hammond's words, "was to Americans a new source of energy, like steam." Yet many citizens failed to grasp this truth. "Every dollar of a bank bill that is issued beyond the quantity of gold and silver in the vaults represents nothing and is therefore a cheat upon somebody," John Adams remarked as late as 1809.

Birth of the Factory

America's industrial revolution was slow in coming. Slater's factory did not signal the disappearance of

the family spinning wheel or the spread of the factory system to other forms of manufacturing. Most
commercial and manufacturing businesses were still
managed by a single owner or a few partners. Methods of distributing goods, keeping records, and accounting remained primitive. Interchangeable firing pins for rifles did not lead at once even to
matching pairs of shoes. More than 15 years were
to pass after the invention of Fitch's steamboat before it was widely accepted.

By the 1770s British manufacturers, especially
those in textiles, had made astonishing progress in
mechanizing their operations, bringing workers together in buildings called factories where waterpower, and later steam, supplied the force to run
new spinning and weaving devices that increased
productivity and reduced labor costs.

Since machine-spun cotton was cheaper and of
better quality than that spun by hand, producers in
other countries were eager to adopt British methods. Americans had depended on Great Britain for
such products until the Revolution cut off supplies;
then the new spirit of nationalism gave impetus to
the development of local industry. A number of
state legislatures offered bounties to anyone who
would introduce the new machinery. The British,
however, guarded their secrets vigilantly. It was illegal to export any of the new machines or to send
their plans abroad. Workers skilled in their construction and use were forbidden to leave the country. These restrictions were effective for a time; the
principles on which the new machines were based
were simple enough, but to construct workable
models without plans was another matter. Although
a number of persons tried to do so, it was not until
Samuel Slater installed his machines in Pawtucket,
Rhode Island, that a successful factory was constructed.

Slater was more than a skilled mechanic. Attracted by stories of the rewards offered in the
United States, he slipped out of England in 1789.
Not daring to carry any plans, he depended on his
memory and his mechanical sense for the complicated specifications of the necessary machines.
When Moses Brown brought him to Rhode Island,
he insisted on scrapping the crude machinery Almy
& Brown had assembled. Then, working in secrecy
with a carpenter who was "under bond not to steal
the patterns nor disclose the nature of the work,"
he built and installed his machinery. In December
1790 the first American factory began production.

It was a humble beginning indeed. Slater's ma-

*Samuel Slater "smuggled a textile mill out of England in his head." Two decades
after its founding, the mill and its surroundings looked like this.*

chines made only cotton thread, which Almy & Brown sold in its Providence store and "put out" to individual artisans, who, working for wages, wove it into cloth in their homes. The machines were tended by a labor force of nine children, for the work was simple and the pace slow. The young operatives' pay ranged from 33 to 67 cents a week, about what a youngster could earn in other occupations.*

The factory was profitable from the start. Slater soon branched out on his own, and others trained by him opened their own establishments. By 1800 seven mills possessing 2,000 spindles were in operation; by 1815, after production had been stimulated by the War of 1812, there were 130,000 spindles turning in 213 factories. Many of the new factories were inefficient, but the well-managed ones earned large profits. Slater began with almost nothing. When he died in 1835 he owned mill properties in Rhode Island, Massachusetts, Connecticut, and New Hampshire in addition to other interests, and by the standards of the day he was a rich man.

Before long the Boston Associates, a group of merchants headed by Francis Cabot Lowell, added a new dimension to factory production. Beginning at Waltham, Massachusetts, where the Charles River provided the necessary waterpower, between 1813 and 1850 they revolutionized textile production. Some early factory owners had set up hand looms in their plants, but the weavers could not keep pace with the whirring spinning jennies. Lowell, after an extensive study of British mills, smuggled the plans for an efficient power loom into America. His Boston Manufacturing Company at Waltham, capitalized at $300,000, combined machine production, large-scale operation, efficient management, and centralized marketing procedures. It concentrated on the mass production of a standardized product.

Lowell's cloth, though plain and rather coarse, was durable and cheap. His profits averaged almost 20 percent a year during the Era of Good Feelings. In 1823 the Boston Associates began to harness the power of the Merrimack River, setting up a new $600,000 corporation at the sleepy village of East Chelmsford, Massachusetts (population 300), where there was a fall of 32 feet in the river. Within three years the town, appropriately renamed Lowell, had 2,000 inhabitants.

The Persistence of the Household System

The efficiency of the Lowell system was obvious, yet it led to no immediate transformation of American manufacturing. While the embargo and the war with Great Britain aided the new factories by limiting foreign competition, they also stimulated nonfactory production. In Monroe's time the household-handicraft-mill complex was still dominant nearly everywhere. Except in the manufacture of textiles, factories employing as many as 50 workers did not exist. Traveling and town-based artisans produced goods ranging from hats, shoes, and other articles of clothing to barrels, clocks, pianos, ships' supplies, cigars, lead pencils, and pottery. Ironworks, brickyards, flour mills, distilleries, and lumberyards could be found even in the most rural parts

An artisan and his apprentices at work at a small pewterer's shop in New York City, pictured in a banner carried by the Society of Pewterers in a procession in New York celebrating the ratification of the Constitution.

---

* This labor pattern persisted for several decades. In 1813 a cotton manufacturer placed the following advertisement in the *Utica* (N.Y.) *Patriot:* "A few sober and industrious families of at least five children each, over the age of eight years are wanted at the Cotton Factory. Widows with large families would do well to attend this notice."

of the country. The historian George Rogers Taylor reports that in and about a single tiny Ohio town in 1815, more than 30 craftsmen of the shoemaker-baker-druggist type plied their trades.

Nearly all these "manufacturers" produced only to supply local needs, but in some instances large industries grew up without advancing to the factory stage. In the neighborhood of the Connecticut town of Danbury, hundreds of small shops turned out hats by handicraft methods. The hats were sold in all sections of the country, the trade being organized by wholesalers. The shoe industry followed a related pattern, with centers of production in Pennsylvania, New Jersey, and especially eastern Massachusetts. Merchants in these regions bought leather in wholesale lots, had it cut to patterns in central workshops, and then distributed it to craftsmen who made the shoes in their homes or shops on a piecework basis. The finished product was returned to the central shops for inspection and packaging and then shipped throughout the United States. Some strange combinations of production techniques appeared, none more peculiar than in the manufacture of stockings. Frequently the feet and legs were knit by machine in separate factories and then "put out" to handworkers who sewed the parts together in their homes.

Since technology affected American industry unevenly, contemporaries found the changes difficult to evaluate. Few people in the 1820s appreciated how profound the impact of the factory system would be. The city of Lowell seemed remarkable and important but not necessarily a herald of future trends. Yet in nearly every field apparently minor changes were being made. Beginning around 1815, small improvements in the design of waterwheels, such as the use of leather transmission belts and metal gears, made possible larger and more efficient machinery in mills and factories. The woolens industry gradually became as mechanized as the cotton. Iron production advanced beyond the stage of the blacksmith's forge and the small foundry only slowly; nevertheless, by 1810 machines were stamping out nails at a third the cost of the hand-forged type, and a few years later sheet iron, formerly hammered out laboriously

Typical of the small factories of the early American Industrial Revolution was this glass-making establishment along the Delaware River near Philadelphia.

by hand, was being produced in efficient rolling mills. At about this time the puddling process for refining pig iron made it possible to use coal for fuel instead of expensive charcoal.

Improvements were made soon after the War of 1812 in the manufacture of paper, glass, and pottery. The commercial canning of sterilized foods in airtight containers began about 1820. The invention in that year of a machine for cutting ice, which reduced the cost by over 50 percent, had equally important effects on urban eating habits.

Corporations

Besides the competition of other types of production and the inability of technology to supply instant solutions to every industrial problem, there were other reasons why the factory took hold so slowly in the United States. Mechanization required substantial capital investment, and capital was chronically in short supply. The modern method of organizing large enterprises, the corporation, was rarely used in this period. Between 1781 and 1801 only 326 corporations were chartered by the states, and only a few of them were engaged in manufacturing.

The general opinion was that only quasi-public projects, such as roads and waterworks, were entitled to the privilege of incorporation. Anyone interested in organizing a corporation had to obtain a special act of a state legislature. And even among businessmen there was a tendency to associate corporations with monopoly, corruption, and the undermining of individual enterprise. In 1820 the economist Daniel Raymond wrote:

> The very object . . . of the act of incorporation is to produce inequality, either in rights, or in the division of property. Prima facie, therefore all money corporations are detrimental to national wealth. They are always created for the benefit of the rich.

Such feelings help to explain why as late as the 1860s most manufacturing was being done by unincorporated companies.

Though the growth of industry did not suddenly revolutionize American life, it reshaped society in various ways. For many years it lessened the importance of foreign commerce. Some relative decline from the lush years immediately preceding Jefferson's embargo was no doubt inevitable, especially in the fabulously profitable reexport trade, but industrial growth reduced the need for foreign products and thus the business of merchants. Only in the 1850s, when the wealth and population of the United States were more than three times what they had been in the first years of the century, did the value of American exports climb back to the levels of 1807. As the country moved closer to self-sufficiency (a point it never reached), nationalistic and isolationist sentiments were subtly augmented. During the embargo and the War of 1812 a great deal of capital had been transferred from commerce to industry; afterward new capital continued to prefer industry, attracted by the high profits and growing prestige of manufacturing. The rise of manufacturing affected farmers too, for as cities grew in size and number, commercial agriculture flourished. Dairy farming, truck gardening, and fruit growing began to thrive around every manufacturing center.

Cotton Revolutionizes the South

By far the most important indirect effect of industrialization occurred in the South, which soon began to produce cotton to supply the new textile factories of Great Britain and New England. The possibility of growing large amounts of this crop in America had not been seriously considered in colonial times, but by the 1780s the demand for raw cotton to feed the voracious British mills was causing many American farmers to experiment with the crop. Most of the world's cotton at this time came from Egypt, India, and the East Indies. The plant was considered tropical, most varieties being unable to survive the slightest frost. Hamilton, who missed nothing that related to the economic growth of the country, reported: "It has been observed . . . that the nearer the place of growth to the equator, the better the quality of the cotton."

Beginning in 1786, "sea island" cotton was grown successfully in the mild, humid lowlands and offshore islands along the coasts of Georgia and South Carolina. This was a high-quality cotton, silky and long-fibered like the Egyptian. But its suscep-

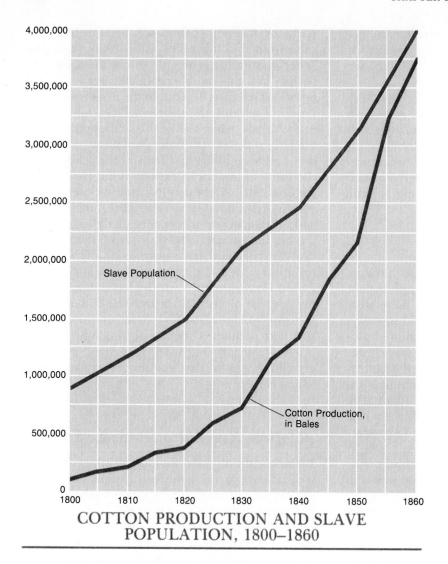

COTTON PRODUCTION AND SLAVE
POPULATION, 1800–1860

tibility to frost severely limited the area of its cultivation. Elsewhere in the South, "green seed," or upland, cotton flourished, but this plant had little commercial value because the seeds could not be easily separated from the lint. When sea island cotton was passed between two rollers, its shiny black seeds simply popped out; with upland cotton, the seeds were pulled through with the lint and crushed, the oils and broken bits destroying the value of the fiber. To remove the seeds by hand was laborious; a slave working all day could clean scarcely a pound of the white fluff. This made it an uneconomical crop. In 1791 the usually sanguine Hamilton admitted in his *Report on Manufactures* that "the extensive cultivation of cotton can, perhaps, hardly be expected."

Early American cotton manufacturers used the sea island variety or imported the foreign fiber, in the latter case paying a duty of 3 cents a pound. However, the planters of South Carolina and Georgia, suffering from hard times after the Revolution, needed a new cash crop. Rice production was not expanding, and indigo, the other staple of the area, had ceased to be profitable when it was no longer possible to claim the British bounty. Cotton seemed an obvious answer. Farmers were experimenting hopefully with varieties of the plant and mulling the problem of how upland cotton could be more easily deseeded.

This was the situation in the spring of 1793, when Eli Whitney was a guest at Mulberry Grove, the plantation of Catherine Greene, widow of General Nathanael Greene, some dozen miles from Savannah.* Whitney had accepted a position as private tutor at 100 guineas a year with a nearby family and had stopped to visit a friend, Phineas Miller, who was overseer of the Greene plantation. While at Mulberry Grove, Whitney, who had never seen a cotton plant before, met a number of the local landowners. To his father he wrote:

> I heard much of the extreme difficulty of ginning Cotton, that is, separating it from its seed. There were a number of very respectable Gentlemen at Mrs. Greene's who all agreed that if a machine could be invented that would clean the Cotton with expedition, it would be a great thing both to the Country and to the inventor.

Whitney thought about the problem for a few days and then "struck out a plan of a machine." He described it to Miller, who enthusiastically offered to finance the invention. Since Whitney had just learned that his job as tutor would pay only 50 guineas, he accepted Miller's proposal.

Within ten days he had solved the problem that had baffled the planters. His "gin" (engine) consisted of a cylinder covered with rows of wire teeth rotating in a box filled with cotton. As the cylinder turned, the teeth passed through narrow slits in a metal grating. Cotton fibers were caught by the teeth and pulled through the slits. The seeds, too thick to pass through the openings, were left behind. A second cylinder, with brushes rotating in the opposite direction to sweep the cotton from the wires, prevented matting and clogging.

This "absurdly simple contrivance" almost instantly transformed southern agriculture. With a gin a slave could clean 50 times as much cotton as by hand; soon larger models driven by mules and horses were available. The machines were so easy to construct (once the basic idea was understood) that Whitney and Miller were never able to enforce their patent rights effectively. Rival manufacturers shamelessly pirated their work, and countless farmers built gins of their own. Cotton production figures tell the story: In 1790 about 3,000 bales (of an average of 500 pounds) were produced in the

United States. In 1793 the total rose to 10,000 bales; two years later, to 17,000; by 1801, to 100,000. The embargo and the War of 1812 temporarily checked expansion, but in 1816 output spurted ahead by more than 25 percent, and in the early 1820s annual production averaged well over 400,000 bales.

Despite this avalanche, the price of cotton remained high. During the 1790s it ranged between 26 and 44 cents a pound, a veritable bonanza. In the next decade the price was lower (15 to 19 cents), but it still provided high profits even for inefficient planters. It was higher again after 1815 and fell below 14 cents only once before 1826. With prices at these levels, profits of $50 an acre were not unusual, and the South boomed.

Upland cotton would grow wherever there were 200 consecutive days without frost and 24 inches of rain. The crop engulfed Georgia and South Carolina and spread north into parts of Virginia. After Andrew Jackson smashed the southwestern Indians during the War of 1812, the rich "Black Belt" area of central Alabama and northern Mississippi and the delta region along the lower Mississippi River were rapidly taken over by the fluffy white staple. In 1821 Alabama alone raised 40,000 bales. Central Tennessee also became important cotton country.

Cotton stimulated the economy of the rest of the nation as well. Most of it was exported, the sale paying for much-needed European products. The transportation, insurance, and final disposition of the crop fell largely into the hands of northern merchants, who profited accordingly. And the surplus corn and hogs of western farmers helped feed the slaves of the new cotton plantations. As Douglass North explained in *The Economic Growth of the United States*, cotton was "the major expansive force" in the economy for a generation, beginning about 1815.

Revival of Slavery

Amid the national rejoicing over this prosperity, one aspect both sad and ominous was easily overlooked. Slavery, a declining or at worst stagnant institution in the decade of the Revolution, was revitalized in the following years.

Libertarian beliefs inspired by the Revolution ran into the roadblock of race prejudice as soon as some of the practical aspects of freedom for blacks

---

* The property, formerly owned by a prominent Georgia Tory, had been given to Greene by the state in gratitude for his having driven out the British during the Revolution.

became apparent. As disciples of John Locke, the Revolutionary generation had a deep respect for property rights; in the last analysis most white Americans placed these rights ahead of the personal liberty of black Americans in their constellation of values. Forced abolition of slavery therefore attracted few recruits. Moreover, the rhetoric of the Revolution had raised the aspirations of blacks. Increasing signs of rebelliousness appeared among them, especially after the slave uprising in Saint Domingue, which culminated, after a great bloodbath, in the establishment of the black Republic of Haiti in 1804. This example of a successful slave revolt filled white Americans with apprehension. Their fears were irrational (Haitian blacks outnumbered whites and mulattoes combined by seven to one) but nonetheless real. And fear led to repression; the exposure of a plot to revolt in Virginia, led by the slave Gabriel, resulted in some three dozen executions even though no actual uprising had occurred.

The mood of the Revolutionary decade had led to the manumission of many slaves; unfortunately, this led many whites to have second thoughts about ending slavery. "If the blacks see all of their color slaves, it will seem to them a disposition of Providence, and they will be content," a Virginia legislator, apparently something of an amateur psychologist, claimed. "But if they see others like themselves free . . . they will repine." As the number of free blacks rose, restrictions on them were everywhere tightened.

In the 1780s many opponents of slavery began to think of solving the "Negro problem" by colonizing freed slaves in some distant region—in the western districts or perhaps in Africa. The colonization movement had two aspects. One, a manifestation of an embryonic black nationalism, reflected the disgust of black Americans with local racial attitudes and their interest in African civilization. Paul Cuffe, a Massachusetts Quaker, managed to finance the emigration of 38 of his fellow blacks to Sierra Leone in 1815, but few others followed. Most influential northern blacks, the most conspicuous among them the Reverend Richard Allen, bishop of the African Methodist Church, opposed the idea vigorously.

The other colonization movement, led by whites, was paternalistic. Some white colonizationists genuinely abhorred slavery. Others could not stomach

living with free blacks; to them colonization was merely a polite word for deportation. Most white colonizationists were conservatives who considered themselves realists. Whether they thought blacks degenerate by nature or the victims of their surroundings, they were sure that American conditions gave them no chance to better their lot and that both races would profit from separation.

The colonization idea became popular in Virginia in the 1790s, but nothing was achieved until after the founding of the American Colonization Society in 1817. The society purchased African land and established the Republic of Liberia. However, despite the cooperation of a handful of black nationalists and the patronage of many important white southerners, including presidents Madison and Monroe and Chief Justice Marshall, it accomplished little. Although some white colonizationists expected ex-slaves to go to Africa as enthusiastic Christian missionaries who would convert and "civilize" the natives, few blacks in fact wished to migrate to a land as alien to their own experience as to their masters'. Only about 12,000 went to Liberia, and the toll taken among them by tropical diseases was large. As late as 1850 the black American population of Liberia was only 6,000.

The cotton boom of the early 19th century acted as a brake on the colonization movement. As cotton production expanded, the need for labor in the South grew apace. The price of slaves doubled between 1795 and 1804. As it rose, the inclination of even the most kindhearted masters to free their slaves began to falter. Although the importation of slaves from abroad had been outlawed by all the states, perhaps 25,000 were smuggled into the country in the 1790s. In 1804 South Carolina reopened the trade, and between that date and 1808, when the constitutional prohibition of importation became effective, some 40,000 were brought in. Thereafter, the miserable traffic in human beings continued clandestinely, though on a very small scale.

Equally obnoxious was the interstate slave trade that resulted from the cotton boom. While it had always been legal for owners to transport their own slaves to a new state if they were settling there, many states forbade, or at least severely restricted, interstate commercial transactions in human flesh. A Virginia law of 1778, for example, prohibited the importation of slaves for purposes of sale, and persons

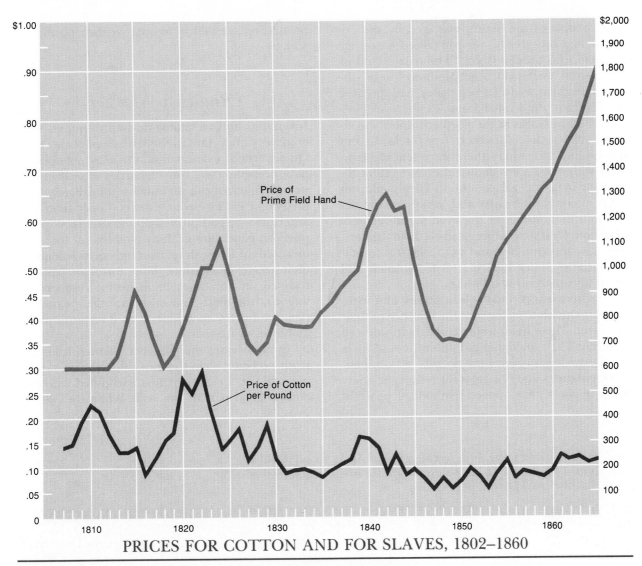

PRICES FOR COTTON AND FOR SLAVES, 1802–1860

The vertical axis on the left shows cents, and the curve for the price of cotton should be read against it; the right vertical axis shows dollars, and the price of slaves should be read against it. These prices are from New Orleans records. According to Conrad and Meyer, the rising trend of slave prices (and a growing slave population) shows the continuing profitability and viability of slavery up to 1860.

entering the state with slaves had to swear that they did not intend to sell them. Once cotton became important, these laws were systematically evaded. There was a surplus of slaves in one part of the United States and an acute shortage in another. A migration from the Upper South to the cotton lands quickly sprang up. Slaves from "free" New York and New Jersey and even from New England began to appear on the auction blocks of Savannah and

Charleston. Early in the Era of Good Feelings, newspapers in New Orleans were carrying reports such as this one: "Jersey negroes appear to be particularly adapted to this market. . . . We have the right to calculate on large importations in the future, from the success which hitherto attended the sale."

By about 1820 the letter of the law began to be changed. Soon the slave trade became an organized business, cruel and shameful, frowned on by the "best" people of the South, managed by the depraved and the greedy, yet patronized by nearly everyone who needed labor. "The native land of Washington, Jefferson, and Madison," one disgusted Virginian told a French visitor, had "become the Guinea of the United States."

The lot of blacks in the northern states was almost as bad as that of southern free blacks. Except in New England, where there were few blacks to begin with, most were denied the vote, either directly or by extralegal pressures. They could not testify in court, intermarry with whites, obtain decent jobs or housing, or get even a rudimentary education. Most states segregated blacks in theaters, hospitals, and churches and on public transportation facilities. They were barred from hotels and restaurants patronized by whites.

Northern blacks could at least protest and try to convince the white majority of the injustice of their treatment. These rights were denied their southern brethren. They could and did publish newspapers and pamphlets, organize for political action, petition legislatures and Congress for redress of grievance—in short, they applied methods of peaceful persuasion in an effort to improve their position in society.

Roads to Market

Inventions and technological improvements were extremely important in the settlement of the West. On superficial examination, this may not seem to have been the case, for the hordes of settlers who struggled across the mountains immediately after the War of 1812 were no better equipped than their ancestors who had pushed up the eastern slopes in previous generations. Many plodded on foot over hundreds of miles, dragging crude carts laden with their meager possessions. More fortunate pioneers traveled on horseback or in heavy, cumbersome wagons, the best known being the hearselike, canvas-topped Conestoga "covered wagons," pulled by horses or oxen.

In many cases the pioneers followed trails and roads no better than those of colonial days—quagmires in wet weather, rutted and pitted with potholes a good part of the year. When they settled

Much of the east-west traffic in the growing United States passed through St. Louis, a vital port on the Mississippi River and the terminus of several western trails. The city looked like this in the 1830s.

down, their way of life was no more advanced than that of the Pilgrims. At first they were creatures of the forest, feeding on its abundance, building their homes and simple furniture with its wood, clothing themselves in the furs of forest animals. They usually planted the first crop in a natural glade; thereafter, year by year, they pushed back the trees with ax and saw and fire until the land was cleared. Any source of power more complicated than an ox was beyond their ken. Until the population of the territory had grown large enough to support town life, settlers were as dependent on crude household manufactures as any earlier pioneer.

The spread of settlement into the Mississippi Valley created challenges that required technological advances if they were to be met. In the social climate of that age in the United States, these advances were not slow in coming. Most were related to transportation, the major problem for westerners. Without economical means of getting their produce to market, western settlers were condemned to lives of crude self-sufficiency. Everyone recognized that an efficient transportation network would increase land values, stimulate domestic and foreign trade, and strengthen the entire economy.

The Mississippi River and its tributaries provided a natural highway for western commerce and communication, but one that had grave disadvantages. Farm products could be floated down to New Orleans on rafts and flatboats, but the descent from Pittsburgh took at least a month. Transportation upstream was out of the question for anything but the lightest and most valuable products, and even for them it was extremely expensive. In any case, the natural flow of trade was between East and West. That is why, from early in the westward movement, much attention was given to building roads linking the Mississippi Valley to the eastern seaboard.

Constructing decent roads over the rugged Appalachians was a formidable task. The steepest grades had to be reduced by cutting through hills and filling in low places, all without modern blasting or earth-moving equipment. Streams had to be bridged. Drainage ditches were essential if the roads were not to be washed out by the first rains, and a firm foundation of stones, topped with a well-crowned gravel dressing, had to be provided if they were to stand up under the pounding of heavy wagons. The skills required for building roads of this quality had been developed in Great Britain and

France, and the earliest American examples, constructed in the 1790s, were similar to good European highways. The first such road, connecting Philadelphia and Lancaster, Pennsylvania, opened to traffic in 1794.

In heavily populated areas the volume of traffic made good roads worth their cost, which ran to as much as $13,000 a mile where the terrain was difficult, though the average was perhaps half that figure. In some cases good roads ran into fairly remote areas. In New York, always a leading state in the movement for improved transportation, an excellent road had been built all the way from Albany to Lake Erie by the time of the War of 1812, and by 1821 the state had some 4,000 miles of good roads.

Transportation and the Government

Most of the improved highways and many bridges were built as business ventures by private interests. Promoters charged tolls, the rates being set by the states. Tolls were collected at gates along the way; hinged poles suspended across the road were turned back by a guard after receipt of the toll. Hence these thoroughfares were known as turnpikes, or simply pikes.

The profits earned by a few early turnpikes, such as the one between Philadelphia and Lancaster, caused the boom in private road building, but even the most fortunate of the turnpike companies did not make much money. Maintenance was expensive, traffic spotty. (Ordinary public roads paralleling turnpikes were sometimes called "shunpikes" because penny-pinching travelers used them to avoid the tolls.) Some states bought stock to bolster weak companies, and others built and operated turnpikes as public enterprises. Local governments everywhere provided considerable support, for every town was eager to develop efficient communication with its neighbors.

Despite much talk about individual self-reliance and free enterprise, local, state, and national governments contributed heavily to the development of what in the jargon of the day were called "internal improvements." They served as "primary entrepreneurs," supplying capital for risky but socially desirable enterprises, with the result that a fascinating mixture of private and public energy went into the building of these institutions. At the federal level even the parsimonious Jeffersonians became deeply involved. In 1808 Secretary of the Treasury Albert Gallatin drafted a comprehensive plan for constructing much-needed roads at a cost of $16 million. This proposal was not adopted, but the government poured money in an erratic and unending stream into turnpike companies and other organizations created to improve transportation.

Logically, the major highways, especially those over the mountains, should have been built by the national government. Strategic military requirements alone would have justified such a program. One major artery, the Old National Road, running from Cumberland, Maryland, to Wheeling, in western Virginia, was constructed by the United States between 1811 and 1818. In time it was extended as far west as Vandalia, Illinois. However, further federal road building was hampered by political squabbles in Congress, usually phrased in constitutional terms but in fact based on sectional rivalries and other economic conflicts. Thus no comprehensive highway program was undertaken in the 19th century.

While the National Road, the New York Pike, and other, rougher trails such as the Wilderness Road into the Kentucky country were adequate for the movement of settlers, they did not begin to answer the West's need for cheap and efficient transportation. Wagon freight rates averaged at least 30 cents a ton-mile around 1815. At such rates, to transport a ton of oats from Buffalo to New York would have cost 12 times the value of the oats! To put the problem another way, four horses could haul a ton and a half of oats about 18 or 20 miles a day over a good road. If they could obtain half their feed by grazing, the horses would still consume about 50 pounds of oats a day. It requires little mathematics to figure out how much oats would be left in the wagon when it reached New York City, almost 400 miles away.

Turnpikes made it possible to transport such goods as clothing, hardware, coffee, and books across the Appalachians, but the expense was considerable. It cost more to ship a ton of freight 300 miles over the mountains from Philadelphia to Pittsburgh than from Pittsburgh to Philadelphia by way of New Orleans, more than ten times as far. Until

the coming of the railroad, which was just being introduced in England in 1825, shipping bulky goods by land over the great distances common in America was uneconomical. Businessmen and inventors concentrated instead on improving water transport, first by designing better boats and then by developing artificial waterways.

"Organs of Communication"

Rafts and flatboats were adequate for downstream travel, but the only practical solution for upstream travel was the steamboat. After John Fitch's work around 1790, a number of others made important contributions to the development of steam navigation. One early enthusiast was John Stevens, a wealthy New Jerseyite, who designed an improved steam boiler for which he received one of the first patents issued by the United States. Stevens got his brother-in-law, Robert R. Livingston, interested in the problem, and the latter used his political influence to obtain an exclusive charter to operate steamboats on New York waters. In 1802, while in France trying to buy New Orleans from Napoleon, Livingston got to know Robert Fulton, a young American artist and engineer who was experimenting with steam navigation, and agreed to finance his work. In 1807, after returning to New York, Fulton constructed the *North River Steam Boat,* famous to history as the *Clermont.*

The *Clermont* measured 142 feet long and 18 feet abeam and drew 7 feet of water. With its towering stack belching black smoke, its side wheels could push it along at a steady 5 miles an hour. Nothing about it was radically new, but Fulton brought the essentials—engine, boiler, paddle wheels, and hull—into proper balance and thereby produced an efficient vessel.

No one could patent a steamboat; soon the new vessels were plying the waters of every navigable river from the Mississippi east. After 1815 steamers were making the run from New Orleans as far as Ohio. By 1820 at least 60 vessels were operating between New Orleans and Louisville, and by the end of the decade there were more than 200 steamers on the Mississippi.

The day of the steamboat had dawned, and although the following generation would experience its high noon, even in the 1820s its major effects

Robert Fulton spent several years in France during the Napoleonic era, trying to interest the government in his inventions. These are plans of one of his early steamboats, which was launched on the Seine in 1803.

were clear. The great Mississippi Valley, in the full tide of its development, was immensely enriched. Produce poured down to New Orleans, which soon ranked with New York and Liverpool among the world's great ports. Only 80,000 tons of freight reached New Orleans from the interior in 1816 and 1817, more than 542,000 tons in 1840 and 1841. Upriver traffic was affected even more spectacularly. Freight charges plummeted, in some cases to a tenth of what they had been after the War of 1812. Around 1818 coffee cost 16 cents a pound more in Cincinnati than in New Orleans, a decade later less than 3 cents more. The Northwest emerged from self-sufficiency with a rush and became part of the national market.

Steamboats were far more comfortable than any contemporary form of land transportation, and competition soon led builders to make them positively luxurious. The *General Pike*, launched in 1819, set the fashion. Marble columns, thick carpets, mirrors, and crimson curtains adorned its cabins and public rooms. Soon the finest steamers were floating palaces where passengers could dine, drink, dance, and gamble in luxury as they sped smoothly to their destinations. Yet raft and flatboat traffic increased. Farmers, lumbermen, and others with goods from upriver floated down in the slack winter season and returned in comfort by steamer after selling their produce—and their rafts as well, for lumber was in great demand in New Orleans. Every January and February, New Orleans teemed with westerners and Yankee sailors, their pockets jingling, bent on a fling

before going back to work. The shops displayed everything from the latest Paris fashions to teething rings made of alligator teeth mounted in silver. During the carnival season the city became one great festival, where every human pleasure could be tasted, every vice indulged. "Have you ever been in New Orleans?" one visiting bard sang in the late 1820s.

> . . . *If not you'd better go,*
> *It's a nation of a queer place; day and night a show!*
> *Frenchmen, Spaniards, West Indians, Creoles, Mustees,*
> *Yankees, Kentuckians, Tennesseeans, lawyers and trustees.*
> *Clergymen, priests, friars, nuns, women of all stains;*
> *Negroes in purple and fine linen, and slaves in rags and chains.*
> *Ships, arks, steamboats, robbers, pirates, alligators,*
> *Assassins, gamblers, drunkards, and cotton speculators;*
> *Sailors, soldiers, pretty girls, and ugly fortunetellers;*
> *Pimps, imps, shrimps, and all sorts of dirty fellows;*
> *White men with black wives, et vice-versa too,*
> *A progeny of all colors—an infernal motley crew!*

The Canal Boom

While the steamboat was conquering western rivers, canals were being constructed that further improved the transportation network. Since the midwestern rivers all emptied into the Gulf of Mexico, they did not provide a direct link with the eastern seaboard. If an artificial waterway could be cut between the great central valley and some navigable stream flowing into the Atlantic, all sections would profit immensely.

Canals were more expensive than roads, but so long as the motive power used in overland transportation was the humble horse, they offered enormous economic advantages to shippers. Because there is less friction to overcome, a team plodding along a towpath could pull a canal barge with a 100-ton load and make better time over long distances than it could pulling a single ton in a wagon on the finest road.

Although canals were as old as Egypt, only about 100 miles of them existed in the United States as late as 1816. Construction costs aside, in a rough and mountainous country canals presented formidable engineering problems. To link the Mississippi Valley and the Atlantic meant somehow circumventing the Appalachian Mountains. Most people thought this impossible.

Mayor De Witt Clinton of New York believed that such a project was feasible in New York State. In 1810, while serving as state canal commissioner, he traveled across central New York and convinced himself that it would be practicable to dig a canal from Buffalo, on Lake Erie, to the Hudson River. The Mohawk Valley cuts through the Appalachian chain just north of Albany, and at no point along the route to Buffalo does the land rise more than 570 feet above the level of the Hudson. Marshaling a mass of technical, financial, and commercial information (and using his political influence cannily), Clinton placed his proposal before the New York legislature. In its defense he was eloquent and farsighted:

> As an organ of communication between the Hudson, the Mississippi, the St. Lawrence, the great lakes of the north and west, and their tributary rivers, [the canal] will create the greatest inland trade ever witnessed. The most fertile and extensive regions of

CANALS AND ROADS, 1820–1850

America will avail themselves of its facilities for a market. All their surplus . . . will concentrate in the city of New York. . . . That city will, in the course of time, become the granary of the world, the emporium of commerce, the seat of manufactures, the focus of great moneyed operations. . . . And before the revolution of a century, the whole island of Manhattan, covered with habitations and replenished with a dense population, will constitute one vast city.

The legislators were convinced, and in 1817 the state began construction along a route 363 miles long, most of it across densely forested wilderness. At the time the longest canal in the United States ran less than 28 miles!

The construction of the Erie Canal, as it was called, was a remarkable accomplishment. The chief engineer, Benjamin Wright, a surveyor-politician from Rome, New York, had had almost no experience with canal building. One of his chief associates, James Geddes, possessed only an elementary school education and knew virtually nothing about surveying. Both learned rapidly by trial and error. Fortunately, Wright proved to be a good organizer and a fine judge of engineering talent. He quickly spotted young men of ability among the workers and pushed them forward. One of his finds, Canvass White, was sent to study British canals. White became an expert on the design of locks; he also discovered an American limestone that could be made into waterproof cement, a vital product in canal construction that had previously been imported at a substantial price from England. Another of Wright's proteges, John B. Jervis, began as an axman, rose in two years to resident engineer in charge of a section of the project, and went on to become perhaps the outstanding American civil engineer of his time. Workers who learned the business digging the "Big Ditch" supervised the construction of dozens of canals throughout the country in later years.

The Erie, completed in 1825, was an immediate financial success. Together with the companion Champlain Canal, which linked Lake Champlain and the Hudson, it brought in over half a million dollars in tolls in its first year. Soon its entire $7 million cost had been recovered, and it was earning profits of about $3 million a year. The effect of this prosperity on New York State was enormous. Buffalo, Rochester, Syracuse, and half a dozen lesser towns along the canal flourished.

Emporium of the Western World

New York City had already become the largest city in the nation, thanks chiefly to its merchants, who had established a reputation for their rapid and orderly way of doing business. In 1818 the Black Ball Line opened the first regularly scheduled freight and passenger service between New York and England. Previously, shipments might languish in port for weeks while a skipper waited for additional cargo. Now merchants on both sides of the Atlantic could count on the Black Ball packets to move their goods between Liverpool and New York on schedule whether or not the transporting vessel had a full cargo. This improvement brought much new business to the port. In the same year New York enacted an auction law requiring that imported goods having been placed on the block could not be withdrawn if a bid satisfactory to the seller was not forthcoming. This too was a boon to businessmen, who could be assured that if they outbid the competition, the goods would be theirs.

Now the canal cemented New York's position as the national metropolis. Most European-manufactured goods destined for the Mississippi Valley entered the country at New York and passed on to the west over the canal. The success of the Erie also sparked a nationwide canal-building boom. Most canals were constructed either by the states, as in the case of the Erie, or as "mixed enterprises" that combined public and private energies.

No state profited as much from this construction as New York, for none possessed New York's geographic advantages. In New England the terrain was so rugged as to discourage all but fanatics. Canals were built connecting Worcester and Northampton, Massachusetts, with the coast, but they were failures financially. The Delaware and Hudson Canal, running from northeastern Pennsylvania across northern New Jersey and lower New York to the Hudson, was completed by private interests in 1828. It managed to earn respectable dividends by barging coal to the eastern seaboard, but it made no attempt to compete with the Erie for the western trade. Pennsylvania, desperate to keep up with New York, engaged in an orgy of construction. In 1834 it completed a complicated system, part canal and part railroad, over the mountains to Pittsburgh. This Mainline Canal cost a staggering sum for that day. With its 177 locks and its cumbersome "in-

A view of New York's Broadway in 1835. The broad avenue was home to many of the large, modern stores that helped make New York City the commercial center of the nation.

clined-plane railroad," it was slow and expensive to operate and never competed effectively with the Erie. Efforts of Maryland to link Baltimore with the West by water failed utterly.

Beyond the mountains there was even greater zeal for canal construction in the 1820s and still more in the 1830s. Once the Erie opened the way across New York, farmers in the Ohio country demanded that links be built between the Ohio River and the Great Lakes so that they could ship their produce by water directly to the East. Local feeder canals seemed equally necessary; with corn worth 20 cents a bushel at Columbus selling for 50 cents at Marietta, on the Ohio, the value of cheap transportation became obvious to Ohio farmers.

Even before the completion of the Erie, Ohio had begun construction of the Ohio and Erie Canal running from the Ohio River to Cleveland. Another, from Toledo to Cincinnati, was begun in 1832. Meanwhile, Indiana had undertaken the 450 mile Wabash and Erie Canal. These canals were well conceived, but the western states overextended themselves building dozens of feeder lines, trying, it sometimes seemed, to supply all farmers west of the Appalachians with water connections from their barns to the New York docks. Politics made such programs almost inevitable, for in order to win support for their pet projects, legislators had to back the schemes of their fellows. The result was frequently financial disaster. There was not enough traffic to pay for all the waterways that were dug. By 1844, some $60 million in state improvement bonds were in default. Nevertheless, the canals benefited both western farmers and the national economy.

Government Aid to Business

Throughout this period both the United States and the states were active in areas that affected the economy directly. Federal banking, tariff, and land legislation had considerable influence on economic expansion. These political activities, which also contributed to the growth of sectional conflicts in the nation, will be considered in Chapter 10; here a number of legal and judicial developments require consideration.

Though prejudice against corporations in the manufacturing field continued, incorporation was such a useful means of bringing together the substantial amounts of capital needed for building roads and canals and for organizing banks and insurance companies that a steadily increasing number of promoters applied for charters. Bills authorizing incorporations became so numerous in

some eastern states that legislators found themselves devoting a disconcertingly large portion of
their time to them. Soon they were tempted to issue
blanket, though restricted, authorizations. In 1809
Massachusetts passed a law establishing strict rules
for all manufacturing corporations in the state. One
rule made shareholders individually liable for their
companies' debts beyond their actual investment.
While still requiring separate authorizations for
each charter, the Massachusetts legislature could
now dispose of applications in a more routine
fashion.

Two years later New York enacted the first general incorporation law, permitting the issuance of
charters without specific legislative action in each
case. Although they held stockholders liable only
"to the extent of their respective shares in the . . .
company," which was the basic privilege sought by
all incorporators, these general charters were not
available to companies capitalized at more than
$50,000, and they ran for only five years. This was
unsatisfactory; after an initial period of enthusiasm
(122 charters were issued between 1811 and 1816),
the law became nearly a dead letter. Other states
did not begin to permit general incorporation until
1837, and businessmen continued to seek, and obtain, special charters for decades thereafter.

Manufacturers in some states received valuable
tax benefits. In Vermont no industrial concern paid
local taxes. A New York law of 1817 exempted textile mills, and in 1823 Ohio extended similar privileges to textile, iron, and glass companies. Manufacturers benefited from the protection granted
inventors by the United States Patent Office, created
in 1790, and the attitude of most courts and juries
toward labor unions and strikes in this period favored employers. Before the end of the 1820s craft
unions had become numerous and active, yet judges
tended to consider strikes unlawful conspiracies and
to find against unions that tried to establish the
closed shop. Though the public's attitude toward
organized labor was beginning to change, the legal
right of unions to exist was not fully established
until the 1840s.

The Marshall Court

The most important legal advantages bestowed on
businessmen in the period were the gift of Chief
Justice John Marshall. Historians have tended to

forget that he had six colleagues on the Supreme
Court, and that is easy to understand. Marshall's
particular combination of charm, logic, and forcefulness made the Court during his long reign, if not
a rubber stamp, remarkably submissive to his view
of the Constitution. Marshall's belief in a powerful
central government explains his tendency to hand
down decisions favorable to manufacturing and
business interests. He also thought that "the business community was the agent of order and progress" and tended to interpret the Constitution in
a way that would advance its interests.

Many important cases came before the Court
between 1819 and 1824, and in each one Marshall's
decision was applauded by most of the business community. The cases involved two major principles:
the "sanctity" of contracts and the supremacy of
federal legislation over the laws of the states. Marshall shared the conviction of the Revolutionary
generation that property had to be protected against
arbitrary seizure if liberty was to be preserved. Contracts between private individuals and between individuals and the government must be strictly enforced, he believed, or chaos will result. He
therefore gave the widest possible application to the
constitutional provision that no state could pass any
law "impairing the Obligation of Contracts."

Two controversies settled in February 1819 illustrate Marshall's views on the subject of contracts.
In *Sturges* v. *Crowninshield* he found a New York
bankruptcy law unconstitutional. States could pass
such laws, he conceded, but they could not make
them applicable to debts incurred before the laws
were passed, for debts were contracts. In *Dartmouth
College* v. *Woodward* he held that a charter granted
by a state was a contract and might not be canceled
or altered without the consent of both parties. Contracts could scarcely be more sacred than Marshall
made them in the Dartmouth College case, which
involved an attempt by New Hampshire to alter the
charter granted to Dartmouth by King George III
in 1769. The state had sought not to destroy the
college but to change it from a private to a public
institution, yet Marshall held that to do so would
violate the contract clause. In the light of this decision, corporations licensed by the states seemed
immune against later attempts to regulate their activities, although, of course, restrictions imposed at
the time of the chartering were not affected. As a
result, states began to spell out the limitations of
corporate charters in greater detail.

*The artist Chester Harding painted
John Marshall in 1828, during the
chief justice's twenty-seventh year on
the Supreme Court. "The unpretentious dignity [and] the sober factual-
ism" of Harding's style (as art historian Oliver Larkin describes it) was
well suited to capturing Marshall's
character.*

Marshall's decisions concerning the division of power between the federal government and the states were even more important. The question of the constitutionality of a national bank, first debated by Hamilton and Jefferson, had not been submitted to the courts during the life of the first Bank of the United States. By the time of the second Bank there were many state banks, and some of them felt that their interests were threatened by the national institution. Responding to pressure from local banks, the Maryland legislature placed an annual tax of $15,000 on "foreign" banks. The Maryland branch of the Bank of the United States refused to pay, whereupon the state brought suit against its cashier, John W. McCulloch. *McCulloch* v. *Maryland* was crucial to the Bank, for five other states had levied taxes on its branches, and others would surely follow suit if the Maryland law were upheld.

Marshall extinguished the threat. The Bank was constitutional, he announced in phrases taken almost verbatim from Hamilton's 1791 memorandum to Washington on the subject; its legality was implied in many of the powers specifically granted to Congress. Full "discretion" must be allowed Congress in deciding exactly how its powers "are to be carried into execution." Since the Bank was legal, the Maryland tax was unconstitutional. Marshall found a "plain repugnance" in the thought of "conferring on one government a power to control the constitutional measures of another." He put this idea in the simplest possible language: "The power to tax involves the power to destroy . . . the power to destroy may defeat and render useless the power to create." The long-range significance of the decision lay in its strengthening of the implied powers of Congress and its confirmation of the Hamiltonian or "loose" interpretation of the Constitution. By establishing the legality of the Bank, it also aided the growth of the economy.

In 1824 Marshall handed down an important decision involving the regulation of interstate commerce. This was the "steamboat case," *Gibbons* v. *Ogden*. In 1815 Aaron Ogden, former United States senator and governor of New Jersey, had purchased the right to operate a ferry between Elizabeth Point, New Jersey, and New York City from Robert Fulton's backer, Robert R. Livingston, who held a New York monopoly of steamboat navigation on the Hudson. When Thomas Gibbons, who held a federal coasting license, set up a competing line, Ogden sued him. Ogden argued in effect that Gibbons could operate his boat (whose captain was Cornelius Vanderbilt, later a famous railroad magnate) on the New Jersey side of the Hudson but had no right to cross into New York waters. After complicated litigation in the lower courts, the case reached the Supreme Court on appeal. Marshall decided in favor of Gibbons, effectively destroying the New York monopoly. A state can regulate commerce that begins and ends in its own territory but not when the transaction involves crossing a state line; then the national authority takes precedence. "The act of Congress," he said, "is supreme; and the law of the state . . . must yield to it."

This decision threw open the interstate steamboat business to all comers, and since an adequate 100-ton vessel could be built for as little as $7,000, dozens of small operators were soon engaged in it. Their competition tended to keep rates low and service efficient, to the great advantage of the country. More important in the long run was the fact that in order to include the ferry business within the federal government's power to regulate inter-

state commerce, Marshall had given the word the widest possible meaning. "Commerce, undoubtedly, is traffic, but it is something more—it is intercourse." By construing the "commerce" clause so broadly, he made it easy for future generations of judges to extend its coverage to include the control of interstate electric power lines and even radio and television transmission.

Many of Marshall's decisions aided the economic development of the country in specific ways, but his chief contribution lay in his broadly national view of economic affairs. When he tried consciously to favor business by making contracts inviolable, his influence was important but limited—and, as it worked out, impermanent. In the steamboat case and in *McCulloch* v. *Maryland,* where he was really deciding between rival property interests, his work was more truly judicial in spirit and far more lasting. In such matters his nationalism enabled him to add form and substance to Hamilton's vision of the economic future of the United States.

Marshall and his colleagues firmly established the principle of judicial limitation on the power of legislatures and made the Supreme Court a vital part of the American system of government. In an age plagued by narrow sectional jealousies, Marshall's contribution was of immense influence and significance, and upon it rests his claim to greatness.

John Marshall died in 1835. Two years later, in the Charles River Bridge case, the court handed down another decision that aided economic development. The state of Massachusetts had built a bridge across the Charles River between Boston and Cambridge that drew traffic from an older, privately owned toll bridge nearby. Since no tolls were collected from users of the state bridge after construction costs were recovered, owners of the older bridge sued for damages on the ground that the free bridge made the stock in their company worthless. They argued that in building the bridge, Massachusetts had violated the contract clause of the Constitution.

The Court, however, now speaking through the new Chief Justice, Roger B. Taney, decided otherwise. The state had a right to place "the comfort and convenience" of the whole community over that of a particular company, Taney declared. "Improvements" that add to public "wealth and property" take precedence. How John Marshall would have voted in this case, in which he would have had to choose between his Dartmouth College and steamboat case arguments, will never be known. But like most of the decisions of the Court that were made while Marshall was chief justice, the Charles River Bridge case advanced the interests of those who favored economic development. Whether they were pursuing political advantage or economic, the Americans of the early 19th century seemed committed to a policy of compromise and accommodation.

Milestones

1790	Samuel Slater sets up first American factory
1793	Eli Whitney invents cotton gin
1807	Robert Fulton's *North River Steam Boat*
1813	Boston Manufacturing Company opens in Waltham, Massachusetts
1816	Second Bank of the United States
	James Monroe elected president
1817	American Colonization Society founded
1819	Dartmouth College case

	(*Dartmouth College* v. *Woodward*)
	Bank case (*McCulloch* v. *Maryland*)
1819–1822	Depression of 1819
1820–1821	Missouri Compromise
1824	Steamboat case (*Gibbons* v. *Ogden*)
1825	J. Q. Adams's presumed "corrupt bargain" with Henry Clay
	Erie Canal completed
1837	*Charles River Bridge* v. *Warren Bridge*

SUPPLEMENTARY READING

Titles marked with an asterisk have been published in paperback.

On the forces changing the American economy and stimulating the development of industry, see Stuart Bruchey, **The Roots of American Economic Growth*** (1965), and D. C. North, **The Economic Growth of the United States*** (1961). G. R. Taylor, **The Transportation Revolution*** (1951), a book far broader in scope than its title indicates, also discusses this subject intelligently. F. J. Turner, **Rise of the New West*** (1906), is still useful on the expansion of the West during the Era of Good Feelings, but see also the appropriate chapters of R. A. Billington, **Westward Expansion** (1967).

On the industrial revolution in America, see A. D. Chandler, Jr., **The Visible Hand: The Managerial Revolution in American Business** (1977), and B. M. Tucker, **Samuel Slater and the Origins of the American Textile Industry** (1984).

On the spread of cotton cultivation in the South, see C. M. Green, **Eli Whitney and the Birth of American Technology*** (1956), and P. W. Gates, **The Farmer's Age** (1960). On the colonization movement, see P. J. Staudenraus, **The African Colonization Movement** (1961).

Taylor's **Transportation Revolution** is the best introduction to the changes in transportation that took place. P. D. Jordan, **The National Road** (1948), is useful, as is George Dangerfield, **Chancellor Robert R. Livingston of New York** (1960), which contains an excellent account of the planning and operation of the *Clermont*.

On the Erie Canal, see R. E. Shaw, **Erie Water West** (1966), Nathan Miller, **The Enterprise of a Free People** (1962), and R. G. Albion, **The Rise of New York Port** (1939). Two works edited by Carter Goodrich, **Government Promotion of American Canals and Railroads,** (1960) and **Canals and American Economic Development** (1961), describe authoritatively the role of government aid in canal construction.

On Marshall, see F. N. Stites, **John Marshall: Defender of the Constitution** (1981). The most important decisions of the Marshall court in this period are discussed in J. A. Garraty (ed.), **Quarrels That Have Shaped the Constitution*** (1987), and R. K. Newmyer, **The Supreme Court Under Marshall and Taney*** (1968).

Jacksonian Democracy

The best government rests on the [whole] people and not on the few, on persons and not on property, on the free development of public opinion and not on authority, . . . the munificent Author of our being has conferred the gifts of mind upon every member of the human race without distinction of outward circumstance.

GEORGE BANCROFT, The Office of the People, *1842*

A t 11 A.M. on March 4, 1829, a bright sunny day, Andrew Jackson, hatless and dressed severely in black, left his quarters at Gadsby's Hotel. Accompanied by a few close associates, he walked up Pennsylvania Avenue to the Capitol. At a few minutes after noon he emerged on the East Portico with the justices of the Supreme Court and other dignitaries. Before a throng of more than 15,000 people he delivered an almost inaudible and thoroughly commonplace inaugural address and then took the presidential oath. The first man to congratulate him was Chief Justice Marshall, who had administered the oath. The second was "Honest George" Kremer, a Pennsylvania congressman best known for the leopardskin coat that he affected, who led the cheering crowd that brushed past the barricade and scrambled up the Capitol steps to wring the new president's hand.

Jackson shouldered his way through the crush, mounted a splendid white horse, and rode off to the White House. A reception had been announced, to which "the officially and socially eligible as defined by precedent" had been invited. The day was unseasonably warm after a hard winter, and the streets of Washington were muddy. As Jackson rode down Pennsylvania Avenue, the crowds that had turned out to see the Hero of New Orleans followed—on horseback, in rickety wagons, and on foot. Nothing could keep them out of the executive mansion, and the result was chaos. Long tables laden with cakes, ice cream, and orange punch had been set up in the East Room, but these scarcely deflected the well-wishers. Jackson was pressed back helplessly as men tracked mud across valuable rugs and clambered up on delicate chairs to catch a glimpse of him. The White House shook with their shouts. Glassware splintered, furniture was overturned, women fainted.

Jackson was a thin old man despite his toughness, and soon he was in danger. Fortunately, friends formed a cordon and managed to extricate him through a rear door. The new president spent his first night in office at Gadsby's.

Only a generation earlier Jefferson had felt obliged to introduce pell-mell to encourage informality in the White House. Now a man whom John Quincy Adams called "a barbarian" held Jefferson's office, and, as one Supreme Court justice complained, "The reign of King 'Mob' seemed triumphant."

"Democratizing" Politics

Jackson's inauguration, and especially this celebration in the White House, symbolized the triumph of "democracy," the achievement of place and station by "the common man." Having been taught by Jefferson that all men are created equal, the Americans of Jackson's day (conveniently ignoring males with black skins, to say nothing of women, regardless of color) found it easy to believe that every person was as competent and as politically important as his neighbor.

The difference between Jeffersonian democracy and the Jackson variety was more one of attitude than of practice. Jefferson had believed that ordinary citizens could be educated to determine right. Jackson insisted that they knew what was right by instinct. Jefferson's pell-mell encouraged the average citizen to hold up his head; by the time of Jackson, the "common man" gloried in ordinariness and made mediocrity a virtue. The slightest hint of distinctiveness or servility became suspect. That President Washington required his footmen to wear uniforms was taken as a matter of course in the 1790s, but the British minister in Jackson's day found it next to impossible to find Americans willing to don his splendid livery. While most middle-class families could still hire people to do their cooking and housework, the word *servant* itself fell out of fashion, replaced by the egalitarian *help.*

The Founding Fathers had not foreseen all the implications of political democracy for a society like the one that existed in the United States. They believed that the ordinary man should have political power in order to protect himself against the superior man, but they assumed that the latter would always lead. The people would naturally choose the best men to manage public affairs. In Washington's day and even in Jefferson's this was generally the case, but the inexorable logic of democracy gradually produced a change. The new western states, unfettered by systems created in a less democratic age, drew up constitutions that eliminated property qualifications for voting and holding office. Many more public offices were made elective rather than appointive. The eastern states revised their own frames of government to accomplish the same purposes.

Even the presidency, designed to be removed from direct public control by the electoral college, felt the impact of the new thinking. By Jackson's time only two states, Delaware and South Carolina, still provided for the choice of presidential electors by the legislature; in all others they were selected by popular vote. The system of permitting the congressional caucus to name the candidates for the presidency came to an end before 1828. Jackson and Adams were put forward by state legislatures, and soon thereafter the still more democratic system of nomination by national party conventions was adopted.

Certain social changes reflected a new way of looking at political affairs. The final disestablishment of churches reveals a dislike of special privilege. The beginnings of the free-school movement, the earliest glimmerings of interest in adult education, and the slow spread of secondary education

all bespeak a concern for improving the knowledge and judgment of the ordinary citizen. The rapid increase in the number of newspapers, their declining prices, and their ever-greater concentration on political affairs indicate that an effort was being made to bring political news to the common man's attention.

All these changes emphasized the idea that every citizen was equally important and the conviction that all should participate actively in government. Officeholders began to stress the fact that they were *representatives* as well as leaders and to appeal more openly and much more intensively for votes. The public responded. At each succeeding presidential election, a larger percentage of the population went to the polls. Roughly 300,000 ballots were cast in 1824, 1.1 million four years later, and 2.4 million in 1840.

As voting became more important, so did competition between the candidates, and this led to changes in the role and structure of political parties. It took money, people, and organized effort to run the campaigns and get out the vote. Parties became powerful institutions; as a result, they attracted voters' loyalties powerfully. This development took place first at the state level and at different times in different states. According to Richard P. McCormick, whose book *The Second American Party System* describes the process, the 1828 election stimulated party formation because instead of several sectional candidates, each dominant in his own region, competing for the presidency, it pitted two nationally known men against each other. This compelled local leaders to make a choice and then to organize their forces in order to convince local voters to accept their judgment. This was especially true in states where neither Adams nor Jackson had a preponderance of backers. Thus the new system established itself much faster in New York and Pennsylvania than in New England, where Adams was strong, or Tennessee, where the native son Jackson had overwhelming support.

Like most institutions, the new parties created bureaucracies to keep them running smoothly. Devoted party workers were rewarded with political office when their efforts were successful. "To the victors belong the spoils," said the New York politician William L. Marcy, and the image, drawn from war and piracy, was appropriate. Although the vigorous wooing of voters constituted a recognition of their importance and commitment to keeping them informed, campaigning—another military term—frequently degenerated into demagoguery. The most effective way to attract the average voter, politicians soon decided, was by flattery.

1828: The New Party System in Embryo

The new system could scarcely have been imagined in 1825 while John Quincy Adams ruled over the White House; Adams was not well equipped either to lead King Mob or to hold it in check. Indeed, it was the battle to succeed Adams that caused the system to develop. The campaign began almost on the day of his selection by the House of Representatives. Jackson felt that he, the man with the largest vote, had been cheated of the presidency in 1824 by "the corrupt bargain" that he believed Adams had made with Henry Clay, and he sought vindication.

Relying heavily on his military reputation and on Adams's talent for making enemies, Jackson avoided taking a stand on issues and on questions where his views might displease one or another faction. The political situation thus became monumentally confused, one side unable to marshal support for its policies, the other unwilling to adopt policies for fear of losing support.

The campaign was disgraced by character assassination and lies of the worst sort. Administration supporters denounced Jackson as a bloodthirsty military tyrant, a drunkard, and a gambler. His wife Rachel, ailing and shy, was dragged into the campaign, her good name heartlessly besmirched. Previously married to a cruel, unbalanced man named Lewis Robards, she had begun living with Jackson before her divorce from Robards had been legally completed. When this fact came to light, she and Jackson had to remarry. Seizing on this incident, an Adams pamphleteer wrote: "Ought a convicted adulteress and her paramour husband be placed in the highest offices of this free and christian land?"

Furious, the Jacksonians (now calling themselves Democrats) replied in kind. They charged that while American minister to Russia, Adams had supplied

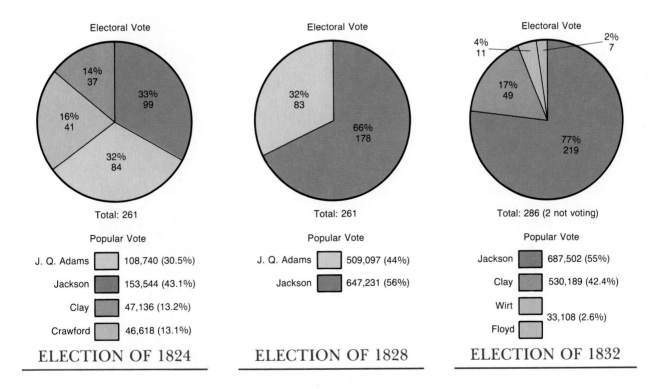

ELECTION OF 1824

ELECTION OF 1828

ELECTION OF 1832

a beautiful American virgin for the delectation of the czar. Discovering that the president had purchased a chess set and a billiard table for the White House, they accused him of squandering public money on gambling devices. They translated his long and distinguished public service into the statistic that he had received over the years a sum equal to $16 for every day of his life in government pay. The great questions of the day were largely ignored.

All this was inexcusable, and both sides must share the blame. But as the politicians noticed when the votes were counted, their efforts had certainly brought out the electorate. *Each* candidate received far more votes than all four candidates had received in the preceding presidential election.

When inauguration day arrived, Adams refused to attend the ceremonies because Jackson had failed to pay the traditional preinaugural courtesy call on him at the White House, but the Old Puritan may have been equally, if unconsciously, motivated by shame at tactics he had countenanced during the campaign. Jackson felt vindication, not shame, but in any case, deep personal feelings were uppermost in everyone's mind at the formal changing of the guard. The real issues, however, remained. Andrew Jackson would now have to deal with them.

The Jacksonian Appeal

Some historians claim that despite his supposed fondness for the common man, Andrew Jackson was not a democrat at all and anything but a consistent friend of the weak and underprivileged. They point out that he was a wealthy land speculator and the owner of a fine Tennessee plantation, the Hermitage, and of many slaves. Before becoming president he had opposed cheap-money schemes and pressed lawsuits against more than 100 individuals who owed him money. Although his supporters liked to cast him as the political heir of Jefferson, he was in many ways like the conservative Washington: a soldier first, an inveterate speculator in western lands, a man with few intellectual interests and only sketchily educated.

Nor was Jackson quite the rough-hewn frontier character he sometimes seemed. True, he could not spell (again, like Washington), he possessed the unsavory habits of the tobacco chewer, and he had a

violent temper, but his manners and life-style were those of a southern planter. His judgment was intuitive yet usually sound; his frequent rages were often feigned, designed to accomplish some carefully thought-out purpose. "He would sometimes extemporize a fit of passion in order to overwhelm an adversary," one contemporary noted, "but his self-command was always perfect." Once, after scattering a delegation of protesters with an exhibition of Jovian wrath, he turned to an observer and said impishly: "They thought I was mad."

It is of small importance to anyone interested in Jacksonian democracy to know exactly how "democratic" Jackson was or how sincere was his interest

A figurehead of Andrew Jackson carved by Laban S. Beecher for the frigate Constitution. *Soon after it was mounted on the ship, an anti-Jackson agitator sawed off the head just below the nose! (It was later neatly mended.) The figurehead is almost 12 feet tall.*

in the welfare of the common man. Whatever his personal convictions, he stood as the symbol for a movement supported by a new, democratically oriented generation. That he was both a great hero and in many ways a most extraordinary person helps explain his mass appeal. He had defeated a mighty British army and killed hosts of Indians, but he acted on hunches and not always consistently, shouted and pounded his fist when angry, put loyalty to old comrades above efficiency when making appointments, distrusted "aristocrats" and all special privilege. Perhaps he was rich, perhaps conservative, but he was a man of the people, born in a frontier cabin, familiar with the problems of the average citizen.

Jackson epitomized many American ideals. He was intensely patriotic, generous to a fault, natural and democratic in manner (at home alike in the forest and in the ballroom of a fine mansion). He admired good horseflesh and beautiful women, yet no sterner moralist ever lived; he was a fighter, a relentless foe, but a gentleman in the best American sense. That some special providence watched over him (as over the United States) appeared beyond argument to those who had followed his career. He seemed, in short, both an average and an ideal American, one the people could identify with and still revere.

For these reasons Jackson drew support from every section and every social class: western farmers and southern planters, urban workers, and bankers and merchants. In this sense he was profoundly democratic—and in the sense, too, that whatever his position on public issues, he believed in equality of opportunity, distrusted entrenched status of every sort, and rejected no free American because of humble origins or inadequate education.

The Spoils System

Jackson took office with the firm intention of punishing the "vile wretches" who had attacked him so viciously during the campaign. (Rachel Jackson died shortly after the election, and her devoted husband was convinced that the indignities heaped on her by Adams partisans had speeded her decline.) The new concept of political office as a reward for victory seemed to justify a housecleaning in Wash-

ington. Henry Clay captured the fears of anti-Jackson government workers. "Among the official corps here there is the greatest solicitude and apprehension," he said. "The members of it feel something like the inhabitants of Cairo when the plague breaks out; no one knows who is next to encounter the stroke of death."

Eager for the "spoils," an army of politicians invaded Washington. There was nothing especially innovative about this invasion, for the principle of filling offices with one's partisans was almost as old as the republic. However, the long lapse of time since the last real political shift, and the recent untypical example of John Quincy Adams, who rarely removed or appointed anyone for political reasons, made Jackson's policy appear revolutionary. His removals were not entirely unjustified, for many government workers had grown senile and others corrupt. A number of officials were found to be short in their accounts; a few were hopeless drunks. Jackson was determined to root out the thieves. Even Adams admitted that some of those Jackson dismissed deserved their fate.

Aside from going along with the spoils system and eliminating crooks and incompetents, Jackson advanced another reason for turning experienced government employees out of their jobs: the principle of rotation. "No man has any more intrinsic right to official station than another," he said. Those who hold government jobs for a long time "are apt to acquire a habit of looking with indifference upon the public interests and of tolerating conduct from which an unpracticed man would revolt." By "rotating" jobholders periodically, more citizens could participate in the tasks of government, and the danger of creating an entrenched bureaucracy would be eliminated. The problem was that the constant replacing of trained workers by novices was not likely to increase the efficiency of the government. Jackson's response to this argument was typical: "The duties of all public officers are . . . so plain and simple that men of intelligence may readily qualify themselves for their performance.

Contempt for expert knowledge and the belief that ordinary Americans can do anything they set their minds to became fundamental tenets of Jacksonian democracy. To apply them to present-day government would be to court disaster, but in the early 19th century it was not so preposterous, because the role that government played in American life was simple and nontechnical.

Furthermore, Jackson did not practice what he preached. By and large his appointees were anything but common men. A majority came from the same social and intellectual elite as those they replaced. As the historian Sidney H. Aronson pointed out, "Circumstances made it difficult for him to locate such common men in the crowd." He did not try to rotate civil servants in the War and Navy departments, where to do so might have been harmful. In general, he left pretty much alone what a modern administrator would call middle management, the backbone of every organization.

Nevertheless, the spoilsmen roamed the capital in force during the spring of 1829, seeking, as the forthright Jackson said, "a tit to suck the treasury pap." Their philosophy was well summarized by a New Yorker: "No d——d rascal who made use of his office . . . for the purpose of keeping Mr. Adams in, and Genl. Jackson out of power is entitled to the least lenity or mercy. . . . Whether or not I shall get anything in the general scramble for plunder, remains to be proven, but I rather guess I shall."

President of All the People

President Jackson was not cynical about the spoils system. As a strong man who intuitively sought to

Jackson's spoils-system policies were repeatedly attacked by opposition cartoonists. "Office Hunters for the Year 1834," for example, portrays the president as a demon dangling the spoils of his office, including banquets, money, weapons, appointments, and—for some obscure reason—millinery, above his greedy supporters.

increase his authority, the idea of making government workers dependent on him made excellent sense. His opponents had pictured him as a simple soldier fronting for a rapacious band of politicians, but he soon proved he would exercise his authority directly. Except for Martin Van Buren, the secretary of state, his Cabinet was not distinguished, and he did not rely on it for advice. He turned instead to an informal "Kitchen Cabinet," which consisted of the influential Van Buren and a few close friends. But these men were advisers, not directors; Jackson was clearly master of his own administration.

More than any earlier president, he conceived of himself as the direct representative of all the people and therefore the embodiment of national power. From Washington to John Quincy Adams, his predecessors together had vetoed only nine bills, always on the ground that they believed the measures unconstitutional. Jackson vetoed 12, some simply because he thought the legislation inexpedient. Yet he had no ambition to expand the scope of federal authority at the expense of the states. Basically he was a Jeffersonian; he favored a "frugal," constitutionally limited national government. Furthermore, he was a poor administrator, given to penny-pinching and lacking in imagination. His strong prejudices and his contempt for expert advice, even in fields such as banking where his ignorance was almost total, did him no credit and the country considerable harm.

Jackson's great success (not merely his popularity) was primarily the result of his personality. A shrewd French observer, Michel Chevalier, after commenting on "his chivalric character, his lofty integrity, and his ardent patriotism," pointed out what was probably the central element in Jackson's appeal. "His tactic in politics, as well as in war," Chevalier wrote in 1824, "is to throw himself forward with the cry of *Comrades, follow me!*" Sometimes he might be wrong, but always he was a leader.

Sectional Tensions Revived

In office Jackson had to say something about western lands, the tariff, and other issues. He tried to steer a moderate course, urging a slight reduction of the tariff and "constitutional" internal improvements. He suggested that once the rapidly disap-

pearing federal debt had been paid off, the surplus revenues of the government might be "distributed" among the states.

Even these cautious proposals caused conflict, so complex were the interrelations of sectional disputes. If the federal government turned its expected surplus over to the states, it could not afford to reduce the price of public land without going into the red. This disturbed westerners, notably Senator Thomas Hart Benton of Missouri, and western concern suggested to southern opponents of the protective tariff an alliance of South and West. The southerners argued that a tariff levied only to raise revenue would increase foreign imports, bring more money into the treasury, and thus make it possible to reduce the price of public land.

The question came up in the Senate in December 1829, when an obscure Connecticut senator, Samuel A. Foot, suggested restricting the sale of government land. Benton promptly denounced the proposal. On January 19, 1830, Senator Robert Y. Hayne of South Carolina, a spokesman for Vice-President Calhoun, supported Benton vigorously, suggesting an alliance of South and West based on cheap land and low tariffs. Daniel Webster then rose to the defense of northeastern interests, cleverly goading Hayne by accusing South Carolina of advocating disunionist policies. Responding to this attack, the South Carolinian, a glib speaker but a rather imprecise thinker, launched into an impassioned exposition of the states' rights doctrine.

Webster then took the floor again and for two days, before galleries packed with the elite of Washington society, cut Hayne's argument to shreds. The Constitution was a compact of the American people, not merely of the states, he insisted, the Union perpetual and indissoluble. Webster made the states' rights position appear close to treason; his "second reply to Hayne" effectively prevented the formation of a West-South alliance.

Jackson Versus Calhoun

The Webster-Hayne debate revived discussion of the idea of nullification. Although southern-born, Jackson had devoted too much of his life to fighting for the entire United States to countenance disunion. Therefore, when the states' rights faction invited him to a dinner to celebrate the anniversary of Jefferson's birth, he came prepared. The evening reverberated with speeches and toasts of a states' rights tenor, but when the president was called on to volunteer a toast, he raised his glass, fixed his eyes on John C. Calhoun, and said: "Our *Federal* Union: It must be preserved!" Calhoun took up the challenge at once. "The Union," he retorted, "next to our liberty, most dear!"

It is difficult to measure the importance of the animosity between Jackson and Calhoun in the crisis to which this clash was a prelude. Calhoun wanted very much to be president. He had failed to inherit the office from John Quincy Adams and had accepted the vice-presidency again under Jackson in the hope of succeeding him at the end of one term, if not sooner, for Jackson's health was known to be frail. Yet Old Hickory showed no sign of passing on or retiring. Jackson also seemed to place special confidence in the shrewd Van Buren, who, as secretary of state, also had claim to the succession.

A silly social fracas in which Calhoun's wife appeared to take the lead in the systematic snubbing of Peggy Eaton, wife of the secretary of war, had estranged Jackson and Calhoun. (Peggy was supposed to have had an affair with Eaton while she was still married to another man, and Jackson, undoubtedly sympathetic because of the attacks he and Rachel had endured, stoutly defended her good name.) Then, shortly after the Jefferson Day dinner, Jackson discovered that in 1818, when he had invaded Florida, Calhoun, then secretary of war, had recommended to President Monroe that Jackson be summoned before a court of inquiry and charged with disobeying orders. Since Calhoun had repeatedly led Jackson to believe that he had supported him at the time, the revelation convinced the president that Calhoun was not a man of honor.

The personal difficulties are worth stressing because Jackson and Calhoun were not far apart ideologically except on the ultimate issue of the right of a state to overrule federal authority. Jackson was a strong president, but he did not believe that the area of national power was large or that it should be expanded. His interests in government economy, in the distribution of federal surpluses to the states, and in interpreting the powers of Congress narrowly were all similar to Calhoun's. Like most westerners, he favored internal improvements, but he preferred that local projects be left to the states. In 1830 he vetoed a bill providing aid for the construction of the Maysville Road because the route was wholly within Kentucky. There were political reasons for this veto, which was a slap at Kentucky's hero, Henry Clay, but it could not fail to please Calhoun.

Indian Removals

The president also took a states' rights position in the controversy that arose between the Cherokee Indians and Georgia. Jackson subscribed to the theory, advanced by Jefferson, that Indians were "savage" because they roamed wild in a trackless wilderness. The "original inhabitants of our forests" were "incapable of self-government," Jackson claimed, ignoring the fact that they had governed themselves without trouble before the whites arrived. If they settled on small farms, they would become "civilized," and all would be well between them and the whites.

Most Indians preferred to maintain their tribal ways, so Jackson pursued a policy of removing them from the path of western settlement. This policy seems heartless to modern critics, but since few Indians were willing to adopt the white way of life, most contemporary whites considered removal the only humane solution if the nation was to continue to expand. Jackson insisted that the Indians receive fair prices for their lands and that the government bear the expense of resettling them. He believed that moving them beyond the Mississippi would protect them from the "degradation and destruction to which they were rapidly hastening . . . in the States."

Many tribes resigned themselves to removal without argument. Between 1831 and 1833 some 15,000 Choctaws migrated from their lands in Mississippi to the region west of Arkansas Territory.

In *Democracy in America*, the Frenchman Alexis de Tocqueville described "the frightful sufferings that attend these forced migrations," and he added sadly that the migrants "have no longer a country, and soon will not be a people." He vividly described a group of Choctaws crossing the Mississippi River at Memphis in the dead of winter.

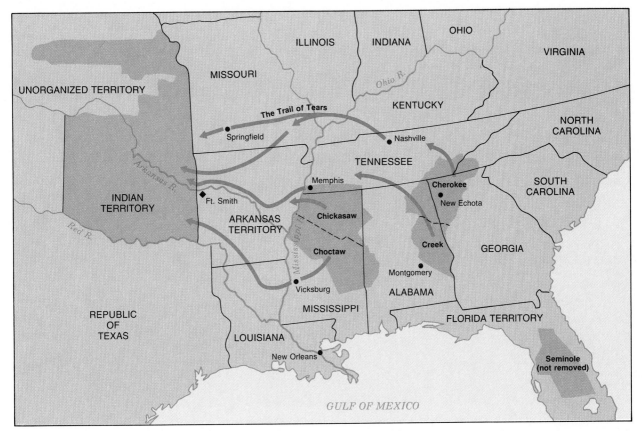

INDIAN REMOVALS

The cold was unusually severe; the snow had frozen hard upon the ground, and the river was drifting huge masses of ice. The Indians had their families with them, and they brought in their train the wounded and the sick, with children newly born and old men upon the verge of death. They possessed neither tents nor wagons, but only their arms and some provisions. I saw them embark to pass the mighty river, and never will that solemn spectacle fade from my remembrance. No cry, no sob, was heard among the assembled crowd; all were silent.

Tocqueville was particularly moved by the sight of an old woman whom he described in a letter to his mother. She was "naked save for a covering which left visible, at a thousand places, the most emaciated figure imaginable. . . . To leave one's country at that age to seek one's fortune in a foreign land, what misery!" "In the whole scene," he went on, "there was an air of ruin and destruction, something which betrayed a final and irrevocable adieu; one couldn't watch without feeling one's heart wrung."

A few tribes, such as Black Hawk's Sac and Fox in Illinois and Osceola's Seminoles in Florida, resisted removal and were subdued by troops. One Indian nation, the Cherokee, sought to hold on to its lands by adjusting to white ways. They took up farming and cattle raising, developed a written language, drafted a constitution, and tried to establish a state within a state in northwestern Georgia. Several treaties with the United States seemed to establish the legality of their government. But Georgia would not recognize the Cherokee Nation. It passed a law in 1828 declaring all Cherokee laws void and the region part of Georgia.

Several hundred Seminole Indians in Florida refused to abandon their tribal lands and move west. Although their leader, Osceola, was treacherously captured in 1837 and soon died in prison, other Seminoles fought on until forced to surrender in 1842; the warriors in this picture are attacking a federal fort. Some Seminoles hid out in the swamps and never gave themselves up.

The Indians challenged this law in the Supreme Court. In *Cherokee Nation* v. *Georgia* (1831) Chief Justice John Marshall had ruled that the Cherokees were "not a foreign state, in the sense of the Constitution" and therefore could not sue in a United States court. However, in *Worcester* v. *Georgia* (1832), a case involving two missionaries to the Cherokees who had not procured licenses required by Georgia law, he ruled that the state could not control the Cherokees or their territory. Later, when a Cherokee named Corn Tassel, convicted in a Georgia court of the murder of another Indian, appealed on the ground that the crime had taken place in Cherokee territory, Marshall declared the Georgia action unconstitutional on the same grounds.

Jackson backed Georgia's position. No independent nation could exist within the United States, he insisted. Georgia thereupon hanged poor Corn Tassel. In 1838, after Jackson had left the White House, the United States forced 15,000 Cherokees to leave Georgia for Oklahoma. About 4,000 of them died on the way; the route has been named the Trail of Tears.

Jackson's willingness to allow Georgia to ignore decisions of the Supreme Court persuaded extreme southern states' righters that he would not oppose the doctrine of nullification should it be formally applied to a law of Congress. They deceived themselves egregiously. Jackson did not challenge Georgia because he approved of the state's position. He spoke of "the poor deluded . . . Cherokees" and called William Wirt, the distinguished lawyer who defended their cause, a "truly wicked" man. Jackson was not one to worry about being inconsistent. When South Carolina revived the talk of nullification in 1832, he acted in quite a different manner.

The Nullification Crisis

The proposed alliance of South and West to reduce the tariff and the price of land had not materialized, partly because Webster had discredited the South in the eyes of western patriots and partly because the planters of South Carolina and Georgia, fearing the competition of fertile new cotton lands in Alabama and Mississippi, opposed the rapid exploitation of the West almost as vociferously as northern manufacturers did. When a new tariff law was passed in 1832, it lowered duties much less than the southerners desired. At once talk of nullifying it began to be heard in South Carolina.

In addition to the economic woes of the up-country cotton planters, the great planter-aristocrats of the rice-growing Tidewater, though relatively prosperous, were troubled by northern criticisms of slavery. In the rice region, blacks outnumbered whites two to one; it was the densest concentration of blacks in the United States. Thousands of these slaves were African-born, brought in during the burst of importations before Congress outlawed the trade in 1808. Controlled usually by overseers of the worst sort, the slaves seemed to their masters like savage beasts straining to rise up against their oppressors. In 1822 the exposure in Charleston of a planned revolt organized by Denmark Vesey, who had bought his freedom with money won in a lottery, had alarmed many whites. News of a far more serious uprising in Virginia led by the slave Nat Turner in 1831, just as the tariff controversy was coming to a head, added to popular concern. Radical South Carolinians saw protective tariffs and agitation against slavery as the two sides of one coin; against both aspects of what appeared to them the tyranny of the majority, nullification seemed the logical defense. Yield on the tariff, editor Henry L. Pinckney of the influential *Charleston Mercury* warned, and "abolition will become the order of the day."

Endless discussions of Calhoun's doctrine after the publication of his "Exposition and Protest" in 1828 had produced much interesting theorizing without clarifying the issue. William H. Freehling, a modern student of the controversy, sums it up aptly: "The theory of nullification was a veritable snarl of contradictions." Admirers of Calhoun praised his "power of analysis & profound philosophical reasonings," but his idea was ingenious rather than profound. Plausible at first glance, it was based on false assumptions: that the Constitution was subject to definitive interpretation; that one party could be permitted to interpret a compact unilaterally without destroying it; that a minority of the nation could reassume its sovereign independence but that a minority of a state could not.

President Jackson was in this respect Calhoun's exact opposite. The South Carolinian's mental gymnastics he brushed aside; intuitively he realized the central reality: If a state could nullify a law of Congress, the Union could not exist. "Tell . . . the Nullifiers from me that they can talk and write resolutions and print threats to their hearts' content," he warned a South Carolina representative when Congress adjourned in July 1832. "But if one drop of blood be shed there in defiance of the laws of the United States, I will hang the first man of them I can get my hands on to the first tree I can find."

The warning was not taken seriously in South Carolina. In October the state legislature provided for the election of a special convention, which, when it met, contained a solid majority of nullifiers. On November 24, 1832, the convention passed an ordinance of nullification prohibiting the collection of tariff duties in the state after February 1, 1833. The legislature then authorized the raising of an army and appropriated money to supply it with weapons.

Jackson quickly began military preparations of his own, telling friends that he would have 50,000 men ready to move in a little over a month. He also made a statesmanlike effort to end the crisis peaceably. First he suggested to Congress that it lower the tariff further. On December 10 he delivered a "Proclamation to the People of South Carolina." Nullification could only lead to the destruction of the Union, he said. "The laws of the United States must be executed. I have no discretionary power on the subject. . . . Those who told you that you might peaceably prevent their execution deceived you." Old Hickory added sternly: "Disunion by armed force is *treason*. Are you really ready to incur its guilt?"

This line of reasoning profoundly shocked even opponents of nullification for two quite different reasons. First of all, it undermined the very basis of states' rights, the belief that sovereignty in the United States had been divided between local and national governments so that local interests could not be dominated by a national majority. Beyond this, Jackson's threat to use force would mean civil war if South Carolina did not back down and possibly the destruction of the Union the president claimed to be defending. Large numbers of people who admired Jackson nonetheless, as Van Buren later wrote, "distrusted his prudence," fearing that he would "commit some rash act." They believed in dealing with the controversy by discussion and compromise.

As a result, in Congress pressure for compromise was tremendous. Administration leaders introduced both a new tariff bill and a Force Bill granting the president additional authority to execute the revenue laws. Calhoun, having resigned as vice-president to accept appointment as senator from South Carolina, led the fight against the Force Bill. Jackson was perfectly willing to see the tariff reduced but insisted that he was determined to enforce the law. As the February 1 deadline approached, he claimed that he could raise 200,000 men if needed to suppress resistance. "Union men, fear not," he said. *"The Union will be preserved."*

Jackson's determination sobered the South Carolina radicals. Their appeal for the support of other southern states fell on deaf ears: All rejected the idea of nullification. The unionist minority in South Carolina added to the radicals' difficulties by threatening civil war if federal authority were defied. Calhoun, though a brave man, was alarmed for his own safety, for Jackson had threatened to "hang him as high as Haman" if nullification were attempted. Observers described him as "excessively uneasy." He was suddenly eager to avoid a showdown.

Ten days before the deadline, South Carolina postponed nullification pending the outcome of the tariff debate. Then Calhoun joined forces with Henry Clay to push a compromise tariff through

As a contemporary observer pictured it, nullification could end only in despotism. Calhoun reaches for a crown as the Constitution and the Union lie dead beneath him. Jackson, at right, restrains one of Calhoun's followers and threatens him and all his ilk with hanging.

Congress. As part of the agreement Congress also passed the Force Bill, mostly as a face-saving device for the president. The compromise reflected the willingness of the North and West to make concessions in the interest of national harmony. Senator Silas Wright of New York, closely affiliated with Van Buren, explained the situation: "People will neither cut throats nor dismember the Union for protection. There is more patriotism and love of country than that left yet. The People will never balance this happy government against ten cents a pound upon a pound of wool."

And so the Union weathered the storm. Having stepped to the brink of civil war, the nation had drawn hastily back. The South Carolina legislature professed to be satisfied with the new tariff (in fact it made few immediate reductions, providing for a gradual lowering of rates over a ten-year period) and repealed the Nullification Ordinance, saving face by nullifying the Force Act, which was now a dead letter. But the radical South Carolina planters were becoming convinced that only secession would protect slavery. The nullification fiasco had proved that they could not succeed without the support of other slave states. Thereafter they devoted themselves ceaselessly to obtaining it.

"The Bank . . . I Will Kill It!"

Jackson's strong stand against South Carolina was the more effective because in the fall of 1832 he had been reelected president. The main issue in this election, aside from Jackson's personal popularity, was the president's determination to destroy the second Bank of the United States. In the "Bank war," Jackson won as complete a victory as in his battle with the nullifiers, yet the effects of his triumph were anything but beneficial to the country.

After *McCulloch* v. *Maryland* had presumably established its legality and the conservative Langdon Cheves had gotten it on a sound footing, the Bank of the United States had flourished. In 1823 Cheves was replaced as president by Nicholas Biddle, who managed it brilliantly. A talented Philadelphian, only 37 when he took over the Bank, Biddle was experienced in literature, the law, and diplomacy as well as in finance. Almost alone in the United States, Biddle realized that his institution could act as a rudimentary central bank, regulating the availability of credit throughout the nation by controlling the lending policies of the state banks. Small banks, possessing limited amounts of gold and silver, sometimes overextended themselves in making large amounts of bank notes available to borrowers in order to earn interest. All this paper money was legally convertible into hard cash on demand, but in the ordinary run of business, people seldom bothered to convert their notes so long as they thought the issuing bank was sound.

Bank notes passed freely from hand to hand and from bank to bank in every section of the country. Eventually much of the paper money of the local banks came across the counter of one or another of the 22 branches of the Bank of the United States. By collecting these notes and presenting them for conversion into specie, Biddle could compel the local banks to maintain adequate reserves of gold and silver—in other words, make them hold their lending policies within bounds. "The Bank of the United States," he explained, "has succeeded in keeping in check many institutions which might otherwise have been tempted into extravagant and ruinous excesses."

Biddle's policies in the 1820s were good for his own institution, which earned substantial profits, for the state banks, and probably for the country. Pressures on local bankers to make loans were enormous. The nation had an insatiable need for capital, and the general mood of the people was optimistic. Everyone wanted to borrow, and everyone expected values to rise, as in general they did. But by making liberal loans to produce merchants, for example, rural bankers indirectly stimulated farmers to expand their output beyond current demand, which eventually led to a decline in prices and an agricultural depression. In every field of economic activity, reckless lending caused inflation and greatly exaggerated the ups and downs of the business cycle. It can be argued, however, that by restricting the lending of state banks, Biddle was slowing the rate of economic growth and that in a predominantly agricultural society an occasional slump was not a large price to pay for rapid economic development.

Biddle's policies acted to stabilize the economy, and many interests, including a substantial percentage of state bankers, supported them. They also provoked a great deal of opposition. In part the opposition originated in pure ignorance: Distrust of paper money did not disappear, and people who disliked all paper saw the Bank as merely the largest (and thus the worst) of many bad institutions. At the other extreme, some bankers chafed under Biddle's restraints because by discouraging them from lending freely, he was limiting their profits. Few financiers realized what Biddle was trying to accomplish. The historian Bray Hammond estimated that in this period no more than one banker in four understood what was happening when he made a loan. What was "sound" banking practice? Honest people disagreed, and many turned against the ideas of Nicholas Biddle.

Bankers who did understand what Biddle was doing also resisted him. New York bankers resented the fact that a Philadelphia institution could wield so much power over their affairs. New York was the nation's largest importing center; huge amounts of tariff revenue were collected there. Yet since this money was deposited to the credit of the Bank of the United States, Biddle controlled it from Philadelphia. Finally, some people objected to the Bank because it was a monopoly. Distrust of chartered corporations as agents of special privilege tended to focus on the Bank, which had a monopoly of public funds but was managed by a private citizen and controlled by a handful of rich men. Biddle's wealth and social position intensified this feeling. Like many brilliant people, he sometimes appeared arrogant. He was unused to criticism and disdainful of ignorant and stupid attacks, failing to see that they were sometimes the most dangerous.

Jackson's Bank Veto

This formidable opposition to the Bank was diffuse and unorganized until Andrew Jackson brought it together. When he did, the Bank was quickly destroyed. Jackson belonged among the ignorant enemies of the institution, a hard-money man suspicious of all commercial banking. "I think it right to be perfectly frank with you," he told Biddle in 1829. "I do not dislike your Bank any more than all banks. But ever since I read the history of the South Sea Bubble I have been afraid of banks."

Jackson's attitude dismayed Biddle. It also mys-

tified him, since the Bank was the country's best defense against a speculative mania like the 18th-century South Sea Bubble, in which hundreds of naive British investors had been fleeced. Almost against his will, Biddle found himself gravitating toward Clay and the new National Republican party, offering advantageous loans and retainers to politicians and newspaper editors in order to build up a following. Thereafter, events moved inevitably toward a showdown, for the president's combative instincts were easily aroused. "The Bank," he told Van Buren, "is trying to kill me, *but I will kill it!*"

Henry Clay, Daniel Webster, and other prominent National Republicans hoped to use the Bank controversy against Jackson. They reasoned that the institution was so important to the country that Jackson's opposition to it would undermine his popularity. They therefore urged Biddle to ask Congress to renew the Bank's charter. The charter would not expire until 1836, but by pressing the issue before the 1832 presidential election, they could force Jackson either to approve the recharter bill or to veto it (which would give candidate Clay a lively issue in the campaign). The banker yielded to this strategy reluctantly, for he would have preferred to postpone the showdown, and a recharter bill passed Congress early in July 1832. Jackson promptly vetoed it.

Jackson's message explaining why he had rejected the bill was immensely popular, but it adds nothing to his reputation as a statesman. Being a good Jeffersonian—and no friend of John Marshall—he insisted that the Bank was unconstitutional. (*McCulloch* v. *Maryland* he brushed aside, saying that as president he had sworn to uphold the Constitution as *he* understood it.) The Bank was inexpedient, he argued. Being a dangerous private monopoly that allowed a handful of rich men to accumulate "many millions" of dollars, the Bank was making "the rich richer and the potent more powerful." Furthermore, many of its stockholders were foreigners: "If we must have a bank . . . it should be *purely American.*" Little that he said made any more sense than this absurdity.*

---

* The country needed all the foreign capital it could attract. Foreigners owned only $8 million of the $35 million stock, and in any case they could not vote their shares.

The "Set To Between Old Hickory and Bully Nick" is pictured in this cartoon of 1834–1835. Jackson seconds are "Little Van" Martin Van Buren and Major Jack Downing; Biddle is seconded by "Long Harry" (Henry Clay) and "Black Dan" Webster.

The most unfortunate aspect of Jackson's veto was that he could have reformed the Bank instead of destroying it. The central banking function was too important to be left in private hands. Biddle once boasted that he could put nearly any bank in the United States out of business simply by forcing it to exchange specie for its bank notes; he thought he was demonstrating his forbearance, but in fact he was revealing a dangerous flaw in the system. When the Jacksonians called him Czar Nicholas, they were not far from the mark. Moreover, private bankers were making profits that in justice belonged to the people, for the government received no interest from the large sums it kept on deposit in the Bank. Jackson would not consider reforms. He set out to smash the Bank of the United States without any real idea of what might be put in its place—a foolhardy act.

Biddle considered Jackson's veto "a manifesto of anarchy," its tone like "the fury of a chained panther biting the bars of his cage." A large majority of the voters, however, approved of Jackson's hard-hitting attack. He was easily reelected president, defeating Clay 219 to 49 in the electoral college.

Buttressed by his election triumph, Jackson acted swiftly. "Until I can strangle this hydra of corruption, the Bank, I will not shrink from my duty," he said. Shortly after the start of his second term, he decided to withdraw the government funds deposited in its vaults. Under the law only the secretary of the treasury could remove the deposits. When Secretary Louis McLane refused to do so, believing that the alternative depositories, the state banks, were less safe, Jackson promptly "promoted" him to secretary of state and appointed William J. Duane, a Pennsylvania lawyer, to the treasury post. Foolishly, he failed to ask Duane his views on the issue before appointing him. Too late he discovered that the new secretary agreed with McLane! It would not be "prudent" to entrust the government's money to "local and irresponsible" banks, Duane said.

Believing that Cabinet officers should obey the president as automatically as a colonel obeys a general, Jackson dismissed Duane, replacing him with Attorney General Roger B. Taney, who had been advising him closely on Bank affairs. Taney carried out the order by depositing new federal receipts in seven state banks in eastern cities while continuing to meet government expenses with drafts on the Bank of the United States.

The situation was confused and slightly unethical. Set on winning the Bank war, Jackson lost sight of his fear of unsound paper money. Taney, however, knew exactly what he was doing. One of the state banks receiving federal funds was the Union Bank of Baltimore. Taney owned stock in this institution, and its president was his close friend. Little wonder that Jackson's enemies were soon calling the favored state banks "pet" banks. This charge was not entirely fair because Taney took pains to see that the deposits were placed in financially sound institutions. Furthermore, by 1836 the government's funds had been spread out reasonably equitably in about 90 banks. But neither was the charge entirely unfair; the administration certainly favored institutions whose directors were politically sympathetic to it.

When Taney began to remove the deposits, the government had $9,868,000 to its credit in the Bank of the United States; within three months the figure fell to about $4 million. Faced with the withdrawal of so much cash, Biddle had to contract his operations. He decided to exaggerate the contraction, pressing the state banks hard by presenting all their notes and checks that came across his counter for conversion into specie and drastically limiting his own bank's business loans. He hoped that the resulting shortage of credit would be blamed on Jackson and that it would force the president to return the deposits. "Nothing but the evidence of suffering . . . will produce any effect," he reasoned.

For a time the strategy appeared to be working. Paper money became scarce, specie almost unobtainable. A serious panic threatened. New York banks were soon refusing to make any loans at all. "Nobody buys; nobody can sell," a French visitor to the city observed. Memorials and petitions poured in on Congress. Worried and indignant delegations of businessmen began trooping to Washington seeking "relief." Clay, Webster, and Calhoun thundered against Jackson in the Senate.

The president would not budge. "I am fixed in my course as firm as the Rocky Mountain," he wrote Vice-President Van Buren. No "frail mortals" who worshiped "the golden calf" could change his mind. To others he swore he would sooner cut off his right arm and "undergo the torture of ten Span-

ish inquisitions" than restore the deposits. When delegations came to him, he roared at them harshly: "Go to Nicholas Biddle. . . . Biddle has all the money!" And in the end—because he was right—business leaders began to take the old general's advice. Pressure on Biddle mounted swiftly, and in July 1834 he suddenly reversed his policy and began to lend money freely. The artificial crisis ended.

Boom and Bust

While the government insisted that its pet banks maintain large reserves, other state banks began to offer credit on easy terms, aided by a large increase in their reserves of gold and silver resulting from causes unconnected with the policies of either the government or Biddle's Bank. A decline in the Chinese demand for Mexican silver led to increased exports of the metal to the United States, and the rise of American interest rates attracted English capital into the country. Heavy English purchases of American cotton at high prices also increased the flow of specie into American banks. These developments caused bank notes in circulation to jump from $82 million in January 1835 to $120 million in December 1836. Bank deposits rose even more rapidly.

Much of the new money flowed into speculation in land; a mania to invest in property swept the country. The increased volume of currency caused prices to soar 15 percent in six months, buoying investors' spirits and making them ever more optimistic about the future. By the summer of 1835 one observer estimated that in New York City, which had about 250,000 residents, enough house lots had been laid out and sold to support a population of 2 million. Chicago at this time had only 2,000 to 3,000 inhabitants, yet most of the land for 25 miles around had been sold and resold in small lots by speculators anticipating the growth of the area. Throughout the West farmers borrowed money from local banks by mortgaging their land, used the money to buy more land from the government, and then borrowed still more money from the banks on the strength of their new deeds.

So long as prices rose, the process could be repeated endlessly. In 1832, while the Bank of the United States still regulated the money supply, federal income from the sale of land was $2.6 million.

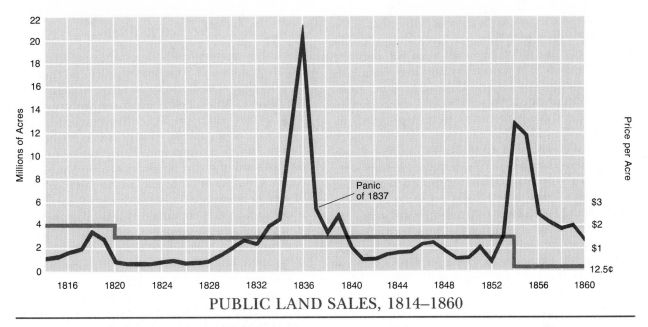

PUBLIC LAND SALES, 1814–1860

The left axis shows millions of acres of public land; the right axis price per acre. The speculative peak of 1836 burst with the Panic of 1837. The size of land parcels offered varied from 160 acres in 1830 to 40 or more acres in 1832 and at later times. Starting in 1830, squatters on public land were allowed to buy it at the minimum price. The 12.5¢ price per acre in 1854 applied to land on the market for 30 years or more.

In 1834 it was $4.9 million; in 1835, $14.8 million. In 1836 it rose to $24.9 million, and the government found itself totally free of debt and with a surplus of $20 million!

Finally Jackson became alarmed by the speculative mania. In the summer of 1836 he issued the Specie Circular, which provided that purchasers must henceforth pay for public land in gold or silver. At once the rush to buy land came to a halt. As demand slackened, prices sagged. Speculators, unable to dispose of lands mortgaged to the banks, had to abandon them to the banks, but the banks could not realize enough on the foreclosed property to recover their loans. Suddenly the public mood changed. Commodity prices tumbled 30 percent between February and May. Hordes of depositors sought to withdraw their money in the form of specie, and soon the banks exhausted their supplies. Panic swept the country in the spring of 1837 as every bank in the nation was forced to suspend specie payments. The boom was over.

Major swings in the business cycle can never be attributed to the actions of a single person, however powerful, but there is no doubt that Jackson's war against the Bank exaggerated the swings of the economic pendulum, not so much by its direct effects as by the impact of the president's ill-considered policies on popular thinking. His Specie Circular did not prevent speculators from buying land—at most it caused purchasers to pay a premium for gold or silver. But it convinced potential buyers that the boom was going to end and led them to make decisions that in fact ended it. Old Hickory's combination of impetuousness, combativeness, arrogance, and ignorance rendered the nation he loved so dearly a serious disservice. He lacked, as Glyndon Van Deusen wrote in *The Jacksonian Era*, "the capacity for that slow and often painful balancing of opposite viewpoints, the fruit of philosophic reflection, which is the characteristic of the man of culture." This was his greatest failing, as a president and as a man.

Jacksonianism Abroad

Jackson's emotional and dogmatic side also influenced his handling of foreign affairs. His patriotism was often so extravagant as to be ludicrous; in less peaceful times he might well have embroiled the country in far bloodier battles than his war with Nicholas Biddle produced. By pushing relentlessly for the solution of minor problems, he won a number of diplomatic successes. Several advantageous reciprocal trade agreements were negotiated, including one with Great Britain that finally opened British West Indian ports to American ships. American claims dating from the Napoleonic wars were pressed vigorously. The most important result of this policy came in 1831, when France agreed to pay about $5 million to compensate for damages to American property during that long conflict.

This settlement, however, led to trouble because the French Chamber of Deputies refused to appropriate the necessary funds. When the United States submitted a bill for the first installment in 1833, it was unable to collect. Jackson at once adopted a belligerent stance, his ire further aroused by a bill for $170,041.18 submitted by Nicholas Biddle for the services of the Bank of the United States in attempting to collect the money. When France ignored the second installment, Jackson sent a blistering message to Congress, full of such phrases as "not to be tolerated" and "take redress into our own hands." He asked for a law "authorizing reprisals upon French property" if the money was not paid.

Jackson's case was ironclad, yet the matter did not merit such vigorous prosecution. Congress wisely took no action. Jackson suspended diplomatic relations with France and ordered the navy readied. The French—in part, no doubt, because they were clearly in the wrong—were insulted by Jackson's manner. Irresponsible talk of war was heard in both countries. Fortunately, the French Chamber finally appropriated the money, Jackson moderated his public pronouncements, and the issue subsided.

Similarly, when a snag delayed the negotiation of the West Indian treaty, Jackson had suggested forcing Great Britain to make concessions by imposing a boycott on trade with Canada. In both cases he showed poor judgment, being ready to take monumental risks to win petty victories. His behavior reinforced the impression held by foreigners that the United States was a rash young country with a chip on its shoulder, pathologically mistrustful of the good faith of European powers.

The Jacksonians

Jackson's personality had a large impact on the shape and tone of American politics and thus with the development of the second party system. When he came to office, nearly everyone professed to be a follower of Jefferson. By 1836 being a Jeffersonian no longer meant much; what mattered was how one felt about Andrew Jackson. He had ridden to power at the head of a diverse political army, but he left behind him an organization with a fairly cohesive, if not necessarily consistent, body of ideas. This Democratic party contained rich citizens and poor, easterners and westerners, abolitionists as well as slaveholders. It was not yet a close-knit national organization, but—always allowing for individual exceptions—the Jacksonians agreed on certain underlying principles. These included suspicion of special privilege and large business corporations, both typified by the Bank of the United States; freedom of economic opportunity, unfettered by private or governmental restrictions; absolute political freedom, at least for white males; and the conviction that any ordinary man is capable of performing the duties of most public offices.

Jackson's ability to reconcile his belief in the supremacy of the Union with his conviction that the area of national authority should be held within narrow limits tended to make the Democrats the party of those who believed that the powers of the states should not be diminished. Tocqueville caught this aspect of Jackson's philosophy perfectly: "Far from wishing to extend Federal power," he wrote, "the president belongs to the party that wishes to limit that power."

Although the radical Locofoco* wing of the party championed the idea, nearly all Jacksonians, like their leader, favored giving the small man his chance—by supporting public education, for example, and by refusing to place much weight on a person's origin, dress, or manners. "One individual is as good as another" (for accuracy we must insert the adjective *white*) was their axiom. This attitude helps explain why immigrants, Catholics, and other minority groups usually voted Democratic. How-

---

* A locofoco was a type of friction match. The name was first applied in politics when a group of New York Jacksonians used these matches to light candles when a conservative faction tried to break up their meeting by turning off the gaslights.

ever, the Jacksonians showed no tendency either to penalize the wealthy or to intervene in economic affairs to aid the underprivileged. The motto "That government is best which governs least" graced the masthead of the chief Jacksonian newspaper, the *Washington Globe,* throughout the era.

Rise of the Whigs

The opposition to Jackson was far less cohesive. Henry Clay's National Republican party provided a nucleus, but Clay never dominated that party as Jackson dominated the Democrats. Its orientation was basically anti-Jackson. It was as though the American people were a great block of granite from which some sculptor had just fashioned a statue of Jackson, the chips scattered about the floor of the studio representing the opposition.

While Jackson was president, the impact of his personality delayed the formation of a true two-party system, but as soon as he surrendered power,

the opposition, taking heart, began to coalesce. Many Democrats could not accept the odd logic of Jacksonian finance. As early as 1834 they, together with the Clay element, the extreme states' righters who followed Calhoun, and other dissident groups, were calling themselves Whigs, the name (harking back to the Revolution) implying patriotic resistance to the tyranny of "King Andrew." This coalition possessed great resources of wealth and talent. Anyone who understood banking was almost obliged to become a Whig unless he was connected with one of Jackson's "pets." Those spiritual descendants of Hamilton who rejected the administration's refusal to approach economic problems from a broadly national perspective also joined in large numbers. Those who found the coarseness and "pushiness" of the Jacksonians offensive were another element in the new party. The anti-intellectual and antiscientific bias of the administration (Jackson rejected proposals for a national university, an observatory, and a scientific and literary institute) drove many well-educated people

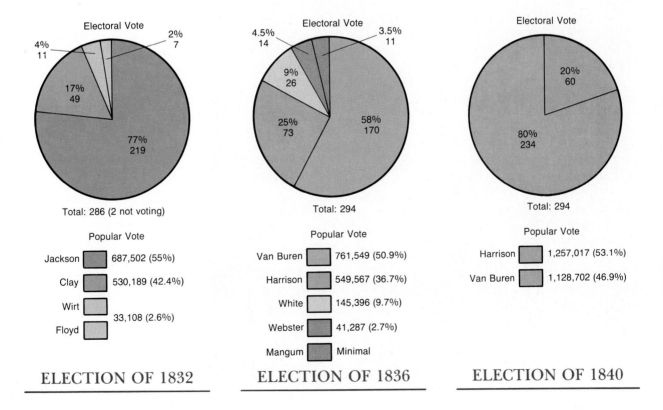

ELECTION OF 1832

Electoral Vote — Total: 286 (2 not voting)
- 77% 219
- 17% 49
- 4% 11
- 2% 7

Popular Vote
- Jackson: 687,502 (55%)
- Clay: 530,189 (42.4%)
- Wirt: 33,108 (2.6%)
- Floyd:

ELECTION OF 1836

Electoral Vote — Total: 294
- 58% 170
- 25% 73
- 9% 26
- 4.5% 14
- 3.5% 11

Popular Vote
- Van Buren: 761,549 (50.9%)
- Harrison: 549,567 (36.7%)
- White: 145,396 (9.7%)
- Webster: 41,287 (2.7%)
- Mangum: Minimal

ELECTION OF 1840

Electoral Vote — Total: 294
- 80% 234
- 20% 60

Popular Vote
- Harrison: 1,257,017 (53.1%)
- Van Buren: 1,128,702 (46.9%)

into the Whig fold. Whig arguments also appealed to ordinary voters who were predisposed to favor strong governments that would check the "excesses" of unrestricted individualism.

The Whigs were slow to develop an effective party organization. They had too many generals and not enough troops. It was hard for them to agree on any issue more complicated than opposition to Jackson. Furthermore, they stood in conflict with the major trend of their age: the glorification of the common man.

Lacking a dominant leader in 1836, the Whigs relied on "favorite sons," hoping to throw the presidential election into the House of Representatives. Daniel Webster ran in New England. For the West and South, Hugh Lawson White of Tennessee, a former friend who had broken with Jackson, was counted on to carry the fight. General William Henry Harrison was supposed to win in the Northwest and to draw support everywhere from those who liked to vote for military heroes. This sorry strategy failed; Jackson's handpicked candidate, Martin Van Buren, won a majority of both the popular and the electoral votes.

An extensive unpaid bill alarms a debtor, one of many who suffered from the tightening of credit that followed the Panic of 1837.

I wish you may get it !!

Sacré bleu, dis is von damn Yankee monkey trick ...

WHO'LL HAVE THE SPECIE ?—

Like the United States, Europe experienced a depression and specie shortage in the late 1830s. France and England, symbolized here by a rooster and bulldog, respectively, asked for American debt payments in hard currency. They were rebuffed by Van Buren, the wily monkey at left.

Martin Van Buren: Jacksonianism Without Jackson

The Red Fox, the Little Magician—Van Buren's brilliance as a political manipulator has tended to obscure his statesmanlike qualities and his engaging personality. High office sobered Van Buren and improved his judgment. He fought the Bank of the United States as a monopoly, but he also opposed irresponsible state banks. New York's Safety Fund System, requiring all banks to contribute to a fund, supervised by the state, to be used to redeem the notes of any member bank that failed, was established largely through his efforts. Van Buren believed in public construction of internal improvements, but he favored state rather than national programs, and he urged a rational approach: Each project must stand on its own as a useful and profitable public utility.

He continued to equivocate spectacularly on the tariff—in his *Autobiography* he described two of his supporters walking home after listening to him talk on the tariff, each convinced that it had been a brilliant speech, but neither having obtained the slightest idea as to where Van Buren stood on the subject—but he was never in the pocket of any special interest group or tariff lobbyist. He accounted himself a good Jeffersonian, tending to prefer state action to federal, but he was by no means doctrinaire. Basically he approached most questions rationally and pragmatically.

Van Buren had outmaneuvered Calhoun easily in the struggle to succeed Jackson, winning the old hero's confidence and serving him well. In 1832 he was elected vice-president and thereafter was conceded to be the "heir apparent." In 1835 the Democratic National Convention nominated him for president unanimously.

Van Buren took office just as the Panic of 1837 struck the country. Its effects were frightening but short-lived. When the banks stopped converting paper money into gold and silver, they outraged conservatives but in effect eased the pressure on the money market: Interest rates declined, and business loans again became relatively easy to obtain. In 1836, at the height of the boom in land sales, Congress had voted to "distribute" the new treasury surplus to the states, and this flow of money, which the states promptly spent, also stimulated the re-vival. Late in 1838 the banks resumed specie pay-ments.

But in 1839 a bumper crop caused a sharp de-cline in the price of cotton. Then a number of state governments that had overextended themselves in road- and canal-building projects were forced to default on their debts. This discouraged investors, particularly foreigners. A general economic de-pression ensued that lasted until 1843.

Van Buren was not responsible for the panic or the depression, but his manner of dealing with economic issues was scarcely helpful. He saw his role as being concerned only with problems plaguing the government, ignoring the economy as a whole. "The less government interferes with private pur-suits the better for the general prosperity," he pon-tificated. As Daniel Webster scornfully pointed out, Van Buren was following a policy of "leaving the people to shift for themselves," one that many Whigs rejected.

Such a hands-off approach to the depression seems foolish by modern standards. Van Buren's refusal to assume any responsibility for the general welfare appears to explode the theory that the Jack-sonians were deeply concerned with the fate of or-dinary citizens. In *The Concept of Jacksonian Democ-racy*, Lee Benson argues that the Whigs, rather than the Democrats, were the "positive liberals" of the era. Benson cites many statements by Whigs about applying "the means of the state boldly and liberally to aid . . . public works."

This approach helps correct past oversimplifi-cations, but it judges the period by the standards of a later age. The country in the 1830s was still mainly agricultural, and for most farmers the de-pression, though serious, did not spell disaster. Moreover, many Jacksonians were perfectly willing to see the states act to stimulate economic growth in bad times—as indeed most states did.

Van Buren's chief goal was finding a substitute for the state banks as a place to keep federal funds. The depression and the suspension of specie pay-ments embarrassed the government along with pri-vate depositors. He soon settled on the idea of "di-vorcing" the government from all banking activities. His independent treasury bill called for the con-struction of government-owned vaults where fed-eral revenues could be stored until needed. To en-sure absolute safety, all payments to the government were to be made in hard cash. After a battle that lasted until the summer of 1840, the Independent Treasury Act passed both the House and the Senate.

Opposition to the Independent Treasury Act had been bitter, and not all of it was partisan. Bank-ers and businessmen objected to the government's withholding so much specie from the banks, which needed all the hard money they could get to support loans that were the lifeblood of economic growth. It seemed irresponsible for the federal government to turn its back on the banks, which so obviously performed a semipublic function. These criticisms made good sense, but through a lucky combination of circumstances, the system worked reasonably well for many years. By creating suspicion in the public mind, officially stated distrust of banks acted as a damper on their tendency to overexpand. No acute shortage of specie developed because heavy agri-cultural exports and the investment of much Eur-opean capital in American railroads beginning in the mid-1840s brought in large amounts of new gold and silver. After 1849 the discovery of gold in Cal-ifornia added another important source of specie. The supply of money and bank credit kept pace roughly with the growth of the economy, but through no fault of the government. "Wildcat" banks proliferated. Fraud and counterfeiting were common, and the operation of everyday business affairs was inconvenienced in countless ways. The disordered state of the currency remained a grave problem until corrected by Civil War banking leg-islation.

The Log Cabin Campaign

It was not his financial policy that led to Van Buren's defeat in 1840. The depression naturally hurt the Democrats, and the Whigs were far better organized than in 1836. The Whigs also adopted a different strategy, cynical but effective. The Jacksonians had come to power on the coattails of a popular general whose views on public questions they concealed or ignored. They had maintained themselves by shout-ing the praises of the common man. Now the Whigs seized on these techniques and carried them to their logical—or illogical—conclusion. Not even bothering to draft a program, and passing over Clay

The 1840 presidential campaign was the first to use circus hoopla and the techniques of mass appeal that came to characterize political contests in the United States. This fanciful drawing adorned the sheet music for "General Harrison's Log Cabin March."

and Webster, whose views were known and therefore controversial, they nominated General William Henry Harrison for president. The Hero of Tippecanoe was counted on to conquer the party created in the image of the Hero of New Orleans. To "balance" the ticket, the Whigs chose a former Democrat, John Tyler of Virginia, an ardent supporter of states' rights, as their vice-presidential candidate.

The Whig argument was specious but effective: General Harrison is a plain man of the people who lives in a log cabin (where the latchstring is always out). Contrast him with the suave Van Buren, luxuriating amid "the Regal Splendor of the President's Palace." Harrison drinks ordinary hard cider and eats hog meat and grits, while Van Buren drinks expensive foreign wines and fattens on fancy concoctions prepared by a French chef. The general's furniture is plain and sturdy; the president dines off gold plates and treads on Royal Wilton carpets that cost the people $5 a yard. In a country where all are equal, the people will reject an aristocrat like "Martin Van Ruin" and put their trust in General Harrison, a simple, brave, honest, public-spirited common man.

Harrison came from a distinguished family, being the son of Benjamin Harrison, a signer of the Declaration of Independence and a former governor of Virginia. He was well educated and in at least comfortable financial circumstances, and he certainly did not live in a log cabin. The Whigs ignored these facts. The log cabin and the cider barrel became their symbols, which every political meeting saw reproduced in a dozen forms. The leading Whig campaign newspaper, edited by a vigorous New Englander named Horace Greeley, was called the *Log Cabin*. Cartoons, doggerel, slogans, and souvenirs were everywhere substituted for argument.

The Democrats used the same methods as the Whigs and were equally well organized, but they had little heart for the fight. The best they could come up with was the fact that their vice-presidential candidate, Richard Mentor Johnson, had killed Tecumseh, not merely defeated him. Van Buren tried to focus public attention on issues, but his voice could not be heard above the huzzahs of the Whigs. When the Whigs chanted "Tippecanoe and Tyler too!" and "Van, Van, is a used-up man" and rolled out another barrel of hard cider, the best the Democrats could come up with was:

Rumpsey, Dumpsey,
Colonel Johnson
Killed Tecumseh.

A huge turnout (four-fifths of the eligible voters) carried Harrison to victory by a margin of almost 150,000. The electoral vote was 234 to 60.

The Democrats had been blown up by their own bomb. In 1828 they had portrayed John Quincy Adams as a bloated aristocrat and Jackson as a simple farmer. The lurid talk of Van Buren dining off golden plates was no different from the stories that made Adams out to be a passionate gambler. If Van Buren was a lesser man than Adams, Harrison was a pale imitation indeed of Andrew Jackson.

The Whigs continued to repeat history by rushing to gather the spoils of victory. Washington was again flooded by office seekers, the political confusion monumental. Harrison had no ambition to be an aggressive leader. He believed that Jackson had misused the veto and professed to put as much emphasis as Washington did on the principle of the separation of legislative and executive powers. This delighted the Whig leaders in Congress, who had had their fill of the "executive usurpation" of Jackson. Either Clay or Webster seemed destined to be the real ruler of the new administration, and soon the two were squabbling over their old general like sparrows over a crust.

At the height of their squabble, less than a month after his inauguration, Harrison fell gravely ill. Pneumonia developed, and on April 4 he died. John Tyler of Virginia, honest and conscientious but doctrinaire, became president of the United States. The political climate of the country changed dramatically. Events began to march in a new direction, one that led ultimately to Bull Run, to Gettysburg, and to Appomattox.

Milestones

1828	Tariff of Abominations
1829–1837	Andrew Jackson's "Kitchen Cabinet"
1830	Daniel Webster's "Second Reply to Hayne"
	Jackson vetoes the Maysville road bill
1831–1838	Removal of southern Indians to Oklahoma
1832	South Carolina Ordinance of Nullification
	Force Act
	Jackson vetoes the Bank recharter bill
1833	Removal of U.S. Treasury funds from the Bank of the United States
	Compromise Tariff Act
1836	Specie Circular
1837–1838	Panic of 1837
1840	Independent Treasury Act
	"Log Cabin" campaign

SUPPLEMENTARY READING

Titles marked with an asterisk have been published in paperback.

On Jackson's presidency, see R. V. Remini, **Andrew Jackson and the Course of American Freedom** (1981) and **Andrew Jackson and the Course of American Democracy** (1984). Alexis de Tocqueville analyzed brilliantly the nature of Jacksonian democracy in **Democracy in America*** (1835–1840). A. M. Schlesinger, Jr., **The Age of Jackson*** (1945), stresses the democratic character of Jacksonianism. D. T. Miller, **Jacksonian Aristocracy** (1967), and two works by Edward Pessen, **Riches, Class and Power Before the Civil War** (1973) and **Jacksonian America*** (1969), describe the growth and extent of economic and class distinctions.

A number of contemporary commentaries by foreigners throw much light on Jacksonian democracy. See especially, in addition to Tocqueville, Frances Trollope, **Domestic Manners of the Americans*** (1832), Michel Chevalier, **Society, Manners and Politics in the United States*** (1961), Harriet Martineau, **Retrospect of Western Travel** (1838) and **Society in America*** (1837), and F. J. Grund, **Aristocracy in America*** (1959). On Jackson's administration of the government and the development of the spoils system, see L. D. White, **The Jacksonians*** (1954), and S. H. Aronson, **Status and Kinship in the Higher Civil Service** (1964); on the development of parties, consult R. P. McCormick, **The Second American Party System*** (1966). On Jackson's Indian policy, refer to F. P. Prucha, **American Indian Policies in the Formative Years*** (1962), B. W. Sheehan, **Seeds of Extinction*** (1973), and R. N. Satz, **American Indian Policy in the Jacksonian Era** (1975).

On the nullification controversy, see R. E. Ellis, **The Union at Risk** (1987), and W. W. Freehling, **Prelude to Civil War: The Nullification Controversy in South Carolina*** (1966), which shows the close relationship between the nullifiers and the slavery issue. The struggle with the Bank is discussed in Bray Hammond, **Banks and Politics in America from the Revolution to the Civil War*** (1957), and J. M. McFaul, **The Politics of Jacksonian Finance** (1972). Peter Temin, **The Jacksonian Economy*** (1969), minimizes the effects of Jackson's policies on economic conditions. Temin also provides an interesting analysis of economic trends throughout the period. T. P. Govan's **Nicholas Biddle*** (1959) is excellent on Biddle's view of banking but too apologetic.

The political and economic ideas of Whigs and Democrats are discussed in Lee Benson, **The Concept of Jacksonian Democracy*** (1961), R. P. Formisano, **The Transformation of Political Culture** (1983), and D. W. Howe, **The Political Culture of the American Whigs** (1980). On the development of the Whig party, in addition to the biographies of leading Whigs, see McCormick's **Second American Party System.** On the Van Buren administration, see John Niven, **Martin Van Buren** (1983), and M. L. Wilson, **The Presidency of Martin Van Buren** (1984). The election of 1840 is treated in R. G. Gunderson, **The Log-Cabin Campaign** (1957), J. A. Garraty, **Silas Wright** (1949), and the biographies of Clay and Webster.

The Making of Middle-Class America

A great democratic revolution is taking place in our midst; everybody sees it, but by no means everybody judges it in the same way. . . . No man on earth can affirm, absolutely and generally, that the new state of societies is better than the old, but it is already easy to see that it is different.

ALEXIS DE TOCQUEVILLE, *1836*

n May 12, 1831, two French aristocrats, Alexis de Tocqueville and Gustave de Beaumont, arrived in New York City from Le Havre on the packet *President*. Their official purpose was to make a study of American prisons for the French government. But they really came, as Tocqueville explained, "to see what a great republic is like."

Tocqueville and Beaumont were only the most insightful of dozens of Europeans who visited the United States during the first half of the 19th century in order to study the "natives." Their visit, for example, overlapped with that of Frances Trollope, whose *Domestic Manners of Americans* (1834) advised English readers that Americans were just as uncouth as they had imagined. A decade later, the English novelist Charles Dickens made what by then had become an almost obligatory pass through this crude outpost of civilization before publishing his report on his "sharp dealing" cousins in *American Notes* (1842). A little later, in a novel, Dickens described the United States as a "Republic . . . full of sores and ulcers."

Tocqueville and Beaumont in America

Unlike Trollope, Dickens, and other uncharitable foreign visitors, Tocqueville and Beaumont did not come to America chock-full of preconceived notions. Both believed that Europe was passing from its aristocratic past into a democratic future. How better to prepare for the change, they believed, than by studying the United States, where democracy was already the "enduring and normal state" of the land. In the nine months they spent in America, they traveled from New York to Boston, then back through New York in order to inspect the state prison at Auburn, then on to Ohio. ("No one has been born there; no one wants to stay there," Tocqueville later said of Ohio.) They examined conditions on the frontier in Michigan Territory, then sailed down the Mississippi River to New Orleans, where they heard an opera good enough to make them imagine they were back in France. They also attended a "Quadroon ball," where, according to Tocqueville, "all the men [were] white, all the women coloured."

From New Orleans they went on to "semibarbarous" Alabama before turning north to Washington, a city that Beaumont declared to be "very ugly." Finally back to New York, whence they sailed for France on February 20, 1832. All told, they had met and interviewed some 250 individuals, ranking from President Jackson—Beaumont insisted on referring to Old Hickory as "Monsieur"—to a number of Chippewa Indians.

It had indeed been a "useful" trip for the two Frenchmen. It resulted in their prison report and in *Marie, ou l'Esclavage aux États Unis* (1835), Beaumont's account of American race problems, cast in the form of a novel. But above all else, the visit provided the material for Tocqueville's classic *De la Démocratie en Amérique*, published in France in 1835 and a year later in an English translation. *Democracy in America* has been the starting point for virtually all subsequent writers who have tried to describe what Tocqueville called "the creative elements" of American institutions.

Tocqueville in Judgment

The gist of *Democracy in America* is contained in the book's first sentence: "No novelty in the United

Among the scores of noted Europeans who visited the United States in its first fifty years, Alexis de Tocqueville is perhaps the best remembered, thanks to his exhaustive and insightful published account of his travels. This lithograph portrait is by Leon Noël.

States struck me more vividly during my stay there than the equality of conditions." Tocqueville meant not that Americans lived in a state of total equality, but that the inequalities that did exist among white Americans were not enforced by institutions or supported by public opinion. Moreover, the inequalities paled when compared with those of Europe. "In America," he concluded, "men are nearer equality than in any other country in the world." The circumstances of one's birth meant little, one's education less, and one's intelligence scarcely anything. Economic differences, while real and certainly "paraded" by those who enjoyed "a pre-eminence of wealth," were transitory. "Such wealth," Tocqueville assured his readers, "is within reach of all."

These sweeping generalizations, however comforting to Americans then and since, are simplifications. Few modern students of Jacksonian America would accept them without qualification. The historian Edward Pessen has pointed out that in the 1830s and 1840s a wide and growing gap existed between the rich and poor in the larger eastern cities. According to Pessen, the wealthiest 4 percent of the population of New York controlled about

half the city's wealth in 1828, about two-thirds in 1845. The number of New Yorkers worth $100,000 or more tripled in that period. A similar concentration of wealth was occurring in Philadelphia and Boston.

Moreover, there was substantial poverty in Jacksonian America that Tocqueville did not recognize. Particularly in the cities, bad times forced many unskilled laborers and their families into dire poverty. Tocqueville took little notice of such inequalities, in part because he was so captivated by the theme of American equality. He also had little interest in how industrialization and urbanization were affecting society. When he did take notice of working conditions, he remarked that wages were higher in America than in Europe and the cost of living was lower, facts obvious to the most obtuse European visitor. Furthermore, as with most foreign visitors, nearly all his contacts were with members of the upper crust. "We hardly see anyone," he acknowledged, "except people of distinction."

Despite his blind spots, Tocqueville realized that America was undergoing some fundamental social changes. These changes, he wrote, were being made by "an innumerable crowd who are . . . not exactly rich nor yet quite poor [and who] have enough property to want order and not enough to excite envy." In his notes he put it even more succinctly: "The whole society seems to have turned into one middle class."

A Restless People

"In America, men never stay still," Tocqueville noted. "Something is almost always provisional about their lives." Other European observers came away equally struck by the restlessness of Americans, without necessarily agreeing that democratic institutions made them so. Frances Trollope thought their "incessant bustling" of a piece with their eating too fast and spitting too often. It stemmed from their "universal pursuit of money," she claimed.

One reason Americans seemed continually on the move was that every year there were more of them. The first federal census in 1790 recorded that there were 3.9 million people in the country. In 1850 there were more than 23 million. The population was doubling every 22 years, just about what Franklin had predicted in 1751! The growth can be

The Dinner Party *was painted around 1825 by Boston artist Henry Sargent. Alexis de Tocqueville tolerated but rarely praised American haute cuisine. After one banquet, he recorded that the dinner represented the infancy of the art: "The vegetables and fish before the meat, the oysters for dessert. In a word, complete barbarism."*

measured geographically by the admission of new states in the 1830s and 1840s: Arkansas in 1836, Michigan in 1837, Florida in 1845, Texas in 1846, and Wisconsin in 1848.

Yet by contemporary European standards, even the settled parts of the United States were sparsely populated in the 1830s and 1840s. But for people accustomed to wide-open spaces, the presence of more than a handful of neighbors was reason enough for moving on. Abraham Lincoln's father Thomas (1778–1851) was typical. He grew up in Kentucky, pioneered in Indiana, and died in Illinois.

The Move to Town

The urge to move had an urban dimension as well. For every "young man" who took the advice of the New York newspaperman Horace Greeley to "go west," several young men and women went instead to town. By the tens of thousands they exchanged the rigors of farming for the uncertain risks and rewards of city life. Boston, New York, and Philadelphia had a combined population of 50,000 at the time of the Revolution. Each expanded rapidly during the first half of the next century. Boston had 40,000 residents in 1820, nearly 140,000 in 1850. Philadelphia grew even more rapidly, from just under 100,000 in 1820 to almost 400,000 in 1850. New York, which had forged ahead of Philadelphia around 1810, grew from 125,000 in 1820 to more than 500,000 in 1850.

However spectacular the growth of the largest cities, the emergence of new towns was more significant. In 1820 the Northeast contained 5 cities with populations above 25,000 and 13 with popu-

Northeast did not occur in the South. There were four cities of respectable size in the region—Mobile, Savannah, Charleston, and Baltimore—and one large city, New Orleans, which had a population of 120,000 in 1850. Yet all were located on the region's perimeter. Neither Virginia nor North Carolina had an urban center of even modest dimensions. Charleston, the oldest and most typically southern city, scarcely grew at all after 1830.

Strangers at the Door

Between 1790 and 1820 the population of the United States more than doubled to 9.6 million. The most remarkable feature of this growth was that it

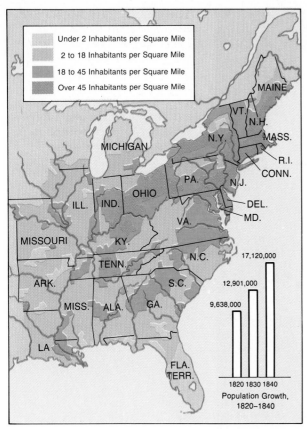

POPULATION DENSITY, 1840

The accelerating westward movement is evident in this map. Arkansas entered the Union in 1836, Michigan in 1837. During the 1830s the population of the nation as a whole increased by nearly one-third. Of the 4.2 million increase, a little over 10 percent were immigrants.

lations above 10,000. Thirty years later, 26 cities had more than 25,000 residents and 62 had more than 10,000.

Even though the Old Northwest remained primarily agricultural, its towns grew as fast as its farms. Pittsburgh, St. Louis, Cincinnati, Louisville, and Lexington attracted settlers in such numbers that by 1850 all but Lexington had populations of over 35,000. Cincinnati, "the Emporium of the West," with a population of 100,000, ranked seventh in the country.

The trek to town that was transforming the

As the balance of rural and urban population began to shift during the years from 1820 to 1860, the number of cities with populations over 100,000 grew from one in 1820—New York—to nine in 1870, including southern and western cities like New Orleans and San Francisco.

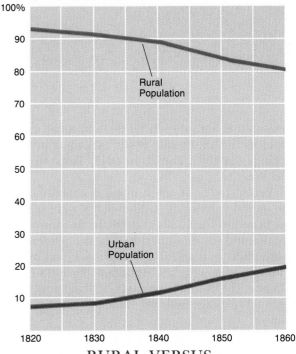

RURAL VERSUS URBAN POPULATION, 1820–1860

resulted almost entirely from natural increase. The birthrate in the early 19th century exceeded 50 per 1,000 population, a rate substantially higher than that of any country in the world today. Fewer than 250,000 immigrants entered the United States between 1790 and 1820. European wars, the ending of the slave trade, and doubts about the viability of the new republic slowed the flow of humanity across the Atlantic to a trickle.

But soon after the final defeat of Napoleon in 1815, immigration began to pick up. In the 1820s some 150,000 European immigrants arrived; in the 1830s, 600,000; in the 1840s, 1.7 million. The 1850 census, the first to make the distinction, estimated that of the nation's population of 23 million, more than 10 percent were foreign-born. In the Northeast the proportion exceeded 15 percent.

Most of this human tide came from Germany and Ireland, but substantial numbers also came from Great Britain and the Scandinavian countries. As with earlier immigrants, many were drawn to America by the prospect of abundant land, high wages, and economic opportunity generally. Some too were attracted by the promise of political and religious freedom. But many came simply because to stay where they were meant to face starvation. This was particularly true of those from Ireland, where a potato blight triggered the flight of tens of thousands. This exodus continued throughout the century, by which time there were more people of Irish origin in America than in Ireland.

Once ashore in New York, Boston, or Philadelphia, most relatively prosperous immigrants pushed directly westward. Others found work in the new factory towns along the route of the Erie Canal, in the lower Delaware Valley southeast of Philadelphia, or along the Merrimack River north of Boston. But most of the Irish immigrants, "the poorest and most wretched population that can be found in the world," one of their priests called them, lacked the means to go west. Aside from the cost of transportation, starting a farm required far more capital than they could raise. Like it or not, they had to settle in the eastern cities.

Viewed in historical perspective, this massive wave of immigration stimulated the American econ-

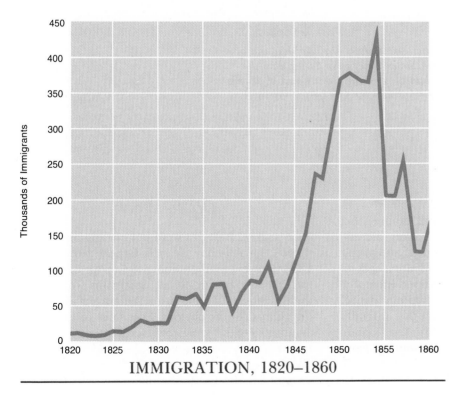

IMMIGRATION, 1820–1860

Immigration before the Civil War was primarily from the northern European countries of Britain, Ireland, and Germany. Between 1820 and 1860, about 800,000 immigrants came from Britain, 3.5 million from Ireland, and 1.5 million from Germany. Famine in Ireland and political upheavals and economic hard times in Germany during the 1840s and 1850s accounted for much of the flow.

*Between 1830 and 1850, some 2.5 million immigrants fled hardship and op-
pression in Europe to settle in the United States. They were packed into the
filthy, airless holds of ships for the transatlantic crossing. Many died of disease.
If they were lucky, passengers such as these aboard the* Cornelius Grinnell
were allowed a few hours on deck.

omy. In the short run, the influx of the 1830s and
1840s depressed living standards and strained the
social fabric. For the first time the nation had acquired a culturally distinctive, citybound, and prop-
ertyless class. The poor Irish immigrants had to
accept whatever wages employers offered them. By
doing so they caused resentment among native
workers, resentment exacerbated by the unfamil-
iarity of the Irish with city ways and by their Roman
Catholic faith, which the Protestant majority associated with European authoritarianism and
corruption.

Off to Work

"It is as if all America were but one gigantic workshop," the Austrian Francis Grund remarked in
1838. However enlightening to European readers,
the fact that practically all Americans worked for
their livings must have struck Americans as a blind-
ing glimpse of the obvious. Ever since John Smith's
assurances to the Jamestown settlers that if they did
not work they would not eat, they had always done
the one to assure themselves of the other. What was
changing in the 1830s was that they worked outside

their homes, if not exactly in "gigantic workshops."

In 1820, despite the growth of cities, three out of every four Americans were still engaged in agriculture. An efficient farming family used the labor of all its members, with chores assigned according to age, strength, and experience. Parents, children, and sometimes grandparents lived in the same house, or in adjoining houses, together with unrelated hired hands, when such existed. Except on large southern plantations run by overseers, farming remained a family enterprise.

By 1850, however, fewer than two out of three workers were farmers, in Massachusetts one of three. Outside the South, the way people earned a living had been transformed.

Until the 1820s and 1830s, the household was also the focus of most nonagricultural pursuits. The typical urban worker was a self-employed artisan. Whether a tailor, shoemaker, printer, baker, or carpenter, he had been apprenticed to a master while still a lad. After five to seven years of training, he became a journeyman and began to earn wages. Eventually, if he was reasonably talented, frugal, and industrious, he could open a shop of his own, take on apprentices, and thus perpetuate the system.

Since an apprentice lived and worked under the same roof as his master and his family, it was natural for the master to have familial as well as occupational authority over him. So intertwined did the life of an apprentice and his master become that the words *employee* and *employer* do not describe the relationship accurately. The historian Sean Wilentz has characterized the preindustrial workshop as "a benevolent hierarchy of skill." Apprentices were sometimes exploited and even physically abused, but just as often strong, personal bonds developed. Some apprentices married one of the master's daughters, thus helping to keep the trade in the family.

Forced reliance on domestically manufactured goods during the embargo and the War of 1812 and the improvements in transportation that were taking place steadily in the 1820s and 1830s prompted many master craftsmen and artisans to expand production. They took on more workers, in some cases as apprentices, more often as relatively unskilled wage earners. Work was broken down into separate simple tasks that the unskilled help could learn easily and repeat endlessly. As a business grew bigger and the division of labor became more complex, the master-turned-businessman spent less time working with his employees and more marketing the product. Elaborate rules evolved regu-

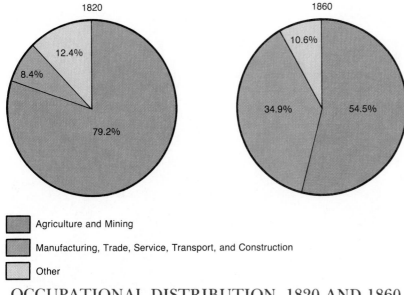

1820

12.4%

8.4%

79.2%

1860

10.6%

34.9%   54.5%

■ Agriculture and Mining

▨ Manufacturing, Trade, Service, Transport, and Construction

□ Other

OCCUPATIONAL DISTRIBUTION, 1820 AND 1860

lating the hours of labor and the on-the-job behavior of workers. Drinking on the job, which in an earlier day had been considered normal and even desirable, was by 1850 almost universally forbidden.

Larger operations required more work space, and the need to locate near suppliers, customers, or a source of waterpower meant that the owner's home could no longer serve as a workplace. During the second quarter of the 19th century, Boston, New York, Philadelphia, and other cities sorted themselves into commercial and residential districts; the residential districts further separated into working-class and employer-class neighborhoods.

Even before the widespread use of machinery, large economies of scale were possible. Until the introduction of sewing machines in the 1850s, shoes were made entirely by hand, yet by the 1830s the shoe manufacturers of Lynn, Massachusetts, had shifted from making finely finished shoes for individual customers to mass-producing the rough brogans worn by slaves and other farmers. Custom-fitted shoes required the attention of a skilled craftsman, but brogans were made by several unskilled laborers, each performing a different function. Only the last handled the finished product.

An Industrial Proletariat?

As the importance of skilled labor declined, so did the ability of workers to influence working conditions. Skilled workers either became employers and

The first mill operations performed only the task of spinning wool, cotton, and other fibers into thread; soon weaving was also mechanized, so that fabric ready to be cut and sewn was manufactured. Note the child at left, working under the spindles where an adult could not stand.

developed entrepreneurial and managerial skills or descended into the mass of wage earners. Simultaneously, the changing structure of work widened the gap between owners and workers and blurred the distinction between skilled and unskilled workers.

These trends might have been expected to generate hostility between workers and employers. To some extent they did. There were strikes for higher wages and to protest work speedups throughout the 1830s and again in the 1850s. Efforts to found unions and to create political organizations dedicated to advancing the interests of workers were also undertaken.

But well into the 1850s Americans displayed few signs of the class solidarity common among European workers. Why America did not produce a self-conscious working class is a question that has long intrigued historians. As with most such large questions, no single answer has been forthcoming. Some historians argue that the existence of the frontier siphoned off displaced and dissatisfied workers. Others believe that ethnic and racial differences kept workers from seeing themselves as a distinct class with common needs and common enemies. Still others have suggested that the influx of needy immigrants willing to accept any job available at almost any wage undercut the organizational efforts of the native-born workers. The fact that the expanding economy created many opportunities for laborers to rise out of the working class was another reason why so few of them developed strong class feelings.

These answers help explain the relative absence of class conflict during the early stages of the industrial revolution in America, but so does the fact that conditions in the early shops and factories represented an improvement for the people who worked in them.

Most factory workers, especially in the textile industry, were drawn from outside the regular labor market. Relatively few hand spinners and weavers became factory workers; indeed, some of them continued to work as they had, for it was many years before the factories could even begin to satisfy the ever-increasing demand for cloth. Nor did immigrants attend the new machines. Instead, the mill owners relied chiefly on women and children. They did so because machines lessened the need for skill

and strength and because the labor shortage made it necessary to tap unexploited sources. By the early 1820s about half the cotton textile workers in the factories were under 16 years of age.

Most people of that generation considered this a good thing. They reasoned that the work was easy and that it kept youngsters busy at useful tasks while providing their families with extra income. Roxanna Foote, whose daughter Harriet Beecher Stowe wrote *Uncle Tom's Cabin*, came from a solid middle-class family in Guilford, Connecticut. Nevertheless, she worked full time before her marriage in her grandfather's small spinning mill. "This spinning-mill was a favorite spot," a relative recalled many years later. "Here the girls often received visitors, or read or chatted while they spun." Roxanna explained her daily regimen as a mill girl matter-of-factly: "I generally rise with the sun, and, after breakfast, take my wheel, which is my daily companion, and the evening is generally devoted to reading, writing, and knitting."

This seems a somewhat idealized picture, or perhaps working for one's grandfather made a difference. Another young girl, Emily Chubbock, later a well-known writer, had a less pleasant recollection of her experience as an 11-year-old factory hand earning $1.25 a week. "My principal recollections . . . are of noise and filth, bleeding hands and aching feet, and a very sad heart." In any case, a society accustomed to seeing the children of fairly well-to-do farmers working full time in the fields was not shocked by the sight of children working all day in mills. In some factories laborers were hired in family units. No member earned very much, but with a couple of adolescent daughters and perhaps a son of 9 or 10 helping out, a family could take home enough to live decently. For most working Americans, then as now, that was success enough.

Instead of hiring children, the Boston Associates developed the Waltham System of employing young, unmarried women in their new textile mills. The young women were lodged in company boardinghouses, which, like college dormitories, became centers of social life and not merely places to eat and sleep. Unlike college dormitories, the boardinghouses were strictly supervised; straitlaced New Englanders did not hesitate to permit their daughters to live in them. The regulations laid down by one company, for example, required that all employees "show that they are penetrated by a laudable love of temperance and virtue." "Ardent spirits" were banished from company property, "games of hazard and cards" prohibited. A 10 P.M. curfew was strictly enforced.

For a generation after the opening of the Merrimack Manufacturing Company in 1823, the thriving factory towns of Lowell, Chicopee, and Manchester provided the background for a remarkable industrial idyll. Young women came from farms all over New England to work for a year or two in the mills. They earned between $2.50 and $3.25 a week, about half of which went for room and board. Some of the remainder they sent home, the rest (what there was of it) they could spend as they wished.

Most of these young women did not have to support themselves. They worked to save for a trousseau, to help educate a younger brother, or simply for the experience and excitement of meeting new people and escaping the confining environment of the farm. "The feeling that at this new work the few hours they had of every-day leisure was entirely their own was a satisfaction to them," one Lowell worker recalled. Anything but an industrial proletariat, they filled the windows of the factories with flowering plants, organized sewing circles, edited their own literary periodicals, and attended lectures on edifying subjects. That such activity was possible on top of a 70-hour workweek is a commentary on both the resiliency of youth and the leisurely pace of these early factories. Dickens, though scarcely enchanted by other American ways, was impressed by his visit to Lowell, which he compared most favorably to "those great haunts of misery," the English manufacturing towns. "They were all well dressed," he wrote of the workers. "They were healthy in appearance, many of them remarkably so, and had the manners and deportment of young women. . . . The rooms in which they worked were as well ordered as themselves."

Life in the mills was not all it might have been. Though they made up 85 percent of the work force, women were kept out of supervisory positions. In 1834 workers in several mills "turned out" to protest cuts in their wages and a hike in board. This work stoppage did not force a reversal of management policy. Another strike two years later in response to a work speedup was somewhat more successful. But when a drop in prices in the 1840s led the owners to introduce new rules designed to increase

production, workers lacked the organizational strength to block them. By then young women of the kind that had flocked to the mills in the 1820s and 1830s were able to find work as schoolteachers or clerks. Mill owners turned increasingly to Irish immigrants to operate their machines.

The Family Recast

The factory system and the growth of cities undermined the importance of home and family as the unit of economic production. This happened first in the cities of the Northeast, then in the West, and eventually wherever nonagricultural jobs occupied a substantial percentage of the work force. More and more people did their work in shops, in offices, or on factory floors. Whether a job was skilled or unskilled, white-collar or blue-collar, or strictly professional, it took the family breadwinner out of the house during working hours six days a week. This did not mean that the family necessarily ceased to be an economic unit. But the labor of the father and any children with jobs came home in the form of cash, thus at least initially in the custody of the individual earners. The social consequences of this change were enormous for the traditional "head of the family" and for his wife and children.

Because he was away so much, the husband had to surrender to his wife some of the power in the family that he had formerly exercised, if for no other reason than that she was always there. The situation bore a superficial resemblance to the relationship of the king of England to the colonies in the 17th century: Whatever the king's power under the law, his authority was limited by his lack of close contact with his colonial "offspring." Perhaps this is what Noah Webster had in mind when he used a similar comparison in describing the ideal father's authority as "like the mild dominion of a limited monarch, and not the iron rule of an austere tyrant." It certainly explains why Tocqueville concluded that "a sort of equality reigns around the domestic hearth" in America. It also explains why American men began to place women on a pedestal, presuming them to be by nature almost saintly, pure of mind and body, selflessly devoted to the care of others.

The new power and prestige that wives and mothers enjoyed was not obtained without cost. Since they were exercising day-to-day control over

Family structure changed as a result of the industrial revolution. Not only did couples have fewer children, but husbands were expected to earn the family's living and concern themselves with worldly business while wives assumed all domestic duties.

household affairs, they were expected to tend only to those affairs. Anything that might take them away from the family hearth was frowned on. Where the typical wife had formerly been a partner in a family enterprise, she now left earning a living entirely to her husband. Time spent away from home or devoted to matters unrelated to the care of husband and family was, according to the new doctrine of "separate spheres," time misappropriated.

This trend widened the gap between the middle and lower classes. For a middle-class wife and mother to take a job or, still worse, to devote herself to any "frivolous" activity outside the home was considered a dereliction of duty. Such an attitude could not possibly develop in families where everyone had to work simply to keep food on the table.

Some women objected to the discrimination implicit in what the historian Barbara Welter has called "the cult of true womanhood." Others escaped its more suffocating aspects by forming close friendships with other women. But most women, including such forceful proponents of women's rights as the educator Catharine Beecher and Sarah Hale, the editor of *Godey's Ladies Book,* subscribed in their writing to the view that a woman's place was in the home. "The formation of the moral and intellectual character of the young is committed mainly to the female hand," Beecher wrote in *A Treatise on Domestic Economy for the Use of Young Ladies.* "The mother forms the character of the future man."

Another reason for the switch in power and influence from husbands to wives was that women began to have fewer children. Here again, the change happened earliest and was most pronounced among families in the rapidly urbanizing Northeast. But the birthrate gradually declined all over the country. People married later than in earlier periods. Long courtships and broken engagements were common, probably because prospective marriage partners were becoming more choosy. On average, women began having their children two or three years later than their mothers had, and they stopped two or three years sooner. Apparently many middle-class couples made a conscious effort to limit family size, even when doing so required sexual abstinence.

Having fewer children led parents to value children more highly, or so it would seem from the additional time and affection they lavished on them. Here again, the mother provided most of both. Child rearing fell within her "sphere" and occupied the time that earlier generations of mothers had devoted to such tasks as weaving, sewing, and farm chores. Not least of these new responsibilities was overseeing the children's education, both secular and religious.

As families became smaller, relations within them became more caring. Parents ceased to think of their children mostly as future workers. The earlier tendency even among loving parents to keep their children at arm's length, yet within reach of the strap, gave way to more intimate relationships. Gone was the Puritan notion that children possessed "a perverse will, a love of what's forbid," and with it the belief that parents were responsible for crushing all juvenile resistance to their authority. In its place arose the view described by Lydia Maria Child in *The Mother's Book* (1831) that children "come to us from heaven, with their little souls full of innocence and peace." Mothers "should not interfere with the influence of angels," Child advised her readers.

Bronson Alcott, another proponent of gentle child-rearing practices, went still further. Children, he insisted, were the moral superiors of their parents. Alcott banished "the rod and all its append-

ages" from his own household, wherein four daughters (one, Louisa May, later the author of *Little Women* and other novels) were raised, and urged other parents to follow his example. "Childhood hath saved me!" he wrote. The English poet William Wordsworth's "Ode on Intimations of Immortality," in which babies entered the world "trailing clouds of glory," served some American parents as a child-rearing manual.

The Second Great Awakening

Belief in the innate goodness of children was of course in direct conflict with the Calvinist doctrine of infant damnation, to which most American Prot-

During the Second Great Awakening, Americans flocked in vast numbers to hear evangelists such as Charles Grandison Finney preach. At huge outdoor camp meetings, which sometimes lasted three or four days and offered a change from the loneliness of frontier life, men and women enthusiastically embraced salvation. "Its sincerity could not be doubted," wrote an English observer after witnessing an emotional conversion at a camp meeting, "but it was the effect of over-excitement, not of sober reasoning."

estant churches formally subscribed. "Of all the impious doctrines which the dark imagination of man ever conceived," Bronson Alcott wrote in his journal, "the worst [is] the belief in original and certain depravity of infant nature." Alcott was far from alone in thinking infant damnation a "debased doctrine," despite its standing as one of the central tenets of orthodox Calvinism.

The inclination to set aside other Calvinist tenets, such as predestination, became more pronounced as a new wave of revivalism took shape in the 1790s. This Second Great Awakening began as a counteroffensive to the deistic thinking and other forms of "infidelity" that New England Congregationalists and southern Methodists alike identified with the French Revolution. Prominent New England ministers, who considered themselves traditionalists but also revivalists, men such as Yale's president, Timothy Dwight, and Dwight's student, the Reverend Lyman Beecher, placed less stress in their sermons on God's arbitrary power over mortals, more on His mercy, love, and "disinterested benevolence." When another of Dwight's students, Horace Bushnell, declared in a sermon on "Christian nurture" in 1844 that Christian parents should prepare their children "for the skies," he meant that parents could contribute to their children's salvation.

Calvinism came under more direct assault from Charles Grandison Finney, probably the most effective of a number of charismatic evangelists who brought the Second Great Awakening to its crest. In 1821 Finney abandoned a promising career as a lawyer and became an itinerant preacher. His most spectacular successes occurred during a series of revivals conducted in towns along the Erie Canal, a region Finney called "the burned-over district" because it had been the site of so many revivals before his own. From Utica, where his revival began in 1826, to Rochester, where it climaxed in 1831, he exhorted his listeners to take their salvation into their own hands. He insisted that people could control their own fate. He dismissed Calvinism as a "theological fiction." Salvation was available to anyone. But the day of judgment was just around the corner; there was little time to waste.

During and after Finney's efforts in Utica, declared conversions increased sharply. In Rochester, church membership doubled in six months. Elsewhere in the country, churches capitalized on the efforts of other evangelists to fill their pews. In 1831 alone, church membership grew by 100,000, an increase according to a New England minister, "unparalleled in the history of the church." The success of the evangelists of the Second Great Awakening stemmed from the timeliness of their assault on Calvinist doctrines, which were ripe for discrediting, and even more from their methods. Finney, for example, consciously set out to be entertaining as well as edifying. The singing of hymns and the solicitation of personal testimonies provided his meetings with emotional release and human interest. Prominent among his innovations was the "anxious bench," where leading members of the community awaited the final prompting from within before coming forward to declare themselves saved.

But the economic changes of the times and the impact of these changes on family life had as important effects on the Second Awakening as even the most accomplished of the evangelists. The growth of industry and commerce that followed the completion of the Erie Canal in 1825, along with the disappearance of undeveloped farmland, led hundreds of young men to leave family farms to seek their fortunes in Utica and other towns along the canal. There, uprooted, uncertain, buffeted between ambition, hope, and anxiety, they found it hard to resist the comfort promised by the revivalists to those who were saved.

But women, and especially the wives of the business leaders of the community, were, as Mary P. Ryan writes, the people "most receptive to the admonitions of the evangelical clergy." Aside from concern for their own salvation, they felt particularly responsible for the Christian education of their children, which fell within their separate sphere. Most of these upper-middle-class women had servants to handle household chores so that they had time and energy to devote to their own and their offsprings' salvation.

Paradoxically, this caused many of them to venture out of that sphere and in doing so they moved further out of the shadow of their husbands. They founded the Oneida County Female Missionary Society, an association that did most of the organizing and a good deal of the financing of the climactic years of the Second Awakening. The Female Missionary Society raised more than $1,000 a year (no small sum at that time) to support the revival in Utica, in its environs, and throughout the burned-over district. "These women," Professor Ryan explains, "orchestrated the revival and devised a sphere for women that had not been anticipated." Apparently without consciously intending to do so, they challenged the authority of the paternalistic, authoritarian churches they so fervently embraced. Then, by mixtures of exhortation, example, and affection, they set out to save the souls of their loved ones, first their children and ultimately their husbands too.

The Era of Associations

Alongside the recast family and the "almost revolutionized" church, a third pillar of the emerging American middle class was the voluntary association. Unlike the other two, it had neither colonial precedents nor contemporary European equivalents. The voluntary association of early 19th-century America was unique. "In France," Tocqueville wrote of this phenomenon, "if you want to proclaim a truth or propagate some feeling . . . you would find the government or in England some territorial magnate." In America, however, "you are sure to find an association."

The leaders of these associations tended to be ministers, lawyers, or merchants, but the rank and file consisted of tradesmen, foremen, clerks, and their wives. Some of these associations were formed around a local cause that some townspeople wished to advance, such as the provision of religious instruction for orphaned children; others were affiliated with associations elsewhere for the purposes of combating some national evil, such as drunkenness. Some, such as the American Board of Commissioners of Foreign Missions, founded in Boston in 1810, quickly became large and complex enterprises. (By 1860 the board had sent 1,250 missionaries into the "heathen world" and raised $8 million to support them.) Others lasted only as long as it took to accomplish a specific good work, such as the construction of a school or a library.

In a sense the associations were assuming functions previously performed in the family, such as caring for old people and providing moral guidance to the young, but without the paternalistic discipline of the old way. They constituted a "benevolent empire," eager to make society over into their members' idea of how God wanted it to be.

Backwoods Utopias

Americans frequently belonged to several associations at the same time, and more than a few made

The simplicity of Shaker life is apparent in this spartan bedroom, with its plain, narrow bed, its washstand, and the hanging pegs which are a practical way of storing articles such as hats, towels, and even a looking glass.

reform their life's work. The most adventuresome tested their reform theories by withdrawing from workaday American society and establishing experimental communities. The communitarian point of view aimed at "commencing a wholesale social reorganization by first establishing and demonstrating its principles completely on a small scale." The first communitarians were religious reformers. In a sense the Pilgrims fall into this category, along with a number of other groups in colonial times, but only in the 19th century did the idea flourish.

One of the earliest significant groups was founded by George Rapp, who brought some 600 Germans to western Pennsylvania in 1804. Rappites renounced marriage and sex and took every word in the Bible literally. They believed that the millennium was at hand; people must have their affairs constantly in order so as to be ready to meet their Maker on short notice. Industrious, pious, and isolated from other Americans by their language and beliefs, the Rappites prospered but had little influence on their neighbors.

More influential were the Shaker communities founded by an Englishwoman, Ann Lee, who came to America in 1774. Mother Ann, as she was called, saw visions that convinced her that Christ would come to earth again as a woman and that she was that woman. With a handful of followers she founded a community near Albany, New York. The group grew rapidly, and after her death in 1784 her movement continued to expand. By the 1830s her followers had established about 20 successful communities.

Like the Rappites, the Shakers practiced celibacy; believing that the millennium was imminent, they saw no reason for perpetuating the human race. Each group lived in a large Family House, the sexes strictly segregated. Property was held in common but controlled by a ruling hierarchy. So much stress was placed on equality of labor and reward and on voluntary acceptance of the rules, however, that the system does not seem to have been oppressive.

The Shaker religion, joyful and fervent, was marked by much group singing and dancing, which provided the members with emotional release from their tightly controlled regimen. An industrious, skillful people, they made a special virtue of simplicity; some of their designs for buildings and, especially, furniture achieved a classic beauty seldom equaled among untutored artisans. Despite their odd customs, the Shakers were universally tolerated and even admired.

There were many other religious colonies, such as the Amana Community, which flourished in New York and Iowa in the 1840s and 1850s, and John Humphrey Noyes's Oneida Community, where the members practiced "complex" marriage—a form of promiscuity based on the principle that every man in the group was married to every woman. They prospered by developing a number of manufacturing skills.

The most important of the religious communitarians was the Mormons. A remarkable Vermont farm boy, Joseph Smith, founded the religion in western New York in the 1820s. Smith saw visions; he claimed to have discovered and translated an ancient text, the Book of Mormon, written in hieroglyphics on plates of gold, which described the adventures of a tribe of Israelites that had populated America from biblical times until their destruction in a great war in A.D. 400. With a small band of followers, Smith established a community in Ohio in 1831. The Mormons' dedication and economic efficiency attracted large numbers of converts, but their unorthodox religious views and their exclusivism, product of their sense of being a chosen people, caused resentment among unbelievers. The Mormons were forced to move first to Missouri and then back to Illinois, where in 1839 they founded the town of Nauvoo.

Nauvoo flourished—by 1844 it was the largest city in the state, with a population of 15,000—but once again the Mormons ran into local trouble. They quarreled among themselves, especially after Smith secretly authorized polygamy (he called it "celestial marriage") and a number of other unusual rites for members of the "Holy Order," the top leaders of the church.* They created a paramilitary organization, the Nauvoo Legion, headed by Smith, envisaging themselves as a semi-independent state within the Union. Smith announced that he was a candidate for president of the United States. Rumors circulated that the Mormons intended to take over the entire Northwest for their "empire." Once

---

* The justification of polygamy, paradoxically, was that marriage was a sacred, eternal state. If a man remarried after his wife's death, eventually he would have two wives in Heaven. Therefore why not on earth?

Persecution forced the Mormons to move from New York to Ohio to Missouri, before settling for a time in Nauvoo, Illinois. In 1830, Mormon leaders were tarred and feathered, as this print shows. Fourteen years later, founder Joseph Smith and his brother Hyrum were arrested by local authorities and murdered in their jail cell by a hostile mob.

again local "gentiles" rose against them; Smith was arrested, then murdered by a mob.

Under a new leader, Brigham Young, the Mormons sought a haven beyond the frontier. In 1847 they marched westward, pressing through the mountains until they reached the desolate wilderness on the shores of Great Salt Lake. There, at last, they established their Zion and began to make their truly significant impact on American history. Irrigation made the desert flourish, precious water wisely being treated as a community asset. Hard, cooperative, intelligently directed effort spelled growth and prosperity; more than 11,000 people were living in the area when it became part of Utah Territory as a result of the Compromise of 1850. In time the communal Mormon settlement broke down, but the religion has remained, along with a distinctive Mormon culture that has been a major force in the shaping of the West. The Mormon church is still by far the most powerful single in-

fluence in Utah and is a thriving organization in many other parts of the United States and in Europe.

Despite their many common characteristics, the religious communities varied enormously; subordination of the individual to the group did not destroy group individualism. Their sexual practices, for example, ranged from the "complex marriage" of the Oneidans through Mormon polygamy and ordinary monogamy to the reluctant acceptance of sexual intercourse by the Amana Community and the absolute celibacy of the Rappites and Shakers. The communities are more significant as reflections of the urgent reform spirit of the age than they are for their accomplishments.

The communities had some influence on reformers who wished to experiment with social organization. When Robert Owen, a British utopian socialist who believed in economic as well as political equality and who considered competition debasing, decided to create an ideal community in America, he purchased the Rappite settlement at New Harmony, Indiana. Owen's advocacy of free love and "enlightened atheism" did not add to the stability of his group or to its popularity among outsiders. The colony was a costly failure.

The American followers of Charles Fourier, a French utopian socialist who proposed that society should be organized in cooperative units called phalanxes, fared better. Fourierism did not seek to tamper with sexual and religious mores. Its advocates included important journalists, such as Horace Greeley of the *New York Tribune* and Parke Godwin of the *New York Evening Post*. In the 1840s several dozen Fourierist colonies were established in the northern and western states. Members worked at whatever tasks they wished and only as much as they wished. Wages were paid according to the "repulsiveness" of the tasks performed; the person who "chose" to clean out a cesspool would receive more than someone hoeing corn or mending a fence or engaging in some task requiring complex skills. As might be expected, none of the communities lasted very long.

The Age of Reform

The communitarians were the most colorful of the reformers, their proposals the most spectacular. More effective, however, were the many individuals who took upon themselves responsibility for caring for the physically and mentally disabled and for the rehabilitation of criminals. The work of Thomas Gallaudet in developing methods for educating deaf people reflects the spirit of the times. Gallaudet's school in Hartford, Connecticut, opened its doors in 1817; by 1851 similar schools for the deaf had been established in 14 states.

Dr. Samuel Gridley Howe did similar work with the blind, devising means for making books with raised letters (Louis Braille's system of raised dots was not introduced until later in the century) that the blind could "read" with their fingers. Howe headed a school for the blind in Boston, the pioneering Perkins Institution, which opened in 1832. Of all that Charles Dickens observed in America, nothing so favorably impressed him as Howe's success in educating 12-year-old Laura Bridgman, who was deaf, mute, and blind. Howe was also interested

in trying to educate the mentally defective, and in other causes, including antislavery. "Every creature in human shape should command our respect," he insisted. "The strong should help the weak, so that the whole should advance as a band of brethren."

One of the most striking aspects of the reform movement was the emphasis reformers placed on establishing special institutions for dealing with social problems. In the colonial period, orphans, indigent persons, the insane, and the feebleminded were usually cared for by members of their own families or boarded in a neighboring household. They remained part of the community. Even criminals were seldom "locked away" for extended jail terms; punishment commonly consisted of whipping, being placed in stocks in the town square, or (for serious crimes) execution. But once persuaded that people were primarily shaped by their surroundings, reformers demanded that deviant and dependent members of the community be taken from their present corrupting circumstances and placed in specialized institutions where they could be trained or rehabilitated. The result, according to the historian David J. Rothman, was "the discovery of the asylum." Almshouses, orphanages, reformatories, prisons, and lunatic asylums sprang up throughout the United States like mushrooms in a forest after a summer rain.

The rationale for this movement was scientific; elaborate statistical reports attested to the benefits that such institutions would bring to both inmates and society as a whole. The motivating spirit of the founders of these asylums was humane, though many of the institutions seem anything but humane to the modern eye. The highly regarded Philadelphia prison system was based on strict solitary confinement, which was supposed to lead culprits to reflect on their sins and then reform their ways. The prison was literally a penitentiary, a place to repent. In fact, the system drove some inmates mad, and soon a rival Auburn system was introduced in New York State that allowed for some social contact among prisoners and for work in shops and stone quarries. Absolute silence was required at all times. The prisoners were herded about in lockstep and punished by flogging for the slightest infraction of the rules. Regular "moral and religious instruction" was provided, which the authorities believed would lead inmates to reform their lives. Tocqueville and Beaumont, in their report on American prisons,

A daguerreotype of Dorothea Lynde Dix, the pioneer reformer who worked to improve the lot of the insane in the United States. She also traveled to Europe, where she urged Queen Victoria and Pope Pius IX to support her efforts.

concluded that the Philadelphia system produced "the deepest impression on the soul of the convict," while the Auburn system made the convict "more conformable to the habits of man in society."

The hospitals for mental patients were intended to cure inmates, not merely to confine them. The emphasis was on isolating them from the pressures of society; on order, quiet, routine; on control but not on punishment. The unfortunates were seen as *de*ranged; the task was to *ar*range their lives in a rational manner. In practice, shortages of trained personnel, niggardly legislative appropriations, and the inherent difficulty of managing violent and irrational patients often produced deplorable conditions in the asylums.

This situation led Dorothea Dix, a woman of almost saintlike selflessness, to devote 30 years of her life to a campaign to improve the care of the insane. She traveled to every state in the Union and as far afield as Turkey and Japan, inspecting asylums and poorhouses. Insane persons in Massachusetts, she wrote in a memorial intended to shock state legislators into action, were being kept in cages

and closets, *"chained, naked, beaten with rods, and lashed into obedience!"* Her reports led to some improvement in conditions in Massachusetts and other states, but in the long run the bright hopes of the reformers were never realized. Institutions founded to uplift the deviant and dependent all too soon lost their reformist intentions and became instead places where society's "misfits" might safely be kept out of sight.

"Demon Rum"

Reformers must of necessity interfere with the affairs of others; thus there is often something of the busybody and the arrogant meddler about them. How they are regarded usually turns on the observer's own attitude toward their objectives. What is to some an unjustified infringement on a person's private affairs is to others a necessary intervention for that person's own good and for the good of society. Consider the temperance movement, the most widely supported and successful reform of the age of reform.

Americans in the 1820s consumed prodigious amounts of alcohol, more than ever before or since. Not that the colonists had been teetotalers. Liquor, mostly in the form of rum or hard apple cider, was cheap and everywhere available; taverns were an integral part of colonial society. There were alcoholics in colonial America, but because neither political nor religious leaders considered drinking dangerous, there was no alcohol "problem." Most doctors recommended the regular consumption of alcohol as healthy. John Adams, certainly the soul of propriety, drank a tankard of hard cider every day for breakfast. Dr. Benjamin Rush's *Inquiry into the Effects of Ardent Spirits* (1784), which questioned the medicinal benefits of alcohol, fell on deaf ears. However, alcohol consumption increased markedly in the early years of the new republic, thanks primarily to the availability of cheap corn and rye whiskey distilled in the new states of Kentucky and Tennessee. In the 1820s the per capita consumption of hard liquor reached 5 gallons, well over twice what it is today. Since small children and many grown people did not drink that much, others obviously drank a great deal more. Many women drank, if mostly at home; and reports of carousing among

14-year-old college freshmen show that youngsters did too. But the bulk of the heavy drinking occurred when men got together, at taverns or grogshops and at work.

Artisans and common laborers regarded their twice-daily "dram" of whiskey as part of their wages. In workshops, masters were expected to halt production periodically to drink with their apprentices and journeymen. Trips to the neighborhood grogshop also figured into the workaday routine. In 1829 Secretary of War John Eaton estimated that three-quarters of the nation's laborers drank at least 4 ounces of distilled spirits a day.

The foundation of the American Temperance Union in 1826 signaled the start of a national crusade against drunkenness. Employing lectures, pamphlets, rallies, essay contests, and other techniques, the union set out to persuade people to "sign the pledge" not to drink liquor. Primitive sociological studies of the effects of drunkenness (reformers were able to show a high statistical correlation between alcohol consumption and crime) added to the effectiveness of the campaign.

In 1840 an organization of reformed drunkards, the Washingtonians, set out to reclaim alcoholics. One of the most effective Washingtonians was John B. Gough, rescued by the organization after seven years in the gutter. "Crawl from the slimy ooze, ye drowned drunkards," Gough would shout, "and with suffocation's blue and livid lips speak out against the drink!"

Revivalist ministers like Charles Grandison Finney argued that alcohol was one of the great barriers to conversion, which helps explain why Utica, a town of fewer than 13,000 residents in 1840, supported four separate temperance societies in that year. Employers all over the country also signed on, declaring their businesses henceforward to be "cold-water" enterprises. Soon the temperance movement claimed a million members.

The temperance people aroused bitter opposition, particularly after they moved beyond calls for restraint to demands for prohibition of all alcohol. German and Irish immigrants, for the most part Catholic, objected to being told by reformers, for the most part Protestant, that their drinking would have to stop. But by the early 1840s the reformers had secured legislation in many states that imposed strict licensing systems and heavy liquor taxes. Local

option laws permitted towns and counties to ban the sale of alcohol altogether.

In 1851 Maine passed the first effective law prohibiting the manufacture and sale of alcoholic beverages. The leader of the campaign was Mayor Neal Dow of Portland, a businessman who became a prohibitionist after seeing the damage done by drunkenness among workers in his tannery. By 1855 a dozen other states had passed laws based on the Maine statute, and the nation's per capita consumption of alcohol had plummeted to 2 gallons a year.

The Abolitionist Crusade

No reform movement of this era was more significant, more ambiguous, or more provocative of later historical investigation than the drive to abolish slavery. That slavery should have been a cause of indignation to reform-minded Americans was inevitable. Humanitarians were outraged by the master's whip and by the practice of disrupting families. Democrats protested the denial of political and civil rights to slaves. Perfectionists of all stripes deplored the fact that slaves had no chance to improve themselves. However, well into the 1820s, the abolitionist cause attracted few followers because there seemed to be no way of getting rid of slavery short of revolution. While a few theorists argued that the Fifth Amendment, which provides that no one may be "deprived of life, liberty, or property, without due process of law," could be interpreted to mean that the Constitution outlawed slavery, the great majority believed that the institution was not subject to federal control.

Particularly in the wake of the Missouri Compromise, antislavery northerners neatly compartmentalized their thinking. Slavery was wrong; they would not tolerate it in their own communities. But since the Constitution obliged them to tolerate it in states where it existed, they felt no responsibility to fight it. The issue was explosive enough even when limited to the question of the expansion of slavery into the territories. People who advocated any kind of forced abolition in states where it was legal were judged irresponsible in the extreme. In 1820 presidential hopeful John Quincy Adams called slavery "the great and foul stain upon the North American

Union." "If the Union must be dissolved," he added, "slavery is precisely the question upon which it ought to break." But Adams expressed these opinions in the privacy of his diary, not in a public speech. Most critics of slavery therefore confined themselves to urging "colonization" or persuading slave owners to treat their property humanely.

One of the few Americans in the 1820s to go further was the Quaker Benjamin Lundy, editor of the Baltimore-based newspaper *The Genius of Universal Emancipation.* Lundy was no fanatic; he urged the use of persuasion in the South rather than interference by the federal government. He also explored the possibility of colonizing free blacks and slaves in Haiti and Canada. But he refused to mince words, and consequently he was subject to frequent harassment.

Even more provocative and less accommodating to local sensibilities was Lundy's youthful assistant, William Lloyd Garrison of Massachusetts. Garrison pronounced himself for "immediate" abolition. When his absolutely unyielding position made continued residence in Baltimore impossible, he returned to Boston, where in 1831 he established his own newspaper, *The Liberator.* "I am in earnest," he announced in the first issue. "I will not equivocate—

Former slave Frederick Douglass was one of the most effective spokesmen of the Massachusetts Anti-Slavery Society in the 1840s.

William Lloyd Garrison founded The Liberator *and edited it for 35 years; the newspaper was one of the nation's leading antislavery publications.*

I will not excuse—I will not retreat a single inch—and I will be heard."

Garrison's position, and that espoused by the New England Anti-Slavery Society, which he organized in 1831, was absolutely unyielding: Slaves must be freed immediately and treated as equals; compensated emancipation was unacceptable, colonization unthinkable. Because the United States government countenanced slavery, Garrison refused to engage in political activity to achieve his ends. Burning a copy of the Constitution—that "agreement with hell"—became a regular feature at Society-sponsored public lectures.

Few white Americans found Garrison's line of argument convincing, and many were outraged by his confrontational tactics. Whenever he spoke in public, he risked being mobbed by what newspaper accounts approvingly described as "gentlemen of property and standing." In 1833 a Garrison meeting in New York City was broken up by colonizationists. Two years later a mob dragged Garrison through the streets of his own Boston. That same day a mob broke up the convention of the New York Anti-Slavery Society in Utica. In 1837 Elijah Lovejoy, a

Garrisonian newspaper editor in Alton, Illinois, first saw his press destroyed by fire and then was himself murdered by a mob. When the proprietors of Philadelphia's Pennsylvania Hall booked an abolitionist meeting in 1838, a mob burned the hall to the ground to prevent the meeting from taking place. The historian Leonard L. Richard has documented more than 100 attacks on abolitionists in the North between 1833 and 1838.

In the wake of this violence some of Garrison's backers had second thoughts about his strategy of immediatism. The wealthy New York businessmen Arthur and Lewis Tappan, who had subsidized *The Liberator,* turned instead to Theodore Dwight Weld, a young minister who was part of Charles Grandison Finney's "holy band" of revivalists. Weld and his followers spoke of "immediate" emancipation "gradually" achieved, and they were willing to engage in political activity to achieve that goal.

In 1840 the Tappans and Weld openly broke with Garrison over the issue of involvement in politics and the participation of female abolitionists as public lecturers. Garrison, ever the radical, supported the women; Weld thought they would needlessly antagonize would-be supporters. The Tappans then organized the Liberty party, which nominated as its presidential candidate James G. Birney, a Kentucky slaveholder who had been converted to evangelical Christianity and abolitionism by Weld. Running on a platform of universal emancipation to be gradually brought about through legislation, Birney received only 7,000 votes.

Many blacks were abolitionists long before the white movement began to attract attention. In 1830 some 50 black antislavery societies existed, and thereafter these groups grew in size and importance, being generally associated with the Garrisonian wing. White abolitionists eagerly sought out black speakers, especially runaway slaves, whose heartrending accounts of their experiences aroused sympathies and who, merely by speaking clearly and with conviction, stood as living proof that blacks were neither animals nor fools.

Frederick Douglass, a former slave who had escaped from Maryland, was one of the most remarkable Americans of his generation. While a bondsman he had received a full portion of beatings and other indignities; but he had been allowed to learn to read and write and to master a trade, opportunities denied the vast majority of slaves. Set-

tling in Boston, he became an agent of the Massachusetts Anti-Slavery Society and a featured speaker at its public meetings.

Douglass was a tall, majestically handsome man who radiated determination and indignation. Slavery, he told white audiences, "brands your republicanism as a sham, your humanity as a base pretense, your Christianity as a lie." In 1845 he published his *Narrative of the Life of Frederick Douglass,* one of the most gripping autobiographical accounts of a slave's life ever written. Douglass insisted that freedom for blacks required not merely emancipation but full equality, social and economic as well as political. Not many white northerners accepted his reasoning, but few who heard him or read his works could afterward maintain the illusion that all blacks were dull-witted or resigned to inferior status.

At first Douglass was, in his own words, "a faithful disciple" of Garrison, prepared to tear up the Constitution and destroy the Union to gain his ends. In the late 1840s, however, he changed his mind, deciding that the Constitution, created to "establish Justice, insure domestic Tranquility . . . and secure the Blessings of Liberty," as its preamble states, "could not well have been designed at the same time to maintain and perpetuate a system of rapine and murder like slavery." Thereafter he fought slavery and race prejudice from within the system, something Garrison was never willing to do.

Garrison's importance cannot be measured by the number of his followers, which was never large. Unlike more moderately inclined enemies of slavery, he recognized that abolitionism was a revolutionary movement, not merely one more middle-class reform. He also understood that achieving racial equality, not merely "freeing" the slaves, was the only way to reach the abolitionists' professed objective: full justice for blacks. And he saw clearly that few whites, even among abolitionists, believed that blacks were their equals.

At the same time, Garrison seemed utterly indifferent to what effect the "immediate" freeing of the slaves would have on the South. He and his followers came close to claiming that all southern whites were villains, all blacks saints. Garrison said he would rather be governed by "the inmates of our penitentiaries" than by southern congressmen, whom he characterized as "desperadoes." The life of the slave owner, he wrote, is "one of unbridled lust, of filthy amalgamation, of swaggering braggadocio, of haughty domination, of cowardly ruffianism, of boundless dissipation, of matchless insolence, of infinite self-conceit, of unequaled oppression, of more than savage cruelty." His followers were no less fanatical in their judgments. "Slavery and cruelty cannot be disjoined," one wrote. "Consequently every slaveholder must be inhuman."

Both Garrison's insights into the limits of northern racial egalitarianism and his blind contempt for southern whites led him to the conclusion that American society was rotten to the core. Hence his refusal to make any concession to the existing establishment, religious or secular. He was hated in the North as much for his explicit denial of the idea that a constitution that supported slavery merited respect as for his implicit denial of the idea that a professed Christian who tolerated slavery for even an instant could hope for salvation. He was, in short, a perfectionist, a trafficker in moral absolutes who wanted his Kingdom of Heaven in the here and now. By contrast, most other American reformers were willing to settle for perfection on the installment plan.

Women's Rights

The question of slavery was related to another major reform movement of the era, the crusade for women's rights. The relationship was personal and ideological, direct and indirect, simple and profound. Superficially, the connection can be explained in this way: Women were as likely as men to find slavery offensive and to protest against it. When they did so, they ran into even more adamant resistance, the prejudices of those who objected to abolitionists being reinforced by their feelings that women should not speak in public or participate in political affairs. Thus female abolitionists, driven by the urgencies of conscience, were almost forced to become advocates of women's rights. "We have good cause to be grateful to the slave," the feminist Abby Kelley wrote. "In striving to strike his irons off, we found most surely, that we were manacled ourselves."

At a more profound level, the reference that abolitionists made to the Declaration of Independence to justify their attack on slavery radicalized women with regard to their own place in society. Were only all men created equal and endowed by

Elizabeth Cady Stanton at the age of 41 with her youngest daughter. In 1848 she helped draft the Declaration Principles, spelling out the injustices of man to woman. The conclusion: "He has endeavored, in every way he could, to destroy her confidence in her own powers, to lessen her self-respect, and to make her willing to lead a dependent and abject life."

God with unalienable rights? For many women the question was a consciousness-raising experience; they began to believe that, like blacks, they were imprisoned from birth in a caste system, legally subordinated and assigned menial social and economic roles that prevented them from developing their full potentialities. Such women considered themselves in a sense worse off than blacks, who had at least the psychological advantage of confronting an openly hostile and repressive society rather than one concealed behind the cloying rhetoric of romantic love.

With the major exception of Margaret Fuller, whose book *Women in the Nineteenth Century* (1844) made a frontal assault on all forms of sexual discrimination, the leading advocates of equal rights for women began their public careers in the abolitionist movement. Among the first were Sarah and Angelina Grimké, South Carolinians who abandoned their native state and the domestic sphere to devote themselves to speaking out against slavery. (In 1841 Angelina married Theodore Dwight Weld.) Male objections to the Grimkés' activities soon made them advocates of women's rights. Similarly, the refusal of delegates to the World Anti-Slavery Convention held in London in 1840 to let women participate in their debates precipitated the decision of two American abolitionists, Lucretia Mott and Elizabeth Cady Stanton, to turn their attention to the women's rights movement.

Slavery aside, there were other aspects of feminist consciousness-raising. Some women rejected the idea that they should confine themselves to a sphere of activity consisting mostly of child rearing and housekeeping. As the historian Nancy Cott has shown, the very effort to enforce this kind of specialization made women aware of their second-class citizenship and thus more likely to be dissatisfied. They lacked not merely the right to vote, of which they did not make a major issue, but if married, the right to own property or to make a will. Lydia Maria Child, a popular novelist, found this last restriction particularly offensive. It excited her "towering indignation" that her husband had to sign her will. David Child was not what today would be called a chauvinist, but, as she explained, "I was indignant for womankind made chattels personal from the beginning of time."

As Lydia Child noted, the subordination of women was as old as civilization. The attack on it came not because of any new discrimination but for the same reasons that motivated reformers against other forms of injustice: belief in progress, a sense of personal responsibility, the conviction that institutions could be changed and that the time for changing them was limited.

When women sought to involve themselves in reform, they became aware of perhaps the most serious handicap that society imposed on them—the conflict between their roles as wives and mothers and their urge to participate in the affairs of the larger world. Elizabeth Cady Stanton has left a striking description of this dilemma. She lived in the 1840s in Seneca Falls, a small town in central New York. Her husband was frequently away on business; she had a brood of growing children and little

domestic help. When, stimulated by her interest in abolition and women's rights, she sought to become active in the movements, her family responsibilities made it almost impossible even to read about them.

"I now fully understood the practical difficulties most women had to contend with," she recalled in her autobiography, *Eighty Years and More* (1898). "The general discontent I felt with woman's portion as wife, mother, housekeeper, physician, and spiritual guide, the chaotic condition into which everything fell without her constant supervision, and the wearied, anxious look of the majority of women, impressed me with the strong feeling that some active measures should be taken." Active measures she took. Together with Lucretia Mott and a few others of like mind, she organized a meeting, the Seneca Falls Convention (July 1848), and drafted the Declaration of Principles, patterned on the Declaration of Independence. "We hold these truths to be self-evident: that all men and women are created equal," it stated, and it went on to list the "injuries and usurpations" of men, just as Jefferson had outlined those of George III.

From this seed the movement grew. During the 1850s a series of national conventions was held, and more and more reformers, including William Lloyd Garrison, joined the cause. Of the recruits, Susan B. Anthony was the most influential, for she was the first to see the need for thorough organization if effective pressure was to be brought to bear on male-dominated society. Her first campaign, mounted in 1854 and 1855 in behalf of a petition to the New York legislature calling for reform of the property and divorce laws, accumulated 6,000 signatures. But the petition did not persuade the legislature to act. Indeed, the feminists achieved very few practical results during the age of reform. Their leaders, however, were persevering types, most of them extraordinarily long-lived. Their major efforts lay in the future.

Despite the aggressiveness of many reformers and the extremity of some of their proposals, little social conflict blighted these years. Most citizens readily accepted the need for improving society and showed a healthy tolerance for even the most harebrained schemes for doing so. When Sylvester Graham, inventor of the graham cracker, traveled up and down the land praising the virtues of hard mattresses, cold showers, and homemade bread, he was mobbed by professional bakers, but otherwise, as his biographer says, "he was the subject of jokes, lampoons, and caustic editorials" rather than violence. Americans argued about everything from prison reform to vegetarianism, from women's rights to phrenology (a pseudoscience much occupied with developing the diagnostic possibilities of measuring the bumps on people's heads). But

they seldom came to blows. Even the abolitionist movement might not have caused serious social strife if the territorial expansion of the late 1840s had not dragged the slavery issue back into politics. When that happened, politics again assumed center stage, public discourse grew embittered, and the first great age of reform came to an end.

Milestones

1774	Ann Lee founds the first Shaker community
1817	Thomas Gallaudet's school for the deaf founded
1820–1850	Rapid increase in European immigration / Rapid growth of cities / Rapid growth of manufacturing
1823	Merrimack Manufacturing Company opens in Lowell, Massachusetts
1826	American Temperance Union founded
1830	Joseph Smith, *The Book of Mormon*
1830s	Second Great Awakening
1830–1850	Utopian communities flourish
1831	William Lloyd Garrison founds *The Liberator*
1831–1832	Alexis de Tocqueville and William Beaumont tour America
1832	Perkins Institution for the Blind founded
1837	The abolitionist Elijah Lovejoy murdered
1843	Dorothea Dix, *Memorial to the Legislature of Massachusetts*
1844	Joseph Smith lynched
1845	Frederick Douglass, *Narrative of the Life of Frederick Douglass*
1847	Mormon migration to the Great Salt Lake
1848	Seneca Falls Convention Declaration of Principles
1851	Maine bans alcoholic beverages

SUPPLEMENTARY READING

Titles marked with an asterisk have been published in paperback.

On Tocqueville and his views of America, Alexis de Tocqueville, **Democracy in America,** (ed.) J. P. Mayer, 1966, "Tocqueville's Travel Notes" in J. P. Mayer (ed.), **Journey to America** (1960), and G. W. Pierson, **Tocqueville and Beaumont in America** (1938). For other visitors' accounts, see Frances Trollope, **Domestic Manners of the Americans** (1832), F. J. Grund, **Aristocracy in America*** (l839), Charles Dickens, **American Notes** (1847), and Harriet Martineau, **Retrospect of Western Travel** (1838). Edward Pessen, **Riches, Class and Power Before the Civil War*** (1973), and Rowland Berthoff, **An Unsettled People*** (1971), offer views different from Tocqueville's.

The growth of cities in the Jacksonian era can be traced in R. C. Wade, **The Urban Frontier*** (1957) and **Slavery in the Cities*** (1964), and in Howard Chudacoff, **The Evolution of American Urban Society*** (1981). A. F. Davis and Mark Halle (eds.), **The Peoples of Philadelphia*** (1973), S. B. Warner, Jr., **The Private City: Philadelphia in Three Periods of Its Growth*** (1968), Oscar Handlin, **Boston's Immigrants*** (1968), and P. R. Knights, **The Plain People of Boston*** (1971), deal with individual cities.

On immigration and ethnicity, see P. T. Knoble, **Paddy and the Republic** (1986), J. P. Dolan, **Immigrant Church: New York's Irish and German Catholics*** (1982), and, generally, Philip Taylor, **The Distant Mirror: European Migration to the United States** (1971), and Stephan Thernstrom (ed.), **Harvard Encyclopedia of American Ethnic Groups** (1980).

On changes in the nature of work in America, consult

A. F. C. Wallace, **Rockdale*** (1978), Alan Dawley, **Class and Community*** (1976), Thomas Dublin, **Women at Work** (1979), and Sean Wilencz, **Chants Democratic** (1984). On the changing place of the family and the changes within it, see M. P. Ryan, **Cradle of the Middle Class: The Family in Oneida, New York*** (1981), Nancy Cott, **The Bonds of Womanhood*** (1977), and Philip Greven, **The Protestant Temperament: Patterns of Child-Rearing, Religious Experience, and the Self in Early America** (1980). On demographic developments, see Walter Nugent, **Structures in American Social History** (1981), and M. A. Vinovskis, **Fertility in Massachusetts from the Revolution to the Civil War** (1981).

The Second Great Awakening has been examined both as a religious phenomenon and as a social one. Still useful are Whitney Cross, **The Burned-over District*** (1950), and Bernard Weisberger, **They Gathered at the River** (1958), but see also William McLoughlin, **Modern Revivalism: Finney to Graham** (1959), Timothy Smith, **Revivalism and Reform** (1965), and P. E. Johnson, **A Shopkeeper's Millennium*** (1978).

On utopianism generally, see Arthur Bestor, **Backwoods Utopias** (1950). N. G. Bringhurst, **Brigham Young and the Expanding American Frontier*** (1985), is informative on the Mormons. R. G. Walters, **American Reformers, 1815–1860*** (1978), is useful. On the social-control implications of reform, see C. S. Griffin, **Their Brothers' Keepers*** (1960), and D. J. Rothman, **Age of the Asylum: Social Order and Disorder in the New Republic*** (1971). Accounts of the temperance movement include Ian Tyrrell, **Sobering Up: From Temperance to Prohibition in Ante-Bellum America** (1979), and W. J. Rorabaugh, **The Alcoholic Republic*** (1979).

For sharply contrasting views of the abolitionist movement, see Stanley Elkins, **Slavery*** (1975), Aileen Kraditor, **Means and Ends in American Abolitionism*** (1967), and Lewis Perry and Michael Fellman (eds.), **Anti-Slavery Reconsidered*** (1979). Biographical accounts include J. L. Thomas, **The Liberator: William Lloyd Garrison*** (1963), Gerda Lerner, **The Grimké Sisters from South Carolina*** (1967), and Nathan Huggins, **Slave and Citizen: The Life of Frederick Douglass*** (1980). On antiabolitionists, see L. L. Richards, **"Gentlemen of Property and Standing"*** (1970).

Two recent interpretive accounts of the history of women and women's rights are Carl Degler, **At Odds: Women and Family in America from the Revolution to the Present*** (1980), and Nancy Woloch, **Women and the American Experience*** (1984). Elizabeth Griffith, **In Her Own Rights: The Life of Elizabeth Cady Stanton** (1984), and K. K. Sklar, **Catharine Beecher** (1973), are solid biographies of important women in the Jacksonian era.

The Way West

In the years after 1815, the lure of cheap land drew hundreds of thousands of pioneers west over the Appalachian mountains. The earliest settlers hauled their possessions along primitive, rutted roads. Once settled, however, the newcomers were not content to live in isolated self-sufficiency. They clamored for better ways to get their produce to markets in the East.

Private entrepreneurs and state governments responded by building roads, canals, and railroads. These "internal improvements" made possible commercial agriculture and spurred the growth of cities in the West. "The spectacle of a young people," marveled a French visitor in 1835, "executing in the short space of fifteen years, a series of works, which the most powerful States of Europe . . . would have shrunk from undertaking, is in truth a noble sight. The advantages which result from these enterprises to the public prosperity are incalculable."

Conestoga wagons, often associated with pioneers on the Oregon Trail, were used by earlier pioneers as well. Left, wagons and cattle jam the Frederick Road leading west from Baltimore. Rapid settlement of the Maryland and Pennsylvania hinterland helped make Baltimore one of the nation's largest cities in the mid-1800s.

The Appalachian mountains presented a daunting barrier to westward travelers. Above, a family on the way to Pittsburgh takes a needed rest and waters its horses. Even with the coming of canals and railroads, crossing the mountains was not easy. In 1837, the Pioneer Fast Line could boast of making the 300-mile trip from Philadelphia to Pittsburgh in "only" 3½ days.

River crossings could be painless or perilous, depending on circumstances. By 1860, Harper's Ferry in the Shenandoah Valley was a well-settled community. Travelers on the Baltimore & Ohio Railroad crossed the Potomac River comfortably over a sturdy covered bridge. (The smokestack on the far side of the river [upper illustration] is the armory made notorious by John Brown's 1859 raid.) Less fortunate travelers are rowed across the Susquehanna River in a flat-bottomed scow (lower illustration).

Starting in 1811, steamboats revolutionized river transportation in the West. Paddlewheelers slashed the cost of shipping goods upstream, thus making the Mississippi and Ohio rivers into two-way thoroughfares. "Steam is crowding our eastern cities with western flour . . . and lading the western steamboats with eastern emigrants and eastern merchandise," wrote an observer in 1841. In the decade after 1840, this busy Mississippi trade transformed St. Louis from a town of 16,000 to a city of 77,000 inhabitants (below). Although the steamboat dominated upriver travel, rafts were still used to ship farm products and bulky goods such as timber and coal downstream (above).

As in colonial times, frontier settlers lived in close contact with Indians. Conflict often resulted. In the West, the Army built forts to protect settlers and maintain order. These outposts were also trading centers where Indians exchanged their furs for manufactured goods of all kinds. Indians camp beside Fort Snelling in Wisconsin in the 1850s.

Emigrants to the Far West had to set out from Missouri in early spring in order to cross the Rockies and Sierras before the first snows of winter. These travelers on the Oregon Trail are fording Medicine Bow Creek in present-day Wyoming. The painting is by Samuel Colman.

Mormons followed the Oregon Trail in the 1840s on their way to the Great Salt Lake. By the 1850s, the Mormons could no longer afford draft animals to pull their wagons, but nevertheless thousands crossed the prairies and the Rockies drawing two-wheeled hand-carts similar to rickshaws (above). Other pioneers, seeking gold, not God, made their way by boat to San Francisco. Below, prospectors in a hurry to reach the diggings squatted in tents on San Francisco's Telegraph Hill.

A Democratic Culture

We have listened too long to the courtly muses of Europe.

RALPH WALDO EMERSON, *1837*

It's good to be shifty in a new country.

J. J. HOOPER, The Adventures of Simon Suggs, *1846*

As the United States grew larger, richer, and more centralized, it began to evolve a more distinctive culture. Still the child of Europe, by mid-century it was clearly the offspring rather than an imitation of the parent society. Jefferson had drawn most of his ideas from classical authors and 17th-century English thinkers. He gave to these doctrines an American cast, as when he stressed the separation of church and state or the pursuit of happiness instead of property in describing the "unalienable rights" of men. But Ralph Waldo Emerson, whose views were roughly similar to Jefferson's and who was also influenced by European thinkers, was an American philosopher. He and his generation drew quite self-consciously on native sources and inspirations. In doing so they described convincingly the emergence of a distinctly democratic culture.

In Search of Native Grounds

Early 19th-century literary groups such as Boston's Anthology Club and the Friendly Club in New York consciously set out to "foster American genius" and to encourage the production of a distinctively American literature. According to the historian Russel B. Nye, in the period between the Revolution and 1830 "every author of note made at least one effort to use American history in a major literary work."

Yet Nye admitted that in nearly every case "nothing of consequence appeared." Of the novelists before 1830, only James Fenimore Cooper made successful use of the national heritage. Beginning with *The Spy* (1821), *The Pioneers* (1823), and *The Last of the Mohicans* (1826), he wrote a long series of tales of Indians and settlers that presented a vivid, if romanticized, picture of frontier life. (Cooper's Indians, Mark Twain quipped, belonged to "an extinct tribe that never existed.") Cooper's work marked a shift from the classicism of the 18th century, which emphasized reason and orderliness in writing, to the romanticism of the early 19th century, with its stress on highly subjective emotional values and its concern for the beauties of nature and the freedom of the individual.

Most novelists of the period slavishly imitated British writers. Some looked to the sentimental novels of Samuel Richardson for a model; others aped satirical writers like Daniel Defoe and Tobias Smollett. Most popular were historical romances done in the manner of the Waverley novels of Sir Walter Scott. None approached the level of the best British writers, and as a result American novelists were badly outdistanced in their own country by the British, both in prestige and popularity. Since foreign copyrights were not recognized in the United States, British books were shamelessly pirated and sold cheaply. Half a million volumes of Scott were sold in America before 1823. American readers benefited but not American writers.

New York City was the literary capital of the country. Its leading light was Washington Irving, whose comical *Diedrich Knickerbocker's History of New York* (1809) made its young author famous on both sides of the Atlantic. Yet Irving soon abandoned the United States for Europe. *The Sketch Book* (1819), which included "Rip Van Winkle" and other well-known tales and legends of the Dutch in the Hudson Valley, was written while the author was residing in Birmingham and London. Outside New York there was much less literary activity. New England was only on the verge of its great literary flowering.

American painting in this period reached a level comparable to that of contemporary European work, but the best received most of their training

In paintings such as Kaaterskill Falls, *artist Thomas Cole captured the splendor of the American landscape. As founder of the Hudson River School, Cole developed a distinctly American style of painting. Like other romantics, he used nature to explore human emotions. But he was also a careful observer of nature, accurately capturing details of tangled underbrush, cascading waters, and individual trees.*

in Europe. Benjamin West, the first and in his day the most highly regarded, went to Europe before the Revolution and never returned; he can scarcely be considered an American. John Singleton Copley, whose stern, straightforward portraits display a more distinctly American character than the work of any of his contemporaries, was a Bostonian. No one so well captured the vigor and integrity of the Revolutionary generation. Charles Willson Peale, after studying under West in London, settled in Philadelphia, where he established a museum containing fossils, stuffed animals, and various natural curiosities as well as paintings. Peale helped found the Pennsylvania Academy of the Fine Arts, and he did much to encourage American painting. Not the

least of his achievements was the production of a large brood of artistic children to whom he gave such names as Rembrandt, Titian, and Rubens. The most talented of Peale's children was (appropriately) Rembrandt, whose portrait of Jefferson, executed in 1800, is one of the finest likenesses of the Sage of Monticello.

Another outstanding artist of this generation was Gilbert Stuart, who is best known for his many studies of George Washington. Stuart studied in England with Benjamin West, and his brush was much in demand in London. He was probably the most technically accomplished of the early American portrait painters. He was fond of painting his subjects with ruddy complexions (produced by means of a judicious mixture of vermilion, purple, and white pigment), which made many of his elderly sitters appear positively cherubic. He once remarked that the pallid flesh tones used by a rival looked "like putrid veal a little blown with green flies."

In general, the painting of the period was less obviously imitative of European models than the national literature. Wealthy merchants, manufacturers, and planters wished their likenesses preserved, and the demand for portraits of the nation's Revolutionary heroes seemed insatiable. Since paintings could not be reproduced as books could be, American artists did a flourishing business. And they remained unmistakably in the European tradition.

Exceptions to this generalization can be found in the work of a number of self-trained artists like Jonathan Fisher, Charles Octavius Cole, and J. William Jennys. These primitive painters supplied rural and middle-class patrons in the same way that Copley and Stuart catered to the tastes of the rich and prominent. Jennys, for example, received $24 in 1801 for portraits of Dr. William Stoddard Williams of Deerfield, Massachusetts, and his wife. Cole specialized in New England sea captains, whom he often painted holding brassbound spyglasses. One historian has discovered traces of more than 20 artisan-painters within the single state of Maine in the 1830s and 1840s. Some of these primitive canvases have great charm and distinction.

The Romantic View of Life

In the western world the romantic movement was a revolt against the bloodless logic of the Age of Reason. It was a noticeable if unnamed point of view in Germany, France, and England as early as the 1780s and in America a generation later; by the second quarter of the 19th century, few intellectuals were unmarked by it. "Romantics" believed that change and growth were the essence of life, for individuals and for institutions. They valued feeling and intuition over pure thought, and they stressed the differences between individuals and societies rather than the similarities. Ardent love of country characterized the movement; individualism, optimism, ingenuousness, and emotion were its bywords. Whereas the Puritans, believing that nearly

everyone was destined to endure the tortures of Hell for all eternity, contemplated death with dread, romantics, assuming that good people would go to Heaven, professed to look forward to death.

Romanticism perfectly fitted the mood of 19th-century America. Interest in raw nature and in primitive peoples, worship of the individual, praise of folk culture, the subordination of intellect to feeling—were these primarily romantic ideas or American ideas? Jacksonian democracy with its self-confidence, careless prodigality, contempt for learning, glorification of the ordinary—was it a product of the American experience or a reflection of a wider world view?

The romantic way of thinking found its fullest American expression in the transcendentalist movement. Transcendentalism, a New England creation, is difficult to describe because it emphasized the indefinable and the unknowable. It was a mystical, intuitive way of looking at life that subordinated facts to feelings. Its literal meaning was "to go beyond the world of the senses," by which the transcendentalists meant the material and observable world. To the transcendentalists, human beings were truly divine because they were part of nature, itself the essence of divinity. Their intellectual capacities did not define their capabilities, for they could "transcend" reason by having faith in themselves and in the fundamental benevolence of the universe. Transcendentalists were complete individualists, seeing the social whole as no more than the sum of its parts. Organized religion, indeed all institutions were unimportant if not counterproductive; what mattered was the single person and that people aspire, stretch *beyond* their known capabilities. Failure resulted only from lack of effort. The expression "Hitch your wagon to a star" is of transcendentalist origin.

Emerson and Thoreau

The leading transcendentalist thinker was Ralph Waldo Emerson. Born in 1803 and educated at Harvard, Emerson became a minister, but in 1832 he gave up his pulpit, deciding that "the profession is antiquated." After traveling in Europe, where he met many romantic writers, including Samuel Taylor Coleridge, William Wordsworth, and (especially important) Thomas Carlyle, he settled in Concord,

Ralph Waldo Emerson was largely responsible for generating the transcendentalist movement, and in a broader sense for fostering romantic thought in the United States.

Massachusetts, to a long career as essayist, lecturer, and sage.

Emerson managed to restore to what he called "corpse-cold" Unitarianism the fervor and purposefulness characteristic of 17th-century Puritanism. His philosophy was at once buoyantly optimistic and rigorously intellectual, self-confident and conscientious. In a notable address at Harvard in 1837, "The American Scholar," he urged Americans to put aside their devotion to things European and seek inspiration in their immediate surroundings. He saw himself as pitting "spiritual powers" against "the mechanical powers and the mechanical philosophy of this time." The new industrial society of New England disturbed him profoundly.

Emerson favored change and believed in progress. It was America's destiny to fulfill "the postponed expectations of the world." Temperamentally, however, he was too serene and too much his own man to fight for the causes other reformers

espoused, and he was too idealistic to accept the compromises that most reformers make to achieve their ends. To abolitionist friends who sought his aid he said: "God must govern his own world. . . . I have quite other slaves to face than those Negroes, to wit, imprisoned thoughts . . . which have no watchman or lover or defender but me."

Because he put so much emphasis on self-reliance, Emerson disliked powerful governments. "The less government we have the better," he said. In a sense he was the prototype of some modern alienated intellectuals, so repelled by the world as it was that he would not actively try to change it. Nevertheless, he thought strong leadership essential, perhaps being influenced in this direction by his friend Carlyle's glorification of the role of great men in history. Emerson also had a strong practical streak. He made his living by lecturing, tracking tirelessly across the country, talking before every type of audience for fees ranging from $50 to several hundreds.

Closely identified with Emerson was his Concord neighbor Henry David Thoreau. After graduating from Harvard in 1837, Thoreau taught school for a time and helped out in a small pencil-making business run by his family. He was a strange man, gentle, a dreamer, content to absorb the beauties of nature almost intuitively, yet stubborn and individualistic to the point of selfishness. "He is the most unmalleable fellow alive," one acquaintance wrote. The hectic scramble for wealth that Thoreau saw all about him he found disgusting—and alarming, for he believed it was destroying both the natural and the human resources of the country.

Like Emerson, Thoreau objected to many of society's restrictions on the individual. "That government is best which governs not at all," he said, going both Emerson and the Jeffersonians one better. He was perfectly prepared to see himself as a majority of one. Emerson reduced him to a phrase when he called him "a born protestant." "When were the good and the brave ever in a majority?" Thoreau asked. "If a man does not keep pace with his companions," he wrote on another occasion, "perhaps it is because he hears a different drummer."

In 1845 Thoreau decided to put to the test his theory that a person need not depend on society for a satisfying existence. He built a cabin at Walden Pond on some property owned by Emerson and lived there alone for two years. He did not try to

WALDEN;

OR,

LIFE IN THE WOODS.

By HENRY D. THOREAU,

AUTHOR OF "A WEEK ON THE CONCORD AND MERRIMACK RIVERS."

I do not propose to write an ode to dejection, but to brag as lustily as chanticleer in the morning, standing on his roost, if only to wake my neighbors up. — Page 92.

BOSTON:
TICKNOR AND FIELDS.
M DCCC LIV.

"I went to the woods," wrote Henry David Thoreau about his purpose in going to Walden Pond, "because I wished to live deliberately, to front only the essential facts of life, and see if I could not learn what it had to teach, and not, when I came to die, to discover that I had not lived." The title page of Walden *shows the cabin that Thoreau built on Emerson's land.*

menting, to prove that *if necessary*, an individual could get along without the products of civilization. He used manufactured plaster in building his Walden cabin, but he also gathered a bushel of clamshells and made a small quantity of lime himself, to prove that it could be done.

At Walden, Thoreau wrote *A Week on the Concord and Merrimack Rivers* (1849), which used an account of a trip he had taken with his brother as a vehicle for a discussion of his ideas about life and literature. He spent much time observing the quiet world around the pond, thinking, and writing in his journal. The best fruit of this period was that extraordinary book *Walden* (1854). Superficially, *Walden* is the story of Thoreau's experiment, moving and beautifully written. It is also an acid indictment of the social behavior of the average American, an attack on unthinking conformity, on subordinating one's own judgment to that of the herd.

The most graphic illustration of Thoreau's confidence in his own values occurred while he was living at Walden. At that time the Mexican War was raging. Thoreau considered the war immoral because it advanced the cause of slavery. To protest, he refused to pay his Massachusetts poll tax. For this he was arrested and lodged in jail, although only for one night because an aunt promptly paid the tax for him. His essay "Civil Disobedience," explaining his view of the proper relation between the individual and the state, resulted from this experience. Like Emerson, however, Thoreau refused to participate in practical reform movements. "I love Henry," one of his friends said, "but I cannot like him; and as for taking his arm, I should as soon think of taking the arm of an elm tree."

Edgar Allan Poe

The work of all the imaginative writers of the period reveals romantic influences, and it is possibly an indication of the affinity of the romantic approach to American conditions that a number of excellent writers of poetry and fiction first appeared in the 1830s and 1840s. Edgar Allan Poe, one of the most remarkable, seems almost a caricature of the romantic image of the tortured genius. Poe was born in Boston in 1809, the son of poor actors who died before he was 3. He was raised by a wealthy Virginian, John Allan.

be entirely self-sufficient: He was not above returning to his family or to Emerson's for a square meal on occasion, and he generally purchased the building materials and other manufactured articles that he needed. Instead he set out, by experi-

Edgar Allan Poe, widely appreciated in his lifetime, inspired generations of later writers with his detective stories and horror tales.

Few persons as neurotic as Poe have been able to produce first-rate work. In college he ran up debts of $2,500 in less than a year and had to withdraw. He won an appointment to West Point but was discharged after a few months for disobedience and "gross neglect of duty." He was a lifelong alcoholic and an occasional taker of drugs. He married a child of 13. Once he attempted to poison himself; repeatedly he was down and out even to the verge of starvation. He was haunted by melancholia and hallucinations. Yet he was an excellent magazine editor, a penetrating critic, a poet of unique if somewhat narrow talents, and a fine short story writer. Although he died at 40, he turned out a large volume of serious, highly original work.

Poe responded strongly to the lure of romanticism. His works abound with examples of wild imagination and fascination with mystery, fright, and the occult. If he did not invent the detective story, he perfected it; his tales "The Murders in the Rue Morgue" and "The Purloined Letter" stressed the thought processes of a clever detective in solving a mystery by reasoning from evidence. Poe was also one of the earliest writers to deal with what are today called science fiction themes, and "The Pit and the Pendulum" and "The Cask of Amontillado" show that he was a master of the horror tale.

Although dissolute in his personal life, when Poe touched pen to paper, he became a disciplined craftsman. The most fantastic passages in his works are the result of careful, reasoned selection; not a word, he believed, could be removed without damage to the whole. And despite his rejection of most of the values prized by middle-class America, Poe was widely read in his own day. His poem "The Raven" won instantaneous popularity when it was published in 1845. Had he been a little more stable, he might have made a good living with his pen— but in that case he might not have written as he did.

Nathaniel Hawthorne

Another product of the prevailing romanticism was Nathaniel Hawthorne of Salem, Massachusetts. Hawthorne was born in 1804. When he was a small child, his father died and his grief-stricken mother became a recluse. Left largely to his own devices, he grew to be a lonely, introspective person. Wandering about New England by himself in summertime, he soaked up local lore, which he drew upon in writing short stories. For a time he lived in Concord, where he came to know most of the leading transcendentalists. However, he disliked the egoism of the transcendental point of view and rejected its bland optimism outright. He called Emerson an "everlasting rejector of all that is," a "seeker for he knows not what."

Hawthorne was fascinated by the past, particularly by the Puritan heritage of New England and its continuing influence on his own generation. He scorned "minute fidelity" to the real world in his fiction, seeking "a severer truth . . . the truth of the human heart." But he was active in politics and an admirer of Andrew Jackson. Three Democratic presidents—Martin Van Buren, James K. Polk, and Franklin Pierce—appointed him to minor political offices.

Hawthorne's early stories, originally published in magazines, were brought together in *Twice-told Tales* (1837). They made excellent use of New England culture and history for background but were concerned chiefly with the struggles of individuals with sin, guilt, and especially the pride and isolation that often afflict those who place too much reliance

Like his contemporaries Emerson and Thoreau, Nathaniel Hawthorne settled in Concord, Massachusetts. As a young man, Hawthorne had isolated himself in order to write. A severe critic of his own work, Hawthorne burned many of his early stories. This portrait of Hawthorne was painted a few years after the publication of Twice-Told Tales, *when he began to emerge from his self-imposed seclusion.*

on their own judgment. His greatest works were two novels written after the Whigs turned him out of his government job in 1849. *The Scarlet Letter* (1850), a grim yet sympathetic analysis of adultery, condemned not the woman, Hester Prynne, but the people who presumed to judge her. *The House of the Seven Gables* (1851) was a gripping account of the decay of an old New England family brought on by the guilt feelings of the current owners of the house, caused by the way their ancestors had cheated the original owners of the property.

Like Poe, Hawthorne was appreciated in his own day and widely read; unlike Poe, he made a modest amount of money from his work. Yet he was never very comfortable in the society he inhabited. He had no patience with the second-rate. And despite

his success in creating word pictures of a somber, mysterious world, he considered America too prosaic a country to inspire good literature. "There is no shadow, no antiquity, no mystery, no picturesque and gloomy wrong, nor anything but a commonplace prosperity," he complained.

Herman Melville

In 1850, while writing *The House of the Seven Gables,* Hawthorne was introduced by his publisher to another writer in the midst of a novel. This was Herman Melville, the book *Moby Dick.* The two became good friends at once, for despite their dissimilar backgrounds, they had a great deal in common. Melville was a New Yorker, born in 1819, one of eight children of a merchant of distinguished lineage. His father, however, lost all his money and died when the boy was 12. Herman left school at 15, worked briefly as a bank clerk, and in 1837 went to sea. For 18 months, in 1841 and 1842, he was crewman on the whaler *Acushnet.* Then he jumped ship in the South Seas. For a time he lived among a tribe of cannibals in the Marquesas; later he made his way to Tahiti, where he idled away nearly a year. After another year at sea he returned to America in the fall of 1844.

Although he had never before attempted serious writing, in 1846 he published *Typee,* an account of his life in the Marquesas. The book was a great success, for Melville had visited a part of the world almost unknown to Americans, and his descriptions of his bizarre experiences suited the taste of a romantic age. Success inspired him to write a sequel, *Omoo* (1847); other books followed quickly.

As he wrote Melville became conscious of deeper powers. In 1849 he began a systematic study of Shakespeare, pondering the bard's intuitive grasp of human nature. Like Hawthorne, Melville could not accept the prevailing optimism of his generation. Unlike his friend, he admired Emerson, seconding the Emersonian demand that Americans reject European ties and develop their own literature. "Believe me," he wrote, "men not very much inferior to Shakespeare are this day being born on the banks of the Ohio." Yet he considered Emerson's vague talk about striving and the inherent goodness of mankind complacent nonsense.

Experience made Melville too aware of the evil

in the world to be a transcendentalist. His novel *Redburn* (1849), based on his adventures on a Liverpool packet, was, as the critic F. O. Matthiessen put it, "a study in disillusion, of innocence confronted with the world, of ideals shattered by facts." Yet Melville was no cynic; he expressed deep sympathy for the Indians and for immigrants, crowded like animals into the holds of transatlantic vessels. He denounced the brutality of discipline in the United States Navy in *White-Jacket* (1850). His essay "The Tartarus of Maids," a moving if somewhat overdrawn description of young women working in a paper factory, protested the subordination of human beings to machines.

Hawthorne, whose dark view of human nature coincided with Melville's, encouraged him to press ahead with *Moby Dick* (1851). This book, Melville said, was "broiled in hellfire." Against the background of a whaling voyage (no better account of whaling has ever been written), he dealt subtly and symbolically with the problems of good and evil, of courage and cowardice, of faith, stubbornness, pride. In Captain Ahab, driven relentlessly to hunt down the huge white whale Moby Dick, which had destroyed his leg, Melville created one of the great figures of literature; in the book as a whole, he produced one of the finest novels written by an American, comparable to the best in any language.

As Melville's work became more profound, it lost its appeal to the average reader, and its originality and symbolic meaning escaped most of the critics. *Moby Dick,* his masterpiece, received little attention, and most of that was unfavorable. He kept on writing until his death in 1891 but was virtually ignored. Only in the 1920s did the critics rediscover him and give him his merited place in the history of American literature. His "Billy Budd, Foretopman," now considered one of his best stories, was not published until 1924.

Walt Whitman

Walt Whitman, whose *Leaves of Grass* (1855) was the last of the great literary works of this brief outpouring of genius, was the most romantic and by far the most distinctly American writer of his age. He was born on Long Island, outside New York City, in 1819. At 13 he left school and became a printer's devil; thereafter he held a succession of newspaper jobs in the metropolitan area. He was an ardent Jacksonian and later a Free Soiler, which got him into hot water with a number of the publishers for whom he worked.

Although genuinely a "common man," thoroughly at home among tradesmen and laborers, he was surely not an ordinary man. Deeply introspective, he read omnivorously, if in a rather disorganized fashion while working out a new, intensely personal mode of expression. During the early 1850s, while employed as a carpenter and composing the poems that made up *Leaves of Grass*, he regularly carried a book of Emerson in his lunch box. "I was simmering, simmering, simmering," he later recalled. "Emerson brought me to a boil." The transcendental idea that inspiration and aspiration are at the heart of all achievement captivated him. A poet could best express himself, he believed, by relying uncritically on his natural inclinations without regard for rigid metrical forms.

Leaves of Grass consisted of a preface, in which Whitman made the extraordinary statement that Americans had "probably the fullest poetical na-

Criticized as undisciplined and pretentious, Walt Whitman expressed a fresh viewpoint on commonplace subjects.

ture" of any people in history, and 12 poems in free verse: rambling, uneven, appearing to most readers shocking both in the commonplace nature of the subject matter and the coarseness of the language. Emerson, Thoreau, and a few others saw a fresh talent in these poems, but most readers and reviewers found them offensive. Indeed, the work was so undisciplined and so much of it had no obvious meaning that it was easy to miss the many passages of great beauty and originality that were scattered throughout.

Part of Whitman's difficulty arose because there was much of the charlatan in his makeup; often his writing did not ring true. He loved to use foreign words and phrases, and since he had no more than a smattering of any foreign language, he frequently sounded pretentious and sometimes downright foolish when he did so. In reality a sensitive, effeminate person, he tried to pose as a great, rough character. (Later in his career he bragged of fathering no less than six illegitimate children, which was assuredly untrue.) He never married, and his work suggests that his strongest emotional ties were with men. Thomas Carlyle once remarked shrewdly that Whitman thought he was a big man because he lived in a big country.

Whitman's work was more authentically American than that of any contemporary. His egoism—he titled one of his finest poems "Song of Myself"—was tempered by his belief that he was typical of all humanity.

> I celebrate myself and sing myself
> And what I assume you shall assume,
> For every atom belonging to me as good belongs to
>   you.

He had a remarkable ear for rendering common speech poetically, for employing slang, for catching the breezy informality of Americans and their faith in themselves.

> Earth! you seem to look for something at my hands,
> Say, old top-knot, what do you want?
> I bequeath myself to the dirt to grow from the grass
>   I love,
> If you want me again look for me under your boot-
>   soles.

Because of these qualities and because in his later work, especially during the Civil War, he occasionally struck a popular chord, Whitman was never as neglected as Melville. When he died in 1892, he was, if not entirely understood, at least widely appreciated.

The Wider Literary Renaissance

Emerson, Thoreau, Poe, Hawthorne, Melville, and Whitman were the great figures of American literature before the Civil War. A number of others, if they lacked genius, were leading literary lights in their day and are still worth reading. One was Henry Wadsworth Longfellow. In 1835, while still in his twenties, Longfellow became professor of modern languages at Harvard. Although he published a fine translation of Dante's *Divine Comedy* and was expert in many languages, his fame came from his poems: "The Village Blacksmith"; "Paul Revere's Ride"; *The Courtship of Miles Standish*, a sentimental tale of Pilgrim days; and *The Song of Hiawatha*, the romantic retelling of an Indian legend. These brought him excellent critical notices and considerable fortune; his work was widely translated and reprinted.

Though musical, polished, and full of vivid images, Longfellow's poetry, like the man, lacked profundity, originality, and force. But it was neither cheap nor trivial. When Longfellow wrote "Life is real! life is earnest! / And the grave is not its goal," he expressed the heartfelt belief of most of his generation. In this sense he captured the spirit of his times better than any of his great contemporaries, better even than Whitman.

Longfellow was the most talented of a group of minor New England writers who collectively gave that region great intellectual vitality. John Greenleaf Whittier, a poet nearly as popular as Longfellow, believed ardently in the abolition of slavery. A few of his poems can still be read with pleasure, among them "The Barefoot Boy," dealing with his rural childhood. Somewhat more weighty was the achievement of James Russell Lowell, the first editor of the *Atlantic Monthly*, founded in Boston in 1857. Lowell's humorous stories written in the New England dialect made an original and influential contribution to the national literature. Dr. Oliver Wendell Holmes, professor of medicine at Harvard, was widely known as a poet and essayist. A few of his poems, such as "The Chambered Nautilus" and "Old Ironsides," are interesting examples of American romantic verse.

So did the important historians of the period, all of them New Englanders. George Bancroft, one of the first Americans to study in Germany, began in 1834 to publish a ten-volume *History of the United States*, based on thorough research. William Hickling Prescott, though nearly blind, wrote extensively on the history of Spain and Spain's American empire, his *Conquest of Mexico* (1843) and *Conquest of Peru* (1847) being his most important works. John Lothrop Motley, another German-trained historian, published his *Rise of the Dutch Republic* in 1856, and Francis Parkman began his great account of the struggle between France and Great Britain for the control of North America with *Conspiracy of Pontiac* in 1851.

The public read these histories avidly. They suited the taste of the times, they were written with a mass audience in mind, and they were thoroughly in the romantic tradition. As David Levin said in his important study *History as Romantic Art*, "They all shared an 'enthusiastic' attitude toward the Past, an affection for grand heroes, an affection for Nature and the 'natural.' "

Southern literature was even more markedly romantic than that of New England. John Pendleton Kennedy of Baltimore wrote several novels with regional historical themes, much in the manner of Sir Walter Scott. Kennedy was also a Whig politician of some importance who served several terms in Congress; in 1852 he became secretary of the navy in the Fillmore Cabinet. The more versatile and influential William Gilmore Simms of South Carolina wrote nearly two dozen novels, several volumes of poetry, and a number of biographies. At his peak in the 1830s he earned as much as $6,000 a year with his pen. *The Partisan* (1835), one of a series of novels dealing with the Revolution, and *The Yemassee* (1835), the story of an early-18th-century Indian war, seem too melodramatic for modern tastes. His portraits of the planter class are too bloodless and reverential to be convincing. His female characters are nearly all pallid and fragile. Only when Simms wrote of frontier life and people did his work possess much power.

Domestic Tastes

Architecture flourished in the northern cities chiefly as a result of the work of Charles Bulfinch and some of his disciples. Bulfinch was influenced by British

The Smithsonian Institution Building, made of red sandstone, is popularly know as "The Castle" because of its eight crenelated towers. Its architect, James Renwick, Jr., also designed New York's Grace Church and Saint Patrick's Cathedral in the popular Gothic Revival style.

architects, but he developed a manner all his own. His "Federal" style gave parts of Boston a dignity and charm equal to the finest sections of London. The State House, numerous other public buildings, and, best of all, many of Bulfinch's private houses—austere yet elegant, solid yet airy and graceful—gave the town a distinction it had lacked before the Revolution.

In the 1830s and 1840s new techniques made it possible to weave colored patterns into cloth by machine, to manufacture wallpaper printed with complicated designs, and to produce rugs and hangings that looked like tapestries. Combined with the use of machine methods in the furniture business, these inventions had a powerful impact on public taste. That impact, at least in the short run, was aesthetically unfortunate. As Russell Lynes writes in his entertaining study *The Tastemakers*, "Styles ran riot. . . . The new chairs and sofas, bedecked with fruit, flowers, and beasties and standing on twisted spindles, crowded into living rooms and parlors."

Wood-turning machinery added to the popularity of the elaborately decorated "Gothic" style of architecture. The irregularity and uniqueness of Gothic buildings suited the prevailing romanticism; their aspiring towers, steeples, and arches and their flexibility (a new wing or extension could always be added without spoiling the effect) made them especially attractive to a people enamored of progress.

A lifelong resident of rural Long Island, William Sidney Mount took everyday life of that corner of America as his inspiration. Eel Spearing at Setauket, *1845, is one of his most characteristic canvases. Mount's subject matter had universal appeal; engravings of his work sold widely in Europe.*

The huge pile of pink masonry of the Smithsonian Institution in Washington, with its nine distinct types of towers, represents American Gothic at its most giddy and lugubrious stage. The building, which was designed in 1846 by James Renwick, confounded generations of architects, but with the passage of time it came to seem the perfect setting for the vast collection of mementos that fill "the nation's attic." "Greek" and "Italian" styles also flourished in this period, the former particularly in the South; elsewhere the Gothic was by all odds the most popular.

Increasingly, Americans of the period were purchasing native art. George Catlin, who painted hundreds of pictures of Indians and their surroundings, all rich in authentic detail, displayed his work before admiring crowds in many cities. Genre painters (artists whose canvases told stories, usually drawn from everyday life), were wildly popular. The best were William Sidney Mount of New York and George Caleb Bingham of Missouri. Rumor had it that Mount received $1,000 for his first important canvas; Bingham's paintings commanded excellent prices; and the public bought engravings of the work of both men in enormous numbers.

The more academic artists of the period were popular as well. The "luminists" and members of the romantic Hudson River school specialized in

Miniature copies of Hiram Powers's The Greek Slave, *Henry James said, stood "exposed under little glass covers" in parlors from Boston to San Francisco.*

grandiose pictures of wild landscapes. In the 1840s Thomas Doughty regularly collected $500 each for his paintings. The works of Asher B. Durand, John Kensett, and Thomas Cole were in demand. The collector Luman Reed commissioned five large Cole canvases for an allegorical series, *The Course of Empire,* and crowds flocked to see another of Cole's series, *The Voyage of Life,* when it was exhibited in New York.

In 1839 the American Art-Union was formed in New York to encourage native art. The Art-Union hit on the ingenious device of selling what were in effect lottery tickets and using the proceeds to purchase paintings, which became the prizes in the lottery. Annual "memberships" sold for $5; 814 people subscribed in 1839, nearly 19,000 ten years later. Soon the Art-Union was giving every member an engraving of one of its principal prizes. The organization had to disband after a New York court outlawed the lottery in 1851, but in 1854 a new Cosmopolitan Art-Union was established in Ohio. In the years before the Civil War it boomed, reaching a peak of 38,000 members and paying as much as $6,000 for an individual work—the sculptor Hiram Powers's boneless female nude, *The Greek Slave.* It also distributed an art magazine and each year gave a young artist a gold medal and $2,000 for foreign study.

The art unions made little effort to encourage innovators, but they were a boon to many artists. The American Art-Union paid out as much as $40,000 for its prizes in a single year. By distributing thousands of engravings and colored prints, they introduced competent American works of art into middle-class homes.

Beginning in the late 1850s, the prints of the firm of Currier and Ives brought a crude but charming kind of art to a still wider audience. Currier and Ives lithographs portrayed horse racing, trains, rural landscapes, and "every tender domestic moment, every sign of national progress, every regional oddity, every private or public disaster from a cut finger to a forest fire." They were issued in very large editions and sold for as little as 15 cents.

Education for Democracy

Except on the edge of the frontier and in the South, most youngsters between the ages of 5 and 10 attended a school for at least a couple of months of the year. These schools, however, were privately run and charged fees. Attendance was not required and fell off sharply once children learned to read and do their sums well enough to get along in day-to-day life. The teachers were usually young men waiting for something better to turn up.

All this changed with the rise of the common school movement. At the heart of the movement was the belief, widely expressed in the first days of the Republic, that a government based on democratic rule must provide the means, as Jefferson put it, to "diffuse knowledge throughout the mass of the people." This meant free tax-supported schools, which all children were expected to attend. It also came to mean that such an educational system should be administered on a statewide basis and that teaching should become a profession that required formal training.

The two most effective leaders of the common school movement were Henry Barnard and Horace Mann. Both were New Englanders, Whigs, trained in the law, and in other ways conservative types. They shared an unquenchable faith in the improvability of the human race through education. Barnard served in educational posts in Connecticut, Rhode Island, and New York in the 1840s and 1850s and as editor of the *American Journal of Education* from 1855 until 1882. Mann drafted the 1837 Massachusetts law creating a state school board, and then became its first secretary. Over the next decade Mann's annual reports carried the case for common schools to every corner of the land. Seldom given to understatement, Mann called common schools "the greatest discovery ever made by man." In his reports he criticized wealthy parents who sent their children to private academies rather than bring them into contact with their poorer neighbors in the local school. He encouraged young women to become teachers while commending them to school boards by claiming that they could get along on lower salaries than men.

By the 1850s every state outside the South provided free elementary schools and supported institutions for training teachers. Many extended the concept of publicly financed education to include high schools, and Michigan and Iowa even established publicly supported colleges.

Historians differ in explaining the success of the common school movement. Some stress the argu-

*The typical one-room schoolhouse could hold up to 80 students. The schoolyard
was a clearing nearby, as artist Henry Inman shows in* Dismissal of School
on an October Afternoon. *Inspired by Horace Mann, the great educational
awakening of the mid-1800s led to such improvements as the first normal
schools to train teachers.*

ments Mann used to win support from employers
by appealing to their need for trained and well-
disciplined workers. Others see the schools as designed to "Americanize" the increasing numbers of
non-English and non-Protestant immigrants who
were flooding into the country. (Force is lent to this
argument by the fact that Catholic bishops in New
York and elsewhere opposed laws requiring Catholic children to attend these "Protestant" schools
and set up their own parochial schools.)

Still other scholars argue that middle-class reformers favored public elementary school on the
theory that they would instill the values of hard
work, punctuality, and submissiveness to authority

in children of the laboring classes. According to this
argument, the reformers favored the new public
high schools mainly because they provided free education for their own children. In truth, almost no
working-class children attended high school, public
or private, until late in the 19th century.

All these reasons played a part in advancing the
cause of the common schools. Yet it remains the
case, as the historians Carl F. Kaestle and Maris
Vinovskis have shown, that the most compelling
argument for common schools was cultural; more
effectively than any other institution, they brought
Americans of different economic circumstances and
ethnic backgrounds into early and mutually bene-

ficial contact with one another. They served the two roles that Mann assigned to them: "the balance wheel of the social machinery" and "the great equalizer."

Engines of Culture

As the population grew and became more concentrated, and as society, especially in the North, was permeated by a middle-class point of view, popular concern for "culture" in the formal sense increased. A largely literate people, committed to the idea of education but not generally well educated, set their hearts on being "refined" and "cultivated." Industrialization made it easier to satisfy this new demand for culture, though the new machines also tended to make the artifacts of culture more stereotyped.

Improved printing techniques reduced the cost of books, magazines, and newspapers. In the 1850s one publisher sold a 50-volume set of Sir Walter Scott for $37.50. The first penny newspaper was the *New York Sun* (1833), but James Gordon Bennett's *New York Herald,* founded in 1835, brought the cheap new journalism to perfection. The *Boston Daily Times* and the *Philadelphia Public Ledger* soon followed. The penny newspapers depended on sensation, crime stories, and society gossip to attract readers, but they covered important national and international news too.

In the 1850s the moralistic and sentimental "domestic" novel entered its prime. The most successful writers in this genre were women, which prompted Hawthorne to complain bitterly that "a d——d mob of scribbling women" was taking over American literature. Typical were Susan Warner's book *The Wide, Wide World* (1850), a sad tale about a pious, submissive girl who cried "more readily and more steadily than any other tormented child in a novel at the time," and Maria Cummins's book *The Lamplighter* (1854), the story of little Gerty, an orphan rescued by a kindly lamplighter, appropriately named Trueman Flint. *The Lamplighter* sold 70,000 copies within a year of publication. The historian Ann Douglas claims in *The Feminization of American Culture* that such novels provided readers (most of whom were women) with the consumer pleasures that today are provided by television soap operas.

Besides reading countless volumes of sentimental nonsense (the books of another novelist, Mary Jane Holmes, sold over a million copies in these years), Americans consumed reams of religious literature. In 1840 the American Tract Society distributed 3 million copies of its publications; in 1855, more than 12 million. The society had hundreds of missionary-salesmen, called colporteurs, who

The Lyceum movement sponsored lectures on every imaginable subject in hundreds of towns. In this lively 1841 caricature, meteorologist James Pollard Espy holds forth to a mixed audience at Clinton Hall in New York City.

fanned out across the country preaching the gospel and selling or giving away religious pamphlets and books. These publications played down denominational differences in favor of a generalized brand of evangelical Christianity. They bore titles such as *Quench Not the Spirit* (over 900,000 copies distributed by 1850) and *The Way to Heaven*. The American Bible Society issued hundreds of thousands of copies of the Old and New Testaments each year. Americans also devoured books on self-improvement, some aimed at uplifting the reader's character, others, which would today be called "how-to-do-it" books, at teaching everything from raising chickens to carving tombstones.

Philanthropists contributed large sums to charity and other good causes; Stephen Girard left $6 million for "educating poor white orphan boys" in his adopted Philadelphia; John Jacob Astor of New York and George Peabody of Massachusetts endowed libraries; John Lowell, son of the pioneer cotton manufacturer, left $500,000 to establish the Lowell Institute in Boston to sponsor free public lectures. In the late 1850s the industrialist Peter Cooper founded the Cooper Institute in New York City, where workers could take free courses in practical subjects. Mechanics' libraries sprang up in every industrial center and attracted so many readers that pressure was soon applied to grant them state funds. In 1848 Massachusetts led the way by authorizing the use of public money to back the Boston Public Library, and soon several states were encouraging local communities to fund tax-supported libraries.

The desire for knowledge and culture in America is well illustrated by the success of the mutual improvement societies known as lyceums. The movement began in Great Britain; in the United States its prime mover was Josiah Holbrook, an itinerant lecturer and sometime schoolmaster from Connecticut. Holbrook founded the first lyceum in 1826 at Millbury, Massachusetts; within five years there were over 1,000 scattered across the country. The lyceums conducted discussions, established libraries, and lobbied for better schools. Soon they began to sponsor lecture series on topics of every sort. Many of the nation's political and intellectual leaders, such as Webster, Emerson, Melville, and Lowell, regularly graced their platforms. So did other, less famous lecturers who in the name of culture pronounced on subjects ranging from "Chemistry Applied to the Mechanic Arts" to a description of the tombs of the Egyptian pharaohs.

The State of the Colleges

Unlike common schools, with their democratic overtones, private colleges had at best a precarious place in Jacksonian America. For one thing, there were too many of them. Any town with pretensions of becoming a regional center felt it had to have a college. Ohio had 25 in the 1850s, Tennessee 16. Many of these institutions were short-lived. Of the 14 colleges founded in Kentucky between 1800 and 1850, only half were still operating in 1860.

The problem of supply was compounded by a demand problem—too few students. Enrollment at the largest, Yale, never topped 400 until the mid-1840s. Higher education was beyond the means of the average family. Although most colleges charged less than half the $55 tuition required by Harvard, that still represented a substantial outlay for most families, wages being what they were. So desperate was the shortage that colleges accepted applicants as young as 11 and 12 and as old as 30.

Once enrolled, students had little worry about making the grade, not least because grades were not given. Since students were hard to come by and classwork was relatively unimportant, discipline was lax. Official authority was frequently challenged, and rioting was known to break out over such weighty matters as the quality of meals. A father who visited his son's college dormitory in 1818 found it inhabited by "half a dozen loungers in a state of oriental lethargy, each stretched out upon two or three chairs, with scarce any indication of life in them [other] than the feeble effort to keep up the fire of their cigarrs."

The typical college curriculum, dominated by the study of Latin and Greek, had almost no practical relevance except for future clergymen. The Yale faculty, most of them ministers, defended the classics as admirably providing for both "the discipline and the furniture of the mind," but these subjects commended themselves to college officials chiefly because they did not require costly equipment or a faculty that knew anything else. Professors spent most of their time in and out of the classroom trying to maintain a semblance of order, "to the exclusion of any great literary undertakings to which their choice might lead them," one explained. "Our country is yet too young for old professors," a Bostonian informed a foreign visitor in the 1830s, "and, besides, they are too poorly paid to induce first rate men to devote themselves to the business of lecturing. . . . We consider professors as secondary men."

Fortunately for the future of higher education, some college officials recognized the need for a drastic overhaul of their institutions. President Francis Wayland of Brown University used his 1842 address, "On the Present Collegiate System," to call for a thorough revamping of the curriculum to make it responsive to the economic realities of American society. This meant more courses in science, economics (where Wayland's own *Elements of Political Economy* might be used), modern history, and applied mathematics; fewer in Hebrew, biblical studies, Greek, and ancient history.

Yale established a separate school of science in 1847, which it hoped would attract serious-minded students and research-minded professors. At Harvard, which also opened a scientific school, students were allowed to choose some of their courses and were compelled to earn grades as a stimulus to study. Colleges in the West and the South began to offer

mechanical and agricultural subjects relevant to their regional economies. Oberlin enrolled four female students in 1837, and the first women's college, the Georgia Female College, opened its doors in 1839.

These reforms slowed the downward spiral of colleges; they did not restore them to the honored place they had enjoyed in the Revolutionary era. Of the first six presidents of the United States, only Washington did not graduate from college. Beginning in 1829, seven of the next eleven did not. In this Presidents Jackson, Van Buren, Harrison, Taylor, Fillmore, Lincoln, and Johnson were like 98 of every 100 white males, all blacks and Indians, and all but a handful of white women in mid-19th-century America. Going to college had yet, in Wayland's words, to "commend itself to the good sense and patriotism of the American people."

Civic Cultures

Unlike the capitals of Europe, which were centers of art and culture, Washington was a cultural backwater, and the politicians seemed content to keep it that way. Whether the United States had *any* cul-

By mid-century, immigrants from Europe and displaced farmers were flooding into American cities, causing tremendous growth. In the Midwest, the rapid expansion of Cincinnati was due in part to its strategic location. This painting, Fourth Street, Cincinnati, *shows the principal downtown artery. The elegant façades attest to the city's prosperity.*

tural center, and if so, where it was, is another matter. Boston, Philadelphia, and New York vied for primacy, but many smaller cities, such as Lexington, Kentucky, the self-proclaimed "Athens of the West," set the tone for the surrounding hinterland.

In the cities members of the "learned professions," especially lawyers, were generally accepted as the arbiters of taste in literature and art. "At the bar or the bench the American aristocracy is found," and there too resides "the most intellectual section of society," the ever-insightful Tocqueville reported. Lawyers came mostly from the upper reaches of the city's economic order, usually from families long in residence.

Emerson only half mockingly called Boston "the hub of the universe," but this was a case when local pride triumphed over his usual good judgment. Boston was indeed the home of the country's leading literary magazine, the *North American Review*, founded in 1815, but Philadelphia had *Graham's*, the country's first illustrated magazine, and *Godey's Ladies Book*, which reached 150,000 subscribers in the 1850s, an enormous number for that date. By 1825 New York's House of Harper, organized in 1817, was the largest book publisher in the nation. Boston was the home of the nation's leading historians, and Philadelphia, with the Pennsylvania Academy of Fine Arts (1815) and the Philadelphia Academy of Music (1857), was conceded by all but blind Bostonians and tin-eared New Yorkers to predominate in artistic and musical matters.

In the West, Cincinnati could point to its seven weekly and two daily newspapers, a literary monthly, a medical journal, and a magazine for teenagers. The first Beethoven symphony ever heard in America was performed in Cincinnati in 1817. By the 1830s such coups had enabled the "Queen City" to replace the "Athens of the West" as the center of trans-Allegheny culture. Having quickly accomplished so much, its boosters reasoned, Cincinnati would soon assume national leadership in cultural matters, as it already had in the processing of pork bellies.

Even smaller cities like Portland, Providence, Hartford, Albany, and Pittsburgh had literary and natural history societies and were regular stops on the lyceum circuit. All in all, American cities had a vitality and diversity that foreign visitors both celebrated and decried. Life in the towns was by some standards crude; many of the people were pushy, crass, and dedicated to the accumulation of wealth. But on this last count, the English novelist Charles Dickens offered some international perspective. "The golden calf they worship," he wrote of Americans in 1841, "is a pigmy compared with the giant effigies set up in other parts of that vast counting-house which lies beyond the Atlantic; and the almighty dollar sinks into something comparatively insignificant amidst a whole Pantheon of better gods."

Scientific Stirrings

Some historians have suggested that American interest in science—and contributions to its advancement—had declined in the early 19th century from the levels achieved during the Revolutionary era. Despite Jefferson's assurances in the 1780s that the United States would soon "produce her full quota of genius," a half century had gone by without a single American scientist even approaching the international recognition accorded Benjamin Franklin.

Tocqueville attributed Americans' indifference to science to their distrust of theory and abstract knowledge. "The purely practical side," he conceded, "is cultivated admirably." Contemporaries cited more pressing needs. "We are a new country," a Boston doctor reminded his son, who wished to pursue a scientific career. "We have, as it were, just landed on these shores; there is a vast deal to be done; and he who will not be doing, must be set down as a drone."

There was progress. State-sponsored geological surveys provided at least temporary livings for the European-trained geologist James Hall and the botanist Asa Gray. (Later, as a Harvard professor, Gray was the leading American advocate of his friend Charles Darwin's theory of natural selection.) Additional jobs opened up with the expansion of the United States Coastal Survey, directed by Benjamin Franklin's great-grandson, Alexander Dallas Bache, in 1843. The opening in 1846 of the Smithsonian Institution in Washington, to which the physicist Joseph Henry was appointed first secretary, helped too. Henry's researches in electromagnetism in the 1830s led to Samuel F. B. Morse's invention of the telegraph, and Bache's lobbying resulted in the founding of the American Association for the Advancement of Science in 1848.

Benjamin Silliman, a Yale scholar, was the country's leading geologist and the moving force behind the American Journal of Science and Arts. *Through such scientific journals, scholars exchanged ideas and knowledge that contributed to scientific advances.*

Yet few Americans pursued science except on a part-time basis. The star sightings and tidal measurements that went into Nathaniel Bowditch's internationally recognized manual, *The New American Practical Navigator,* had to be made in his spare time. He made his living as an actuary in an insurance company. Maria Mitchell, America's best-known 19th-century woman scientist, won international celebrity and a gold medal from the king of Denmark for calculating the position of a new comet in 1847. She was employed as a librarian in Nantucket when she made the calculations.

For all the practical obstacles in the way of doing serious science in Jacksonian America, its near-wilderness circumstances sometimes provided those on the lookout with unexpected targets of opportunity. An almost literal case in point is that of Dr. William Beaumont. In 1822, while serving as an army surgeon in upstate New York, Beaumont was called to attend to Alexis St. Martin, a 19-year-old Canadian woodsman who had been shot by accident. The shell, fired from no more than 3 feet away, had blasted a hole in his chest the size of a grapefruit; it had blown away the sixth rib, fractured the fifth, and left protruding a portion of his lung "as large as a turkey's egg." There was also something else sticking out. "What at first view I could not believe possible," Beaumont recorded in his diary, "on closer observation, I found to be actually the stomach with a puncture in the protruding portion large enough to receive my forefinger, and through which a portion of the food he had taken for breakfast had come out and lodged in his clothing."

Believing the patient to be a goner, Dr. Beaumont did what he could to administer relief and dress the wound. But the young man survived, exposed stomach and all. Eventually a flap formed over the opening in the stomach, but it could be pushed back, exposing the inner workings of the organ. After St. Martin recovered, Beaumont took him into his household and began studying how he digested food.

Over the next decade Beaumont performed hundreds of experiments testing the relative digestibility of foods and analyzing the chemical properties of gastric juices. His *Experiments and Observations on the Gastric Juices and the Physiology of Digestion* (1833), though largely ignored in the United States, won him a reputation among European physiologists as the world's leading expert on the human gastric system. His fame, however, did not prevent his army superiors, perhaps resenting the time he was diverting from his official duties, from forcing him to resign in 1840. St. Martin then returned to Canada, where he married, fathered four children, and died at the ripe age of 83.

American Humor

The clash between the desire of a few for a "high" culture and the simpler tastes of the majority led

James Fenimore Cooper to conclude that Americans would be forever "wanting in most of the high tastes, and consequently in the high enjoyments." But other writers were not so sure, and some, rather than despair over the cultural incongruities, found in them a rich source of humor.

They were hardly the first to do so. The comic potential in juxtaposing high ideals and low reality had been exploited by the Greek playwright Aristophanes; by Rabelais, the creator of *Gargantua;* and by Cervantes in *The Adventures of Don Quixote*—all, incidentally, works available in mid-century America. William Byrd and Benjamin Franklin had both used the differences between the pretensions of colonial sophisticates and the ways of common folk to good comic effect. But the possibilities of this kind of humor were greatly enlarged in the Jacksonian era. Where else was there a country theoretically based on equality whose inhabitants were so strikingly varied?

One of the first writers to exploit the comic aspects of Jacksonian democracy was Seba Smith, a newspaperman from Portland, Maine. Smith's fictional creation, Major Jack Downing, was a Jackson man from a part of the country suspicious of both the general's politics and his intelligence. Smith had Major Downing accompany the president on his 1833 tour of New England, which included, among other adventures, an appearance at Harvard to receive an honorary degree. In the presence of so many learned gentlemen with political views contrary to his own, Downing advised the president "jest to say nothing, but look as knowing as any of them." Which was exactly what Jackson did, even when faced by snickering "sassy students." "The General stood it out like a hero," the major assured his readers, "and got through very well."

A writer who turned the possibilities of "Down East" humor to more telling satirical effect was James Russell Lowell, author of the *Bigelow Papers,* which began appearing in 1847. Lowell juxtaposed Hosea Biglow, a Yankee farmer of "homely common-sense heated up by conscience," and Birdofredum Sawin, a scoundrel hoping to turn a profit on his patriotism. When approached by a recruiting officer, Hosea Biglow set his opposition to the Mexican War (actually Lowell's) to verse:

> *They may talk o' Freedom's airy*
> *Till they're pupple in the face,—*
> *It's a grand gret cemetary*

> *For the barthrights of our race;*
> *They jest want this Californy*
> *So's to lug new slave-states in*
> *To abuse ye, an' to scorn ye,*
> *An' to plunder ye like sin.*

Birdofredum, in contrast, signed up to fight in Mexico, where he lost an eye, a leg, and his left arm. When he returned home he ran for political office. As to his platform:

> *Ef, wile you're 'lectioneerin round, some curus*
>   *chaps should beg*
> *To know my views o' state affairs, jest answer*
>   *WOODEN LEG!*
> *Ef they aint settisfied with thet, an' kin o' pry an'*
>   *doubt*
> *An' ax fer sutthin' deffynit, jest say ONE EYE*
>   *PUT OUT!*

The Old Southwest provided another locale for juxtaposing the genteel and the vulgar. Life in the region provided chroniclers with more than enough violence to capture the attention of their "gentle readers." Violence figures prominently in Augustus Baldwin Longstreet's story "The Fight," in which one Ransy Sniffle, "who, in his earlier days, had fed copiously upon red clay and blackberries," promoted a wrestling match between two toughs, Bill and Bob. After provoking both to do battle, Ransy sat back to enjoy the slaughter. And slaughter it was. Bob, the victor, "entirely lost his left ear and a large piece of his left cheek." As for Bill, he

presented a hideous spectacle. About a third of his nose, at the lower extremity, was bit off, and his face so swelled and bruised that it was difficult to discover anything of the human visage, much more the fine features which he carried into the fight.

Johnson J. Hooper's creation Simon Suggs was the ultimate frontier rogue as confidence man. Whether engaged in horse swapping or faking a conversion experience at a camp meeting in order to steal the collection basket, Suggs lived by the maxim "It is good to be shifty in a new country." He was not alone in this opinion. In a new country, it made sense not to take oneself too seriously. While the outcome of the nation's experiment in combining democracy and cultural aspiration remained in doubt, most Americans took their laughs where they could find them.

Milestones

1827–1838	John Audubon, *Birds of America*
1834	George Bancroft, *History of the United States*
1835	James Gordon Bennett's *New York Herald* founded
1836	John Lowell endows Lowell Institute public lectures
1837	Ralph Waldo Emerson's Harvard lecture, "The American Scholar"
	Oberlin College enrolls the first women students
1837–1848	Horace Mann serves as secretary of the Massachusetts Board of Education
1839	Establishment of the American Art Union
1842–1843	Herman Melville lives in the South Pacific
1843	Hiram Powers, *The Greek Slave* (sculpture)
1845	Edgar Allan Poe, "The Raven"
1845–1846	Henry David Thoreau lives at Walden Pond
1846	Smithsonian Institution opens
1847	James Russell Lowell, *Bigelow Papers*
1848	American Association for the Advancement of Science founded
1850	Nathaniel Hawthorne, *The Scarlet Letter*
1851	Herman Melville, *Moby Dick*
	Francis Parkman, *The Conspiracy of Pontiac*
1854	Thoreau, *Walden*
1855–1892	Walt Whitman, *Leaves of Grass* (various editions)
1857	*Atlantic Monthly* first published
1859	Peter Cooper founds Cooper Institute

SUPPLEMENTARY READING

Titles marked with an asterisk have been published in paperback.

Useful surveys of cultural and intellectual currents in this period are Merle Curti, **The Growth of American Thought** (1951), R. B. Nye, **Society and Culture in America*** (1974), and Rush Welter, **The Mind of America, 1820–1860*** (1975). See also Richard Hofstadter, **Anti-intellectualism in American Life*** (1963), and Stow Persons, **The Decline of American Gentility** (1975), for a more critical assessment. F. O. Mattheissen, **American Renaissance** (1941), remains valuable.

On transcendentalism, see Perry Miller (ed.), **The American Transcendentalists** (1957). Two books by Joel Porte, **Emerson and Thoreau: Transcendentalists in Conflict** (1966) and **Representative Man: Ralph Waldo Emerson in His Time*** (1979), cover the transcendentalist "community." For a critical appraisal, see Quentin Anderson, **The Imperial Self** (1971).

On American literature, Van Wyck Brooks, **The Flowering of New England*** (1936), remains a readable survey. Alfred Kazin, **On Native Grounds*** (1942), is more critically disposed. David Levin, **History as Romantic Art** (1959), is excellent on the era's historians and their approaches to their craft.

On the cultural life of the South, see Clement Eaton, **The Mind of the Old South*** (1964), and Drew Faust, **A Sacred Circle** (1977). On education, see L. A. Cremin, **American Education: The National Experience*** (1980), and C. F. Kaestle, **Pillars of the Republic** (1983); see also Jonathan Messerli, **Horace Mann** (1972). M. B. Katz, in **The Irony of Early School Reform*** (1968), questions the motives of the reformers; Diane Ravitch, in **The Revisionists Revised*** (1978), challenges Katz. C. F. Kaestle and Maris Vinovskis, **Education and Social Change** (1980), is excellent.

Popular culture is discussed in Carl Bode, **The American Lyceum*** (1956) and **The Anatomy of Popular Culture** (1959), and Russell Lynes, **The Tastemakers*** (1954). Ann Douglas, **The Feminization of American Culture** (1977), is excellent on the pervasiveness and impact of sentimental literature. Neil Harris, **The Artist in American Society*** (1966), puts art in its social setting. See also

Barbara Novak, **Nature and Culture: American Landscape Painting** (1980).

The standard sources for the history of American colleges remain Richard Hofstadter, **Academic Freedom in the Age of the College** (1955), and Fred Rudolph, **The American College and University** (1961). But see also David Allmendinger, **Paupers and Scholars** (1975), R. A. McCaughey, "The Transformation of American Academic Life," in **Perspectives in American History** (1975), Ronald Story, **The Forging of an Aristocracy** (1980), and

Colin Burke, **American Collegiate Populations** (1982).

Scientific activities are examined in G. H. Daniels, **American Science in the Age of Jackson** (1968), W. H. Goetzmann, **Exploration and Empire*** (1967), William Stanton, **The Great United States Exploring Expedition** (1975), and A. H. Dupree, **Science in the Federal Government** (1957).

On American humor before the Civil War, see K. S. Lynn (ed.), **The Comic Tradition in America*** (1958), and Constance Rourke, **American Humor** (1931).

Expansion and Slavery

Were other reasoning wanting in favor of now elevating this question . . . it is surely to be found, found abundantly, in . . . the fulfilment of our manifest destiny to overspread the continent allotted by Providence for the free development of our yearly multiplying millions.

JOHN L. O'SULLIVAN, *1845*

President John Tyler was a thin, rather delicate-appearing man with pale blue eyes and a long nose. Courteous, tactful, soft-spoken, he gave the impression of being weak, an impression reinforced by his professed belief that the president should defer to Congress in the formulation of policy. This was a false impression; John Tyler was stubborn and proud, and these characteristics combined with an almost total lack of imagination to make him worship consistency, as so many second-raters do. He had turned away from Jackson because of the aggressive way the president had used his powers of appointment and the veto, but he also disagreed with Henry Clay and the northern Whigs about the Bank, protection, and federal internal improvements. Being a states' rights southerner, he considered such measures unconstitutional. Nevertheless, he was prepared to cooperate with Clay as the leader of what he called the "more immediate representatives" of the people, the members of Congress. But he was not prepared to be Clay's puppet. He asked all of Harrison's Cabinet to remain in office.

Tyler's Troubles

Tyler and Clay did not get along, and for this Clay was chiefly to blame. He behaved in an overbearing manner that was out of keeping with his nature, probably because he resented having been passed over by the Whigs in 1840. (When news of Harrison's nomination reached him in Washington, he was half drunk. His face darkened. "I am the most unfortunate man in the history of parties," he said, "always run . . . when sure to be defeated, and now betrayed for a nomination when I, or anyone, would be sure of an election.") He considered himself the real head of the Whig party and intended to exercise his leadership.

In Congress, Clay announced a comprehensive program that ignored Tyler's states' rights view of the Constitution. Most important was his plan to set up a new Bank of the United States. A bill to repeal the Independent Treasury Act caused no difficulty, but when Congress passed a new Bank bill, Tyler vetoed it. The entire Cabinet except Secretary of State Webster thereupon resigned in protest.

Abandoned by the Whigs, Tyler attempted to build a party of his own. He failed to do so, and for the remainder of his term the political squabbling in Washington was continuous. Clay wanted to distribute the proceeds from land sales to the states, presumably to bolster their sagging finances but actually to reduce federal revenues in order to justify raising the tariff. To win western votes for distribution, he agreed to support the Preemption Act of 1841 legalizing the right of squatters to occupy unsurveyed land and to buy it later at $1.25 an acre without bidding for it at auction. However, the southerners insisted on an amendment pledging that distribution would be stopped if the tariff were raised above the 20 percent level, and when the Whigs blithely tried to push a high tariff through Congress without repealing the Distribution Act, Tyler vetoed the bill. Finally, the Distribution Act was repealed and Tyler signed the new Tariff Act of 1842, raising duties to about the levels of 1832.

The Webster-Ashburton Treaty

Webster's decision to remain in the Cabinet was motivated in part by his desire to settle the boundary between Maine and New Brunswick. The intent of

John Tyler posed for a daguerreotypist about 1850, after he had retired from public life. Tyler voted in favor of Virginia's secession ordinance in 1861.

the peace treaty of 1783 had been to award the United States all land in the area drained by rivers flowing into the Atlantic rather than the St. Lawrence, but the wording was obscure and the old maps conflicting. The issue became critical in 1838 when Canadians began cutting timber in the Aroostook Valley, which was claimed by the United States. When Maine sent an agent to remonstrate with the lumberjacks, he was arrested. Maine and New Brunswick each called up militia and the "Aroostook war" followed. No one was killed, yet the danger of a real war was great. Acting with admirable restraint, Van Buren sent General Winfield Scott to the area, and Scott managed to arrange a truce.

In 1842 the British sent a new minister, Lord Ashburton, to the United States to try to settle all outstanding disputes. Ashburton, head of a London banking house that had large investments in the United States, made an ideal ambassador. He and Webster easily worked out a compromise boundary. The British cared relatively little about the Aroos-

took Valley timber but needed part of the territory to the north to build a military road connecting Halifax and Quebec. Webster, who thought any settlement desirable simply to eliminate a possible cause of war, willingly agreed.

The problem of placating Maine and Massachusetts, which wanted every acre of the land in dispute, Webster solved in an extraordinary manner. It was known that during the peace negotiations ending the Revolution, Franklin had marked the boundary between Maine and Canada on a map with a heavy red line, but no one could find the Franklin map. Webster obtained an old map of the area and had someone mark off in red a line that followed the British version of the boundary. He showed this document to representatives of Maine and Massachusetts, convincing them that they had better agree to his compromise before the British got wind of it and demanded the whole region! It later came out that the British had a true copy of the Franklin map, which showed that the entire area rightfully belonged to the United States.

Webster's generosity made excellent sense. Lord Ashburton, gratified by having obtained the strategic territory, made concessions elsewhere along the Canadian and American border. The Senate ratified the Webster-Ashburton Treaty in August 1842. Its importance, more symbolic than practical, was nonetheless great. British dependence on foreign foodstuffs was increasing; America's need for British capital was rising. War, or even unsettled affairs, would have injured vital business relations and produced no compensating gains.

The Texas Question

The settlement with Great Britain won support in every section of the United States, but the same could not be said for Tyler's attempt to annex the Republic of Texas, for this involved the question of slavery. In the Transcontinental Treaty of 1819 with Spain, the boundary of the United States had been drawn in such a way as to exclude Texas. This seemed unimportant at the time, yet within months of ratification of the treaty in February 1821, Americans led by Stephen F. Austin had begun to settle in the area, by then part of an independent Mexico. Cotton flourished on the fertile Texas plains, and the Mexican authorities offered free land to groups of settlers. By 1830 there were some 20,000 white Americans in Texas, about 2,000 slaves, and only a few thousand Mexicans.

President John Quincy Adams had offered Mexico $1 million for Texas, and Jackson was willing to pay $5 million, but Mexico would not sell. Nevertheless, the flood of American settlers alarmed the Mexican authorities. The immigrants apparently felt no loyalty to Mexico. Most were Protestants, though Mexican law required that all immigrants be Catholics; few attempted to learn more than a few words of Spanish. When Mexico outlawed slavery, they evaded the law by "freeing" their slaves and then signing them to lifetime contracts as indentured servants. In 1830 Mexico prohibited further immigration of Americans into Texas, though again the law proved impossible to enforce.

As soon as the Mexican government began to restrict them, the Texans began to seek independence. In 1835 a series of skirmishes escalated into a full-scale rebellion. The Mexican president, Antonio López de Santa Anna, marched north with 6,000 soldiers to subdue the rebels. Late in February 1836 he reached San Antonio.

A force of 187 men under Colonel William B. Travis held the city. They took refuge behind the stout walls of a former mission called the Alamo. For ten days they beat off Santa Anna's assaults, inflicting terrible casualties on the attackers. Finally, on March 6, the Mexicans breeched and scaled the walls. Once inside they killed everyone, even the wounded, then soaked the corpses in oil and burned them. Among the dead were the legendary Davy Crockett and Jim Bowie, inventor of the Bowie knife.

After the Alamo and a similar slaughter at another garrison at Goliad, southeast of San Antonio, peaceful settlement of the dispute between Texas and Mexico was impossible. Meanwhile, on March 2, 1836, Texas had declared its independence. Sam Houston, a former congressman and governor of Tennessee and an experienced Indian fighter, was placed in charge of the rebel army. For a time Houston retreated before Santa Anna's troops, who greatly outnumbered his own. At the San Jacinto River he took a stand. On April 21, 1836, shouting "Forward! Charge! Remember the Alamo! Remember Goliad!" his troops routed the Mexican army, which soon retreated across the Rio Grande. In October, Houston was elected president of the Republic of Texas, and a month later a plebiscite revealed that an overwhelming majority favored annexation by the United States.

President Jackson hesitated. To take Texas might lead to war with Mexico. Assuredly it would stir up the slavery controversy. On his last day in office he recognized the republic, but he made no move to accept it into the Union, nor did his successor, Van Buren. Texas thereupon went its own way, which involved developing friendly ties with Great Britain. An independent Texas suited British tastes perfectly, for it could provide an alternative

By 1834, "Anglos," or immigrants from the United States, greatly outnumbered Spanish-speaking settlers in Texas. When the demands of Texans for a separate state within Mexico were rejected, tensions with the Mexican government increased. Soon after hostilities erupted in 1835, this rebel force led by Stephen Austin captured Fort San Antonio de Bexar.

supply of raw cotton and a market for manufactures unfettered by tariffs.

These events caused alarm in the United States, especially among southerners, who dreaded the possibility that a Texas dominated by Great Britain might abolish slavery. As a southerner, Tyler shared these feelings; as a beleaguered politician, spurned by the Whigs and held in contempt by most Democrats, he saw in annexation a chance to revive his fortunes. When Webster resigned as secretary of state in 1843, Tyler replaced him with a fellow Virginian, Abel P. Upshur, whom he ordered to seek a treaty of annexation. The South was eager to take Texas, and in the West and even the Northeast the patriotic urge to add such a magnificent new territory to the national domain was great. Counting noses, Upshur convinced himself that the Senate would approve annexation by the necessary two-thirds majority. He negotiated a treaty in February 1844, but before he could sign it he was killed by the accidental explosion of a cannon on U.S.S. *Princeton* during a weapons demonstration.

To ensure the winning of Texas, Tyler appointed John C. Calhoun secretary of state. This was a blunder; by then Calhoun was so closely associated with the South and with slavery that his appointment alienated thousands of northerners who might otherwise have welcomed annexation. Suddenly Texas became a hot political issue. Clay and Van Buren, who seemed assured of the 1844 Whig and Democratic presidential nominations, promptly announced that they opposed annexation, chiefly on the grounds that it would probably

lead to war with Mexico. With a national election in the offing, northern and western senators refused to vote for annexation, and in June the Senate rejected the treaty, 35 to 16. The Texans were angry and embarrassed, the British eager again to take advantage of the situation.

Manifest Destiny

The Senate, Clay, and Van Buren had all misinterpreted public opinion. John C. Calhoun, whose world was so far removed from that of the average citizen, in this case came much closer to comprehending the mood of the country than any of its other leaders.

For two centuries Americans had been gradually conquering a continent. The first colonists had envisaged a domain extending from the Atlantic to the Pacific, though they had not realized the immensity of the New World. By the time their descendants came to appreciate its size, they had been chastened by the experience of battling the Indians for possession of the land and then laboriously developing it. The Revolution and its aftermath of nationalism greatly stimulated expansion, and then, before the riches of trans-Appalachia had even been inventoried, Jefferson had stunned the country with Louisiana, an area so big that the mere thought of it left Americans giddy.

The westward march from the 17th century to the 1840s had seemed fraught with peril, the prize golden but attainable only through patient labor and fearful hardships. Wild animals and wild men, mighty forests and mighty foreign powers beset the path. John Adams wrote of "conquering" the West "from the trees and rocks and wild beasts." He was "enflamed" by the possibilities of "that vast scene which is opening in the West," but to win it the United States would have to "march *intrepidly* on."

Quite rapidly (as historians measure time) the atmosphere changed. Each year of national growth increased the power and confidence of the people, and every forward step revealed a wider horizon. Now the West seemed a ripe apple, to be picked almost casually. Where pioneers had once stood in awe before the majesty of the Blue Ridge, then hesitated to venture from the protective shadows of the forest into the open prairies of Illinois, they now shrugged their shoulders at great deserts and began to talk of the Rocky Mountains as "mere molehills" along the road to the Pacific. After 200 years of westward expansion had brought them as far as Missouri and Iowa, Americans perceived their destined goal. *The whole continent was to be theirs!* Theirs to exploit, and theirs to make into one mighty nation, a land of opportunity, a showcase to display the virtues of democratic institutions, living proof that Americans were indeed God's chosen people. A New York journalist, John L. O'Sullivan, captured the new mood in a sentence. Nothing must interfere, he wrote in 1845, with "the fulfillment of our *manifest destiny* to overspread the continent allotted by Providence for the free development of our yearly multiplying millions."

The politicians did not sense the new mood in 1844; even Calhoun, who saw the acquisition of Texas as part of a broader program, was thinking of balancing sectional interests rather than of national expansion. In fact, the expansion, stimulated by the natural growth of the population and by a revived flood of immigration, was going on in every section and with little regard for political boundaries. New settlers rolled westward in hordes. Between 1830 and 1835 some 10,000 entered "foreign" Texas, and this was a trickle compared to what the early 1840s were to bring.

Life on the Trail

The romantic myths attached by later generations to this mighty human tide have obscured the ad-

justments forced on the pioneers and focused attention on the least significant of the dangers they faced and the hardships they endured. For example, Indians could, of course, be deadly enemies, but pioneers were more likely to complain that the Indians they encountered were dirty, lazy, and thieving than to worry about the danger of Indian attack. Women tended to fear their strangeness, not their actual behavior. Far more dangerous was the possibility of accidents on the trail, particularly to children, and also unsanitary conditions and exposure to the elements.

"Going west" had always been laborious, but in the 1840s the distances covered were longer by far and the comforts and conveniences of "civilization" that had to be left behind, being more extensive than those available to earlier generations, tended to be more painful to surrender. Moving west disrupted the new pattern of family life; there were few, if any, "separate spheres" on the trail and relatively few in frontier settlements, at least in the first years. "Far from city marketplaces and factories," the historian Julie Roy Jeffries writes, "the pioneer family had to become self-sufficient. Much of the model of appropriate female behavior had to be disregarded." Women learned to load wagons, pitch tents, chase stray cattle. Men, for their part, had to keep an eye on children and help with tasks like cooking and washing.

Travel on the plains west of the Mississippi was especially taxing for women. Guidebooks promised them that "regular exercise, in the open air . . . gives additional vigor and strength." But the books did not prepare them for having to collect dried buffalo dung for fuel, for the heat and choking dust of summer, for enduring a week of steady rain, for the monotony, the dirt, the cramped quarters. Caring for an infant or a 2-year-old in a wagon could be torture week after week on the trail, for there were limits to what the average husband could or would do on the way west. In their letters and journals pioneer women mostly complained of being bone weary and about the difficulties of day-to-day existence. "It is impossible to keep anything clean," one recorded, and it is not hard to envisage the difficulty of doing so while living for weeks on end on the trail. "Oh dear," another wrote in her journal, "I do so want to get there it is now almost four months since we have slept in a house." What sort of a house a pioneer family would actually sleep in when they reached their destination is a question this woman did not record, which was probably fortunate for her peace of mind.

California and Oregon

By 1840 many Americans had settled far to the west in California, which was unmistakably Mexican territory, and in the Oregon country, jointly claimed by the United States and Great Britain, and it was to these distant regions that the pioneers were going in increasing numbers as the decade progressed. California was a sparsely settled land of some 7,000 Spanish-speaking ranchers and a handful of "Anglo" settlers from the United States. Until the 1830s, when their estates were broken up by the anticlerical Mexican government, 21 Catholic missions, stretching north from San Diego to San Francisco, controlled more than 30,000 Indian converts, who were little better off than slaves. Richard Henry Dana, a Harvard College student, sailed around South America to California as an ordinary seaman on the brig *Pilgrim* in 1834. His account of that voyage in *Two Years Before the Mast* (1840) contains a fine description of what life was like in the region: "There is no working class (the Indians being practically serfs and doing all the hard work) and every rich man looks like a grandee, and every poor scamp like a broken-down gentleman."

Oregon, a vaguely defined area between California and Russian Alaska, proved still more alluring to Americans. Captain Robert Gray had sailed up the Columbia River in 1792, and Lewis and Clark had visited the region on their great expedition. In 1811 John Jacob Astor's Pacific Fur Company had established trading posts on the Columbia. Two decades later Methodist, Presbyterian, and Catholic missionaries began to find their way into the Willamette Valley, a green land of rich soil, mild climate, and tall forests teeming with game. Gradually a small number of settlers followed, until by 1840 there were about 500 Americans in the Willamette area.

In the early 1840s, fired by the spirit of manifest destiny, the country suddenly burned with "Oregon fever." In dozens upon dozens of towns, societies were founded to collect information and organize groups to make the march to the Pacific. Land hunger (stimulated by glowing reports from the scene) drew the new migrants most powerfully, but the patriotic concept of manifest destiny gave the trek across the 2,000 miles of wilderness separating Oregon from the western edge of American settlement in Missouri the character of a crusade. In 1843 nearly 1,000 pioneers made the long trip.

The Oregon Trail began at the western border of Missouri and followed the Kansas River and the perverse, muddy Platte ("a mile wide and six inches deep") past Fort Laramie to the Rockies. It crossed the Continental Divide by the relatively easy South Pass, veered south to Fort Bridger, on Mexican soil, and then ran north and west through the valley of the Snake River and eventually, by way of the Columbia, to Fort Vancouver, a British post guarding the entrance to the Willamette Valley.

"Oregon Fever" swept the country in the mid-1840s, setting thousands of emigrants on the Oregon Trail. People full of hope assembled in wagon trains at jumping-off places along the Missouri River. Their optimism often turned to despair as they faced the hardships of the journey, from fording rivers to hauling wagons by ropes, chains, and pulleys over steep rocky ridges.

Over this tortuous path wound the canvas-covered caravans with their scouts and their accompanying herds. Each group became a self-governing community on the march, with regulations democratically agreed on "for the purpose of keeping good order and promoting civil and military discipline." Most of the travelers consisted of young families, some from as far away as the East Coast cities, more from towns and farms in the Ohio Valley. Few could be classified as poor because the cost of the trip for a family of four was about $600, no small sum at that time. (The faster and less fatiguing trip by ship around South America cost about $600 per person.)

For large groups Indians posed no great threat (though constant vigilance was necessary), but the

The Old Spanish Trail was the earliest of the trails west. Part of it was mapped in 1776 by a Franciscan missionary. The Santa Fe Trail came into wide use after 1823. The Oregon Trail was pioneered by trappers and missionaries. The Mormon Trail was first traversed in 1847, while the Oxbow Route, developed under a federal mail contract, was used from 1858 to 1861.

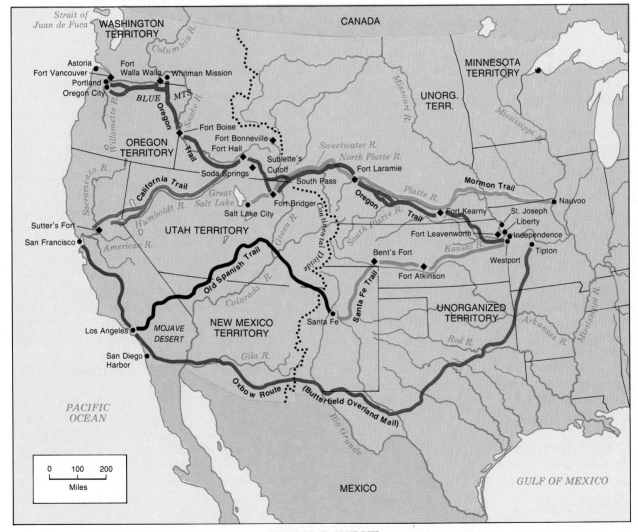

TRAILS WEST

five-month trip was full of labor, discomfort, and uncertainty; in the words of the historian David Lavender, a "remorseless, unending, weather scoured, nerve-rasping plod on and on and on and on, foot by aching foot." And at the end lay the regular tasks of pioneering. The spirit of the trail-blazers is caught in an entry from the diary of James Nesmith:

> Friday, October 27.—Arrived at Oregon City at the falls of the Willamette.
>
> Saturday, October 28.—Went to work.

Behind the dreams of the Far West as an American Eden lay the commercial importance of the three major West Coast harbors: San Diego, San Francisco, and the Strait of Juan de Fuca leading into Puget Sound. Eastern merchants considered these harbors the keys to the trade of the Orient. That San Diego and San Francisco were Mexican and the Puget Sound district was claimed by Great Britain only heightened their desire to possess them. As early as 1835, Jackson tried to buy the San Francisco region. Even Calhoun called San Francisco the future New York of the Pacific and proposed buying all of California from Mexico.

The Election of 1844

In the spring of 1844 expansion did not seem likely to affect the presidential election. The Whigs nominated Clay unanimously and ignored Texas in their party platform. When the Democrats gathered in convention at Baltimore in May, Van Buren appeared to have the nomination in his pocket. He too wanted to keep Texas out of the campaign. That a politician of Van Buren's caliber, controlling the party machinery, could be upset at a national convention seemed unthinkable. But upset he was, for the southern delegates rallied round the Calhoun policy of taking Texas to save it for slavery. "I can beat Clay and Van Buren put together on this issue," Calhoun boasted. "They are behind the age." With the aid of a few northern expansionists the southerners forced through a rule requiring that the choice be by a two-thirds majority. This Van Buren could not muster. After a brief deadlock, a "dark horse," James K. Polk of Tennessee, swept the convention.

Polk was a good Jacksonian; his supporters called him "Young Hickory." He opposed high tariffs and was dead set against establishing another national bank. But he believed in taking Texas, and he favored expansion generally. To mollify the Van Burenites, the convention nominated Senator Silas Wright of New York for vice-president, but Wright was Van Buren's friend and equally opposed to annexation. When the word was flashed to him in Washington over the new "magnetic telegraph" that Samuel F. B. Morse had just installed between the convention hall in Baltimore and the Capitol, he refused to run. The delegates then picked an annexationist, George M. Dallas of Pennsylvania. The Democratic platform demanded that Texas be "reannexed" (implying that it had been part of the Louisiana Purchase) and that all of Oregon be "reoccupied" (suggesting that the joint occupation of the region with Great Britain, which had been agreed to in the Convention of 1818, be abrogated).

Texas was now in the campaign. When Clay sensed the new expansionist sentiment of the voters, he tried to hedge on his opposition to annexation, but by doing so he probably lost as many votes as he gained. The election was extremely close. The campaign followed the pattern established in 1840, with stress on parades, mass meetings, and slogans. Polk carried the country by only 38,000 of 2.7 million votes. In the electoral college the vote was 170 to 105.

The decisive factor in the contest was the Liberty party, an antislavery splinter group organized in 1840. Only 62,000 voters supported candidate James G. Birney, a "reformed" Kentucky slaveholder, but nearly 16,000 of them lived in New York, most in the western part of the state, a Whig stronghold. Since Polk carried New York by barely 5,000, the votes for Birney probably cost Clay the state. Had he won New York's 36 electoral votes, he would have been elected, 141 to 134.

Polk's victory was nevertheless taken as a mandate for expansion. Tyler promptly called on Congress to take Texas by joint resolution, which would avoid the necessity of obtaining a two-thirds majority in the Senate. This was done a few days before Tyler left the White House. Under the resolution, if the new state agreed, as many as four new states might be carved from its territory. Polk accepted this arrangement, and in December 1845 Texas became a state.

Polk as President

President Polk, a slightly built, erect man with grave, steel-gray eyes, was approaching 50. His mind was not of the first order, for he was too tense and calculating to allow his intellect free rein, but he was an efficient, hard worker with a strong will and a tough skin, qualities that stood him in good stead in the White House, and he made politics his whole life. It was typical of the man that he developed a special technique of handshaking in order better to cope with the interminable reception lines that every leader has to endure. "When I observed a strong man approaching," he once explained, "I generally took advantage of him by . . . seizing him

"This is the House That Polk Built" is the title of this 1846 cartoon directed against the president. Polk hatches his eggs and schemes for territorial expansion, reducing the tariff, and gaining fame that make up a house of cards. Contrary to the cartoonist's view, Polk succeeded in his expansionist goals, presiding over the triumph of Manifest Destiny.

by the tip of his fingers, giving him a hearty shake, and thus preventing him from getting a full grip upon me." In four years in office he was away from his desk in Washington for a total of only six weeks.

Polk was uncommonly successful in doing what he set out to do as president. He persuaded Congress to lower the tariff of 1842 and to restore the independent treasury. He opposed federal internal improvements and managed to have his way. He made himself the spokesman of American expansion by committing himself to obtaining, in addition to Texas, both Oregon and the great Southwest. Here again, he succeeded.

Oregon was the first order of business. In his inaugural address Polk stated the American claim to the entire region in the plainest terms, but he informed the British minister in Washington, Richard Pakenham, that he would accept a boundary following the 49th parallel to the Pacific. Pakenham rejected this proposal without submitting it to London, and Polk thereupon decided to insist again on the whole area. When Congress met in December 1845, he asked for authority to give the necessary one year's notice for abrogating the 1818 treaty of joint occupation. "The only way to treat John Bull," he told one congressman, "was to look him straight in the eye." Following considerable discussion, Congress complied, and in May 1846 Polk notified Great Britain that he intended to terminate the joint occupation.

The British then decided to compromise. Officials of the Hudson's Bay Company had become alarmed by the rapid growth of the American settlement in the Willamette Valley. By 1845 there were some 5,000 people there, whereas the country north of the Columbia contained no more than 750 British subjects. A clash between the groups could have but one result. The company decided to shift its base from the Columbia to Vancouver Island. And British experts outside the company reported that the Oregon country could not possibly be defended in case of war. Thus when Polk accompanied the one-year notice with a hint that he would again consider a compromise, the British foreign secretary, Lord Aberdeen, hastily suggested Polk's earlier proposal, dividing the Oregon territory along the 49th parallel. Polk, abandoning his belligerent attitude, agreed. The treaty followed that line from the Rockies to Puget Sound, but Vancouver Island, which extends below the line, was left entirely to the British, so that both nations retained free use of the Strait of Juan de Fuca. Although some northern Democrats accused Polk of treachery because he had failed to fight for all of Oregon, the treaty so obviously accorded with the national interest that the Senate approved it by a large majority in June 1846. Polk was then free to take up the Texas question in earnest.

War with Mexico

One reason for the popularity of the Oregon compromise was that the country was already at war with Mexico and wanted no trouble with Great Britain. The war had broken out in large measure because of the expansionist spirit, and the confidence born of its overwhelming advantages of size and wealth, which certainly encouraged the United States to bully Mexico. Mexican pride was also involved. Texas had been independent for the better part of a decade, and Mexico had made no serious effort to reconquer it; nevertheless, Mexico promptly broke off diplomatic relations when the United States annexed the republic.

Polk, who was ready to fight if he could not obtain what he wanted by negotiation, ordered General Zachary Taylor into Texas to defend the border. However, the location of that border was in dispute. Texas claimed the Rio Grande; Mexico insisted that the boundary was the Nueces River, which emptied into the Gulf about 150 miles to the north. Taylor reached the Nueces in July 1845 with about 1,500 troops and crossed into the disputed territory. He stopped on the southern bank at Corpus Christi, not wishing to provoke the Mexicans by marching to the Rio Grande.

In November, Polk sent an envoy, John Slidell,

The general public obtained glimpses of the war through popular lithographs like this by Currier & Ives. The Mexican soldiers (in green) seem to be powerless, despite their cannons, against the onslaught of "Gringos" in blue.

on a secret mission to Mexico to try to obtain the disputed territory by negotiation. Mexico was in default on some $2 million owed American citizens for losses suffered during political upheavals in the country. Polk authorized Slidell to cancel this debt in return for recognition of the annexation of Texas and acceptance of the Rio Grande boundary. The president also empowered him to offer as much as $30 million if Mexico would sell the United States all or part of New Mexico and California.

It would have been to Mexico's long-range advantage to have made a deal with Slidell. The area Polk wanted, lying in the path of American expansion, was likely to be engulfed as Texas had been, without regard for the actions of the American or Mexican governments. Polk assumed that his tough stance would compel the Mexicans to give in. But the Mexican government refused to receive Slidell. The president, General Mariano Paredes, promptly reaffirmed his country's claim to all of Texas. In March 1846 Slidell returned to Washington convinced that the Mexicans would not negotiate until they had been "chastised."

Polk had already ordered Taylor to advance to the Rio Grande. By March 28 the army, swelled to about 4,000, was drawn up on the north bank of the river, across from the Mexican town of Matamoros. When a Mexican force crossed the river on April 25 and attacked an American mounted patrol, Polk had his pretext. His message to Congress treated the matter as a fait accompli: "War exists," he stated flatly. He asked for authority not merely to drive the Mexicans back but to prosecute the war to "a speedy and successful termination." Congress accepted this reasoning and without actually declaring war voted to raise and supply an additional 50,000 troops.

From the first battle, the outcome of the Mexican War was never in doubt. At Palo Alto, north of the Rio Grande, 2,300 Americans scattered a Mexican force more than twice their number. Then, hotly pursuing, 1,700 Americans routed 7,500 Mexicans at Resaca de la Palma. Fewer than 50 United States soldiers lost their lives in these engagements, while Mexican losses in killed, wounded, and captured exceeded 1,000. Within a week of the outbreak of hostilities, the Mexicans had been driven across the Rio Grande and General Taylor had his troops firmly established on the southern bank.

The Mexican army was poorly equipped and, despite a surfeit of high-ranking officers, poorly led. The well-supplied American forces had a hard core of youthful West Pointers eager to make their reputations and regulars trained in Indian warfare to provide the leadership needed to turn volunteer soldiers into first-rate fighting men. Yet Mexico was a large, rugged country with few decent roads; conquering it proved to be a formidable task.

To the Halls of Montezuma

President Polk insisted not only on directing grand strategy (he displayed real ability as a military planner) but on supervising hundreds of petty details, down to the purchase of mules and the promotion of enlisted men. But he allowed party considerations to control his choice of generals. This partisanship caused unnecessary turmoil in army ranks. He wanted, as Thomas Hart Benton said, "a small war, just large enough to require a treaty of peace, and not large enough to make military reputations dangerous for the presidency."

Unfortunately for Polk, both Taylor and Winfield Scott, the commanding general in Washington, were Whigs. Polk, who tended to suspect the motives of anyone who disagreed with him, feared that one or the other would make political capital of his popularity as a military leader. The examples of his hero, Jackson, and of General Harrison loomed large in Polk's thinking.

Polk's attitude was narrow, almost unpatriotic, but not unrealistic. Zachary Taylor was not a brilliant soldier. He had joined the army in 1808 and made it his whole life. He cared so little for politics that he had never bothered to cast a ballot in an election. Polk believed that he lacked the "grasp of mind" necessary for high command, and General Scott complained of his "comfortable, laborsaving contempt for learning of every kind." But Taylor commanded the love and respect of his men (they called him Old Rough and Ready and even Zack), and he knew how to deploy them in the field. He had won another victory against a Mexican force three times larger than his own at Buena Vista in February 1847.

The dust had barely settled on the field of Buena Vista when Whig politicians began to pay Taylor court. "Great expectations and great consequences rest upon you," a Kentucky politician explained to him. "People everywhere begin to talk of converting you into a political leader, when the War is done."

Polk's concern was heightened because domestic opposition to the war was growing. Many northerners feared that the war would lead to the expansion of slavery. Others—among them an obscure Illinois congressman named Abraham Lincoln—felt that Polk had misled Congress about

the original outbreak of fighting and that the United States was the aggressor. The farther from the Rio Grande one went in the United States, the less popular "Mr. Polk's war" became; in New England opposition was almost as widespread as it had been to "Mr. Madison's war" in 1812.

Polk's design for prosecuting the war consisted of three parts. First, he would clear the Mexicans

American naval power proved a decisive factor in the Mexican War. The Pacific Squadron, under John D. Sloat and Robert F. Stockton, secured California, and a 200-vessel fleet conveyed Winfield Scott's army to Veracruz. The light salmon-colored area was later ceded to the United States by Texas.

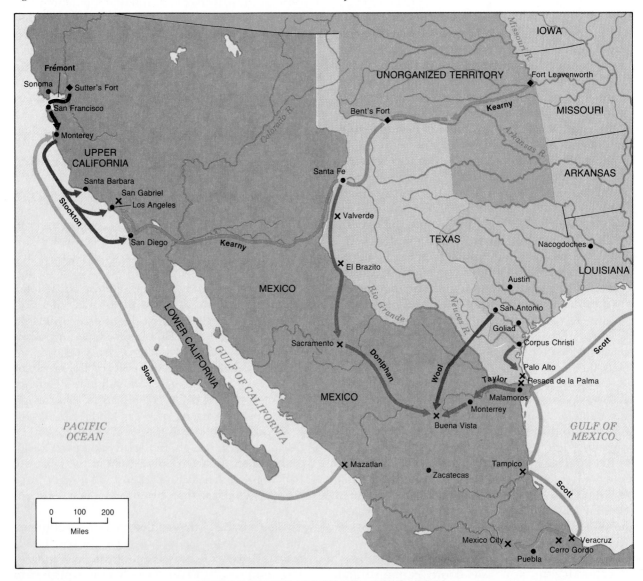

THE MEXICAN WAR, 1846–1848

from Texas and occupy the northern provinces of Mexico. Second, he would take possession of California and New Mexico. Finally, he would march on Mexico City. Proceeding west from the Rio Grande, Taylor swiftly overran Mexico's northern provinces. In June 1846, American settlers in the Sacramento Valley seized Sonoma and raised the Bear Flag of the Republic of California. Another group, headed by Captain John C. Frémont, leader of an American exploring party that happened to be in the area, clashed with the Mexican authorities around Monterey, California, and then joined with the Sonoma rebels. A naval squadron under Commodore John D. Sloat captured Monterey and San Francisco in July 1846, and a squadron of cavalry joined the other American units in mopping-up operations around San Diego and Los Angeles. By February 1847 the United States had won control of nearly all of Mexico north of the capital city.

The campaign against Mexico City was the most difficult of the war. Fearful of Taylor's growing popularity and entertaining certain honest misgivings about his ability to oversee a complicated campaign, Polk put Winfield Scott in charge of the offensive. He tried to persuade Congress to make Thomas Hart Benton a lieutenant general so as to have a Democrat in nominal control, but the Senate had the good sense to vote down this absurd proposal.

About Scott's competence no one entertained a doubt. But he seemed even more of a threat to the Democrats than Taylor, because he had political ambitions as well as military ability. In 1840 the Whigs had considered running him for president. Scion of an old Virginia family, Scott stood nearly 6½ feet tall; in uniform his presence was commanding. He was intelligent, even-tempered, and cultivated, if somewhat pompous. After a sound but not spectacular record in the War of 1812, he had added to his reputation by helping to modernize military administration and strengthen the professional training of officers. The vast difference between the army of 1812 and that of 1846 was chiefly his doing. On the record, and despite the politics of the situation, Polk had little choice but to give him this command.

Scott landed his army south of Veracruz, Mexico, on March 9, 1847, laid siege to the city, and obtained its surrender in less than three weeks with the loss of only a handful of his 10,000 men. Marching westward through hostile country, he maintained effective discipline, avoiding atrocities that might have inflamed the countryside against him. Finding his way blocked by well-placed artillery and a large army at Cerro Gordo, where the national road rose steeply toward the central highlands, Scott outflanked the Mexican position and then carried it by storm, capturing more than 3,000 prisoners and much equipment. By mid-May he had advanced to Puebla, only 80 miles southeast of Mexico City.

After delaying until August for the arrival of reinforcements, he pressed on, won two hard-fought victories at the outskirts of the capital, and on September 14 hammered his way into the city. In every engagement the American troops had been outnumbered, yet they always exacted a far heavier toll from the defenders than they themselves were forced to pay. In the fighting on the edge of Mexico City, for example, Scott's army sustained about 1,000 casualties, for the Mexicans defended their capital bravely. But 4,000 Mexicans were killed or wounded in the engagements, and 3,000 (including eight generals, two of them former presidents of the republic) were taken prisoner. No less an authority than the duke of Wellington, the conqueror of Napoleon, called Scott's campaign the most brilliant of modern times.

The Treaty of Guadalupe Hidalgo

The Mexicans were thoroughly beaten, but they refused to accept the situation. As soon as the news of the capture of Veracruz reached Washington, Polk sent Nicholas P. Trist, chief clerk of the State Department, to accompany Scott's army and to act as peace commissioner after the fall of Mexico City. Trist possessed impeccable credentials as a Democrat, for he had married a granddaughter of Thomas Jefferson and had served for a time as secretary to Andrew Jackson. Long residence as United States consul at Havana had given him an excellent command of Spanish.

Trist joined Scott at Veracruz in May. The two men took an instant dislike to each other. Scott considered it a "personal dishonor" to be asked to defer to what he considered a State Department flunky, and his feelings were not salved when Trist sent him an officious 30-page letter discoursing on the nature of his assignment. However, Scott was eager to end the war and realized that a petty quarrel with the president's emissary would not advance that objec-

This 1846 daguerreotype is the earliest known American war photograph. U.S. General John E. Wool poses with his staff in Saltillo, Mexico.

tive. Trist fell ill, and Scott sent him a jar of guava marmalade; after that they became good friends.

Because of the confused state of affairs following the fall of Mexico City, Trist was unable to open negotiations with Mexican peace commissioners until January 1848. Polk, unable to understand the delay, became impatient. Originally he had authorized Trist to pay $30 million for New Mexico, Upper and Lower California, and the right of transit across Mexico's narrow isthmus of Tehuantepec. Now, observing the disorganized state of Mexican affairs, he began to consider demanding more territory and paying less for it. He summoned Trist home.

Trist, with Scott's backing, ignored the order. He realized that unless a treaty was arranged soon, the Mexican government might disintegrate, leaving no one in authority to sign a treaty. He dashed off a 65-page letter to the president, in effect refusing to be recalled, and proceeded to negotiate. Early in February the Treaty of Guadalupe Hidalgo was completed. By its terms Mexico accepted the Rio Grande as the boundary of Texas and ceded New Mexico and Upper California to the United States. In return the United States agreed to pay Mexico $15 million and to take on the claims of American citizens against Mexico, which by that time amounted to another $3.25 million.

When he learned that Trist had ignored his orders, the president seethed. Trist was "contemptibly base," he thought, an "impudent and unqualified scoundrel." He ordered Trist placed under arrest and fired from his State Department job.* Yet Polk had no choice but to submit the treaty to the Senate, for to have insisted on more territory would have meant more fighting, and the war had become increasingly unpopular. The relatively easy military victory made some people ashamed that their country was crushing a weaker neighbor. Abolitionists, led by William Lloyd Garrison, called it an "invasion . . . waged solely for the detestable and horrible purpose of extending and perpetuating American slavery." The Senate, subject to the same pressures as the president, ratified the agreement by a vote of 38 to 14.

The Fruits of Victory

The Mexican War, won quickly and at relatively small cost in lives and money, brought huge ter-

---

* Trist was retired to private life without being paid for his time in Mexico. In 1870, when he was on his deathbed, Congress finally awarded him $14,299.20.

ritorial gains. The Pacific Coast from south of San Diego to the 49th parallel and all the land between the coast and the Continental Divide had become the property of the American people. Immense amounts of labor and capital would have to be invested before this new territory could be made to yield its bounty, but the country clearly had the capacity to accomplish the job.

In this atmosphere came what seemed a sign from the heavens. In January 1848, while Scott's veterans rested on their victorious arms in Mexico City, a mechanic named James W. Marshall was building a sawmill on the American River in the Sacramento Valley east of San Francisco. One day, while supervising the deepening of the millrace, he noticed a few flecks of yellow in the bed of the stream. These he gathered up and tested. They were pure gold.

Other strikes had been made in California and been treated skeptically or as matters of local curiosity; since the days of Jamestown, too many pioneers had run fruitlessly in search of El Dorado, and too much fool's gold had been passed off as the real thing. Yet this discovery produced an international sensation. The gold was real and plentiful—$200 million of it was extracted in four years—but equally important was the fact that everyone was ready to believe the news. The gold rush reflected the heady confidence inspired by Guadalupe Hidalgo; it seemed the ultimate justification of manifest destiny. Surely an era of continental prosperity and harmony had dawned.

Slavery: The Fire Bell in the Night Rings Again

Prosperity came in full measure but harmony did not, for once again expansion brought the nation face to face with the divisive question of slavery. This giant chunk of North America, most of it vacant, its future soon to be determined—should it be slave or free? The question, in one sense, seems hardly worth the national crisis it provoked. Slavery appeared to have little future in New Mexico, less in California and Oregon. Why did the South fight so hard for the right to bring slaves into a region so poorly suited to their exploitation?

Narrow partisanship provides part of the explanation. In districts where slavery was en-trenched, a congressman who watched over the institution with the eyes of Argus, ever ready to defend it against the most trivial slight, usually found himself a popular hero. In the northern states, the representatives who were vigilant in what they might describe as "freedom's cause" seldom regretted it on election day. But slavery raised a moral question. Most Americans tried to avoid confronting this truth; as patriots they assumed that any sectional issue could be solved by compromise. However, while the majority of whites had little respect for blacks, slave or free, few persons, northern or southern, could look upon the ownership of one human being by another as simply an alternative form of economic organization and argue its merits as they would those of the protective tariff or a national bank. Twist the facts as they might, slavery was either right or it was wrong; being on the whole honest and moral, they could not, having faced that truth, stand by unconcerned while the question was debated.

The question could come up in Congress only indirectly, for the Constitution did not give the federal government any control over slavery in the states. But Congress had complete control in the territories. Therefore, the fact that slavery had no future in the Mexican cession was unimportant—in fact, for the foes of slavery it was an advantage. By attacking slavery where it did not and probably never could exist, they could conceal from the slave-holders—and perhaps even from themselves—their hope ultimately to extinguish the institution.

Slavery had complicated the Texas problem from the start, and it beclouded the future of the Southwest even before the Mexican flag had been stripped from the staffs at Santa Fe and Los Angeles. The northern, Van Burenite wing of the Democratic party had become increasingly uneasy about the proslavery cast of Polk's policies, which were unpopular in their part of the country. Once it became likely that the war would bring new territory into the Union, these northerners felt compelled to try to check the president and to assure their constituents that they would resist the admission of further slave territory. On August 8, 1846, during the debate on a bill appropriating money for the conduct of the war, Democratic Congressman David Wilmot of Pennsylvania introduced an amendment that provided "as an express and fundamental condition to the acquisition of any territory from the Republic of Mexico" that "neither slavery nor involuntary servitude shall ever exist in any part of said territory, except for crime, whereof the party shall first be duly convicted."

The Wilmot Proviso passed the House, where northern congressmen outnumbered southern, but lost in the Senate, where southerners held the balance. To counter it, Calhoun, again senator from South Carolina, introduced resolutions in February 1846 that argued that Congress had no right to bar slavery from any territory; since territories belonged to all the states, slave and free, all should have equal rights in them. From this position it was only a step (soon taken) to demanding that Congress guarantee the right of slave owners to bring slaves into the territories and establish federal slave codes in the territories. Most northerners considered this proposal as repulsive as southerners found the Wilmot Proviso.

Calhoun's resolutions could never pass the House of Representatives, and Wilmot's proviso had no chance in the Senate. Yet their very existence threatened the Union; as Senator Benton remarked, they were like the blades of a pair of scissors, ineffective separately, an efficient cutting tool taken together.

To resolve the territorial problem, two compromises were offered. One, eventually backed by President Polk, would extend the Missouri Compromise line to the Pacific. The majority of southerners were willing to go along with this scheme, but most northerners would no longer agree to the reservation of *any* new territory for slavery. The other possibility, advocated by Senator Lewis Cass of Michigan, called for organizing new territories without mention of slavery, thus leaving it to local settlers, through their territorial legislatures, to determine their own institutions. Cass's "popular sovereignty," known more vulgarly as "squatter sovereignty," had the superficial merit of appearing to be democratic. Its virtue for the members of Congress, however, was that it allowed them to escape the responsibility of deciding the question themselves.

The Election of 1848

One test of strength occurred in August, before the 1848 presidential election. After six months of acrimonious debate, Congress passed a bill barring slavery from Oregon. The test, however, proved little. If it required half a year to settle the question for Oregon, how could an answer ever be found for California and New Mexico? Plainly the time had come, in a democracy, to go to the people. The coming presidential election seemed to provide an ideal opportunity.

The opportunity was missed. The politicians of parties hedged, fearful of losing votes in one section or another. With the issues blurred, the electorate had no real choice. That the Whigs should behave in such a manner was perhaps to be expected of the party of "Tippecanoe and Tyler too," but in 1848 they outdid even their 1840 performance, nominating Zachary Taylor for president. They chose the general despite his lack of political sophistication and after he had flatly refused to state his opinion on any current subject. The party offered no platform. Taylor was a brave man and a fine general; the Democrats had mistreated him; he was a common, ordinary fellow, unpretentious and warmhearted. Such was the Whig "argument." Taylor's contribution to the campaign was so naive as to be pathetic. "I am a Whig, *but not an ultra Whig*. . . . If elected . . . I should feel bound to administer the government untrammeled by party schemes."

The Democratic party had little better to offer. All the drive and zeal characteristic of it in the Jackson period had gradually seeped away. Polk's espousal of Texas's annexation had driven many northerners from its ranks. Individuals like James Buchanan of Pennsylvania, Polk's secretary of state, and William L. Marcy of New York, his secretary of war—cautious, cynical politicians interested chiefly in getting and holding office—now came to the fore in northern Democratic politics.

The Democratic nominee was Lewis Cass, the father of popular sovereignty, but the party did not endorse that or any other solution to the territorial question. Cass was at least an experienced politician, having been governor of Michigan Territory, secretary of war, minister to France, and senator. Nevertheless, his approach to life was exemplified by an annoying habit he displayed at Washington social functions: A teetotaler, he would circulate among the guests with a glass in hand, raising it to his lips repeatedly but never swallowing a drop.

The Van Buren wing of the Democratic party was known as the Barnburners to call attention to their radicalism—supposedly they would burn down the barn to get rid of the rats. The Barn-burners could not stomach Cass, in part because he was willing to countenance the extension of slavery into new territories, in part because he had led the swing to Polk in the 1844 Democratic convention. Combining with the antislavery Liberty party, they formed the Free Soil party and nominated Van Buren.

Van Buren knew he could not be elected, but he believed the time had come to take a stand. "The minds of nearly all mankind have been penetrated by a conviction of the evils of slavery," the onetime "Fox" and "Magician" declared. The Free Soil party polled nearly 300,000 votes, about 10 percent of the total, in a very dull campaign. Offered a choice

between the honest ignorance of Taylor and the cynical opportunism of Cass, the voters—by a narrow margin—chose the former, Taylor receiving 1.36 million votes to Cass's 1.22 million. Taylor carried 8 of the 15 slave states and 7 of the 15 free states, proof that the sectional issue had been avoided.

The Gold Rush

It was now clear that the question of slavery in the territories had to be faced. The discovery of gold had brought an army of prospectors into California. By the summer of 1848 San Francisco had become almost a ghost town, and an estimated two-thirds

The hard road to El Dorado was sketched by J. Goldsborough Bruff, a Washington, D.C., draftsman who led a company "to see the elephant" (in the phrase of the day) in 1849. Two self-portraits from Bruff's diary neatly sum up the journey, with pencil notes reading as follows. Leaving Home (No. 1): "D——n your $3, when one can make $100 a day easy." Arrival in California (No. 5): "The mule understands breaking better than being broke . . . 40 miles more without fodder! rather tight, but then the jig's up and I'll soon have my pile! so I'll drive on." The sign on the tree reads "Only 40 mi. to the Settlements. Flour $2.25 lb."

of the adult males of Oregon had hastened south to the gold fields. After President Polk confirmed the "extraordinary character" of the strike in his annual message of December 1848, there was no containing the gold seekers. During 1849 some 25,000 Americans made their way to California from the East by ship; more than 55,000 others crossed the continent by overland routes. About 8,000 Mexicans, 5,000 South Americans, and numbers of Europeans joined the rush.

The rough limits of the gold country had been quickly marked out. For 150 miles and more along the western slope of the Sierra stretched the great mother lode. Along the expanse any stream or canyon, any ancient gravel bed might conceal a treasure in nuggets, flakes, or dust. Armed with pickaxes and shovels, with washing pans, even with knives and spoons, the eager prospectors hacked and dug and sifted, each accumulating a horde, some great, some small, of gleaming yellow metal.

The impact on the region was enormous. Between 1849 and 1860 about 200,000 people, nearly all of them males, crossed the Rockies to California and thousands more reached California by ship. Almost overnight the Spanish-American population was reduced to the status of a minority. Disregarding justice and reason alike, the newcomers from the East, as one observer noted, "regarded every man but a native [North] American as an interloper." They referred to people of Latin American origin as "greasers" and sought by law and by violence to keep them from mining for gold. Even the local Californians (now American citizens) were discriminated against. The few free blacks in California and the several thousand more who came in search of gold were treated no better. As for the far larger Indian population, it was almost wiped out. There were about 150,000 Indians in California in the mid-1840s but only 35,000 in 1860.

The ethnic conflict was only part of the problem. Rough, hard men, separated from women, lusting for gold in a strange wild country where fortunes could be made in a day, gambled away in an hour, or stolen in an instant—the situation demanded the establishment of a territorial government. President Taylor appreciated this, and in his gruff, simplehearted way he suggested an uncomplicated answer: Admit California directly as a state, letting the Californians decide for themselves about slavery. The rest of the Mexican Cession could be formed

into another state. No need for Congress, with its angry rivalries, to meddle at all, he believed. In this way the nation could avoid the divisive effects of sectional debate.

The Californians reacted favorably to Taylor's proposal. They were overwhelmingly opposed to slavery, though not for humanitarian reasons. On the contrary, they tended to look upon blacks as they did Mexicans and feared that if slavery were permitted, white gold seekers would be disadvantaged. "They would be unable," one delegate to the California constitutional convention predicted, "to compete with the bands of negroes who would be set to work under the direction of capitalists. It would become a monopoly." By October 1849 they had drawn up a constitution that outlawed slavery, and by December the new state government was functioning.

At this the South stood aghast. Taylor was the owner of a large plantation and many slaves; southerners had assumed (without bothering to ask) that he would fight to keep the territories open to slavery. To admit California would destroy the balance between free and slave states in the Senate; to allow all the new land to become free would doom the South to wither in a corner of the country, surrounded by hostile free states. Should that happen, how long could slavery sustain itself even in South Carolina? Radicals were already saying that the South would have to choose between secession and surrender. Taylor's plan played into the hands of extremists.

The Compromise of 1850

This was no longer a squabble over territorial governments. With the Union itself at stake, Henry Clay rose to save the day. He had been as angry and frustrated when the Whigs nominated Taylor as he was when they passed him over for Harrison. Now, well beyond 70 and in ill health, he put away his ambition and his resentment and for the last time concentrated his remarkable vision on a great, multifaceted national problem. California must be free and soon admitted to the Union, but the South must have some compensation. For that matter, why not seize the opportunity to settle every outstanding sectional conflict related to slavery? Clay wondered long and hard, drew up a plan, then consulted his

*Two leading lights of the day, Clay and Webster, as they looked at about the time
they played major roles in the Compromise of 1850. The daguerreotype of Clay
dates from the late 1840s; that of Webster from 1851, a year before his death.
Both are by the noted Boston firm of Southworth and Hawes.*

old Whig rival Webster and obtained his general
approval. On January 29, 1850, he laid his proposal,
"founded upon mutual forbearance," before the
Senate. A few days later he defended it on the floor
of the Senate in the last great speech of his life.

California should be brought directly into the
Union as a free state, he argued. The rest of the
Southwest should be organized as a territory without mention of slavery: The southerners would retain the right to bring slaves there, while in fact
none would do so. "You have got what is worth
more than a thousand Wilmot Provisos," Clay
pointed out to his northern colleagues. "You have
nature on your side." Empty lands in dispute along
the Texas border should be assigned to New Mexico
Territory, Clay continued, but in exchange the
United States should take over Texas's preannex-
ation debts. The slave trade should be abolished in
the District of Columbia (but not slavery itself), and
a more effective federal fugitive slave law should
be enacted and strictly enforced in the North.

Clay's proposals occasioned one of the most
magnificent debates in the history of the Senate.

Every important member had his say. Calhoun, perhaps even more than Clay, realized that the future
of the nation was at stake and that his own days
were numbered (he died four weeks later). Too feeble to deliver his speech himself, he sat impassive,
wrapped in a great cloak, while Senator James M.
Mason of Virginia read it to the crowded Senate.
Calhoun thought his plan would save the Union,
but his speech was an argument for secession; he
demanded that the North yield completely on every
point, ceasing even to discuss the question of slavery.
Clay's compromise was unsatisfactory; he himself
had no other to offer. If you will not yield, he said
to the northern senators, "let the States . . . agree
to separate and part in peace. If you are unwilling
we should part in peace, tell us so, and we shall
know what to do."

Three days later, on March 7, Daniel Webster
took the floor. He too had begun to fail; the brilliant
volubility and the thunder were gone, and when he
spoke his face was bathed in sweat and there were
strange pauses in his delivery. But his argument was
lucid. Clay's proposals should be adopted. Since the

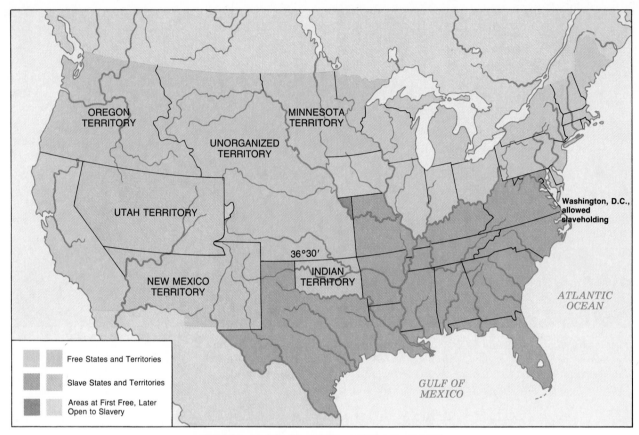

FREE AND SLAVE AREAS, 1850

This map and the map on the facing page show different aspects of the Compromise of 1850. Here, the two shades of salmon and the two shades of green show clearly the distribution of slave and free areas. The Utah and New Mexico territories were allowed to choose to be either free or slave, as their own constitutions determined.

future of all the territories had already been fixed by geographic and economic factors, the Wilmot Proviso was unnecessary. The North's constitutional obligation to yield fugitive slaves, he said, braving the wrath of New England abolitionists, was "binding in honor and conscience." (A cynic might say that once again Webster was placing property rights above human rights.) The Union, he continued, could not be sundered without bloodshed. At the thought of the dread possibility, the old fire flared: "Peaceable secession!" Webster exclaimed, "Heaven forbid! Where is the flag of the republic to remain? Where is the eagle still to tower?"

The debate did not end with the aging giants.

Every possible viewpoint was presented, argued, rebutted, rehashed. Senator William H. Seward of New York, a new Whig leader, close to Taylor's ear, caused a stir while arguing against concessions to the slave interests by saying that despite the constitutional obligation to return fugitive slaves, a "higher law" than the Constitution, the law of God, forbade anything that countenanced the evil of slavery.

The majority clearly favored some compromise, but nothing could have been accomplished without the death of President Taylor on July 9. Obstinate, probably resentful because few people paid him half the heed they paid Clay and other prominent mem-

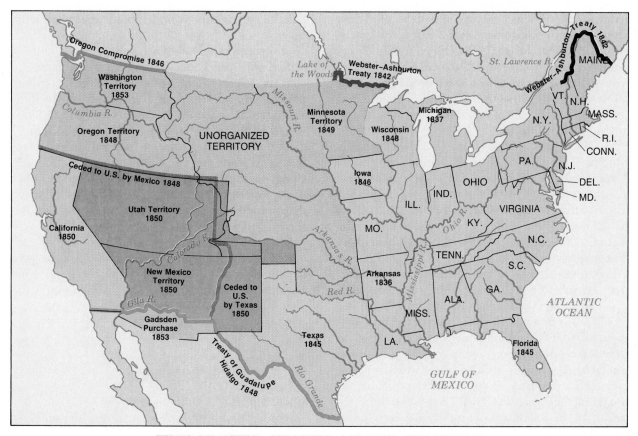

THE UNITED STATES AT MID-CENTURY

This map indicates the provisions of the Compromise of 1850 that applied to the Mexican Cession. Beginning with the annexation of Texas in 1845 and ending with the Gadsden Purchase in 1853 (to furnish a route for a southern transcontinental railroad), the United States acquired more than 869 million acres of territory. With the Gadsden Purchase, the geographical expansion of the continental United States was completed.

bers of Congress, he had insisted on his own plan to bring both California and New Mexico directly into the Union. When Vice-President Millard Fillmore succeeded him, the deadlock between the White House and Capitol Hill was broken. Even so, each part of the compromise had to be voted on separately, for too many stubborn congressmen were willing to overturn the whole plan because they objected to specific parts of it. Senator Benton, for example, announced against Clay's omnibus bill because he objected to the fugitive slave provision and the Texas boundary settlement.

The final congressional maneuvering was man-

aged by another relative newcomer, Senator Stephen A. Douglas of Illinois, who took over when Washington's summer heat prostrated the exhausted Clay. Partisanship and economic interests complicated Douglas's problem. According to rumor, Clay had persuaded an important Virginia newspaper editor to back the compromise by promising him a $100,000 government printing contract. This inflamed many southerners. New York merchants, fearful of the disruption of their southern business, submitted a petition bearing 25,000 names in favor of compromise, a document that had a favorable effect in the South. The prospect of the federal government's paying the debt of Texas made ardent compromisers of a horde of speculators. Between February and September, Texas bonds rose erratically from 29 to over 60, while men like W. W. Corcoran, whose Washington bank held more than $400,000 of these securities, entertained legislators and supplied lobbyists with large amounts of cash.

In the Senate and then in the House, tangled combinations pushed through the separate measures, one by one. California became the thirty-first state. The rest of the Mexican Cession was divided into two territories, New Mexico and Utah, each to be admitted to the Union when qualified, "with or without slavery as [its] constitution may prescribe." Texas received $10 million to pay off its debt in return for accepting a narrower western boundary. The slave trade in the District of Columbia was abolished as of January 1, 1851. The Fugitive Slave Act of 1793 was amended to provide for the appointment of federal commissioners with authority to issue warrants, summon posses, and compel citizens under pain of fine or imprisonment to assist in the capture of fugitives. Accused fugitives could not testify in their own defense. They were to be returned to the South without jury trial merely upon the submission of an affidavit by their "owner."

Only 4 senators and 28 representatives voted for all these bills. The two sides did not meet somewhere in the middle as is the case with most compromises. Each bill passed because those who preferred it outnumbered those opposed. In general, the Democrats gave more support to the compromise than the Whigs, but party lines never held firmly. In the Senate, for example, 17 Democrats and 15 Whigs voted to admit California as a free state. A large number of congressmen absented themselves when parts of the settlement unpopular in their home districts came to a vote; 21 senators and 36 representatives failed to commit themselves on the new fugitive slave bill. Senator Jefferson Davis of Mississippi voted for the fugitive slave measure and the bill creating Utah Territory, remained silent on the New Mexico bill, and opposed the other measures. Senator Salmon P. Chase of Ohio, an abolitionist, supported only the admission of California and the abolition of the slave trade.

In this piecemeal fashion the Union was preserved. The credit belongs mostly to Clay, whose original conceptualization of the compromise enabled lesser minds to understand what they must do.

Everywhere sober and conservative citizens sighed with relief. Mass meetings throughout the country "ratified" the result. Hundreds of newspapers gave the compromise editorial approval. In Washington patriotic harmony reigned. "You would suppose that nobody had ever thought of disunion," Webster wrote. "All say they always meant to stand by the Union to the last." When Congress met again in December, it seemed that party asperities had been buried forever. "I have determined never to make another speech on the slavery question," Senator Douglas told his colleagues. "Let us cease agitating, stop the debate, and drop the subject." If this were done, he predicted, the compromise would be accepted as a "final settlement." With this bit of wishful thinking the year 1850 passed into history.

Milestones

1835 Fall of the Alamo mission

1837 United States recognizes the Republic of Texas

1840 Richard Henry Dana, *Two Years Before the Mast*

1841 Vice-President John Tyler becomes president
Preemption Act grants "squatters' rights"

1842 Webster-Ashburton Treaty determines Maine boundary

1843 Oregon Trail opens

1845 Texas annexed
John L. O'Sullivan coins the expression *manifest destiny*

1846 Oregon boundary dispute settled
War with Mexico
House of Representatives adopts the Wilmot Proviso

1847 General Winfield Scott captures Mexico City

1848 Discovery of gold at Sutter's Mill, California
Treaty of Guadalupe Hidalgo

1850 Compromise of 1850

SUPPLEMENTARY READING

Titles marked with an asterisk have been published in paperback.

G. G. Van Deusen, **The Jacksonian Era*** (1959), provides a convenient summary of the period. On the Tyler administration, see R. J. Morgan, **A Whig Embattled: The Presidency Under John Tyler** (1954).

On diplomatic affairs, see P. A. Varg, **United States Foreign Relations, 1820–1860** (1979), and D. M. Pletcher, **The Diplomacy of Annexation: Texas, Oregon, and the Mexican War** (1973).

The new expansionism is discussed in A. K. Weinberg, **Manifest Destiny*** (1935), and in two works by Frederick Merk, **Manifest Destiny and Mission in American History*** (1963) and **The Monroe Doctrine and American Expansionism** (1966). H. N. Smith, **Virgin Land*** (1950), is also important for an understanding of this subject. The course of western development is treated in R. A. Billington, and Martin Ridge, **The Far Western Frontier*** (1982). On Oregon, see David Lavender, **Westward Vision*** (1963), J. R. Jeffrey, **Frontier Women** (1979), J. D. Unruh, **The Plains Across** (1979), Sandra Myres (ed.), **Ho for California! Women's Overland Diaries** (1980), and Francis Parkman's classic account, **The Oregon Trail*** (1849).

On the election of 1844, see J. C. N. Paul, **Rift in the Democracy*** (1961). The standard biography of Polk is C. G. Sellers, **James K. Polk** (1957–1966), but see also P. H. Bergeron, **The Presidency of James K. Polk** (1987). N. A. Graebner, **Empire on the Pacific** (1955), is the fullest analysis of the factors influencing the Oregon boundary compromise.

There are a number of good brief accounts of the Mexican War, including R. W. Johannsen, **To the Halls of Montezuma** (1987), and O. A. Singletary, **The Mexican War*** (1960). J. H. Schroeder, **Mr. Polk's War** (1973), discusses American opposition to the conflict. For details on the discovery of gold in California, in addition to the works by Billington and Ridge already mentioned, see R. W. Paul, **California Gold: The Beginning of Mining in the Far West*** (1947). On the treatment of Mexicans and blacks, see R. F. Heize and A. J. Almquist, **The Other Californians*** (1971), and R. M. Lapp, **Blacks in Gold Rush California** (1977).

The fullest study of the Compromise of 1850 is Holman Hamilton, **Prologue to Conflict*** (1964). See also the biographies of Clay, Calhoun, and Webster cited in earlier chapters, R. W. Johannsen, **Stephen A. Douglas** (1973), Holman Hamilton, **Zachary Taylor** (1951), and A. O. Craven, **The Growth of Southern Nationalism** (1953).

The Sections Go Their Ways

It is a great mistake to suppose that disunion can be effected by a single blow. The cords which bind these states together in one common Union are far too numerous and powerful for that. Disunion must be the work of time.

JOHN C. CALHOUN, *March 4, 1850*

A nation growing as rapidly as the United States in the middle decades of the 19th century changed continually in hundreds of ways. It was developing a national economy marked by the dependence of each area on all the others, the production of goods in one region for sale in all, the increased specialization of agricultural and industrial producers, and the growth in size of units of production.

Cotton remained the most important southern crop and the major American export. However, manufacturing in the Northeast and the railroads, which revolutionized transportation and communication, became the mainsprings of economic growth. The continuing westward movement of agriculture had significant new effects. American foreign commerce changed radically, and the flood of European immigration had an impact on manufacturing, town life, and farming.

The South

The South was less affected than the other sections by urbanization, European immigration, the transportation revolution, and industrialization. The region remained predominantly agricultural; cotton was still king, slavery the most distinctive southern institution. But important changes were occurring. Cotton continued to march westward until by 1859 fully 1.3 million of the 4.3 million bales grown in the United States came from beyond the Mississippi. In the Upper South, Virginia held its place as the leading tobacco producer, but states beyond the Appalachians were raising more than half the crop. The introduction of Bright Yellow, a mild variety of tobacco that (miraculously) grew best in poor soil, gave a great stimulus to production. The older sections of Maryland, Virginia, and North Carolina shifted to the kind of diversified farming usually associated with the Northeast. By 1849 the wheat crop of Virginia was worth twice as much as the tobacco crop.

In the time of Washington and Jefferson, progressive Virginia planters had experimented with crop rotation and fertilizers. In the mid-19th century, Edmund Ruffin introduced the use of marl, an earth rich in calcium, to counteract the acidity of worn-out tobacco fields. Ruffin discovered that dressings of marl, combined with the use of fertilizers and with proper drainage and plowing methods, doubled and even tripled the yield of corn and wheat. In the 1840s some southerners began to import Peruvian guano, a high-nitrogen fertilizer of bird droppings, which increased yields. Others experimented with contour plowing to control erosion and with improved breeds of livestock, new types of plows, and agricultural machinery.

The Economics of Slavery

The increased importance of cotton in the South strengthened the hold of slavery on the region. The price of slaves rose until by the 1850s a prime field hand was worth as much as $1,800, roughly three times the cost in the 1820s. While the prestige value of owning this kind of property affected prices, the rise chiefly reflected the increasing value of the South's agricultural output. "Crop value per slave" jumped from less than $15 early in the century to more than $125 in 1859.

In the cotton fields of the Deep South, slaves brought several hundred dollars per head more than in the older regions; thus the tendency to sell them "down the river" continued. Mississippi took in some 10,000 slaves a year throughout the period; by 1830 the black population of the state exceeded the white. Slave trading became a big business. There were about 50 dealers in Charleston in the 1850s and 200 in New Orleans. The largest traders were Isaac Franklin and John Armfield, who collected slaves from Virginia and Maryland at their "model jail" in Alexandria and shipped them by land

and sea to a depot near Natchez. Each of the partners cleared half a million dollars before retiring, and some smaller operators did proportionately well.

The impact of the trade on the slaves was frequently disastrous. Husbands were often separated from wives, parents from children. This was somewhat less likely to happen on large, well-managed plantations than on small farms, but it was common enough everywhere. Because the business was so profitable, the prejudice against slave traders abated as the price of slaves rose. Men of high social status became traders, and persons of humble origin who had prospered in the trade had little difficulty in

Not surprisingly, the areas of greatest cotton production were also the areas of the highest proportion of slaves in the population. Note the concentrations of both in the Piedmont, the Alabama Black Belt, and the lower Mississippi Valley, and the relative absence of both in the Appalachian Mountains.

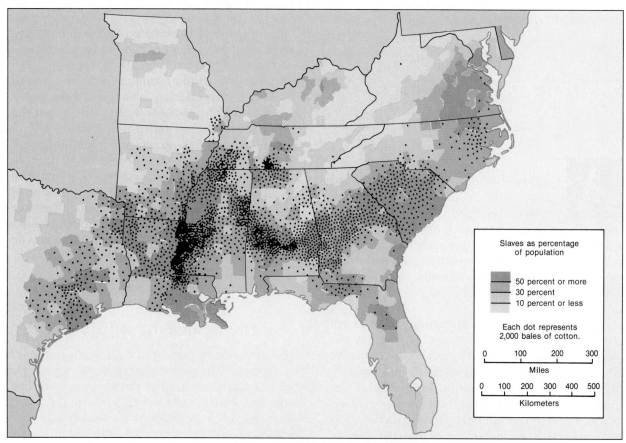

COTTON AND SLAVES IN THE SOUTH, 1860

buying land and setting up as respectable planters.

As blacks became more expensive, the ownership of slaves became more concentrated. In 1860 only about 46,000 of the 8 million white residents of the slave states had as many as 20. When one calculates the cost of 20 slaves and the land to keep them profitably occupied, it is easy to understand why this figure is so small. The most efficient size of a plantation worked by gangs of slaves ranged between 1,000 and 2,000 acres. In every part of the South the majority of farmers cultivated no more than 200 acres, in many sections less than 100 acres. On the eve of the Civil War only one white family in four owned any slaves at all. A few large plantations and many small farms—this was the pattern.

There were few genuine economies of scale in

These reportorial views of slavery were sketched by a young Austrian, Franz Hölzlhuber, who toured the South between 1856 and 1860. Above is a rice plantation on the Arkansas River. The slaves at right, harvesting sugar cane in Louisiana, are dressed in striped garb to discourage attempts at escape.

southern agriculture. Small farmers grew the staple crops, and many of them owned a few slaves, often working beside them in the fields. These yeomen farmers were hardworking, self-reliant, and moderately prosperous, quite unlike the "poor white trash" of the pine barrens and the remote valleys of the Appalachians who scratched a meager subsistence from substandard soils and lived in ignorance and squalor.

Well-managed plantations yielded annual profits of 10 percent and more, and in general, money invested in southern agriculture earned at least a modest return. Considering the way the work force was exploited, this is hardly surprising. Recent estimates indicate that after allowing for the cost of land and capital, the average plantation slave "earned" cotton worth $78.78 in 1859. It cost masters about $32 a year to feed, clothe, and house a slave. In other words, almost 60 percent of the product of slave labor was expropriated by the masters.

The South failed to develop locally owned marketing and transportation facilities, and for this slavery was at least partly responsible. In 1840 *Hunt's Merchant Magazine* estimated that it cost $2.85 to move a bale of cotton from the farm to a seaport and that additional charges for storage, insurance, port fees, and freight to a European port exceeded $15. Middlemen from outside the South commonly earned most of this money. New York capitalists gradually came to control much of the South's cotton from the moment it was picked, and a large percentage of the crop found its way into New York warehouses before being sold to manufacturers. The same middlemen supplied most of the foreign goods that the planters purchased with their cotton earnings.

Southerners complained about this state of affairs but did little to correct it. Capital tied up in the ownership of labor could not be invested in anything else, and social pressures in the South militated against investment in trade and commerce. Ownership of land and slaves yielded a kind of psychic income not available to any middleman. As one British visitor pointed out, the southern blacks were "a nonconsuming class." Still more depressing, under slavery the enormous reservoir of intelligence and skill that the blacks represented was almost entirely wasted. Many slave artisans worked on the plantations, and a few free blacks made their way in the South remarkably well, but the amount of

talent unused, energy misdirected, and imagination smothered can only be guessed.

Foreign observers in New England frequently noted the alertness and industriousness of ordinary laborers and attributed this, justifiably, to the high level of literacy. Nearly everyone in New England could read and write. Correspondingly, the stagnation and inefficiency of southern labor could be attributed in part to the high degree of illiteracy, for over 20 percent of *white* southerners could not read or write, another tragic squandering of human resources.

Antebellum Plantation Life

There was never any such thing as a "typical" plantation, but it is possible to describe, in a general way, what a medium-to-large operation employing 20 or more slaves was like in the two decades preceding the Civil War. Such a plantation was more like a small village than a northern-type agricultural unit, and in another way more like a self-sufficient colonial farm than a 19th-century commercial operation, although its major activity involved producing cotton or some other cash crop.

In addition to the master's house with its complement of barns and stables, there would usually be a kitchen, a smoke house, a wash house, a home for the overseer should one be employed, perhaps a schoolhouse, a gristmill, a forge, and of course the slave quarters, off at a distance (but not too far) from the center.

Slaveholding families were also quite different from northern families of similar status, in part because they were engaged in agriculture and in part because of their so-called peculiar institution. Husbands and wives did not function in separate spheres to nearly the same extent, though their individual functions were different and gender-related.

Although planter families purchased their fine clothes, furniture, and china, as well as other manufactured products such as sewing machines, cooking utensils, books, and musical instruments, plantations were busy centers of household manufacture, turning out most of the clothing of slaves except for shoes and the everyday clothing of their own children, along with bedding and other textiles. Spinning, weaving, and sewing were women's work, both for whites and blacks. Nearly all the food con-

Profits from cash crops allowed successful planters to build graceful homes like this one on the Mississippi River. The "Big House," in which the master and his family lived, might be a splendid mansion that offered imported luxuries, or a much simpler, plain wooden dwelling.

sumed was raised on the land; only tea and coffee and a few other food items were commonly purchased.

The master was in general charge and his word was law—the system was literally paternalistic. But his wife nearly always had immense responsibilities. Running the household meant supervising the servants (and punishing them when necessary, which often meant wielding a lash), nursing the sick, taking care of the vegetable and flower gardens, planning meals, and seeing to the education of her own children and the training of young slaves. It could also involve running the entire plantation on the frequent occasions when her husband was away on business. At the same time, her role entailed being a "southern lady," refined, graceful, supposedly untroubled by worldly affairs.

Most slaveholding women had to learn all these things by doing; in general, southern women married while still in their teens and had been given little or no training in the household arts. Unmarried "young ladies" had few responsibilities beyond caring for their own rooms and persons and perhaps such "ladylike" tasks as arranging flowers.

The majority of the slaves of both sexes were field hands who labored on the land from dawn to dusk. Household servants and artisans, indeed any slave other than small children and the aged and infirm, might be called on for such labor when needed. Slave women were expected to cook for their own families and do other chores after working in the fields.

Children, free and slave, were cared for by slaves, the former by household servants, the latter usually by an elderly woman, perhaps with the help of a girl only a little older than the children. Infants were brought to their mothers in the fields for nursing several times a day, for after a month or two at most, slave mothers were required to go back to work. Slave children were not put to work until they were 6 or 7 and until they were about 10 were given only small tasks such as feeding the chickens or minding a smaller child. Black and white youngsters played together and were often cared for by the same nursemaid.

Slave cabins were simple and crude; most consisted of a single room, dark, with a fireplace for cooking and heat. Usually the flooring was raised above ground level, though some were set on the bare earth. Though certainly Spartan, these quarters compared favorably with those of European peasants of the time and the poorest white American farmers. And as Elizabeth Fox-Genovese explains in *Within the Plantation Household*, they were "primarily places to sleep, take shelter, and eat the last meal of the day," and "did not harbor the real life of slave families, much less the slave community."

The Sociology of Slavery

It is difficult to generalize about the peculiar institution because so much depended on the individual master's behavior. Owners exercised power over their human possessions "as absolute . . . as the Khan of Tartary." Asked about how slave "criminals" were dealt with, an ex-slave reported: "I ain't heard nothin' 'bout no jails. . . . What they done was 'most beat de life out of de niggers to make 'em behave." Yet most owners provided adequate clothing, housing, and food for their slaves. Only a fool or a sadist would fail to take care of such valuable property. However, vital statistics indicate that infant mortality among slaves was twice the white rate, life expectancy at least five years less. One student of this subject, Richard Sutch, concludes: "The returns from slavery were maximized by using force to extract the maximum amount of work from the slaves while providing them only with sufficient food, shelter, clothing, and health care to keep them healthy and hard working."

On balance, it is significant that the United States was the only nation in the Western Hemisphere where the slave population grew by natural increase. After the ending of the slave trade in 1808, the black population increased at nearly the same rate as the white. Put differently, during the entire period from the founding of Jamestown to the Civil War, only a little more than half a million slaves were imported into the country, about 5 percent of the number of Africans carried by slavers to the New World. Yet in 1860 there were about 4 million blacks in the United States.

Most owners felt responsibilities toward their slaves, and slaves were dependent on and in some ways imitative of white values. However, powerful fears and resentments, not always recognized, existed on both sides. The plantation environment forced the two races to live in close proximity. From this circumstance could arise every sort of human relationship. One planter, using the appropriate pseudonym Clod Thumper, could write: "Africans are nothing but brutes, and they will love you better for whipping, whether they deserve it or not." Another, describing a slave named Bug, could say: "No one knows but myself what feeling I have for him. Black as he is we were raised together." One southern white woman tended a dying servant with "the kindest & most unremitting attention." Another, discovered crying after the death of a slave she had repeatedly abused, is said to have explained her grief by complaining that she "didn't have nobody to whip no more."

Such diametrically conflicting sentiments often existed within the same person. And almost no white southerners had any difficulty exploiting the labor of slaves for whom they felt genuine affection.

Slaves were without rights; they developed a distinctive way of life by attempting to resist oppression and injustice while accommodating themselves to the system. Their marriages had no legal status, but their partnerships seem to have been as loving and stable as those of their masters. Certainly they were acutely conscious of family relationships and responsibilities.

Slave religion, on the surface an untutored form of Christianity tinctured with some African survivals, seemed to most slave owners a useful instrument for teaching meekness and resignation and for providing harmless emotional release, which it sometimes was and did. However, religious meetings, secret and open, provided slaves with the opportunity to organize, which led at times to rebellions and more often to less drastic ways of resisting white domination. Religion also sustained the slaves' sense of their own worth as beings made in the image of

God, and it taught them, therefore, that while human beings can be enslaved in body, their spirits cannot be enslaved without their consent.

Nearly every white observer claimed that slaves were congenitally lazy; George Washington, for example, wrote that "when an overlooker's back is turned, the most of them will slight their work, or be idle altogether." Sarah Gayle, an admirable woman capable of showing real concern for her servants, could convince herself that her "indulgence" had made them all "idle and full of complaints," a charge that her journal, in which she described the activities of her household, totally disproves. If the typical slave was indeed lazy, it can be explained as a rational response to forced, uncompensated labor. As one planter confessed, slaves "are not stimulated to care and industry as white people are, who labor for themselves." "Laziness" was also a reflection of a peasantlike view of the world, one that was a product of their surroundings, not of their servile status. The historian Eugene D. Genovese says that owners might have liked their slaves to behave like clock-punching factory workers, but plantations were not factories, and no one, least of all the masters, punched a clock. "Do as I say, not as I do," is not an effective way of teaching anything. Moreover, it must be remembered that under slavery the "overlooker's back" was rarely turned. Slaves worked long and hard, whatever their innate tendencies might have been.

Observing that slaves often seemed happy and were only rarely overtly rebellious, whites persuaded themselves that most blacks accepted the system without resentment and indeed preferred slavery to the uncertainties of freedom. There was much talk about "loyal and faithful servants." The Civil War, when slaves flocked to the Union lines once assured of freedom and fair treatment, would disabuse them of this illusion.

As slaves rose in price and as northern opposition to the institution grew more vocal, the system hardened perceptibly. Southerners made much of the danger of insurrection. When a plot was uncovered or a revolt took place, instant and savage reprisals resulted. In 1822, after the conspiracy of Denmark Vesey was exposed by informers, 37 slaves were executed and another 30-odd deported, although no overt act of rebellion had occurred. After an uprising in Louisiana, 16 blacks were decapitated, their heads left to rot on poles along the Mississippi as a grim warning.

The Nat Turner revolt in Virginia in 1831 was the most sensational of the slave uprisings; 57 whites lost their lives before it was suppressed. Southerners treated runaways almost as brutally as rebels, though they posed no real threat to whites. The authorities tracked down fugitives with bloodhounds and subjected captives to merciless lashings.

After the Nat Turner revolt, interest in doing away with slavery vanished in the white South. The southern states made it increasingly difficult for masters to free their slaves; during 1859 only about 3,000 in a slave population of nearly 4 million were given their freedom.

Slavery did not flourish in urban settings, and cities did not flourish in societies where slavery was important. Most southern cities were small, and within them, slaves made up a small fraction of the labor force. The existence of slavery goes a long way toward explaining why the South was so rural and why it had so little industry. Blacks were much harder to supervise and control in urban settings. More important, as the historian Barbara Jeanne Fields has explained, there was a "profound basis for antagonism between slavery and urban development." Individual slaves were successfully employed in southern manufacturing plants, but they made up only an insignificant fraction of the South's small industrial labor supply. Wherever there was industrial development, the proportion of slaves in the population was declining.

Southern whites considered the existence of free blacks undesirable, no matter where they lived. The mere fact that they could support themselves disproved the notion that blacks were by nature childlike and shiftless, unable to work efficiently without white guidance. From the whites' point of view, free blacks set a bad example for slaves. At a minimum, the sight of "a vile and lazy free negro lolling in the sun-shine" might make slaves envious. Still worse, it might encourage them to try to escape, and worst of all, the free blacks might help them do so.

Many southern states passed laws aimed at forcing free blacks to emigrate, but these laws were not well enforced. There is ample evidence that the white people of, say, Maryland would have liked to get rid of the state's large free-black population. Free blacks were barred from occupations in which

Slave traders continued to smuggle their cargoes to America long after importation was outlawed. This engraving of the deck of the Wildfire *upon the ship's capture at Key West was published in* Harper's Weekly *in June 1860.*

such a person was ever charged with the possession of contraband goods.

Psychological Effects of Slavery

The injustice of slavery needs no proof; less obvious is the fact that it had a corrosive effect on the personalities of southerners, slave and free alike. By "the making of a human being an animal without hope," the system bore heavily on all slaves' sense of their own worth. Some found the condition absolutely unbearable. They became the habitual runaways who collected whip scars like medals, the "loyal" servants who struck out in rage against a master knowing that the result would be certain death, and the leaders of slave revolts.

Denmark Vesey of South Carolina, even after buying his freedom, could not stomach the subservience demanded of slaves by the system. When he saw Charleston slaves step into the gutter to make way for whites, he taunted them: "You deserve to remain slaves!" For years he preached resistance to his fellows, drawing his texts from the Declaration of Independence and the Bible and promising help from black Haiti. So vehemently did he argue that some of his followers claimed they feared Vesey more than their masters, even more than God. He planned his uprising for five years, patiently working out the details, only to see it aborted at the last moment when a few of his recruits lost their nerve and betrayed him. For Denmark Vesey, death was probably preferable to living with such rage as his soul contained.

Yet Veseys were rare. Most slaves appeared, if not contented, at least resigned to their fate. Many seemed even to accept the whites' evaluation of their inherent abilities and place in society. Of course, in most instances it is impossible to know whether or not this apparent subservience was feigned in order to avoid trouble.

Slaves had strong family and group attachments and a complex culture of their own, maintained, so to speak, under the noses of their masters. By a mixture of subterfuge, accommodation, and passive resistance, they erected subtle defenses against exploitation, achieving a sense of community that helped sustain the psychic integrity of individuals. But slavery discouraged, if it did not extinguish, independent judgment and self-reliance. These

they might cause trouble—no free black could be the captain of a ship, for example—and they were required by law to find a "respectable" white person who would testify as to their "good conduct and character." But whites did not try very hard to expel them, as Professor Fields has shown, because they needed their labor.

Some unscrupulous southerners engaged in smuggling blacks from Africa. About 54,000 slaves were brought to America illegally after the trade was outlawed in 1808, not a very large number relative to the slave population. British, French, Portuguese, and American naval vessels patrolled the African coast continuously. The American navy alone seized more than 50 suspected slavers in the two decades before 1860. However, the fast, shark-like pirate cruisers were hard to catch, and the anti-slave-trade laws were imperfectly worded and unevenly enforced. Many accounts tell of slaves in America long after 1808 with filed teeth, tattoos, and other signs of African origin, yet no one owning

In the 1800s, a few artists recorded scenes of slave life. Benjamin Latrobe called this watercolor "Preparation for the enjoyment of a fine Sunday." In their limited free time, slaves attended religious services, sang, danced, and relaxed with friends and family.

qualities are difficult enough to develop in human beings under the best circumstances; when every element in white society encouraged slaves to let others do their thinking for them, to avoid questioning the status quo, to lead a simple, animal existence, many did so willingly enough. Was this not slavery's greatest shame?

Slavery also warped the whites. Professor Fox-Genovese has shown how slaveholders developed contradictory stereotypes of slave nature. They described black men either as "Sambos" (lazy and subservient) or "Bucks" (superpotent and aggressive), females either as "Mammys" (nurturing and faithful) or "Jezebels" (wanton and seductive). The Sambo image enabled idle slave owners to exact labor from their slaves by brute force and justify their cruel whips by arguing that *black* men were

inherently lazy. Buck, Fox-Genovese argues, was a reversal of the white ideal of a southern cavalier, morally inferior, thus properly kept in bondage. And by picturing black men as sexual threats to white women, slaveholders could avoid facing the fact that they could and often did take advantage of their power to avail themselves of black women. (Estimates of the proportion of the slave population fathered by whites range from 4 to 8 percent.) As for Jezebel, that stereotype "legitimated the wanton behavior of white men by proclaiming black women to be lusty wenches in whom sexual impulse overwhelmed all restraint." By contrast, Mammy was a way that whites "displaced [black women's normal] sexuality into nurture" and "potential hostility into sustenance and love."

The harm done to the slaves by such mental

distortions is obvious. More obscure is the effect on the masters: Self-indulgence is perhaps only contemptible; self-delusion is pitiable and ultimately destructive.

Probably the large majority of owners respected the most fundamental personal rights of their slaves. Indeed, so far as sexual behavior is concerned, there are countless known cases of lasting relationships based on love and mutual respect between owners and what law and the community defined as their property. But the psychological injury inflicted on whites by slavery can be demonstrated without resort to Freudian insights. By associating working for others with servility, it discouraged many poor southerners from hiring out to earn a stake. It provided the weak, the shiftless, and the unsuccessful with a scapegoat that made their own miserable state easier to bear but harder to escape.

More subtly, the patriarchal nature of the slave system reinforced the already existing tendency toward male dominance over wives and children typical of the larger society. For men of exceptional character, the responsibilties of ownership could be ennobling, but for hotheads, alcoholics, or others with psychological problems, the power could be brutalizing, with terrible effects on the whole plantation community, whites and blacks alike.

Aside from its fundamental immorality, slavery caused basically decent people to commit countless petty cruelties. "I feel badly, got very angry and whipped Lavinia," one Louisiana woman wrote in her diary. "O! for government over my temper." But for slavery, she would surely have had better self-control. Similar, though again more subtle, was the interaction of the institution with the American tendency to brag and bluster. "You can manage ordinary niggers by lickin' 'em and by givin' 'em a taste of hot iron once in a while when they're extra ugly," one uncouth Georgian was heard to say at a slave auction shortly before the Civil War. "But if a nigger ever sets himself up against me, I can't never have any patience with him. I just get my pistol and shoot him right down; and that's the best way." With the price of slaves as high as it was, this was probably just talk, but bad talk, harmful to speaker and listener alike. Northern braggarts, perforce, were less objectionable.

Still, braggarts are inconsequential in most social situations; historians need seldom pay them much

heed. However, the finest white southerners were often warped by the institution. Even those who abhorred slavery sometimes let it corrupt their thinking: "I consider the labor of a breeding woman as no object, and that a child raised every 2 years is of more profit than the crop of the best laboring man." This cold calculation came from the pen of the author of the Declaration of Independence.

Manufacturing in the South

Although the temper of southern society discouraged business and commercial activities, considerable manufacturing developed. Small flour and lumber mills flourished. Iron and coal were mined in Virginia, Kentucky, and Tennessee. In the 1850s the Tredegar Iron Works in Richmond did an annual business of about $1 million.

The availability of the raw material and the abundance of waterpower along the Appalachian slopes made it possible to manufacture textiles profitably in the South. By 1825 a thriving factory was functioning at Fayetteville, North Carolina, and soon others sprang up elsewhere in North Carolina and in adjoining states. William Gregg's factory, at Graniteville, South Carolina, established in 1846, was a constant moneymaker. An able propagandist as well as a good businessman, Gregg saw the textile business not only as a source of profit but also as a device for improving the lot of the South's poor whites. He worked hard to weaken the southern prejudice against manufacturing and made his plant a model of benevolent paternalism similar to that of the early mills of Lowell. As with every other industry, however, southern textile manufacturing amounted to very little when compared with that of the North. Gregg employed only about 300 textile workers in 1850, the whole state of South Carolina fewer than 900. Lowell, Massachusetts, had more spindles turning in 1860 than the entire South.

Less than 15 percent of all the goods manufactured in the United States in 1860 came from the South; the region did not really develop an industrial society. Its textile manufacturers depended on the North for machinery, for skilled workers and technicians, for financing, and for insurance. When the English geologist Charles Lyell visited New Orleans in 1846, he was astounded to discover that the thriving city supported not a single book publisher.

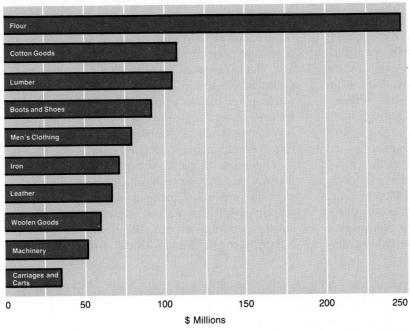

The leading American industries as listed in the 1860 census of manufacturers are ranked here by value of product. The boot and shoe industry employed the most workers—123,000. Next were cotton goods and men's clothing, each with just under 115,000 workers.

TEN LEADING MANUFACTURED PRODUCTS, 1860

Even a local guidebook that he purchased bore a New York imprint.

The Northern Industrial Juggernaut

The most obvious change in the North in the decades before the Civil War was the rapid growth of industry. The best estimates suggest that immediately after the War of 1812, the United States was manufacturing annually less than $200 million worth of goods. In 1859 the northeastern states alone produced $1.27 billion of the national total of almost $2 billion.

Manufacturing expanded in so many directions that it is difficult to portray or to summarize its evolution. The factory system made great strides. The development of rich anthracite coal fields in Pennsylvania was particularly important in this connection. The coal could be floated cheaply on canals to convenient sites and used to produce both heat for smelting and metalworking and steam power to drive machinery. Steam permitted greater flexibility in locating factories and in organizing work within them, and since waterpower was already being used

to capacity, steam was essential for the expansion of output.

American industry displayed a remarkable receptivity to technological change. In *March of the Iron Men*, Roger Burlingame provides a long list of inventions and processes developed between 1825 and 1850, including—besides such obviously important items as the sewing machine, the vulcanization of rubber, and the cylinder press—the screw-making machine, the friction match, the lead pencil, and an apparatus for making soda water. A society in flux put a premium on resourcefulness; an environment that offered so much freedom to the individual encouraged experimentation. The expanding market inspired businessmen to use new techniques. With skilled labor always in short supply, the pressure to substitute machines for trained hands was great.

In the 1820s a foreign visitor noted: "Everything new is quickly introduced here, and all the latest inventions. . . . The moment an American hears the word *invention* he pricks up his ears." Twenty years later a Frenchman wrote: "If they continue to work with the same ardor, they will soon have nothing more to desire or to do. All the mountains will be flattened, the valleys filled, all matter rendered productive." By 1850 the United States led the world in the manufacture of goods that required the use of precision instruments, and in certain industries the country was well on the way toward modern mass production methods. American clocks, pistols, rifles, and locks were outstanding.

The American exhibits at the London Crystal Palace Exhibition of 1851 so impressed the British that they sent two special commissions to the United States to study manufacturing practices. After visiting the Springfield Arsenal, where a worker took apart ten muskets, each made in a different year, mixed up the parts, and then reassembled the guns, each in perfect working order, the British investigators placed a large order for gunmaking ma-

chinery. They also hired a number of American technicians to help organize what became the Enfield rifle factory. They were amazed by the lock and clock factories of New England and by the plants where screws, files, and similar metal objects were turned out in volume by automatic machinery. Instead of resisting new laborsaving machines, the investigators noted, "the workingmen hail with satisfaction all mechanical improvements."

Invention alone does not account for the industrial advance. Every year new natural resources were discovered and made available by the westward march of settlement, and the expansion of agriculture produced an ever-larger supply of raw materials for the mills and factories. Of the ten leading

The 1853 New York Crystal Palace Exhibition celebrated American ingenuity in manufacturing and agriculture. The huge glass and iron building shown in this color lithograph was modeled on London's Crystal Palace. The exhibits displayed impressive examples of American inventions and industrial progress. The building was gutted by fire in 1856.

industries in 1860, eight (flour milling, cotton textiles, lumber, shoes, men's clothing, leather, woolen goods, and liquor) relied on farm products for their raw materials.

In the 1850s the earlier prejudice against the corporation began to break down; by the end of the decade the northern and northwestern states had all passed general incorporation laws. Of course, the corporate device made possible larger accumulations of capital. While the federal government did not charter business corporations, two actions of Congress illustrate the shift in public attitudes. In 1840 a group of scientists sought a federal charter for a National Institution for the Promotion of Science. They were turned down on constitutional grounds; if Congress "went on erecting corporations in this way," one legislator said, "they would come, at last, to have corporations for everything." In 1863, however, the bill creating the National Academy of Science went through both houses without debate.

Industrial growth led to a great increase in the demand for labor. The effects, however, were mixed. Skilled artisans, technicians, and toolmakers earned good wages and found it relatively easy to set themselves up first as independent craftsmen, later as small manufacturers. The expanding frontier drained off much agricultural labor that might otherwise have been attracted to industry, and the thriving new towns of the West absorbed large numbers of eastern artisans of every kind. At the same time, the pay of an unskilled worker was never enough to support a family decently, and the new machines weakened the bargaining power of artisans by making skill less important.

Many other forces acted to stimulate manufacturing. As discussed earlier, immigration increased rapidly in the 1830s and 1840s. An avalanche of strong backs, willing hands, and keen minds descended on the country from Europe. European investors poured large sums into the booming American economy, and the savings of millions of Americans and the great hoard of new California gold added to the supply of capital. Improvements in transportation, the growth of the population, the absence of internal tariff barriers, and the relatively high per capita wealth of the people all meant an ever-expanding market for manufactured goods.

Self-generated Expansion

The pace of the advance is best explained by the many interactions that industrial activity produced. The cotton textile business was clearly the most important example. Samuel Slater built his first machines in his own little plant, but soon the industry spawned dozens of companies devoted to the manufacture of looms, spinning frames, and other machines. They in turn stimulated the growth of machine-tool production, metalworking companies, and eventually the mining and refining of iron. "For a considerable . . . period," George S. Gibb wrote in *Textile Machinery Building in New England, 1813–1849,* "the manufacture of textile machinery appears to have been America's greatest heavy goods industry. . . . From the textile mills and the textile machine shops came the men who supplied most of the tools for the American Industrial Revolution."

Other examples abound. The invention of the sewing machine in 1846 by Elias Howe (who got his early training in a Lowell cotton-machine factory) resulted in the creation of the ready-made clothing industry. The sewing machine also revolutionized the shoe industry, speeding the trend toward factory production and triggering the same kind of secondary growth that occurred in the textile business. The new agricultural machinery business, besides stimulating other industries, made possible a huge expansion of farm production, which stimulated economic growth still more.

A Nation of Immigrants

Rapid industrialization influenced American life in countless ways, none more significant than its effect on the character of the work force and consequently on the structure of society. The jobs created by industrial expansion attracted European immigrants by the tens of thousands. It is a truism that America is a nation of immigrants—even the ancestors of the Indians came to the New World from Asia. But only with the development of nationalism, that is, with the establishment of the independent United States, did the word *immigrant,* meaning a foreign-born resident, come into existence.

The "native" population (native in this case

BOOM AND BUST IN THE EARLY REPUBLIC, 1790–1860

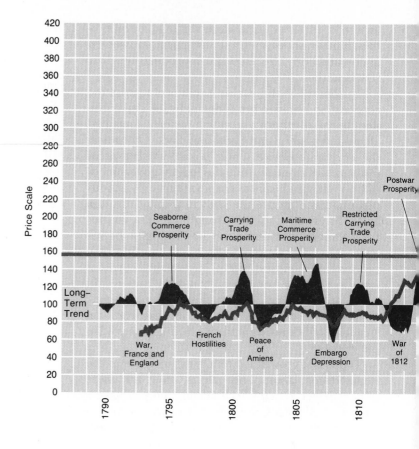

The price scale on the left axis applies to the blue line and shows changes in wholesale commodity prices as they rise above and fall below the base line of 100. During most of this era, wholesale prices were depressed. The base line of 100 is also the long-term trend line for the United States economy as a whole. The peaks and valleys above and below the long-term trend line give a general sense of boom and bust periods. The right axis and green line show, for comparison, the price of a year's tuition at Harvard College. In 1790 it was $24, but by 1860 it had risen to $104.

meaning those whose ancestors had come from Europe rather than the only true native Americans, the Indians) tended to look down on immigrants, and many of the immigrants, in turn, developed prejudices of their own. The Irish, for example, disliked the blacks, with whom they often competed for work. One Irish leader in the old country, Daniel O'Connell, admitted that the American Irish were "among the worst enemies of the colored race." And of course blacks responded with equal bitterness. "Every hour sees us elbowed out of some employment to make room for some newly arrived emigrant from the Emerald Isle, whose hunger and color entitle him to special favor," one of them complained. Antiblack prejudice was less noticeable among other immigrant groups but by no means absent; most immigrants adopted the views of the local majority, which was in every area unfriendly to blacks.

Social and racial rivalries aside, unskilled immigrants caused serious disruptions of economic patterns wherever they appeared. Their absorption

into the factories of New England speeded the disintegration of the system of hiring young farm women. Already competition and technical advances in the textile industry were increasing the pace of the machines and reducing the number of skilled workers needed to run them. Fewer young farm women were willing to work under these conditions. Recent immigrants, who required less "coddling" and who seemed to provide the mills with a "permanent" working force, replaced the women in large numbers. By 1860 Irish immigrants alone made up more than 50 percent of the labor force in the New England mills.

How Wage Earners Lived

The influx of immigrants does not entirely explain the low standard of living of industrial workers during this period. Low wages and the crowding that resulted from the swift expansion of city populations produced slums that would make the most

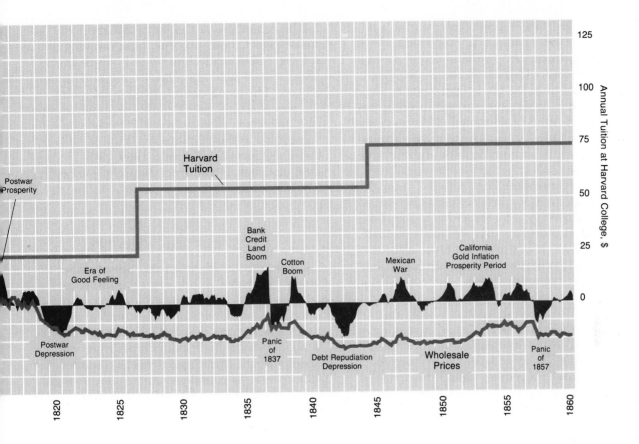

noisome modern ghetto seem a paradise. A Boston investigation in the late 1840s described one district as "a perfect hive of human beings . . . huddled together like brutes." In New York tens of thousands of the poor lived in dark, rank cellars, those in the waterfront districts often invaded by high tides. Tenement houses like great gloomy prisons rose back to back, each with many windowless rooms and often without heat or running water.

Out of doors, city life for the poor was almost equally squalid. Slum streets were littered with garbage and trash. Recreational facilities were almost nonexistent; work on Central Park in New York City, the first important urban park in the country, was not begun until the mid-1850s. Police and fire protection in the cities were pitifully inadequate. "Urban problems" were less critical than a century later only because they affected a smaller part of the population; for those who experienced them, they were, all too often, crushing. In the mid-1850s large numbers of children in New York scrounged a bare existence by begging and scavenging. They took shelter at night in coal bins and empty barrels.

In the early factory towns, most working families maintained small vegetable gardens and a few chickens; low wage rates did not necessarily reflect a low standard of living. But in the new industrial slums even a blade of grass was unusual. In 1851 the editor Horace Greeley's *New York Tribune* published a minimum weekly budget for a family of five. The budget, which allowed nothing for savings, medical bills, recreation, or other amenities (Greeley did include 12 cents a week for newspapers), came to $10.37. Since the weekly pay of a factory hand seldom reached $5, the wives and children of most male factory workers also had to labor in the factories merely to survive. And child labor in the 1850s differed fundamentally from child labor in the 1820s. The pace of the machines had become much faster by then, and the working environment more depressing.

Relatively few workers belonged to unions, but federations of craft unions sprang up in some cities, and during the boom that preceded the Panic of

1837, a National Trades Union representing a few northeastern cities managed to hold conventions. Early in the Jackson era, "workingmen's" political parties enjoyed a brief popularity, occasionally electing a few local officials. These organizations were made up mostly of skilled craftsmen, professional reformers, and even businessmen. They soon expired, destroyed by internal bickering over questions that had little or nothing to do with working conditions.

The depression of the late 1830s led to the demise of most trade unions. Nevertheless, skilled workers improved their lot somewhat in the 1840s and 1850s. The working day declined gradually from about 12½ hours to 10 or 11 hours. Many states passed 10-hour laws and laws regulating child labor, but they were poorly enforced. Most states, however, enacted effective mechanic's lien laws, giving workers first call on the assets of bankrupt and defaulting employers, and the Massachusetts court's decision in the case of *Commonwealth* v. *Hunt* (1842), establishing the legality of labor unions, became a judicial landmark when other state courts followed the precedent.

The flush times of the early 1850s caused the union movement to revive. Many strikes occurred, and a few new national organizations appeared. However, most unions were local institutions, weak and with little control over their membership. The Panic of 1857 dealt the labor movement another body blow. Thus there was no trend toward the general unionization of labor between 1820 and the Civil War.

For this the workers themselves were partly responsible: Craftsmen took little interest in unskilled workers except to keep them down. Few common laborers considered themselves part of a permanent working class with different objectives from those of their employers. Although hired labor had existed throughout the colonial period, it was only with the growth of factories and other large enterprises that significant numbers of people worked for wages. To many, wage labor seemed almost un-American, a violation of the republican values of freedom and independence that had triumphed in the Revolution. Jefferson's professed dislike of urban life was based in part on his fear that people who worked for wages would be so beholden to their employers that they could not act independently.

This republican value system, along with the fluidity of society, the influx of job-hungry immigrants, and the widespread employment of women and children in unskilled jobs, made labor organization difficult. The assumption was that nearly anyone who was willing to work could eventually escape from the wage-earning class. "If any continue through life in the condition of the hired laborer," Abraham Lincoln declared in 1859, "it is . . . because of either a dependent nature which prefers it, or improvidence, folly, or singular misfortune."

Progress and Poverty

Any investigation of American society before the Civil War reveals a paradox that is obvious but difficult to resolve. The United States was a land of opportunity, a democratic society with a prosperous, expanding economy and few class distinctions. Its people had a high standard of living in comparison with the citizens of European countries. Yet within this rich, confident nation there existed a class of miserably underpaid and depressed unskilled workers, mostly immigrants, who were worse off materially than nearly any southern slave. The literature is full of descriptions of needleworkers earning 12 cents a day, of women driven to prostitution because they could not earn a living decently, of hunger marches and soup kitchens, of disease and crime and people sunk into apathy by hopeless poverty. In 1848 more than 56,000 New Yorkers, about a quarter of the population, were receiving some form of public relief. A police drive in that city in 1860 brought in nearly 500 beggars.

The middle-class majority seemed indifferent to or at best unaware of these conditions. Reformers conducted investigations, published exposés, and labored to help the victims of urbanization and industrialization. They achieved little. Great fires burned in these decades to release the incredible energies of America. The poor were the ashes, sifting down silent and unnoticed beneath the dazzle and the smoke. While the industrial revolution was making the United States the most prosperous nation in the world, it was also creating, as the historian Robert H. Bremner has said, "a poverty problem, novel in kind and alarming in size." Industrialization produced poverty and riches (in Marxist terminology, a proletarian class and an aristocracy of capitalists). Tenements sprang up cheek by jowl with the urban palaces of the new rich and the tree-lined streets of the prosperous middle class.

Economic opportunities were great, and taxation was minimal. Little wonder that as the generations passed, the rich got richer. Industrialization accelerated the process and by stimulating the immigration of masses of poor workers skewed the social balance still further. Society became more stratified, and differences in wealth and status among citizens grew greater. But the ideology of egalitarian democracy held its own. By the mid-19th century, Americans were convinced that all men were equal, and indeed all *white* men had equal political rights. Socially and economically, however, the distances between top and bottom were widening. This situation endured for the rest of the century, and in some respects it still endures.

Foreign Commerce

Changes in the pattern of foreign commerce were less noticeable than those in manufacturing but were nevertheless significant. After increasing erratically during the 1820s and 1830s, both imports and exports leapt forward in the next 20 years. The nation remained primarily an exporter of raw materials and an importer of manufactured goods, and in most years it imported more than it exported. Cotton continued to be the most valuable export, in 1860 accounting for a record $191 million of total exports of $333 million. Despite America's own thriving industry, textiles still held the lead among imports, with iron products second. As in earlier days, Great Britain was both the best customer of the United States and its leading supplier.

The success of sailing packets, those "square-riggers on schedule," greatly facilitated the move-

Whaling voyages could last for three years as ships scoured the oceans for sperm whales. Once whales were sighted, crews in whaleboats chased and killed their prey. Here, a carcass has been towed back to the whaler to be stripped of blubber and other valuable parts. The blubber was boiled down into oil. The oil from one sperm whale could fill 45 barrels.

ment of passengers and freight. Fifty-two packets were operating between New York and Europe by 1845, and many more plied between New York and other American ports. The packets accelerated the tendency for trade to concentrate in New York and to a lesser extent in Philadelphia, Baltimore, and New Orleans. The commerce of Boston and smaller New England towns like Providence and New Haven, which had flourished in earlier days, now languished.

New Bedford and a few other southern New England towns shrewdly saved their prosperity by concentrating on whaling, which boomed between 1830 and 1860. The supply of whales seemed unlimited—as indeed it was, given the primitive hunting techniques of the age of sail. By the mid-1850s, with sperm oil selling at more than $1.75 a gallon and the country exporting an average of $2.7 million worth of whale oil and whalebone a year, New Bedford boasted a whaling fleet of well over 300 vessels and a population approaching 25,000.

The whalers ranged the oceans of the world; they lived a hard, lonely life punctuated by moments of exhilaration when they sighted the great mammoths of the deep and drove the harpoon home. They also made magnificent profits. To clear 100 percent in a single voyage was merely routine.

The increase in the volume and value of trade and its concentration at larger ports had a marked effect on the construction of ships. By the 1850s the average vessel was three times the size of those built 30 years earlier. Startling improvements in design, culminating in the long, sleek, white-winged clipper ships, made possible speeds previously undreamed of. Appearing just in time to supply the need for fast transportation to the California gold fields, the clippers cut sailing time around Cape Horn to San Francisco from five or six months to three, the record of 89 days being held jointly by the *Andrew Jackson* and Donald McKay's famous *Flying Cloud*. Another McKay-designed clipper, *Champion of the Seas*, once logged 465 nautical miles in 24 hours, far in excess of the best efforts of modern yachts. To achieve such speeds, cargo capacity had to be sacrificed, making clippers uneconomical for carrying the bulky produce that was the mainstay of commerce. But for specialty goods, in their brief heyday the clippers were unsurpassed. Hong Kong merchants, never known for extravagance, willingly

paid 75 cents a cubic foot to ship tea by clipper to London even though slower vessels charged only 28 cents. In the early 1850s clippers sold for as much as $150,000; with decent luck a ship might earn its full cost in a voyage or two.

Steam Conquers the Atlantic

The reign of the clipper ship was short. Like so many other things, ocean commerce was being mechanized. Steamships conquered the high seas more slowly than the rivers because early models were unsafe in rough waters and uneconomical. A riverboat could take on fuel along its route, whereas an Atlantic steamer had to carry tons of coal across the ocean, thereby reducing its capacity for cargo. However, by the late 1840s, steamships were capturing most of the passenger traffic, mail contracts, and first-class freight. These vessels could not keep up with the clippers in a heavy breeze, but their average speed was far greater, especially on the westward voyage against the prevailing winds. Steamers were soon crossing the Atlantic in less than ten days. Nevertheless, for very long voyages, such as the 15,000-mile haul around South America to California, fast-sailing ships held their own for many years.

The steamship, and especially the iron ship, which had greater cargo-carrying capacity and was stronger and less costly to maintain, took away the advantages that American shipbuilders had held since colonial times. American lumber was cheap, but the British excelled in iron technology. Although the United States invested about $14.5 million in subsidies for the shipping industry, the funds were not employed intelligently and did little good. In 1858 government efforts to aid shipping were abandoned.

The combination of competition, government subsidy, and technological advance drove down shipping rates. Between the mid-1820s and the mid-1850s the cost of moving a pound of cotton from New York to Liverpool fell from 1 cent to about a third of a cent. Transatlantic passengers could obtain the best accommodations on the fastest ships for under $200, good accommodations on slower packets for as little as $75.

Rates were especially low for European emi-

Commerce on the lower Mississippi depended heavily on steamboats, because railroads were far less extensive in the South than in the North.

grants willing to travel to America on cargo vessels. By the 1840s at least 4,000 ships were engaged in carrying bulky American cotton and Canadian lumber to Europe. On their return trips with manufactured goods they had much unoccupied space, which they converted into rough quarters for passengers. Conditions on these ships were crowded, gloomy, and foul. Frequently, epidemics took a fearful toll among steerage passengers. On one crossing of the ship *Lark*, 158 of 440 passengers died of typhus.

Yet without this cheap means of transportation, thousands of poor immigrants would simply have remained at home. Bargain freight rates also help explain the clamor of American manufacturers for high tariffs, for transportation costs added relatively little to the price of European goods.

Canals and Railroads

Another dramatic change was the shift in the direction of the nation's internal commerce and its immense increase. From the time of the first settlers in the Mississippi Valley, the Great River had controlled the flow of goods from farm to market. The completion of the Erie Canal in 1825 heralded a shift, speeded by the feverish canal construction of the following decade. In 1830 there were 1,277 miles of canal in the United States; by 1840 there were 3,326 miles.

Each year saw more western produce moving to market through the canals. In 1845 the Erie was still drawing over two-thirds of its west-east traffic from within New York, but by 1847, despite the fact that this local business held steady, more than half of its traffic came from west of Buffalo, and by 1851 more than two-thirds. The volume of western commerce over the Erie in 1851 amounted to more than 20 times what it had been in 1836, while the value of western goods reaching New Orleans in this period increased only $2\frac{1}{2}$ times.

The expanding traffic and New York's enormous share of it caused businessmen in other eastern cities whose canal projects had been unsuccessful to respond promptly when a new means of transport, the railroad, became available. The first railroads were built in England in the 1820s. In 1830 the first American line, the ambitiously named Baltimore and Ohio Railroad, carried 80,000 passengers over a 13-mile stretch of track. By 1833 Charleston, South Carolina, had a line reaching 136 miles to Hamburg, on the Savannah River. Two years later the cars began rolling on the Boston and

Worcester Railroad. The Panic of 1837 slowed construction, but by 1840 the United States had 3,328 miles of track, equal to the canal mileage and nearly double the railroad mileage of all Europe.

The first railroads did not compete with the canals for intersectional traffic. The through connections needed to move goods economically over great distances materialized slowly. Of the 6,000 miles of track operating in 1848, nearly all lay east of the Appalachians, and little of it had been coordinated into railroad systems. The intention of most early builders had been to monopolize the trade of surrounding districts, not to establish connections with competing centers. Frequently, railroads used tracks of different widths deliberately to prevent other lines from tying into their tracks.

Engineering problems held back growth. Steep grades and sharp curves—unavoidable in many parts of the country if the cost of the roads was not to be prohibitive—required more powerful and flexible engines than yet existed. Sparks from wood-burning locomotives caused fires. Wooden rails topped with strap iron wore out quickly and broke loose under the weight and vibration of heavy cars. In time the iron T rail and the use of crossties set in loose gravel to reduce vibration increased the durability of the tracks and made possible heavier, more efficient equipment. Modifications in the design of locomotives enabled the trains to negotiate sharp curves. Engines that could burn hard coal appeared, thereby eliminating the danger of starting fires along the right-of-way and reducing fuel costs.

Between 1848 and 1852 railroad mileage nearly doubled. Three years later it had doubled again, and by 1860 the nation had 30,636 miles of track. During this extraordinary burst of activity, four companies drove lines of gleaming iron from the Atlantic seaboard to the great interior valley. In 1851 the Erie, longest road in the world with 537 miles of track, linked the Hudson River north of New York City with Dunkirk on Lake Erie. Late the next year the Baltimore and Ohio reached the Ohio River at Wheeling, and in 1853 a banker named Erastus Corning consolidated eight short lines connecting Albany and Buffalo to form the New York Central. Finally, in 1858 the Pennsylvania Railroad completed a line across the mountains from Philadelphia to Pittsburgh.

In the states beyond the Appalachians, building went on at an even more feverish pace. In the 1850s builders in Ohio laid more than 2,300 miles of track, in Illinois more than 2,600, in Wisconsin nearly 900. By 1855 passengers could travel from Chicago or St. Louis to the East Coast at a cost of $20 to $30, the trip taking, with luck, less than 48 hours. A generation earlier such a trip required two to three weeks. Construction was slower in the South: Mississippi laid about 800 miles, Alabama 600.

Financing the Railroads

Railroad building required immense amounts of labor and capital at a time when many other demands for these resources existed. Immigrants or (in the South) slaves did most of the heavy work. Raising the necessary money proved a more complex task.

Private investors supplied about three-quarters of the money invested in railroads before 1860, more than $800 million in the 1850s alone. Much of this capital came from local merchants and businessmen and from farmers along the proposed rights-of-way. Funds were easy to raise because subscribers seldom had to lay out the full price of their stock at one time; instead they were subject to periodic "calls" for a percentage of their commitment as construction progressed. If the road made money, much of the additional mileage could be paid for out of earnings from the first sections built. The Utica and Schenectady Railroad, one of the lines that became part of the New York Central, was capitalized in 1833 at $2 million (20,000 shares at $100). Only $75 per share was ever called; in 1844 the road had been completed, shares were selling at $129, and shareholders were receiving handsome cash dividends.

The Utica and Schenectady was a short road in a rich territory; for less favorably situated lines, stocks were hard to sell. Of the lines connecting the seaboard with the Middle West, the New York Central alone needed no public aid, chiefly because it ran through prosperous, well-populated country and across level terrain. The others were all "mixed enterprises," drawing about half their capital from state and local governments.

Public aid took many forms. Towns, counties, and the states themselves lent money to railroads and invested in their stock. Special privileges, such as exemption from taxation and the right to condemn property, were often granted, and in a few cases states built and operated roads as public corporations.

As with earlier internal improvement proposals, federal financial aid to railroads was usually blocked in Congress by a combination of eastern and southern votes. But in 1850 a scheme for granting federal lands to the states to build a line from Lake Michigan to the Gulf of Mexico passed both houses. The main beneficiary was the Illinois Central Railroad, which received a 200-foot right-of-way and alternate strips of land along the track 1 mile wide and 6 miles deep, a total of almost 2.6 million acres. By mortgaging this land and by selling portions of it to farmers, the Illinois Central raised nearly all the $23.4 million it spent on construction. The success of this operation led to additional grants of almost 20 million acres in the 1850s, benefiting more than 40 railroads. Far larger federal grants were made after the Civil War, when the transcontinental lines were built.

Frequently, the capitalists who promoted railroads were more concerned with making money out of the construction of the lines than with operating them. The banker Erastus Corning was a good railroad man; his lines were well maintained and efficiently run. Yet he was also mayor of Albany, an important figure in state and national politics, and a manufacturer of iron. He accepted no salary as president of the Utica and Schenectady, "asking only that he have the privilege of supplying all the rails, running gear, tools and other iron and steel articles used." When he could not himself produce rails of the proper quality, he purchased them in England, charging the railroad a commission for his services. Corning's actions led to stockholder complaints, and a committee was appointed to investigate. He managed to control this group easily enough, but it did report that "the practice of buying articles for the use of the Railroad Company from its own officers might in time come to lead to abuses of great magnitude." The prediction proved all too accurate in the generation following the Civil War.

Corning, it must be emphasized, was honest enough; his mistake, if mistake it was, lay in overestimating his own impartiality a little. Others in the business were unashamedly crooked and avidly took advantage of the public passion for railroads.

ILLINOIS CENTRAL RAILROAD COMPANY
OFFER FOR SALE
ONE MILLION ACRES OF SUPERIOR FARMING LANDS,
IN FARMS OF
40, 80 & 160 acres and upwards at from $8 to $12 per acre.
THESE LANDS ARE
NOT SURPASSED BY ANY IN THE WORLD.
THEY LIE ALONG
THE WHOLE LINE OF THE CENTRAL ILLINOIS RAILROAD,
For Sale on LONG CREDIT, SHORT CREDIT and for CASH, they are situated near TOWNS,
VILLAGES, SCHOOLS and CHURCHES.

This Illinois Central advertisement offers land for sale along its right of way. By encouraging settlement, railroads helped develop the lands beyond the Appalachians. By mid-century, a network of rail lines crisscrossed the Northeast and Midwest, hauling freight and passengers between rural and urban areas.

Some officials issued stock to themselves without paying for it and then sold the shares to gullible investors. Others manipulated the books of their corporations and set up special construction companies and paid them exorbitant returns out of railroad assets. These practices did not become widespread until after the Civil War, but all of them first sprang up in the period now under discussion. At the same time that the country was first developing a truly national economy, it was also producing its first really big-time crooks.

Railroads and the Economy

The effects of so much railroad construction were profound. Though the main reason that farmers put more land under the plow was an increase in the price of agricultural products, the railroad helped determine just what land was used and how profitably it could be farmed. Much of the fertile prairie through which the Illinois Central ran had been available for settlement for many years before 1850, but development had been slow because it was remote from navigable waters and had no timber. In 1840 the three counties immediately northeast of Springfield had a population of about 8,500. They produced about 59,000 bushels of wheat and 690,000 bushels of corn. In the next decade the region grew slowly by the standards of that day: The three counties had about 14,000 people in 1850 and produced 71,000 bushels of wheat and 2.2 million bushels of corn. Then came the railroad and with it an agricultural revolution. By 1860 the population of the three counties had soared to over 38,000, wheat production had topped 550,000 bushels, and corn 5.7 million bushels. "Land-grant" railroads such as the Illinois Central stimulated agricultural expansion by advertising their lands widely and selling farm sites at low rates on liberal terms.

Access to world markets gave the farmers of the upper Mississippi Valley an incentive to increase output. Land was plentiful and cheap, but farm labor was scarce; consequently, agricultural wages rose sharply, especially after 1850. New tools and machines appeared in time to ease the labor shortage. First came the steel plowshare, invented by John Deere, a Vermont-born blacksmith who had moved to Illinois in 1837. The prairie sod was tough and sticky, but Deere's smooth metal plows cut through it easily. In 1839 Deere turned out ten such plows in his little shop in Moline, Illinois. By 1857 he was selling 10,000 a year.

Still more important was the perfection of the mechanical reaper, for wheat production was limited more by the amount that farmers could handle during the brief harvest season than by the acreage they could plant and cultivate. The major figure in the development of the reaper was Cyrus Hall McCormick. McCormick's horse-drawn reaper bent the grain against the cutting knife and then deposited it neatly on a platform, whence it could easily be raked into windrows. With this machine, two workers could cut 14 times as much wheat as with scythes.

McCormick prospered, but despite his patents, he could not keep other manufacturers out of the business. Competition led to continual improvement of the machines and kept prices within the reach of most farmers. Installment selling added to demand. By 1860 nearly 80,000 reapers had been sold; their efficiency helps explain why wheat output rose by nearly 75 percent in the 1850s.

The railroad had an equally powerful impact on American cities. The eastern seaports benefited, and so did countless intermediate centers, such as Buffalo and Cincinnati. But no city was affected more profoundly by railroads than Chicago. In 1850 not a single line had reached there; five years later it was terminal for 2,200 miles of track and controlled the commerce of an imperial domain. By extending half a dozen lines west to the Mississippi, it drained off nearly all the river traffic north of St. Louis. The Illinois Central sucked the expanding output of the prairies into Chicago as well. Most of this freight went eastward over the new railroads or on the Great Lakes and the Erie Canal. Nearly 350,000 tons of shipping plied the lakes by 1855.

The railroads, like the textile industry, stimulated other kinds of economic activity. They transformed agriculture, as we have seen; both real estate values and buying and selling of land increased whenever the iron horse puffed into a new district. The railroads spurred regional concentration of industry and an increase in the size of business units. Their insatiable need for capital stimulated the growth of investment banking. The complexity of their operations made them, as the historian Alfred

Cyrus McCormick invented his mechanical reaper on his father's farm in Virginia. However, he built his first factory in Chicago in 1847 and was soon supplying reapers to the rapidly expanding farms of the Midwest. The McCormick Reaper Factory, above, helped make Chicago the capital of the farm-machinery industry.

D. Chandler, Jr., writes, "the first modern business enterprises," the first to employ large numbers of salaried managers and to develop "a large internal organizational structure with carefully defined lines of responsibility."

Although they apparently did not have much effect on general manufacturing before the Civil War, the roads consumed nearly half the nation's output of bar and sheet iron in 1860. Probably more labor and more capital were occupied in economic activities resulting from the development of railroads than in the roads themselves—another way of saying that the railroads were immensely valuable internal improvements.

The proliferation of trunk lines and the competition of the canal system (for many products the slowness of canal transportation was not a serious handicap) led to a sharp decline in freight and passenger rates. Periodically, railroads engaged in "wars" to capture business. At times a person could travel from New York to Buffalo for as little as

$4; anthracite was being shipped from the Pennsylvania mines to the coast for $1.50 a ton. The Erie Canal reduced its toll charges by more than two-thirds in the face of railroad competition, and the roads in turn cut rates drastically until, on the eve of the Civil War, it cost less than 1 cent per ton-mile to send produce through the canal and only slightly more than 2 cents a mile on the railroads. By that time one could ship a bushel of wheat from Chicago to New York by railroad for less than 35 cents.

Cheap transportation had a revolutionary effect on western agriculture. Farmers in Iowa could now raise grain to feed the factory workers of Lowell and even of Manchester, England. Two-thirds of the meat consumed in New York City was soon arriving by rail from beyond the Appalachians. The center of American wheat production shifted westward to Illinois, Wisconsin, and Indiana. When the Crimean War (1853–1856) and European crop failures increased foreign demand, these regions boomed. Success bred success for farmers and for the railroads. Profits earned carrying wheat enabled the roads to build feeder lines that opened up still wider areas to commercial agriculture and made it easy to bring in lumber, farm machinery, household furnishings, and the settlers themselves at low cost.

Railroads and the Sectional Conflict

Increased production and cheap transportation boosted the western farmer's income and standard of living. The days of isolation and self-sufficiency, even for the family on the edge of the frontier, rapidly disappeared. Pioneers quickly became operators of businesses and, to a far greater extent than their forbears, consumers, buying all sorts of manufactured articles that their ancestors had made for themselves or done without. This had its cost. Like southern planters, they now became dependent on middlemen and lost some of their feeling of self-reliance. Overproduction became a problem. It began to take more capital to buy a farm, for as profits increased, so did the price of land. Machinery was an additional expense. The proportion of farm laborers and tenants increased.

The linking of East and West had fateful effects on politics. The increased ease of movement from section to section and the ever-more-complex social and economic integration of East and West stimulated nationalism and thus became a force for the preservation of the Union. Without the railroads and canals, Illinois and Iowa would scarcely have dared to side against the South in 1861. When the Mississippi ceased to be essential to them, citizens of the upper valley could afford to be more hostile to slavery and especially to its westward extension. Economic ties with the Northeast reinforced cultural connections.

The South might have preserved its influence in the Northwest if it had pressed forward its own railroad-building program. It failed to do so. There were many southern lines but nothing like a southern system. As late as 1856 one could get from Memphis to Richmond or Charleston only by very indirect routes. As late as 1859 the land-grant road extending the Illinois Central to Mobile, Alabama,

was not complete, nor did any economical connection exist between Chicago and New Orleans.

This state of affairs could be accounted for in part by the scattered population of the South, the paucity of passenger traffic, the seasonal nature of much of the freight business, and the absence of large cities. Southerners placed too much reliance on the Mississippi: The fact that traffic on the river continued heavy throughout the 1850s blinded them to the precipitous rate at which their relative share of the nation's trade was declining. But the fundamental cause of the South's backwardness in railroad construction was the attitude of its leaders. Southerners of means were no more interested in commerce than in industry; their capital found other outlets.

The Economy on the Eve of the Civil War

Between the mid-1840s and the mid-1850s the United States experienced one of the most remarkable periods of growth in the history of the world. Every economic indicator surged forward: manufacturing, grain and cotton production, population, railroad mileage, gold production, sales of public land. The building of the railroads stimulated business, and by making transportation cheaper, the completed lines energized the nation's economy. The American System that Henry Clay had dreamed of arrived with a rush just as Clay was passing from the scene.

Inevitably, this growth caused dislocations that were aggravated by the boom psychology that once again infected the popular mind. In 1857 there was a serious collapse. The return of Russian wheat to the world market after the Crimean War caused grain prices to fall. This checked agricultural expansion, which hurt the railroads and cut down on the demand for manufactures. Unemployment increased. Frightened depositors started runs on banks, most of which had to suspend specie payments.

People called this abrupt downturn the Panic of 1857. Yet the vigor of the economy was such that the bad times did not last long. The upper Mississippi Valley suffered most, for so much new land

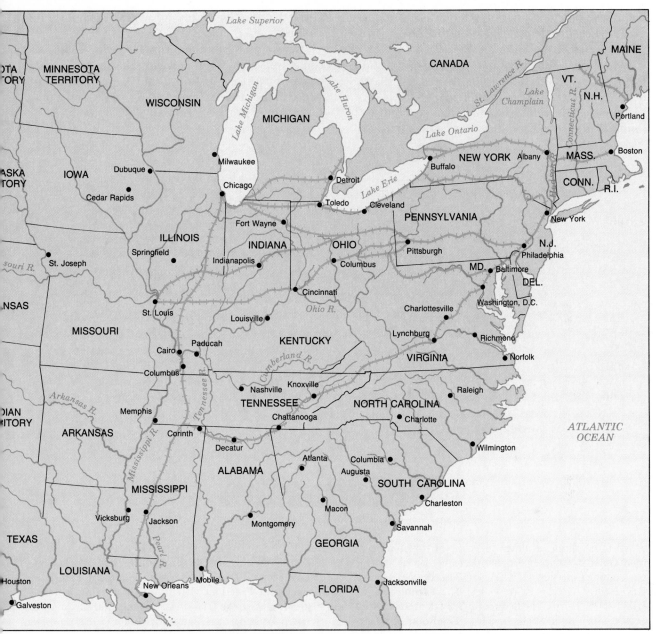

PRIMARY RAILROADS, 1860

*This map shows trunk lines (lines carrying through traffic) in operation in
1860. Certain towns and cities owed their spectacularly rapid growth to the railroad, Chicago being an outstanding example. The map suggests the strong influence of the railroads on the expansion and economic prosperity of smaller cities
such as Fort Wayne, Milwaukee, and Nashville. At the outbreak of the Civil
War in 1861, the relative lack of railroads in the South was a bad omen for the
Confederacy. Note especially the gap at Chattanooga.*

had been opened up that supplies of farm produce greatly exceeded demand. Elsewhere conditions improved rapidly.

The South, somewhat out of the hectic rush to begin with, was affected very little by the collapse of 1857, for cotton prices continued high. This gave planters the false impression that their economy was immune to such violent downturns. Some began to argue that the South would be better off out of the Union.

Before a new national upward swing could become well established, however, the sectional crisis between North and South shook people's confidence in the future. Then the war came, and a new set of forces shaped economic development.

Milestones

1808	Congress bans further importation of slaves
1822	"Conspiracy" of Denmark Vesey
1825	Erie Canal completed
1830	Baltimore and Ohio Railroad begins operation
1831	Nat Turner's slave uprising
1837	Cyrus Hall McCormick opens reaper factory in Chicago
1839	John Deere begins manufacturing steel plows
1840–1857	Boom in manufacturing, railroad construction, and foreign commerce
1842	*Commonwealth* v. *Hunt* establishes the legality of unions
1846	Elias Howe invents the sewing machine
1850	Congress grants land to aid construction of the Illinois Central Railroad
1854	Clipper ship *Flying Cloud* sails from New York to San Francisco in 89 days
1857	Brief economic depression (Panic of 1857)

SUPPLEMENTARY READING

Titles marked with an asterisk have been published in paperback.

Most of the volumes dealing with economic developments mentioned in Chapter 8 continue to be useful for this period. See especially G. R. Taylor, **The Transportation Revolution*** (1951), P. W. Gates, **The Farmer's Age*** (1960), D. C. North, **The Economic Growth of the United States*** (1961), and Stuart Bruchey, **The Roots of American Economic Growth*** (1965). On the Panic of 1857, see J. L. Huston, **The Panic of 1857 and the Coming of the Civil War** (1987).

An excellent survey of the antebellum South is Clement Eaton, **The Growth of Southern Civilization*** (1961). For more detailed coverage, see Gavin Wright, **The Political Economy of the Cotton South** (1978).

The literature on slavery is extensive and of high quality. See especially K. M. Stampp, **The Peculiar Institution*** (1956), E. D. Genovese, **Roll, Jordan, Roll*** (1975), Elizabeth Fox-Genovese, **Within the Plantation House-** hold* (1988), J. W. Blassingame, **The Slave Community*** (1972), L. W. Levine, **Black Culture and Black Consciousness** (1977), H. G. Gutman, **The Black Family in Slavery and Freedom** (1976), and Catharine Clinton, **Plantation Mistress** (1984). Among specialized volumes, Bertram Wyatt-Brown, **Southern Honor** (1982), and Ira Berlin, **Slaves Without Masters** (1975), provide important information about free blacks. On slave insurrections, E. D. Genovese, **From Rebellion to Revolution** (1979), and S. B. Oates, **The Fires of Jubilee: Nat Turner's Fierce Rebellion** (1975), are excellent. R. C. Wade, **Slavery in the Cities*** (1964), contains much interesting material, as does W. K. Scarborough, **The Overseer** (1966).

On industrial developments, in addition to the books mentioned in Chapter 9, see H. J. Habbakuk, **American and British Technology in the Nineteenth Century*** (1962), and Nathan Rosenberg, **Technology and Amer-**

ican **Economic Growth** (1972). On labor history, see Thomas Dublin, **Women at Work** (1977), R. A. Mohl, **Poverty in New York** (1971), and B. M. Wertheimer, **We Were There** (1977). For detals on workingmen's political activities, see Edward Pessen, **Most Uncommon Jacksonians*** (1967).

Immigration is dealt with in M. A. Jones, **American Immigration*** (1960), poverty in R. H. Bremner, **From the Depths*** (1956), and in Mohl's **Poverty in New York.** Taylor's **Transportation Revolution** is outstanding on de-velopments in commerce and communication. J. F. Stover, **Iron Road to the West** (1978), provides a good survey of railroad building in the 1850s. Among the specialized studies of railroad development are T. C. Cochran, **Railroad Leaders** (1953), P. W. Gates, **The Illinois Central Railroad and its Colonization Work** (1934), E. C. Kirkland, **Men, Cities, and Transportation** (1948), and Albert Fishlow, **American Railroads and the Transformation of the Ante-Bellum Economy** (1965).

XV

The Coming of the Civil War

"A house divided against itself cannot stand." I believe this government cannot endure permanently half slave and half free. I do not expect the Union to be dissolved; I do not expect the house to fall; but I do expect it will cease to be divided. It will become all one thing, or all the other.

ABRAHAM LINCOLN, *June 17, 1858*

The political settlement between North and South that Henry Clay designed in 1850 lasted only four years. One specific event wrecked it, but it was probably doomed in any case. Americans continued to migrate westward by the thousands, and as long as slaveholders could carry their human property into federally controlled territories, northern resentment would smolder. Slaves continued to seek freedom in the North, and the stronger federal Fugitive Slave Act did not guarantee their capture and return. Abolitionists intensified their propaganda.

The Slave Power Comes North

The new fugitive slave law encouraged more southerners to try to recover escaped slaves. Something approaching panic reigned in the black communities of northern cities after its passage. Thousands of blacks, not all of them former slaves, fled to Canada, but many remained. A few were arrested, generally without incident. However, not all the captives were in fact runaways, and northerners frequently refused to stand aside while these people were dragged off in chains.

Shortly after the passage of the act, a New Yorker, James Hamlet, was seized, convicted, and rushed off to slavery in Maryland without even being allowed to communicate with his wife and children. The New York black community was outraged, and with help from white neighbors it swiftly raised $800 to buy his freedom. In 1851 Euphemia Williams, who had lived for years as a free woman in Pennsylvania, was seized, her presumed owner claiming also her six children, all Pennsylvania-born. A federal judge released the Williamses, but the case caused alarm in the North.

Abolitionists often interfered with the enforcement of the law. When two Georgians came to Boston to reclaim William and Ellen Craft, admitted fugitives, a "vigilance committee" forced them to return home empty-handed. The Crafts prudently—or perhaps in disgust—decided to leave the United States for England. Early in 1851 a Virginia agent captured Frederick "Shadrach" Wilkins, a waiter in a Boston coffeehouse. While Wilkins was being held for deportation, a mob of blacks broke into the courthouse and freed him. That October a slave named Jerry, who had escaped from Missouri, was arrested in Syracuse, New York. Within minutes the whole town had the news. Crowds surged through the streets, and when night fell, a mob smashed into the building where Jerry was being held and spirited him away to safety in Canada.

Such incidents exacerbated sectional feelings. Southerners accused the North of reneging on one of the main promises made in the Compromise of 1850, while the sight of harmless human beings being hustled off to a life of slavery disturbed many northerners who were not abolitionists. Although most white northerners were probably not prepared to break it, in some states the Fugitive Slave Act became virtually unenforceable. Massachusetts passed a strong personal liberty law. When a newspaperman in Wisconsin was convicted of raising a mob to free a captured runaway, the state supreme court declared the Fugitive Slave Act unconstitutional and released him. After long delays the United States Supreme Court overruled this decision (*Ableman* v. *Booth*, 1859), but in the meantime the act was a dead letter in Wisconsin and in other states as well. In all, in the decade of the act's existence, about 300 fugitives were returned to their owners. In the process far larger numbers of white northerners got an eyewitness view of the heart-lessness of slavery.

"Uncle Tom's Cabin"

Tremendously important in increasing sectional tensions and bringing home the evils of slavery to still more people in the North was Harriet Beecher Stowe's novel *Uncle Tom's Cabin* (1852). Stowe was neither a professional writer nor an abolitionist, and she had almost no firsthand knowledge of slavery. But her conscience had been roused by the Fugitive Slave Act. In gathering material for the book, she depended heavily on abolitionist writers, many of whom she knew. She dashed it off quickly; as she later recalled, it seemed to write itself. Nevertheless, *Uncle Tom's Cabin* was an enormous success: 10,000

A poster advertising Uncle Tom's Cabin *in 1852, the year of its publication. The following year, Stowe published* A Key to Uncle Tom's Cabin, *intended to provide documentary evidence in support of disputed details of her indictment of slavery.*

copies were sold in a week, 300,000 in a year. It was translated into dozens of languages. Dramatized versions were staged in countries throughout the world.

Harriet Beecher Stowe was hardly a distinguished writer; it was her approach to the subject that explains the book's success. Her tale of the pious, patient slave Uncle Tom, the saintly white child Eva, and the callous slave driver Simon Legree appealed to an audience far wider than that reached by the abolitionists. She avoided the self-righteous, accusatory tone of most abolitionist tracts and did not seek to convert readers to belief in racial equality. Many of her southern white characters were fine, sensitive people, while the cruel Simon Legree was a transplanted Connecticut Yankee. There were many heartrending scenes of pain, self-sacrifice, and heroism. The story proved especially effective on the stage: The slave Eliza crossing the frozen Ohio River to freedom, the death of Little Eva, Eva and Tom ascending to Heaven—these scenes left audiences in tears.

Southern critics pointed out, correctly enough, that Stowe's picture of plantation life was distorted, her slaves atypical. They called her a "coarse, ugly, long-tongued woman" and accused her of trying to "awaken rancorous hatred and malignant jealousies" that would undermine national unity. Most northerners, having little basis on which to judge the accuracy of the book, tended to discount southern criticism as biased. In any case, *Uncle Tom's Cabin* raised questions that transcended the issue of accuracy. Did it matter if every slave was not as kindly as Uncle Tom, as determined as George Harris? What if only one white master was as evil as Simon Legree? No earlier white American writer had looked at slaves as people.

Uncle Tom's Cabin touched the hearts of millions. Some became abolitionists; others, still hesitating to step forward, asked themselves as they put the book down: Is slavery just?

"Young America"

Clearly, a distraction was needed to help keep the lid on sectional troubles. Some people hoped to find one in foreign affairs. The spirit of manifest destiny explains this in large part; once the United States had reached the Pacific, expansionists began to think of transmitting the dynamic, democratic spirit of the United States to other countries by aiding local revolutionaries, opening up new markets, perhaps even annexing foreign lands.

This "Young America" spirit was partly emotional, a mindless confidence that democracy would triumph everywhere, that public opinion was "stronger than the Bayonet." At the time of the European revolutions of 1848, Americans talked freely about helping the liberals in their struggles against autocratic governments. Horace Greeley's *New York Tribune* predicted that Europe would soon become "one great and splendid Republic . . . and we shall all be citizens of the world." When the Austrians crushed a rebellion in Hungary, Secretary of State Daniel Webster addressed an insulting note full of vague threats to the Austrian chargé d'affaires in Washington. Hungarian revolutionary hero Louis Kossuth visited the United States in search of aid in 1851 and 1852; President Fillmore put U.S.S. *Mississippi* at his disposal, and great crowds turned out to cheer him.

The United States had no intention of going to war to win independence for the Hungarians, as Kossuth soon learned to his sorrow. However, the same democratic-expansionist sentiment led to dreams of conquests in the Caribbean area. In 1855 a freebooter named William Walker, backed by an American company engaged in transporting migrants to California across Central America, seized control of Nicaragua and elected himself president. He was ousted two years later but made repeated attempts to regain control until, in 1860, he died before a Honduran firing squad. Another would-be dictator, "General" George W. L. Bickley, claiming that he was disturbed by that "crookedest of all boundary lines, the Rio Grande," tried to organize an expedition to conquer Mexico.

Though many northerners suspected them of engaging in plots to obtain more territory for slavery, Walker and Bickley were primarily adventurers trying to use the prevailing mood of buoyant expansionism for selfish ends. But there were reasons unreleated to slavery why Central America suddenly seemed important. The rapid development of California created a need for improved communication with the West Coast. A canal across Central America would cut weeks from the sailing time between New York and San Francisco. In 1850 Secretary of State John M. Clayton and the British minister to the United States, Henry Lytton Bulwer, negotiated a treaty providing for the demilitarization and joint Anglo-American control of any canal across the isthmus.

As this area assumed strategic importance to the

MASTER JONATHAN TRIES TO SMOKE A CUBA, BUT IT DOESN'T AGREE WITH HIM!!

Despite opposition from European nations, expansionists in the United States believed Cuba should become an American possession. In 1850, a small private army left New Orleans for Cuba. The invaders were soon forced to flee. In this Punch *cartoon, the British delight in the failure of Master Jonathan—the United States—to seize Cuba.*

United States, the desire to obtain Cuba grew stronger. In 1854 President Franklin Pierce instructed his minister to Spain, Pierre Soulé of Louisiana, to offer $130 million for the island. Since Soulé was a hotheaded bungler, the administration arranged for him first to confer in Belgium with the American ministers to Great Britain and France, James Buchanan and John Y. Mason, to work out a plan for persuading Spain to sell. Out of this meeting came the Ostend Manifesto, a confidential dispatch to the State Department suggesting that if Spain refused to sell Cuba, "the great law of self-preservation" might justify "wresting" it from Spain by force.

News of the manifesto leaked out, and it had to be published. Northern opinion was outraged by this "slaveholders' plot." Europeans claimed to be shocked by such "dishonorable" and "clandestine" diplomacy. The government had to disavow the manifesto, and any hope of obtaining Cuba or any other territory in the Caribbean vanished.

The expansionist mood of the moment also explains President Fillmore's dispatching an expedition under Commodore Matthew C. Perry to try for commercial concessions in the isolated kingdom of Japan in 1852. Perry's expedition was a great success. The Japanese, impressed by American naval power, agreed to establish diplomatic relations. In 1858 an American envoy, Townsend Harris, negotiated a commercial treaty that opened to American ships six Japanese ports heretofore closed to foreigners. President Pierce's negotiation of a Canadian reciprocity treaty with Great Britain in 1854 and an unsuccessful attempt, also made under

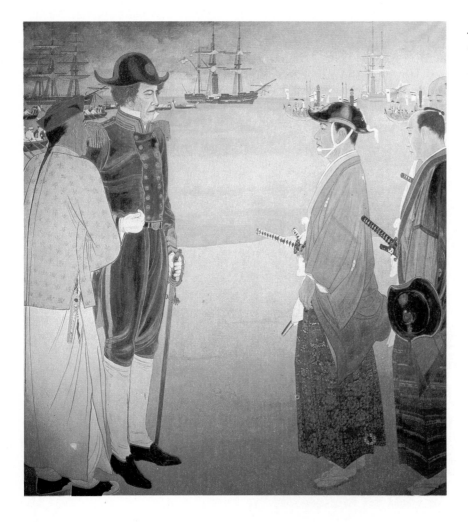

Japanese artist Gessan Ogata painted this watercolor of Commodore Perry's "First landing at Kurihama, July 14, 1853." The "black ships" of Perry's squadron are in the background.

Pierce, to annex the Hawaiian Islands are further demonstrations of the assertive foreign policy of the period.

The Little Giant

The most prominent spokesman of the Young America movement was Stephen A. Douglas. The senator from Illinois was the Henry Clay of his generation. Like Clay at his best, Douglas was able to see the needs of the nation in the broadest perspective. He held a succession of state offices before being elected to Congress in 1842 at the age of 29. After only two terms in the House, he was chosen United States senator.

Douglas succeeded at almost everything he attempted. His law practice was large and prosperous. He dabbled in Chicago real estate and made a fortune. Politics suited him to perfection. Rarely has a man seemed so closely attuned to his time and place in history. Although very short, he had powerful shoulders, a large head, strong features, and deep-set, piercing eyes. His high forehead was made to appear even bolder by the way he wore his hair, swept back in a pompadour and draped over his collar. His appearance was so imposing that friends called him "the Little Giant." "I live with my con-stituents," he once boasted, "drink with them, lodge with them, pray with them, laugh, hunt, dance, and work with them. I eat their corn dodgers and fried bacon and sleep two in a bed with them." Yet he was no mere backslapper. He read widely, wrote poetry, financed a number of young American artists, served as a regent of the Smithsonian Institution, and was interested in scientific farming.

The foundations of Douglas's politics were expansion and popular sovereignty. He had been willing to fight for all of Oregon in 1846, and he supported the Mexican War to the hilt, in sharp contrast to his one-term Illinois colleague in Congress, Abraham Lincoln. That local settlers should determine their own institutions was, to his way of thinking, axiomatic. Arguments over the future of slavery in the territories he believed a foolish waste of energy and time since he was convinced that natural conditions would keep the institution out of the West.

The main thing, he insisted, was to get on with the development of the United States. Let the nation build railroads, acquire new territory, expand its trade. He believed slavery "a curse beyond computation" for both blacks and whites, but he refused to admit that any moral issue was involved. He cared not, he boasted, whether slavery was voted up or voted down. This was not really true, but the question was interfering with the rapid exploitation of

"By God, sir, I made James Buchanan, and by God, sir, I will unmake him!" Stephen A. Douglas remarked with characteristic exaggeration during the debate over Kansas.

the continent. Douglas wanted it settled so that the country could concentrate on more important matters.

Douglas's success in steering the Compromise of 1850 through Congress added to his reputation. In 1851, he set out to win the Democratic presidential nomination, reasoning that since he was the brightest, most imaginative, and hardest-working Democrat around, he had every right to press his claim.

This brash aggressiveness proved his undoing. He expressed open contempt for James Buchanan and said of his other chief rival, Lewis Cass, who had won considerable fame while serving as minister to France, that his "reputation was beyond the C."

At the 1852 Democratic convention Douglas had no chance. Cass and Buchanan killed each other off, and the delegates finally chose a dark horse, Franklin Pierce of New Hampshire. The Whigs, rejecting the colorless Fillmore, nominated General Winfield Scott, who was known as Old Fuss and Feathers "because of his punctiliousness in dress and decorum." In the campaign both sides supported the Compromise of 1850. The Democrats won an easy victory, 254 electoral votes to 42.

So handsome a triumph seemed to ensure stability, but in fact it was a prelude to political chaos. The Whig party was crumbling fast. The "Cotton" Whigs of the South, alienated by the antislavery sentiments of their northern brethren, were flocking into the Democratic fold. In the North the radical "Conscience" Whigs and the "Silver Gray" faction that was undisturbed by slavery found themselves more and more at odds with each other. Congress fell overwhelmingly into the hands of proslavery southern Democrats, a development profoundly disturbing to northern Democrats as well as to Whigs.

The Kansas-Nebraska Act

Franklin Pierce was a youthful-appearing 48 when he took office. He was generally well liked by politicians. His career had included service in both houses of Congress. Alcohol had become a problem for him in Washington, however, and in 1842 he had resigned from the Senate and returned home to try to best the bottle, a struggle in which he was

successful. His law practice boomed, and he added to his reputation by serving as a brigadier general during the Mexican War. Though his nomination for president came as a surprise, once made, it had appeared perfectly reasonable. Great things were expected of his administration, especially after he surrounded himself with men of all factions: To balance his appointment of a radical states' rights Mississippian, Jefferson Davis, as secretary of war, for example, he named a conservative northerner, William L. Marcy of New York, as secretary of state.

Only a strong leader, however, can manage a ministry of all talents, and that President Pierce was not. He followed, as the historian Allan Nevins put it, a "policy of smiling on everybody but specially favoring both ends against the middle." The ship of state was soon drifting; Pierce seemed incapable of holding firm the helm.

This was the situation in January 1854 when Senator Douglas, chairman of the Committee on Territories, introduced what looked like a routine bill organizing the land west of Missouri and Iowa as Nebraska Territory. Since settlers were beginning to trickle into the area, the time had arrived to set up a civil administration. But Douglas also acted because a territorial government was essential to railroad development. As a director of the Illinois Central line and as a land speculator, he hoped to make Chicago the terminus of a transcontinental railroad, but construction could not begin until the route was cleared of Indians and brought under some kind of civil control.

Southerners, wishing to bring the transcontinental line to Memphis or New Orleans, pointed out that a right-of-way through organized territory already existed across Texas and New Mexico Territory. In 1853 the United States minister to Mexico, James Gadsden, a prominent southern railroad executive, had engineered the purchase of more than 29,000 square miles of Mexican territory south of the Gila River, which provided an easy route through the mountains for such a railroad. Douglas, whose vision of the economic potentialities of the nation was Hamiltonian, would have been willing to support the construction of two or even three transcontinental railroads, but he knew that Congress would not go that far. In any case, he believed that the Nebraska region must be organized promptly.

The Gadsden Purchase was signed on July 4, 1854, at Mesilla, New Mexico Territory, in a formal ceremony attended by local residents. This painting was executed by a Mesilla native to commemorate the event on its 75th anniversary.

The powerful southern faction in Congress would not go along with Douglas's proposal as it stood. The railroad question aside, Nebraska would presumably become a free state, for it lay north of latitude 36°30′ in a district from which slavery had been excluded by the Missouri Compromise. Under pressure from the southerners, led by Senator David R. Atchison of Missouri, Douglas agreed first to divide the region into two territories, Kansas and Nebraska, and then—a fateful concession—to repeal the part of the Missouri Compromise that excluded slavery from land north of 36°30′. Whether the new territories should become slave or free, he argued, should be left to the decision of the settlers in accordance with the democratic principle of popular sovereignty. The fact that he might advance his presidential ambitions by making concessions to the South must have influenced Douglas too, as must the local political situation in Missouri, where slaveholders feared being "surrounded" on three sides by free states.

Douglas's miscalculation of northern sentiment was monumental. It was one thing to apply popular sovereignty to the new territories in the Southwest, quite another to apply it to a region that had been part of the United States for half a century and free soil for 34 years. Word that the area was to be opened to slavery caused an indignant outcry; many moderate opponents of slavery were radicalized. A group of abolitionist congressmen issued what they called their "Appeal of the Independent Democrats" (actually, all were Free Soilers and Whigs) denouncing the Kansas-Nebraska bill as "a gross violation of a sacred pledge" and calling for a campaign of letter writing, petitions, and public meetings to prevent its passage. The unanimity and force of the northern public's reaction was like nothing in America since the days of the Stamp Act and the Intolerable Acts.

But protests could not defeat the bill. Southerners in both houses backed it regardless of party. Douglas, at his best when under attack, pushed it with all his power. The authors of the "Appeal," he charged, were "the pure unadulterated representatives of Abolitionism, Free Soilism, [and] Niggerism." President Pierce added whatever force the administration could muster. As a result, the northern Democrats split, and the bill became law late in May 1854. In this manner the nation took the greatest single step in its march toward the abyss of secession and civil war.

The repeal of the Missouri Compromise struck the North like a slap in the face—at once shameful and challenging. Presumably the question of slavery in the territories had been settled forever; now, seemingly without justification, it had been reopened. Two days after the Kansas-Nebraska bill passed the House of Representatives, Anthony Burns, a slave who had escaped from Virginia by stowing away on a ship, was arrested in Boston. A mob tried to free him but was thrown back by federal agents. President Pierce ordered the Boston district attorney to "incur any expense" to enforce the law, and he sent a revenue cutter to Boston to carry Burns back to Virginia. Troops were rushed to the scene to restrain the swelling crowds.

Burns was returned to his master, but it required two companies of artillery and 1,000 police and marines to get him aboard ship. As the grim parade marched past buildings festooned with black crepe, the crowd screamed, "Kidnappers! Kidnappers!" at the soldiers. Estimates of the cost of returning this single slave to his owner ran as high as $100,000. In previous cases Boston's conservative leaders,

Whig to a man, had tended to hold back; after the Burns incident, they were thoroughly radicalized. "We went to bed one night old fashioned . . . Whigs," one of them explained, "and waked up stark mad Abolitionists."

Know-Nothings and Republicans

There were 91 free-state Democrats in the House of Representatives when the Kansas-Nebraska Act was passed, only 25 after the next election. With the Whig party already moribund, dissidents flocked to two new parties.

One was the American, or "Know-Nothing," party, so called because it grew out of a secret society whose members used the password "I don't know." The Know-Nothings were primarily nativists—immigration was soaring in the early 1850s, and the influx of poor foreigners was causing genuine social problems. Crime was on the rise in the cities along with drunkenness and other "diseases of poverty."

Several emotion-charged issues related to the fact that a large percentage of the immigrants were Irish and German Catholics also troubled the Know-Nothings. Questions such as public financing of parochial schools, lay control of church policies, the prohibition of alcoholic beverages, and increasing the time before an immigrant could apply for citizenship (the Know-Nothings favored 21 years) were matters of major importance to them. Since these were divisive issues, the established political parties tried to avoid them; hence the development of the new party.

The American party was important in the South as well as in the North, and while most Know-Nothings disliked blacks and considered them inherently inferior beings, they tended to adopt the dominant view of slavery in whichever section they were located. In the North most opposed the Kansas-Nebraska Act.

Operating often in tacit alliance with the antislavery forces (dislike of slavery did not prevent many abolitionists from being prejudiced against Catholics and immigrants), the northern Know-Nothings won a string of local victories in 1854 and elected more than 40 congressmen.

Far more significant in the long run was the

KIDNAPPING AGAIN!!

A MAN WAS STOLEN LAST NIGHT BY THE

Fugitive Slave Bill COMMISSIONER!

HE WILL HAVE HIS

MOCK TRIAL

ON SATURDAY, MAY 27, AT 9 O'CLOCK,

In the Kidnapper's 'Court,' before the Hon. Slave Bill Commissioner,

AT THE COURT HOUSE, IN COURT SQUARE.

SHALL BOSTON STEAL ANOTHER MAN?

Thursday, May 25, 1854.

Anthony Burns, the subject of this Boston poster, was the third runaway slave to be seized and returned to the South under the hated Fugitive Slave Act of 1850. The Burns case galvanized public opinion just when Congress was debating the Kansas-Nebraska Act. The passage of that bill further outraged northerners.

formation of the Republican party, which was made up of former Free Soilers, Conscience Whigs, and "Anti-Nebraska" Democrats. The American party was a national organization, but the Republican party was purely sectional. It sprang up spontaneously throughout the Old Northwest and caught on with a rush in New England.

Republicans presented themselves as the party of freedom. They were not abolitionists (though most abolitionists were soon voting Republican), but they insisted that slavery be kept out of the territories. They believed that if America was to remain a land of opportunity, free white labor must have exclusive access to the West. Thus the party appealed not only to voters who disapproved of slavery, but also to those who wished to keep blacks—free or slave—out of their states. In 1854 the Republicans won over 100 seats in the House of Representatives and control of many state governments.

The Whig party had almost disappeared in the northern states and the Democratic party had been gravely weakened, but it was unclear how these two new parties would fare. The Know-Nothing party had the superficial advantage of being a nationwide

organization, but where slavery was concerned, this was anything but advantageous. And many northerners who disliked slavery were troubled by the harsh Know-Nothing policies toward immigrants and Catholics. If the Know-Nothings were in control, said former Whig congressman Abraham Lincoln in 1855, the Declaration of Independence would read "all men are created equal, except negroes, *and foreigners, and catholics.*"

"Bleeding Kansas"

Still the furor might have died down if settlement of the new territories had proceeded in an orderly manner. Almost none of the settlers who flocked to Kansas owned slaves, and relatively few of them were primarily interested in the slavery question. Most had a low opinion of blacks. ("I kem to Kansas to live in a free state," one northerner explained. "I don't want niggers a-trampin' over my grave.") Like nearly all frontier settlers, they wanted land and local political office, lucrative government contracts, and other business opportunities.

By 1855, civil war had erupted in Kansas as bands of proslavery settlers fought free staters. Northerners and southerners contributed to the agony of "Bleeding Kansas" by sending money and arms to those who supported their views. In this sketch, free staters fire on the proslavery settlement of Hickory Point near Leavenworth.

When Congress opened the gates to settlement in May 1854, none of the land in the territory was available for sale. Treaties extinguishing Indian titles had yet to be ratified, and public lands had not been surveyed. In July, Congress authorized squatters to occupy unsurveyed federal lands, but much of this property was far to the west of the frontier and practically inaccessible. The situation led to confusion over property boundaries, to graft and speculation, and to general uncertainty, thereby exacerbating the difficulty of establishing an orderly government.

The legal status of slavery in Kansas became the focus of all these conflicts. Both northern abolitionists and southern defenders of slavery were determined to have Kansas. They made of the territory first a testing ground and then a battlefield, thus exposing the fatal flaw in the Kansas-Nebraska Act and the idea of popular sovereignty. The law said that the people of Kansas were "perfectly free" to decide the slavery question. But the citizens of territories were not entirely free because territories were not sovereign political units. The act had created a political vacuum, which its vague statement that the settlers must establish their domestic institutions "subject . . . to the Constitution" did not begin to fill. When should the institutions be established? Was it democratic to let a handful of first

comers make decisions that would affect the lives of the thousands soon to follow? The virtues of the time-tested system of congressional control established by the Northwest Ordinance became fully apparent only when the system was discarded.

More serious was the fact that outsiders, North and South, refused to permit Kansans to work out their own destiny. The contest for control began at once. The New England Emigrant Aid Society was formed, with grandiose plans for transporting antislavery settlers to the area. The society transported only a handful of New Englanders to Kansas. Yet the New Englanders were very conspicuous, and the society helped many middle western antislavery settlers to make the move.

In doing so, it stirred southerners to action. The proslavery forces enjoyed several advantages in this struggle. The first inhabitants in frontier regions nearly always came from lands immediately to the east. In this case they were proslavery Missourians. When word spread that "foreigners" from New England were seeking to "steal" Kansas, many Missourians rushed to protect their "rights." "If we win we carry slavery to the Pacific Ocean," Senator Atchison boasted.

In November 1854 an election was held in Kansas to pick a territorial delegate to Congress. A large band of Missourians crossed over specifically to vote

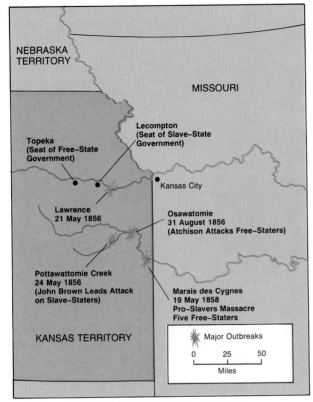

"BLEEDING KANSAS"

night. They dragged five unsuspecting men from their rude cabins and murdered them. This slaughter brought men on both sides to arms by the hundreds. As Brown's biographer, Stephen B. Oates, has written, "Kansas was in complete chaos." Armed bands, one led by Brown himself, "prowled the countryside, shooting at one another and looting."

Brown and his followers escaped capture and were never indicted for the murders, but pressure from federal troops eventually forced him to go into hiding. He finally left Kansas in October 1856. By that time some 200 persons had lost their lives.

A certain amount of violence was normal in any frontier community, but it suited the political interests of the Republicans to make the situation in Kansas seem worse than it was. Exaggerated accounts of "bleeding Kansas" filled the pages of northern newspapers. The Democrats were also partly to blame, for although residents of nearby states often tried to influence elections in new territories, the actions of the border ruffians made a mockery of the democratic process.

However, the main responsibility for the Kansas tragedy must be borne by the Pierce administration. Under popular sovereignty, the national government was supposed to see that elections were orderly and honest. Instead, the president acted as a partisan. When the first governor of the territory objected to the manner in which the proslavery legislature had been elected, Pierce replaced him with a man who backed the southern group without question.

for a proslavery candidate and elected him easily. In March 1855 some 5,000 "border ruffians" again descended on Kansas and elected a territorial legislature. A census had recorded 2,905 eligible voters, but 6,307 votes were cast. The legislature promptly enacted a slave code and laws prohibiting abolitionist agitation. Antislavery settlers refused to recognize this regime and held elections of their own. By January 1856 two governments existed in Kansas, one based on fraud, the other extralegal.

By denouncing the free-state government located at Topeka, President Pierce encouraged the proslavery settlers to assume the offensive. In May, 800 of them sacked the antislavery town of Lawrence. An extremist named John Brown then took the law into his own hands in retaliation. By his reckoning, five Free Soilers had been killed by proslavery forces. In May 1856, together with six companions (four of them his sons), Brown stole into a settlement on Pottawatomie Creek in the dead of

Making a Senator a Martyr

As counterpoint to the fighting in Kansas there arose an almost continuous cacophony in the halls of Congress. Red-faced legislators traded insults and threats. Epithets like "liar" were freely tossed about. Prominent in these angry outbursts was a new senator, Charles Sumner of Massachusetts. Brilliant, learned, and articulate, Sumner had made a name for himself in New England as a reformer interested in the peace movement, prison reform, and the abolition of slavery. He possessed great magnetism and was, according to the tastes of the day, an accomplished orator, but he suffered inner torments of a complex nature that warped his personality. He was egotistical and humorless. His un-

A well-known contemporary drawing gives a dramatic view of Brooks caning Sumner. Beneath Sumner's left hand is a scroll inscribed "Kansas." The cartoon's title is "Southern Chivalry—Argument versus Clubs."

yielding devotion to his principles was less praiseworthy than it seemed on casual examination, for it resulted from his complete lack of respect for the principles of others. Reform movements evidently provided him with a kind of emotional release; he became combative and totally lacking in objectivity when espousing a cause.

In the Kansas debates Sumner displayed an icy disdain for his foes. Colleagues threatened him with assassination, called him a "filthy reptile" and a "leper." He was impervious to such hostility. In the spring of 1856 he loosed a dreadful blast titled "The Crime Against Kansas." Characterizing administration policy as tyrannical, imbecilic, absurd, and infamous, he demanded that Kansas be admitted to the Union at once as a free state. Then he began a long and intemperate attack on both Douglas and the elderly Senator Andrew P. Butler of South Carolina, who was not present to defend himself.

Sumner described Butler as a "Don Quixote" who had taken "the harlot, slavery" as his mistress, and he spoke scornfully of "the loose expectoration" of Butler's speech. This was an inexcusable reference to the uncontrollable drooling to which the elderly senator was subject. While he was still talking, Douglas, who shrugged off most political name-calling as part of the game, was heard to mutter, "That damn fool will get himself killed by some other damn fool."

Such a "fool" quickly materialized in the person of Congressman Preston S. Brooks of South Carolina, a nephew of Senator Butler. Since Butler was absent from Washington, Brooks, who was probably as mentally unbalanced as Sumner, assumed the responsibility of defending his kinsman's honor. A southern romantic par excellence, he decided that caning Sumner would reflect his contempt more effectively than challenging him to a duel. Two days after the speech, Brooks entered the Senate as it adjourned. Sumner remained at his desk writing. After waiting with exquisite punctilio until a talkative woman in the lobby had left so that she would be spared the sight of violence, Brooks walked up to Sumner and rained blows on his head with a gutta-percha cane until he fell, unconscious and bloody, to the floor. "I . . . gave him about 30 first-rate stripes," Brooks later boasted. "Towards the last he bellowed like a calf. I wore my cane out completely but saved the head which is gold." The physical damage suffered by Sumner was relatively superficial, but the incident so affected him psychologically that he was unable to return to his seat in Congress until 1859.

Both sides made much of this disgraceful incident. When the House censured him, Brooks resigned, returned to his home district, and was triumphantly reelected. A number of well-wishers sent him souvenir canes. Northerners viewed the affair as illustrating the brutalizing effect of slavery on southern whites and made a hero of Sumner.

Buchanan Tries His Hand

Such was the atmosphere surrounding the 1856 presidential election. The Republican party now dominated much of the North. It nominated John C. Frémont, "the Pathfinder," one of the heroes of the conquest of California during the Mexican War. Frémont fitted the Whig tradition of presidential candidates: a popular military man with almost no political experience. Unlike Taylor and Scott, however, he was sound and articulate on the issue of slavery in the territories. Although citizens of diverse interests had joined the party, Republicans expressed their objectives in one simple slogan: "Free soil, free speech, and Frémont."

The Democrats cast aside the ineffectual Pierce, but they did not dare nominate Douglas because he had raised such a storm in the North. They settled on James Buchanan, chiefly because he had been out of the country serving as minister to Great Britain during the long debate over Kansas! The American party nominated ex-president Fillmore, a choice the remnants of the Whigs endorsed. Walt Whitman had been an ardent Democrat. But the party's stand on slavery in the territories disgusted him. In 1856 he wrote a poem, "The 18th Presidency," denouncing both Buchanan and Fillmore:

> Two galvanized old men, close on
> the summons to depart this life
> . . . relics and proofs of the little
> political bargains . . .

In the campaign, the Democrats concentrated on denouncing the Republicans as a sectional party that threatened to destroy the Union. On this issue they carried the day. Buchanan won only a minority of the popular vote, but he had strength in every section. He got 174 electoral votes to Frémont's 114 and Fillmore's 8. The significant contest took place in the populous states just north of slave territory—Pennsylvania, Ohio, Indiana, and Illinois. Buchanan carried all but Ohio, though by narrow margins.

James Buchanan "never made a witty remark, never wrote a memorable sentence, and never showed a touch of distinction," according to historian Allan Nevins.

No one could say that James Buchanan lacked political experience. He had been elected to the Pennsylvania legislature in 1815 when only 24. He served for well over 20 years in Congress and had been minister to Russia, then Polk's secretary of state, then minister to Great Britain under Pierce.

Personally, Buchanan was a bundle of contradictions. Dignified in bearing and by nature cautious, he could consume enormous amounts of liquor without showing the slightest sign of inebriation. A big, heavy man, he was nonetheless remarkably graceful and light on his tiny feet, of which he was inordinately proud. He wore a very high collar to conceal a scarred neck, and because of an eye defect he habitually carried his head to one side and slightly forward, which gave him, as his biographer says, "a perpetual attitude of courteous deference and attentive interest" that sometimes led individuals to believe they had won a greater share of his attention and support than was actually the case. In fact he was extremely stubborn and sometimes vindictive.

Buchanan was popular with women and attracted to them as well, but although he contemplated marriage on more than one occasion, he never took the final step. Over the years many strong men in politics had, like Walt Whitman, held him in contempt. Yet he was patriotic, conscientious, and moderate. While Republican extremists called him a "Doughface"—they believed he lacked the force of character to stand up against southern extremists—many voters in 1856 thought he had the qualities necessary to steer the nation to calmer waters.

The Court's Turn

Before Buchanan could fairly take the Kansas problem in hand, an event occurred that drove another deep wedge between North and South. Back in 1834 Dr. John Emerson of St. Louis joined the army as a surgeon and was assigned to duty at Rock Island, Illinois. Later he was transferred to Fort Snelling, in Wisconsin Territory. In 1838 he returned to Missouri. Accompanying him on these travels was his body servant, Dred Scott, a slave. In 1846, after Emerson's death, Scott and his wife Harriet, whom he had married while in Wisconsin, with the help of a friendly lawyer brought suit in the Missouri courts for their liberty, arguing that residence in Illinois, where slavery was barred under the Northwest Ordinance, and in Wisconsin Territory, where the Missouri Compromise outlawed it, had made them free.

The future of Dred and Harriet Scott mattered not at all to the country or the courts; at issue was the question of whether Congress or the local legislatures had the power to outlaw slavery in the territories. After many years of litigation, the case reached the Supreme Court. On March 6, 1857, two days after Buchanan's inauguration, the high tribunal acted. Free or slave, the Court declared, blacks were not citizens; therefore, Scott could not sue in a federal court. This was dubious legal logic because many blacks were accepted as citizens in some states when the Constitution was drafted and ratified, and Article 4, Section 2, says that "the citizens of each state shall be entitled to all privileges and immunities of citizens in the several states." But it settled Scott's fate.

However, the Court went further. Since the plaintiff had returned to Missouri, the laws of Illinois no longer applied to him. His residence in Wisconsin Territory—this was the most controversial part of the decision—did not make him free because the Missouri Compromise was unconstitutional. According to the Bill of Rights (the Fifth Amendment), the federal government cannot deprive any person of life, liberty, or property without due process of law.* Therefore, Chief Justice Roger B. Taney reasoned, "An Act of Congress which deprives a person . . . of his liberty or property merely because he came himself or brought his property into a particular Territory . . . could hardly be dignified with the name of due process of law."

The Dred Scott decision has been widely criticized on legal grounds. Each justice filed his own opinion, and in several important particulars there was no line of argument that any five of the nine agreed on. Some critics have reasoned that the justices should not have gone beyond the minimum of argument necessary to settle the case, and many have made much of the fact that a majority of the justices were southerners. It would be going too far, however, to accuse them of plotting to extend slavery. They were trying to settle the vexing question of slavery in the territories once and for all. If this objective could only be accomplished by fuzzy reasoning, it would not be the first or the last time in the history of jurisprudence that an important result rested on shaky logic.

In addition to invalidating the already repealed Missouri Compromise, the decision threatened Douglas's principle of popular sovereignty, for if Congress could not exclude slaves from a territory, how could a mere territorial legislature do so? Until statehood was granted, slavery seemed as inviolate as freedom of religion or speech or any other civil liberty guaranteed by the Constitution. Where formerly freedom (as guaranteed in the Bill of Rights) was a national institution and slavery a local one, now, according to the Court, slavery was nationwide, excluded only where states had specifically abolished it.

The irony of employing the Bill of Rights to keep blacks in chains did not escape northern critics. Now

---

* Some state constitutions had similar provisions, but the slave states obviously did not.

slaves could be brought into Minnesota Territory, even into Oregon. In his inaugural address Buchanan had sanctimoniously urged the people to accept the forthcoming ruling, "whatever this may be," as a final settlement. Many assumed (indeed, it was true) that he had put pressure on the Court to act as it did and that he knew in advance of his speech what the decision would be. If this "greatest crime in the judicial annals of the Republic" was allowed to stand, northerners argued, the Republican party would have no reason to exist: Its program had been declared unconstitutional! The Dred Scott decision convinced thousands that the South was engaged in an aggressive attempt to extend the peculiar institution so far that it could no longer be considered peculiar.

The Lecompton Constitution

Kansas soon provided a test for northern suspicions. Initially Buchanan handled the problem of Kansas well by appointing Robert J. Walker as governor. Although he was from Mississippi, Walker had no desire to foist slavery on the territory against the will of its inhabitants. He was a small man but a courageous one, patriotic, vigorous, tough-minded, much like Douglas in temper and belief. A former senator and Cabinet member, he had more political stature by far than any previous governor of the territory.

The proslavery leaders in Kansas had managed to convene a constitutional convention at Lecompton, but the Free Soil forces had refused to participate in the election of delegates. When this rump body drafted a proslavery constitution and then refused to submit it to a fair vote of all the settlers, Walker denounced its work and hurried back to Washington to explain the situation to Buchanan.

The president refused to face reality. His prosouthern advisers were clamoring for him to "save" Kansas. Instead of rejecting the Lecompton constitution, he asked Congress to admit Kansas to the Union with this document as its frame of government.

Buchanan's decision brought him head-on against Stephen A. Douglas, and the repercussions of their clash shattered the Democratic party. Principle and self-interest (an irresistible combination)

forced Douglas to oppose the leader of his party. If he stood aside while Congress admitted Kansas, not only would he be abandoning popular sovereignty, but he would be committing political suicide as well. He was up for reelection to the Senate in 1858. All but one of the 56 newspapers in Illinois had declared editorially against the Lecompton constitution; if he supported it, defeat was certain. In a dramatic confrontation at the White House, he and Buchanan argued the question at length, tempers rising. Finally, the president tried to force him into line. "Mr. Douglas," he said, "I desire you to remember that no Democrat ever yet differed from an Administration of his own choice without being crushed." "Mr. President," Douglas replied contemptuously, "I wish you to remember that General Jackson is dead!" And he stalked out of the room.

Buchanan then compounded his error by putting tremendous political pressure on Douglas, cutting off his Illinois patronage on the eve of his reelection campaign. Of course Douglas persisted, openly joining the Republicans in the fight. Congress rejected the Lecompton bill.

Meanwhile, the extent of the fraud perpetrated at Lecompton became clear. In October 1857 a new legislature had been chosen in Kansas, antislavery voters participating in the balloting. It ordered a referendum on the Lecompton constitution in January 1858. The constitution was overwhelmingly rejected; this time the proslavery settlers boycotted the test. When Buchanan persisted in pressing Congress to admit Kansas under the Lecompton constitution, Congress ordered another referendum. To slant the case in favor of approval, the legislators stipulated that if the constitution was voted down, Kansas could not be admitted into the Union until it had a population of 90,000. Nevertheless, the Kansans rejected it by a ratio of six to one.

More than opposition to slavery influenced this vote, for by 1858 most Kansans were totally alienated from the Democratic administration in Washington because of its bungling and corrupt management of the public lands. After delaying sales unconscionably, Buchanan suddenly put 8 million acres up for auction in 1858. Squatters on this land were faced, in the midst of a depression, with finding $200 in cash to cover the minimum price of their quarter sections or losing their improvements. Local protests forced a delay of the sales, but Kansans by the thousands were convinced that Buchanan had thrown the land on the market out of pique at their rejection of the Lecompton constitution.

The Emergence of Lincoln

These were dark days. During the Panic of 1857 northerners put the blame for the hard times on the southern-dominated Congress, which had just reduced tariff duties to the lowest levels in nearly half a century. As prices plummeted and unemployment rose, they attributed the collapse to foreign competition and accused the South of having sacrificed the prosperity of the rest of the nation for its selfish advantage. The South in turn read in its relative immunity from the depression proof of the superiority of the slave system, which further stimulated the running sectional debate about the relative merits of free and slave labor.

Dissolution threatened the Union. To many Americans, Stephen A. Douglas seemed to offer the best hope of preserving it. For this reason unusual attention was focused on his campaign for reelection to the Senate in 1858. The importance of the contest and Douglas's national prestige put great pressure on the Republicans of Illinois to nominate someone who would make a good showing against him. The man they chose was Abraham Lincoln.

After a towering figure has passed from the stage, it is always difficult to discover what he was like before his rise to prominence. This is especially true of Lincoln, who changed greatly when power, responsibility, and fame came to him. Lincoln was not unknown in 1858, but his public career had not been distinguished. He was born in Kentucky in 1809, and the story of his early life can be condensed, as he once said himself, into a single line from Gray's *Elegy:* "The short and simple annals of the poor." His illiterate father, Thomas Lincoln, was a typical frontier wanderer. When Abraham was 7 the family moved to Indiana. In 1830 they pushed west again into southern Illinois. The boy received almost no formal schooling.

However, Lincoln had a good mind, and he was extremely ambitious. He cut loose from his family, made a trip to New Orleans, and for a time managed a general store in New Salem, Illinois. In 1834, when barely 25, he won a seat in the Illinois legislature

as a Whig. Meanwhile, he studied law and was admitted to the bar in 1836.

Lincoln remained in the legislature until 1842, displaying a perfect willingness to adopt the Whig position on all issues. In 1846 he was elected to Congress. While not engaged in politics he worked at the law, maintaining an office in Springfield and following the circuit, taking a variety of cases, few of much importance. He earned a decent but by no means sumptuous living. After one term in Congress, marked by his partisan opposition to Polk's Mexican policy, his political career petered out. He seemed fated to pass his remaining years as a small-town lawyer.

Even during this period Lincoln's personality was extraordinarily complex. His bawdy sense of humor and his endless fund of stories and tall tales made him a legend first in Illinois and then in Washington. He was admired in Illinois as an expert axman and a champion wrestler. He was thoroughly at home with toughs like the "Clary's Grove Boys" of New Salem and in the convivial atmosphere of a party caucus. But in a society where most men drank heavily, he never touched liquor. And he was subject to periods of melancholy so profound as to appear almost psychopathic. Friends spoke of him as having "cat fits," and he wrote of himself in the early 1840s: "I am now the most miserable man living. If what I felt were equally distributed to the whole human family, there would not be one cheerful face on earth."

In a region swept by repeated waves of religious revivalism, Lincoln managed to be at once a man of calm spirituality and a skeptic without appearing offensive to conventional believers. He was a party wheelhorse, a corporation lawyer, even a railroad lobbyist, yet his reputation for integrity was stainless.

The revival of the slavery controversy in 1854 stirred Lincoln deeply. No abolitionist, he had tried to take a "realistic" view of the problem. The Kansas-Nebraska bill led him to see the moral issue more clearly. "If slavery is not wrong, nothing is wrong," he stated with the directness and simplicity of expression for which he later became famous. Compromises made in the past for the sake of sectional harmony had always sought to preserve as much territory as possible for freedom. Yet unlike most Free Soilers, he did not blame the southerners for

How Lincoln aged during his term of office is evident when one compares Alexander Hesler's portrait, taken on June 3, 1860, with one by an unnamed photographer taken on April 10, 1865.

slavery. "They are just what we would be in their situation," he confessed.

The moderation of his position combined with its moral force won Lincoln many admirers in the great body of citizens who were trying to reconcile their low opinion of blacks and their patriotic desire to avoid an issue that threatened the Union with their growing conviction that slavery was sinful. Anything that aided slavery was wrong, Lincoln argued. But before casting the first stone, northerners should look into their own hearts: "If there be a man amongst us who is so impatient of [slavery] as a wrong as to disregard its actual presence among us and the difficulty of getting rid of it suddenly in a satisfactory way . . . that man is misplaced if he is on our platform." And Lincoln confessed:

> If all earthly power were given to me, I should not know what to do as to the existing institution. But . . . [this] furnishes no more excuse for permitting slavery to go into our free territory than it would for reviving the African slave trade.

Thus Lincoln was at once compassionate toward the slave owner and stern toward the institution. "A house divided against itself cannot stand," he warned. "I believe this government cannot endure permanently half slave and half free." Without minimizing the difficulties or urging a hasty or ill-considered solution, Lincoln demanded that the people look toward a day, however remote, when not only Kansas but the entire country would be free.

The Lincoln-Douglas Debates

As Lincoln developed these ideas, his reputation grew. In 1855 he almost won the Whig nomination for senator. He became a Republican shortly thereafter, and in June 1856, at the first Republican National Convention, he received 110 votes for the vice-presidential nomination. He seemed the logical man to pit against Douglas in 1858.

In July, Lincoln challenged Douglas to a series

The Lincoln-Douglas debates began in June 1858 with Lincoln's "House Divided" speech and lasted until October. At rallies such as the one announced in this poster, the tall, awkward "Rail Splitter" challenged the "Little Giant" to thoroughly examine the slavery question.

gestures and bold, exaggerated arguments. He did not hesitate to call "Honest Abe" a liar. Lincoln, on his part, was slow and deliberate of speech, his voice curiously high-pitched. He seldom used gestures or oratorical tricks, trying rather to create an impression of utter sincerity to add force to his remarks.

The two employed different political styles each calculated to project a particular image. Douglas epitomized efficiency and success. He dressed in the latest fashion, favoring flashy vests and the finest broadcloth. He was a glad-hander and a heavy drinker—apparently he died of cirrhosis of the liver. Ordinarily he arrived in town in a private railroad car, to be met by a brass band, then to ride at the head of a parade to the appointed place.

Lincoln appeared before the voters as a man of the people. He wore ill-fitting black suits and a stovepipe hat—repository for letters, bills, scribbled notes, and other scraps—that exaggerated his great height. He presented a worn and rumpled appearance, partly because he traveled from place to place on day coaches, accompanied by only a few advisers. When local supporters came to meet him at the station, he preferred to walk with them through the streets to the scene of the debate.

Lincoln and Douglas maintained a high intellectual level in their speeches, but these were political debates. They were seeking not to influence future historians (who have nonetheless pondered their words endlessly) but to win votes. They tended to exaggerate their differences, which were not in fact enormous. Neither wanted to see slavery in the territories or thought it economically efficient, and neither sought to abolish it by political action or by force. Both believed blacks congenitally inferior to whites, though Douglas took more pleasure in expounding on supposed racial differences than Lincoln did.

Douglas's strategy was to make Lincoln look like an abolitionist. He accused the Republicans of favoring racial equality and refusing to abide by the decision of the Supreme Court in the Dred Scott case. Himself he pictured as a heroic champion of democracy, attacked on one side by the "black" Republicans and on the other by the Buchananites, yet ready to fight to his last breath for popular sovereignty.

Lincoln tried to picture Douglas as proslavery and a defender of the Dred Scott decision. "Slavery is an unqualified evil to the negro, to the white man,

of seven debates. The senator accepted. The debates were well attended and widely reported, for the idea of a direct confrontation between candidates for an important office captured the popular imagination.

The choice of the next senator lay, of course, in the hands of the Illinois legislature. Technically, Douglas and Lincoln were campaigning for candidates for the legislature who were pledged to support them for the Senate seat. They presented a sharp physical contrast that must have helped voters sort out their differing points of view. Douglas was short and stocky, Lincoln long and lean. Douglas gave the impression of irrepressible energy. While speaking, he roamed the platform; he used broad to the soil, and to the State," he said. "Judge Douglas," he also said, "is blowing out the moral lights around us, when he contends that whoever wants slaves has a right to hold them."

However, Lincoln often weakened the impact of his arguments, being perhaps too eager to demonstrate his conservatism. The historian David M. Potter drew a nice distinction in Lincoln's position between "what he would do for the slave" and "what he would do for the Negro." "All men are created equal," he would say on the authority of the Declaration of Independence, only to add: "I am not, nor ever have been, in favor of bringing about in any way the social and political equality of the white and black races." He opposed allowing blacks to vote, to sit on juries, to marry whites, even to be citizens. He predicted the "ultimate extinction" of slavery, but when pressed he predicted that it would not occur "in less than a hundred years at the least." He took a fence-sitting position on the question of abolition in the District of Columbia and stated flatly that he did not favor repeal of the Fugitive Slave Act.

In the debate at Freeport, a town northwest of Chicago near the Wisconsin line, Lincoln asked Douglas if, considering the Dred Scott decision, the people of a territory could exclude slavery before the territory became a state. Unhesitatingly Douglas replied that they could, simply by not passing the local laws essential for holding blacks in bondage. "It matters not what way the Supreme Court may hereafter decide as to the abstract question," he said. "The people have the lawful means to introduce or exclude it as they please, for the reason that slavery cannot exist . . . unless it is supported by local police regulations."

This argument saved Douglas in Illinois. The Democrats carried the legislature by a narrow margin, whereas it is almost certain that if Douglas had accepted the Dred Scott decision outright, the balance would have swung to the Republicans. But the so-called Freeport Doctrine cost him heavily two years later when he made his bid for the Democratic presidential nomination. "It matters not what way the Supreme Court may hereafter decide"—southern extremists would not accept a man who suggested that the Dred Scott decision could be circumvented, though in fact Douglas had only stated the obvious.

Probably Lincoln had not thought beyond the senatorial election when he asked the question; he was merely hoping to keep Douglas on the defensive and perhaps injure him in southern Illinois, where considerable proslavery sentiment existed. In any case, defeat did Lincoln no harm politically. He had more than held his own against one of the most formidable debaters in politics, and his distinctive personality and point of view had impressed themselves on thousands of minds. Indeed, the defeat revitalized his political career.

The campaign of 1858 marked Douglas's last triumph, Lincoln's last defeat. Elsewhere the elections in the North went heavily to the Republicans. When the old Congress reconvened in December, northern-sponsored economic measures (a higher tariff, the transcontinental railroad, river and harbor improvements, a free homestead bill) were all blocked by southern votes.

Whether the South could continue to prevent the passage of this legislation in the new Congress was problematical. In early 1859 even many moderate southerners were uneasy about the future. The radicals, made panicky by Republican victories and their own failure to win in Kansas, spoke openly of secession if a Republican was elected president in 1860. Lincoln's "house divided" speech was quoted out of context, while Douglas's Freeport Doctrine added to southern woes. When Senator William H. Seward of New York spoke of an "irrepressible conflict" between freedom and slavery, southerners became still more alarmed.

Naturally they struck back. Led by such self-described "fire-eaters" as William L. Yancey of Alabama and Senators Jefferson Davis of Mississippi, John Slidell of Louisiana, and James H. Hammond of South Carolina, they demanded a federal slave code for the territories and talked of annexing Cuba and reviving the African slave trade.

John Brown's Raid

In October 1859 John Brown, the scourge of Kansas, made his second contribution to the unfolding sectional drama. Gathering a group of 18 followers, white and black, he staged an attack on Harpers Ferry, Virginia, a town on the Potomac River upstream from Washington. Having boned up on guerrilla tactics, he planned to seize the federal arsenal there; arm the slaves, whom he thought would

The image of John Brown as martyr was memorialized in art as well as in song and story. Here is a sentimental interpretation, The Last Moments of John Brown, *painted in 1884 by American genre artist Thomas Hovenden.*

flock to his side; and then establish a black republic in the mountains of Virginia.

Simply by overpowering a few night watchmen, Brown and his men occupied the arsenal and a nearby rifle factory. They captured several hostages, one of them Colonel Lewis Washington, a great-grandnephew of George Washington. But no slaves came forward to join them. Federal troops commanded by Robert E. Lee soon trapped Brown's men in an engine house of the Baltimore and Ohio Railroad. After a two-day siege in which the attackers picked off ten of his men, Brown was captured.

No incident so well illustrates the role of emotion and irrationality in the sectional crisis as John Brown's raid. Over the years before his Kansas escapade, Brown had been a drifter, horse thief, and swindler, several times a bankrupt—a failure in everything he attempted. His maternal grandmother, his mother, and five aunts and uncles were certifiably insane, as were 2 of his 20 children and many collateral relatives. After his ghastly Pottawatomie murders it should have been obvious to anyone that he was both fanatical and mentally unstable: Some of the victims were hacked to bits. Yet numbers of high-minded northerners, including Emerson and Thoreau, had supported him and his antislavery "work" after 1856. Some—among them Franklin B. Sanborn, a teacher; Thomas Wentworth Higginson, a clergyman; and the merchant George

L. Stearns—contributed knowingly to his Harpers Ferry enterprise. After Brown's capture, Emerson, in an essay called "Courage," called him "a martyr" who would "make the gallows as glorious as the cross."

Southerners reacted to Harpers Ferry with equal irrationality, some with a rage similar to Brown's. Dozens of hapless northerners in the southern states were arrested, beaten, or driven off. One, falsely suspected of being an accomplice of Brown, was lynched.

Brown's fate lay in the hands of the Virginia authorities. Ignoring his obvious derangement, they charged him with treason, conspiracy, and murder. He was speedily convicted and sentenced to death by hanging.

Yet "Old Brown" had still one more contribution to make to the developing sectional tragedy. Despite the furor he had created, cool heads everywhere called for calm and denounced his attack. Most Republican politicians repudiated him. Even execution would probably not have made a martyr of Brown had he behaved like a madman after his capture. Instead, an enormous dignity descended on him as he lay in his Virginia jail awaiting death. Whatever his faults, he truly believed in racial equality. He addressed blacks who worked for him as "Mister" and arranged for them to eat at his table and sit with his family in church. This conviction served him well in his last days. "If it is deemed necessary that I should forfeit my life for the furtherance of the ends of justice, and mingle my blood further with the blood of . . . millions in this slave country whose rights are disregarded by wicked, cruel, and unjust enactments," he said before the judge pronounced sentence, "I say, let it be done."

This John Brown, with his patriarchal beard and sad eyes, so apparently incompatible with the bloody terrorist of Pottawatomie and Harpers Ferry, led thousands in the North to ignore his past and treat him almost as a saint.

And so Brown became to the North a hero and to the South a symbol of northern ruthlessness. The historian C. Vann Woodward put it this way: "Paranoia continued to induce counterparanoia, each antagonist infecting the other reciprocally, until the vicious spiral ended in war." Soon, as the popular song had it, Brown's body lay "a-mould-ering in the grave," and the memory of his bloody act did indeed go "marching on."

The Election of 1860

By 1860 the nation was teetering on the brink of disunion. Radicals North and South were heedlessly provoking one another. When a disgruntled North Carolinian, Hinton Rowan Helper, published *The Impending Crisis of the South* (1857), an attempt to demonstrate statistically that slavery was ruining the South's economy and corrupting its social structure, the Republicans flooded the country with an abridged edition, though they knew that southerners considered the book an appeal for social revolution. "I have always been a fervid Union man," one southerner wrote in 1859, "but I confess the [northern] endorsement of the Harpers Ferry outrage and Helper's infernal doctrine has shaken my fidelity."

Extremism was more evident in the South, and to any casual observer that section must have seemed the aggressor in the crisis. Yet even in demanding the reopening of the African slave trade, southern radicals believed that they were defending themselves against attack. They felt surrounded by hostility. The North was growing at a much faster rate; if nothing was done, they feared, a flood of new free states would soon be able to amend the Constitution and emancipate the slaves. John Brown's raid, with its threat of an insurrection like Nat Turner's, reduced them to a state of panic.

When legislatures in state after state in the South cracked down on freedom of expression, made the manumission of slaves illegal, banished free blacks, and took other steps that northerners considered blatantly provocative, the advocates of these policies believed that they were only defending the status quo. Perhaps, by seceding from the Union, the South could raise a dike against the tide of abolitionism. Secession also provided an emotional release, a way of dissipating tension by striking back at criticism.

Stephen A. Douglas was probably the last hope of avoiding a rupture between North and South. But when the Democrats met at Charleston, South Carolina, in April 1860 to choose a presidential candidate, the southern delegates would not support him unless he promised not to disturb slavery in the territories. Indeed, they went further in their demands. The North, William L. Yancey of Alabama insisted, must accept the proposition that slavery was not merely tolerable but right. Of course, the northerners would not go so far. "Gentlemen of the South," said Senator George E. Pugh of Ohio in replying to Yancey, "you mistake us—you mistake us! We will not do it!" When southern proposals were voted down, most of the delegates from the Deep South walked out and the convention adjourned without naming a candidate.

In June the Democrats reconvened at Baltimore. Again they failed to reach agreement. The two wings then met separately, the northerners nominating Douglas, the southerners John C. Breckinridge of Kentucky, Buchanan's vice-president. On the question of slavery in the territories, the northerners promised to "abide by the decision of the Supreme Court," which meant, in effect, that they stood for Douglas's Freeport Doctrine. The southerners announced their belief that neither Congress nor any territorial government could prevent citizens from settling "with their property" in any territory.

Meanwhile, the Republicans, who met in Chicago in mid-May, had drafted a platform attractive to all classes and all sections of the northern and western states. For manufacturers they proposed a high tariff, for farmers a homestead law providing free land for settlers. Internal improvements "of a National character," notably a railroad to the Pacific, should receive federal aid. No restrictions should be placed on immigration. As to slavery in the territories, the Republicans did not equivocate: "The normal condition of all the territory of the United States is that of freedom." Neither Congress nor a local legislature could "give legal existence to Slavery in any Territory."

In choosing a presidential candidate the Republicans displayed equally shrewd political judgment. Senator Seward was the front-runner, but he had taken too extreme a stand and appeared unlikely to carry the crucial states of Pennsylvania, Indiana, and Illinois. He led on the first ballot but could not get a majority. Then the delegates began to look closely at Abraham Lincoln. His thoughtful and moderate views on the main issue of the times and his formidable debating skills attracted many, and so did his political personality. "Honest Abe,"

the "Railsplitter," a man of humble origins (born in a log cabin), self-educated, self-made, a common man but by no means an ordinary man—the combination seemed unbeatable.

It also helped that Lincoln was from a crucial state and had an excellent team of convention managers. Taking advantage of the fact that the convention was meeting in Lincoln's home state, they packed the gallery with leather-lunged Chicago ward heelers assigned the task of shouting for their man. They also made a series of deals with the leaders of other state delegations to win additional votes. "I authorize no bargains and will be bound by none," Lincoln telegraphed the convention. "Lincoln ain't here and don't know what we have to meet," one of his managers remarked—and proceeded to trade off two Cabinet posts for the votes of key states.

On the second ballot Lincoln drew shoulder to shoulder with Seward; on the third he was within two votes of victory. Before the roll could be called again, delegates began to switch their votes, and in a landslide, soon made unanimous, Lincoln was nominated.

A few days earlier the remnants of the American and Whig parties had formed the Constitutional Union party and nominated John Bell of Tennessee for president. "It is both the part of patriotism and of duty," they resolved, "to recognize no political principle other than the Constitution of the country, the union of the states, and the enforcement of the laws." Ostrichlike, the Constitutional Unionists ignored the conflicts rending the nation. Only in the border states, where the consequences of disunion were sure to be most tragic, did they have any following.

With four candidates in the field, no one could win a popular majority, but it soon became clear that Lincoln was going to be elected. Breckinridge had most of the slave states in his pocket and Bell would run strong in the border regions, but the populous northern and western states had a majority of the electoral vote, and there the choice lay between the Republicans and the Douglas Democrats. In such a contest the Republicans, with their attractive economic program and their strong stand against slavery in the territories, were sure to come out on top.

Lincoln avoided campaigning and made no public statements. Douglas, recognizing the certainty of Lincoln's victory, accepted his fate and for the first

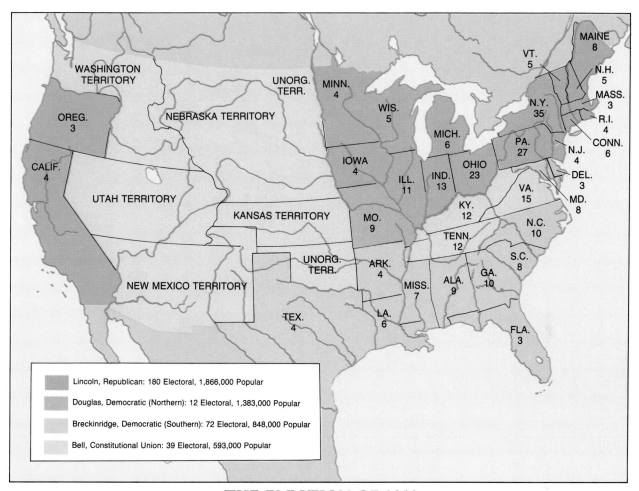

Lincoln, Republican: 180 Electoral, 1,866,000 Popular

Douglas, Democratic (Northern): 12 Electoral, 1,383,000 Popular

Breckinridge, Democratic (Southern): 72 Electoral, 848,000 Popular

Bell, Constitutional Union: 39 Electoral, 593,000 Popular

THE ELECTION OF 1860

time in his career rose above ambition. "We must try to save the Union," he said. "I will go South." In the heart of the Cotton Kingdom, he appealed to the voters to stand by the Union whoever was elected. He was the only candidate to do so; the others refused to remind the people that their election might result in secession and civil war.

When the votes were counted, Lincoln had 1,866,000, almost a million fewer than the combined total of his three opponents, but he swept the North and West, which gave him 180 electoral votes and the presidency. Douglas received 1,383,000 votes, so distributed that he carried only Missouri and part of New Jersey. Breckinridge, with 848,000 popular votes, won most of the South; Bell, with 593,000, carried Virginia, Tennessee, and Ken-

tucky. Lincoln was thus a minority president, but his title to the office was unquestionable. Even if his opponents could have combined their popular votes in each state, Lincoln would have won.

The Secession Crisis

Only days after Lincoln's victory, the South Carolina legislature ordered an election of delegates to a convention to decide the state's future course. On December 20 the convention voted unanimously to secede, basing its action on the logic of Calhoun. "The State of South Carolina has resumed her position among the nations of the world," the delegates announced.

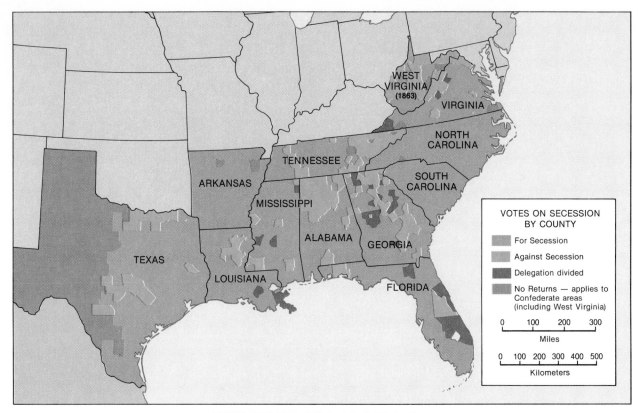

THE VOTE FOR SECESSION

A comparison of this map with the one on page 360 shows the minimal support for secession in the mainly nonslave mountain areas of the Appalachians. The strong antisecession sentiment in mountainous areas of Virginia eventually led several counties there to break from Virginia in 1863 and form the new state of West Virginia.

By February 1, 1861, the six other states of the Lower South had followed suit. A week later, at Montgomery, Alabama, a provisional government of the Confederate States of America was established. Virginia, Tennessee, North Carolina, and Arkansas did not leave the Union but announced that if the federal government attempted to use force against the Confederacy, they too would secede.

Why were southerners willing to wreck the Union their grandfathers had put together with so much love and labor? No simple explanation is possible. The danger that the expanding North would overwhelm them was for neither today nor tomorrow. Lincoln had assured them that he would re-spect slavery where it existed. The Democrats had retained control of Congress in the election; the Supreme Court was firmly in their hands as well. If the North did try to destroy slavery, secession would perhaps be a logical tactic, but why not wait until the threat materialized? To leave the Union meant abandoning the very objectives for which the South had been contending for over a decade: a share of the federal territories and an enforceable fugitive slave law.

One reason why the South rejected this line of thinking was the tremendous economic energy generated in the North, which seemed to threaten the South's independence. As one southerner complained at a commercial convention in 1855:

From the rattle with which the nurse tickles the ear of the child born in the South to the shroud which covers the cold form of the dead, everything comes from the North. We rise from between sheets made in Northern looms, and pillow's of Northern feathers, to wash in basins made in the North. . . . We eat from Northern plates and dishes; our rooms are swept with Northern brooms, our gardens dug with Northern spades . . . and the very wood which feeds our fires is cut with Northern axes, helved with hickory brought from Connecticut and New York.

Secession, southerners argued, would "liberate" the South and produce the kind of balanced economy that was proving so successful in the North. Moreover, the mere possibility of emancipation was a powerful force for secession. "We must either submit to degradation, and to the loss of property worth four billions," the Mississippi convention declared, "or we must secede."

The years of sectional conflict, the growing northern criticism of slavery, perhaps even an unconscious awareness that this criticism was well founded, had undermined and in many cases destroyed the patriotic feelings of southerners. Because of the constant clamor set up by New England antislavery groups, the South tended to identify all northerners as "Yankee abolitionists" and to resent them with increasing passion. "I look upon the whole New England race as a troublesome unquiet set of meddlers," one Georgian wrote. In addition, a Republican president would not need the consent of Congress to flood the South with unfriendly federal officials—abolitionists and perhaps even blacks. Such a possibility most southerners found unsupportable. Fear approaching panic swept the region.

Although states' rights provided the rationale for leaving the Union, and southerners expounded the strict constructionist interpretation of the Constitution with great ingenuity, the economic and emotional factors were far more basic. The Lower South decided to go ahead with secession regardless of the cost. "Let the consequences be what they may," an Atlanta newspaper proclaimed. "Whether the Potomac is crimsoned in human gore, and Pennsylvania Avenue is paved ten fathoms in depth with mangled bodies . . . the South will never submit."

Not every slave owner could contemplate secession with such bloodthirsty equanimity. Some believed that the risks of war and slave insurrection were too great. Others retained a profound loyalty to the United States. Many accepted secession only after the deepest examination of conscience. Lieutenant Colonel Robert E. Lee of Virginia was typical of thousands. "I see only that a fearful calamity is upon us," he wrote during the secession crisis. "There is no sacrifice I am not ready to make for the preservation of the Union save that of honour. If a disruption takes place, I shall go back in sorrow to my people & share the misery of my native state."

In the North there was a foolish but understandable reluctance to believe that the South really intended to break away. President-elect Lincoln was inclined to write off secession as a bluff designed to win concessions he was determined not to make. He also showed lamentable political caution in refusing to announce his plans or to cooperate with the outgoing Democratic administration before his inauguration.

In the South there was an equally unrealistic expectation that the North would not resist secession forcibly. The "Yankees" were timid materialists who would neither bear the cost nor risk their lives to prevent secession. It was commonly believed that "a lady's thimble will hold all the blood that will be shed."

President Buchanan recognized the seriousness of the situation but professed himself powerless. Secession, he said, was illegal, but the federal government had no legal way to prevent it. (This was the same dilemma that had surfaced during the nullification crisis but as Senator Douglas had reminded him, Buchanan was no Andrew Jackson.) He urged making concessions to the South yet lacked the forcefulness to take the situation in hand. Of course, he faced unprecedented difficulties. His term was about to run out, and since he could not commit his successor, his influence was minuscule. Yet a bolder president would have denounced secession in uncompromising terms. Instead Buchanan vacillated between compromise and aimless drift.

Appeasers, well-meaning believers in compromise, and those prepared to fight to preserve the Union were alike incapable of effective action. A group of moderates headed by Henry Clay's disciple, Senator John J. Crittenden of Kentucky, proposed a constitutional amendment in which slavery would be "recognized as existing" in all territories south of latitude 36°30′. The amendment also promised that no future amendment would tamper with the institution in the slave states and offered other guarantees to the South. But Lincoln refused to consider any arrangement that would open new territory to slavery. "On the territorial question," he wrote, "I am inflexible." The Crittenden Compromise got nowhere.

The new southern Confederacy set vigorously to work drafting a constitution, choosing Jefferson Davis as provisional president, seizing arsenals and other federal property within its boundaries, and preparing to dispatch diplomatic representatives to enlist the support of foreign powers. Buchanan bumbled helplessly in Washington. And out in Illinois, Abraham Lincoln juggled Cabinet posts and grew a beard.

Milestones

1850	Compromise of 1850	**1856**	Caning of Senator Charles
	Clayton-Bulwer Treaty with		Sumner in the Senate
	Great Britain		Pottawatomie Massacre
1851–1860	Northern resistance to	**1856–1858**	Unrest in Kansas Territory
	enforcement of the Fugitive		("bleeding Kansas")
	Slave Act	**1857**	Dred Scott case (*Dred Scott* v.
1852	Harriet Beecher Stowe, *Uncle*		*Sandford*)
	Tom's Cabin		Panic of 1857
	Commodore Matthew Perry	**1858**	Lincoln-Douglas debates
	opens Japan to U.S. trade	**1859**	John Brown's raid on Harpers
1853	Gadsden Purchase		Ferry
1854	Ostend Manifesto	**1860**	South Carolina secedes from
	Kansas-Nebraska Act repeals		the Union
	Missouri Compromise	**1861**	Confederate States of America
1855	William Walker seizes power in		established
	Nicaragua		Lincoln rejects the Crittenden
			Compromise

SUPPLEMENTARY READING

Titles marked with an asterisk have been published in paperback.

The events leading to the Civil War have been analyzed by dozens of historians. Allan Nevins provides the fullest and most magisterial treatment in **The Ordeal of the Union** (1947) and **The Emergence of Lincoln*** (1950). An excellent briefer summary is D. M. Potter, **The Impending Crisis*** (1976). See also W. J. Cooper, Jr., **Liberty and Slavery: Southern Politics to 1860** (1983), Michael Holt, **The Political Crisis of the 1850s** (1978), and R. H. Sewell, **Ballots for Freedom: Antislavery Politics** (1976). Eric Foner, **Free Soil, Free Labor, Free Men*** (1970), is an excellent analysis of Republican ideas and policies.

On the enforcement of the Fugitive Slave Act, see S. W. Campbell, **The Slave Catchers** (1970), and T. D. Morris, **Free Men All: The Personal Liberty Laws** (1974). Everyone should read Harriet Beecher Stowe's **Uncle**

Tom's Cabin.* R. F. Wilson, **Crusader in Crinoline** (1941), is a satisfactory biography of Stowe, and E. L. McKitrick (ed.), **Slavery Defended*** (1963), contains a typical southern review of **Uncle Tom's Cabin.** Two studies stress the antiblack feelings of whites in the western states and their relation to the sectional crisis: E. H. Berwanger, **The Frontier Against Slavery*** (1967), and V. J. Voegeli, **Free But Not Equal*** (1967).

For details on foreign policy in the 1850s, see C. H. Brown, **Agents of Manifest Destiny** (1980), R. E. May, **The Southern Dream of a Caribbean Empire** (1974), and P. S. Klein, **President James Buchanan** (1962). D. S. Spencer, **Louis Kossuth and Young America** (1977), is also worth reading.

On Stephen A. Douglas, see R. W. Johannsen, **Stephen**

A. **Douglas** (1973). Nevins is particularly good on the Kansas controversy, but see also J. A. Rawley, **Race and Politics: "Bleeding Kansas"** (1969), and P. W. Gates, **Fifty Million Acres: Conflicts over Kansas Land Policy*** (1954).

Sumner's role in the deepening crisis is brilliantly discussed in David Donald, **Charles Sumner and the Coming of the Civil War** (1960). Klein's life of Buchanan is careful and judicious. On the Dred Scott case, see D. E. Fehrenbacher, **The *Dred Scott* Case** (1978).

The best modern biographies of Lincoln are B. P Thomas, **Abraham Lincoln** (1952), and S. B. Oates, **With Malice Toward None*** (1977). On his early career, see D. E. Fehrenbacher, **Prelude to Greatness*** (1962). W. E. Gienapp, **The Origins of the Republican Party** (1987), is a good recent study. S. B. Oates, **To Purge This Land with Blood** (1970), is a good biography of John Brown, but Nevins's **Ordeal of the Union** provides the finest account of the raid on Harpers Ferry. R. F. Nichols, **The Disruption of American Democracy*** (1948), describes the breakup of the Democratic party and the election of 1860. On the secession crisis and the outbreak of the Civil War, consult S. A. Channing, **Crisis of Fear*** (1970), and J. L. Roark, **Masters Without Slaves*** (1977).

XVI

The War to Save the Union

If the thing is pressed I think Lee will surrender.

    GENERAL PHILIP SHERIDAN *to General Ulysses S. Grant,*
April 6, 1865

Let the thing be pressed.

    PRESIDENT ABRAHAM LINCOLN *to Generals Grant and*
Sheridan, April 7, 1865

The nomination of Lincoln had succeeded brilliantly for the Republicans, but was his election a good thing for the country? As the inauguration approached, many Americans had their doubts. Honest Abe was a clever politician who had spoken well about the central issue of the times, but would he act decisively in this crisis? His behavior as president-elect was not reassuring. He spent much time closeted with politicians. Was he too obtuse to understand the grave threat to the Union posed by secession? People remembered uneasily that he had never held executive office, that his congressional career had been short and undistinguished. When he finally uprooted himself from Springfield in February 1861, his occasional speeches en route to Washington were vague, almost flippant. He kissed babies, shook hands, mouthed platitudes. Some people thought

it downright cowardly that he let himself be spirited in the dead of night through Baltimore, where feeling against him ran high.

Cabinet Making

Everyone waited tensely to see whether Lincoln would oppose secession with force, but Lincoln seemed concerned only with organizing his Cabinet. The final slate was not ready until the morning of inauguration day, and shrewd observers found it alarming, for the new president had chosen to construct a "balanced" Cabinet representing a wide range of opinion instead of putting together a group of harmonious advisers who could help him face the crisis.

William H. Seward, the secretary of state, was the ablest and best known of the appointees. Despite his reputation for radicalism, the hawk-nosed, chinless, tousle-haired Seward hoped to conciliate the South and was thus in bad odor with the radical wing of the Republican party. In time Seward proved himself Lincoln's strong right arm, but at the start he badly underestimated the president and expected to dominate him. Senator Salmon P. Chase, a bald, square jawed antislavery leader from Ohio, whom Lincoln named secretary of the treasury, represented the radicals. Chase was humorless and vain but able; he detested Seward, agreeing with him only in thinking Lincoln a weakling. Many of the president's other selections worried thoughtful people.

Lincoln's inaugural address was conciliatory but firm. Southern institutions were in no danger from his administration. Secession, however, was illegal, the Union "perpetual." "A husband and wife may be divorced," Lincoln said, employing one of his homely and, by the Victorian standards of the day, slightly risqué metaphors, "but the different parts of our country cannot. . . . Intercourse, either amicable or hostile, must continue between them." His tone was calm and warm. His concluding words catch the spirit of the inaugural perfectly:

> I am loath to close. We are not enemies, but friends. We must not be enemies. Though passion may have strained, it must not break, our bonds of affection. The mystic chords of memory, stretching from every battlefield and patriot grave to every living heart . . .

415

will yet swell the chorus of the Union when again touched, as surely they will be, by the better angels of our nature.

Fort Sumter: The First Shot

While denying the legality of secession, Lincoln had taken a temporizing position. The Confederates had seized most federal property in the Deep South. Lincoln admitted frankly that he would not attempt to reclaim this property. However, two strongholds, Fort Sumter, on an island in Charleston harbor, and Fort Pickens, at Pensacola, Florida, were still in loyal hands. Most Republicans did not want to surrender them without a show of resistance. To do so, one wrote, would be to convert the American eagle into a "debilitated chicken."

Yet to reinforce the forts might mean bloodshed that would make reconciliation impossible. After weeks of indecision, Lincoln took the moderate step of sending a naval expedition to supply the beleaguered Sumter garrison with food. Unwilling to permit this, the Confederates opened fire on the fort on April 12 before the supply ships arrived. After holding out for 34 hours, Major Robert Anderson and his men surrendered.

The attack precipitated an outburst of patriotic indignation in the North. Lincoln issued a call for 75,000 volunteers, and this caused Virginia, North Carolina, Arkansas, and Tennessee to secede. After years of crises and compromises, the nation chose to settle the great quarrel between the sections by force of arms.

Southerners considered Lincoln's call for troops an act of naked aggression. When the first Union regiment tried to pass through Baltimore in mid-April, it was attacked by a mob. The prosouthern chief of police telegraphed the Maryland state's attorney: "Streets red with blood. Send . . . for the riflemen to come, without delay. Fresh hordes will be down on us to-morrow." The chief and the mayor of Baltimore then ordered the railroad bridges connecting Baltimore with the northern states destroyed. Order was not restored until Union troops occupied key points in the city.

The southerners were seeking to exercise what a later generation would call the right of self-determination. How, they asked, could the North square its professed belief in democracy with its refusal to permit the southern states to leave the Union when a majority of their citizens wished to do so?

Lincoln took the position that secession was a rejection of democracy. If the South could refuse to abide by the result of an election in which it had freely participated, then everything that monarchists and other conservatives had said about the instability of republican governments would be proved true. "The central idea of secession is the essence of anarchy," he said. The United States must "demonstrate to the world" that "when ballots have been fairly and constitutionally decided, there can be no successful appeal except to ballots themselves, at succeeding elections."

This was the proper ground to take, both morally and politically. A war against slavery would not have been supported by a majority of northerners. Slavery was the root cause of secession but not of the North's determination to resist secession, which resulted from the people's commitment to the Union. Although abolition was to be one of the major results of the Civil War, the war was fought for nationalistic reasons, not to destroy slavery. Lincoln made this plain when he wrote in response to an editorial by Horace Greeley urging immediate emancipation: "I would save the Union. . . . If I could save the Union without freeing any slave, I would do it; and if I could save it by freeing all the slaves, I would do it; and if I could do it by freeing some and leaving others alone, I would also do that." He added, however, "I intend no modification of my oft-expressed personal wish that all men, everywhere, could be free."

The Blue and the Gray

In any test between the United States and the Confederacy, the former possessed tremendous advantages. There were more than 20 million people in the northern states (excluding Kentucky and Missouri, where opinion was divided) but only 9 million in the South, of whom about 3.5 million were slaves the whites hesitated to trust with arms. The North's economic capacity to wage war was even more preponderant. It was manufacturing nine times as much as the Confederacy (including 97 percent of the nation's firearms) and had a far larger and more efficient railroad system than the South. Northern control of the merchant marine and the navy made possible a blockade of the Confederacy, a particularly potent threat to a region so dependent on foreign markets.

The Confederates discounted these advantages. Many doubted that public opinion in the North would sustain Lincoln if he attempted to meet secession with force. Northern manufacturers needed southern markets, and merchants depended heavily on southern business. Many western farmers were still sending their produce down the Mississippi. War would threaten the prosperity of all these groups, southerners maintained. Should the North try to cut Europe off from southern cotton, the powers, particularly Great Britain, would descend on the land in their might, force open southern ports, and provide the Confederacy with the means of defending itself forever. "You do not dare to make war on cotton," Senator Hammond of South Carolina had taunted his northern colleagues in 1858. "No power on earth dares to make war upon it. Cotton is king."

The Confederacy also counted on certain military advantages. The new nation need only hold what it had; it could fight a defensive war, less costly in men and material and of great importance in maintaining morale and winning outside sympathy. Southerners would be defending not only their social institutions but also their homes and families.

To some extent the South benefited from superior military leadership. Both armies relied on West Pointers for their top commanders. Since most professionals followed the decisions of their home states when the war broke out, about 300 West Pointers became northern officers, about 180 southern. Among officers of lesser rank, the southerners probably excelled in the first years of the struggle, for the military tradition was strong in the South, and many young men had attended military academies, which were far more numerous in the South than in the North. Luck played a part too; the Confederacy quickly found a great commander, while the highest-ranking northern generals in the early stages of the war proved either bungling or indecisive. In battle after battle Union armies were defeated by forces of equal or smaller size.

There was little to distinguish the enlisted men of the two sides. After reading thousands of letters written by Union and Confederate soldiers, the historian Bell I. Wiley concluded that if they were all

tossed in the air and identifying marks removed, "it would be impossible to know which were written by Rebs, which by Yanks." Since northern and southern common soldiers were so much alike, superior generalship clearly made some difference.

Both sides faced massive difficulties in organizing for a war long feared but never properly anticipated. After southern defections, the regular army consisted of only 13,000 officers and enlisted men, far too few to absorb the 186,000 who had joined the colors by early summer. Recruiting was left to the states, each being assigned a quota; there was little central organization. Natty companies of "Fire Zouaves" and "Garibaldi Guards" in gorgeous uniforms rubbed shoulders with slovenly units composed of toughs and criminals and with regiments of farm boys from Iowa, Illinois, and Michigan. Unlike later conflicts in which men from all parts of the country were mixed in each regiment, Civil War units were recruited locally. Men in each company tended to have known one another or had friends in common in civilian life. But few knew even the rudiments of soldiering. The hastily composed high command, headed by the elderly Winfield Scott, debated grand strategy endlessly while regimental commanders lacked decent maps of Virginia.

The Whig prejudice against powerful presidents was part of Lincoln's political heritage; conse-

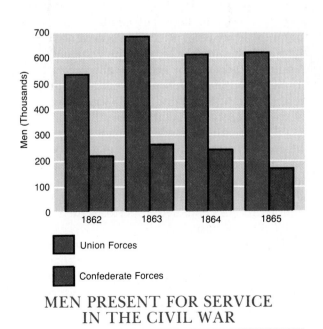

MEN PRESENT FOR SERVICE
IN THE CIVIL WAR

quently at the start he did not display the firmness of Jackson or Polk in his dealings with Congress and his Cabinet. But his strength lay in his ability to think problems through, accept their implications, and then to act unflinchingly. Anything but a tyrant by nature, he boldly exceeded the conventional limits of presidential power in the emergency, expanding the army without congressional authorization, suspending the writ of habeas corpus, even emancipating the slaves when he thought military necessity demanded that action. Yet he also displayed remarkable patience and depth of character: He would willingly accept snubs and insults in order to advance the cause. He kept a close check on every aspect of the war effort, but found time for thought too. His young secretary John Nicolay reported seeing him sit sometimes for a whole hour like "a petrified image," lost in contemplation.

Gradually Lincoln's stock rose—first with men like Seward, who saw him close up and experienced both his steel and his gentleness, then with the people at large, who sensed his compassion, his humility, his wisdom. He was only 52 when he became president, and already people were calling him Old Abe. Before long they would call him Father Abraham.

The Confederacy faced far greater problems than the North, for it had to create an entire administration under pressure of war, with the additional handicap of the states' rights philosophy to which it was committed. The Confederate constitution explicitly recognized the sovereignty of the states and contained no broad authorization for laws designed to advance the general welfare. State governments repeatedly defied the central administration, located at Richmond after Virginia seceded, even with regard to military affairs.

Of course, the Confederacy made heavy use of the precedents and administrative machinery taken over from the United States. The government quickly decided that all federal laws would remain in force until specifically repealed, and many former federal officials continued to perform their duties under the new auspices.

The call to arms produced a turnout in the Confederacy perhaps even more impressive than that in the North; by July 1861 about 112,000 men were under arms. As in the North, men of every type enlisted, and morale was high. Some wealthy re-

cruits brought slave servants with them to care for their needs in camp, cavalrymen supplied their own horses, and many men arrived with their own shotguns and hunting rifles. Ordinary militia companies sporting names like Tallapoosa Thrashers, Cherokee Lincoln Killers, and Chickasaw Desperadoes marched in step with troops of "character, blood, and social position" bearing names like Richmond Howitzers and Louisiana Zouaves. ("Zouave" mania swept both North and South, prospective soldiers evidently considering broad sashes and baggy breeches the embodiment of military splendor.)

President Jefferson Davis represented the best type of southern planter, noted for his humane treatment of his slaves. In politics he had pursued a somewhat unusual course. While senator from Mississippi, he opposed the Compromise of 1850 and became a leader of the southern radicals. After Pierce made him secretary of war, however, he took a more nationalistic position, one close to that of Douglas. Davis supported the transcontinental railroad idea and spoke in favor of the annexation of Cuba and other Caribbean areas. He rejected Doug-

Jefferson Davis sat for this portrait in 1863 in his mansion in Richmond. It is the only wartime portrait from life of the Confederate president.

las's position during the Kansas controversy but tried to close the breach that Kansas had opened in Democratic ranks. After the 1860 election he supported secession only reluctantly, preferring to give Lincoln a chance to prove that he meant the South no harm.

Davis was courageous, industrious, and intelligent, but he was rather too reserved and opinionated to make either a good politician or a popular leader. As president he devoted too much time to details, failed to delegate authority, and (unlike Lincoln) was impatient with garrulous and dull-witted people, types political leaders frequently have to deal with. Being a graduate of West Point, he fancied himself a military expert, but he was a mediocre military thinker. Unlike Lincoln, he quarreled frequently with his subordinates, held grudges, and allowed personal feelings to distort his judgment. "If anyone disagrees with Mr. Davis," his wife Varina Davis admitted, "he resents it and ascribes the difference to the perversity of his opponent."

The Test of Battle: Bull Run

"Forward to Richmond!" "On to Washington!" Such shouts propelled the opposing armies into battle long before they were properly trained. On July 21 at Manassas Junction, Virginia, some 20 miles below Washington, on a branch of the Potomac called Bull Run, 30,000 men under General Irvin McDowell attacked a roughly equal force of Confederates commanded by the "Napoleon of the South," Pierre G. T. Beauregard. McDowell swept back the Confederate left flank. Victory seemed sure. Then a Virginia brigade under Thomas J. Jackson rushed to the field by rail from the Shenandoah Valley in the nick of time, held doggedly to a key hill, and checked the advance. (A South Carolina general, seeking to rally his own men, pointed to the hill and shouted: "Look, there is Jackson with his Virginians, standing like a stone wall against the enemy." Thus "Stonewall" Jackson received his nickname.)

The southerners then counterattacked, driving the Union soldiers back. As often happens with green troops, retreat quickly turned to rout. McDowell's men fled toward the defenses of Washington, abandoning their weapons, stumbling through lines of supply wagons, trampling foolish

sightseers who had come out to watch the battle. Panic engulfed Washington. Richmond exulted. Both sides expected the northern capital to fall within hours.

The inexperienced southern troops were too disorganized to follow up their victory. Casualties on both sides were light, and the battle had little direct effect on anything but morale. Southern confidence soared, while the North began to realize how immense the task of subduing the Confederacy would be.

After Bull Run, Lincoln devised a broader, more systematic strategy for winning the war. The navy would clamp a tight blockade on all southern ports. In the West operations designed to gain control of the Mississippi would be undertaken. (This was part of General Scott's "Anaconda Plan," designed to starve the South into submission.) More important, a new army would be mustered at Washington to invade Virginia. Congress promptly authorized the enlistment of 500,000 three-year volunteers. To lead this army and—after General Scott's retirement in November—to command the Union forces, Lincoln appointed a 34-year-old major general, George B. McClellan.

McClellan was the North's first military hero. Units under his command had driven the Confederates from the pro-Union western counties of Virginia, clearing the way for the admission of West Virginia as a separate state in 1863. The fighting had been on a small scale, but McClellan, an incurable romanticizer and something of an egomaniac, managed to inflate its importance. "You have annihilated two armies," he proclaimed in a widely publicized message to his troops. Few northerners noticed that they had "annihilated" only about 250 Confederates.

Despite his penchant for self-glorification, McClellan possessed solid qualifications for command. One was experience. After graduation from West Point in 1846, he had served in the Mexican War. During the Crimean War he spent a year in the field, talking with British officers and studying fortifications. McClellan had a fine military bearing, a flair for the dramatic, and the ability to inspire troops. He was a talented administrator and organizer. He liked to concoct bold plans and dreamed of striking swiftly at the heart of the Confederacy to capture Richmond, Nashville, even New Orleans.

A hasty pencil sketch by an unknown artist captures the panic that swept the Union ranks after the defeat at Bull Run. The scene is the main road leading through Centerville to Washington.

Yet he was sensible enough to insist on massive logistic support, thorough training for the troops, iron discipline, and meticulous staff work before making a move.

Paying for the War

After Bull Run, this policy was exactly right. By the fall of the year a real army was taking shape along the Potomac: disciplined, confident, adequately supplied. Northern shops and factories were producing guns, ammunition, wagons, uniforms, shoes, and the countless other supplies needed to fight a great war. Most manufacturers operated on a small scale, but with the armed forces soon wearing out 3 million pairs of shoes and 1.5 million uniforms a year and with men leaving their jobs by the hundreds of thousands to fight, the tendency of industry to mechanize and to increase the size of the average manufacturing unit became ever more pronounced.

At the beginning of the war Secretary of the Treasury Salmon P. Chase underestimated how much the war would cost. He learned quickly. In August 1861 Congress passed an income tax law (3 percent on incomes over $800, which effectively exempted ordinary wage earners) and assessed a direct tax on the states. Loans amounting to $140 million were authorized. As the war dragged on and expenses mounted, new excise taxes on every imaginable product and service were passed, and still further borrowing was necessary. In 1863 the banking system was overhauled.

During the war the federal government borrowed a total of $2.2 billion and collected $667 million in taxes, slightly over 20 percent of its total expenditures. These unprecedentedly large sums proved inadequate. Some obligations were met by printing paper money unredeemable in coin. About $431 million in "greenbacks"—the term distinguished this fiat money from the redeemable yellowback bills—were issued during the course of the war.

Public confidence in all paper money vacillated with each change in the fortunes of the Union armies.

On balance, the heavy emphasis on borrowing and currency inflation was expensive but not irresponsible. In a country still chiefly agricultural, people had relatively low cash incomes and therefore could not easily bear a heavy tax load. Many Americans considered it reasonable to expect future generations to pay part of the dollar cost of saving the Union when theirs was contributing so heavily in labor and blood.

Politics as Usual

Partisan politics was altered by the war but not suspended. The secession of the southern states left the Republicans with large majorities in both houses of Congress. Most Democrats supported measures necessary for the conduct of the war but objected to the way the Lincoln administration was conducting it. The sharpest conflicts came when slavery and race relations were under discussion, the Democrats adopting a conservative stance and the Republicans dividing into Moderate and Radical wings. Political divisions on economic issues such as

This painting by David G. Blythe shows Lincoln chained by political enemies to strict constitutionality while he fights the dragon of rebellion. Tammany Democrats, led by New York's Mayor Fernando Wood, were among the Northerners who opposed the war and called for peace at any price.

tariffs and land policy tended to cut across party lines and, so far as the Republicans were concerned, to bear little relation to slavery and race.

As the war progressed, the Radical faction became increasingly influential. In 1861 the most prominent Radical senator was Charles Sumner, finally recovered from his caning by Preston Brooks and brimful of hatred for slaveholders. In the House, Thaddeus Stevens of Pennsylvania was the rising power. Sumner and Stevens were uncompromising on all questions relating to slaves; they insisted not merely on abolition but on granting full political and civil rights to blacks. Moderate Republicans objected vehemently to treating blacks as equals and opposed making abolition a war aim, and even many of the so-called Radicals disagreed with Sumner and Stevens on race relations. Senator Benjamin Wade of Ohio, for example, was a lifelong opponent of slavery, yet he had convinced himself that blacks (he habitually called them "niggers") had a distinctive and unpleasant smell. He considered the common white prejudice against blacks perfectly understandable. But prejudice, he maintained, gave no one the right "to do injustice to anybody"; he insisted that blacks were at least as intelligent as whites and were entitled not merely to freedom but to full political equality.

At the other end of the political spectrum stood the so-called Peace Democrats. These "Copperheads" (apparently the reference was not to the poisonous snake but to an earlier time when some hard-money Democrats wore copper pennies around their necks) opposed all measures in support of the war. They hoped to win control of Congress and force a negotiated peace. Few were actually disloyal, but their activities at a time when thousands of men were risking their lives in battle infuriated many northerners.

Lincoln treated dissenters with a curious mixture of repression and tolerance. He suspended the writ of habeas corpus in critical areas and applied martial law freely. Over 13,000 persons were arrested and held without trial, many, as it later turned out, unjustly. The president argued that the government dared not stand on ceremony in a national emergency. His object, he insisted, was not to punish but to prevent. Arbitrary arrests were rarely, if ever, made for purely political purposes, and free elections were held as scheduled throughout the war.

The federal courts compiled an admirable rec-

ord in defending civil liberties, though when in conflict with the military, they could not enforce their decrees. In *Ex parte Merryman* (1861), Chief Justice Taney held General George Cadwalader in contempt for failing to produce a prisoner for trial when ordered to do so, but Cadwalader went unpunished and the prisoner continued to languish behind bars. After the war, in *Ex parte Milligan* (1866), the Supreme Court declared illegal the military trials of civilians in areas where the regular courts were functioning, but by that time the question was of only academic interest.

The most notorious domestic foe of the administration was the Peace Democrat Congressman Clement L. Vallandigham of Ohio. There were two rebellions in progress, Vallandigham claimed, "the Secessionist Rebellion" and "the Abolitionist Rebellion." "I am against both," he added. In 1863, after he had made a speech urging that the war be ended by negotiation, Vallandigham was seized by the military and thrown into jail. But Lincoln ordered him released and banished to the Confederacy. Once at liberty, Vallandigham moved to Canada, from which refuge he ran unsuccessfully for governor of Ohio.

Vallandigham was a zealot who "chose to ignore expediency," as his biographer put it. "Perish offices," he once said, "perish life itself, but do the thing that is right." In 1864 he returned to Ohio. Although he campaigned against Lincoln in the presidential election, he was not molested. As the historian David Herbert Donald has written, Lincoln was not a dictator. Throughout the conflict, "the harshness of war regulations was often tempered by leniency."

Behind Confederate Lines

The South also revised its strategy after Bull Run. Though it might have been wiser to risk everything on a bold invasion of the North, President Davis relied primarily on a strong defense to wear down the Union's will to fight. In 1862 the Confederate Congress passed a conscription act that permitted the hiring of substitutes and exempted many classes of people (including college professors, druggists, and mail carriers) whose work could hardly have been deemed essential. A provision deferring one slave owner or overseer for every plantation of 20 or more slaves led many to grumble about "a rich man's war and a poor man's fight."

Although the Confederacy did not develop a two-party system, there was plenty of internal political strife. Southern devotion to states' rights and individual liberty (for white men) caused endless trouble. Conflicts were continually erupting between Davis and southern governors jealous of their prerogatives as heads of "sovereign" states.

Finance was the Confederacy's most vexing problem. The blockade made it impossible to raise much money through tariffs. The Confederate Congress passed an income tax together with many excise taxes but all told covered only 2 percent of its needs by taxation. The most effective levy was a tax in kind, amounting to one-tenth of each farmer's production. The South borrowed as much as it could ($712 million), even mortgaging cotton undeliverable because of the blockade, in order to gain European credits. But it relied mainly on printing paper currency; over $1.5 billion poured from the presses during the war. Considering the amount issued, this currency held its value well until late in the war, when the military fortunes of the Confederacy began to decline. Then the bottom fell out, and by early 1865 the Confederate dollar was worth less than 2 cents in gold.

Outfitting the army strained southern resources to the limit. Large supplies of small arms (some 600,000 weapons during the entire war) came from Europe through the blockade, along with other valuable matériel. As the blockade became more efficient, however, it became increasingly difficult to obtain European goods. The Confederates did manage to build a number of munitions plants, and they captured huge amounts of northern arms. No battle was lost because of a lack of guns or other military equipment, though shortages of shoes and uniforms handicapped the Confederate forces on some occasions.

Foreign policy loomed large in Confederate thinking, for the "cotton is king" theory presupposed that the great powers would break any northern blockade to get cotton for their textile mills. Southern expectations were not realized, however. The European nations would have been delighted to see the United States broken up, but none was prepared to support the Confederacy directly. The attitude of Great Britain was decisive. The cutting off of cotton did not hit the British as hard as the

South had hoped. They had a large supply on hand when the war broke out, and when that was exhausted, alternative sources in India and Egypt took up part of the slack. Furthermore, British crop failures necessitated the importation of large amounts of northern wheat, providing a powerful reason for not antagonizing the United States. The fact that most ordinary people in Great Britain favored the North also influenced British policy.

Several times the two nations came to the brink of war. In November 1861 U.S.S. *San Jacinto* stopped a British vessel, the *Trent,* on the high seas and forcibly arrested two Confederate envoys, James M. Mason and John Slidell, who were en route to London. This violation of international law would probably have led to war had not Lincoln decided to turn the southerners loose. In 1862 two powerful cruisers, the *Florida* and the *Alabama,* were built for the Confederates in English shipyards under the most transparent of subterfuges. Despite American protests, they were permitted to put to sea and were soon wreaking havoc among northern merchant ships. When two ironclad "rams" were also built in Britain for the Confederates, the United States made it clear that it would declare war if the ships were delivered. The British government then confiscated the vessels, avoiding a showdown.

Charles Francis Adams, the American minister in London, ably handled the many vexing problems that arose. However, the military situation determined British policy; once the North obtained a clear superiority on the battlefield, the possibility of intervention vanished.

War in the West: Shiloh

After Bull Run no heavy fighting took place until early 1862. Then, while McClellan continued his deliberate preparations to attack Richmond, Union forces in the West, led by a shabby, cigar-smoking West Pointer named Ulysses S. Grant, invaded Tennessee from a base at Cairo, Illinois. Making effective use of armored gunboats, Grant captured Forts Henry and Donelson, strongholds on the Tennessee and Cumberland rivers in northern Tennessee, taking 14,000 prisoners. Next he marched toward Corinth, Mississippi, an important railroad junction.

To check Grant's advance, the Confederates

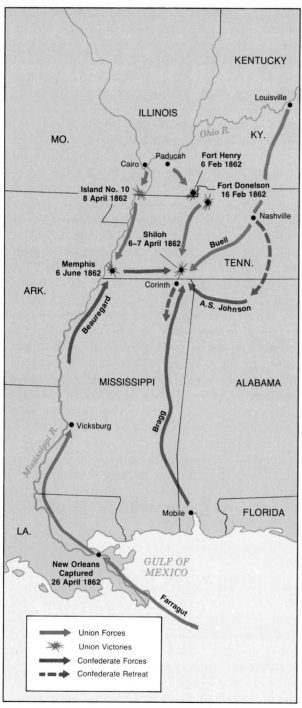

WAR IN THE WEST, 1862

The bloody battle at Shiloh in April of 1862 left Vicksburg, and thus control of the Mississippi, in Southern hands.

massed 40,000 men under Albert Sidney Johnston. On April 6, while Grant slowly concentrated his forces, Johnston struck suddenly at Shiloh, 20 miles north of Corinth. Some Union soldiers were caught half-dressed, others in the midst of brewing their morning coffee. A few died in their blankets. "We were more than surprised," one Illinois officer later admitted. "We were astonished." However, Grant's men stood their ground. At the end of a day of ghastly carnage, the Confederates held the advantage, but fresh Union troops poured in during the night, and on the second day of battle the tide turned. The Confederates fell back toward Corinth, exhausted and demoralized.

Grant was so shaken by the unexpected attack and appalled by his losses that he allowed the enemy to escape. This cost him the fine reputation he had won in capturing Fort Henry and Fort Donelson. He was relieved of his command. Although Corinth eventually fell and New Orleans was captured by a naval force under the command of Captain David Farragut, Vicksburg, key to control of the Mississippi, remained firmly in Confederate hands. A great opportunity had been lost.

Shiloh had other results. The staggering casualties shook the confidence of both belligerents. More Americans fell there in two days than in all the battles of the Revolution, the War of 1812, and the Mexican War combined. Union losses exceeded 13,000 out of 63,000 engaged; the Confederates lost 10,699, including General Johnston. Technology in the shape of more accurate guns that could be fired far more rapidly than the muskets of earlier times and more powerful artillery were responsible for the carnage. Gradually the generals began to reconsider their tactics and to experiment with field fortifications and other defensive measures. And the people, North and South, stopped thinking of the war as a romantic test of courage and military guile.

McClellan, the Reluctant Warrior

In Virginia, General McClellan, after unaccountable delays, was finally moving against Richmond. Instead of trying to advance across the difficult terrain of northern Virginia, he transported his army by water to the tip of the peninsula formed by the York and James rivers in order to attack Richmond from the southeast. After the famous battle (March 9, 1862) between U.S.S. *Monitor* and the Confederate *Merrimack,* the first fight in history between armored warships, control of these waters was securely in northern hands.

While McClellan's plan alarmed many congressmen because it seemed to leave Washington relatively unprotected, it simplified the problem of keeping the army supplied in hostile country. But McClellan now displayed the weaknesses that even-

tually ruined his career. His problems were both intellectual and psychological. Basically, he approached tactical questions in the manner of a typical 18th-century general. He considered war a kind of gentlemanly contest (similar to chess with its castles and knights) in which maneuver, guile, and position determined victory. He saw the Civil War not as a mighty struggle over fundamental beliefs but as a sort of complex game that commanders played at a leisurely pace and for limited stakes. He believed it more important to capture Richmond than to destroy the army protecting it. With their capital in

After the first battle at Bull Run, in July of 1861, there was little action until the following spring, when McClellan launched his Peninsula campaign. The battle of Antietam was the culmination of the fighting in the summer of 1862.

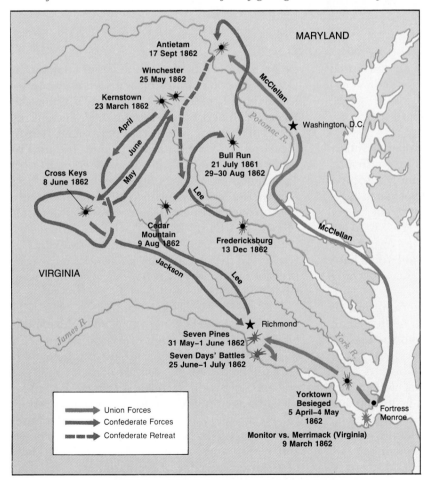

WAR IN THE EAST, 1861–1862

In the Peninsula campaign, the cautious McClellan faced the South's most brilliant generals, Robert E. Lee and Thomas J. "Stonewall" Jackson. During the Seven Days Battle as McClellan moved on Richmond, Lee attacked Union supply lines. This sketch by Alfred Waud shows McClellan's retreat after the failed attempt to take Richmond.

northern hands, surely the southerners (outwitted and outmaneuvered by a brilliant general) would acknowledge defeat and agree to return to the Union. The idea of crushing the South seemed to him wrongheaded and uncivilized.

Beyond this, McClellan was temperamentally unsuited for a position of so much responsibility. Beneath the swagger he was profoundly insecure. He talked like Napoleon, but he did not like to fight. He called repeatedly for more men; when he got them, he demanded still more. He knew how to get ready, but he was never ready in his own mind. What was said of another Union general would have been better said of McClellan: He was "watching the enemy as fast as he can."

McClellan began the Peninsula campaign in mid-March. Proceeding deliberately, he floated an army of 112,000 men down the Potomac and by May 14 had established a base at White House Landing, less than 25 miles from Richmond. A swift thrust might have ended the war quickly, but McClellan delayed, despite the fact that he had 80,000 men in striking position and large reserves. As he pushed forward slowly, the Confederates caught part of his force separated from the main body by the rain-swollen Chickahominy River and attacked. The Battle of Seven Pines was indecisive yet resulted in more than 10,000 casualties.

At Seven Pines the Confederate commander, General Joseph E. Johnston, was severely wounded; leadership of the Army of Northern Virginia then passed to Robert E. Lee. Although a reluctant supporter of secession, Lee was a superb soldier. During the Mexican War his gallantry under fire inspired General Scott to call him the bravest man in the army; another officer rhapsodized over his "daring reconnaissances pushed up to the cannon's mouth." He also had displayed an almost instinctive mastery of tactics. Admiral Raphael Semmes, who accompanied Scott's army on the march to Mexico City, recalled in 1851 that Lee "seemed to receive impressions intuitively, which it cost other men much labor to acquire."

Lee was McClellan's antithesis. McClellan seemed almost deliberately to avoid understanding his foes, acting as though every southern general was an Alexander. Lee, a master psychologist on the battlefield, took the measure of each Union general and devised his tactics accordingly. Where McClellan was complex, egotistical, perhaps even unbalanced, Lee was courtly, tactful, and entirely without McClellan's vainglorious belief that he was a man of destiny. Yet on the battlefield Lee's boldness skirted the edge of foolhardiness.

To relieve the pressure on Richmond, Lee sent General "Stonewall" Jackson, soon to be his most trusted lieutenant, on a diversionary raid in the Shenandoah Valley, west of Richmond and Washington. Jackson struck hard and swiftly at scattered Union forces in the region, winning a number of battles and capturing vast stores of equipment. Lincoln dispatched 20,000 reserves to the Shenandoah to check him—to the dismay of McClellan, who wanted the troops to attack Richmond from the north. But after Seven Pines, Lee ordered Jackson back to Richmond. While Union armies streamed toward the valley, Jackson slipped stealthily between them. On June 25 he reached Ashland, directly north of the Confederate capital.

Before that date McClellan had possessed clear numerical superiority yet had only inched ahead; now the advantage lay with Lee and the very next day he attacked. For seven days the battle raged. Lee's plan was brilliant but too complicated for an army yet untested: the full weight of his force never hit the northern army at any one time. Nevertheless, the shock was formidable. McClellan, who excelled in defense, fell back, his lines intact, exacting a fearful toll. Under difficult conditions he managed to transfer his troops to a new base on the James River at Harrison's Landing, where the guns of the navy could shield his position. Again the loss of life was terrible: Northern casualties totaled 15,800, those of the South nearly 20,000.

Lee Counterattacks: Antietam

McClellan was still within striking distance of Richmond, in an impregnable position with secure supply lines and 86,000 soldiers ready to resume battle. Lee had absorbed heavy losses without winning any significant advantage. Yet Lincoln was exasperated with McClellan for having surrendered the initiative and, after much deliberation, reduced his authority by placing him under General Henry W. Halleck. Halleck called off the Peninsula campaign and ordered McClellan to move his army from the James to the Potomac, near Washington. He was to join General John Pope, who was gathering a new army between Washington and Richmond.

It is possible, as James McPherson suggests in his gripping account of the war, *Battle Cry of Freedom*, that if McClellan had persisted and captured Richmond, the war might have ended and the Union been restored without the abolition of slavery, since

Lee in 1863, by Julian Vannerson. "So great is my confidence in General Lee," Stonewall Jackson remarked, "that I am willing to follow him blind-folded."

at that point the North was still fighting for union, not for freedom for the slaves. Ironically, as McPherson puts it, "by defeating McClellan, Lee assured a prolongation of the war until it destroyed slavery." Of course, no one expressed this idea at the time.

For the president to have lost confidence in McClellan was understandable. Nevertheless, to allow Halleck to pull back the troops was a bad mistake. When they withdrew, Lee seized the initiative. With typical decisiveness and daring, he marched rapidly north. Late in August his Confederates drove General Pope's confused troops from the same ground, Bull Run, where the first major engagement of the war had been fought.

Thirteen months had passed since the first failure at Bull Run, and despite the expenditure of thousands of lives, the Union army stood as far from Richmond as ever. Dismayed by Pope's incompetence, Lincoln turned in desperation back to McClellan. When his secretary protested that McClellan had expressed contempt for the president, Lincoln replied gently: "We must use what tools we have."

While McClellan was regrouping the shaken Union Army, Lee once again took the offensive. He realized that no number of individual southern triumphs could destroy the enormous material advantages of the North. Unless some dramatic blow, delivered on northern soil, persuaded the people of the United States that military victory was impossible, the South would surely be crushed in the long run by the weight of superior resources. Lee therefore marched rapidly northwest around the defenses of Washington.

Acting with even more than his usual boldness, Lee divided his army of 60,000 into a number of units. One, under Stonewall Jackson, descended on weakly defended Harpers Ferry, capturing more than 11,000 prisoners. Another pressed as far north as Hagerstown, Maryland, nearly to the Pennsylvania line. McClellan pursued with his usual deliberation until a captured dispatch revealed to him Lee's dispositions. Then he moved a bit more swiftly, forcing Lee to stand and fight on September 17 at Sharpsburg, Maryland, between the Potomac and Antietam Creek.* On a field that offered Lee

no room to maneuver, 70,000 Union soldiers clashed with 40,000 Confederates. When darkness fell, more than 22,000 lay dead or wounded on the bloody field.

Although casualties were evenly divided and the Confederate lines remained intact, Lee's position was perilous. His men were exhausted. McClellan had not yet thrown in his reserves, and new federal units were arriving hourly. A bold northern general would have continued the fight without respite through the night. One of ordinary aggressiveness would have waited for first light and then struck with every soldier who could hold a rifle, for with the Potomac at his back, Lee could not retreat under fire without inviting disaster. McClellan, however, did nothing. For an entire day, while Lee scanned the field in futile search of some weakness in the Union lines, he held his fire. That night the Confederates slipped back across the Potomac into Virginia.

Lee's invasion had failed; his army had been badly mauled; the gravest threat to the Union in the war had been checked. But McClellan had let victory slip through his fingers. Soon Lee was back behind the defenses of Richmond, rebuilding his army.

Once again, this time finally, Lincoln dismissed McClellan from his command.

The Emancipation Proclamation

Antietam, though hardly the victory he had hoped for, gave Lincoln the excuse he needed to take a step that changed the character of the war decisively. When the fighting started, fear of alienating the border states was reason enough for not making emancipation a war aim. However, pressures to act against the South's peculiar institution mounted steadily. Slavery had divided the nation; now it was driving northerners to war within themselves. Love of country led them to fight to save the Union, but fighting aroused hatreds and caused many to desire to smash the enemy. Sacrifice, pain, and grief made abolitionists of many who had no love for blacks—they sought to free the slave only to injure the master.

To make abolition an object of the war might encourage the slaves to revolt, but Lincoln dis-

---

* Southerners tended to identify battles by nearby towns, northerners by bodies of water. Thus Manassas and Bull Run, Sharpsburg and Antietam, Murfreesboro and Stone's River, and so on.

claimed this objective. Nevertheless, the possibility existed. Already the slaves seemed to be looking to the North for freedom: Whenever Union troops invaded Confederate territory, slaves flocked into their lines.

As the war progressed, the Radical faction in Congress gradually chipped away at slavery. In April 1862 the Radicals pushed through a bill abolishing slavery in the District of Columbia; two months later another measure outlawed it in the territories; in July the Confiscation Act "freed" all slaves owned by persons in rebellion against the

The genesis of the Emancipation Proclamation seen from diametrically opposed viewpoints. The drawing at left is by Adalbert Johann Volck, a Baltimore dentist and vitriolic propagandist for the Confederate cause. A satanic Lincoln, one foot on the Constitution, is inspired by a portrait of John Brown with a halo and a depiction of the alleged excesses of the Saint Domingue slave revolt of the 1790s. David Gilmour Blythe, a staunch administration supporter, left no doubt in his painting (below) that the sources of Lincoln's inspiration were of a much higher order.

United States. In fighting for these measures and in urging general emancipation, some Radicals made statements harshly critical of Lincoln; but while he carefully avoided being identified with them or with any other faction, the president was never very far from their position. He resisted emancipation because he feared it would divide the country and injure the war effort, not because he personally disapproved. Indeed, he frequently offered Radical pressure as an excuse for doing what he wished to do on his own.

Lincoln would have preferred to see slavery done away with by state law, with compensation for slave owners and federal aid for former slaves willing to leave the United States. He tried repeatedly to persuade the loyal slave states to adopt this policy, but without success. By the summer of 1862 he was convinced that for military reasons and to win the support of liberal opinion in Europe, the government should make abolition a war aim. "We must free the slaves or be ourselves subdued," he explained to a member of his Cabinet. He delayed temporarily, fearing that a statement in the face of military reverses would be taken as a sign of weakness. The "victory" at Antietam Creek gave him his opportunity, and on September 22 he made public the Emancipation Proclamation. After January 1, 1863, it said, all slaves in areas in rebellion against the United States "shall be then, thenceforward, and forever free."

No single slave was freed directly by Lincoln's announcement, which did not apply to the border states or to those sections of the Confederacy, like New Orleans and Norfolk, Virginia, already controlled by federal troops. The proclamation differed in philosophy, however, from the Confiscation Act in striking at the institution, not at the property of rebels. Henceforth every Union victory would speed the destruction of slavery without regard for the attitudes of individual masters.

Some of the president's advisers thought the proclamation inexpedient, and others considered it illegal. Lincoln justified it as a way to weaken the enemy. The proclamation is full of phrases like "as a fit and necessary war measure" and "warranted by the Constitution upon military necessity."

Southerners considered the Emancipation Proclamation an incitement to slave rebellion—as one of them put it, an "infamous attempt to . . . convert the quiet, ignorant, and dependent black son of toil into a savage incendiary and brutal murderer." Most antislavery groups thought it did not go far enough. Lincoln "is only stopping on the edge of Niagara, to pick up a few chips," one abolitionist declared. "He and they will go over together." Foreign opinion was mixed: Liberals tended to applaud, conservatives to react with alarm or contempt.

As Lincoln anticipated, the proclamation had a subtle but continuing impact in the North. Its immediate effect was to aggravate racial prejudices. Millions of whites disapproved of slavery yet abhorred the idea of equality for blacks. David Wilmot, for example, insisted that his famous proviso was designed to preserve the territories for whites rather than to weaken slavery, and as late as 1857 the people of Iowa rejected black suffrage by a vote of 49,000 to 8,000. To some, emancipation seemed to herald an invasion of the North by blacks who would compete for jobs, drive down wages, commit crimes, spread diseases, and eventually destroy the "purity" of the white race. The word *miscegenation* was coined in 1863 by David G. Croly, an editor of the *New York World,* directly as a result of the Emancipation Proclamation. Its original meaning was "the mingling of the white and black races on the continent *as a consequence of the freedom of the latter.*" Of course, the fact of miscegenation in its current, more general meaning long antedated the freeing of any slave.

The Democrats spared no effort to make political capital of these fears and prejudices even before Lincoln's Emancipation Proclamation, and they made large gains in the 1862 election, especially in the Northwest. So strong was antiblack feeling that most of the Republican politicians who defended emancipation did so with racist arguments. Far from encouraging southern blacks to move north, they claimed, the ending of slavery would lead to a mass migration of northern blacks to the South.

When the Emancipation Proclamation began actually to free slaves, the government pursued a policy of "containment," that is, of keeping the ex-slaves in the South. Panicky fears of an inundation of blacks subsided in the North. Nevertheless, emancipation remained a cause of social discontent. In March 1863, volunteering having fallen off, Congress passed a conscription act. The law applied to all men between 20 and 45, but it allowed draftees to hire substitutes and even to buy exemption for $300, provisions that were patently unfair to the poor. During the remainder of the war 46,000 men were actually drafted, whereas 118,000 hired substitutes, and another 161,000 "failed to report." Conscription represented an enormous expansion of national authority, since in effect it gave the government the power of life and death over individual citizens.

Negrophobia and the Draft Riots

After the passage of the Conscription Act, draft riots erupted in a number of cities. By far the most serious disturbance occurred in New York City in July 1863. Many workers resented conscription in principle and were embittered by the $300 exemption fee (which represented a year's wages). The idea of being forced to risk their lives to free slaves who would then, they believed, compete with them for jobs infuriated them. On July 13 a mob attacked the office where the names of conscripts were being drawn. Most of the rioters were poor Irish Catholic laborers who resented both the blacks and the middle-class Protestant whites who seemed to them responsible for the special attention blacks were suddenly receiving. For four days the city was an inferno. Public buildings, shops, and private residences were put to the torch. What began as a protest against the draft became an assault on blacks and the well-to-do. It took federal troops and the temporary suspension of the draft in the city to put an end to the rioting. By the time order was restored over 100 people (most of them rioters) had lost their lives.

The Emancipation Proclamation does not entirely account for the draft riots. The new policy neither reflected nor triggered a revolution in white thinking about the race question. Its significance was subtle but real; both the naive view that Lincoln freed the slaves on January 1, 1863, and the cynical one that his action was a mere propaganda trick are incorrect. Northern hostility to emancipation arose from fear of change more than from hatred of blacks, while liberal disavowals of any intention to treat blacks as equals were in large measure designed to quiet this fear. To a degree the racial backlash that the proclamation inspired reflected the public's awareness that a change, frightening but irreversible, *had occurred*.

Most white northerners did not surrender their comforting belief in black inferiority, and Lincoln was no exception. Yet Lincoln was evolving. He talked about deporting ex-slaves to the tropics, but he did not send any there. And he began to receive black leaders in the White House and to allow black groups to hold meetings on the grounds.

Many other Americans were changing too. The brutality of the New York riots horrified many white citizens. Over $40,000 was swiftly raised to aid the victims, and some conservatives were so appalled by the Irish rioters that they began to talk of giving blacks the vote. The influential *Atlantic Monthly* commented: "It is impossible to name any standard . . . that will give a vote to the Celt and exclude the negro."

The Emancipated People

To blacks, both slave and free, the Emancipation Proclamation served as a beacon. Even if it failed immediately to liberate one slave or to lift the burdens of prejudice from one black back, it stood as a promise of future improvement. "I took the proclamation for a little more than it purported," Frederick Douglass recalled in his autobiography, "and saw in its spirit a life and power far beyond its letter." Lincoln was by modern standards a racist, but his most militant black contemporaries respected him deeply. The *Anglo-African,* an uncompromising black newspaper (the position of which is revealed in an 1862 editorial that asked: "Poor, chicken-hearted, semi-barbarous Caucasians, when will you learn that "the earth was made for MAN?"), referred in 1864 to Lincoln's "many noble acts" and urged his reelection. Douglass said of him: "Lincoln was not . . . either our man or our model. In his interests, in his association, in his habits of thought and in his prejudices, he was a white man." Nevertheless, Douglass described Lincoln as "one whom I could love, honor, and trust without reserve or doubt."

As for the slaves of the South, after January 1, 1863, whenever the "Army of Freedom" approached, they laid down their plows and hoes and flocked to the Union lines in droves. "We-all knows about it," one black confided to a northern clergyman early in 1863. "Only we darsen't let on. We *pretends* not to know." Such behavior came as a shock to the owners. "[The slaves] who loved us best—as we thought—were the first to leave us," one planter mourned. Talk of slave "ingratitude" increased. Instead of referring to their workers as "servants" or "my black family," many owners began to describe them as "slaves" or "niggers."

Black Soldiers

A revolutionary shift occurred in white thinking about using black men as soldiers. Although they had fought in the Revolution and in the Battle of New Orleans during the War of 1812, a law of 1792 barred blacks from the army. During the early stages of the rebellion, despite the eagerness of thousands of free blacks to enlist, the prohibition remained in force. By 1862, however, the need for manpower was creating pressure for change. In August Secretary of War Edwin M. Stanton authorized the military government of the captured South Carolina sea islands to enlist slaves in the area. After the Emancipation Proclamation specifically authorized the enlistment of blacks, the governor of Massa-

chusetts moved to organize a black regiment, the famous Massachusetts 54th. Swiftly thereafter, other states began to recruit black soldiers, and in May 1863 the federal government established a Bureau of Colored Troops to supervise their enlistment. By the end of the war one soldier in eight in the Union army was black.

Enlisting large numbers of black soldiers changed the war from a struggle to save the Union to a kind of revolution. "Let the black man . . . get an eagle on his button and a musket on his shoulder," wrote Frederick Douglass, "and there is no power on earth which can deny that he has earned the right to citizenship."

Black soldiers were segregated and commanded by white officers. For example, the Massachusetts 54th regiment was commanded by Colonel Robert Gould Shaw of Boston, called by one admirer "the very type and flower of the Anglo-Saxon race." At first black soldiers received only $7 a month, about half what white soldiers were paid. But they soon proved themselves in battle; of the 180,000 who served in the Union army, 37,000 were killed, a rate of loss about 40 percent higher than that among

The Emancipation Proclamation allowed free blacks to enlist in the Union army. By late 1863, the Union had 58 black regiments. The skepticism of white commanders soon faded as black troops proved their bravery under fire. Here, soldiers from the 22nd U.S. Colored Troops charge an enemy position outside Petersburg in June 1864.

white troops. Their bravery under fire convinced thousands of northern white soldiers that blacks were not by nature childish or cowardly.

Southerners were another matter. There is no doubt that black soldiers were cruelly mistreated in Confederate prison camps. Still worse, many black captives were killed on the spot. After overrunnng the garrison of Fort Pillow on the Mississippi River, the Confederates massacred several dozen black soldiers, along with their white commander. Lincoln was tempted to order reprisals, but he and his advisers realized that this would have been both morally wrong (two wrongs never make a right) and likely to lead to still more atrocities. "Blood can not restore blood," Lincoln said in his usual direct way.

Antietam to Gettysburg

It was well that Lincoln seized on Antietam to release his proclamation; had he waited for a more impressive victory, he would have waited nearly a year. To replace McClellan, he chose General Ambrose E. Burnside, best known to history for his magnificent side-whiskers (originally called burnsides, later, at first jokingly, sideburns). Burnside was a corps commander, but he lacked the self-confidence essential to anyone who takes responsibility for major decisions. He knew his limitations and tried to avoid high command, but patriotism and his sense of duty compelled him, when pressed, to accept leadership of the Army of the Potomac. He prepared to march on Richmond.

Unlike McClellan, Burnside was aggressive—too aggressive. He planned to ford the Rappahannock River at Fredericksburg. Supply problems and bad weather delayed him until mid-December, giving Lee time to concentrate his army in impregnable positions behind the town. Although he had more than 120,000 men against Lee's 75,000, Burnside should have called off the attack when he saw Lee's advantage; instead he ordered the troops forward. Crossing the river over pontoon bridges, his divisions occupied Fredericksburg. Then, in wave after wave, they charged the Confederate defense line while Lee's artillery riddled them from nearby Marye's Heights. Watching the battle from his command post on the heights, General Lee was deeply moved. Turning to General James Longstreet, he

GETTYSBURG CAMPAIGN, 1863

Gettysburg, in July of 1863, marked the turning point of the war; after it the South never again tried to invade the North.

said: "It is well that war is so terrible—we should grow too fond of it!"

On December 14, the day following this futile assault, General Burnside, tears streaming down his cheeks, ordered the evacuation of Fredericksburg. Shortly thereafter, General Joseph Hooker replaced him.

Unlike Burnside, "Fighting Joe" Hooker was ill-tempered, vindictive, and devious. In naming him to command the Army of the Potomac, Lincoln sent him a letter that was a measure of his desperation but is now famous for what it reveals of the president's character:

> I think that during Gen. Burnside's command of the Army, you have taken counsel of your ambition, and thwarted him as much as you could, in which you did

a great wrong to the country. . . . I have heard, in such a way as to believe it, of you, recently saying that both the Army and the Government need a Dictator. Of course it is not *for* this, but in spite of it, that I have given you the command. Only those generals who gain successes, can set up dictators. What I now ask of you is military success, and I will risk the dictatorship. . . . Beware of rashness, but with energy and sleepless vigilance, go forward, and give us victories.

Hooker proved no better than his predecessor, but his failings were more like McClellan's than Burnside's. By the spring of 1863 he had 125,000 men ready for action. Late in April he forded the Rappahannock and quickly concentrated at Chancellorsville, about 10 miles west of Fredericksburg. His army outnumbered the Confederates by more than two to one; he should have forced a battle at once. Instead he delayed, and while he did, Lee sent Stonewall Jackson's corps of 28,000 men across tangled countryside to a position directly athwart Hooker's unsuspecting flank. At 6 P.M. on May 2, Jackson attacked.

Completely surprised, the Union right crumbled, brigade after brigade overrun before it could wheel to meet Jackson's charge. At the first sound of firing, Lee had struck along the entire front to impede Union troop movements. If the battle had begun earlier in the day, the Confederates might have won a decisive victory; as it happened, nightfall brought a lull, and the next day the Union troops rallied and held their ground. Heavy fighting continued until May 5, when Hooker abandoned the field and retreated in good order behind the Rappahannock.

Chancellorsville cost the Confederates dearly, for their losses, in excess of 12,000, were almost as heavy as the North's and harder to replace. They also lost Stonewall Jackson, struck down by the bullets of his own men while returning from a reconnaissance. Nevertheless, the Union army had suffered another fearful blow to its morale.

Lee knew that time was still on the side of the North; to defend Richmond was not enough. Already federal troops in the West were closing in on Vicksburg, threatening to cut Confederate communications with Arkansas and Texas. Now was the time to strike, while the morale of the northern people was at low ebb. With 75,000 soldiers he crossed the Potomac again, a larger Union force

dogging his right flank. By late June his army had fanned out across southern Pennsylvania in a 50-mile arc from Chambersburg to the Susquehanna. Gray-clad soldiers ranged 50 miles northwest of Baltimore, within 10 miles of Harrisburg.

As Union soldiers had been doing in Virginia, Lee's men destroyed property and commandeered food, horses, and clothing wherever they could find them. They even seized a number of blacks and sent them south to be sold as slaves. On July 1 a Confederate division looking for shoes in the town of Gettysburg clashed with two brigades of Union cavalry northwest of the town. Both sides sent out calls for reinforcements. Like iron filings drawn to a magnet, the two armies converged. The Confederates won control of the town, but the Union army, now commanded by General George G. Meade, took a strong position on Cemetery Ridge, a hook-shaped stretch of high ground just to the south. Lee's men occupied Seminary Ridge, a parallel position. On this field the fate of the Union was probably decided. For two days the Confederates attacked Cemetery Ridge, pounding it with the heaviest artillery barrage ever seen in America and sweeping bravely up its flanks in repeated assaults. During General George E. Pickett's famous charge, a handful of his men actually reached the Union lines, but reserves drove them back. By nightfall on July 3 the Confederate army was spent and bleeding, the Union lines unbroken.

The following day was the Fourth of July. The two weary forces rested on their arms. Had the Union army attacked in force, the Confederates might have been crushed, but just as McClellan had hesitated after Antietam, Meade let opportunity pass. On July 5 Lee retreated to safety. For the first time he had been clearly bested on the field of battle.

Lincoln Finds His General: Vicksburg

On that same Independence Day, far to the west, federal troops won another great victory. When General Halleck was called east in July 1862, Ulysses S. Grant reassumed command of the Union troops. Grant was one of the most controversial officers in the army. At West Point he had compiled an indifferent record, ranking 21st in a class of 39. During the Mexican War he served well, but when he was later assigned to a lonely post in Oregon, he took to drink and was forced to resign his commission. Thereafter he was by turns a farmer, a real estate agent, and a clerk in a leather goods store. In 1861, approaching 40, he seemed well into a life of frustration and mediocrity.

The war gave him a second chance. Back in service, however, his reputation as a ne'er-do-well and his unmilitary bearing worked against him, as did the heavy casualties suffered by his troops at Shiloh. Yet the fact that he knew how to manage a large army and win battles did not escape Lincoln. According to tradition, when a gossip tried to poison the president against Grant by referring to his drinking, Lincoln retorted that if he knew what brand Grant favored, he would send a barrel of it to some of his other generals.* Grant never used alcohol as a substitute for courage. "Old Ulysses," one of his soldiers said, "he don't scare worth a damn."

Grant's major aim was to capture Vicksburg, a city of tremendous strategic importance. Together with Port Hudson, a bastion north of Baton Rouge, Louisiana, it guarded a 150-mile stretch of the Mississippi. The river between these points was inaccessible to federal gunboats. So long as Vicksburg remained in southern hands, the trans-Mississippi region could send men and supplies to the rest of the Confederacy.

Vicksburg sits on a high bluff overlooking a sharp bend in the river. When it proved unapproachable from either the west or the north, Grant devised an audacious scheme for getting at it from the east. He descended the Mississippi from Memphis to a point a few miles north of the city. Then, leaving part of his force behind to create the impression that he planned to attack from the north, he crossed the west bank and slipped quickly southward. Recrossing the river below Vicksburg, he abandoned his communications and supply lines and struck at Jackson, the capital of Mississippi. In a series of swift engagements his troops captured Jackson, cutting off the army of General John C. Pemberton, defending Vicksburg, from other Con-

In outward appearance, Ulysses S. Grant was an unlikely leader. Despite his neatness in the formal portrait, Grant usually wore a sloppy, tobacco-stained uniform, and he had a reputation as a drunkard. During the war, critics pressed Lincoln to replace Grant, but the president replied, "I can't spare this man. He fights!"

federate units. Turning next on Pemberton, Grant defeated him in two decisive battles, Champion's Hill and Big Black River, and drove him inside the Vicksburg fortifications. By mid-May the city was under siege. Grant applied relentless pressure, and on July 4 Pemberton surrendered. With Vicksburg in Union hands, federal gunboats could range the entire length of the Mississippi.* Texas and Arkansas were for all practical purposes lost to the Confederacy.

---

* Lincoln denied having said this, pointing out that it was a version of a remark about General James Wolfe attributed to King George II. When a critic claimed that Wolfe was a madman, the King is said to have replied: "I wish he would bite some of the others."

---

* Port Hudson, isolated by Vicksburg's fall, surrendered on July 9.

VICKSBURG CAMPAIGN, 1863

When Vicksburg fell to the Union troops on July 4, 1863, the Mississippi River was reopened to the free passage of Federal forces.

Lincoln had disliked Grant's plan for capturing Vicksburg. Now he generously confessed his error and placed Grant in command of all federal troops west of the Appalachians. Grant promptly took charge of the fighting around Chattanooga, where Confederate advances, beginning with the Battle of Chickamauga (September 19–20), were threatening to develop into a major disaster for the North. Shifting corps commanders and bringing up fresh units, he won another decisive victory at Chattanooga in a series of battles ending on November 25, 1863. This cleared the way for an invasion of Georgia. Suddenly this unkempt, stubby little man, who looked more like a tramp than a general, emerged as the military leader the North had been so desperately seeking. In March 1864 Lincoln summoned him to Washington, named him lieutenant general, and gave him supreme command of the armies of the United States.

Economic and Social Effects, North and South

Though much blood would yet be spilled, by the end of 1863 the Confederacy was on the road to defeat. Northern military pressure, gradually increasing, was eroding the South's most precious resource: manpower. An ever-tightening naval blockade was reducing its economic strength. Shortages developed that, combined with the flood of currency pouring from the presses, led to drastic inflation. By 1864 an officer's coat cost $2,000 in Confederate money, cigars sold for $10 each, butter was $25 a pound, and flour went for $275 a barrel. Wages rose too, but not nearly as rapidly.

The southern railroad network was gradually wearing out, the major lines maintaining operations only by cannibalizing less vital roads. Imported products such as coffee disappeared; even salt became scarce. Efforts to increase manufacturing were only moderately successful because of the shortage of labor, capital, and technical knowledge. In general, southern prejudice against centralized authority prevented the Confederacy from making effective use of its scarce resources. Even blockade running was left in private hands until 1864. Precious cargo space that should have been reserved for medical supplies and arms was often devoted to high-priced luxuries.

In the North, after a brief depression in 1861 caused by the uncertainties of the situation and the loss of southern business, the economy flourished. Government purchases greatly stimulated certain lines of manufacturing, the railroads operated at close to capacity and with increasing efficiency, the farm machinery business boomed because so many farmers left their fields to serve in the army, and bad harvests in Europe boosted agricultural prices.

Congress passed a number of economic measures long desired but held up in the past by southern opposition. The Homestead Act (1862) gave 160 acres to any settler who would farm the land for five years. The Morrill Land Grant Act of the same year provided the states with land at the rate of 30,000 acres for each member of Congress to support state agricultural colleges. Various tariff acts raised the duties on manufactured goods to an average rate of 47 percent in order to protect domestic manufacturers from foreign competition. The Pacific Railway Act (1862) authorized subsidies in land and money for the construction of a transcontinental railroad. And the National Banking Act of 1863 gave the country, at last, a uniform currency. Under this act, banks could obtain federal charters by investing at least one-third of their capital in United States bonds. They might then issue currency up to 90 percent of the value of those bonds. A 10 percent tax on the issues of state banks drove state bank notes out of circulation.

All these laws stimulated the economy. Whether the overall economic effect of the Civil War on the Union was beneficial is less clear. Since it was fought mostly with rifles, light cannon, horses, and wagons, it had much less effect on heavy industry than later wars would have. Although the economy grew, it did so more slowly during the 1860s than in the decades preceding and following. Prices soared beginning in 1862, averaging about 80 percent over the 1860 level by the end of the war. As in the South, wages did not keep pace. This did not make for a healthy economy; nor did the fact that there were chronic shortages of labor in many fields, shortages aggravated by a sharp drop in the number of immigrants entering the country.

As the war dragged on and the continuing inflation eroded purchasing power, resentment on the part of workers deepened. During the 1850s iron moulders, cigarmakers, and some other crafts had formed national unions. This trend continued through the war years. There were many strikes. Inflation and shortages encouraged speculation and fostered a selfish, materialistic attitude toward life. Many contractors took advantage of wartime confusion to sell the government shoddy goods. By 1864 cotton was worth $1.90 a pound in New England. It could be had for 20 cents a pound in the South. Though it was illegal to traffic in the staple across the lines, unscrupulous operators did so and made huge profits. "Cotton was the great corrupter of the Civil War," the historian James McPherson has written.

Yet the war undoubtedly hastened industrialization and laid the basis for many other aspects of modern civilization. It posed problems of organization and planning, both military and civilian, that challenged the talents of creative persons and thus led to a more complex and efficient economy. The mechanization of production, the growth of large corporations, the creation of a better banking system, and the emergence of business leaders attuned

to these conditions would surely have occurred in any case, for industrialization was under way long before the South seceded. Nevertheless, the war greatly speeded all these changes.

Women in Wartime

Many southern women took over the management of farms and small plantations when their menfolk went off to war. Others became volunteer nurses, and after an initial period of resistance, the Confederate army began to enlist women in the medical corps. At least two female nurses, Captain Sally Tompkins and Kate Cumming, left records of their experiences that throw much light on how the wounded were treated during the war. Other southern women worked as clerks in newly organized government departments.

Large numbers of women also contributed to the northern war effort. As in the South, farm women went out into fields to plant and harvest crops, aided in many instances by new farm machinery. Many others took jobs in textile factories; in establishments making shoes, uniforms, and other supplies for the army; and in government agencies. But as was usually the case, the low wages traditionally paid women acted as a brake on wage increases for their male colleagues.

Besides working in factories and shops and on farms, northern women, again like their southern counterparts, aided the war effort more directly. Elizabeth Blackwell, the first American woman doctor of medicine, had already founded the New York Infirmary for Women and Children. After war broke out she helped set up what became the United States Sanitary Commission, an organization of women dedicated to improving sanitary conditions at army camps, supplying hospitals with volunteer nurses, and raising money for medical supplies. Many thousands of women volunteers took part in Sanitary Commission, YMCA, and similar programs.

An additional 3,000-odd women served as regular army nurses during the conflict. At the start the high command of both armies resisted the efforts of women to help, but necessity and a grudging recognition of the competence of these women gradually brought the generals around. The "proper sphere" of American women was expand-

Despite enormous difficulties, Elizabeth Blackwell managed to complete medical school and become the first woman doctor in the United States. During the Civil War, she organized the Women's Central Association of Relief, which trained nurses for war work. Women such as Dorothea Dix and Clara Barton in the North and Sally Tompkins in the South nursed sick and wounded soldiers.

ing, another illustration of the modernizing effect of the war.

Grant in the Wilderness

Grant's strategy as supreme commander was simple, logical, and ruthless. He would attack Lee and try to capture Richmond. General William Tecumseh Sherman would drive from Chattanooga toward Atlanta, Georgia. Like a lobster's claw, the two armies could then close to crush all resistance. Early in May 1864 Grant and Sherman commenced operations, each with more than 100,000 men.

Grant marched the Army of the Potomac directly into the tangled wilderness area south of the Rappahannock, where Hooker had been routed a year earlier. Lee, having only 60,000 men, forced the battle in the roughest possible country, where Grant found it difficult to make efficient use of his larger force. For two days (May 5–6) the Battle of the Wilderness raged. When it was over, the North had sustained another 18,000 casualties, far more than the Confederates. But unlike his predecessor, Grant did not fall back after being checked, nor did he expose his army to the kind of devastating counterattack at which Lee was so expert. Instead he shifted his troops to the southeast, attempting to outflank the Confederates. Divining his intent, Lee rushed his divisions southeastward and disposed them behind hastily erected earthworks in well-placed positions around Spotsylvania Court House. Grant attacked. After five more days, at a cost to the Union army of another 12,000 men, the Confederate lines were still intact.

Grant had grasped the fundamental truth that the war could be won only by grinding the South down beneath the weight of numbers. His own losses of men and equipment could be replaced; Lee's could not. When critics complained of the cost, he replied doggedly that he intended to fight on in the same manner if it took all summer. Once more he pressed southeastward in an effort to outflank the enemy. At Cold Harbor, 9 miles from Richmond, he found the Confederates once more in strong defenses. He attacked. It was a battle as foolish and nearly as one-sided as General Pakenham's assault on Jackson's line outside New Orleans in 1815. "At Cold Harbor," the forthright Grant confessed in his memoirs, "no advantage whatever was gained to compensate for the heavy losses we sustained."

Sixty thousand casualties in less than a month! The news sent a wave of dismay through the North. There were demands that "Butcher" Grant be removed from command. Lincoln, however, stood firm. Although the price was fearfully high, Grant was gaining his objective. At Cold Harbor, Lee had to fight without a single regiment in general reserve while Grant's army was larger than at the start of the offensive. When Grant next swung around his flank, striking south of the James River toward Petersburg, Lee had to rush his troops to that city to hold him.

As Grant pushed southward, both Union and Confederate armies took heavy casualties. At Cold Harbor, Grant lost 12,000 men. This photograph, taken from a church steeple, shows Union commanders planning the attack on Cold Harbor. Grant, standing at left, leans over the back of a wooden pew to study the map held by another officer.

As the Confederates dug in, Grant put Petersburg under siege. Soon both armies had constructed complicated lines of breastworks and trenches, running for miles in a great arc south of Petersburg, much like the fortifications that would be used in France in World War I. Methodically the Union forces extended their lines, seeking to weaken the Confederates and cut the rail connections supplying Lee's troops and the city of Richmond. Grant could not overwhelm him, but by late June, Lee was

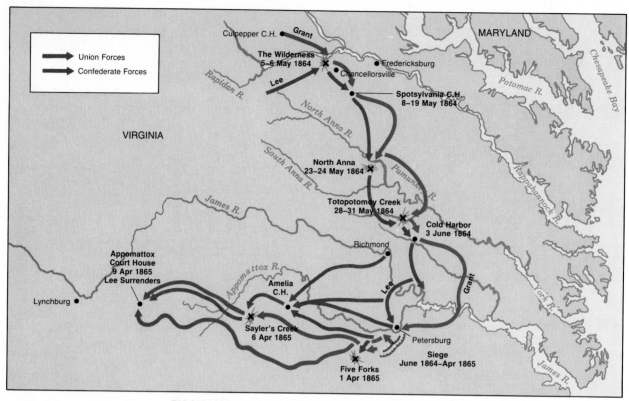

WAR ENDS IN VIRGINIA, 1864–1865

Grant's repeated and costly attempts (60,000 casualties the first month) to out-flank Lee are detailed here. At Five Forks the long seige of Petersburg was bro-ken; Richmond was evacuated. A week later, Lee surrendered.

pinned to earth. Moving again would mean having to abandon Richmond—tantamount, in southern eyes, to surrender.

Sherman in Georgia

The summer of 1864 saw the North submerged in pessimism. The Army of the Potomac held Lee at bay but appeared powerless to defeat him. In Georgia, General Sherman inched forward methodically against the wily Joseph E. Johnston, but when he tried a direct assault at Kennesaw Mountain on June 27, he was thrown back with heavy casualties. In July Confederate raiders under General Jubal Early dashed suddenly across the Potomac from the Shenandoah Valley to within 5 miles of Washington before being turned back. A draft call for 500,000 additional men did not improve the public temper. Huge losses and the absence of a decisive victory

were taxing the northern will to continue the fight.

In June, Lincoln had been renominated on a National Union ticket, with the Tennessee Unionist Andrew Johnson, a former Democrat, as his running mate. He was under attack not only from the Democrats, who nominated General McClellan and came out for a policy that might almost be characterized as peace at any price, but also from the Radical Republicans, many of whom had wished to dump him in favor of Secretary of the Treasury Chase.

Then, almost overnight, the atmosphere changed. On September 2 General Sherman's army fought its way into Atlanta. When the Confederates countered with an offensive northward toward Tennessee,* Sherman did not follow. Instead he aban-

---

* This force was crushed before Nashville in December by a Union army under General George Thomas.

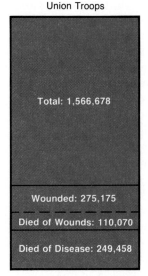

Union Troops

Total: 1,566,678

Wounded: 275,175

Died of Wounds: 110,070

Died of Disease: 249,458

Confederate Troops

Total: 1,082,119

Wounded: 100,000

Died of Wounds: 94,000

Died of Disease: 164,000

CASUALTIES OF THE CIVIL WAR

The Union death rate was 23 percent, the Confederate rate 24 percent. In general, twice as many soldiers were killed by disease as were killed by bullets.

doned his communications with Chattanooga and marched unopposed through Georgia, "from Atlanta to the sea."

Far more completely than most military men of his generation, Sherman believed in total war—in appropriating or destroying everything that might help the enemy continue the fight. The march through Georgia had many objectives besides conquering territory. One obvious one was economic, the destruction of southern resources. "[We] must make old and young, rich and poor feel the hard hand of war," Sherman said. Before taking Atlanta he wrote his wife: "We have devoured the land. . . . All the people retire before us and desolation is behind. To realize what war is one should follow our tracks."

Another object of Sherman's march was psychological. "If the North can march an army right through the South," he told General Grant, southerners will take it "as proof positive that the North can prevail." This was certainly true of Georgia's blacks, who flocked to the invaders by the thousands, women and children as well as men, all cheering mightily when the soldiers put their former masters' homes to the torch. "They pray and shout and mix up my name with Moses," Sherman explained.

Sherman's victories staggered the Confederacy and the anti-Lincoln forces in the North. In November the president was easily reelected, 212 electoral votes to 21. The country was determined to carry on the struggle.

At last the South's will to resist began to crack. Sherman entered Savannah on December 22, having denuded a strip of Georgia 60 miles wide. Early in January 1865 he marched northward, leaving behind "a broad black streak of ruin and desolation—the fences all gone; lonesome smoke-stacks, surrounded by dark heaps of ashes and cinders, marking the spots where human habitations had stood." In February his troops captured Columbia, South Carolina. Soon they were in North Carolina, advancing relentlessly. In Virginia, Grant's vise grew daily tighter, the Confederate lines thinner and more ragged.

To Appomattox Court House

On March 4 Lincoln took the presidential oath and delivered his second inaugural address. Photographs taken at about this time show how four years of war had marked him. Somehow he had become both gentle and steel-tough, both haggard and inwardly calm. With victory sure, he spoke for tolerance, mercy, and reconstruction. "Let us judge not," he said after stating again his personal dislike of slavery, "that we be not judged." He urged all Americans to turn without malice to the task of mending the damage and to make a just and lasting peace between the sections.

Now the Confederate troops around Petersburg could no longer withstand the federal pressure. Desperately Lee tried to pull his forces back to the Richmond and Danville Railroad at Lynchburg, but the swift wings of Grant's army enveloped them. Richmond fell on April 3. With fewer than 30,000 effectives to oppose Grant's 115,000, Lee recognized the futility of further resistance. On April 9 he and Grant met by prearrangement at Appomattox Court House.

It was a scene at once pathetic and inspiring. Lee was noble in defeat, Grant, despite his rough-hewn exterior, sensitive and magnanimous in victory. "I met you once before, General Lee, while we were serving in Mexico," Grant said after they had shaken hands. "I have always remembered your appearance, and I think I should have recognized you anywhere." They talked briefly of that earlier war, and then, acting on Lincoln's instructions, with which he was in full accord, Grant outlined his terms. All that would be required was that the Confederate soldiers lay down their arms. They could return to their homes in peace. When Lee hinted (he was too proud to ask outright for the concession) that his men would profit greatly if allowed to retain possession of their horses, Grant agreed to let them do so.

Costs and Prospects

And so the war ended. It had cost the nation more than 600,000 lives, nearly as many as in all other American wars combined. The story of one of the

The war was a private as well as a public agony. Countless families lost fathers, brothers, husbands, and sons who fell in battle or died of wounds and disease. Before leaving home, men sat for formal photographs, leaving these bittersweet reminders for their families. This Union private poses with his Colt revolver and saber.

lost thousands must stand for all, Union and Confederate. Jones Budbury, a tall, 19-year-old redhead, was working in a Pennsylvania textile mill when the war broke out, and he enlisted at once. His regiment first saw action at Bull Run. He took part in McClellan's Peninsula campaign. He fought at Second Bull Run, at Chancellorsville, and at Gettysburg. A few months after Gettysburg he was wounded in the foot and spent some time in an army hospital. By the spring of 1864 he had risen through the ranks to first sergeant and his hair had turned gray. In June he was captured and sent to Andersonville military prison, but he fell ill and the Confederates released him. In March 1865 he was back with his regiment in the lines besieging Richmond. On April 6, three days before Lee's surrender, Jones Budbury was killed while pursuing Confederate units near Sailor's Creek, Virginia.

The war also caused enormous property losses, especially in the Confederacy. All the human and material destruction explains the eroding hatred and bitterness that the war implanted in millions of hearts. The corruption, the gross materialism, and the selfishness generated by wartime conditions were other disagreeable by-products of the conflict. Such sores fester in any society, but the Civil War bred conditions that inflamed and multiplied them. The war produced many examples of charity, self-sacrifice, and devotion to duty as well, yet if the general moral atmosphere of the postwar generation can be said to have resulted from the experiences of 1861–1865, the effect overall was bad.

What had been obtained at this price? Slavery was dead. Paradoxically, while the war had been fought to preserve the Union, after 1865 the people tended to see the United States not as a union of states but as a nation. After Appomattox, secession was almost literally inconceivable. In a strictly political sense, as Lincoln had predicted from the start, the northern victory heartened friends of republican government and democracy throughout the world. A better-integrated society and a more technically advanced and productive economic system also resulted from the war.

The Americans of 1865 estimated the balance between cost and profit according to their individual fortunes and prejudices. Only the wisest realized that no final accounting could be made until the people had decided what to do with the fruits of victory. That the physical damage would be repaired no one could reasonably doubt; that even the loss

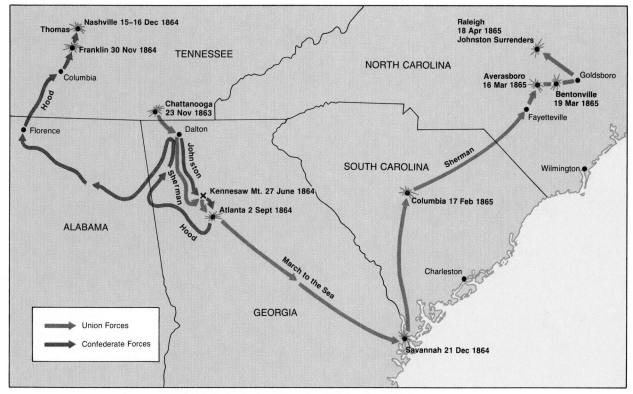

THE WAR MOVES SOUTH, 1863–1865

Confederate John B. Hood's "forlorn hope" offensive toward Nashville failed to deter Sherman from marching through Georgia. Joseph E. Johnston could offer little resistance to Sherman's drive through the Carolinas.

of human resources would be restored in short order was equally apparent. But would the nation make good use of the opportunities the war had made available? What would the ex-slaves do with freedom? How would whites, northern and southern, react to emancipation? To what end would the new technology and social efficiency be directed? Would the people be able to forget the recent past and fulfill the hopes for which so many brave soldiers had given their "last full measure of devotion"?

The cost of total war was evident throughout the South after Sherman's armies moved through Georgia and the Carolinas. Photographs documented stark scenes of destruction like this one taken by George W. Barnard showing the ruined railroad depot at Charleston, South Carolina.

Milestones

1861	Confederates attack Fort Sumter; Lincoln calls for 75,000 volunteers		Congress passes the Homestead, Morrill Land Grant, and Pacific Railway acts
	First Battle of Bull Run		Battle of Fredericksburg
	Lincoln appoints George B. McCllelan commander of the Union army	**1863**	Congress passes the Conscription and National Banking acts
	Ex parte Merryman		Draft riots in New York City
	Trent Affair		Battle of Chancellorsville
1862	Confederate Congress passes Conscription Act		Battle of Gettysburg
			Siege and capture of Vicksburg
	Battle of Shiloh	**1864**	Battle of the Wilderness
	Robert E. Lee named commander of the Army of Northern Virginia		Battle of Spottsylvania Court House
	Seven Days' Battle for Richmond		Battle of Cold Harbor
			Capture of Atlanta
	Second Battle of Bull Run		Sherman's March through Georgia; capture of Savannah
	Battle of Antietam; McClellan relieved of his command	**1864–1865**	Siege of Petersburg
	Lincoln issues the Emancipation Proclamation	**1865**	Capture of Columbia, South Carolina
			Lee surrenders to Grant at Appomattox Court House

SUPPLEMENTARY READING

Titles marked with an asterisk have been published in paperback.

The best recent survey of the Civil War period is J. M. McPherson, **Battle Cry of Freedom** (1988), but Allan Nevins's eight-volume **Ordeal of the Union** (1947–1971), continues to be valuable, both as an account of the fighting and as an analysis of political, social, and economic developments. J. G. Randall, **Lincoln, the President*** (1945–1955), is an excellent scholarly study (the last volume of this work was completed after Randall's death by R. N. Current). Political and constitutional problems are dealt with in H. M. Hyman, **A More Perfect Union** (1973). Lincoln's dealings with the Radicals have been extensively investigated. H. L. Trefousse, **The Radical Republicans: Lincoln's Vanguard for Racial Justice*** (1969), which praises Lincoln's management of the Radicals and minimizes his differences with them, is a good summary, but see also A. G. Bogue, **The Earnest Men: Republicans in the Civil War Senate** (1981), F. L. Klement, **The Cop-**

perheads in the Middle West (1960), and J. H. Silbey, **A Respectable Minority: The Democratic Party in the Civil War Era*** (1977).

For the movement to make abolition a war aim and the reaction to it, see J. M. McPherson, **The Struggle for Equality*** (1964), G. M. Frederickson, **The Inner Civil War*** (1965), and V. J. Voegeli, **Free but Not Equal: The Midwest and the Negro During the Civil War*** (1967).

The activities and attitudes of blacks during the war are summarized in D. T. Cornish, **The Sable Arm: Negro Troops in the Union Army*** (1956), L. F. Litwak, **Been in the Storm So Long** (1979), B. J. Fields, **Slavery and Freeedom on the Middle Ground** (1985), C. L. Mohr, **On the Threshold of Freedom** (1986), and Benjamin Quarles, **The Negro in the Civil War*** (1969). On the New York draft riots, see Adrian Cook, **The Armies of the Streets** (1974).

For aspects of economic and social history, see P. W. Gates, **Agriculture and the Civil War** (1965), M. E. Massey, **Bonnet Brigades: American Women and the Civil War** (1966), and R. P. Sharkey, **Money, Class, and Party.**

E. M. Thomas, **The Confederate Nation** (1979), is a good survey. The fullest biography of Jefferson Davis is Hudson Strode, **Jefferson Davis** (1955–1965).

The voluminous literature on the military history of the Civil War can only be sampled. K. P. Williams, **Lincoln Finds a General** (1949–1952), is exhaustive and judicious. T. H. Williams, **Lincoln and His Generals*** (1952), is briefer and more lively. See also three books by Bruce Catton: **Mr. Lincoln's Army*** (1951), **Glory Road*** (1952), and **A Stillness at Appomattox*** (1953). The famous **Battles and Leaders of the Civil War,** written during the 1880s by participants, is available in condensed form edited by Ned Bradford (1956). B. I. Wiley, in both **The Life of Billy Yank*** (1952) and **The Life of Johnny Reb** (1943), discusses the role of the common soldier. For the naval side of the conflict, see R. S. West, Jr., **Mr. Lincoln's Navy** (1957).

Among the biographies of Civil War generals the following are especially noteworthy: W. S. McFeely, **Grant** (1981), S. W. Sears, **George B. McClellan** (1988), Lloyd Lewis, **Sherman, Fighting Prophet** (1932), D. S. Freeman, **R. E. Lee** (1934–1935), and Frank Vandiver, **Mighty Stonewall** (1957). U. S. Grant's, **Personal Memoirs*** (1885) should not be missed.

The diplomacy of the Civil War period is covered in D. P. Crook, **The North, the South, and the Powers** (1974), M. B. Duberman, **Charles Francis Adams*** (1961), and F. L. Owsley and H. C. Owsley, **King Cotton Diplomacy** (1959).

American Lives:
Three Families in the Post–Civil War South

The Village Post Office

William La Fayette Black, a Confederate veteran, was a citizen of Harlan, a small community in a remote section of northern Alabama. He farmed a considerable acreage, but his main business was running the Harlan general store. His wife Martha was the village postmistress.

In his store Black sold farm tools, seed, coffee, tobacco, cloth, and all sorts of other goods. Most of his customers were white farmers; slightly more than 10 percent were black. Some owned their own land, and some were tenants or sharecroppers. (Unlike many southern merchants, Black made a point of treating black customers fairly.)

Local farmers had to buy things on credit because they had many expenses and little money during the planting and growing seasons. They gave Black a lien on their fall crops as security for what they needed during the spring and summer.

Black was therefore an important person in the community. People gathered in his store to talk about politics and crop prospects, to gossip, and perhaps to play a game of checkers. Farmers could scarcely exist without the credit he advanced them, and in hard times he readily carried them as long as possible. It was in his interest to do so, because it was always possible that low prices or a crop failure would hurt him almost as much as the debtors. Still, he also had to borrow to run his business; over the years he accumulated a great deal of land when people who owed him money went bankrupt.

However, the Blacks' life-style was far from easy. Their home was originally a one-room log cabin. As the family grew Black added to it until by 1889 there were four bedrooms and a kitchen as well as the original building. But the house had no cellar. It stood a foot or so above the ground resting on stone pillars. Hogs, chickens, dogs, and cats took shelter beneath it. The house was drafty, heated only by a single stone fireplace. There was no running water.

Black sometimes worked in the fields along with his sons and his tenants. They grew corn, wheat, oats, and of course cotton, which was their cash crop. They worked hard. During the winter they cleared woodland, uprooted stumps, and mended fences and equipment. After plowing and planting, there were the usual tasks of hoeing out weeds and ultimately harvesting the grain. Then in the fall they picked and ginned the cotton. Besides doing the cooking and other household tasks, Martha Black and her daughters milked the family cows, spun cotton, and wove cotton and wool into cloth for the family's use.

In 1889 the Blacks moved to Ashland, a larger town. Black purchased a more substantial house and a part interest in another general store. His partner was a power in the local Democratic party. Black himself was what he called "a Grover Cleveland Democrat." He would have nothing to do with the Populists, who were strong in many sections of Alabama.

When he died in 1900, Black left an estate valued at $25,000. One of his sons, Hugo, became a justice of the United States Supreme Court.

Samuel and Patsy McLeod owned a small cotton farm near Mayesville, South Carolina. The McLeods had been born slaves. Some of their 17 children had been sold away from them. After the war Patsy McLeod continued to work as a cook for her former master. Her wages, carefully saved, had helped make it possible for the family to buy five acres of cotton land.

The McLeod's "Homestead"

McLeod and his sons had then built a log house on the property, which the McLeods proudly christened "The Homestead." It was very small (especially for such a large family) and lacking in conveniences. The floor was of dirt and the two windows had shutters, but no glass panes. The children slept in bunk beds built against the walls. A solid brick fireplace supplied heat. A kitchen with its own chimney was later attached to the cabin.

Gradually the McLeods improved the property, building a barn and other outbuildings. Each fall they took their cotton to the farm of a white neighbor, where it was ginned and baled. Patsy McLeod spun some of this cotton and wove the thread to make shirts and underwear for the family. Shoes and most of their other clothes had to be purchased in the town of Sumter, which was 12 miles from the farm. Shopping in Sumter was an all-day trip by horse and wagon, but exciting for the children whose turn it was to accompany Samuel McLeod on such an expedition.

The McLeods were industrious and thrifty. Everyone worked on the farm. The youngest children gathered fruits and vegetables and fed and tended the animals. Others fished and hunted in the steams and woods of the area. The oldest boys worked for wages on nearby farms and what they earned helped pay for more land. Some of this land was too swampy for growing cotton, so the McLeods began to grow rice also.

Most of the McLeod children had little formal education, but Mary, the fifteenth child, born in 1875, was sent to a school for blacks operated by the Presbyterian Church near Mayesville, where the pupils learned to read by studying the Bible. Mary went into teaching and eventually founded a school of her own in Florida. She gradually elevated what began as an elementary school first to high school, then to junior college status. It finally became Bethune-Cookman College, a four-year liberal arts institution.

Simon Baruch emigrated to the United States from East Prussia in 1855, when he was 15. He came to Camden, South Carolina, because two friends from his hometown had started a business there. With their help he was able to go to medical school and become a doctor. He served in the Confederate army during the Civil War, then married Isabelle Wolfe. Isabelle's parents had been wealthy, but their home and property (along with nearly everything in the Camden area) had been destroyed by General Sherman's army during the late stages of the war.

Dr. Baruch was a tall, dignified man, very formal. His son Bernard claimed that despite the heat of South Carolina summers, he had never seen his father in shirtsleeves. But Baruch was a typical country doctor. He made his rounds in the countryside, treating both white and black patients. Times were hard in South Carolina during Reconstruction. Since money was scarce, Baruch often had to accept payment in goods—a cord of wood, perhaps, or some cotton or corn. Isabelle Baruch helped out by giving piano lessons for 25 cents an hour.

Gradually things improved. There was never a great deal of money but the Baruchs lived well. They had a large house, servants, and three acres of land on which Baruch ran a genuine farm in miniature. He raised cotton, corn, vegetables, and even sugarcane, which his servants refined into brown sugar for the family's use.

Although he was less prejudiced than most white southerners, Baruch detested the "Black Republican" government that controlled South Carolina in the 1870s. He joined the Ku Klux Klan. His children went to a small private school, but in their free time they mingled freely with black children. Many years later Bernard Baruch wrote: "What a cruel thing it was when I grew old enough to appreciate the gulf that separated the white and black races!" He did not add that it must have seemed much more cruel to the black children than to him.

In 1880 Dr. Baruch gave up his practice in South Carolina and moved the family to New York City.

Reconstruction and the South

No great social revolution ever took place without causing great temporary loss and inconvenience.

THE NATION, *1867*

The experiment has totally failed.

THE NATION, *1871*

This is socialism.

THE NATION, *1874*

O n April 5, 1865, Abraham Lincoln visited Richmond. The fallen capital lay in ruins, sections blackened by fire, but the president was able to walk the streets unmolested and almost unattended. Everywhere black people crowded around him worshipfully; some fell to their knees as he passed, crying "Glory, Hallelujah," hailing him as a messiah. But even white townspeople seemed to have accepted defeat without resentment.

A few days later, in Washington, Lincoln delivered an important speech on Reconstruction, urging compassion and open-mindedness. On April 14 he held a Cabinet meeting at which postwar readjustment was considered at length. That evening, while Lincoln was watching a performance of the play *Our American Cousin* at Ford's Theater, a half-mad actor, John Wilkes Booth, slipped into his box and shot him in the back of the head with a small pistol. Early the next morning, without having regained consciousness, Lincoln died.

The murder was part of a complicated plot organized by die-hard prosoutherners. Seldom have fanatics displayed so little understanding of their own interests, for with Lincoln perished the South's best hope for a mild peace. After his body had been taken home to Illinois, the national mood hardened; apparently the awesome drama was still unfolding; retribution and a final humbling of the South were inevitable.

Presidential Reconstruction

Despite its bloodiness, the Civil War had caused less intersectional hatred than might have been expected. Although civilian property was often seized or destroyed, the invading armies treated the southern population with remarkable forbearance, both during the war and after Appomattox. While he was ensconced in Richmond behind Lee's army, northerners boasted that they would "hang Jeff Davis to a sour apple tree," and when he was captured in Georgia in May 1865, he was at once clapped into irons preparatory to being tried for treason and murder. But feeling against Davis subsided quickly. In 1867 the military turned him over to the civil courts, which released him on bail. He was never brought to trial. A few other Confederate officials spent short periods behind bars, but the only southerner executed for war crimes was Major Henry Wirz, the commandant of Andersonville military prison.

The legal questions related to bringing the defeated states back into the Union were extremely complex. Since southerners believed that secession was legal, logic should have compelled them to argue that they were out of the Union and would thus have to be formally readmitted. Northerners should have taken the contrary position, for they had fought to prove that secession was illegal. Yet the people of both sections did just the opposite. Senator Charles Sumner and Congressman Thaddeus Stevens, in 1861 uncompromising expounders of the theory that the Union was indissoluble, now insisted that the Confederate states had "committed suicide" and should be treated like "conquered provinces." Lincoln believed the issue a "pernicious abstraction" and tried to ignore it.

The process of readmission began in 1862, when Lincoln reappointed provisional governors for those parts of the South that had been occupied by federal troops. On December 8, 1863, he issued a proclamation setting forth a general policy. With the exception of high Confederate officials and a few other special groups, all southerners could reinstate themselves as United States citizens by taking a simple loyalty oath. When, in any state, a number equal to ten percent of those voting in the 1860 election had taken this oath, they could set up a state government. Such governments had to be republican in form, must recognize the "permanent freedom" of the slaves, and must provide for black education. The plan, however, did not require that blacks be given the right to vote.

The "ten percent plan" reflected Lincoln's lack of vindictiveness and his political wisdom. He realized that any government based on such a small minority of the population would be, as he put it, merely "a tangible nucleus which the remainder . . . may rally around as fast as it can," a sort of puppet regime, like the paper government established in those sections of Virginia under federal control.* The regimes established under this plan in Tennessee, Louisiana, and Arkansas bore, in the president's mind, the same relation to finally reconstructed states that an egg bears to a chicken. "We shall sooner have the fowl by hatching it than by smashing it," he remarked. He knew that eventually representatives of the Southern states would again be sitting in Congress, and he wished to lay the groundwork for a strong Republican party in the section. Yet he realized that Congress had no intention of seating representatives from the "ten percent" states at once.

The Radicals in Congress disliked the ten percent plan, partly because of its moderation and partly because it enabled Lincoln to determine Union policy toward the recaptured regions. In July 1864 they passed the Wade-Davis bill, which provided for constitutional conventions only after a *majority* of the voters in a Southern state had taken a loyalty oath. Confederate officials and anyone who had "voluntarily borne arms against the United States" were barred from voting in the election or serving at the convention. Besides prohibiting slavery, the new state constitutions would have to repudiate Confederate debts. Lincoln disposed of the Wade-Davis bill with a pocket veto, and there matters stood when Andrew Johnson became president following the assassination.

Andrew Johnson, as recorded by Matthew Brady's camera in 1865. Johnson, Charles Dickens reported, radiated purposefulness but no "genial sunlight."

Lincoln had picked Johnson for a running mate in 1864 because he was a border-state Unionist Democrat and something of a hero as a result of his courageous service as military governor of Tennessee. From origins even more lowly than Lincoln's, Johnson had risen to be congressman, governor of Tennessee, and United States senator. He was able and ambitious but fundamentally unsure of himself, as could be seen in his boastfulness and stubbornness. His political strength came from the poor whites and yeomen farmers of eastern Tennessee, and he was fond of extolling the common man and attacking "stuck-up aristocrats."

Thaddeus Stevens called Johnson a "rank demagogue" and a "damned scoundrel," and it is true that he was a masterful rabble-rouser. But few politicians of his generation labored so consistently in behalf of small farmers. Free homesteads, public education, absolute social equality—such were his objectives. The father of communism, Karl Marx, a close observer of American affairs at this time, wrote approvingly of Johnson's "deadly hatred of the oligarchy."

---

* By approving the separation of the western counties that had refused to secede, this government provided a legal pretext for the creation of West Virginia.

Johnson was a Democrat, but because of his record and his reassuring penchant for excoriating southern aristocrats, the Republicans in Congress were ready to cooperate with him. "Johnson, we have faith in you," said Senator Ben Wade, author of the Wade-Davis bill, the day after Lincoln's death. "By the gods, there will be no trouble now in running the government!"

Johnson's reply, "Treason must be made infamous," delighted the Radicals, but the president proved temperamentally unable to work with them. As Eric L. McKitrick has shown in *Andrew Johnson and Reconstruction,* Johnson was an "outsider," a "lone wolf" in every way. Like Randolph of Roanoke, his antithesis intellectually and socially, opposition was his specialty; he soon alienated every powerful Republican in Washington.

Radical Republicans listened to Johnson's diatribes against secessionists and the great planters and assumed that he was antisouthern. Nothing could have been further from the truth. He had great respect for states' rights and he shared most of his poor white Tennessee constituents' contempt of blacks. "Damn the negroes, I am fighting these traitorous aristocrats, their masters," he told a friend during the war. "I wish to God," he said on another occasion, "every head of a family in the United States had one slave to take the drudgery and menial service off his family."

The new president did not want to injure or humiliate all southerners. He issued an amnesty proclamation only slightly more rigorous than Lincoln's. It assumed, correctly enough, that with the war over most southern voters would freely take the loyalty oath; thus it contained no ten percent clause. More classes of Confederates, including those who owned taxable property in excess of $20,000, were excluded from the general pardon. By the time Congress convened in December 1865, all of the southern states had organized governments, ratified the Thirteenth Amendment abolishing slavery, and elected senators and representatives. Johnson promptly recommended these new governments to the attention of Congress.

Republican Radicals

Peace found the Republicans in Congress no more united than they had been during the war. A small

Matthew Brady's photograph of the stalwart radical Republican, Thaddeus Stevens. Stevens served in the House from 1859 until his death in 1868.

group of "ultra" Radicals were demanding immediate and absolute civil and political equality for blacks; they should be given, for example, the vote, a plot of land, and access to a decent education. Senator Sumner led this faction. A second group of Radicals, headed by Thaddeus Stevens in the House and Ben Wade in the Senate, agreed with the ultras' objectives but were prepared to accept half a loaf if necessary to win the support of less radical colleagues.

Nearly all Radicals distinguished between the "natural" God-given rights described in the Declaration of Independence, and social equality. "Equality," said Stevens, "does not mean that a negro shall sit in the same seat or eat at the same table with a white man. That is a matter of taste which every man must decide for himself." This did not reflect personal prejudice in Stevens's case. When he died, he was buried in a black cemetery. Here is his epitaph, written by himself: "I repose in this quiet and secluded spot, not from any natural preference for solitude, but finding other cemeteries limited as to race, by charter rules, I have chosen this that I might illustrate in my death the principles which I advocated through a long life, equality of man before his Creator."

The moderate Republicans wanted to protect ex-slaves from exploitation and guarantee their basic rights but were unprepared to push for full political equality. A handful of Republicans sided with the Democrats in support of Johnson's approach, but all the rest insisted at least on the minimum demands of the moderates. Thus Johnsonian Reconstruction was doomed.

Johnson's proposal had no chance in Congress for reasons having little to do with black rights. The Thirteenth Amendment had the effect of increasing the representation of the southern states in Congress because it made the Three-fifths Compromise meaningless. Henceforth those who had been slaves would be counted as whole persons in apportioning seats in the House of Representatives. If Congress seated the southerners, the balance of power might swing to the Democrats. To expect the Republicans to surrender power in such a fashion was unrealistic. Former Copperheads gushing with extravagant praise for Johnson put them instantly on guard.

In addition, the ex-Confederates were not overflowing with goodwill toward their conquerors. A minority would have nothing to do with amnesties and pardons:

> Oh, I'm a good old rebel,
> Now that's just what I am;
> For the "fair land of freedom,"
> I do not care a dam.
> I'm glad I fit against it—
> I only wish we'd won
> And I don't want no pardon
> For anything I done.

Southern voters had further provoked northern resentment by their choice of congressmen. Georgia elected Alexander H. Stephens, vice-president of the Confederacy, to the Senate, although he was still in a federal prison awaiting trial for treason! Several dozen men who had served in the Confederate Congress had been elected to either the House or the Senate, together with four generals and many other high officials. It was understandable that southern people would select locally respected and experienced leaders, but it was equally reasonable that these choices would sit poorly with northerners.

Finally, the so-called Black Codes enacted by southern governments to control former slaves alarmed the North. These varied in severity from state to state. When seen in historical perspective, even the strictest codes represented a considerable improvement over slavery. Most permitted blacks to sue and to testify in court, at least in cases involving members of their own race. Blacks were allowed to own certain kinds of property; marriages were made legal; other rights were guaranteed. However, blacks could not bear arms, be employed in occupations other than farming and domestic service, or leave their jobs without forfeiting back pay. The Louisiana code required them to sign labor contracts for the year during the first ten days of January. A similar rule was put into effect in Mississippi, where, in addition, drunkards, vagrants, beggars, "common night-walkers," and even persons who "misspend what they earn" and who could not pay the stiff fines assessed for such misbehavior were to be "hired out . . . at public outcry" to the white persons who would take them for the shortest period in return for paying the fines. Such laws, apparently designed to get around the Thirteenth Amendment, outraged northerners.

For all these reasons the Republicans in Congress rejected Johnsonian Reconstruction. Quickly they created a joint committee on Reconstruction, headed by Senator William P. Fessenden of Maine, a moderate, to study the question of readmitting the southern states.

The committee held public hearings that produced much evidence of the mistreatment of blacks. Colonel George A. Custer, stationed in Texas, testified: "It is of weekly, if not of daily occurrence that Freedmen are murdered." The nurse Clara Barton told a gruesome tale about a pregnant woman who had been brutally whipped. Others described the intimidation of blacks by poor whites. The hearings strengthened the hands of the Radicals, who had been claiming all along that the South was perpetuating slavery under another name.

President Johnson's attitude speeded the swing toward the Radical position. While the hearings were in progress, Congress passed a bill expanding and extending the Freedmen's Bureau, which had

Agents of the Freedmen's Bureau helped defend former slaves against white attacks and provided them with food, clothing, and medical care. They also set up schools. However, hostility toward the activities of the Freedmen's Bureau was widespread. In 1866, during a race riot in Memphis, mobs killed 46 blacks and burned this Freedmen's schoolhouse.

been established in March 1865 to care for refugees. The bureau, a branch of the War Department, was already exercising considerable coercive and supervisory power in the South. Now Congress sought to add to its authority in order to protect the black population. Although the bill had wide support, Johnson vetoed it, arguing that it was an unconstitutional extension of military authority in peacetime. Congress then passed a Civil Rights Act that, besides declaring specifically that blacks were citizens of the United States, denied the states the power to restrict their rights to testify in court, to make contracts for their labor, and to hold property. In other words, it put teeth in the Thirteenth Amendment.

Once again the president refused to go along, although his veto was sure to drive more moderates into the arms of the Radicals. On April 9, 1866, Congress repassed the Civil Rights Act by a two-thirds majority, the first time in American history that a major piece of legislation became law over the veto of a president. This event marked a revolution in the history of Reconstruction, indeed, in federal-state relations, north as well as south. Thereafter Congress, not President Johnson, had the upper hand.

In the clash between the president and Congress, Johnson was his own worst enemy. His language was often intemperate, his handling of opponents inept, his analysis of southern conditions incorrect. He had assumed that the small southern farmers who made up the majority in the Confederacy shared his prejudices against the planter class. They did not, as their choices in the postwar elections demonstrated. In fact, Johnson's hatred of the southern aristocracy may have been based more on jealousy than on principle. Under the Reconstruction plan, persons excluded from the blanket amnesty could apply individually for the restoration of their rights. When wealthy and socially prominent southerners flocked to Washington, hat in hand, he found their flattery and humility exhilarating. He issued pardons wholesale. "I did not expect to keep out all who were excluded from the amnesty," he explained. "I intended they should sue for pardon, and so realize the enormity of their crime."

The president misread northern opinion. He believed that Congress had no right to pass laws affecting the South before southern representatives had been readmitted to Congress. However, in the light of the refusal of most southern whites to grant any real power or responsibility to the freedmen (an attitude that Johnson did not condemn), the public would not accept this point of view. Johnson placed his own judgment over that of the overwhelming majority of northern voters, and this was a great error, morally and tactically. By encouraging southerners to resist efforts to improve the lot of blacks, Johnson played into the hands of northern extremists.

The Radicals encountered grave problems in fighting for their program. Northerners might object to the Black Codes and to seating "rebels" in Congress, but few believed in racial equality. Between 1865 and 1868 Wisconsin, Minnesota, Connecticut, Nebraska, New Jersey, Ohio, Michigan, and Pennsylvania all rejected bills granting blacks the vote.

The Radicals were in effect demanding not merely equal rights for freedmen but extra rights; not merely the vote but special protection of that right against the pressure that southern whites would surely apply to undermine it. This idea flew in the face of conventional American beliefs in equality before the law and individual self-reliance. Such protection would involve interference by the federal government in local affairs, a concept at variance with American practice. Events were to show that the Radicals were correct—that what amounted to a political revolution in state-federal relations was essential if blacks were to achieve real equality. But in the climate of that day their proposals encountered bitter resistance, and not only from southerners.

Thus, while the Radicals sought partisan advantage in their battle with Johnson and sometimes played on war-bred passions in achieving their ends, they were taking large political risks in defense of genuinely held principles. One historian has aptly called them the "moral trustees" of the Civil War.

The Fourteenth Amendment

In June 1866 Congress submitted to the states a new amendment to the Constitution. The Fourteenth Amendment was, in the context of the times, a truly radical measure. Never before had newly freed slaves been granted significant political rights. For example, in the British Caribbean sugar islands, where slavery had been abolished in the 1830s, stiff property qualifications and poll taxes kept freedmen from voting. The Fourteenth Amendment was also a milestone along the road to the centralization of political power in the United States because it

reduced the power of all the states. In this sense it confirmed the great change wrought by the Civil War: the growth of a more complex, more closely integrated social and economic structure requiring closer national supervision. Few people understood this aspect of the amendment at the time.

First the amendment supplied a broad definition of American citizenship: "All persons born or naturalized in the United States, and subject to the jurisdiction thereof, are citizens of the United States and of the State wherein they reside." Obviously this included blacks. Then it struck at discriminatory legislation like the Black Codes: "No State shall make or enforce any law which shall abridge the privileges or immunities of citizens of the United States; nor shall any State deprive any person of life, liberty, or property, without due process of law." The next section attempted to force the southern states to permit blacks to vote. If a state denied the vote to any class of its adult male citizens, its representation was to be reduced proportionately. Under another clause, former federal officials who had served the Confederacy were barred from holding either state or federal office unless specifically pardoned by a two-thirds vote of Congress. Finally, the Confederate debt was repudiated.

While the amendment did not specifically outlaw segregation or prevent a state from disfranchising blacks, the southern states would have none of it. Without them the necessary three-fourths majority of the states could not be obtained.

President Johnson vowed to make the choice between the Fourteenth Amendment and his own policy the main issue of the 1866 congressional elections. He embarked on "a swing around the circle" to rally the public to his cause. He failed dismally. Northern women objected to the implication in the amendment that black men were more fitted to vote than white women, but a large majority of northern voters was determined that blacks must have at least formal legal equality. The Republicans won better than two-thirds of the seats in both houses, together with control of all of the northern state governments. Johnson emerged from the campaign discredited, the Radicals stronger and determined to have their way. The southern states, Congressman James A. Garfield of Ohio said in February 1867, have "flung back into our teeth the magnanimous offer of a generous nation. It is now our turn to act."

The Reconstruction Acts

Had the southern states been willing to accept the Fourteenth Amendment, coercive measures might have been avoided. Their recalcitrance and continuing indications that local authorities were persecuting blacks finally led to the passage, on March 2, 1867, of the First Reconstruction Act. This law divided the former Confederacy—exclusive of Tennessee, which had ratified the Fourteenth Amendment—into five military districts, each controlled by

Johnson tried to turn public opinion against the Radicals' plan for Reconstruction. He toured the country, stumping for the Constitution with the same speech at every stop. His efforts failed as mobs greeted him with the cry, "Shut up, Johnson." This Harper's Weekly *cartoon reflects public criticism of Johnson as a parrot repeating a single word.*

a major general. It gave these officers almost dictatorial power to protect the civil rights of "all persons," maintain order, and supervise the administration of justice. To rid themselves of military rule, the former states were required to adopt constitutions guaranteeing blacks the right to vote and disfranchising broad classes of ex-Confederates. If the new constitutions proved satisfactory to Congress, and if the new governments ratified the Fourteenth Amendment, their representatives would be admitted to Congress and military rule ended. Johnson's veto of the act was easily overridden.

Although drastic, the Reconstruction Act was so vague that it proved unworkable. Military control was easily established. But in deference to moderate Republican views, the law had not spelled out the process by which the new constitutions were to be drawn up. Southern whites preferred the status quo, even under army control, to enfranchising blacks and retiring their own respected leaders. They made no effort to follow the steps laid down in the law. Congress therefore passed a second act requiring the military authorities to register voters and supervise the election of delegates to constitutional conventions. A third act further clarified procedures.

Still white southerners resisted. The laws required that the constitutions be approved by a majority of the registered voters. Simply by staying away from the polls, whites prevented ratification in state after state. At last, in March 1868, a full year after the First Reconstruction Act, Congress changed the rules again. The constitutions were to be ratified by a majority of the voters. In June 1868, Arkansas, having fulfilled the requirements, was readmitted to the Union, and by July a sufficient number of states had ratified the Fourteenth Amendment to make it part of the Constitution. But it was not until July 1870 that the last southern state, Georgia, qualified to the satisfaction of Congress.

Congress Takes Charge

To carry out this program in the face of determined southern resistance required singlemindedness over a long period to an extent seldom demonstrated by an American legislature. The persistence resulted in part from the suffering and frustrations of the war years. The refusal of the South to accept the spirit of even the mild reconstruction designed by Johnson goaded the North to ever more overbearing efforts to bring the ex-Confederates to heel. President Johnson's stubbornness also influenced the Republicans. They became obsessed with the need to defeat him. The unsettled times and the large Republican majorities, always threatened by the possibility of a Democratic resurgence if "unreconstructed" southern congressmen were readmitted, sustained their determination.

These considerations led Republicans to attempt a kind of grand revision of the federal government, one that almost destroyed the balance between judicial, executive, and legislative power established in 1789. A series of measures passed between 1866 and 1868 increased the authority of Congress over the army, over the process of amending the Constitution, and over Cabinet members and lesser appointive officers. Even the Supreme Court was affected. Its size was reduced and its jurisdiction over civil rights cases limited. Finally, in a showdown caused by emotion more than by practical considerations, the Republicans attempted to remove President Johnson from office.

Johnson was a poor president and out of touch with public opinion, but he had done nothing to merit ejection from office. While he had a low opinion of blacks, his opinion was so widely shared by whites that it is unhistorical to condemn him as a reactionary on this ground. Johnson believed that he was fighting to preserve constitutional government. He was honest and devoted to duty, and his record easily withstood the most searching examination. When Congress passed laws taking away powers granted him by the Constitution, he refused to submit.

The chief issue was the Tenure of Office Act of 1867, which prohibited the president from removing officials who had been appointed with the consent of the Senate without first obtaining Senate approval. In February 1868 Johnson "violated" this act by dismissing Secretary of War Edwin M. Stanton, who had been openly in sympathy with the Radicals for some time. The House, acting under the procedure set up in the Constitution for removing the president, promptly impeached him before the bar of the Senate, Chief Justice Salmon P. Chase presiding.

The trial was conducted in a partisan and vindictive manner. Johnson's lawyers easily established that he had removed Stanton only in an effort to prove the Tenure of Office Act unconstitutional. They demonstrated that the act did not protect Stanton to begin with, since it gave Cabinet members tenure "during the term of the President by whom they may have been appointed," and Stanton had been appointed in 1862, during Lincoln's first term!

Nevertheless the Radicals pressed the charges (11 separate articles) relentlessly. To the argument that Johnson had committed no crime, the learned Senator Sumner retorted that the proceedings were "political in character" rather than judicial. Thaddeus Stevens, directing the attack on behalf of the House, warned the senators that although "no corrupt or wicked motive" could be attributed to Johnson, they would "be tortured on the gibbet of everlasting obloquy" if they did not convict him. Tremendous pressure was applied to the handful of Republican senators who were unwilling to disregard the evidence.

Seven of them resisted to the end, and the Senate failed by a single vote to convict Johnson. This was probably fortunate. Had he been forced from office on such flimsy grounds, the independence of the executive might have been permanently weakened. Then the legislative branch would have become supreme.

The Fifteenth Amendment

The failure of the impeachment did not affect the course of Reconstruction. The president was acquitted on May 16, 1868. A few days later, the Republican National Convention nominated General Ulysses S. Grant for the presidency. At the Democratic convention Johnson had considerable support, but the delegates nominated Horatio Seymour, a former governor of New York. In November Grant won an easy victory in the electoral college, 214 to 80, but the popular vote was close: 3 million to 2.7 million. Although he would probably have carried the electoral college in any case, Grant's margin in the popular vote was supplied by southern blacks enfranchised under the Reconstruction Acts, about 450,000 of whom supported him. A majority of white voters probably preferred Sey-

The black vote helped Grant win five former Confederate states in the election of 1868. Although Republicans had avoided supporting suffrage for blacks during the campaign, they changed course after their victory and proposed the Fifteenth Amendment. In this cartoon, Grant, standing on shore, advises white Southerners to accept black suffrage.

mour. Since many citizens undoubtedly voted Republican because of personal admiration for General Grant, the election statistics suggest that a substantial white majority opposed the policies of the Radicals.

The Reconstruction Acts and the ratification of the Fourteenth Amendment achieved the purpose of enabling black southerners to vote. The Radicals, however, were not satisfied; despite the unpopularity of the idea in the North, they wished to guarantee the right of blacks to vote in every state. Another amendment seemed the only way to accomplish this objective, but passage of such an amendment appeared impossible. The Republican platform in the 1868 election had smugly distinguished between blacks voting in the South ("demanded by every consideration of public safety, of gratitude, and of justice") and in the North (where the question "properly belongs to the people").

However, after the election had demonstrated how important the black vote could be, Republican strategy shifted. Grant had carried Indiana by less than 10,000 votes and lost New York by a similar number. If blacks in these and other closely divided states had voted, Republican strength would have been greatly enhanced.

Suddenly Congress blossomed with suffrage amendments. After considerable bickering over details, the Fifteenth Amendment was sent to the states for ratification in February 1869. It forbade all the states to deny the vote to anyone "on account of race, color, or previous condition of servitude." Once again nothing was said about denial of the vote on the basis of sex, which caused feminists such as Elizabeth Cady Stanton to be even more outraged than they had been by the Fourteenth Amendment.

Most southern states, still under federal pressure, ratified the amendment swiftly. The same was true in most of New England and in some western states. Bitter battles were waged in Connecticut, New York, Pennsylvania, and the states immediately north of the Ohio River, but by March 1870 most of them had ratified the amendment and it became part of the Constitution.

The debates occasioned by these contests show that partisan advantage was not the only reason why voters approved black suffrage at last. The unfairness of a double standard of voting, North and South, the contribution of black soldiers during the war, and the hope that by passing the amendment the strife of Reconstruction could finally be ended all played a part.

When the Fifteenth Amendment went into effect, President Grant called it "the greatest civil change and . . . the most important event that has occurred since the nation came to life." The American Anti-Slavery Society formally dissolved itself, its work apparently completed. "The Fifteenth Amendment confers upon the African race the care of its own destiny," Radical Congressman James A.

Garfield wrote proudly after the amendment was ratified. "It places their fortunes in their own hands."

Many of the celebrants lived to see the amendment subverted in the South. That it could be evaded by literacy tests and other restrictions was apparent at the time and may even have influenced some persons who voted for it. But a stronger amendment—one, for instance, that positively granted the right to vote to all men and put the supervision of elections under national control—could not have been ratified.

"Black Republican" Reconstruction: Scalawags and Carpetbaggers

The Radicals had at last succeeded in imposing their will upon the South. Throughout the region former slaves had real political influence; they voted, held office, and exercised the "privileges" and enjoyed the "immunities" guaranteed them by the Fourteenth Amendment. Almost to a man they voted Republican.

The spectacle of blacks not five years removed from slavery in positions of power and responsibility attracted much attention at the time and has since been examined exhaustively by historians. The subject is controversial, but certain facts are beyond argument. Black officeholders were neither numerous nor inordinately influential. None was ever elected governor of a state; fewer than a dozen and a half during the entire period served in Congress. Blacks held many minor offices and were influential in southern legislatures, although (except in South Carolina) they never made up the majority. Certainly they did not share the spoils of office in proportion to their numbers.

The real rulers of the "black Republican" governments were white, the "scalawags"—southerners willing to cooperate with the Republicans because they accepted the results of the war and to advance their own interests—and the "carpetbaggers"—northerners who went to the South as idealists to help the freed slaves, as employees of the federal government, or more commonly as settlers hoping to improve themselves.

The scalawags were by far the more numerous. A few were prewar politicians or well-to-do planters, men such as the Mississippi planter John L. Alcorn and Joseph E. Brown, the Confederate governor of Georgia. General James Longstreet, one of Lee's most important lieutenants, was another prominent southerner who cooperated with the Republicans. But most were people who had supported the Whig party before the secession crisis and who saw the

During Reconstruction, fourteen blacks won election to the House of Representatives and two, Hiram Revels and Blanche K. Bruce, served in the Senate. Revels, at far left, won the Mississippi Senate seat that Jefferson Davis had once held. He later became president of Alcorn University. Congressman R. Brown Elliot, at far right, had been educated at Eton in England.

Republicans as the logical successors of the Whigs.

The carpetbaggers were a particularly varied lot. Most had mixed motives for coming south and personal gain was certainly among them. But so were opposition to slavery and the belief that blacks deserved to be treated decently and given a chance to get ahead in the world. Among the most admirable of the carpetbaggers was Adelbert Ames of Maine, who was governor of Mississippi in 1874–1875. Ames was, in the words of historian Richard N. Current, "about as pure and incorruptible a governor as Mississippi or any other state is likely ever to have."

Many northern blacks became carpetbaggers: former Union soldiers, missionaries from northern black churches, and also teachers, lawyers, and other members of the small northern black professional class. Many of these became officeholders, but like southern black politicans their influence was limited.

That blacks should fail to dominate southern governments is certainly understandable. They lacked experience in politics and were mostly poor and uneducated. They were nearly everywhere a minority. Those blacks who held office during Reconstruction tended to be better educated and more prosperous than most southern blacks. In his interesting analysis of black South Carolina politicians, Thomas Holt shows that a disproportionate number of them had been free before the war. Of those freed by the Thirteenth Amendment, a large percentage had been house servants or artisans, not field hands. Mulatto politicians were also disproportionately numerous and (as a group) more conservative and economically better off than other black leaders.

In South Carolina and elsewhere, blacks proved in the main able and conscientious public servants, able because the best tended to rise to the top in such a fluid situation, and conscientious because most of those who achieved importance sought eagerly to demonstrate the capacity of their race for self-government. Even at the local level, where the quality of officials was usually poor, there was little difference in the degree of competence displayed by white and black officeholders. In power, the blacks were not vindictive; by and large they did not seek to restrict the rights of ex-Confederates.

Not all black legislators and administrators were paragons of virtue. In South Carolina, despite their control of the legislature, they broke up into factions repeatedly and failed to press for laws that would improve the lot of poor black farm workers. In *The Prostrate South* (1874), James S. Pike, a northern newspaperman, wrote: "The rule of South Carolina should not be dignified with the name of government. It is the installation of a huge system of brigandage." Like many northern commentators, Pike exaggerated the immorality and incompetence of the blacks, but waste and corruption were common in Reconstruction governments. Half the budget of Louisiana in some years went for salaries and "mileage" for representatives and their staffs. One Arkansas black took $9,000 from the state for repairing a bridge that had cost only $500 to build. A South Carolina legislator was voted an additional $1,000 in salary after he lost that sum betting on a horse race.

However, the corruption must be seen in perspective. The big thieves were nearly always white; blacks got mostly crumbs. Furthermore, graft and callous disregard of the public interest characterized government in every section and at every level during the decade after Appomattox. Big-city bosses in the North embezzled sums that dwarfed the most brazen southern frauds. The New York City Tweed Ring probably made off with more money than all the southern thieves, black and white, combined. While the evidence does not justify the southern corruption, it suggests that the unique features of Reconstruction politics—black suffrage, military supervision, carpetbagger and scalawag influence—do not explain it.

The "black Republican" governments displayed qualities that grew directly from the ignorance and political inexperience of the former slaves. There was a tragicomic aspect to the South Carolina legislature during these years, its many black members—some dressed in old frock coats, others in rude farm clothes—rising to points of order and personal privilege without reason, discoursing ponderously on subjects they did not understand. But those who complained about the ignorance and irresponsibility of blacks conveniently forgot that the tendency of 19th-century American democracy was away from educational, financial, or any other restrictions on the franchise. Thousands of white southerners were as illiterate and uncultured as the freedmen, yet no one suggested depriving them of the ballot.

In fact, the Radical southern governments ac-

The Freedmen's Bureau established 4,329 schools, attended by some 250,000 ex-slaves, in the postwar South. Harper's Weekly *artist Alfred Waud sketched a Freedmen's Bureau school in Vicksburg, Mississippi, in 1866. Many of the teachers were white women from the North.*

complished a great deal. They spent money freely but not entirely wastefully. Tax rates zoomed, but the money financed the repair and expansion of the South's dilapidated railroad network, rebuilt crumbling levees, and expanded social services. Before the Civil War, as Eric Foner points out in *Reconstruction: America's Unfinished Revolution,* "slavery had sharply curtailed the scope of public authority" because the slaves were governed by private individuals (their owners) far more than by the state. The planters possessed a disproportionate share of political as well as economic power, and they spent relatively little public money on education and public services of all kinds. During Reconstruction an enormous gap had to be filled, and it took money to fill it. The Freedmen's Bureau made a start, and northern religious and philanthropic organizations did important work. Eventually, however, the state governments established and supported hospitals, asylums, and systems of free public education that, while segregated, greatly benefited everyone, whites as well as blacks. Much state money was also spent on economic development: land reclamation, repairing and expanding the war-ravaged railroads, maintaining levees.

The former slaves grasped eagerly at the opportunities to learn. Nearly all appreciated the im-

mense importance of knowing how to read and write; the sight of elderly men and women poring laboriously over elementary texts beside their grandchildren was common everywhere. Schools and other institutions were supported chiefly by property taxes, and these, of course, hit well-to-do white farmers hard. Hence much of the complaining about the "extravagance" of Reconstruction governments concealed selfish objections to paying for public projects. Eventually the benefits of expanded government services to the entire population became clear, and when white supremacy was reestablished, most of the new services remained in force, and the corruption and inefficiency inherited from the carpetbagger governments continued.

The Ravaged Land

The South's grave economic problems complicated the rebuilding of its political system. The section had never been as prosperous as the North, and wartime destruction left it desperately poor by any standard. In the long run the abolition of slavery released immeasurable quantities of human energy previously stifled, but the immediate effect was to create confusion. Freedom to move without a pass, to "see the world," was one of the ex-slaves' most cherished benefits of emancipation. Understandably, many at first equated legal freedom with freedom from having to earn a living, a tendency reinforced for a time by the willingness of the Freedmen's Bureau to provide rations and other forms of relief in war-devastated areas. Most, however, soon accepted the fact that they must earn a living; a small plot of land of their own ("40 acres and a mule") would complete their independence.

This objective was forcefully supported by the relentless Congressman Thaddeus Stevens, whose hatred of the planter class was pathological. "The property of the chief rebels should be seized," he stated. If the lands of the richest "70,000 proud, bloated and defiant rebels" were confiscated, the federal government would obtain 394 million acres. Every adult male ex-slave could easily be supplied with 40 acres. The beauty of his scheme, Stevens insisted, was that "nine-tenths of the (southern) people would remain untouched." Dispossessing the great planters would make the South "a safe republic," its lands cultivated by "the free labor of intelligent citizens." If the plan drove the planters into exile, "all the better."

Although Stevens's figures were faulty, many Radicals agreed with him. "We must see that the freedmen are established on the soil," Senator Sumner declared. "The great plantations, which have been so many nurseries of the rebellion, must be broken up, and the freedmen must have the pieces." Stevens, Sumner, and others who wanted to give land to the freedmen weakened their case by associating it with the idea of punishing the former rebels; the average American had too much respect for property rights to support a policy of confiscation.

Aside from its vindictiveness, the extremists' view was simplistic. Land without tools, seed, and other necessities would have done the freedmen little good. Congress did throw open 46 million acres of poor-quality federal land in the South to blacks under the Homestead Act, but few settled upon it. Establishing former slaves on small farms with adequate financial aid would have been of incalculable benefit to them and to the nation. This would have been practicable, but it was not done.

The former slaves therefore had to work out their destiny within the established framework of southern agriculture. White planters, influenced by the precipitous decline of sugar production in Jamaica and other Caribbean islands that had followed the abolition of slavery there, expected them to be incapable of self-directed effort. If allowed to become independent farmers, they would either starve to death or descend into barbarism. Of course the blacks did neither. True, the output of cotton and other southern staples declined precipitously after slavery was abolished. Observers soon came to the conclusion that a free black produced much less than a slave had produced. "You can't get only about two-thirds as much out of 'em now as you could when they were slaves," an Arkansas planter complained.

However, the decline in productivity was not caused by the *inability* of free blacks to work independently. What happened was that since they now held, in the pithy phrase of the economist Robert Higgs, "property rights over their own bodies," they chose no longer to work like slaves. They let their children play instead of forcing them into the fields. Mothers devoted more time to child care and housework, less to farm labor. Elderly blacks worked less.

Noting these changes, white critics spoke scornfully of black laziness and shiftlessness. "You cannot make the negro work without physical compulsion," was the common view. As the economic historians Roger Ransom and Richard Sutch have said, the perfectly reasonable desire of ex-slaves to devote more time to leisure was "taken as 'evidence' to support racist characterizations of blacks as lazy, incompetent, and unwilling to work." A leading southern magazine complained in 1866 that black women now expected their husbands "to support them in idleness." It would never have made such a comment about white housewives. Ransom and Sutch also point out that, while working less, emancipated blacks were far better off materially than under slavery. Their earnings brought them almost 30 percent more than the value of the subsistence provided by their former masters.

The family life of ex–slaves was changed in other ways. Male authority increased when husbands became true heads of families. (Under slavery the ultimate responsibility for providing for women and children was the master's.) When blacks became citizens, the men acquired rights and powers denied to all women, such as the right to hold public office and serve on juries. Similarly, black women became more like white women, devoting themselves to separate "spheres" where their lives revolved around housekeeping and child rearing.

Sharecropping and the Crop Lien System

Before the passage of the Reconstruction Acts, plantation owners tried to farm their land with gang labor, the same system as before, only now paying wages to the ex-slaves. This method did not work well for two entirely different reasons. Money was scarce, and capital, never adequate even before the collapse of the Confederacy, accumulated slowly. Interest rates were extremely high. This situation made it difficult for landowners to pay their laborers in cash. More important, blacks did not like working for wages because it kept them under the direction of whites and thus reminded them of slavery. They wanted to be independent, to manage not merely their free time but their entire lives for themselves. Since the voluntary withdrawal of so much black labor from the work force had produced a shortage, the blacks had their way. "I had to yield," one planter admitted, "or lose my labor."

Quite swiftly, a new agricultural system known as sharecropping emerged. Instead of cultivating the land by gang labor as in antebellum times, plant-

ers broke up their estates into small units and established on each a black family. The planter provided housing, agricultural implements, draft animals, seed, and other supplies, and the family provided labor. The crop was divided between them, usually on a fifty-fifty basis. If the landlord supplied only land and housing, the laborer got a larger share. This was called share tenancy.

Sharecropping gave blacks the day-to-day control of their lives that they craved and the hope of earning enough to buy a small farm. But few achieved this ambition because whites resisted their efforts adamantly. As late as 1880 blacks owned less than 10 percent of the agricultural land in the South, although they made up more than half of the region's farm population. Mississippi actually prohibited the purchase of farmland by blacks.

Many white farmers in the South were also trapped by the sharecropping system and by white efforts to keep blacks in a subordinate position. New fencing laws kept them from grazing livestock on undeveloped land, a practice common before the Civil War. But the main cause of southern rural poverty for whites as well as blacks was the lack of enough capital to finance the sharecropping system. Like their colonial ancestors, the landowners had to borrow against October's harvest to pay for April's seed. Thus the crop-lien system developed,

After the Civil War, most blacks worked as sharecroppers on land owned by whites. In this photograph, black sharecroppers pick cotton, a major cash crop of the South. Because the price for cotton remained low, sharecroppers often fell into debt and were tied to the land almost as tightly as under slavery.

and to protect their investments, lenders insisted that the grower concentrate on readily marketable cash crops: tobacco, sugar, and especially cotton.

The system injured everyone. Diversified farming would have reduced the farmers' need for cash, preserved the fertility of the soil, and, by placing a premium on imagination and shrewdness, aided the best of them to rise in the world. Under the crop-lien system, both landowner and sharecropper depended on credit supplied by local bankers, merchants, and storekeepers for everything from seed, tools, and fertilizer to overalls, coffee, and salt. Crossroads stores proliferated, and a new class of small merchants appeared. The prices of goods sold on credit were high, adding to the burden borne by the rural population. The small southern merchants were almost equally victimized by the system, for they also lacked capital, bought goods on credit, and had to pay high interest rates.

Seen in broad perspective, the situation is not difficult to understand. The South, drained of every resource by the war, was competing for funds with the North and West, both vigorous and expanding and therefore voracious consumers of capital. Reconstruction, in the literal sense of the word, was accomplished chiefly at the expense of the standard of living of the producing classes. The crop-lien system and the small storekeeper were only agents of an economic process dictated by national, perhaps even worldwide, conditions.

This does not mean that the South's economy was paralyzed by the shortage of capital or that recovery and growth did not take place. But compared with the rest of the country, progress was slow. Just before the Civil War cotton harvests averaged about 4 million bales. During the conflict, output fell to about half a million, and the former Confederate states did not enjoy a 4-million-bale year again until 1870. Only after 1874 did the crop begin to top that figure consistently. In contrast, national wheat production in 1859 was 175 million bushels and in 1878, 449 million. About 7,000 miles of railroad were built in the South between 1865 and 1879; in the rest of the nation nearly 45,000 miles of track were laid.

In manufacturing the South made important gains after the war. The tobacco industry, stimulated by the sudden popularity of the cigarette, expanded rapidly. Virginia and North Carolina tobacco towns like Richmond, Lynchburg, and

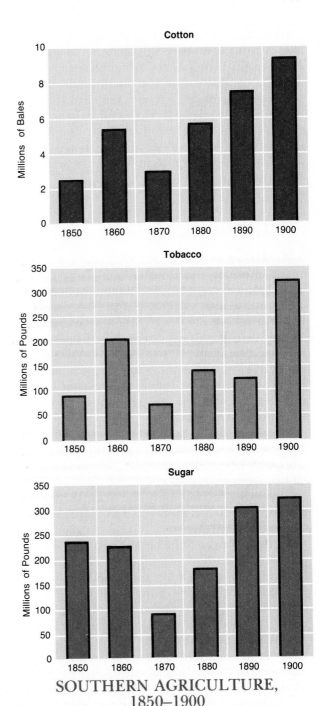

SOUTHERN AGRICULTURE, 1850–1900

Cotton production recovered to its prewar level by 1880, but tobacco and sugar production lagged. Not until 1900 did tobacco growers have a better year than they had in 1860. The years following 1870 saw a general downward trend in wholesale prices for farm commodities. (Statistics are for the 11 states of the Confederacy.)

Durham flourished. The exploitation of the coal and iron deposits of northeastern Alabama in the early 1870s made a boom town of Birmingham. The manufacture of cotton cloth increased, productive capacity nearly doubling between 1865 and 1880. Yet the mills of Massachusetts alone had eight times the capacity of the entire South in 1880. Despite the increases, the South's share of the national output of manufactured goods declined sharply during the Reconstruction era.

The White Counterrevolution

Radical southern governments could sustain themselves only so long as they had the support of a significant proportion of the white population, for except in South Carolina and Louisiana, the blacks were not numerous enough to win elections alone. The key to survival lay in the hands of the wealthy merchants and planters, mostly former Whigs. People of this sort had nothing to fear from black economic competition. Taking a broad view, they could see that improving the lot of the former slaves would benefit all classes.

Southern white Republicans used the Union League of America, a patriotic club founded during the war, to control the black vote. Employing secret rituals, exotic symbols, and other paraphernalia calculated to impress unsophisticated people, they enrolled the freedmen in droves and marched them to the polls en masse.

Powerless to check the League by open methods, dissident southerners established a number of secret terrorist societies, bearing such names as the Ku Klux Klan, the Knights of the White Camelia, and the Pale Faces. The most notorious of these organizations was the Klan, which was organized in Tennessee in 1866. At first it was purely a social club, but by 1868 it had been taken over by vigilante types dedicated to driving blacks out of politics, and it was spreading rapidly across the South. Sheet-clad night riders roamed the countryside, frightening the impressionable and chastising the defiant. Klansmen, using a weird mumbo jumbo and claiming to be the ghosts of Confederate soldiers, spread horrendous rumors and published broadsides designed to persuade the freedmen that it was unhealthy for them to participate in politics:

Niggers and Leaguers, get out of the way,
We're born of the night and we vanish by day.
No rations have we, but the flesh of man—
And love niggers best—the Ku Klux Klan;
We catch 'em alive and roast 'em whole,
Then hand 'em around with a sharpened pole.
Whole Leagues have been eaten, not leaving a man,
And went away hungry—the Ku Klux Klan. . . .

When intimidation failed, the Klansmen resorted to force. After being whipped by one group in Tennessee, a recently elected justice of the peace reported: "They said they had nothing particular against me . . . but they did not intend any nigger to hold office." In hundreds of cases the KKK murdered their opponents, often in the most gruesome manner.

Congress struck at the Klan with three Force Acts (1870–1871), which placed elections under federal jurisdiction and imposed fines and prison sentences on persons convicted of interfering with any citizen's exercise of the franchise. Troops were dispatched to areas where the Klan was strong, and by 1872 the federal authorities had arrested enough Klansmen to break up the organization.

Nevertheless the Klan contributed substantially to the destruction of Radical regimes in the South. Its depredations weakened the will of white Republicans (few of whom really believed in racial equality), and it intimidated many blacks, who gave up trying to exercise their rights. The fact that the army had to be called in to suppress it was a glaring illustration of the weakness of the Reconstruction governments.

Gradually it became respectable to intimidate black voters. Beginning in Mississippi in 1874, terrorism spread through the South. Instead of hiding behind masks and operating in the dark, these terrorists donned red shirts, organized into military companies, and paraded openly. Mississippi redshirts seized militant blacks and whipped them publicly. Killings were frequent. When blacks dared to fight back, heavily armed whites easily put them to rout. In other states similar results followed.

Terrorism fed on fear, fear on terrorism. White violence led to fear of black retaliation and thus to even more brutal attacks. The slightest sign of resistance came to be seen as the beginning of race war, and when the blacks suffered indignities and persecutions in silence, the awareness of how much they must resent the mistreatment made them appear more dangerous still. Thus self-hatred was displaced, guilt suppressed, aggression justified as self-defense, individual conscience submerged in the animality of the mob.

Before long the blacks learned to stay home on election day. One by one, "Conservative" parties—Democratic in national affairs—took over southern state governments. Intimidation was only a partial explanation of this development. The increasing solidarity of whites, northern and southern, was equally significant.

The North had subjected the South to control from Washington while preserving state sovereignty in the North itself. In the long run this discrimination proved unworkable. Many northerners had supported the Radical policy only out of irritation with President Johnson. After his retirement their enthusiasm waned. The war was fading into the past and with it the worst of the anger it had generated.

Northern voters could still be stirred by references to the sacrifices Republicans had made to save the Union and by reminders that the Democratic party was the organization of rebels, Copperheads, and the Ku Klux Klan. "If the Devil himself were at the helm of the ship of state," wrote the novelist Lydia Maria Child in 1872, "my conscience would not allow me to aid in removing him to make room for the Democratic party." Yet emotional appeals could not convince northerners that it was still necessary to maintain a large army in the South. In 1869 the occupying forces were down to 11,000 men. After Klan disruption and intimidation had made a farce of the 1874 elections in Mississippi, Governor Ames appealed to Washington for help. President Grant's attorney general, Edwards Pierrepont, refused to act. "The whole public are tired out with these autumnal outbreaks in the South," he told Ames. "Preserve the peace by the forces of your own state."

Nationalism was reasserting itself. Had not Washington and Jefferson been Virginians? Was not Andrew Jackson Carolina-born? Since most northerners had little real love or respect for blacks, their interest in racial equality flagged once they felt reasonably certain that blacks would not be reenslaved if left to their own devices in the South.

Another, much subtler force was also at work. The prewar Republican party had stressed the common interest of workers, manufacturers, and farmers in a free and mobile society, a land of equal opportunity where all could work in harmony. Southern whites had insisted that laborers must be disciplined if large enterprises were to be run efficiently. By the 1870s, as large industrial enterprises developed in the northern states, the thinking of business leaders changed—the southern argument began to make sense to them, and they became more sympathetic to the southern demand for more control over "their" labor force.

Grant as President

Other matters occupied the attention of northern voters. The expansion of industry and the rapid development of the West, stimulated by a new wave of railroad building, loomed more important to many than the fortunes of ex-slaves. Beginning in 1873, when a stock market panic struck at public confidence, economic difficulties plagued the country for nearly a decade. Heated controversies arose over tariff policy, with western agricultural interests seeking to force reductions from the high levels established during the war, and over the handling of the wartime greenback paper money, with debtor groups and many manufacturers favoring further expansion of the supply of dollars and conservative merchants and bankers arguing for retiring the greenbacks in order to return to a "sound" currency.

More damaging to the Republicans was the failure of Ulysses S. Grant to live up to expectations as president. Qualities that had made Grant a fine military leader for a democracy—his dislike of political maneuvering and his simple belief that the popular will could best be observed in the actions of Congress—made him a poor chief executive. When Congress failed to act on his suggestion that the quality of the civil service needed improvement, he announced meekly that if Congress did nothing, he would assume the country did not want anything done. Grant was honest, but his honesty was of the naive type that made him the dupe of unscrupulous friends and schemers.

His most serious weakness as president was his failure to deal effectively with economic and social problems, but the one that injured him and the Republicans most was his inability to cope with government corruption. Grant did not cause the corruption, nor did he participate in the remotest way in the rush to "fatten at the public trough," as the reformers of the day might have put it. But he did nothing to prevent the scandals that disgraced his administration. Out of a misplaced belief in the

sanctity of friendship, he protected some of the worst culprits and allowed calculating tricksters to use his good name and the prestige of his office to advance their own interests at the country's expense.

The worst of the scandals—such as the Whiskey Ring affair, which implicated Grant's private secretary, Orville E. Babcock, and cost the government millions in tax revenue, and the defalcations of Secretary of War William W. Belknap in the management of Indian affairs—did not become public knowledge during Grant's first term. However, in 1872 Republican reformers, alarmed by rumors of corruption and disappointed by Grant's failure to press for civil service reform, organized the Liberal Republican party and nominated Horace Greeley, the able but eccentric editor of the *New York Tribune,* for president.

The Liberal Republicans were mostly well educated, socially prominent types—editors, college presidents, and economists, along with a sprinkling of businessmen and politicians. Their liberalism was of the *laissez faire* variety; they were for low tariffs and sound money, and against what they called "class legislation," meaning measures benefiting particular groups, whether labor unions or railroad companies or farm organizations. Nearly all had supported Reconstruction at the start, but by the early 1870s most were including southern blacks among the special interests that ought to be left to their own devices. Their observation of urban corruption and of unrestricted immigration led them to disparage universal suffrage, which, one of them said, "can only mean in plain English the government of ignorance and vice."

The Democrats also nominated Greeley in 1872, although he had devoted his political life to flailing the Democratic party in the *Tribune.* That surrender to expediency, together with Greeley's temperamental unsuitability for the presidency, made the campaign a fiasco for the reformers. Grant triumphed easily, with a popular majority of nearly 800,000.

Nevertheless, the defection of the Liberal Republicans hurt the Republican party in Congress. In the 1874 elections, no longer hampered as in the presidential contest by Greeley's notoriety and Grant's fame, the Democrats carried the House of Representatives. It was clear that the days of military rule in the South were ending. By the end of 1875 only three southern states—South Carolina, Flor-

In 1872, Republicans who opposed Grant's renomination bolted the party and nominated Horace Greeley. These Liberal Republicans—some of them former Radicals—sought to conciliate the South. In this cartoon, Thomas Nast, a Grant supporter, condemns the actions of Greeley and Charles Sumner as they push a black man to shake hands with a Klan member and a Copperhead.

ida, and Louisiana—were still under Republican control.

The Republican party in the South was "dead as a doornail," a reporter noted. He reflected the opinion of thousands when he added: "We ought to have a sound sensible republican . . . for the next President as a measure of safety; but only on the condition of absolute noninterference in Southern local affairs, for which there is no further need or excuse."

The Disputed Election of 1876

Against this background the presidential election of 1876 took place. Since corruption in government was the most widely discussed issue, the Republicans passed over their most attractive political personality, the dynamic James G. Blaine, Speaker of the House of Representatives, who had been connected with some chicanery involving railroad securities. Instead they nominated Governor Rutherford B. Hayes of Ohio, a former general with an unsmirched reputation. The Democrats picked Governor Samuel J. Tilden of New York, a wealthy lawyer who had attracted national attention for his part in breaking up the Tweed Ring in New York City.

In November early returns indicated that Tilden had carried New York, New Jersey, Connecticut, Indiana, and all the southern states, including Louisiana, South Carolina, and Florida, where Republican regimes were still in control. This seemed to give him 203 electoral votes to Hayes's 165, and a popular plurality in the neighborhood of 250,000 out of more than 8 million votes cast. However, Republican leaders had anticipated the possible loss of Florida, South Carolina, and Louisiana and were prepared to use their control of the election machinery in those states to throw out sufficient Democratic ballots to alter the results if doing so would change the national outcome. Realizing that the electoral votes of those states were exactly enough to elect their man, they telegraphed their henchmen on the scene, ordering them to go into action. The local Republicans then invalidated Democratic ballots in wholesale lots and filed returns showing Hayes the winner. Naturally the local Democrats protested vigorously and filed their own returns.

The Constitution provides (Article II, section 1) that presidential electors must meet in their respective states to vote and forward the results to "the Seat of the Government." There, it adds, "the President of the Senate shall, in the Presence of the Senate and House of Representatives, open all the Certificates, and the Votes shall then be counted." But who was to do the counting? The House was Democratic, the Senate Republican; neither would agree to allow the other to do the job. On January 29, 1877, scarcely a month before inauguration day, Congress created an electoral commission to decide the disputed cases. The commission consisted of five senators (three Republicans and two Democrats), five representatives (three Democrats and two Republicans), and five justices of the Supreme Court (two Democrats, two Republicans, and one "independent" judge, David Davis). Since it was a foregone conclusion that the others would vote for their party no matter what the evidence, Davis would presumably swing the balance in the interest of fairness.

But before the commission met, the Illinois legislature elected Davis senator! He had to resign from the Court and the commission. Since independents were rare even on the Supreme Court, no neutral was available to replace him. The vacancy went to Associate Justice Joseph P. Bradley of New Jersey, a Republican.

Evidence presented before the commission revealed a disgraceful picture of election shenanigans. On the one hand, in all three disputed states Dem-

ocrats had clearly cast a majority of the votes; on the other, it was unquestionable that many blacks had been forcibly prevented from voting.

In truth, both sides were shamefully corrupt. Lew Wallace, a northern politician later famous as the author of the novel *Ben Hur,* visited Louisiana and Florida shortly after the election. "It is terrible to see the extent to which all classes go in their determination to win," he wrote his wife from Florida. "Money and intimidation can obtain the oath of white men as well as black to any required statement. . . . If we win, our methods are subject to impeachment for possible fraud. If the enemy win, it is the same thing." The governor of Louisiana was reportedly willing to sell his state's electoral votes for $200,000. The Florida election board was supposed to have offered itself to Tilden for the same price. "That seems to be the standard figure," Tilden remarked ruefully.

Most modern authorities take the view that in a fair election the Republicans would have carried South Carolina and Louisiana but that Florida would have gone to Tilden, giving him the election, 188 electoral votes to 181. In the last analysis, this opinion has been arrived at simply by counting white and black noses: blacks were in the majority in South Carolina and Louisiana. Amid the tension and confusion of early 1877, however, even a Solomon would have been hard pressed to judge rightly amid the rumors, lies, and contradictory statements, and the electoral commission was not composed of Solomons. The Democrats had some hopes that Justice Bradley would be sympathetic to their case, for he was known to be opposed to harsh Reconstruction policies. On the eve of the commission's decision in the Florida controversy, he was apparently ready to vote in favor of Tilden. But the Republicans subjected him to tremendous political pressure. When he read his opinion on February 8, it was for Hayes. Thus, by a vote of 8 to 7, the commission awarded Florida's electoral votes to the Republicans.

The rest of the proceedings were routine. The commission assigned all the disputed electoral votes (including one in Oregon where the Democratic governor had seized on a technicality to replace a single Republican elector with a Democrat) to Hayes.

With the spitefulness common to rejected suitors, the Democrats assailed Bradley until, as *The New York Times* put it, he seemed like "a middle-aged St. Sebastian, stuck full of Democratic darts." Unlike Sebastian, however, Bradley was protected from the arrows by the armor of his Republican faith.

To such a level had the republic of Jefferson and John Adams descended. Democratic institutions, shaken by the South's refusal to go along with the majority in 1860 and by the suppression of civil rights during the rebellion, and further weakened by military intervention and the intimidation of blacks in the South during Reconstruction, now seemed a farce. According to Tilden's campaign manager, angry Democrats in 15 states, chiefly war veterans, were readying themselves to march on Washington to force the inauguration of Tilden. Tempers flared in Congress, where some spoke om-

inously of a filibuster that would prevent the recording of the electoral vote and leave the country, on March 4, with no president at all.

The Compromise of 1877

Fortunately, forces for compromise had been at work behind the scenes in Washington for some time. Although northern Democrats threatened to fight to the last ditch, many southern Democrats were willing to accept Hayes if he would promise to remove the troops and allow the southern states to manage their internal affairs by themselves. Ex-Whig planters and merchants who had reluctantly abandoned the carpetbag governments and who sympathized with Republican economic policies hoped that by supporting Hayes they might con-

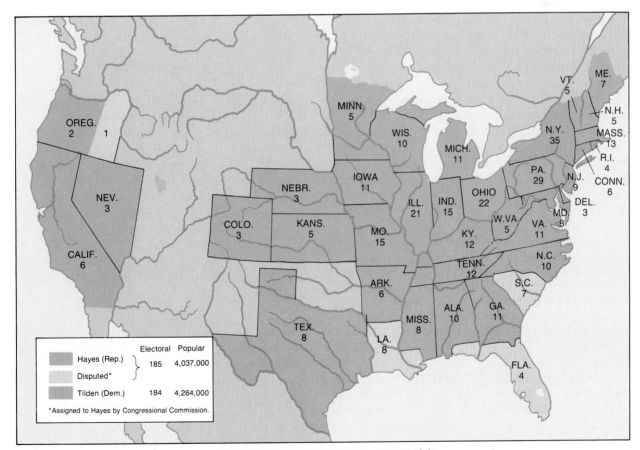

THE COMPROMISE OF 1877

tribute to the restoration of the two-party system that had been destroyed in the South during the 1850s. Ohio Congressman James A. Garfield urged Hayes to find "some discreet way" of showing these southerners that he favored "internal improvements." Hayes replied: "Your views are so nearly the same as mine that I need not say a word."

Tradition has it that a great compromise between the sections was worked out during a dramatic meeting at the Wormley Hotel* in Washington on February 26. Actually, as C. Vann Woodward has demonstrated in his important book *Reunion and Reaction*, the negotiations were long-drawn-out and informal, and the Wormley conference was but one of many. With the tacit support of many Democrats, the electoral vote was counted by the president of the Senate on March 2, and Hayes was declared elected, 185 votes to 184.

Like all compromises, this agreement was not entirely satisfactory; like most, it was not honored in every detail. Hayes recalled the last troops from South Carolina and Louisiana in April. He appointed a former Confederate general, David M. Key of Tennessee, postmaster general and delegated to him the congenial task of finding southerners willing to serve their country as officials of a Republican administration. But the alliance of ex-Whigs and northern Republicans did not flourish; the South remained solidly Democratic. The major significance of the compromise, one of the great intersectional political accommodations of American history, has been well summarized by Professor Woodward:

> The Compromise of 1877 marked the abandonment of principles and force and a return to the traditional ways of expediency and concession. It wrote an end to Reconstruction and recognized a new regime in the South. More profoundly than Constitutional amendments and wordy statutes it shaped the future of four million freedmen and their progeny for generations to come.

For most of the former slaves, this future was to be bleak. Forgotten in the North, manipulated and then callously rejected by the South, rebuffed by the Supreme Court, voiceless in national affairs,

they and their descendants were condemned in the interests of sectional harmony to lives of poverty, indignity, and little hope. Meanwhile, the rest of the United States continued its golden march toward wealth and power.

Milestones

1863	Lincoln announces "Ten Percent Plan" for Reconstruction
Mar. 1865	Establishment of the Freedmen's Bureau
Apr. 1865	General Lee surrenders at Appomattox Court House
Apr. 1865	Assassination of Abraham Lincoln, Andrew Johnson becomes President
May 1865	Johnson's Amnesty plan
Dec. 1865	Thirteenth Amendment ratified
1865–1866	Enactment of Black Codes by southern states
Apr. 1866	Civil Rights Act passed over Johnson's veto
Sept. 1866	Johnson campaigns for his Reconstruction policy
Mar. 1867	First Reconstruction Act
Feb. 1868	House of Representatives impeaches Johnson
Mar. 1868	Fourth Reconstruction Act
May 1868	Senate acquits Johnson
July 1868	Fourteenth Amendment ratified
Nov. 1868	Ulysses S. Grant elected President
1868–1872	Ku Klux Klan in action
Mar. 1870	Fifteenth Amendment ratified
1870–1871	Force (Ku Klux Klan) Acts destroys Klan
1872	Liberal Republican party nominates Horace Greeley for President
Nov. 1872	Grant reelected President
1876	Disputed presidential election
Feb. 1877	Electoral Commission awards disputed votes to Rutherford B. Hayes
	Hayes agrees to Compromise of 1877

---

* Ironically, the hotel was owned by James Wormley, reputedly the wealthiest black in Washington.

SUPPLEMENTARY READING

Titles marked with an asterisk have been published in paperback.

The finest of many excellent overviews of the Reconstruction Era is Eric Foner's **Reconstruction: America's Unfinished Revolution*** (1988). The older approach to the period, stressing the excesses of black-influenced governments and criticizing the Radicals, derives from the seminal work of W. A. Dunning, **Reconstruction, Political and Economic*** (1907). W. E. B. Du Bois, **Black Reconstruction in America*** (1935) was the pioneering counterattack against the Dunning view. See also Eric Foner, **Politics and Ideology in the Age of the Civil War** (1980), and Foner's **Nothing But Freedom*** (1984).

Lincoln's ideas about Reconstruction are analyzed in W. B. Hesseltine, **Lincoln's plan of Reconstruction*** (1960), and in many of the Lincoln volumes mentioned in earlier chapters. Albert Castel, **The Presidency of Andrew Johnson** (1979), is a balanced recent account. On Johnson's battle with the congressional Radicals, see H. L. Trefousse, **The Radical Republicans: Lincoln's Vanguard for Racial Justice*** (1969), E. L. McKitrick, **Andrew Johnson and Reconstruction*** (1960), and M. L. Benedict, **The Impeachment and Trial of Andrew Johnson** (1973). A number of biographies provide information helpful in understanding the Radicals. These include David Donald, **Charles Sumner and the Rights of Man** (1970), B. P. Thomas and H. M. Hyman, **Stanton** (1962), R. N. Current, **Old Thad Stevens** (1942), and H. L. Trefousse, **Benjamin Franklin Wade** (1963). J. M. McPherson, **The Struggle for Equality: Abolitionists and the Negro in the Civil War and Reconstruction*** (1964), is also valuable. On the Fourteenth Amendment, see Joseph James, **The Framing of the Fourteenth Amendment*** (1956); on the Fifteenth Amendment, see William Gillette, **The Right to Vote: Politics and the Passage of the Fifteenth Amendment*** (1965).

Conditions in the South during Reconstruction are discussed in R. H. Abbott, **The Republican Party and the South** (1986), Michael Perman, **Reunion Without Compromise** (1973), H. N. Rabinowitz, **Race Relations in the Urban South** (1978), J. L. Roark, **Masters Without Slaves** (1977), and Leon Litwack, **Been in the Storm Too Long** (1979).

For state studies, see W. L. Rose, **Rehearsal for Reconstruction: The Port Royal Experiment*** (1964), Thomas Holt, **Black over White: Negro Political Leadership in South Carolina** (1977), W. C. Harris, **The Day of the Carpetbagger: Republican Reconstruction in Mississippi** (1979) and Joel Williamson, **After Slavery: The Negro in South Carolina During Reconstruction*** (1965). See also Joel Williamson, **The Crucible of Race: Black-White Relations in the American South Since Emancipation** (1984), a psychoanalytical interpretation of racism. G. R. Bentley, **A History of the Freedmen's Bureau** (1955), discusses the work of that important organization, but see also W. S. McFeely, **Yankee Stepfather: General O. O. Howard and the Freedmen*** (1968). On the Ku Klux Klan, see G. C. Rable, **But There Was No Peace*** (1984), and A. W. Trelease, **White Terror: The Ku Klux Klan Conspiracy and Southern Reconstruction** (1971).

On the economic and social effects of Reconstruction, see G. D. Jaynes, **Branches Without Roots: Genesis of the Black Working Class** (1986), R. L. Ransom and Richard Sutch, **One Kind of Freedom: The Economic Consequences of Emancipation*** (1977), Robert Higgs, **Competition and Coercion: Blacks in the American Economy, 1865–1914** (1977), and C. F. Oubre, **Forty Acres and a Mule** (1978). F. A. Shannon, **The Farmer's Last Frontier*** (1945), is also a useful text on southern agriculture. For the growth of industry, see J. F. Stover, **The Railroads of the South** (1955).

On Grant's presidency, see W. S. McFeely, **Grant** (1981); Allan Nevins, **Hamilton Fish: The Inner History of the Grant Administration** (1936), and Matthew Josephson, **The Politicos*** (1938), contain much additional information. On the Republican reform movement, see J. G. Sproat, **"The Best Men": Liberal Reformers in the Gilded Age*** (1968), and M. B. Duberman, **Charles Francis Adams*** (1961). For the disputed election of 1876 and the compromise following it, consult C. V. Woodward, **Reunion and Reaction*** (1951), and K. I. Polakoff, **The Politics of Inertia: The Election of 1876 and the End of Reconstruction** (1973). William Gillette, **Retreat from Reconstruction** (1980), is also an important study.

PORTFOLIO FOUR
Blacks in Slavery and Freedom

It is much easier to generalize about what life was like for American blacks under slavery than for free people of that time. Indeed, the fact that the restrictions imposed upon slaves reduced drastically their possibilities for individual development and self-expression was the basic injustice of the slave system. Nevertheless, as these illustrations show, the institution affected its victims in many different ways. Seen from this perspective, the ending of slavery expanded the ability of individual blacks to "be themselves." Even after more than a century, however, the possibilities open to the average black are still more limited than those available to the average white. Finally ending this discrimination is one of the major tasks our society faces today.

The three views of slave life on this page throw different lights on "the peculiar institution." Edwin White, an academic painter, titled his carefully humble yet dignified portrayal of a quite moment Thoughts of Liberia. Actually, few blacks ever returned to Africa in spite of colonization efforts by well-meaning groups.

In 1862, T. H. O'Sullivan made this extraordinary photograph of five generations of a slave family. All were born on the plantation of J. J. Smith in Beaufort, South Carolina.

A Northern visitor, George Fuller, traveled through Alabama in 1858 to observe the conditions under which slaves lived. He sketched this woman, her skirts hitched up and the reins of a plantation mule looped around her neck, plowing a field. In the background are a cotton gin (the building on stilts) and a cotton press, which was used to compress the ginned cotton into bales for shipping.

473

Before 1860, many of the free blacks of the northern states lived in cities and towns. For most, the church was the center of community life. This 1853 scene from Frank Leslie's Illustrated Newspaper *shows a prayer meeting in the African Church of Cincinnati, Ohio.*

Thomas "Daddy" Rice was a popular vaudeville star in the pre–Civil War years. He introduced the character "Jim Crow" in a song-and-dance blackface act ("Wheel a-bout and turn a-bout/And jump . . . Jim Crow") based on the antics of a black stable boy he claimed to have seen. His "Jump Jim Crow" act helped launch the popular minstrel shows of the 19th century. Unfortunately, they also promoted the stereotype of the shiftless black man. The term Jim Crow *later came to be applied to the system of Southern segregation laws and customs in the late 19th century.*

Slaves, of course, could be bought and sold at their owners' discretion, like any piece of property. Edwin Taylor's 1852 painting **American Slave Market** catches a sense of the mundane way that most owners viewed the trade in human beings. With the slave went a bill of sale. Below is a receipt covering the sale of "a Negro man by the name of Ned about 38 or 40 years of age which negro I warrant to be a slave for life" for $800. The note in the upper right corner, added by the buyer's great-grandson, comments that Ned was reputed to be a good cabinet maker.

My Great Grand Father Jas. Benson Zachry Old Henry County, Present Newton County. This slave was reputed to be a good cabin maker.

Columbus 95th May 1842

Received of James B Zachry by the hands of John Morton Eight Hundred dollars in full consideration for a Negro Man by the name of Ned about 38 or 40 years of age which negro I warrant to be a slave for life & to be sound & well both in body & mind & I also warrant him against the Claims of Myself my heirs or against the Claim of any other person or persons Whomsoever given under my hand and seal this day and year above written

Henry Morton
Jois B. well

Stephen Wall Seal

475

Reconstruction meant a new set of accommodations to freedom within an older social order. Winslow Homer's tense painting, A Visit from the Old Mistress, *conveys a feeling of the complex relationships that developed between newly freed blacks and their former owners.*

For most former slaves, day-to-day activity in the rural South remained a round of planting, cultivating, and harvesting. For example, the way that hogs were slaughtered and the meat cured or made into sausage did not change. Some blacks, however, did not stay on the land, but instead worked in individual settings, such as this tobacco-processing plant in Danville, Virginia, where men, women, and children were employed stripping tobacco.

In the Wake of War

It may be metaphorically said that natural selection is daily and hourly scrutinizing, throughout the world, the slightest variations; rejecting those that are bad, preserving and adding up all that are good; silently and insensibly working, whenever and wherever opportunity offers.

Charles Darwin, The Origin of Species, *1859*

The way for people to gain their reasonable rights is not by voluntarily throwing them away.

W. E. B. Du Bois, Of Mr. Booker T. Washington and Others, *1903* hen Americans turned from fighting and making weapons to more constructive occupations, they transformed their agriculture, trade, manufacturing, mining, and means of communication. Immigration increased rapidly. Cities grew in size and number, exerting on every aspect of life an influence at least as pervasive as that exercised on earlier generations by the frontier. More and more Americans were flocking to the towns and cities, supporting themselves by laboring at machines or by scratching accounts in ledgers. At the same time farm production rose to new heights, invigorated by new marketing methods and the increased use of machinery. Railroad construction stimulated and unified the economy, helping to make possible still larger and more efficient enterprises. The flow of gold and silver from western mines excited people's imaginations and their avarice, while petroleum, the "black gold" discovered in Pennsylvania shortly before the war, gave rise to a new industry soon to become one of the most important in the nation. These developments amounted to more than a mere change of scale; they altered the structure of the economy and the society.

The American Commonwealth

Most students of the subject have concluded that the political history of the United States in the last quarter of the 19th century was singularly divorced from the meaningful issues of that day. On the rare occasions that important, supposedly controversial measures were debated, they excited far less argument than they merited. A graduated income tax, the greatest instrument for orderly economic and social change that a democratic society has devised, was enacted during the Civil War, repealed after that conflict, reenacted in 1894 as part of the maneuvering over tariff reform, and then declared unconstitutional in 1895 without causing much more than a ripple in the world of partisan politics. This was typical; as the English observer James Bryce noted in the late 1880s, the politicians were "clinging too long to outworn issues" and "neglecting to discover and work out new principles capable of solving the problems which now perplex the country." Congress, another critic wrote, "does not solve the problems, the solution of which is demanded by the life of the nation."

"Root, Hog, or Die"

After Appomattox, the immense resources of the United States, combined with the high value most Americans assigned to work and achievement, made the people strongly materialistic.

After the failures of Reconstruction, Americans seemed even more enamored with material values. They were tired of sacrifice, eager to act for themselves. They professed to believe strongly in a government policy of noninterference, or laissez faire. " 'Things regulate themselves' . . . means, of course, that God regulates them by his general laws," Professor Francis Bowen of Harvard wrote in his *American Political Economy* (1870).

Impressed by such logic, people now tolerated the grossest kind of waste and seemed to care little about corruption in high places, so long as no one interfered with their personal pursuit of profit. Mark Twain, raised in an earlier era, called this the

Gilded Age, dazzling on the surface, base metal below.

Certain intellectual currents encouraged the exploitative drives of the people. Charles Darwin's *Origin of Species* was published in 1859, and by the 1870s his theory of evolution was beginning to influence opinion in the United States. That nature had ordained a kind of inevitable progress, governed by the natural selection of the individual organisms best adapted to survive in a particular environment, seemed eminently reasonable to most Americans, for it fitted well with their own experiences. "Let the buyer beware; that covers the whole business," the sugar magnate Henry O. Havemeyer explained to an investigating committee. "You cannot wet-nurse people from the time they are born until the time they die. They have to wade and get stuck, and that is the way men are educated."

Yale professor William Graham Sumner sometimes used the survival-of-the-fittest analogy in teaching undergraduates. "Professor," one student asked Sumner, "don't you believe in any government aid to industries?" "No!" Sumner replied, "It's root, hog, or die." The student persisted: "Suppose some professor of political science came along and took your job away from you. Wouldn't you be sore?" "Any other professor is welcome to try," Sumner answered promptly. "If he gets my job, it is my fault. My business is to teach the subject so well that no one can take the job away from me." Sumner's argument described what came to be known as social Darwinism, the belief that human business and social relationships were governed by the Darwinian principle that the "fittest" will always "survive" if allowed to exercise their capacities without restriction.

Few businessmen were directly influenced by Darwin's ideas. Most eagerly accepted any aid they could get from the government; many were active in philanthropy; some felt a deep sense of social responsibility. Nevertheless, most were sincere individualists. They believed in competition, being convinced that the nation would prosper most if all people were free to seek their personal fortunes by their own methods.

The Shape of Politics

A succession of weak presidents presided over the White House. Although the impeachment pro-

ceedings against Andrew Johnson had failed, Congress dominated the government. Within Congress, the Senate generally overshadowed the House of Representatives. In his novel *Democracy* (1880), the cynical Henry Adams wrote that the United States had a "government of the people, by the people, for the benefit of Senators." Critics called the Senate a "rich man's club," and it did contain many millionaires. However, the true sources of the Senate's influence lay in the long tenure of many of its members (which enabled them to master the craft of politics), in the fact that it was small enough to encourage real debate and in its long-established reputation for wisdom, intelligence, and statesmanship.

The House of Representatives, by contrast, was one of the most disorderly and inefficient legislative bodies in the world. As I make my notes, one reporter wrote in 1882 while sitting in the House gallery,

> I see a dozen men reading newspapers with their feet on their desks. . . . The vile odor of . . . tobacco . . . rises from the two-for-five-cents cigars in the mouths of the so-called gentlemen below. . . . They chew, too! Every desk has a spittoon of pink and gold china beside it to catch the filth from the statesman's mouth.

An infernal din rose from the crowded chamber. Desks slammed; members held private conversations, hailed pages, shuffled from place to place, clamored for the attention of the Speaker—all while some poor orator tried to discuss the question of the moment. Speaking in the House, one writer said, was like trying to address the crowd on a passing Broadway bus from the curb in front of the Astor House in New York.

The great political parties professed undying enmity to each other, but they seldom took clearly opposing positions on the questions of the day. Democrats were separated from Republicans more by accidents of geography, religious affiliation, ethnic background, and emotion than by economic issues.

The fundamental division between Democrats and Republicans was sectional, a result of the Civil War. The South, after the political rights of blacks had been drastically circumscribed, became heavily Democratic. Most of New England was solidly Republican. Elsewhere the two parties stood in fair balance, although the Republicans tended to have the advantage.

The personalities of political leaders often dic-

Joseph Keppler's 1890 Puck *cartoon "None but Millionaires Need Apply—The Coming Style of Presidential Election," comments acidly on the low status of the presidency. The tag* Eight Pieces With This Set *on the chief executive's chair refers to the Cabinet. As the examples in this chapter show, the late 19th century was a heyday for political cartoonists.*

tated the voting patterns of individuals and groups. In the 1884 presidential election, the banker J. P. Morgan voted Democratic because he admired Grover Cleveland, while Irish-Americans, traditionally Democrats, cast thousands of ballots for Republican James G. Blaine. In the 1892 contest in which Cleveland defeated Benjamin Harrison, a prominent steel manufacturer wrote to his even more prominent competitor, Andrew Carnegie: "I am very sorry for President Harrison, but I cannot see that our interests are going to be affected one way or the other." And Carnegie replied: "We have nothing to fear. . . . Cleveland is [a] pretty good fellow. Off for Venice tomorrow."

The balance of political power after 1876 was almost perfect—"the most spectacular degree of equilibrium in American history." Between 1856 and 1912 the Democrats elected a president only twice (1884 and 1892), but most contests were extremely close. Majorities in both the Senate and the House fluctuated continually. Between 1876 and 1896 the "dominant" Republican party controlled both houses of Congress and the presidency at the same time for only one two-year period.

Issues of the Gilded Age

Four questions obsessed politicians in these years. One was the "bloody shirt." The term, which became part of the language after a Massachusetts con-

gressman dramatically displayed to his colleagues in the House the bloodstained shirt of an Ohio carpetbagger who had been flogged by terrorists in Mississippi, referred to the tactic of reminding the electorate of the northern states that the men who had taken the South out of the Union and precipitated the Civil War had been Democrats and that they and their descendants were still Democrats. "Every man that endeavored to tear down the old flag," a Republican orator proclaimed in 1876, "was a Democrat. Every man that tried to destroy this nation was a Democrat. . . . The man that assassinated Abraham Lincoln was a Democrat. . . . Soldiers, every scar you have on your heroic bodies was given you by a Democrat."

Every scoundrel or incompetent who sought office under the Republican banner waved the bloody shirt in order to divert the attention of northern voters from his own shortcomings.

Waving the bloody shirt was related intimately to the issue of the rights of blacks. Throughout this period Republicans vacillated between trying to build up their organization in the South by appealing to black voters—which required them to make sure that blacks in the South could vote—and trying to win conservative white support by stressing economic issues such as the tariff. When the former strategy seemed wise, they waved the bloody shirt with vigor; in the latter case, they piously announced that the blacks' future was "as safe in the hands of one party as it is in the other."

The question of veterans' pensions also bore a close relationship to the bloody shirt. Following the Civil War, Union soldiers founded the Grand Army of the Republic. By 1890 the organization had a membership of more than 400,000. The GAR put immense pressure on Congress, first for aid to veterans with service-connected disabilities, then for those with any disability, and eventually for all former Union soldiers.

The tariff was another perennial issue in post–Civil War politics. Manufacturers desired protective tariffs to keep out competing products, and a majority of their workers were convinced that wage levels would fall if goods produced by cheap foreign labor entered the United States untaxed. Many farmers supported protection, though almost no competing agricultural products were being imported. Congressman William McKinley of Ohio, who reputedly could make reciting a tariff schedule sound like poetry, stated the majority opinion in the clearest terms: High tariffs foster the growth of

Uncle Sam walks the floor with a fretful "Infant Industries," saying "I guess he won't stop howling till I give him enough Protection Soothing Syrup to burst him!" An 1896 Puck *cartoon by Louis Dalrymple.*

industry and thus create jobs. "Reduce the tariff and labor is the first to suffer," he said.

The Democrats professed to believe in moderation, yet whenever party leaders tried to revise the tariff downward, Democratic congressmen from industrial states like Pennsylvania and New York sided with the Republicans. Every new tariff bill became an occasion for logrolling, lobbying, and outrageous politicking rather than for sane discussion and careful evaluation of the public interest.

A third political question in this period was currency reform. During the Civil War, it will be recalled, the government, faced with obligations it could not meet by taxing or borrowing, suspended specie payments and issued about $450 million in paper money. The greenbacks did not command the full confidence of a people accustomed to money readily convertible into gold or silver. Greenbacks seemed to threaten inflation, for how could one trust the government not to issue them in wholesale lots to avoid passing unpopular tax laws? Thus when the war ended, strong sentiment developed for withdrawing the greenbacks from circulation and returning to a bullion standard.

Beginning during Reconstruction, prices declined sharply. The deflation increased the real income of bondholders and other creditors but injured debtors. Farmers were particularly hard hit, for many of them had borrowed heavily during the wartime boom to finance expansion.

Here was a question of real significance. However, the major parties refused to confront each other over the currency question. While Republicans professed to be the party of sound money, most western Republicans favored expansion of the currency. And while one wing of the Democrats flirted with the Greenbackers, the conservative, or "Bourbon," Democrats favored deflation as much as Republicans did.

In 1874 a bill to increase the supply of greenbacks was defeated in a Republican-dominated Congress only by the veto of President Grant. The next year Congress voted to resume specie payments, but in order to avoid a party split on the question, the Republicans agreed to allow $300 million in greenbacks to remain in circulation and to postpone actual resumption of specie payments until 1879.

Under various administrations, steps were taken to increase or decrease the amount of money in circulation, but the net effect on the economy was not significant. Few politicians before 1890 considered monetary policy as a device for influencing economic development.

The final major political issue of these years was civil service reform. That the federal bureaucracy needed overhauling nearly everyone agreed. As American society grew larger and more complex, the government necessarily took on more functions. The need for professional administration increased. The number of federal employees rose from 53,000 in 1871 to 256,000 at the end of the century. Corruption flourished; waste and inefficiency were the normal state of affairs. "The federal system . . . was generally undistinguished," the historian Leonard D. White concluded after an exhaustive study of the period. "Nobody, whether in Congress or in the executive departments, seemed able to rise much above the handicraft office methods that were cumbersome even in the simpler days of the Jacksonians."

Every honest observer could see the need for reform, but the politicians argued that patronage was the lifeblood of politics, that parties could not function without armies of loyal political workers, and that the workers expected and deserved the rewards of office when their efforts were crowned with victory at the polls. Typical was the attitude of the New York assemblyman who, according to Theodore Roosevelt, had "the same idea about Public Life and the Civil Service that a vulture has of a dead sheep."

Blacks After Reconstruction

Minorities were treated with callousness and contempt in the postwar decades. That the South would deal harshly with the former slaves once federal control was relaxed probably should have been expected. Men like Governor Wade Hampton of South Carolina had promised to respect black civil rights. "We . . . will secure to every citizen, the lowest as well as the highest, black as well as white, full and equal protection in the enjoyment of all his rights under the Constitution," Hampton said in 1877. This pledge was not kept.

President Hayes had urged blacks to trust southern whites. A new Era of Good Feelings had dawned, he announced after making a goodwill tour of the South shortly after his inauguration. By December

1877 he had been sadly disillusioned. "By state legislation, by frauds, by intimidation, and by violence of the most atrocious character, colored citizens have been deprived of the right of suffrage," he wrote in his diary. However, he did nothing to remedy the situation. Frederick Douglass called Hayes's policy "sickly conciliation."

Hayes's successors in the 1880s did no better. "Time is the only cure," President Garfield said, thereby confessing that he had no policy at all. President Arthur gave federal patronage to antiblack groups in an effort to split the Democratic South. In President Cleveland's day, blacks had scarcely a friend in high places, North or South. In 1887 Cleveland explained to a correspondent why he opposed "mixed schools." Expert opinion, the president said, believed "that separate schools were of much more benefit for the colored people." Hayes, Garfield, and Arthur were Republicans, Cleveland a Democrat; party made little difference. Both parties subscribed to hypocritical statements about equality and constitutional rights, and neither did anything to implement them.

For a time blacks were not totally disfranchised in the South. Rival white factions tried to manipulate them, and corruption flourished as widely as in the machine-dominated wards of the northern cities. In the 1890s, however, the southern states, led by Mississippi, began to deprive blacks of the vote despite the Fifteenth Amendment. Poll taxes raised a formidable economic barrier, one that also disfranchised many poor whites. Literacy tests completed the work; a number of states provided a loophole for illiterate whites by including an "understanding" clause whereby an illiterate person could qualify by demonstrating an ability to explain the meaning of a section of the state constitution when an election official read it to him. Blacks who attempted to take the test were uniformly declared to have failed it.

In Louisiana, 130,000 blacks voted in the election of 1896. Then the law was changed. In 1900 only 5,000 votes were cast by blacks. With unctuous hypocrisy, white southerners insisted that they loved "their" blacks dearly and wished only to protect them from "the machinations of those who would use them only to further their own base ends." "We take away the Negroes' votes," a Louisiana politician explained, "to protect them just as we would protect a little child and prevent it from injuring itself with sharp-edged tools."

Practically every Supreme Court decision after 1877 that affected blacks somehow "nullified or curtailed" their rights, Professor Rayford W. Logan writes. In *Hall* v. *De Cuir* (1878) the Court even threw out a state law forbidding segregation on riverboats, arguing that it was an unjustifiable interference with interstate commerce. The *Civil Rights Cases* (1883) declared the Civil Rights Act of 1875 unconstitutional. Blacks who were refused equal accommodations or privileges by hotels, theaters, and other privately owned facilities had no recourse in law, the Court announced. The Fourteenth Amendment guaranteed their civil rights against invasion by the states, not by individuals.

Finally, in *Plessy* v. *Ferguson* (1896), the Court ruled that even in places of public accommodation, such as railroads and, by implication, schools, segregation was legal so long as facilities of equal quality were provided. "If one race be inferior to the other socially, the Constitution of the United States cannot put them upon the same plane." In a noble dissent in the Plessy case, Justice John Marshall Harlan protested this line of argument. "Our Constitution is color-blind," he said. "The arbitrary separation of citizens, on the basis of race . . . is a badge of servitude wholly inconsistent with civil freedom and the equality before the law established by the Constitution." Alas, more than half a century was to pass before the Court came around to Harlan's reasoning and reversed the Plessy decision. Meanwhile, total segregation was imposed throughout the South. Separate schools, prisons, hospitals, recreational facilities, and even cemeteries were provided for blacks, and these were almost never equal to those available to whites.

Most northerners supported the government and the Court. Social Darwinist ideas seemed to demonstrate that since there were physiological differences between whites and blacks and since the whites were in control of the country, they were the "fittest" by nature. Newspapers presented a stereotyped, derogatory picture of blacks, no matter what the circumstances. Northern magazines repeatedly made blacks the butt of crude jokes. "The Negro's day is over," the tough-minded William Graham Sumner explained. "He is out of fashion."

The restoration of white rule abruptly halted the progress in public education for blacks that the Reconstruction governments had made. Church groups and private foundations such as the Peabody Fund and the Slater Fund, financed chiefly by northern philanthropists, supported black schools after

Frances Benjamin Johnston, the first black woman photographer of note, documented Tuskegee Institute's activities in the early years of the century. Here students help with building construction about 1900.

1877, among them two important experiments in vocational training, Hampton Institute and Tuskegee Institute.

These schools had to overcome considerable resistance and suspicion in the white community; they survived only because they taught a docile, essentially subservient philosophy, preparing students to accept second-class citizenship and become farmers and craftsmen. Since proficiency in academic subjects might have given the lie to the southern belief that blacks were intellectually inferior to whites, such subjects were avoided.

The southern insistence on segregating the public schools, buttressed by the "separate but equal" decision of the Supreme Court in *Plessy* v. *Ferguson,* imposed a crushing financial burden on poor, sparsely settled communities, and the dominant opinion that blacks were not really educable did not encourage these communities to make special efforts in their behalf.

Booker T. Washington and the Atlanta Compromise

Since nearly all contemporary biologists, physicians, and other supposed experts on race were convinced that blacks were inferior beings, educated northerners generally accepted black inferiority as fact. James Bryce, whose study of the United States at this time, *The American Commonwealth* (1888), has become a classic, saw many Americans of this type and absorbed their social Darwinist point of view. Negroes, Bryce wrote, were inherently docile, pliable, submissive, lustful, childish, impressionable, emotional, heedless, and "unthrifty." They had "no capacity for abstract thinking, for scientific inquiry, or for any kind of invention." Being "unspeakably inferior," they were "unfit to cope with a superior race."

Like Bryce, most Americans did not especially wish blacks ill; they simply refused to consider them quite human and consigned them complacently to oblivion, along with the Indians, who were also dismissed as racially inferior by Darwinians. A vicious circle was established. By denying blacks decent educational opportunities and good jobs, the dominant race could use the blacks' resultant ignorance and poverty to justify the inferior facilities offered them.

Southern blacks reacted to this deplorable situation in a variety of ways. Some sought redress in racial pride and what would later be called black nationalism. Some became so disaffected that they tried to revive the African colonization movement. "Africa is our home," insisted Bishop Henry M. Turner, a huge, plainspoken man who had served as an army chaplain during the war and as a member of the Georgia legislature during Reconstruction. "Every man that has the sense of an animal must see there is no future in this country for the Negro." Another militant, T. Thomas Fortune, editor of the New York *Age* and founder of the Afro-American League (1887), called on blacks to demand full civil rights, better schools, and fair wages and to fight against discrimination of every sort. "Let us stand up like men in our own organization," he urged. "If others use . . . violence to combat our peaceful arguments, it is not for us to run away from violence."

Militancy and black separatism won few adherents among southern blacks. For one thing, life was better than it had been under slavery. According to the most conservative estimates, the living standard of the average southern black more than doubled between 1865 and 1900. But the forces of repression were extremely powerful. The late 19th century saw more lynchings in the South than any other period of American history. This helps explain the tactics of Booker T. Washington, one of the most extraordinary Americans of that generation.

Washington had been born a slave in Virginia in 1856. Laboriously he obtained an education, supporting himself while a student by working as a janitor. In 1881, with the financial help of northern philanthropists, he founded Tuskegee Institute in Alabama. His experiences convinced Washington that blacks must lift themselves by their own bootstraps but that they must also accommodate themselves to white prejudices. A persuasive speaker and a brilliant fund-raiser, he soon developed a national reputation as a "reasonable" champion of his race. (In 1891 Harvard awarded him an honorary degree.)

In 1895 Washington made a now-famous speech to a mixed audience in Atlanta. To the blacks he said: "Cast down your bucket where you are," by which he meant stop fighting segregation and second-class citizenship and concentrate on learning useful skills. "Dignify and glorify common labor," he urged. "Agitation of questions of racial equality is the extremest folly." Progress up the social and economic ladder would come not from "artificial forcing" but from self-improvement. "There is as much dignity in tilling a field as in writing a poem."

Washington asked the whites of what he called "our beloved South" to lend the blacks a hand in their efforts to advance themselves. If you will do so, he promised, you will be "surrounded by the most patient, faithful, law-abiding, and unresentful people that the world has seen."

This so-called Atlanta Compromise delighted white southerners and won Washington financial support in every section of the country. He became one of the most powerful men in the United States, consulted by presidents, in close touch with business and philanthropic leaders, and capable of influencing in countless unobtrusive ways the fate of millions of blacks.

Blacks responded to the compromise with mixed feelings. Accepting Washington's approach might relieve them of many burdens and dangers and bring them considerable material assistance. Obsequiousness might, like discretion, be the better part of valor. But the cost was high in surrendered personal dignity and lost hopes of obtaining real justice.

Washington's career illustrates the terrible dilemma that American blacks have always faced: the choice between confrontation and accommodation. This choice was particularly difficult in the late 19th century.

Washington chose accommodation. It is easy to condemn him as a toady but difficult to see how, at that time, a more aggressive policy could have succeeded. One can even interpret the Atlanta Compromise as a subtle form of black nationalism; in a way, Washington was not urging blacks to accept inferiority and racial slurs but to ignore them. His own behavior lends force to this view, for his method of operating was indeed subtle, even devious. In public he minimized the importance of civil and political rights and accepted separate but equal facilities—if they were truly equal. Behind the scenes he lobbied against restrictive measures, marshaled large sums of money to fight test cases in the courts, and worked hard in northern states to organize the black vote and make sure that black political leaders got a share of the spoils of office. As one black militant put it, Washington knew the virtue of "sa-

gacious silence." He may not, in retrospect, seem an admirable man, but he was a useful one. His defects point up more the unlovely aspects of the age than those of his own character.

The West After the Civil War

The West displayed these aspects of the age, and a number of others, in heightened form. Many parts of the region had as large a percentage of foreign-born residents as the populous eastern states—nearly a third of all Californians were foreign-born, as were more than 40 percent of Nevadans and over half the residents of Idaho and Arizona. There were, of course, large populations of Spanish-speaking Americans of Mexican origin all over the Southwest. Chinese and Irish laborers were pouring into California by the thousands, and there were substantial numbers of Germans in Texas. Germans, Scandinavians, and other Europeans were also important on the high plains east of the Rockies.

Although the image of the West as a land of great open spaces is accurate enough, the region contained several bustling cities. San Francisco, with a population approaching 250,000 in the late 1870s, had long outgrown its role as a rickety boomtown where the forty-niners bought supplies and squandered whatever wealth they had sifted from the streams of the Sierra. It was still an important warehouse and supply center, but it was also the commercial and financial heart of the Pacific Coast and a center of light manufacturing, food processing, and machine shops. Denver, San Antonio, and Salt Lake City were far smaller but growing rapidly and equally "urban."

There was, in short, no one West, no typical westerner. If the economy was predominantly agricultural and extractive, it was also commercial and entering the early stages of industrial development. The seeds of such large enterprises as Wells Fargo, Levi Strauss, and half a dozen important department store empires were sown in the immediate postwar decades.

Above all, however, the West epitomized the social Darwinist, "every man for himself" psychology of post-Reconstruction American society. In 1879 several thousand southern blacks suddenly migrated to western Kansas. When asked why, one of their leaders replied: "The white people [in the

South] treat our people so bad . . . that it is impossible for them to stand it." But their treatment in Kansas was not much better, certainly not better than the way blacks were treated in the northern states. California had been a free state from the moment of its entry into the Union as part of the Compromise of 1850, but it treated its black citizens poorly, even refusing to ratify the Fifteenth Amendment.

Beginning in the mid-1850s, a steady flow of Chinese migrated to the United States, most of them to the West Coast region. About four or five thousand a year came until the negotiation of the Burlingame Treaty of 1868, the purpose of which was to provide cheap labor for railroad construction crews. Thereafter the annual influx more than doubled, though before 1882 it exceeded 20,000 only twice. When the railroads were completed the Chinese, who were hardworking and willing to work for low wages, began to compete with native workers. A great cry of resentment went up on the West Coast. Riots broke out in San Francisco in 1877. Bigots called Chinese workers "groveling worms" and described them as "more slavish and brutish than the beasts that roam the fields." When the

Construction crew laying tracks along the west slope of the Cascades in 1885. By then, such physically demanding and socially isolated work had largely devolved upon the most recently arrived immigrants, as seems the case here.

migration suddenly increased in 1882 to nearly 40,000, the protests reached such a peak that Congress passed a law prohibiting all Chinese immigration for ten years. Later legislation extended the ban indefinitely.

Chinese immigrants created genuine social problems. Most did not intend to remain in the United States and therefore made little effort to accommodate themselves to American ways. Their supposed attachment to gambling, opium, and prostitutes—over 90 percent of the Chinese in America in the 1880s were men—alarmed respectable citizens. But the westerners' attitude toward the Chinese differed only in degree from their attitude toward the Mexicans who flocked into the Southwest to work as farm laborers and to help build railroads.

The Plains Indians

"Whites," the historian Rodman Paul wrote, "did not shed their old attitudes when they crossed into a new country." His generalization applies with special force to the way the westerners dealt with Indians. For 250 years the Indians had been driven back steadily, yet on the eve of the Civil War they still inhabited roughly half the United States. By the time of Hayes's inauguration, however, the Indians had been shattered as independent peoples, and in another decade the survivors were penned up on reservations, the government committed to a policy of extinguishing their way of life.

In 1860 the survivors of most of the eastern tribes were living peacefully in what is now Oklahoma. In California the forty-niners had made short work of the local tribes. Elsewhere in the West—in the deserts of the Great Basin between the Sierra and the Rockies, in the mountains themselves, and on the semiarid, grass-covered plains between the Rockies and the edge of white civilization in eastern Kansas and Nebraska—nearly a quarter of a million Indians dominated the land.

By far the most important lived on the High Plains. From the Blackfeet of southwestern Canada and the Sioux of Minnesota and the Dakotas to the Cheyenne of Colorado and Wyoming and the Comanche of northern Texas, the plains tribes possessed a generally uniform culture. All lived by hunting the hulking American bison, or buffalo, which ranged over the plains by the millions. The buffalo provided the Indians with food, clothing, even shelter, for the famous Indian tepee was covered with hides. On the treeless plains, dried buffalo dung was used for fuel. The buffalo was also an important symbol in Indian religion.

Although they seemed the epitome of freedom, pride, and self-reliance, the plains Indians had begun to fall under the sway of white power. They eagerly adopted the products of the more technically advanced culture—cloth, metal tools, weapons, cheap decorations. However, the most important thing the whites gave them had nothing to do with technology: It was the horse.

The geological record shows that the genus *Equus* was native to America, but it had become extinct in the Western Hemisphere long before Cortés brought the first modern horses to America in the 16th century. Multiplying rapidly thereafter, the animals soon roamed wild from Texas to the Argentine. By the 18th century the Indians of the plains had made them a vital part of their culture.

Horses thrived on the plains, and so did their masters. Mounted Indians could run down buffalo instead of stalking them on foot. They could move more easily over the country and fight more effectively too. They could acquire and transport more possessions and increase the size of their tepees, for horses could drag heavy loads heaped on A-shaped frames (called *travois* by the French), whereas earlier Indians had only dogs to depend on as pack animals. The frames of the travois, when disassembled, served as poles for tepees. The Indians also adopted modern weapons: the cavalry sword, which they particularly admired, and the rifle. Both added to their effectiveness as hunters and fighters. However, like the whites' liquor and diseases, horses and guns caused problems. The buffalo herds began to diminish, and warfare became bloodier and more frequent.

In a familiar and tragic pattern, the majority of the western tribes greeted the first whites to enter their domains in a friendly fashion. Lewis and Clark and their handful of companions crossed and recrossed the entire region without a single clash with the Indians they encountered. As late as the 1830s, white hunters and trappers ranged freely over most of the West, trading with the Indians and often marrying Indian women. Settlers pushing cross-country toward Oregon in the 1840s met with relatively little trouble.

An Oglala Sioux named Kills Two painted this portrayal of "An Indian Horse Dance." Horses were vital to survival for the Sioux, as their inclusion in such ceremonies demonstrates.

After the start of the gold rush, the need to link the East with California meant that the tribes were pushed aside. Deliberately, the government in Washington prepared the way. In 1851 Thomas Fitzpatrick, an experienced mountain man, scout for the first large group of settlers to Oregon in 1841 and for American soldiers in California during the Mexican War, summoned a great "council" of the tribes. About 10,000 Indians gathered that September at Horse Creek, 37 miles east of Fort Laramie, in what is now Wyoming.

The Indians respected Fitzpatrick, who had recently married a woman who was half Indian. At Horse Creek he persuaded each tribe to accept definite limits to its hunting grounds. In return the Indians were promised gifts and annual payments. This policy, known as "concentration," was designed to cut down on intertribal warfare and—far more important—to enable the government to negotiate separately with each tribe. It was the classic strategy of divide and conquer.

Although it made a mockery of diplomacy to treat with Indian tribes as though they were European powers, the United States maintained that each tribe was a sovereign nation, to be dealt with as an equal in solemn treaties. Both sides knew that this was not the case. Tribal chiefs had only limited power; young braves frequently refused to respect agreements made by their elders.

Indian Wars

The government showed little interest in honoring agreements with Indians. No sooner had the Kansas-Nebraska bill become law than the Kansas, Omaha, Pawnee, and Yankton Sioux tribes began to feel pressure for further concessions of territory. Other trouble developed in the Sioux country. Thus it happened that in 1862, after federal troops had been pulled out of the West for service against the Confederacy, most of the plains Indians rose up against the whites. For five years intermittent but bloody clashes kept the entire area in a state of alarm.

This was guerrilla warfare, with all its horror and treachery. In 1864 a party of Colorado militia fell upon an unsuspecting Cheyenne community at Sand Creek and killed an estimated 450. "Kill and scalp all, big and little," Colonel J. M. Chivington, a minister in private life, told his men. "Nits make lice." A white observer described the scene: "They were scalped, their brains knocked out; the men used their knives, ripped open women, clubbed little children, knocked them in the head with their guns, beat their brains out, mutilated their bodies in every sense of the word." General Nelson A. Miles called this Chivington Massacre the "foulest and most unjustifiable crime in the annals of America," but it was no worse than many incidents in earlier conflicts with Indians and not very different from what was later to occur in guerrilla wars involving American troops in the Philippines and, more recently, in Vietnam.

In turn the Indians slaughtered dozens of isolated white families, ambushed small parties, and fought many successful skirmishes against troops and militia. They achieved their most notable triumph in December 1866, when the Oglala Sioux,

under their great chief Red Cloud, wiped out a party of 82 soldiers under Captain W. J. Fetterman. Red Cloud fought ruthlessly, but only when goaded by the construction of the Bozeman Trail, a road through the heart of the Sioux hunting grounds in southern Montana.*

In 1867 the government tried a new strategy. The concentration policy had evidently not gone far enough. All the plains Indians would be confined to two small reservations, one in the Black Hills of Dakota Territory, the other in Oklahoma, and forced to become farmers. At two great conclaves held in 1867 and 1868 at Medicine Lodge Creek and Fort Laramie, the principal chiefs yielded to the government's demands.

Many Indians refused to abide by these agreements. With their whole way of life at stake, they raged across the plains like a prairie fire—and were almost as destructive.

That a relative handful of "savages," without central leadership or plan, could hold off the cream of the army, battle-hardened in the Civil War, can be explained by the character of the vast, trackless country and the ineptness of many American military commanders. Indian leadership was also poor in that few chiefs were capable of organizing a campaign or following up an advantage. But the Indians made superb guerrillas. Every observer called them the best cavalry soldiers in the world. Armed with stubby, powerful bows capable of driving an arrow clear through a bull buffalo, they were a fair match for troops equipped with carbines and Colt revolvers. Expertly they led pursuers into ambushes, swept down on unsuspecting supply details, and stole up on small parties the way a mountain lion stalks a grazing lamb. Trouble flared here one week, another week somewhere else, perhaps 500 miles away. No less an authority than General William Tecumseh Sherman testified that a mere 50 Indians could often "checkmate" 3,000 soldiers.

If one concedes that no one could reverse the direction of history or stop the invasion of Indian lands, some version of the small-reservation policy would probably have been best for the Indians. Had they been guaranteed a reasonable amount of land and adequate subsidies and allowed to maintain

---

* Fetterman had boasted that with 80 cavalrymen he could ride the entire length of the Bozeman Trail. When he tried, however, he blundered into an ambush.

their way of life, they might have accepted the situation and ceased to harry the whites.

Whatever chance that policy had was weakened by the government's maladministration of Indian affairs. In dealing with Indians, 19th-century Americans displayed a grave lack of talent for administration. After 1849 the Department of the Interior supposedly had charge of tribal affairs. Most of its agents systematically cheated the Indians. One, heavily involved in mining operations on the side, diverted goods intended for his charges to his private ventures. When an inspector looked into his records, he sold him shares in a mine. That worthy in turn protected himself by sharing some of the loot with the son of the commissioner of Indian affairs. "No branch of the national government is so spotted with fraud, so tainted with corruption . . . as this Indian Bureau," Congressman Garfield charged in 1869.

At about this time a Yale paleontologist, Othniel C. Marsh, who wished to dig for fossils on the Sioux reservation, asked Red Cloud for permission to enter his domain. The chief agreed on condition that Marsh, whom the Indians called Big Bone Chief, take back with him samples of the moldy flour and beef that government agents were supplying to his people. Appalled by what he saw on the reservation, Professor Marsh took the rotten supplies directly to President Grant and prepared a list of charges against the agents. General Philip Sheridan was no lover of Indians. "The only good Indians I ever saw," he said in an oft-quoted remark, "were dead." But he understood why they behaved as they did. "We took away their country and their means of support, broke up their mode of living, their habits of life, introduced disease and decay among them, and it was for this and against this that they made war. Could anyone expect less?"

In 1869 Congress created a nonpolitical Board of Indian Commissioners to oversee Indian affairs, but the bureaucrats in Washington stymied the commissioners at every turn. "Their recommendations were ignored, . . . gross breaking of the law was winked at, and . . . many matters were not submitted to them at all," the biographer of one commissioner has written. "They decided that their task was as useless as it was irritating."

But in 1874 gold was discovered in the Black Hills Indian reservation. By the next winter thousands of miners had invaded the reserved area.

Comanche, the only survivor on the army's side at the Battle of Little Bighorn. His rider was among the 264 cavalrymen who perished with General Custer that June afternoon in 1876.

Already alarmed by the approach of crews building the Northern Pacific Railroad, the Sioux once again went on the warpath. Joining with nontreaty tribes to the west, they concentrated in the region of the Bighorn River, in southern Montana Territory.

The summer of 1876 saw three columns of troops in the field against them. The commander of one column, General Alfred H. Terry, sent ahead a small detachment of the Seventh Cavalry under Colonel George A. Custer with orders to locate the Indians' camp and then block their escape route into the inaccessible Bighorn Mountains. Custer was vain and rash, and vanity and rashness were grave handicaps when fighting Indians. Grossly underestimating the number of the Indians, he decided to attack directly with his tiny force of 264 men. At the Little Bighorn late in June he found himself surrounded by 2,500 Sioux under Rain-in-the-Face, Crazy Horse, and Sitting Bull. He and all his men died on the field.

Because it was so one-sided, "Custer's Last Stand" was not a typical battle, though it may be taken as symbolic of the Indian warfare of the period in the sense that it was characterized by bravery, foolhardiness, and a tragic waste of life. The battle greatly heartened the Indians, but it did not gain them their cause. That autumn, short of rations and hard-pressed by overwhelming numbers of soldiers, they surrendered and returned to the reservation.

The Destruction of Tribal Life

Thereafter, the fighting slackened. For this the building of transcontinental railroads and the destruction of the buffalo were chiefly responsible. An estimated 13 to 15 million head had roamed the plains in the mid-1860s. Then the slaughter began. Thousands were butchered to feed the gangs of laborers engaged in building the Union Pacific Railroad. Thousands more fell before the guns of sportsmen. Buffalo hunting became a fad, and a brisk demand developed for buffalo rugs and mounted buffalo heads. The railroads contributed to the decimation of the buffalo by running excursion trains for hunters; even the shameful practice of gunning down the beasts directly from the cars was allowed. In 1871 and 1872 the Grand Duke Alexis of Russia headed a gigantic hunt, supported by "Buffalo Bill" Cody, most famous of the pro-

fessional buffalo killers, the Seventh United States Cavalry under General Sheridan, and hundreds of Indians.

The discovery in 1871 of a way to make commercial use of buffalo hides completed the tragedy. In the next three years about 9 million head were killed; after another decade the animals were almost extinct. No more efficient way could have been found for destroying the plains Indians. The disappearance of the bison left them starving, homeless, purposeless.

By 1887 the tribes of the mountains and deserts beyond the plains had also given up the fight. Typical of the heartlessness of the government's treatment of these peoples was that afforded the Nez Percé of Oregon and Idaho, who were led by the remarkable Chief Joseph. After outwitting federal troops in a campaign across more than 1,000 miles of rough country, Joseph finally surrendered in October 1877. The Nez Percé were then settled on "the malarial bottoms of the Indian Territory" in far-off Oklahoma. The last Indians to abandon the unequal battle were the relentless Apaches of the Southwest, who finally yielded upon the capture of their leader, Geronimo, in 1886.

By the 1880s the advance of whites into the plains had become, in the words of one congressman, as irresistible "as that of Sherman's to the sea." Greed for land lay behind the pressure, but large numbers of disinterested people, including most of those who deplored the way the Indians had been treated in the past, believed that the only practical way to solve the "Indian problem" was to persuade the Indians to abandon their tribal culture and live on family farms. The "wild" Indian must be changed into a "civilized" member of "American" society.

To accomplish this goal Congress passed the Dawes Severalty Act of 1887. Tribal lands were to be split up into individual allotments. To keep speculators from wresting the allotments from the Indians while they were adjusting to their new way of life, the land could not be disposed of for 25 years. Funds were to be appropriated for educating and training the Indians, and those who accepted allotments, took up residence "separate from any tribe," and "adopted the habits of civilized life" were to be granted United States citizenship.

The sponsors of the Severalty Act thought they were effecting a fine humanitarian reform. "We must throw some protection over [the Indian]," Sen-

Preparing to surrender to General Crook, Geronimo (mounted, left) and Natiche stand with their respective sons and Geronimo's grandson; the sons wear ceremonial paint. This photograph was taken in the Sierra Madre mountains of Mexico in 1886, just before the surrender.

ator Henry L. Dawes declared. "We must hold up his hand." But the law had disastrous results in the long run. It assumed that Indians could be transformed into small agricultural capitalists by an act of Congress. It weakened what was left of the Indians' culture without enabling them to adapt to white ways. Moreover, unscrupulous whites systematically tricked many Indians into leasing their allotments for a pittance, and local authorities often taxed Indian lands at excessive rates. In 1934, after about 86 million of the 138 million acres assigned under the Dawes Act had passed into white hands, the government returned to a policy of encouraging tribal ownership of Indian lands.

Exploiting Mineral Wealth in the West

Americans had long regarded the West as a limitless treasure to be grasped as rapidly as possible, and after 1865 they engrossed its riches still faster and in a wider variety of ways. From the mid-1850s to the mid-1870s thousands of gold-crazed prospectors fanned out through the Rockies, panning every stream and hacking furiously at every likely out-

cropping from the Fraser River country of British Columbia to Tucson in southern Arizona, from the eastern slopes of the Sierra to the Great Plains.

Gold and silver were scattered throughout the area, though usually too thinly to make mining profitable. Whenever anyone made a "strike," prospectors, the vast majority utterly without previous experience but driven by what a mining journal of the period called an "unhealthy desire" for sudden wealth, flocked to the site, drawn by rumors of streambeds gleaming with gold-rich gravel and of nuggets the size of men's fists. For a few months the area teemed with activity. Towns of 5,000 or more sprang up overnight; improvised roads were crowded with people and supply wagons. Claims were staked out along every stream and gully. Then, usually, expectations faded in the light of reality: high prices, low yields, hardship, violence, and deception. The boom collapsed, and the towns died as quickly as they had risen. A few would have found wealth, the rest only backbreaking labor and disappointment—until tales of another strike sent them dashing feverishly across the land on another golden chase.

In the spring of 1858 it was on the Fraser River in Canada that the horde descended, 30,000 Californians in the vanguard. The following spring, Pikes Peak in Colorado attracted the pack, experienced California prospectors ("yonder siders") mixing with "greenhorns" from every corner of the globe. In June 1859 came the finds in Nevada, where the famous Comstock Lode yielded ores worth nearly $4,000 a ton. In 1861, while men in the settled areas were laying down their tools to take up arms, the miners were racing to the Idaho panhandle, hoping to become millionaires overnight. The next year the rush was to the Snake River valley, in 1863 and 1864 to Montana. From 1874 to 1876 the Black Hills in the heart of the Sioux lands were inundated with prospectors.

In a sense the Denvers, Aurarias, Virginia Cities, Orofinos, and Gold Creeks of the West during the war years were harbingers of the attitudes that flourished in the East in the age of President Grant and his immediate successors. The miners enthusiastically adopted the get-rich-quick philosophy, willingly enduring privations and laboring hard, always with the object of striking it rich. The idea of reserving any part of the West for future generations never entered their heads.

The sudden prosperity of the mining towns attracted every kind of shady character—according to one forty-niner, "rascals from Oregon, pickpockets from New York, accomplished gentlemen from Europe, interlopers from Lima and Chile, Mexican thieves, gamblers from no particular spot, and assassins manufactured in Hell." Gambling dens, dance halls, saloons, and brothels mushroomed wherever precious metal was found.

Law enforcement was a constant problem. Gold and silver dominated people's thoughts and dreams, and few paid much attention to the means employed in accumulating this wealth. Storekeepers charged outrageous prices; claim holders "salted" worthless properties with nuggets in order to swindle gullible investors. Ostentation characterized the successful, braggadocio those who failed. During the administration of President Grant, Virginia City, Nevada, was at the peak of its vulgar prosperity. It had 25 saloons before it had 4,000 people. By the 1870s its mountainside site was disfigured by ugly, ornate mansions where successful mine operators ate from fine china and swilled champagne as though it were water.

In 1873, after the discovery of the Big Bonanza, a seam of rich ore more than 50 feet thick, the future of Virginia City seemed boundless. Other discoveries shortly thereafter indicated to optimists that the mining boom in the West would continue indefinitely. The finds in the Black Hills district in 1875 and 1876, heralding deposits yielding eventually $100 million, led to the mushroom growth of Deadwood, home of Wild Bill Hickok, Deadwood Dick, Calamity Jane, and such lesser-known characters as California Jack and Poker Alice. In Deadwood, according to the historian Ray Allen Billington, "the faro games were wilder, the hurdy-gurdy dance halls noisier, the street brawls more common, than in any other western town." New strikes in Colorado in 1876 and 1877 caused the town of Leadville to boom; in 1880 there were 30,000 people in

Nat Love, a cowboy who earned the name of "Deadwood Dick" throughout the Dakotas in the 1880s for his prowess with a lariat. His autobiography, published in 1907, attests to the role blacks played in the settling of the Wild West.

the area. However, this was the last important flurry to ruffle the mining frontier. The West continued to yield much gold and silver, especially silver, but big corporations produced nearly all of it. The mines around Deadwood were soon controlled by one large company, Homestake Mining.

This is the culminating irony of the history of the mining frontier: Shoestring prospectors, independent and enterprising, made the key discoveries. They established local institutions and supplied the West with much of its color and folklore. But the stockholders of large corporations, many of whom had never seen a mine, made off with the lion's share of the wealth. Those whose worship of gold was direct and incessant, the prospectors who peopled the mining towns and gave the frontier its character, mostly died poor, still seeking a prize as elusive if not as illusory as the pot of gold at the end of the rainbow.

The mining of gold and silver was not essentially different from the mining of coal and iron. To operate profitably, large capital investments, heavy machinery, railroads, and hundreds of skilled workers (mostly "deep" miners from Cornwall, in England) were required. Henry Comstock, the prospector who gave his name to the Comstock Lode,

was luckier than most, but he sold his claims to the lode for a pittance, disposing of what became one valuable mine for $40 and receiving only $10,000 for his share of the fabulous Ophir, the richest concentration of gold and silver ever found. More typical of the successful mine owner was George Hearst, senator from California and father of the newspaper tycoon William Randolph Hearst, who, by shrewd speculations, obtained large blocks of stock in mining properties scattered from Montana to Mexico.

Though marked by violence, fraud, greed, and shattered hopes, the gold rushes had valuable results. The most obvious was the new metal itself, which bolstered the financial position of the United States during and after the Civil War. Quantities of European goods needed for the war effort and for postwar economic development were paid for with the yield of the new mines. Gold and silver also caused a great increase of interest in the West. A valuable literature appeared, part imaginative, part reportorial, describing the mining camps and the life of the prospectors. These works fascinated contemporaries (as they have continued to fascinate succeeding generations when adapted to the motion picture and to television). Mark Twain's *Roughing*

An idealized engraving of the interior of a gold mine in Nevada in the 1870s. Neither prospectors like Henry Comstock nor those who dug these mines figured prominently among those enriched by them.

It (1872), based in part on his experiences in the Nevada mining country, is the most famous example of this literature.

Each new strike and rush, no matter how ephemeral, brought permanent settlers along with the prospectors: farmers, cattlemen, storekeepers, teamsters, lawyers, and ministers. The boomtowns had to import everything from bread, meat, and liquor to building materials and tools of every sort. Without the well-worn trails blazed by earlier hunters and migrants headed for Oregon and California and of freighting companies equipped to haul heavy loads over long distances, the towns could not have existed. Some of the gold seekers saw from the start that a better living could be made supplying the needs of prospectors than looking for the elusive metal. Others, failing to find mineral wealth, took up whatever occupation they could rather than starve or return home empty-handed. In every mining town—along with the saloons and brothels—schools, churches, and newspaper offices sprang up.

The philosopher Josiah Royce (1855–1916), the son of forty-niners, grew up in a California mining town and in San Francisco. Many years later, while teaching at Harvard, he wrote a book about life in the camps. "The romantic degradation of the early mining life, with its . . . inevitable brutality and its resulting loathsome corruption, gave place to the commonplace industries of the later mining days," he recalled.

The mines also speeded the political organization of the West. Colorado and Nevada became territories in 1861, Arizona and Idaho in 1863, Montana in 1864. Although Nevada was admitted before it had 60,000 residents (in 1864, to ratify the Thirteenth Amendment and help reelect Lincoln), most of these territories did not become states for decades. But thanks to the miners, the framework for future development was established early.

The Land Bonanza

While the miners were engrossing the mineral wealth of the West, other interests were snapping up the region's choice farmland. The Homestead Act of 1862 had presumably ended the reign of the speculator and the large landholder. An early amendment to the act even prevented husbands and wives from filing separate claims. The West, land reformers had assumed, would soon be dotted with 160-acre family farms.

They were doomed to disappointment. Most landless Americans were too poor to become farmers even when they could obtain land without cost. The expense of moving a family to the ever-receding frontier exceeded the means of many, and the costs of hoes and scythes, harvesting machines, fencing, and housing presented a formidable barrier. As for the industrial workers for whom the free land was supposed to provide a "safety valve," they had neither the skills nor the inclination to become farmers. Homesteaders usually came from districts not far removed from frontier conditions, and despite the intent of the law, speculators often managed to obtain large tracts. They hired men to stake out claims, falsely swear that they had fulfilled the conditions laid down in the law for obtaining legal title, and then deed the land over to their employers.

Furthermore, 160 acres was not enough for raising livestock or for the kind of commercial agriculture that was developing west of the Mississippi. Congress made a feeble attempt to make larger holdings available to homesteaders by passing the Timber Culture Act of 1873, which permitted individuals to claim an additional 160 acres if they would agree to plant a quarter of it with trees within ten years. This law proved helpful to some farmers in Kansas, Nebraska, and the Dakotas. Nevertheless, fewer than 25 percent of the 245,000 who took up land under it obtained final title to the property. Raising large numbers of seedlings on the plains was a difficult task.

While futilely attempting to make a forest of parts of the treeless plains, the government permitted private interests to gobble up and destroy many of the great forests that clothed the slopes of the Rockies and the Sierra. The Timber and Stone Act of 1878 allowed anyone to acquire a quarter section of forest land for $2.50 an acre if it was "unfit for civilization." This laxly drawn measure enabled lumber companies to obtain thousands of acres by hiring dummy entrymen, whom they marched in gangs to the land offices, paying them a few dollars for their time after they had signed over their claims.

Had the land laws been more precisely drafted, it is still unlikely that the policy of granting free land to small homesteaders would have succeeded. Aside from the built-in difficulties faced by small-scale ag-

*The crews of five combines stopped during the wheat harvest on a bonanza
farm in northern California to have their picture taken. Combines such as these
reaped, threshed, cleaned, and bagged grain in a single operation.*

riculturalists, frontier farmers of the 1870s and
1880s had to grapple with novel problems. The soil
was rich, but the climate, especially in the semiarid
regions beyond the 98th meridian of longitude,
made agriculture frequently difficult and often impossible. Blizzards, floods, grasshopper plagues,
and prairie fires caused repeated heartaches, but
periodic drought and searing summer heat were
the worst hazards.

At the same time, the flat immensity of the land,
combined with newly available farm machinery and
the development of rail connections with the East,
encouraged the growth of enormous corporation-
controlled "bonanza" farms. One such organization
was the railroad-owned empire managed by Oliver
Dalrymple in Dakota Territory, which cultivated
25,000 acres of wheat in 1880. Dalrymple employed
200 pairs of harrows to prepare his soil, 125 seeders
to sow his seed, and 155 binders to harvest his crop.

Bonanza farmers could buy supplies wholesale
and obtain concessions from railroads and proces-
sors; even the biggest organizations could not cope
with prolonged drought, however, and most of the
bonanza outfits failed in the dry years of the late
1880s. Wise farmers who diversified their crops and
cultivated their land intensively fared better in the

long run, though even they could not hope to earn
a profit in really dry years.

Despite the hazards of plains agriculture, the
region became the breadbasket of America in the
decades following the Civil War. By 1889 Minnesota
topped the nation in wheat production, and ten
years later four of the five leading wheat states lay
west of the Mississippi. The plains also accounted
for large percentages of the nation's other cereal
crops, together with immense quantities of beef,
pork, and mutton.

Like other exploiters of the nation's resources,
farmers took whatever they could from the soil with
little heed for preserving its fertility and preventing
erosion. The consequent national loss was less
apparent because it was diffuse and slow to
assume drastic proportions, but it was nonetheless
real.

Western Railroad Building

Further exploitation of land resources by private
interests resulted from the government's policy of
subsidizing western railroads. Here was a clear illustration of the conflict between the idea of the

West as a national heritage to be disposed of to deserving citizens and the concept of the region as a cornucopia pouring forth riches to be gathered up and carted off by anyone powerful and determined enough to take them. When it came to a choice between giving a particular tract to railroads or to homesteaders, the homesteaders nearly always lost out.

Unless the government had been willing to build the transcontinental lines itself—and this was unthinkable in an age dominated by belief in individual exploitation—some system of subsidy was essential. Private investors would not hazard the huge sums needed to lay tracks across hundreds of miles of rugged, empty country when traffic over the road could not possibly produce profits for many years. It might appear that subsidizing construction by direct outlays of public funds would have been adopted, but that idea had few supporters. Most voters were wary of entrusting the dispensing of large sums to politicians. Grants of land seemed a sensible way of financing construction. The method avoided direct outlays of public funds, for the companies could pledge the land as security for bond issues or sell it directly for cash. Moreover, land and railroad values were intimately linked in contemporary thinking. "The occupation of new land and the building of new mileage go hand in hand," the *Commercial and Financial Chronicle* explained in 1886.

There could be no great or continuous opening up of new territory without the necessary facilities in the way of railroads. On the other hand, most new mileage on the borders of our Western territory is prosecuted with the idea and expectation that it is to pave the way for an accession of new settlers and an extension of the area of land devoted to their uses.

In many cases the value of the land granted might be recovered by the government when it sold other lands in the vicinity, for such properties would certainly be worth more after transportation facilities to eastern markets had been constructed. "Why," the governor of one eastern state asked in 1867, "should private individuals be called upon to make a useless sacrifice of their means, when railroads can be constructed by the unity of public and private interests, and made profitable to all?"

About 49 million acres were given to various lines indirectly in the form of grants to the states, but the most lavish gifts of the public domain were those made directly to builders of intersectional trunk lines. These roads received more than 155 million acres, although about 25 million acres reverted to the government because some companies failed to lay the required miles of track. About 75 percent of this land went to aid the construction of four transcontinental railroads: the Union Pacific–Central Pacific line, running from Nebraska to San Francisco, completed in 1869; the Atchison, Topeka and Santa Fe, running from Kansas City to Los

Railroads expanded using bridges and trestles to cross inhospitable terrain that had presented problems for horse and wagon. This bridge east of Santa Fe, New Mexico, was completed in 1880.

Angeles by way of Santa Fe and Albuquerque, completed in 1883; the Southern Pacific, running from San Francisco to New Orleans by way of Yuma and El Paso, completed in 1883; and the Northern Pacific, running from Duluth, Minnesota, to Portland, Oregon, completed in 1883.

The Pacific Railway Act of 1862 established the pattern for these grants. It gave the builders of the Union Pacific and Central Pacific railroads 5 square miles of public land on each side of their right of way for each mile of track laid. The land was allotted in alternate sections, forming a pattern like a checkerboard, the squares of one color representing railroad property, the other government property. Presumably this arrangement benefited the entire nation since half the land close to the railroad remained in public hands.

However, whenever grants were made to railroads, the adjacent government lands were not opened to homesteaders, on the theory that free land in the immediate vicinity of a line would prevent the road from disposing of its properties at good prices. Since, in addition to the land granted the railroads, a wide zone of "indemnity" lands was reserved to allow the roads to choose alternative sites to make up for land that settlers had already taken up within the checkerboard, homesteading was in fact prohibited near land-grant railroads. Grants per mile of track ranged from five alternate sections on each side of the track to the Union and Central Pacific to 40 sections to the Northern Pacific. In the latter case, when the indemnity zone was included, homesteaders were barred from an area 100 miles wide, all the way from Lake Superior to the Pacific. More than 20 years after receiving its immense grant, the Northern Pacific was still attempting to keep homesteaders from filing in the indemnity zone. President Cleveland finally put a stop to this in 1887, saying that he could find "no evidence" that "this vast tract is necessary for the fulfillment of the grant."

Historians have argued at length about the fairness of the land-grant system. No railroad corporation waxed fat directly from the sale of its lands, which were sold at prices averaging between $2 and $5 an acre. Collectively the roads have taken in between $400 million and $500 million from this source, but only over the course of a century. Land-grant lines did a great deal to encourage the growth of the West by advertising their property and by providing cheap transportation for prospective set-

tlers and efficient shipping services for farmers. They were required by law to carry troops and handle government business free or at reduced rates, which saved the government millions over the years. At the same time the system imposed no effective restraints on how the railroads used the funds raised with federal aid. Being able to lay track with money obtained from land grants, the operators tended to be extravagant and often downright corrupt.

The Union Pacific was built by a construction company, the Crédit Mobilier, which was owned by the promoters. These men awarded themselves contracts at prices that assured the Crédit Mobilier of fat profits. When Congress threatened to investigate the Union Pacific in 1868, Oakes Ames, a stockholder in both companies who was also a member of Congress, sold key congressmen and government officials over 300 shares of Crédit Mobilier stock at a price far below its real value. "I have found," Ames said, "there is no difficulty in inducing men to look after their own property."

When these transactions were exposed, the House of Representatives censured Ames, but such was the temper of the times that neither he nor most of his associates believed that he had done anything wrong. According to the president of one western railroad, congressmen frequently tried to use their influence to get railroad land at bargain prices. "Isn't there a discount?" they would ask. "Surely you can give the land cheaper to a friend. . . ." The railroads seldom resisted this type of pressure.

The construction of the Central Pacific in the 1860s illustrates how the system encouraged extravagance. The line was controlled by four businessmen, Collis P. Huntington ("scrupulously dishonest" but an excellent manager); Leland Stanford, a Sacramento grocer and politican; Mark Hopkins, a hardware merchant; and Charles Crocker, a hulking, relentless driver of men who had come to California during the gold rush and made a small fortune as a merchant. The Central Pacific and the Union Pacific were given, in addition to their land grants, loans in the form of government bonds—from $16,000 to $48,000 for each mile of track laid, depending on the difficulty of the terrain. The two competed for the subsidies, the Central Pacific building eastward from Sacramento, the Union Pacific westward from Nebraska. Each put crews to work grading and laying track, bringing up supplies over the already completed road. The

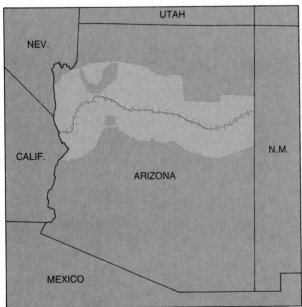

On the contemporary map (upper), the Atlantic and Pacific Railroad land grant in Arizona appears as shaded squares on a checkerboard. The grant cut a 100-mile-wide swath across the entire territory (lower).

Union Pacific employed Civil War veterans and Irish immigrants; the Central, Chinese immigrants.

This plan favored the Union Pacific. While the Central Pacific was inching upward through the gorges and granite of the mighty Sierra, the Union Pacific was racing across the level plains, laying 540 miles of track between 1865 and 1867. Once beyond the Sierra, the Central Pacific would have easy going across the Nevada-Utah plateau country, but by then it might be too late to prevent the Union Pacific from making off with most of the government aid.

Crocker managed the Central Pacific construction crews. He wasted huge sums by working through the winter in the High Sierra. Often the men labored in tunnels dug through 40-foot snowdrifts to get at the frozen ground. To speed construction of the Summit Tunnel, Crocker had a shaft cut down from above so that crews could work out from the middle as well as in from each end. In 1866, over the most difficult terrain, he laid 28 miles of track—at a cost of more than $280,000 a mile. Experts later estimated that 70 percent of this sum could have been saved had speed not been a factor. Such prodigality made economic sense to Huntington, Stanford, Hopkins, and Crocker because of the profits they were making through the construction company and because of the gains they could count on once they reached the flat country beyond the Sierra, where construction costs would amount to only half the federal aid.

Crocker's herculean efforts paid off. The mountains were conquered, and then the crews raced across the Great Basin to Salt Lake City and beyond.

The meeting of the rails—the occasion of a national celebration—took place at Promontory, north of Ogden, Utah, on May 10, 1869. Leland Stanford drove the final ceremonial golden spike with a silver hammer.* The Union Pacific had built 1,086 miles of track, the Central 689 miles.

In the long run the wasteful way in which the Central Pacific was built hurt the road severely. It was ill-constructed, over grades too steep and around curves too sharp, and burdened with debts that were too heavy. Such was the fate of nearly all the railroads constructed with the help of government subsidies.

The only transcontinental built without land grants was the Great Northern, running from St. Paul, Minnesota, to the Pacific. Spending private capital, its guiding genius, James J. Hill, was compelled to build economically and to plan carefully. As a result, his was the only transcontinental line to weather the depression of the 1890s without going into bankruptcy.

The Cattle Kingdom

While miners were digging out the mineral wealth of the West and railroaders were taking possession of much of its land, another group was exploiting endless acres of its grass. For 20 years after the Civil War, cattlemen and sheep raisers dominated huge areas of the High Plains, making millions of dollars by grazing their herds on lands they did not own.

Columbus brought the first cattle to the New World in 1493, on his second voyage, and later *conquistadores* took them to every corner of Spain's American empire. Mexico proved to be so well suited to raising cattle that many were allowed to roam free. They multiplied rapidly, and by the late 18th century what is now southern Texas harbored enormous herds. The beasts interbred with nondescript "English" cattle, brought into the area by settlers from the United States, to produce the Texas longhorn. Hardy, wiry, ill-tempered, and fleet, with horns often attaining a spread of 6 feet, these animals were far from ideal as beef cattle and almost as hard to capture as wild horses. But they

existed in southern Texas by the million, most of them unowned.

The lack of markets and transportation explains why Texas cattle were lightly regarded. But conditions were changing. Industrial growth in the East was causing an increase in the urban population and a consequent rise in the demand for food. At the same time, the expansion of the railroad network made it possible to move cattle cheaply over long distances. As the iron rails inched across the plains, astute cattlemen began to do some elementary figuring. Longhorns could be had locally for $3 to $4 a head. In the northern cities they would bring ten times that much, perhaps even more. Why not round them up and herd them northward to the railroads, allowing them to feed along the way on the abundant grasses of the plains?

In 1866 a number of Texans drove large herds northward toward Sedalia, Missouri, railhead of the Missouri Pacific. This route took the herds through wooded and settled country and across Indian reservations, which provoked many difficulties. At the same time Charles Goodnight and Oliver Loving successfully drove 2,000 head in a great arc west to New Mexico Territory and then north to Colorado.

The next year the drovers, inspired by a clever young Illinois cattle dealer named Joseph G. McCoy and other entrepreneurs, led their herds north by a more westerly route, across unsettled grasslands, to the Kansas Pacific line at Abilene, Kansas, which McCoy described as "a very small, dead place, consisting of about one dozen log huts." They earned excellent profits, and during the next five years about 1.5 million head made the "long drive" over the Chisholm Trail to Abilene, where they were sold to ranchers, feedlot operators, and the agents of eastern meat packers. Other shipping points sprang up as the railroads pushed westward. According to the best estimates, 10 million head were driven north before the practice ended in the mid-1880s.

The technique of the long drive, which involved guiding herds of two or three thousand cattle slowly across as much as a thousand miles of country, produced the American cowboy, renowned in song, story, and on film. Half a dozen of these men could control several thousand steers. Mounted on wiry ponies, they would range alongside the herd, keeping the animals on the move but preventing stampedes, allowing them time to rest yet steadily pressing them toward the yards of Abilene.

---

* A mysterious "San Francisco jeweler" passed among the onlookers, taking orders for souvenir watch chains that he proposed to make from the spike at $5 each.

THE WEST: CATTLE, RAILROADS, AND MINING, 1850–1893

The cowboy's life was far more prosaic than it appears in modern legend, consisting mainly of endless hours on the trail surrounded by thousands of bellowing beasts. Cowboys were a mixed lot: Mexican *vaqueros* and blacks made up about a third of them, but there were many local Texans, Civil War veterans, former miners, and, in the words of Theodore Roosevelt, "wild spirits from every land." They virtually lived on horseback, for their work kept them far from human habitation for months on end.

Most, accustomed to solitude, were indeed "strong, silent men." They were courageous—and expert marksmen, too, for they lived amid many dangers and had to know how to protect themselves. Few grew rich, yet like the miners they were true representatives of their time—determinedly individualistic, contemptuous of authority, crude, devoted to coarse pleasures.

The major "cattle towns," Abilene, Wichita, Ellsworth, Dodge City, and Caldwell, had their full share of saloons, gambling dens, and "dance houses" patronized by cowboys and by other transients bent on having a good time. Most were young, male, and single. Violence punctuated their activities, but tales of individual desperadoes and gangs of outlaws "shooting up" cattle towns and terrorizing honest citizens are fictitious. Police forces were well organized. Indeed, the "respectable" town residents tended to urge leniency for lawbreakers because of the money they and their fellows brought to the towns. A careful check of the records by the historian Robert Dykstra revealed that between 1870 and 1885 there were only 45 homicides in these five towns, and some of them had nothing to do with the cattle trade.

Open-Range Ranching

Soon cattlemen discovered that the hardy Texas stock could survive the winters of the northern plains. Attracted by the apparently limitless forage, they began to bring up herds to stock the vast regions where the buffalo had so recently roamed. Introducing pedigreed Hereford bulls, they improved the stock without weakening its resistance to harsh conditions. By 1880 some 4.5 million head had spread across the sea of grass that ran from Kansas to Montana and west to the Rockies.

The prairie grasses offered cattlemen a bonanza almost as valuable as the gold mines. Open-range ranching required actual ownership of no more than a few acres along some watercourse. In this semiarid region, control of water enabled a rancher to dominate all the surrounding area back to the divide separating his range from the next stream without investing a cent in the purchase of land. His cattle, wandering freely on the public domain, fattened on grass owned by all the people, to be turned into beefsteak and leather for the profit of the rancher.

Theoretically, anyone could pasture stock on the open range, but without access to water it was impossible to do so. "I have 2 miles of running water," a cattleman said in testifying before the Public Land Commission. "That accounts for my ranch being where it is. The next water from me in one direction is 23 miles; now no man can have a ranch between these two places. I have control of the grass, the

same as though I owned it." By having his cowhands take out homestead claims along watercourses in his region, a rancher could greatly expand the area he dominated. In the late 1870s one Colorado cattle baron controlled an area roughly the size of Connecticut and Rhode Island even though he owned only 105 small parcels that totaled about 15,500 acres.

Generally a group of ranchers acted together, obtaining legal title to the lands along the bank of a stream and grazing their cattle over the area drained by it. The herds became thoroughly intermixed, each owner's being identified by an individual brand mark. Every spring and fall the ranchers staged a great roundup, driving in all the cattle to a central place, separating them by the brands, culling steers for shipment to market, and branding new calves.

With the demand for meat rising and transportation cheap, princely fortunes could be made in a few years. Capitalists from the East and from Europe began to pour funds into the business. Eastern "dudes" like Theodore Roosevelt, a young New York assemblyman who sank over $50,000 into his Elkhorn Ranch in Dakota Territory in 1883, bought up cattle as a sort of profitable hobby. (Roosevelt, clad in buckskin and bearing a small armory of rifles and six-shooters, made quite a splash in Dakota, but not as a rancher.)

Unlike other exploiters of the West's resources, the ranchers did not at first injure or reduce any public resource. Grass eaten by their stock renewed itself annually, the soil enriched by the droppings of the animals. Furthermore, ranchers poached on the public domain because there was no reasonable way for them to obtain legal possession of the large areas necessary to raise cattle on the plains. Federal land laws made no allowance for the special conditions of the semiarid West. "Title to the public lands [of the West] cannot be honestly acquired under the homestead laws," S. E. Burdett, commissioner of the General Land Office, reported in 1875. "A system of sale should be authorized in accordance with the necessities of the situation."

Such a system was soon devised by Major John Wesley Powell, later the director of the United States Geological Survey. His *Report on the Lands of the Arid Region of the United States* (1879) suggested that western lands be divided into three classes: irrigable lands, timber lands, and "pasturage" lands. On the pasturage lands the "farm unit" ought to be at least 2,560 acres (four sections), Powell urged. Groups of these units should be organized into "pasturage districts" in which the ranchers "should have the right to make their own regulations for the division of lands, the use of the water . . . and for the pasturage of lands in common or in severalty."

Barbed-Wire Warfare

Congress refused to change the land laws in any basic way, and this had two harmful effects. First, it encouraged fraud: Those who could not get title to enough land honestly turned to subterfuge. The Desert Land Act (1877) allowed anyone to obtain 640 acres in the arid states for $1.25 an acre provided the owner irrigated part of it within three years. More than 2.6 million acres were taken up under the act, and according to the best estimate, about 95 percent of the claims were fraudulent—no sincere effort was made to irrigate the land.

Second, overcrowding became a problem that led to serious conflicts, even killings, because no one had uncontestable title to the land. The leading ranchers banded together in cattlemen's associations to deal with overcrowding and with such problems as quarantine regulations, water rights, and thievery. In most cases these associations devised effective and sensible rules, but their functions would better have been performed by the government, as such matters usually are.

To keep other ranchers' cattle from the sections of the public domain they considered their own, the associations and many individuals began to fence huge areas. This was possible only because of the invention in 1874 of barbed wire by Joseph F. Glidden, an Illinois farmer. By the 1880s thousands of miles of the new fencing had been strung across the plains, often across roads and in a few cases around entire communities. "Barbed-wire wars" resulted, fought by rancher against rancher, cattleman against sheepman, herder against farmer. The associations tried to police their fences and to punish anyone who cut their wire. Signs posted along lonely stretches gave dire warnings to trespassers. "The Son of a Bitch who opens this fence had better look

In 1885 masked Nebraskans seeking access to water posed for photographer S. D. Butcher, who captioned the picture "Settlers taking the law in their own hands: cutting 15 miles of the Brighton Ranch fence."

out for his scalp," one such sign announced, another fine statement of the philosophy of the age.

By stringing so much wire the cattlemen were unwittingly destroying their own way of doing business. On a truly open range, cattle could fend for themselves, instinctively finding water during droughts, drifting safely downwind before blizzards. Barbed wire prevented their free movement. During winter storms these slender strands became as lethal as high-tension wires; the drifting cattle piled up against them and died by the thousands. "The advent of barbed wire," Walter Prescott Webb wrote in his classic study *The Great Plains* (1931), "brought about the disappearance of the open, free range and converted the range country into the big-pasture country."

The boom times were ending. Overproduction was driving down the price of beef; expenses were on the rise; many sections of the range were badly overgrazed. The dry summer of 1886 left the stock in such poor condition as winter approached that the *Rocky Mountain Husbandman* urged its readers to sell their cattle despite the prevailing low prices rather than "endanger the whole herd by having the range overstocked."

Some ranchers took this advice; those who did not made a fatal error. Winter that year arrived early and with unparalleled fury. Blizzards raged and temperatures plummeted far below zero. Cattle crowded into low places only to be engulfed in giant snowdrifts; barbed wire took a fearful toll. When spring finally came, the streams were choked with rotting carcasses. Between 80 and 90 percent of all cattle on the range were dead.

That cruel winter finished open-range cattle raising. The large companies were bankrupt; many independent operators, Roosevelt among them, became discouraged and sold out. When the industry revived, it was on a smaller, more efficiently organized scale. Cattle raising, like mining before it, ceased to be an adventure in rollicking individualism and became a business.

By the late 1880s the bonanza days of the West were over. No previous frontier had caught the imagination of Americans so completely as the Great West, with its heroic size, its awesome emptiness, its massive, sculptured beauty. Now the frontier was no more. Most of what Professor Webb called the "primary windfalls" of the region—the furs, the precious metals, the forests, the cattle, and the grass—had been snatched up by firstcomers and by individuals already wealthy. Big companies were taking over all the West's resources. The nation was becoming more powerful, richer, larger, and its economic structure more complex and diversified as the West yielded its treasures. But the East, especially eastern industrialists and financiers, increasingly dominated the economy of the nation.

Milestones

1859	Charles Darwin's *Origin of Species*
	Comstock Lode discovered
1864	Chivington Massacre
1869	Union Pacific Railroad completed
	Board of Indian Commissioners established
1873	Timber Culture Act
1875	Civil Rights Act
1876	Battle of the Little Bighorn
1877	Desert Land Act
1878	Timber and Stone Act
1879	Major Powell's *Report on the Lands of the Arid Region*
	Specie payments resumed
1881	Tuskegee Institute founded
1883	*Civil Rights Cases*
1886–1887	Blizzards put an end to open-range ranching
1887	Dawes Severalty Act
1888	James Bryce's *American Commonwealth*
1890–1900	Blacks deprived of the vote in the South
1895	Booker T. Washington's Atlanta Compromise speech
1896	*Plessy* v. *Ferguson* sanctions segregation

SUPPLEMENTARY READING

Titles marked with an asterisk have been published in paperback.

Three superb analyses of the political system of the period were written by men who studied it firsthand: James Bryce, **The American Commonwealth*** (1888), Woodrow Wilson, **Congressional Government*** (1886), and Moisei Ostrogorski, **Democracy and the Organization of Political Parties*** (1902). Morton Keller, **Affairs of State** (1977), is an interesting analysis of public life in the period.

The issues of post-Reconstruction politics are discussed in S. P. Hirshson, **Farewell to the Bloody Shirt*** (1962), Allen Weinstein, **Prelude to Populism: Origins of the Silver Issue** (1970), Irwin Unger, **The Greenback Era*** (1964), Milton Friedman and A. J. Schwartz, **A Monetary History of the United States*** (1963), and W. T. K. Nugent, **Money and American Society** (1968).

The economic, political, and legal ideas current in this period are covered in Sidney Fine, **Laissez Faire and the General Welfare State*** (1956), and J. W. Hurst, **Law and the Conditions of Freedom in the Nineteenth-Century United States*** (1956). C. D. Warner and Mark Twain, **The Gilded Age*** (1873), is a useful and entertaining contemporary impression. On social Darwinism, see R. C. Bannister, **Social Darwinism** (1979).

Western development is covered in R. A. Billington and Martin Ridge, **Westward Expansion** (1982), and in R. W. Paul, **The Far West and the Great Plains** (1988), which puts more emphasis on social aspects of the subject. Gunther Barth, **Instant Cities** (1975), deals with the development of San Francisco and Denver. On the Indians, general works include W. E. Washburn, **The Indian in America*** (1975), and W. T. Hagan, **American Indians*** (1961). Of more specialized books, the following are useful: F. G. Roe, **The Indian and the Horse** (1955), R. W. Mardock, **The Reformers and the American Indian** (1971), R. M. Utley, **Frontier Regulars: The United States Army and the Indian*** (1973); and F. P. Prucha, **The Great Father: The U.S. Government and the American Indians** (1984).

On the fate of other minority groups, see R. W. Logan, **The Negro in American Life and Thought: The Nadir*** (1954), Joel Williamson, **The Crucible of Race** (1984), L. R. Harlan, **Booker T. Washington*** (1972), C. V. Woodward, **The Strange Career of Jim Crow*** (1966), Gunther Barth, **Bitter Strength: A History of the Chinese in the United States** (1964), and John Higham, **Strangers in the Land*** (1955). On the mining frontier consult R. W. Paul, **Mining Frontiers of the Far West*** (1963), W. T. Jackson, **Treasure Hill: Portrait of a Silver Mining Camp*** (1963), Paula Petric, **No Step Backward: Women and Family on the Rocky Mountain Frontier** (1987) and D. A. Smith, **Rocky Mountain Mining Camps*** (1967). Mark Twain, **Roughing It*** (1872), is a classic contemporary account, and W. H. Goetzmann, **Exploration and Empire** (1966), throws much light on all aspects of western development. F. A. Shannon, **The Farmer's Last Frontier*** (1945), is excellent on all questions relating to post–Civil War agriculture. Bonanza farming is described in H. M. Drache, **The Day of the Bonanza** (1964).

The development of transcontinental railroads is discussed in R. E. Riegel, **The Story of the Western Railroads*** (1926), O. O. Winther, **The Transportation Frontier*** (1964), and G. R. Taylor and I. D. Neu, **The American Railroad Network** (1956). See also David Lavender, **The Great Persuader** (1970), Albro Martin, **James J. Hill and the Opening of the Northwest** (1976), R. G. Athearn, **Union Pacific Country*** (1971), and L. L. Waters, **Steel Rails to Santa Fe** (1950).

On cattle ranching on the plains, a good account is Lewis Atherton, **The Cattle Kings*** (1961), but see also Don Worcester, **The Chisholm Trail** (1980). On the cowboy and his life, see J. B. Frantz and J. E. Choate, **The American Cowboy** (1955), and R. R. Dykstra, **The Cattle Towns*** (1968). W. P. Webb, **The Great Plains*** (1931), is a fascinating analysis of the development of a unique civilization on the plains.

American Lives:
Clement Vann Rogers and George William Norris

Clem Rogers

C lem Rogers was part Cherokee Indian on both sides. He was born in Indian Territory in 1839, shortly after President Andrew Jackson had forced the Cherokee to migrate there from their ancestral lands in Georgia. Although he was proud of his Indian blood, Rogers lived more like the whites than the Indians. He never learned to speak Cherokee, though he was able to understand the language. His grandfather had actually settled in the region well before the tribe was forced there by Jackson.

The Rogers family had prospered in the Territory and Clem had been given a "white" education. But his father died when he was very young and after his mother remarried, Clem did not get along with his stepfather. When he was 16, his mother gave him enough cattle and horses to get started as a rancher, as well as two slaves (the Cherokee had adopted slavery along with other customs of their white Georgia neighbors).

Under Cherokee law, anyone could occupy and use any tribal land not already being used by another person; Clem settled in Cooweescoowee County, 30 miles south of the Kansas border. There he married Mary America Schrimsher, who was also part Cherokee.

When the Civil War broke out, Clem Rogers joined the Cherokee Mounted Rifles, a Confederate regiment commanded by Chief Stand Watie, one of the signers of the treaty in which the Cherokee had agreed to leave Georgia. He took part in a series of raids and engagements along the Kansas border and emerged from the war a captain.

When he returned from the war, Rogers found his ranch run down, his cattle missing. Of course his slaves were now free. He began anew, first as a laborer, then transporting freight by wagon from Missouri to Texas. With profits from this business he bought cattle and began ranching again. Gradually he extended his holdings of cattle. Reportedly he was the first rancher in the district to fence his land with barbed wire. By 1875 he had a substantial seven-room house with great stone chimneys surrounded by a white picket fence that enclosed Mary America's impressive flower gardens. He was also said to own the only piano in the county. The cowboys Rogers hired to work his cattle lived in a bunkhouse behind his home.

Clem Rogers was tough, shrewd, and ambitious. He was also something of a character. While his son Will was still learning to talk he taught him a number of "cuss words" and trained the baby to let loose with them when Clem snatched his bottle out of his mouth. He continued to prosper, buying cattle in Texas, fattening them on his tribal ranch, and then sending them off, several thousand head each year, to the slaughterhouses of St. Louis. He also raised fine horses and grew substantial amounts of corn and wheat.

By the late 1880s, however, the same forces that were putting an end to open range ranching on the northern plains were also affecting Indian

Beaver City, ca. 1890

Territory. In 1889 the Missouri Pacific Railroad laid track directly across land Rogers had been using for grazing and fenced its right of way with wire. This cut Rogers off from half the natural feed he needed to maintain his operation. At the same time the federal government opened a large section of the Territory to white homesteaders, who poured in by the thousands. Almost two million acres were claimed by these "Boomers" in a single day.

Rogers responded by shifting more of his land from cattle to wheat. He also improved his herds by replacing Texas longhorns with shorthorn steers. These required more care, but they produced greater amounts of higher quality beef. In 1895 he sold out, moved to Claremore, Oklahoma, and became vice president of a bank. He was also involved in politics, being a power in Cherokee affairs. In 1907 he was a delegate to the convention that drafted the state's constitution when Oklahoma was admitted to the Union.

The same forces that influenced the career of Clem Rogers affected in a somewhat different way the career of a young lawyer named George W. Norris. Norris, born in 1861, grew up on a farm in Ohio, taught school for a year, and then earned a law degree at what later became Valparaiso University in Indiana. In 1885 he moved to Beaver City, a farm town in southwestern Nebraska, to open an office.

That part of the country was booming. There was plenty of rain in western Nebraska and Kansas and the corn crop was enormous. Beaver City had only about a thousand residents but it was growing fast and prospering because of the business of the farmers of the region. It had two newspapers and two banks. A high school and a court house had been built recently. There was a flour mill and even a hotel.

Norris rented two rooms in a building near the court house, one to serve as his office, the other as his living quarters. At first he did not have much legal business and took on all sorts of jobs to earn money. He became an agent for the banks and for individuals interested in lending money to farmers and local businessmen. He also sold life insurance, and even applied for a job selling typewriters, but the manufacturer of this recently perfected invention turned him down for the understandable reason that he did not know how to type.

Norris's law practice gradually developed, a high point coming when the Burlington and Missouri Railroad made him its local attorney. He began to acquire farm properties, and he put up a two-story building in town, renting space to the Furnas County Bank and other businesses. He took another big step up the economic and social ladder when he married Pluma Lashley, daughter of Beaver City's leading businessman. When the elder Lashley died shortly thereafter, he left the Norrises the town flour mill.

However, western Nebraska was ravaged by drought in the early 1890s and the dry cycle had a crushing effect on farmers and most local enterprises. Norris's moneylending business shrank to almost nothing. The Furnas County Bank and other tenants of his office building failed. He avoided losing the flour mill only by borrowing money from friends.

In this situation he turned to politics merely to earn a living. In 1892 he was elected prosecuting attorney of the county on the Republican ticket; in 1895 district judge; in 1902 member of Congress.

After five terms in the House of Representatives, Norris was elected to the Senate, a place he was to hold for the next 30 years.

507

XIX

An Industrial Giant

You know how often I had not an unbroken night's sleep, worrying about how it was all coming out. All the fortune I have made has not served to compensate for the anxiety of that period. . . . If I had foreseen the future I doubt whether I would have had the courage to go on.

JOHN D. ROCKEFELLER

Our organization does not consist of idealists. . . . I look first to cigars.

ADOLPH STRASSER, *president of the Cigar Makers Union, 1883*

W hen the Civil War began, the country's industrial output, though important and increasing, did not approach that of the major European powers. By the end of the century the United States had become far and away the colossus among world manufacturers, dwarfing the production of Great Britain and Germany. The world had never seen such rapid economic growth. Modern economists estimate that the output of goods and services in the country (the gross national product, or GNP) increased by 44 percent between 1874 and 1883 and continued to expand in succeeding years. This growth was not confined to the Northeast. Wisconsin, for example, underwent a major transformation between 1873 and 1893; an economy based on grain and lumber became a mainly urban-centered industrial economy.

Industrial Growth: An Overview

American manufacturing flourished for many reasons. New natural resources were discovered and exploited steadily, thereby increasing opportunities. These opportunities in turn attracted the brightest and most energetic of a vigorous and expanding population. The growth of the country added constantly to the size of the national market, and protective tariffs shielded that market from foreign competition. Yet foreign capital entered the market freely, in part because tariffs kept out so many foreign goods. The dominant spirit of the time encouraged businessmen to maximum effort by emphasizing progress, glorifying material wealth, and justifying aggressiveness. European immigrants provided the additional labor needed by expanding industry; 2.5 million arrived in the 1870s, twice that number in the 1880s.

It was a period of rapid advances in basic science, and technicians created a bountiful harvest of new machines, processes, and power sources that increased productivity in many industries and created new industries as well. In agriculture there were what one contemporary expert called "an endless variety of cultivators," better harvesters and binding machines, and combines capable of threshing and bagging 450 pounds of grain a minute. An 1886 report of the Illinois Bureau of Labor Statistics claimed that "new machinery has displaced fully 50 percent of the muscular labor formerly required to do a given amount of work in the manufacture of agricultural implements."

As a result of improvements in the milling of grain, packaged cereals appeared on the American breakfast table. The commercial canning of food, spurred by the "automatic line" canning factory, expanded so rapidly that by 1887 a writer in *Good Housekeeping* magazine could say: "Housekeeping is getting to be ready made, as well as clothing." The Bonsack cigarette-rolling machine created a new industry that changed the habits of millions. George B. Eastman created another with his development of mass-produced roll photographic film and the simple but efficient Kodak camera. The perfection of the typewriter by the Remington company in the

1880s revolutionized the way office work was performed.

Railroads: The First Big Business

In 1866, returning from his honeymoon in Europe, 30-year-old Charles Francis Adams, Jr., grandson and great-grandson of presidents, full of ambition and ready, as he put it, to confront the world "face to face," looked about in search of a career. "Surveying the whole field," he later explained, "I fixed on the railroad system as the most developing force and the largest field of the day, and determined to attach myself to it." Adams's judgment was acute: For the next 25 years the railroads were probably the most significant element in American economic development, railroad executives the most powerful people in the country.

Railroads were important first as an industry in themselves. Less than 35,000 miles of track existed when Lee laid down his sword at Appomattox. In 1875 railroad mileage exceeded 74,000 and the skeleton of the network was complete. Over the next two decades the skeleton was fleshed out. In 1890 the mature but still growing system took in over $1 billion in passenger and freight revenues. (The federal government's income in 1890 was only $403 million.) The value of railroad properties and equipment was more than $8.7 billion. The national railroad debt of $5.1 billion was almost five times the national debt of $1.1 billion! By 1900 the nation had 193,000 miles of track.

The emphasis in railroad construction after 1865 was on organizing integrated systems. The lines had high fixed costs: taxes, interest on their bonds, maintenance of track and rolling stock, salaries of office personnel. A short train with half-empty cars required nearly as many workers and as much fuel to operate as a long one jammed with freight or passengers. To earn profits, the railroads had to carry as much traffic as possible. They therefore spread out feeder lines to draw business to their main lines the way the root network of a tree draws water into its trunk.

Before the Civil War, as we have seen, passengers and freight could travel by rail from beyond Chicago and St. Louis to the Atlantic Coast, but only after the war did true interregional trunk lines appear. In 1861, for example, the New York Central ran from Albany to Buffalo. One could proceed from Buffalo to Chicago, but on a different company's trains. In 1867 the Central passed into the hands of "Commodore" Cornelius Vanderbilt, who had made a large fortune in the shipping business. Vanderbilt already controlled lines running from Albany to New York City; now he merged these properties with the Central. In 1873 he integrated the Lake Shore and Michigan Southern into his empire, and two years later the Michigan Central. At his death in 1877 the Central operated a network of over 4,500 miles of track between New York City and most of the principal cities of the Middle West.

While Vanderbilt was putting together the New York Central complex, Thomas A. Scott was fusing roads to Cincinnati, Indianapolis, St. Louis, and Chicago to his Pennsylvania Railroad, which linked Pittsburgh and Philadelphia. In 1871 the Pennsylvania obtained access to New York; soon it reached Baltimore and Washington. By 1869 another important system, the Erie, extended from New York to Cleveland, Cincinnati, and St. Louis. Soon thereafter it too tapped the markets of Chicago and other cities. In 1874 the Baltimore and Ohio also obtained access to Chicago.

The transcontinentals were trunk lines from the start; the emptiness of the western country would have made short lines unprofitable, and builders quickly grasped the need for direct connections to eastern markets and thorough integration of feeder lines.

The dominant system builder of the Southwest was Jay Gould, a soft-spoken, unostentatious-looking man who was in fact ruthless, cynical, and aggressive. Another railroad president once called Gould a "perfect eel." Gould took over the Kansas Pacific, running from Denver to Kansas City, and consolidated it with the Union Pacific and the Missouri Pacific, a line from Kansas City to St. Louis. Often he put together such properties merely to unload them on other railroads at a profit, but his grasp of the importance of integration was sound.

In the Northwest, Henry Villard, a German-born ex-newspaperman, constructed another great complex based on his control of the Northern Pacific. James J. Hill controlled the Great Northern system, still another western network.

The Civil War had highlighted the need for through railroad connections in the South. Shortly

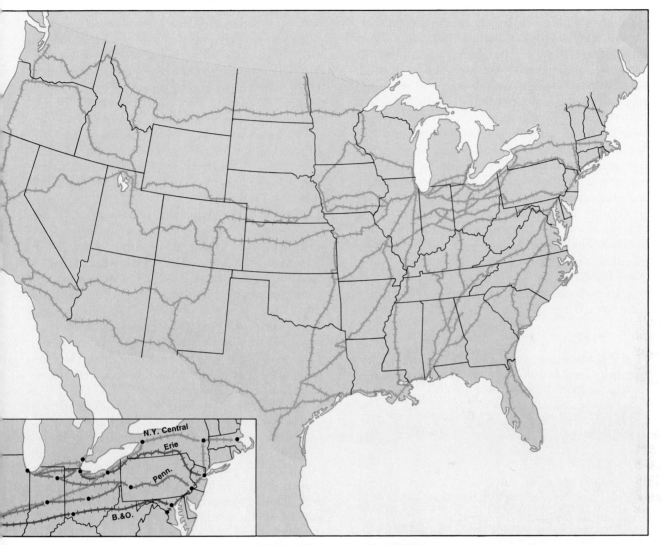

N.Y. Central

Erie

Penn.

B.&O.

PRIMARY RAILROADS, 1890

By 1890 trunk lines spanned the country, supplemented by networks of smaller feeder lines. The inset shows the trunk lines of four major companies that dominated rail service in the Northeast and linked up with western lines at Chicago and St. Louis.

after the conflict the Chesapeake and Ohio opened a direct line from Norfolk, Virginia, to Cincinnati. By the late 1880s, the Richmond and West Point Terminal Company controlled an 8,558-mile network. Like other southern trunk lines such as the Louisville and Nashville and the Atlantic Coast Line, this system was controlled by northern capitalists.

The trunk lines interconnected and thus had to standardize many of their activities. This in turn led to the standardization of other aspects of life. The present system of time zones was developed in 1883 by the roads. The standard track gauge (4 feet $8\frac{1}{2}$ inches) was established in 1886. Standardized car-coupling and braking mechanisms, standard signal systems, even standard methods of accounting were essential to the effective functioning of the network.

The lines sought to work out fixed rates for carrying different types of freight, charging more for valuable manufactured goods than for bulky products like coal or wheat, and they agreed to permit rate concessions to shippers when necessary to avoid hauling empty cars. In other words, they charged what the traffic would bear. However, by the 1880s the men who ran the railroads had come to recognize the advantages of cooperating with one another in order to avoid "senseless" competition. Railroad management was becoming a kind of profession, with certain standard ways of doing things, even with its own professional journals and with regional organizations such as the Eastern Trunk Line Association and the Western Traffic Association.

The railroads stimulated the economy indirectly. Like foreign commerce and the textile industry in

Widely distributed circular encouraging easterners to migrate to Iowa and Nebraska in 1873. Such advertisements were not noted for their accuracy.

earlier times, they served as a "multiplier," speeding development. In 1869 they bought $41.6 million worth of cars and locomotives; in 1889, $90.8 million. Their purchases created thousands of jobs and led to countless technological advances.

Because of their voracious appetite for traffic, railroads in sparsely settled regions and in areas with undeveloped resources devoted much money and effort to stimulating local economic growth. The Louisville and Nashville, for instance, was a prime mover in the expansion of the iron industry in Alabama in the 1880s.

To speed the settlement of new regions, the land-grant railroads sold land cheaply and on easy terms, for sales meant future business as well as current income. They offered reduced rates to travelers interested in buying farms and set up "bureaus of immigration" that distributed elaborate brochures describing the wonders of the new country. Their agents greeted immigrants at the eastern ports and tried to steer them to railroad property. They sent agents who were usually themselves immigrants—often ministers—all over Europe to recruit prospective settlers.

Technological advances in railroading accelerated economic development in complex ways. In 1869 George Westinghouse invented the air brake. By enabling an engineer to apply the brakes to all cars simultaneously (formerly each car had to be braked separately by its own conductor or brakeman), this invention made possible revolutionary increases in the size of trains and the speed at which they could operate safely. The sleeping car, invented in 1864 by George Pullman, now came into its own.

To pull the heavier trains, more powerful locomotives were needed. They in turn produced a call for stronger and more durable rails to bear the additional weight. Steel, itself reduced in cost because of technological developments, supplied the answer, for steel rails outlasted iron many times despite the use of much heavier equipment.

A close tie developed between the railroads and the nation's telegraph network, dominated by the Western Union Company. Commonly the roads allowed Western Union to string wires along their rights of way, and they transported telegraphers and their equipment without charge. In return they received free telegraphic service, important for efficiency and safety.

Iron, Oil, and Electricity

The transformation of iron manufacturing affected the nation almost as much as railroad development. Output rose from 920,000 tons in 1860 to 10.3 million tons in 1900, but the big change came in the development of ways to mass-produce steel. In its pure form (wrought iron) the metal is tough but relatively soft. Ordinary cast iron, which contains large amounts of carbon and other impurities, is hard but brittle. Steel, which contains 1 or 2 percent carbon, combines the hardness of cast iron with the toughness of wrought iron. For nearly every purpose—structural girders for bridges and buildings,

Minnesota's Mesabi Range (shown in 1899) was developed largely with Rockefeller money. It shipped 4,000 tons of iron ore in 1892 and within a decade tripled that amount—an increase reflected in the graph.

railroad track, machine tools, boiler plate, barbed wire—steel is immensely superior to other kinds of iron.

But steel was so expensive to manufacture that it could not be used for bulky products until the invention in the 1850s of the Bessemer process, perfected independently by Henry Bessemer, an Englishman, and William Kelly of Kentucky. Bessemer and Kelly discovered that a stream of air directed into a mass of molten iron caused the carbon and other impurities to combine with oxygen and burn off. When measured amounts of carbon, silicon, and manganese were then added, the brew became steel. What had been a rare metal could now be produced by the hundreds and thousands of tons. The Bessemer process and the open-hearth method, a slower but more precise technique that enabled producers to sample the molten mass and thus control quality closely, were introduced commercially in the 1860s. In 1870 77,000 tons of steel were manufactured. Such growth would have been impossible but for the huge supplies of iron ore in the United States and the coal necessary to fire the furnaces that refined it. In the 1870s the great iron fields rimming Lake Superior began to yield their treasures. The enormous iron concentrations of the Mesabi region made a compass needle spin like a top. Mesabi ores could be mined with steam shovels, almost like gravel.

Pittsburgh, surrounded by vast coal deposits, became the iron and steel capital of the country, the Minnesota ores reaching it by way of steamers on the Great Lakes and rail lines from Cleveland. Other cities in Pennsylvania and Ohio were important producers, and a separate complex, centering on Birmingham, Alabama, developed to exploit local iron and coal fields.

The petroleum industry expanded even more spectacularly than iron and steel. Edwin L. Drake drilled the first successful well in Pennsylvania in 1859. During the Civil War production ranged between 2 million and 3 million barrels a year. By 1890 the figure had leaped to about 50 million barrels.

Before the invention of the gasoline engine and the automobile, the most important petroleum product was kerosene, which was burned in lamps. Refiners heated crude oil in large kettles and, after the volatile elements had escaped, condensed the kerosene in coils cooled by water. The heavier petroleum tars were discarded.

Technological advances came rapidly. By the early 1870s, refiners had learned how to "crack" petroleum by applying high temperatures to the crude in order to rearrange its molecular structure, thereby increasing the percentage of kerosene yielded. By-products such as naphtha, gasoline (used in vaporized form as an illuminating gas), rhigolene (a local anesthetic), cymogene (a coolant for refrigerating machines), and many lubricants and waxes began to appear on the market. At the same time a great increase in the supply of crude oil drove prices down, especially after the German-born chemist Herman Frasch perfected a method for removing sulfur from low-quality petroleum.

These circumstances put a premium on refining efficiency. Larger plants that used expensive machinery and employed skilled technicians became more important. In the mid-1860s only three refineries in the country could process 2,000 barrels of crude a week; a decade later plants capable of handling 1,000 barrels a day were common.

Two other important new industries were the telephone and electric light businesses. Both were typical of the period, being products of technical advances and intimately related to the growth of a high-speed, urban civilization that put great stress on communication. The telephone was invented in 1876 by Alexander Graham Bell, who had been led to the study of acoustics through his interest in the education of the deaf. The invention soon proved its practical value. By 1900 there were almost 800,000 phones in the country, twice the total for all Europe. The American Telephone and Telegraph Company, a consolidation of over 100 local systems, dominated the business.

When Western Union realized the importance of the telephone, it tried for a time to compete with Bell by developing a machine of its own. The man it commissioned to devise this machine was Thomas A. Edison, but Bell's patents proved unassailable. Edison had already made a number of contributions toward solving what he called the "mysteries of electrical force," including a multiplex telegraph capable of sending four messages over a single wire at the same time. At Menlo Park, New Jersey, he built the prototype of the modern research laboratory, where specific problems could be attacked

Edison patented the phonograph in 1878, budgeting $18 for its invention. He was photographed in his laboratory on June 16, 1888, at 5:30 A.M., working on a wax cylinder model.

on a mass scale by a team of trained specialists. During his lifetime he took out more than 1,000 patents, covering machines as varied as the phonograph, the motion picture projector, the storage battery, and the mimeograph.

Edison's most significant achievement was the incandescent lamp, or electric light bulb. Others before Edison had experimented with the idea of producing light by passing electricity through a filament in a vacuum. Always, however, the filaments quickly burned out. Edison tried hundreds of fibers before producing, in 1879, a carbonized filament that would glow brightly in a vacuum tube for as long as 170 hours without crumbling. At Christmastime he decorated the grounds about his laboratory with a few dozen of the new lights. People flocked by the thousands to see this miracle of the "Wizard of Menlo Park." The inventor boasted that soon he would be able to illuminate entire towns, even great cities like New York.

He was true to his promise. In 1882 his Edison Illuminating Company opened a power station in New York and began to supply current for lighting to 85 consumers, including *The New York Times* and the banking house of J. P. Morgan and Company. Soon central stations were springing up everywhere until, by 1898, there were about 3,000 in the country.

The substitution of electric for steam power in factories was as liberating as steam for waterpower before the Civil War. Small, safe electric motors replaced dangerous and cumbersome mazes of belts and wheels. The electric power industry expanded rapidly. By the early years of the 20th century almost 6 billion kilowatt-hours of electricity were being produced annually. Yet this was only the beginning.

Competition and Monopoly: The Railroads

During the post–Civil War era, expansion in industry went hand in hand with concentration. The principal cause of this trend, aside from the obvious economics resulting from large-scale production and the growing importance of expensive machinery, was the downward trend of prices after 1873. The deflation, which resulted mainly from the failure of the money supply to keep pace with the rapid increase in the volume of goods produced, affected agricultural goods as well as manufactures, and it lasted until 1896 or 1897.

Contemporaries believed they were living through a "great depression." That label is misleading, for output expanded almost continuously, and at a rapid rate, until 1893, when production slumped and a true depression struck the country. Falling prices, however, kept a steady pressure on profit margins, and this led to increased production and thus to intense competition for markets. According to economists, competition advanced the public interest by keeping prices low and assuring the most efficient producer the largest profit. Up to a point, it accomplished these purposes in the years after 1865, but it also caused side effects that injured both the economy and society as a whole. Railroad managers, for instance, found it impossible to enforce "official" rate schedules and maintain their regional associations once competitive pressures mounted. In 1865 it had cost from 96 cents to $2.15 per 100 pounds, depending on the class of freight, to ship goods from New York to Chicago. In 1888 rates ranged from 35 cents to 75 cents.

Competition cut deeply into railroad profits, causing the lines to seek desperately to increase volume. They did so chiefly by reducing rates still more, on a selective basis. They gave rebates (secret reductions below the published rates) to large shippers in order to capture their business. The granting of discounts to those who shipped in volume made economic sense: It was easier to handle freight in carload lots than in smaller units. So intense was the battle for business, however, that the roads often made concessions to big customers far beyond what the economics of bulk shipment justified. In the 1870s the New York Central regularly reduced the rates charged important shippers by 50 to 80 percent. One large Utica dry goods merchant received a rate of 9 cents while others paid 33 cents. Two big New York City grain merchants paid so little that they soon controlled the grain business of the entire city.

Railroad officials disliked rebating but found no way to avoid the practice. "Notwithstanding my horror of rebates," the president of a New England trunk line told one of his executives in discussing the case of a brick manufacturer, "bill at the usual rate, and rebate Mr. Cole 25 cents a thousand." In extreme cases the railroads even gave large shippers drawbacks, which were rebates on the business of the shippers' competitors! Besides rebating, railroads issued passes to favored shippers, built sidings at the plants of important companies without charge, and gave freely of their landholdings to attract businesses to their territory. "The force of competition," a railroad man explained, "is one that no carrying corporation can withstand and before which the managing officers of a corporation are

helpless." James F. Joy of the Chicago, Burlington, and Quincy made the same point more bluntly: "Unless you prepare to defend yourselves," he advised the president of the Michigan Central, "you will be boarded by pirates in all quarters." A person trying to run a railroad honestly, wrote Charles Francis Adams, Jr., in *Railroads: Their Origin and Problems* (1879), would be like Don Quixote tilting at a windmill.

To make up for losses forced on them by competitive pressures, railroads charged higher rates at way points along their tracks where no competition existed. Frequently it cost more to ship a product a short distance than a longer one. Rochester, New York, was served only by the New York Central. In the 1870s it cost 30 cents to transport a barrel of flour from Rochester to New York City, a distance of 350 miles. At the same time flour could be shipped from Minneapolis to New York, a distance of well over 1,000 miles, for only 20 cents a barrel. One Rochester businessman told a state investigating committee that he could save 18 cents a hundredweight by sending goods to St. Louis by way of New York, where several carriers competed for the traffic, even though, in fact, the goods might come back through Rochester over the same tracks on the way to St. Louis!

Although cheap transportation stimulated the economy, few people benefited from cutthroat competition. Small shippers—and all businessmen in cities and towns with limited rail outlets—suffered; railroad discrimination speeded the concentration of industry in large corporations located in major centers. The instability of rates even troubled interests like the middle western flour millers who benefited from the competitive situation, for it hampered planning. Nor could manufacturers who received rebates be entirely happy, since few could be sure that some other producer was not getting a larger reduction.

Probably the worst sufferers were the roads themselves. The loss of revenue resulting from rate cutting, combined with inflated debts, put most of them in grave difficulty when faced with a downturn in the business cycle. In 1876 two-fifths of all railroad bonds were in default; three years later 65 lines were bankrupt. Wits called Samuel J. Tilden, the 1876 Democratic presidential candidate, the "Great Forecloser" because of his work reorganizing bankrupt railroads at this time.

Edward Steichen's memorable photograph of J. Pierpont Morgan, taken in 1906. Looking the formidable Morgan in the eye, Steichen said, was like facing the headlights of an onrushing express train.

Since the public would not countenance bankrupt railroads going out of business, these companies were placed in the hands of court-appointed receivers. The receivers, however, seldom provided efficient management and had no funds at their disposal for new equipment.

During the 1880s the major roads responded to these pressures by building or buying lines in order to create interregional systems. These were the first giant corporations, capitalized in the hundreds of millions of dollars. Their enormous cost led to another wave of bankruptcies when a true depression struck in the 1890s.

The consequent reorganizations brought most of the big systems under the control of financiers, notably J. Pierpont Morgan, and such other private

bankers as Kuhn, Loeb of New York and Lee, Higginson of Boston. The economic historian A. D. Noyes described in 1904 what the bankers did:

> Bondholders were requested to scale down interest charges, receiving new stock in compensation, while the shareholders were invited to pay a cash assessment, thus providing a working fund. [The bankers] combined to guarantee that the requisite money should be raised. They too were paid in new stock. . . . Though the total capital issues were increased, fixed charges were diminished and a sufficient fund for road improvement and new equipment was provided.

Critics called the reorganizations "Morganizations." Representatives of the bankers sat on the board of every line they saved, and their influence was predominant. They consistently opposed rate wars, rebating, and other competitive practices. In effect, control of the railroad network became centralized, even though the companies maintained their separate existences and operated in a seemingly independent manner. When Morgan died in 1913, "Morgan men" dominated the boards of the New York Central; the Erie; the New York, New Haven and Hartford; the Southern; the Père Marquette; the Atchison, Topeka and Santa Fe; and many other lines.

Competition and Monopoly: Steel

The iron and steel industry was also intensely competitive. Despite the trend toward higher production, demand varied erratically from year to year, even from month to month. In good times producers built new facilities, only to suffer heavy losses when demand declined. The forward rush of technology put a tremendous emphasis on efficiency; expensive plants quickly became obsolete. Improved transportation facilities allowed manufacturers in widely separated places to compete with one another.

The kingpin of the industry was Andrew Carnegie. Carnegie was born in Scotland, and came to the United States in 1848 at the age of 12. His first job, as a bobbin boy in a cotton mill, brought him $1.20 a week, but his talents fitted the times perfectly, and he rose rapidly: to Western Union messenger boy, to telegrapher, to private secretary, to railroad manager. He saved his money, made some shrewd investments, and by 1868 had an income of $50,000 a year.

At about this time he decided to specialize in the iron business. Carnegie possessed great talent as a salesman, boundless faith in the future of the country, an uncanny knack for choosing topflight subordinates, and enough ruthlessness to survive in the iron and steel jungle. Where other steelmen built new plants in good times, he preferred to expand in bad times, when it cost far less to do so. During the 1870s, he later recalled, "many of my friends needed money. . . . [I] bought out five or six of them. That is what gave me my leading interest in this steel business."

Carnegie grasped the importance of technological improvements. Slightly skeptical of the Bessemer process at first, once he became convinced of its practicality, he adopted it enthusiastically. In 1875 he built the J. Edgar Thomson Steel Works, named after a president of the Pennsylvania Railroad, his biggest customer. He employed chemists and other specialists and was soon making steel from iron oxides that other manufacturers had discarded as waste. He was a merciless competitor. When a plant manager announced, "We broke all records for making steel last week," Carnegie replied, "Congratulations! Why not do it every week?" Carnegie sold rails by paying "commissions" to railroad purchasing agents, and he was not above reneging on a contract if he thought it profitable and safe to do so.

By 1890 the Carnegie Steel Company dominated the industry, and its output increased nearly tenfold during the next decade. Profits soared. Alarmed by his increasing control of the industry, the makers of finished steel products such as barbed wire and tubing began to combine and to consider entering the primary field. Carnegie, his competitive temper aroused, threatened to turn to finished products himself. A colossal steel war seemed imminent.

However, Carnegie longed to retire in order to devote himself to philanthropic work. He believed that great wealth entailed social responsibilities and that it was a disgrace to die rich. When J. P. Morgan approached him through an intermediary with an offer to buy him out, he assented readily. In 1901 Morgan put together United States Steel, the

Andrew Carnegie in later life. His phenomenal rags-to-riches career was one of the real-life models for Horatio Alger's dime novels on the theme "poor boy makes good."

"world's first billion-dollar corporation." This combination included all the Carnegie properties, the Federal Steel Company (Carnegie's largest competitor), and such important fabricators of finished products as the American Steel and Wire Company, the American Tin Plate Company, and the National Tube Company. Vast reserves of Minnesota iron ore and a fleet of Great Lakes ore steamers were also included. U.S. Steel was capitalized at $1.4 billion, about twice the value of its component properties but not necessarily an overestimation of its profit-earning capacity. The owners of Carnegie Steel received $492 million, of which $250 million went to Carnegie himself.

Competition and Monopoly: Oil

The pattern of fierce competition leading to combination and monopoly is well illustrated by the history of the petroleum industry. Irresistible pressures pushed the refiners into a brutal struggle to dominate the business. Production of crude oil, subject to the uncertainties of prospecting and drilling, fluctuated constantly and without regard for need. In general, output surged far ahead of demand.

By the 1870s the chief oil-refining centers were Cleveland, Pittsburgh, Baltimore, and the New York City area. Of these, Cleveland was the fastest-growing, chiefly because the New York Central and Erie railroads competed fiercely for its oil trade and the Erie Canal offered an alternative route.

The Standard Oil Company of Cleveland, founded in 1870 by a 31-year-old merchant named John D. Rockefeller, emerged as the giant among the refiners. Rockefeller exploited every possible technical advance and employed fair means and foul to persuade competitors either to sell out or to join forces. By 1879 he controlled 90 percent of the nation's oil-refining capacity along with a network of oil pipelines and large reserves of petroleum in the ground.

Standard Oil emerged victorious from the competitive wars because Rockefeller and his associates were the toughest and most imaginative fighters as well as the most efficient refiners in the business. In addition to obtaining from the railroads a 10 percent rebate and drawbacks on its competitors' shipments, Standard Oil cut prices locally to force small independents to sell out or face ruin. Since kerosene was sold in grocery stores, Standard supplied its own outlets with meat, sugar, and other products at artificially low prices to help crush the stores that handled other brands of kerosene. The company employed spies to track down the customers of independents and offer them oil at bargain prices. Bribery was also a Standard practice; the reformer Henry Demarest Lloyd quipped that the company had done everything to the Pennsylvania legislature except refine it. Although a bold planner and a daring taker of necessary risks, Rockefeller was far too orderly and astute to enjoy the free-swinging battles that plagued his industry. Born in an upstate New York village in 1839, he settled in Cleveland in 1855 and became a produce merchant. During the Civil War he invested in a local refinery and by 1865 was engaged full time in the oil business.

Like Carnegie, Rockefeller was an organizer; he knew little about the technology of petroleum. His

A regally attired John D. Rockefeller, astride a barrel from his Standard Oil refinery, his crown encircled by the railroads he controlled. His actual attire was considerably less conspicuous.

forte was meticulous attention to detail: Stories are told of his ordering the number of drops of solder used to seal oil cans reduced from 40 to 39 and of his insisting that the manager of one of his refineries account for 750 missing barrel bungs. Not miserliness but a profound grasp of the economies of large-scale production explains this behavior.

Rockefeller competed ruthlessly not primarily to crush other refiners but to persuade them to join with him, to share the business peaceably and rationally so that all could profit. Competition was obsolescent, he argued, though no more effective competitor than he ever lived.

Having achieved his monopoly, Rockefeller stabilized and structured it by creating a new type of business organization, the trust. Standard Oil was an Ohio corporation, prohibited by state law from owning plants in other states or holding stock in out-of-state corporations. As Rockefeller and his associates took over dozens of companies with facilities scattered across the country, serious legal and managerial difficulties arose. How could these many organizations be integrated with Standard Oil of Ohio?

A rotund, genial little Pennsylvania lawyer named Samuel C. T. Dodd came up with an answer to this question in 1879.* The stock of Standard of Ohio and of all the other companies that the Rockefeller interests had swallowed up was turned over to nine trustees, who were empowered to "exercise general supervision" over all the properties. Stockholders received in exchange trust certificates, on which dividends were paid. This seemingly simple device brought order to the petroleum business. Competition almost disappeared; prices steadied; profits skyrocketed. By 1892 John D. Rockefeller was worth over $800 million.

The Standard Oil Trust was not a corporation. It had no charter, indeed no legal existence at all. For many years few people outside the organization knew that it existed. The form they chose persuaded Rockefeller and other Standard Oil officials that without violating their consciences, they could deny under oath that Standard Oil of Ohio owned or controlled other corporations "directly or indirectly through its officers or agents." The trustees controlled these organizations—and Standard of Ohio too!

After Standard Oil's duplicity was revealed during a New York investigation in 1888, the word *trust,* formerly signifying a fiduciary arrangement for the protection of the interests of individuals incompetent or unwilling to guard them themselves, became a synonym for *monopoly.* However, from the company's point of view, monopoly was not the purpose of the trust—that had been achieved before the device was invented. Centralization of the management of diverse and far-flung operations in the interest of efficiency was its chief function. Standard Oil headquarters in New York became the brain of a complex network where information from salaried managers in the field was collected and digested, where top managerial decisions were made, and

* The trust formula was not "perfected" until 1882.

whence orders went out to armies of drillers, refiners, scientists, and salesmen.

Competition and Monopoly: Utilities and Retailing

That utilities such as the telephone and electric lighting industries tended to form monopolies is not difficult to explain, for in such fields competition involved costly duplication of equipment and, particularly in the case of the telephone, loss of service efficiency. However, competitive pressures were strong in the early stages of their development. Since these industries depended on patents, Bell and Edison had to fight mighty battles in the courts with rivals seeking to infringe on their rights. When Edison first announced his electric light, capitalists, engineers, and inventors flocked to Menlo Park. He proudly revealed to them the secrets of his marvelous lamp. Many hurried away to turn this information to their own advantage, thinking the "Wizard" a naive fool. When they invaded the field, the law provided Edison with far less protection than he had expected. "My electric light inventions have brought me no profits, only forty years of litigation," Edison later complained. A patent, he said bitterly, was "simply an invitation to a lawsuit."

The attitude of businessmen toward the rights of inventors and industrial pioneers is illustrated by an early advertisement of the Westinghouse Company:

> We regard it as fortunate that we have deferred entering the electrical field until the present moment. Having thus profited by the public experience of others, we enter ourselves for competition, hampered by a minimum of expense for experimental outlay. . . . In short, our organization is free, in large measure, of the load with which [other] electrical enterprises seem to be encumbered. The fruit of this . . . we propose to share with the customer.

Competition in the electric lighting business raged for some years among Edison, Westinghouse, and another corporation, the Thomson-Houston Electric Company, which was operating 870 central lighting stations by 1890. In 1892 the Edison and Thomson-Houston companies merged, forming General Electric, a $35 million corporation. There-

The glove counter in Rike's Department Store, Dayton, Ohio, 1893. Ferns on the stairs, ornate wall decorations, and an abundance of help distinguished this store from its bargain-basement competition.

after, General Electric and Westinghouse maintained their dominance in the manufacture of bulbs and electrical equipment as well as in the distribution of electrical power.

The pattern of competition leading to dominance by a few great companies was repeated in many businesses. In life insurance an immense expansion took place after the Civil War, stimulated by the development of a new type of group policy, the "tontine," by Henry B. Hyde of the Equitable Life Company.* High-pressure salesmanship prevailed; agents gave rebates to customers by shaving their own commissions; companies stole "crack" agents from their rivals and raided new territories. They sometimes invested as much as 96 percent of the first year's premiums into obtaining new business. By 1900, after three decades of fierce competition, three giants dominated the industry—Equitable, New York Life, and Mutual Life, each with approximately $1 billion of insurance in force.

In retailing, the period saw the growth of urban department stores. In 1862 Alexander T. Stewart

had built an eight-story emporium in New York City that covered an entire block and employed 2,000 persons. John Wanamaker in Philadelphia and Marshall Field in Chicago headed similar establishments by the 1880s, and there were others. These department stores were run like factories. They advertised heavily, stressing low prices, efficient service, and money-back guarantees. High volume made for large profits. Here is how one of Field's biographers described his methods:

> His was a one-price store, with the price plainly marked on the merchandise. Goods were not misrepresented, and a reputation for quality merchandise and for fair and honest dealing was built up. . . . Courtesy toward customers was an unfailing rule. Stocks of goods were bought at wholesale for cash in anticipation of consumer demand and then a demand for them was created.

Americans' Reactions to Big Business

The expansion of industry and its concentration in fewer and fewer hands changed the way many people felt about the role of government in economic and social affairs. The fact that Americans

---

* A tontine policy paid no dividends for a stated period of years. The heirs of a policyholder who died received the face value but no dividends. At the end of the tontine period, survivors collected not only their own dividends but also those of the unfortunates who had died or permitted their policies to lapse. This was psychologically appealing, since it stressed living rather than dying and added an element of gambling to insurance.

disliked powerful governments in general and strict regulation of the economy in particular had never meant that they objected to all government activity in the economic sphere. Banking laws, tariffs, internal-improvement legislation, and the granting of public land to railroads are only the most obvious of the economic regulations enforced in the 19th century by both the federal government and the states. Americans saw no contradiction between government activities of this type and the free enterprise philosophy, for such laws were intended to release human energy and thus increase the area in which freedom could operate. Tariffs stimulated industry and created new jobs, railroad grants opened up new regions for development, and so on. As J. W. Hurst has written in a thought-provoking study, *Law and the Conditions of Freedom in the Nineteenth-Century United States* (1956), the people "resort to law to enlarge the options open to private individual and group energy."

The growth of huge industrial and financial organizations and the increasing complexity of economic relations frightened people yet made them at the same time greedy for more of the goods and services the new society was turning out. To many, the great new corporations and trusts resembled Frankenstein's monster—marvelous and powerful but a grave threat to society. The astute James Bryce described the changes in *The American Commonwealth* (1888):

> Modern civilization . . . has become more exacting. It discerns more benefits which the organized power of government can secure, and grows more anxious to attain them. Men live fast, and are impatient of the slow working of natural laws. . . . There are benefits which the law of supply and demand do not procure. Unlimited competition seems to press too hard on the weak. The power of groups of men organized by incorporation as joint-stock companies, or of small knots of rich men acting in combination, has developed with unexpected strength in unexpected ways, overshadowing individuals and even communities, and showing that the very freedom of association which men sought to secure by law . . . may, under the shelter of the law, ripen into a new form of tyranny.

To some extent public fear of the industrial giants reflected concern about monopoly. If Standard Oil dominated oil refining, it might raise prices inordinately at vast cost to consumers. Charles Francis

Adams, Jr., expressed this feeling in the 1870s: "In the minds of the great majority, and not without reason, the idea of any industrial combination is closely connected with that of monopoly, and monopoly with extortion."

Although in isolated cases monopolists did raise prices unreasonably, generally they did not. On the contrary, prices tended to fall until by the 1890s a veritable "consumer's millennium" had arrived. Far more important in causing resentment was the fear that the monopolists were destroying economic opportunity and threatening democratic institutions. It was not the wealth of tycoons like Carnegie and Rockefeller and Morgan so much as their influence that worried people. In the face of the growing disparity between rich and poor, could republican institutions survive? "The belief is common," wrote Charles Francis Adams's brother Henry as early as 1870, "that the day is at hand when corporations . . . swaying power such as has never in the world's history been trusted in the hands of mere private citizens . . . will ultimately succeed in directing government itself."

Some observers believed either autocracy or a form of revolutionary socialism to be almost inevitable. In 1890 former president Hayes pondered "the wrong and evils of the money-piling tendency of our country, which is changing laws, government, and morals and giving all power to the rich" and decided that he was going to become a "nihilist." Campaigning for the governorship of Texas in 1890, James S. Hogg, a staunch conservative, said: "Within a few years, unless something is done, most of the wealth and talent of our country will be on one side, while arrayed on the other will be the great mass of the people, composing the bone and sinew of this government." John Boyle O'Reilly, a liberal Catholic journalist, wrote in 1886: "There is something worse than Anarchy, bad as that is; and it is irresponsible power in the hands of mere wealth." William Cook, a New York lawyer, warned in *The Corporation Problem* (1891) that "colossal aggregations of capital" were "dangerous to the republic."

These were typical reactions of responsible citizens to the rise of industrial combinations. Less thoughtful Americans sometimes went much further in their hatred of entrenched wealth. In 1900 Eddie Cudahy, son of a prominent member of the Beef Trust, was kidnapped. His captor, Pat Crowe, received $25,000 ransom but was apprehended. Crowe's guilt was clear: "I want to start right by confessing in plain English that I was guilty of the kidnapping," he wrote. Yet a jury acquitted him, presumably on the theory that it was all right to rob a member of the Beef Trust.

As criticism mounted, business leaders rose to their own defense. Rockefeller described in graphic terms the chaotic conditions that plagued the oil industry before the rise of Standard Oil:

> It seemed absolutely necessary to extend the market for oil . . . and also greatly improve the process of refining so that oil could be made and sold cheaply, yet with a profit. We proceeded to buy the largest and best refining concerns and centralized the administration of them with a view to securing greater economy and efficiency.

Carnegie, in an essay published in 1889, insisted that the concentration of wealth was necessary if humanity was to progress, softening this "Gospel of Wealth" by insisting that the rich must use their money "in the manner which . . . is best calculated to produce the most beneficial results for the community." The rich man was merely a trustee for his "poorer brethren," Carnegie said, "bringing to their service his superior wisdom, experience, and ability to administer." Lesser tycoons echoed these arguments.

The voices of the critics were louder if not necessarily more influential. Many clergymen denounced unrestrained competition, which they considered un-Christian. The new class of professional economists (the American Economic Association was founded in 1885) tended to repudiate laissez faire. State aid, Richard T. Ely of Johns Hopkins University wrote, "is an indispensable condition of human progress."

Reformers: George, Bellamy, Lloyd

The popularity of a number of radical theorists reflects public feeling in the period. In 1879 Henry George, a California newspaperman, published *Progress and Poverty*, a forthright attack on the maldistribution of wealth in the United States. George argued that labor was the true and only source of

capital. Observing the speculative fever of the West, which enabled landowners to reap profits merely by holding property while population increased, George proposed a property tax that would confiscate this "unearned increment." The value of land depended on society and should belong to society; allowing individuals to keep this wealth was the major cause of the growing disparity between rich and poor, George believed.

George's "single tax," as others called it, would bring in so much money that no other taxes would be necessary, and the government would have plenty of funds to establish new schools, museums, theaters, and other badly needed social and cultural services. Though the single tax was never adopted, George's ideas attracted enthusiastic attention. Single tax clubs sprang up throughout the nation, and *Progress and Poverty* became a best-seller.

Even more spectacular was the reception afforded *Looking Backward, 2000–1887*, a utopian novel written in 1888 by Edward Bellamy. This book, which sold over a million copies in its first few years, described a future America that was completely socialized, all economic activity carefully planned. Bellamy compared 19th-century society to a lumbering stagecoach on which the favored few rode in comfort while the mass of the people hauled them along life's route. Occasionally one of the toilers managed to fight his way onto the coach; whenever a rider fell from it, he had to join the multitude dragging it along.

Such, Bellamy wrote, was the working of the vaunted American competitive system. He suggested that the ideal socialist state, in which all citizens shared equally, would arrive without revolution or violence. The trend toward consolidation would continue, he predicted, until one monster trust controlled all economic activity. At this point everyone would realize that nationalization was essential.

A third influential attack on monopoly was that of Henry Demarest Lloyd, whose *Wealth Against Commonwealth* appeared in 1894. Lloyd, a journalist of independent means, devoted years to preparing a denunciation of the Standard Oil Company. Marshaling masses of facts and vivid examples of Standard's evildoing, he assaulted the trust at every point. Although in his zeal Lloyd sometimes distorted and exaggerated the evidence to make his indictment more effective—"Every important man

THE AGE OF GIANT ENTERPRISE, 1861–1920

This is the second of three price graphs; the first appeared in Chapter 14, pages 372–373. The price scale on the left axis applies to the blue line. It shows changes in wholesale commodity prices as they vary around the base line/trend line of 100. In the 45 years after 1870, wholesale prices were consistently below par, regardless of the periods of relative prosperity and depression shown by the solid peaks and valleys. The green line, scaled to the right axis, shows as a contrast what the retail price of a dozen eggs was between 1870 and 1920. This line reflects the wholesale price line.

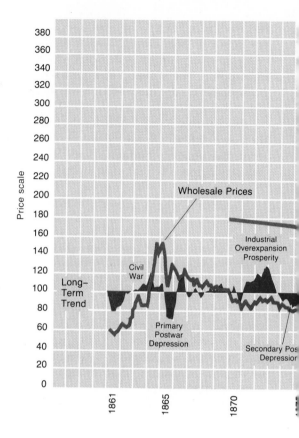

in the oil, coal and many other trusts ought today to be in some one of our penitentiaries," he wrote in a typical overstatement—as a polemic his book was peerless. His forceful but uncomplicated arguments and his copious references to official documents made *Wealth Against Commonwealth* utterly convincing to thousands. The book was more than an attack on Standard Oil. Lloyd denounced the application of Darwin's concept of survival of the fittest to economic and social affairs, and he condemned laissez faire policies as leading directly to monopoly.

The popularity of these books indicates that the trend toward monopoly in the United States worried many people. But despite the drastic changes suggested in their pages, none of these writers questioned the underlying values of the middle-class majority. They insisted that reform could be accomplished without serious inconvenience to any individual or class. In *Looking Backward* Bellamy pictured the socialists of the future gathered around a radiolike gadget in a well-furnished parlor listening to a minister delivering an inspiring sermon.

Nor did most of their millions of readers seriously consider trying to apply the reformers' ideas. Henry George ran for mayor of New York City in 1886 and lost narrowly to Abram S. Hewitt, a wealthy iron manufacturer, but even if he had won, he would have been powerless to apply the single tax to metropolitan property. The national discontent was apparently not as profound as the popularity of these works might suggest. If John D. Rockefeller became the bogeyman of American in-

dustry because of Lloyd's attack, no one prevented him from also becoming the richest man in the United States.

Reformers: The Marxists

By the 1870s the ideas of Marxian socialists were beginning to penetrate the United States, and in 1877 a Marxist Socialist Labor party was founded. Laurence Gronlund in *The Cooperative Commonwealth* (1884) made the first serious attempt to explain to Americans the ideas Marx expressed in *Das Kapital* (*Capital*), not yet translated into English.

Capitalism, Gronlund claimed, contained the seeds of its own destruction. The state ought to own all the means of production. Competition was "Established Anarchy," middlemen were "parasites," and speculators were "vampires." "Capital and Labor," he wrote in one of the rare humorous lines in his book, "are just as harmonious as roast beef and a hungry stomach." Yet like other harsh critics of that day, Gronlund expected the millennium to arrive in a peaceful, orderly manner. The red flag

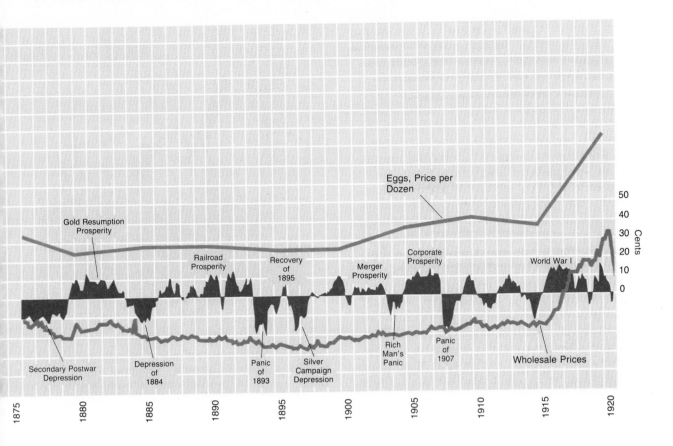

Gold Resumption Prosperity

Eggs, Price per Dozen

Railroad Prosperity

Recovery of 1895

Merger Prosperity

Corporate Prosperity

World War I

Cents

50
40
30
20
10
0

Secondary Postwar Depression

Depression of 1884

Panic of 1893

Silver Campaign Depression

Rich Man's Panic

Panic of 1907

Wholesale Prices

1875 1880 1885 1890 1895 1900 1905 1910 1915 1920

of socialism, he said, "has no relation to blood." The movement could accommodate "representatives of all classes," even "thoughtful" middlemen parasites.

The leading voice of the Socialist Labor party, Daniel De Leon, editor of the party's weekly, *The People,* was a different type. He was born in the West Indies, son of a Dutch army doctor stationed in Curaçao, and educated in Europe. He emigrated to the United States in the 1870s, where he was progressively attracted by the ideas of Henry George, then Edward Bellamy and the Knights of Labor, and finally Marx. Personally mild-mannered and kindly, when he put pen to paper, he became a doctrinaire revolutionary. He excoriated the AFL and the Knights of Labor in *The People,* insisting that industrial workers could improve their lot only by adopting socialism and joining the Socialist Labor party. He paid scant attention, however, to the practical needs or even to the opinions of rank-and-file working people. The labor historian Philip Taft aptly characterized him as a "verbal revolutionary." In 1891 he was the Socialist Labor party's candidate for governor of New York.

Government Reactions to Big Business: Railroad Regulation

Political action related to the growth of big business came first on the state level and dealt chiefly with the regulation of railroads. Even before the Civil War, a number of New England states established railroad commissions to supervise lines within their borders; by the end of the century 28 states had such boards.

Strict regulation was largely the result of agitation by the National Grange of the Patrons of Husbandry. The Grange, founded in 1867 by Oliver H. Kelley, was created to provide social and cultural benefits for isolated rural communities. As it spread and grew in influence—14 states had Granges by 1872, and membership reached 800,000 in 1874—the movement became political too. "Granger" candidates, often not themselves farmers (many local businessmen resented such railroad practices as rebating), won control of a number of state legislatures in the West and the South. Railroad regulation invariably followed, for farmers' eagerness for inter-

nal improvements tended to turn to disillusionment
after the lines were built. Intense competition might
reduce rates between major centers like Chicago and
New York and Philadelphia, but most western farm
districts were served by only one railroad. In 1877,
for example, the freight charges of the Burlington
road were almost four times as high west of the
Missouri as they were east of the river. It cost less
to ship wheat from Chicago to Liverpool, England,
than from some parts of the Dakotas to Minneapolis.

Granger-controlled legislatures tried to eliminate this kind of discrimination. The Illinois
Granger laws were typical. They established "reasonable" maximum rates and outlawed "unjust" discrimination. The legislature also set up a commission to enforce the laws and punish violators.

The railroads protested, insisting that they were
being deprived of property without due process of
law. In *Munn* v. *Illinois* (1877), a case that involved
a grain elevator whose owner had refused to comply
with a state warehouse act, the Supreme Court upheld the constitutionality of this kind of act. Any
business that served a public interest, such as a railroad or a grain warehouse, was subject to state control, the justices ruled. Legislatures might fix maximum charges; if the charges seemed unreasonable
to the parties concerned, they should direct their
complaints to the legislatures or to the voters, not
to the courts.

Regulation of the railroad network by the individual states was inefficient, and in some cases the
commissions were incompetent and even corrupt.
When the Supreme Court, in the Wabash case
(1886), declared unconstitutional an Illinois regulation outlawing the long-and-short-haul evil, federal action became necessary. The Wabash, St. Louis
and Pacific Railroad had charged 25 cents per 100
pounds for shipping goods from Gilman, Illinois,
to New York City and only 15 cents from Peoria,
which was 86 miles farther from New York. Illinois
judges had held this to be illegal, but the Supreme
Court decided that Illinois could not regulate interstate shipments.

Congress filled the gap created by the Wabash
decision in 1887 by passing the Interstate Commerce Act. All charges made by railroads "shall be
reasonable and just," the act stated. Rebates, drawbacks, the long-and-short-haul evil, and other competitive practices were declared unlawful, and so
were their monopolistic counterparts, pools and

*A Thomas Nast cartoon ridiculing the willingness of
the United States Senate—the "Senatorial Round-
House"—to do the bidding of the railroad lobbyists during the debates that led to the Interstate Commerce Act
of 1888.*

traffic-sharing agreements. Railroads were required
to publish schedules of rates and forbidden to
change them without due public notice. Most important, the law established the Interstate Commerce Commission (ICC), the first federal regulatory board, to supervise the affairs of railroads,
investigate complaints, and issue cease and desist
orders when the roads acted illegally.

The Interstate Commerce Act broke new
ground, yet it was neither radical nor particularly
effective. Its terms were contradictory, some having
been designed to stimulate, others to penalize competition. The chairman of the commission soon
characterized the law as an "anomaly." It sought,
he said, to "enforce competition" at the same time
that it outlawed "the acts and inducements by which
competition is ordinarily effected."

The new commission had less power than the
law seemed to give it. It could not fix rates, only
bring the roads to court when it considered rates
unreasonably high. Such cases could be extremely
complicated; applying the law was "like cutting a

path through a jungle." With the truth so hard to determine and the burden of proof on the commission, the courts in nearly every instance decided in favor of the railroads.

State regulatory commissions also fared poorly in the Supreme Court in the last years of the century. Overruling part of their 1877 decision in *Munn* v. *Illinois*, the justices declared in *Chicago, Milwaukee and St. Paul Railroad Company* v. *Minnesota* (1890) that the reasonableness of rates was "eminently a question for judicial investigation." In a Texas case, *Reagan* v. *Farmers' Loan and Trust Company* (1894), the Court held that it had the "power and duty" to decide if rates were "unjust and unreasonable" even when the state legislature itself had established them. Nevertheless, by describing so clearly the right of Congress to regulate private corporations engaged in interstate commerce, the Interstate Commerce Act challenged the philosophy of laissez faire. Later legislation made the commission more effective. The commission also served as the model for a host of similar federal administrative authorities, such as the Federal Communications Commission (1934).

Government Reactions to Big Business: The Sherman Antitrust Act

As with railroad legislation, the first antitrust laws originated in the states, but they were southern and western states with relatively little industry, and most of the statutes were vaguely worded and ill-enforced. Federal action came in 1890 with the passage of the Sherman Antitrust Act. Any combination "in the form of trust or otherwise" that was "in restraint of trade or commerce among the several states, or with foreign nations" was declared illegal. Persons forming such combinations were subject to fines of $5,000 and a year in jail. Individuals and businesses suffering losses because of actions that violated the law were authorized to sue in the federal courts for triple damages.

Where the Interstate Commerce Act sought to outlaw the excesses of competition, the Sherman Act was supposed to restore competition. If businessmen joined together to "restrain" (monopolize) trade in a particular field, they should be punished and their deeds undone. "The great thing this bill does," Senator George Frisbie Hoar of Massachusetts explained, "is to extend the common-law principle . . . to international and interstate commerce." This was important because the states ran into legal difficulties when they tried to use the common law to restrict corporations engaged in interstate activities.

But the Sherman Act was rather loosely worded—Thurman Arnold, a modern authority, once said that it made it "a crime to violate a vaguely stated economic policy." Critics have argued that the congressmen were more interested in quieting the public clamor for action against the trusts than in actually breaking up any of the new combinations. Quieting the clamor was certainly one of their objectives. However, they were trying to solve a new problem and were not sure how to proceed. A law with teeth too sharp might do more harm than good. Most Americans assumed that the courts would deal with the details, as they always had in common-law matters.

In fact the Supreme Court quickly emasculated the Sherman Act. In *United States* v. *E. C. Knight Company* (1895) it held that the American Sugar Refining Company had not violated the law by taking over a number of important competitors. Although the Sugar Trust now controlled about 98 percent of all sugar refining in the United States, it was not restraining trade. "Doubtless the power to control the manufacture of a given thing involves in a certain sense the control of its disposition," the Court said in one of the greatest feats of judicial understatement of all time. "Although the exercise of that power may result in bringing the operation of commerce into play, it does not control it, and affects it only incidentally and indirectly."

If the creation of the Sugar Trust did not violate the Sherman Act, it seemed unlikely that any other combination of manufacturers could be convicted under the law. In *The History of the Last Quarter Century in the United States* (1896), E. Benjamin Andrews, president of Brown University, delivered a strong indictment of trusts. "The crimes to which some of them resorted to crush out competition were unworthy of civilization," he wrote. Yet he referred only obliquely to the Sherman Act, dismissing it as "obviously ineffectual" and "of little avail."

However, in several cases in 1898 and 1899 the Supreme Court ruled that agreements to fix prices or divide markets did violate the Sherman Act. These decisions precipitated a wave of outright mergers in which a handful of large companies swallowed up hundreds of smaller ones. Presumably mergers were not illegal. When, some years after his retirement, Andrew Carnegie was asked by a committee of the House of Representatives to explain how he had dared to participate in the formation of the U.S. Steel Corporation, he replied: "Nobody ever mentioned the Sherman Act to me, that I remember."

The Union Movement

At the time of the Civil War, only a small percentage of the American work force was organized, and most union members were cigarmakers, printers, carpenters, and other skilled artisans, not factory hands. Aside from ironworkers, railroad workers, and miners, few industrial laborers belonged to unions. Nevertheless, the union was the workers' response to the big corporation: a combination designed to eliminate competition for jobs and to provide efficient organization for labor.

After 1865 the growth of national craft unions, which had been stimulated by labor dissatisfaction during the Civil War, quickened perceptibly. In 1866 a federation of these organizations, the National Labor Union, was founded and by the early 1870s many new trades, notably in railroading, had been unionized.

Most of the leaders of these unions were visionaries who were out of touch with the practical needs and aspirations of workers. They opposed the wage system, strikes, and anything that increased the laborers' sense of being members of the working class. A major objective was the formation of worker-owned cooperatives.

Far more remarkable was the Knights of Labor, a curious organization founded in 1869 by a group of Philadelphia garment workers headed by Uriah S. Stephens. Like so many labor organizers of the period, Stephens was a reformer of wide interests rather than a man dedicated to the specific problems of industrial workers. He, his successor Terence V. Powderly, and many other leaders of the Knights would have been thoroughly at home in the labor organizations of the Jacksonian era. Like the Jacksonians, they supported political objectives that had

A black delegate introduces Terrence V. Powderly at a Knights of Labor convention held in Richmond. At one point the union had some 60,000 black members.

no direct connection with working conditions, such as currency reform and the curbing of land speculation. They rejected the idea that workers must resign themselves to remaining wage earners. By pooling their resources, workingmen could advance up the economic ladder and enter the capitalist class. "There is no good reason," Powderly wrote in his autobiography, *The Path I Trod*, "why labor cannot, through cooperation, own and operate mines, factories, and railroads." The leading Knights saw no contradiction between their denunciation of "soulless" monopolies and "drones" like bankers and lawyers and their talk of "combining all branches of trade in one common brotherhood." Such muddled thinking led the Knights to attack the wage system and to frown on strikes as "acts of private warfare."

If the Knights had one foot in the past, they also had one foot in the future. They supported some startlingly advanced ideas. Rejecting the traditional grouping of workers by crafts, they developed a concept closely resembling modern industrial unionism. They welcomed blacks (though mostly in segregated locals), women, and immigrants, and they accepted unskilled workers as well as artisans. The eight-hour day was one of their basic demands, their argument being that increased leisure would give workers time to develop more cultivated tastes and higher aspirations. Higher pay would inevitably follow.

The growth of the union, however, had little to do with ideology. Stephens had made the Knights a secret organization with an elaborate ritual. Under his leadership, as late as 1879 it had fewer than 10,000 members. Under Powderly, secrecy was discarded. Between 1882 and 1886 successful strikes by local "assemblies" against western railroads, including one against the hated Jay Gould's Missouri Pacific, brought recruits by the thousands. Mem-

An anarchist group printed 20,000 of these bilingual handbills on the day of the Haymarket bombing in Chicago in 1886.

bership passed 42,000 in 1882, hit 110,000 in 1885, and the next year soared beyond 700,000. Alas, sudden prosperity was too much for the Knights. The union's national leadership was unable to control local groups. A number of poorly planned strikes failed dismally, and the public was alienated by sporadic acts of violence and intimidation. Disillusioned recruits began to drift away.

Circumstances largely fortuitous caused the collapse of the organization. By 1886 the movement for the eight-hour day had gained wide support among workers, including many who did not belong to unions. Several hundred thousand (estimates vary) were on strike in various parts of the country by May of that year. In Chicago, a center of the eight-hour movement, about 80,000 workers were involved, and a small group of anarchists was trying to take advantage of the excitement to win support.

When a striker was killed in a fracas at the McCormick Harvesting Machine Company, the anarchists called a protest meeting on May 4, at Haymarket Square. Police intervened to break up the meeting, and someone—whose identity has never been established—hurled a bomb into their ranks. Seven policemen were killed and many others injured.

The American Federation of Labor

Though the anarchists were the immediate victims of the resulting public indignation and hysteria—seven were condemned to death and four eventually executed—organized labor, especially the Knights, suffered heavily. No tie between the Knights and the bombing could be established, but the union had been closely connected with the eight-hour agitation, and the public tended to associate it with violence and radicalism. Its membership declined as suddenly as it had risen, and soon it ceased to exist as a force in the labor movement.

The Knights' place was taken by the American Federation of Labor, a combination of national craft unions established in 1886. In a sense the AFL was a reactionary organization. Its principal leaders, Adolph Strasser and Samuel Gompers of the Cigarmakers Union, were, like the founders of the Knights of Labor, originally interested in utopian social reforms. They even toyed with the idea of forming a workingmen's political party. Experience, however, soon led them to concentrate on organizing skilled workers and fighting for "bread and butter" issues such as higher wages and shorter hours. "Our organization does not consist of idealists," Strasser explained to a congressional committee. "We do not control the production of the world. That is controlled by the employers. . . . I look first to cigars."

The AFL accepted the fact that most workers would remain wage earners all their lives and tried to develop in them a sense of common purpose and pride in their skills and station. Strasser and Gompers paid great attention to building a strong organization of dues-paying members committed to unionism as a way of improving their lot. Rank-and-file AFL members were naturally eager to win wage increases and other benefits, but most also valued their unions for the companionship they provided, the sense of belonging to a group. In other words, despite statements such as Strasser's, unions, in and out of the AFL, were a kind of club as well as a means of defending and advancing their members' material interests.

The chief weapon of the federation was the strike, which it used to win concessions from employers and to attract recruits. Gompers, president of the AFL almost continuously from 1886 until his death in 1924, encouraged workers to make "intelligent use of the ballot" to advance their interests. The federation worked for such things as eight-hour, employers' liability, and mine safety laws, but it avoided direct involvement in politics. "I have my own philosophy and my own dreams," Gompers once told a left-wing French politician, "but first and foremost I want to increase the workingman's welfare year by year. . . . The French workers waste their economic force by their political divisions."

Gompers's approach to labor problems produced solid, if unspectacular, growth for the AFL. Unions with a total of about 150,000 members formed the federation in 1886. By 1892 membership had reached 250,000, and in 1901 it passed the million mark.

Labor Militancy Rebuffed

The stress of the AFL on the strike weapon reflected rather than caused the increasing militancy of labor.

Workers felt themselves threatened from all sides: the growing size and power of their corporate employers, the substitution of machines for human skills, the invasion of foreign workers willing to accept substandard wages. At the same time they had tasted some of the material benefits of industrialization and had learned the advantages of concerted action.

The average employer behaved like a tyrant when dealing with his workers. He discharged them arbitrarily when they tried to organize unions; he hired scabs to break strikes; he frequently failed to provide the most rudimentary protections against injury on the job. Some employers, Carnegie, for example, professed to approve of unions, but almost none would bargain with labor collectively. To do so, they argued, would be to deprive workers of their freedom to contract for their own labor in any way they saw fit.

The industrialists of the period were not all ogres; they were as alarmed by the rapid changes of the times as their workers, and since they had more at stake materially, they were probably more frightened by the uncertainties. Deflation, technological change, and intense competition kept even the most successful under constant pressure.

The thinking of most employers was remarkably confused. They considered workers who joined unions "disloyal," and at the same time they treated labor as a commodity to be purchased as cheaply as possible. "If I wanted boiler iron," Henry B. Stone, a railroad official, explained, "I would go out on the market and buy it where I could get it cheapest, and if I wanted to employ men, I would do the same." Yet Stone was furious when the men he had "bought" joined a union. When labor was scarce, employers resisted demands for higher wages by arguing that the price of labor was controlled by its productivity; when it was plentiful, they justified reducing wages by referring to the law of supply and demand.

Thus capital and labor were often spoiling for a fight, frequently without fully understanding why. When labor troubles developed, they tended to be bitter, even violent. In 1877 a great railroad strike convulsed much of the nation. It began on the Baltimore and Ohio system in response to a wage cut and spread to other eastern lines and then throughout the West until about two-thirds of the railroad mileage of the country had been shut down. Vio-

After the collapse of his American Railway Union in 1897, Eugene V. Debs (shown here addressing a Socialist party gathering) devoted himself to politics.

lence broke out, rail yards were put to the torch, and dismayed and frightened businessmen formed militia companies to patrol the streets of Chicago and other cities. Eventually President Hayes sent federal troops to the trouble spots to restore order, and the strike collapsed. There had been no real danger of revolution, but the violence and destruction of the strike had been without precedent in America.

The disturbances of 1877 were a response to a business slump, those of the next decade a response to good times. Twice as many strikes occurred in 1886 as in any previous year. Even before the Haymarket bombing centered the country's attention on labor problems, the situation had become so disturbing that President Grover Cleveland, in the first presidential message devoted to labor problems, had urged Congress to create a voluntary arbitration board to aid in settling labor disputes—a remarkable suggestion for a man of Cleveland's conservative, laissez faire approach to economic issues.

In 1892 a violent strike broke out among silver miners at Coeur d'Alene, Idaho, and a far more important clash shook Andrew Carnegie's Home-

stead steel plant near Pittsburgh when strikers attacked 300 private guards brought in to protect strikebreakers. Seven guards were killed at Homestead, and the rest were forced to "surrender" and march off ignominiously. The Homestead affair was part of a struggle between capital and labor in the steel industry. The steelmen insisted that the workers were holding back progress by resisting technological advances, while the workers believed that the company was refusing to share the fruits of more efficient operation fairly. The strike was precipitated by the decision of company officials to crush the union at all costs. The final defeat, after a five-month walkout, of the 24,000-member Amalgamated Association of Iron and Steel Workers, one of the most important elements in the AFL, destroyed unionism as an effective force in the steel industry and set back the progress of organized labor all over the country.

As in the case of the Haymarket bombing, the activities of radicals on the fringe of the dispute turned the public against the steelworkers. The boss of Homestead was Henry Clay Frick, a tough-minded foe of unions who was determined to "teach our employees a lesson." Frick made the decision to bring in strikebreakers and to employ Pinkerton detectives to protect them. During the course of the strike, Alexander Berkman, an anarchist, burst into Frick's office and attempted to assassinate him. Frick was only slightly wounded, but the attack brought him much sympathy and unjustly discredited the strikers.

The most important strike of the period took place in 1894. It began when the workers at George Pullman's Palace Car factory outside Chicago walked out in protest against wage cuts. (While reducing wages, Pullman insisted on holding the line on rents in the company town of Pullman; when a delegation called on him to remonstrate, he refused to give in and had three of the leaders fired.) Some Pullman workers belonged to the American Railway Union, headed by Eugene V. Debs. After the strike had dragged along for weeks, the union voted to refuse to handle trains with Pullman cars. The union was perfectly willing to handle mail trains, but the owners refused to run trains unless they were made up of a full complement of cars.

When Pullman cars were added to mail trains, the workers refused to move them. The resulting railroad strike tied up trunk lines running in and out of Chicago. The railroad owners appealed to President Cleveland to send troops to preserve order. On the pretext that the soldiers were needed to ensure the movement of the mails, Cleveland agreed. When Debs defied a federal injunction to end the walkout, he was jailed for contempt, and the strike was broken.

Whither America, Whither Democracy?

Each year more of the nation's wealth and power seemed to fall into fewer hands. As with the railroads, other industries were coming to be influenced, if not completely dominated, by bankers. The firm of J. P. Morgan and Company controlled many railroads; the largest steel, electrical, agricultural machinery, rubber, and shipping companies; two life insurance companies; and a number of banks. By 1913 Morgan and the Rockefeller National City Bank group between them could name 341 directors to 112 corporations worth over $22.2 billion. The "Money Trust," a loose but potent fraternity of financiers, seemed fated to become the ultimate monopoly.

Centralization unquestionably increased efficiency, at least in industries that used a great deal of expensive machinery to turn out goods for the mass market and in those where close coordination of output, distribution, and sales was important. The public benefited immensely from the productive efficiency of the new empires. Living standards rose. But the trend toward giantism raised doubts. With ownership falling into fewer hands, what would be the ultimate effect of big business on American democracy? What did it mean for ordinary people when a few tycoons possessed huge fortunes and commanded such influence even on the Congress and the courts?

The crushing of the Pullman strike demonstrated the power of the courts to break strikes by issuing injunctions. And the courts seemed concerned only with protecting the interests of the rich and powerful. Particularly ominous for organized labor was the fact that the federal government based its request for the injunction that broke the strike on the Sherman Antitrust Act, arguing that the American Railway Union was a combination in restraint of trade. An indirect result of the Pullman strike was that while serving his sentence for con-

tempt, Eugene Debs was visited by a number of prominent socialists who sought to convert him to their cause. One gave him a copy of Karl Marx's *Capital*, which he found too dull to finish, but he did read *Looking Backward* and *Wealth Against Commonwealth*. In 1897 he became a socialist.

Milestones	
1859	First oil well drilled in Pennsylvania
1868	Carnegie Steel Company formed
1869	George Westinghouse invents the air brake
	Knights of Labor founded
1870	Standard Oil Company formed
1870–1890	Railroad trunk lines completed
1876	Alexander Graham Bell invents the telephone
1877	Great Railroad Strike
	Munn v. *Illinois* upholds state regulatory laws
1879	Thomas Edison invents the electric light
	Henry George's *Progress and Poverty*
1884	*The Cooperative Commonwealth* by Laurence Gronlund
1886	Haymarket bombing
	American Federation of Labor founded
1887	Interstate Commerce Act
1888	Edward Bellamy's *Looking Backward*
1889	Andrew Carnegie's "Gospel of Wealth"
1890	Sherman Antitrust Act
1892	Homestead strike
	General Electric Company formed
1894	Pullman strike
	Henry Demarest Lloyd's *Wealth Against Commonwealth*
1895	*United States* v. *E. C. Knight Company* weakens Sherman Act
1901	U.S. Steel Corporation formed

SUPPLEMENTARY READING

Titles marked with an asterisk have been published in paperback.

Of works dealing with industrial growth, E. C. Kirkland, **IndustryComes of Age*** (1961), is the best general introduction, but see also Stuart Bruchey, **Growth of the American Economy** (1975). Matthew Josephson, **The Robber Barons*** (1934), is highly critical but provocative. A. D. Chandler, Jr., **The Visible Hand** (1977), covers the way businesses were organized and managed. On technological developments, see H. J. Habakkuk, **American and British Technology in the Nineteenth Century*** (1962), and W. P. Strassmann, **Risk and Technological Innovation** (1959).

On the railroad industry, consult A. D. Chandler, Jr., **Railroads: The Nation's First Big Business** (1965), J. F. Stover, **American Railroads*** (1961), T. C. Cochran, **Railroad Leaders** (1953), and Julius Grodinsky, **Transcontinental Railway Strategy** (1962).

The iron and steel business is discussed in detail in J. F. Wall, **Andrew Carnegie** (1970), and Peter Temin, **Iron and Steel in Nineteenth-Century America** (1964), an economic analysis. On the oil industry, see Carl Solberg, **Oil Power*** (1976), a good survey, and for more detail, H. F. Williamson and A. R. Daum, **The American Petroleum Industry: Age of Illumination** (1959), and Allan Nevins, **Study in Power: John D. Rockefeller** (1953).

The electrical industry is discussed in an excellent study, H. C. Passer, **The Electrical Manufacturers** (1953), and in an equally good biography, Matthew Josephson, **Edison*** (1959). About the telephone, see John Brooks, **Telephone** (1976), and R. V. Bruce, **Alexander Graham Bell** (1973).

Many of these volumes deal with the problems of competition and monopoly. See also, however, Gabriel Kolko, **Railroads and Regulation*** (1965), which is critical of both railroad leaders and government policy. J. D. Rockefeller, **Random Reminiscences of Men and Events** (1909), makes the case for Standard Oil, while H. D. Lloyd, **Wealth Against Commonwealth** (1894), attacks the trust mercilessly.

For discussion of the radical critics, see J. L. Thomas, **Alternative Americas: Henry George, Edward Bellamy, Henry Demarest Lloyd** (1983), H. H. Quint, **The Forging of American Socialism** (1964), L. G. Seretan, **Daniel De Leon: The Odyssey of an American Marxist** (1979), and also the radicals' own writings.

On the growth of unions, see David Montgomery, **Beyond Equality** (1967), G. N. Grob, **Workers and Utopia** (1961), Harold Livesay, **Samuel Gompers and Organized Labor in America** (1978), and Nick Salvatore, **Eugene V. Debs** (1982). The important strikes and labor violence of the period are covered in R. V. Bruce, **1877: Year of Violence** (1959), Paul Arvich, **The Haymarket Tragedy** (1984), Leon Wolff, **Lockout** (1965), and Almont Lindsey, **The Pullman Strike** (1942).

The background of government regulation of industry is treated in Sidney Fine, **Laissez Faire and the General-Welfare State*** (1956), and J. A. Garraty, **The New Commonwealth*** (1968). Other useful volumes include Ari and Olive Hoogenboom, **A History of the ICC*** (1976), H. B. Thorelli, **The Federal Antitrust Policy** (1954), and G. W. Miller, **Railroads and the Granger Laws** (1971).

American Lives:
The Steltzles and the Smiths

New York's Lower East Side

Dora Uhlendorf was the daughter of a baker who had emigrated to New York City from Germany before the Civil War. The family settled on the Lower East Side and developed a prosperous business. When she grew up Dora married John Steltzle, a brewer, but misfortune struck, first when the Steltzle brewery failed, and then when John Steltzle died.

Dora's parents had objected to her marrying Steltzle, so she was determined not to ask them for help. Instead she moved with her five children to cheap quarters on the Lower East Side. There, as her son Charles later recalled, she spent "many years in a hand-to-hand battle with all the horrors of poverty, asking favors of no one."

The family lived in a series of tenements, usually on the top floor where the rent was lowest. Frequently the bedrooms had no outside windows; the only ventilation was a window on a dark hallway, the only running water from a faucet in the hall. Such places were unbearably hot in summer; the Steltzles spent many such nights on the roof. The tenements were also extremely noisy, the din created by crying children, squabbling neighbors, drunks, and children at play.

Dora Steltzle worked day and night in these dingy apartments sewing bathrobes for a local manufacturer for about $2 a dozen, a task that took, on average, three days. "We children soon learned to do a great many things for ourselves, because she was always sewing, sewing, sewing," Charles explained. When the bathrobe business was slow, Dora took in washing. At such times the family subsisted chiefly on stale rolls.

Charles went to school until he was 11, but by the time he was eight he was working too. He earned 50 cents a week stripping tobacco leaves from their stems in a tenement sweatshop, sold newspapers, and peddled oranges and candles door to door. A high point was the summer of 1879, when he got a job in a restaurant. His chief memory of this (perhaps distorted by the passage of many years) involved consuming unfinished portions of cake and ice cream left by departing diners.

Despite its hardships, in later life Charles Steltzle insisted that his boyhood had been a happy one. In summer he and his friends swam in the East River, blissfully ignoring passing ferries. He belonged to a club, "the Orchard Street gang," whose members sat around on old boxes dreaming of "going out West to shoot Indians and eat bear meat." He learned by experience to respect the "human qualities" of the local Tammany Hall politicos, who made it their business to know the social and economic needs of everyone in their district. "The reformers live uptown and . . . seem to be in business for the purpose of taking privileges away from the people, rather than furnishing them with jobs, and coal, and food," he explained. "It is by helping in such matters as these that Tammany Hall gains influence."

Charles Steltzle became a Presbyterian minister, preaching the social gospel and working with slum children and labor groups.

The Steltzles came "down" to the Lower East Side from a better neighborhood. At the same time Alfred E. and Catherine Mulvehill Smith and their three children were also living in the district, but in a part that was far from a slum. Alfred was of German and Italian descent, while Catherine's parents were Irish. Alfred Smith, a Civil War veteran, owned a modest trucking business. The family lived in a comfortable flat near the southern tip of Manhattan Island. Since they were Catholics, the children went to the local

Swimming in the East River

parochial school, which was run by the Christian Brothers order.

In 1886 Alfred Smith died and the family's fortunes turned sharply downward. His widow went to work in an umbrella factory. Two years later, 14-year-old Alfred Jr. had to drop out of school. He went to work as a "chaser," or errand boy, first of a series of such jobs. By the early 1890s he was working in the bustling Fulton Fish Market, supplying restaurants and stores and earning $12 a week.

The Smiths were firm supporters of the Democratic party and of Tammany Hall, the local Democratic machine. In their ward the "boss" was Tom Foley, a big, friendly man with a large black moustache. Young Alfred got to know Foley because he often stopped in at a saloon owned by Foley for a glass of beer. For a time he served as a kind of assistant to the boss, and became one of his most enthusiastic supporters. Later in life he had fond memories of watching the boss walking through the crowded streets of the Lower East Side handing out pennies and nickels to passing children. "When they got a nickel they thought it was Sunday," he recalled.

In 1894 Smith supported Foley in a factional dispute within Tammany and was rewarded with a job serving subpoenas at an annual salary of $800, substantial pay for that time. In 1903 he was elected to the state Assembly, the start of a career that included four terms as governor of New York and the 1928 Democratic presidential nomination.

Fulton's Fish Market in the 1880s

XX

American Society in the Industrial Age

There is in all the past nothing to compare with the rapid changes now going on in the civilized world. . . . Industrial changes imply social changes and necessitate political changes. Progressive societies outgrow institutions as children outgrow clothes.

HENRY GEORGE, Social Problems (*1883*)

The industrialization that followed the Civil War profoundly affected every aspect of American life. New machines, improvements in transportation and communication, the appearance of the great corporation with its uncertain implications for the future—all made deep impressions on the shape and indeed the very character of American society. The growth of cities and the influx of tens of thousands of immigrants who knew little about urban life and who neither spoke nor understood English had large effects on the lives they led and the world they inhabited.

Middle-Class Life

In so large and diverse a country as the United States, it is hard to generalize about how people lived and worked and how they fared while doing so. Some, as we have just seen, became fabulously wealthy in the new industrial society, in no small part because neither the federal government nor the states taxed their incomes.

Members of the professions and the large and diffuse groups of shopkeepers, small manufacturers, skilled craftsmen, and established farmers that made up the middle class lived in varying degrees of comfort. A family with an annual income of $1,000 in the 1880s would have no need to skimp on food, clothing, or shelter. According to the best modern estimates, about a quarter of the families in the cities employed at least one full-time servant.

In such families, husbands and wives continued to maintain their separate spheres, the men going off to their shops and offices, the women devoting their main energies to caring for (or at least supervising the care of) children and household. Middle-class women maintained the trend toward having fewer children. The children in a family of this type, though treasured, were carefully supervised. Much stress was placed on their being "little ladies and gentlemen," meaning having good manners and doing what their elders told them to do. This was the era of Victorian prudery, so in most families "young people" (today we would call them teenagers) were closely chaperoned when in the company of "members of the opposite sex." Upward-striving parents were much concerned about the status and prospects of their children's marriage partners, but it was no longer considered proper to interfere with the "course of true love" for any materialistic or purely social reason.

Wage Earners

Wage earners felt the full force of the industrial tide in countless ways—some beneficial, others not. As manufacturing and mining became more important, the number of workers in these fields multiplied rapidly: from 885,000 in 1860 to more than 3.2 million in 1890. Though workers lacked much sense of solidarity, they exerted a far greater influence on society at the turn of the century than they had in the years before the Civil War.

More efficient methods of production enabled them to increase their output, making possible a rise in their standard of living. The working day still tended to approximate the hours of daylight, but it was shortening perceptibly by the 1880s in many occupations. In 1860 the average had been

11 hours, but by 1880 only one worker in four labored more than ten hours, and radicals were beginning to talk about eight hours as a fair day's work.

This generalization, however, conceals some important differences. Skilled industrial workers—such types as railroad engineers and conductors, machinists, and iron molders—were quite well off in most cases. But unskilled laborers still could not earn enough to maintain a family decently by their own efforts alone.

James H. Ducker's *Men of the Steel Rails*, a study of the work force of the Atchison, Topeka and Santa Fe Railroad, throws much light on working conditions and workers' attitudes at this time. Ordinary track laborers were paid from $1.00 to $1.25 a day, whereas engineers received three times that amount or more. In addition, many of the better-paid workers picked up additional sums, some by legitimate means, such as renting spare rooms to other workers, some by practices ranging from shady to flagrantly criminal.

Railroad management tried to discipline the labor force by establishing rules for each job category, but it had difficulty enforcing them. "There were many schemes to avoid work and evade regulations," Ducker reports. Drunkenness on the job was a constant problem. Many conductors were said to be "color blind," the expression referring not to any physical defect or to their lack of racial prejudice but to their inability to tell the difference between the road's money and their own. Baggage and freight handlers frequently made off with goods ranging from a few cigars or a bottle of whiskey to entire shipments of merchandise. According to Ducker, transient workers, called "boomers," had "a deserved reputation as rowdies who cared more for drink than decorum, cards than church, lust than love." Other workers, of course, were law-abiding, hardworking family men.

Industrialization created problems for workers beyond the obvious one of earning enough money to support themselves. By and large, skilled workers, always better off than the unskilled, improved their positions relatively, despite the increased use of machinery. Furthermore, when machines took the place of human skills, jobs became monotonous. Mechanization undermined both the artisans' pride and their bargaining power vis-à-vis their employers. As expensive machinery became more important, the worker seemed of necessity less important.

Machines more than workers controlled the pace of work and its duration. The time clock regulated the labor force more rigidly than the most exacting foreman. The length of the workday may have declined, but the pace of work and the danger involved in working around heavy, high-speed machinery increased accordingly.

As businesses grew larger, personal contact between employer and hired hand tended to disappear. Relations between them became less human, more businesslike and ruthless. However, large enterprises usually employed a higher percentage of managerial and clerical workers than smaller companies, thus providing opportunities for more blue-collar workers to rise in the industrial hierarchy. But the trend toward bigness made it more difficult for workers to rise from the ranks of labor to become themselves manufacturers, as Andrew Carnegie, for example, had done during the Civil War era.

Another problem for workers was that industrialization tended to accentuate swings of the business cycle. On the upswing, something approaching full employment existed, but in periods of depression, unemployment became a problem that affected workers without regard for their individual abilities. It is significant that the word *unemployment* (though not, of course, the condition itself) was a late-19th-century invention.

Working Women

Women continued to be a significant part of the industrial working force. But now many more of them were working outside their homes; the factory had almost completely replaced the household as the seat of manufacturing. At least half of all working women were domestic servants; textile mills and the "sewing trades" accounted for a large percentage of the rest. But in all fields women were paid substantially lower wages than men.

Women found many new types of work in these years, a fact commented on by *The New York Times* as early as 1869. They made up the overwhelming majority of salespersons and cashiers in the big new department stores. Partly because of the persistence of the "cult of true womanhood" into the postwar era, managers considered women more polite, easier to control, and more honest than male workers, all qualities especially valuable in the huge empo-

In a society that still believed that the sexes should maintain "separate spheres," the new profession of nursing was viewed as particularly suited to women. Doctoring was reserved for men.

riums. Over half of the more than 1,700 employees in A. T. Stewart's New York store were women.

Educated, middle-class women also dominated the new profession of nursing, which developed alongside the expanding medical profession and the establishment of large urban hospitals. To nearly all doctors, to most men, and indeed to many women of that day, nursing seemed the perfect female profession, since it required the same characteristics that women were thought to have by nature: selflessness, cleanliness, kindliness, tact, sensitivity, and submissiveness to male control. "It seemed obvious," the historian Charles Rosenberg writes in *The Care of Strangers,* "that women were better suited than men to nursing." Typical was this remark of a contemporary authority: "Since God could not care for all the sick, he made women to nurse." Why it had not occurred to the Lord to make more women physicians, or for that matter members of other prestigious professions like law and the clergy, this man did not explain, probably because it had not occurred to him either.

Middle-class women did replace men as teachers in most of the nation's grade schools, and they also replaced men as clerks, secretaries, and operators of the new typewriters in goverment departments and in business offices. Most men with the knowledge of spelling and grammar that these positions required had better opportunities and were uninterested in office work, so women high school graduates, of whom there was an increasing number, filled the gap.

Both department store clerks and "typewriters" (as they were called) earned more money than unskilled factory workers, and working conditions were more pleasant. According to one advertisement of the period, a "Type-Writer" was an ideal Christmas present for "deserving" young women. "No invention has opened for women so broad and easy an avenue to profitable and suitable employment." Opportunities for promotion for women, however, were rare; managerial posts in these fields remained almost exclusively in the hands of men.

Farmers

Long the backbone of American society, independent farmers and the agricultural way of life were rapidly being left behind in the race for wealth and status. The number of farmers and the volume of agricultural production continued to rise, but agriculture's relative place in the national economy was declining. Between 1860 and 1890 the number of farms rose from 2 million to 4.5 million; wheat output leaped from 173 million bushels to 449 million, cotton from 5.3 million bales to 8.5 million. The rural population increased from 25 million to 40.8 million. Yet industry was expanding far faster, and the urban population, quadrupling in the period, would soon overtake and pass that of the countryside.

Along with this relative decline, farmers suffered a decline in status. Compared to middle-class city dwellers, they seemed provincial and behind the times. People in the cities began to refer to farmers as "rubes," "hicks," and "hayseeds" and to view them with bemused tolerance or even contempt.

This combination of circumstances angered and frustrated farmers. Waves of radicalism swept the agricultural regions, giving rise to demands for social and economic experiments that played a major role in breaking down rural laissez faire prejudices. As we have seen, in the 1870s pressure from the Patrons of Husbandry produced legislation regulating railroads and warehouses. This Granger movement also led to many cooperative experiments in the marketing of farm products and in the purchase of machinery, fertilizers, and other goods.

Not all farmers were affected by economic developments in the same way. Because of the steady decline of the price level, those in newly settled regions were usually worse off than those in older areas, since they had to borrow money to get started and were therefore burdened with fixed interest charges that became harder to meet each year. In the 1870s farmers in Illinois and Iowa suffered most, which accounts for the strength of the Granger movement in that region. Except as a purely social organization, the Grange had little importance in the eastern states, where rapidly expanding urban markets made farmers relatively prosperous. A typical eastern farm family raising wheat and other grains and perhaps some livestock worked hard but made a good living. Such a family might employ a neighbor's daughter to help with housework, milking, and similar chores and a hired hand whose work was mainly in the fields.

By the late 1880s farmers in the old Middle West had also become better established. Even when prices dipped and a general depression gripped the country, they were able to weather the bad times nicely by taking advantage of lower transportation costs, better farm machinery, and new fertilizers and insecticides to increase output and by shifting from wheat to the production of corn, oats, hogs, and cattle, which had not declined so drastically in price.

On the agricultural frontier from Texas to the Dakotas, and through the states of the old Confederacy, farmers were less fortunate. The burdens of the crop-lien system kept thousands of southern farmers in penury, while on the plains life was a succession of hardships. The first settlers in western Kansas, Nebraska, and the Dakotas took up land along the rivers and creeks where they found enough timber for home building, fuel, and fencing. Later arrivals had to build houses of the tough prairie sod and depend on hay, sunflower stalks, and buffalo dung for fuel.

Frontier farm families had always had to work hard and endure the hazards of storm, drought, and insect plagues, along with isolation and loneliness. But all these burdens were magnified on the prairies and the high plains. Hamlin Garland, a writer who grew up on a farm in Iowa, described conditions in graphic and moving terms in his autobiography, *A Son of the Middle Border* (1890), and in *Main-Travelled Roads* (1891). Life was particularly hard for farm women, who in addition to child care and housework performed endless farm chores— milking cows, feeding livestock, raising vegetables, and so on. "I . . . am set and running every morning at half-past four o'clock, and run all day, often until half-past eleven P. M.," one farm woman explained. "Is it any wonder I have become slightly demoralized?"

On the plains, women also had to endure drab, cheerless surroundings without the companionship of neighbors or the respites and stimulations of social life. After Hamlin Garland's mother read the grim discussions of women's lot in *Main-Travelled Roads*, she wrote him: "You might have said more, but I'm glad you didn't. Farmers' wives have enough to bear as it is."

Working-Class Family Life

Early social workers who visited the homes of industrial laborers in this period reported enormous

A Minnesota farming family photographed in front of their house in 1895. Winters must have been lonely times on the Northern Plains.

differences in the standards of living of people engaged in the same line of work, differences related to such variables as health, intelligence, the wife's ability as a homemaker, the degree of the family's commitment to middle-class values, and pure luck. Some families spent most of their income on food; others saved substantial sums even when earning no more than $400 or $500 a year. Family incomes varied greatly among workers who received similar hourly wages, depending on the steadiness of employment and on the number of family members holding jobs.

Consider the cases of two Illinois coal miners, each decent, hardworking union men with large families, each earning $1.50 a day in 1883. One was out of work nearly half the year; his income in 1883 was only $250. He, his wife, and their five children, aged 3 to 19, lived in a two-room tenement. They existed almost exclusively on a diet of bread and salt meat. Nevertheless, as an investigator reported, their home was neat and clean, and three of the children were attending school.

The other miner, father of four children, worked full time and brought home $420 in 1883. He owned a six-room house and an acre of land, where the family raised vegetables. Their food bill for the year was more than ten times that of the family just described. Two admirable families, probably similar in social attitudes and perhaps in political loyalties, but possessed of very different standards of living.

The cases of two families headed by railroad brakemen provide a different kind of variation. One man brought home only $360 to house and feed a wife and eight children. Here is the report of a state official who interviewed the family: "Clothes ragged, children half-dressed and dirty. They all sleep in one room regardless of sex. . . . The entire concern is as wretched as could be imagined. Father is shiftless. . . . Wife is without ambition or industry."

The other brakeman and his wife had only two children, and he earned $484 in 1883. They owned a well-furnished house, kept a cow, and raised vegetables for home consumption. Although they were far from rich, they managed to put aside enough for insurance, reading matter, and a few small luxuries.

Working-Class Attitudes

Social workers and government officials made many efforts in the 1880s and 1890s to find out how working people felt about all sorts of matters connected with their jobs. Their reports reveal a wide spectrum of opinion. To the question, asked of two Wisconsin carpenters, "What new laws, in your opinion, ought to be enacted?" one replied: "Keep down strikes and rioters. Let every man attend to his own business." But the other answered: "Complete nationalization of land and all ways of transportation. Burn all government bonds. A graduated income tax. . . . Abolish child labor and [pass] any other act that capitalists say is wrong."

Every variation of opinion between these extremes was expressed by working people in many sections and in many kinds of work. In 1881 a female textile worker in Lawrence, Massachusetts, said to an interviewer: "If you will stand by the mill, and see the people coming out, you will be surprised to see the happy, contented look they all have."

Despite such remarks and the general improvement in living standards, it is clear if only from the large number of bitter strikes of the period that dissatisfaction was widespread among industrial workers. Writing in 1885, the labor leader Terence V. Powderly reported that "a deep-rooted feeling of discontent pervades the masses." A few years later a Connecticut official conducted an informal survey of labor opinion in the state and found a "feeling of bitterness" and "distrust of employers" to be endemic.

The discontent had many causes. For some workers, poverty was still the chief problem, but for others, rising aspirations triggered discontent. Workers were confused about their destiny; the tradition that no one of ability need remain a hired hand died hard. They wanted to believe their bosses and the politicians when those worthies voiced the old slogans about a classless society and the community of interest of capital and labor. "Our men," William Vanderbilt of the New York Central said in 1877, "feel that, although I . . . may have my millions and they the rewards of their daily toil, still we are about equal in the end. If they suffer, I suffer, and if I suffer, they cannot escape." "The poor," another conservative spokesman said a decade later, "are not poor because the rich are rich." Instead "the service of capital" softened their lot and gave them many benefits.

Statements such as these, though self-serving, were essentially correct. The rich were growing richer and more people were growing rich, but or-

dinary workers were better off too. However, the gap between the very rich and the ordinary citizen was widening. "The tendency . . . is toward centralization and aggregation," the Illinois Bureau of Labor Statistics reported in 1886. "This involves a separation of the people into classes, and the permanently subordinate status of large numbers of them."

Mobility: Social, Economic, and Educational

To study mobility in a large industrial country is extraordinarily difficult. Americans in the late 19th century believed their society offered great opportunities for individual advancement, and to prove it they pointed to men like Andrew Carnegie and to other poor boys who accumulated large fortunes. How general the rise from rags to riches (or even to modest comfort) was is another question.

Americans had been on the move, mostly westward, since the colonial period, but studies of census records, such as those of Stephan Thernstrom, show that there was considerable geographic mobility in urban areas throughout the last half of the 19th century and into the 20th. Most investigations reveal that only about half the people recorded in one census were still in the same place ten years later; as Thernstrom puts it, "transiency was part of the American way of life. . . . The country had an enormous reservoir of footloose men, who could be lured to new destinations when opportunity beckoned."

In most of the cities studied, mobility was accompanied by some economic and social improvement. On the average, about a quarter of the manual laborers traced rose to middle-class status during their lifetimes, and the sons of manual laborers were still more likely to improve their place in society. In New York City about a third of the Italian and Jewish immigrants of the 1890s had risen from unskilled to skilled jobs a decade later. Even in Newburyport, Massachusetts, a town that was something of an economic backwater, most laborers made some progress, though far fewer rose to skilled or white-collar positions than in more prosperous cities.

Such progress was primarily the result of the

economic growth the nation was experiencing and of the energy and ambition of the people, native-born and immigrant alike, who were pouring into the cities in such numbers. But the public education system gave an additional boost to the upwardly mobile.

The history of American education after about 1870 reflects the impact of social and economic change. Although Horace Mann, Henry Barnard, and others had laid the foundations for state-supported school systems earlier in the century, most of these systems became compulsory only after the Civil War, when the growth of cities provided the concentration of population and financial resources necessary for economical mass education. In the 1860s about half the children in the country were getting some formal education, but this did not mean that half the children were attending school at any one time. Sessions were short, especially in rural areas, and many teachers were poorly trained. President Calvin Coolidge noted in his autobiography that the one-room school he attended in rural Vermont in the 1880s was open only in slack seasons when the 20-odd students were not needed in the fields. "Few, if any, of my teachers reached the standard now required," he wrote, adding that his own

younger sister had obtained a teaching certificate and actually taught a class when she was only 12.

Attendance in the public schools increased from 6.8 million in 1870 to 15.5 million in 1900, a remarkable expansion even when allowance is made for the growth of the population. More remarkable still, during a time when prices were declining steadily, public expenditures for education nearly quadrupled. A typical elementary school graduate, at least in the cities, could count on having studied, besides the traditional "three Rs," history, geography, a bit of science, drawing, and physical training.

Industrialization created many demands for vocational and technical training; both employers and unskilled workers quickly grasped the possibilities. Science courses were taught in some of the new high schools, but secondary education was still assumed to be only for those with special abilities and youths whose families did not require that they immediately become breadwinners. As late as 1890 fewer than 300,000 of the 14.3 million children attending public and private schools had progressed beyond the eighth grade, and nearly a third of these were attending private institutions.

In 1880 Calvin M. Woodward opened the Manual Training School in St. Louis, and soon a number

An 1890s classroom with 40-plus kids, all about the same age, from the same economic and social circumstances, and set to the same assignment by a woman teacher. The urban public school had arrived.

of similar schools were offering courses in carpentry, metalwork, sewing, and other crafts. Woodward thought of vocational training as part of a broad general education rather than as preparation for a specific occupation, but by 1890, 36 cities had established purely vocational public high schools.

Because manual training attracted the backing of industrialists, organized labor was at first suspicious of the new trend. One union leader called trade schools "breeding schools for scabs and rats." Fortunately, the usefulness of such training soon became evident to the unions; by 1910 the AFL was lobbying side by side with the National Association of Manufacturers for more trade schools.

Education certainly helped young people to rise in the world, but progress from rags to real riches was far from common. Carnegies were rare. A study of the family backgrounds of 200 late-19th-century business leaders revealed that nearly all of them grew up in well-to-do middle-class families. They were far better educated than the general run, and most were members of one or another Protestant church.

More than the absence of real opportunity, the unrealistic expectations inspired by the rags-to-riches myth explains why so many workers, even when expressing dissatisfaction with life as it was, continued to subscribe to such middle-class values as hard work and thrift—that is, they continued to hope. Professor Thernstrom notes that hundreds of poor people in Newburyport, by practicing what he calls "ruthless underconsumption," gradually accumulated enough money to buy their own homes and provide for themselves in their old age.

The "New" Immigration

Industrial expansion increased the need for labor, and this in turn powerfully stimulated immigration. Between 1866 and 1915 about 25 million foreigners entered the United States. Industrial growth alone does not explain the influx. The launching in 1858 of the English liner *Great Eastern*, which measured nearly 700 feet from stem to stern and weighed about 19,000 tons, opened a new era in transatlantic travel. Although most immigrants traveled in steerage, which was cramped and almost totally lacking in amenities, the Atlantic crossing, once so hazardous, became safe and speedy with the perfection of the steamship. Competition between the great packet lines such as Cunard, North German Lloyd, and Holland-America drove down the cost of the passage, and advertising by the lines further stimulated traffic.

"Push" pressures as well as these "pull" factors had much to do with this "new" immigration. Improvements in transportation produced unexpected and disruptive changes in the economies of many European countries. Cheap wheat from the United States, Russia, and other parts of the world poured into Europe, bringing disaster to farmers from England and the Scandinavian countries to Italy, Greece, and Russia. The spreading industrial revolution and the increased use of farm machinery led to the collapse of the peasant economy of central and southern Europe. For rural inhabitants this meant the loss of self-sufficiency, the fragmentation of landholdings, unemployment, and, for many, the decision to make a new start in the New World.

Political and religious persecutions pushed still others into the migrating stream, but the main reason for immigration remained the desire for economic betterment. "In America," a British immigrant reported, "you get pies and puddings."

While immigrants continued to people the farms of America, industry absorbed an ever-increasing number of the newcomers. In 1870 one industrial worker in three was foreign-born. When congressional investigators examined 21 major industries early in the new century, they discovered that well over half of the labor force had not been born in the United States.

Most of the new millions entered the country by way of New York City. A Serbian immigrant, Michael Pupin, later a distinguished physicist at Columbia University, has left a moving description of what it was like. He arrived in 1874 on the Hamburg-American liner *Westphalia* amid a horde of other newcomers. Disembarking at Hoboken, he was taken by tug to the immigration reception center at Castle Garden on the southern tip of Manhattan Island. He confessed to the authorities that he had only 5 cents to his name and knew no Americans except—by reputation—Franklin, Lincoln, and Harriet Beecher Stowe. But he explained in eloquent phrases why he wanted to live in the land of liberty rather than in the Austro-Hungarian Empire.

The officials conferred briefly, then admitted

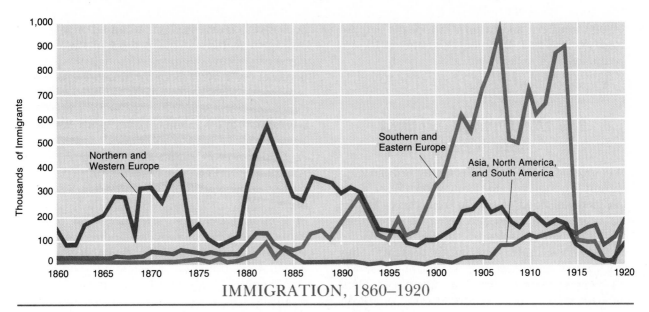

IMMIGRATION, 1860–1920

In this graph Germany is counted as a part of northern and western Europe. Note the tide of "new" immigration from southern and eastern Europe in the early 1900s, and how it plummeted during World War I.

him. After a good breakfast, supplied by the immigration authorities, someone from the Castle Garden Labor Bureau offered him a job as a farmhand in Delaware. Within 24 hours of his arrival he had reached his destination, ready to go to work.

Before 1882, when—in addition to the Chinese—criminals, idiots, lunatics, and persons liable to become public charges were excluded, entry into the United States was almost unrestricted. Indeed, until 1891 the Atlantic Coast states, not the federal government, exercised whatever controls were imposed on newcomers. Even when federally imposed, medical inspection was perfunctory. Public Health officials boasted that with "one glance" at each arrival, the inspectors could "take in six details, namely the scalp, face, neck, hands, gait and general condition, both mental and physical." Only those who failed this "test" were examined more closely. On average, only one immigrant in 50 was ultimately rejected.

Private agencies, philanthropic and commercial, served as a link between the new arrivals and employers looking for labor. Until the Foran Act of 1885 outlawed the practice, a few companies brought in skilled workers under contract, advancing them passage money and collecting it in in-

stallments from their paychecks, a system somewhat like the indentured servitude of colonial times. Numerous nationality groups assisted (and sometimes exploited) their compatriots by organizing "immigrant banks" that recruited labor in the old country, arranged transportation, and then housed the newcomers in boardinghouses in the United States while finding them jobs. The *padrone* system of the Italians and Greeks was typical. The *padrone*, a sort of contractor who agreed to supply gangs of unskilled workers to companies for a lump sum, usually signed on immigrants unfamiliar with American wage levels at rates that assured him a healthy profit.

Beginning in the 1880s, the spreading effects of industrialization in Europe caused a shift in the sources of American immigration from northern and western to southern and eastern sections of the Continent. In 1882 when a total of 789,000 immigrants entered the United States, more than 350,000 came from Great Britain and Germany, only 32,000 from Italy, and fewer than 17,000 from Russia. In 1907—the all-time peak year, with 1,285,000 immigrants—Great Britain and Germany supplied fewer than half as many as they had 25 years earlier, while Russia and Italy were supplying 11 times as many as before. Up to 1880, only about

200,000 southern and eastern Europeans had migrated to America. Between 1880 and 1910, approximately 8.4 million arrived.

The Old Immigrants and the New

Of course, Michael Pupin was not an ordinary immigrant. Though he came from eastern Europe, he preceded the flood of people from there, and he was more sophisticated and better educated than most. The new immigrants, like the "old" Irish of the 1840s and 1850s, were mostly peasants. They also seemed more than ordinarily clannish; southern Italians typically called all people outside their families *forestieri*, "foreigners." Old-stock Americans thought them harder to assimilate, and in fact many were. Some Italian immigrants, for example, were unmarried men who had come to the United States to earn enough money to buy a farm back home. Such people made hard and willing workers but were not much concerned with being part of an American community.

The "birds of passage" formed a substantial minority, but the immigrant who saved in order to bring his wife and children or his younger brothers and sisters to America was more typical. In addition, thousands of immigrants came as family groups and intended to remain. Some, like the eastern European Jewish migrants, were refugees who were almost desperately eager to become Americans, though of course they retained and nurtured much of their traditional culture.

Cultural differences among immigrants were often large and had important effects on their relations with native-born Americans and with other immigrant groups. Italians who settled in the city of Buffalo, the historian Virginia Yans-McLaughlin has shown, adjusted relatively smoothly to urban industrial life because of their close family and kinship ties. Poverty, unemployment, female jobholding outside the home, and other traumas that might have been expected to disrupt family relationships apparently had little effect. Polish immigrants in Buffalo, having different traditions, found adjustment more difficult.

German-American and Irish-American Catholics had different attitudes that caused them to clash over such matters as the policies of the Catholic University in Washington. Although (or perhaps because) the Haymarket anarchists were German-born, in 1887 one prominent German-American denounced the Knights of Labor as a hotbed of radicalism—and was said to have claimed that it was dominated by "Irish ignoramuses." Controversies erupted between Catholic and Protestant German-Americans, between Greek-American groups supporting various political factions in their homeland, and so on.

Confused by such differences and conflicts, many Americans of longer standing concluded, wrongly but understandably, that the new immigrants were incapable of becoming good citizens and should be kept out. During the 1880s large numbers of social workers, economists, and church leaders, worried by the problems that arose when so many poor immigrants flocked into cities already bursting at the seams, began to believe that some restriction should be placed on the incoming human tide. The directors of charitable organizations, which bore the burden of aiding the most unfortunate immigrants, complained that their resources were being exhausted by the needs of the flood.

Social Darwinists and people obsessed with pseudoscientific ideas about "racial purity" also found the new immigration alarming. Misunderstanding the findings of the new science of genetics, they attributed the social problems associated with mass immigration to supposed physiological characteristics of the newcomers. Forgetting that earlier Americans had accused pre–Civil War Irish and German immigrants of similar deficiencies, they decided that the peoples of southern and eastern Europe were racially (and therefore permanently) inferior to "Nordic" and "Anglo-Saxon" types and ought to be kept out.

Workers, fearing the competition of people with low living standards and no bargaining power, spoke out against the "enticing of penniless and unapprised immigrants . . . to undermine our wages and social welfare." In 1883 the president of the Amalgamated Iron and Steel Workers told a Senate committee that Hungarian, Polish, Italian, and other immigrants "can live where I think a decent man would die; they can live on . . . food that other men would not touch." A Wisconsin iron-

Contemporary cartoonists reflected the "new nativist" attitude toward unrestricted immigration. Frank Beard's 1885 drawing shows anarchists, socialists, and members of the Mafia arriving from the sewers of Europe and being resisted by Columbia and her watchdogs "Law" and "Order."

worker put it this way: "Immigrants work for almost nothing and seem to be able to live on wind—something I can not do."

Employers were not disturbed by the influx of people with strong backs willing to work hard for low wages. Nevertheless, by the late 1880s many of them were alarmed about the supposed radicalism of the immigrants. The Haymarket bombing focused attention on the handful of foreign-born extremists in the country and loosed a flood of unjustified charges that "anarchists and communists" were dominating the labor movement. Nativism, which had waxed in the 1850s under the Know-Nothing banner and waned during the Civil War, now flared up again, and for similar reasons. Denunciations of "longhaired, wild-eyed, bad-smelling, atheistic, reckless foreign wretches," of "Europe's human and inhuman rubbish," of the

"cutthroats of Beelzebub from the Rhine, the Danube, the Vistula and the Elbe" crowded the pages of the nation's press. The Grand Army of the Republic, an organization of Civil War veterans, grumbled about foreign-born radicals.

These nativists, again like the pre–Civil War variety, disliked Catholics and other minority groups more than immigrants as such. The largest nativist organization of the period, the American Protective Association, founded in 1887, existed primarily to resist what its members called the "Catholic menace." The Protestant majority treated new immigrants as underlings, tried to keep them out of the best jobs, and discouraged their efforts to climb the social ladder. This prejudice functioned only at the social and economic levels. But nowhere in America did prejudice lead to interference with religious freedom in the narrow sense. And neither labor leaders nor important industrialists, despite their misgivings about immigration, took a broadly antiforeign position.

After the Exclusion Act of 1882 and the almost meaningless 1885 ban on importing contract labor, no further restrictions were imposed on immigration until the 20th century. Strong support for a literacy test for admission developed in the 1890s, pushed by a new organization, the Immigration Restriction League. Since there was much more illiteracy in the southeastern quarter of Europe than in the northwestern, such a test would discriminate without seeming to do so on national or racial grounds. A literacy test bill passed both houses of Congress in 1897, but President Cleveland vetoed it. Such a "radical departure" from the "generous and free-handed policy" of the past, Cleveland said, was unjustified. He added, perhaps with tongue in cheek, that a literacy requirement would not keep out "unruly agitators," who were only too adept at reading and writing.

out the national transportation network. But by the final decades of the century, the expansion of industry had become the chief cause of city growth. Thus the urban concentration continued; in 1890 one person in three lived in a city, by 1910 nearly one in two.

A steadily increasing proportion of the urban population was made up of immigrants. In 1890 the foreign-born population of Chicago almost equaled the total population of Chicago in 1880; a third of all Bostonians and a quarter of all Philadelphians had been born abroad, and four out of five residents of New York City were either immigrants themselves or the children of immigrants.

After 1890 the immigrant concentration became even more dense. The migrants from eastern and southern Europe lacked the resources to travel to the agriculturally developing regions (to say nothing of the sums necessary to acquire land and farm equipment). As the concentration progressed, it fed

The Expanding City and Its Problems

Americans who favored restricting immigration made much of the fact that so many of the newcomers crowded into the cities, aggravating problems of housing, public health, crime, and immorality. Immigrants concentrated in the cities because the jobs created by expanding industry were located there. So, of course, did native-born Americans; the proportion of urban dwellers had been steadily increasing since about 1820.

It is important to keep in mind that population density is not necessarily related to the existence of large cities. In the late 19th century there were areas in Asia as large as the United States that were as densely populated as Belgium and England yet overwhelmingly rural. The United States by any standard was sparsely populated, but well before the Civil War it had become one of the most urban nations in the world.

Industrialization does not entirely explain the growth of 19th-century cities. All the large American cities began as commercial centers, and the development of huge metropolises such as New York and Chicago would have been impossible with-

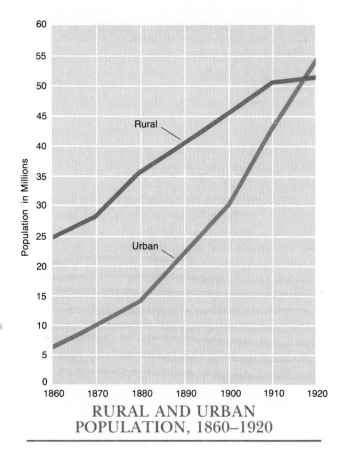

RURAL AND URBAN
POPULATION, 1860–1920

on itself, for all the eastern cities developed many ethnic neighborhoods, in each of which immigrants of one nationality congregated. Lonely, confused, often unable to speak English, the Italians, the Greeks, the Polish and Russian Jews, and other immigrants tended to settle where their predecessors had settled. Eager to maintain their traditional culture, they supported "national" churches and schools. Newspapers in their native languages flourished, as did social organizations of all sorts. Each great American city became a Europe in microcosm where it sometimes seemed that every language in the world but English could be heard. New York, the great entrepôt, had Italian, Polish, Greek, Jewish, and Bohemian quarters, even a Chinatown.

Although ethnic neighborhoods were crowded, unhealthy, and crime-ridden and many of the residents were desperately poor, they were not ghettos in the European sense, for those who lived there were not compelled by law to remain. Thousands "escaped" yearly to better districts. American ghettos were places where hopes and ambitions were fulfilled, where people worked hard and endured hardships in order to improve their own lot and that of their children.

Observing the immigrants' attachment to "foreign" values and institutions, numbers of native-born citizens accused the newcomers of resisting Americanization and blamed them for urban problems. The immigrants were involved in these problems, but the rapidity of urban expansion explains the troubles associated with city life far more fully than the high percentage of foreigners.

The Urban Infrastructure

The cities were suffering from growing pains. Sewer and water facilities frequently could not keep pace with skyrocketing needs. By the 1890s the tremendous growth of Chicago had put such a strain on its sanitation system that the Chicago River had become virtually an open sewer, and the city's drinking water contained such a high concentration of germ-killing chemicals that it tasted like creosote. In the 1880s all the sewers of Baltimore emptied into the sluggish Back Basin, and according to the journalist H. L. Mencken, every summer the city smelled "like a billion polecats." Fire protection became less and less adequate, garbage piled up in the streets faster

than it could be carted away, and the streets themselves crumbled beneath the pounding of heavy traffic. Urban growth proceeded with such speed that new streets were laid out more rapidly than they could be paved. Chicago had more than 1,400 miles of dirt streets in 1890.

People poured into the great cities faster than housing could be built to accommodate them. The influx into areas already densely packed in the 1840s became unbearable as rising property values and the absence of zoning laws conspired to make builders utilize every possible foot of space, squeezing out light and air ruthlessly in order to wedge in a few additional family units.

Substandard living quarters aggravated other evils such as disease and the disintegration of family life with its attendant mental anguish, crime, and juvenile delinquency. The bloody New York riots of 1863, though sparked by dislike of the Civil War draft and of blacks, reflected the bitterness and frustration of thousands jammed together amid filth and threatened by disease. A citizens' committee seeking to discover the causes of the riots expressed its amazement after visiting the slums "that so much misery, disease, and wretchedness can be huddled together and hidden . . . unvisited and unthought of, so near our own abodes." New York City created the Metropolitan Health Board in 1866, and a state tenement house law the following year made a feeble beginning at regulating city housing. Another law in 1879 placed a limit on the percentage of lot space that could be covered by new construction and established minimum standards of plumbing and ventilation. The magazine *Plumber and Sanitary Engineer* sponsored a contest to pick the best design for a tenement that met these specifications. The winner of the competition was James E. Ware, whose plan for a "dumbbell" apartment house managed to crowd 24 to 32 four-room apartments onto a plot of ground measuring only 25 by 100 feet. Oscar Handlin elaborates in *The Uprooted:*

The feat was accomplished by narrowing the building at its middle so that it took on the shape of a dumbbell. The indentation was only two-and-a-half feet wide and varied in length from five to fifty feet; but, added to the similar indentations on the adjoining houses, it created on each side an air-shaft five feet wide. . . . The stairs, halls, and common water closets were cramped into the narrow center of the building so that almost the whole of its surface was available for living quarters.

Despite efforts at reform, in 1890 more than 1.4 million persons were living on Manhattan Island, and in some sections the population density exceeded 900 persons per acre. Jacob Riis, a reporter, captured the horror of the crowded warrens in his classic study of life in the slums, *How the Other Half Lives* (1890):

> Be a little careful, please! The hall is dark and you might stumble. . . . Here where the hall turns and dives into utter darkness is . . . a flight of stairs. You can feel your way, if you cannot see it. Close? Yes! What would you have? All the fresh air that enters these stairs comes from the hall-door that is forever slamming. . . . The sinks are in the hallway, that all the tenants may have access—and all be poisoned alike

by their summer stenches. . . . Here is a door. Listen! That short, hacking cough, that tiny, helpless wail—what do they mean? . . . The child is dying of measles. With half a chance it might have lived; but it had none. That dark bedroom killed it.

The unhealthiness of the tenements was notorious; one noxious corner of New York became known as the "lung block" because of the prevalence of tuberculosis among its inhabitants. In 1900 three out of five babies born in one poor district of Chicago died before their first birthday. Equally frightening was the impact of overcrowding on the morals of the tenement dweller. The number of prison inmates in the United States increased by 50 percent in the 1880s, and the homicide rate nearly tripled, most of the rise occurring in cities. Driven into the streets by the squalor of their homes, slum youths formed gangs bearing names like Alley Gang, Rock Gang, and Hell's Kitchen Gang. From petty thievery and shoplifting they graduated to housebreaking, bank robbery, and murder. According to Jacob Riis, when the leader of the infamous Whyo Gang, convicted of murder, confessed his sins to a prison chaplain, "his father confessor turned pale . . . though many years of labor as chaplain of the Tombs had hardened him to such rehearsals."

Slums bred criminals—the wonder was that they bred so few. They also drove well-to-do residents into exclusive sections and to the suburbs. From Boston's Beacon Hill and Back Bay to San Francisco's Nob Hill, the rich retired into their cluttered mansions and ignored conditions in the poorer parts of town.

Modernizing the Cities

As American cities grew larger and more crowded, thereby aggravating a host of social problems, practical forces operated to bring about improvements. Once the relationship between polluted water and disease was fully understood, everyone saw the need for decent water and sewage systems. It is true that some businessmen profited from corrupt dealings with the city machines, but more of them wanted efficient and honest government in order to reduce their tax bills. City dwellers of all classes resented dirt, noise, and ugliness, and in many communities public-spirited groups formed societies to plant

An alley known as "Bandit's Roost," on New York's Lower East Side, photographed for the New York Sun *in 1887 by police reporter Jacob Riis, himself an immigrant. "What sort of an answer, think you, would come from these tenements to the question 'Is life worth living?'" Riis asked in his book* How the Other Half Lives.

trees, clean up littered areas, and develop recreational facilities. When one city undertook improvements, others tended to follow suit, spurred on by local pride and the booster spirit.

Gradually, the basic facilities of urban living were improved. Streets were paved, first with cobblestones and wood blocks and then with smoother, quieter asphalt. Gaslight, then electric arc lights, and finally Edison's incandescent lamps brightened the cities after dark, making law enforcement easier, stimulating nightlife, and permitting factories and shops to operate after sunset.

Urban transportation underwent enormous changes. Until the 1880s, horse-drawn cars running on tracks set flush with the street were the main means of urban public transportation. In 1860 New York City's horsecars were carrying about 100,000 passengers a day. But horsecars had serious drawbacks. Enormous numbers of horses were needed, and feeding and stabling the animals was costly. Their droppings (10 pounds per day per horse) became a major source of urban pollution. That is why the invention of the electric trolley car in the 1880s put an end to horsecar transportation. Trolleys were cheaper and less unsightly than horsecars and quieter than steam-powered trains.

A retired naval officer, Frank J. Sprague, installed the first practical electric trolley line in Richmond, Virginia, in 1887 and 1888. At once other cities seized upon the trolley. Lines soon radiated outward from the city centers, bringing commuters and shoppers from the residential districts to the business district. Without them the big-city department stores could not have flourished as they did. By 1895 some 850 lines were busily hauling city dwellers over 10,000 miles of track, and mileage tripled in the following decade. As with other new enterprises, control of street railways quickly became centralized until a few big operators controlled the trolleys of more than 100 eastern cities and towns.

Streetcars changed the character of big-city life. Before their introduction, urban communities were limited by the distances people could conveniently walk to work. The "walking city" could not easily extend more than 2½ miles from its center. Streetcars increased this radius to 6 miles or more, which meant that the area of the city expanded enormously. Dramatic population shifts resulted as the better-off moved away from the center in search of

However noisy and unsightly their overhead rails, the electric trolleys represented a tremendous improvement in the urban environment over their waste-discharging predecessors when introduced in the 1880s.

air and space, abandoning the crumbling, jam-packed older neighborhoods to the poor. Thus economic segregation speeded the growth of ghettos. Older peripheral towns that had maintained some of the self-contained qualities of village life were swallowed up, becoming metropolitan centers. The village of Medford, Massachusetts, outside Boston, had 11,000 residents in 1890 when the first trolley line from the city center reached it. By 1905 its population had reached 23,000.

As time passed, each new area, originally peopled by rising economic groups, tended to become crowded and then to deteriorate. By extending their tracks beyond the developed areas, the streetcar companies further speeded suburban growth because they assured developers, bankers, builders, and middle-class home buyers of efficient transport to the center of town. By keeping fares low (5 cents a ride was standard) the lines enabled poor people to "escape" to the countryside on holidays. Kenneth T. Jackson traces the pattern in *Crabgrass Frontier:* "First, streetcar lines were built out to existing villages. . . . These areas subsequently developed into large communities. Second, the tracks actually created residential neighborhoods where none had existed before."

Los Angeles, according to Professor Jackson, "provides the premier example of the confluence of street railway entrepreneurs and real-estate development." Henry E. Huntington, a nephew of the railroad baron Collis P. Huntington, built his Pacific Electric Railway into a vast network of lines primarily to aid in selling homesites on lands he had purchased cheaply before the tracks were laid.

The combined activities of real estate developers, trolley operators, and efficient builders made home ownership possible for people of modest means. "For the first time in the history of the world," Jackson writes, "middle-class families . . . could reasonably expect to buy a detached home on an accessible lot in a safe and sanitary environment."

Advances in bridge design, notably the perfection of the steel-cable suspension bridge by John A. Roebling, aided the ebb and flow of metropolitan populations. The Brooklyn Bridge, described by a poet as "a weird metallic Apparition . . . the cables, like divine messages from above . . . cutting and dividing into innumerable musical spaces the nude

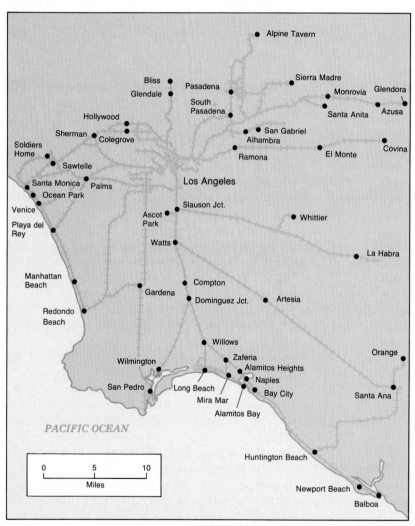

By the early 1900s, a street railway network radiated from the settled parts of central Los Angeles for 30 miles and more. Henry Huntington claimed that the Los Angeles and Pacific Electric system "extended into the open country, ahead of, and not behind, the population. . . ." Data from Fogelson, The Fragmented Metropolis.

LOS ANGELES AREA
STREET RAILWAY NETWORK, 1909

immensity of the sky," was Roebling's triumph. Completed in 1883 at a cost of $15 million, it was soon carrying more than 33 million passengers a year over the East River between Manhattan and Brooklyn.

Even the high cost of urban real estate, which spawned the tenement, produced some beneficial results in the long run. Instead of crowding squat structures cheek by jowl on 25-foot lots, architects began to build upward. The introduction of iron-skeleton construction, which freed the walls from bearing the immense weight of a tall building, was the work of a group of Chicago architects who had been attracted to the metropolis of the Middle West by opportunities to be found amid the ashes of the great fire of 1871. The group included William Le Baron Jenney, John A. Holabird, Martin Roche, John W. Root, and Louis H. Sullivan. Jenney's Home Insurance Building, completed in 1885, was the first metal-frame edifice. Height alone, however, did not satisfy these innovators; they sought a form that would reflect the structure and purpose of their buildings.

Their leader was Louis Sullivan. Architects must discard "books, rules, precedents, or any such educational impediments" and design functional buildings, he argued. A tall building "must be every inch a proud and soaring thing, rising in sheer exultation . . . from bottom to top . . . a unit without a single dissenting line." Sullivan's Wainwright Building in St. Louis and his Prudential Building in Buffalo, both completed in the early 1890s, combined beauty, modest construction costs, and efficient use of space in trailblazing ways. Soon a "race to the skies" was on in the great cities of America, and the words *skyscraper* and *skyline* entered the language.

The remarkable White City built for the Chicago World's Fair of 1893 by Daniel H. Burnham, with its broad vistas and acres of open space, led to a national City Beautiful movement, the most lasting result of which was the development of many public parks. The landscape architect Frederick Law Olmsted, designer of New York's Central Park, was a leading figure in the movement.

But efforts to relieve the congestion in slum dis-

Designed by Daniel H. Burnham for the Chicago's World Fair in 1893, "White City" inspired other architects with its ideal of uncongested and visually satisfying urban living. The results, still visible, were mixed.

tricts made little headway. In Brooklyn, Alfred T. White established Home Buildings, a 40-family model tenement in 1877; eventually he expanded the experiment to include 267 apartments. Each unit had plenty of light and air and contained its own sink and toilet. Ellen Collins developed a smaller project in Manhattan's Fourth Ward in the 1890s. These model tenements were self-sustaining, but of necessity they yielded only modest returns. The landlords were essentially philanthropists; their work had no significant impact on urban housing in the 19th century.

Leisure Activities: More Fun and Games

By bringing together large numbers of people, cities made possible many kinds of social activity difficult or impossible to maintain in rural areas. Cities remained unsurpassed as centers of artistic and intellectual life. New York was the outstanding example, as seen in its many theaters and in the founding of the American Museum of Natural History (1870), the Metropolitan Museum of Art (1870), and the Metropolitan Opera (1883), but other cities were equally hospitable to such endeavors. Boston's Museum of Fine Arts, for example, was founded in 1870, the Boston Symphony in 1881.

Of course, less sophisticated forms of recreation also flourished in the urban environment. It is only a slight exaggeration to say that crowded urban centers had a saloon on every corner; during the last third of the 19th century the number of saloons in the country tripled. Saloons were strictly male working-class institutions, usually decorated with pictures and other mementos of sports heroes, the bar perhaps under the charge of a retired pugilist.

For workingmen the saloon was a kind of club, a place to meet friends, exchange news and gossip, gamble, and eat, as well as to drink beer and whiskey. Saloons also flourished because factory owners and other employers of large numbers of workers tended to forbid the consumption of alcohol on their premises. In addition, the gradual reduction of the workday left men with more free time, which may explain why vaudeville and burlesques, the latter described by one straight-laced critic as a "disgrace-ful spectacle of padded legs juggling and tight-laced wriggling," also proliferated.

Calvinist-inspired opposition to sports as a frivolous waste of valuable time was steadily evaporating, replaced among the upper and middle classes by the realization that games like golf and tennis were "healthy occupation[s] for mind and body." Bicycling became a fad, both as a means of getting from place to place in the ever-expanding cities and as a form of exercise and recreation.

Many of the new streetcar companies built picnic grounds and amusement parks at their outer limits. In good weather thousands seeking to relax after a hard day's work flocked to these "trolley parks" to enjoy a fresh-air meal or patronize the shooting galleries, merry-go-rounds, and "freak shows."

The postwar era also saw the first important development of spectator sports, again because cities provided the concentrations of population necessary to support them. Curious relationships developed between upper- and working-class interests and between competitive sports as pure enjoyment for players and spectators and sports as something to bet on. Horse racing had strictly upper-class origins, but racetracks attracted huge crowds of ordinary people more intent on picking a winner than on improving the breed.

Professional boxing offers an even better example. It was in a sense a hobby of the rich, who sponsored favorite gladiators, offered prizes, and often wagered large sums on the matches. But the audiences were made up overwhelmingly of young working-class males, from whose ranks most of the fighters emerged. The gambling and also the brutality of the bloody, bare-knuckle character of the fights caused many communities to outlaw boxing, a fact that added to the appeal of the sport for some.

The first widely popular pugilist was the legendary "Boston Strong Boy," John L. Sullivan, who became heavyweight champion in 1882 by disposing of one Paddy Ryan in nine rounds. Sullivan was an immensely powerful man whose idea of fighting, according to his biographer, "was simply to hammer his opponent into unconsciousness," something he did repeatedly during his ten-year reign. Sullivan became an international celebrity and made and lost large sums during this period. He was also the beneficiary of patronage in such forms as a diamond belt worth $10,000 presented to him by some of his admirers. Yet boxing remained a raffish, clandestine occupation. One of Sullivan's important fights took place in France, on the estate of Baron Rothschild, yet when it ended both he and his opponent were arrested.

Three major team games, baseball, football, and basketball, developed in something approaching their modern form during the last quarter of the century. Various forms of what became baseball were played long before that time. Organized teams, in most cases made up of upper-class amateurs, first emerged in the 1840s, but the game only became truly popular during the Civil War, when it was a major form of camp recreation for the troops.

After the war professional teams began to appear (the first, the Cincinnati Red Stockings, paid players between $800 and $1,400 for the season), and in 1876 teams in eight cities formed the National League. The American League followed in 1901. After a brief period of rivalry, the two leagues made peace in 1903, the year of the first World Series.

Organized play led to codification of the rules and improvements in technique and strategy, for example, the development of "minor" leagues, impartial umpires calling balls and strikes and ruling on close plays, the use of both catcher's masks and padded gloves, and the invention of various kinds of curves and other erratic pitches (often enhanced by "doctoring" the ball). As early as the 1870s, baseball was being called the "national game" and losing all upper-class connotations. Important games attracted crowds in the tens of thousands; betting became a problem. Despite its urban origins, its broad green fields and dusty basepaths gave the game a rural character that has only recently begun to fade.

Nobody "invented" baseball, but both football and basketball owe their present form to individuals. James Naismith's invention of basketball is undisputed. In 1891, while a student at a YMCA school, he attached peach baskets to the edge of an elevated running track in the gymnasium and drew up what are still the basic rules of the game. The first basketball was a soccer ball. The game was popular from the start, but since it was played indoors, it was not an important spectator sport until much later.

Football was not created by one person in the way that basketball was; it evolved out of English rugby. For many decades it remained almost en-

Thomas Eakins's Baseball Players Practicing, *painted in 1875, one year before the organization of the National League. The relative similarity of the batter's stance to that favored today suggests the timelessness of this national pastime.*

tirely a college sport and thus was played almost entirely by upper- and middle-class types. (Organized collegiate sports dated back to before the Civil War; the first intercollegiate matches were rowing races between Harvard and Yale students.)

The first intercollege football game occurred when Princeton defeated Rutgers in 1869, and by the 1880s college football had become extremely popular. Much of the game's modern character was the work of Walter Camp, the athletic director and football coach at Yale. Camp cut the size of teams from 15 to 11, and he invented the scrimmage line, the four-down system, and the key position of quarterback. He publicized the game in a series of books, ranging from *How to Coach a Team* (1886) to *Jack Hall at Yale* (1909). Camp's prestige was such that when he named his first All America team after the 1889 season, no one challenged his judgment. Well into the 20th century, the players that Camp selected were *the* All Americans.

Camp claimed that amateur sports like football taught the value of hard work, cooperation, and fair play. His practice was more questionable. He is known to have recruited players who could not meet Yale's academic standards and to have found means of putting money in his players' pockets. At Yale and elsewhere all the problems that emphasis on athletic achievement poses for modern institutions of higher education existed in microcosm well before 1900.

Spectator sports had little appeal to women at this time and indeed for decades thereafter. And few women participated in organized athletics. Sports were "manly" activities; a woman might ride a bicycle, play croquet and perhaps a little tennis, but to display any concentrated interest in excelling in a sport was considered unfeminine.

Religious Responses to Industrial Society

The modernization of the great cities was not solving most of the social problems of the slums. As this fact became clear, a number of urban religious leaders began to take a hard look at the situation. Traditionally, American churchmen had insisted that where sin was concerned, there were no extenuating circumstances. To the well-to-do they preached the virtues of thrift and hard work; to the poor they extended the possibility of a better existence in the next world; to all they stressed one's responsibility for one's own behavior—and thus for one's own salvation. Such a point of view brought meager comfort to residents of slums. Consequently, the churches lost influence in the poorer sections. Furthermore, as better-off citizens followed the streetcar lines out from the city centers, their church leaders followed them.

In New York 17 Protestant congregations abandoned the depressed areas of Lower Manhattan between 1868 and 1888. Catering thereafter almost entirely to middle-class and upper-class worshipers, the pastors tended to become even more conservative. No more strident defender of reactionary ideas existed than the pastor of Brooklyn's fashionable Plymouth Congregational Church, Henry Ward Beecher. Beecher, a younger brother of Harriet Beecher Stowe, the author of *Uncle Tom's Cabin*, attributed poverty to the improvidence of laborers who, he claimed, squandered their wages on liquor and tobacco. "No man in this land suffers from poverty," he said, "unless it be more than his fault—unless it be his sin." The best check on labor unrest was a plentiful supply of cheap immigrant labor, he told President Hayes. Unions were "the worst form of despotism and tyranny in the history of Christendom."

An increasing proportion of the residents of the blighted districts were Catholics, and the Roman church devoted much effort to distributing alms, maintaining homes for orphans and old people, and other forms of social welfare. But church leaders seemed unconcerned with the social causes of the blight; they were deeply committed to the idea that sin and vice were personal, poverty an act of God. They deplored the rising tide of crime, disease, and destitution among their coreligionists, yet they failed to see the connection between these evils and the squalor of the slums. "Intemperance is the great evil we have to overcome," wrote the president of the leading Catholic charitable organization, the Society of St. Vincent de Paul. "It is the source of the misery for at least three-fourths of the families we are called upon to visit and relieve." The church, according to the historian Aaron I. Abell, "seemed oblivious to the bearing of civil legislation on the course of moral and social reform." Instead it invested much money and energy in chimerical at-

Perhaps the most widely admired of middle-class urban ministers of his day, Henry Ward Beecher also became the best known when a member of his Brooklyn congregation in 1874 charged him with adultery. A jury exonerated him.

tempts to colonize poor city dwellers in the West.

Like conservative Protestant clergymen, the Catholic hierarchy tended to be at best neutral toward organized labor. Cardinal James Gibbons spoke favorably of the Knights of Labor in 1886 after the Haymarket bombing, but he took a dim view of strikes. The clergy's attitude changed somewhat after Pope Leo XIII issued his encyclical *Rerum novarum* (1891). This statement criticized the excesses of capitalism, including the "greed of unchecked competition"; it defended the right of labor to form unions and stressed the duty of government to care for the poor. Workers were entitled to wages that would guarantee their families a reasonable and frugal comfort, Leo declared, and they committed no sin by seeking government aid to get it. Concrete

action by American Catholics, however, was slow in coming, probably because of the conservatism of the clergy and the parochial concerns of lay leaders.

The conservatism of most Protestant and Catholic clergymen did not prevent some earnest preachers from working directly to improve the lot of the city poor. Some followed the path blazed by Dwight L. Moody, a lay evangelist who became famous throughout America and Great Britain in the 1870s. A gargantuan figure weighing nearly 300 pounds, Moody conducted a vigorous campaign to persuade the denizens of the slums to cast aside their sinful ways. He went among them full of enthusiasm and God's love and made an impact no less powerful than that of George Whitefield during the Great Awakening of the 18th century or Charles Grandison Finney in the first part of the 19th. The evangelists founded mission schools in the slums and tried to provide spiritual and recreational facilities for the unfortunate. They were prominent in the establishment of American branches of the Young Men's Christian Association (1851) and the Salvation Army (1880).

However, the evangelists paid little heed to the causes of urban poverty and vice, believing that faith in God would enable the poor to transcend the material difficulties of life. For a number of Protestant clergymen who had become familiar with the slums, a different approach seemed called for. Slum conditions caused the sins and crimes of the cities; the wretched human beings who committed them could not be blamed, these ministers argued. They began to preach a "Social Gospel" that focused on improving living conditions rather than on saving souls. If people were to lead pure lives, they must have enough to eat, decent homes, and opportunities to develop their talents. Social Gospelers advocated civil service reform, child labor legislation, regulation of big corporations, and heavy taxes on incomes and inheritances.

The most influential preacher of the Social Gospel was probably Washington Gladden. At first Gladden, who was raised on a Massachusetts farm, had opposed all government interference in social and economic affairs, but his experiences as a minister in Springfield, Massachusetts, and Columbus, Ohio, exposed him to the realities of life in industrial cities, and his views changed. In *Applied Christianity* (1886) and in other works he defended labor's right to organize and strike and denounced the idea that supply and demand should control wage rates. He favored factory inspection laws, strict regulation of public utilities, and other reforms.

Gladden never questioned the basic values of capitalism. By the 1890s a number of ministers had gone all the way to socialism. The Reverend William D. P. Bliss of Boston, for example, believed in the kind of welfare state envisioned by Edward Bellamy in *Looking Backward*. He founded the Society of Christian Socialists (1889) and edited a radical journal, *The Dawn*. In addition to nationalizing industry, Bliss and other Christian Socialists advocated government unemployment relief programs, public housing and slum clearance projects, and other measures designed to aid the city poor.

Nothing so well reveals the receptivity of the public to the Social Gospel as the popularity of Charles M. Sheldon's novel *In His Steps* (1896), one of America's all-time best-sellers. Sheldon, a minister in Topeka, Kansas, described what happened in the mythical city of Raymond when a group of leading citizens decided to live truly Christian lives, asking themselves, "What would Jesus do?" before adopting any course of action. Naturally the tone of Raymond's society was immensely improved, but basic social reforms followed quickly. The Rectangle, a terrible slum area "too dirty, too coarse, too sinful, too awful for close contact," became the center of a great reform effort. One of Raymond's "leading society heiresses" undertook a slum clearance project, and a concerted attack was made on drunkenness and immorality. The moral regeneration of the entire community was soon accomplished.

The Settlement Houses

Although millions read *In His Steps*, its effect, and that of other Social Gospel literature, was merely inspirational. On the practical level, a number of earnest souls began to grapple with slum problems by organizing what were known as settlement houses. These were community centers located in poor districts that provided guidance and services to all who would use them. The settlement workers, most of them idealistic, well-to-do young people, lived in the houses and were active in neighborhood affairs.

The prototype of the settlement house was London's Toynbee Hall, founded in the early 1880s;

the first American example was the Neighborhood Guild, opened on the Lower East Side of New York in 1886 by Dr. Stanton Coit. By the turn of the 20th century 100 had been established, the most famous being Jane Addams's Hull House in Chicago (1889), Robert A. Woods's South End House in Boston (1892), and Lillian Wald's Henry Street Settlement in New York (1893).

Though some men were active in the movement, the most important settlement house workers were women fresh from college—the first generation of young women to experience the trauma of having developed their capacities only to find that society offered them few opportunities to use them. The settlements provided an outlet for their hopes and energies, and they seized on it avidly. An English social reformer who visited Hull House around the turn of the century described the residents as "strong-minded energetic women, bustling about their various enterprises" and "earnest-faced self-subordinating and mild-mannered men who slide from room to room apologetically."

The settlement workers tried to interpret American ways to the new immigrants and to create a community spirit in order to teach, in the words of one of them, "right living through social relations." Unlike most charity workers, who acted out of a sense of upper-class responsibility toward the unfortunate, they expected to benefit morally and intellectually themselves by experiencing a way of life far different from their own and by obtaining "the first-hand knowledge the college classroom cannot give." Lillian Wald, a nurse by training, explained the concept succinctly in *The House on Henry Street* (1915): "We were to live in the neighborhood, . . . identify ourselves with it socially, and, in brief, contribute to it our citizenship."

Lillian Wald and other settlement workers soon discovered that practical problems absorbed most of their energies. They agitated for tenement house laws, regulation of the labor of women and children, and better schools. They employed private resources to establish playgrounds in the slums, along with libraries, classes in everything from child nutrition and home management to literature and arts and crafts, social clubs, and day-care centers. When they observed that many poor families were so occupied with the struggle to survive that they were neglecting or even abandoning their children, they tried to place the children in foster homes in the country.

In Boston, Robert A. Woods organized clubs to get the youngsters of the South End off the streets, helped establish a restaurant where a meal could be had for 5 cents, acted as an arbitrator in labor disputes, and lobbied for laws tightening up the franchises of public utility companies. In Chicago, Jane Addams developed an outstanding cultural program that included classes in music and art and an excellent "little theater" group. Hull House soon boasted a gymnasium, a day nursery, and several social clubs. Addams also worked tirelessly and effectively for improved public services and for social legislation of all kinds. She even got herself appointed garbage inspector in her ward and hounded local landlords and the garbage contractor until something approaching decent service was established.

A few critics considered the settlement houses mere devices to socialize the unruly poor by teaching them the "punctilios of upper-class propriety," but almost everyone appreciated their virtues. By the end of the century the Catholics, laggard in entering the arena of practical social reform, were joining the movement, partly because they were losing many communicants to socially minded Protestant churches. The first Catholic-run settlement house was founded in 1898 in an Italian district of New York. Two years later Brownson House in Los Angeles, catering chiefly to Mexican immigrants, opened its doors.

With all their accomplishments, the settlement houses seemed to be fighting a losing battle. "Private beneficence," Jane Addams wrote of Hull House, "is totally inadequate to deal with the vast numbers of the city's disinherited." As a tropical forest grows faster than a handful of men armed with machetes can cut it down, so the slums, fed by an annual influx of hundreds of thousands, blighted new areas more rapidly than the intrepid settlement house workers could clean up old ones. It became increasingly apparent that the wealth and authority of the state must be brought to bear in order to keep abreast of the problem.

Civilization and Its Discontents

As the 19th century died, the majority of the American people—especially the comfortably well-off, the residents of small towns, the shopkeepers, some farmers, and skilled workers—remained confirmed

This portrait of Jane Addams was completed in 1896 by Alice Kellog Tyler, who worked as an artist at Hull House.

optimists and uncritical admirers of their civilization. However, blacks, immigrants, and others who failed to share equitably in the good things of life, along with a growing number of humanitarian reformers, found little to cheer about and much to lament in their increasingly industrialized society. Giant monopolies flourished despite federal restrictions. The gap between rich and poor appeared to be widening, while the slum spread its poison and the materially successful made a god of their success. Human values seemed in grave danger of being crushed by impersonal forces typified by the great corporations.

In 1871 Walt Whitman, usually so full of extravagant praise for the American way of life, had called his fellow countrymen the "most materialistic and money-making people ever known."

I say we had best look our times and lands searchingly in the face, like a physician diagnosing some deep disease. Never was there, perhaps, more hollowness of heart than at present, and here in the United States.

By the late 1880s a well-known journalist could write to a friend: "The wheel of progress is to be run over the whole human race and smash us all." Others noted an alarming jump in the national divorce rate and an increasing taste for all kinds of luxury. "People are made slaves by a desperate struggle to keep up appearances," a Massachusetts commentator declared, and the economist David A. Wells expressed concern over statistics showing that heart disease and mental illness were on the rise. These "diseases of civilization," Wells explained, were "one result of the continuous mental and nervous activity which modern high-tension methods of business have necessitated."

Wells was a prominent liberal, but pessimism was no monopoly of liberals. A little later, Senator Henry Cabot Lodge of Massachusetts, himself a millionaire, complained of the "lawlessness" of the "modern and recent plutocrat" and his "disregard of the rights of others." Lodge spoke of "the enormous contrast between the sanguine mental attitude prevalent in my youth and that, perhaps wiser, but certainly darker view, so general today." His onetime Harvard professor, Henry Adams, was still more critical of the moneygrubbers. "All one's friends," he complained, along with church and university leaders and other educated people, "had joined the banks to force submission to capitalism."

Of course, intellectuals often tend to be critical of the world they live in, whatever its nature; Thoreau denounced materialism and the worship of progress in the 1840s as vigorously as any late-19th-century prophet of gloom. But the voices of the dissatisfied were rising. Despite the many benefits that industrialization had made possible, it was by no means clear around 1900 that the American people were really better off under the new dispensation.

Milestones

1858	English liner *Great Eastern* launched
1876	National Baseball League founded
1880	Salvation Army founded
1880s	"New immigration" begins
1882	John L. Sullivan wins heavyweight boxing championship
	Chinese Exclusion Act
1883	Brooklyn Bridge completed
1885	Foran Contract Labor Act
1887	American Protective Association founded
1888	First urban electric streetcar system
1889	Jane Addams founds Hull House
	Walter Camp's first All America football team
1890	Jacob Riis, *How the Other Half Lives*
	Calvin Woodward opens his Manual Training School
1891	Pope Leo XIII issues *Rerum novarum* encyclical
1896	Charles M. Sheldon, *In His Steps*

SUPPLEMENTARY READING

Titles marked with an asterisk have been published in paperback.

An enormous number of books deal with the social history of late-19th-century America. J. A. Garraty, **The New Commonwealth*** (1968), treats most of the subjects covered in this chapter; A. M. Schlesinger's classic study, **The Rise of the City** (1933), provides a wealth of information about social trends. See also the appropriate sections of Steven Mintz and Susan Kellogg, **Domestic Revolutions: A Social History of the American Family** (1988), and C. N. Degler, **At Odds: Women and the Family in America** (1980).

Henry Adams, **The Education of Henry Adams*** (1918), is a fascinating if highly personal view of the period, and James Bryce, **The American Commonwealth*** (1888), while primarily a political analysis, contains a great deal of information about social conditions, as does D. A. Wells, **Recent Economic Changes** (1889).

On industrial workers, see David Montgomery, **Beyond Equality*** (1967), J. E. Drucker, **Men of the Steel Rails** (1983), Walter Licht, **Working on the Railroad** (1984), and H. G. Gutman, **Work, Culture, and Society in Industrializing America*** (1977). J. A. Garraty (ed.), **Labor and Capital in the Gilded Age*** (1968), provides a convenient selection of testimony from the great 1883 Senate investigation of that subject, while David Brody, **Steelworkers in America*** (1960), and Stephan Thernstrom, **Poverty and Progress: Social Mobility in a Nineteenth-Century City** (1964), throw much light on the lives of workingmen. S. M. Rothman, **Woman's Proper Place** (1978), discusses the new job opportunities for women. Thernstrom's book **The Other Bostonians** (1973) is a brilliant analysis of social and geographic mobility and an excellent summary of work on these important topics. Businessmen's attitudes are covered in T. C. Cochran, **Railroad Leaders** (1953), and E. C. Kirkland, **Dream and Thought in the Business Community** (1956).

On immigration, see M. A. Jones, **American Immigration*** (1960), and John Higham, **Send These to Me*** (1975). Oscar Handlin, **The Uprooted*** (1951), describes the life of the new immigrants somewhat romantically but with sensitivity, while John Higham, **Strangers in the Land*** (1955), stresses the reactions of native-born Americans to successive waves of immigration. Moses Rischin, **The Promised City: New York's Jews*** (1962), Thomas Kessner, **The Golden Door: Italian and Jewish Immigrant Mobility** (1977), Humbert Nelli, **The Italians of Chicago*** (1970), Virginia Yans-McLaughlin, **Family and Community: Italian Immigrants in Buffalo** (1977), and T. N. Brown, **Irish-American Nationalism** (1966), are important monographs.

A brief interpretive history of urban development is C. N. Glaab and A. T. Brown, **A History of Urban America*** (1967). K. T. Jackson, **Crabgrass Frontier** (1985), is a pioneering history of suburban development, and J. C. Teaford, **The Unheralded Triumph** (1984), gives weight to the accomplishments of the cities as well as their inadequacies. On the growing pains of American cities, consult R. H. Bremner, **From the Depths*** (1956), Jacob Riis, **How the Other Half Lives*** (1890), and Roy Lubove, **The Progressives and the Slums** (1962). Urban architecture is discussed in J. E. Burchard and Albert Bush-Brown, **The Architecture of America*** (1961). S. B. Warner, Jr., **Streetcar Suburbs** (1962), is an interesting study of Boston's development that is full of suggestive ideas about late-19th-century growth.

On the early development of intercollegiate sports, see R. A. Smith, **Sports and Freedom: The Rise of Big-Time College Athletics** (1988). The response of religion to industrialism is discussed in H. F. May, **Protestant Churches and Industrial America*** (1949), A. I. Abell, **American Catholicism and Social Action** (1960), and Arthur Mann, **Yankee Reformers in the Urban Age*** (1954). For details of the settlement house movement, see A. F. Davis, **Spearheads for Reform** (1967), Davis's **American Heroine** (1973), a life of Jane Addams, and two classic personal accounts, Jane Addams, **Twenty Years at Hull House*** (1910), and Lillian Wald, **The House on Henry Street** (1915).

PORTFOLIO FIVE
The New Immigrants

A great many immigrants in the late 1800s and early 1900s settled in large East Coast cities, especially New York. This 1886 watercolor of Baxter Street is a reasonably realistic sketch of an area in New York's infamous Five Points slum. The sketch was done for a stage set used in a comedy about Irish immigrants.

Starting in 1892, Ellis Island in New York Harbor was the processing center for immigrants. The newcomers often had to wait hours before being cleared for entry into the United States. Many were from southern and eastern Europe. Lewis Hine photographed this Italian mother and child waiting to be admitted.

Part of the processing was a medical examination. Below a doctor checks a group of women with her stethoscope. The eye chart on the back wall is in Cyrillic (the Russian alphabet).

Once cleared at Ellis Island, the immigrants often found their way to neighborhoods in New York City where people from their mother countries had already settled. Orchard St. (left) in Manhattan was a bustling shopping area for the eastern European Jewish community, with food and clothing sold out of storefronts and off pushcarts in the street. Mulberry Bend (below) was in the heart of the Italian district of Manhattan's Lower East Side.

Living conditions in the tenements that lined these streets could be appalling. The boy at lower left fills a basin at a communal faucet, which was the tenants' only source of water for cooking, laundry, and bathing.

Getting a job was the first priority for immigrants, since most arrived with little money or other resources. This New York employment agency, photographed by Lewis Hine in 1910, posted available jobs in construction and coal mining in places as far away as West Virginia.

For some families the workplace was the same tenement room in which they ate and slept. The garment industry, employing a largely Jewish immigrant work force, relied on "home work" and paid workers by the garment (the piece) rather than by the hour.

Levi Strauss (1830–1902) was not a "new" immigrant, having emigrated to New York from Bavaria in 1847. He peddled clothing and household items until 1853, when he booked passage on a clipper ship bound for San Francisco. He had planned to sell dry goods to the gold prospectors, including canvas for tents and wagon covers, but he found that what the miners needed most was sturdy work clothes. So he hired a tailor to sew the canvas into trousers—he later switched to blue-dyed denim—and soon "those pants of Levi's" became famous. By the 1870s Strauss's copper-riveted Model 501 Double X blue jeans and denim overalls were an established American institution, as this ad from the period shows.

Levi Strauss's success was repeated by many of the "new" immigrants. A sampling of people who achieved their ambitions in various fields in their adopted country appears on the facing page.

Jacob Riis (1849–1914)
From Denmark in 1870.
*Journalist and photographer. Author
of* How the Other Half Lives *(1890),
an exposé of immigrant life
in the slums.*

Mother Frances Xavier Cabrini
(1850–1917)
From Italy in 1889.
*Roman Catholic saint, canonized in
1946. Founded convents, schools,
orphanages, and hospitals.*

Emma Goldman
(1869–1940)
From Russia in 1885.
*Lecturer, editor, and anarchist activist.
Founder of* Mother Earth, *anarchist journal.
See "American Lives" portrait, page 638.*

Felix Frankfurter (1882–1965)
From Austria in 1894.
*Harvard law professor, 1914–1939.
Supreme Court justice, 1939–1962.
A founder of the American Civil
Liberties Union.*

Sidney Hillman (1887–1946)
From Lithuania in 1907.
*Labor leader. President of
Amalgamated Clothing Workers of
America, 1914–1946. Active in
Roosevelt's New Deal.*

Irving Berlin (1888–1989)
From Russia in 1893.
*Songwriter. Composed nearly one
thousand songs, including "God
Bless America," "White Christmas,"
and "Alexander's Ragtime Band," his
first big hit in 1911.*

XXI

Intellectual and Cultural Trends

These natural ordermakers, whether amateurs or officials, came to the front immediately. There seemed to be no possibility which there was not some one there to think of, or which within twenty-four hours was not in some way provided for. . . . California education has, of course, made the thought of all possible recuperation easy.

WILLIAM JAMES, *eyewitness account of the San Francisco earthquake, 1906*

I ndustrialization altered the way Americans thought at the same time that it transformed their ways of making a living. Technological advances revolutionized the communication of ideas more drastically than they did the transportation of goods or the manufacture of steel. The materialism that permeated American attitudes toward business also affected contemporary education and literature, while Charles Darwin's theory of evolution influenced American philosophers, lawyers, and historians profoundly.

New ideas about how children should be educated and what they should be taught emerged along with new methods of communicating information to adults. As American society became more complex, the need for specialized training increased, boosting the importance of higher education. Americans began to make significant contributions both in the so-called hard sciences, such as chemistry and physics, and in relatively new soft social sciences, such as psychology, political science, and sociology. A new literary flowering comparable to the renaissance of the 1840s and 1850s occurred in the 1870s and 1880s. By the end of the 19th century America had finally emerged intellectually from the shadow of Europe.

The Pursuit of Knowledge

Improvements in public education and the needs of an increasingly complex society for every type of intellectual skill caused a veritable revolution in how knowledge was discovered, disseminated, and put to use. Observing the effects of formal education on their children, many older people were eager to experience some of its benefits. Nothing so well illustrates the desire for new information as the rise of the Chautauqua movement, founded by John H. Vincent, a Methodist minister, and Lewis Miller, an Ohio manufacturer of farm machinery. Vincent had charge of Sunday schools for the Methodist church. In 1874 he and Miller organized a two-week summer course for Sunday school teachers on the shores of Lake Chautauqua in New York. Besides instruction, they offered good meals, evening songfests around the campfire, and a relaxing atmosphere— all for $6 for the two weeks.

The 40 young teachers who attended were delighted with the program, and soon the leafy shore of Lake Chautauqua became a city of tents each summer as thousands poured into the region from all over the country. The founders expanded their offerings to include instruction in literature, science, government, and economics. Famous authorities, including, over the years, six presidents of the United States, came to lecture to open-air audiences on every subject imaginable. Eventually Chautauqua even offered correspondence courses leading over a four-year period to a diploma. Books were written specifically for the program, and a monthly magazine, *The Chautauquan,* was published.

Such success provoked imitation, and by 1900 there were about 200 Chautauqua-type organizations. Intellectual standards in these programs varied greatly; musicians (good and bad), homespun humorists, inspirational lecturers, and assorted quacks shared the platform with prominent divines and scholars. Moneymaking undoubtedly motivated many of the entrepreneurs who operated the centers, all of which, including the original Chautauqua, reflected the prevailing tastes of the American people—diverse, enthusiastic, uncritical, and shallow. Nevertheless, the movement provided opportunities for thousands seeking stimulation and intellectual improvement. Still larger numbers profited from the proliferation of public libraries. Private donors, led by the ironmaster Andrew Carnegie, contributed millions to the cause. In 1900 over 1,700 libraries in the United States had collections of more than 5,000 volumes.

Newspapers were an even more important means for disseminating information and educating the masses. Here new technology supplied the major incentive for change. The development by Richard Hoe and Stephen Tucker of the web press (1871), which printed simultaneously on both sides of paper fed into it from large rolls, and Ottmar Mergenthaler's linotype machine (1886), which cast rows of type as needed directly from molten metal, cut printing costs dramatically. Machines for making paper out of wood pulp reduced the cost of newsprint to a quarter of what it had been in the 1860s. By 1895 machines were printing, cutting, and folding 32-page newspapers at a rate of 24,000 an hour.

The telegraph and transoceanic cables wrought a similar transformation in the gathering of news. Press associations, led by the New York Associated Press, flourished; the syndicated article appeared; and a few publishers—Edward W. Scripps was the first—began to amass chains of newspapers.

Population growth and better education created an ever-larger demand for printed matter. At the same time, the integration of the economy enabled manufacturers to sell their goods all over the country. Advertising became important, and sellers soon learned that newspapers and magazines were excellent means of placing their products before millions of eyes. Advertising revenues soared just when new machines and general expansion were making publishing an expensive business. The day of the journeyman printer-editor ended. Rich men such as the railroad magnate Jay Gould and the mining tycoon George Hearst invested heavily in newspapers in the post–Civil War decades.

Rich publishers tended to be conservative, but reaching the masses meant lowering intellectual and cultural standards, appealing to emotions, and adopting popular, sometimes radical, causes. Cheap, mass-circulation papers had first appeared in the 1830s and 1840s, the most successful being the *Sun*, the *Herald*, and the *Tribune* in New York, the *Philadelphia Public Ledger*, and the *Baltimore Sun*. None of them much exceeded a circulation of 50,000 before the Civil War. The first publisher to reach a truly massive audience was Joseph Pulitzer,

a Hungarian-born immigrant who made a first-rate paper of the *St. Louis Post-Dispatch*. In 1883 Pulitzer bought the *New York World*, a sheet with a circulation of perhaps 20,000. Within a year he was selling 100,000 copies daily, and by the late 1890s the *World*'s circulation regularly exceeded 1 million.

Pulitzer achieved this brilliant success by casting a wide net. To the masses he offered bold, black headlines devoted to crime (ANOTHER MURDERER TO HANG), scandal (VICE ADMIRAL'S SON IN JAIL), catastrophe (TWENTY-FOUR MINERS KILLED), society and the theater (LILY LANGTRY'S NEW ADMIRER), together with feature stories, political cartoons, comics, and pictures. For the educated and affluent he provided better political and financial coverage than the most respectable New York journals. Pulitzer made the *World* a crusader for civic improvement by attacking

John Singer Sargent's 1905 portrait of Joseph Pulitzer. Upon his death six years later, Pulitzer's will provided for the endowment of the Columbia School of Journalism and the establishment of Pulitzer Prizes for journalism, letters, and other categories.

Publishing challenger to Joseph Pulitzer in the 1890s, William Randolph Hearst, here depicted in 1906 as a member of Congress, and his newspapers remained a not always constructive force in national politics well into the 1930s.

political corruption, monopoly, and slum problems.

"The *World* is the people's newspaper," Pulitzer boasted, and in the sense that it interested men and women of every sort, he was correct. Pulitzer's methods were quickly copied by competitors, especially William Randolph Hearst, who purchased the *New York Journal* in 1895 and soon outdid the *World* in sensationalism. But no other newspaperman of the era approached Pulitzer in originality, boldness, and the knack of reaching the masses without abandoning seriousness of purpose and basic integrity.

Magazine Journalism

Growth and ferment also characterized the magazine world. In 1865 there were about 700 magazines in the country; by the turn of the century, more than 5,000. Until the mid-1880s, few of the new magazines were in any way unusual. A handful of serious periodicals, such as the *Atlantic Monthly, Harper's,* and *The Century,* staid in tone and conservative in political caste, dominated the field. Articles on current affairs, a good deal of fiction and poetry, and historical and biographical studies filled their pages. Although they had great influence, none approached a mass circulation because of the limited size of the upper-middle-class audience they aimed at. *The Century* reached a peak in the 1880s of about 250,000 when it published a series of articles on Civil War battles by famous commanders, but it could not sustain that level. A circulation of 100,000 was considered good for such magazines.

The leading publisher of magazines directed at the average citizen in the 1860s and 1870s was Frank Leslie. His periodicals bore such titles as *Frank Leslie's Chimney Corner, Frank Leslie's Illustrated Newspaper,* and *Frank Leslie's Jolly Joker.* Leslie specialized in illustrations of current events (he put as many as 34 engravers to work on a single picture in order to bring it out quickly) and on providing what he frankly admitted was "mental pabulum"—a combination of cheap romantic fiction, old-fashioned poetry, jokes, and advice columns. Some of his magazines sold as many as 300,000 copies per issue.

After about 1885 new serious magazines such as *The Forum* (1886) and *The Arena* (1889) emphasized hard-hitting articles on controversial subjects by leading experts. The weekly *Literary Digest* (1890) offered summaries of press opinion on current events, and the *Review of Reviews* (1891) provided monthly commentary on the news.

Even more startling changes revolutionized the mass-circulation field. In 1889 Edward W. Bok became editor of the *Ladies' Home Journal.* Besides advice columns ("Ruth Ashmore's Side Talks with Girls"), he offered articles on child care, gardening, and interior decorating, published fine contemporary novelists, and commissioned public figures, such as Presidents Grover Cleveland and Benjamin Harrison, to discuss important questions. He printed colored reproductions of art masterpieces—the invention of cheap photoengraving was of enormous significance in the success of mass-circulation magazines—and crusaded for women's suffrage, conservation, and other reforms. Bok did more than cater to public tastes; he created new tastes.

Bok and his many competitors reached millions

of readers. Like Pulitzer in the newspaper field, they found ways of interesting rich and poor, the cultivated and the ignorant. Using the new printing technology to cut costs and drawing heavily on advertising revenues, they sold their magazines for 10 or 15 cents a copy and still made fortunes.

Colleges and Universities

The same forces that were affecting the dissemination of information were also altering higher education and professional training. The number of colleges rose from about 350 to 500 between 1878 and 1898, and the student body roughly tripled. Despite this growth, less than 2 percent of the college-age population attended college, but the aspirations of the nation's youth were rising, and more and more parents had the financial means necessary for fulfilling them.

More significant than the expansion of the colleges were the alterations in their curricula and in the atmosphere on the average campus. In 1870 most colleges were still small, limited in their offerings, intellectually stagnant. The ill-paid professors were seldom scholars of stature. Thereafter, change came like a flood tide. State universities proliferated; the federal government's land-grant program in support of training in "agriculture and the mechanic arts," established under the Morrill Act of 1862, came into its own; wealthy philanthropists poured fortunes into old institutions and founded new ones; professional schools of law, medicine, education, business, journalism, and other specialties increased in number.

In the forefront of reform was Harvard, the oldest and most prestigious college in the country. In the 1860s it possessed an excellent faculty, but teaching methods were antiquated, and the curriculum had remained almost unchanged since the colonial period. In 1869, however, a dynamic president, the chemist Charles W. Eliot, introduced the elective system, gradually eliminating required courses and expanding offerings in such areas as modern languages, economics, and the laboratory sciences.

Eliot also encouraged the faculty to experiment with new teaching methods, and he brought in professors with original minds and new ideas. One was Henry Adams, grandson of John Quincy Adams, who made the study of medieval history a true intellectual experience. "Mr. Adams roused the spirit

of inquiry and controversy in me," one student later wrote.

Under Eliot's guidance the standards of the medical school were raised. In the law school, Christopher Columbus Langdell introduced the case method of study. In some respects Eliot went too far—the elective system encouraged superficiality and laxness in many students—but on balance he transformed Harvard from a college, "a place to which a young man is sent," to a university, a place "to which he goes."

An even more important development in higher education was the founding of Johns Hopkins in 1876. This university was one of many established in the period by wealthy industrialists; its benefactor, the Baltimore merchant Johns Hopkins, had made his fortune in the Baltimore and Ohio Railroad. Its distinctiveness, however, was due to the vision of Daniel Coit Gilman, its first president.

Gilman modeled Johns Hopkins on the German universities, where meticulous research and freedom of inquiry were the guiding principles. In staffing the institution, he sought scholars of the highest reputation, scouring Europe as well as America in his search for talent and offering outstanding men high salaries for that time—up to $5,000 for a professor, roughly ten times the income of a skilled artisan. At the same time, he employed a number of relatively unknown but brilliant younger scholars, such as Herbert Baxter Adams, whom he made an associate in history on the strength of his excellent doctoral dissertation at the University of Heidelberg. Gilman promised his teachers good students and ample opportunity to pursue their own research (which explains why so many Hopkins professors repeatedly turned down attractive offers from other universities).

Johns Hopkins specialized in graduate education. In the generation after its founding, it turned out a remarkable percentage of the most important scholars in the nation, including Woodrow Wilson in political science, John Dewey in philosophy, Frederick Jackson Turner in history, and John R. Commons in economics. The seminar conducted by Herbert Baxter Adams was particularly productive; the Adams-edited *Johns Hopkins Studies in Historical and Political Science*, consisting of the doctoral dissertations of his students, was "the mother of similar studies in every part of the United States."

The success of Johns Hopkins did not stop the migration of American scholars to Europe; more than 2,000 matriculated at German universities during the 1880s. But as Hopkins graduates took up professorships at other institutions and as scholars trained elsewhere adopted the Hopkins methods, true graduate education became possible in most sections of the country.

The example of Johns Hopkins encouraged other wealthy individuals to endow universities offering advanced work. Clark University in Worcester, Massachusetts, founded by Jonas Clark, a merchant and real estate speculator, opened its doors in 1889. Its president, G. Stanley Hall, had been a professor of psychology at Hopkins, and he built the new university in that institution's image. More important was John D. Rockefeller's creation, the University of Chicago (1892). The president of the University of Chicago, William Rainey Harper, was a brilliant biblical scholar—he received his Ph.D. from Yale at the age of 18—and an imaginative administrator.

Like Daniel Coit Gilman, Harper sought top-flight scholars for his faculty. He offered such high salaries that he was besieged with over 1,000 applications. Armed with Rockefeller dollars, he "raided" the best institutions in the nation. He decimated the faculty of the new Clark University—"an act of wreckage," the indignant President Hall complained, "comparable to anything that the worst trust ever attempted against its competitors." Chicago offered first-class graduate and undergraduate education. During its first year there were 120 instructors for fewer than 600 students, and despite fears that the mighty tycoon Rockefeller would force his social and economic views on the institution, academic freedom was the rule.

State and federal aid to higher education expanded rapidly. The Morrill Act, granting land to each state at a rate of 30,000 acres for each senator and representative, provided the endowments that gave many important modern universities, such as Illinois, Michigan State, and Ohio State, their start. While the federal assistance was earmarked for specific subjects, the land-grant institutions offered a full range of courses, and all received additional state funds. They were coeducational from the start, and most developed professional schools and experimented with extension work and summer programs.

Typical of the better state institutions was the University of Michigan, which reached the top rank among the nation's universities during the presidency of James B. Angell (1871–1909). Like Eliot at Harvard, Angell expanded the undergraduate curriculum and strengthened the law and medical schools. He encouraged graduate studies, seeking to make Michigan "part of the great world of scholars," and sought ways in which the university could serve the general community.

Important advances were made in women's higher education beginning with Vassar College, which opened its doors to 300 women students in 1865. Wellesley and Smith, both founded in 1875, completed the so-called Big Three women's colleges. These three, the already established Mount Holyoke, and Bryn Mawr (1885), Barnard (1889), and Radcliffe (1893) became known as the Seven Sisters.

The only professional careers easily available to women graduates were nursing, teaching, and the new area called social work. Nevertheless, the remarkable women that these institutions trained were conscious of their uniqueness and determined to demonstrate their capabilities. Fewer than 40 percent of the first few generations of women graduates ever married. "Sending a daughter to college," the historian William H. Chafe writes, was "like letting the genie out of the bottle."

Not all the changes in higher education were beneficial. The elective system led to superficiality; students gained a smattering of knowledge of many subjects and mastered none. Intensive graduate work often produced narrowness of outlook and research monographs on trivial subjects. Attempts to apply the scientific method in fields such as history and economics often enticed students into making smug claims to objectivity and definitiveness that from the nature of the subjects they could not even approach in their work.

The gifts of rich industrialists sometimes came with strings, and college boards of trustees tended to be dominated by businessmen who sometimes attempted to impose their own social and economic beliefs on faculty members. Few professors actually lost their positions because their views offended trustees, but at many institutions trustees exerted constant nagging pressures that limited academic freedom and scholarly objectivity. At state colleges, politicians often interfered in academic affairs, even treating professorships as part of the patronage system.

Thorstein Veblen pointed out in his caustic study *The Higher Learning in America* (1918) that "the in-

A geology field trip in the 1880s sets out from the administration building of Smith College. Along with their picks and hammers, the young women carry baskets that look as though they might contain lunch.

trusion of businesslike ideals, aims and methods" harmed the universities in countless subtle ways. Size alone—the verbose Veblen called it "an executive weakness for spectacular magnitude"—became an end in itself, and the practical values of education were exalted over the humanistic. At many institutions professors came to be regarded as mere hired hands. In 1893 the members of the faculty of Stanford University were officially classified as personal servants of Mrs. Leland Stanford, widow of the founder. This was done in good cause—the Stanford estate was tied up in probate court and the ruling made it possible to pay professors out of Mrs. Stanford's allowance for household expenses—but that such a procedure was even conceivable must have appalled the scholarly world.

As the number of college graduates increased and as colleges ceased being primarily training institutions for clergymen, the influence of alumni on educational policies began to make itself felt—not always happily. Campus social activities became more important. Fraternities proliferated. Interest in organized sports first appeared as a laudable outgrowth of the general expansion of the curriculum, but soon athletic contests were playing a role all out of proportion to their significance. After football evolved as the leading intercollegiate sport it became a source of revenue that many colleges dared not neglect. Since students, alumni, and the public demanded winning teams, college administrators stooped to subsidizing student athletes, in extreme cases employing players who were not students at all. One exasperated college president quipped that the B.A. degree was coming to mean Bachelor of Athletics. Thus higher education reflected American values, with all their strengths and weaknesses.

Scientific Advances

Much has been made of the crassness of late-19th-century American life, yet the period produced intellectual achievements of the highest quality. If the business mentality dominated society, and if the great barons of industry, exalting practicality over theory, tended to look down on the life of the mind, intellectuals, quietly pondering the problems of their generation, nonetheless created works that affected the country as profoundly as the achievements of industrial organizers like Rockefeller and Carnegie and technicians like Edison and Bell.

In pure science America produced a number of outstanding figures in these years. The giant among them, whose contributions some experts rank with those of Newton, Darwin, and Einstein, was Josiah Willard Gibbs, professor of mathematical physics at Yale from 1871 to 1903. Gibbs created an entirely new science, physical chemistry, and made possible the study of how complex substances respond to changes in temperature and pressure. Purely theoretical at the time, Gibbs's ideas led to vital advances in metallurgy and in the manufacture of plastics, drugs, and other products. Gibbs is often used to illustrate the supposed indifference of the age to its great minds, but this is hardly fair; he was a shy, self-effacing man who cared little for the spotlight or for collecting disciples. He published his major papers in the obscure *Transactions of the Connecticut Academy of Arts and Sciences*. Furthermore, he was so far ahead of his time that only a handful of specialists had a glimmering of the importance of his work.

Of lesser but still major significance was the work of Albert A. Michelson of the University of Chicago, who made the first accurate measurements of the speed of light. Michelson's research helped prepare the way for Einstein's theory of relativity; in 1907 he became the first American scientist to win a Nobel Prize.

The New Social Sciences

In the social sciences, the achievements of the leading thinkers were closely connected to the practical issues of the age. The application of the theory of evolution to every aspect of human relations, the impact of industrialization on society—such topics were of intense concern to economists, sociologists, and historians. An understanding of Darwin increased the already strong interest in studying the development of institutions and their interactions. Controversies over trusts, slum conditions, and other problems drew scholars out of their towers and into practical affairs.

Social scientists were impressed by the progress being made in the physical and biological sciences. They eagerly applied the scientific method to their own specialties, hoping thereby to arrive at objective truths in fields that were by nature essentially subjective.

Among the economists, something approaching a revolution took place in the 1880s. The classical school, which maintained that immutable natural laws governed all human behavior and used the insights of Darwin only to justify unrestrained competition and laissez faire, was challenged by a group of young economists who argued that as times changed, economic theories and laws must be modified in order to remain relevant. Richard T. Ely, another of the scholars who made Johns Hopkins a font of new ideas in the 1880s, summarized the thinking of this group in 1885. The state, Ely proclaimed, is "an educational and ethical agency whose positive aid is an indispensable condition of human progress." Laissez faire was outmoded and dangerous. Economic problems were basically moral problems; their solution required "the united efforts of Church, state and science." The proper way to study these problems was by analyzing actual conditions, not by applying abstract laws or principles.

This approach produced the so-called institutionalist school of economics, whose members made detailed, on-the-spot investigations of labor unions, sweatshops, factories, and mines. The study of institutions, they believed, would lead to both theoretical insights and practical social reform. John R. Commons, one of Ely's students at Johns Hopkins and later professor of economics at the University of Wisconsin, was the outstanding member of this school. His ten-volume *Documentary History of American Industrial Society* (1910–1911) reveals the institutionalist approach at its best.

A similar revolution struck sociology in the mid-1880s. Prevailing opinion up to that time rejected the idea of government interference with the organization of society. The influence of the English social Darwinist Herbert Spencer, who objected even to public schools and the postal system, was immense. Spencer and his American disciples, among them Edward L. Youmans, editor of *Popular Science Monthly*, twisted Darwin's ideas to mean that society could be changed only by the force of evolution, which moved with cosmic slowness. "You and I can do nothing at all," Youmans told the reformer Henry George. "It's all a matter of evolution. Perhaps in four or five thousand years evolution may have carried men beyond this state of things."

Such a point of view made little sense in America, where society was changing rapidly and the range of government social and economic activity was expanding. It was first challenged by an obscure scholar employed by the U.S. Geological Survey, Lester Frank Ward. In *Dynamic Sociology* (1883) Ward assailed the Spencerians for ignoring the possibility of "the improvement of society by cold calculation." In *The Psychic Factors of Civilization* (1893) he blasted the "law of competition." Human progress, he argued, consisted of "triumphing little by little over this law," for example, by interfering with biological processes through the use of medicines to kill harmful bacteria.

Government regulation of the economy offered another illustration of how people could control the environment. "Nothing is more obvious today," Ward wrote in 1895, "than the signal inability of capital and private enterprise to take care of themselves unaided by the state." Society must indeed evolve, but it would evolve through careful social planning. Like the new economists, Ward emphasized the practical and ethical sides of his subject. Sociologists should seek "the betterment of society," he said, "Dynamic Sociology aims at the organization of happiness." Ward's arguments yielded few concrete results before 1900, but they ultimately demolished social Darwinism and laid the theoretical basis for the modern welfare state.

Similar currents of thought influenced other social sciences. In *Systems of Consanguinity* (1871) the pioneer anthropologist Lewis Henry Morgan developed a theory of social evolution and showed how kinship relationships reflected and affected tribal institutions. The new political scientists were also evolutionists and institutionalists. The Founding Fathers, living in a world dominated by Newton's concept of the universe as an immense, orderly machine, had conceived of the political system as an impersonal set of institutions and principles—a government of laws rather than of men. Nineteenth-century thinkers (John C. Calhoun is the best example) concerned themselves with abstractions, such as states' rights, and ignored the extralegal aspects of politics, such as parties and pressure groups. In the 1880s political scientists began to employ a different approach. In his doctoral dissertation at Johns Hopkins, *Congressional Govern-*

ment (1885), Woodrow Wilson analyzed the American political system. He concluded that the real locus of authority lay in the committees of Congress, which had no constitutional basis at all. Wilson was by no means a radical, but he viewed politics as a dynamic process and offered no theoretical objection to the expansion of state power. "Every means," he wrote in *The State* (1889), "by which society may be perfected through the instrumentality of government . . . ought certainly to be diligently sought."

Progressive Education

Traditionally, American teachers had emphasized the three Rs and relied on strict discipline and rote learning. Typical of the pedagogues of the period was the Chicago teacher, described by a reformer in the 1890s, who told her students firmly: "Don't stop to think; tell me what you know!" Yet new ideas were attracting attention. According to a German educator, Johann Friedrich Herbart, teachers could best arouse the interest of their students by relating new information to what they already knew; good teaching called for professional training, psychological insight, enthusiasm, and imagination, not merely facts and a birch rod. At the same time, evolutionists were pressing for a kind of education that would help children to "survive" by adapting to the demands of their environment.

Forward-looking educators seized on these ideas because dynamic social changes were making the old system increasingly inadequate. Settlement house workers discovered that slum children needed training in handicrafts, good citizenship, and personal hygiene as much as in reading and writing. They were appalled by the local schools, which suffered from the same ills—filth, overcrowding, rickety construction—that plagued the tenements and by school systems that were controlled by machine politicians who doled out teaching positions to party hacks and other untrained persons. They argued that playgrounds, nurseries, kindergartens, and adult education programs were essential in communities where most women worked and many people lacked much formal education. "We are impatient with the schools which lay all stress on reading and writing," Jane Addams declared. This type of education "fails to give the child any clew to the life about him."

The philosopher who summarized and gave direction to these forces was John Dewey, a professor at the University of Chicago. Dewey was concerned with the implications of evolution—indeed, of all science—for education. Essentially, his approach was ethical. Was the nation's youth being properly prepared for the tasks it faced in the modern world? In 1896, together with his wife Harriet, Dewey founded the Laboratory School to put his educational ideas to the test. Three years later he published *The School and Society*, describing and defending his theories.

"Education," Dewey insisted, was "the fundamental method of social progress and reform." To seek to improve conditions merely by passing laws was "futile." Moreover, in an industrial society the family no longer performed many of the educational functions it had carried out in an agrarian society. Farm children learn about nature, about work, about human character in countless ways denied to children in cities. The school can fill the gap by becoming "an embryonic community . . . with types of occupations that reflect the life of the larger society." At the same time, education should center on the child, and new information should be related to what the child already knows. Children's imaginations, energies, and curiosity are tools for broadening their outlooks and increasing their stores of information. Finally, the school should become an instrument for social reform, "saturating" children with the "spirit of service" and helping to produce a "society which is worthy, lovely, and harmonious." Education, in other words, ought to build character and teach good citizenship as well as transmit knowledge.

The School and Society created a stir, and Dewey immediately assumed leadership of what in the next generation was called progressive education. Although the gains made in public education before 1900 were more quantitative than qualitative and the philosophy dominant in most schools was not very different at the end of the century from that prevailing in Horace Mann's day, change was in the air.

Law and History

Even jurisprudence, by its nature conservative and rooted in tradition, felt the pressure of evolutionary thought and the new emphasis on studying insti-

On joining the faculty of the University of Chicago in 1894, John Dewey, a child of rural Vermont, took up the challenge of adapting American education practices and ideals to the rapidly urbanizing society that he saw all about him. His subsequent move to Columbia University's Teachers College in 1904 only reinforced his commitment to "progressive education."

tutions as they actually are. In 1881 Oliver Wendell Holmes, Jr., published *The Common Law*. Rejecting the ideas that judges should limit themselves to the mechanical explication of statutes and that law consisted only of what was written in law books, Holmes argued that "the felt necessities of the time" rather than precedent should determine the rules by which people are governed. "The life of the law has not been logic; it has been experience," he wrote. "It is revolting," he added on another occasion, "to have no better reason for a rule of law than that it was laid down in the time of Henry IV."

Holmes went on to a long and brilliant judicial career during which he repeatedly stressed the right of the people, through their elected representatives, to deal with contemporary problems in any reasonable way, unfettered by outmoded conceptions of the proper limits of government authority. Like the societies they regulated, laws should evolve as times and conditions changed, he said.

This way of reasoning caused no sudden reversal of judicial practice. Holmes's most notable opinions as a judge tended to be dissents. But his philosophy reflected the best thinking of the late 19th century, and his influence has grown with every decade of the 20th.

The new approach to knowledge did not always advance the cause of liberal reform. Historians in the graduate schools became intensely interested in studying the origins and evolution of political institutions. They concluded, after much "scientific" study of old charters and law codes, that the roots of democracy were to be found in the customs of the ancient tribes of northern Europe. This theory of the Teutonic origins of democracy, which has since been thoroughly discredited, fitted well with the prejudices of people of British stock, and it provided ammunition for those who favored restricting immigration and for those who argued that blacks were inferior beings.

Out of this work, however, came an essentially

Appointed to the Supreme Court in 1902 by his friend Theodore Roosevelt, Oliver Wendell Holmes, Jr., remained there for 29 years and seven presidents. His opinions, often in dissent, regularly called on his colleagues to exercise judicial restraint and allow elected officials to carry out their democratic responsibilities.

democratic concept, the frontier thesis of Frederick Jackson Turner, still another scholar trained at Johns Hopkins. Turner's essay "The Significance of the Frontier in American History" (1893) argued that the frontier experience, through which every section of the country had passed, had affected the thinking of the people and the shape of American institutions. The isolation of the frontier and the need during each successive westward advance to create civilization anew account, Turner wrote, for the individualism of Americans and the democratic character of their society. Nearly everything unique in our culture could be traced to the existence of the frontier, he claimed.

Life on the frontier was not as democratic as Turner believed, and his thesis certainly does not "explain" American development as completely as he said it did. Nevertheless, his work showed how important it was to investigate the evolution of institutions, and it encouraged historians to study social and economic, as well as purely political, subjects. If the claims of the new historians to objectivity and definitiveness were absurdly overstated, their emphasis on thoroughness, exactitude, and impartiality did much to raise standards in the profession. Perhaps the finest product of the new scientific school, a happy combination of meticulous scholarship and literary artistry, was Henry Adams's nine-volume *History of the United States During the Administrations of Jefferson and Madison.*

Realism in Literature

When what Mark Twain called the Gilded Age began, American literature was dominated by the romantic mood. All the important writers of the 1840s and 1850s except Hawthorne, Thoreau, and Poe were still living. Longfellow stood at the height of his fame, and the lachrymose Susan Warner—"tears on almost every page"—continued to turn out stories in the style of her popular *Wide, Wide World.* Romanticism, however, had lost its creative force; most writing in the decade after 1865 was sentimental trash pandering to the preconceptions of middle-class readers. Magazines like the *Atlantic Monthly* overflowed with stories about fair ladies worshiped from afar by stainless heroes, women coping selflessly with drunken husbands, and poor but honest youths rising through various combinations of virtue and assiduity to positions of wealth and influence. Most writers of fiction tended to ignore the eternal conflicts inherent in human nature.

The patent unreality, even dishonesty, of contemporary fiction eventually caused a reaction. The most important forces giving rise to the Age of Realism were those that were transforming every other aspect of American life: industrialism, with its associated complexities and social problems; the theory of evolution, which made people more aware of the force of the environment and the basic conflicts of existence; the new science, which taught dispassionate, empirical observation. Novelists undertook the examination of slum life, the conflict between capital and labor, and political corruption. They created multidimensional characters, depicted persons of every social class, used dialect and slang to capture the flavor of particular types, and fashioned painstaking descriptions of the surroundings into which they placed their subjects.*

Mark Twain

Easy as it was to romanticize the West, that region lent itself to the realistic approach as well. Almost of necessity, novelists writing about the West described coarse characters from the lower levels of society and dealt with crime and violence. It would have been difficult indeed to write a genteel romance about a mining camp. The outstanding figure of western literature, the first great American realist, was Mark Twain.

Twain was born Samuel L. Clemens in 1835. He grew up in Hannibal, Missouri, on the banks of the Mississippi. After mastering the printer's trade and working as a riverboat pilot, he went west to Nevada in 1861. The wild, rough life of Virginia City fascinated him, but prospecting got him nowhere, and he became a reporter for the *Territorial Enterprise.* Soon he was publishing humorous stories about the local life under the nom de plume Mark Twain. In 1865, while working in California, he wrote "The Celebrated Jumping Frog of Calaveras County," a story that brought him national recognition. A tour of Europe and the Holy Land in 1867–1868 led to *The Innocents Abroad* (1869), which made him famous.

---

* The romantic novel did not disappear. General Lew Wallace's *Ben Hur* (1880) and Frances Hodgson Burnett's *Little Lord Fauntleroy* (1886) were best-sellers.

Twain's greatness stemmed from his keen reportorial eye and ear, his eagerness to live life to the fullest, his marvelous sense of humor, and his ability to be at once in society and outside it, to love humanity yet be repelled by human vanity and perversity. He epitomized the zest and adaptability of his age and also its materialism. No contemporary pursued the almighty dollar more assiduously. An inveterate speculator, he made a fortune with his pen and lost it in foolish business ventures. He wrote tirelessly and endlessly about America and Europe, about his own times and the feudal past, about tourists, slaves, tycoons, cracker-barrel philosophers— and human destiny. He was equally at home and equally successful on the Great River of his childhood, in the mining camps, and in the eastern bourgeois society of his mature years. But every prize slipped through his fingers. Twain died a dark pessimist, surrounded by adulation yet alone, an alien and a stranger in the land he loved and knew so well.

Twain excelled every contemporary in the portrayal of character. In his biting satire *The Gilded Age* (1873) he created that magnificent mountebank Colonel Beriah Sellers, purveyor of eyewash ("the Infallible Imperial Oriental Optic Liniment") and false hopes, ridiculous, unscrupulous, but lovable. In *Huckleberry Finn* (1884), his masterpiece, his portrait of the slave Jim, loyal, patient, naive, yet withal a man, is unforgettable. When Huck takes advantage of Jim's credulity merely for his own amusement, the slave turns from him coldly and says: "Dat truck dah is trash; en trash is what people is dat puts dirt on de head er dey fren's en makes 'em ashamed." And there is Huck Finn himself, full of devilry, romantic, amoral—up to a point—and at bottom the complete realist. When Miss Watson tells him he can get anything he wants by praying for it, he makes the effort, is disillusioned, and concludes: "If a body can get anything they pray for, why don't Deacon Winn get back the money he lost on pork? . . . Why can't Miss Watson fat up? No, I says to myself, there ain't nothing in it."

Whether directly, as in *The Innocents Abroad* and in his fascinating account of the world of the river pilot, *Life on the Mississippi* (1883), or when transformed by his imagination in works of fiction such as *Tom Sawyer* (1876) and *A Connecticut Yankee in King Arthur's Court* (1889), Mark Twain always put much of his own experience and feeling into his work. A story, he told a fellow author, "must be

Mark Twain, in a photograph (left) taken five years before his death in 1910, was both a satirist of American optimism in his writings and its victim in misguided business ventures that brought him to the brink of bankruptcy. He is caricatured (right) riding his "Celebrated Jumping Frog of Calaveras County" in this 1872 cartoon by English artist Frederick Waddy.

written with the blood out of a man's heart." His innermost confusions, the clash between his recognition of the pretentiousness and meanness of human beings and his wish to be accepted by society, added depths and overtones to his writing that together with his comic genius give it lasting appeal. He could not rise above the sentimentality and prudery of his generation entirely, for these qualities were part of his nature. He never dealt effectively with sexual love, for example, and often, even in *Huckleberry Finn,* contrived to end his tales on absurdly optimistic notes that ring false after so many brilliant pages portraying life as it is. Rough and uneven like the man himself, his works catch more of the spirit of the age he named than those of any other writer.

William Dean Howells

Twain's realism was far less self-conscious than that of his longtime friend William Dean Howells. Like Twain, Howells, who was born in Ohio in 1837, had little formal education. He learned the printer's trade from his father and became a reporter for the *Ohio State Journal.* In 1860 he wrote a campaign biography of Lincoln and was rewarded with an appointment as consul in Venice. His sketches in *Venetian Life* (1866) were a product of this experience. After the Civil War he worked briefly for *The Nation* in New York and then moved to Boston, where he became editor of the *Atlantic Monthly.* In 1886 he returned to New York as editor of *Harper's.*

A long series of novels and much literary criticism poured from Howells's pen over the next 30 years. He was not at first a critic of society, being content to write about what he called the "smiling aspects" of life. Realism to Howells meant concern for the complexities of individual personalities and faithful description of the genteel, middle-class world he knew best. But he had a sharp eye, an open mind, and a social conscience. Gradually he became aware of the problems that industrialization had created. In 1885, in *The Rise of Silas Lapham,* he dealt with some of the ethical conflicts faced by businessmen in a competitive society. The harsh public reaction to the Haymarket bombing in 1886 stirred him, and he threw himself into a futile campaign to prevent the execution of the anarchist suspects. Thereafter he moved rapidly toward the left; soon he was calling himself a socialist. "After fifty years of optimistic content with 'civilization' . . . I now abhor it, and feel that it is coming out all wrong in the end, unless it bases itself anew on a real equality," he wrote. But he added immediately: "Meanwhile I wear a fur-lined overcoat, and live in all the luxury my money can buy."

Howells was more than a reformer, more than an inventor of utopias like Edward Bellamy, though he admired Bellamy and wrote a utopian novel of his own, *A Traveller from Altruria* (1894). In *A Hazard of New Fortunes* (1890) he attempted to portray the whole range of metropolitan life, weaving the destinies of a dozen interesting personalities from diverse sections and social classes. The book represents a triumph of realism in its careful descriptions of various sections of New York and the ways of life of rich and poor, in the intricacy of its characters, and in its rejection of sentimentality and romantic love. "A man knows that he can love and wholly cease to love, not once merely, but several times," the narrator says, "but in regard to women he cherishes the superstition of the romances that love is once for all, and forever."

Howells was also the most influential critic of his time. He helped bring the best contemporary foreign writers, including Tolstoy, Dostoyevski, Ibsen, and Zola, to the attention of readers in the United States, and he encouraged many important young American novelists, among them Stephen Crane, Theodore Dreiser, Frank Norris, and Hamlin Garland.

Some of these writers went beyond Howells's realism to what they called naturalism. Many, like Twain and Howells, began as newspaper reporters.

Working for a big-city daily in the 1890s was sure to teach anyone a great deal about the dark side of life. Naturalist writers believed that the human being was essentially an animal, a helpless creature whose fate was determined by environment. Their world was Darwin's world—mindless, without mercy or justice. They wrote chiefly about the most primitive emotions—lust, hate, greed. In *Maggie, A Girl of the Streets* (1893) Stephen Crane described the seduction, degradation, and eventual suicide of a young woman, all set against the background of a sordid slum; in *The Red Badge of Courage* (1895) he captured the pain and humor of war. In *McTeague* (1899) Frank Norris told the story of a brutal, dull-witted dentist who murdered his greed-crazed wife with his bare fists.

Such stuff was too strong for Howells, yet he recognized its importance and befriended the younger writers in many ways. He found a publisher for *Maggie* after it had been rejected many times, and he wrote appreciative reviews of the work of Garland and Norris. Even Theodore Dreiser, who was contemptuous of Howells's writings and considered him hopelessly middle-class in point of view, appreciated his aid and praised his influence on American literature. Dreiser's first novel, *Sister Carrie* (1900), treated sex so forthrightly that it was withdrawn after publication.

Henry James

Henry James was very different in spirit and background from the tempestuous naturalists. Born to wealth and reared in a cosmopolitan atmosphere, James spent most of his mature life in Europe, writing novels, short stories, plays, and volumes of criticism. Although far removed from the world of practical affairs, he was preeminently a realist, determined, as he once said, "to leave a multitude of pictures of my time" for the future to contemplate. He admired the European realists and denounced the "floods of tepid soap and water which under the name of novels are being vomited forth" by the romancers. "All life belongs to you," he told his fellow novelists. "There is no impression of life, no manner of seeing it and feeling it, to which the plan of the novelist may not offer a place."

While he preferred living in the cultivated surroundings of London high society, James yearned for the recognition of his fellow Americans almost as avidly as Mark Twain. However, he was incapable of modifying his rarefied, overly subtle manner of writing. Most serious writers of the time admired his books, and he received many honors, but he never achieved widespread popularity. His major theme was the clash of American and European cultures, his primary interest the close-up examination of wealthy, sensitive, yet often corrupt persons in a cultivated but far from polite society.

James dealt with social issues such as feminism and the difficulties faced by artists in the modern world, but he subordinated them to his interest in his subjects as individuals. *The American* (1877) told the story of the love of a wealthy American in Paris for a French noblewoman who rejected him because her family disapproved of his "commercial" background. *The Portrait of a Lady* (1881) described the disillusionment of an intelligent woman married to a charming but morally bankrupt man and her eventual decision to remain with him nonetheless. *The Bostonians* (1886) was a complicated and psychologically sensitive study of the varieties of female behavior in a seemingly uniform social situation.

James's reputation, greater today than in his lifetime, rests more on his highly refined accounts of the interactions of individuals and their environment and his masterful commentaries on the novel as a literary form than on his ability as a storyteller. Few major writers have been more long-winded, more prone to circumlocution. Yet few have been so dedicated to their art, possessed of such psychological penetration, or so successful in producing a large body of important work.

Realism in Art

American painters responded to the times as writers did, but with one difference: Despite the new concern for realism, the romantic tradition retained its vitality. Preeminent among the realists was Thomas Eakins, who was born in Philadelphia in 1844. Eakins studied in Europe in the late 1860s and was influenced by the great realists of the 17th century, Velázquez and Rembrandt. Returning to America in 1870, he passed the remainder of his life teaching and painting in Philadelphia.

The scientific spirit of the age suited Eakins perfectly. He mastered human anatomy; some of his finest paintings, such as *The Gross Clinic* (1875), are graphic illustrations of surgical operations. He was an early experimenter with motion pictures, using the camera to capture exactly the attitudes of human beings and animals in action. Like his friend Walt Whitman, whose portrait is one of his greatest achievements, Eakins gloried in the ordinary. But he had none of Whitman's weakness for sham and self-delusion. His portraits are monuments to his integrity. Never would he touch up or soften a likeness to please his sitter. When the Union League of Philadelphia commissioned a canvas of Rutherford B. Hayes, Eakins showed the president working in his shirtsleeves, which scandalized the club fathers. His work was no mere mirror reflecting surface values. His study of six men bathing (*The Swimming Hole*) is a stark portrayal of nakedness; his surgical scenes catch the tenseness of a situation without descending into sensationalism.

Winslow Homer, a Boston-born painter best known for his brilliant watercolors, was also influenced by realist ideas. Homer was a lithographer as well as a master of the watercolor medium, yet he had had almost no formal training. Indeed, he was contemptuous of academicians and refused to go abroad to study. Aesthetics seemed not to concern him at all; he liked to shock people by referring to his profession as "the picture line." His concern for accuracy was so intense that in preparation for painting *The Life Line* (1884) he made a trip to Atlantic City to observe the handling of a breeches buoy. "When I have selected [a subject]," he said, "I paint it exactly as it appears."

During the Civil War, Homer worked as an artist-reporter for *Harper's Weekly,* and he continued to do magazine illustrations for some years thereafter. He roamed America, painting scenes of southern farm life, Adirondack campers, and, after about 1880, magnificent seascapes and studies of fishermen and sailors.

Homer's work contains romantic elements. His *Gulf Stream* (1899), showing a sailor on a small, broken boat menaced by an approaching waterspout and a school of sharks, and his *Fox Hunt* (1893), in which huge, ominous crows hover over a fox at bay, express his interest in the violence and drama of raw nature, a distinctly romantic theme. However, his approach, even in these works, was utterly prosaic. When some women complained about the fate of the black sailor in *Gulf Stream,* Homer wrote his dealer sarcastically: "Tell these ladies that the unfortunate Negro . . . will be rescued and returned

Thomas Eakins's interest in science was as great as his interest in art. In the early 1880s he collaborated with the photographer Eadweard Muybridge in serial-action photographic experiments and later devised a special camera for his anatomical studies; this is one of his pictures taken with the Marey wheel.

to his friends and home, and live happily ever after."

The outstanding romantic painter of the period was Albert Pinkham Ryder, a strange, neurotic genius haunted by the mystery and poetry of the sea. Ryder was born in New Bedford, Massachusetts, in 1847, during that city's heyday as a whaling port and spent most of his mature years in New York City, living and working in a dirty, cluttered attic studio. He typified the solitary romantic—brooding, eccentric, otherworldly, mystical. His heavily glazed paintings of dark seas and small boats "bathed in an atmosphere of golden luminosity" beneath a pale moon, weird canvases like *The Race Track* (*Death on a Pale Horse*), which shows a specter carrying a scythe riding on an empty track under an ominous sky, radiate a strange magic.

The careers of Eakins, Homer, and Ryder show that the late-19th-century American environment was not uncongenial to first-rate artists. Nevertheless, at least two major American painters aban-

doned native shores for Europe. One was James A. McNeill Whistler, whose portrait of his mother, which he called *Arrangement in Grey and Black,* is probably the most famous canvas ever painted by an American. Whistler left the United States in 1855 when he was 21 and spent most of his life in Paris and London. "I shall come to America," he announced grandly, "when the duty on works of art is abolished!"

Whistler made a profession of eccentricity, but he was a talented and versatile artist. Some of his portraits are triumphs of realism, while his misty studies of the London waterfront are thoroughly romantic in conception. Paintings such as "Whistler's Mother" represent still another expression of his talent. Spare and muted in tone, they are more interesting as precise arrangements of color and space than as images of particular objects; they had considerable influence on the course of modern art.

The second important expatriate artist was Mary Cassatt, daughter of a wealthy Pittsburgh banker

The impact of Eakins's photographic experiments (see figure on previous page) can be seen in The Swimming Hole, *painted in 1883. Eakins was then director of the Pennsylvania Academy's art school.*

and sister of Alexander J. Cassatt, who was president of the Pennsylvania Railroad around the turn of the century. She went to Paris as a tourist and dabbled in art like many conventional young socialites, then was caught up in the impressionist movement and decided to become a serious painter. Her work is more French than American and was little appreciated in the United States before the First World War. When once she returned to America for a visit, the *Philadelphia Public Ledger* reported: "Mary Cassatt, sister of Mr. Cassatt, president of the Pennsylvania Railroad, returned from Europe yesterday. She has been studying painting in Paris, and owns the smallest Pekinese dog in the world."

If Mary Cassatt was unappreciated and if Whistler had reasons for considering Americans uncul-

tured, it remains true that interest in art was considerable. Museums and art schools increased in number, and settlement house workers put on exhibitions that attracted enthusiastic crowds. Wealthy patrons gave countless commissions to portrait painters and poured fortunes into collecting. Martin A. Ryerson, with money made in lumber, bought the works of the French impressionists when few Americans understood their importance. Charles L. Freer of the American Car and Foundry Company was a specialist in oriental art. John G. Johnson, a successful corporation lawyer, covered the walls of his Philadelphia mansion with Italian primitives, accumulated before anyone else appreciated them. Other enthusiasts, notably the banker J. P. Morgan, employed experts to help them put together their collections. Nor were the advanced painters of the day rejected by wealthy patrons. Though Eakins's work was undervalued, he received many important commissions. Some of Homer's canvases commanded thousands of dollars, and so did those of the radical Whistler.

The Pragmatic Approach

It would have been remarkable indeed if the intellectual ferment of the late 19th century had not affected contemporary ideas about the meaning of life, the truth of revealed religion, moral values, and similar fundamental problems. In particular, the theory of evolution, so important in altering contemporary views of science, history, and social relations, produced significant changes in American thinking about religious and philosophical questions.

Evolution posed an immediate challenge to religion: If Darwin was correct, the biblical account of the creation was obviously untrue and the idea that the human race had been formed in God's image was highly unlikely. A bitter controversy erupted, described by President Andrew D. White of Cornell University in *The Warfare of Science with Theology in Christendom* (1896). While millions continued to believe in the literal truth of the Bible, among intellectuals, lay and clerical, victory went to the evolutionists because in addition to the arguments of the geologists and the biologists, scholars were throwing light on the historical development of the Bible, showing it to be of human rather than divine origin.

Evolution did not undermine the faith of any large percentage of the population. If the account of the Creation in Genesis could not be taken literally, the Bible remained a repository of wisdom and inspiration. Such books as John Fiske's *Outlines of Cosmic Philosophy* (1874) provided religious persons with the comforting thesis that evolution, while true, was merely God's way of ordering the universe—as the liberal preacher Washington Gladden put it, "a most impressive demonstration of the presence of God in the world."

The effects of Darwinism on philosophy were less dramatic but in the end more significant. Fixed systems and eternal verities were difficult to justify in a world that was constantly evolving. By the early 1870s a few philosophers had begun to reason that

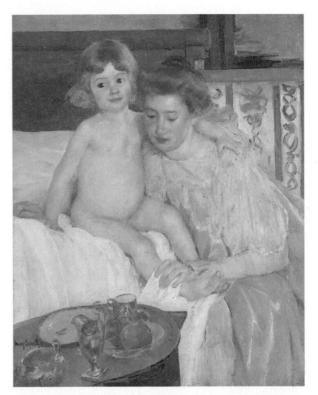

Now widely recognized as one of America's finest impressionist painters, Mary Cassatt found her talent ignored in this country during her lifetime. She portrayed mothers and children with a grace and tenderness that (some would say) only a woman artist could convey.

ideas and theories mattered little except when applied to specifics. "Nothing justifies the development of abstract principles but their utility in enlarging our concrete knowledge of nature," wrote Chauncey Wright, secretary of the American Academy of Arts and Sciences. In "How to Make Our Ideas Clear" (1878), Wright's friend Charles S. Peirce, an amazingly versatile and talented albeit obscure thinker, argued that concepts could be fairly understood only in terms of their practical effects. Once the mind accepted the truth of evolution, Peirce believed, logic required that it accept the impermanence even of scientific laws. There was, he wrote, "an element of indeterminacy, spontaneity, or absolute chance in nature."

This startling philosophy, which Peirce called pragmatism, was presented in more understandable language by William James, brother of the novelist. James was one of the most remarkable persons of his generation. Educated in London, Paris, Bonn, and Geneva—as well as at Harvard—he studied painting, participated in a zoological expedition to South America, took a medical degree, and was a professor at Harvard successively of comparative anatomy, psychology, and philosophy. His *Principles of Psychology* (1890) may be said to have established that discipline as a modern science. His *Varieties of Religious Experience* (1902), which treated the subject from both psychological and philosophical points of view, helped thousands of readers to reconcile their religious faith with their increasing knowledge of psychology and the physical universe.

Although he was less rigorous a logician than Peirce, James's wide range and his verve and imagination as a writer made him by far the most influential philosopher of his time. He rejected the deterministic interpretation of Darwinism and all other one-idea explanations of existence. Belief in free will was one of his axioms; environment might influence survival, but so did the *desire* to survive, which existed independent of surrounding circumstances. Even truth was relative; it did not exist in the abstract but *happened* under particular circumstances. What a person thought helped to make thought occur or come true. The mind, James wrote in a typically vivid phrase, has "a vote" in determining truth. Religion was true, for example, because people were religious.

The pragmatic approach inspired much of the reform spirit of the late 19th century and even more of that of the early 20th. James's hammer blows shattered the laissez faire extremism of Herbert Spencer. In "Great Men and Their Environment" (1880) he argued that social changes were brought about by the actions of geniuses whom society had selected and raised to positions of power, rather than by the impersonal force of the environment. Such reasoning fitted the preconceptions of rugged individualists yet encouraged those dissatisfied with society to work for change. Educational reformers like John Dewey, the institutionalist school of economists, settlement house workers, and other reformers adopted pragmatism eagerly.

Yet pragmatism brought Americans face to face with somber problems. Though relativism made them optimistic, it bred insecurity, for there could be no certainty, no comforting reliance on any eternal value in the absence of absolute truth. Pragmatism also seemed to suggest that the end justified the means, that what worked was more important than what ought to be. At the time of James's death in 1910, the *Commercial and Financial Chronicle* pointed out that the pragmatic philosophy was helpful to businessmen in making decisions. By emphasizing practice at the expense of theory, the new

William James (with the beard) and his novelist brother Henry James in a warm photographic portrait taken around 1900.

philosophy encouraged materialism, anti-intellectualism, and other unlovely aspects of the American character. And what place had conventional morality in such a system? Perhaps pragmatism placed too much reliance on the free will of human beings, ignoring their capacity for selfishness and self-delusion.

The people of the new century found pragmatism a heady wine. They would quaff it freely and enthusiastically—down to the bitter dregs.

Milestones

1865 Vassar College founded
1869 Charles W. Eliot becomes president of Harvard
1874 Chautauqua movement begins
1876 Johns Hopkins University founded
1881 Oliver Wendell Holmes, Jr., *The Common Law*
1883 Joseph Pulitzer purchases the *New York World*

1886 Ottmar Mergenthaler invents the linotype machine
William Dean Howells becomes editor of *Harper's*
1889 Edward W. Bok becomes editor of the *Ladies' Home Journal*
1890 William James, *Principles of Psychology*
1893 Frederick Jackson Turner, "The Significance of the Frontier in American History"
1899 John Dewey, *The School and Society*

SUPPLEMENTARY READING

Titles marked with an asterisk have been published in paperback.

All the surveys of American intellectual history deal extensively with this period. See, for example, Louis Hartz, **The Liberal Tradition in America*** (1955), and Clinton Rossiter, **Conservatism in America*** (1962). P. A. Carter, **The Spiritual Crisis of the Gilded Age** (1971), and H. S. Commager, **The American Mind*** (1950), contain much interesting information, and there are useful essays on aspects of the subject in H. W. Morgan (ed.), **The Gilded Age: A Reappraisal*** (1970), Ray Ginger, **The Age of Excess*** (1965), is also stimulating.

The best treatment of the Chautauqua movement is Victoria Case and R. O. Case, **We Called It Culture** (1948). Trends in the history of journalism are discussed in B. A. Weisberger, **The American Newspaperman** (1961), George Juergens, **Joseph Pulitzer and the *New York World*** (1966), and W. A. Swanberg, **Citizen Hearst*** (1961).

On higher education, see L. R. Veysey, **The Emergence of the American University*** (1965), E. A. Green, **Mary Lyon and Mount Holyoke** (1979), Hugh Hawkins, **Pioneer: A History of the Johns Hopkins University** (1960), and Hawkins's **Between Harvard and America: The Educational Leadership of Charles W. Eliot** (1972). Thorstein Veblen, **The Higher Learning in America*** (1918), is full of stimulating opinions.

For developments in American science, see the excellent essay by P. F. Boller, Jr., in H. W. Morgan (ed.), **The Gilded Age*** (1970). A good general introduction to the work of the social scientists is Sidney Fine, **Laissez Faire and the General-Welfare State** (1957), but see also Richard Hofstadter, **Social Darwinism in American Thought*** (1944), and Jurgen Herbst, **The German Historical School in American Scholarship** (1965). As to trends in educational theory, see L. A. Cremin, **American Education: The Metropolitan Experience** (1988). On Twain, see Justin Kaplan, **Mr. Clemens and Mark Twain*** (1966); on Howells, see E. H. Cady, **The Realist at War** (1958); on James, see Leon Edel, **Henry James*** (1953–1962).

Two good sources on pragmatism are Hofstadter's **Social Darwinism** and Bruce Kuklick, **The Rise of American Philosophy** (1977).

American Lives:
The Johnson Family of Nebraska

Settlers entering Nebraska

Jens Johnson was 22 when he emigrated to the United States from Denmark in 1849. He made his way west to Madison, Wisconsin, where he worked at odd jobs while accumulating enough money to buy a wagon, horses, and a plow. He married a young Norwegian woman in Madison. They were able to get a small farm in the western part of the state, where they began to raise a family. When the Civil War broke out, Johnson volunteered. He fought all through the war without a scratch, serving under Grant at Shiloh and Vicksburg, later under Sherman "from Atlanta to the Sea." Jens thought Grant showed little regard for his men and dismissed him as "a butcher." But he greatly admired Sherman.

Shortly after he returned to Wisconsin his wife died of tuberculosis, leaving him with four young children, all girls. He packed them into a covered wagon with all his worldly goods and set out for Nebraska, where in the northeastern part of the state, he took up a quarter section under the Homestead Act. They lived in a tent made from the cover of the wagon until he built a house.

In 1867, Johnson met Edel Maria Bille, a recently arrived Danish woman who was living with her aunt on a nearby farm, and soon persuaded her to marry him. They had four children, three of them boys. For years the family lived almost entirely on what their farm produced. They grew wheat, corn, and vegetables and raised cattle, sheep, pigs, and chickens, as well as horses. They had plenty of wood for the fire and for fencing on their own property. Wild berries for jams grew in abundance.

Jens had his wheat ground at a nearby mill, the miller doing the job in exchange for a quarter of the flour. He slaughtered an occasional cow or some pigs, kept the meat frozen in winter, then smoked or salted the rest when the warm weather came. He kept a large store of wool from his sheep, which the women used to knit stockings, mittens, and sweaters for the family.

Of course the Johnsons had to have money to buy things like sugar and coffee, or manufactured goods such as shoes, dishes, and wire for fences. To pay for these things they sold some butter and eggs, or perhaps a cow in the nearby town of Homer. It was a life of hard, endless

Family farm in northeastern Nebraska

labor; even the smallest children contributed. But the Johnsons saw what they were doing not as working but as living. Time was their money, a kind, after all, that had to be spent one way or another. They had little real money, but little need for it, and everyone felt needed.

That part of Nebraska was being settled by people of many backgrounds. First the New Englanders, who had arrived during the struggle over slavery in the territories that resulted from the passage of the Kansas-Nebraska Act. Many veterans had arrived, like Jens Johnson, after the Civil War. One of his friends was a Swede who had come to America to escape a jail term for having killed a deer that was eating his crops. There was a group of Germans, including a rather odd former philosophy professor named Winkhaus, who was said to be "brain-broke" from having spent too much time thinking. The district contained settlers from Ireland too, as well as a large Danish community.

It was by no means an ideal community. The native-born settlers disliked the immigrants, for some reason especially the Danes. The Protestants distrusted the Irish because they were Catholics. The local Republican politicians waved the bloody shirt, while most of the hardworking farmers expressed contempt for the politicians, claiming that they were being governed by "a wasp's nest of crooks and scoundrels."

The only public school in the area was open from December through February. The teachers were inexperienced. Much stress was placed on memory, especially on learning to spell. The oldest of the Johnson boys, Alvin, remembered struggling to master the following sentence: "Bill Wright, the mill wright, can't write 'rite' right." The boys dreamed of going west; a branch of the Oregon Trail ran past the farm and canvas-topped prairie schooners were still to be seen going by in the 1870s.

In the late 1880s Jens Johnson turned management of the farm over to his three sons. They decided to change it from a self-sufficient, "farming-as-a-way-of-life" enterprise to a business. They cleared more land in order to grow more corn and oats. They raised as many hogs and cattle as possible, intending to sell them to meat packers. But the pigs were wiped out by hog cholera and chinch bugs destroyed the entire crop of oats. Eventually they began to turn a profit but, as Alvin later wrote, by 1892 they had done "more worrying than my father did in all his life."

Eventually, all the Johnsons left the farm. Two of the older girls got jobs in the Indian Service, another taught school for a time then moved to New York to study medicine at Cornell. The two younger sons became lawyers. Alvin became a college professor and eventually the founder and director of the New School for Social Research. Jens and Edel Johnson sold the farm, moved to a nearby town, then to California, where they spent their last years.

A country school

Politics: Local, State, and National

"What a pity he is so dreadfully senatorial," said Mrs. Lee.
"Otherwise I rather admire him."

   "Now he is settling down to his work," continued Carrington. "See
how he dodges all the sharp issues. . . . What a genius the fellow has
for leading a party."

HENRY ADAMS, Democracy, *1880*

The ordinary American voter does not object to mediocrity. He has a
lower conception of the qualities requisite to make a statesman than
those who direct public opinion in Europe have.

JAMES BRYCE, Why Great Men Are Not
Chosen President, *1888*

boards of experts, once broad policies have been laid down by Congress, but in the 19th century, specialists had not yet arrived at this conclusion. Reformers could thunder self-righteously against the spoils system, but how could political parties exist without it? Young economists like Richard T. Ely and Henry Carter Adams were insisting that laissez faire was outmoded, but no one had yet devised the techniques and instruments that would have to be used if the economy was to be measured and managed effectively by a central authority. The embryonic social sciences had not even collected the statistical information necessary for efficient direction of the economy. If the politicians steered clear of the "real" issues, they did so as much out of a healthy respect for their own ignorance as out of any desire to avoid controversy.

T he major American parties have nearly always avoided clear-cut stands on controversial questions in order to appeal to as wide a segment of the electorate as possible, but in the last quarter of the 19th century, their equivocations assumed abnormal proportions. This was due in part to the precarious balance of power between them: Neither dared declare itself too clearly on any question lest it drive away more voters than it attracted.

The rapid pace of social and economic change also militated against political decisiveness. No one in or out of politics had as yet devised effective solutions for many current problems. When party leaders tried to deal with the money question, they discovered that the bankers and the professional economists were as confused as the public at large. "We dabble in theories of our own and clutch convulsively at the doctrines of others," a Philadelphia banker confessed. "From the vast tract of mire by which the subject is surrounded, overlaid, and besmeared, it is almost impossible to arrive at anything like a fair estimate of its real nature." How could mere politicians act rationally or consistently in such circumstances?

The parties stumbled badly when they confronted the tariff problem because tariffs in a complex industrial economy are not susceptible to determination by counting noses. Modern experience has shown that they are better arrived at by impartial

Politicial Decision Making: Ethnic and Religious Issues

The major parties had national committees, and delegates met in national conventions every four years to select their presidential candidates and draft "platforms," but they remained essentially separate state organizations. Professionals spent far more time dealing with local people and local issues than they did thinking about tariffs and money policy and other matters of broad national concern. They had to understand how different kinds of people felt about such matters if they wanted to win their support. In many parts of the country, that meant entering a veritable maze of diverse and often conflicting interests. People's ethnic backgrounds, their religious affiliations, whether they lived in cities or on farms, how they felt about the Civil War, and countless aspects of their lives that had no apparent relationship to national political issues affected whether they voted Republican or Democratic.

The politicians of the period were not shy about explaining why people voted the way they did. Senator George Frisbie Hoar of Massachusetts, for example, offered such an analysis in an 1889 magazine article. The Republicans, he wrote, were

the men who do the work of piety and charity in our churches . . . who administer our school systems . . . who own and till their own farms . . . who perform skilled labor . . . who went to the war . . . who paid the debt, and kept the currency sound, and saved the nation's honor.

The Democrats, he went on, were "the old slave-owner and slave-driver, the saloon-keeper, the ballot-box-stuffer, the Kuklux, the criminal class of the great cities, and men who cannot read or write."

Despite the partisan character of Hoar's analysis, it contained an element of truth; a more disinterested observer, James Bryce, wrote in *The American Commonwealth* that at least in the North, "the best people" were Republicans, whereas a "vast ignorant fluctuating mass of people" were Democrats. But if Hoar or even Bryce were correct, the Republicans would have swept the northern states at every election, which they assuredly did not.

In any case, it was (and it remains) even more difficult to discover *why* people voted one way or the other in the decades after the Civil War. People of Irish descent tended to vote Democratic, but whether they did so because they lived in cities or because they were Roman Catholics or because they believed that most Americans of British descent voted Republican was not always clear.

Plausible generalizations break down when examined closely. Northerners were Republicans, southerners Democrats; Catholics were Democrats, Protestants Republicans; German-Americans voted Democratic, Americans of Scandinavian descent Republican. All these statements and many others like them are subject to a multitude of exceptions. And of course they conflict one with another. They offer little guidance for predicting how, for example, a German Lutheran living in Tennessee would vote.

Detailed analyses of local elections in districts where people of particular religious and ethnic backgrounds lived suggest that Protestants who belonged to churches that emphasized ritual and the passive acceptance of authority tended to vote Democratic; those who worshiped in churches where the stress was on simple services, personal piety, and the importance of being "saved" usually voted Republican. Middle western German Lutherans were "ritualists," and many did tend to vote for Democrats. But as Paul Kleppner has explained in *The Cross of Culture,* "Not all German Lutherans were equally ritualistic," and numbers of them voted for Republicans.

Local and state issues also interacted with religious and ethnic backgrounds to affect political attitudes. Prohibition, public education, and other matters subject to state and local control that seemed to have little or no relation to religion were in fact questions on which voters split along religious and ethnic lines. All these tangles influenced the way political leaders devised their strategies and chose candidates for office. And how voters felt about local issues almost invariably affected how they voted in national elections.

City Government

City governments were influenced by the religious and ethnic character of the inhabitants and further complicated by the special problems of late-19th-century urban life: rapid, helter-skelter growth; the influx of European immigrants; the need to develop costly transportation, sanitation, and other public-utility systems; and the crime and corruption that the size, confusion, and anonymity incidental to urban existence fostered.

The movement to the suburbs of large numbers of middle-class city people who might have been expected to supply the political leadership needed to deal with these problems created a vacuum of sorts, a vacuum that was filled by political bosses, with their informal but powerful "machines."

The immigrants who flocked into American cities in the 1880s and early 1890s made up much of the "vast ignorant fluctuating mass" that Bryce was referring to in his description of party alignments. They were largely of peasant stock, and having come from societies unacquainted with the blessings of democracy, they had no experience with representative government. The tendency of urban workers to move frequently in search of better jobs further lessened the likelihood that they would develop political influence independently.

Furthermore, the difficulties of life in the slums bewildered and often overwhelmed newcomers, both native and foreign-born. Hopeful, but passive and naive, they could hardly be expected to take a broad view of social problems when so beset by personal ones. This enabled shrewd urban politicians—most of them in this period of Irish origin, the Irish being the firstcomers among the migrants and, according to mobility studies, more likely to stay put—to take command of the city masses and march them in obedient phalanxes to the polls.

Most city machines were loose-knit neighborhood organizations headed by ward bosses, not tightly geared hierarchical bureaucracies ruled by a single leader. "Big Tim" Sullivan of New York's Lower East Side and "Hinky Dink" Kenna of Chicago were typical of the breed. People like Sullivan and Kenna performed many useful services for what they liked to think of as their constituents. They found jobs for new arrivals and distributed food and other help to all in bad times. Anyone in trouble with the law could obtain at least a hearing from the ward boss, and often, if the crime was venial or due to ignorance, the difficulty was quietly "fixed" and the culprit was sent off with a word of caution. Sullivan provided turkey dinners for 5,000 or more derelicts each Christmas, distributed new shoes to the poor children of his district on his birthday, and arranged summer boat rides and picnics for young and old alike. At any time of year the victim of some sudden disaster could turn to the local clubhouse for help. Informally, probably without consciously intending to do so, the bosses educated the immigrants in the complexities of American civilization, helping them to leap the gulf between the almost medieval society of their origins and the modern industrial world.

The price of such aid—the bosses were not altruists—was unquestioning political support, which the bosses converted into cash. In New York, Sullivan levied tribute on gambling, had a hand in the liquor business, and controlled the issuance of peddlers' licenses. When he died in 1913, he was reputedly worth $1 million. Yet he and others like him were immensely popular; 25,000 grieving constituents followed Big Tim's coffin on its way to the grave.

Though he served a useful social function, the typical boss was not a reformer. Surveying the role of the Irish in New York City politics, the sociologist (later senator) Daniel Patrick Moynihan noted that despite their successes, the bosses "did not know what to do with power. . . . They never thought of politics as an instrument of social change."

The more visible and better-known city bosses played even less socially justifiable roles than the ward bosses. Their principal technique for extracting money from the public till was the kickback. To get city contracts, suppliers were made to pad their bills and, when paid for their work with funds from the city treasury, turn over the excess to the poli-

Thomas Nast's devastating assaults on the Tweed Ring, printed in Harper's Weekly, *helped bring about the ring's demise. In this cartoon Tweed and his fellow vultures cower under the storm against them. Tweed offered Nast a $500,000 bribe to stop the cartoon.*

ticians. Similarly, operators of streetcar lines, gas and electricity companies, and other public utilities were compelled to pay huge bribes to obtain favorable franchises.

The most notorious of the 19th-century city bosses was William Marcy Tweed, whose "Tweed Ring" extracted tens of millions of dollars from New York City during the brief period from 1869 to 1871. Tweed was swiftly jailed. More typical was Richard Croker, who ruled New York's Tammany Hall organization from the mid-1880s to the end of the century. Croker held a number of local offices, but his power rested on his position as chairman of the Tammany Hall finance committee. Although more concerned than Tweed with the social and economic services that machines provided, Croker was primarily a corrupt political manipulator; he accumulated a large fortune and owned a $200,000 mansion and a stable of racehorses, one of which was good enough to win the English Derby.

Despite their welfare work and their popularity, most bosses were essentially thieves. Efforts to romanticize them as the Robin Hoods of industrial society grossly distort the facts. However, the system developed and survived because too many middle-class city dwellers were indifferent to the fate of the poor. Except during occasional reform waves, few tried to check the rapaciousness of the politicos.

Many substantial citizens shared at least indirectly in the corruption. The owners of tenements were interested in crowding as many rent payers as possible into their buildings. Utility companies seeking franchises preferred a system that enabled them to buy favors. Honest citizens who had no selfish stake in the system and who were repelled by the sordidness of city government were seldom sufficiently concerned to do anything about it. When young Theodore Roosevelt decided to seek a political career in 1880, his New York socialite friends laughed in his face. They told him, Roosevelt wrote in his autobiography, "that politics were 'low'; that the organizations were not controlled by 'gentlemen'; that I would find them run by saloon-keepers, horse-car conductors, and the like."

Many so-called urban reformers resented the boss system mainly because it gave political power to people who were not "gentlemen" or, as one reformer put it, to a "proletarian mob" of "illiterate peasants, freshly raked from Irish bogs, or Bohemian mines, or Italian robber nests." A British visitor in Chicago struck at the root of the urban problem of the era. "Everybody is fighting to be rich," he said, "and nobody can attend to making the city fit to live in."

Republicans and Democrats

As for national politics, with the Democrats invincible in the South and the Republicans predominant in New England and most of the states beyond the Mississippi, the outcome of presidential elections was usually determined in a handful of populous states: New York (together with its satellites, New Jersey and Connecticut), Ohio, Indiana, and Illinois. The fact that opinion in these states on important questions such as the tariff and monetary policy was divided and that every imaginable religious and ethnic interest was represented in the electorate goes far to explain why the parties hesitated to commit themselves on issues. In every presidential election, Democrats and Republicans concentrated their heaviest guns on these states. Of the 18 Democrats and Republicans nominated for president in the nine elections between 1868 and 1900, only three were not from New York, Ohio, Indiana, or Illinois, and all three lost.

Partisanship was intense in these states. A story is told of a Democrat from a town in Illinois who was trying to persuade a doctor he knew to settle there. He admitted that the town already had five doctors, more than enough to care for the medical needs of the populace. But all five were Republicans. "If you come here you can commence all the Democratic practice," he assured the doctor. There are, he added sagely, "a set of public men here that will do what they can for you." Campaigns were conducted in a carnival atmosphere, entertainment being substituted for serious debate. Large sums were spent on brass bands, barbecues, uniforms, and banners. Speakers of national reputation were imported to attract crowds, and spellbinders noted for their leather lungs—this was before the day of the loudspeaker—and their ability to rouse popular emotions were brought in to address mass meetings.

With so much depending on so few, the level of political morality was abysmal. Mudslinging, character assassination, and plain lying were standard practice; bribery was routine. Drifters and other dissolute citizens were paid in cash—or more often in free drinks—to vote the party ticket. The names of persons long dead were solemnly inscribed in voting registers, their suffrages exercised by impostors. During the 1880 campaign the Democratic national chairman, hearing that the Republicans were planning to transport Kentuckians into Indiana to vote illegally in that crucial state, urged Indiana Democrats to "check this outrageous fraud." Then, perhaps seeking an easier solution to the problem, he added: "If necessary . . . keep even with them." Since, as this incident demonstrates, both parties indulged in these tactics, their efforts often canceled one another's, yet certain presidents were made and unmade in this sordid fashion.

The Men in the White House

The leading statesmen of the period showed as little interest in important contemporary questions as the party hacks who made up the rank and file of their organizations. Consider the presidents.

Rutherford B. Hayes, president from 1877 to 1881, came to office with a distinguished record. He attended Kenyon College and Harvard Law School before settling down to practice in Cincinnati. Although he had a family to support, he volunteered for service within weeks after the first shell fell on Fort Sumter. "A just and necessary war," he called it in his diary. "I would prefer to go into it if I knew I was to die . . . than to live through and after it without taking any part."

Hayes was wounded at South Mountain on the eve of Antietam, and later served under Sheridan in the Shenandoah Valley campaign of 1864. En-

tering the army as a major, he emerged a major general. In 1864 he was elected to Congress; four years later he became governor of Ohio, serving three terms altogether. The Republicans nominated him for president in 1876 because of his reputation for honesty and moderation, and his election, made possible by the Compromise of 1877, seemed to presage an era of sectional harmony and political probity.

Outwardly Hayes had a sunny disposition; inwardly, in his own words, he was sometimes "nervous to the point of disaster." Despite his geniality, he was utterly without political glamour. He played down the tariff issue whenever possible, favoring protection in principle but refusing to become a mere spokesman for local interests. On the money question he was conservative. He cheerfully approved the resumption of gold payments in 1879 and vetoed bills to expand the currency. He ac-

In this 1880 campaign lithograph by Currier & Ives, "Farmer Garfield" uses a scythe made of honesty, ability, and patriotism to cut a swath to the White House through brush infested by snakes with names like Falsehood and Malice. One snake bears the countenance of Garfield's predecessor, Hayes.

counted himself a civil service reformer, being opposed to the collection of political contributions from federal officeholders.

Since Hayes saw himself more as a caretaker than a leader, he believed that Congress should assume the main responsibility for solving national problems. One historian writes that he showed "no capacity for such large-minded leadership as might have tamed the political hordes and aroused the enthusiasm, or at least the interest, of the public."

Hayes complained about the South's failure to treat blacks decently after the withdrawal of federal troops, but he took no action. He worked harder for civil service reform yet failed to achieve the "thorough, rapid, and complete" change he had promised. In most matters, he was content to "let the record show that he had made the requests."

Hayes's successor, James A. Garfield, was cut down by an assassin's bullet four months after his inauguration. Even in that short time, however, his ineffectiveness had been demonstrated. Garfield grew up in poverty on an Ohio farm. When the Civil War broke out, he helped organize a volunteer regiment and soon proved himself an excellent battlefield commander. He fought at Shiloh and later at Chickamauga. In two years he rose from lieutenant colonel to major general. In 1863 he won a seat in Congress, where his oratorical and managerial skills brought him to prominence in the affairs of the Republican party.

Garfield was studious and industrious, and he had wide-ranging interests. His weakness was indecisiveness—what an admirer described as a "want of certainty."

He did not enjoy waving the bloody shirt, but when hard pressed politically—as when his name was linked with the Crédit Mobilier railroad scandal—he would lash out at the South in an effort to distract the voters. In theory he was inclined toward low tariffs. Nevertheless, he would not sacrifice the interests of Ohio manufacturers for a mere principle.

Similarly, though eager to improve the efficiency of the government and resentful of the "intellectual dissipation" resulting from time wasted listening to the countless appeals of office seekers, he often wilted under pressure from the spoilsmen. Only on fiscal policy did he take a firm stand: He opposed categorically all inflationary schemes.

Political patronage proved to be Garfield's undoing. The Republican party in 1880 was split into two factions, the "Stalwarts" and the "Half-Breeds." The Stalwarts, led by New York Senator Roscoe Conkling, believed in the blatant pursuit of the spoils of office. The Half-Breeds did not disagree but behaved more circumspectly, hoping to attract the support of independents. Competition for office was the main reason for their rivalry.

Garfield had been a compromise choice at the 1880 Republican convention. His election precipitated a great battle over patronage, the new president standing in a sort of no-man's-land between the factions. He did stand up to the most grasping politicians, resisting in particular the demands of Senator Conkling. By backing the investigation of a post office scandal and by appointing a Half-Breed collector of the Port of New York, he infuriated the Stalwarts. In July 1881 an unbalanced Stalwart lawyer named Charles J. Guiteau shot Garfield in the Washington railroad station. After lingering for weeks, the president died on September 19.

The assassination of Garfield elevated Chester A. Arthur to the presidency. Arthur was a New York lawyer. An abolitionist, he became an early convert to the Republican party and rose rapidly in its local councils. In 1871 Grant gave him the juiciest political plum in the country, the collectorship of the Port of New York, which he held until removed by Hayes in 1878 for refusing to keep his hands out of party politics.

The vice-presidency was the only elective position that Arthur had ever held. Before Garfield's death, he had paid little attention to questions like the tariff and monetary policy, being content to take in fees ranging upward of $50,000 a year as collector of the port and to oversee the operations of the New York customs office, with its hordes of clerks and laborers. (During Arthur's tenure, the novelist Herman Melville was employed as an "outdoor inspector" by the Custom House.) Of course, Arthur was an unblushing defender of the spoils system, though in fairness it must be said that he was personally honest and an excellent administrator.

The tragic circumstances of his elevation to the presidency sobered Arthur considerably. Although he was a genial, convivial man, perhaps overly fond of good food and flashy clothes, he comported himself with great dignity as president. He handled patronage matters with restraint, and he gave at least nominal support to the movement for civil service reform, which had been strengthened by the public's indignation at the assassination of Garfield. In 1883 Congress passed the Pendleton Act, "classifying" about 10 percent of all government jobs and creating the bipartisan Civil Service Commission to administer competitive examinations for these positions. The law made it illegal to force officeholders to make political contributions and empowered the president to expand the list of classified positions at his discretion.

Many politicians resented the new system—one senator denounced it as "un-American"—but the Pendleton Act opened a new era in government administration. The results have been summed up by the historian Ari Hoogenboom:

> An unprofessional civil service became more professionalized. Better-educated civil servants were recruited and society accorded them a higher place. . . . Local political considerations gave way in civil servants' minds to the national concerns of a federal office. Business influence and ideals replaced those of the politician.

Arthur urged the appointment of a nonpartisan commission to study tariff rates and to suggest rational reductions; when such a commission was created, he urged Congress to adopt its recommendations. He came out for federal regulation of railroads several years before the passage of the Interstate Commerce Act.

As an administrator Arthur was systematic, thoughtful, businesslike, and at the same time cheerful and considerate. Just the same, he too was a political failure. He made no real attempt to push his program through Congress, instead devoting most of his energies to a futile effort to build up his personal following in the Republican party by distributing favors. But the Stalwarts would not forgive his "desertion," and the reform element could not forget his past. At the 1884 convention the politicos shunted him aside.

The election of 1884 brought the Democrat Grover Cleveland to the White House. Cleveland grew up in western New York. After studying law, he settled in Buffalo. Though somewhat lacking in the social graces and in intellectual pretensions, he had a basic integrity that everyone recognized; when

A portrait of Grover Cleveland by the artist Anders Zorn. The well-fed look was the trademark of most politicians of that era.

a group of reformers sought a candidate for mayor in 1881, he was a natural choice. His success in Buffalo led to his election as governor of New York in 1882.

In the governor's chair his no-nonsense attitude toward public administration endeared him to civil service reformers at the same time that his basic conservatism pleased businessmen. When he vetoed a popular bill to force a reduction of the fares charged by the New York City elevated railway on the grounds that it was an unconstitutional violation of the company's franchise, his stock soared. Here was a man who cared more for principle than the adulation of the multitude, a man of courage, honest, hardworking, and eminently sound. The Democrats nominated him for president in 1884.

The election revolved around personal issues, for the platforms of the parties were almost identical. On the one hand, the Republican candidate, the dynamic James G. Blaine, had an immense following, but his reputation had been soiled by the publication of the "Mulligan letters," which connected him with the corrupt granting of congressional favors to the Little Rock and Fort Smith Railroad. On the other hand, it came out during the campaign that Cleveland, a bachelor, had fathered an illegitimate child. Instead of debating public issues, the Republicans chanted the ditty

> *Ma! Ma! Where's my pa?*
> *Gone to the White House,*
>   *Ha! Ha! Ha!*

to which the Democrats countered

> *Blaine, Blaine, James G. Blaine,*
> *The continental liar from the State of Maine.*

Blaine lost more heavily in the mudslinging than Cleveland, whose quiet courage in saying, "Tell the truth," when his past was brought to light contrasted favorably with Blaine's glib and unconvincing denials. A significant group of eastern Republicans, known as Mugwumps, campaigned for the Democrats.* However, Blaine ran a strong race against a general pro-Democratic trend; Cleveland won the election by fewer than 25,000 votes. The change of 600 ballots in New York would have given that state, and the presidency, to his opponent.

As a Democrat, Cleveland had no stomach for refighting the Civil War. Civil service reformers overestimated his commitment to their cause, for he believed in rotation in office. He would not summarily dismiss Republicans, but he thought that when they had served four years, they "should as a rule give way to good men of our party." He did, however, insist on honesty and efficiency regardless of party. As a result, he made few poor appointments.

Cleveland had little imagination and too narrow a conception of his powers and duties to be a successful president. His appearance perfectly re-

flected his character: a squat, burly man weighing well over 200 pounds, he could defend a position against heavy odds, yet he lacked flexibility. He took a fairly broad view of the powers of the federal government, but he thought it unseemly to put pressure on Congress, believing in "the entire independence of the executive and legislative branches."

Toward the end of his term Cleveland bestirred himself and tried to provide constructive leadership on the tariff question. The government was embarrassed by a large revenue surplus, which Cleveland hoped to reduce by cutting the duties on necessities and on raw materials used in manufacturing. He devoted his entire annual message of December 1887 to the tariff, thereby focusing public attention on the subject. When worried Democrats reminded him that an election was coming up and that the tariff might cause a rift in the organization, he replied simply: "What is the use of being elected or re-elected, unless you stand for something?"

The House of Representatives, dominated by southern Democrats, passed a bill reducing many duties, but the measure, known as the Mills bill, was flagrantly partisan: It slashed the rates on iron products, glass, wool, and other items made in the North and left those on southern goods almost untouched. The Republican-controlled Senate rejected the Mills bill, and the issue was left to be settled by the voters at the 1888 election.

In that contest, Cleveland obtained a plurality of the popular vote, but his opponent, Benjamin Harrison, grandson of President William Henry Harrison, carried most of the key northeastern industrial states by narrow margins, thereby obtaining a comfortable majority in the electoral college, 233 to 168.

Although intelligent and able, Harrison was too reserved to make a good politician. He did not suffer fools gladly and kept even his most important advisers at arm's length. One observer called him a "human iceberg." During the Civil War, he fought under Sherman at Atlanta and won a reputation as a stern, effective disciplinarian. In 1876 he ran unsuccessfully for governor of Indiana, but in 1881 he was elected to the Senate.

Harrison believed ardently in protective tariffs, stating firmly, if illogically, that he was against "cheaper costs" because cheaper costs seemed "necessarily to involve a cheaper man and woman under

---

* The Mugwumps considered themselves reformers, but on social and economic questions nearly all of them were very conservative. They were sound-money proponents and advocates of laissez faire. Reform to them consisted almost entirely of doing away with corruption and making the government more efficient.

PUT YOUR APPLICATION IN THE SLOT AND GET AN OFFICE.

President Benjamin Harrison swapping political office for electioneering support as depicted by a cartoonist, a practice that civil service reformers insisted corrupted national politics. In point of fact, "Little Ben" was among the least given to patronage appointments among post–Civil War presidents.

the coat." His approach to fiscal policy was conservative, though he was freehanded in the matter of veterans' pensions. He would not use "an apothecary's scale," he said, "to weigh the rewards of men who saved the country." No more flamboyant waver of the bloody shirt existed.

Harrison professed to favor civil service reform, but a biographer, Father Harry J. Sievers, admits that he fashioned a "singularly unimpressive" record on the question. He appointed the vigorous young reformer Theodore Roosevelt to the Civil Service Commission and then proceeded to undercut him systematically. Before long the frustrated Roosevelt was calling the president a "cold blooded, narrow minded, prejudiced, obstinate, timid old psalm singing Indianapolis politician."

Under Harrison, Congress distinguished itself by expending, for the first time in a period of peace, more than $1 billion in a single session. It raised the tariff to an all-time high. The Sherman Antitrust Act was passed; so was the Silver Purchase Act, authorizing the government to coin large amounts of that metal, a measure much desired by mining interests and those favoring inflation. A "force" bill providing for federal control of elections as a means of protecting the right of southern blacks to vote, a right increasingly under attack, passed the House only to be filibustered to death in the Senate.

Harrison had little to do with the fate of any of these measures. By and large he failed, as one historian has said, to give the people "magnetic and responsive leadership." The Republicans lost control of Congress in 1890, and two years later Grover Cleveland swept back into power, defeating Harrison by more than 350,000 votes.

Congressional Leaders

Among the lesser politicians of the period, the most outstanding was James G. Blaine of Maine, who served in Congress from 1863 to 1881, first in the House and then in the Senate. Blaine had many of the qualities that mark a great leader: personal dynamism, imagination, political intuition, oratorical ability, and a broad view of the national interest. President Lincoln spotted him when he was a freshman congressman, calling him "one of the brightest men in the House" and "one of the coming men of the country."

Blaine was essentially a reasonable man, a member of the moderate Republican faction during Reconstruction. He favored sound money without opposing inflexibly every suggestion for increasing the volume of the currency. He supported the protective system yet advocated reciprocity agreements to increase trade. He adopted a moderate and tolerant attitude toward the South. Almost alone among the politicians of his generation, he was deeply interested in foreign affairs. His personal warmth captivated thousands.

That Blaine, though perennially an aspirant, never became president was in part a reflection of his abilities and his participation in so many controversial affairs. Naturally, he aroused jealousies and made many enemies. But some inexplicable flaw marred his character. He had a streak of reck-

Parodying a popular painting of the day depicting a beautiful Greek courtesan being unveiled before Athenian statesmen, Puck's *Bernhard Fillam drew James G. Blaine revealed to Republican leaders in 1884. The "Mulligan letters" receive prominent display among the tattoos, and Blaine's renowned personal magnetism is labeled as a fraud.*

lessness entirely out of keeping with his reasonable position on most issues. He showered contempt on civil service reformers, characterizing them as "noisy but not numerous, . . . ambitious but not wise, pretentious but not powerful." The scandal of the Mulligan letters made a dark blot on his record. Blaine moved though history amid cheers and won a host of spectacular if petty triumphs, yet his career was barren, essentially tragic.

Roscoe Conkling's was another remarkable but empty career. Handsome, colorful, companionable, and dignified, Conkling served in Congress almost continuously from 1859 to 1881 and was a great power, dominating the complex politics of New York for many years. Such was his prestige that two presidents offered him a seat on the Supreme Court. Yet no measure of importance was attached to his name; he squandered his energies in acrimonious personal quarrels, caring only for partisan advantage.

Dozens of other figures might be mentioned; the following are representative types.

Congressman William McKinley of Ohio was the most personally attractive. He was a man of simple honesty, nobility of character, quiet warmth—and a politician to the core. The tariff was McKinley's special competence, the principle of protection his guiding star. The peak of his career still lay in the future in the early 1890s.

Another Ohioan, John Sherman, brother of the famous Civil War general, accomplished the remarkable feat of holding national office continuously from 1855 to 1898. He had a deserved reputation for expertise in financial matters. However, he was colorless and stiff, and altogether too willing to compromise his beliefs for political advantage.

Sherman gave his name (and not much else) to the Antitrust Act of 1890 and to other important legislation, but in retrospect he left little mark on the history of the country despite his long service.

Thomas B. Reed, Republican congressman from Maine, was a witty, widely read man but ultraconservative and cursed with a sharp tongue that he could never curb. Reed coined the famous definition of a statesman: "a politician who is dead." When one pompous politico said in his presence that he would rather be right than president, Reed advised him not to worry, since he would never be either. In 1890 Reed was elected Speaker of the House and quickly won the nickname "Czar" because of his autocratic way of expediting business. Since the Republicans had only a paper-thin majority, the Democrats attempted to block action on partisan measures by refusing to answer to their names on quorum calls. Reed coolly ordered the clerk to re-

cord them as present and proceeded to carry on the business of the House. His control became so absolute that Washington jokesters said that representatives dared not breathe without his permission. Reed had large ambitions and the courage of his convictions, but his vindictiveness kept him from exercising a constructive influence on his times.

Agricultural Discontent

The vacuity of American politics may well have stemmed from the complacency of the middle-class majority. The country was growing; no foreign enemy threatened it; the poor were mostly recent immigrants, blacks, and others with little influence, easily ignored by those in comfortable circumstances. However, one important group in society suffered increasingly as the years rolled by: the

The western land boom reached a climax on April 22, 1889, when parts of Oklahoma were opened to settlers. With a few hours, nearly 2 million acres were claimed by hordes of "boomers." This photograph was taken a few weeks later in the boom town of Guthrie, whose sign painter was working overtime.

farmers. Out of their travail came the force that finally, in the 1890s, brought American politics face to face with the problems of the age.

Immediately after the Civil War, wheat sold at nearly $1.50 a bushel, and in the early 1870s it was still worth well over a dollar. By the mid-1890s the average price stood in the neighborhood of 60 cents. Cotton, the great southern staple, which sold for more than 30 cents a pound in 1866 and 15 cents in the early 1870s, at times in the 1890s fell below 6 cents.

The tariff on manufactured goods appeared to aggravate the farmers' predicament, and so did the domestic marketing system, which enabled a multitude of middlemen to gobble up a large share of the profits of agriculture. The shortage of credit, particularly in the South, was an additional burden. Furthermore, the improvements in transportation that made it practicable for farmers in Australia, Canada, Russia, and Argentina to sell their produce in western European markets increased the competition faced by Americans seeking to dispose of surplus produce abroad.

Throughout the mid-1880s farmers on the plains had experienced boom conditions. Adequate rainfall produced bountiful harvests, credit was available, and property values rose rapidly. In the 1880s the population of Kansas increased by 43 percent, that of Nebraska by 134 percent, that of the Dakotas by 278 percent. This agricultural expansion contributed to the destruction of open-range cattle raising and changed the economy of cattle towns like Dodge City, which came to depend more on farmers than on cowboys and ranchers for business.

Speculative booms occur periodically in every frontier district; like all others, this one collapsed when settlers and investors took a more realistic look at the prospects of the region. In this case special circumstances turned the slump into a catastrophe. A succession of dry years shattered the hopes of the farmers. The downward swing of the business cycle in the early 1890s completed the devastation. Settlers who had paid more for their lands than they were worth and borrowed money at high interest rates to do so found themselves squeezed relentlessly. Thousands lost their farms and returned eastward, penniless and dispirited. The population of Nebraska increased by fewer than 4,000 persons in the entire decade of the 1890s.

The Populist Movement

The agricultural depression triggered a new outburst of farm radicalism, the Alliance movement. Alliances were organizations of farmers' clubs, most of which had sprung up during the bad times of the late 1870s. The first Knights of Reliance group was founded in 1877 in Lampasas County, Texas. As the Farmers Alliance, this organization gradually expanded in northeastern Texas, and after 1885 it spread rapidly throughout the cotton states. Alliance leaders stressed cooperation. Their co-ops bought fertilizer and other supplies in bulk and sold them at fair prices to members. They sought to market their crops cooperatively but could not raise the necessary capital from banks—with the result that some of them began to question the workings of the American financial and monetary system. They became economic and social radicals in the process. In the northern regions a similar though less influential alliance movement developed.

The alliances adopted somewhat differing policies, but all agreed that agricultural prices were too low, that transportation costs were too high, and that something was radically wrong with the nation's financial system. "There are three great crops raised in Nebraska," an angry rural editor proclaimed in 1890. "One is a crop of corn, one is a crop of freight rates, and one a crop of interest. One is produced by farmers who by sweat and toil farm the land. The other two are produced by men who sit in their offices and behind their bank counters and farm the farmers." All agreed on the need for political action if the lot of the agriculturalist was to be improved.

Although the state alliances of the Dakotas and Kansas joined the Southern Alliance in 1889, for a time local prejudices and conflicting interests prevented the formation of a single national organization. Northern farmers mostly voted Republican, southerners Democratic, and resentments created during the Civil War lingered in all sections. Cotton-producing southerners opposed the protective tariff; most northerners, fearing the competition of foreign grain producers, favored it. Railroad regulation and federal land policy seemed vital questions to northerners; financial reform loomed most important in southern eyes. Northerners were receptive to the idea of forming a third party, while southerners, wedded to the one-party system, pre-

Mary Elizabeth Lease was a prominent Populist noted for her rallying cry to "raise less corn and more hell."

ate a new national party. By uniting southern and western farmers, they succeeded in breaking the sectional barrier erected by the Civil War. If they could recruit industrial workers, perhaps a real political revolution could be accomplished. In February 1892, farm leaders, representatives of the Knights of Labor, and various professional reformers, some 800 in all, met at St. Louis, organized the People's, or Populist, party, and issued a call for a national convention to meet at Omaha in July.

That convention nominated General James B. Weaver of Iowa for president (with a one-legged Confederate veteran as his running mate) and drafted a platform that called for a graduated income tax and national ownership of railroads and the telegraph and telephone systems. It also advocated a "subtreasury" plan that would permit farmers to hold nonperishable crops off the market when prices were low. Under this proposal, the government would make loans in the form of greenbacks to farmers, secured by crops held in storage in federal warehouses. When prices rose, the farmers could sell their crops and repay the loans. To combat deflation further, the platform demanded the unlimited coinage of silver and an increase in the money supply "to no less than $50 per capita."

To make the government more responsive to public opinion, the Populists urged the adoption of the initiative and referendum procedures and the election of United States senators by popular vote. To win the support of industrial workers, their platform denounced the use of Pinkerton detectives in labor disputes and backed the eight-hour day and the restriction of "undesirable" immigration.

The Populists created, in the phrase of the historian Lawrence Goodwyn, "a multi-sectional institution of reform." They were not, however, revolutionaries. They saw themselves not as a persecuted minority but as a victimized majority betrayed by what would a century later be called the establishment. They were at most ambivalent about the free enterprise system, and they tended to attribute social and economic injustices not to built-in inequities in the system but to nefarious conspiracies organized by selfish interests in order to subvert the system.

The appearance of the new party was the most exciting and significant aspect of the presidential campaign of 1892, which saw Harrison and Cleveland refighting the election of 1888. The Populists

ferred working to capture local Democratic machines.

The farm groups entered local politics in the 1890 elections. Convinced of the righteousness of their cause, they campaigned with tremendous fervor. The results were encouraging. In the South, Alliance-sponsored gubernatorial candidates won in Georgia, Tennessee, South Carolina, and Texas; eight southern legislatures fell under Alliance control, and 44 congressmen and 3 senators committed to Alliance objectives were sent to Washington. In the West, Alliance candidates swept Kansas and captured a majority in the Nebraska legislature and enough seats in Minnesota and South Dakota to hold the balance of power between the major parties.

Such success, coupled with the reluctance of the Republicans and Democrats to make concessions to their demands, encouraged Alliance leaders to creput forth a host of colorful spellbinders: Tom Watson, a Georgia congressman whose temper was such that on one occasion he administered a beating to a local planter with the man's own riding crop; William A. Peffer, a senator from Kansas whose long beard and grave demeanor gave him the look of a Hebrew prophet; "Sockless Jerry" Simpson of Kansas, unlettered but full of grass-roots shrewdness and wit, a former Greenbacker and an admirer of the single-tax doctrine of Henry George; Ignatius Donnelly, the "Minnesota Sage," who claimed to be an authority on science, economics, and Shakespeare (he believed that Francis Bacon wrote the plays) and whose widely read novel, *Caesar's Column* (1891), pictured an America of the future wherein

a handful of plutocrats tyrannized masses of downtrodden workers and serfs.

In the one-party South, Populist strategists sought to wean black farmers away from the ruling Democratic organization. Their competition forced the "subsidies" paid for black votes up to as much as a dollar—two days' wages. Southern black farmers had their own Colored Alliance, and even before 1892 their leaders had worked closely with the white alliances. Nearly 100 black delegates had attended the Populist convention at St. Louis. Of course, the blacks would be useless to the party if they could not vote; therefore, white Populist leaders opposed the southern trend toward disfranchising blacks and called for full civil rights for all.

Jeremiah "Sockless Jerry" Simpson speaking at a political debate in Kansas in 1892. Like many Populists, a flamboyant campaigner, Simpson earned his nickname by using the claim that he wore no socks against his well-dressed opponent for a congressional seat.

In the Northwest, the Populists assailed the "bankers' conspiracy" in unbridled terms. Ignatius Donnelly, running for governor of Minnesota, wrote another futuristic political novel, *The Golden Bottle*, and made 150 speeches, vowing to make the campaign "the liveliest ever seen" in the state.

The results proved disappointing. Tom Watson lost his seat in Congress, and Donnelly ran a poor third in the Minnesota gubernatorial race. The Populists did sweep Kansas. They elected numbers of local officials in other western states and cast over a million votes for General Weaver. But the effort to unite white and black farmers in the South failed miserably. Conservative Democrats, while continuing with considerable success to attract black voters, played on racial fears cruelly, insisting that the Populists sought to undermine white supremacy. Since most white Populists saw the alliance with blacks as at best a marriage of convenience, this argument had a deadly effect. Elsewhere, even in the old centers of the Granger movement, the party made no significant impression. Urban workers remained aloof.

By standing firmly for conservative financial policies, Cleveland attracted considerable Republican support and won a solid victory over Harrison in the electoral college, 277 to 145. Weaver's electoral vote was 22.

Showdown on Silver

One conclusion that politicians reached after analyzing the 1892 returns was that the money question, particularly the controversy over the coinage of silver, was of paramount interest to the voters. Despite the wide-ranging appeal of the Populist platform, most of Weaver's strength came from the silver-mining states. By contrast, Cleveland's strong stand for gold proved popular in the Northwest.

In truth, the issue of gold versus silver was superficial; the important question was what, if anything, should be done to check the deflationary spiral. The declining price level benefited bondholders and other people with fixed incomes and injured debtors. Industrial workers profited from deflation except during periods of depression, when unemployment rose—which helps explain why the Populists made little headway among them. Southern farmers, who were prisoners of the crop-lien system,

and farmers in the plains states were hit hard by the downward trend.

By the early 1890s, discussion of federal monetary policy revolved around the coinage of silver. Traditionally, the United States had been on a bimetallic standard. Both gold and silver were coined, the number of grains of each in the dollar being adjusted periodically to reflect the commercial value of the two metals. An act of 1792 established a 15:1 ratio—371.25 grains of silver and 24.75 grains of gold were each worth $1 at the Mint. In 1834 the ratio was changed to 16:1 and in 1853 to 14.8:1, the latter reduction in the value of gold reflecting the new discoveries in California. This ratio slightly undervalued silver. In 1861, for example, the amount of silver bullion in a dollar was worth $1.03 in the open market, so no one took silver to the Mint for coinage. However, an avalanche of silver from the mines of Nevada and Colorado gradually depressed the price until, around 1874, it again became profitable for miners to coin their bullion. Alas, when they tried to do so, they discovered that the Coinage Act of 1873, taking account of the fact that no silver had been presented to the Mint in years, had demonetized the metal.

The silver mines denounced this "Crime of '73," and inflationists, who wanted more money put into circulation regardless of its base, joined them in demanding a return to bimetallism. Conservatives, still fighting the battle against greenback paper money, resisted strongly. The result was a series of compromises. In 1878 the Bland-Allison Act authorized the purchase of $2 million to $4 million of silver a month at the market price, but this had little inflationary effect because the government consistently purchased the minimum amount. The commercial price of silver continued to fall; in 1890 its ratio to gold was 20:1. In that year the Sherman Silver Purchase Act required the government to buy 4.5 million *ounces* of silver monthly, but in the face of increasing supplies, the price of silver fell still further. The ratio reached 26:1 in 1893 and 32:1 in 1894.

The compromises satisfied no one. Silver miners grumbled because their bullion brought in only half what it had in the early 1870s. Debtors noted angrily that because of the general decline in prices, the dollars they used to meet their obligations were worth more than twice as much as in 1865. Advocates of the gold standard feared that unlimited silver coinage would be authorized, "destroying the value of the dollar." When a financial panic brought on by the collapse of the London banking house of Baring Brothers ushered in a severe industrial depression, the confidence of both silverites and "gold bugs" was further eroded.

President Cleveland believed that the controversy over silver had caused the depression by shaking the confidence of the business community and that all would be well if the country returned to a single gold standard. He summoned a special session of Congress, and by exerting immense political pressure he obtained the repeal of the Sherman Silver Purchase Act in October 1893. All that this accomplished was to split the Democratic party, its southern and western wings deserting him almost to a man.

During 1894 and 1895, while the nation floundered in the worst depression it had ever experienced, a series of events further undermined public confidence. In the spring of 1894 several "armies" of the unemployed, the most imposing led by Jacob S. Coxey, an eccentric Ohio businessman, marched on Washington to demand relief. Coxey wanted the government to undertake a program of federal public works and to authorize local communities to exchange non-interest-bearing bonds with the Treasury for $500 million in paper money, the funds to be used to hire unemployed workers to build roads. The scheme, Coxey claimed, would pump money into the economy, provide work for the jobless, and benefit the entire nation by improving transportation facilities.

When Coxey's group of demonstrators, perhaps 500 in all, reached Washington, he and two other leaders were arrested for trespassing on the grounds of the Capitol. Their followers were dispersed by club-wielding policemen. This callous treatment convinced many Americans that the government had little interest in the suffering of the people, an opinion strengthened when Cleveland, in July 1894, used federal troops to crush the Pullman strike.

The next year the Supreme Court handed down several reactionary decisions. In *United States* v. *E. C. Knight Company* it refused to employ the Sherman Antitrust Act to break up the Sugar Trust. In *Pollock* v. *Farmers' Loan and Trust Company* it invalidated a federal income tax law despite the fact that a similar measure levied during the Civil War had been upheld by the Court in *Springer* v. *United States* (1881).

Finally, the Court denied a writ of habeas corpus to Eugene V. Debs of the American Railway Union, who was languishing in prison for disobeying a federal injunction during the Pullman strike.

On top of these indications of official conservatism came a desperate financial crisis. Throughout 1894 the Treasury's supply of gold dwindled as worried citizens exchanged greenbacks (now convertible into gold) for hard money and foreign investors cashed in large amounts of American securities. The government tried to sell bonds for gold to bolster the reserve, but since most investors purchased the bonds with gold-backed paper money, in effect withdrawing gold from the Treasury and then returning it for the bonds, the gold reserve continued to melt away. Early in 1895 it touched a low point of $41 million.

At this juncture a syndicate of bankers headed by J. P. Morgan turned the tide by underwriting a $62 million bond issue, guaranteeing that half the gold would come from Europe. This caused a great public outcry; the spectacle of the nation being saved from bankruptcy by a private banker infuriated millions.

These events, together with the continuing depression, discredited the Cleveland administration. "I haven't got words to say what I think of that old bag of beef," Governor "Pitchfork Ben" Tillman of South Carolina, who had resolutely resisted the Populists in 1892, told a local audience two years later. "If you send me to the Senate, I promise I won't be bulldozed by him."

As the presidential election of 1896 approached, with the Populists demanding unlimited coinage of silver at a ratio of 16:1, the major parties found it impossible to continue straddling the money question. The Populist vote had increased by 42 percent in the 1894 congressional elections. Southern and western Democratic leaders feared that they would lose their following unless Cleveland was repudiated. Western Republicans, led by Senator Henry M. Teller of Colorado, were threatening to bolt to the Populists unless their party came out for silver coinage. After a generation of political equivocation, the major parties had to face an important issue squarely.

The Republicans, meeting to choose a candidate at St. Louis in June 1896, announced for the gold standard. "We are unalterably opposed to every measure calculated to debase our currency or impair the credit of our country," the platform declared. "We are therefore opposed to the free coinage of silver. . . . The existing gold standard must be maintained." The party then nominated Ohio's William McKinley for president. McKinley, best known for his staunch advocacy of the protective tariff yet highly regarded by labor, was expected to run strongly in the Middle West and the East.

The Democratic convention met in July at Chicago. The pro-gold Cleveland element made a hard fight, but the silverites swept them aside. The high point came when a youthful Nebraskan named William Jennings Bryan spoke for silver against gold, for western farmers against the industrial East. Bryan's every sentence provoked ear-shattering applause.

We have petitioned and our petitions have been scorned; we have entreated, and our entreaties have been disregarded; we have begged, and they have

Portraits of William Jennings Bryan with his wife and children, along with the text of the "cross of gold" speech, appeared on this typically colorful campaign poster for the 1896 campaign.

mocked when our calamity came. We beg no longer we entreat no more; we petition no more. We defy them!

The crowd responded like a great choir to Bryan's oratorical cues. "Burn down your cities and leave our farms," he said, "and your cities will spring up again as if by magic; but destroy our farms and the grass will grow in the streets of every city in the country." He ended with a marvelous figure of speech that set the tone for the coming campaign. "You shall not press down upon the brow of labor this crown of thorns," he warned, bringing his hands down suggestively to his temples. "You shall not crucify mankind upon a cross of gold!" Dramatically, he extended his arms to the side, the very figure of the crucified Christ.

The convention promptly adopted a platform calling for "the free and unlimited coinage of both silver and gold at the present legal ratio of 16 to 1" and went on to nominate Bryan, who was barely 36, for president.

This action put tremendous pressure on the Populists. If they supported Bryan, they risked losing their party identity; if they nominated another candidate, they would ensure McKinley's election. Those more concerned with immediate political advantage, especially officeholders and aspirants, took the former position. Those (mostly old Alliance members raised in the cooperative movement) who considered free silver a minor issue and a poor substitute for the subtreasury plan as an approach to the deflation problem, rejected "fusion" with the Democrats. "The Democratic idea of fusion," Tom Watson complained, is "that we play Jonah while they play whale." In part because the delegates could not find a person of stature willing to become a candidate against him, the Populist convention nominated Bryan, seeking to preserve the party identity by substituting Watson for the Democratic vice-presidential nominee, Arthur Sewall of Maine.

The Election of 1896

Never did a presidential campaign raise such intense emotions. The Republicans from the silver-mining states swung solidly behind Bryan. The gold Democrats refused to accept the decision of the Chi-

Cartoon satirizing the predicament of Democrats like New York's Governor David B. Hill, who found their party aligned with the Populists in the 1896 presidential election. More than sartorial adjustments were required of such conservative politicos.

cago convention. Cleveland professed to be "so dazed by the political situation that I am in no condition for speech or thought on the subject." Many others adopted the policy of Governor David B. Hill of New York, who said, "I am a Democrat still—very still." The extreme gold bugs, calling themselves National Democrats, nominated their own candidate, 79-year-old Senator John M. Palmer of Illinois. Palmer ran only to injure Bryan. "Fellow Democrats," he announced, "I will not consider it any great fault if you decide to cast your vote for William McKinley."

At the start the Republicans seemed to have everything in their favor. Bryan's youth and relative lack of political experience—two terms in the House—contrasted unfavorably with McKinley's distinguished war record, his long service in Congress and as governor of Ohio, and his reputation for honesty and good judgment. The severe depression operated in favor of the party out of power, although by repudiating Cleveland, the Democrats escaped much of the burden of explaining away his errors. The newspapers came out almost unanimously for the Republicans. Important Democratic papers such as the *New York World*, the *Boston Herald*, the *Baltimore Sun*, the *Chicago Chronicle*, and the *Richmond Times* supported McKinley editorially and even slanted news stories against the Democrats. The *New York Times* accused Bryan of being insane, his affliction being variously classified as "paranoia querulenta," "graphomania," and "oratorical monomania." The Democrats had very little money and few well-known speakers to fight the campaign.

But Bryan proved a formidable opponent. Casting aside tradition, he took to the stump personally, traveling 18,000 miles and making over 600 speeches. He was one of the greatest of orators. A big, handsome man with a voice capable of carrying without strain to the far corners of a great hall yet equally effective before a cluster of auditors at a rural crossroads, he projected an image of absolute sincerity without appearing fanatical or argumentative. At every major stop on his tour, huge crowds assembled. In Minnesota he packed the 10,000-seat St. Paul Auditorium, while thousands milled in the streets outside.

His energy was amazing, and his charm and good humor were unfailing. At one whistle stop, while he was shaving in his compartment, a small group outside the train began clamoring for a glimpse of him. Flinging open the window and beaming through the lather, he shook hands cheerfully with each of the admirers. Everywhere he hammered away at the money question. Yet he did not totally neglect other issues. He was defending, he said, "all the people who suffer from the operations of trusts, syndicates, and combines."

McKinley's campaign was managed by a new type of politician, Marcus Alonzo Hanna, an Ohio businessman. In a sense Hanna was a product of the Pendleton Civil Service Act. When deprived of the contributions of officeholders, the parties turned to business for funds, and Hanna was one of the first leaders with a foot in both camps. Politics fascinated him, and despite his wealth and wide interests, he was willing to labor endlessly at the routine work of political organization.

Hanna aspired to be a kingmaker and early fastened on McKinley, whose charm he found irresis-

tible, as the vehicle for satisfying his ambition. He spent about $100,000 of his own money on the pre-convention campaign. His attitude toward the candidate, one mutual friend observed, was "that of a big, bashful boy toward the girl he loves."

Before most Republicans realized how effective Bryan was on the stump, Hanna perceived the danger and sprang into action. Since the late 1880s the character of political organization had been changing. The Civil Service Act was also cutting down on the number of jobs available to reward campaign workers. At the same time, the new mass-circulation newspapers and the nationwide press associations were increasing the pressure on candidates to speak openly and often on national issues. This trend put a premium on party organization and consistency—the old political trick of speaking out of one side of the mouth to one audience and out the other to another no longer worked very well. The old military metaphors of political discourse, the terms *campaign* and *spoils* and *standard bearer*, remained, but others more businesslike became popular: *boss, machine, lobbyist*.

As the federal government became more involved in economic issues, business interests found more reason to be concerned about national elections and were more willing to spend money in behalf of candidates whose views they approved. In the campaign of 1888 the Republicans had set up a businessman's "advisory board" to raise money and stir up enthusiasm for Benjamin Harrison.

Hanna understood what was happening to politics. Certain that money was the key to political power, he raised an enormous campaign fund. When businessmen hesitated to contribute, he pried open their purses by a combination of persuasiveness and intimidation. Banks and insurance companies were "assessed" a percentage of their assets, big corporations a share of their receipts, until some $3.5 million had been collected.

Hanna disbursed these funds with efficiency and imagination. He sent 1,500 speakers into the doubtful districts and blanketed the land with 250 million pieces of campaign literature, printed in a dozen languages. "He has advertised McKinley as if he were a patent medicine," Theodore Roosevelt, never at a loss for words, exclaimed.

Incapable of competing with Bryan as a swayer of mass audiences, McKinley conducted a "front-porch campaign." This technique dated from the first Harrison-Cleveland election, when Harrison regularly delivered off-the-cuff speeches to groups of visitors representing special interests or regions in his hometown of Indianapolis. The system conserved the candidate's energies and enabled him to avoid the appearance of seeking the presidency too openly—which was still considered bad form—and at the same time allowed him to make headlines throughout the country.

Guided by the masterful Hanna, McKinley brought the front-porch method to perfection. Superficially, the proceedings were delightfully informal. From every corner of the land, groups representing various regions, occupations, and interests descended on McKinley's unpretentious frame house in Canton, Ohio. Gathering on the

Beginning with his acceptance of the presidential nomination, William McKinley mounted his campaign from his front porch in Canton, Ohio.

lawn—the grass was soon reduced to mud, the fence stripped of pickets by souvenir hunters—the visitors paid their compliments to the candidate and heard him deliver a brief speech, while beside him on the porch his aged mother and adoring invalid wife listened with rapt attention. Then there was a small reception, during which the delegates were given an opportunity to shake their host's hand.

Despite the air of informality, these performances were carefully staged. The delegations arrived on a tightly coordinated schedule worked out by McKinley's staff and the railroads, which operated cut-rate excursion trains to Canton from all over the nation. McKinley was fully briefed on the special interests and attitudes of each group, and the speeches of delegation leaders were submitted in advance. Often his secretary amended these remarks, and on occasion McKinley wrote the visitors' speeches himself. His own talks were carefully prepared, each calculated to make a particular point. All were reported fully in the newspapers. Thus without moving from his doorstep, McKinley met thousands of people from every section of the country.

These tactics worked admirably. On election day McKinley carried the East; the Middle West including even Iowa, Minnesota, and North Dakota; and the Pacific Coast states of Oregon and California. Bryan won in the South, the plains states, and the Rocky Mountain region. McKinley collected 271 electoral votes to Bryan's 176, the popular vote being 7,036,000 to 6,468,000.

The Meaning of the Election

The sharp sectional division marked the failure of the Populist effort to unite northern and southern farmers and also the triumph of the industrial part of the country over the agricultural. Business and financial interests voted solidly for the Republicans, fearing that a Democratic victory would bring economic chaos. When a Nebraska landowner tried to float a mortgage during the campaign, a loan company official wrote him: "If McKinley is elected, we think we will be in the market, but we do not care to make any investments while there is an uncertainty as to what kind of money a person will be paid back in."

Other social and economic interests were far

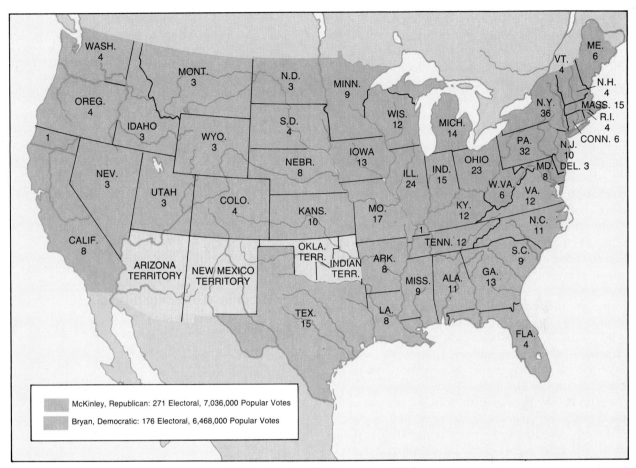

McKinley, Republican: 271 Electoral, 7,036,000 Popular Votes

Bryan, Democratic: 176 Electoral, 6,468,000 Popular Votes

THE ELECTION OF 1896

from being united. Many thousands of farmers voted for McKinley, as his success in states such as North Dakota, Iowa, and Minnesota proved. In the East and in the states bordering the Great Lakes, the agricultural depression was not severe, and farm radicalism was almost nonexistent.

A preponderance of the labor vote also went to the Republicans. In part this resulted from the tremendous pressures that many industrialists applied to their workers. "Men," one manufacturer announced, "vote as you please, but if Bryan is elected . . . the whistle will not blow Wednesday morning." Some companies placed orders for materials subject to cancellation if the Democrats won. Yet coercion was not a major factor, for McKinley was highly regarded in labor circles. While governor of Ohio,

he had advocated the arbitration of industrial disputes and backed a law fining employers who refused to permit workers to join unions. During the Pullman strike he had sent his brother to try to persuade George Pullman to deal fairly with the strikers. He had invariably based his advocacy of high tariffs on the argument that American wage levels would be depressed if foreign goods could enter the country untaxed. Mark Hanna too had the reputation of always giving his employees a square deal. The Republicans carried nearly all the large cities, and in closely contested states such as Illinois and Ohio this made the difference between victory and defeat.

During the campaign, some frightened Republicans had laid plans for fleeing the country if Bryan were elected, and belligerent ones, such as Theodore Roosevelt, then police commissioner of New York City, readied themselves to meet the "social revolutionaries" on the battlefield. Victory sent such people into transports of joy. Most conservatives concluded that the way of life they so fervently admired had been saved for all time.

However heartfelt, such sentiments were not founded on fact. With workers standing beside capitalists and with the farm vote split, it cannot be said that the election divided the nation class against class or that McKinley's victory saved the country from revolution.

Far from representing a triumph for the status quo, the election marked the coming of age of modern America. The battle between gold and silver, which everyone had considered so vital, had little real significance. The inflationists seemed to have been beaten, but new gold discoveries in Alaska and South Africa and improved methods of extracting gold from low-grade ores soon led to a great expansion of the money supply. In any case, within two decades the system of basing the volume of currency on bullion had been abandoned. Bryan and the "political" Populists who supported him, supposedly the advance agents of revolution, were oriented more toward the past than the future; their ideal was the rural America of Jefferson and Jackson.

McKinley, for all his innate conservatism, was capable of looking ahead toward the new century. His approach was national where Bryan's was basically parochial. Though never daring and seldom imaginative, he was able to deal pragmatically with current problems. Before long, as the United States became increasingly an exporter of manufactures, he would even modify his position on the tariff. And no one better reflected the spirit of the age than Mark Hanna, the outstanding political realist of his generation. Far from preventing change, the outcome of the election of 1896 made possible still greater changes as the United States moved into the 20th century.

Milestones

1873 Congress suspends the coining of silver ("Crime of '73")

1877 Farmers Alliance movement begins

1878 Bland-Allison Act

1879 Greenback paper money made convertible into gold

1881 President Garfield assassinated

1883 Pendleton Civil Service Act

1887 Interstate Commerce Act
Cleveland's tariff message

1890 Sherman Silver Purchase Act

1892 People's (Populist) party founded

1893 Panic of 1893

1894 Coxey's Army marches to Washington to demand relief

1895 Supreme Court declares federal income tax unconstitutional (*Pollock v. Farmers' Loan and Trust Company*)
J. P. Morgan raises $62 million in gold for the Treasury

1896 William Jennings Bryan, "Cross of Gold" speech

SUPPLEMENTARY READING

Titles marked with an asterisk have been published in paperback.

The political history of this period is covered in lively and controversial fashion in Matthew Josephson, **The Politicos*** (1938), and more solidly and sympathetically in H. W. Morgan, **From Hayes to McKinley** (1969). H. U. Faulkner, **Politics, Reform, and Expansion*** (1959), treats the politics of the 1890s in some detail, and Samuel McSeveney, **The Politics of Depression: Political Behavior in the Northeast** (1972), and C. V. Woodward, **Origins of the New South*** (1951), are important regional studies. J. A. Garraty, **The New Commonwealth*** (1968), attempts to trace the changing character of the political system after 1877.

There are three superb analyses of the political system of the period written by men who studied it firsthand: James Bryce, **The American Commonwealth*** (1888), Woodrow Wilson, **Congressional Government*** (1886), and Moisei Ostrogorski, **Democracy and the Organization of Political Parties*** (1902). Morton Keller, **Affairs of State** (1977), is an interesting analysis of public life in the period. L. D. White, **The Republican Era*** (1958), is an excellent study of the government in that period. D. J. Rothman, **Politics and Power: The United States Senate*** (1966), analyzes the shifting structure of the upper house.

J. C. Teaford, **The Unheralded Triumph: City Government** (1984), B. C. Campbell, **Representative Democracy** (1980), R. J. Jensen, **The Winning of the Midwest** (1971), and Paul Kleppner, **The Cross of Culture** (1977), are important studies of the character of state and local politics.

The issues of post-Reconstruction politics are discussed in S. P. Hirshson, **Farewell to the Bloody Shirt*** (1962), Allen Weinstein, **Prelude to Populism: Origins of the Silver Issue** (1970), Irwin Unger, **The Greenback Era*** (1964), W. T. K. Nugent, **Money and American Society** (1968), Geoffrey Blodgett, **The Gentle Reformers** (1966), J. G. Sproat, **"The Best Men": Liberal Reformers in the Gilded Age** (1968), Ari Hoogenboom, **Outlawing the Spoils** (1961), and in several essays in H. W. Morgan (ed.), **The Gilded Age*** (1970).

Among biographies of political leaders, the following are especially worth consulting: Ari Hoogenboom, **The Presidency of Rutherford B. Hayes** (1988), Allan Peskin, **Garfield** (1978), F. C. Reeves, **Gentleman President: Chester A. Arthur** (1978), J. D. Doenecke, **The Presidency of James A. Garfield and Chester A. Arthur** (1981), Allan Nevins, **Grover Cleveland** (1932), H. S. Merrill, **Bourbon Leader: Grover Cleveland and the Democratic Party*** (1957), H. J. Sievers, **Benjamin Harrison** (1952–1968), H. E. Socolovsky and A. B. Spetter, **The Presidency of Benjamin Harrison** (1987), and H. W. Morgan, **William McKinley and His America** (1963).

On the farmers' problems, see F. A. Shannon, **The Farmer's Last Frontier*** (1945), J. D. Hicks, **The Populist Revolt*** (1931), and Theodore Saloutos, **Farmer Movements in the South*** (1960). Populism has been the subject of intensive study. Richard Hofstadter, **The Age of Reform*** (1955), takes a dim view of populism as a reform movement, while Norman Pollack, **The Populist Response to Industrial America** (1962), pictures it as a radical one. W. T. K. Nugent, **The Tolerant Populists** (1963), leans in Pollack's direction but is more restrained. Lawrence Goodwyn, **Democratic Promise: The Populist Movement in America** (1976), calls it "a people's movement of mass democratic aspiration." R. W. Cherny, **Populism, Progressivism, and the Transformation of Nebraska Politics** (1981), Sheldon Hackney, **Populism to Progressivism in Alabama** (1969), and Steven Hahn, **The Roots of Southern Populism** (1983), are more than local studies.

On the depression of the 1890s, consult Charles Hoffman, **The Depression of the Nineties** (1970), Carlos Schwantes, **Coxey's Army** (1985), Stanley Buder, **Pullman** (1967), and Nick Salvatore, **Eugene V. Debs** (1982). On Bryan and the election of 1896, see P. W. Glad, **The Trumpet Soundeth** (1960), R. W. Cherny, **A Righteous Cause: William Jennings Bryan** (1985), S. L. Jones, **The Presidential Election of 1896** (1964), R. F. Durden, **The Climax of Populism** (1965), and P. W. Glad, **McKinley, Bryan, and the People*** (1964). On McKinley, consult L. L. Gould, **The Presidency of William McKinley** (1980), and Herbert Croly, **Marcus Alonzo Hanna** (1912), the best life of Hanna.

From Isolation to Empire

You furnish the pictures and I'll furnish the war.

WILLIAM RANDOLPH HEARST *to Frederic Remington, 1898*

I walked the floor of the White House night after night until midnight; and I am not ashamed to tell you, gentlemen, that I went down on my knees and prayed Almighty God for light and guidance more than one night. And one night late it came to me. . . . There was nothing left for us to do but to take them all, and to educate the Filipinos, and uplift and Christianize them.

PRESIDENT WILLIAM McKINLEY *explaining to Methodist churchmen his decision to favor annexation of the Philippine Islands, 1899*

A mericans have always been somewhat ambivalent in their attitudes toward other nations, and at no time was this more clearly the case than in the decades following the Civil War. Occupied with exploiting the West and building their great industrial machine, they gave little thought to foreign affairs. Benjamin Harrison reflected a widely held belief when he said during the 1888 presidential campaign that the United States was "an apart nation" and so it should remain. James Bryce made the same point in *The American Commonwealth*. "Happy America," he wrote, stood "apart in a world of her own . . . safe even from menace."

The historian David W. Pletcher has called the period the "awkward age" of American diplomacy, a time when the foreign service was "amateurish" and "spoils-ridden," when policy was either nonexistent or poorly planned, when treaties were clumsily drafted and state secrets ill kept. "The general idea of the diplomatic service," one reporter commented at this time, "is that it is a soft berth for wealthy young men who enjoy court society." The *New York Sun,* an important newspaper, suggested in the 1880s that the State Department had "outgrown its usefulness" and ought to be abolished.

America's Divided View of the World

Late-19th-century Americans never ignored world affairs entirely. They had little direct concern for what went on in Europe, but their interest in Latin America was great and growing, in the Far East only somewhat less so. Economic developments, especially shifts in foreign commerce resulting from industrialization, strengthened this interest with every passing year. Whether one sees isolation or expansion as the hallmark of American foreign policy after 1865 depends on the part of the world one looks at.

The disdain of the people of the United States for Europe rested on several historical foundations. Faith in the unique character of American civilization—and the converse of that belief, suspicion of Europe's supposedly aristocratic and decadent society—formed the chief basis of this isolation. Bitter memories of indignities suffered during the Revolution and the Napoleonic wars and anger at the hostile attitude of the great powers toward the United States during the Civil War strengthened it, as did the dislike of Americans for the pomp and punctilio of European monarchies. Also important was the undeniable truth that the United States was practically invulnerable to European attack and at the same time incapable of mounting an offensive against any European power. In turning their backs on Europe, Americans were taking no risk and passing up few opportunities—hence their indifference.

When occasional disagreements with one or another of the great powers erupted, the United States pressed its claims hard. It insisted, for example, that Great Britain pay for the loss of some 100,000 tons of American shipping sunk by Confederate cruisers that had been built in British yards during the rebellion. Some politicians even demanded that the British pay for the entire cost of the war after the Battle of Gettysburg—some $2 billion—on the grounds that without British backing, the Confederacy would have collapsed at about that point. However, the controversy never became critical, and in 1871 the two nations signed the Treaty of Washington, agreeing to arbitrate the so-called *Alabama* claims. The next year the judges awarded the United States $15.5 million for the ships and cargoes that had been destroyed.

In the 1880s a squabble developed with Ger-

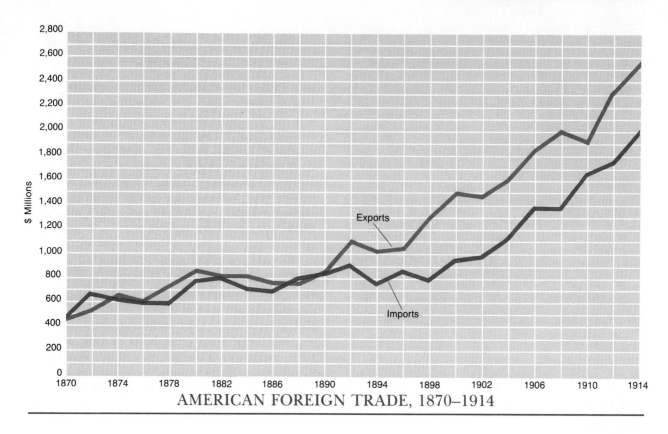

AMERICAN FOREIGN TRADE, 1870–1914

many, France, and a number of other countries over their banning of American pork products, ostensibly because some uninspected American pork was discovered to be diseased. The affair produced a great deal of windy oratory denouncing European autocracy and led to threats of economic retaliation. Congress eventually provided for the inspection of meat destined for export, and in 1891 the European nations lifted the ban. Similarly, there were repeated alarms and outbursts of anti-British feeling in the United States in connection with Great Britain's treatment of Ireland—all motivated chiefly by the desire of politicians to appeal to Irish-American voters.

Origins of the Large Policy

The nation's interests elsewhere in the world gradually increased. During the Civil War, France had established a protectorate over Mexico, installing the Archduke Maximilian of Austria as emperor.

In 1866 Secretary of State William H. Seward demanded that the French withdraw, and the government moved 50,000 soldiers to the Rio Grande. Fearing American intervention, among other reasons, the French pulled their troops out that winter, whereupon nationalist rebels seized and executed Maximilian. Shortly thereafter, at Seward's instigation, the United States purchased Alaska from Russia for $7.2 million, thereby ridding the continent of another foreign power.

That same year, 1867, the aggressive Seward acquired the Midway Islands in the western Pacific, which had been discovered in 1859 by an American naval officer, N. C. Brooks. Seward also made overtures toward annexing the Hawaiian Islands, and he looked longingly at Cuba. In 1870 President Grant submitted to the Senate a treaty annexing the Dominican Republic. He applied tremendous pressure in an effort to obtain ratification, thus forcing a "great debate" on extracontinental expansion. Expansionists stressed the wealth and resources of the country, the markets it would provide, even its "salubrious climate." But the arguments of the opposition proved more persuasive. The distance of the Dominican Republic from the continent, its crowded, dark-skinned population of what one congressman called "semi-civilized, semi-barbarous men who cannot speak our language," made annexation appear unattractive. The treaty was rejected. Prevailing opinion was well summarized by a Philadelphia newspaper: "The true interests of the American people will be better served . . . by thorough and complete development of the immense resources of our existing territory than by any rash attempts to increase it."

But the internal growth that preoccupied Americans eventually led them to look outward. By the late 1880s the country was exporting a steadily increasing share of its agricultural and industrial production. Exports, only $450 million in 1870, passed the billion-dollar mark early in the 1890s.

The character of foreign trade was also changing. Manufactures loomed ever more important among exports. American steelmakers could compete with British producers anywhere in the world. In 1900 one firm received a large order for steel plates from a Glasgow shipbuilder, and another won contracts for structural steel to be used in constructing bridges for the Uganda Railroad in British East Africa. When a member of Parliament questioned the colonial secretary about the latter deal, the secretary replied: "Tenders [bids] were invited in the United Kingdom . . . [but] one of the American tenders was found to be considerably the lowest in every respect and was therefore accepted." When American industrialists became conscious of their ability to compete with Europeans in far-off markets, they took more interest in world affairs, particularly during periods of depression, when domestic consumption fell.

Shifting intellectual currents further altered attitudes. Darwin's theories, applicable by analogy to international relations, gave the concept of manifest destiny a new plausibility. Darwinists like the historian John Fiske argued that the American government was so clearly the world's "fittest" that it was destined to spread peacefully over "every land on the earth's surface." In *Our Country* (1885) Josiah Strong found racist and religious justifications for expansionism, again based on the theory of evolution. The Anglo-Saxon race, centered now in the United States, possessed "an instinct or genius for

colonization," Strong claimed. "God, with infinite wisdom and skill is training the Anglo-Saxon race for . . . the final competition of races." Christianity, he added, had developed "aggressive traits calculated to impress its institutions upon mankind." Soon American civilization would "move down upon" Mexico and all Latin America, and "out upon the islands of the sea, over upon Africa and beyond." "Can anyone doubt," Strong asked, "that the result of this . . . will be 'the survival of the fittest'?"*

The completion of the conquest of the West encouraged Americans to consider expansion beyond the seas. "For nearly 300 years the dominant fact in American life has been expansion," declared Frederick Jackson Turner, propounder of the frontier thesis. "That these energies of expansion will no longer operate would be a rash prediction." Turner and writers who advanced other expansionist arguments were much influenced by foreign thinking. European liberals had tended to disapprove of colonial ventures, but in the 1870s and 1880s many of them were changing their minds. English liberals in particular began to talk and write about the "superiority" of English culture, to describe the virtues of the "Anglo-Saxon race," to stress a "duty" to spread Christianity among the heathen, and to advance economic arguments for overseas expansion.

European ideas were reinforced for Americans by their observations of the imperialist activities of the European powers in what would today be called underdeveloped areas. By swallowing up most of Africa and biting off bits and pieces of the crumbling empire of China, the French, British, Germans, and other colonizers inspired some Americans to advocate joining the feast before all the choice morsels had been digested. "While the great powers of Europe are steadily enlarging their colonial domination in Asia and Africa," James G. Blaine said in 1884, "it is the especial province of this country to improve and expand its trade with the nations of America." While Blaine emphasized commerce, the excitement and adventure of overseas enterprises appealed to many people even more than the economic possibilities or any sense of obligation to fulfill a supposed national, religious, or racial destiny.

---

* In later writings Strong insisted that by "fittest" he was referring to "social efficiency," not "mere strength."

Finally, military and strategic arguments were advanced to justify adopting a "large" policy. The powerful Union army had been demobilized rapidly after Appomattox; in the 1880s only about 25,000 men were under arms, their chief occupation fighting Indians in the West. Half the navy had been scrapped after the war, and the remaining ships were obsolete. While other nations were building steam-powered iron warships, the United States still depended on wooden sailing vessels.

The decrepit state of the navy vexed many of its officers and led one of them, Captain Alfred Thayer Mahan, to develop a startling theory about the importance of sea power. He explained his theory in *The Influence of Sea Power upon History* (1890) and *The Influence of Sea Power upon the French Revolution and Empire* (1892). According to Mahan, history proved that a nation with a powerful navy and the overseas bases necessary to maintain it would

be invulnerable in war and prosperous in time of peace. Applied to the current American situation, this meant that in addition to building a modern fleet, the United States should obtain a string of coaling stations and bases in the Caribbean, annex the Hawaiian Islands, and cut a canal across Central America. A more extensive colonial empire might follow, but these bases and the canal they would protect were essential first steps to ensure America's future as a great power.

Writing at a time when the imperialist-minded European nations showed signs of extending their influence in South America and the Pacific islands, Mahan attracted many influential disciples. One was Congressman Henry Cabot Lodge of Massachusetts. Lodge had married into a navy family and was intimate with the head of the new Naval War College, Commodore Stephen B. Luce. He helped push through Congress in 1883 an act authorizing the building of three steel warships, and he consistently advocated expanding and modernizing the fleet. Elevated to the Senate in 1893, Lodge pressed for expansionist policies, basing his arguments on Mahan's strategic concepts. "Sea power," he proclaimed, "is essential to the greatness of every splendid people." Lodge's friend Theodore Roosevelt was another ardent supporter of the "large" policy, but he had little influence until McKinley appointed him assistant secretary of the navy in 1897.

The Course of Empire in the Pacific

The interest of the United States in the Pacific and the Far East began in the late 18th century, when the first American merchant ship dropped anchor in Canton harbor. After the Treaty of Wanghia (1844), American merchants in China enjoyed many privileges, and trade expanded rapidly. Missionaries began to flock to the country; in the late 1880s, over 500 were living there.

The Hawaiian Islands were an important way station on the route to China, and by 1820 merchants and missionaries were making contacts there. As early as 1854 a movement to annex the islands existed, though it foundered because Hawaii insisted on being admitted to the Union as a state. Commodore Perry's expedition to Japan led to the

A 1904 photograph of Admiral Alfred Thayer Mahan, a leading advocate of sea power and proponent of naval expansionism. His views found favor among such imperialist-minded Republicans as Henry Cabot Lodge and Theodore Roosevelt.

signing of a commercial treaty (1858) that opened several Japanese ports to American traders.

The United States pursued a policy of cooperating with the European powers in expanding commercial opportunities in the Far East. In Hawaii the tendency was to claim a special position but to accept the fact that Europeans also had interests in the islands. This state of affairs did not change radically following the Civil War. Despite Chinese protests over the exclusion of their nationals from the United States after 1882, American commercial privileges in China were not disturbed. American influence in Hawaii increased; the descendants of missionary families, most of them engaged in raising sugar, dominated the Hawaiian monarchy. In 1875 a reciprocity treaty admitted Hawaiian sugar to the United States free of duty in return for a promise to yield no territory to a foreign power. When this treaty was renewed in 1887, the United States obtained the right to establish a naval base at Pearl Harbor. In addition to occupying Midway Island, America obtained a foothold in the Samoan Islands in the South Pacific.

During the 1890s American interest in the Pacific area steadily intensified. Conditions in Hawaii had much to do with this. The McKinley Tariff Act of 1890, discontinuing the duty on raw sugar and compensating American producers of cane and beet sugar by granting them a bounty of 2 cents a pound, struck Hawaiian sugar growers hard, for it destroyed the advantage they had gained in the reciprocity treaty. The following year the death of the complaisant King Kalakaua brought Queen Liliuokalani, a determined nationalist, to the throne. Placing herself at the head of a "Hawaii for the Hawaiians" movement, she abolished the existing constitution under which the white minority had pretty much controlled the islands and attempted to rule as an absolute monarch. The resident Americans then staged a coup. In January 1893, with the connivance of the United States minister, John L. Stevens, who ordered 150 marines from the cruiser *Boston* into Honolulu, they deposed Queen Liliuokalani and set up a provisional government. Stevens recognized their regime at once, and the new government sent a delegation to Washington to seek a treaty of annexation.

In the closing days of the Harrison administration such a treaty was negotiated and sent to the Senate, but when Cleveland took office in March,

he withdrew it. The new president disapproved of the way American troops had been used to overthrow the queen. He sent a special commissioner, James H. Blount, to Hawaii to investigate. When Blount reported that the native Hawaiians opposed annexation, the president dismissed Stevens and attempted to restore Queen Liliuokalani. Since the provisional government was by that time firmly entrenched, this could not be accomplished peacefully. Because Cleveland was unwilling to use force against the Americans in the islands, however much he objected to their actions, he found himself unable to do anything. The revolutionary government of Hawaii remained in power, independent yet eager to be annexed.

The Hawaiian debate continued sporadically over the next four years. It provided a thorough airing of the question of overseas expansion. Fears that another power—Great Britain or perhaps Japan—might step into the void created by Cleveland's refusal to act alarmed those who favored annexation. When the Republicans returned to power in 1897, a new annexation treaty was negotiated, but domestic sugar producers now threw their weight against it, and the McKinley administration could not obtain the necessary two-thirds majority in the Senate. Finally, in July 1898, after the outbreak of the Spanish-American War, Congress annexed the islands by joint resolution, a procedure requiring only a simple majority vote.

The Course of Empire in Latin America

Most of the arguments for extending American influence in the Pacific applied more strongly to Central and South America, where the United States had much larger economic interests and where the strategic importance of the region was clear. Furthermore, the Monroe Doctrine had long conditioned the American people to the idea of acting to protect national interests in the Western Hemisphere.

As early as 1869 President Grant had come out for an American-owned canal across the isthmus of Panama, in spite of the fact that the United States had agreed in the Clayton-Bulwer Treaty with Great Britain (1850) that neither nation would "obtain or maintain for itself any exclusive control" over an interoceanic canal. In 1880, when the French engineer Ferdinand de Lesseps organized a company to build a canal across the isthmus, President Hayes announced that the United States would not permit a European power to control such a waterway. "The policy of the country is a canal under American control," he announced, another blithe disregard of the Clayton-Bulwer agreement.

In 1889 a pan-American conference met in Washington to discuss hemisphere problems. Secretary of State James G. Blaine hoped to use this meeting to obtain a reciprocity agreement with the Latin American countries, for the United States was importing about three times as much from them as they were purchasing in America. However, the delegates accomplished nothing beyond the establishment of the International Bureau—later known as the Pan-American Union—to promote commercial and cultural exchange. The conference was nevertheless significant, for it marked the first effort by the United States to assume the leadership of the nations of the hemisphere.

At the Washington meeting the United States posed as a friend of peace; Blaine's proposals included a general arbitration treaty to settle hemisphere disputes. A minor disagreement with the Republic of Chile in 1891 soon demonstrated that the country could quickly be brought to the verge of war with one of its southern neighbors. Anti-*Yanqui* feeling was high in Chile, chiefly because the United States had refused to sell arms to the current government during the revolution that had brought it to power. In October a group of sailors from the U.S.S. *Baltimore* on shore leave in Valparaiso was set upon by a mob. Two of the sailors were killed and more than a dozen injured. President Harrison, furious at what he called an "insult . . . to the uniform of the United States sailors," demanded "prompt and full reparation." When the Chilean authorities delayed in supplying an appropriate apology and issued a statement that "imputed untruth and insincerity" on Harrison's part, the president sent to Congress a special message virtually inviting it to declare war. Faced with this threat, Chile backed down, offering the required apology and agreeing to pay damages to the sailors. Chile's humiliation destroyed much of the goodwill engendered by the Pan-American Conference.

When Cleveland returned to power in 1893, the possibility of trouble in Latin America seemed remote, for he had always opposed imperialistic ventures. The Latin American diplomatic colony in Washington greeted him warmly after its experience with Harrison. Yet scarcely two years later the United States was again on the verge of war in South America, this time as a result of a crisis in Venezuela, and before this issue was settled, Cleveland had made the most powerful claim to American hegemony in the hemisphere ever uttered.

The tangled borderland between Venezuela and British Guiana had long been in dispute, Venezuela demanding more of the region than it was entitled to and Great Britain submitting exaggerated claims and imperiously refusing to submit the question to arbitration. What made a crisis of the controversy was the political situation in the United States. A minor incident in Nicaragua, where the British had temporarily occupied the port of Corinto to force compensation for injuries to British subjects in that country, had alarmed American supporters of the Monroe Doctrine. Cleveland had avoided involvement, and along with his refusal to take Hawaii, the incident had angered expansionists. With his party rapidly deserting him because of his stand on the silver question and with the election of 1896 approaching, the president desperately needed a popular issue.

There was considerable latent anti-British feeling in the United States. By taking the Venezuelan side in the boundary dispute, Cleveland would be defending a weak neighbor against a great power, a position certain to evoke a popular response. "Turn this Venezuela question up or down, North, South, East or West, and it is a winner," one Democrat advised the president.

Cleveland did not resist the temptation to intervene. In July 1895 he ordered Secretary of State Richard Olney to send a near-ultimatum to the British. By occupying the disputed territory, Olney insisted, Great Britain was invading Venezuela and violating the Monroe Doctrine. Quite gratuitously, he went on to boast: "To-day the United States is practically sovereign on this continent, and its fiat is law upon the subjects to which it confines its interposition." Unless Great Britain responded promptly by agreeing to arbitration, the president would call the question to the attention of Congress.

The note threatened war, but the British ignored it for months. They did not take the United States seriously as a world power, and with reason, for the American navy, although expanding, could not hope to stand up against the British, who had 50 battleships, 25 armored cruisers, and many smaller vessels. When Lord Salisbury, the prime minister and foreign secretary, finally replied, he rejected outright the argument that the Monroe Doctrine had any status under international law and refused to arbitrate what he called the "exaggerated pretentions" of the Venezuelans.

If Olney's note had been belligerent, this reply was supercilious and sharp to the point of asperity. Cleveland was furious. On December 17, 1895, he asked Congress for authority to appoint an American commission to determine the correct line between British Guiana and Venezuela. When that had been done, he added, the United States should "resist by every means in its power" the appropriation by Great Britain of any territory "we have determined of right belongs to Venezuela." Congress responded at once, unanimously appropriating $100,000 for the boundary commission. Popular approval was almost universal.

In Great Britain, government and people suddenly awoke to the seriousness of the situation. No one wanted a war with the United States over a remote patch of tropical real estate. In Europe, Britain was concerned about German economic competition and the increased military power of that nation. In addition, Canada would be terribly vulnerable to American attack in the event of war. The immense potential strength of the United States could no longer be ignored. Why make an enemy of a nation of 70 million, already the richest industrial power in the world? To fight with the United States, the British colonial secretary realized, "would be an absurdity as well as a crime."

Great Britain agreed to arbitrate the boundary. The war scare subsided; soon Olney was talking about "our inborn and instinctive English sympathies" and offering "to stand side by side and shoulder to shoulder with England in . . . the defence of human rights." When the boundary tribunal awarded nearly all the disputed region to Great Britain, whatever ill feeling the surrender may have occasioned in that country faded away. Instead of leading to war, the affair marked the beginning of an era of Anglo-American friendship. It had the unfortunate effect, however, of adding to the long-held American conviction that the nation could get what it wanted in international affairs by threat and bluster—a dangerous illusion.

The Cuban Revolution

On February 10, 1896, scarcely a week after Venezuela and Great Britain had signed the treaty ending their dispute, General Valeriano Weyler arrived in Havana from Spain to take up his duties as governor of Cuba. His assignment to this post was occasioned by the guerrilla warfare that Cuban nationalist rebels had been waging for almost a year. Weyler, a tough and ruthless soldier, set out to administer Cuba with "a salutary rigor." He began herding the rural population into wretched "reconcentration" camps in order to deprive the rebels of food and recruits. Resistance in Cuba hardened.

The United States had been interested in Cuba since the time of John Quincy Adams and, were it not for northern opposition to adding more slave territory, might well have obtained the island in one way or another before 1860. When the Cubans revolted against Spain in 1868, considerable support for intervening on their behalf developed. Hamilton Fish, Grant's secretary of state, resisted this sentiment, and Spain managed to pacify the rebels in 1878 by promising reforms. But change was slow in coming; slavery was not abolished until 1886. The worldwide depression of the 1890s hit the Cuban economy hard, and when an American tariff act in 1894 jacked up the rate on Cuban sugar by 40 percent, thus cutting off Cuban growers from the American market, the resulting distress precipitated another revolt.

Public sympathy in the United States went to the Cubans, who seemed to be fighting for liberty and democracy against an autocratic Old World power. Most American newspapers supported the Cubans; labor unions, veterans' organizations, many Protestant clergymen, and important politicians in both major parties demanded that the United States aid the rebel cause. Rapidly increasing American investments in Cuban sugar plantations, now approaching $50 million, were endangered by the fighting and by the social chaos sweeping across the island. Cuban propagandists in the United States played on American sentiments cleverly. When reports, often exaggerated, of the cruelty of "Butcher" Weyler and the horrors of his reconcentration

Instability in Latin America led many to speculate that the United States would play an increasingly dominant role in the region. In Louis Dalrymple's 1895 cartoon, Uncle Sam wins the affections of the damsel Cuba as Spanish misrule and native insurgency lay waste to each other.

camps filtered into America, the cry for action intensified. In April 1896 Congress adopted a resolution suggesting that the revolutionaries be granted the rights of belligerents. Since this would have been akin to formal recognition, Cleveland would not go that far, but he did exert diplomatic pressure on Spain to remove the causes of the rebels' complaints, and he offered the services of his government as mediator. The Spanish rejected the suggestion.

For a time the issue subsided. The election of 1896 deflected American attention from Cuba, and then McKinley refused to take any action that might disturb Spanish-American relations. Business interests—except those with holdings in Cuba—backed McKinley, for they feared that a crisis would upset the economy, which was just beginning to pick up after the depression. In Cuba, General Weyler made some progress toward stifling rebel resistance.

American expansionists, however, continued to demand intervention, and the press, especially Joseph Pulitzer's *New York World* and William Randolph Hearst's *New York Journal*, competing fiercely to increase circulation, kept resentment alive with tales of Spanish atrocities. McKinley remained adamant. Although he warned Spain that Cuba must be pacified, and soon, his tone was friendly and he issued no ultimatum. A new government in Spain relieved the situation by recalling Weyler and promising the Cubans partial self-government. In a message to Congress in December 1897, McKinley urged that Spain be given "a reasonable chance to realize her expectations" in the island. McKinley was not insensitive to Cuba's plight—though not a rich man, he made an anonymous contribution of $5,000 to the Red Cross Cuban relief fund—but he genuinely wanted to avoid intervention.

His hopes were doomed, primarily because

Spain failed to "realize her expectations." The fighting in Cuba continued. When riots broke out in Havana in January 1898, McKinley ordered the battleship *Maine* to Havana harbor to protect American citizens.

Shortly thereafter, Hearst's *New York Journal* printed a letter written to a friend in Cuba by the Spanish minister in Washington, Dupuy de Lôme. The letter had been stolen by a spy. De Lôme, an experienced but arrogant diplomat, failed to appreciate McKinley's efforts to avoid intervening in Cuba. In the letter he characterized the president as a *politicastro,* or "small-time politician," which was a gross error, and a "bidder for the admiration of the crowd," which was equally insulting though somewhat closer to the truth. Americans were outraged, and de Lôme's hasty resignation did little to soothe their feelings.

Then, on February 15, the *Maine* exploded and sank in Havana harbor, 260 of its crew perishing in the disaster. Interventionists in the United States accused Spain of having destroyed the ship and clamored for war. The willingness of Americans to blame Spain indicates the extent of anti-Spanish opinion in the United States by 1898. No one has ever discovered what actually happened. A naval court of inquiry decided that the vessel had been sunk by a submarine mine, but it now seems more likely that an internal explosion destroyed the *Maine.* The Spanish government could hardly have been foolish enough to commit an act that would probably bring American troops into Cuba.

With admirable courage, McKinley refused to panic, but he could not resist the wishes of millions of citizens that something be done to stop the fighting and allow the Cubans to determine their own fate. Spanish pride and Cuban patriotism had taken the issue of peace or war out of the president's hands. Spain could not put down the rebellion, and it would not yield to the nationalists' increasingly extreme demands. To have granted independence to Cuba might have caused the Madrid government to fall, might even have led to the collapse of the monarchy, for the Spanish public was in no mood to surrender. The Cubans, sensing that the continuing bloodshed aided their cause, refused to give the Spanish regime room to maneuver. After the *Maine* disaster, Spain might have agreed to an armistice had the rebels asked for one, and in the resulting negotiations it might well have given up the island. The rebels refused to make the first move. The fighting continued, bringing the United States every day closer to intervention.

The president faced a dilemma. Most business interests of the country, to which he was particularly sensitive, opposed intervention. His personal feelings were equally firm. "I have been through one war," he told a friend. "I have seen the dead piled up, and I do not want to see another." Congress, however, seemed determined to act. When he submitted a restrained report on the sinking of the *Maine,* the Democrats in Congress, even most of those who had supported Cleveland's policies, gleefully accused him of timidity. Vice-President Garret A. Hobart warned him that the Senate could not be held in check for long; should Congress declare war on its own, the administration would be discredited.

McKinley spent a succession of sleepless nights; sedatives brought him no repose. Finally, early in April, the president drafted a message asking for authority to use the armed forces "to secure a full and final termination of hostilities" in Cuba.

At the last moment the Spanish government seemed to yield; it ordered its troops in Cuba to cease hostilities. McKinley passed this information on to Congress along with his war message, but he gave it no emphasis and did not try to check the march toward war. To seek further delay would have been courageous but not necessarily wiser. Merely to stop fighting was not enough. The Cuban nationalists now insisted on full independence, and the Spanish politicians were unprepared to abandon the last remnant of their once-great American empire. If the United States took Cuba by force, the Spanish leaders might save their political skins; if they meekly surrendered the island, they were done for.

The "Splendid Little" Spanish-American War

On April 20 Congress, by joint resolution, recognized the independence of Cuba and authorized the use of the armed forces to drive out the Spanish. An amendment proposed by Senator Henry M. Teller disclaiming any intention of adding Cuban territory to the United States passed without opposition. Four days later Spain declared war on the United States.

The Spanish-American War was fought to free

Cuba, but the first action took place on the other side of the globe, in the Philippine Islands. Weeks earlier, Assistant Secretary of the Navy Theodore Roosevelt had alerted Commodore George Dewey, who was in command of the United States Asiatic Squadron located at Hong Kong, to move against the Spanish base at Manila if war came. Dewey had acted promptly, drilling his gun crews, taking on supplies, giving his gleaming white ships a coat of battle-gray paint, and establishing secret contacts with the Filipino nationalist leader, Emilio Aguinaldo. When word of the declaration of war reached him, he steamed from Hong Kong across the South China Sea with four cruisers and two gunboats. On the night of April 30 he entered Manila Bay, and at daybreak he opened fire on the Spanish fleet at 5,000 yards. His squadron made five passes, each time reducing the range; when the smoke had cleared, all ten of Admiral Montojo's ships had been destroyed. Not a single American was killed in the engagement.

Dewey immediately asked for troops to take and hold Manila, for now that war had been declared, he could not return to Hong Kong or put in at any other neutral port. McKinley took the fateful step of dispatching some 11,000 soldiers and additional naval support. On August 13 these forces, assisted by Filipino irregulars under Aguinaldo, captured Manila.

Meanwhile, in the main theater of operations, the United States had won a swift and total victory, though more because of the weakness of the Spanish armed forces than because of the power or efficiency of the American. When the war began, the regular army consisted of about 28,000 men. This tiny force was bolstered by 200,000 hastily enlisted volunteers. In May an expeditionary force gathered at Tampa, Florida. That hamlet was inundated by the masses

A woman recruiting officer, accompanied by a military band, urging enlistments in New York City at the outbreak of the Spanish-American War. Patriotism, at least, was not seen as gender-specific.

of men and supplies that descended on it. Entire regiments sat without uniforms or weapons while hundreds of freight cars jammed with equipment lay forgotten on sidings. Army management was abominable, rivalry between commanders a serious problem. Aggressive units like the regiment of "Rough Riders" raised by Theodore Roosevelt, now a lieutenant colonel of volunteers, scrambled for space and supplies, shouldering aside other units to get what they needed. "No words could describe . . . the confusion and lack of system and the general mismanagement of affairs here," the angry Roosevelt complained.

Since a Spanish fleet under Admiral Pascual Cervera was known to be in Caribbean waters, no invading army could safely embark until the fleet could be located. On May 29, American ships found Cervera at Santiago harbor, on the eastern end of Cuba, and established a blockade. In June a 17,000-man expeditionary force commanded by General William Shafter landed at Daiquiri, east of Santiago, and pressed quickly toward the city, handicapped more by its own bad staff work than by the enemy, though the Spanish troops resisted bravely. The Americans sweated through Cuba's torrid summer in heavy wool winter uniforms, ate "embalmed beef" out of cans, and fought mostly with old-fashioned rifles using black-powder cartridges that marked the position of each soldier with a puff of smoke whenever he pulled the trigger. On July 1 they broke through undermanned Spanish defenses and stormed San Juan Hill, the intrepid Roosevelt in the van. ("Are you afraid to stand up while I am on horseback?" Roosevelt demanded of one soldier.)

With Santiago harbor in range of American artillery, Admiral Cervera had to run the blockade. On July 3 his black-hulled ships, flags proudly flying, steamed forth from the harbor and fled westward along the coast. Like hounds after rabbits, five American battleships and two cruisers, commanded by Rear Admiral William T. Sampson and Commodore Winfield Scott Schley, ran them down. In four hours the entire Spanish force was destroyed by a hail of 8-inch and 13-inch projectiles. Damage to the American ships was superficial; only one seaman lost his life in the engagement.

The end then came abruptly. Santiago surrendered on July 17. A few days later other United States troops completed the occupation of Puerto Rico. On August 12, one day before the fall of Manila, Spain agreed to get out of Cuba and to cede Puerto Rico and the island of Guam in the Marianas to the United States. The future of the Philippines was to be settled at a formal peace conference, convening in Paris on October 1.

Developing a Colonial Policy

Although the Spanish resisted surrendering the Philippines at Paris, they had been so thoroughly defeated that they had no choice. The decision hung rather on the outcome of a conflict over policy within the United States. The war, won at so little cost militarily, produced problems far larger than those it solved.* The nation had become a great power in the world's eyes. The United States, a French diplomat wrote a few years later, "is seated at the table where the great game is played, and it cannot leave it." European leaders had been impressed by the forcefulness of Cleveland's diplomacy in the Venezuela boundary dispute and by the efficiency the navy displayed in the war. The annexation of Hawaii and other overseas bases intensified their conviction that the United States was serious about becoming a major force in international affairs.

But were the American people determined to exercise that force? The debate over taking the Philippine Islands throws much light on their attitudes. The imagination of Americans had been captured by the trappings of empire, not by its essence. It was titillating to think of a world map liberally sprinkled with American flags and of the economic benefits that colonies might bring, but most citizens were not prepared to join in a worldwide struggle for power and influence. They entered blithely upon adventures in far-off regions without facing the implications of their decision.

Since the United States (in the Teller Amendment) had abjured any claim to Cuba, even though expansionists had long desired the island, logic dictated that a similar policy be applied to the Philippines, a remote land few Americans had ever thought about before 1898. But expansionists were

---

* More than 5,000 Americans died as a result of the conflict, but fewer than 400 fell in combat. The others were mostly victims of yellow fever, typhoid, and other diseases.

*As the Monroe Doctrine became more significant around the turn of the century,
chauvinistic cartoonists used it to taunt European powers. In this example, from a
1901 issue of* Puck, *the European chickens complain, "You're not the only rooster
in South America!" to which Uncle Sam retorts, "I was aware of that when I
cooped you up!"*

eager to annex the entire archipelago. Even before
he had learned to spell the name, Senator Lodge
was saying that "the Phillipines (*sic*) mean a vast
future trade and wealth and power," offering the
nation a greater opportunity "than anything that
has happened . . . since the annexation of Louisiana."

President McKinley adopted a more cautious
stance, but he too favored "the general principle of
holding on to what we can get." A speaking tour of
the Middle West in October 1898, during which he
experimented with varying degrees of commitment
to expansionism, convinced him that the public
wanted the islands. Business opinion had shifted
dramatically during the war. Business leaders were
now calling the Philippines the gateway to the markets of the Far East.

The Anti-imperialists

An important minority objected strongly to the
United States acquiring overseas possessions. Persons as different in interest and philosophy as the
tycoon Andrew Carnegie and the labor leader Samuel Gompers, the venerable Republican Senator
George Frisbie Hoar of Massachusetts and "Pitchfork Ben" Tillman, the southern Democratic firebrand, together with the writers Mark Twain and
William Dean Howells, the reformers Lincoln Steffens and Jane Addams, and the educators Charles
W. Eliot of Harvard and David Starr Jordan of Stanford united in opposing the annexation of the Philippines.

The anti-imperialists insisted that since no one
would consider statehood for the Philippines, it

would be unconstitutional to annex them. It was a violation of the spirit of the Declaration of Independence to govern a foreign territory without the consent of its inhabitants, Senator Hoar argued; by taking over "vassal states" in "barbarous archipelagoes" the United States was "trampling . . . on our own great Charter, which recognizes alike the liberty and the dignity of individual manhood."

McKinley was not insensitive to this appeal to idealism and tradition, which was the fundamental element in the anti-imperialist argument, but he rejected it for several reasons. Many people who opposed Philippine annexation were neither idealists nor constitutional purists. Partisanship led numbers of Democrats to object. Other anti-imperialists were governed by racial and ethnic prejudices, as Senator Hoar's statement indicates. They opposed not expansion as such—Carnegie, for example, was eager to have Canada added to the Union—but expansion that brought under the American flag people whom they believed unfit for American citizenship. Labor leaders particularly feared the competition of "the Chinese, the Negritos, and the Malays" who presumably would flood into the United States if the Philippines were taken.

More compelling to McKinley was the absence of any practical alternative to annexation. Public opinion would not sanction restoring Spanish authority in the Philippines or allowing some other power to have them. That the Filipinos were sufficiently advanced and united socially to form a stable government if granted independence seemed unlikely. Senator Hoar believed that "for years and for generations, and perhaps for centuries, there would have been turbulence, disorder and revolution" in the islands if they were left to their own devices.

Strangely—for he was a kind and gentle man—Hoar faced this possibility with equanimity. McKinley was unable to do so. The president searched the depths of his soul and could find no solution but annexation. Of course, the state of public feeling made the decision easier. And he probably found the idea of presiding over an empire appealing. Certainly the commercial possibilities did not escape him. In the end it was with a heavy sense of responsibility that he ordered the American peace commissioners to insist on acquiring the Philippines. To salve the feelings of the Spanish, the United States agreed to pay $20 million for the archipelago, but it was a forced sale, accepted by Spain under duress.

The peace treaty faced a hard battle in the United States Senate, where a combination of partisan politics and anticolonialism made it difficult to amass the two-thirds majority necessary for ratification. McKinley had shrewdly appointed three senators, including one Democrat, to the peace commission. This predisposed many members of the upper house to approve the treaty, but the vote was close. William Jennings Bryan, titular head of the Democratic party, could probably have prevented ratification had he urged his supporters to vote nay. Although he was opposed to taking the Philippines, he did not do so. To reject the treaty would leave the United States technically at war with Spain and the fate of the Philippines undetermined; better to accept the islands and then grant them independence. The question should be decided, Bryan said, "not by a minority of the Senate but by a majority of the people" at the next presidential election. Perplexed by Bryan's stand, a number of Democrats allowed themselves to be persuaded by the expansionists' arguments and by McKinley's judicious use of patronage; the treaty was ratified in February 1899 by a vote of 57 to 27.

The Philippine Rebellion

The national referendum that Bryan had hoped for never materialized. Bryan himself confused the issue in 1900 by making free silver a major plank in his platform, thereby driving conservative anti-imperialists into McKinley's arms. Moreover, early in 1899 the Filipino nationalists under Aguinaldo, furious because the United States would not withdraw, rose in rebellion. A savage guerrilla war resulted, one that cost far more in lives and money than the "splendid little" Spanish-American conflict.

Like all conflicts waged in tangled terrain chiefly by small, isolated units surrounded by a hostile civilian population, neither side displayed much regard for the "rules" of war. Goaded by sneak attacks and instances of cruelty to captives, American soldiers, most of whom had little respect for Filipinos to begin with, responded in kind. Civilians were rounded up, prisoners were tortured, property was

Emilio Aguinaldo, who commanded Filipino insurgents who worked with Commodore Dewey to help overthrow Spanish rule of the Philippines in 1898. He later took up arms against the United States in a brutal three-year struggle when President McKinley opposed granting independence to the islands.

destroyed. Horrible tales of rape, arson, and murder by United States troops filtered into the country, providing ammunition for the anti-imperialists. "You seem to have about finished your work of civilizing the Filipinos," Andrew Carnegie wrote angrily to one of the American peace commissioners. "About 8,000 of them have been completely civilized and sent to Heaven. I hope you like it." In fact, far more than 8,000 Filipinos lost their lives during the conflict, which raged for three years. More than 70,000 American soldiers had to be sent to the islands before the resistance was crushed, and about as many of them lost their lives as had perished in the Cuban conflict.

In 1899, before the fighting started, McKinley had sent a commission to the Philippines to study the problem. The committee attributed the revolt to the ambitions of the nationalist leaders and recommended that the Philippines be granted independence at an indefinite future date. The following year the president sent another commission, this one headed by William Howard Taft, a federal judge, to establish a government. Taft, a warm-hearted, affable man, took an instant liking to the Filipinos, and his policy of encouraging them to participate in the territorial government attracted many converts. In July 1901 he became the first civilian governor of the Philippines, though the rebellion went on for many months.

Actually, McKinley's reelection in 1900 settled the Philippine question so far as most Americans were concerned. Anti-imperialists still claimed that it was unconstitutional to take over territories without the consent of the local population. Their reasoning, though certainly not specious, was unhistorical. No American government had seriously considered the wishes of the American Indians, the French and Spanish settlers in Louisiana, or the Eskimos of Alaska when it had seemed in the national interest to annex new lands.

Cuba and the United States

Nevertheless, grave constitutional questions arose as a result of the acquisitions that followed the Spanish-American War. McKinley acted with remarkable independence in handling the problems involved in expansion. He set up military governments in Cuba, Puerto Rico, and the Philippines without specific congressional authority. But eventually both Congress and the Supreme Court took a hand in shaping colonial policy. In 1900 Congress passed the Foraker Act, establishing a civil government for Puerto Rico. It did not give the Puerto Ricans either American citizenship or full local self-government, and it placed a tariff on Puerto Rican products imported into the United States.

The tariff provision was promptly challenged in the courts on the grounds that Puerto Rico was part of the United States, but in *Downes* v. *Bidwell* (1901) the Supreme Court upheld the legality of the duties. In this and other "insular cases" the reasoning of the judges was more than ordinarily difficult to follow. ("We suggest, without intending to decide, that there may be a distinction between certain natural rights enforced in the Constitution . . . and what may be termed artificial or remedial rights," the Downes opinion held.) The effect, however, was clear: The Constitution did not follow the flag; Congress could act toward the colonies almost as it pleased. A colony, one dissenting justice said, could be kept "like a disembodied shade, in an indeterminate state of ambiguous existence for an indefinite period."

While the most heated arguments raged over Philippine policy, the most difficult colonial problems concerned the relationship between the United States and Cuba, for there idealism and self-interest clashed painfully. Despite the desire of most Americans to get out of Cuba, an independent government could not easily be created. Order and prosperity did not automatically appear when the red and gold ensigns of Spain were hauled down from the flagstaffs of Havana and Santiago.

The insurgent government was feeble, corrupt, and oligarchic, the Cuban economy in a state of collapse, life chaotic. The first Americans entering Havana found the streets littered with garbage and the corpses of horses and dogs. All public services were at a standstill; it seemed essential for the United States, as McKinley said, to give "aid and direction" until "tranquillity" could be restored.

As soon as American troops landed in Cuba, trouble broke out between them and the populace. Most American soldiers viewed the ragged, half-starved insurgents as "thieving dagoes" and displayed an unfortunate race prejudice against their dark-skinned allies. The novelist Stephen Crane, who covered the war for Pulitzer's *World*, reported: "Both officers and privates have the most lively contempt for the Cubans. They despise them."

General Shafter did not help matters. He believed the Cubans "no more fit for self-government than gun-powder is for hell," and he used the insurgents chiefly as labor troops. After the fall of Santiago, he refused to let rebel leaders participate in the formal surrender of the city. This infuriated the proud and idealistic Cuban commander, General Calixto Garcia.

When McKinley established a military government for Cuba late in 1898, it was soon embroiled with local leaders. Then an eager horde of American promoters descended on Cuba in search of profitable franchises and concessions. Congress put a stop to this exploitation by forbidding all such grants as long as the occupation continued.

The problems were indeed knotty, for no strong local leader capable of uniting Cuba appeared. Even Senator Teller, father of the Teller Amendment, expressed concern lest "unstable and unsafe" elements gain control of the country. European leaders expected that the United States would eventually annex Cuba, and many Americans, including General Leonard Wood, who became military governor in December 1899, considered this the best solution. The desperate state of the people, the heavy economic stake of Americans in the region, and its strategic importance militated against withdrawal.

In the end the United States did withdraw, after doing a great deal to modernize sugar production, improve sanitary conditions, establish schools, and restore orderly administration. In November 1900 a Cuban constitutional convention met at Havana and proceeded without substantial American interference or direction to draft a frame of government. The chief restrictions imposed by this document on Cuba's freedom concerned foreign relations; at the insistence of the United States, it authorized American intervention whenever necessary "for the reservation of Cuban independence" and "the maintenance of a government adequate for the protection of life, property, and individual liberty." Cuba had to promise to make no treaty with a foreign power compromising its independence and to grant naval bases on its soil to the United States.

This arrangement, known as the Platt Amendment, was accepted, after some grumbling, by the Cubans. It had the support of most American opponents of imperialism. The amendment was a true compromise; as David F. Healy, a leading student of Cuban-American relations, has said, "It promised to give the Cubans real internal self government . . . and at the same time to safeguard American interests." In May 1902 the United States turned over the reins of government to the new republic. The next year the two countries signed a reciprocity treaty tightening the economic bonds between them.

True friendship did not result. Although American troops occupied Cuba only once, in 1906, and then at the specific request of Cuban authorities, the United States repeatedly used the threat of intervention to coerce the Cuban government. American economic penetration proceeded rapidly and without regard for the well-being of the Cuban peasants, many of whom lived in a state of peonage on great sugar plantations. Nor did their good intentions make up for the tendency of Americans to consider themselves innately superior to the Cubans and to overlook the fact that Cubans did not always wish to adopt American customs and culture. The reform program instituted during the occupation was marred by attempts to apply American standards at every step. The new schools used American textbooks that had been translated into Spanish without adapting the material to the experience of Cuban children. General Wood considered the Cubans "inert" because they showed little interest in his plans to grant a large measure of self-government to municipal authorities. He failed to understand that the people were accustomed to a centralized system with decision making concentrated in Havana. Wood complained that the Cubans were mired in "old ruts," yet the same charge might well have been leveled at him, though he was an efficient and energetic administrator.

The United States in the Caribbean

If the purpose of the Spanish-American War had been to bring peace and order to Cuba, the Platt Amendment was a logical step. The same purpose soon necessitated a further extension of the principle, for once the United States accepted the role of protector and stabilizer in part of the Caribbean, it seemed desirable, for the same economic, strategic, and humanitarian reasons, to supervise the entire region.

The Caribbean countries were economically underdeveloped, socially backward, politically unstable, and desperately poor. Everywhere, a few families owned most of the land and dominated social and political life. Most of the people were uneducated peasants, many of them little better off than slaves. Rival cliques of wealthy families struggled for power, force being the usual method of effecting a change in government. Most of the meager income of the average Caribbean state was swallowed up by the military or diverted into the pockets of the current rulers.

Cynicism and fraud poisoned relations between most of these nations and the great powers. European merchants and bankers systematically cheated their Latin American customers, who in

turn frequently refused to honor their obligations. Foreign bankers floated Caribbean bond issues on outrageous terms, while revolutionary Caribbean governments annulled concessions and repudiated debts with equal disdain for honest business dealing.

Because these countries were weak, the powers tended to intervene whenever their nationals were cheated or when chaotic conditions endangered the lives and property of foreigners. In one notorious instance Germany sent two warships to Port-au-Prince, Haiti, and by threatening to bombard the town compelled the Haitian government to pay $30,000 in damages to a German citizen who had been arrested and fined for allegedly assaulting a local policeman.

In 1902, shortly after the United States had pulled out of Cuba, trouble erupted in Venezuela, where a dictator, Cipriano Castro, was refusing to honor debts owed the citizens of European nations. To force Castro to pay up, Germany and Great Britain established a blockade of Venezuelan ports and destroyed a number of Venezuelan gunboats and harbor defenses. Under American pressure the Europeans agreed to arbitrate the dispute. For the first time, European powers had accepted the broad implications of the Monroe Doctrine. The British prime minister, Arthur Balfour, went so far as to state publicly that "it would be a great gain to civilization if the United States were more actively to interest themselves in making arrangements by which these constantly recurring difficulties . . . could be avoided."

By this time Theodore Roosevelt had become president of the United States, and he quickly capitalized on the new European attitude. In 1903 the Dominican Republic defaulted on bonds totaling some $40 million. When European investors urged their governments to intervene, Roosevelt announced that under the Monroe Doctrine the United States could not permit foreign nations to intervene in Latin America. But, he added, Latin American nations should not be allowed to escape their obligations. "If we intend to say 'Hands off,' . . . sooner or later we must keep order ourselves," he told Secretary of War Elihu Root.

The president did not want to make a colony of the Dominican Republic. "I have about the same desire to annex it as a gorged boa constrictor might have to swallow a porcupine wrong-end-to," he said. He therefore arranged for the United States to take charge of the Dominican customs service—the one

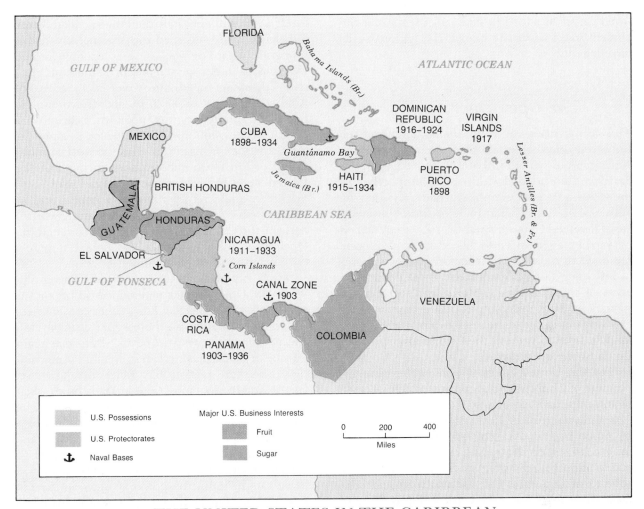

THE UNITED STATES IN THE CARIBBEAN

Puerto Rico was ceded by Spain after the Spanish-American War; the Virgin Islands were bought from Denmark; and the Canal Zone was leased from Panama. The ranges of dates following Cuba, Dominican Republic, Haiti, Nicaragua, and Panama cover those years during which the United States either had troops in occupation or, in some other way (such as financial), had a protectorate relationship with that country.

reliable source of revenue in that poverty-stricken country. Fifty-five percent of the customs duties would be devoted to debt payment, the remainder turned over to the Dominican government to care for its internal needs. Roosevelt defined his policy, known as the Roosevelt Corollary to the Monroe Doctrine, in a message to Congress in December 1904. "Chronic wrongdoing" in Latin America, he stated with his typical disregard for the subtleties of complex affairs, might require outside interven-tion. Since, under the Monroe Doctrine, no other nation could step in, the United States must "ex-ercise . . . an international police power."

In the short run this policy worked admirably. Dominican customs were honestly collected for the first time, and the country's finances were put in order. The presence of American warships in the area provided a needed measure of political stabil-ity. In the long run, however, the Roosevelt Cor-ollary caused a great deal of resentment in Latin

America, for it added to nationalist fears that the United States wished to exploit the region for its own benefit.

The Open Door Policy

The insular cases, the Platt Amendment, and the Roosevelt Corollary established the framework for American policy both in Latin America and in the Far East. Coincidental with the Cuban rebellion of the 1890s, a far greater upheaval had convulsed the ancient empire of China. In 1894 and 1895 Japan easily defeated China in a war over Korea. Alarmed by Japan's aggressiveness, the European powers hastened to carve out for themselves new spheres of influence along China's coast. After the annexation of the Philippines, McKinley's secretary of state, John Hay, urged on by businessmen fearful of losing out in the scramble to exploit the Chinese market, tried to prevent the further absorption of China by the great powers.

For the United States to join in the dismemberment of China was politically impossible because of anti-imperialist feeling, so Hay sought to protect American interests by clever diplomacy. In a series of "Open Door" notes (1899) he asked the powers to agree to respect the trading rights of all countries and to impose no discriminatory duties within their spheres of influence. Chinese tariffs should continue to be collected in these areas and by Chinese officials.

The replies to the Open Door notes were at best noncommittal, yet Hay blandly announced in March 1900 that the powers had "accepted" his suggestions! Thus he could claim to have prevented the breakup of the empire and protected the right of Americans to do business freely in its territories. In reality nothing had been accomplished; the imperialist nations did not extend their political control of China only because they feared that by doing so they might precipitate a major war among themselves. Nevertheless, Hay's action marked a revolutionary departure from the traditional American policy of isolation, a bold advance into the complicated and dangerous world of international power politics.

Within a few months of Hay's announcement, the Open Door policy was put to the test. Chinese nationalists, angered by the spreading influence of foreign governments, launched the so-called Boxer Rebellion. They swarmed into Peking and drove foreigners within the walls of their legations, which were placed under siege. For weeks, until an international rescue expedition (which included 2,500 American soldiers) broke through to free them, the fate of the foreigners was unknown. Fearing that the Europeans would use the rebellion as a pretext for further expropriations, Hay sent off another round of Open Door notes announcing that the United States believed in the preservation of "Chinese territorial and administrative entity" and in "the principle of equal and impartial trade with all parts of the Chinese Empire." This broadened the Open Door policy to include all China, not merely the European spheres of influence.

Hay's diplomacy was superficially successful. While the United States maintained no important military force in the Far East, American business and commercial interests there were free to develop and to compete with Europeans'. But once again European jealousies and fears rather than American cleverness were responsible. When the Japanese, mistrusting Russian intentions in Manchuria, asked Hay how he intended to implement his policy, he replied meekly that the United States was "not prepared . . . to enforce these views on the east by any demonstration which could present a character of hostility to any other power." The United States was being caught up in the power struggle in the Far East without having faced the implications of its actions.

In time the country would pay a heavy price for this unrealistic attitude, but in the decade following 1900 its policy of diplomatic meddling unbacked by bayonets worked fairly well. Japan attacked Russia in a quarrel over Manchuria, smashing the Russian fleet in 1905 and winning a series of battles on the mainland. Japan was not prepared for a long war, however, and suggested to President Roosevelt that an American offer to mediate would be received favorably.

Eager to preserve the nice balance in the Far East, which enabled the United States to exert influence without any significant commitment of force, Roosevelt accepted the hint. In June 1905 he invited the belligerents to a conference at Portsmouth, New Hampshire. At the conference the Japanese won title to Russia's sphere around Port Arthur and a free hand in Korea, but when they

A rendering of a multinational assault on antiforeign Chinese militants—Boxers—who held Americans captive in Peking in 1900. A detachment of American Marines is at the left of the picture.

demanded Sakhalin Island and a large money indemnity, the Russians balked. Unwilling to resume the war, the Japanese settled for half of Sakhalin and no money.

The Treaty of Portsmouth was unpopular in Japan, and the government managed to place the blame on Roosevelt, who had supported the compromise. Ill feeling against Americans increased in 1906 when the San Francisco school board, responding to local opposition to the influx of cheap labor from Japan, instituted a policy of segregating oriental children in a special school. Japan protested, and President Roosevelt persuaded the San Franciscans to abandon segregation in exchange for his pledge to cut off further Japanese immigration. He accomplished this through a "Gentlemen's Agreement" (1907) in which the Japanese promised not to issue passports to laborers seeking to come to America. Discriminatory legislation based specifically on race was thus avoided. However, the atmosphere between the two countries remained charged. Japanese resentment at American race prejudice was great; many Americans talked fearfully of the "yellow peril."

Theodore Roosevelt was preeminently a realist in foreign relations. "Don't bluster," he once said. "Don't flourish a revolver, and never draw unless you intend to shoot." In the Far East he failed to follow his own advice. He considered the situation in that part of the world fraught with peril. The Philippines, he said, were "our heel of Achilles," indefensible in case of a Japanese attack. He suggested privately that the United States ought to "be prepared for giving the islands independence . . . much sooner than I think advisable from their own standpoint."

Yet even though Roosevelt did not increase appreciably American naval and military strength in the Orient, neither did he stop trying to influence the course of events in the area, and he took no step toward withdrawing from the Philippines. He sent the fleet on a world cruise to demonstrate its might to Japan but knew well that this was mere bluff. "The 'Open Door' policy," he warned his successor, "completely disappears as soon as a powerful nation determines to disregard it." Nevertheless he allowed the belief to persist in the United States that the nation could influence the course of Far Eastern history without risk or real involvement.

The Isthmian Canal

In the Caribbean region American policy centered on building an interoceanic canal across Central America. Expanding interests in Latin America and the Far East made a canal necessary, a truth pointed up during the war with Spain by the two-month voyage of the U.S.S. *Oregon* around South America from California waters to participate in the action against Admiral Cervera's fleet at Santiago. The first step was to get rid of the old Clayton-Bulwer Treaty with Great Britain, which barred the United States from building a canal on its own. In 1901 Lord Pauncefote, the British ambassador, and Secretary of State John Hay negotiated an agreement abrogating the Clayton-Bulwer pact and giving America the right to build, and by implication fortify, a transisthmian waterway. The United States agreed in turn to maintain any such canal "free and open to the vessels of commerce and of war of all nations."

One possible canal route lay across the Colombian province of Panama, where the French-controlled New Panama Canal Company had taken over the franchise of the old De Lesseps company. Only 50 miles separated the oceans in Panama. The terrain, however, was rugged and unhealthy. Though the French company had sunk much money into the project, it had little to show for its efforts aside from some rough excavations. A second possible route ran across Nicaragua. This route was about 200 miles long but was relatively easy, since much of it traversed Lake Nicaragua and other natural waterways.

President McKinley appointed a commission to study the alternatives. It reported that the Panamanian route was technically superior but recommended building in Nicaragua because the New Panama Canal Company was asking $109 million for its assets, which the commission valued at only $40 million. Lacking another potential purchaser, the French company lowered its price to $40 million, and after a great deal of clever propagandizing by Philippe Bunau-Varilla, a French engineer with heavy investments in the company, President Roosevelt settled on the Panamanian route.

In January 1903 Secretary of State Hay negotiated a treaty with Tomás Herrán, the Colombian chargé d'affaires in Washington. In return for a 99-year lease on a zone across Panama 6 miles wide, the United States agreed to pay Colombia $10 mil-

The Panama Canal under construction. Cutting the path between the seas consumed more than 61 million pounds of dynamite and the lives of hundreds of workers, most of whom were black laborers from Barbados and Jamaica.

lion and an annual rent of $250,000. The Colombian senate, however, unanimously rejected this treaty, in part because it did not adequately protect Colombian sovereignty over Panama and in part because it hardly seemed fair that the New Panama Canal Company should receive $40 million for its frozen assets and Colombia only $10 million. The government demanded $15 million directly from the United States, plus $10 million of the company's share.

A little more patience might have produced a mutually satisfactory settlement, but Roosevelt regarded the Colombians as highwaymen who were "mad to get hold of the $40,000,000 of the Frenchmen." ("You could no more make an agreement with the Colombian rulers," Roosevelt later remarked, "than you could nail currant jelly to a wall.") When Panamanians, egged on by the French company, staged a revolution in November 1903, Roosevelt ordered the cruiser *Nashville* to Panama. Colombian government forces found themselves looking down the barrels of the guns of the *Nashville* and shortly thereafter eight other American warships. The revolution succeeded.

Roosevelt instantly recognized the new Republic of Panama. Secretary Hay and the new Panamanian minister, Bunau-Varilla, then negotiated a treaty granting the United States a zone 10 miles wide in perpetuity, on the same terms as those rejected by Colombia. Within the Canal Zone the United States could act as "the sovereign of the territory . . . to the entire exclusion of . . . the Republic of Panama." The United States guaranteed the independence of the republic. The New Panama Canal Company then received its $40 million.

Historians have condemned Roosevelt for his actions in this shabby affair, and with good reason. It was not that he fomented the revolution, for he did not. Separated from the government at Bogotá by an impenetrable jungle, the people of Panama province had long wanted to be free of Colombian rule. Since an American-built canal would bring a flood of dollars and jobs to the area, they were prepared to take any necessary steps to avoid having the United States shift to the Nicaraguan route. Nor was it that Roosevelt prevented Colombia from suppressing the revolution. He sinned, rather, in his disregard of Latin American sensibilities. He referred to the Colombians as "dagoes" and insisted smugly that he was defending "the interests of collective civilization" when he overrode their opposition to his plans. "They cut their own throats," he said. "They tried to hold us up; and too late they have discovered their criminal error."

If uncharitable, Roosevelt's analysis was not entirely inaccurate, yet it did not justify his haste in taking Panama under his wing. "Have I defended myself?" Roosevelt asked Secretary of War Root. "You certainly have, Mr. President," Root retorted. "You were accused of seduction and you have conclusively proved that you were guilty of rape." Throughout Latin America, especially as nationalist sentiments grew stronger, Roosevelt's intolerance and aggressiveness in the canal incident bred resentment and fear.

In 1921 the United States made amends by giving Colombia $25 million. Colombia in turn recognized the independence of the Republic of Panama, but Panama was independent only in name because the United States controlled the canal. Meanwhile, the first vessels passed through the canal in 1914—and American hegemony in the Ca-

ribbean expanded. Yet even in that strategically vital area there was more show than substance to American strength. The navy ruled Caribbean waters largely by default, for it lacked adequate bases in the region. In 1903, as authorized by the Cuban constitution, the United States obtained an excellent site for a base at Guantanamo Bay, but before 1914 Congress appropriated only $89,000 to develop it.

The tendency was to try to influence outlying areas without actually controlling them. Roosevelt's successor, William Howard Taft, called this policy "dollar diplomacy," his reasoning being that economic penetration would bring stability to underdeveloped areas and power and profit to the United States without the government's having to commit troops or spend public funds.

Under Taft the State Department won a place for American bankers in an international syndicate engaged in financing railroads in Manchuria. When Nicaragua defaulted on its foreign debt in 1911, the department arranged for American bankers to reorganize Nicaraguan finances and manage the customs service. Although the government truthfully insisted that it did not "covet an inch of territory south of the Rio Grande," dollar diplomacy provoked further apprehension in Latin America. Efforts to establish similar arrangements in Honduras, Costa Rica, and Guatemala all failed. In Nicaragua orderly administration of the finances did not bring internal peace. In 1912 some 2,500 American marines and sailors had to be landed to put down a revolution.

Economic penetration proceeded briskly. American investments in Cuba reached $500 million by 1920, and smaller but significant investments were made in the Dominican Republic and in Haiti. In Central America the United Fruit Company accumulated large holdings in banana plantations, railroads, and other ventures. Other firms plunged heavily in Mexico's rich mineral resources.

Non-Colonial Imperial Expansion

The United States deserves fair marks for effort in its foreign relations following the Spanish-American War, barely passing marks for performance, and failing marks for results. If one defines imperialism narrowly as a policy of occupying and governing foreign lands, American imperialism lasted for an extremely short time. With trivial exceptions, all the American colonies—Hawaii, the Philippines, Guam, Puerto Rico, the Guantanamo base, and the Canal Zone—were obtained between 1898 and 1903. In retrospect it seems clear that the urge to own colonies was only fleeting; the legitimate questions raised by the anti-imperialists and the headaches connected with the management of overseas possessions soon produced a change of policy.

The objections of protectionists to the lowering of tariff barriers, the shock of the Philippine insurrection, and a growing conviction that the costs of colonial administration outweighed the profits affected American thinking. Hay's Open Door notes (which anti-imperialists praised highly) marked the beginning of the retreat from imperialism thus defined, while the Roosevelt Corollary and dollar diplomacy signaled the consolidation of a new policy. Elihu Root summarized this policy as it applied to the Caribbean nations (and by implication to the rest of the underdeveloped world) in 1905: "We do not want to take them for ourselves. We do not want any foreign nations to take them for themselves. We want to help them."

Yet imperialism can be given a broader definition. The historian William Appleman Williams, a sharp critic, has described 20th-century American foreign policy as one of "non-colonial imperial expansion." Its object was to obtain profitable American economic penetration of underdeveloped areas without the trouble of owning and controlling them. Its subsidiary aim was to encourage these countries to "modernize," that is, to remake themselves in the image of the United States. The Open Door policy, in Williams's view, was not unrealistic and by no means a failure—indeed, it was too successful. He criticized American policy not because it did not work or because it led to trouble with the powers but because of its harmful effects on underdeveloped countries.

Examined from this perspective, the Open Door policy, the Roosevelt Corollary, and dollar diplomacy make a single pattern of exploitation, "tragic" rather than evil, according to Williams, because its creators were not evil but only of limited vision. They did not recognize the contradictions in their ideas and values. They saw American expansion as beneficial to all concerned—and not exclusively in materialistic terms. They genuinely believed that they were exporting democracy along with capitalism and industrialization.

Williams probably goes too far in arguing that American statesmen consciously planned their foreign policy in these terms. American economic interests in foreign nations expanded enormously in the 20th century, but diplomacy had relatively little to do with this. Western industrial society (not merely American) was engulfing the rest of the world, as it continues to engulf it. Yet he is correct in pointing out that western economic penetration has had many unfortunate results for the nonindustrial nations. It is also true that Americans were particularly, though not uniquely, unimpressed by the different social and cultural patterns of people in far-off lands and insensitive to the wishes of such people to develop in their own ways.

Both the United States government and American businessmen showed little interest in finding out what the people of Cuba wanted from life. They assumed that the Cubans wanted what everybody (read "Americans") wanted and, if by some strange chance this was not the case, that it was best to give it to them anyway. Dollar diplomacy had as its objectives the avoidance of violence and the economic development of Latin America; it paid small heed to how peace was maintained or how the fruits of development were distributed. The policy was self-defeating, for long-run stability depended on the support of the people, and this was seldom forthcoming.

By the eve of World War I the United States had become a world power and had assumed what it saw as a duty to guide the development of many countries with traditions far different from its own. The American people, however, did not understand what these changes involved. While they stood ready to extend their influence into distant lands, they did so blithely, with little awareness of the implications of their behavior for themselves or for other peoples. The national psychology, if such can be said to exist, remained fundamentally isolationist. Americans understood that their wealth and numbers made their nation strong and that geography made it practically invulnerable. Thus they proceeded to do what they wanted to do in foreign affairs, limited more by their humanly flexible consciences than by any rational analysis of the probable consequences. This policy seemed safe enough—in 1914.

Milestones

1850	Clayton-Bulwer Canal Treaty		Spanish-American War breaks out
1858	Commercial treaty with Japan		Battle of Manila Bay
1867	Alaska purchased from Russia		Battle of San Juan Hill
1871	Treaty of Washington, settling the *Alabama* claims		Annexation of Hawaii
1875	Hawaiian reciprocity treaty	**1899**	Open Door notes
1885	Josiah Strong, *Our Country*	**1900**	Platt Amendment to the Cuban constitution
1889	First Pan-American Conference	**1901**	Hay-Pauncefote Canal Treaty
1890	A. T. Mahan, *The Influence of Sea Power*		Supreme Court decides *Insular Cases* on control of colonies
1891	*Baltimore* crisis with Chile	**1902**	Venezuela bond dispute
1893	Queen Liliuokalani of Hawaii overthrown	**1904**	Roosevelt Corollary to the Monroe Doctrine
1895	Venezuela boundary dispute	**1907**	"Gentlemen's Agreement" with Japan
1898	*Maine* explodes in Havana harbor		

SUPPLEMENTARY READING

Titles marked with an asterisk have been published in paperback.

For an overview of post–Civil War diplomatic history, see Milton Plesur, **America's Outward Thrust*** (1971), and D. M. Pletcher, **The Awkward Years** (1962). J. A. S. Grenville and G. B. Young, **Politics, Strategy, and American Diplomacy: Studies in Foreign Policy** (1966), throws light on many aspects of the period. Walter La Feber, **The New Empire** (1963), presents a forceful but somewhat overstated argument on the extent of expansionist sentiment, especially on the part of American businessmen. Contemporary attitudes are reflected in Josiah Strong, **Our Country** (1885) and A. T. Mahan, **The Influence of Sea Power upon History*** (1890), provides the clearest presentation of Mahan's thesis.

On Hawaiian annexation, see Mere Tate, **The United States and the Hawaiian Kingdom** (1965). On the Spanish-American War, see D. F. Trask, **The War with Spain in 1898** (1981), H. W. Morgan, **America's Road to Empire*** (1965), E. R. May, **Imperial Democracy*** (1961), L. L. Gourd, **The Presidency of William McKinley** (1980), and Orestes Ferrara, **The Last Spanish War** (1937).

On imperialism, see David Healy, **U.S. Expansionism: The Imperialist Urge in the 1890's** (1970), E. R May, **American Imperialism: A Speculative Essay** (1968), and W. A. Williams, **The Tragedy of American Diplomacy*** (1962). R. L. Beisner, **Twelve Against Empire: The Anti-imperialists*** (1968), contains lively and thoughtful sketches of leading foes of expansion. See also E. B. Thompkins, **Anti-imperialism in the United States** (1970). For details of colonial problems, see Leon Wolff, **Little Brown Brother** (1961), and R. E. Welch, Jr., **Response to Imperialism** (1979), on the Philippines; D. F. Healy, **The United States in Cuba** (1963); and D. G. Munro, **Intervention and Dollar Diplomacy in the Caribbean** (1964). David McCullough, **The Path Between the Seas** (1977), is an excellent history of the Panama Canal. Other useful volumes include Thomas McCormick, **China Market*** (1967), H. C. Hill, **Roosevelt and the Caribbean** (1927), R. E. Osgood, **Ideals and Self-interest in America's Foreign Relations*** (1953), and G. F. Kennan, **American Diplomacy*** (1951).

American Lives:

Emma Goldman

Emma Goldman in the 1890s

In January of 1886 a 16-year-old Jewish girl named Emma Goldman arrived in New York City from St. Petersburg, Russia, where her parents ran a grocery store. As soon as she had been examined by immigration officials she hurried on to Rochester, New York, where her half-sister lived. Emma was extremely independent-minded. Her father had tried to make her get married when she was 15, saying when she protested that "all a Jewish daughter needs to know is how to prepare *gefülte* fish, cut noodles fine, and give the man plenty of children." She had flatly refused to marry. "I wanted to study, to know life, to travel," she explained years later. She had also found the harsh government of the Czar unbearable. Finally, she and an older sister left for America. Like most immigrants, they expected the United States, "the land of opportunity," to be a kind of paradise on earth.

At first Emma lived with her half-sister's family and got a job in a factory sewing coats for $2.50 a week. Since she paid her sister $1.50 a week for room and board and needed 60 cents a week for carfare, she had only 40 cents for all her other needs. But when she asked her employer for more money he simply told her to "look for work elsewhere." This she did, finding a job at another factory that paid $4 a week.

The next year she married Jacob Kirshner, another Russian immigrant, but they did not get along and were soon divorced. Then she moved to New Haven, Connecticut, where she worked in a corset factory. In 1889 she moved to New York City. There she fell in with a group of radicals, most of them either socialists or anarchists. She herself was by this time an ardent anarchist, convinced by her experiences with the darker aspects of American capitalism that *all* governments repressed individual freedom and should simply be abolished.

In New York Emma fell in love with another Russian-born radical, Alexander Berkman. They started a kind of commune with another couple, sharing everything equally. Emma worked at home sewing shirts. Alexander found a job making cigars.

Next, Goldman and Berkman moved back to New Haven, where she started a cooperative dressmaking shop. Then the couple moved to Springfield, Massachusetts, where, with Berkman's cousin, an artist, they opened a photography studio. When this business failed they borrowed $150 and opened an ice cream parlor.

Nearly all immigrants of that period retained their faith in the promise of American life even after they discovered that the streets were not paved with gold and that the people and the government were not as perfect as they had expected when they arrived. But Emma Goldman was so disappointed by the United States that she became even more radical than she had been in Czarist Russia. The harsh punishment meted out to the anarchists who were accused of the Haymarket bombing shocked her deeply.

In 1892 when she and Berkman learned of the bloody battle of Pinkertons and strikers during the Homestead steel strike, they closed the ice cream parlor and went to New York. They decided to assassinate Henry Clay Frick, the arch-villain of the Homestead drama. First they tried to manufacture a bomb, but that proved to be beyond their powers. Berkman then went to Pittsburgh where, posing as a representative of an agency that provided strikebreakers, he got into

Frick's office and shot him. For this crime he was sentenced to 14 years in prison.

The next year Goldman was herself arrested and sentenced to a year in jail after making an "incendiary" speech urging unemployed workers to distrust politicians and demand government relief. Thereafter she was taken up by important native-born radicals and soon was preaching anarchism to ordinary workers rather than to other radical immigrant groups. She got to know Lillian Wald and other New York settlement workers, but while she respected their motives, she disparaged their methods. It did little good to teach the poor good table manners, she said, if they did not have enough food to eat. Next she studied nursing in Vienna for a year. When she returned, she worked as a midwife among the New York poor, an experience that made her an outspoken advocate of birth control. She also helped organize a theatrical group, managed a touring group of Russian actors, and lectured on theatrical topics.

In 1906 Goldman founded *Mother Earth*, an anarchist journal. When Alexander Berkman was released from prison later that year, she made him its editor. *Mother Earth* attacked governments, organized religion, and private property. Goldman believed in a primitive form of communism in which all would share equally and no one would have power over anyone else. She was convinced that the result would be world peace and universal prosperity.

By this time Emma Goldman had become a celebrity. As Berkman noted, she "had become a woman of the world." He was disturbed by what he called "the foreign element in the circle she had gathered around her," but it was foreign only from his still narrowly Russian immigrant's perspective. Over the next decade she campaigned for freedom of speech all over the United States and in Canada, and lectured in support of birth control. At one point she developed a joint subscription plan covering *Mother Earth* and the *American Journal of Eugenics*, a magazine that advocated the use of contraception. In 1915 she deliberately courted arrest by describing methods of contraception at public lectures before large audiences. Men, she reported, showed great interest, but women "snicker and giggle and pretend to be shocked." Eventually she was arrested, convicted, and sentenced to a brief jail term.

With Alexander Berkman in 1917

Goldman's biographer, Richard Drinnan, has described her as "one of the significant women in the years before the First World War." The outbreak of that conflict, and especially American entry in it, seemed to her a calamity beyond measure. When Congress passed a conscription act, she, Berkman, and a few other radicals organized the No-Conscription League, not so much to persuade men to resist the draft as to provide aid and comfort to anyone who did so.

After American entry into World War I, both she and Berkman were convicted of conspiring to persuade men not to register for the draft. She was sentenced to two years in federal prison and in 1919 she and Berkman were deported to Russia.

Of course "Red Emma" Goldman was not a typical American, but she was in many ways a typical American immigrant. She held on to the culture of the old country; most of her close friends in the United States were Russians. But at the same time she learned English and quickly became familiar with American ways. She worked hard and developed a number of valuable skills. Gradually she moved up the economic ladder: from sweatshop laborer, to factory work, to running a shop, to nursing, to lecturing, and to editing a magazine. And while she was critical of the government and economic system of the United States, she was a typical immigrant also in insisting that she was an American patriot. "The kind of patriotism we represent," she said during her trial in 1917, "is the kind of patriotism which loves America with open eyes."

Progressivism: The Age of Reform

The true friend of property, the true conservative, is he who insists that property shall be the servant and not the master of the commonwealth. . . . The citizens of the United States must effectively control the mighty commercial forces which they have themselves called into being.

THEODORE ROOSEVELT, *1910*

T he period bounded roughly by the end of the Spanish-American War and American entry into World War I is usually called the Progressive Era. Like all such generalizations about complex subjects, this title involves a great simplification. Whether *progressive* is taken to mean "tending toward change" or "improvement" or is merely used to suggest an attitude of mind, it was neither a unique nor a universal characteristic of the early years of the 20th century. Progressive elements had existed in earlier periods and did not disappear when the first American soldiers took ship for France. In important ways the progressivism of the time was a continuation of the response to industrialism that began after the Civil War, a response that has not ended. Historians have scoured the sources trying to define and explain the Progressive Era, without satisfying everyone. Nevertheless, the term *progressive* provides a useful de-

scription of this exciting and significant period of American history.

Roots of Progressivism

The progressives were never a single group seeking a single objective. The movement sprang from many sources. One was the fight against corruption and inefficiency in government, which began with the Liberal Republicans of the Grant era and was continued by the Mugwumps of the 1880s. The struggle for civil service reform was only the first skirmish in this battle; the continuing power of corrupt political machines and the growing influence of corporations and their lobbyists on municipal and state governments outraged thousands of citizens and led them to seek ways of purifying politics and making the machinery of government at all levels responsive to the majority rather than to special-interest groups.

Progressivism also had roots in the effort to regulate and control big business, which characterized the Granger and Populist agitation of the 1870s and 1890s. The failure of the Interstate Commerce Act to end railroad abuses and of the Sherman Antitrust Act to check the growth of large corporations became increasingly apparent after 1900. The return of prosperity after the depression of the 1890s encouraged reformers by removing the inhibiting fear, so influential in the 1896 presidential campaign, that an assault on the industrial giants might lead to the collapse of the economy.

Between 1897 and 1904 the trend toward concentration in industry accelerated. Such new giants as Amalgamated Copper (1899), U.S. Steel (1901), and International Harvester (1902) attracted most of the attention, but even more alarming were the overall statistics. In a single year (1899) more than 1,200 firms were absorbed in mergers, the resulting combinations being capitalized at $2.2 billion. By 1904 there were 318 industrial combinations in the country, with an aggregate capital of $7.5 billion. People who considered bigness inherently evil demanded that the huge new "trusts" be broken up or at least strictly controlled.

Settlement house workers and other reformers concerned about the welfare of the urban poor made up a third battalion in the progressive army. This was an area in which women made the most important contributions. The working and living conditions of slum dwellers remained abominable, and the child labor problem was particularly acute; in 1900 about 1.7 million children under the age of 16 were working full time—more than the membership of the American Federation of Labor. In addition, laws regulating the hours and working conditions of women in industry were far from adequate, and almost nothing had been done, despite the increased use of dangerous machinery in the factories, to enforce safety rules or to provide compensation or insurance for workers injured on the job. As the number of professionally competent social workers grew, the movement for social welfare legislation gained momentum.

All these tendencies may be summed up in Robert H. Wiebe's phrase, "the search for order." America was becoming more urban, more industrial, more mechanized, more centralized—in short, more complex. This trend put a premium on efficiency and cooperation. It seemed obvious to the progressives that people must become more socially minded, the economy more carefully organized.

By attracting additional thousands of sympathizers to the general cause of reform, the return of prosperity after 1896 fueled the progressive movement. Good times made the average person more tolerant and generous. So long as profits were on the rise, the average employer did not object if labor improved its position too. Middle-class Americans who had been prepared to go to the barricades in the event of a Bryan victory in 1896 became conscience-stricken when they compared their own comfortable circumstances with those of the "huddled masses" of immigrants and native poor.

Giant industrial and commercial corporations threatened not so much the economic well-being as the ambitions and sense of importance of the middle class. What owner of a small mill or shop could now hope to rise to the heights attained by Carnegie or merchants like John Wanamaker and Marshall Field? The growth of large labor organizations worried such types. In general, character and moral values seemed less influential; organizations—cold, impersonal, heartless—were coming to control business, politics, and too many other aspects of life.

This development led historian Richard Hofstadter to suggest still another explanation of the progressive movement. Numbers of moderately prosperous businessmen, together with members of the professions and other educated people, felt threatened by the increasing power and status of the new tycoons, many of them coarse, domineering, and fond of vulgar display. The antics of machine politicians who made a mockery of the traditions of duty, service, and patriotism associated with statesmanship also troubled them. Comfortably well-off, middle-level businessmen lived in what seemed like genteel poverty compared to a Rockefeller or a Morgan.

Protestant pastors accustomed to the respect and deference of their flocks found their moral leadership challenged by materialistic vestrymen who did not even pay them decent salaries. College professors worried about their institutions falling under the sway of wealthy trustees who had little interest in or respect for learning. Lawyers had been "the aristocracy of the United States," James Bryce recalled in 1905; they were now merely "a part of the great organized system of industrial and financial enterprise."

Such people could support reform measures without feeling that they were being very radical because the intellectual currents of the time harmonized with their ideas of social improvement and the welfare state. The new doctrines of the social scientists, the Social Gospel religious leaders, and the philosophers of pragmatism provided a salubrious climate for progressivism. Many of the thinkers who formulated these doctrines in the 1880s and 1890s turned to the task of putting them into practice in the new century. Their number included the economist Richard T. Ely, the philosopher John Dewey, and the Baptist clergyman Walter Rauschenbusch, who, in addition to his many books extolling the Social Gospel, was active in civic reform movements.

The Muckrakers

As the diffuse progressive army gradually formed its battalions, a new journalistic fad brought the movement into focus. For many years magazines had been publishing articles discussing current political, social, and economic problems. Henry Demarest Lloyd's first blast at the Standard Oil monopoly appeared in the *Atlantic Monthly* in 1881. Over the years the tempo and forcefulness of this

One of McClure's *most effective "muckrakers," Ida Tarbell brought to her investigative journalism the well-trained mind of an historian and the indignation of a daughter whose father was done in by the interests, specifically the Standard Oil Company.*

type of literature increased. Then, in the fall of 1902, *McClure's* began two particularly hard-hitting series of articles, one on Standard Oil by Ida Tarbell, the other on big-city political machines by Lincoln Steffens. These articles provoked much comment. When the editor, S. S. McClure, decided to include in the January 1903 issue an attack on labor gangsterism in the coal fields along with installments of the Tarbell and Steffens series, he called attention to the circumstance in a striking editorial.

Something was radically wrong with the "American character," McClure wrote. These articles showed that large numbers of American employers, workers, and politicians were fundamentally immoral. Lawyers were becoming tools of big business, judges were permitting evildoers to escape justice, the churches were materialistic, educators seemed incapable of understanding what was happening.

"There is no one left; none but all of us," McClure concluded. "We have to pay in the end."

McClure's editorial loosed a chain reaction. The issue sold out quickly. Thousands of readers found their own vague apprehensions brought into focus, some becoming active in progressive movements, more lending passive support.

Other editors jumped to adopt the McClure formula. A small army of professional writers soon flooded the periodical press with denunciations of the insurance business, the drug business, college athletics, prostitution, sweatshop labor, political corruption, and dozens of other subjects. This type of article inspired Theodore Roosevelt, with his gift for vivid language, to compare the journalists to "the Man with the Muck-Rake" in John Bunyan's *Pilgrim's Progress*, whose attention was so fixed on the filth at his feet that he could not notice the "celestial crown" that was offered him in exchange. Roosevelt's characterization grossly misrepresented the literature of exposure, but the label *muckraking* was thereafter affixed to the type. Despite its literal connotations, *muckraker* became a term of honor.

The Progressive Mind

Progressives sought to arouse the conscience of "the people" in order to "purify" American life. They were convinced that human beings were by nature decent, well-intentioned, and kind. (After all, the words *human* and *humane* have the same root.) Unlike many earlier reformers, they believed that the source of society's evils lay in the structure of its institutions, not in the weaknesses or sinfulness of individuals. Therefore local, state, and national government must be made more responsive to the will of decent citizens who stood for the traditional virtues. Then the government must act; whatever its virtues, laissez-faire was obsolete. Businessmen, especially big businessmen, must be compelled to behave fairly, their acquisitive drives curbed in the interests of justice and equal opportunity for all. The weaker elements in society—women, children, the poor, the infirm—must be protected against unscrupulous power.

Despite its fervor and democratic rhetoric, progressivism was paternalistic, moderate, and often softheaded. Typical reformers of the period oversimplified complicated issues and treated their personal values as absolute standards of truth and morality. Thus progressives often acted at cross-purposes; at times some were even at war with themselves. This accounts for the diffuseness of the movement. Cutthroat business practices were criticized by great tycoons seeking to preserve their own positions and by small operators trying to protect themselves against the tycoons. But many tycoons and small operators considered themselves progressives; the former wanted federal regulation of big business and the latter strict enforcement of the antitrust laws, both legitimate "progressive" objectives.

Many progressives who desired to improve the living standards of industrial workers rejected the proposition that workers could help themselves best by organizing powerful national unions. They found it difficult to cooperate with actual working people, who seemed to them unrefined and narrow-minded. Union leaders favored government action to outlaw child labor and restrict immigration but

adopted a laissez-faire attitude toward wages-and-hours legislation; they preferred to win these objectives through collective bargaining, thereby justifying their own existence. Many who favored "municipal socialism" (public ownership of streetcar lines, waterworks, and other local utilities) adamantly opposed national ownership of railroads. Progressives stressed individual freedom yet gave strong backing to the drive to deprive the public of its right to drink alcoholic beverages. Few progressives worked more assiduously than Congressman George W. Norris of rural Nebraska for reforms that would increase the power of the ordinary voter, such as the direct primary and popular election of senators, yet Norris characterized the mass of urban voters as "the mob."

The progressives never challenged the fundamental principles of capitalism, nor did they attempt a basic reorganization of society. They would have little to do with the socialist brand of reform. Wisconsin was the most progressive of states, but its leaders never cooperated with the Socialist party of Milwaukee. When socialists threatened to win control of Los Angeles in 1911, California progressives made common cause with reactionary groups in order to defeat them. Many progressives were anti-immigrant, and only a handful had anything to offer blacks, surely the most exploited group in American society.

A good example of the relatively limited radicalism of most progressives is offered by the experiences of progressive artists. Early in the century a number of painters, including Robert Henri, John Sloan, and George Luks, tried to develop a distinctively American style. They turned to city streets and the people of the slums for their models, and they depended more on inspiration and inner conviction than careful craftsmanship to achieve their effects.

These so-called ashcan artists were individualists, yet they supported political and social reform and were caught up in the progressive movement. Sloan was a socialist; Henri claimed to be an anarchist. Most saw themselves as rebels. But artistically the ashcan painters were not very advanced. Their idols were long-dead European masters such as Hogarth, Goya, and Daumier. They were uninfluenced by the outburst of Postimpressionist activity then taking place in Europe. To their dismay, when they included canvases by European painters

A George Luks portrait of a coal miner, 1924, an impressive example of the "ashcan" school of American painting, which typically combined working-class subject matter and social conscience.

like Matisse and Picasso in a show of their own works they put on at the 69th Regiment Armory in New York City in 1913, the Europeans got all the attention.

"Radical" Progressives: The Wave of the Future

There were, of course, some people whose views were more fundamentally radical. The hard times of the 1890s and the callous reactions of conservatives to the victims of that depression pushed many toward Marxian socialism. In 1900 the labor leader Eugene V. Debs ran for president on the Socialist ticket. He polled fewer than 100,000 votes. When he ran again four years later he got more

than 400,000. Labor leaders hoping to organize unskilled workers in heavy industry were increasingly frustrated by the craft orientation of the American Federation of Labor, and some saw in socialism a way to win rank-and-file backing.

In 1905 Debs; William "Big Bill" Haywood, of the Western Federation of Miners; Mary Harris "Mother" Jones, a former organizer for the United Mine Workers; Daniel De Leon, of the Socialist Labor party; and a few others organized a new union, the Industrial Workers of the World. The IWW was openly anticapitalist. The preamble to its constitution began: "The working class and the employing class have nothing in common."

But the IWW never attracted many ordinary workers. Haywood, its most prominent leader, was usually a general in search of an army. His forte was attracting attention to spontaneous strikes by unorganized workers, not the patient recruiting of workers and the pursuit of practical goals. Shortly after the founding of the IWW, he was charged with complicity in the murder of an antiunion governor of Colorado after an earlier strike but was acquitted. In 1912 he was closely involved in a bitter and at times bloody strike of textile workers in Lawrence, Massachusetts, which was settled with some benefit to the strikers, and in a strike the following winter and spring by silk workers in Paterson, New Jersey, that was a failure.

Other "advanced" European ideas affected the thinking and behavior of progressive intellectuals. Sigmund Freud's psychoanalytical theories attracted numbers of Americans, especially after G. Stanley Hall invited Freud and some of his disciples to lecture at Clark University in 1909. Not many progressives actually read *The Interpretation of Dreams* or any of Freud's other works, none of which was translated into English before 1909, but many picked up enough of the vocabulary of psychoanalysis to discourse impressively about the significance of slips of the tongue, sublimation, and infant sexuality.

Some saw in Freud's ideas reason to effect a "revolution of manners and morals" that would have shocked (or at least embarrassed) Freud, who was personally quite conventional. They advocated easy divorce, trial marriage, and doing away with the double standard in all matters relating to sex. They rejected Victorian reticence and what they incorrectly identified as "puritan" morality out of hand, and they called for programs of sex education, especially the dissemination of information about methods of birth control.

Most large cities boasted groups of these "bohemian" thinkers, by far the most famous being the one centered in New York City's Greenwich Village. It was, Thomas Bender writes in *New York Intellect*, "a happy collaboration of 'revolutionary' writers and artists . . . at one time or another, almost every man or woman of the Village rebellion." The dancer Isadora Duncan, the photographer Alfred Stieglitz, the novelist Floyd Dell, several of the ashcan artists, and the playwright Eugene O'Neill rubbed shoulders with Big Bill Haywood of the IWW, the anarchist Emma Goldman, the psychoanalyst A. A. Brill, the militant feminist advocate of birth control

The impact of The Silent War, *a 1906 novel by John Ames Mitchell that dealt with the growing class struggle in America, was enhanced by William Balfour-Ker's graphic illustration,* From the Depths.

Margaret Sanger, Max Eastman, editor of their organ, *The Masses*, and John Reed, a young Harvard graduate who was soon to become famous for his eyewitness account of the Russian Revolution, *Ten Days That Shook the World*.

Goldman, Haywood, Sanger, and a few others in this group were genuine radicals who sought basic changes in bourgeois society, but despite much talk, most of the Greenwich Village intellectuals displayed what their historian Leslie Fishbein calls "a highly personalistic concern" for their own interests. *The Masses* described itself as "a revolutionary and not a reform magazine . . . a magazine whose final policy is to do as it pleases." Nearly all of them came from middle-class backgrounds. They found the far-different world of the Italian and Jewish immigrants of the Village and its surrounding neighborhoods charming. But they did not become involved in the immigrants' lives the way the settlement house workers did. Their influence on their own times, therefore, was limited. "Do as I say, not as I do" is not an effective way to change minds. They are historically important, however, because many of them were genuinely creative people and because many of the ideas and practices they advocated were adopted by later generations.

The creative writers of the era, applying the spirit of progressivism to the realism they had inherited from Howells and the naturalists, tended to adopt an optimistic tone. The poet Ezra Pound, for example, at this time talked grandly of an American Renaissance and fashioned a new kind of poetry called imagism, which, while not appearing to be realistic, abjured all abstract generalizations and concentrated on concrete word pictures to convey meaning. "Little" magazines and experimental theatrical companies sprang to life by the dozen, each convinced that it would revolutionize its art. The poet Carl Sandburg, the best-known representative of the "Chicago school," denounced the local plutocrats but sang the praises of the city they had made: "Hog Butcher for the World," "City of the Big Shoulders."

Most writers eagerly adopted Freudian psychology without understanding it. Freud's teachings seemed only to mean that they should cast off the restrictions of Victorian prudery; they ignored his essentially dark view of human nature. Theirs was an "innocent rebellion," exuberant and rather muddleheaded.

Political Reform: Cities First

To most "ordinary" progressives, political corruption and inefficiency lay at the root of the evils plaguing American society, and nowhere were corruption and inefficiency more obvious than in the nation's cities. Two characteristics of urban life are its anonymity and its complexity. These qualities help explain why slavery did not flourish in cities, which was undoubtedly a good thing, but also why the above-named vices did flourish, which was not good at all. As the cities grew, their antiquated and boss-ridden administrations became more and more disgraceful. Consider the example of San Francisco. After 1901, a shrewd lawyer named Abe Ruef ruled one of the most powerful and dissolute political machines in the nation. Only one kind of paving material was used on San Francisco's streets, and Ruef was the lawyer for the company that supplied it. When the gas company asked for a rate increase of 10 cents per 100 cubic feet, Ruef, who was already collecting $1,000 a month from the company as a "retainer," demanded and got an outright bribe of $20,000. A streetcar company needed city authorization to install overhead trolley wires; Ruef's approval cost the company $85,000. Prostitution flourished, with Ruef and his henchmen sharing in the profits. There was a brisk illegal trade in liquor licenses and other favors.

Similar conditions existed in dozens of communities. For his famous muckraking series for *McClure's*, Lincoln Steffens visited St. Louis, Minneapolis, Pittsburgh, New York, Chicago, and Philadelphia and found them all riddled with corruption.

Beginning in the late 1890s progressives mounted a massive assault on dishonest and inefficient urban governments. In San Francisco a group headed by Fremont Older, a newspaperman, and Rudolph Spreckels, a wealthy sugar manufacturer, broke the machine and lodged Ruef in jail. In Toledo, Ohio, Samuel M. "Golden Rule" Jones won election as mayor in 1897 and succeeded in arousing the citizenry against the corruptionists. Other important progressive mayors were Tom L. Johnson of Cleveland, whose administration Lincoln Steffens called the best in the United States; Seth Low and later John P. Mitchell of New York; and Hazen S. Pingree of Detroit.

City reformers could seldom destroy the machines without changing urban political institutions. Some cities obtained "home rule" charters that gave them greater freedom from state control in dealing with local matters. Many created research bureaus that investigated government problems in a scientific and nonpartisan manner. A number of middle-sized communities (Galveston, Texas, was the prototype) experimented with a system that integrated executive and legislative powers in the hands of a small elected commission, thereby concentrating responsibility and making it easier to coordinate complex activities. Out of this experiment came the city manager system, under which the commissioners appointed a professional manager to administer city affairs on a nonpartisan basis. Dayton, Ohio, which adopted the plan after the town was devastated by a flood in 1913, offers the best illustration of the city manager system in the Progressive Era.

Once the political system had been made responsive to the desires of the people, the progressives hoped to use it to improve society itself. Many cities experimented with "gas and water socialism," taking over public utility companies and operating them as departments of the municipal government. Under "Golden Rule" Jones, Toledo established a minimum wage for city employees, built playgrounds and golf courses, and moderated its harsh penal code. Mayor Seth Low improved New York's public transportation system and obtained passage of the tenement house law of 1901. Mayor Tom Johnson forced a fare cut to 3 cents on the Cleveland street railways.

Political Reform: The States

To carry out this kind of change required the support of state legislatures, since all municipal government depends on the authority of a sovereign state. Such approval was often difficult to obtain—local bosses were usually entrenched in powerful state machines, and most legislatures were controlled by rural majorities insensitive to urban needs. Therefore, the progressives had to strike at inefficiency and corruption at the state level too.

During the first decade of the new century, Wisconsin, the progressive state par excellence, was transformed by Robert M. La Follette, one of the most remarkable figures of the age. La Follette was born in Primrose, Wisconsin, in 1855. He had served

Robert M. La Follette speaking to Wisconsin farmers in 1897. After six years as governor of the state, he won election to the Senate, serving four terms.

three terms as a Republican congressman (1885–1891) and developed a reputation as an uncompromising foe of corruption before being elected governor in 1900. That the people would always do the right thing if properly informed and inspired was the fundamental article of his political faith. "Machine control is based upon misrepresentation and ignorance," La Follette said. "Democracy is based upon knowledge." His own career seemed to prove his point, for in his repeated clashes with the conservative Wisconsin Republican machine, he won battle after battle by vigorous grass-roots campaigning.

Despite the opposition of railroad and lumbering interests, Governor La Follette obtained a direct primary system for nominating candidates, a corrupt practices act, and laws limiting campaign expenditures and lobbying activities. In power he became something of a boss himself. He made ruthless use of patronage, demanded absolute loyalty of his subordinates, and often stretched, or at least oversimplified, the truth when presenting complex issues to the voters.

La Follette was a consummate showman who never rose entirely above rural prejudices. He was prone to scent a nefarious "conspiracy" organized by "the interests" behind even the mildest opposition to his proposals. But he was devoted to the cause of honest government. Realizing that some state functions called for specialized technical knowledge, he used commissions and agencies to handle such matters as railroad regulation, tax assessment, conservation, and highway construction. Wisconsin established a legislative reference library to assist lawmakers in drafting bills. For work of this kind, La Follette called on the faculty of the University of Wisconsin, enticing top-notch economists and political scientists into the public service and drawing freely on the advice of such outstanding social scientists as Richard T. Ely, John R. Commons, and E. A. Ross.

The success of what became known as the Wisconsin Idea led other states to adopt similar programs. Reform administrations swept into office in Iowa and Arkansas (1901), Oregon (1902), Minnesota, Kansas, and Mississippi (1904), New York and Georgia (1906), Nebraska (1909), New Jersey and Colorado (1910). In some cases the reformers were Republicans, in others Democrats, but in all the example of Wisconsin was influential. By 1910 15 states had established legislative reference services, most of them staffed by personnel trained in Wisconsin. The direct primary system became almost universal.

Some states went beyond Wisconsin in striving to make their governments responsive to the popular will. In 1902 Oregon began to experiment with the initiative, a system by which a bill could be forced on the attention of the legislature by popular petition, and the referendum, a method for allowing the electorate to approve measures rejected by their representatives and to repeal measures that the legislature had passed. Eleven states, most of them in the West, legalized these devices by 1914.

State Social Legislation

The first state laws aimed at social problems long antedated the Progressive Era, but most were either so imprecise as to be unenforceable or, like the Georgia law "limiting" textile workers to 11 hours a day, so weak as to be ineffective. In 1874 Massachusetts restricted the working hours of women and children to ten per day, and by the 1890s many other states, mostly in the East and Middle West, had followed suit. Illinois passed an eight-hour law for women workers in 1893. A New York law of 1882 struck at the sweatshops of the slums by prohibiting the manufacture of cigars on premises "occupied as a house or residence."

As part of this trend, some states established special rules for workers in hazardous industries. In the 1890s several states limited the hours of railroad workers on the grounds that fatigue sometimes caused railroad accidents. Utah restricted miners to eight hours in 1896. In 1901 New York finally enacted an effective tenement house law, greatly increasing the area of open space on building lots and requiring toilets for each apartment, better ventilation systems, and more adequate fireproofing.

Before 1900 the collective impact of such legislation was not impressive. Powerful manufacturers and landlords often succeeded in defeating the bills or rendering them innocuous. The federal system further complicated the task of obtaining effective legislation.

The Fourteenth Amendment to the Constitution, although enacted to protect the civil rights of blacks, imposed a revolutionary restriction on the states by forbidding them to "deprive any person of life, liberty, or property without due process of law." Since much state social legislation represented new uses of police power that conservative judges considered dangerous and unwise, the Fourteenth Amendment gave them an excuse to overturn the laws on the grounds that they deprived someone of liberty or property.

As stricter and more far-reaching laws were enacted, many judges, sensing what they took to be a trend toward socialism and regimentation, adopted an increasingly narrow interpretation of state police power. The United States Supreme Court upheld the Utah mining law of 1896 (*Holden* v. *Hardy*, 1898), but in 1905 it declared in the case of *Lochner* v. *New York* that a New York ten-hour act for bakers deprived the bakers of the liberty of working as long as they wished and thus violated the Fourteenth Amendment. Justice Oliver Wendell Holmes, Jr., wrote a famous dissenting opinion in this case. If the people of New York believed that the public health was endangered by bakers working long hours, he reasoned, it was not the Court's job to overrule them. "A constitution is not intended to embody a particular economic theory, whether of paternalism . . . or of laissez faire," Holmes said. "The word 'liberty,' in the Fourteenth Amendment, is perverted when it is held to prevent the natural outcome of a dominant opinion."

Nevertheless, the progressives continued to battle for legislation based on police power. Women played a particularly important part in these struggles. Sparked by the National Child Labor Committee, organized in 1904, reformers over the next ten years obtained laws in nearly every state banning the employment of young children and limiting the hours of older ones. Many of these laws were poorly enforced, yet when Congress passed a federal child labor law in 1916, the Supreme Court, in *Hammer* v. *Dagenhart* (1918), declared it unconstitutional.*

By 1917 nearly all the states had placed limitations on the hours of women industrial workers, and about ten had set minimum wage standards for women. But once again federal action that would have extended such regulation to the entire country did not materialize. A minimum wage law for women in the District of Columbia was overturned by the Court in *Adkins* v. *Children's Hospital* (1923).

Laws protecting workers against on-the-job accidents were also enacted by many states. Disasters like the 1911 fire in New York City, in which nearly

---

* A second child labor law, passed in 1919, was also thrown out by the Court, and a child labor amendment, submitted in 1924, failed to achieve ratification by the necessary three-quarters of the states.

150 women perished because the Triangle shirt-waist factory had no fire escapes, led to the passage of stricter municipal building codes and factory inspection acts. By 1910 most states had modified the common-law principle that a worker accepted the risk of accident as a condition of employment and was not entitled to compensation if injured unless it could be proved that the employer had been negligent. Gradually the states adopted accident insurance plans, and some began to grant pensions to widows with small children. Most manufacturers favored such measures, if for no other reason than that they regularized procedures and avoided costly lawsuits.

The passage of so much state social legislation sent conservatives scurrying to the Supreme Court for redress. Such persons believed that no government had the power to deprive either workers or employers of the right to negotiate any kind of labor contract they wished. The decision of the Supreme Court in *Lochner* v. *New York* seemed to indicate that the justices would adopt this point of view. But when an Oregon law limiting women laundry workers to ten hours a day was challenged in *Muller* v. *Oregon* (1908), Florence Kelley and Josephine Goldmark of the Consumers' League persuaded Louis D. Brandeis to defend the statute before the Court.

The Consumers' League, whose slogan was "investigate, agitate, legislate," was probably the most effective of the many women's reform organizations of the period. With the aid of League researchers, Brandeis prepared a remarkable brief stuffed with economic and sociological evidence indicating that long hours damaged both the health of individual women and the health of society. This nonlegal evidence greatly impressed the justices. "It may not be amiss," they declared, "to notice . . . expressions of opinion from other than judicial sources" in determining the constitutionality of such laws. "Woman's physical structure, and the functions she performs in consequence thereof, justify special legislation," they concluded. After 1908 the right of states to protect women, children, and workers performing dangerous and unhealthy tasks by special legislation was widely accepted. The use of the "Brandeis brief" technique to demonstrate the need for such legislation became standard practice.

Progressives also launched a massive, if ill-coordinated, attack on problems related to monopoly. The variety of regulatory legislation passed by

the states between 1900 and 1917 was almost infinite. Wisconsin created a powerful railroad commission staffed with nonpartisan experts; it enacted a graduated income tax and strengthened the state tax commission, which then proceeded to force corporations to bear a larger share of the cost of government; it overhauled the laws regulating insurance companies and set up a small state-owned life insurance company to serve as a yardstick for evaluating the rates of private companies. In 1911, besides creating an industrial commission to enforce the state's labor and factory legislation, Wisconsin progressives established a conservation commission, headed by Charles R. Van Hise, president of the University of Wisconsin.

A similar spate of legislation characterized the brief reign of Woodrow Wilson as governor of New Jersey (1911–1913). Urged on by the relentless Wilson, the legislature created a public utility commission with authority to evaluate the properties of railroad, gas, electric, telephone, and express companies and to fix rates and set standards for these corporations. The legislature enacted storage and food inspection laws, and in 1913 it passed seven bills (the "Seven Sisters" laws) tightening the state's loose controls over corporations, which had won New Jersey the unenviable reputation of being "the mother of trusts." Economic reforms in other states were less spectacular but impressive in the mass. In New York an investigation of the big life insurance companies led to comprehensive changes in the insurance laws and put Charles Evans Hughes, who had conducted the investigation, in the governor's chair. In Iowa stiff laws regulating railroads were passed in 1906. In Nebraska the legislature created a bank deposit insurance system in 1909. Minnesota levied an inheritance tax and built a harvesting machine factory to compete with the harvester trust. Georgia raised the taxes on corporations.

Political Reform in Washington

On the national level the Progressive Era saw the culmination of the struggle for women's suffrage. The shock occasioned by the failure of the Thirteenth and Fourteenth amendments to give women the vote resulted in a split among feminists. One group, the American Women's Suffrage Association, focused on the vote question alone. The more

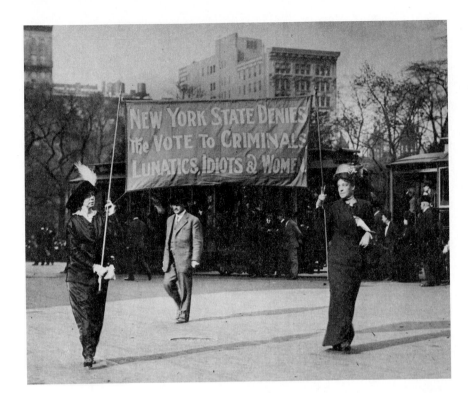

A banner in a 1911 women's suffrage parade carries one of the longest-standing arguments in favor of women getting the vote.

radical National Women's Suffrage Association, led by Elizabeth Cady Stanton and Susan B. Anthony, concerned itself with many issues of importance to women as well as the suffrage. The NWSA put the immediate interests of women ahead of everything else. It was deeply involved in efforts to unionize women workers, yet it did not hesitate to urge women to be strikebreakers if they could get better jobs by doing so.

Aside from their lack of unity, feminists were handicapped in the late 19th century by Victorian sexual inhibitions, which most of their leaders shared. Even under the best of circumstances, dislike of male-dominated society was hard enough to separate from dislike of men. At a time when sex was an unmentionable topic in polite society and sexual feelings were often deeply repressed, some of the most militant advocates of women's rights probably did not understand their own feelings. Most feminists, for example, opposed contraception, insisting that birth control by any means other than abstinence would encourage what they called masculine lust. The Victorian idealization of female "purity" and the popular image of women as the revered guardians of home and family further confused many reformers. And the trend of 19th-century scientific thinking influenced by the Darwinian concept of biological adaptation led to the conclusion that the female personality was different from that of the male and that the differences were inherent, not culturally determined.

These ideas and prejudices enticed feminists into a logical trap. If women were morally superior to men—a tempting conclusion—giving women the vote would improve the character of the electorate. Society would benefit because politics would become less corrupt, war a thing of the past. "City housekeeping has failed," said Jane Addams of Hull House in arguing for the reform of municipal government, "partly because women, the traditional housekeepers, have not been consulted."

The trouble with this argument (aside from the fact that opponents could easily demonstrate that in states where women did vote, governments were no better or worse than elsewhere) was that it surrendered the principle of equality. In the long run this was to have serious consequences for the women's movement, though the immediate effect of the

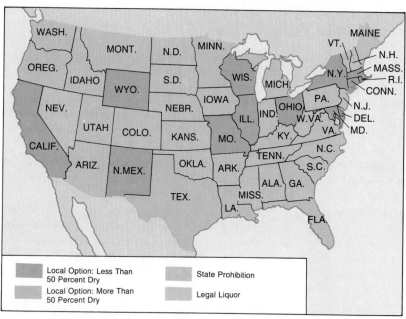

SUFFRAGE AND PROHIBITION, 1917

*These maps give a sense of the state-by-state progress of women's suffrage
and prohibition by 1917. The Eighteenth Amendment, enforcing national prohibition, passed in 1919; the Nineteenth Amendment, allowing
women the right to vote, in 1920. Both amendments were a culmination
of reform efforts before and during the Progressive Era. The original
1917 version of the temperance map referred to the three "wet" states—
New Jersey, Pennsylvania, and Nevada—as "Booze States."*

purity argument was probably to advance the suffragists' cause.

By the early 20th century there were signs of progress. In 1890 the two major women's groups combined as the National American Women's Suffrage Association. Stanton and Anthony were the first two presidents of the association, but new leaders were emerging, the most notable being Carrie Chapman Catt, a woman who combined superb organizing abilities and political skills with commitment to broad social reform. The NAWSA made winning the right to vote its main objective and concentrated on a state-by-state approach. By 1896 Wyoming, Utah, Colorado, and Idaho had been won over to women's suffrage.

The burgeoning of the progressive movement helped as middle-class recruits of both sexes adopted the cause. California voted for women's suffrage in 1911 after having defeated the proposal some years earlier, and several other states fell into line. For the first time, large numbers of working-class women began to agitate for the vote.

The suffragists then shifted the campaign back to the national level, the lead taken by a new organization, the Congressional Union, headed by Alice Paul. After some hesitation the NAWSA began to campaign for a constitutional amendment, which won congressional approval in 1918. By 1920 the necessary three-quarters of the states had ratified the Nineteenth Amendment; the long fight was over.

The progressive drive for political democracy also found expression in the Seventeenth Amendment to the Constitution, ratified in 1913, which required the popular election of senators. And a group of "insurgent" congressmen managed to reform the House of Representatives by limiting the power of the Speaker. During the early years of the century, operating under the system established in the 1890s by "Czar" Thomas B. Reed, Speaker Joseph G. Cannon exercised tyrannical authority, appointing the members of all committees and controlling the course of legislation. Representatives could seldom obtain the floor without obtaining the Speaker's consent. In 1910 the insurgents, led by George W. Norris, stripped Cannon of his control over the House Rules Committee. Thereafter, appointments to committees were determined by the entire membership, acting through party caucuses. This change was thoroughly progressive. "We want

the House to be representative of the people and each individual member to have his ideas presented and passed on," Norris explained.

No other important alterations of the national political system were made during the Progressive Era. Although some 20 states passed presidential primary laws, the cumbersome method of electing presidents was not changed.

Theodore Roosevelt: Cowboy in the White House

On September 6, 1901, an anarchist named Leon Czolgosz shot President McKinley during a public reception at the Pan-American Exposition at Buffalo, New York. Eight days later McKinley died and Theodore Roosevelt became president of the United States. His ascension to the presidency marked the beginning of a new era in national politics.

Although only 42, by far the youngest president in the nation's history up to that time, Roosevelt brought solid qualifications to the office. Son of a well-to-do New York merchant of Dutch ancestry, he had graduated from Harvard in 1880 and studied law briefly at Columbia, though he did not complete his degree. In addition to political experience that included three terms in the New York assembly, six years on the United States Civil Service Commission, two years as police commissioner of New York City, another as assistant secretary of the navy, and a term as governor of New York, he had been a rancher in Dakota Territory and a soldier in the Spanish-American War. He was also a well-known historian: His *Naval War of 1812* (1882), begun during his undergraduate days at Harvard, and his four-volume *Winning of the West* (1889–1896) were valuable works of scholarship, and he had written two popular biographies and other books as well. Politically, he had always been a loyal Republican. He rejected the Mugwump heresy in 1884, despite his distaste for Blaine, and during the tempestuous 1890s he vigorously denounced populism, Bryanism, and "labor agitators."

Nevertheless, Roosevelt's elevation to the presidency alarmed many conservatives, and not without reason. He did not fit their conception, based on a composite image of the chief executives from Hayes to McKinley, of what a president should be like. He seemed too undignified, too energetic, too outspoken, too unconventional. It was one thing to have operated a cattle ranch, another to have captured a gang of rustlers at gunpoint; one thing to have run a metropolitan police force, another to have roamed New York slums in the small hours to catch patrolmen fraternizing with thieves and prostitutes; one thing to have commanded a regiment, another to have killed a Spaniard personally.

Roosevelt had been a sickly child, plagued by asthma and poor eyesight, and he seems to have spent much of his adult life compensating for the sense of inadequacy that these troubles bred in him. He repeatedly carried his displays of physical stamina and personal courage, and his love of athletics and big-game hunting, to preternatural lengths. Henry Adams, who watched Roosevelt's development over the years with a mixture of fear and amusement, said that he was "pure act."

Once, while fox hunting, Roosevelt fell from his horse, cutting his face severely and breaking his left arm. Instead of waiting for help or struggling to some nearby house to summon a doctor, he clambered back on his horse and resumed the chase. "I was in at the death," he wrote next day. "I looked pretty gay, with one arm dangling, and my face and clothes like the walls of a slaughter house." That evening, after his arm had been set and put in splints, he attended a dinner party.

Roosevelt worshiped aggressiveness and was extremely sensitive to any threat to his honor as a gentleman. When another young man showed some slight interest in Roosevelt's fiancée, he sent for a set of French dueling pistols. His teachers found him an interesting student, for he was intelligent and imaginative, if rather annoyingly argumentative. "Now look here, Roosevelt," one Harvard professor finally said to him, "let me talk. I'm running this course."

Few individuals have rationalized or sublimated

Theodore Roosevelt in full oratorical flight. No wonder journalists were captivated by him; even when proceeding cautiously, which was most of the time as president, he brought life to national politics.

their feelings of inferiority as effectively as Roosevelt, and to such good purpose. And few have been more genuinely warmhearted, more full of spontaneity, more committed to the ideals of public service and national greatness. As a political leader he was energetic and hard-driving. Conservatives and timid souls, sensing his aggressiveness even when he held it in check, distrusted Roosevelt's judgment, fearing he might go off half-cocked in some crisis. In fact his judgment was nearly always sound; responsibility usually tempered his aggressiveness.

When Roosevelt was first mentioned as a running mate for McKinley in 1900, he wrote: "The Vice Presidency is a most honorable office, but for a young man there is not much to do." As president it would have been unthinkable for him to preside over a caretaker administration devoted to maintaining the status quo. However, the reigning Republican politicos, basking in the sunshine of the prosperity that had contributed so much to their victory in 1900, distrusted anything suggestive of change.

Had Roosevelt been the impetuous hothead that conservatives feared, he would have plunged ahead without regard for their feelings and influence. Instead he moved slowly and often got what he wanted by using his executive power rather than by persuading Congress to pass new laws. His domestic program included some measure of control of big corporations, more power for the Interstate Commerce Commission, and the conservation of natural resources. By consulting congressional leaders and following their advice not to bring up controversial matters like the tariff and currency reform, he obtained a modest budget of new laws.

The Newlands Act (1902) funneled the proceeds from land sales in the West into federal irrigation projects. The Department of Commerce and Labor, which was to include a Bureau of Corporations with authority to investigate industrial combines and issue reports was established. The Elkins Railroad Act of 1903 strengthened the Interstate Commerce Commission's hand against the railroads by making the receiving as well as the granting of rebates illegal and by forbidding the roads to deviate in any way from their published rates.

Roosevelt and Big Business

Roosevelt soon became known as a trustbuster, and in the sense that he considered the monopoly prob-

Roosevelt, the trust-busting lion tamer, whips beef, oil, steel, and other trusts into shape as they emerge from their Wall Street den.

lem the most pressing issue of the times, this was accurate to an extent. But he did not believe in breaking up big corporations indiscriminately. Regulation seemed the best way to deal with large corporations because, he said, industrial giantism "could not be eliminated unless we were willing to turn back the wheels of modern progress."

With Congress unwilling to pass a stiff regulatory law, Roosevelt resorted to the Sherman Act to get at the problem. Although the Supreme Court decision in the Sugar Trust case seemed to have emasculated that law, in 1902 he ordered the Justice Department to bring suit against the Northern Securities Company.

He chose his target wisely. The Northern Securities Company controlled the Great Northern, the Northern Pacific, and the Chicago, Burlington and Quincy railroads. It had been created in 1901 after a titanic battle on the New York Stock Exchange between the forces of J. P. Morgan and James J. Hill and those of E. H. Harriman, who was associated with the Rockefeller interests. In their efforts to obtain control of the Northern Pacific, the rivals had forced its stock up to $1,000 a share, ruining many speculators and threatening to cause a panic.

Neither side could win a clear-cut victory, so they decided to put the stock of all three railroads into a holding company owned by the two groups. Since Harriman already controlled the Union Pacific and the Southern Pacific, a virtual monopoly of western railroads was effected. The public had been alarmed, for the merger seemed to typify the rapaciousness of the tycoons.

The announcement of the suit caused consternation in the business world. Morgan rushed to the White House. "If we have done anything wrong," he said to the president, "send your man to my man and they can fix it up." Roosevelt was not fundamentally opposed to this sort of agreement, but it was too late to compromise in this instance. Attorney General Philander C. Knox pressed the case vigorously, and in 1904 the Supreme Court ordered the dissolution of the Northern Securities Company.

Roosevelt then ordered suits against the meat packers, the Standard Oil Trust, and the American Tobacco Company. His stock among progressives rose, yet he had not embarrassed the conservatives in Congress by demanding new antitrust legislation.

The president went out of his way to assure cooperative corporation magnates that he was not against size per se. His Bureau of Corporations followed a policy of "obtaining hearty co-operation rather than arousing (the) antagonism of business and industrial interests." At a White House conference in 1905, Roosevelt and Elbert H. Gary, chairman of the board of U.S. Steel, reached a "gentlemen's agreement" whereby Gary promised "to cooperate with the Government in every possible way." The Bureau of Corporations would conduct an investigation of U.S. Steel, Gary allowing it full access to company records. Roosevelt in turn promised that if the investigation revealed any corporate malpractices, he would allow Gary to set matters right voluntarily, thereby avoiding an antitrust suit. He reached a similar agreement with the International Harvester Company two years later.

There were limits to the effectiveness of such arrangements. Standard Oil agreed to a similar détente and then reneged, refusing to turn over vital records to the bureau. The Justice Department brought suit against the company under the Sherman Act, and eventually it was broken up at the order of the Supreme Court. Roosevelt would have preferred a more binding kind of regulation, but when he asked for laws giving the government supervisory authority over big combinations, Congress refused to act.

Square Dealing

Roosevelt made remarkable use of his executive power during the anthracite coal strike of 1902. In June the United Mine Workers, led by John Mitchell, laid down their picks and demanded higher wages, an eight-hour day, and recognition of the union. Most of the anthracite mines were owned by railroads. Two years earlier the miners had won a 10 percent wage increase in a similar strike, chiefly because the owners feared that labor unrest might endanger the election of McKinley. Now the coal companies were dead set against further concessions; when the men walked out, they shut down their properties and prepared to starve the strikers into submission.

The strike dragged on through summer and early fall. The miners conducted themselves with great restraint, avoiding violence and offering to submit their claims to arbitration. As the price of anthracite soared with the approach of winter, sentiment in their behalf mounted.

The owners' spokesman, George F. Baer of the Reading Railroad, proved particularly inept at public relations. Baer stated categorically that God was on the side of management, but when someone suggested asking an important Roman Catholic prelate to arbitrate the dispute, he replied icily: "Anthracite mining is a business and not a religious, sentimental or academic proposition."

Roosevelt shared the public's sympathy for the miners, and the threat of a coal shortage alarmed him. Early in October he summoned both sides to a conference in Washington and urged them as patriotic Americans to sacrifice any "personal consideration" for the "general good." His action enraged the coal operators, for they believed he was trying to force them to recognize the union. They refused even to speak to the UMW representatives at the conference and demanded that Roosevelt end the

A silent procession of striking coal miners makes an orderly demonstration at Shenandoah, Pennsylvania, during the 1902 coal strike.

strike by force and bring suit against the union under the Sherman Act. Mitchell, aware of the immense prestige that Roosevelt had conferred on the union by calling the conference, cooperated fully with the president.

The attitudes of management and the union further strengthened public support for the miners. Even former president Grover Cleveland, who had used federal troops to break the Pullman strike, said that he was "disturbed and vexed by the tone and substance of the operators' deliverances." Encouraged by this state of affairs, Roosevelt took a bold step: He announced that unless a settlement was reached promptly, he would order federal troops

into the anthracite regions, not to break the strike but to seize and operate the mines.

The threat of government intervention brought the owners to terms. A Cabinet member, Elihu Root, worked out the details with J. P. Morgan, whose firm had major interests in the Reading and other railroads, while cruising the Hudson River on Morgan's yacht. The miners would return to the pits, and all issues between them and the coal companies would be submitted for settlement to a commission appointed by Roosevelt. Both sides accepted the arrangement, and the men went back to work. In March 1903 the commission granted the miners a 10 percent wage increase and a nine-hour day.

To the public the incident seemed a perfect illustration of the progressive spirit—in Roosevelt's words, everyone had received a "square deal." In fact the results were by no means so clear-cut. The miners gained relatively little, and the companies lost still less, for they were not required to recognize the United Mine Workers and the commission also recommended a 10 percent increase in the price of coal, ample compensation for the increased wage costs. The president was the main winner. The public acclaimed him as a fearless, imaginative, public-spirited leader. Without calling on Congress for support, he had expanded his own authority and hence that of the federal government. His action marked a major forward step in the evolution of the modern presidency.

T.R.: President in His Own Right

By reviving the Sherman Act, settling the coal strike, and pushing moderate reforms through Congress, Roosevelt ensured that he would be reelected president in 1904. Progressives, if not yet captivated, were at least pleased by his performance. Conservative Republicans offered no serious objection. Sensing that Roosevelt had won over the liberals, the Democrats nominated a conservative, Judge Alton B. Parker of New York, and bid for the support of eastern industrialists.

This strategy failed, for businessmen continued to eye the party of Bryan with intense suspicion. They preferred, as the *New York Sun* put it, "the impulsive candidate of the party of conservatism to the conservative candidate of the party which the business interests regard as permanently and dangerously impulsive." Despite his resentment at Roosevelt's attack on the Northern Securities Company, J. P. Morgan contributed $150,000 to the Republican campaign. Other tycoons gave with equal generosity. Roosevelt swept the country, carrying even the normally Democratic border states of Maryland and Missouri.

Encouraged by the landslide and the increasing militancy of progressives, Roosevelt pressed for more reform legislation. His most imaginative proposal was a plan to make the District of Columbia a model progressive community. He suggested child labor and factory inspection laws and a slum clear-

ance program, but Congress refused to act. Likewise, his request for a minimum wage for railroad workers was rejected.

He had greater success when he proposed still another increase in the power of the Interstate Commerce Commission. Rebating remained a serious problem. With progressive state governors demanding federal action and farmers and manufacturers, especially in the Middle West, clamoring for relief against discriminatory rates, Roosevelt was ready by 1905 to make railroad legislation his major objective. The ICC should be empowered to fix rates, not merely to challenge unreasonable ones. It should have the right to inspect the private records of the railroads, since fair rates could not be determined unless the true financial condition of the roads was known.

Because these proposals struck at rights that businessmen considered sacrosanct, many congressmen balked. But Roosevelt applied presidential pressure, and in June 1906 the Hepburn bill became law. It gave the commission the power to inspect the books of railroad companies, to set maximum rates (once a complaint had been filed by a shipper), and to control sleeping car companies, owners of oil pipelines, and other firms engaged in transportation. Railroads could no longer issue passes freely—an important check on their political influence. In all, the Hepburn Act made the ICC a more powerful and more active body. Though it did not outlaw judicial review of ICC decisions, thereafter those decisions were seldom overturned by the courts.

Congress also passed meat inspection and pure food and drug legislation. In 1906 Upton Sinclair published *The Jungle*, a devastating exposé of the filthy conditions in the Chicago slaughterhouses. Sinclair was more interested in writing a socialist tract than he was in meat inspection, but his book, a best-seller, raised a storm against the packers. After Roosevelt read *The Jungle*, he sent two officials to Chicago to investigate. Their report was so shocking, he said, that its publication would "be well-nigh ruinous to our export trade in meat." He threatened to release the report, however, unless Congress acted. After a hot fight, the meat inspection bill passed. The Pure Food and Drug Act, forbidding the manufacture and sale of adulterated and fraudulently labeled products, rode through Congress on the coattails of this measure.

Before the passage of the Pure Food and Drug Act in 1906, manufacturers were free to use any ingredients they chose. Many "tonics" kept their promises of increased vigor by delivering doses of cocaine, alcohol, or other narcotics.

Roosevelt has probably received more credit than he deserves for these laws. He had never been deeply interested in pure food legislation, and he considered Dr. Harvey W. Wiley, chief chemist of the Department of Agriculture and the leader of the fight for this reform, something of a crank. He compromised with opponents of meat inspection cheerfully, despite his loud denunciations of the evils under attack. "As now carried on the (meatpacking) business is both a menace to health and an outrage on decency," he said. "No legislation that is not drastic and thoroughgoing will be of avail." Yet he went along with the packers' demand that the government pay the costs of inspection, though he believed that "the only way to secure efficiency is by the imposition upon the packers of a fee." Nevertheless, the end results were positive and in line with his conception of the public good.

To advanced liberals Roosevelt's achievements seemed limited when placed beside his professed objectives and his smug evaluations of what he had done. How could he be a reformer and a defender of established interests at the same time? Roosevelt found no difficulty in holding such a position. As one historian has said, "He stood close to the center and bared his teeth at the conservatives of the right and the liberals of the extreme left."

Tilting Left

As the progressive movement advanced, Roosevelt advanced with it. He never accepted all the ideas of what he called its "lunatic fringe," but he took steadily more liberal positions. He always insisted that he was not hostile to business interests, but when those interests sought to exploit the national domain, they had no more implacable foe. Conservation of natural resources was dear to his heart and probably his most significant achievement as president. He placed some 150 million acres of forest lands in federal reserves, and he strictly enforced the laws governing grazing, mining, and lumbering. When his opponents attached to an important appropriations bill a rider prohibiting the creation of further reserves without the approval of Congress, Roosevelt transferred an additional 17 million acres to the reserve before signing the bill. In 1908 he organized a National Conservation Conference, attended by 44 governors and 500 others, to discuss conservation matters. As a result of this meeting, most states created conservation commissions.

As Roosevelt became more liberal, conservative Republicans began to balk at following his lead. The sudden panic that struck the financial world in October 1907 speeded the trend. Government policies had no direct bearing on the panic, which began with a run on several important New York trust companies and spread to the Stock Exchange when speculators found themselves unable to borrow money to meet their obligations. In the emergency, Roosevelt authorized the deposit of large amounts of government cash in New York banks. He informally agreed to the acquisition of the Tennessee Coal and Iron Company by U.S. Steel when the bankers told him that the purchase was necessary to end the panic. In spite of his efforts, conservatives insisted on referring to the financial collapse as "Roosevelt's panic," and they blamed the president for the depression that followed on its heels.

Roosevelt, however, turned left rather than right. In 1908 he came out in favor of federal income and inheritance taxes, stricter regulation of interstate corporations, and reforms designed to help industrial workers. He denounced "the speculative folly and the flagrant dishonesty" of "malefactors of great wealth," further alienating conservative, or Old Guard, Republicans, who resented the attacks on their integrity implicit in Roosevelt's statements. When the president began criticizing the courts, the last bastion of conservatism, he lost all chance of obtaining further reform legislation. As he said himself, during his last months in office "stagnation continued to rage with uninterrupted violence."

William Howard Taft: The Listless Progressive

But Roosevelt remained popular and politically powerful. Before his term ended, he chose William Howard Taft, his secretary of war, to succeed him and easily obtained Taft's nomination. William Jennings Bryan was again the Democratic candidate. Campaigning on Roosevelt's record, Taft carried the country by well over a million votes, defeating Bryan 321 to 162 in the electoral college.

Taft was intelligent, experienced, and public-spirited; he seemed ideally suited to carry out Roosevelt's policies. Born in Cincinnati in 1857, educated at Yale, he had served as an Ohio judge, as solicitor general of the United States under Benjamin Harrison, and then as a federal circuit court judge before accepting McKinley's assignment to head the Philippine Commission in 1900. His suc-

Taft was the first presidential golfer, playing enthusiastically despite his bulk. He ended his career happily as a chief justice of the Supreme Court.

cess as civil governor of the Philippines led Roosevelt to make him secretary of war in 1904.

Taft supported the Square Deal loyally. This, together with his mentor's ardent endorsement, won him the backing of most progressive Republicans. Yet the Old Guard liked him too; although outgoing, he had none of the Roosevelt impetuosity and aggressiveness. His genial personality and his obvious desire to avoid conflict appealed to moderates.

However, Taft lacked the physical and mental stamina required of a modern chief executive. Though not lazy, he weighed over 300 pounds and needed to rest this vast bulk more than the job allowed. He liked to eat in leisurely fashion, to idle away mornings on the golf course, to take an afternoon nap. Campaigning bored him; speech making seemed a useless chore. The judicial life was his real love; intense partisanship dismayed and confused him. He was too reasonable to control a coalition and not ambitious enough to impose his will on others. He found extremists irritating and persistent people (including his wife) difficult to resist. He supported many progressive measures, but he never absorbed the progressive spirit.

Taft honestly desired to carry out most of Roosevelt's policies. He enforced the Sherman Act vigorously and continued to expand the national forest reserves. He signed the Mann-Elkins Act of 1910, which empowered the Interstate Commerce Commission to suspend rate increases without waiting for a shipper to complain and established the Commerce Court to speed the settlement of railroad rate cases. An eight-hour day for all persons engaged in work on government contracts, mine safety legislation, and several other reform measures received his approval. He even summoned Congress into special session specifically to reduce tariff duties—something that Roosevelt had not dared to attempt.

But Taft had been disturbed by Roosevelt's sweeping use of executive power. "We have got to work out our problems on the basis of law," he insisted. Whereas Roosevelt had excelled at maneuvering around congressional opposition and at finding ways to accomplish his objectives without waiting for Congress to act, Taft adamantly refused to use such tactics. His restraint was in many ways admirable, but it reduced his effectiveness.

In case after case, Taft's lack of vigor and his political ineptness led to trouble. In the matter of the tariff, he favored downward revision. When the special session met in 1909, the House promptly passed a bill that was in line with his desires. But Senate protectionists restored the high rates of the Act of 1897 on most items. A group of insurgent senators, led by Robert La Follette of Wisconsin, fought these changes desperately, producing masses of statistics to show that the proposed schedules on cotton goods, woolens, and other products were unreasonably high. They were fighting the president's battle, yet Taft did little to help them. He signed the final Payne-Aldrich measure and called it "the best (tariff) bill that the Republican party ever passed." His attitude dumbfounded the progressives.

In 1910 Taft got into difficulty with the conservationists. Though he believed in husbanding natural resources carefully, he did not like the way Roosevelt had circumvented Congress in adding to the forest reserves. He demanded, and eventually obtained, specific legislation to accomplish this purpose. The issue that aroused the conservationists concerned the integrity of his secretary of the interior, Richard A. Ballinger. A less than ardent conservationist, Ballinger returned to the public domain certain waterpower sites that the Roosevelt administration had withdrawn on the legally questionable grounds that they were to become ranger stations. Ballinger's action alarmed Chief Forester Gifford Pinchot, the darling of the conservationists. When Pinchot learned that Ballinger intended to validate the shaky claim of mining interests to a large tract of coal-rich land in Alaska, he launched an intemperate attack on the secretary.

In the Ballinger-Pinchot controversy, Taft felt obliged to support his own man. The coal lands dispute was complex, and Pinchot's charges were exaggerated. It was certainly unfair to call Ballinger "the most effective opponent the conservation policies have yet had." When Pinchot, whose own motives were partly political, persisted in criticizing Ballinger, Taft dismissed him. He had no choice under the circumstances, but a more adept politician might have found some way of avoiding a showdown.

Breakup of the Republican Party

One ominous aspect of the Ballinger-Pinchot affair was that Pinchot was a close friend of Theodore Roosevelt. After Taft's inauguration, Roosevelt had gone off to hunt big game in Africa, bearing in his baggage an autographed photograph of his protégé and a touching letter of appreciation, in which the new president said: "I can never forget that the power I now exercise was a voluntary transfer from you to me." For months, as he trudged across Africa, guns blazing, Roosevelt was out of touch with affairs in the United States. As soon as he emerged from the wilderness in March 1910, bearing more than 3,000 trophies, including 9 lions, 5 elephants, and 13 rhinos, he was caught up in the squabble between the progressive members of his party and its titular head. Pinchot met him in Italy, laden with injured innocence and a packet of angry letters from various progressives. His intimate friend Senator Henry Cabot Lodge, essentially a conservative, barraged him with messages, the gist of which was that Taft was lazy and inept and that Roosevelt should prepare to become the "Moses" who would guide the party "out of the wilderness of doubt and discontent" into which Taft had led it.

Roosevelt hoped to steer a middle course, but

Pinchot's complaints impressed him. Taft had decided to strike out on his own, he concluded. "No man must render such a service as that I rendered Taft and expect the individual . . . not in the end to become uncomfortable and resentful," he wrote Lodge sadly. Taft sensed the former president's coolness and was offended. He was egged on by his ambitious wife, who wanted him to stand clear of Roosevelt's shadow and establish his own reputation.

Perhaps the resulting rupture was inevitable. The Republican party was dividing into two factions, the progressives and the Old Guard. Forced

Political cartoonists came of age during the Progressive Era, not least because of such easily caricatured presidents as the frenetic T.R. and the outsized Taft.

THE DISPUTED CHAIR

T. R. TO TAFT: "I only lent it to you, anyway"

to choose between them, Taft threw in his lot with the Old Guard. Roosevelt backed the progressives. Speaking at Osawatomie, Kansas, in August 1910, he came out for a comprehensive program of social legislation, which he called the New Nationalism. Besides attacking "special privilege" and the "unfair money-getting" practices of "lawbreakers of great wealth," he called for a broad expansion of federal power. "The betterment we seek must be accomplished," he said, "mainly through the National Government."

The final break came in October 1911, when the president ordered an antitrust suit against U.S. Steel. Roosevelt, of course, opposed breaking up large corporations. "The effort at prohibiting all combination has substantially failed," he said in his New Nationalism speech. "The way out lies . . . in completely controlling them." Taft was prepared to enforce the Sherman Act "or die in the attempt." But what angered Roosevelt was Taft's emphasis in the suit on U.S. Steel's absorption of the Tennessee Coal and Iron Company, which Roosevelt had unofficially authorized during the panic of 1907. The government's antitrust brief made Roosevelt appear to have been either an abettor of monopoly or, far worse, a fool who had been duped by the steel corporation. Early in 1912 he declared himself a candidate for the Republican presidential nomination.

Roosevelt plunged into the preconvention campaign with typical energy. He was almost uniformly victorious in states that held presidential primaries, carrying even Ohio, Taft's home state. However, the president controlled the party machinery and entered the national convention with a small majority of the delegates. Since some Taft delegates had been chosen under questionable circumstances, the Roosevelt forces challenged the right of 254 of them to their seats. The Taft-controlled credentials committee, paying little attention to the evidence, gave all but a few of the disputed seats to the president, who then won the nomination on the first ballot.

Had Roosevelt swallowed his resentment and bided his time, Taft would almost certainly have been defeated in the election, and the 1916 Republican nomination would have been Roosevelt's for the asking. But he was understandably outraged by the ruthless manner in which the Taft "steamroller" had overridden his forces. When his leading supporters urged him to organize a third party, and

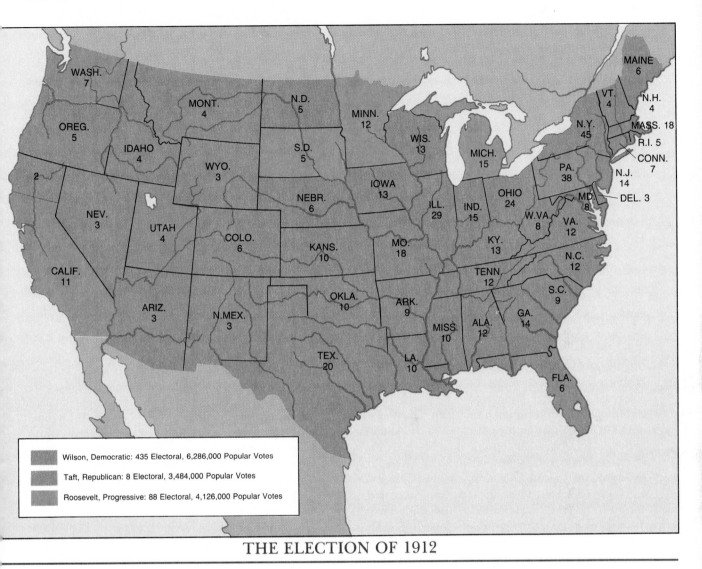

Wilson, Democratic: 435 Electoral, 6,286,000 Popular Votes

Taft, Republican: 8 Electoral, 3,484,000 Popular Votes

Roosevelt, Progressive: 88 Electoral, 4,126,000 Popular Votes

THE ELECTION OF 1912

The fourth largest vote getter in the election of 1912 was Eugene V. Debs of the Socialist party, who gained about 900,000 popular votes (or approximately 6 percent of the total popular vote), but no electoral vote.

when two of them, George W. Perkins, formerly a partner of the banker J. P. Morgan, and the publisher Frank Munsey, offered to finance the campaign, Roosevelt agreed to make the race.

In August, amid scenes of hysterical enthusiasm, the first convention of the Progressive party met at Chicago and nominated him for president. Announcing that he felt "as strong as a bull moose," Roosevelt delivered a stirring "confession of faith," calling for strict regulation of corporations, a tariff commission, national presidential primaries, minimum wage and workers' compensation laws, the elimination of child labor, and many other reforms.

The Election of 1912

The Democrats made the most of the opportunity offered by the Republican schism. Had they nominated a conservative or allowed Bryan a fourth chance, they would probably have ensured Roosevelt's election. Instead, after battling through 46 ballots at their convention in Baltimore, they nominated Woodrow Wilson, who had achieved a remarkable liberal record as governor of New Jersey.

Although as a political scientist Wilson had criticized the status quo and taken a pragmatic approach to the idea of government regulation of the economy, he had objected strongly to Bryan's brand of politics. In 1896 he voted for the Gold Democratic party candidate for president. But by 1912, influenced partly by ambition and partly by the spirit of the times, he had been converted to progressivism. He called his brand of reform the New Freedom.

The federal government could best advance the cause of social justice, Wilson reasoned, by eradicating the special privileges that enabled the "interests" to flourish. Where Roosevelt had lost faith in competition as a way of protecting the public against monopolies, Wilson insisted that competition could be restored. The government must break up the great trusts, establish fair rules for doing business, and subject violators to stiff punishments. Thereafter, the free enterprise system would protect the public from exploitation without destroying individual initiative and opportunity. "If America is not to have free enterprise, then she can have freedom of no sort whatever," he said. Although rather vague, this argument appealed to thousands of voters who found the growing power of large corporations frightening but who hesitated to make the thoroughgoing commitment to government control of business that Roosevelt was advocating.

Roosevelt's reasoning was perhaps theoretically more sound.

Laissez faire made less sense than it had in earlier times. The complexities of the modern world seemed to call for a positive approach, a plan, the close application of human intelligence to social and economic problems. As Herbert Croly insisted in *The Promise of American Life* (1909), the time had come to employ Hamiltonian means to achieve Jeffersonian ends.

Roosevelt dismissed Wilson's New Freedom as "rural toryism," but being less drastic and more in line with American experience than the New Nationalism, it had much to recommend it. The danger that selfish individuals would use the power of the state for their own ends had certainly not disappeared, despite the efforts of progressives to make

government more responsive to popular opinion. Any considerable expansion of national power would increase the danger and probably create new difficulties. Managing so complicated an enterprise as an industrialized nation was sure to be a formidable task. Furthermore, individual freedom of opportunity merited the toleration of a certain amount of inefficiency.

To choose between the New Nationalism and the New Freedom, between the dynamic Roosevelt and the idealistic Wilson, was indeed difficult. Thousands grappled with this problem before going to the polls, but partisan politics determined the outcome of the election. Taft got the hard-core Republican vote but lost the progressive wing of the GOP to Roosevelt. Wilson had the solid support of both conservative and liberal Democrats. As a result, Wilson won an easy victory in the electoral college, receiving 435 votes to Roosevelt's 88 and Taft's 8. The popular vote was Wilson, 6,286,000; Roosevelt, 4,126,000; and Taft, 3,484,000.

If partisan politics had determined the winner, the election was nonetheless an overwhelming endorsement of progressivism. The temper of the times was shown by the 897,000 votes given Eugene Debs, who was again the Socialist candidate. Altogether, professed liberals amassed over 11 million of the 15 million ballots cast. Wilson was a minority president, but he took office with a clear mandate to press forward with further reforms.

Wilson: The New Freedom

No man ever rose more suddenly or spectacularly in American politics than Woodrow Wilson. In the spring of 1910 he was president of Princeton University; he had never held or even run for public office. In the fall of 1912 he was president-elect of the United States. Yet if his rise was meteoric, in a very real sense he had devoted his life to preparing for it. He was born in Staunton, Virginia, in 1856, the son of a Presbyterian minister. As a student he became interested in political theory, dreaming of representing his state in the Senate. He studied law solely because he thought it the best avenue to public office, and when he discovered that he did not like legal work, he took a doctorate at Johns Hopkins in political science.

For years Wilson's political ambitions appeared

He instituted the preceptorial system, which placed the students in close intellectual and social contact with their teachers. He attracted outstanding young scholars to the Princeton faculty.

In time Wilson's educational ideas and his overbearing manner of applying them got him in trouble with some of Princeton's alumni and trustees. Though his university career was wrecked, the controversies, in which he appeared to be championing democracy and progress in the face of reactionary opponents, brought him at last to the attention of the politicians. Then, in a great rush, came power and fame.

Wilson was an immediate success as president. Since Roosevelt's last year in office, Congress had been almost continually at war with the executive branch and with itself. Legislative achievements had been relatively few. Now a small avalanche of important measures received the approval of the lawmakers. In October 1913 the Underwood Tariff brought the first significant reduction of duties since before the Civil War. Food products, wool, iron and steel, shoes, agricultural machinery, and other items that could be produced more cheaply in the United States than abroad were placed on the free list. Rates on most other goods were cut substantially, the object being to equalize foreign and domestic costs. To compensate for the expected loss of revenue, the act provided for a graduated tax on personal incomes.*

Two months later the Federal Reserve Act gave the country a central banking system for the first time since Jackson destroyed the Bank of the United States. The measure divided the nation into 12 banking districts, each under the supervision of a Federal Reserve bank, a sort of bank for bankers. All national banks in each district and any state banks that wished to participate had to invest 6 percent of their capital and surplus in the reserve bank, which was empowered to exchange (the technical term is *rediscount*) paper money, called Federal Reserve notes, for the commercial and agricultural paper that member banks took in as security from borrowers. The volume of currency was no longer at the mercy of the supply of gold or any other particular commodity.

Woodrow Wilson, presiding over the 1906 Princeton commencement, with steel magnate cum *educational philanthropist Andrew Carnegie firmly in tow.*

doomed to frustration. He taught at Bryn Mawr, then at Wesleyan, finally at his alma mater, Princeton. He wrote several influential books, among them *Congressional Government* and *The State,* and achieved an outstanding reputation as a teacher and lecturer. In 1902 he was chosen president of Princeton and soon won a place among the nation's leading educators. He revised the curriculum, introducing many new subjects and insisting that students pursue an organized and integrated course of study.

---

* The Sixteenth Amendment, ratified in February 1913, authorized the imposition of a federal income tax.

The crown and nerve center of the system was the Federal Reserve Board in Washington, which appointed a majority of the directors of the Federal Reserve banks and had some control over rediscount rates (the commission charged by the reserve banks for performing the rediscounting function). The board provided a modicum of public control over the banks, but the effort to weaken the power of the great New York banks by decentralizing the system proved ineffective. Nevertheless, a true central banking system was created.

When inflation threatened, the reserve banks could raise the rediscount rate, discouraging borrowing and thus reducing the amount of money in circulation. In bad times it could lower the rate, making it easier to borrow and injecting new dollars into the economy. Much remained to be learned about the proper management of the money supply, but the nation finally had a flexible yet safe currency.

In 1914 Congress passed two important laws affecting corporations. One created the Federal Trade Commission to replace Roosevelt's Bureau of Corporations. In addition to investigating corporations and publishing reports, this nonpartisan board could issue cease and desist orders against "unfair" trade practices brought to light through its research. The law did not define the term *unfair*, and the commission's rulings could be taken on appeal to the federal courts, but the FTC was nonetheless a powerful instrument for protecting the public against the trusts.

The second measure, the Clayton Antitrust Act, made certain specific business practices illegal, including price discrimination that tended to foster monopoly; "tying" agreements, which forbade retailers from handling the products of a firm's competitors; and the creation of interlocking directorates as a means of controlling competing companies. The act exempted labor unions and agricultural organizations from the antitrust laws and curtailed the use of injunctions in labor disputes. The officers of corporations could be held individually responsible if their companies violated the antitrust laws.

The Democrats controlled both houses of Congress for the first time since 1890 and were eager to make a good record, but Wilson's imaginative and aggressive use of presidential power was decisive. He called the legislators into special session in April 1913 and appeared before them to lay out his program; he was the first president to address Congress in person since John Adams. Then he

followed the course of administration bills closely. He had a private telephone line installed between the Capitol and the White House. Administration representatives haunted the cloakrooms and lobbies of both houses. Cooperative congressmen began to receive notes of praise and encouragement, recalcitrant ones stern demands for support, often pecked out on the president's own portable typewriter. When lobbyists tried to frustrate his plans for tariff reform by bringing pressure to bear on key senators, he made a dramatic appeal to the people. "The public ought to know the extraordinary exertions being made by the lobby in Washington," he told reporters. "Only public opinion can check and destroy it." The voters responded so strongly that the Senate passed the tariff bill substantially as Wilson desired it.

Wilson explained his success by saying, only half humorously, that running the government was child's play for anyone who had managed the faculty of a university. Responsible party government was his objective; he expected individual Democrats to support the decisions of the party majority, and his idealism never prevented him from awarding the spoils of office to city bosses and conservative congressmen, so long as they supported his program. Nor did his career as a political theorist make him rigid and doctrinaire. In practice the differences between his New Freedom and Roosevelt's New Nationalism tended to disappear. The Underwood Tariff and the Clayton Antitrust Act fitted the philosophy Wilson had expounded during the campaign, but the Federal Trade Commission represented a step toward the kind of regulated economy that Roosevelt advocated. So did the Federal Reserve system.

There were limits to Wilson's progressivism, limits imposed partly by his temperament and partly by his philosophy. He objected as strenuously to laws granting special favors to farmers and workers as to those benefiting the tycoons. When a bill was introduced in 1914 making low-interest loans available to farmers, he refused to support it. "It is unwise and unjustifiable to extend the credit of the Government to a single class of the community," he said. He considered the provision exempting unions from the antitrust laws equally unsound. Nor would he push for a federal law prohibiting child labor; such a measure would be unconstitutional, he believed. He also refused to back the constitutional amendment giving the vote to women.

By the end of 1914 the Wilsonian record, on balance, was positive but distinctly limited. The president believed that the major progressive goals had been achieved; he had no plans for further reform. Many other progressives thought that a great deal more remained to be done.

The Progressives and Minority Rights

On one important issue, race relations, Wilson was distinctly reactionary. With a mere handful of exceptions, the progressives exhibited strong prejudices against nonwhite people and against certain categories of whites as well. Many were as unsympathetic to immigrants from Asia and eastern and southern Europe as any of the "conservative" opponents of immigration in the 1880s and 1890s. The Gentlemen's Agreement excluding Japanese immigrants was reached in 1907 at the height of the progressive movement. In the same year, Congress appointed a commission headed by Senator William Dillingham of Vermont to study the immigration question. The Dillingham Commission labored for more than two years and brought forth a 41-volume report that led in 1913 to a bill restricting the number of newcomers to be admitted and reducing especially the influx from eastern and southern Europe. Only the outbreak of war in Europe in 1914, which cut immigration to a trickle, prevented the passage of this measure.

American Indians were also affected by the progressives' racial attitudes. Where the sponsors of the Dawes Act had assumed that Indians were inherently capable of adopting the ways of "civilized" people, in the progressive period the tendency was to write Indians off as fundamentally inferior and to assume that they would make second-class citizens at best. Francis Leupp, Theodore Roosevelt's commissioner of Indian affairs, put it this way in a 1905 report: "If nature has set a different physical stamp upon different races of men it is fair to assume that the variation . . . is manifested in mental and moral traits as well. . . . Nothing is gained by trying to undo nature's work." A leading muckraker, Ray Stannard Baker, who was far more sympathetic to blacks than most progressives, dismissed Indians as pathetic beings, "eating, sleeping, idling, with no more thought of the future than a white man's child."

In 1902 Congress passed the Dead Indian Land Act, which made it easier for Indians to sell allotments that they had inherited, and in 1906 another law further relaxed restrictions on land sales. Efforts to improve the education of Indian children continued, but most progressives assumed that only vocational training would benefit them. Theodore Roosevelt knew from his experiences as a rancher in Dakota Territory that Indians could be as energetic and capable as whites, but he considered these "exceptional." As for the rest, it would be many generations before they could be expected to "move forward" enough to become "ordinary citizens," Roosevelt believed. "The Indian stirred little controversy among the leading political warriors of the progressive era," a recent scholar writes.

To say that blacks did not fare well at the hands of progressives would be a gross understatement. Populist efforts to unite white and black farmers in the southern states had led to the imposition of further repressive measures. Segregation became more rigid, white opposition to black voting more monolithic. In 1900 the body of a Mississippi black was dug up by order of the state legislature and reburied in a segregated cemetery; in Virginia in 1902 the daughter of Robert E. Lee was arrested for riding in the black section of a railroad car. "Insult is being added to injury continually," a black journalist in Alabama complained. "Have those in power forgotten that there is a God?"

Many progressive women, still smarting from the insult to their sex entailed in the Fourteenth and Fifteenth amendments and eager to attract southern support for their campaign for the vote, adopted racist arguments. They contrasted the supposed corruption and incompetence of black voters with their own "purity" and intelligence. Southern progressives of both sexes argued that disfranchising blacks would reduce corruption by removing from unscrupulous white politicians the temptation to purchase black votes!

The typical southern attitude toward the education of blacks was summed up in a folk proverb: "When you educate a Negro, you spoil a good field hand." In 1910, only about 8,000 black children in the entire South were attending high schools. Despite the almost total suppression of black rights, lynchings continued to occur; between 1900 and 1914 more than 1,100 blacks were murdered by mobs, most (but not all) in the southern states. In the rare cases where local prosecutors brought the lynchers to trial, juries almost without exception brought in verdicts of not guilty.

Booker T. Washington was shaken by this trend, but he could find no way to combat it. The times were passing him by. He appealed to his white southern "friends" for help but got nowhere. Increasingly he talked about the virtues of rural life, the evils of big cities, and the uselessness of higher education for black people. By the turn of the century a number of young, well-educated blacks, most of them northerners, were breaking away from his accommodationist leadership.

Black Militancy

Wlliam E. B. Du Bois was the most prominent of the militants. Du Bois was born in Great Barrington, Massachusetts, in 1868. His father, a restless wanderer of Negro and French Huguenot stock, abandoned the family, and young William grew up on the edge of poverty. Neither accepted nor openly rejected by the overwhelmingly white community, he devoted himself to his studies, showing such bril-

A striking likeness of W. E. B. Du Bois drawn by Winold Reiss when Du Bois was in his fifties.

liance that his future education was assured by scholarships: to Fisk University, then to Harvard, then to the University of Berlin. In 1895 Du Bois became the first American black to earn a Ph.D. in history from Harvard; his dissertation, *The Suppression of the African Slave Trade* (1896), remains a standard reference.

Personal success and "acceptance" by whites did not make the proud and sensitive Du Bois complacent. Outraged by white racism and the willingness of many blacks to settle for second-class citizenship, he set out to make American blacks proud of their color—"Beauty is black," he said—and of their African origins and culture.

Like Washington, Du Bois wanted blacks to lift themselves by their own bootstraps. They must establish their own businesses, run their own newspapers and colleges, write their own literature; they must preserve their identity rather than seek to amalgamate themselves into a society that offered them only crumbs and contempt. At first he cooperated with Washington, but in 1903, in an essay, "Of Mr. Booker T. Washington and Others," he subjected Washington's "attitude of adjustment and submission" to polite but searching criticism. Washington had asked blacks to give up political power, civil rights, and the hope of higher education, not realizing that "voting is necessary to modern manhood, that . . . discrimination is barbarism, and that black boys need education as well as white boys." Washington "apologizes for injustice," Du Bois charged. "He belittles the emasculating effects of caste distinctions, and opposes the higher training and ambitions of our brightest minds." Du Bois deemed this totally wrong. "The way for a people to gain their reasonable rights is not by voluntarily throwing them away."

Du Bois was not an uncritical admirer of the ordinary American black. He believed that "immorality, crime, and laziness" were common vices. Quite properly, he blamed the weaknesses of blacks on the treatment afforded them by whites, but his approach to the solution of racial problems was frankly elitist. "The Negro race," he wrote, "is going to be saved by its exceptional men," what he called the "talented tenth" of the black population. After describing in vivid detail how white mistreatment had corrupted his people, Du Bois added loftily: "A saving remnant continually survives and persists, continually aspires, continually shows itself in thrift and ability and character." As the historian Benjamin Quarles has said, Du Bois was "uncomfortable in the presence of the rank and file."

Whatever his prejudices, Du Bois exposed both the weaknesses of Washington's strategy and the callousness of white American attitudes. Accommodation was not working. Washington was praised, even lionized by prominent southern whites, yet when Theodore Roosevelt invited him to a meal at the White House, they exploded with indignation, and Roosevelt, although not personally prejudiced, meekly backtracked, never repeating his "mistake." He defended his record by saying, "I have stood as valiantly for the rights of the negro as any president since Lincoln," which, sad to relate, was true enough.

Not mere impatience but despair led Du Bois and a few like-minded blacks to meet at Niagara Falls in July 1905 and to issue a stirring list of demands: the unrestricted right to vote, an end to every kind of segregation, equality of economic opportunity, higher education for the talented, equal justice in the courts, and an end to trade-union discrimination. This Niagara Movement did not attract mass support, but it did stir the consciences of some whites, many of them the descendants of abolitionists, who were also becoming disenchanted by the failure of accommodation to provide blacks with real opportunity.

In 1909, the centennial of the birth of Abraham Lincoln, a group of these liberals, including the newspaperman Oswald Garrison Villard (grandson of William Lloyd Garrison), the social worker Jane Addams, the philosopher John Dewey, and the novelist William Dean Howells, founded the National Association for the Advancement of Colored People (NAACP). The organization was dedicated to the eradication of racial discrimination. Its leadership was predominantly white in the early years, but Du Bois became a national officer and the editor of its journal, *The Crisis*.

A turning point had been reached. After 1909 virtually every important leader, white and black alike, rejected the Washington approach. More and more, blacks turned to the study of their past in an effort to stimulate pride in their heritage. In 1915 Carter G. Woodson founded the Association for the Study of Negro Life and History; the following year he began editing the *Journal of Negro History,* which became the major organ for the publishing of scholarly studies on the subject.

This militancy produced few results in the Pro-

gressive Era. Theodore Roosevelt behaved no differently from earlier Republican presidents; he courted blacks when he thought it advantageous, turned his back when he did not. When he ran for president on the Progressive ticket in 1912, he pursued a "lily-white" policy, hoping to break the Democrats' monopoly in the South. By trusting in "(white) men of justice and of vision," Roosevelt argued in the face of decades of experience to the contrary, "the colored men of the South will ultimately get justice."

The southern-born Wilson was actively antipathetic to blacks. During the 1912 campaign he appealed to them for support and promised to "assist in advancing the interest of their race" in every possible way. Once elected, he refused even to appoint a privately financed commission to study the race problem. Southerners dominated his administration and Congress; as a result, blacks were further degraded. No less than 35 blacks in the Atlanta post office lost their jobs. In Washington employees in many government offices were rigidly segregated, and those who objected were summarily discharged.

These actions stirred such a storm that Wilson backtracked a little. But he never abandoned his belief that segregation was in the best interests of both races. "Wilson . . . promised a 'new freedom,' " one newspaperman complained. "On the contrary we are given a stone instead of a loaf of bread." Even Booker T. Washington admitted that his people were more "discouraged and bitter" than at any time in his memory.

Du Bois, who had supported Wilson in 1912, attacked administration policy in *The Crisis*. In November 1914 the militant editor of the *Boston Guardian,* William Monroe Trotter, a classmate of Du Bois at Harvard and a far more caustic critic of the Washington approach, led a delegation to the White House to protest the segregation policy of the government. When Wilson accused him of blackmail, Trotter lost his temper, and an ugly confrontation resulted. The mood of black leaders had changed completely.

By this time the Great War had broken out in Europe. Soon its effects would be felt by every American, by blacks perhaps more than by any other group. In November 1915, a year almost to the day after Trotter's clash with Wilson, Booker T. Washington died. One era had ended; a new one was beginning.

Milestones

1890 National American Women's Suffrage Association founded

1900 Robert La Follette elected governor of Wisconsin

1901 President McKinley assassinated

1902 National coal strike

Oregon adopts initiative system for proposing legislation

1904 *Northern Securities* case revives the Sherman Antitrust Act

National Child Labor Committee established

1905 Industrial Workers of the World founded

1906 Hepburn Act strengthens Interstate Commerce Commission

Upton Sinclair, *The Jungle*

1907 U.S. Steel absorbs the Tennessee Coal and Iron Company

1908 Theodore Roosevelt convenes the National Conservation Conference

Muller v. *Oregon* upholds the law limiting the working hours of women

1909 Herbert Croly, *The Promise of American Life*

National Association for the Advancement of Colored People founded

1910 Ballinger-Pinchot affair

1911 Roosevelt's New Nationalism speech

1912 Roosevelt runs for president on the Progressive party ticket

1913 Sixteenth Amendment authorizes federal income taxes

Seventeenth Amendment provides for direct election of U.S. senators

Underwood Tariff

Federal Reserve Act

1914 Federal Trade Commission Act

Clayton Antitrust Act

1920 Nineteenth Amendment guarantees women the right to vote

SUPPLEMENTARY READING

Titles marked with an asterisk have been published in paperback.

The political history of the Progressive Era is surveyed in G. E. Mowry, **The Era of Theodore Roosevelt*** (1958), and A. S. Link, **Woodrow Wilson and the Progressive Era*** (1954). Important interpretations of progressivism include Richard Hofstadter, **The Age of Reform*** (1955), Gabriel Kolko, **The Triumph of Conservatism*** (1963), J. M. Cooper, Jr., **The Warrior and the Priest: Theodore Roosevelt and Woodrow Wilson** (1983), D. W. Grantham, **Southern Progressivism** (1983), and R. H. Wiebe, **Businessmen and Reform*** (1962).

The role of muckraking journalism is considered in D. M. Chalmers, **The Social and Political Ideas of the Muckrakers*** (1964), and Peter Lyon, **Success Story: The Life and Times of S. S. McClure** (1963).

On the radicals, see Leslie Fishbein, **Rebels in Bohemia** (1982), Thomas Bender, **New York Intellectuals** (1987), H. F. May, **The End of American Innocence*** (1964), and N. G. Hale, **Freud and the Americans** (1971).

State and local progressivism are considered in G. E. Mowry, **The California Progressives*** (1951), R. S. Max-well, **La Follette and the Rise of Progressivism in Wisconsin** (1956), H. L. Warner, **Progressivism in Ohio** (1964), Sheldon Hackney, **Populism to Progressivism in Alabama** (1969), Z. L. Miller, **Boss Cox's Cincinnati*** (1968), J. D. Buenker, **Urban Liberalism and Progressive Reform** (1973), G. B. Tindall, **The Emergence of the New South** (1967), and C. V. Woodward, **Origins of the New South*** (1951). The struggle for women's suffrage is described in A.S. Kraditor, **The Ideas of the Woman Suffrage Movement*** (1981). See also W. L. O'Neill, **Everyone Was Brave: The Rise and Fall of Feminism in America*** (1969), and C. N. Degler, **At Odds** (1980). Books treating special aspects of progressivism include A. F. Davis, **Spearheads for Reform: The Social Settlements and the Progressive Movement*** (1967), Melvin Dubofsky, **When Workers Organize** (1968), Samuel Haber, **Efficiency and Uplift** (1964), James Weinstein, **The Corporate Ideal and the Liberal State** (1981), J. H. Timberlake, **Prohibition and the Progressive Movement*** (1963), Albro Martin, **Enterprise Denied: Origins** of the Decline of American Railroads (1971), Ruth Rosen, **The Lost Sisterhood** (1982), and W. L. O'Neill, **Divorce in the Progressive Era** (1967). On blacks, see C. F. Kellogg, **NAACP: A History of the National Association for the Advancement of Colored People*** (1970), E. M. Rudwick, **W. E. B. Du Bois*** (1960), and J. T. Kirby, **Darkness at the Dawning: Race and Reform in the Progressive South** (1972). On the treatment of Indians, consult F. E. Hoxie, **A Final Promise: The Campaign to Assimilate the Indians** (1984).

W. H. Harbaugh, **Power and Responsibility*** (1961), is the soundest scholarly treatment of Roosevelt's career. G. W. Chessman, **Theodore Roosevelt and the Politics of Power*** (1969), is a good brief account, and J. M. Blum, **The Republican Roosevelt*** (1954), is a brilliant analysis of his political philosophy and his management of the presidency.

On Taft, see D. F. Anderson, **William Howard Taft: A Conservative's Conception of the Presidency** (1973), and P. E. Coletta, **The Presidency of William Howard Taft** (1973). The breakup of the Republican party and the history of the Progressive party are discussed in J. A. Garraty, **Right-hand Man: The Life of George W. Perkins** (1960).

The standard biography of Wilson, still incomplete, is A. S. Link, **Wilson** (1947–1965). Two brief biographies are J. M. Blum, **Woodrow Wilson and the Politics of Morality*** (1956), and J. A. Garraty, **Woodrow Wilson*** (1956).

Women in the Workplace

"Look! the boss has a **WOMAN** to write his letters"

It used to be argued that the "liberation" of American women occurred in the 1920s with the emergence of the "flapper," with her short skirts, bobbed hair, and fondness for cigarettes, alcohol, and other forms of what was quaintly described as "making whoopee." The flapper phenomenon was explained by referring to the disillusionment that affected people after the World War, and to the passage of the women's suffrage amendment, which, by giving women political power, was thought to have opened the way for the achievement of full equality.

It is now clear that flappers were the exception rather than the rule in the 1920s, that they were by no means as liberated as they and others thought, and that, in any case, the struggle for true equality of the sexes was far from over. Furthermore, much more significant changes in the lives of women were taking place at that time than those associated with what the flappers were doing, or even with the right to vote.

None of these changes was more important than the fact that increasing numbers of women were holding down full-time jobs. The trend toward taking up work outside the home began to accelerate in the prewar years and has, of course, continued into the present day. But what happened to working women in the 1920s marked a kind of turning point.

In the 1890s, a new female secretary in an office might be the butt of wisecracks from the male help (see opposite page), but more and more educated middle-class women were venturing into the world of work outside the home. This 1908 visiting nurse, climbing over the tenement rooftops of New York's Lower East Side on her way to see patients who were too sick to visit a clinic, was perhaps more venturesome than most.

Women had, of course, worked in mills and factories and as domestics for a very long time. Working children, like the little girl tending textile machinery above, were common. Their plight was a serious concern to muckraking writers and photographers like Lewis Hine. Black women (left) often found it impossible even to get industrial jobs, and had to settle for domestic work as maids and cooks.

Many immigrant women worked in garment industry sweatshops. In 1911, the tragic fire at the Triangle Shirtwaist Co., which caused workers to leap to their deaths (top), gave impetus to labor organizations such as Women's Trade Union League and the International Ladies' Garment Workers Union (ILGWU). The Women's League sponsored demonstrations (note the sign on the right of the lower photo: "Do You Want Fire Protection? Organize") and pushed for better pay and conditions for women workers.

ONE OF THE
THOUSAND
Y.M.C.A. GIRLS
IN FRANCE

United
War Work
Campaign
Nov. 11th to 18th

American entry into World War I brought great changes to the lives of women workers. A few went to France with YMCA units and other service organizations that ran field kitchens, hospitals, and recreation programs for American troops (above). Even privileged young women such as the Vassar College group at left took cooking lessons in a patriotic spirit, to help on the home front.

Other women took jobs formerly held by men who had joined the army. For example, they served as welders in munitions plants (bottom), as streetcar conductors (lower left), and as car cleaners on the Northern Pacific Railroad (right).

Reginald Marsh's painting Subway, 14th St. *(1930) catches the turbulent, competitive spirit of rush-hour New York in which women were no longer "protected," in the Victorian sense, from the realities of working life.*

Woodrow Wilson and the Great War

It is a fearful thing to lead this great people into war, into the most terrible and disastrous of all wars, civilization itself seeming to be in the balance. But the right is more precious than peace, and we shall fight for the things which we have always carried nearest our hearts—for democracy.

WOODROW WILSON, *War Message to Congress, April 2, 1917*

oodrow Wilson's approach to foreign relations was well intentioned and idealistic but somewhat confused. He knew that the United States had no wish to injure any foreign state and assumed that all nations would recognize this fact and cooperate. He wanted to help other countries, especially the republics of Latin America, achieve stable democratic governments and improve the living conditions of their people. Imperialism was, in his eyes, immoral. At the same time, he felt obliged to sustain and protect American interests abroad. The maintenance of the Open Door in China and the completion of the Panama Canal were as important to him as they had been to Theodore Roosevelt.

Wilson's view of nations with traditions different from those of the United States was shortsighted and provincial. His attitude resembled that of 19th-century Christian missionaries: He wanted to spread the gospel of American democracy, to lift and enlighten the unfortunate and the ignorant—but in his own way. "I am going to teach the South American republics to elect good men!" he told one British diplomat.

Missionary Diplomacy

Wilson set out to raise the moral tone of American foreign policy by denouncing dollar diplomacy. Encouraging bankers to lend money to countries like China, he said, implied the possibility of "forcible interference" if the loans were not repaid, and that would be "obnoxious to the principles upon which the government of our people rests." To seek special economic concessions in Latin America was "unfair" and "degrading." The United States would deal with Latin American nations "upon terms of equality and honor."

In certain small matters Wilson succeeded in conducting American diplomacy on this idealistic basis. He withdrew the government's support of the international consortium that was arranging a loan to develop Chinese railroads, and American bankers pulled out. When the Japanese attempted, in the notorious Twenty-one Demands (1915), to reduce China almost to the status of a Japanese protectorate, he persuaded them to modify their conditions slightly. Congress had passed a law in 1912 exempting American coastal shipping from the payment of tolls on the Panama Canal in spite of a provision in the Hay-Pauncefote Treaty with Great Britain guaranteeing that the canal would be available to the vessels of all nations "on terms of entire equality." Wilson insisted that Congress repeal the law. He also permitted Secretary of State William Jennings Bryan to negotiate conciliation treaties with 21 nations. The distinctive feature of these agreements was the provision for a "cooling off" period of one year, during which signatories agreed, in the event of a dispute, not to engage in hostilities.

Where more vital interests were concerned, Wilson sometimes failed to live up to his promises. Because of the strategic importance of the Panama Canal, he was unwilling to tolerate "unrest" anywhere in the Caribbean. Within months of his inauguration he was pursuing the same tactics that circumstances had forced on Roosevelt and Taft. The Bryan-Chamorro Treaty of 1914, which gave the United States an option to build a canal across Nicaragua, made that country virtually an American protectorate and served to maintain in power an unpopular dictator, Adolfo Díaz.

A much more serious example of missionary diplomacy occurred in Mexico. In 1911 a liberal coalition overthrew the dictator Porfirio Díaz, who had been exploiting the resources and people of Mexico for the benefit of a small class of wealthy landowners, clerics, and military men since the 1870s. Francisco Madero became president.

Madero, a wealthy landowner apparently influenced by the progressive movement in the United States, was committed to economic reform and the drafting of a democratic constitution. Unfortunately, he was weak-willed and a terrible administrator. Conditions in Mexico deteriorated rapidly, and less than a month before Wilson's inauguration, one of Madero's generals, Victoriano Huerta, seized power and had his former chief murdered. Huerta was an unabashed reactionary, but he was committed to maintaining the stability that foreign investors desired. Most of the European powers promptly recognized his government.

The American ambassador, together with important American financial and business interests in Mexico and in the United States, urged Wilson to do so too, but he refused. His sympathies were all with the government of Madero, whose murder had horrified him. "I will not recognize a government of butchers," he said. This was unconventional; nations do not ordinarily consider the means by which a foreign regime has come to power before deciding to establish diplomatic relations.

Wilson brought enormous pressure to bear against Huerta. He dragooned the British into withdrawing recognition. He dickered with other Mexican factions. He demanded that Huerta hold free elections as the price of American mediation in the continuing civil war. Huerta would not yield an inch. Indeed, he drew strength from Wilson's effort to oust him, for even his enemies resented American interference in Mexican affairs. Frustration, added to his moral outrage, weakened Wilson's judgment. He subordinated his wish to let the Mexicans solve their own problems to his desire to destroy Huerta.

The tense situation exploded in April 1914, when a small party of American sailors was arrested in the port of Tampico, Mexico. When the Mexican government refused to supply the apology demanded by the sailors' commander, Wilson fastened on the affair as an excuse for sending troops into Mexico.

The invasion took place at Veracruz, whence Winfield Scott had launched the assault on Mexico City in 1847. Instead of meekly surrendering the city, the Mexicans resisted tenaciously, suffering

Francisco "Pancho" Villa, Mexican insurrectionary, border bandit, and thorn in President Wilson's side, in 1920, after his capture by the Mexican Army.

400 casualties before falling back. This bloodshed caused dismay throughout Latin America and failed to unseat Huerta.

At this point, Argentina, Brazil, and Chile offered to mediate the dispute. Wilson accepted, Huerta also agreed, and the conferees met at Niagara Falls, Ontario, in May. Although no settlement was reached, Huerta, hard pressed by Mexican opponents, abdicated. On August 20, 1914, General Venustiano Carranza entered Mexico City in triumph.

Carranza favored representative government, but he proved scarcely more successful than the tyrant Huerta in controlling the country. One of his own generals, Francisco "Pancho" Villa, rose against him and seized control of Mexico City.

Wilson now made a monumental blunder. Villa professed to be willing to cooperate with the United States, and Wilson, taking him at his word, gave him his support. However, Villa was little more than an ambitious bandit with no other objective than personal power. Carranza, though no radical, was committed to social reform. Fighting back, he drove the Villistas into the northern provinces.

Wilson finally realized the extent of Carranza's influence in Mexico, and in October 1915 he recognized the Carranza government. Still his Mexican troubles were not over. Early in 1916 Villa, seeking to undermine Carranza by forcing the United States to intervene, stopped a train in northern Mexico and killed 16 American passengers in cold blood. Then he crossed into New Mexico and burned the town of Columbus, killing 19. Having learned his lesson, Wilson would have preferred to bear even this assault in silence, but public opinion forced him to send American troops under General John J. Pershing across the border in pursuit of Villa.

Villa proved impossible to catch. Cleverly, he drew Pershing deeper and deeper into Mexico, and this alarmed Carranza, who insisted that the Americans withdraw. Several clashes occurred between Pershing's men and Mexican regulars, and for a brief period in June 1916 war seemed imminent. Wilson now acted bravely and wisely. Early in 1917 he recalled Pershing's force, leaving the Mexicans to work out their own destiny.

Missionary diplomacy in Mexico had produced mixed but in the long run beneficial results. By opposing Huerta, Wilson had surrendered to his prejudices, yet he had also helped the real revolutionaries even though they opposed his acts. His bungling bred anti-Americanism in Mexico, but by his later restraint in the face of stinging provocations, he permitted the constitutionalists to consolidate their power.

Outbreak of the Great War

On June 28, 1914, in the Austro-Hungarian provincial capital of Sarajevo, Gavrilo Princip, a young student, assassinated the Archduke Franz Ferdinand, heir to the imperial throne. Princip was a member of the Black Hand, a Serbian terrorist organization. He was seeking to further the cause of Serbian nationalism. Instead his rash act precipitated a general European war. Within little more than a month, following a complex series of diplomatic challenges and responses, two great coalitions, the Central Powers (chiefly Germany and Aus-

tria-Hungary) and the Allied Powers (chiefly Great Britain, France, and Russia), were locked in a brutal struggle that brought one era in world history to a close and inaugurated another.

The outbreak of what contemporaries were soon to call the Great War caught Americans psychologically unprepared; few understood the significance of what had happened. President Wilson promptly issued a proclamation of neutrality and asked the nation to be "impartial in thought." Of course, no one, not even the president, had the superhuman self-control that this request called for, but the almost unanimous reaction of Americans, aside from dismay, was that the conflict did not concern them. They were wrong, for this was a world war, and Americans were sure to be affected by its outcome.

There were good reasons, aside from a failure to understand the significance of the struggle, why

Antiwar protesters marching in the May Day parade, 1916, when the war in Europe had been under way for 20 months and the entry of the United States was still opposed by most politicians.

the United States sought to remain neutral. Over a third of its 92 million inhabitants were either European-born or the children of European immigrants. Sentimental ties bound them to the lands of their ancestors. American involvement would create new internal stresses in a society already strained by the task of assimilating so many diverse groups. War was also an affront to the prevailing progressive spirit, which assumed that human beings were reasonable, high-minded, and capable of settling disputes peaceably. Along with the traditional American fear of entanglement in European affairs, these were ample reasons for remaining aloof.

Though most Americans hoped to keep out of the war, nearly everyone was partial to one side or the other. People of German or Austrian descent, about 8 million in number, and the nation's 4.5 million Irish-Americans, motivated chiefly by hatred of the British, sympathized with the Central Powers. The majority of the people, however, influenced by bonds of language and culture, preferred an Allied victory, and when the Germans launched a mighty assault across neutral Belgium in an effort to outflank the French armies, this unprovoked attack on a tiny nation whose neutrality the Germans had previously agreed to respect caused a great deal of anti-German feeling.

As the war progressed, the Allies cleverly exploited American prejudices by such devices as publishing exaggerated tales of German atrocities against Belgian civilians. A supposedly impartial study of these charges by the widely respected James Bryce, author of *The American Commonwealth,* portrayed the Germans as ruthless barbarians. The Germans also conducted a propaganda campaign in the United States, but they labored under severe handicaps and won few converts.

Freedom of the Seas

Propaganda did not basically alter American attitudes; far more important were questions rising out of trade and commerce. Under international law, neutrals could trade freely with any belligerent. Americans were prepared to do so, but because the British fleet dominated the North Atlantic, they could not. The situation was similar to the one that had prevailed during the Napoleonic wars. The British declared nearly all commodities, even food-

stuffs, to be contraband of war. They set limits on exports to neutral nations such as Denmark and the Netherlands so that those countries could not transship supplies to Germany. They forced neutral merchant ships into Allied ports in order to search them for goods headed for the enemy. Many cargoes were confiscated, often without payment. American firms that traded with the Central Powers were "blacklisted," which meant that no British subject could deal with them. When these policies caused protests in America, the British answered that in a battle for survival, they dared not adhere to old-fashioned rules of international law.

Had the United States insisted that Great Britain abandon these "illegal" practices, as the Germans demanded, no doubt it could have had its way. The British foreign secretary, Sir Edward Grey, later admitted: "The ill-will of the United States meant certain defeat. The object of diplomacy, therefore, was to secure the maximum of blockade that could be enforced without a rupture with the United States." It is ironic that an embargo, which failed so ignominiously in Jefferson's day, would have been almost instantly effective if applied at any time after 1914, for American supplies were vital to the Allies.

Though British tactics frequently exasperated Wilson, he never considered taking such a drastic step. He faced a dilemma. To allow the British to make the rules meant siding against the Central Powers. Yet to insist on the old rules (which had never been obeyed in wartime) meant siding against the Allies because that would have deprived them of much of the value of their naval superiority. Nothing the United States might do would be truly impartial.

Wilson's own sentiments made it doubly difficult for him to object strenuously to British practices. No American admired British institutions and culture more extravagantly. "Everything I love most in the world is at stake," he confessed privately to the British ambassador. A German victory "would be fatal to our form of Government and American ideals."

In any event, the immense expansion of American trade with the Allies made an embargo unthinkable. While commerce with the Central Powers fell to a trickle, that with the Allies soared from $825 million in 1914 to over $3.2 billion in 1916. An attempt to limit this commerce would have raised a storm; to have eliminated it would have

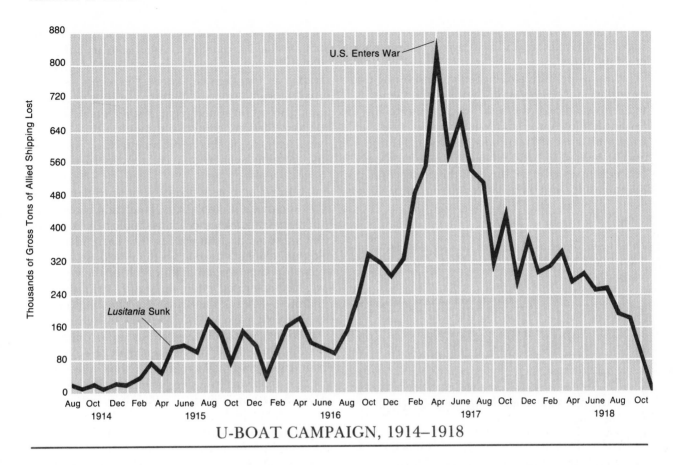

U-BOAT CAMPAIGN, 1914–1918

caused a catastrophe. Munitions makers and other businessmen did not want the United States to enter the war. Neutrality suited their purposes admirably.

Britain and France soon exhausted their ready cash and by early 1917 had borrowed well over $2 billion. Although these loans violated no principle of international law, they fastened the United States more closely to the Allies' cause.

During the first months of the Great War, the Germans were not especially concerned about neutral trade or American goods because they expected to crush the Allied armies quickly. When their first swift thrust into France was blunted along the Marne River and the war became a bloody stalemate, they began to challenge the Allies' control of the seas. Unwilling to risk their battleships and cruisers against the much larger British fleet, they resorted to a new weapon, the submarine, commonly known as the U-boat (for *Unterseeboot*).

German submarines played a role in World War I not unlike that of American privateers in the Rev-

olution and the War of 1812: They ranged the seas stealthily in search of merchant ships. However, submarines could not operate under the ordinary rules of war, which required that a raider stop its prey, examine its papers and cargo, and give the crew and passengers time to get off in lifeboats before sending it to the bottom. When surfaced, U-boats were vulnerable to the deck guns that many merchant ships carried; they could even be sunk by ramming, once they had stopped and put out a boarding party. Therefore, they commonly launched their torpedoes from below the surface without warning. The result was often a heavy loss of life on the torpedoed ships.

In February 1915 the Germans declared the waters surrounding the British Isles a zone of war and announced that they would sink without warning all enemy merchant ships encountered in the area. Since Allied vessels sometimes flew neutral flags to disguise their identity, neutral ships entering the zone would do so at their own risk. This statement was largely bluff, for the Germans had only a handful of submarines at sea; but they were feverishly building more.

Wilson—perhaps too hurriedly, considering the importance of the question—warned the Germans that he would hold them to "strict accountability" for any loss of American life or property resulting from violations of "acknowledged (neutral) rights on the high seas." He did not distinguish clearly between losses incurred through the destruction of *American* ships and those resulting from the sinking

Three weeks before the Lusitania *was torpedoed, this notice appeared in the classified sections of Washington newspapers.*

NOTICE!

TRAVELLERS intending to embark on the Atlantic voyage are reminded that a state of war exists between Germany and her allies and Great Britain and her allies; that the zone of war includes the waters adjacent to the British Isles; that, in accordance with formal notice given by the Imperial German Government, vessels flying the flag of Great Britain, or of any of her allies, are liable to destruction in those waters and that travellers sailing in the war zone on ships of Great Britain or her allies do so at their own risk.

IMPERIAL GERMAN EMBASSY
WASHINGTON, D. C., APRIL 22, 1915.

of other vessels. If he meant to hold the Germans responsible for injuries to Americans on *belligerent* vessels, he was changing international law as arbitrarily as the Germans were. Secretary of State Bryan, who opposed Wilson vigorously on this point, stood on sound legal ground when he said, "A ship carrying contraband should not rely upon passengers to protect her from attack—it would be like putting women and children in front of an army."

Correct or not, Wilson's position reflected the attitude of most Americans. It seemed barbaric to them that defenseless civilians should be killed without warning, and they refused to surrender their "rights" as neutrals to cross the North Atlantic on any ship they wished. The depth of their feeling was demonstrated when, on May 7, 1915, the submarine *U-20* sank the British liner *Lusitania* off the Irish coast. Nearly 1,200 persons, including 128 Americans, lost their lives in this catastrophe.

The torpedoing of the *Lusitania* caused as profound and emotional a reaction in the United States as that following the destruction of the *Maine* in Havana harbor. Wilson, like McKinley in 1898, was shocked, but he kept his head. He demanded that Germany disavow the sinking, indemnify the victims, and promise to stop attacking passenger vessels. When the Germans quibbled about these points, he responded with further diplomatic correspondence rather than with an ultimatum.

In one sense this was sound policy. The Germans pointed out that they had published warnings in American newspapers saying they considered the *Lusitania* subject to attack, that the liner was carrying munitions, and that on past voyages it had flown the American flag as a *ruse de guerre*. It would have been difficult politically for the German government to have backed down before an American ultimatum; however, after dragging the controversy out for nearly a year, it apologized and agreed to pay an indemnity. After the torpedoing of the French channel steamer *Sussex* in March 1916 had produced another stiff American protest, the Germans at last promised, in the *Sussex* pledge, to stop sinking merchant ships without warning.

Had Wilson forced a showdown in 1915, he would have alienated a large segment of American opinion. Even his relatively mild notes resulted in the resignation of Secretary of State Bryan, who believed it unneutral to treat German violations of international law differently from Allied violations—and Bryan reflected the feelings of thousands.*

Yet if Wilson had sought a declaration of war over the *Lusitania,* a majority of Congress and the country would probably have gone along, and in that event the dreadful carnage in Europe would have ended much sooner. This is the reasoning of hindsight, yet such a policy would have been logical, given Wilson's assumptions about the justice of the Allied cause and America's stake in an Allied victory.

In November 1915 Wilson at last began to press for increased military and naval expenditures. Nevertheless, he continued to vacillate. He dispatched a sharp note protesting Allied blacklisting of American firms, and to his confidant, Colonel Edward M. House, he called the British "poor boobs."

The Election of 1916

Part of Wilson's confusion in 1916 resulted from the political difficulties he faced in his fight for reelection. He had won the presidency in 1912 only because the Republican party had split in two. Now Theodore Roosevelt, the chief defector, had become so incensed by Wilson's refusal to commit the United States to the Allied cause that he was ready to support almost any Republican in order to guarantee the president's defeat. At the same time, many progressives were complaining about Wilson's unwillingness to work for further domestic reforms. Unless he could find additional support, he seemed likely to be defeated.

He attacked the problem by wooing the progressives. In January 1916 he appointed Louis D. Brandeis to the Supreme Court. In addition to being an advanced progressive, Brandeis was Jewish, the first American of that religion appointed to the Court. Wilson's action won him many friends among people who favored fair treatment for minority groups. In July he bid for the farm vote by signing the Farm Loan Act to provide low-cost loans based on agricultural credit. Shortly thereafter, he approved the Keating-Owen Child Labor Act, barring goods manufactured by the labor of children

under 16 from interstate commerce, and a workers' compensation act for federal employees. He persuaded Congress to pass the Adamson Act, establishing an eight-hour day for railroad workers, and he modified his position on the tariff by approving the creation of a tariff commission.

Each of these actions represented a sharp reversal. In 1913 Wilson had considered Brandeis too radical even for a Cabinet post. The new farm, labor, and tariff laws were all examples of the kind of "class legislation" he had refused to countenance in 1913 and 1914. As the historian Arthur S. Link has pointed out, Wilson was putting into effect "almost every important plank of the Progressive platform of 1912." His actions paid spectacular political dividends when Roosevelt refused to run as a Progressive and came out for the Republican nominee, Associate Justice Charles Evans Hughes. The Progressive convention then endorsed Hughes, who had compiled a fine liberal record as governor of New York, but many of Roosevelt's 1912 supporters felt that he had betrayed them and voted for Wilson.

The key issue in the campaign was American policy toward the warring powers. Wilson intended to stress preparedness, which he was now wholeheartedly supporting. However, during the Democratic convention, the delegates shook the hall with cheers whenever orators referred to the president's success in keeping the country out of the war. One spellbinder, referring to the *Sussex* pledge, announced that the president had "wrung from the most militant spirit that ever brooded above a battlefield an acknowledgement of American rights and an agreement to American demands," and the convention erupted in a demonstration that lasted more than 20 minutes. Thus "He Kept Us Out of War" became the Democratic slogan.

To his credit, Wilson made no promises. "I can't keep the country out of war," he told one member of his Cabinet. "Any little German lieutenant can put us into the war at any time by some calculated outrage." His attitude undoubtedly cost him the votes of extremists on both sides, but it won the backing of thousands of moderates.

The combination of progressivism and the peace issue placed the Democrats on substantially equal terms with the Republicans; thereafter, personal factors probably tipped the balance. Hughes was very stiff and an ineffective speaker; he offended a number of important politicians, especially in cru-

---

* Wilson appointed Robert Lansing, counselor of the State Department, to succeed Bryan.

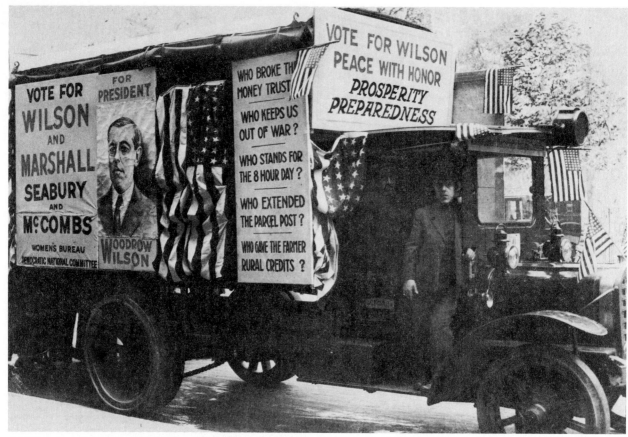

A Wilson campaign truck offered New York City voters a convenient summary of the 1916 Democratic platform. The eight-hour-day plank refers to the president's support of a federal law for railroad workers.

cial California, where he inadvertently snubbed the popular progressive governor, Hiram Johnson; and he equivocated on a number of issues. Nevertheless, on election night he appeared to have won, having carried nearly all the East and Middle West. Late returns gave Wilson California, however, and with it victory by the narrow margin of 277 to 254 in the electoral college. He led Hughes in the popular vote, 9.1 million to 8.5 million.

The Road to War

Encouraged by his triumph, appalled by the continuing slaughter on the battlefields, fearful that the United States would be dragged into the holocaust, Wilson made one last effort to end the war by ne-

gotiation. In 1915 and again in 1916 he had sent his friend Colonel House on a secret mission to London, Paris, and Berlin to try to mediate among the belligerents. Each had proved fruitless, but, after another long season of bloodshed, perhaps the powers would listen to reason.

Wilson's own feelings were more genuinely neutral than at any other time during the war, for the Germans had stopped sinking merchant ships without warning and the British had irritated him repeatedly by their arbitrary restrictions on neutral trade. He drafted a note to the belligerents asking them to state the terms on which they would agree to lay down their arms. Unless the fighting ended soon, he warned, neutrals and belligerents alike would be so ruined that peace would be meaningless.

When neither side responded encouragingly, Wilson, on January 22, 1917, delivered a moving, prophetic speech aimed, as he admitted, at "the people of the countries now at war" more than at their governments. Any settlement imposed by a victor, he declared, would breed hatred and more wars. There must be a "peace without victory" based on the principles that all nations were equal and that every nationality group should determine its own form of government. He mentioned, albeit vaguely, disarmament and freedom of the seas, and he suggested the creation of some kind of international organization to preserve world peace. "There must be not a balance of power, but a community of power," he said, and he added, "I am speaking for the silent mass of mankind everywhere."

This noble appeal met a tragic fate. The Germans had already decided to renounce the *Sussex* pledge and unleash their submarines against all vessels headed for Allied ports. After February 1, any ship in the war zone would be attacked without warning. Possessing more than 100 U-boats, the German military leaders had convinced themselves that they could starve the British people into submission and reduce the Allied armies to impotence by cutting off the flow of American supplies. The United States would probably declare war, but the Germans believed that they could overwhelm the Allies before the Americans could get to the battlefields in force.

In *Tiger at the Gates,* the French playwright Jean Giraudoux makes Ulysses say, while attempting to stave off what he considers an inevitable war with the Trojans: "The privilege of great men is to view catastrophe from a terrace." This is not always true, but in 1917, after the German military leaders had made their decision, events moved relentlessly, almost uninfluenced by the actors who presumably controlled the fate of the world:

February 3: S.S. *Housatonic* torpedoed. Wilson announces to Congress that he has severed diplomatic relations with Germany. Secretary of State Lansing hands the German ambassador, Count von Bernstorff, his passport. *February 24:* Walter Hines Page, United States ambassador to Great Britain, transmits to the State Department an intercepted German dispatch (the "Zimmermann telegram") revealing that Germany has proposed a secret alliance with Mexico, Mex-

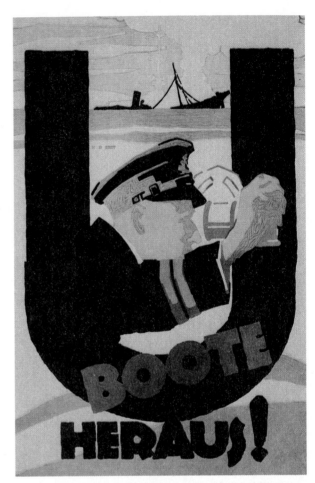

"U-Boote Heraus!" (*"U-boats go get 'em!"*) A German poster aimed at encouraging their submarine crews.

ico to receive, in the event of war with the United States, "the lost territory in Texas, New Mexico, and Arizona." *February 25:* Cunard liner *Laconia* torpedoed, two American women perish. *February 26:* Wilson asks Congress for authority to arm American merchant ships. *March 1:* Zimmermann Telegram released to the press. *March 4:* President Wilson takes oath of office, beginning his second term. Congress adjourns without passing the armed ship bill, the measure having been filibustered to death by antiwar senators. Wilson characterizes the filibusterers, led by Senator Robert M. La Follette, as "a little group of willful men, representing no opinion but their own." *March 9:* Wilson, acting under his executive powers, orders the arming of American merchantmen. *March 12:* Revolutionary provisional government established in Russia. *Algonquin* torpedoed. *March 15:* Czar Nicholas II *of Russia abdicates. March 16: City of Memphis, Illinois, Vigilancia torpedoed. March 21: New York World,* a leading Democratic newspaper, calls for declaration of war on Germany. Wilson summons Congress to convene in a special session on April 2. *March 25:* Wilson calls up the National Guard. *April 2:* Wilson asks Congress to declare war. Germany is guilty of "throwing to the winds all scruples of humanity," he says. America must fight, not to conquer, but for "peace and justice. . . . The world must be made safe for democracy." *April 4, 6:* Congress declares war—the vote, 82–6 in the Senate, 373–50 in the House.

The bare record conceals Wilson's agonizing search for an honorable alternative to war. To admit that Germany posed a threat to the United States meant confessing that interventionists had been right all along. To go to war meant, besides sending innocent Americans to their deaths, allowing "the spirit of ruthless brutality [to] enter into the very fibre of our national life."

The president's Presbyterian conscience tortured him relentlessly. He lost sleep, appeared gray and drawn. When someone asked him which side he hoped would win, he answered petulantly, "Neither." "He was resisting," Secretary of State Lansing recorded, "the irresistible logic of events." In the end Wilson could satisfy himself only by giving intervention an idealistic purpose. The war had become a threat to humanity. Unless the United States threw its weight into the balance, western civilization itself might be destroyed. Out of the long bloodbath must come a new and better world. The war must be fought to end, for all time, war itself. Thus in the name not of vengeance and victory but of justice and humanity he sent his people into battle.

Mobilizing the Economy

America's entry into the Great War determined its outcome. The Allies were running out of money and supplies; their troops, decimated by nearly three years in the trenches, were disheartened and rebellious. In February and March 1917 U-boats sent over a million tons of Allied shipping to the bottom of the Atlantic. The outbreak of the Russian Revolution in March 1917, at first lifting the spirits of the western democracies, led to the Bolshevik takeover under Lenin. The Russian armies collapsed; by December 1917 Russia was out of the

war and the Germans were moving masses of men and equipment from the eastern front to France. Without the aid of the United States, it is likely that the war would have ended in 1918 on terms dictated from Berlin. Instead, American men and supplies helped contain the Germans' last drives and then push them back to final defeat.

It was a close thing, for the United States entered the war little better prepared to fight than it had been in 1898. The conversion of American industry to war production had to be organized and carried out without prearrangement. What the historian Harvey A. De Weerd has called "absurdly large" goals were set, far beyond what the army could use. Confusion and waste resulted. The hurriedly designed shipbuilding program was an almost total fiasco. The gigantic Hog Island yard, which employed at its peak over 34,000 workers, completed its first vessel after the war ended. Airplane, tank, and artillery construction programs, all too large to begin with, developed too slowly to affect the war. The big guns that backed up American soldiers in 1918 were made in France and Great Britain; of the 8.8 million rounds of artillery ammunition fired by American troops, only about 8,000 were manufactured in the United States. Congress authorized the manufacture of 20,000, but only a handful, mostly British-designed planes made in America, got to France.

"America," writes David M. Kennedy in *Over Here,* "was no 'arsenal of democracy' in World War I; the American doughboy in France was typically transported in a British ship, wore a steel helmet modeled on the British Tommy's, and fought with French ordnance." American pilots such as the great "ace" Captain Eddie Rickenbacker flew British Sopwiths and De Havillands or French Spads and Nieuports. Theodore Roosevelt's son Quentin was shot down while flying a Spad over Château-Thierry in July 1918.

The problem of mobilization was complicated. It took Congress six weeks of hot debate merely to decide on conscription. Only in September 1917, nearly six months after the declaration of war, did the first draftees reach the training camps, and it is hard to see how Wilson could have speeded this process appreciably. He wisely supported the professional soldiers, who insisted that he resist the appeals of politicians who wanted to raise volunteer units, even rejecting, at considerable political cost,

Theodore Roosevelt's offer to raise an entire army division.

Wilson was a forceful and inspiring war leader once he grasped what needed to be done. He displayed both determination and unfailing patience in the face of frustration and criticism. Raising an army was only a small part of the job. The Allies had to be supplied with food and munitions, and immense amounts of money had to be collected.

After several false starts Wilson placed the task in the hands of the War Industries Board (WIB). The board was given almost dictatorial power to allocate scarce materials, standardize production, fix prices, and coordinate American and Allied purchasing. Evaluating the mobilization effort raises interesting historical questions. The antitrust laws were suspended and producers were encouraged, even compelled, to cooperate with one another. Government regulation went far beyond what the New Nationalists had envisaged in 1912.

As for the New Freedom variety of laissez faire, it had no place in a wartime economy. The nation's railroads, strained by immensely increased traffic, became progressively less efficient. A monumental tie-up in December 1917 and January 1918 finally persuaded Wilson to appoint Secretary of the Treasury William G. McAdoo director-general of the railroads, with power to run the roads as a single system. McAdoo's Railroad Administration pooled all railroad equipment, centralized purchasing, standardized accounting practices, and raised wages and passenger rates.

Wilson accepted the kind of government-in-dustry agreement developed under Theodore Roosevelt that he had denounced in 1912. Prices were set by the WIB at levels that allowed large profits— U.S. Steel, for example, despite high taxes, cleared over half a billion dollars in two years. It is at least arguable that producers would have turned out just as much even if compelled to charge lower prices.

At the start of the war, army procurement was decentralized and inefficient—as many as eight bureaus were purchasing material in competition with one another. One official bought 1,200 typewriters, stacked them in the basement of a government building, and announced proudly to his superior: "There is going to be the greatest competition for typewriters around here, and I have them all."

Mobilization required close cooperation between business and the military. However, the army resisted cooperating with civilian agencies, being, as the historian Paul Koistiner writes, "suspicious of, and hostile toward, civilian institutions." Wilson finally compelled the War Department to place officers on WIB committees, and when the army discovered that its interests were not injured by the system, the foundation was laid for what was later to be known as the "industrial-military complex," the alliance between business and military leaders that was to cause so much controversy after World War II.

The history of industrial mobilization was the history of the entire home-front effort in microcosm: Prodigies were performed, but the task was so gigantic and unprecedented that a full year passed before an efficient system had been devised, and many unforeseen results occurred.

The problem of mobilizing agricultural resources was solved more quickly, and this was fortunate because in April 1917 the British had on hand only a six-week supply of food. As food administrator Wilson appointed Herbert Hoover, a mining engineer who had headed the Belgian Relief Commission earlier in the war. Acting under powers granted by the Lever Act of 1917, Hoover set the price of wheat at $2.20 a bushel in order to encourage production. He established a government corporation to purchase the entire American and Cuban sugar crop, which he then doled out to American and British refiners. To avoid rationing he organized a campaign to persuade consumers to conserve food voluntarily. One slogan ran "If U fast U beat U boats," another "Serve beans by all means."

"Wheatless Mondays" and "meatless Tuesdays" were the rule, and although no law compelled their observance, the public responded patriotically. Boy Scouts dug up backyards and vacant lots to plant vegetable gardens; chefs devised new recipes to save on scarce items; restaurants added horsemeat, rabbit, and whale steak to their menus and doled out butter and sugar to customers in minuscule amounts. Mothers pressured their children to "Hooverize" their plates. Chicago residents were so successful in making use of leftovers that the volume of raw garbage in the city declined from 12,862 tons to 8,386 tons per month.

Without subjecting its own citizens to serious inconvenience, the United States increased food ex-

Wartime belt-tightening inspired new business ventures for a few entrepreneurs. GET AC-QUAINTED—CUT DOWN YOUR MEAT BILLS AND BUY HORSE MEAT, *urges the sign at right.*

ports from 12.3 million tons to 18.6 million tons. Farmers, of course, profited greatly: Their real income went up nearly 30 percent between 1915 and 1918.

Workers in Wartime

With the army siphoning so many men from the labor market and with immigration reduced to a trickle, unemployment disappeared and wages rose. Although the cost of living soared, imposing hardships on people with fixed incomes, the boom produced unprecedented opportunities.

Americans, always a mobile people, pulled up their roots in record numbers. Disadvantaged groups, especially blacks, were particularly attracted by jobs in big-city factories. Early in the conflict, the government began regulating the wages and hours of workers building army camps and manufacturing uniforms. In April 1918 Wilson created the National War Labor Board, headed by former president Taft and Frank P. Walsh, a prominent lawyer, to settle labor disputes. The board considered more than 1,200 cases and prevented many strikes. The War Labor Policies Board, chaired by Felix Frankfurter of the Harvard Law School, set wages-and-hours

standards for each major war industry. Since these were determined in consultation with employers and representatives of labor, they speeded the unionization of workers by compelling management, even in antiunion industries like steel, to deal with labor leaders. Union membership rose by 2.3 million during the war.

However, the wartime emergency roused the public against strikers; some conservatives even demanded that war workers be conscripted just as soldiers were. While he opposed strikes that impeded the war effort, Wilson set great store in preserving the individual worker's freedom of action. It would be "most unfortunate . . . to relax the laws by which safeguards have been thrown about labor," he said. "We must accomplish the results we desire by organized effort rather than compulsion."

Trends in the steel industry reflect the improvement of the lot of labor in wartime. Wages of unskilled steelworkers more than doubled. Thousands of southern blacks flocked into the steel towns. Union organizers made inroads in many plants, and by the summer of 1918 they were preparing an all-out effort to unionize the industry. If the world was to be made safe for democracy, they argued, there must be "economic democracy [along] with political democracy."

Paying for the War

Wilson managed the task of financing the war effectively. The struggle cost the United States about $33.5 billion, not counting pensions and other postwar expenses. About $7 billion of this was lent to the Allies,* but since this money was spent largely in America, it contributed to the national prosperity.

Over two-thirds of the cost of the war was met by borrowing. Five Liberty and Victory Loan drives, spurred by advertising, parades, and other appeals to patriotism, persuaded the people to open their purses. Industrialists, eager to inculcate in their employees a sense of personal involvement in the war effort, conducted campaigns in their plants. Some went so far as to threaten "A Bond or Your Job," but more typical was the appeal of the managers of the Gary, Indiana, plant of U.S. Steel, who published bond advertisements in six languages in order to reach their immigrant workers.

In addition to borrowing, the government collected about $10.5 billion in taxes during the war. A steeply graduated income tax took more than 75 percent of the incomes of the wealthiest citizens. A 65 percent excess-profits tax and a 25 percent inheritance tax were also enacted. Thus while many individuals made fortunes out of the war, its cost was distributed far more equitably than that of the Civil War. Americans also contributed generously to philanthropic agencies engaged in war work. Most notable, perhaps, was the great 1918 drive of the United War Work Council, an interfaith religious group, which raised over $200 million mainly to finance recreational programs for the troops overseas.

Propaganda and Civil Liberties

Wilson was preeminently a teacher and preacher, a specialist in the transmission of ideas and ideals. He excelled at mobilizing public opinion and inspiring Americans to work for the better world he hoped would emerge from the war. In April 1917 he created the Committee on Public Information (CPI), headed by the journalist George Creel. Soon 75,000 speakers were deluging the country with

---

* In 1914 Americans owed foreigners about $3.8 billion. By 1919 Americans *were owed* $12.5 billion by Europeans alone.

propaganda prepared by hundreds of CPI writers. They pictured the war as a crusade for freedom and democracy, the Germans as a bestial people bent on world domination.

A large majority of the nation supported the war enthusiastically. But thousands of persons—German-Americans and Irish-Americans, for example; people of pacifist leanings such as Jane Addams, the founder of Hull House; and some who thought both sides in the war were wrong—still opposed American involvement. Creel's committee and a

In 1917 the Germania Life Insurance Building in St. Paul was renamed the Guardian Building; since Germania herself could not be disguised, down she came.

number of unofficial "patriotic" groups allowed their enthusiasm for the conversion of the hesitant to become suppression of dissent. Persons who refused to buy war bonds were often exposed to public ridicule and even assault. People with German names were persecuted without regard for their views; some school boards outlawed the teaching of the German language; sauerkraut was renamed "liberty cabbage." Opponents of the war of unquestionable patriotism were subjected to coarse abuse. A cartoonist pictured Senator Robert La Follette, who opposed entering the war, receiving an Iron Cross from the German militarists, and the faculty of his own University of Wisconsin voted to censure him.

Wilson, "a friend of free speech in theory," David M. Kennedy has written, "was its foe in fact." He signed the Espionage Act of 1917, which imposed fines of up to $10,000 and jail sentences ranging to 20 years on persons convicted of aiding the enemy or obstructing recruiting, and he authorized the postmaster general to ban from the mails any material that seemed treasonable or seditious.

In May 1918, again with Wilson's approval, Congress passed the Sedition Act, which made "saying anything" to discourage the purchase of war bonds a crime, with the proviso that investment counselors could still offer "bona fide and not disloyal advice" to clients. The law also made it illegal to "utter, print, write, or publish any disloyal, profane, scurrilous, or abusive language" about the government, the Constitution, or the uniform of the army or navy. Socialist periodicals such as *The Masses* were suppressed, and Eugene V. Debs was sentenced to ten years in prison for making an antiwar speech. Ricardo Flores Magón, an anarchist, was sentenced to 20 years in jail for publishing a statement criticizing Wilson's Mexican policy, an issue that had nothing to do with the war.

These laws went far beyond what was necessary to protect the national interest. Citizens were jailed for suggesting that the draft law was unconstitutional and for criticizing private organizations like the Red Cross and the YMCA. One woman was sent to prison for writing, "I am for the people, and the government is for the profiteers."

The Supreme Court upheld the constitutionality of the Espionage Act in *Schenck* v. *United States* (1919), a case involving a man who had mailed circulars to draftees urging them to refuse to report for induction into the army. Free speech has its limits, Justice Oliver Wendell Holmes, Jr., explained. No one has the right to cry, "Fire!" in a crowded theater. When there is a "clear and present danger" that a particular statement would threaten the national interest, it can be repressed by law. In peacetime Schenck's circulars would be permissible, but not in time of war.

The "clear and present danger" doctrine did not prevent judges and juries from interpreting the Espionage and Sedition acts broadly, and while in many instances their decisions were overturned by higher courts, this usually did not occur until after the war. The wartime hysteria far exceeded anything that happened in Great Britain and France. In 1916 the French novelist Henri Barbusse published *Le Feu (Under Fire)*, a graphic account of the horrors and purposelessness of trench warfare. In one chapter Barbusse described a pilot flying over the trenches on a Sunday, observing French and German soldiers at Mass in the open fields, each worshiping the same God. Yet *Le Feu* circulated freely in France and even won the coveted Prix Goncourt.

Wartime Reforms

The American mobilization experience was part and product of the Progressive Era. The work of the progressives at the national and state levels in expanding government functions in order to deal with social and economic problems provided precedents and conditioned the people for the all-out effort of 1917 and 1918. Social and economic planning and the management of huge business operations by public boards and committees got their first practical tests. College professors, technicians, and others with complex skills entered government service en masse. The federal government for the first time entered actively such fields as housing and labor relations.

Many progressives believed that the war was creating the sense of common purpose that would stimulate the people to act unselfishly to benefit the poor and to eradicate social evils. Patriotism and public service seemed at last united. Secretary of War Newton D. Baker, a prewar urban reformer, expressed this attitude in supporting a federal child labor law: "We cannot afford, when we are losing boys in France, to lose children in the United States."

Men and women of this sort worked for a dozen causes only remotely related to the war effort. The women's suffrage movement was brought to fruition, as was the campaign against alcohol. Both the Eighteenth Amendment, outlawing alcoholic beverages, and the Nineteenth, giving women the vote, were adopted at least in part because of the war. Reformers began to talk about health insurance. The progressive campaign against prostitution and venereal disease gained strength, winning the enthusiastic support both of persons worried about inexperienced local girls being seduced by the soldiers and of those concerned lest prostitutes lead innocent soldiers astray. One of the latter type claimed to have persuaded "over 1,000 fallen women" to promise not to go near any army camps.

The effort to wipe out prostitution around military installations was a cause of some misunderstanding with the Allies, who provided licensed facilities for their troops as a matter of course. When the premier of France graciously offered to supply prostitutes for American units in his country, Secretary Baker is said to have remarked: "For God's sake . . . don't show this to the President or he'll stop the war." Apparently Baker had a rather peculiar sense of humor. After a tour of the front in France, he assured an American women's group that life in the trenches was "far less uncomfortable" than he had thought and that not a single American doughboy was "living a life which he would not be willing to have [his] mother see him live."

Efforts by young women such as these in war gardens were meant not only to keep the boys "over there" well supplied with vegetables, but also to make those in the United States feel part of the struggle to make the world safe for democracy.

Women and Blacks in Wartime

Although a number of prominent feminists were pacifists, most supported the war enthusiastically, moved by patriotism and the belief that opposition to the war would doom their hopes of gaining the vote. They also expected that the war would open up many kinds of high-paying jobs to women. To some extent it did; about a million women replaced men in uniform, but the numbers actually engaged in war industries were small (about 6,000 found jobs making airplanes, for example), and the gains were fleeting. When the war ended, most women who were engaged in industrial work either left their jobs voluntarily or were fired to make room for returning veterans. Some women went overseas as nurses, and a few served as ambulance drivers and YMCA workers.

Most unions were unsympathetic to the idea of enrolling women, and the government did little to encourage women to do more for the war effort than prepare bandages, knit warm clothing for soldiers, participate in food conservation programs, and encourage people to buy war bonds. There was a Women in Industry Service in the Department of Labor and a Woman's Committee of the Council of National Defense, but both served primarily as window dressing for the Wilson administration. The final report of another wartime agency, issued in 1919, admitted that few women war workers had been paid as much as men and that women had been promoted more slowly than men, were not accepted by unions, and were discharged promptly when the war ended.

The wartime "great migration" of southern blacks to northern cities where jobs were available brought them important economic benefits. Actually, the emigration of blacks from the former slave states began with emancipation, but the mass exodus that many people had expected was slow to materialize. Between 1870 and 1890 only about 80,000 blacks moved to northern cities. Compared with the influx from Europe and from northern farms, this was a trivial number. The black portion of the population of New York City, for example, fell from over 10 percent in 1800 to under 2 percent in 1900.

Around the turn of the century, as the first post-slavery generation reached maturity and as southern repression increased, the northward movement quickened—about 200,000 blacks migrated between 1890 and 1910. Then, after 1914, the war boom drew blacks north in a flood. Agents of northern manufacturers flocked into the Cotton Belt to recruit them in wholesale lots. "Leave the benighted land," the *Chicago Defender*, a newspaper with a considerable circulation in southern states, urged. "Get out of the South." Half a million made the move between 1914 and 1919. The black population of New York rose from 92,000 to 152,000, that of Chicago from 44,000 to 109,000, that of Detroit from 5,700 to 41,000.

Life for the newcomers was difficult; many whites resented them; workers feared them as potential strikebreakers yet refused to admit them into their unions. In East St. Louis, Illinois, where employers had brought in large numbers of blacks in an attempt to discourage local unions from striking for higher wages, a bloody riot erupted during the summer of 1917 in which nine whites and an undetermined number of blacks were killed. As in peacetime, the Wilson administration was at worst antagonistic and at best indifferent to blacks' needs and aspirations.

Nevertheless, the blacks who moved north during the war were, as a group, infinitely better off, materially and psychologically, than those they left behind. They earned good wages and were accorded at least some human rights. They were not treated by the whites as equals, or even in most cases entirely fairly, but they could vote, send their children to decent schools, and within reasonable limits do and say what they pleased without fear of humiliation or physical attack.

There were two black regiments in the regular army and a number of black national guard units when the war began, and once these outfits were brought up to combat strength, no more volunteers were accepted. Indeed, at first no blacks were conscripted; southerners in particular found the thought of giving large numbers of blacks guns and teaching them how to use them most disturbing. Blacks were, however, soon drafted, and once they were, a larger proportion of them than whites were taken. One Georgia draft board exempted more than 500 of 815 white registrants and only 6 of the 202 blacks in its jurisdiction before its members were relieved of their duties. After a riot in Texas in which black soldiers killed 17 white civilians, black recruits were dispersed among many camps for training to lessen the possibility of trouble.

In the service, all blacks were placed in segregated units. Only a handful were commissioned officers. Most, even those sent overseas, were assigned to labor battalions, working as stevedores and common laborers. But many fought and died for the country. Altogether about 200,000 served in France. There were black Red Cross nurses in France, and some blacks held relatively high posts in government agencies in Washington, the most important being Emmett J. Scott, who was special assistant for Negro affairs in the War Department.

W. E. B. Du Bois supported the war wholeheartedly. He praised Wilson for making, at last, a strong statement against lynching, which had in-

THE WESTERN FRONT, 1918

creased to a shocking extent during the previous decade. He even went along with the fact that the handful of black officer candidates were trained in a segregated camp: "Let us," he wrote in *The Crisis,* "while the war lasts, forget our special grievances and close ranks shoulder to shoulder with our fellow citizens and the allied nations that are fighting for democracy."

Many blacks condemned Du Bois's accommodationism (which he promptly abandoned when the war ended), but most saw the war as an opportunity to demonstrate their patriotism and prove their worth. For the moment the prevailing mood was one of optimism. "We may expect to see the walls of prejudice gradually crumble"—this was the common attitude of blacks in 1917 and 1918. If winning the war would make the world safe for democracy, surely blacks in the United States would be better off when it was won. Whether or not this turned out to be so was (and still is) a matter of opinion.

"Over There"

All activity on the home front had one ultimate objective: defeating the Central Powers on the bat-

American infantrymen of the 1st Division under shell fire outside Exermont, in the Ardennes Forest, France, in the waning days of the Great War.

tlefield. This was accomplished. The navy performed with special distinction. In April 1917, German submarines sank more than 870,000 tons of Allied shipping; after April 1918, monthly losses never reached 300,000 tons. The decision to send merchant ships across the Atlantic in convoys screened by destroyers made the reduction possible. Checking the U-boats was essential because of the need to transport American troops to Europe. Slightly more than 2 million soldiers made the voyage safely. Those who crossed on fast ocean liners were in little danger so long as the vessel maintained high speed and followed a zigzag course, a lesson learned from the *Lusitania*, whose captain had neglected both these precautions. Those who traveled on slower troop transports benefited from the protection of destroyers and also from the fact that the Germans concentrated on attacking supply ships. They continued to believe that inexperienced American soldiers would not be a major factor in the war.

The first units of the American Expeditionary Force (AEF), elements of the regular army commanded by General John J. Pershing, reached Paris on Independence Day in 1917. They took up positions on the front near Verdun in October. Not until the spring of 1918, however, did the "doughboys" play a significant role in the fighting, though their mere presence boosted French and British morale.

Pershing, as commander of the AEF, insisted on maintaining his troops as independent units; he would not allow them to be filtered into the Allied armies as reinforcements. This was part of a perhaps unfortunate general policy that reflected America's isolationism. (Wilson always referred to the other nations fighting Germany as "associates," not as "allies.")

In March 1918 the Germans launched a great spring offensive, their armies strengthened by thousands of veterans from the Russian front. By late May they had reached a point on the Marne River near the town of Château-Thierry, only 50 miles from Paris. Early in June the AEF fought its first major engagements, driving the Germans back from Château-Thierry and Belleau Wood.

In this fighting only about 27,500 Americans saw action, and they suffered appalling losses. Nevertheless, when the Germans advanced again in the direction of the Marne in mid-July, 85,000 Amer-

icans were in the lines that withstood their charge. Then, in the major turning point of the war, the Allied armies counterattacked. Some 270,000 Americans participated, helping to flatten the German bulge between Reims and Soissons. By late August the American First Army, 500,000 strong, was poised before the Saint-Mihiel salient, a deep extension of the German lines southeast of Verdun. On September 12 this army, buttressed by French troops, struck and in two days wiped out the salient.

Late in September began the greatest American engagement of the war. No fewer than 1.2 million doughboys drove forward west of Verdun into the Argonne Forest. For over a month of indescribable horror they inched ahead through the tangle of the Argonne and the formidable defenses of the Hindenburg line, while to the west, French and British armies staged similar drives. In this one offensive the AEF suffered 120,000 casualties. Finally, on November 1, they broke the German center and raced toward the vital Sedan-Mézières railroad. On November 11, with Allied armies advancing on all fronts, the Germans signed the armistice, ending the fighting.*

Preparing for Peace

On November 11, 1918, the fighting ended, but the shape of the postwar world remained to be determined. European society had been shaken to its foundations. Confusion reigned. People wanted peace yet burned for revenge. Millions faced starvation. Other millions were disillusioned by the seemingly purposeless sacrifices of four years of horrible war. Communism—to some an idealistic promise of human betterment, to others a commitment to rational economic and social planning, to still others a danger to individual freedom, toleration, and democracy—having conquered Russia, threatened to envelop Germany and much of the

---

* American losses in the war amounted to 112,432 dead and 230,074 wounded. More than half of the deaths, however, resulted from disease. Though severe, these casualties were trivial compared with those of the other belligerents. British Commonwealth deaths amounted to 947,000, French to 1.38 million, Russian to 1.7 million, Italian to 460,000. Among the Central Powers, Germany lost 1.8 million men, Austria-Hungary 1.2 million, Turkey 325,000. In addition, about 20 million were wounded.

defunct Austro-Hungarian Empire, perhaps even the victorious Allies. How could stability be restored? How could victory be made worth its enormous cost?

Woodrow Wilson had grasped the significance of the war while most statesmen still thought that triumph on the battlefield would settle everything automatically. As early as January 1917 he had realized that victory would be wasted if the winners permitted themselves the luxury of vengeance. Such a policy would disrupt the balance of power and lead to economic and social chaos. American participation in the struggle had not blurred his vision. The victors must build a better society, not punish those they believed had destroyed the old.

In a speech to Congress on January 8, 1918, Wilson outlined a plan, known as the Fourteen Points, designed to make the world "fit and safe to live in." The peace treaty should be negotiated in full view of world opinion, not in secret. It should guarantee the freedom of the seas to all nations, in war as in peacetime. It should tear down barriers to international trade, provide for a drastic reduction of armaments, and establish a colonial system that would take proper account of the interests of the native peoples concerned. European boundaries should be redrawn so that no substantial group would have to live under a government not of its own choosing.

More specifically, captured Russian territory should be restored, Belgium evacuated, Alsace-Lorraine returned to France, the heterogeneous nationalities of Austria-Hungary accorded autonomy. Italy's frontiers should be adjusted "along clearly recognizable lines of nationality," the Balkans made free, Turkey divested of its subject peoples, an independent Polish state (with access to the Baltic Sea) created. To oversee the new system, Wilson insisted, "a general association of nations must be formed under specific covenants for the purpose of affording mutual guarantees of political independence and territorial integrity to great and small states alike."

Wilson's Fourteen Points for a fair peace lifted the hopes of people everywhere. After the guns fell silent, however, the vagueness and inconsistencies in his list became apparent. Complete national self-determination was impossible in Europe; there were too many regions of mixed population for every group to be satisfied. Self-determination, like the war itself, fostered the spirit of nationalism that Wilson's dream of international organization, a league of nations, was designed to de-emphasize. Furthermore, the Allies had made territorial commitments to one another in secret treaties that ran counter to the principle of self-determination, and they were not ready to give up all claim to Germany's colonies. Freedom of the seas in wartime posed another problem; the British flatly refused to accept the idea. In every Allied country, millions rejected the idea of a peace without indemnities. They expected to make the enemy pay for the war, hoping, as Sir Eric Geddes, first lord of the Admiralty, said, to squeeze Germany "as a lemon is squeezed—until the pips squeak."

Wilson assumed that the practical benefits of his program would compel opponents to fall in line. He had the immense advantage of seeking nothing for his own country and the additional strength of being leader of the one important nation to emerge from the war richer and more powerful than it had been in 1914.

Yet this combination of altruism, idealism, and power was his undoing; it intensified his tendency to be overbearing and undermined his judgment. He had never found it easy to compromise. Once, when he was president of Princeton, he got into an argument over some abstract question with a professor while shooting a game of pool. To avoid acrimony, the professor finally said: "Well, Doctor Wilson, there are two sides to every question." "Yes," Wilson answered, "a right side and a wrong side." Now, believing that the fate of humanity hung on his actions, he was unyielding. Always a preacher, he became in his own mind a prophet—almost, one fears, a kind of god.

In the last weeks of the war Wilson proved to be a brilliant diplomat, first dangling the Fourteen Points before the German people to encourage them to overthrow Kaiser Wilhelm II and sue for an armistice, then sending Colonel House to Paris to persuade Allied leaders to accept the Fourteen Points as the basis for the peace. When the Allies raised objections, House made small concessions, but by hinting that the United States might make a separate peace with Germany, he forced them to agree. Under the armistice, Germany had to withdraw behind the Rhine River and surrender its submarines, together with quantities of munitions and other materials. In return it received the assurance of the Allies that the Wilsonian principles would prevail at the Paris peace conference.

Wilson then came to a daring decision: He would personally attend the conference, which convened on January 12, 1919, at Paris, as a member of the United States Peace Commission. This was a precedent-shattering step, for no president had ever left American territory while in office. (Taft, who had a summer home on the St. Lawrence River in Canada, never vacationed there during his term, believing that to do so would be unconstitutional.)

Wilson probably erred in going to Paris, but not because of the novelty or possible illegality of the act. By going, he was turning his back on obvious domestic problems. Western farmers believed that they had been discriminated against during the war, since wheat prices had been controlled while southern cotton had been allowed to rise unchecked from 7 cents a pound in 1914 to 35 cents in 1919. The administration's drastic tax program had angered many businessmen. Labor, despite its gains, was restive in the face of reconversion to peacetime conditions.

Wilson had increased his political difficulties by making a partisan appeal for the election of a Democratic Congress in 1918. Republicans, who had in many instances supported his war program more loyally than the Democrats, considered the action a gross affront. The appeal failed; the Republicans won majorities in both houses. Wilson appeared to have been repudiated at home at the very moment that he set forth to represent the nation abroad. Most important, Wilson intended to break with the isolationist tradition and bring the United States into a league of nations. Such a revolutionary change would require explanation; he should have undertaken a major campaign to convince the American people of the wisdom of this step.

Wilson also erred in his choice of the other commissioners. He selected Colonel House, Secretary of State Lansing, General Tasker H. Bliss, and Henry White, a career diplomat. These men were thoroughly competent, but only White was a Republican, and he had no stature as a politician. Since the peace treaty would have to be ratified by the Senate, Wilson should have given that body some representation on the commission, and since the Republicans would have a majority in the new Senate, a Republican senator, or someone who had the full confidence of the Republican leadership, should

have been appointed. (The wily McKinley had named three senators to the American delegation to the peace conference after the Spanish-American War.)

The Paris Peace Conference

Wilson arrived in Europe a world hero. He toured England, France, and Italy briefly and was greeted ecstatically almost everywhere. The reception tended to increase his sense of mission and to convince him, in the fashion of a typical progressive, that whatever the European politicians might say about it, "the people" were behind his program.

When the conference settled down to its work, control quickly fell into the hands of the so-called Big Four: Wilson, Prime Minister David Lloyd George of Great Britain, Premier Georges Clemenceau of France, and Prime Minister Vittorio Orlando of Italy. Wilson stood out in this group but did not dominate it. His principal advantage in the negotiations was his untiring industry. He alone of the leaders tried to master all the complex details of the task.

The 78-year-old Clemenceau cared only for one thing: French security. He viewed Wilson cynically, saying that since mankind had been unable to keep God's Ten Commandments, it was unlikely to do better with Wilson's Fourteen Points. Lloyd George's approach was pragmatic and almost cavalier. He sympathized with much that Wilson was trying to accomplish but found the president's frequent sermonettes about "right being more important than might, and justice being more eternal than force" incomprehensible. "If you want to succeed in politics," Lloyd George advised a British statesman, "you must keep your conscience well under control." Orlando, clever, cultured, a believer in international cooperation but inflexible where Italian national interests were concerned, was not the equal of his three colleagues in influence. He left the conference in a huff when they failed to meet all his demands.

The conference labored from January to May 1919 and finally brought forth the Versailles Treaty. American liberals whose hopes had soared at the thought of a peace based on the Fourteen Points found the document abysmally disappointing.

The "Big Four" at the Hotel Crillon in Paris. First row, from the left: Orlando of Italy, Lloyd George of Great Britain, Clemenceau of France, and Wilson of the United States.

The peace settlement failed to carry out the principle of self-determination completely. It gave Italy a large section of the Austrian Tyrol, though the area contained 200,000 people who considered themselves Austrians. Other German-speaking groups were incorporated into the new states of Poland and Czechoslovakia. Japan was allowed to take over the Chinese province of Shantung, and the Allies swallowed up all the German colonies in Africa and the Far East.

The victors forced Germany to accept responsibility for having caused the war—an act of senseless vindictiveness as well as a gross oversimplification—and to sign a "blank check," agreeing to pay for all damage to civilian properties and even future pensions and other indirect war costs. This reparations bill, as finally determined, amounted to $33 billion. Instead of attacking imperialism, the treaty attacked German imperialism; instead of seeking a new international social order based on liberty and democracy, it created a great-power entente designed to crush Germany and to exclude Bolshevist Russia from the family of nations. It said nothing about freedom of the seas, the reduction of tariffs, or disarmament. To those who had taken Wilson's "peace without victory" speech and the Fourteen

Points literally, the Versailles Treaty seemed an abomination.

The complaints of the critics were individually reasonable, yet their conclusions were not entirely fair. The new map of Europe left fewer people on "foreign" soil than in any earlier period of history. Though the Allies seized the German colonies, they were required, under the mandate system, to render to the League of Nations annual accounts of their stewardship and to prepare the inhabitants for eventual independence. Above all, Wilson had persuaded the powers to incorporate the League of Nations in the treaty.

Wilson expected the League of Nations to make up for all the inadequacies of the Versailles Treaty. Once the League had begun to function, problems like freedom of the seas and disarmament would solve themselves, he argued, and the relaxation of trade barriers would surely follow. The League would arbitrate international disputes, act as a central body for registering treaties, and employ military and economic sanctions against aggressor nations. Each member promised (Article 10) to protect the "territorial integrity" and "political independence" of all other members. No great power could be made to go to war against its will, but Wilson emphasized that all were *morally* obligated to carry out League decisions. By any standard, Wilson had achieved a remarkably moderate peace, one full of hope for the future. Except for the war guilt clause and the heavy reparations imposed on Germany, he could be justly proud of his work.

The Senate and the League of Nations

When Wilson returned from France, he finally directed his attention to the task of winning public approval of his handiwork. A large majority of the people probably favored the League of Nations in principle, though few understood all its implications or were entirely happy with every detail. Wilson had persuaded the Allies to accept certain changes in the original draft to mollify American opposition. No nation could be forced to accept a colonial mandate, and "domestic questions" such as the Monroe Doctrine, tariffs, and immigration were excluded from League control.

Many senators found these modifications insufficient. Even before the peace conference ended, 37 Republican senators signed a round-robin, devised by Henry Cabot Lodge of Massachusetts, opposing Wilson's League and demanding that the question of an international organization be put off until "the urgent business of negotiating peace terms with Germany" had been completed. Wilson rejected this suggestion icily. Further alterations were out of the question. "Anyone who opposes me . . . I'll crush!" he told one Democratic senator. "I shall consent to nothing. The Senate must take its medicine." Thus the stage was set for a monumental test of strength between the president and the Republican majority in the Senate.

Partisanship, principle, and prejudice clashed mightily in this contest. A presidential election loomed. Should the League prove a success, the Republicans wanted to be able to claim a share of the credit, but Wilson had refused to allow them to participate in drafting the document. This predisposed all of them to favor changes. Politics aside, genuine alarm at the possible sacrifice of American sovereignty to an international authority led many Republicans to urge modification of the League covenant, or constitution. Personal dislike of Wilson

President and Mrs. Woodrow Wilson during the Versailles Peace Conference in 1919. Clearly, something did not smell right.

and his high-handed methods motivated others. Yet the noble purpose of the League made many reluctant to reject it entirely. The intense desire of the people to have an end to the long war made GOP leaders hesitate before voting down the Versailles Treaty, and they could not reject the League without rejecting the treaty.

Wilson could count on the Democratic senators almost to a man, but he had to win over many Republicans to obtain the two-thirds majority necessary for ratification. Republican opinion divided roughly into three segments. At one extreme were some dozen "irreconcilables," led by the shaggy-browed William E. Borah of Idaho, an able and kindly person of progressive leanings but an uncompromising isolationist. Borah claimed that he would vote against the League even if Jesus Christ returned to earth to argue in its behalf, and most of his followers were equally inflexible. At the other extreme stood another dozen "mild" reservationists who were in favor of the League but who hoped to alter it in minor ways, chiefly for political purposes. In the middle were the "strong" reservationists, senators willing to go along with the League only if American sovereignty were fully protected and it was made clear that their party had played a major role in fashioning the final document.

Senator Lodge, the leader of the Republican opposition, was a haughty, rather cynical, intensely partisan individual. He possessed a keen intelligence, a mastery of parliamentary procedure, and, as chairman of the Senate Foreign Relations Committee, a great deal of power. Although not an isolationist, he had little faith in the League. He also had a profound distrust of Democrats, especially Wilson, whom he considered a hypocrite and a coward. The president's pious idealism left him cold. While perfectly ready to see the country participate actively in world affairs, Lodge insisted that its right to determine its own best interests in every situation be preserved. He had been a senator since 1893 and an admirer of senatorial independence since early manhood. When a Democratic president tried to ram the Versailles Treaty down the Senate's throat, he fought him with every weapon he could muster.

A skeptical view of the League of Nations in London's Punch. *The dove of peace looks askance at Wilson's hefty olive branch, asking "Isn't this a bit thick?"*

Lodge belonged to the strong reservationist faction. His own proposals, known as the Lodge Reservations, 14 in number to match Wilson's Fourteen Points, limited the United States' obligations to the League and stated in unmistakable terms the right of Congress to decide when to honor these obligations. Some of the reservations were mere quibbles. Others, such as the provision that the United States would not endorse Japan's seizure of Chinese territory, were included mainly to embarrass Wilson by pointing up compromises he had made at Versailles. The most important reservation applied to Article 10 of the League covenant, which committed signatories to protect the political independence and territorial integrity of all member nations. Wilson had rightly called Article 10 "the heart of the Covenant." One of Lodge's reservations made it inoperable so far as the United States was concerned "unless in any particular case the Congress . . . shall by act or joint resolution so provide."

Lodge performed brilliantly, if somewhat unscrupulously, in uniting the three Republican factions behind his reservations. He got the irreconcilables to agree to them by conceding their right to vote against the final version in any event, and he held the mild reservationists in line by modifying some of his demands and stressing the importance of party unity. Reservations—as distinct from amendments—would not have to win the formal approval of other League members. In addition, the Lodge proposals dealt forthrightly with the problem of reconciling traditional concepts of national sovereignty with the new idea of world cooperation. Supporters of the League could accept them without sacrifice of principle. Wilson, however, refused to agree. "Accept the Treaty with the Lodge reservations?" the president snorted when a friendly senator warned him that he must accept a compromise. "Never! Never!"

This foolish intransigence seems almost incomprehensible in a man of Wilson's intelligence and political experience. In part his hatred of Lodge accounts for it, in part his faith in his League. His physical condition in 1919 also played a role. At Paris he had suffered a violent attack of indigestion that was probably a symptom of a minor stroke. Thereafter, many observers noted small changes in his personality, particularly increased stubbornness and a loss of good judgment. Instead of making concessions, the president set out early in September on a nationwide speaking tour to rally support for the League. Though some of his speeches were brilliant, they had little effect on senatorial opinion, and the effort drained his last physical reserves. On September 25, after an address in Pueblo, Colorado, he collapsed. The rest of the trip had to be canceled. A few days later, in Washington, he suffered a severe stroke that partially paralyzed his left side.

For nearly two months the president was almost totally cut off from affairs of state, leaving supporters of the League leaderless while Lodge maneuvered the reservations through the Senate. Gradually, popular attitudes toward the League shifted. Organized groups of Italian-, Irish-, and German-Americans, angered by what they considered unfair treatment of their native lands in the Versailles Treaty, clamored for outright rejection. The arguments of the irreconcilables persuaded many citizens that Wilson had made too sharp a break with America's isolationist past and that the Lodge Reservations were therefore necessary. Other issues connected with the reconversion of society to a peacetime basis increasingly occupied the public mind.

A coalition of Democratic and moderate Republican senators could easily have carried the treaty. That no such coalition was organized was Wilson's fault. Lodge obtained the simple majority necessary to add his reservations to the treaty merely by keeping his own party united. When the time came for the final roll call on November 19, Wilson, bitter and emotionally distraught, urged the Democrats to vote for rejection. "Better a thousand times to go down fighting than to dip your colours to dishonourable compromise," he explained to his wife. Thus the amended treaty failed, 35 to 55, the irreconcilables and the Democrats voting against it. Lodge then allowed the original draft without his reservations to come to a vote. Again the result was defeat, 38 to 53. Only one Republican cast a ballot for ratification.

Dismayed but not yet crushed, friends of the League in both parties forced reconsideration of the treaty early in 1920. Neither Lodge nor Wilson would yield an inch. Lodge, who had little confidence in the effectiveness of any league of nations, was under no compulsion to compromise. Wilson, who believed that the League was the world's best

hope, did have such a compulsion. Yet he would not compromise either.

As the British historian Robert Skidelsky has written, "The architect of the Treaty's defeat in Congress was Wilson himself." His behavior is further evidence of his physical and mental decline. Probably he was incompetent to perform the duties of his office. Had he died or stepped down, the treaty, with reservations, would almost certainly have been ratified. When the Senate balloted again in March, half the Democrats voted for the treaty with the Lodge Reservations. The others, mostly southern party regulars, joined the irreconcilables. Together they mustered 35 votes, 7 more than the one-third that meant defeat.

Demobilization

To win the war, the nation had accepted drastic regulation of the economy in order to increase production and improve social efficiency. When the war ended, the government, in Wilson's words, "took the harness off" at once, blithely assuming that the economy could readjust itself without direction. The army was hastily demobilized, pouring millions of veterans into the job market without plan. All society seemed in flux. When the War Department sent letters to the next of kin of 30,000 soldiers buried in France, 12,000 of the letters were returned as undeliverable. No person of the name on the envelope lived at the indicated address. Nearly all controls established by the War Industries Board and other agencies were dropped overnight. Billions of dollars' worth of war contracts were canceled.

Business boomed in 1919 as consumers spent wartime savings on automobiles, homes, and other goods that had been in short supply during the conflict. But temporary shortages caused inflation; by 1920 the cost of living stood at more than twice the level of 1913.

Inflation in turn produced labor trouble. The unions, grown strong during the war, struck for wage increases. Over 4 million workers, one out of five in the labor force, were on strike at some time during 1919. Work stoppages aggravated shortages, triggering further inflation and more strikes. Then came one of the most precipitous economic declines

During the Red Scare, radical cartoonist William Gropper sharply criticized the tactics of Attorney General Palmer. These drawings appeared in The Liberator *early in 1920. At left, Palmer's agents warn, "Clear the road there, boys—we got a dangerous Red." At right, a suspect faces a loutish, unsympathetic audience.*

in American history. Between July 1920 and March 1922, prices, especially agricultural prices, plummeted. Unemployment soared. Thus the unrealistic attitude of the Wilson government toward the complexities of economic readjustment caused considerable unnecessary strife.

The Red Scare

Far more serious than the economic losses were the social effects of these difficulties. Everyone wanted peace, but wartime tensions did not subside; apparently people continued to need some release for the aggressive drives they had formerly focused on the Germans. Most Americans found strikes frustrating and drew invidious comparisons between the lot of the unemployed soldier who had risked his life for a dollar a day and that of the striker who had drawn fat wages during the war in perfect safety.

The activities of radicals in the labor movement led millions of Americans to associate unionism and strikes with the new threat of communist world revolution. Although there were only a relative handful of communists in the United States, Russia's experience persuaded many people that a tiny minority of ruthless revolutionaries could take over a

nation of millions if conditions were right. Communists appointed themselves the champions of workers; labor unrest attracted them magnetically. When strikes broke out, some accompanied by violence, many people interpreted them as communist-inspired preludes to revolution. Louis Wiley, an experienced *New York Times* reporter, told a friend at this time that anarchists, socialists, and radical labor leaders were "joining together with the object of overthrowing the American Government through a bloody revolution and establishing a Bolshevist republic."

Organized labor in America had seldom been truly radical. The Industrial Workers of the World (IWW) had made little impression in most industries. But some labor leaders had been attracted to socialism, and many Americans failed to distinguish between the common ends sought by communists and socialists and the entirely different methods by which they proposed to achieve those ends. When a general strike paralyzed Seattle in February 1919, the fact that a procommunist had helped organize it sent shivers down countless conservative spines. When the radical William Z. Foster began a drive to organize the steel industry at about this time, the fears became more intense. In September 1919 a total of 343,000 steelworkers walked off their jobs, and in the same month the Boston police struck.

Violence marked the steel strike, and the suspension of police protection in Boston led to looting and fighting that ended only when Governor Calvin Coolidge (who might have prevented the strike had he acted earlier) called out the National Guard.

During the same period a handful of terrorists caused widespread alarm by attempting to murder various prominent persons, including John D. Rockefeller, Justice Oliver Wendell Holmes, Jr., and Attorney General A. Mitchell Palmer. Although the terrorists were anarchists and anarchism had little in common with communism, many citizens lumped all extremists together and associated them with a monstrous assault on society.

What aroused the public even more was the fact that most radicals were not American citizens. Wartime fear of alien saboteurs easily transformed itself into peacetime terror of foreign radicals. In place of Germany, the enemy became the lowly immigrant, usually an Italian or a Jew or a Slav and usually an industrial worker. In this muddled way, radicalism, unionism, and questions of racial and national origins combined to make many Americans believe that their way of life was in imminent danger. That few immigrants were radicals, that most workers had no interest in communism, and that the extremists themselves were faction-ridden and irresolute did not affect conservative thinking. From all over the country came demands that radicals be ruthlessly suppressed. Thus the "Red Scare" was born.

Attorney General Palmer was the key figure in the resulting purge. He had been a typical progressive, a supporter of the League of Nations and such reforms as women's suffrage and child labor legislation. But pressure from Congress and his growing conviction that the communists really were a menace led him to join the "red hunt." Soon he was saying of the radicals: "Out of the sly and crafty eyes of many of them leap cupidity, cruelty, insanity, and crime; from their lopsided faces, sloping brows, and misshapen features may be recognized the unmistakable criminal type."

In August 1919, Palmer established within the Department of Justice the General Intelligence Division, headed by J. Edgar Hoover, to collect information about clandestine radical activities. In November, Justice Department agents swooped down on the meeting places in a dozen cities of an anarchist organization known as the Union of Russian Workers. More than 650 persons, many of them unconnected with the union, were arrested, but in only 43 cases could evidence be found to justify deportation.

Nevertheless, the public reacted so favorably that Palmer, thinking now of winning the 1920 Democratic presidential nomination, planned an immense roundup of communists. He obtained 3,000 warrants, and on January 2, 1920, his agents, reinforced by local police and self-appointed vigilantes, struck simultaneously in 33 cities. Palmer's biographer, Stanley Coben, has described the "Palmer raids" vividly:

> There was a knock on the door, the rush of police. In meeting houses, all were lined up to be searched; those who resisted often suffered brutal treatment. . . . Police searched the homes of many of those arrested; books and papers, as well as many people found in these residences, were carried off to headquarters. Policemen also sought those whose names appeared on seized membership lists; they captured many of these suspects in bed or at work, searching their homes, confiscating their possessions, almost always without warrants.

About 6,000 persons were taken into custody, many of them citizens and therefore not subject to the deportation laws, many others unconnected with any radical cause. Some were held incommunicado for weeks while the authorities searched for evidence against them. In a number of cases, individuals who went to visit prisoners were themselves thrown behind bars on the theory that they too must be communists. Hundreds of suspects were jammed into filthy "bullpens," beaten, and forced to sign "confessions."

The public tolerated these wholesale violations of civil liberties because of the supposed menace of communism. Gradually, however, protests began to be heard, first from lawyers and liberal magazines, then from a wider segment of the population. No revolutionary outbreak had taken place. Of 6,000 seized in the Palmer raids, only 556 proved liable to deportation. The widespread ransacking of communists' homes and meeting places produced mountains of inflammatory literature but only three pistols.

Palmer, attempting to maintain the crusade, announced that the radicals planned a gigantic terrorist demonstration for May Day 1920. In New York and other cities, thousands of police were placed on round-the-clock duty; federal troops stood by anxiously. But the day passed without even a rowdy meeting. Suddenly Palmer appeared ridiculous. The Red Scare swiftly subsided.

The Election of 1920

Wilson still hoped for vindication at the polls in the presidential election, which he sought to make a "great and solemn referendum" on the League. He would have liked to run for a third term, but in his enfeebled condition, he attracted no support among Democratic leaders. The party nominated James M. Cox of Ohio.

Cox favored joining the League, but the election did not produce the referendum on the new organization that Wilson desired. The Republicans, whose candidate was another Ohioan, Senator Warren G. Harding, equivocated shamelessly on the issue. The election turned on other matters, largely emotional. Disillusioned by the results of the war, many Americans had had their fill of idealism. They wanted, apparently, to end the long period of moral uplift and reform agitation that had begun under Theodore Roosevelt and return to what Harding called "normalcy."

To the extent that the voters were expressing opinions on Wilson's League, their response was overwhelmingly negative. Senator Harding had been a strong reservationist, yet he swept the country, winning over 16.1 million votes to Cox's 9.1 million. In July 1921, Congress formally ended the war with the Central Powers by passing a joint resolution.

The defeat of the League was a tragedy both for Wilson, whose crusade for a world order based on peace and justice ended in failure, and for the world, which was condemned by the result to endure another still more horrible and costly war. Perhaps this dreadful outcome could not have been avoided. Had Wilson compromised and Lodge behaved like a statesman instead of a politician, America would have joined the League, but it might well have failed to respond when called on to meet its obligations. As events soon demonstrated, the League powers acted pusillanimously and even dishonorably when challenged by aggressor nations.

Yet it might have been different had the Senate ratified the Versailles Treaty. What was lost when the treaty failed in the Senate was not peace but the possibility of peace, a tragic loss indeed.

Milestones

1914 United States invades Veracruz, Mexico War breaks out in Europe	United States declares war on the Central Powers Herbert Hoover named Food Administrator Bernard Baruch named head of the War Industries Board
1915 U-boat torpedoes the *Lusitania* United States recognizes the Carranza government in Mexico	
1916 Louis D. Brandeis named to the Supreme Court Adamson Act gives railroad workers the eight-hour day "Pancho" Villa burns Columbus, New Mexico	**1918** Sedition Act Republicans gain control of both houses of Congress Armistice ends the Great War
1917 Wilson's "Peace Without Victory" speech Germany resumes unrestricted submarine warfare	**1919** Steel strike Red Scare, climaxing in Palmer raids Paris Peace Conference Senate rejects Versailles Treaty **1920** Senate rejects Versailles Treaty

SUPPLEMENTARY READING

Titles marked with an asterisk have been published in paperback.

Wilson's handling of foreign relations is discussed in several volumes by A. S. Link: **Wilson** (1947), **Woodrow Wilson and the Progressive Era*** (1954), and **Wilson the Diplomatist*** (1957). R. H. Ferrell, **Woodrow Wilson and World War I*** (1985), is an up-to-date survey of the period. See also N. G. Levin, Jr., **Woodrow Wilson and World Politics*** (1968). Latin American affairs under Wilson are treated in D. G. Munro, **Intervention and Dollar Diplomacy in the Caribbean** (1964).

For details of America's entry into the Great War, see E. R. May, **The World War and American Isolation*** (1959), and E. H. Buehrig, **Woodrow Wilson and the Balance of Power** (1955).

The war on the home front is covered in D. M. Kennedy, **Over Here: The First World War and American Society** (1980), and more briefly in W. E. Leuchtenburg, **The Perils of Prosperity*** (1958). A good account of military preparation is H. A. De Weerd, **President Wilson Fights His War** (1968). Other useful volumes include R. D. Cuff, **The War Industries Board** (1973); Charles Gilbert, **American Financing of World War I** (1970); S. L. Vaughn, **Holding Fast the Inner Lines** (1980), which deals with the Committee on Public Information; M. I. Urofsky, **Big Steel and the Wilson Administration** (1969); Donald Johnson, **The Challenge to American Freedoms** (1963); David Brody, **Steelworkers in America*** (1960); D. R. Beaver, **Newton D. Baker and the American War Effort** (1966); and S. W. Livermore, **Politics is Adjourned: Woodrow Wilson and the War Congress*** (1966).

On American military participation, consult De Weerd, **President Wilson Fights His War.** Laurence Stallings, **The Doughboys*** (1963), is a good popular account of the American army in France. See also F. E. Vandiver, **Black Jack: The Life and Times of John J. Pershing** (1977). On blacks in the army, see A. E. Barbeau and F. Henri, **The Unknown Soldiers** (1974).

On the peace settlement, in addition to the biographies of Wilson, consult A. J. Mayer, **Politics and Diplomacy of Peacemaking** (1967), T. A. Bailey, **Woodrow Wilson and the Lost Peace*** (1944) and **Woodrow Wilson and the Great Betrayal*** (1945), J. A. Garraty, **Henry Cabot Lodge** (1953), and Ralph Stone, **The Irreconcilables*** (1970).

On radicalism and the Red Scare, see R. K. Murray, **The Red Scare*** (1955), Stanley Coben, **A. Mitchell Palmer** (1963), David Brody, **The Steel Strike of 1919*** (1965), and R. L. Friedheim, **The Seattle General Strike*** (1965). On the election of 1920, see Wesley Bagby, **The Road to Normalcy*** (1962), Burl Noggle, **Into the Twenties** (1974), and R. K. Murray, **The Harding Era** (1969).

Postwar Society and Culture: Change and Adjustment

In the spring of '27 something bright and alien flashed across the sky. A young Minnesotan who seemed to have nothing to do with his generation did a heroic thing and for a moment people set down their glasses in the country clubs and speakeasies and thought of their old best dreams.

F. SCOTT FITZGERALD *on Lindbergh's flight to Paris*

T he Great War seemed to many who lived through it a turning point in history, the real division separating the 19th from the new 20th century. Actually most of what seemed new to the people of the 1920s had begun well before 1917, and the changes they noticed were still going on. They were in the midst of new social, cultural, and economic forces, forces that were to shape their lives and those of their children and grandchildren.

Closing the Gates

The ending of the Red Scare did not signal the disappearance of xenophobia. It was perhaps inevitable and possibly wise that some limitation be placed on the entry of immigrants into the United States after the war. An immense backlog of prospective migrants had piled up during the conflict, and the desperate postwar economic condition of Europe led hundreds of thousands to seek better circumstances in the United States. Immigration increased from 110,000 in 1919 to 430,000 in 1920

and 805,000 in 1921, with every prospect of continuing to rise.

In 1921 Congress, reflecting widespread prejudice against eastern and southern Europeans, passed an emergency act establishing a quota system. Each year 3 percent of the number of foreign-born residents of the United States in 1910 (about 350,000 persons) might enter the country. Each country's quota was based on the number of its nationals in the United States in 1910. This meant that only a relative handful of the total would be from southern and eastern Europe. In 1924 the quota was reduced to 2 percent and the base year shifted to 1890, thereby lowering further the proportion of southern and eastern Europeans admitted.

In 1929 Congress established a system that allowed only 150,000 immigrants a year to enter the country. Each national quota was based on the supposed origins of the entire white population of the United States in 1920, not merely on the foreign-born. Here is an example of how the system worked:

$$\frac{\text{Italian quota}}{150,000} = \frac{\text{Italian-origin population, 1920}}{\text{White population, 1920}}$$

$$\frac{\text{Italian quota}}{150,000} = \frac{3,800,000}{95,500,000}$$

Italian quota = 6,000 (approximately)

Presumably this method would preserve the status quo; in fact it heavily favored immigrants from Great Britain. The system was complicated and unscientific, for no one could determine with accuracy the "origins" of millions of citizens.

The law reduced actual immigration to far below 150,000 a year. British immigration between 1931 and 1939, for example, amounted to only 23,000 even though the annual British quota was over 65,000. Meanwhile, hundreds of thousands of southern and eastern Europeans waited for admission.

The United States had closed the gates. The National Origins Act caused the foreign-born percentage of the population to fall from about 13 percent in 1920 to 4.7 percent in 1970. Instead of an open, cosmopolitan society eager to accept, in Emma Lazarus's stirring line, the "huddled masses yearning to breathe free," America now became

Immigrants entering the United States through New York City's Ellis Island. When immigration to the United States surged again after the war, restrictionists moved quickly to convince Congress to reject the traditional policy of unlimited immigration in favor of strict national quotas.

committed to preserving a homogeneous, "Anglo-Saxon" population.

Distaste for immigrants from eastern Europe, many of whom were Jewish, expanded into a more general anti-Semitism in the 1920s. American Jews, whether foreign-born or native, were subject to increasing discrimination, not because they were slow in adopting American ways but because, being ambitious and hardworking as immigrants were supposed to be, many of them were getting ahead in the world more rapidly than expected. Prestigious colleges like Harvard, Yale, and Columbia that had in the past admitted Jews based on their academic records now imposed unofficial but effective quotas. Medical schools also established quotas, and no matter how talented, most young Jewish lawyers and bankers could find places only in so-called Jewish firms.

New Urban Social Patterns

The census of 1920 revealed that for the first time a majority of Americans (54 million in a population of 106 million) lived in "urban" rather than "rural" places. These figures are somewhat misleading when applied to the study of social attitudes because the census classified anyone in a community of 2,500 or more as urban. Of the 54 million "urban" residents in 1920, over 16 million lived in villages and towns of fewer than 25,000 persons, and the evidence suggests strongly that a large majority of them held ideas and values more like those of rural citizens than like those of city dwellers. But the truly urban Americans, the one person in four who lived in a city of 100,000 or more—and particularly the nearly 16.4 million who lived in metropolises of at least half a million—were increasing steadily in number and influence. More than 19 million persons moved from farms to cities in the 1920s, and the population living in centers of 100,000 or more increased by about a third.

Being a city dweller meant far more than changing one's physical surroundings. It affected family structure, educational opportunities, and dozens of other aspects of human existence. Indeed, since most of the changes in the relations of husbands, wives, and children that had occurred in the 19th century were related to the fact that people were leaving farms to work in towns and cities, these trends continued and were intensified in the early 20th century as more and more people settled in urban centers. In addition, couples continued to marry more out of love and physical attraction than for social position or economic advantage or to please parents. In each successive decade, people married slightly later and had slightly fewer children.

Earlier differences between working-class and

middle-class family structures persisted. In 1920 about a quarter of the American women who were working were married, but less than 10 percent of all married women were working. Middle-class married women who worked were nearly all either childless or highly paid professionals who were able to employ servants. Most male skilled workers now earned enough to support a family in modest comfort so long as they could work steadily, but an unskilled laborer still could not. Wives in most such families helped out, usually by taking in laundry or doing piecework sewing for jobbers.

However, there were important variations in the roles of wives of different ethnic backgrounds. Those who could not speak English well had difficulty obtaining work. Italian immigrant women rarely worked outside the home even if childless. Irish-American wives often found jobs as domestics or, if better educated, as nurses, telephone operators, or clerks. Out of necessity, a far larger proportion of black women, married or single, worked than white women, but they could rarely find better-paying jobs than domestic service. Compulsory education and state child labor laws kept an increasing percentage of the children of the unskilled out of the job market into their mid-teens, but many found odd jobs, and some evaded the laws.

By the 1920s the concept of the "companionate" family had emerged. In such families, husbands and wives would deal with each other as equals, which under existing conditions meant sharing housework and child care, downplaying male authority, and stressing mutual satisfaction in sexual and other matters. They should be friends and lovers, not merely housekeepers, earners of money, and producers of children. Procreation did not have to be the main purpose of matrimony, but if there were children, they should be left as free as possible to develop in their own way; rigid discipline was limiting and therefore wrong. By contrast, advocates of companionate relationships believed that there was nothing particularly sacred about marriage; divorce should be made easier for couples that did not get along, provided they did not have children.

Much attention was given at this time to "scientific" child raising. Child-care experts (a new breed) agreed that routine medical examinations and good nutrition were of central importance, but they were divided about how the socialization and psychological development of the young should be handled. One school stressed rigid training: Children should not be spoiled by indulgence, toilet training should begin early in infancy, thumb sucking should be suppressed, too much kissing could turn male youngsters into "mama's boys." "Children are made not born," John B. Watson, a former president of the American Psychological Association who was also a vice-president of the important J. Walter Thompson advertising agency, explained in *The Psychological Care of Infant and Child* (1928). "Never hug and kiss them, never let them sit in your lap. If you must, kiss them once on the forehead when they say good night."

The other school favored a more permissive approach. Toilet training could wait; parents should pay attention to their children's expressed needs, not impose a generalized set of rules upon them. In *The Companionate Marriage* (1927), Benjamin B. Lindsey, a juvenile court judge, suggested a kind of trial marriage, a period during which a young couple could get used to each other before undertaking to raise a family. By practicing contraception, such couples could separate without doing serious damage to anyone if they decided to end the relationship. If the relationship remained firm and loving, it would become a traditional marriage, and their children would grow up in a loving environment that would help them to become warm, well-adjusted adults.

Lindsey was one among many self-appointed experts who advocated more freedom for young people and open discussion of all questions related to sex. He was most concerned about the welfare of children, whose natural sexuality, he insisted, was being stupidly repressed by Victorian prudes. Others put more emphasis on married women's rights and the injustice of the double standard. Still others were interested in breaking down 19th-century sexual taboos for all people, married or single.

The Younger Generation

All of these matters were of particular concern to young adults—the generation born around the turn of the century that had grown up before and during the Great War. That war had raised their hopes for the future and its outcome dashed them. Now the narrowness and prudery of so many of their elders and the stuffy conservatism of nearly all politicians seemed not merely old-fashioned but ludicrous. The actions of red-baiters and reactionaries led them to exaggerate the importance of their right to express themselves in bizarre ways. Their models and indeed some of their leaders were the prewar Greenwich Village bohemians.

The 1920s has been dubbed the Jazz Age, the era of "flaming youth," when young people danced to syncopated "African" rhythms, careened about the countryside in automobiles in search of pleasure and forgetfulness, and made gods of movie stars and professional athletes. This view of the period bears some resemblance to reality. "Younger people," one observer noted in 1922, were attempting "to create a way of life free from the bondage of

In his many illustrations for magazines such as Life *and* McClure's, *John Held, Jr., captured the spirit of the roaring twenties and the new sense of freedom expressed in flapper-style clothing and freer relations between the sexes.*

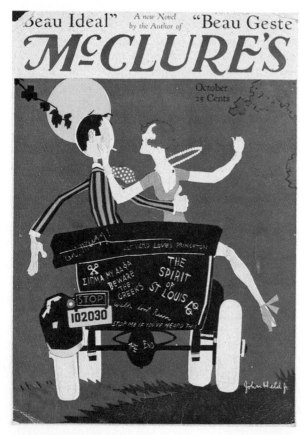

an authority that has lost all meaning." But the resemblance is only superficial; they certainly appreciated having a good time, and like any generation moving from adolescence to maturity, the young people of the 1920s were eager to understand the world and make their way in it. They were more unconventional than their grandparents primarily because they were adjusting to more profound and more rapid changes in their world than their grandparents could have imagined.

Beliefs that only the avant garde had held before the war became commonplaces. In other words, trends barely perceptible during the Progressive Era now reached avalanche proportions. This was particularly noticeable in relationships between the sexes. The historian Beth L. Bailey has shown how this relates to courtship. In the late 19th century a typical young man "paid a call" on a female friend. He met and conversed with her parents, perhaps over coffee and cookies. The couple remained at home, the parents nearby if not actually participating in what was essentially a social (one might say, public) event held in a private place.

By the 1920s paying calls was being replaced by dating; the young man called only to "pick up" his date, the two to go off, free of parental supervision, for whatever diversion they wished. Unlike a call, Professor Bailey explains, a date was "a private act in the public world."

Dating developed many conventions out of keeping with the trend toward freedom in sexual matters of which it was a part. A man asked a woman for a date because dating meant going somewhere and spending money, and the man was expected to do the transporting and pay the bill. This made the woman doubly dependent; under the old system, *she* provided the refreshments, and there was no taboo against her doing the inviting.

But there is no question that for the young people of the 1920s, relations between the sexes were becoming more relaxed and uninhibited. Respectable young women smoked cigarettes, something previously done in public only by prostitutes and bohemian types. They cast off their heavy corsets, wore lipstick and "exotic" perfumes, and shortened both their hair and their skirts, the latter rising steadily from instep to ankle to calf to knee and beyond as the decade progressed.

Freudian psychology and the more accessible ideas of the British "sexologist" Havelock Ellis reached steadily deeper into the popular psyche. According to A. A. Brill, the chief American popularizer of Freud's theories, the sex drive was irrepressible. "Love and sex are the same thing," he wrote. "The urge is there, and whether the individual desires it or no, it always manifests itself."* Since sex was "the central function of life," Ellis argued, it must be "simple and natural and pure and good." Bombarded by these exciting ideas and by erotic books and movies, to say nothing of their own inclinations, young people found casting off their inhibitions more and more tempting.

Conservatives bemoaned what they described as the breakdown of moral standards, the fragmentation of the family, and the decline of parental authority—all with some reason. Nevertheless, society was not collapsing. Much of the rebelliousness of the young, like their particular styles of dress, was faddish, in a sense a kind of youthful conformity. This was particularly true of college students, every aspect of whose extracurricular life (which was consuming a steadily larger share of most students' time and energy to begin with) was governed by elaborate rituals. In *The Damned and the Beautiful*, Paula S. Fass has shown how such matters as fraternity and sorority initiations, proms, attendance at Saturday afternoon football games, styles of dress, and college slang, seemingly aspects of independence and free choice, were nearly everywhere shaped and controlled by peer pressure.

But young people's new ways of relating to one another, while influenced by the desire to conform, were not mere fads and were not confined to people under 30. This can be seen most clearly in the birth control movement, the drive to legalize the use of contraceptives.

The "New" Woman

The young people of the 1920s were more open about sex and perhaps more sexually precocious than the young had been before the war. This does not mean that most of them engaged in sexual intercourse before marriage or that they tended to

marry earlier. Single young people might "believe in" birth control, but relatively few (at least by modern standards) had occasion to practice it. Contraception was a concern of married people, particularly married women.

The leading American proponent of birth control in the 1920s, and the person who coined the term, was Margaret Sanger, one of the less self-centered Greenwich Village bohemians. Before the war she was a political radical, a friend of Eugene Debs, Big Bill Haywood, and Emma Goldman. Gradually, however, her attention focused on the plight of the poor women she encountered while working as a nurse; many of these women were burdened by large numbers of children yet knew nothing about contraception. Sanger began to write articles and pamphlets designed to enlighten them, but when she did so she ran afoul of the Comstock Act of 1873, an antiobscenity law that banned the distribution of information about contraception from the mails. She was frequently in trouble with the law, but she was persistent to the edge of fanaticism. In 1921 she founded the American Birth Control League and two years later a research center.

The medical profession, though wary of the issue, gave some support to the birth control movement, as did the eugenicists, who claimed that unless the fecundity of "unfit" types (people others might describe simply as poor) was curbed, "race suicide" would result. Sanger accepted support wherever it could be found; by the end of the decade she was no longer on the cutting edge of the movement or even a very radical feminist. But by that time resistance to the use of contraception was crumbling. However, the Supreme Court did not determine that the right to use contraceptives was guaranteed by the Constitution until the 1960s.

Other sex-based restrictions and limitations that were of particular importance to women also seemed to be breaking down. The divorce laws had been modified in most states. More women were taking jobs, attracted by the expanding demand for clerks, typists, salespeople, receptionists, telephone operators, and similar service-oriented occupations. Over 10.6 million women were working by the end of the decade, compared to 8.4 million in 1920. The Department of Labor's Women's Bureau, outgrowth of a wartime agency, was founded in 1920 and was soon conducting investigations of the work-

---

* The historian John C. Burnham claims that Brill's "preoccupation with the grossly sexual and his insensitivity to intellectual subtleties gave much of American psychoanalysis both a sensational and simplistic tendency."

ing conditions women faced in different industries and how various laws affected them.

But most of these gains were illusory. Relaxation of the strict standards of sexual morality did not eliminate the double standard. More women worked, but most of the jobs they held were still menial or of a kind that few men wanted: domestic service, elementary school teaching, clerical work, selling behind a counter. One of the worst blows fell in 1923 when in the case of *Adkins* v. *Children's Hospital*, the Supreme Court declared a federal law that limited the hours of work for women in the District of Columbia unconstitutional.

Where they competed for jobs with men, women usually received much lower wages. Women's Bureau studies demonstrated this repeatedly, yet when the head of the bureau, Mary Anderson, tried to get employers to raise women's wages, most of them first claimed that the men had families to support, and when she reminded them that many female employees also had family responsibilities, they told her that there was a "tacit understanding" that women were to make less than men. "If I paid them the same," one employer said, "there would be a revolution." Efforts to get the American Federation of Labor to take up the issue met with failure; few of the unions in the federation admitted women.

The number of women college graduates con-

Mass-produced and mass-marketed clothing became readily available to most Americans for the first time in the 1920s, as this young saleswoman's wares attest.

tinued to expand, but the colleges placed more emphasis on subjects like home economics that seemed designed to make them better housewives rather than professional nutritionists or business executives. As one Vassar College administrator (a woman!) said, colleges should provide "education for women along the lines of their chief interests and responsibilities, motherhood and the home."

The 1920s proved disillusioning to feminists, who now paid a price for their single-minded pursuit of the right to vote in the Progressive Era. After the ratification of the Nineteenth Amendment, Carrie Chapman Catt was exultant. "We are no longer petitioners," she announced, "but free and equal citizens." Many activists, assuming the battle won, lost interest in agitating for change. They believed that the suffrage amendment had given them the one weapon needed to achieve whatever women still lacked. In fact, it soon became apparent that women did not vote as a bloc. Many, perhaps most, married women voted for the candidates their husbands supported.

When radical feminists discovered that voting did not automatically bring true equality, they founded the Women's party and began campaigning for an equal rights amendment. Their leader, Alice Paul, a dynamic if somewhat fanatical person, disdained specific goals such as disarmament, an end to child labor, and liberalized birth control. Total equality for women was the one objective. The party considered protective legislation governing the hours and working conditions of women discriminatory. This caused the so-called social feminists, who believed that children and working women needed the protection provided by such laws, to break away.

The Women's party never attracted a wide following, but only partly because of the split with the social feminists. Many of the younger radical women, like the bohemians of the Progressive Era, were primarily concerned with their personal freedom to behave as they wished; politics did not interest them. But a more important reason was that nearly all the radicals failed to see that questions of gender—the attitudes that men and women *were taught* to take toward each other, not immutable physical or psychological differences—stood in the way of true sexual equality. Many more women joined the more moderate League of Women Voters, which attempted to mobilize support for a broad spectrum of reforms, some of which had no specific connection with the interests of women as such. The entire women's movement lost momentum. The battle for the equal rights amendment persisted through the 1930s, but it was lost. By the end of that decade the movement was moribund.

Popular Culture: Movies and Radio

The postwar decade saw immense changes in popular culture. Unlike the literary flowering of the era, these changes seemed in tune with the times, not a reaction against them. This was true in part because they were products as much of technology as of human imagination.

The first motion pictures were made around 1900, but the medium only came into its own after the Great War. The early films, such as the eight-minute epic *The Great Train Robbery* (1903), were brief, action-packed, and unpretentious. Professional actors and most educated people viewed them with amused contempt. But their success was instantaneous with recent immigrants and many other slum dwellers. In 1912 there were nearly 13,000 movie houses in the United States, more than 500 in New York City alone. Many of these places were converted stores called nickelodeons because the admission charge was only 5 cents.

In the beginning the mere recording of movement seemed to satisfy the public, but success led to rapid technical and artistic improvements and consequently to more cultivated audiences. David W. Griffith's 12-reel *Birth of a Nation* (1915) was a particularly important breakthrough in both areas, though Griffith's sympathetic treatment of the Ku Klux Klan of Reconstruction days angered blacks and white liberals.

By the mid-1920s the industry, centered in Hollywood, California, was the fourth largest in the nation in capital investment. Films moved from the nickelodeons to converted theaters. So large was the audience that movie "palaces" seating several thousand people sprang up in the major cities. *Daily* ticket sales averaged more than 10 million. With the introduction of talking movies, *The Jazz Singer* (1927) being the first of significance, and color films a decade later, the motion picture reached technological maturity. Costs and profits mounted; by

Man against machine: Charlie Chaplin duels a folding Murphy bed in the film One A.M.

the 1930s, million-dollar productions were common.

Many movies were still tasteless trash catering to the prejudices of the multitude. Sex, crime, war, romantic adventure, broad comedy, and luxurious living were the main themes, endlessly repeated in predictable patterns. Popular actors and actresses tended to be either handsome, talentless sticks or so-called character actors who were typecast over and over again as heroes, villains, comedians. The stars attracted armies of adoring fans and received thousands of dollars a week for their services. Critics charged that the movies were destroying the legitimate stage (which experienced a sharp decline), corrupting the morals of youth, and glorifying the materialistic aspects of life.

Nevertheless, the motion picture made positive contributions to American culture. Beginning with the work of Griffith, filmmakers created an entirely new theatrical art, using close-ups to portray character and heighten tension and broad panoramic shots to transcend the limits of the stage. They employed, with remarkable results, special lighting effects, the fade-out, and other techniques impossible in the live theater. Movies enabled dozens of established actors to reach wider audiences and developed many first-rate new ones. As the medium matured, it produced many dramatic works of high quality. At its best the motion picture offered a breadth and power of impact superior to anything on the traditional stage.

Charlie Chaplin was the greatest film star of the era. His characterization of the sad-eyed little tramp with his toothbrush moustache and his cane, tight frock coat, and baggy trousers became famous throughout the world. Chaplin's films were superficially unpretentious; they seemed even in the 1920s old-fashioned, aimed at the lower-class audiences that had first found the movies magical. But his work proved both universally popular and enduring; he was perhaps the greatest comic artist of all time. The animated cartoon, perfected by Walt Disney, was a lesser but significant cinematic achievement; Mickey Mouse, Donald Duck, and other Disney cartoon characters gave endless delight to millions of children.

Even more pervasive than the movies in its effects on the American people was radio. Wireless transmission of sound was developed in the late 19th century by many scientists in Europe and the United States. An American, Lee De Forest, working in the decade before the Great War, devised the key improvements that made long-distance broadcasting possible. During the war radio was put to important military uses and was strictly controlled, but immediately thereafter the airwaves were thrown open to everybody.

Radio was briefly the domain of hobbyists, thousands of "hams" broadcasting in indiscriminate fashion. Even under these conditions, the manufacture of radio equipment became a big business. In 1920 the first commercial station (KDKA in Pittsburgh) began broadcasting, and by the end of 1922 over 500 stations were in operation. In 1926 the National Broadcasting Company, the first continentwide network, was created.

It took little time for broadcasters to discover the power of the new medium. When one pioneer interrupted a music program to ask listeners to phone in requests, the station received 3,000 calls in an hour. The immediacy of radio explained its tremendous impact. As a means of communicating the latest news, it had no peer; beginning with the broadcast of the 1924 presidential nominating conventions, all major public events were covered "live." Advertisers seized on radio too; it proved to be as effective a way to sell soap as to transmit news.

Advertising had mixed effects on broadcasting. The sums paid by businesses for airtime made possible elaborate entertainments performed by the finest actors and musicians, all without cost to listeners. However, advertisers hungered for mass markets. They preferred to sponsor programs of little intellectual content, aimed at the lowest tastes and utterly uncontroversial. And good and bad alike, programs were constantly interrupted by irritating pronouncements extolling the supposed virtues of one commercial product or another.

In 1927 Congress limited the number of stations and parceled out wavelengths to prevent interference. Further legislation in 1934 established the Federal Communications Commission, with power to revoke the licenses of stations that failed to operate in the public interest. But the FCC placed no effective controls on programming or on advertising practices.

The Golden Age of Sports

The extraordinary popularity of sports in the postwar period can be explained in a number of ways. People had more money to spend and more free time to fill. Radio was bringing suspenseful, play-by-play accounts of sports contests into millions of homes, thus encouraging tens of thousands to want to see similar events with their own eyes. New means of persuasion developed by advertisers to sell lipstick, breakfast cereal, and refrigerators were applied with equal success to sporting events and to the athletes who participated in them.

There had been great athletes before; indeed, probably the greatest all-around athlete of the 20th century was Jim Thorpe, a Sac and Fox Indian who won both the pentathalon and the decathalon at the 1912 Olympic Games, made Walter Camp's All America football team in 1912 and 1913, then played major league baseball for several years before becoming a pioneer founder of and player in the National Football League. But what truly made the 1920s a golden age was a coincidence—the emergence in a few short years of a remarkable collection of what today would be called superstars.

In football there was the University of Illinois's Harold "Red" Grange, who averaged over 10 yards a carry during his college career and who in one incredible quarter during the 1924 game between Illinois and Michigan carried the ball four times and scored a touchdown each time, gaining in the process 263 yards. In prize fighting, heavyweight champion Jack Dempsey, the "Manassas Mauler," knocked out a succession of challengers in bloody battles only to be deposed in 1927 by "Gentleman Gene" Tunney, who gave him a 15-round boxing lesson and then, according to Tunney's own account, celebrated by consuming "several pots of tea."

During the same years William "Big Bill" Tilden dominated tennis, winning the men's singles title every year from 1920 to 1925 along with nearly every other tournament he entered. Beginning in 1923, Robert T. "Bobby" Jones ruled over the world of golf with equal authority, his climactic achievement being his capturing of the amateur and open championships of both the United States and Great Britain in 1930.

A few women athletes dominated their sports during this Golden Age in similar fashion. In tennis

Gertrude Ederle being greased before the start of her 1926 swim across the English Channel. She not only made it, but in faster time than any of the four men who had preceded her.

Helen Wills was three times United States singles champion and the winner of the women's singles at Wimbledon eight times in the late 1920s and early 1930s. The swimmer Gertrude Ederle, holder of 18 world's records by the time she was 17, swam the English Channel on her second attempt in 1926. She was not only the first woman to do so, but she did it faster than any of the four men who had previously made it across.

However, the sports star among stars was "the Sultan of Swat," baseball's Babe Ruth.* Ruth not only dominated baseball, he changed it from a game ruled by pitchers and low scores to one where hitting was more greatly admired. Originally himself a brilliant pitcher, his incredible hitting ability made him more valuable in the outfield, where he could play every day. Before Ruth, John "Home Run" Baker was the most famous slugger; his greatest home run total was 12, achieved shortly before the World War. Ruth hit 29 in 1919 and 54 in 1920, his first year

with the New York Yankees. By 1923 he was so feared that he was given a base on balls more than half the times he appeared at the plate.

The achievements of these and other outstanding athletes had a cumulative effect. New stadiums were built, and they were filled by "the largest crowds that ever witnessed athletic sports since the fall of Rome." Record crowds paying unprecedented sums attended all sorts of events.

Football was the preeminent school sport. At many colleges football afternoons came to resemble religious rites both in their formality, with their cheerleaders and marching bands, and in the fervor of the crowds. A national magazine titled a 1928 article "The Great God Football," and the editor of a college newspaper denounced "disloyal" students who took seats in the grandstand where they could see what was happening on the field rather than encouraging the team by doing their bit in the student cheering section in the end zone.

Tens of thousands of men and women took up tennis, golf, and swimming. The turkey trot, a popular prewar dance, led in the next decade to what one historian called "an imitative swarm of hops,

---

* His full name was George Herman Ruth, but everyone used the nickname "Babe," given him early in his career.

wriggles, squirms, glides and gallops named after all the animals in the menagerie."

Urban-Rural Conflicts: Fundamentalism

These were buoyant times for people in tune with the times—the young, the devil-may-care, factory workers with money in their pockets, many different types. Nearly all of them were city people. However, the tensions and hostilities of the 1920s also found expression in ways related to an older rift in American society, the conflict between the urban and the rural way of life. To many among the scattered millions who tilled the soil and among the millions who lived in towns and small cities, the new city-oriented culture seemed sinful, overly materialistic, and unhealthy. To them change was something to be resented and resisted.

In Baptism in Kansas (1928), *John Stewart Curry viewed sympathetically the sincerity and depth of feeling that marked the revival of religious fundamentalism in much of rural America during the 1920s. Curry was a leader of the rural regionalist painters, seeking, he said, to show the "struggle of man against nature."*

Yet there was no denying its fascination. Made even more aware of the appeal of the city by radio and the automobile, farmers and townspeople coveted the comfort and excitement of city life at the same time that they condemned its vices. Rural society proclaimed the superiority of its ways at least in part to protect itself from temptation. Change, omnipresent in the postwar world, must be resisted even at the cost of individualism and freedom.

One expression of this intolerance was a resurgence of religious fundamentalism. Although it was especially prevalent among Baptists and Methodists, fundamentalism was primarily an attitude of mind, profoundly conservative, rather than a religious idea. Fundamentalists rejected the theory of evolution, indeed, all knowledge about the origins of the universe and the human race that had been discovered during the 19th century.

Urban sophisticates tended to dismiss fundamentalists as boors and hayseed fanatics, yet the persistence of old-fashioned ideas was understandable. In rural areas where educational standards were low and culture was relatively static, old ideas remained unchallenged. The power of reason, so obvious in a technologically advanced society, seemed much less obvious to rural people. Farmers, living in close contact with the capricious, elemental power of nature, tended to have more respect for the force of divine providence than city folk. Beyond this, the majesty and beauty of the King James translation of the Bible, the only book in countless rural homes, made it extraordinarily difficult for many persons to abandon their belief in its literal truth.

What made crusaders of the fundamentalists, however, was their resentment of modern urban culture. While in some cases they harassed liberal ministers, their religious attitudes had little public significance; their efforts to impose their views on public education were another matter. The teaching of evolution must be prohibited, they insisted. Throughout the early 1920s they campaigned vigorously for laws banning discussion of Darwin's theory in textbooks and classrooms.

Their greatest asset in this unfortunate crusade was William Jennings Bryan. Age had not improved the "Peerless Leader." After leaving Wilson's Cabinet in 1915, he devoted much time to religious and moral issues, but without applying himself conscientiously to the study of these difficult questions. He went about the country charging that "they"—meaning the mass of educated Americans—had "taken the Lord away from the schools." He denounced the use of public money to undermine Christian principles, and he offered $100 to anyone who would admit to being descended from an ape. His immense popularity in rural areas assured him a wide audience, and no one came forward to take his money.

The fundamentalists won a minor victory in 1925, when Tennessee passed a law forbidding instructors in the state's schools and colleges to teach "any theory that denies the story of the Divine Creation of man as taught in the Bible." Although the bill passed both houses by big majorities, most legislators voted aye only because they dared not expose themselves to charges that they disbelieved the Bible. Educators in the state, hoping to obtain larger school appropriations from the legislature, hesitated to protest. Governor Austin Peay, an intelligent and liberal-minded man, feared to veto the bill lest he jeopardize other measures he was backing. "Probably the law will never be applied," he predicted when he signed it. Even Bryan, who used his influence to obtain passage of the measure, urged—unsuccessfully—that it include no penalties.

Upon learning of the passage of this act, the American Civil Liberties Union announced that it would finance a test case challenging its constitutionality if a Tennessee teacher would deliberately violate the statute. Urged on by friends, John T. Scopes, a young biology teacher in Dayton, reluctantly agreed and did teach that man was descended from other primates. He was arrested. A battery of nationally known lawyers came forward to defend him; the state obtained the services of Bryan himself. The so-called "Monkey Trial" became an overnight sensation.

Clarence Darrow, chief counsel for the defendant, stated the issue clearly. "Scopes isn't on trial," he said, "civilization is on trial. The prosecution is opening the doors for a reign of bigotry equal to anything in the Middle Ages. No man's belief will be safe if they win." The comic aspects of the trial obscured this issue. Big-city reporters like H. L. Mencken of the *Baltimore Evening Sun* flocked to Dayton to make sport of the fundamentalists. Scopes's conviction was a foregone conclusion; after the jury rendered its verdict, the judge fined him $100.

Nevertheless, the trial exposed both the stupidity

and the danger of the fundamentalist position. The high point came when Bryan agreed to testify as an expert witness on the Bible. In a sweltering courtroom, both men in shirtsleeves, the lanky, rough-hewn Darrow cross-examined the aging champion of fundamentalism, mercilessly exposing his child-like faith and his abysmal ignorance. Bryan admitted to believing that Eve had been created from Adam's rib and that a whale had swallowed Jonah. "I believe in a God that can make a whale and can make a man and make both do what He pleases," he explained.

The Monkey Trial ended badly for nearly everyone concerned. Scopes moved away from Dayton; the judge, John Raulston, was defeated when he sought reelection; Bryan died in his sleep a few days after the trial. But fundamentalism continued to flourish, not only in the nation's backwaters but also in many cities, brought there by rural people in search of work. In retrospect, even the heroes of the Scopes trial—science and freedom of thought—seem somewhat less stainless than they did to liberals at the time. The account of evolution in the textbook used by Scopes was far from satisfactory, yet it was advanced as unassailable fact. The book also contained statements that to the modern mind seem at least as bigoted as anything that Bryan said at Dayton. In a section on the "races of man," for example, it described Caucasians as "the highest type of all . . . represented by the civilized white inhabitants of Europe and America."

Urban Rural Conflicts: Prohibition

The conflict between the countryside and the city was fought on many fronts, and in one sector the rural forces achieved a quick victory. This was the prohibition of the manufacture, transportation, and sale of alcoholic beverages by the Eighteenth Amendment, ratified in 1919. Although there were some big-city advocates of prohibition, the Eighteenth Amendment, in the words of the historian Andrew Sinclair, marked a triumph of the "Corn Belt over the conveyor belt."

The temperance movement had been important since the Age of Jackson; it was a major issue in many states during the Gilded Age, and by the Progressive Era many reformers were eager to prohibit drinking entirely. Indeed, prohibition was a typical progressive reform, moralistic, backed by the middle class, aimed at frustrating "the interests"—in this case, the distillers.

The World War aided the prohibitionists by increasing the need for food. The Lever Act of 1917 outlawed the use of grain in the manufacture of alcoholic beverages, primarily as a conservation measure. The prevailing dislike of foreigners helped the dry cause still more, as beer drinking was associated with Germans. State and local laws had made a large part of the country dry by 1917. National prohibition became official in January 1920.

This "experiment noble in purpose," as Herbert Hoover called it, achieved a number of socially desirable results. It reduced the national consumption of alcohol from 2.6 gallons per capita in the period just before the war to under one gallon in the early 1930s. Arrests for drunkenness fell off sharply, as did deaths from alcoholism. Fewer workers squandered their wages on drink. If the drys had been willing to legalize beer and wine, the experiment might have worked. Instead, by insisting on total abstinence, they drove thousands of moderates to violate the law. Strict enforcement became impossible, especially in the cities.

In areas where sentiment favored prohibition strongly, liquor remained difficult to find. Elsewhere, anyone with sufficient money could obtain it easily. Smuggling became a major business, *bootlegger* a household word. Private individuals busied themselves learning how to manufacture "bathtub gin." Many druggists issued prescriptions for alcohol with a free hand. The manufacture of wine for religious ceremonies was legal; consumption of sacramental wine jumped by 800,000 gallons during the first two years of prohibition. The saloon disappeared, replaced by the speakeasy, a supposedly secret bar or club, operating under the benevolent eye of the local police.

That the law was often violated does not mean that it was ineffective any more than violations of laws against theft and murder mean that those laws are ineffective. Although gangsters such as Alphonse "Scarface Al" Capone of Chicago were engaged in the liquor traffic, their "organizations" existed before the passage of the Eighteenth Amendment. But prohibition widened already serious rifts in the social fabric of the country. Besides

Ben Shahn's Prohibition Alley *is a richly symbolic summary of the seamier side of the "noble experiment." Under a diagram of the workings of a still, bootleggers stack whiskey smuggled in by ship, an operation eyed by Chicago gangster Al Capone. At lower left is a victim of gang warfare; at lower right, patrons outside a speakeasy.*

undermining public morality by encouraging hypocrisy, it almost destroyed the Democratic party as a national organization; Democratic immigrants in the cities hated it, but southern Democrats sang its praises (often while continuing to drink—the humorist Will Rogers quipped that Mississippi would vote dry "as long as the voters could stagger to the polls").

The hypocrisy of prohibition had a particularly deleterious effect on politicians, a class seldom famous for candor. Congressmen catered to the demands of the powerful lobby of the Anti-Saloon League yet failed to grant adequate funds to the Prohibition Bureau. Nearly all the prominent leaders, Democrat and Republican, from Wilson and La Follette to Hoover and Franklin D. Roosevelt, equiv-

ocated shamelessly on the liquor question. By the end of the decade almost every competent observer recognized that prohibition needed at least to be overhauled, but the well-organized and powerful dry forces rejected all proposals for modifying it.

The Ku Klux Klan

The most horrible manifestation of the social malaise of the 1920s was the revival of the Ku Klux Klan. This new Klan, founded in 1915 by William J. Simmons, a former preacher, admitted only native-born white Protestants. The distrust of foreigners, blacks, Catholics, and Jews implicit in this regulation explains why it flourished in the social climate that spawned religious fundamentalism, immigration restriction, and prohibition. In 1920 two unscrupulous publicity agents, Edward Y. Clarke and Elizabeth Tyler, got control of the movement and organized a massive membership drive, diverting a major share of the initiation fees into their own pockets. In a little over a year they enrolled 100,000 recruits, and by 1923 they claimed the astonishing total of 5 million.

Simmons gave his society trappings and mystery calculated to attract gullible and bigoted persons who yearned to express their frustrations and hostilities without personal risk. Klansmen masked themselves in white robes and hoods and enjoyed a childish mumbo jumbo of magnificent-sounding titles and dogmas (kleagle, klaliff, kludd; kloxology, kloran). They burned crosses in the night, organized mass demonstrations to intimidate people they disliked, and put pressure on employers to fire black workers from better-paying jobs.

The Klan had relatively little appeal in the Northeast or in metropolitan centers in other parts of the country, but it found many members in middle-sized cities and in the small towns and villages of middle western and western states like Indiana and Oregon. The scapegoats in such regions were immigrants, Jews, and especially Catholics. The rationale was an urge to return to an older, supposedly finer America and to stamp out all varieties of nonconformity. Klansmen "watched everybody," themselves safe from observation behind their masks and robes. They persecuted gamblers, "loose" women, violators of the prohibition laws, and anyone who happened to differ from them on religious questions or who belonged to a "foreign race."

The very success of the Klan led to its undoing. Factionalism sprang up, and rival leaders squabbled over the large sums that had been collected from the membership. The cruel and outrageous behavior of the organization roused both liberals and conservatives in every part of the country. And of course its victims joined forces against their tormentors. When the powerful leader of the Indiana Klan, a middle-aged reprobate named David C. Stephenson, was convicted of assaulting and causing the death of a young woman, the rank and file aban-

A Ku Klux Klan initiation ceremony, photographed in Kansas in the 1920s. During its peak influence at mid-decade, Klan endorsement was essential to political candidates in many areas of the West and Midwest. Campaigning for reelection in 1924, an Indiana congressman testifies, "I was told to join the Klan, or else."

doned the organization in droves. The Klan remained influential for a number of years, contributing to the defeat of the Catholic Alfred E. Smith in the 1928 presidential election, but it ceased to be a dynamic force after 1924. By 1930 it had only some 9,000 members.

Sacco and Vanzetti

The excesses of the fundamentalists, the xenophobes, the Klan, the red-baiters, and the prohibitionists disturbed American intellectuals profoundly. More and more they became alienated, bitter, and contemptuous of the people who appeared to control the country. Yet their alienation came at the very time that society was growing more dependent on brains and sophistication. This compounded the confusion and disillusionment characteristic of the period.

Nothing demonstrates this fact so clearly as the Sacco-Vanzetti case. In April 1920 two men in South Braintree, Massachusetts, killed a paymaster and a guard in a daring daylight robbery of a shoe factory. Shortly thereafter, Nicola Sacco and Bartolomeo Vanzetti were charged with the crime, and in 1921 they were convicted of murder. Sacco and Vanzetti were anarchists and Italian immigrants. Their trial was a travesty of justice. The presiding judge, Webster Thayer, conducted the proceedings like a prosecuting attorney; privately he referred to the defendants as "those anarchist bastards."

The case became a cause célèbre. Prominent persons throughout the world protested, and for years Sacco and Vanzetti were kept alive by efforts to obtain a new trial. Vanzetti's quiet dignity and courage in the face of death wrung the hearts of millions. "You see me before you, not trembling," he told the court. "I never commit a crime in my life. . . . I am so convinced to be right that if you could execute me two times, and if I could be reborn two other times, I would live again and do what I have done already." When, in August 1927, the two were at last electrocuted, the disillusionment of American

Vanzetti (left) and Sacco were led into court handcuffed in April 1927 to hear the death sentence pronounced. They were electrocuted in August of that year, six years after their conviction.

intellectuals with current values was profound. Some historians, impressed by modern ballistic studies of Sacco's gun, now suspect that he, at least, may have been guilty. Nevertheless, the truth and the shame remain: Sacco and Vanzetti paid with their lives for being radicals and aliens, not for any crime.

Literary Trends

The literature of the 1920s reflects the disillusionment of the intellectuals. The prewar period had been an age of hopeful experimentation in the world of letters. But the historian Henry F. May has shown that the Progressive Era writers, along with most other intellectuals, were beginning to abandon this view by about 1912. The wasteful horrors of the World War and then the antics of the fundamentalists and the cruelty of the red-baiters and the Klan turned them into critics of society. Among the many writers shaken by the execution of Sacco and Vanzetti were the poet Edna St. Vincent Millay, the playwright Maxwell Anderson, and the novelists Upton Sinclair and John Dos Passos. After the war the poet Ezra Pound dropped his talk of an American Renaissance and wrote instead of a "botched civilization." The soldiers of the Great War, he said,

walked eye-deep in hell
believing in old men's lies, then unbelieving
came home, home to a lie,
home to deceits,
home to old lies and new infamy . . .

Yet out of this negativism came a literary flowering of major importance. The herald of the new day was Henry Adams, whose autobiography, *The Education of Henry Adams,* was published posthumously in 1918. Adams's disillusionment long antedated the war, but his description of late-19th-century corruption and materialism and his warning that industrialism was crushing the human spirit beneath the weight of its machines appealed powerfully to those whose pessimism was newborn. Soon hundreds of bright young men and women were referring to themselves, with almost maudlin self-pity, as the "lost generation."

The symbol of the lost generation, in his own mind as well as to his contemporaries and to later critics, was F. Scott Fitzgerald. Born to modest wealth in St. Paul, Minnesota, in 1896, Fitzgerald attended Princeton and served in the army during the World War. He rose to sudden fame in 1920 when he published *This Side of Paradise,* a somewhat sophomoric novel that appealed powerfully to college students and captured the fears and confusions of the lost generation. In *The Great Gatsby* (1925), a more mature work, Fitzgerald dissected a modern millionaire—coarse, unscrupulous, jaded, in love with another man's wife. Gatsby's tragedy lay in his dedication to a woman who, Fitzgerald made clear, did not merit his passion. He lived in "the service of a vast, vulgar, meretricious beauty," and in the end he understood this himself.

The tragedy of *The Great Gatsby* was related to Fitzgerald's own. Pleasure-loving and extravagant, he squandered the money earned by *This Side of Paradise.* When *The Great Gatsby* failed to sell as well, he turned to writing potboilers. "I really worked hard as hell last winter," he told the critic Edmund Wilson, "but it was all trash and it nearly broke my heart." While some of his later work, particularly *Tender Is the Night* (1934), was first-class, he descended into the despair of alcoholism and ended his days as a Hollywood scriptwriter.

Many young American writers and artists became expatriates in the 1920s. They flocked to Rome, Berlin, and especially Paris, where they could live cheaply and escape what seemed to them the "conspiracy against the individual" prevalent in their own country. The *quartier latin* along the left bank of the Seine was a large-scale Greenwich Village in those days. Writers, artists, and eccentrics of every sort lived there. Some made meager livings as journalists, translators, and editors, perhaps turning an extra dollar from time to time by selling a story or a poem to an American magazine or a painting to a tourist.

Ernest Hemingway was the most talented of the expatriates. He had served in the Italian army during the war and been grievously wounded (in spirit as well as in body). He settled in Paris in 1922 to write. His first novel, *The Sun Also Rises* (1926), portrayed the café world of the expatriate and the rootless desperation, amorality, and sense of outrage at life's meaninglessness that obsessed so many in those years. In *A Farewell to Arms* (1929) he drew on his military experiences to describe the confusion and horror of war.

Hemingway's books were best-sellers, and he became a legend in his own time, but his style rather than his ideas explains his towering reputation. Few novelists have been such self-conscious craftsmen or as capable of suggesting powerful emotions and action in so few words. Mark Twain and Stephen Crane were his models, Gertrude Stein, a quirky, revolutionary genius, his teacher. But his style was his own, direct, simple, taut, spare:

> I went out the door and down the hall to the room where Catherine was to be after the baby came. I sat in a chair there and looked at the room. I had the paper in my coat that I had bought when I went out for lunch and I read it . . . . After a while I stopped reading and turned off the light and watched it get dark outside. (*A Farewell to Arms*)

This kind of writing, evoking rather than describing emotion, fascinated readers and inspired hundreds of imitators; it has made a permanent mark on world literature. What Hemingway had to say was of less universal interest—he was an unabashed, rather muddled romantic, an adolescent emotionally. He wrote about bullfights, hunting and fishing, violence; while he did so with masterful penetration, these themes placed limits on his work that he never transcended. The critic Alfred Kazin summed Hemingway up in a sentence: "He brought a major art to a minor vision of life."

Although neither was the equal of Hemingway or Fitzgerald, two other writers of the 1920s deserve mention: H. L. Mencken and Sinclair Lewis. Each reflected the distaste of intellectuals for the climate of the times. Mencken, a Baltimore newspaperman and founder of one of the great magazines of the era, the *American Mercury*, was a thoroughgoing cynic. He coined the world *booboisie* to define the complacent, middle-class majority, and he fired superbly witty broadsides at fundamentalists, prohibitionists and "Puritans." "Puritanism," he once said, "is the haunting fear that someone, somewhere, may be happy."

Contrasting images of two literary stars of the "lost generation": (left) F. Scott Fitzgerald as the thoughtful, introspective artist, and (right) Ernest Hemingway, sportsman and man of action.

But Mencken was never indifferent to the many aspects of American life that aroused his contempt. Politics at once fascinated and repelled him, and he assailed the statesmen of his generation with magnificent impartiality:

BRYAN: "If the fellow was sincere, then so was P. T. Barnum. . . . He was, in fact, a charlatan, a mountebank, a zany without sense or dignity."

WILSON: "The bogus Liberal. . . . A pedagogue thrown up to 1,000 diameters by a magic lantern."

HARDING: "The numskull, Gamaliel. . . . the Marion stonehead. . . . The operations of his medulla oblongata . . . resemble the rattlings of a colossal linotype charged with rubber stamps."

COOLIDGE: "A cheap and trashy fellow, deficient in sense and almost devoid of any notion of honor—in brief, a dreadful little cad."

HOOVER: "Lord Hoover is no more than a pious old woman, a fat Coolidge. . . . He would have made a good bishop."

As these examples demonstrate, Mencken's diatribes, though amusing, were not profound. In perspective he seems more a professional iconoclast than a constructive critic; like both Fitzgerald and Hemingway, he was something of a perennial adolescent. However, he consistently supported freedom of expression of every sort.

Sinclair Lewis was probably the most popular American novelist of the 1920s. Like Fitzgerald, his first major work brought him instant fame and notoriety—and for the same reason. *Main Street* (1920) portrayed the smug ignorance and bigotry of the American small town so accurately that even Lewis's victims recognized themselves; his title became a symbol for provinciality and middle-class meanness of spirit. In *Babbitt* (1922) he created an image of the businessman of the 1920s, gregarious, a "booster," blindly orthodox in his political and social opinions, a slave to every cliché, and full of loud self-confidence, but underneath the surface a bumbling, rather timid fellow who would have liked to be better than he was but dared not try.

Lewis went on to dissect the medical profession in *Arrowsmith* (1925), religion in *Elmer Gantry* (1927), fascism in *It Can't Happen Here* (1935). Although his indictment of contemporary society rivaled Mencken's in savagery, Lewis was not a cynic. Superficially as objective as an anthropologist, he remained at heart committed to the way of life he was assaulting. His remarkable powers of observation depended on his identification with the society he described. He was frustrated by the fact that his victims, recognizing themselves in his pages, accepted his criticisms with remarkable good temper and, displaying the very absence of intellectual rigor that he decried, cheerfully sought to reform.

Lacking Mencken's ability to remain aloof, Lewis tended to value his own work in terms of its popular reception. He craved the good opinion and praise of his fellows. When he was awarded the Pulitzer Prize for *Arrowsmith*, he petulantly refused it because it had not been offered earlier. He politicked shamelessly for a Nobel Prize, which he received in 1930, the first American author to win this honor.

Lewis was preeminently a product of the 1920s. When times changed, he could no longer portray society with such striking verisimilitude; none of his later novels approached the level of *Main Street* and *Babbitt*. When critics noticed this, Lewis became bewildered, almost disoriented. He died in 1951 a desperately unhappy man.

The "New Negro"

Even more than for white liberals, the postwar reaction had brought despair for many blacks. Aside from the barbarities of the Klan, they suffered from the postwar middle-class hostility to labor (and from the persistent reluctance of organized labor to admit black workers to its ranks). The increasing presence of southern blacks in northern cities also caused conflict. Some 393,000 settled in New York, Pennsylvania, and Illinois in the 1920s, most of them in New York City, Philadelphia, and Chicago. The black population of New York City more than doubled between 1920 and 1930.

In earlier periods blacks in northern cities had tended to live together but in small neighborhoods scattered over large areas. Now the tendency was toward concentration in what came to be called ghettos. Harlem, a white middle-class residential section of New York City as late as 1910, had 50,000 blacks in 1914, 73,000 in 1920, and nearly 165,000 in 1930.

The restrictions of ghetto life produced a vicious circle of degradation. Population growth and segregation caused a desperate housing shortage; rents in Harlem doubled between 1919 and 1927. Since the average black worker was unskilled and ill paid, tenants were forced to take in boarders. Landlords converted private homes into rooming houses and allowed their properties to fall into disrepair. The process of decay was speeded by the influx of what the black sociologist E. Franklin Frazier called "ignorant and unsophisticated peasant people" from the rural South, who were inexperienced in city living. These conditions caused disease and crime rates to rise sharply.

Even in small northern cities where they made up only a tiny proportion of the population, blacks were treated badly. When Robert S. Lynd and Helen M. Lynd made their classic sociological analysis of "Middletown" (Muncie, Indiana), they discovered that although black and white children attended the same schools, the churches, the larger movie houses, and other places of public accommodation were segregated. The local YMCA had a gymnasium where high school basketball was played, but the secretary refused to allow any team with a black player to use it. Even the news in Muncie was segregated. Local papers chronicled the affairs of the black community—roughly 5 percent of the population—under the heading "In Colored Circles."

Coming after the hopes inspired by wartime gains, the disappointments of the 1920s produced a new militancy among many blacks. In 1919 W. E. B. Du Bois wrote in The Crisis: "We are cowards and jackasses if . . . we do not marshal every ounce of our brain and brawn to fight . . . against the forces of hell in our own land." He increased his commitment to black nationalism, organizing a series of Pan-African Conferences in an effort—futile, as it turned out—to create an international black movement.

Du Bois never made up his mind whether to work for integration or black separatism. Such ambivalence never troubled Marcus Garvey, a West Indian whose Universal Negro Improvement Association attracted hundreds of thousands of followers in the early 1920s. Garvey had nothing but contempt for whites, for light-skinned blacks like Du Bois, and for organizations such as the NAACP, which sought to bring whites and blacks together to fight segregation and other forms of prejudice. "Back to Africa" was his slogan; the black man must "work out his salvation in his motherland." (Paradoxically, Garvey's ideas won the enthusiastic sup-

port of the Ku Klux Klan and other white racist groups.)

Garvey's message was naive, but it served to build racial pride among the masses of poor and unschooled blacks. He dressed in elaborate braided uniforms, wore a plumed hat, drove about in a limousine. Both God and Christ were black, he insisted. He organized black businesses of many sorts, including a company that manufactured black dolls. He established a corps of Black Cross nurses and a Black Star steamship line to transport blacks back to Africa.

More sophisticated black leaders like Du Bois detested Garvey, whom they thought something of a charlatan. His motives are at this distance unclear, and part of his troubles resulted only from his being a terrible businessman. In 1923 his steamship line went into bankruptcy. He was convicted of defrauding the thousands of his supporters who had invested in its stock and was sent to prison. Nevertheless, his message, if not his methods, helped to create the "New Negro," proud of being black and prepared to resist both white mistreatment and white ideas. "Up you mighty race, you can accomplish what you will!"

The ghettos produced compensating advantages for blacks. One effect, not fully used until later, was to increase their political power by enabling them to elect representatives to state legislatures and to Congress and to exert considerable influence in closely contested elections. More immediately, city life stimulated self-confidence; despite their horrors, the ghettos offered economic opportunity, political rights, and freedom from the everyday debasements of life in the South. The ghetto was a black world where black men and women could be themselves.

Black writers, musicians, and artists found in the ghettos both an audience and the "spiritual emancipation" that unleashed their capacities. Jazz, the great popular music of the age, was largely the creation of black musicians working in New Orleans before the turn of the century. By the 1920s it had spread throughout the country and to most of the rest of the world. White musicians and white audiences took it up; in a way, it became a force for racial tolerance and understanding.

Jazz meant improvisation, and both players and audiences experienced in it a kind of liberation. Jazz was the music of the 1920s in part because it ex-

Beginning in the late 1930s, black artist Jacob Lawrence painted a series of powerful "picture-narratives" dealing with the black experience in America. This painting, of Southern blacks crowding onto northbound trains during World War I, is the first of a 60-panel narrative that Lawrence titled The Migration of the Negro.

pressed the desire of so many people to break with tradition and throw off conventional restraints. Surely this helps to explain why it was so important to blacks.

Harlem, the largest black city in the world, became in the 1920s a cultural capital, center of the "Harlem Renaissance." Black newspapers and magazines flourished along with theatrical companies and libraries. Du Bois opened *The Crisis* to young writers and artists, and a dozen "little" magazines sprang up. Langston Hughes, one of the best poets of the era, described the exhilaration of his first arrival in this city within a city, a "magnet" for every black intellectual and artist. "Harlem! I . . . dropped my bags, took a deep breath, and felt happy again."

With some exceptions, black writers like Hughes did not share in the disillusionment that afflicted so many white intellectuals. The persistence of prejudice angered them and made them militant. But to be militant one must be at some level hopeful, and this they were. Sociologists and psychologists (for whom the ghettos were rich social laboratories) were demonstrating that environment rather than heredity was preventing black economic progress. Together with the achievements of creative blacks, which for the first time were being appreciated by large numbers of white intellectuals, these discoveries seemed to herald the eventual disappearance of race prejudice. The black, Alain Locke wrote in *The New Negro* (1925), "lays aside the status of beneficiary and ward for that of a collaborator and participant in American civilization." Alas, as Locke and other black intellectuals were soon to discover, this prediction, like so many made in the 1920s, did not come to pass.

The "New Era"

Despite the turmoil of the times and the dissatisfactions expressed by some of the nation's best minds, the 1920s was an exceptionally prosperous decade. Business boomed, real wages rose, unemployment declined. The United States was as rich as all Europe; perhaps 40 percent of the world's total wealth lay in American hands. Little wonder that business leaders and other conservatives described the period as a "new era."

The prosperity rested on many bases, one of which was the friendly, hands-off attitude of the federal government, which bolstered the confidence of the business community. The Federal Reserve Board kept interest rates low, a further stimulus to economic growth. Pent-up wartime demand helped to power the boom; the construction business in particular profited from a series of extremely busy years. The continuing mechanization and rationalization of industry provided a more fundamental stimulus to the economy. From heavy road-grading equipment and concrete mixers to devices for making cigars and glass tubes, from pneumatic tools to the dial telephone, machinery was replacing human hands at an ever more rapid rate. Industrial output almost doubled between 1921 and 1929 without any substantial increase in the industrial labor force. Greater use of power, especially of electricity, also encouraged expansion—by 1929 the United States was producing more electricity than the rest of the world combined.

Most important, American manufacturing was experiencing a remarkable improvement in efficiency. The method of breaking down the complex processes of production into many simple operations and the use of interchangeable parts were 19th-century innovations; in the 1920s they were adopted on an almost universal scale. The moving assembly line, which carried the product to the worker, perfected by Henry Ford in his automobile plant in the decade before World War I, speeded production and reduced costs. In ten years the hourly output of Ford workers quadrupled. The time-and-motion studies of Frederick W. Taylor, developed early in the century, were applied in hundreds of factories after the war. Taylor's method was to make careful analyses of each step and movement in the manufacturing process. Then workers would be taught exactly how best to perform each function. Taylor described his system as "enforced standardization" made possible by the "enforced cooperation" of workers. "Taylorism" alarmed some union leaders, but no one could deny the effectiveness of "scientific shop management" methods.

The Age of the Consumer

The growing ability of manufacturers to produce goods meant that great effort had to be made to create new consumer demands. Advertising and salesmanship were raised almost to the status of fine arts. Bruce Barton, one of the advertising geniuses of the era, wrote a best-selling book, *The Man Nobody Knows* (1925), in which he described Jesus as the "founder of modern business," the man who "picked up twelve men from the bottom ranks . . . and forged them into an organization that conquered the world." In 1930 no less a personage than Eleanor Roosevelt, wife of the governor of New York, gave a testimonial for a leading breakfast cereal, which had, she said, "undoubtedly played its part" in building the "robust physique" of her teenage son, John.

Producers concentrated on making their goods more attractive and on changing models frequently to entice buyers into the market. The practice of selling goods on the installment plan helped bring expensive items within the reach of the masses. Inventions and technological advances created new or improved products: radios, automobiles, electric appliances such as vacuum cleaners and refrigerators, gadgets like cigarette lighters, new forms of entertainment like motion pictures. These influences interacted in much the way the textile industry in the early 19th century and the railroad industry after the Civil War had been the "multipliers" of their times.

Undoubtedly, the automobile had the single most important impact on the nation's economy in the 1920s. Although well over a million cars a year were being regularly produced by 1916, the real expansion of the industry came after 1921. Output reached 3.6 million in 1923 and fell below that figure only twice during the remainder of the decade. By 1929 some 23 million private cars clogged the highways, an average of nearly one per family.

The auto industry gave birth to industries that manufactured tires and spark plugs and other products. It consumed immense quantities of rubber, paint, glass, nickel, and petroleum products. It triggered a gigantic road-building program: The 387,000 miles of paved roads in the United States in 1921 grew to 662,000 miles in 1929. Thousands of persons found employment in filling stations, roadside stands, and other businesses catering to the motoring public. The tourist industry profited, and the shift of population from the cities to the suburbs was accelerated.

The automobile made life more mobile yet also more encapsulated. It changed recreational patterns and family life. It created a generation of tinkerers and amateur mechanics and explorers. In addition, it profoundly affected the way Americans thought. It gave them a freedom never before imagined. The owner of the most rickety jalopy could travel farther, faster, and far more comfortably than a monarch of old with his blooded steeds and gilded coaches.

These benefits were real and priceless. But cars came to have a symbolic significance that was equally important; they gave their owners a feeling of power and status similar to that which owning a horse gave to a medieval knight. According to some authorities, the typical American cared more about owning an automobile than about owning a home.

In time there were undesirable, even dangerous results of the automotive revolution: roadside scenery disfigured by billboards, gas stations, and other enterprises aimed at satisfying the traveler's needs; horrendous traffic jams; soaring accident rates; air pollution; the neglect of public transportation, which was an important cause of the deterioration of inner cities. All these disadvantages were noticed during the 1920s, but in the springtime of the new industry they were discounted. The automobile seemed an unalloyed blessing, part toy, part tool, part symbol of American freedom, prosperity, and individualism.

According to his biographer, Allan Nevins, Henry Ford's complex personality included the characteristics of "a wry, cross-grained, brilliant adolescent." Here, on a summer outing, Ford poses as a western badman.

Henry Ford

The person most responsible for the growth of the automobile industry was Henry Ford, a self-taught mechanic from Greenfield, Michigan. Ford was not a great inventor or one of the true automobile pioneers. He was not even the first person to man-ufacture a good low-priced car (that was the achievement of Ransom E. Olds, producer of the "Merry Oldsmobile"). He had two brilliant insights. The first was, in his words, "Get the prices down to the buying power." Through mass production, cars could be made cheaply enough to put them within reach of the ordinary citizen. In 1908 he designed the Model T Ford, a simple, tough box on wheels. In a year he proved his point by selling 11,000 Model

Ts. Thereafter, relentlessly cutting costs and increasing efficiency by installing the assembly-line system, he expanded production at an unbelievable rate. By 1925 he was turning out more than 9,000 cars a day, one approximately every 10 seconds, and the price of the Model T had been reduced to below $300.

Ford grasped the importance of high wages in stimulating output (and selling more automobiles). This was his second insight. The assembly line simplified the laborer's task and increased the pace of work; at the same time it made each worker much more productive. Jobs became boring and fatiguing, and absenteeism and labor turnover developed into serious problems. To combat this, in 1914 Ford established the $5 day, an increase of about $2 over prevailing wages. The rate of turnover in his plant fell 90 percent, and although critics charged that he recaptured his additional labor costs by speeding up the line, his policy had a revolutionary effect on wage rates. Later he raised the minimum to $6 and then to $7 a day.

Ford's profits soared along with sales; since he owned the entire company, he became a billionaire. He also became an authentic folk hero: His homespun style, his dislike of bankers and sophisticated society, and his intense individualism endeared him to millions. He stood as a symbol of the wonders of the American system—he had given the nation a marvelous convenience at a low price, at the same time enriching himself and raising the living standards of his thousands of employees.

Unfortunately, Ford had the defects of his virtues in full measure. He paid high wages but tyrannized his workers. He refused to deal with any union and employed spies to investigate the private lives of his help and gangsters and bully boys to enforce plant discipline. When he discovered a worker driving any car but a Ford, he had him dismissed. So close was the supervision in the factory that workers devised the "Ford whisper," a means of talking without moving the lips.

Success made Ford stubborn. The Model T remained essentially unchanged for nearly 20 years. Other companies, notably General Motors, were soon turning out better vehicles for very little more money. Customers, increasingly affluent and style-conscious, began to shift to Chevrolets and Chryslers. Finally, in 1927, Ford shut down all operations for 18 months in order to retool for the Model A.

His competitors rushed in during this period to fill the vacuum. Although his company continued to make a great deal of money, Ford never regained the dominant position he had held for so long.

Ford was enormously uninformed, yet—because of his success and the praise the world heaped on him—he did not hesitate to speak out on subjects far outside his area of competence, from the evils of drink and tobacco to medicine and international affairs. He developed political ambitions and published virulent anti-Semitic propaganda. He said he would not give 5 cents for all the art in the world.

While praising his talents as a manufacturer, historians have not dealt kindly with Ford the man, in part no doubt because he once said, "History is more or less the bunk."

The Airplane

Henry Ford was also an early manufacturer of airplanes, and though the airplane industry was not economically important in the 1920s, its development in that decade laid the basis for changes in life-styles and attitudes at least as momentous as those produced by the automobile. The invention of the internal combustion gasoline engine, with its extremely high ratio of power to weight, made the airplane possible, which explains why the early experiments with "flying machines" took place at about the same time that the prototypes of the modern automobile were being manufactured. Wilbur and Orville Wright made their famous flight at Kitty Hawk, North Carolina, in 1903, five years before Ford produced his Model T. Another pair of brothers, Malcolm and Haimes Lockheed, built their Model G, one of the earliest commercial planes (commercial in the sense that they used it to take passengers up at $5 a ride) in 1913.

The World War speeded the advance of airplane technology, and most of the planes built in the 1920s were intended for military use. Practical commercial air travel was long delayed. Aerial acrobats, parachute jumpers, wing walkers, and other "daredevils" who put on shows at county fairs and similar places where crowds gathered were the principal civilian aviators of the 1920s. They "barnstormed" from town to town, living the same kind of inbred, encapsulated lives that circus people did, their chief rewards being the sense of independence and pride

A boyish-looking Charles A. Lindbergh during his flying apprenticeship as a stunt pilot in 1925, two years before his solo flight across the Atlantic.

that the successful performance of their highly skilled but risky trade provided.

The great event of the decade for aviation, still an achievement that must strike awe in the hearts of reflective persons, was Charles A. Lindbergh's nonstop flight from New York to Paris in May 1927. It took more than 33 hours for Lindbergh's single-engine *Spirit of St. Louis* to cross the Atlantic, a formidable physical achievement for the pilot as well as an example of skill and courage. When the public learned that the intrepid "Lucky Lindy" was handsome, modest, uninterested in converting his new fame into cash, and a model of propriety (he neither drank nor smoked), his role as an American hero was assured. It was a role Lindbergh detested—one biographer has described him as "by nature solitary"—but could not avoid.

Lindbergh's flight enormously increased public interest in flying, but it was a landmark in aviation technology as well. The day of routine passenger flights was at last about to dawn. In July 1927, a mere two months after the *Spirit of St. Louis* touched down at Le Bourget Field in France, William E. Boeing of Boeing Air Transport began flying passengers and mail between San Francisco and Chicago, using the M-40, a plane of his own design and manufacture. Early in 1928 he changed the company name to United Aircraft and Transport. Two years later Boeing produced the first all-metal low-wing plane, and in 1933 the twin-engine 247, called

by the historian John B. Rae "the first genuinely modern transport airplane."

In retrospect the postwar era seems even more a period of transition than it appeared to most people at the time. Rarely had the old become the new so swiftly, and rarely had the two existed side by side in such profusion. Creativity and reaction, hope and despair, freedom and repression—the modern world in all its unfathomable complexity was emerging.

Milestones

1908 Henry Ford begins production of Model T automobile

1914 Ford establishes the $5 day for auto workers

1919 Eighteenth Amendment outlaws alcoholic beverages

Nineteenth Amendment grants women the vote

1920 Sinclair Lewis, *Main Street*

F. Scott Fitzgerald, *This Side of Paradise*

First commercial radio station, KDKA, begins broadcasting

1921 Margaret Sanger founds the American Birth Control League

1923 Supreme Court overturns the law limiting hours of work for women

1925 Scopes trial in Dayton, Tennessee

1926 Gertrude Ederle swims the English Channel

Ernest Hemingway, *The Sun Also Rises*

1927 Babe Ruth hits 60 home runs

Charles A. Lindbergh flies solo from New York to Paris

Sacco and Vanzetti executed

The Jazz Singer first sound motion picture

Jack Dempsey loses heavyweight boxing title to Gene Tunney

1930 Bobby Jones wins the U.S. and British amateur and open golf titles

SUPPLEMENTARY READING

Titles marked with an asterisk have been published in paperback.

A comprehensive survey of the 1920s is J. D. Hicks, **Republican Ascendancy*** (1960); W. E. Leuchtenburg, **The Perils of Prosperity*** (1958), is equally broad in coverage and more interpretive. See also Geoffrey Perrett, **America in the Twenties** (1982), P. A. Carter, **Another Part of the Twenties** (1977), and John Braeman et al. (eds.), **Change and Continuity: The Twenties** (1968). F. L. Allen, **Only Yesterday*** (1931), is a modern classic, oriented especially toward social history.

Nativism and immigration restriction are covered in M. A. Jones, **American Immigration*** (1960), and John Higham, **Strangers in the Land*** (1955). On changes in the family, see Steven Mintz and Susan Kellogg, **Domestic**

Revolutions (1988); on other social trends, see John D'Emilio and Estelle Freedman, **Intimate Matters** (1988), N. G. Hale, **Freud and the Americans** (1971), Paula Fass, **The Damned and the Beautiful** (1977), and D. M. Brown, **Setting a Course: American Women in the 1920s** (1987). The "new" woman is discussed in William Chafe, **The American Woman** (1972), S. M. Rothman, **Women's Proper Place** (1975), and Nancy Woloch, **Women and the American Experience** (1971). Women workers are dealt with in W. D. Wandersee, **Women's Work and Family Values** (1981). On popular culture, see Russell Lynes, **The Tastemakers*** (1954), Robert Sklar, **Movie-made America** (1976), S. J. Douglas, **Inventing American**

Broadcasting (1987), and P. T. Rosen, **The Modern Stentors: Radio Broadcasting and the Federal Government** (1980).

Fundamentalism is treated in N. F. Furniss, **The Fundamentalist Controversy** (1954), the Monkey Trial in Lawrence Levine, **Defender of the Faith** (1965). The most thoughtful history of prohibition is Andrew Sinclair, **Prohibition: The Era of Excess*** (1962), but see also J. R. Gusfield, **Symbolic Crusade** (1963), and N. H. Clark, **Deliver Us from Evil*** (1976). On the Klan, consult D. M. Chalmers, **Hooded Americanism*** (1965), K. T. Jackson, **The Ku Klux Klan in the City*** (1967), and A. S. Rice, **The Ku Klux Klan in American Politics** (1961).

Sacco and Vanzetti are dealt with sympathetically in all surveys of the period, but Francis Russell, **Tragedy in Dedham** (1962), casts doubt on their innocence.

For the history of blacks, see Gilbert Osofsky, **Harlem: The Making of a Ghetto*** (1965), E. D. Cronon, **Black Moses: The Story of Marcus Garvey*** (1955), and N. I. Huggins, **Harlem Renaissance*** (1971).

The literature of the 1920s is analyzed in Alfred Kazin, **On Native Grounds*** (1942), and F. J. Hoffman, **The Twenties*** (1955). On Fitzgerald, see Arthur Mizener, **The Far Side of Paradise*** (1951); on Hemingway, C. H. Baker, **Hemingway*** (1956); on Mencken, W. R. Manchester, **Disturber of the Peace*** (1951); on Lewis, Mark Schorer, **Sinclair Lewis*** (1961).

The New Era is treated in the general books on the 1920s and in E. W. Hawley, **The Great War and the Search for a Modern Order*** (1979), Daniel Horowitz, **The Morality of Spending** (1985), S. M. Jacoby, **Employing Bureaucracy** (1985), and Roland Marchand, **Advertising the American Dream** (1985).

On Henry Ford, see Allan Nevins and F. E. Hill, **Ford** (1954–1957), and Keith Sward, **The Legend of Henry Ford*** (1948). J. B. Rae, **The American Automobile Industry** (1984), J. J. Flink, **The Car Culture** (1975), and D. L. Lewis and Lawrence Goldstein (eds.), **The Automobile and American Culture** (1984), are full of interesting material.

American Painting, 1920–1960

EDWARD HOPPER *Early Sunday Morning* (1930)

Edward Hopper's aim as an artist was "the most exact transcription" of his "most intimate impressions." With concentrated simplicity, he painted an essence of the American scene, conveying an eerie sense of loneliness. He displayed little interest in foreign artistic trends.

JOHN MARIN *Sun Spots* (1920)

John Marin's watercolor Sun Spots *shows the influence of modern French artists such as Monet and Picasso. In his cityscapes and landscapes, Marin used simplified, scattered shapes to paint nature's "warring, pushing, pulling" forces.*

GEORGIA O'KEEFFE *Cow Skull: Red, White, and Blue* (1931)

In the 1920s Georgia O'Keeffe, America's premier woman painter, moved to the southwest. Like Hopper, she ignored European influences and found her way to artistic abstraction through observation of her desert surroundings.

THOMAS HART BENTON *Romance* (1931/32)

The most controversial and probably the most influential of the so-called regional painters was Thomas Hart Benton. A violently opinionated Populist, Benton denounced the entire modern movement in painting as "dirt." His main subject was his native Missouri, as exemplified in this touching 1931 scene.

737

REGINALD MARSH *Twenty Cent Movie* (1936)

MARK ROTHKO *Number 10* (1950)

BEN SHAHN *Willis Avenue Bridge* (1940)

In the 1930s a group of artists now known as social realists used their work to probe into the lives of ordinary people. Reginald Marsh haunted run-down New York neighborhoods during the depression to record his impressions of bums, honky-tonks, and subways. In Twenty Cent Movie *(top) the front of a seedy movie house pulses with color and action. Ben Shahn is well-known for his powerfully sympathetic portrayals of the abandoned, the homeless, the crippled, and the derelict (bottom).*

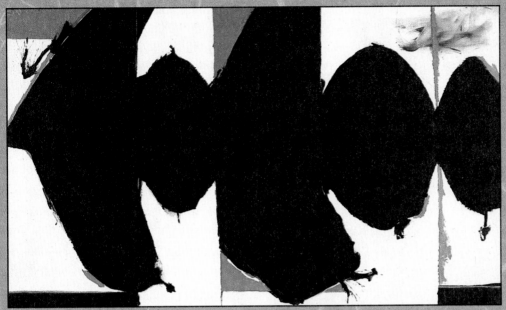

ROBERT MOTHERWELL *Elegy to the Spanish Republic 108* (1965/67)

WILLEM DE KOONING *Women and Bicycle* (1952/53)

Abstract expressionism burst on the art scene in the decade following 1945. Some works, such as Robert Motherwell's Elegy to the Spanish Republic *(above), used actual places and events as a starting point for abstract comment. Mark Rothko pioneered "color-field abstraction," the subtle interaction of areas of color (opposite page). Willem de Kooning, an action painter like Jackson Pollock (see page 887), did a famous series of canvases on the theme of women (right).*

JASPER JOHNS *Target with Four Faces* (1955)

Op and pop artists turned from the emotionalism of most abstract expressionism to a cool and more detached approach. Josef Albers's Homage to the Square: Apparition (*below*) was one of his long series of canvases studying the variations of color and dimension possible within one simple design. Jasper Johns, in Target with Four Faces (*left*), a precursor of pop art, used a repetitively simple and easily identified symbol, the target.

Whatever the art fashion of the moment, representational art is always in demand. The commercial uses of such work are everywhere. And serious easel painting retains a durable human appeal. The modern persistence of the realist tradition is best demonstrated by the work of Andrew Wyeth (*opposite page*), whose paintings portray in careful detail the people and places he knows best.

JOSEF ALBERS *Homage to the Square: Apparition* (1959)

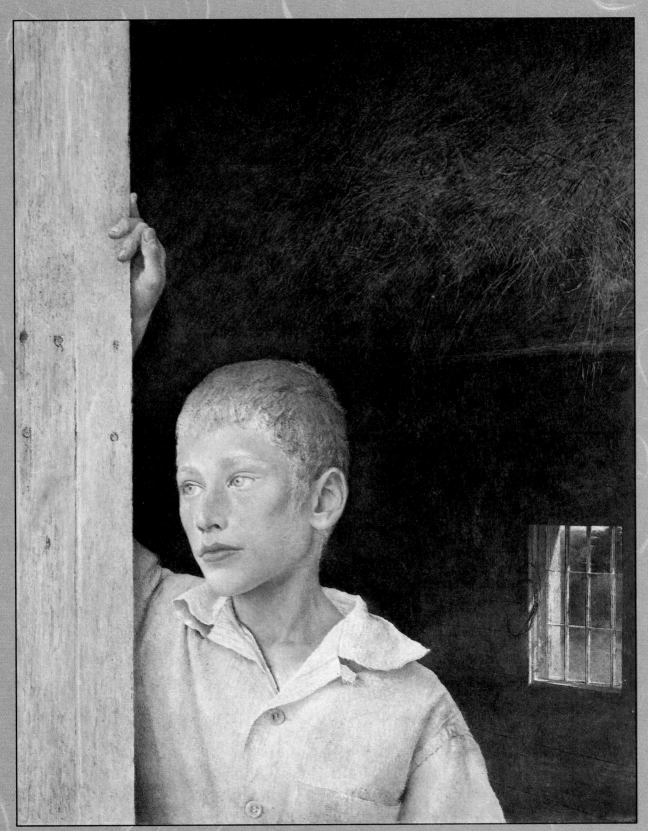

ANDREW WYETH *Albert's Son* (1959)

XXVII

The New Era, 1921–1933

All we can hope to assure the individual through government is liberty, justice, intellectual welfare, equality of opportunity, and stimulation to service.

HERBERT HOOVER, American Individualism, *1922*

I do not approve of stealing, but if I had to make a choice between stealing and starving, I would surely not choose to starve.

DANIEL WILLARD, *president of the Baltimore & Ohio Railroad, 1928*

T he men who presided over the government of the United States from 1921 to 1929 were Warren G. Harding of Ohio and Calvin Coolidge of Massachusetts. Harding was a newspaperman by trade, publisher of the *Marion Star,* with previous political experience as a legislator and lieutenant governor in his home state and as a United States senator. No president, before or since, looked more like a statesman; few were less suited for running the country. Coolidge was a taciturn, extremely conservative New Englander with a long record in Massachusetts politics climaxed by his inept but much admired suppression of the Boston police strike while governor. Harding referred to him as "that little fellow from Massachusetts." Coolidge preferred to follow public opinion and hope for the best. "Mr. Coolidge's genius for inactivity is developed to a very high point," the correspondent Walter Lippmann wrote. "It is a grim, determined, alert inactivity, which keeps Mr. Coolidge occupied constantly."*

---

* Coolidge was physically delicate, being plagued by chronic stomach trouble. He required 10 or 11 hours of sleep a day.

"Normalcy"

Harding won the 1920 Republican nomination because the party convention could not decide between General Leonard Wood, who represented the Roosevelt progressives, and Frank Lowden, governor of Illinois. His genial nature and lack of strong convictions made him attractive to many of the politicos after eight years of the headstrong Wilson. During the campaign he exasperated sophisticates by his ignorance and imprecision. He coined the famous vulgarism *normalcy* as a substitute for the word *normality*, referred, during a speech before a group of actors, to Shakespeare's play *Charles the Fifth,* and committed numerous other blunders. "Why does he not get a private secretary who can clothe . . . his 'ideas' in the language customarily used by educated men?" one Boston gentleman demanded of Senator Lodge, who was strongly supporting Harding. Lodge, ordinarily a stickler for linguistic exactitude, replied acidly that he found Harding a paragon by comparison with Wilson, "a man who wrote English very well without ever saying anything." A large majority of the voters, untroubled by the candidate's lack of erudition, shared Lodge's confidence that he would be a vast improvement over Wilson.

Harding has often been characterized as lazy and incompetent. In fact, he was hardworking and politically shrewd; his major weaknesses were indecisiveness and an unwillingness to offend. He turned the most important government departments over to efficient administrators of impeccable reputation: Charles Evans Hughes, the secretary of state; Herbert Hoover in the Commerce Department; Andrew Mellon in the Treasury; and Henry C. Wallace in Agriculture. He kept track of what these men did but seldom initiated policy in their areas. However, Harding gave many lesser offices, and a few of major importance, to the unsavory "Ohio Gang" headed by Harry M. Daugherty, whom he made attorney general.

The president was too kindly, too well-intentioned, and too unambitious to be dishonest. He appointed corruptionists like Daugherty, Secretary of the Interior Albert B. Fall, Director of the Mint "Ed" Scobey, and Charles R. Forbes, head of the new Veterans Bureau, out of a sense of personal obligation or because they were old friends who shared his taste for poker and liquor. Before 1921

Said President Harding's mother of her son's accommodating ways, "I'm only grateful Warren wasn't born a girl."

he had enjoyed officeholding; he was adept at mouthing platitudes, a loyal party man who seldom questioned the decisions of his superiors. In the lonely eminence of the White House, whence, as President Harry Truman later said, the buck cannot be passed, he found only misery. "The White House is a prison," he complained. "I can't get away from the men who dog my footsteps. I am in jail."

"Regulating" Business

Secretary of the Treasury Mellon, multimillionaire banker and master of the aluminum industry, dominated administration domestic policy. Mellon set out to lower the taxes of the rich, reverse the low-tariff policies of the Wilson period, return to the laissez faire philosophy of McKinley, and reduce the national debt by cutting expenses and administrating the government more efficiently.

In principle his program had considerable merit. Tax rates designed to check consumer spending in time of war and to raise the huge sum needed to defeat the Central Powers were undoubtedly ham-

pering economic expansion in the early 1920s. Certain industries that had sprung up in the United States during the Great War were suffering from German and Japanese competition now that the fighting had ended. Rigid regulation necessary during a national crisis could well be dispensed with in peacetime. And efficiency and economy in government are always desirable.

Yet Mellon carried his policies to unreasonable extremes. He proposed eliminating inheritance taxes and reducing the tax on high incomes by two-thirds, but he opposed lower rates for taxpayers earning less than $66,000 a year, apparently not realizing that economic expansion required greater mass consumption as well. Freeing the rich from "oppressive" taxation, he argued, would enable them to invest more in potentially productive enterprises, the success of which would create jobs for ordinary people. Little wonder that Mellon's admirers called him the greatest secretary of the treasury since Alexander Hamilton.

Although the Republicans had large majorities in both houses of Congress, Mellon's proposals were too reactionary to win unqualified approval. Congress passed the Budget and Accounting Act (1921), creating a director of the budget to assist in preparing a unified budget and a comptroller general to audit government accounts. A general budget had long been needed; previously, Congress had dealt with the requirements of each department separately, trusting largely to luck that income and expenditures would balance at year's end. Mellon's tax and tariff program ran into stiff opposition from middle western Republicans and southern Democrats, who combined to form the so-called farm bloc. The revival of European agriculture after the World War cut the demand for American farm produce just when the increased use of fertilizers and machinery was boosting output. As in the era after the Civil War, farmers found themselves burdened with heavy debts while their income dwindled. In the decade after 1919 their share of the national income fell by nearly 50 percent. The farm bloc represented a kind of conservative populism, economic grievances combining with a general prejudice against "Wall Street financiers" and rich industrialists to unite agriculture against "the interests."

Mellon epitomized everything the farm bloc disliked. Rejecting his more extreme suggestions, it pushed through the Revenue Act of 1921, which abolished the excess-profits tax and cut the top income tax rate from 73 percent to 50 percent but raised the tax on corporate profits slightly and left inheritance taxes untouched. Three years later Congress cut the maximum income tax to 40 percent, reduced taxes on lower incomes significantly, and raised inheritance levies.

Congress also overhauled Mellon's tariff proposals. It placed heavy duties on agricultural products in 1921. The Fordney-McCumber Tariff of 1922 granted more than adequate protection to the "infant industries" (rayon, china, toys, and chemicals) yet held to the Wilsonian principle of moderate protection for most industrial products. Agricultural machinery and other items used by farmers remained on the free list.

Mellon nevertheless succeeded in balancing the budget and reducing the national debt by an average of over $500 million a year. So committed were the Republican leaders to retrenchment that they even resisted the demands of veterans, organized in the politically potent American Legion, for an "adjusted compensation" bonus. Arguing, not entirely without reason, that they had served for a pittance while war workers had been drawing down high wages, the veterans sought grants equal to $1.00 a day for their period in uniform ($1.25 for time overseas). Congress responded sympathetically, but Harding and Coolidge both vetoed bonus bills in the name of economy. Finally, in 1924, a compromise bill granting the veterans paid-up life insurance policies was passed over Coolidge's veto.

That the business community heartily approved the policies of Harding and Coolidge is not surprising. Both presidents were uncritical advocates of the business point of view. "We want less government in business and more business in government," Harding pontificated, to which Coolidge added, "The business of the United States is business." Harding and Coolidge used their power of appointment to convert regulatory bodies like the Interstate Commerce Commission and the Federal Reserve Board into pro-business agencies that ceased almost entirely to restrict the activities of the industries they were supposed to be controlling. The ICC became almost the reverse of what it had been in the Progressive Era. The Federal Trade Commission, in the words of one bemused academic, seemed to be trying to commit hara-kiri.

The Harding Scandals

At least Mellon was honest. The Ohio Gang used its power in the most corrupt way imaginable. Jesse Smith, a crony of Attorney General Daugherty, was what today would be called an influence peddler. When he was exposed in 1923, he committed suicide. Charles R. Forbes of the Veterans Bureau siphoned millions of dollars appropriated for the construction of hospitals into his own pocket. When he was found out, he fled to Europe. Later he returned, stood trial, and was sentenced to two years in prison. His assistant, Charles F. Cramer, committed suicide. Daugherty himself was implicated in the fraudulent return of German assets seized by the alien property custodian to their original owners. He escaped imprisonment only by refusing to testify on the ground that he might incriminate himself. Thomas W. Miller, the alien property custodian, was sent to jail for accepting a bribe.

The worst scandal involved Secretary of the Interior Albert B. Fall, a former senator. In 1921 Fall arranged with the complaisant secretary of the navy, Edwin Denby, for the transfer to the Interior Department of government oil reserves being held for the future use of the navy. He then leased these properties to private oil companies. Edward L. Doheny's Pan-American Petroleum Company got the Elk Hills reserve in California; the Teapot Dome reserve in Wyoming was turned over to Harry F. Sinclair's Mammoth Oil Company. When critics protested, Fall explained that it was necessary to develop the Elk Hills and Teapot Dome properties because adjoining private drillers were draining off the navy's oil. Nevertheless, in 1923 the Senate ordered a full-scale investigation, conducted by Senator Thomas J. Walsh of Montana. It soon came out that Doheny had "lent" Fall $100,000 in hard cash, handed over secretly in a "little black bag." Sinclair had given Fall over $300,000 in cash and negotiable securities.

Although the three culprits escaped conviction on the charge of conspiring to defraud the government, Sinclair was sentenced to nine months in jail for contempt of the Senate and for tampering with a jury, and Fall was fined $100,000 and given a year in prison for accepting a bribe. In 1927 the Supreme Court revoked the leases, and the two reserves were returned to the government.

The public still knew little of the scandals when,

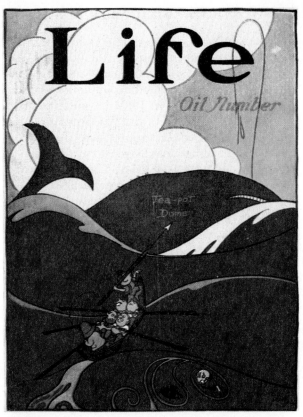

"Thar she blows!!" proclaims the cover of the humor magazine Life's *"oil number" in March 1924, as an honest citizen prepares to harpoon the Teapot Dome conspiracy. A guilty-looking politician has bailed out and is trying to swim clear of the impending fracas.*

in June 1923, Harding left Washington on a speaking tour that included a visit to Alaska. His health was poor and his spirits were low, for he had begun to understand how his "Goddamn friends" had betrayed him. On the return trip from Alaska, he came down with what his physician, an incompetent crony whom he had made surgeon general of the United States, diagnosed as ptomaine poisoning resulting from his having eaten a tainted Japanese crab. In fact the president had suffered a heart attack. He died in San Francisco on August 2.

Few presidents have been more deeply mourned by the people at the moment of their passing. Harding's kindly nature, his very ordinariness, increased his human appeal. Three million people viewed his coffin as it crossed the country. When the scandals came to light, sadness turned to scorn and contempt. The poet e. e. cummings came closer to catching the final judgment of Harding's contemporaries than any historian has:

> *the first president to be loved by his*
> *bitterest enemies" is dead*
> *the only man woman or child who wrote*
> *a simple declarative sentence with seven*
> *   grammatical*
> *errors "is dead"*
> *beautiful Warren Gamaliel Harding*
> *"is" dead*
> *he's*
> *"dead"*
> *if he wouldn't have eaten them Yapanese Craps*
> *somebody might hardly never not have been*
> *   unsorry, perhaps*

Coolidge Prosperity

Had he lived, Harding might well have been defeated in 1924 because of the scandals. Vice-President Coolidge, unconnected with the troubles and not the type to surround himself with cronies of any kind, seemed the ideal person to clean out the corruptionists. After he had replaced Attorney General Daugherty with Harlan Fiske Stone, dean of the Columbia University Law School, the scandals ceased to be a serious political handicap for the Republicans.

Coolidge soon became the darling of the conservatives. His admiration for businessmen and his devotion to laissez faire knew no limit. "The man who builds a factory builds a temple," he said in all seriousness. "The Government can do more to remedy the economic ills of the people by a system of rigid economy in public expenditures than can be accomplished through any other action." Andrew Mellon, whom he kept on as secretary of the treasury, became his mentor in economic affairs.

Coolidge won the 1924 Republican nomination easily. The Democrats, badly split, required 103 ballots to choose a candidate. The southern wing, dry, anti-immigrant, pro-Klan, had fixed on William G. McAdoo, Wilson's secretary of the treasury. The eastern, urban, wet element supported Governor Alfred E. Smith of New York, child of the slums, a Catholic who had compiled a distinguished record in the field of social welfare legislation. After days

However accurate the point that his policies and those of big business were harmonious, the image of "Silent Cal" Coolidge playing a saxophone for the benefit of a Charleston-dancing "flapper" is sheer cartoonist license.

of futile politicking, the party compromised on John W. Davis, a conservative corporation lawyer closely allied with the Morgan banking interests.

Dismayed by the conservatism of Coolidge and Davis, Robert M. La Follette, backed by the farm bloc, the Socialist party, the American Federation of Labor, and numbers of intellectuals, entered the race as the candidate of a new Progressive party. The Progressives adopted a neopopulist platform calling for the nationalization of railroads, the direct election of the president, the protection of labor's right to bargain collectively, and other reforms.

The situation was almost exactly the opposite of 1912, when one conservative had run against two liberals and had been swamped. Coolidge received 15.7 million votes, Davis 8.4 million, La Follette 4.8 million. In the electoral college La Follette won only

his native Wisconsin; Coolidge defeated Davis, 382 to 136. Conservatism was clearly the dominant mood of the country.

While Coolidge reigned, complacency was the order of the day. "The country," the president reported to Congress in 1928, "can regard the present with satisfaction, and anticipate the future with optimism."

Peace Without a Sword

Presidents Harding and Coolidge handled foreign relations in much the same way as they managed domestic affairs. Harding deferred to senatorial prejudice against executive domination in the area and let his secretary of state, Charles Evans Hughes, make policy. Coolidge adopted a similar course. In directing foreign relations, they faced the obstacle of a resurgent isolationism. The same forces of war-bred hatred, postwar disillusionment, and fear of communist subversion that produced the Red Scare at home led Americans to back away from close involvement in world affairs. The bloodiness and apparent senselessness of the Great War convinced millions that the only way to be sure it would not happen again was to "steer clear" of "entanglements." That these famous words had been used by Washington and Jefferson in vastly different contexts did not deter the isolationists of the 1920s from attributing to them the same authority they gave to Scripture. Yet far-flung American economic interests and the need for both raw materials for industry and foreign markets for America's growing surpluses of agricultural and manufactured goods made close attention to and involvement in developments all over the world unavoidable.

Isolationist sentiments therefore did not deter the government from seeking to advance American interests abroad. The Open Door concept remained predominant; the State Department worked to uncover opportunities in underdeveloped countries for exporters and investors, hoping both to stimulate the American economy and to bring stability to "backward" nations. While this policy sometimes aroused local resentments because of the tendency of the United States to support entrenched elites while the masses of peasants and city workers lived in poverty, it also resulted in a further retreat from active interventionism.

The first important diplomatic event of the period revealed a great deal about American foreign policy after the World War. During the war Japan had greatly increased its influence in the Far East, especially in Manchuria, the northeastern province of warlord-dominated China. To maintain the Open Door in China, it would be necessary to check Japanese expansion. But there was little hope of restoring the old spheres of influence, which the mass of Chinese people bitterly resented. In addition, Japan, the United States, and Great Britain were engaged in expensive naval building programs, a competition none of them really wanted but from which no one dared withdraw unilaterally.

In November 1921, hoping to reach a general agreement with China, Japan, and the Europeans that would keep China open to the commerce of all and slow the armaments race, Secretary of State Hughes convened a conference in Washington. By the following February the Washington Conference had drafted three major treaties and a number of lesser agreements.

In the Five-Power Treaty, the United States, Great Britain, France, Japan, and Italy agreed to stop building battleships for ten years and to reduce their fleets of capital ships to a fixed ratio, with Great Britain and the United States limited to 525,000 tons, Japan to 315,000 tons, and France and Italy to 175,000 tons. The new ratio was expected to produce a balance of forces in the Pacific.

The Four-Power Treaty, signed by the United States, Great Britain, Japan, and France, committed these nations to respect one another's interests in the islands of the Pacific and to confer in the event that any other country launched an attack in the area.

All the conferees signed the Nine-Power Treaty, agreeing to respect China's independence and to maintain the Open Door. On the surface, this was of monumental importance to the United States, since it seemed to mean that Japan had given up its territorial ambitions on the Asian mainland and that both the Japanese and the Europeans had formally endorsed the Open Door concept.

By taking the lead in drafting these agreements, the United States regained some of the moral influence it had lost by not joining the League of Nations. The treaties, however, were uniformly toothless. The signers of the Four-Power pact agreed only to consult in case of aggression in the

Pacific; they made no promises to help one another or to restrict their own freedom of action. As President Harding assured the Senate, there was "no commitment to armed force, no alliance, no written or moral obligation to join in defense."

The naval disarmament treaty said nothing about the number of other warships that the powers might build, about the far more important question of land and air forces, or about the underlying industrial and financial structures that controlled the ability of the nations to make war. In addition, the 5:5:3 ratio actually enabled the Japanese to dominate the western Pacific. It made the Philippine Islands undefendable and exposed Hawaii to possible attack. In a sense these American bases became hostages of Japan. Yet Congress was so unconcerned about Japanese sensibilities that it refused to grant any immigration quota to Japan under the National Origins Act of 1924, even though the formula as applied to other nations would have allowed only 100 Japanese a year to enter the country. The law, Secretary Hughes warned, produced in Japan "a sense of injury and antagonism instead of friendship and cooperation."

Hughes did not think war a likely result, but Japanese resentment of "white imperialism" played into the hands of the military party in that nation. Many Japanese army and navy officers considered war with the United States inevitable. "The emotional resentment against America," Akira Iriye writes in *Across the Pacific*, "was reinforced by a more sophisticated view of future Japanese-American conflict that was advocated by some army strategists."

As for the key Nine-Power Treaty, Japan did not abandon its territorial ambitions in China, and China remained so riven by conflict among the warlords and so resentful of the "imperialists" that the economic advantages of the Open Door turned out to be small indeed.

The United States entered into all these agreements without realizing their full implications and not really prepared to play an active part in Far Eastern affairs. "We have no favorites in the present dog fight in China," the head of the Far Eastern division of the State Department wrote of the civil war going on there in 1924. "They all look alike to us." The Japanese soon realized that the United States would not do much to defend its interests in China. The result, in Professor Iriye's words, was "a new image of America, as a country that delighted in moralism . . . but that was not likely to challenge Japan with force."

The Peace Movement

The Americans of the 1920s wanted peace but would neither surrender their prejudices and dislikes nor build the defenses necessary to make it safe to indulge these passions. "The people have had all the war, all the taxation, and all the military service that they want," President Coolidge announced in 1925.

Peace societies flourished, among them the Carnegie Endowment for International Peace, designed "to hasten the abolition of war, the foulest blot upon our civilization," and the Woodrow Wilson Foundation, aimed at helping "the liberal forces of mankind throughout the world . . . who intend to promote peace by the means of justice." In 1923 Edward W. Bok, retired editor of the *Ladies' Home Journal*, offered a prize of $100,000 for the best workable plan for preserving international peace. He was flooded with suggestions. Former Assistant Secretary of the Navy Franklin D. Roosevelt drafted one while recovering from an attack of infantile paralysis. Such was the temper of the times that he felt constrained to include in the preamble this statement:

We seek not to become involved as a nation in the purely regional affairs of groups of other nations, nor to give to the representatives of other peoples the right

Leaders of the Women's International League for Peace and Freedom assembled at the end of World War I to argue in favor of U.S. participation in a worldwide peace organization such as the League of Nations. Jane Addams is in front, fourth from left; at her left is Mrs. Robert La Follette, wife of the Wisconsin senator.

to compel us to enter upon undertakings calling for a leading up to the use of armed force without our full and free consent, given through our constitutional procedure.

So great was the opposition to international co-operation that the United States refused to accept membership on the World Court, although this tribunal could settle disputes only when the nations involved agreed. Probably a majority of the American people favored joining the court, but its advocates were never able to persuade two-thirds of the Senate to ratify the necessary treaty. Too many peace lovers believed that their goal could be attained simply by pointing out the moral and practical disadvantages of war.

The culmination of this illusory faith in preventing war by criticizing it came with the signing of the Kellogg-Briand Pact in 1928. The treaty was born in the fertile brain of French Foreign Minister Aristide Briand, who was eager to collect allies against possible attack by a resurgent Germany. In 1927 Briand proposed to Secretary of State Frank B. Kellogg that their countries agree never to go to war with each other. Kellogg found the idea as repugnant as any conventional alliance, but American isolationists and pacifists found the suggestion fascinating. They plagued Kellogg with demands that he negotiate such a treaty.

To extricate himself from this situation, Kellogg suggested that the pact be broadened to include all nations. Now Briand was angry. Like Kellogg, he saw how meaningless such a treaty would be, especially when Kellogg insisted that it be hedged with a proviso that "every nation is free at all times . . . to defend its territory from attack and it alone is competent to decide when circumstances require war in self-defense." Nevertheless, Briand too found public pressures irresistible. In August 1928, at Paris, diplomats from 15 nations bestowed on one another an "international kiss," condemning "recourse to war for the solution of international controversies" and renouncing war "as an instrument of national policy." Seldom has so unrealistic a promise been made by so many intelligent people. Yet most Americans considered the Kellogg-Briand Pact a milestone in the history of civilization: The Senate, habitually so suspicious of international commitments, ratified it 85 to 1.

The Good Neighbor Policy

The conflict betweeen the desire to avoid foreign entanglements and the desire to advance American economic interests is well illustrated by events in Latin America. "Yankeephobia" had long been a chronic condition south of the Rio Grande. The continued presence of marines in Central America fed this ill feeling, as did the failure of the United States to enter the League of Nations (which all but four Latin American nations had joined). Basic, of course, was the objection to being controlled by foreigners, whether directly when troops were employed or through the economic domination involved in dollar diplomacy. The immense wealth and power of the "Colossus of the North" and the feeling of most Latin Americans that the wielders of this strength had little respect for the needs and values of their southern neighbors were further causes of distrust. However, the evident desire of the United States to limit its international involvements had a gradually mollifying effect on Latin American opinion.

In dealing with this part of the world, Harding and Coolidge performed neither better nor worse than Wilson had. In the face of continued radicalism and instability in Mexico, which caused Americans with interests in land and oil rights to suffer heavy losses, President Coolidge acted with forbearance. His appointment of Dwight W. Morrow, a patient, sympathetic ambassador, resulted in an improvement in Mexican-American relations. The Mexicans were able to complete their social and economic revolution in the 1920s without significant interference by the United States.

Under Coolidge's successor, Herbert Hoover, the United States began at last to treat Latin American nations as equals. Hoover reversed Wilson's policy of trying to teach them "to elect good men." The Clark Memorandum (1930), written by Undersecretary of State J. Reuben Clark, disassociated the right of intervention in Latin America from the Roosevelt Corollary. The corollary had been an improper extension of the Monroe Doctrine, Clark declared. The right of the United States to intervene depended rather on "the doctrine of self-preservation."

The distinction seemed slight to Latin Americans, but since it seemed unlikely that the existence of the United States could be threatened in the area, it was important. By 1934 the marines who had been occupying Nicaragua, Haiti, and the Dominican Republic had all been withdrawn and the United States had renounced the right to intervene in Cuban affairs, thereby abrogating the Platt Amendment to the Cuban constitution. Unfortunately, the United States did little to try to improve social and economic conditions in the Caribbean region, so the underlying envy and resentment of "rich Uncle Sam" did not disappear.

The Totalitarian Challenge

The futility and danger of isolationism were exposed in September 1931 when the Japanese, long dominant in Chinese Manchuria, marched in an army and converted it into a puppet state they named Manchukuo. This violated both the Kellogg-Briand and Nine-Power pacts. China, now controlled by General Chiang Kai-shek, appealed to the League of Nations and to the United States for help. Neither would intervene. When League officials asked about the possibility of American cooperation in some kind of police action, President Hoover refused to consider either economic or military reprisals. The United States was not a world policeman, he said. The Nine-Power and Kellogg-Briand treaties were "solely moral instruments."

The League sent a commission to Manchuria to investigate. Henry L. Stimson, Hoover's secretary of state, announced that the United States would never recognize the legality of seizures made in violation of American treaty rights. This so-called Stimson Doctrine served only to irritate the Japanese.

In January 1932 Japan attacked Shanghai, the bloody battle marked by the indiscriminate bombing of residential districts. When the League of Nations at last officially condemned their aggressions, the Japanese withdrew from the organization and extended their control of northern China. The lesson of Manchuria was not lost on Adolf Hitler, who became chancellor of Germany on January 30, 1933.

It is easy, in surveying the diplomatic events of 1920–1929, to condemn the United States and the European democracies for their unwillingness to stand up for principles, their refusal to resist when Japan and later Germany and Italy embarked on the aggressions that led to World War II. It is also proper to place some of the blame for the troubles of the era on the same powers: They controlled much of the world's resources and were primarily interested in holding on to what they had.

War Debts and Reparations

The democracies did not take a strong stand against Japan in part because they were quarreling about other matters. Particularly divisive was the controversy over war debts—what Germany owed the Allies and what the Allies owed the United States. The United States had lent more than $10 billion to its comrades in arms. Since most of this money had been spent on weapons and other supplies in the United States, it might well have been considered part of America's contribution to the war effort. The public, however, demanded full repayment—with

A merciless France demands war reparations from Germany in this Los Angeles Times *cartoon from 1922. American aid to the German economy had little effect in the face of Germany's enormous reparations costs.*

interest. "These were loans, not contributions," Treasury Secretary Mellon firmly declared. Even when the Foreign Debt Commission scaled down the interest rate from 5 percent to about 2 percent, the total, to be repaid over a period of 62 years, amounted to more than $22 billion.

Repayment of such a sum was virtually impossible. In the first place, the money had not been put to productive use. Dollars lent to build factories or roads might be expected to earn profits for the borrower, but those devoted to the purchase of shells only destroyed wealth. Furthermore, the American protective tariff reduced the ability of the Allies to earn the dollars needed to pay the debts.

The Allies tried to load their obligations to the United States, along with the other costs of the war, on the backs of the Germans. They demanded reparations amounting to $33 billion. If this sum were collected, they declared, they could rebuild their economies and obtain the international exchange needed to pay their debts to the United States. But Germany was reluctant even to try to pay such huge reparations, and when Germany defaulted, so did the Allies.

Everyone was bitterly resentful: the Germans because they felt they were being bled white; the Americans, as Senator Hiram Johnson of California would have it, because the wily Europeans were treating the United States as "an international sucker"; the Allies because, as the French said, *l'oncle Shylock* (a play on the names Uncle Sam and Shylock, the moneylender in Shakespeare's *Merchant of Venice*) was demanding his pound of flesh with interest. "If nations were only business firms," Clemenceau wrote to President Coolidge in 1926, "bank notes would determine the fate of the world. . . . Come see the endless lists of dead in our villages."

Everyone shared the blame: the Germans because they resorted to a runaway inflation that reduced the mark to less than one trillionth of its prewar value, at least in part in hopes of avoiding their international obligations; the Americans because they refused to recognize the connection between the tariff and the debt question; the Allies because they made little effort to pay even a reasonable proportion of their obligations.

In 1924 an international agreement, the Dawes Plan, provided Germany with a $200 million loan designed to stabilize its currency. Germany agreed to pay about $250 million a year in reparations. In 1929 the Young Plan further scaled down the reparations bill. In practice, the Allies paid the United States about what they collected from Germany. Since Germany got the money largely from private American loans, the United States would have served itself and the rest of the world far better had it written off the war debts at the start. In any case, in the late 1920s Americans stopped lending money to Germany, the Great Depression struck, Germany defaulted on its reparations payments, and the Allies then gave up all pretense of meeting their obligations to the United States. The last token payments were made in 1933. All that remained was a heritage of mistrust and hostility.

The Election of 1928

Meanwhile, dramatic changes had occurred in the United States. The climax of Coolidge prosperity came in 1928. The president—somewhat cryptically, as was his wont—decided not to run again, and Secretary of Commerce Hoover, whom he detested, easily won the Republican nomination. Hoover was the intellectual leader, almost the philosopher, of the New Era. He spoke and wrote of "progressive individualism." American capitalists, he believed, had learned to curb their selfish instincts. Voluntary trade associations could create "codes of business practice and ethics that would eliminate abuses and make for higher standards."

Although stiff and uncommunicative and entirely without experience in elective office, Hoover made an admirable candidate in 1928. His roots in the Middle West and West (Iowa-born, he was raised in Oregon and educated at Stanford University in California) neatly balanced his outstanding reputation among eastern business tycoons. He took a "modern" approach to both capital and labor; businessmen should cooperate with one another and with their workers too. He opposed both union busting and trustbusting. His career as a mining engineer had given him a wide knowledge of the world, yet he had become highly critical of Europe—which disarmed the isolationists, who might otherwise have suspected that his long years abroad had made him an effete cosmopolite.

The Democrats, having had their fill of factionalism in 1924, could no longer deny the nomination to Governor Al Smith. Superficially, Smith was

Hoover's antithesis. Born and raised in New York's Lower East Side slums, affable, witty, determinedly casual of manner, he had been schooled in machine politics by Tammany Hall. Smith was a Catholic, Hoover a Quaker; Smith was a wet, whereas Hoover supported prohibition; Smith dealt easily with people of every race and nationality, while Hoover had little interest in and less knowledge of blacks and immigrants. However, like Hoover, Smith managed to combine a basic conservatism with humanitarian concern for the underprivileged. As adept in administration as Hoover, he was equally uncritical of the American capitalist system.

Unwilling to challenge the public's complacent view of Coolidge prosperity, the Democrats adopted a conservative platform. Smith appointed John J. Raskob, a wealthy automobile executive, to manage his campaign. Franklin D. Roosevelt, who ran for governor of New York at Smith's urging in 1928, charged that Hoover's expansion of the functions of the Department of Commerce had been at least mildly socialistic. This strategy failed miserably. Nothing Smith could do or say was capable of convincing many businessmen that he was a better choice than Hoover. His Catholicism, his brashness, his criticism of prohibition, his machine connections, and his urban background hurt him in rural areas, especially in the normally Democratic South.

In the election Hoover won a smashing triumph, 444 to 87 in the electoral college, 21.4 million to 14 million in the popular vote. All the usually Democratic border states and even North Carolina, Florida, and Texas went to the Republicans, along with the entire West and the Northeast save for Massachusetts and Rhode Island.

After this defeat the Democratic party appeared on the verge of extinction. Nothing could have been further from the truth. The religious question and his big-city roots had hurt Smith, but the chief reason he lost was prosperity—and the good times were soon to end. Hoover's overwhelming victory also concealed a political realignment that was taking place. Working-class voters in the cities, largely Catholic and unimpressed by Coolidge prosperity, had swung heavily to the Democrats. In 1924 the 12 largest cities had been solidly Republican; in 1928 all went Democratic. In agricultural states like Iowa, Smith ran far better than Davis had in 1924, for Coolidge's vetoes of bills designed to raise farm prices had caused considerable resentment. A new

Herbert Hoover relaxing during the 1928 presidential campaign. "That man has been offering me advice for the last five years," President Coolidge said of his Secretary of Commerce, "all of it bad."

coalition of urban workers and dissatisfied farmers was in the making.

Economic Problems

The American economic system of the 1920s had grave flaws. Certain industries did not share in the good times. The coal business, suffering from the competition of petroleum, entered a period of decline. The production of cotton and woolen cloth also lagged because of the competition of new synthetics, principally rayon. The industry began to be plagued by falling profit margins and chronic unemployment.

The movement toward consolidation in industry, somewhat checked during the latter part of the Progressive Era, resumed; by 1929 a mere 200 corporations controlled nearly half the nation's corporate assets. General Motors, Ford, and Chrysler turned out nearly 90 percent of all American cars and trucks. Four tobacco companies produced over 90 percent of the cigarettes. One percent of all financial institutions controlled 46 percent of the nation's banking business. Even retail merchandising, traditionally the domain of the small shopkeeper, reflected the trend. The A&P food chain expanded from 400 stores in 1912 to 17,500 in 1928. The Woolworth chain of five-and-ten-cent stores experienced similar growth.

Most large manufacturers, aware that bad public relations resulting from the unbridled use of monopolistic power outweighed any immediate economic gain, sought stability and "fair" prices rather than the maximum profit possible at the moment. "Regulated" competition was the order of the day, oligopoly the typical situation. The trade association movement flourished; producers formed voluntary organizations to exchange information, discuss policies toward government and the public, and "administer" prices in their industry. Usually the largest corporation, such as U.S. Steel in the iron and steel business, became the "price leader," its competitors, some themselves giants, following slavishly.

The success of the trade associations depended in part on the attitude of the federal government, for such organizations might well have been attacked under the antitrust laws. Their defenders argued that the associations made business more efficient and prevented violent gyrations of prices and production. President Harding accepted this line of reasoning. Secretary of Commerce Hoover put the facilities of his department at the disposal of the associations. "We are passing from a period of extremely individualistic action into a period of associational activities," Hoover stated. After Coolidge became president, the Antitrust Division of the Justice Department itself encouraged the trade associations to cooperate in ways that had previously been considered violations of the Sherman Act.

Even more important to the trade associations were the good times. With profits high and markets expanding, the most powerful producers could afford to share the bounty with smaller, less efficient competitors.

The weakest element in the economy was agriculture. Farm prices slumped and farmers' costs mounted. Besides having to purchase expensive machinery in order to compete, farmers confronted high foreign tariffs and in some cases quotas on the importation of foodstuffs. As crop yields per acre rose, chiefly because of the increased use of chemical fertilizers, agricultural prices fell further.

Despite the efforts of the farm bloc, the government did little to improve the situation. President Harding opposed direct aid to agriculture as a matter of principle. "Every farmer is a captain of industry," he declared. "The elimination of competition among them would be impossible without sacrificing that fine individualism that still keeps the farm the real reservoir from which the nation draws so many of the finest elements of its citizenship." During his administration Congress strengthened the laws regulating railroad rates and grain exchanges and made it easier for farmers to borrow money, but it did nothing to increase agricultural income. Nor did the high tariffs on agricultural produce have much effect. Being forced to sell their surpluses abroad, farmers found that world prices depressed domestic prices despite the tariff wall.

In 1921 George N. Peek, a plow manufacturer from Moline, Illinois, advanced a scheme to "make the tariff effective for agriculture." The federal government, Peek suggested in "Equality for Agriculture," should buy up the surplus American production of wheat.* This additional demand would cause domestic prices to rise. Then the government could sell the wheat abroad at the lower world price. It could recover its losses by assessing an "equalization fee" on the wheat farmers.

Peek's plan had flaws. If the price of staples rose, farmers would tend to increase their output. Yet this problem might have been solved by imposing production controls. It was certainly a promising idea; hundreds of organizations in the Farm Belt endorsed it. Farm bloc congressmen took it up, and in 1927 the McNary-Haugen bill was passed, only to be vetoed by President Coolidge. Although he raised a number of practical objections, Coolidge based his opposition chiefly on constitutional and philosophical grounds. "A healthy economic condition is best maintained through a free play of competition," he insisted, ignoring the fact that the scheme had been devised precisely because competition was proving unhealthy for American farmers. Congress passed a similar bill in 1928, and again Coolidge rejected it.

Thus while most economic indicators reflected an unprecedented prosperity, the boom time rested on unstable foundations. The problem was mainly

---

* He soon extended his plan to cover cotton and other staples.

one of maldistribution of resources. Productive capacity raced ahead of buying power. Too large a share of the profits were going into too few pockets. The 27,000 families with the highest annual incomes in 1929 received as much money as the 11 million with annual incomes of under $1,500, the minimum sum required at that time to maintain a family decently. High earnings and low taxes permitted huge sums to pile up in the hands of individuals who did not invest the money productively. A good deal of it went into stock market speculation, which led to the "big bull market" and eventually to the Great Depression.

The Crash of 1929

In the spring of 1928, prices on the New York Stock Exchange, already at a historic high, began to surge ahead. As the presidential campaign gathered momentum, the market increased its upward pace, stimulated by the candidates' efforts to outdo each other in praising the marvels of the American economic system. "Glamour" stocks skyrocketed—Radio Corporation of America rose from under 100 to 400 between March and November. A few conservative brokers expressed alarm, warning that most stocks were grossly overpriced. The majority scoffed at such talk. "Be a bull on America," they urged. "Never sell the United States short."

During the first half of 1929, stock prices climbed still higher. A mania for speculation swept the country, thousands of small investors putting their savings into common stocks.

In September the market wavered. Amid volatile fluctuations, stock averages eased downward. Most analysts contended that the Exchange was "digesting" previous gains. A Harvard economist expressed the prevailing view when he said that stock prices had reached a "permanently high plateau" and would soon resume their advance.

On October 24 a wave of selling sent prices spinning. Nearly 13 million shares changed hands—a record. Bankers and politicians rallied to check the decline, as they had during the panic of 1907 (see page 659). J. P. Morgan, Jr., rivaled the efforts of his father in that earlier crisis. President Hoover assured the people that "the business of the country . . . is on a sound and prosperous basis." But on October 29, the bottom seemed to drop out. More

James Rosenberg, an attorney and amateur artist, sketched this grim view of the Wall Street financial district, October 29, 1929 ("Black Tuesday"), as a Day of Judgment.

than 16 million shares were sold, prices plummeting. The boom was over.

Hoover and the Depression

The collapse of the stock market did not cause the depression; stocks rallied late in the year, and business activity did not begin to decline significantly until the spring of 1930. The Great Depression was a worldwide phenomenon caused chiefly by economic imbalances resulting from the chaos of the Great War. In the United States too much wealth had fallen into too few hands, with the result that consumers were unable to buy all the goods produced. The trouble came to a head mainly because of the easy-credit policies of the Federal Reserve Board and the Mellon tax structure, which favored the rich. Its effects were so profound and prolonged because the politicians (and for that matter the professional economists) did not fully understand what was happening or what to do about it.

The chronic problem of underconsumption operated to speed the downward spiral. Unable to rid themselves of mounting inventories, manufacturers closed plants and laid off workers, thereby causing demand to shrink further. Automobile output fell from 4.5 million units in 1929 to 1.1 million in 1932. When Ford closed his Detroit plants in 1931, some 75,000 workers lost their jobs, and the decline in auto production affected a host of suppliers and intermediaries as well.

The financial system cracked under the strain. More than 1,300 banks closed their doors in 1930, another 3,700 during the next two years. Each failure deprived thousands of persons of funds that might have been used to buy goods; when the Bank of the United States in New York City became insolvent in December 1930, all 400,000 depositors found their savings immobilized. And of course the industrial depression worsened the depression in agriculture by further reducing the demand for American foodstuffs. Every economic indicator reflected the collapse. New investments declined from $10 billion in 1929 to $1 billion in 1932, and national income fell from over $80 billion to under $50 billion in the same brief period. Unemployment, under 1 million at the height of the boom, rose to at least 13 million.

President Hoover was an intelligent man, experienced in business matters and knowledgeable in economics. Treasury Secretary Mellon believed that the economy should be allowed to slide unchecked until the cycle had found its bottom. "Let the slump liquidate itself," Mellon urged. "Liquidate labor, liquidate stocks, liquidate the farmers. . . . People will work harder, live a more moral life. Values will be adjusted, and enterprising people will pick up the wrecks from less competent people." Hoover realized that such a policy would cause unbearable hardship for millions. He rejected Mellon's advice to let the depression run its course.

Hoover's program for ending the depression evolved gradually. At first he called on businessmen to maintain prices and wages. The government should cut taxes in order to increase consumers' spendable income, institute public works programs to stimulate production and create jobs for the un-

employed, lower interest rates to make it easier for businesses to borrow in order to expand, and make loans to banks and industrial corporations threatened with collapse and to homeowners unable to meet mortgage payments. The president also proposed measures making it easier for farmers to borrow money, and he suggested that cooperative farm marketing schemes designed to solve the problem of overproduction be supported by the government. He called for an expansion of state and local relief programs and urged all who could afford it to give more to charity. Above all he tried to restore public confidence. The economy was basically healthy; the depression was only a minor downturn; prosperity was "just around the corner."

In other words, Hoover rejected classical economics. Indeed, many laissez faire theorists attacked his handling of the depression. The English economist Lionel Robbins, writing in 1934, criticized Hoover's "grandiose buying organizations" and his efforts to maintain consumer income "at all costs." Numbers of "liberal" economists, however, praised the Hoover program.

Though Hoover's plans were theoretically sound, they failed to check the economic slide, in part because of curious limitations in his conception of how they should be implemented. He placed far too much reliance on his powers of persuasion and the willingness of citizens to act in the public interest without legal compulsion. He urged manufacturers to maintain wages and keep their factories in operation, but the manufacturers, under the harsh pressure of economic realities, soon slashed wages and curtailed output sharply. He permitted the Federal Farm Board (created under the Agricultural Marketing Act of 1929) to establish semipublic stabilization corporations with authority to buy up surplus wheat and cotton, but he refused to countenance crop or acreage controls. The stabilization corporations poured out hundreds of millions of dollars without checking falling agricultural prices because farmers increased production faster than the corporations could buy up the excess for disposal abroad.

Hoover resisted proposals to shift responsibility from state and local agencies to the federal government, despite the fact—soon obvious—that they lacked the resources to cope with the emergency. By 1932 the federal government, with Hoover's approval, was spending $500 million a year on public works projects, but because of the decline in state and municipal construction, the total public outlay fell nearly $1 billion below what it had been in 1930. More serious was his refusal, on constitutional grounds, to allow federal funds to be used for the relief of individuals. State and municipal agencies and private charities must take care of the needy, he contended.

Unfortunately, the depression was drying up the sources of private charities just as the demands on these organizations were expanding. State and municipal agencies were swamped at a time when their capacities to tax and borrow were shrinking. By 1932 more than 40,600 Boston families were on relief (compared with 7,400 families in 1929); in Chicago 700,000 persons—40 percent of the work force—were unemployed. Only the national government possessed the power and the credit to deal adequately with the crisis.

Yet Hoover would not act. He set up a committee to coordinate local relief activities but insisted on preserving what he called "the principles of individual and local responsibility." For the federal government to take over relief would "lead to the superstate where every man becomes the servant of the state and real liberty is lost."

Federal loans to businessmen were constitutional, he believed, because the money could be put to productive use and eventually repaid. When drought destroyed the crops of farmers in the South and Southwest in 1930, the government lent them money to buy seed and even food for their livestock, but Hoover would permit no direct relief for the farmers themselves. In 1932 he approved the creation of the Reconstruction Finance Corporation to lend money to banks, railroads, and insurance companies. The RFC represented an important extension of national authority, yet it was thoroughly in line with Hoover's philosophy. Its loans, secured by solid collateral, were commercial transactions, not gifts; the agency did almost nothing for individuals in need of relief. The same could be said of the Glass-Steagall Banking Act of 1932, which eased the tight credit situation by permitting Federal Reserve banks to accept a wider variety of commercial paper as security for loans. The public grew increasingly resentful of the president's doctrinaire adherence to principle while breadlines lengthened and millions of willing workers searched fruitlessly for jobs.

As time passed and the depression worsened, Hoover put more stress on the importance of balancing the federal budget, reasoning that since citizens had to live within their limited means in hard times, the government should set a good example. This policy was counterproductive; by reducing its expenditures, the government made the depression worse. The policy was also impossible to carry out because in fact the government's income fell precipitously, creating what the economist Herbert Stein has called "fiscal stimulation by inadvertence." By June 1931 the budget was nearly $500 million in the red.

Hoover understood the value of pumping money into a stagnant economy. He might have made a virtue of necessity. The difficulty lay in the fact that nearly all "informed" opinion believed that a balanced budget was essential to recovery. The most prestigious economists insisted on it; so did business leaders, labor leaders, and even most socialists. In 1932, when the House of Representatives refused to vote a tax increase, the Democratic Speaker compelled reconsideration of the bill by asking all "who do not want to balance the budget to rise." Not a single member did so. As late as 1939 a public opinion poll revealed that over 60 percent of the people (even 57.5 percent of the unemployed) favored reducing government expenditures in order to balance the budget. When Hoover said, "prosperity cannot be restored by raids on the public Treasury," he was mistaken, but it is equally wrong to criticize him for failing to understand what almost no one understood in the 1930s.

Hoover can, however, be faulted for allowing his anti-European prejudices to interfere with the implementation of his program. In 1930 Congress passed the Hawley-Smoot Tariff Act, which raised duties on most manufactured products to prohibitive levels. Hoover signed it cheerfully. The new tariff made it impossible for European nations to earn the dollars they needed to continue making payments on their World War I debts to the United States, and it helped bring on a financial collapse in Europe in 1931. In that year Hoover wisely proposed a one-year moratorium on all international obligations. But the efforts of Great Britain and many other countries to save their own skins by devaluing their currencies in order to encourage foreigners to buy their goods led him to blame them for the depression itself. He seemed unable to grasp what should have been obvious to a person of his intelligence: that high American tariffs made currency devaluation almost inevitable in Europe and that the curtailment of American investment on the Continent as a result of the depression had dealt a staggering blow to the economies of all the European nations.

Much of the contemporary criticism of Hoover and a good deal of that heaped on him by later historians was unfair. Yet his record as president shows that he was too rigidly wedded to a particular theory of government to cope effectively with the problems of the day. Since these problems were in a sense insoluble—no one possessed enough knowledge and intelligence to understand entirely what was wrong or enough authority to enforce the proper corrective measures—flexibility and a willingness to experiment were essential to any program aimed at restoring prosperity. Hoover lacked these qualities. He was his own worst enemy, being too uncompromising to get on well with the politicians and too aloof to win the confidence and affection of ordinary people. As Joan Hoff Wilson has noted, he refused "to backslap, fraternize with local supporters, kiss babies." He had too much faith in himself and his plans. When he failed to achieve the results he anticipated, he attracted, despite his devotion to duty and his concern for the welfare of the country, not sympathy but scorn.

Hitting Bottom

During the spring of 1932, as the economy sounded the depths, thousands of Americans faced starvation. In Philadelphia during an 11-day period when no relief funds were available, hundreds of families existed on stale bread, thin soup, and garbage. In the nation as a whole, only about one-quarter of the unemployed were receiving any public aid. In Birmingham, Alabama, landlords in poor districts gave up trying to collect rents, preferring, one Alabama congressman told a Senate committee, "to have somebody living there free of charge rather than to have the house . . . burned up for fuel" by scavengers. Many people were evicted, and they often gathered in ramshackle communities constructed of packing boxes, rusty sheet metal, and similar refuse on swamps, garbage dumps, and other waste-

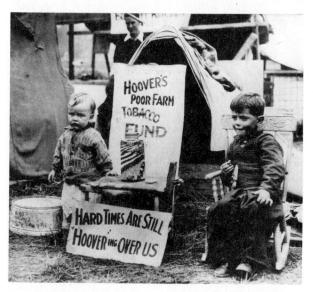

Just as Republican presidents took credit for everything that went well in the 1920s, all that went wrong after the 1929 crash was blamed on their party leader.

land. People began to call these places "Hoovervilles."

Thousands of tramps roamed the countryside begging and scavenging for food. At the same time, food prices fell so low that farmers burned corn for fuel. In Iowa and Nebraska farmers organized Farm Holiday movements, refusing to ship their crops to market in protest against 31-cent-a-bushel corn and 38-cent wheat. They blocked roads and rail lines, dumped milk, overturned trucks, and established picket lines to enforce their boycott. The world seemed to have been turned upside down. Professor Felix Frankfurter of the Harvard Law School remarked only half humorously that henceforth the terms B.C. and A.D. would mean "Before Crash" and "After Depression."

The national mood ranged from apathy to resentment. In 1931 federal immigration agents and local groups in the Southwest began rounding up Mexican-Americans and deporting them. Some of those returned to Mexico had entered the United States illegally; others had come in properly. Unemployed Mexicans were ejected because they might become public charges, those with jobs because they were presumably taking bread from the mouths of citizens. "Capitalism is dying," the phi-

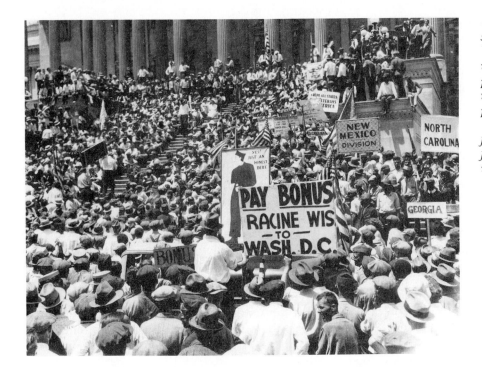

Unemployed veterans on the steps of the Capitol Building, Washington, July 5, 1932, where they demanded early payment of their bonus as a means of combatting the depression. Some 7000 of these "bonus marchers" were later forcibly evicted by the army from their encampment in nearby Anacostia Flats.

losopher Reinhold Niebuhr remarked in 1932, "and . . . it ought to die."

In June and July 1932 some 20,000 veterans marched on Washington to demand immediate payment of their "adjusted compensation" bonuses. When Congress rejected their appeal, 2,000 of them refused to leave, settling in a jerry-built camp of shacks and tents at Anacostia Flats, a swamp bordering the Potomac. President Hoover, alarmed, charged incorrectly that the "Bonus Army" was largely composed of criminals and radicals and sent troops into the Flats to disperse it with bayonets, tear gas, and tanks. The task was accomplished amid much confusion; fortunately, no one was killed. The protest had been aimless and not entirely justified, yet the spectacle of the United States government chasing unarmed veterans with tanks appalled the nation.

The unprecedented severity of the depression led some persons to favor radical economic and political changes. The disparity between the lots of the rich and the poor, always a challenge to democracy, became more striking and engendered considerable bitterness. "Unless something is done to provide employment," two labor leaders warned Hoover, "disorder . . . is sure to arise. . . . There is a grow-

ing demand that the entire business and social structure be changed because of the general dissatisfaction with the present system."

The Communist party gained few converts among farmers and industrial workers, but a considerable number of intellectuals, alienated by the trends of the 1920s, responded positively to the communists' emphasis on economic planning and the total mobilization of the state to achieve social goals. Even the cracker-barrel humorist Will Rogers was impressed by reports of the absence of serious unemployment in Russia. "All roads lead to Moscow," the former muckraker Lincoln Steffens wrote.

Victims of the Depression

Depression is a word used by economists but also by psychologists, and the depression of the 1930s had profound psychological effects on its victims as well as the obvious economic ones. Almost without exception, people who lost their jobs first searched energetically for new ones, but when they remained unemployed for more than a few months, they sank gradually into apathy. E. Wight Bakke, a Yale sociologist who interviewed hundreds of unemployed men in the United States and England during the depression, described the final stage of decline as "permanent readjustment," by which he meant that the long-term jobless simply gave up. The settlement house worker Lillian Wald came to a similar conclusion. Unemployed people at her famous Henry Street settlement, she noticed, had lost both "ambition and pride."

Simple discouragement alone does not explain why so many of the jobless reacted this way. People who had worked all their adult lives often became ashamed of themselves when they could not find a job. Professor Bakke reported that half the unemployed people in New Haven that he interviewed never applied for public assistance no matter how desperate their circumstances. A purely physiological factor was often involved as well. When money ran low, people had to cut down on relatively expensive foods like fruit, meat, and dairy products. In New York City, for example, milk consumption fell by a million quarts a day. In nutritional terms they consumed more carbohydrates and less food rich in energy-building vitamins and proteins. Listlessness (another word for apathy) often resulted.

This psychological depression helps explain why the unemployed were not, in general, very radical. There were meetings and protest marches and also

strikes, but the former were usually organized by people who were not themselves unemployed, and strikers, almost by definition, are people who are refusing to work, not those who have no job to quit. According to the historian Charles H. Trout, when radicals tried to organize protests among unemployed men in Boston, the men "did not take to the streets or plead for a revision of the system, but instead throngs milled outside the Municipal Employment Bureau in the Micawber-like hope that something would turn up."

The depression affected the families of the jobless in many ways. It caused a dramatic drop in the birthrate, from 27.7 per 1,000 population in 1920 to 18.4 per 1,000 in the early 1930s, the lowest in American history. Sometimes it strengthened family ties. Some unemployed men spent more time with their children and helped their wives with cooking and housework. Others, however, became impatient when their children demanded attention, refused to help around the house, sulked, or took to drink.

The influence of wives in families struck by unemployment tended to increase, and in this respect women suffered less psychologically from the depression. They were usually too busy trying to make ends meet to become apathetic. But the way they

A bread line in Chicago. The Great Depression, an English observer said, "outraged and baffled" the nation that took it as "an article of faith . . . that America, somehow, was different from the rest of the world."

used this influence varied. Some wives were sympathetic, others scornful when the "breadwinner" came home with empty hands. When the wife of an unemployed man managed to find a job, the result could be either gratitude and pride or bitter resentment on the man's part, resentment or a sense of liberation on the woman's.

Children often caused strains in families. Parental authority declined when there was less money available to supply children's needs. Some youngsters became angry when their allowance was cut or when told that they could not have something that they particularly wanted. Some adolescents found part time jobs to help out. Others refused to go to school. The truest generalization about the effects of the depression on family relations is probably the most obvious one: Where relationships were close and loving, they became stronger; where they were not, the results could be disastrous.

The Election of 1932

As the end of his term approached, President Hoover seemed to grow daily more petulant and pessimistic. The depression, coming after 12 years of Republican rule, probably ensured a Democratic victory in any case, but his attitude as the election neared alienated many voters and turned defeat into rout.

Confident of victory, the Democrats chose Governor Franklin Delano Roosevelt of New York as their presidential candidate. Roosevelt owed his nomination chiefly to his success as governor. Under his administration, New York had led the nation in providing relief for the needy and had enacted an impressive program of old-age pensions, unemployment insurance, and conservation and public power projects. In 1928, while Hoover was carrying New York against Smith by a wide margin, Roosevelt won election by 25,000 votes. In 1930 he swept the state by a 700,000-vote majority, double the previous record. He also had the advantage of the Roosevelt name (he was a distant cousin of the inimitable T.R.), and his sunny, magnetic personality contrasted favorably with that of the glum and colorless Hoover.

Roosevelt was far from being a radical. Although he had supported the League of Nations while campaigning for the vice-presidency in 1920, during the ensuing decade he had not seriously challenged the basic tenets of Coolidge prosperity. He never had much difficulty adjusting his views to prevailing attitudes. For a time he even served as head of the American Construction Council, a trade association. Indeed, his life before the depression gave little indication that he understood the aspirations of ordinary people or had any deep commitment to social reform.

Roosevelt was born to wealth and social status in Dutchess County, New York, in 1882. Pampered in childhood by a doting yet domineering mother, he was educated at the exclusive Groton School and then at Harvard, where he proceeded, as his biographer Frank Freidel has written, "from one extracurricular triumph to another." Ambition as much as the desire to render public service motivated his career in politics; even after an attack of polio in 1921 left him badly crippled in both legs, he refused to abandon his hopes for high office. During the 1920s he was a hardworking member of the liberal wing of his party. He supported Smith for president in 1924 and 1928.

To some observers Roosevelt seemed rather a lightweight intellectually. When he ran for the vice-presidency, the *Chicago Tribune* commented: "If he is Theodore Roosevelt, Elihu Root is Gene Debs, and Bryan is a brewer." Twelve years later many critics judged him too irresolute, too amiable, too eager to please all factions to be a forceful leader. Herbert Hoover thought he was "ignorant but well-meaning," and the political analyst Walter Lippmann, in a now-famous observation, called him "a pleasant man who, without any important qualifications for the job, would very much like to be President."

Despite his physical handicap—he could walk only a few steps, and then only with the aid of steel braces and two canes—Roosevelt was a marvelous campaigner. He traveled back and forth across the country, radiating confidence and good humor even when directing his sharpest barbs at the Republicans. Like every great political leader, he took as much from the people as he gave them, understanding the causes of their confusion, sensing their needs. "I have looked into the faces of thousands of Americans," he told a friend. "They have the frightened look of lost children. . . . They are saying: 'We're caught in something we don't understand; perhaps this fellow can help us out.' "

Voters responded in a similar manner. "The people," one member of the Hoover administration

A vigorous-looking Franklin D. Roosevelt campaigning for the presidency in 1932. His vice-presidential running mate, John N. Garner, and the conveniently placed post, allowed the handicapped candidate to stand when greeting voters along the way.

noted, "seem to be lifting eager faces to Franklin Roosevelt, having the impression that he is talking intimately to them." But this man then added: "I am glad of his enthusiasm and buoyance but it cannot escape the sense that he really does not understand the full meaning of his own recitations."

Roosevelt soaked up information and ideas from a thousand sources—from professors like Raymond Moley and Rexford Tugwell of Columbia, from politicians like the Texan vice-presidential candidate John N. Garner, from social workers, businessmen, and lawyers. To those seeking specific answers to the questions of the day, he was seldom satisfying. On such vital matters as farm policy, the tariff, and government spending, he equivocated, contradicted himself, or remained silent.

Aided by hindsight, historians have discovered portents of much of his later program in his campaign speeches. These pronouncements, buried among dozens of conflicting generalities, often passed unnoticed at the time. He said, for example:

> If starvation and dire need on the part of any of our citizens make necessary the appropriation of additional funds which would keep the budget out of balance, I shall not hesitate to . . . ask the people to authorize the expenditure of that additional amount.

In the same speech, however, he called for steep cuts in federal spending and a balanced budget, and he castigated Hoover for presiding over "the greatest spending administration in peace time in our history."

Nevertheless, Roosevelt's basic position was unmistakable. There must be a "re-appraisal of values," a "new deal." Instead of adhering to conventional limits on the extent of federal power, the government should do whatever was necessary to protect the unfortunate and advance the public good. Lacking concrete answers, Roosevelt advocated a point of view rather than a plan: "The country needs bold, persistent experimentation. It is common sense to take a method and try it. If it fails, admit it frankly and try another. But above all, try something."

The popularity of this approach was demonstrated in November. Hoover, who had lost only eight states in 1928, won only six, all in the Northeast, in 1932. Roosevelt amassed 22.8 million votes to Hoover's 15.8 million and carried the electoral college, 472 to 59.

During the interval between the election and Roosevelt's inauguration in March 1933, the Great Depression reached its nadir. The holdover "lame duck" Congress, last of its kind, proved incapable of effective action.* President Hoover, perhaps understandably, hesitated to institute changes without the cooperation of his successor. Roosevelt, for equally plausible reasons, refused to accept responsibility before assuming power officially. The nation, curiously apathetic in the face of so much suffering, drifted aimlessly, like a sailboat in a flat calm.

---

* The Twentieth Amendment (1933) provided for convening new Congresses in January instead of the following December. It also advanced the date of the president's inauguration from March 4 to January 20.

Milestones

1921 Budget and Accounting Act
  Washington Disarmament Conference
1922 Fordney-McCumber Tariff protecting
  "infant industries"
1923 President Harding dies; Coolidge
  becomes president
  Teapot Dome and other "Harding
  scandals" exposed
1924 Dawes Plan restructures German
  reparations payments
  National Origins Act establishes
  immigration quotas
1927 McNary-Haugen farm relief bill
  vetoed by President Coolidge
1928 Kellogg-Briand Treaty outlaws war as
  "an instrument of national policy"

1929 New York Stock Exchange crash ends
  "big bull market"
  Young Plan further reduces German
  reparations
1930 Clark Memorandum renounces the
  Roosevelt Corollary to the Monroe
  Doctrine
  Hawley-Smoot Tariff raises duties on
  foreign manufactures
1931 Japanese invade Manchuria
  Hoover Moratorium on war debts
1932 Bonus Marchers in Washington
  dispersed by troops
  Reconstruction Finance Corporation
  created
  Franklin D. Roosevelt elected president

SUPPLEMENTARY READING

Titles marked with an asterisk have been published in paperback.

The political history of the 1920s is surveyed in J. D. Hicks, **Republican Ascendancy*** (1960), and R. K. Murray, **The Politics of Normalcy*** (1973), and more fully in Murray, **The Harding Era** (1969). See also E. W. Hawley, **The Great War and the Search for a Modern Order*** (1979). The labor history of the postwar decade is discussed in Irving Bernstein, **The Lean Years*** (1960), and R. H. Zieger, **Republicans and Labor** (1969).

The best brief biography of Harding is Andrew Sinclair, **The Available Man*** (1965); and D. R. McCoy, **Calvin Coolidge: The Quiet President** (1967), is the best life of Coolidge. David Burner, **The Politics of Provincialism: The Democratic Party in Transition*** (1968), discusses the evolution of the Democratic party in the 1920s. R. F. Himmelberg, **The Origins of the National Recovery Act*** (1976), is good on the trade associations.

Diplomatic developments are summarized in Selig Adler, **The Uncertain Giant*** (1965). See also Akira Iriye, **After Imperialism** (1965) and **Across the Pacific** (1967), and T. H. Buckley, **The United States and the Washington Conference** (1970). Charles De Benedetti, **Origins of the Modern American Peace Movement** (1978) deals effectively with antiwar sentiment, and J. H. Wilson, **American Business and Foreign Policy*** (1971), is an important study of American interest in foreign markets in the 1920s.

On isolationism, see R. A. Divine, **The Reluctant Belligerent** (1965) and **The Illusion of Neutrality** (1962), and Manfred Jonas, **Isolationism in America** (1966). On Latin American relations, see I. F. Gellman, **Good Neighbor Diplomacy** (1979).

Farm discontent is covered in Theodore Saloutos and J. D. Hicks, **Twentieth-Century Populism: Agricultural Discontent in the Middle West*** (1951), and G. C. Fite, **George N. Peek and the Fight for Farm Parity** (1954). On the election of 1928, see Oscar Handlin, **Al Smith and His America** (1958), and E. A. Moore, **A Catholic Runs for President** (1956).

For details on the stock market crash, see Robert Sobel, **The Great Bull Market*** (1968), and J. K. Galbraith, **The Great Crash*** (1961). Hoover's role is analyzed in A. U. Romasco, **The Poverty of Abundance*** (1965), M. L. Fausold, **The Presidency of Herbert Hoover** (1985), Joan Hoff Wilson, **Herbert Hoover: Forgotten Progressive*** (1975), and A. M. Schlesinger, Jr., **The Crisis of the Old Order** (1957). L. V. Chandler, **America's Greatest Depression*** (1970), is a good introduction to the economic problems, but see also C. H. Trout, **Boston, the Great Depression, and the New Deal** (1977), M. A. Bernstein, **The Great Depression** (1987), and J. A. Garraty, **The Great Depression*** (1986), which puts American developments in world perspective.

XXVIII

The New Deal, 1933–1941

I have been having an interesting time here. . . . Washington seems much more intelligent and cheerful than under any recent Administration, but . . . nothing really makes much sense, because Roosevelt has no real policy.

EDMUND WILSON, *critic, 1934*

The royalists of the economic order have conceded that political freedom was the business of government, but they have maintained that economic slavery was nobody's business.

FRANKLIN D. ROOSEVELT, *1936*

The Hundred Days

Something drastic had to be done. The most conservative business leaders were as ready for government intervention as the most advanced radicals. Partisanship, though not disappearing, was for once subordinated to broad national needs. A sign of this change came in February, even before Roosevelt took office, when Congress submitted the Twenty-first Amendment, putting an end to prohibition, to the states. Before the year was out the necessary three-quarters of the states had ratified it. The prohibition era was over.

But it was unquestionably Franklin D. Roosevelt who provided the spark that reenergized the American people. His inaugural address, delivered in a raw mist beneath dark March skies, reassured the country and at the same time stirred it to action. "The only thing we have to fear is fear itself." "Our true destiny is not to be ministered unto but to minister to ourselves and to our fellow men." "This Nation asks for action, and action now." "I assume unhesitatingly the leadership of this great army of our people." Many such lines punctuated the brief address, which concluded with a stern pledge:

> In the event that Congress shall fail . . . I shall not evade the clear course of duty that will then confront me. I shall ask the Congress for the one remaining instrument to meet the crisis—broad Executive power to wage a war against the emergency.

A s the date of Franklin Roosevelt's inauguration approached, the banking system disintegrated—no word less strong portrays the extent of the collapse. Starting in the rural West and spreading to major cities like Detroit and Baltimore, a financial panic swept the land. Depositors lined up before the doors of even the soundest institutions, desperate to withdraw their savings. Hundreds of banks were forced to close. In February, to check the panic, the governor of Michigan declared a "bank holiday," shutting every bank in the state for eight days. Maryland, Kentucky, California, and a number of other states followed suit; by inauguration day, four-fifths of the states had suspended all banking operations.

The inaugural captured the heart of the country; almost half a million letters of congratulation poured into the White House. When Roosevelt summoned Congress into special session on March 9, the legislators outdid one another to enact his proposals into law. "I had as soon start a mutiny in the face of a foreign foe as . . . against the program of the President," one representative declared. In the following "Hundred Days" (Congress adjourned on June 16), an impressive body of legislation was placed on the statute books. Opposition, in the sense of an organized group committed to resisting the administration, simply did not exist.

Roosevelt had the power and the will to act but no comprehensive plan of action. He and his eager congressional collaborators proceeded in a dozen directions at once, sometimes wisely, sometimes not, often at cross-purposes with themselves and one another. One of the first administration measures was the Economy Act, which reduced the salaries of federal employees by 15 percent and cut various veterans' benefits. Such belt-tightening measures could only make the depression worse.

Although Roosevelt never entirely got over the urge to economize in hard times, most of the New Deal programs were designed to stimulate the economy. Untangling the national financial mess was the most immediate task. On March 5 Roosevelt declared a nationwide bank holiday and placed an embargo on the exportation of gold. Within hours after it convened, Congress passed an emergency banking bill confirming these measures, outlawing the hoarding of gold, and giving the president broad power over the operations of the Federal Reserve system.

To explain the complexities of the banking problem to the public, Roosevelt delivered the first of his "fireside chats" over a national radio network. "I want to talk for a few minutes with the people of the United States about banking," he explained. His warmth and steadiness reassured millions of listeners. A plan for reopening the banks under Treasury Department licenses was devised, and soon most of them were functioning again, public confidence in their solvency restored. This solved the immediate problem, but inadvertently (or so it seemed) it also determined that banks should remain private institutions; many experts were urging that the banks be nationalized, a step that would probably have been easily accomplished at that critical moment. Reform, not revolutionary change, had been decided on at the very start of Roosevelt's presidency.

In April, Roosevelt took the country off the gold standard, hoping thereby to cause prices to rise. Before the session ended, Congress established the Federal Deposit Insurance Corporation (FDIC) to guarantee bank deposits. It also forced the separation of investment banking and commercial banking concerns while extending the power of the Federal Reserve Board over both types of institutions, and it created the Home Owners Loan Corporation (HOLC) to refinance mortgages and prevent foreclosures. It passed a Federal Securities Act requiring promoters to make public full financial information

Well-wishers greet the president at Warm Springs, Georgia, in 1933. The Roosevelt "magic," unfeigned and inexhaustible, amazed his associates. "I have never had contact with a man who was loved as he is," reported Secretary of the Interior Harold L. Ickes.

about new stock issues and giving the Federal Trade Commission the right to regulate such transactions.*

After Congress adjourned, the government began buying gold on the open market. When this policy failed to push up the price of gold, Congress in January 1934 passed the Gold Reserve Act, which gave the president the power to fix the price of gold by proclamation. Roosevelt promptly set the price at $35 an ounce, an increase of about 40 percent.

The National Recovery Administration

Problems of unemployment and industrial stagnation had high priority during the Hundred Days. Congress appropriated $500 million for relief of the needy, and it created the Civilian Conservation Corps to provide jobs for men between the ages of 18 and 25 in reforestation and other conservation projects. To stimulate industry, Congress passed one of its most controversial measures, the National Industrial Recovery Act (NIRA). Besides establishing the Public Works Administration with authority to spend $3.3 billion, this law permitted manufacturers to draw up industrywide codes of "fair business practices." Under the law producers could agree to raise prices and limit production without violating the antitrust laws. The law gave workers the protection of minimum wage and maximum hours regulations and guaranteed them the right "to organize and bargain collectively through representatives of their own choosing," an immense stimulus to the union movement.

The NIRA was a variant on the idea of the corporate state. This concept envisaged a system of industrywide organizations of capitalists and workers (supervised by the government) that would resolve conflicts internally, thereby avoiding wasteful economic competition and dangerous social clashes. It was an outgrowth of the trade association idea, although Hoover, who had supported voluntary associations, denounced it because of its compulsory aspects. It was also similar to experiments being carried out by the fascist dictator Benito Mussolini

in Italy and by the Nazis in Adolf Hitler's Germany. It did not, of course, turn America into a fascist state, but it did herald an increasing concentration of economic power in the hands of interest groups, both industrialists' organizations and labor unions.

The act created a government agency, the National Recovery Administration (NRA), to supervise the drafting and operation of the business codes. Drafting posed difficult problems, first because each industry insisted on tailoring the agreements to its special needs and second because most manufacturers were unwilling to accept all the provisions of Section 7a of the law dealing with the rights of labor. While thousands of employers agreed to the pledge "We Do Our Part" in order to receive the Blue Eagle symbol of NRA, many were more interested in the monopolistic aspects of the act than in boosting wages and encouraging unionization. In practice, the codes were drawn up by the largest manufacturers in each industry.

The effects of NIRA were both more and less than the designers of the system had intended. In a sense it tried to accomplish the impossible—to change the nature of business ethics and control the everyday activities of millions of individual enterprises. At the practical level, it did not end the depression. There was a brief upturn in the spring of 1933, but the expected revival of industry did not take place; in nearly every case the dominant producers in each industry used their power to raise prices and limit production rather than to hire more workers and increase output.

Beginning with the cotton textile code, however, the agreements succeeded in doing away with the centuries-old problem of child labor in industry. They established the principle of federal regulation of wages and hours and led to the organization of thousands of workers, even in industries where unions had seldom been significant. Within a year John L. Lewis's United Mine Workers expanded from 150,000 members to half a million. About 100,000 automobile workers joined unions, as did a comparable number of steelworkers.

Labor leaders used the NIRA to persuade workers that the popular president wanted them to join unions—something of an overstatement. In 1935, because the conservative and craft-oriented AFL had displayed little enthusiasm for enrolling unskilled workers on an industrywide basis, John L. Lewis, together with officials of the garment trade

---

* In 1934 this task was transferred to the new Securities and Exchange Commission, which was given broad authority over the activities of stock exchanges.

unions, formed the Committee for Industrial Organization (CIO) and set out to rally workers in each of these mass-production industries into one union without regard for craft lines, a far more effective method of organization. The AFL expelled these unions, however, and in 1938 the CIO became the Congress of Industrial Organizations. Soon it rivaled the AFL in size and importance.

The Agricultural Adjustment Administration

Roosevelt was more concerned about the plight of the farmers than that of any other group because he believed that the nation was becoming overcommitted to industry. The Agricultural Adjustment Act of May 1933, combined compulsory restrictions on production with government subsidies to growers of wheat, cotton, tobacco, pork, and a few other staple crops. The money for these payments was raised by levying processing taxes on middlemen such as flour millers. The object was to lift agricultural prices to "parity" with industrial prices, the ratio in most cases being based on the levels of 1909–1914, when farmers had been reasonably prosperous. In return for withdrawing part of their land from cultivation, farmers received "rental" payments from the Agricultural Adjustment Administration (AAA).

Since the 1933 crops were growing when the law was passed, Secretary of Agriculture Henry A. Wallace, son of Harding's secretary of agriculture and himself an experienced farmer and plant geneticist, decided to pay farmers to destroy the crops in the field. Cotton planters plowed up 10 million acres, receiving $100 million in return. Six million baby pigs and 200,000 pregnant sows were slaughtered. Such ruthlessness appalled observers, particularly when they thought of the millions of hungry Americans who could have eaten all that pork.

Thereafter, limitation of acreage proved sufficient to raise some agricultural prices considerably. Tobacco farmers benefited, and so did those who raised corn and hogs. The price of wheat also rose, though more because of bad harvests than the AAA program. But dairy farmers and cattlemen were hurt by the law, as were the railroads (which had less freight to haul) and, of course, consumers. Many

farmers insisted that NRA was raising the cost of manufactured goods more than AAA was raising the prices they received for their crops. "While the farmer is losing his pants to his creditors," one Iowan complained, "NRA is rolling up his shirt. [Soon] we'll have a nudist colony."

A far more serious weakness of the program was its failure to assist tenant farmers and sharecroppers, many of whom lost their livelihoods completely when owners took land out of production to obtain AAA payments. Yet acreage restrictions and mortgage relief helped thousands. The law was a remarkable attempt to bring order to the chaotic agricultural economy. One New Deal official called it "the greatest single experiment in economic planning under capitalist conditions ever attempted by a democracy in times of peace." This was an overstatement. The AAA was a drastic change of American policy, but foreign producers of coffee, sugar, tea, rubber, and other staples had adopted the same techniques of restricting output and subsidizing growers well before the United States did.

The Tennessee Valley Authority

Another striking achievement of the Hundred Days was the creation of the Tennessee Valley Authority (TVA). During World War I the government had constructed a hydroelectric plant at Muscle Shoals, Alabama, to provide power for factories manufacturing synthetic nitrate explosives. After 1920, farm groups and public power enthusiasts, led by Senator George W. Norris of Nebraska, had blocked administration plans to turn these facilities over to private capitalists, but their efforts to have the site operated by the government had been defeated by presidential vetoes.

Roosevelt wanted to have the entire Tennessee Valley area incorporated into a broad experiment in social planning. Besides expanding the hydroelectric plants at Muscle Shoals and developing nitrate manufacturing in order to produce cheap fertilizers, he envisioned a coordinated program of soil conservation, reforestation, and industrialization.

Over the objections of private power companies, led by Wendell L. Willkie of the Commonwealth and Southern Corporation, Congress passed the TVA Act in May 1933. This law created a board authorized to build dams, power plants, and trans-

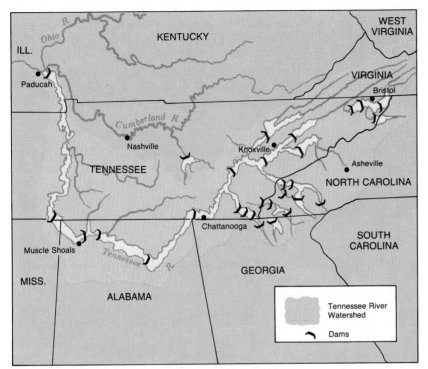

THE TENNESSEE VALLEY AUTHORITY

mission lines and to sell fertilizers and electricity to individuals and local communities. The board could undertake flood control, soil conservation, and reforestation projects and improve the navigation of the river. TVA never became the comprehensive regional planning organization some of its sponsors had anticipated, but it improved the standard of living of millions of inhabitants of the valley. In addition to producing electricity and fertilizers and providing a "yardstick" whereby the efficiency—and thus the rates—of private power companies could be tested, it took on other functions, ranging from the eradication of malaria to the development of recreational facilities.

The New Deal Spirit

By the end of the Hundred Days the country had made up its mind about Roosevelt's New Deal, and despite the vicissitudes of the next decade, it never really changed it. A large majority labeled the New Deal a solid success. Considerable recovery had taken place, but more basic was the fact that Roosevelt, recruiting an army of forceful officials to staff the new government agencies, had infused his administration with a spirit of bustle and optimism. Dozens of people who lived through those stirring times have left records that reveal the New Deal spirit. The director of the presidential Secret Service unit, returning to the White House on inauguration day after escorting Herbert Hoover to the railroad station, found the executive mansion "transformed during my absence into a gay place, full of people who oozed confidence."

"Come at once to Washington," Senator Robert La Follette, Jr., son of "Fighting Bob," telegraphed Donald Richberg, an old Theodore Roosevelt progressive. "Great things are under way." "I have been in a constant spin of activity," another New Dealer wrote a friend. "I feel as if I were alive all over, and that this cockeyed world is taking us somewhere." Justice Harlan Fiske Stone of the Supreme Court recorded: "Never was there such a change in the transfer of government."

Although Roosevelt was not much of an intellectual, his openness to suggestion made him eager to draw on the ideas and energies of experts of all sorts. New Deal agencies soon teemed with college professors and young lawyers without political experience.

The New Deal lacked any consistent ideological base. Though the so-called Brains Trust (a group headed by Raymond Moley, a Columbia political scientist, that included Columbia economists Rexford G. Tugwell and Adolf A. Berle, Jr., and a number of others) attracted a great deal of attention, theorists never impressed Roosevelt. His New Deal drew on the old populist tradition, as seen in its antipathy to bankers and its willingness to adopt schemes for inflating the currency; on the New Nationalism of Theodore Roosevelt in its dislike of competition and its de-emphasis of the antitrust laws; and on the ideas of social workers trained in the Progressive Era. Techniques developed by the Wilsonians also found places in the system: Louis D. Brandeis had considerable influence on Roosevelt's financial reforms, and New Deal labor policy grew directly out of the experience of the War Labor Board of 1917–1918.

Within the administrative maze that Roosevelt created, rival bureaucrats battled to enforce their views. The "spenders," led by Tugwell, clashed with advocates of strict economy, who gathered around Lewis Douglas, director of the budget. Blithely disregarding logically irreconcilable differences, Roosevelt mediated between the factions. Washington became a battleground for dozens of special interest groups: the Farm Bureau Federation, the unions, the trade associations, the silver miners. William E. Leuchtenburg has described New Deal policy as "interest-group democracy"; another historian, Ellis W. Hawley, called it "counterorganization" policy aimed at creating "monopoly power" among groups previously unorganized, such as farmers and industrial workers. While, as Leuchtenburg says, the system was superior to that of Roosevelt's predecessors—who had allowed one interest, big business, to predominate—it slighted the unorganized majority. NRA aimed frankly at raising the prices paid by consumers of manufactured goods; the AAA processing tax came ultimately from the pocketbooks of ordinary citizens.

The Unemployed

At least 9 million persons were still without work in 1934 and hundreds of thousands of them were in real need. Here is the recollection of Malcolm Little, later famous as the radical black leader Malcolm X.

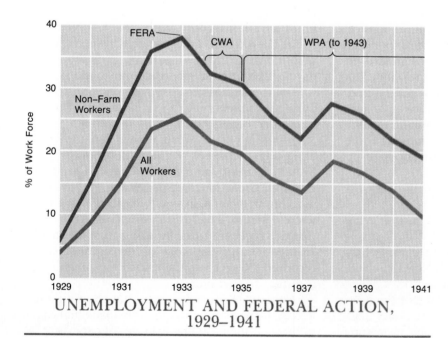

Unemployment of non-farm workers reached nearly 40 percent by early 1933. The Federal Employment Relief Act (FERA) of May 1933 was followed by the Civil Works Administration (CWA) later that year, and in turn by the Works Progress Administration (WPA) in April of 1935.

UNEMPLOYMENT AND FEDERAL ACTION, 1929–1941

By 1934, we really began to suffer. This was about the worst depression year, and no one we knew had enough to eat or live on. . . . There was a bakery where, for a nickel, a couple of us children would buy a tall flour sack of day-old bread and cookies. . . . But there were times when there wasn't even a nickel and we would be so hungry we were dizzy. My mother would boil a big pot of dandelion greens and we would eat that.

Yet the Democrats confounded the political experts, including their own, by increasing their already large majorities in both houses of Congress in the 1934 elections. All the evidence indicates that most of the jobless continued to support the administration. Their loyalty can best be explained by Roosevelt's unemployment policies.

In May 1933 Congress had established the Federal Emergency Relief Administration and given it $500 million to be dispensed through state relief organizations. Roosevelt appointed Harry L. Hopkins, an eccentric but brilliant and dedicated social worker, to direct the FERA. Hopkins insisted that the unemployed needed jobs, not handouts. In November he persuaded Roosevelt to create the Civil Works Administration, and within a month he put more than 4 million persons to work building and repairing roads and public buildings, teaching, dec-

orating the walls of post offices with murals, and applying their special skills in dozens of other ways.

The cost of this program frightened Roosevelt—Hopkins spent about $1 billion in less than five months—and he soon abolished the CWA. But an extensive public works program was continued throughout 1934 under FERA. Despite charges that many of the projects were "boondoggles," thousands of roads, bridges, schools, and other structures were built or refurbished.

After the 1934 elections, Roosevelt committed himself to the Hopkins approach. In May 1935 he put Hopkins in charge of the Works Progress Administration (WPA). By the time this agency was disbanded in 1943 it had spent $11 billion and found employment for 8.5 million persons. Besides building public works, the WPA developed the Federal Theater Project, which put thousands of actors, directors, and stagehands to work; the Federal Writers' Project, which turned out valuable guidebooks, collected local lore, and published about 1,000 books and pamphlets; and the Federal Art Project, which employed needy painters and sculptors. In addition, the National Youth Administration created part-time jobs for more than 2 million high school and college students.

WPA did not reach all the unemployed. At no

Otherwise unemployed workers removing curbstones in a street-widening project. WPA undertakings extended from carving nature trails in wilderness regions of the Far West to constructing bridges in the heart of New York City.

time during the New Deal years did unemployment fall below 10 percent of the work force, and in some places it was much higher. Unemployment in Boston, for instance, ranged between 20 and 30 percent throughout the 1930s. Like so many New Deal programs, WPA did not go far enough, chiefly because Roosevelt could not escape his fear of unbalancing the budget drastically. Halfway measures did not provide the massive stimulus the economy needed. The president also hesitated to undertake projects that might compete with private enterprises for fear of offending business. Yet his caution did him no good politically; the business interests he sought to placate were becoming increasingly hostile to the New Deal.

Literature in the Depression

Some American novelists found Soviet communism attractive and wrote "proletarian" novels in which ordinary workers were the heroes, and stylistic niceties gave way to the rough language of the street and the factory. Most of these books were of little artistic merit, and none achieved great commercial success. The best of the depression writers avoided the party line, though they were critical of many aspects of American life. One was John Dos Passos, author of the trilogy *U.S.A.* (1930–1936).

Dos Passos came from a well-to-do family of Portuguese descent. He was educated at Harvard and drove an ambulance in France during the Great War. *U.S.A.* was a massive intricately constructed work with an anticapitalist and deeply pessimistic point of view. It portrayed American society between 1900 and 1930 in broad perspective, interweaving the stories of five major characters and a galaxy of lesser figures. Throughout the narrative Dos Passos scattered capsule sketches of famous people, ranging from Andrew Carnegie and William Jennings Bryan to the movie idol Rudolph Valentino and the architect Frank Lloyd Wright. He included "newsreel" sections recounting events of the period and "camera eye" sections in which he revealed his personal reactions to the passing parade.

Dos Passos's method was relentless, cold, methodical—utterly realistic. He had no sympathy for his characters or their world. *U.S.A.* was a monument to the despair and anger of liberals confronting the Great Depression. After the depression, however, Dos Passos rapidly abandoned his radical views.

The novel that best portrayed the desperate plight of the millions impoverished by the depression was *The Grapes of Wrath* (1939) by John Steinbeck, which described the fate of the Joads, an Oklahoma farm family driven by drought and bad times to abandon their land and become migratory laborers in California. Steinbeck captured the patient bewilderment of the downtrodden, the brutality bred of fear that characterized their exploiters, and the furious resentments of the radicals of the 1930s. He depicted the parching blackness of the Oklahoma dust bowl, the grandeur of California, the backbreaking toil of the migrant fruit pickers, and the ultimate indignation of a people repeatedly degraded. "In the eyes of the hungry there is a growing wrath. In the souls of the people the grapes of wrath are filling and growing heavy, growing heavy for the vintage."

Like so many other writers of the decade, Steinbeck was an angry man. "There is a crime here that goes beyond denunciation," he wrote. He had the compassion that Dos Passos lacked, and this quality raised *The Grapes of Wrath* to the level of great tragedy. In other works, such as *Tortilla Flat* (1935) and *The Long Valley* (1938), Steinbeck described the life of California cannery workers and ranchers with moving warmth without becoming overly sentimental.

Although his work was less political than that of Dos Passos or Steinbeck, Thomas Wolfe, a passionate, intensely troubled young man of vast but undisciplined talents, sought to describe the kaleidoscopic character of American life, the limitless variety of the nation. "I will know this country when I am through as I know the palm of my hand, and I will put it on paper and make it true and beautiful," he boasted.

During the last ten years of his short life Wolfe wrote four novels: *Look Homeward, Angel* (1929), *Of Time and the River* (1935), and two published posthumously, *The Web and the Rock* (1939) and *You Can't Go Home Again* (1940). All were autobiographical and to some extent repetitious, for he was an unabashed egoist. Nevertheless, he was a superb interpreter of contemporary society. He crammed his pages with unforgettable vignettes—a train hurtling across the New Jersey meadows in the dark, a young woman clutching her skirt on a windswept corner, a group of derelicts huddled for shelter in a public toilet on a frigid night. And no writer caught more clearly the frantic pace and confusion of the great cities, the despair of the depression, the divided nature of human beings, their fears and hopes, their undirected, uncontrollable energy.

William Faulkner, probably the finest modern American novelist, responded to the era in still another way. Born in 1897, within a year of Fitzgerald and Hemingway, like Wolfe he attained literary maturity only in the 1930s. After service in the Canadian air force in World War I, he returned to his native Mississippi, working at a series of odd jobs and publishing relatively inconsequential poetry and fiction. Suddenly, between 1929 and 1932, he burst into prominence with four major novels: *The Sound and the Fury, As I Lay Dying, Sanctuary,* and *Light in August.*

Faulkner created a local world, Yoknapatawpha County, and peopled it with some of the most remarkable characters in American fiction—among

Accepting the Nobel Prize in literature, Faulkner spoke of a lifelong attempt "to create out of the materials of the human spirit something which did not exist before."

"I am completely partisan," Steinbeck wrote. "Every effort I can bring to bear is . . . at the call of the common working people."

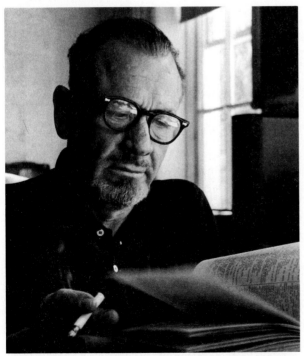

them the Sartoris family, typical of the old southern aristocracy worn down at the heels, and the Snopes clan, shrewd, unscrupulous, boorish representatives of the new day. He pictured the South's poverty and its pride, its dreadful racial problem, the guilt and obscure passions plaguing white and black alike. No contemporary excelled him as a commentator on the multiple dilemmas of modern life. His characters are possessed, driven to pursue high ideals yet weighted down with their awareness of their inadequacies and their sinfulness. They are imprisoned in their surroundings, no matter how they may strive to escape them. The French novelist Simone de Beauvoir caught this aspect of Faulkner's work when she wrote that he "offered us a glimpse of fascinating depths . . . in those secret, shameless fires that rage in the bellies of men and women alike."

Faulkner, like Dos Passos, was essentially a pessimist. His characters continually experienced emotions too intense to be bearable, often too profound and too subtle for the natures he had given them. Nevertheless, his stature was beyond question, and unlike so many other novelists of the period, he maintained a high level in his later years. He was awarded the 1949 Nobel Prize for literature.

The Extremists

Roosevelt's moderation provoked extremists both on the left and on the right. The most formidable was Louisiana's Senator Huey Long, the "Kingfish." Raised on a farm in northern Louisiana, Long was successively a traveling salesman, a lawyer, state railroad commissioner, governor, and, after 1930, United States senator. By 1933 he ruled Louisiana with the absolutism of an oriental monarch. Long was controversial in his day, and so he has remained. He was certainly a demagogue. Yet the plight of all poor people concerned him deeply. More important, he tried to do something about it.

Long did not question segregation or white supremacy, nor did he suggest that Louisiana blacks should be allowed to vote. He used the word *nigger* with total unself-consciousness, even when addressing northern black leaders. But he treated black-baiters with scathing contempt. When Hiram W. Evans, imperial wizard of the Ku Klux Klan, announced his intention to campaign against him in Louisiana, Long told reporters: "Quote me as saying that that Imperial bastard will never set foot in Louisiana, and that when I call him a sonofabitch I am not using profanity, but am referring to the circumstances of his birth."

As a reformer, Long stood in the populist tradition; he hated bankers and "the interests." He believed that poor people, regardless of color, should have a chance to earn a decent living and get an education. His arguments were simplistic, patronizing, possibly insincere, but effective. "Don't say I'm working for niggers," he told one northern journalist. "I'm for the poor man—all poor men. Black and white, they all gotta have a chance. . . . 'Every Man a King'—that's my slogan."

Raffish, totally unrestrained, yet shrewd—a fellow southern politician called him "the smartest lunatic I ever saw"—Long had supported the New Deal at the start. But partly because he thought Roosevelt too conservative and partly because of his

Senator Huey Long in a typical energetic speaking pose. Both his politics and his flamboyant, grass-roots style were in the Populist tradition.

own ambition, he soon broke with the administration. While Roosevelt was probably more hostile to the big financiers than to any other interest, Long denounced him as "a phoney" and a stooge of Wall Street. "I can take him," he boasted in a typical sally. "His mother's watching him, and she won't let him go too far, but I ain't got no mother left, and if I had, she'd think anything I said was all right."

By 1935 Long's "Share Our Wealth" movement had a membership of over 4.6 million. His program called for the confiscation of family fortunes of more than $5 million and a tax of 100 percent on incomes of over $1 million a year. The money would be used to buy every family a "homestead" (a house, a car, and other necessities) and provide an annual family income of $2,000 to $3,000, plus old-age pensions, educational benefits, and veterans' pensions. As the 1936 election approached, he planned to organize a third party to split the liberal vote. He assumed that the Republicans would win the election and so botch the job of fighting the depression that he could sweep the country in 1940.

Less powerful than Long but more widely influential was Father Charles E. Coughlin, the "Radio Priest," a genial Irishman of Canadian birth. Coughlin in 1926 began broadcasting a weekly religious message over station WJR in Detroit. His mellifluous voice and orotund rhetoric won him a huge national audience, and the depression gave him a secular cause. In 1933 he had been an eager New Dealer, but his dislike of New Deal financial policies—he believed that inflating the currency would end the depression—and his need for ever more sensational ideas to hold his radio audience led him to turn against the New Deal. By 1935 he was calling Roosevelt a "great betrayer and liar."

Although Coughlin's National Union for Social Justice was especially appealing to Catholics, it attracted people of every faith, particularly in the lower-middle-class districts of the big cities. Some of his talks caused more than a million people to send him messages of congratulation; contributions amounting to $500,000 a year flooded his headquarters. Coughlin attacked bankers, New Deal

Father Charles Coughlin, the "Radio Priest," whose weekly program reached 30–45 million listeners nationwide, photographed in Detroit as he promoted his National Union for Social Justice.

planners, Roosevelt's farm program, and the alleged sympathy of the administration for communists and Jews, both of which Coughlin denounced in his weekly talks. His program resembled fascism more than any leftist philosophy, but he posed a threat, especially in combination with Long, to the continuation of Democratic rule.

Another rapidly growing movement alarmed the Democrats in 1934 and 1935: Dr. Francis E. Townsend's campaign for "old-age revolving pensions." Townsend, a retired California physician, colorless and low-key, had an oversimplified and therefore appealing "solution" to the nation's troubles. The pitiful state of thousands of elderly persons, whose job prospects were even dimmer than those of the mass of the unemployed, he found shocking. He advocated paying every person 60 years of age and over a pension of $200 a month, the only conditions being that the pensioners not hold jobs and that they spend the entire sum within 30 days. Their purchases, he argued, would stimulate production, thereby creating new jobs and revitalizing the economy. A stiff transactions tax, collected whenever any commodity changed hands, would pay for the program.

Economists quickly pointed out that with about 10 million persons eligible for the Townsend pensions, the cost would amount to $24 billion a year—roughly half the national income. But among the elderly the scheme proved extremely popular. Townsend Clubs, their proceedings conducted in the spirit of revivalist camp meetings, flourished everywhere, and the *Townsend National Weekly* reached a circulation of over 200,000. Although most Townsendites were anything but radical politically, their plan, like Long's Share Our Wealth scheme, would have revolutionized the distribution of wealth in the country. The movement marked the emergence of a new force in American society. With medical advances lengthening the average life span, the percentage of old people in the population was rising. The breakdown of close family ties in an increasingly mobile society now caused many of these citizens to be cast adrift to live out their last years poor, sick, idle, and alone.

With the possible exception of Long, the extremists had little understanding of practical affairs. (It could be said that Townsend knew what to do with money but not how to get it and Coughlin knew how to get money but not what to do with it.) Collectively they represented a threat to Roosevelt; their success helped to make the president see that he must move boldly to restore good times or face serious political trouble in 1936.

Political imperatives had much to do with his decision, and the influence of Justice Brandeis and his disciples, notably Felix Frankfurter, was great. They urged Roosevelt to abandon his pro-business programs, especially NRA, and stress restoring competition and taxing corporations more heavily. The fact that most businessmen were turning away from him encouraged the president to accept this advice; so did the Supreme Court's decision in *Schechter* v. *United States* in May 1935, which declared the National Industrial Recovery Act unconstitutional. (The case involved the provisions of the NRA Live Poultry Code; the Court voided the act on the grounds that Congress had delegated too much legislative power to the code authorities and that the defendants, four brothers engaged in slaughtering chickens in New York City, were not engaged in interstate commerce.)

The Second New Deal

Existing laws had failed to end the depression. Extremists were luring away some of Roosevelt's supporters, and conservatives had failed to appreciate his moderation. The voters, heartened by the partial success of early New Deal measures, had responded by further increasing the Democrats' control of Congress in the 1934 elections and were clamoring for further reforms. But the Supreme Court had declared many key New Deal measures unconstitutional. For these many reasons, Roosevelt in June launched what historians call the Second New Deal.

There followed the "Second Hundred Days," one of the most productive periods in the history of American legislation. The National Labor Relations Act—commonly known as the Wagner Act—restored the labor guarantees wiped out by the Schechter decision. It gave workers the right to bargain collectively and prohibited employers from interfering with union organizational activities in their factories. The National Labor Relations Board (NLRB) was established to supervise plant elections and designate successful unions as official bargaining agents when a majority of the workers approved. It was difficult to force some big corporations to bargain "in good faith," as the law required, but the NLRB could conduct investigations of employer practices and issue cease and desist orders when "unfair" activities came to light.

The Social Security Act of August 1935 set up a system of old-age insurance, financed partly by a tax on wages (paid by workers) and partly by a tax on payrolls (paid by employers). It created a state-federal system of unemployment insurance, similarly financed. Liberal critics considered this social security system inadequate because it did not cover agricultural workers, domestics, self-employed per-

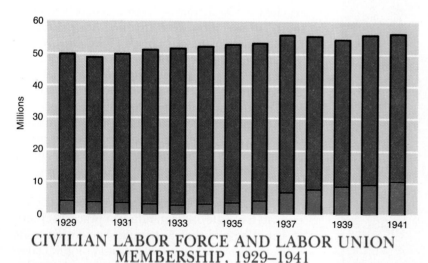

CIVILIAN LABOR FORCE AND LABOR UNION MEMBERSHIP, 1929–1941

The green portion of the vertical bars represents the number of civilian labor force workers in unions, as against the total work force. Union membership more than doubled in the years from 1937 to 1941, from less than 5 million to more than 10 million.

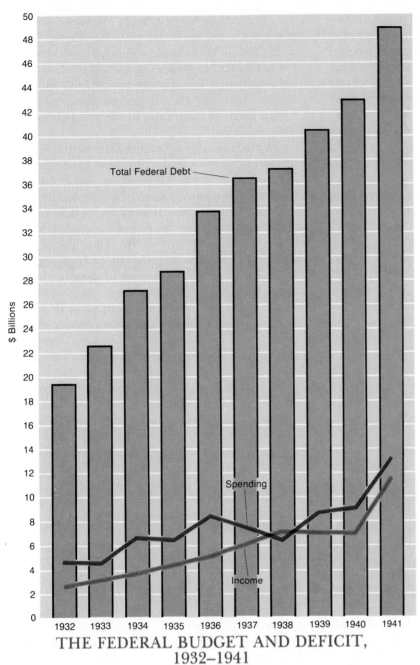

The gap between the blue (income) line and the red (spending) line shows the deficit each year for the ten years between 1932 and 1941, and the bars show how the total debt increased to almost $43 billion by 1941. According to Keynes, such deficits help to stimulate a lagging economy.

Total Federal Debt

Spending

Income

$ Billions

1932 1933 1934 1935 1936 1937 1938 1939 1940 1941

THE FEDERAL BUDGET AND DEFICIT,
1932–1941

sons, and some other groups particularly in need of its benefits. Health insurance was not included, and because the size of pensions depended on the amount earned, the lowest-paid workers could not count on much support after reaching the age of 65. Yet the law was of major significance. Over the years the pension payments were increased and the classes of workers covered expanded.

Among other important laws enacted at this time were a new banking act and a public utility act. The former strengthened the control of the Federal Reserve Board (renamed the Board of Governors) over member banks and over commercial credit and interest rates. The Public Utility Holding Company Act outlawed the pyramiding of control of gas and electricity companies through the use of holding companies and gave federal commissions the power to regulate the rates and financial practices of these companies. The hotly debated "death sentence" clause of this law provided for the dismemberment of all utility complexes more than twice removed from the actual operating companies and authorized the Securities and Exchange Commission to break up smaller ones that could not demonstrate that their existence served some socially useful purpose.

The Rural Electrification Administration (REA), created by executive order, also began to function during this remarkable period. REA lent money at low interest rates to utility companies and to farmer cooperatives interested in bringing electricity to rural areas. When REA went into operation, only one farm in ten had electricity; by 1950 only one in ten did not.

Another important measure was the Wealth Tax Act of August 1935, which, while not the "soak the rich" measure both its supporters and its opponents claimed, raised taxes on large incomes considerably. Estate and gift taxes were also increased. Stiffer taxes on corporate profits reflected the Brandeis group's desire to penalize corporate giantism. Much of the opposition to other New Deal legislation arose from the fact that after these changes in the tax laws were made, the well-to-do had to bear a larger share of the cost of *all* government activities.

Whether the Second New Deal was more radical than the First depends largely on the vantage point from which it is considered. Measures like the Social Security Act had greater long-range effect on American life than the legislation of the first Hundred Days but were fundamentally less revolutionary than laws like the National Industrial Recovery Act and the Agricultural Adjustment Act, which attempted to establish a planned economy. As Arthur M. Schlesinger, Jr., has observed:

> Where the First New Deal contemplated government, business, and labor marching hand in hand toward a brave new society, the Second New Deal proposed to revitalize the tired old society. . . . The First New Deal characteristically told business what it must do. The Second New Deal characteristically told business what it must *not* do.

This distinction escaped most of Roosevelt's critics, particularly the businessmen, who felt the impact of his assault on existing conditions most directly. Even if in theory NIRA threatened the free enterprise system, it was less objectionable to manufacturers than laws that increased their taxes and forced them to contribute to old-age pensions for their workers.

Herbert Hoover epitomized the attitude of conservatives when he called the New Deal "the most stupendous invasion of the whole spirit of Liberty that the nation has witnessed." Undoubtedly, many opponents of the New Deal sincerely believed that it was undermining the foundations of American freedom. The cost of the New Deal also alarmed them. By 1936 some members of the administration had fallen under the influence of the British economist John Maynard Keynes, who argued that the world depression could be conquered if governments would deliberately unbalance their budgets by reducing interest rates and taxes and increasing expenditures in order to stimulate consumption and investment.

Roosevelt never accepted Keynes's theories; he conferred with the economist in 1934 but could not grasp the "rigmarole of figures" with which Keynes deluged him. Nevertheless, the imperatives of the depression forced him to spend more than the government was collecting in taxes; thus he adopted in part the Keynesian approach. Conservative businessmen considered him financially irresponsible, and the fact that deficit spending seemed to be good politics made them seethe with rage.

The Election of 1936

The election of 1936 loomed as a showdown. "America is in peril," the Republican platform declared. The GOP candidate, Governor Alfred M. Landon of Kansas, was a former follower of Theodore Roosevelt, a foe of the Ku Klux Klan in the 1920s, and a believer in government regulation of business. But he was a poor speaker, colorless, and handicapped by the reactionary views of many of his backers. Against Roosevelt's charm and political astuteness, Landon's arguments—chiefly that he could administer the government more efficiently than the president—made little impression. He won the support of some anti–New Deal Democrats, among them two former presidential candidates, Al Smith and John W. Davis, but this was not enough.

The radical fringe put a third candidate in the field, Congressman William Lemke of North Dakota, who ran on the Union party ticket. Father Coughlin, denouncing Roosevelt as the "dumbest man ever to occupy the White House," rallied his National Union for Social Justice behind Lemke; Francis Townsend also supported him. However, the extremists were losing ground by 1936. Huey Long had fallen victim to an assassin in September 1935, and his organization was taken over by a blatantly demagogic rightist, Gerald L. K. Smith. The New Deal, Smith said in 1936, was led by "a slimy group of men culled from the pink campuses of America." The Townsendites fell under a cloud because of rumors that some of their leaders had their fingers in the organization's treasury. Father Coughlin's slanderous assaults on Roosevelt caused a backlash; a number of American Catholic prelates denounced him, and the Vatican issued an unofficial but influential rebuke. Lemke got only 892,000 votes.

Roosevelt did not win in 1936 because of the inadequacies of his foes. Having abandoned his efforts to hold the businessmen, whom he now denounced as "economic royalists," he appealed for the votes of workers and the underprivileged. The new labor unions gratefully poured thousands of dollars into the campaign to reelect him. Black voters switched to the Democratic party in record numbers. Farmers liked Roosevelt because of his evident concern for their welfare. When the Supreme Court declared the Agricultural Adjustment Act unconstitutional (*United States* v. *Butler*, 1936), he immediately rushed through a new law, the Soil Conservation and Domestic Allotment Act, which accomplished the same objective by paying farmers to divert land from commercial crops to soil-building plants like clover and soybeans. Countless elderly persons backed Roosevelt out of gratitude for the Social Security Act. Homeowners were grateful for his program guaranteeing mortgages—eventually about 20 percent of all urban private dwellings were refinanced by the Home Owners Loan Corporation—and for the Federal Housing Administration, which, beginning in 1934, made available low-cost, long-term loans for modernizing old buildings and constructing new ones. A modest upturn, which raised industrial output to the levels of

1930, played into Roosevelt's hands. For the first time since 1931, U.S. Steel was showing a profit.

On election day the country gave the president a tremendous vote of confidence. He carried every state but Maine and Vermont. The Republicans elected only 89 members of the House of Representatives, and their strength in the Senate fell to 16, an all-time low. Both Roosevelt's personality and his program had captivated the land. He seemed irresistible, the most powerfully entrenched president in the history of the United States.

Roosevelt and the "Nine Old Men"

On January 20, in his second inaugural, Roosevelt spoke of the plight of millions of citizens "denied the greater part of what the very lowest standards of today call the necessities of life." A third of the nation, he added without exaggeration, was "ill-housed, ill-clad, ill-nourished." He interpreted his landslide victory as a mandate for further reforms, and with his prestige and his immense congressional majorities, nothing appeared to stand in his way—nothing, that is, except the Supreme Court.

Throughout Roosevelt's first term the Court had stood almost immovable against increasing the scope of federal authority and broadening the general power of government, state as well as national, to cope with the exigencies of the depression. Of the nine justices, only Louis Brandeis, Benjamin N. Cardozo, and Harlan Fiske Stone viewed the New Deal sympathetically. Four others—James C. McReynolds, Willis Van Devanter, Pierce Butler, and George Sutherland—were intransigent reactionaries. Chief Justice Charles Evans Hughes and Justice Owen J. Roberts, though more open-minded, tended to side with the reactionaries on many questions.

Much of the early New Deal legislation, pushed through Congress at top speed during the Hundred Days, had been drafted without proper regard for the Constitution. Even the liberal justices considered the National Industrial Recovery Act unconstitutional (the Schechter decision was a unanimous one). The Court had also voided the federal Guffey-Snyder Act, establishing minimum wages in the coal industry, and a New York minimum wage law, thereby creating, as Roosevelt remarked, a "no man's land" where neither national nor state government could act. The conservative majority had adopted what Roosevelt called a "horse-and-buggy" interpretation of the commerce clause of the Constitution, closing off one of the most important avenues for expanding federal power.

Worse, the reactionaries on the Court seemed governed by no consistent constitutional philosophy; they tended to limit the police power of the states when wages-and-hours laws came before them and to interpret it broadly when state laws restricting civil liberties were under consideration. In 1937 all the major measures of the Second Hundred Days appeared doomed. The Wagner Act had little chance of winning approval, experts predicted. Lawyers were advising employers to ignore the Social Security Act, so confident were they that the Court would declare it unconstitutional.

In a New York Herald Tribune *cartoon titled "No Boost for the Administration Make-up Department," a court-packing wolf in the sheep's clothing of a court "reform" bill acts surprised when halted by a gun-toting Senate.*

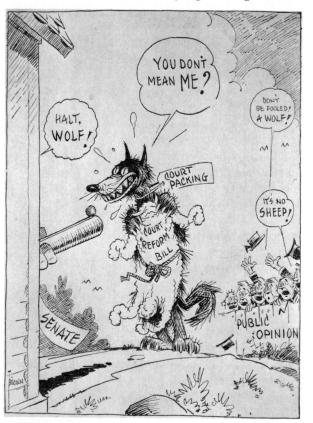

Facing this situation, Roosevelt decided to ask Congress to shift the balance on the Court by increasing the number of justices, thinly disguising the purpose of his plan by making it part of a general reorganization of the judiciary. A member of the Court reaching the age of 70 would have the option of retiring at full pay. Should such a justice choose not to retire, the president was to appoint an additional justice, up to a maximum of six, in order to ease the burden of work for the aged jurists who remained on the bench.

Roosevelt knew that this measure would run into resistance, but he expected that the huge Democratic majorities in Congress could override any opposition and that the public would back him solidly. No astute politician had erred so badly in estimating the effects of an action since Stephen A. Douglas introduced the Kansas-Nebraska bill in 1854.

Although polls showed the public fairly evenly divided on the "court-packing" bill, the opposition was vocal and influential. To the expected denunciations of conservatives were added the complaints of liberals fearful that the principle of court packing might in the future be used to subvert civil liberties. What, Senator Norris asked, would have been the reaction if a man like Harding had proposed such a measure? Opposition in Congress was immediate and intense; many who had cheerfully supported every New Deal bill came out against the plan. The press denounced it, and so did most local bar associations. Chief Justice Hughes released a devastating critique; even the liberal Brandeis—the oldest judge on the Court—rejected the bill out of hand. And many voters felt that Roosevelt had tried to trick them. The 1936 Democratic platform had spoken only of a possible amendment "clarifying" the Court's power, and Roosevelt had studiously avoided the issue during the campaign.

For months Roosevelt stubbornly refused to concede defeat, but in July 1937, he had to yield. Minor administrative reforms of the judiciary were enacted, but the size of the Court remained unchanged.

The struggle did save the legislation of the Second New Deal. Alarmed by the threat to the Court, Justices Hughes and Roberts, never entirely committed to the conservative position, beat a strategic retreat on a series of specific issues. While the debate was raging in Congress, they sided with the liberals in upholding first a minimum wage law of the state of Washington that was little different from the New York act the Court had recently rejected, then the Wagner Act, then the Social Security Act. In May, Justice Van Devanter retired, and Roosevelt replaced him with Senator Hugo Black of Alabama, a New Dealer. The conservative justices thereupon gave up the fight, and soon Roosevelt was able to appoint enough new judges to give the Court a large pro–New Deal majority. No further measure of significance was declared unconstitutional during his presidency.

The Court fight hurt Roosevelt severely. His prestige never fully recovered. Conservative Democrats who had feared to oppose him because of his supposedly invulnerable popularity took heart and began to join with the Republicans on key issues. When the president summoned a special session of Congress in November 1937 and submitted a program of "must" legislation, not one of his bills was passed.

The New Deal Winds Down

The Court fight marked the beginning of the end of the New Deal. Social and economic developments contributed to its decline, and the final blow originated in the area of foreign affairs. With unemployment high, wages low, and workers relatively powerless against their employers, most Americans had liked New Deal labor legislation and sympathized with the industrial unions whose growth it stimulated. The NRA, the Wagner Act and the CIO's organizing of such industries as steel and automobiles changed the power structure within the economy. What amounted to a revolution in the lives of wage earners had occurred. Aside from the obvious changes—higher wages, shorter hours, paid vacations, insurance of various kinds—unionization had meant fair methods of settling disputes about work practices and a measure of job security based on seniority for tens of thousands of workers. The CIO in particular had done much to increase the influence of labor in politics and to bring blacks and other minorities into the labor movement.

In 1937 a series of "sit-down strikes" broke out, beginning at the General Motors plant in Flint, Michigan. Striking workers barricaded themselves inside the factories; when police and strikebreakers tried to dislodge them, they drove them off with

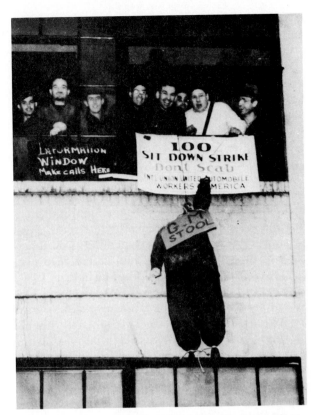

A group of sit-down strikers inside the Chevrolet plant in Flint, Michigan, looking out. They are hanging a "G-M stool" in effigy. The sign directly above the dummy reminds fellow workers: "Don't Scab."

barrages of soda bottles, tools, spare parts, and crockery. The tolerant attitude of the Roosevelt administration assured the strikers that the government would not intervene. "It is illegal," Roosevelt said of the General Motors strike, "but shooting it out . . . [is not] the answer. . . . Why can't those fellows in General Motors meet with the committee of workers?" Fearful that all-out efforts to clear their plants would result in the destruction of expensive machinery, most employers capitulated to the workers' demands. All the automobile manufacturers but Henry Ford quickly came to terms with the United Automobile Workers.

The major steel companies, led by U.S. Steel, recognized the CIO and granted higher wages and a 40-hour workweek. The auto and steel unions alone boasted more than 725,000 members by late 1937; other CIO units conquered numerous industries, including rubber and textiles. These gains and the aggressive way in which the unions pursued their objectives gave many members of the middle class second thoughts about the fairness of labor's demands. Sit-down strikes, the disregard of unions for the "rights" of nonunion workers, and the violence that accompanied some strikes seemed to some not merely unreasonable but a threat to social order. The enthusiasm of such people for all reform cooled rapidly.

While the sit-down strikes and the Court fight were going on, the New Deal suffered another heavy blow. Business conditions had been gradually improving since 1933. Heartened by the trend, Roosevelt, who had never fully grasped the importance of government spending in stimulating recovery, cut back sharply on the relief program in June 1937, with disastrous results. Between August and October the economy slipped downward like sand through a chute. Stock prices plummeted; unemployment rose by 2 million; industrial production slumped. This "Roosevelt recession" further damaged the president's reputation, and for many months he aggravated the situation by adopting an almost Hoover-like attitude. "Everything will work out all right if we just sit tight and keep quiet," he actually said.

While the president hesitated, rival theorists within his administration warred. The Keynesians, led by WPA head Harry Hopkins, Marriner Eccles of the Federal Reserve, and Secretary of the Interior Harold Ickes, clamored for stepped-up government spending. The conservatives, led by Treasury Secretary Henry Morgenthau, Jr., advocated retrenchment. Perhaps confused by the conflict, Roosevelt seemed incapable of decisive action. When Keynes offered him "some bird's eye impressions" of the recession in February 1938, urging "large scale recourse to . . . public works and other investments aided by Government funds," Roosevelt sent him only a routine acknowledgment drafted by Morgenthau.

In April 1938 Roosevelt finally committed himself to heavy deficit spending. At his urging Congress passed a $3.75 billion public works bill. Two major pieces of legislation were also enacted at about this time. A new AAA program in February 1938 set marketing quotas and acreage limitations for growers of staples like wheat, cotton, and tobacco and authorized the Commodity Credit Corporation

to lend money to farmers on their surplus crops. The surpluses were to be stored by the government; when prices rose, farmers could repay the loans, reclaim their produce, and sell it on the open market, thereby maintaining an "ever-normal granary."

The second measure, the Fair Labor Standards Act, abolished child labor and established a national minimum wage of 40 cents an hour and a maximum workweek of 40 hours, with time and a half for overtime. Although the law failed to cover many of the poorest-paid types of labor, its passage meant wage increases for 750,000 workers. In later years many more classes of workers were brought within its protection, and the minimum wage was repeatedly increased.

These measures further alienated conservatives without dramatically improving economic conditions. The resistance of many Democratic congressmen to additional economic and social "experiments" hardened. As the 1938 elections approached, Roosevelt decided to go to the voters in an effort to strengthen party discipline and re-energize the New Deal. He singled out a number of conservative Democratic senators, notably Walter F. George of Georgia, Millard F. Tydings of Maryland, and "Cotton Ed" Smith of South Carolina, and tried to "purge" them by backing other Democrats in the primaries.

The purge failed. Southern voters liked Roosevelt but resented his interference in local politics. Smith dodged the issue of liberalism by stressing the question of white supremacy, Tydings emphasized Roosevelt's "invasion" of Maryland. In Georgia the president's enemies compared his campaign against George to General Sherman's march across the state during the Civil War. All three senators were easily renominated and then reelected in November. In the nation at large, the Republicans made important gains for the first time since Roosevelt had taken office. The Democrats maintained nominal control of both houses of Congress, but the conservative coalition, though unable to muster the votes to do away with accomplished reforms, succeeded in blocking additional legislation.*

---

* The so-called conservative coalition was never a well-organized group. Its membership shifted from issue to issue; it had no real leaders and no long-range plans.

Significance of the New Deal

After World War II broke out in 1939, the Great Depression was swept away on a wave of orders from the beleaguered European democracies. For this prosperity, Roosevelt received much undeserved credit. His New Deal had not returned the country to full employment. Despite the aid given the jobless, the generation of workers born between 1900 and 1910 who entered the 1930s as unskilled laborers had their careers permanently stunted by the depression. Far fewer rose to middle-class status than at any time since the 1830s and 1840s. Roosevelt's willingness to experiment with different means of combating the depression made sense because no one really knew what to do; however, his uncertainty about the ultimate objectives of the New Deal was counterproductive. He vacillated between seeking to stimulate the economy through deficit spending and trying to balance the budget; between a narrow "America first" economic nationalism and a broad-gauged international approach; between regulating monopolies and trustbusting; between helping the underprivileged and bolstering the al-

ready strong. At times he acted on the assumptions that the United States had a "mature" economy and that the major problem was overproduction. At other times he appeared to think that the answer to the depression was more production. He could never make up his mind whether to try to rally liberals to his cause without regard for party or to run the government as a partisan leader, conciliating the conservative Democrats.

Roosevelt's fondness for establishing new agencies to deal with specific problems vastly increased the federal bureaucracy, indirectly added to the influence of lobbyists, and made it more difficult to monitor government activities. His cavalier attitude toward constitutional limitations on executive power, which he justified as being necessary in a national emergency, set in motion trends that so increased the prestige and authority of the presidency that the balance among the executive, legislative, and judicial branches was threatened.

Yet these are criticisms after the fact; they ignore what one historian has called the "sense of urgency and haste" that made the New Deal "a mixture of accomplishment, frustration, and misdirected ef-

The proliferation of federal agencies during the New Deal inspired cartoonists. In this example, Swift's Gulliver is tied down by the Lilliputian Brain Trusters.

fort." On balance, the New Deal had an immense constructive impact. By 1939 the country was committed to the idea that the federal government should accept responsibility for the national welfare and act to meet specific problems in every necessary way. What was most significant was not the proliferation of new agencies or the expansion of federal power; these were continuations of trends already a century old when the New Deal began. The importance of the "Roosevelt revolution" was that it removed the issue from politics. "Never again," the Republican presidential candidate was to say in 1952, "shall we allow a depression in the United States."

Because of New Deal decisions, many formerly unregulated areas of American life became subject to federal authority: the stock exchange, agricultural prices and production, labor relations, old-age pensions, relief of the needy. If the New Deal failed to end the depression, it effected changes that have—so far, at least—prevented later economic declines from becoming catastrophes. By encouraging the growth of unions, the New Deal probably helped workers obtain a larger share of the profits of industry. By putting a floor under the income of many farmers, it checked the decline of agricultural living standards, though not that of the agricultural population. The social security program, with all its inadequacies, lessened the impact of bad times on an increasingly large proportion of the population and provided immense psychological benefits to all.

Among other important social changes, the TVA and the New Deal rural electrification program made farm life literally more civilized. Urban public housing, though never undertaken on a massive scale, helped rehabilitate some of the nation's worst slums. Government public power projects, such as the giant Bonneville and Grand Coulee dams in the Pacific Northwest, were only the most spectacular part of a comprehensive New Deal program to develop the nation's natural resources. Exploitation of the natural resources of the West was checked, and a start was made toward the proper national management of the land and water of the region, along with its petroleum, lumber, and other resources. The NIRA and later labor legislation forced employers to reexamine their role in American life and to become more socially conscious. The WPA art and theater programs widened the horizons of

millions. All in all, the spirit of the New Deal heightened the people's sense of community, revitalized national energies, and stimulated the imagination and creative instincts of countless citizens.

Women New Dealers: The Network

Largely because of the influence of Eleanor Roosevelt and Molly Dewson, head of the Women's Division of the Democratic National Committee and a major force in that party, the Roosevelt administration employed far more women in positions of importance than any earlier one. Secretary of Labor Frances Perkins was the first woman appointed to a Cabinet post, but she was no token choice, having been active in labor relations for more than 20 years as secretary of the Consumers' League during the

Workers at the Carnegie Steel Company plant in Pittsburgh give a warm welcome to Frances Perkins, FDR's secretary of labor. She had been a prominent social worker and reformer in the Progressive Era.

progressive period, as a factory inspector immediately after the war, and as a member and then chair of the New York State Industrial Commission. As secretary of labor she helped draft New Deal labor legislation and kept Roosevelt informed on various labor problems outside the government.

In addition to Perkins, there were dozens of other women New Dealers. Molly Dewson and Eleanor Roosevelt headed an informal but effective "network"—women in key posts who kept in touch constantly, always seeking to place reform-minded women in government jobs. (According to the historian William Chafe, "Washington seemed like a perpetual convention of social workers as women . . . [took] on government assignments.") Dewson also won a larger influence for Democratic women in conventions and campaigns and a larger share of the spoils that came with victory. Between 1932 and 1938 the number of women postmasters increased by 50 percent.

As for Eleanor Roosevelt, through her newspaper column, "My Day," and as a speaker on public issues, she became a major force in her own right, both as a politician and as a stateswoman. She perceived herself, the historian Tamara Hareven has written, as "an ombudsman with the increasingly bureaucratized and impersonal (federal) government." Her influence on her husband and thus on the New Deal was large, especially in the area of civil rights, where the administration needed constant prodding.

She was particularly identified with efforts to obtain better treatment for blacks, in and out of government. The *Chicago Defender,* an influential black newspaper, noted that she "stood like the Rock of Gibraltar against pernicious encroachments on the rights of minorities." (A disgruntled southerner made the same point differently: "She goes around telling the Negroes they are as good as anyone else.")

Blacks During the New Deal

The shift of black voters from the Republican to the Democratic party during the New Deal years was one of the most dramatic and significant in American history. The cause was not the depression itself, although it hit blacks especially hard. In 1932, when things were at their worst, fewer blacks de-

fected from the Republican party than the members of any other traditionally Republican group. Four years later, however, blacks voted for Roosevelt in overwhelming numbers.

Blacks supported the New Deal for the same reasons that whites did, but how the New Deal affected blacks in general and racial attitudes specifically are more complicated questions. Claiming that he dared not antagonize southern congressmen, whose votes he needed for his recovery programs, Roosevelt did nothing about civil rights before 1941 and little thereafter.

Many of the early New Deal programs treated blacks as second-class citizens. They were often paid at lower rates than whites under NRA codes (and so joked sardonically that NRA stood for "Negro Run Around" and "Negroes Ruined Again"). The early farm programs shortchanged black tenant farmers and sharecroppers. Blacks got far fewer appointments in the Civilian Conservation Corps than their numbers warranted, and those who were accepted were assigned to all-black camps. TVA developments were rigidly segregated, and almost no blacks got jobs in TVA offices. New Deal urban housing projects inadvertently but nonetheless effectively increased the concentration of blacks in particular neighborhoods. The Social Security Act, by excluding agricultural laborers and domestic servants, did nothing for hundreds of thousands of poor black workers or for Mexican-American farmhands in the Southwest. In 1939 unemployment was twice as high among blacks as among whites, and whites' wages were double the level of blacks' wages.

The fact that members of racial minorities got less than they deserved did not keep most of them from becoming New Dealers: Half a loaf was more than any American government had given blacks since the time of U. S. Grant. As one black minister explained, "[Negroes] have never been so crazy as to wait for things to be perfect."

Aside from the direct benefits, blacks profited in other ways. Secretary of the Interior Harold L. Ickes appointed Charles Forman as a special assistant assigned "to keep the government honest when it came to race." In 1936 Roosevelt appointed Mary McLeod Bethune, founder of Bethune-Cookman College, as head of the Division of Negro Affairs in the National Youth Administration (NYA), a post that enabled her to develop educational and oc-

*Black sharecroppers evicted from their tenant farms were photographed by
Arthur Rothstein along a Missouri road in 1939. Rothstein was one of a group
of outstanding photographers who created a unique "sociological and economic
survey" of the nation between 1936 and 1942 under the aegis of the Farm
Security Administration.*

cupational training programs for disadvantaged
black youngsters. Bethune, along with Forman, another black lawyer in Ickes's department, named
William Hastie, and a few others made up an informal "Black Cabinet" that lobbied throughout the
Washington bureaucracy on behalf of better opportunities for blacks.

In the labor movement, the new CIO unions
recruited black members, and this was particularly
significant because these unions were organizing
industries—steel, automobiles, and mining, among
others—that employed large numbers of blacks.
Thus while black Americans suffered horribly during the depression, New Deal efforts to counteract
its effects brought them some relief and a measure
of hope. And this became increasingly true with the
passage of time. During Roosevelt's second term,
blacks found far less to criticize than in his first.

A New Deal for Indians

As in many other matters, New Deal policy toward
American Indians built on early trends but carried
them further. During the Harding and Coolidge
administrations, more Indian land had passed into
the hands of whites, and agents of the Bureau of
Indian Affairs had tried to suppress any element
of Indian culture that they considered "pagan" or
"lascivious." In 1924 Congress finally granted citizenship to all Indians, but whites still generally
agreed that Indians should be treated as wards of
the state. Assimilation had failed; indeed, tribal cultures had proved remarkably enduring. Indian languages and religious practices, patterns of family
life, arts and crafts—all had resisted generations of
efforts to "civilize" the tribes.

Government policy took a new direction in 1933

when President Roosevelt named John Collier commissioner of Indian affairs. In the 1920s Collier had studied the Indians of the Southwest and was appalled by what he had learned. He became executive secretary of the American Indian Defense Association and in 1925 editor of a reform-oriented magazine, *American Indian Life.* By the time he was appointed commissioner, the depression had reduced about a third of the 320,000 Indians living on reservations to penury.

Collier was convinced that something should be done to revive the spirits of these people. He favored a pluralistic approach, seeking to help the Indians preserve their ancient cultures but also (somewhat contradictorily) to help them earn more money and make use of modern medical advances and modern techniques of soil conservation. He was particularly eager to encourage the revival of tribal governments that could function as community service centers and represent the Indians in dealings with the federal bureaucracy.

In part because of Collier's urging, Congress passed the Indian Reorganization Act of 1934. This law did away with the Dawes Act allotment system and enabled Indians to establish tribal governments with powers like those of cities, and it encouraged, but did not require, Indians to return individually owned lands to tribal control. In various ways about 4 million of the 90 million acres of Indian land lost under the allotment system were returned to the tribes. In addition, Harry Hopkins made special efforts to see that needy Indians who were not living on reservations got relief aid. There was also a special Indian division of the Civilian Conservation Corps that organized work for Indians right on their reservations.

New Deal Indian policy was controversial among Indians as well as among other groups. Some critics charged Collier with trying to turn back the clock. Others attacked him as a segregationist and claimed that he was trying to restore "pagan" religious practices and convert the Indians to communism. Still others objected to his employing professional anthropologists with supposedly "advanced" ideas.

In truth the problem was more complicated than Collier had imagined. Indians who owned profitable allotments, such as those in Oklahoma who held valuable oil and mineral rights, did not relish turning their land over to tribal control. In New Mexico, the Navajos, whose lands had relatively little com-

mercial value, nonetheless voted decisively against going back to the communal system. All told, 77 of 269 tribes voted against communal holdings. Nevertheless, like so many of its programs, the New Deal's Indian policy marked an important and necessary shift of perspective, a bold effort to deal constructively with a long-standing national problem.

The Role of Roosevelt

How much of the credit for New Deal policies belongs personally to Franklin D. Roosevelt is debatable. He had little to do with many of the details and some of the broad principles behind the New Deal. His knowledge of economics was skimpy, his understanding of many social problems superficial, his political philosophy distressingly vague. The British leader Anthony Eden described him as "a conjurer, skillfully juggling with balls of dynamite, whose nature he failed to understand," and the historian David Brody writes perceptively of Roosevelt's "unreflective acceptance" of the basic structure of American society.

Nevertheless, every aspect of the New Deal bears the brand of Roosevelt's remarkable personality. Brain Truster Rexford Tugwell has left one of the best-balanced judgments of the president. "Roosevelt was not really very much at home with ideas," Tugwell explained. He preferred to stick with what he already knew. But he was always open to new facts, and something within him "forbade inaction when there was something to be done." Roosevelt's political genius constructed the coalition that made the program possible; his humanitarianism made it a reform movement of major significance. Although considered by many a terrible administrator because he encouraged rivalry among his subordinates, assigned different agencies overlapping responsibilities, failed to discharge many incompetents, and frequently put off making difficult decisions, he was in fact one of the most effective chief executives in the nation's history. His seemingly haphazard practice of dividing authority among competing administrators unleashed the energies and sparked the imagination of his aides, which gave the ponderous federal bureaucracy a remarkable flexibility and élan.

Like Andrew Jackson, Roosevelt maximized his role as leader of all the people. His informal bi-

Eleanor and Franklin D. Roosevelt, with their son, Franklin, Jr., at the family home in Hyde Park, New York. While the Roosevelts' family life was far from idyllic, White House reporters generally respected their right to privacy.

weekly press conferences kept the public in touch with developments and him in tune with popular thinking. He made the radio an instrument for communicating with the masses in the most direct way imaginable: His fireside chats convinced millions that he was personally interested in each citizen's life and welfare, as in a way he was. At a time when the size and complexity of the government made it impossible for any one person to direct the nation's destiny, Roosevelt managed the minor miracle of personifying that government to 130 million people. Under Hoover, a single clerk was able to handle the routine mail that flowed into the office of the president from ordinary citizens. Under Roosevelt, the task required a staff of 50.

While the New Deal was still evolving, contemporaries recognized Roosevelt's right to a place beside Washington, Jefferson, and Lincoln among the great presidents. The years have not altered their judgment. Yet as his second term drew toward its close, some of his most important work still lay in the future.

The Triumph of Isolationism

Franklin Roosevelt was at heart an internationalist, but his highest priority was to end the depression, and like most world leaders in the 1930s, he placed revival of his own country's limping economy ahead of general world recovery. In April 1933 he took the United States off the gold standard, hoping that devaluing the dollar would make it easier to sell American goods abroad. The following month a World Economic Conference was held in London. Delegates from 64 nations sought ways to increase world trade, perhaps by a general reduction of tariffs and the stabilization of currencies. After flirting with the idea of currency stabilization, Roosevelt threw a bombshell into the conference by announcing that the United States would not return to the gold standard. His decision increased international ill feeling, and the conference collapsed. The German financier Hjalmar Schacht announced smugly that Roosevelt was adopting the maxim of the great *Führer,* Adolf Hitler: "Take your economic fate in your own hands."

Against this background, vital changes in American foreign policy took place. Unable to persuade the country to take positive action against aggressors, internationalists like Secretary of State Stimson had begun in 1931 to work for a discretionary arms embargo law, to be applied by the president in time of war against whichever side had broken the peace. By early 1933 Stimson had obtained Hoover's backing for an embargo bill, as well as the support of President-elect Roosevelt. First the munitions manufacturers and then the isolationists pounced on it, and in the resulting debate it was amended to make the embargo apply impartially to *all* belligerents.

Instead of providing an effective if essentially negative weapon for influencing international affairs, a blanket embargo would intensify America's ostrichlike isolationism. Stimson's policy would have permitted arms shipments to China but not to Japan, which might have discouraged the Japanese from attacking. As amended, the embargo would have automatically applied to both sides, thus removing the United States as an influence in the conflict. While Roosevelt accepted the change, the internationalists in Congress did not, and when they withdrew their support, the measure died.

The attitude of the munitions makers, who opposed both forms of the embargo, led to a series of studies of the industry. The most important was a Senate investigation (1934–1936) headed by Gerald P. Nye of North Dakota. Nye was convinced that "the interests" had conspired to drag America into World War I; his investigation was more an inquisition than an honest effort to discover what American bankers and munitions makers had been doing

between 1914 and 1918. The committee's staff, ferreting through subpoenaed records, uncovered sensational facts about the lobbying activities and profits of various concerns. The Du Pont company's earnings, for example, had soared from $5 million in 1914 to $82 million in 1916. When one senator suggested to Irénée Du Pont that he was displaying a somewhat different attitude toward war than most citizens, Du Pont replied coolly: "Yes; perhaps. You were not in the game, or you might have a different viewpoint."

Munitions makers had profited far more from neutrality than from American participation in the war, but the Nye report convinced millions of citizens that the bankers who had lent the Allies money and the "merchants of death" who had sold them arms had tricked the country into war and that the "mistake" of 1917 must never be repeated.

While the Nye committee labored, Walter Millis published *The Road to War: America, 1914–1917* (1935). In this best-seller Millis advanced the thesis that British propaganda, the heavy purchases of American supplies by the Allies, and Wilson's differing reactions to violations of neutral rights by Germany and Great Britain had drawn the United States into a war it could and should have steered clear of. Thousands found Millis's logic convincing.

These developments led in 1935 to what the historian Robert A. Divine has called the "triumph of isolation." The danger of another world war mounted steadily as Germany, Italy, and Japan repeatedly resorted to force to achieve their expansionist aims. In March 1935 Hitler instituted universal military training. In May, Mussolini massed troops in Italian Somaliland, using a trivial border clash as a pretext for threatening the ancient kingdom of Ethiopia.

Congress responded by passing the Neutrality Act of 1935, which forbade the sale of munitions to all belligerents whenever the president should proclaim that a state of war existed. Americans who took passage on belligerent ships after such a proclamation had been issued would do so at their own risk. Roosevelt would have preferred a discretionary embargo or no new legislation at all, but he dared not arouse the ire of the isolationists by vetoing the bill.

In October 1935 Italy invaded Ethiopia, and Roosevelt invoked the new neutrality law. Secretary of State Cordell Hull asked American exporters to support a "moral embargo" on the sale of oil and

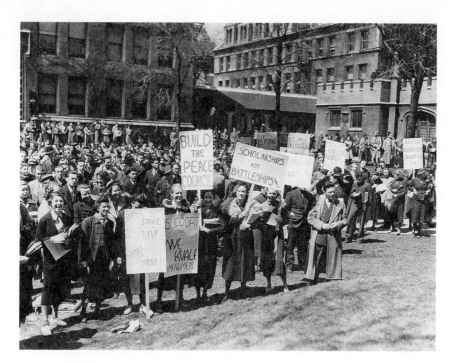

College campuses in the 1930s were often the scenes of organized protests against any governmental action that might increase the possibility of the United States going to war again. The faculty and students of the University of Chicago, pictured here in a 1937 demonstration, were particularly vocal in their isolationist sentiments.

other products not covered by the act. His plea was ignored; oil shipments to Italy tripled between October and January. Italy quickly overran and annexed Ethiopia. In February 1936 Congress passed a second neutrality act forbidding all loans to belligerents.

The next summer, civil war broke out in Spain. The rebels, led by the reactionary General Francisco Franco and strongly backed by Italy and Germany, sought to overthrow the somewhat leftist Spanish Republic. Here, clearly, was a clash between democracy and fascism, and the neutrality laws did not apply to civil wars. However, Roosevelt now became more fearful of involvement than some isolationists. (Senator Nye, for example, favored selling arms to the Spanish government.) The president believed that American interference might cause the conflict in Spain to become a global war, and he was wary of antagonizing the substantial number of American Catholics who were sympathetic to the Franco regime. He warned the Glenn L. Martin aircraft company that selling warplanes to the Spanish Republic "would not be in line with the policy of this government," and at his urging Congress passed another neutrality act broadening the arms embargo to cover civil wars.

Isolationism now reached its peak. A public opinion poll revealed in March 1937 that 94 percent of the people thought American policy should be directed at keeping out of all foreign wars rather than trying to prevent wars from breaking out. In April, Congress passed still another neutrality law. It continued the embargo on munitions and loans, forbade Americans to travel on belligerent ships, and gave the president discretionary authority to place the sale of other goods to belligerents on a cash-and-carry basis. In theory this would preserve the nation's profitable foreign trade without the risk of war; in fact it played into the hands of the aggressors. While German planes and cannons were turning the tide in Spain, the United States was denying the hard-pressed Spanish loyalists even a case of cartridges.

"With every surrender the prospects of a European war grow darker," Claude G. Bowers, the American ambassador to Spain, warned. The *New York Herald Tribune* pointed out that the neutrality legislation was literally reactionary—designed to keep the United States out of the war of 1914–1918, not the conflict looming on the horizon. President Roosevelt, in part because of domestic problems such as the Supreme Court packing struggle and

An American volunteer joining the Loyalist ranks in Spain in 1937. Although the American government remained officially neutral during the Spanish Civil War, hundreds of Americans joined the Lincoln Brigade to help the leftist Loyalists against General Franco and his fascist allies.

the wave of sit-down strikes and in part because of his own vacillation, seemed to have lost control over the formulation of American foreign policy. The American people, like wild creatures before a forest fire, were rushing in blind panic from the conflagration.

War Again in Europe

There were limits beyond which Americans would not go. In July 1937 the Japanese again attacked China, pressing ahead on a broad front. Roosevelt believed that invoking the neutrality law would only help the well-armed Japanese. Taking advantage of the fact that neither side had formally declared war, he allowed the shipment of arms and supplies to both sides.

Then the president went further. Speaking at Chicago in October, he condemned nations—he mentioned none by name—who were "creating a state of international anarchy and instability from which there is no escape through mere isolation or neutrality." The way to deal with "the epidemic of

world lawlessness" was to "quarantine" it. Evidently Roosevelt had no specific plan in mind; nevertheless, the quarantine speech produced a windy burst of isolationist rhetoric that forced him to back down. "It's a terrible thing," he said, "to look over your shoulder when you are trying to lead—and to find no one there."

Roosevelt came gradually to the conclusion that resisting aggression was more important than keeping out of war, but when he did, his fear of the isolationists led him at times to be less than candid in his public statements. Hitler's annexation of Austria in March 1938 caused him deep concern. The Nazis' vicious anti-Semitism had caused many of Germany's 500,000 Jewish citizens to seek refuge abroad. Now 190,000 Austrian Jews were under Nazi control. When Roosevelt learned that the Germans were burning synagogues, expelling Jewish children from schools, and otherwise mistreating innocent people, he said that he "could scarcely believe that such things could occur." But public opinion opposed changing the immigration law so that more refugees could be admitted, and the president did nothing.

In September 1938 Hitler demanded that Czechoslovakia cede the German-speaking Sudetenland region to the Reich. British prime minister Neville Chamberlain and French premier Edouard Deladier, in a conference with Hitler at Munich, yielded to Hitler's threats and promises and persuaded the Czechs to surrender the Sudetenland. Roosevelt failed again to speak out. But when the Nazis seized the rest of Czechoslovakia in March 1939, Roosevelt called for "methods short of war" to demonstrate America's determination to resist the aggressor.

When Hitler threatened Poland in the spring of 1939, demanding the free city of Danzig and the Polish Corridor separating East Prussia from the rest of Germany, and again when Mussolini invaded Albania, Roosevelt urged Congress to repeal the 1937 neutrality act so that the United States could sell arms to Britain and France in the event of war.

Congress refused. "Captain," Vice-President Garner told Roosevelt after counting noses in the Senate, "you haven't got the votes," and the president, perhaps unwisely, accepted this judgment and did not press the issue.

In August 1939 Germany and Russia signed a

A 1938 German poster glorifying Adolf Hitler with the slogan: "One people, one nation, one leader."

nonaggression pact, prelude to their joint assault on Poland. On September 1 Hitler's troops invaded Poland, at last provoking Great Britain and France to declare war. Roosevelt immediately summoned Congress into special session and again asked for repeal of the arms embargo. In November, in a vote that followed party lines closely, the Democratic majority pushed through a law permitting the sale of arms and other contraband on a cash-and-carry basis. Short-term loans were authorized, but American vessels were forbidden to carry any products to the belligerents. Since the Allies controlled the seas, cash-and-carry gave them a tremendous advantage.

The German attack on Poland effected a basic change in American thinking. Keeping out of the war remained an almost universal hope, but preventing a Nazi victory became the ultimate, if not always conscious, objective of many citizens. In

Roosevelt's case it was perfectly conscious, though he dared not express his feelings candidly because of isolationist strength in Congress and the country. He moved slowly, responding to rather than directing the course of events.

Cash-and-carry did not stop the Nazis. Poland fell in less than a month; then, after a winter lull that cynics called the "phony war," Hitler loosed his armored divisions. Between April 9 and June 22 he taught the world the awful meaning of *Blitzkrieg:* "lightning war." Denmark, Norway, the Netherlands, Belgium, and France were successively overwhelmed. The British army, pinned against the sea at Dunkirk, saved itself from annihilation only by fleeing back across the English Channel. After the French submitted to his harsh terms on June 22, Hitler controlled nearly all of western Europe.

Roosevelt responded to these disasters in a number of ways. In the fall of 1939, reacting to warnings from Albert Einstein and other scientists that the Germans were trying to develop an atomic bomb, he committed federal funds to a top secret atomic energy program. Even as the British and French were falling back, he sold them, without legal authority, surplus government arms. When Italy entered the war against France, the president called the invasion a stab in the back. During the first five months of 1940 he asked Congress to appropriate over $4 billion for national defense. To strengthen national unity, he named Henry L. Stimson secretary of war* and another Republican, Frank Knox, secretary of the navy.

After the fall of France, Hitler attempted to bomb and starve the British into submission. The epic air battles over England during the summer of 1940 ended in a decisive defeat for the Nazis, but the Royal Navy, which had only about 100 destroyers, could not control German submarine attacks on shipping. Far more destroyers were needed. In this desperate hour, Prime Minister Winston Churchill, who had replaced Chamberlain in May 1940, asked Roosevelt for 50 old American destroyers to fill the gap.

The navy had 240 destroyers in commission and more than 50 under construction. But direct loan or sale of the vessels would have violated both international and American laws. Any attempt to obtain new legislation would have aroused fears that

---

* Stimson had held this post from 1911 to 1913 in the Taft Cabinet.

the United States was going down the path that had led it into World War I. Long delay if not outright defeat would have resulted. Roosevelt therefore arranged to "trade" the destroyers for six British naval bases in the Caribbean. In addition, Great Britain leased bases in Bermuda and Newfoundland to the United States.

The destroyers-for-bases deal was one of Roosevelt's masterful achievements as a statesman and as a politician. It helped save Great Britain, and at the same time it circumvented isolationist prejudices, since the president could present it as a shrewd bargain that bolstered America's defenses. A string of island bastions in the Atlantic was more valuable than 50 old destroyers.

Lines were hardening throughout the world. In September 1940, despite last-ditch isolationist resistance, Congress enacted the first peacetime draft in American history. Some 1.2 million draftees were summoned for one year of service, and 800,000 reservists were called to active duty. That same month Japan signed a mutual-assistance pact with Germany and Italy. This Rome-Berlin-Tokyo axis fused the conflicts in Europe and Asia, turning the struggle into a global war.

A Third Term for FDR

In the midst of these events the 1940 presidential election took place. Why Roosevelt decided to run for a third term is a much-debated question. Partisanship had something to do with it, for no other Democrat seemed so likely to carry the country. Nor would the president have been human had he not been tempted to hold on to power, especially in such critical times. His conviction that no one else could keep a rein on the isolationists was probably decisive. In any case, he was easily renominated. Vice-President Garner, who had become disenchanted with Roosevelt and the New Deal, did not seek a third term; at Roosevelt's dictation, the party chose Secretary of Agriculture Henry A. Wallace to replace him.

The leading Republican candidates were Senator Robert A. Taft of Ohio, son of the former president, and District Attorney Thomas E. Dewey of New York, who had won fame as a "racket buster" and political reformer. Taft was considered conservative and lacking in political glamour; Dewey, barely 38, seemed too young and inexperienced.

Instead the Republicans nominated the darkest of dark horses, Wendell L. Willkie of Indiana, the utility magnate who had led the fight against the TVA in 1933.

Despite his political inexperience and Wall Street connections, Willkie, an energetic, charming, openhearted man, made an appealing candidate. His rough-hewn rural manner (one Democrat called him "a simple, barefoot Wall Street lawyer") won him wide support in farm districts. Willkie had difficulty, however, finding issues on which to oppose Roosevelt. Good times were at last returning. The New Deal reforms were too popular and too much in line with his own thinking to invite attack. He believed as strongly as the president that America could no longer ignore the Nazi threat.

In the end Willkie focused his campaign on Roosevelt's conduct of foreign relations. A preponderance of the Democrats favored all-out aid to Britain, while most Republicans still wished to avoid foreign entanglements. But the crisis was causing many persons to shift sides. Among interventionists, organizations like the Committee to Defend America by Aiding the Allies, headed by Republican William Allen White, and the small but influential Century Group contained members of both parties. So did the isolationist America First Committee, led by Robert E. Wood of Sears, Roebuck and the famous aviator Charles A. Lindbergh.

Wendell Willkie, just after his nomination by the Republican party for the presidency in 1940. Combining rural beginnings, Wall Street success, and a disarming grin, he gave hope of being a more formidable challenger to FDR than Alf Landon had been four years earlier.

While rejecting the isolationist position, Willkie charged that Roosevelt intended to make the United States a participant in the war. "If you reelect him," he told one audience, "you may expect war in April 1941," to which Roosevelt retorted (disingenuously, since he knew he was not a free agent in the situation), "I have said this before, but I shall say it again and again and again: Your boys are not going to be sent into any foreign wars." In November, Roosevelt carried the country handily, though by a smaller majority than in 1932 or 1936. The popular vote was 27 million to 22 million, the electoral count 449 to 82.

The Undeclared War

The election encouraged Roosevelt to act more boldly. When Prime Minster Winston Churchill informed him that the cash-and-carry system would no longer suffice because Great Britain was rapidly exhausting its financial resources, he decided at once to provide the British with whatever they needed. Instead of proposing to lend them money, a step certain to evoke memories of the vexatious war debt controversies, he devised the lend-lease program, one of his most ingenious and imaginative creations.

First he delivered a fireside chat that stressed the evil intentions of the Nazis and the dangers that a German victory would create for America. Aiding Britain should be looked at simply as a form of self-defense. "As planes and ships and guns and shells are produced," he said, American defense experts would decide "how much shall be sent abroad and how much shall remain at home." Encouraged by favorable public response to the radio talk, Roosevelt went to Congress in January 1941 with a plan calling for the expenditure of $7 billion for war materials that the president could sell, lend, lease, exchange, or transfer to any country whose defense he deemed vital to that of the United States. After two months of debate, Congress gave him what he had asked for.

Although the wording of the Lend-Lease Act obscured its immediate purpose, the saving of Great Britain, the president was frank in explaining his plan. He did not minimize the dangers involved, yet his mastery of practical politics was never more in evidence. To counter Irish-American prejudices against the English, he pointed out that the Irish

Republic would surely fall under Nazi domination if Hitler won the war. He coupled his demand for heavy military expenditures with his enunciation of the idealistic "Four Freedoms"—freedom of speech, freedom of religion, freedom from want, and freedom from fear—for which, he said, the war was being fought.

After the enactment of lend-lease, aid short of war was no longer seriously debated. The American navy began to patrol the North Atlantic, shadowing German submarines and radioing their locations to British warships and planes. In April 1941 United States forces occupied Greenland; in May the president declared a state of unlimited national emergency. After Hitler invaded the Soviet Union in June, Roosevelt moved slowly, for anti-Soviet feeling in the United States was intense.* But it was obviously to the nation's advantage to help any country that was resisting Hitler's armies. In November $1 billion in lend-lease aid was put at the disposal of the Russians.

Meanwhile, the Americans occupied Iceland in July 1941, and Congress extended the draft law in August—by the margin of a single vote in the House of Representatives. In September the German submarine *U-652* fired a torpedo at the destroyer *Greer* in the North Atlantic. The *Greer,* which had provoked the attack by tracking *U-652* and flashing its position to a British plane, avoided the torpedo and dropped 19 depth charges in an effort to sink the submarine.

Roosevelt (nothing he ever did provided more ammunition for his critics) announced that the *Greer* had been innocently "carrying mail to Iceland." He called the U-boats "the rattlesnakes of the Atlantic" and ordered the navy to "shoot on sight" any German craft in the waters south and west of Iceland and to convoy merchant vessels as far as that island. After the sinking of the destroyer *Reuben James* on October 30, Congress voted to allow the arming of American merchant ships and to permit them to carry cargoes to Allied ports. For all practical purposes, though not yet officially, the United States had gone to war.

---

* During the 1930s Russia took a far firmer stand against the fascists than any other power, but after joining Hitler in swallowing up Poland, it attacked and defeated Finland during the winter of 1939–1940 and annexed the Baltic states. These acts practically destroyed the small communist movement in the United States.

Milestones

New Deal Agencies

1933 Civilian Conservation Corps (CCC)
Federal Emergency Relief
Administration (FERA)
Agricultural Adjustment
Administration (AAA)
Tennessee Valley Authority (TVA)
Home Owners Loan Corporation
(HOLC)
National Recovery Administration
(NRA)
Federal Deposit Insurance
Corporation (FDIC)
Public Works Administration (PWA)

Civil Works Administration (CWA)
1934 Securities and Exchange Commission
(SEC)
Federal Communications Commission
(FCC)
Federal Housing Administration
(FHA)
1935 Works Progress Administration
(WPA)
Resettlement Administration (RA)
Rural Elecrification Administration
(REA)
National Youth Administration (NYA)
National Labor Relations Board
(NLRB)

SUPPLEMENTARY READING

Titles marked with an asterisk have been published in paperback.

Of the many biographies of Roosevelt, see especially Frank Freidel, **Franklin D. Roosevelt** (1990), and J. M. Burns, **Roosevelt: The Lion and the Fox*** (1956). On Eleanor Roosevelt, see J. P. Lash, **Eleanor and Franklin*** (1971), and Lois Scharf, **Eleanor Roosevelt: First Lady of American Liberalism** (1987). J. T. Patterson, **Congressional Conservatism and the New Deal*** (1967), is a solid study of congressional politics. On the Brains Trust, see E. A. Rosen, **Hoover, Roosevelt, and the Brains Trust** (1977).

Useful special studies of the New Deal include M. H. Leff, '**The Limits of Symbolic Reform: The New Deal and Taxation** (1984), Richard Lowitt, **The New Deal in the West** (1984), V. L. Perkins, **Crisis in Agriculture: The AAA and the New Deal** (1969), D. E. Conrad, **The Forgotten Farmers** (1965), E. W. Hawley, **The New Deal and the Problem of Monopoly*** (1966), Roy Lubove, **The Struggle for Social Security** (1968), J. D. Matthews, **The Federal Theatre** (1967), C. H. Trout, **Boston, the Great Depression, and the New Deal** (1977), Barbara Blumberg, **The New Deal and the Unemployed** (1979), B. F. Schwartz, **The Civil Works Administration** (1984), Irving Bernstein, **Turbulent Years** (1970), J. S. Olson, **Saving Capitalism** (1988), and Sidney Fine, **Sit Down: The General Motors Strike** (1969). On constitutional questions,

see P. L. Murphy, **The Constitution in Crisis Times*** (1972).

For the activities of the "radical fringe," consult D. R. McCoy, **Angry Voices: Left-of-Center Politics in the New Deal Era** (1958), and D. H. Bennett, **Demagogues in the Depression** (1969). On Huey Long, see T. H. Williams, **Huey Long: A Biography** (1969). On blacks during the 1930s, see Raymond Wolters, **Negroes and the Great Depression*** (1970), N. J. Weiss, **Farewell to the Party of Lincoln** (1983), and Harvard Sitkoff, **A New Deal for Blacks*** (1978); on women, see W. H. Chafe, **The American Woman*** (1972), and Susan Ware, **Beyond Suffrage: Women in the New Deal** (1981) and **Partner and I** (1987), a life of Molly Dewson. On New Deal Indian policy, see K. R. Philip, **John Collier's Crusade for Indian Reform** (1977) and J. S. Olson and Raymond Wilson, **Native Americans in the 20th Century** (1984).

On isolationism and the events leading to the United States' entering the Second World War, see R. A. Divine, **The Reluctant Belligerent*** (1965), brief but comprehensive, and **The Illusion of Neutrality*** (1962), Waldo Heinrichs, **Threshold of War*** (1988), T. R. Fehrenbach, **F.D.R.'s Undeclared War** (1967), W. S. Cole, **Roosevelt and the Isolationists** (1983), and W. F. Kimball, **The Most Unsordid Act** (1969), on lend-lease.

War and Peace

BRUTUS: *I do believe that these applauses are*
For some new honours that are heaped on Caesar.

CASSIUS: *Why, man, he doth bestride the narrow world*
Like a Colossus . . .

WILLIAM SHAKESPEARE, Julius Caesar

ONE GI: *Now we have the world by the tail.*

ANOTHER: *Now we are all sons of bitches.*

A-bomb test site blockhouse, Alamogordo, N.M., July 16, 1945

By December 1941 the United States was in fact at war, but it is hard to see how a formal declaration could have come about had it not been for Japan. Japanese-American relations had worsened steadily after Japan resumed its war on China in 1937. As they extended their control, the invaders systematically froze out American and other foreign business interests. They declared that the Open Door policy was obsolete. Roosevelt retaliated by lending money to China and asking American manufacturers not to sell airplanes to Japan. In July 1940 Congress placed exports of aviation gasoline and certain types of scrap iron to Japan under a licensing system; in September all sales of scrap were banned. After the creation of the Rome-Berlin-Tokyo axis, Roosevelt extended the embargo to include machine tools and other items. The Japanese pushed ahead relentlessly despite the economic pressures.

The Road to Pearl Harbor

Neither the United States nor Japan wanted war. Roosevelt considered Germany a far the more dangerous enemy and was alarmed by the possibility of engaging in a two-front war. In the spring of 1941 Secretary of State Hull conferred in Washington with the Japanese ambassador, Kichisaburo Nomura, in an effort to resolve their differences. Hull showed little appreciation of the political and military situation in the Far East. He demanded that Japan withdraw from China and promise not to attack the Dutch and French colonies in Southeast Asia. How he expected to get Japan to give up its conquests without either making concessions or going to war is not clear.

Japan might well have accepted limited annexations in the area in return for the removal of American trade restrictions, but Hull seemed bent on converting the Japanese to pacifism by exhortation. He insisted on total withdrawal, to which even the moderates in Japan would not agree. When Hitler invaded the Soviet Union, thereby removing the threat of Russian intervention in the Far East, Japan decided to occupy Indochina even at the risk of war with the United States. Roosevelt retaliated in July 1941 by freezing Japanese assets in the United States and clamping an embargo on oil.

Now the war party in Japan assumed control. Nomura was instructed to tell Hull that his country would refrain from further expansion if the United States and Great Britain would cut off all aid to China and lift the economic blockade. Japan promised to pull out of Indochina once "a just peace" had been established with China. When the United States rejected these demands, the Japanese prepared to assault the Dutch East Indies, British Malaya, and the Philippines. To immobilize the United States Pacific Fleet, they planned a surprise aerial raid on the Hawaiian naval base at Pearl Harbor.

An American cryptanalyst, Colonel William F. Friedman, had cracked the Japanese diplomatic code; the government therefore had good reason to believe that war was imminent. But in the hectic rush of events, both military and civilian authorities failed to make effective use of the information collected. They expected the blow to fall somewhere in Southeast Asia, possibly in the Philippines.

The garrison at Pearl Harbor was alerted against "a surprise aggressive move in any direction." The commanders there, Admiral Husband E. Kimmel and General Walter C. Short, believing an attack impossible, took precautions only against Japanese sabotage. Thus when planes from Japanese aircraft carriers swooped down on Pearl Harbor on the morning of December 7, they found easy targets. In less than two hours they reduced the Pacific Fleet to a smoking ruin: two battleships destroyed, six others heavily battered, nearly a dozen lesser vessels put out of action. More than 150 planes were wrecked; over 2,300 servicemen were killed and 1,100 wounded.

Never had American arms suffered a more devastating or shameful defeat. The official blame was placed chiefly on Admiral Kimmel and General Short. They might well have been more alert, but responsibility for the disaster was widespread. Military and civilian officials in Washington had failed to pass on all that they knew to Hawaii or even to one another. Further, the crucial intelligence about the coming attack that the code breakers provided was mixed with masses of other information and was extremely difficult to evaluate.

On December 8 Congress declared war on Japan. Formal war with Germany and Italy was still not inevitable—isolationists were far more ready to resist the "yellow peril" in Asia than to fight in Europe. The Axis powers, however, honored their treaty obligations to Japan and on December 11 declared war on the United States. America was now fully engaged in the great world conflict.

Mobilizing the Home Front

War placed immense strains on the American economy and produced immense results. About 15 million men and women entered the armed services; they, and in part the millions more in Allied uniforms, had to be fed, clothed, housed, and supplied with equipment ranging from typewriters and paper clips to rifles and grenades, tanks and airplanes. Congress granted wide emergency powers to the president. It refrained from excessive meddling in administrative problems and in military strategy. However, though the Democrats retained control of both houses throughout the war, their margins were relatively narrow. A coalition of conservatives in both parties frequently prevented the president from having his way and exercised close control over expenditures.

Roosevelt was an inspiring war leader but not a very good administrator. Any honest account of the war on the home front must reveal glaring examples of confusion, inefficiency, and pointless bickering. The squabbling and waste characteristic of the early New Deal period made relatively little difference— what mattered then was raising the nation's spirits and keeping people occupied; efficiency was less than essential, however desirable. In wartime the nation's fate, perhaps that of the entire free world, depended on delivering weapons and supplies to the battlefronts.

The confusion attending economic mobilization can easily be overstressed. Nearly all Roosevelt's basic decisions were sensible and humane: to pay a large part of the cost of the war by collecting taxes rather than by borrowing and to base taxation on ability to pay, to ration scarce raw materials and consumer goods, and to regulate prices and wages. If these decisions were not always translated into action with perfect effectiveness, they always operated in the direction of efficiency and the public good.

Roosevelt's greatest accomplishment was his inspiring of businessmen, workers, and farmers with a sense of national purpose. In this respect his function duplicated his earlier role in fighting the depression, and he performed it with even greater success.

A sense of tremendous economic expansion caused by the demands of war can most easily be grasped by examining official statistics of production. In 1939 the United States was still mired in the Great Depression. The gross national product amounted to about $91.3 billion. In 1945, after allowing for changes in the price level, it was $166.6 billion. More specifically, manufacturing output nearly doubled, and agricultural output rose 22 percent. In 1939 the United States turned out fewer than 6,000 airplanes; in 1944, more than 96,000. Shipyards produced 237,000 tons of vessels in 1939, 10 million tons in 1943.

Wartime experience proved that the Keynesian economists were correct in saying that government spending would spark economic growth. About 8 million people were unemployed in June 1940. After Pearl Harbor, unemployment practically disappeared, and by 1945 the civilian work force had increased by nearly 7 million. Military mobilization had begun well before December 1941, by which time 1.6 million men were already under arms. Economic mobilization proceeded much more slowly, mainly because the president refused to centralize authority. For months after Pearl Harbor various civilian agencies squabbled with the military over everything from the allocation of scarce raw materials to the technical specifications of weapons. Roosevelt refused to settle these conflicts as only he could have.

The War Economy

Yet by early 1943 the nation's economic machinery had been converted to a wartime footing and was functioning smoothly. Supreme Court Justice James F. Byrnes resigned from the Court to become a sort of "economic czar." His Office of War Mobilization had complete control over the issuance of priorities and over prices. Rents, food prices, and wages were strictly regulated, and items in short supply were rationed to consumers. Wages and prices had soared during 1942, but after April 1943 they leveled off. Thereafter the cost of living scarcely changed until controls were lifted after the war.

Expanded industrial production together with conscription caused a labor shortage that increased the bargaining power of workers. At the same time, the national emergency required some limitation on the workers' right to take advantage of this power. After Pearl Harbor, Roosevelt created a National War Labor Board to arbitrate disputes and stabilize wage rates, and he banned all changes in wages without NWLB approval. In the "Little Steel" case in July 1942, the NWLB laid down the rule that wage increases should not normally exceed 15 percent of the rates of January 1941, a figure roughly in line with the increase in the cost of living since that date.

Prosperity and stiffer government controls added significantly to the strength of organized labor; indeed, the war had more to do with institutionalizing industrywide collective bargaining than the New Deal period. As workers recognized the benefits of union membership, they flocked into the organizations. Strikes declined sharply, but some crippling work stoppages did occur. In May 1943 the government seized the coal mines after John L. Lewis's United Mine Workers walked out of the pits. This strike led Congress to pass, over Roosevelt's veto, the Smith-Connally War Labor Disputes Act,

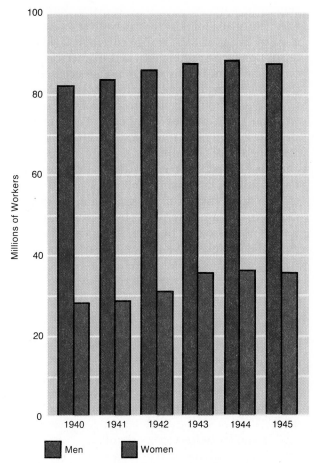

MEN AND WOMEN IN THE LABOR FORCE, 1940–1945

In 1940, about 75 percent of workers in the labor force—82 million—were men, and the other 25 percent—28 million—were women. By the end of World War II, in 1945, nearly 8 million more women had entered the work force, as against 5 million more men. The balance of the labor force had shifted to roughly 70 percent men, 30 percent women.

which gave the president the power to take over any war plant threatened by a strike and outlawed strikes against seized plants. Although strikes continued to occur—the loss in hours of labor zoomed to 38 million in 1945—when Roosevelt asked for a labor draft law, Congress refused to go along.

Wages and prices remained in fair balance. Overtime work fattened paychecks, and a new stress in labor contracts on paid vacations, premium pay for night work, and various forms of employer-subsidized health insurance were added benefits. The war effort had almost no adverse effect on the standard of living of the average citizen, a vivid demonstration of the productivity of the American economy. The manufacture of automobiles ceased, and pleasure driving became next to impossible because of gasoline rationing, but most civilian activities went on much as they had before Pearl Harbor. Because of the need to conserve cloth, skirts were shortened, cuffs disappeared from men's trousers, and the vest passed out of style. Plastics replaced metals in toys, containers, and other products. Although items such as meat, sugar, and shoes were rationed, they were doled out in amounts adequate for the needs of most persons. Americans had both guns and butter; belt-tightening of the type experienced by the other belligerents was unnecessary.

The federal government spent twice as much money between 1941 and 1945 as in its entire previous history. This made heavy borrowing necessary. The national debt, which stood at less than $49 billion in 1941, increased by more than that amount each year between 1942 and 1945 and totaled nearly $260 billion when the war ended. However, more than 40 percent of the total was met by taxation, a far larger proportion than in any earlier war.

This policy helped to check inflation by siphoning off money that would otherwise have competed for scarce consumer goods. Heavy excise taxes on amusements and luxuries further discouraged spending, as did the government's war bond campaigns, which persuaded patriotic citizens to lend part of their income to Uncle Sam. High taxes on incomes (up to 94 percent) and on excess profits (95 percent), together with a limit of $25,000 a year after taxes on salaries, convinced the people that no one was profiting inordinately from the war effort.

The income tax, which had never before touched the mass of white-collar and industrial workers, was extended downward until nearly everyone had to pay it. To ensure efficient collection of the relatively small sums paid by most persons, Congress adopted the payroll-deduction system proposed by Beardsley Ruml, chairman of the Federal Reserve Bank of New York. Employers withheld the taxes owed by workers from their paychecks and turned the money over to the government.

The steeply graduated tax rates combined with a general increase in the income of workers and farmers effected a substantial shift in the distribution of wealth in the United States. The poor became richer, while the rich, if not actually poorer, collected a smaller proportion of the national income. The wealthiest 1 percent of the population had received 13.4 percent of the national income in 1935 and 11.5 percent in 1941. In 1944 this group received 6.7 percent.

War and Social Change

Enormous social effects stemmed from this shift, but World War II altered the patterns of American life in so many ways that it would be wrong to ascribe the transformations to any single source. Never was the population more fluid. The millions who put on uniforms found themselves transported first to training camps in every section of the country and then to battlefields scattered from Europe and Africa to the far reaches of the Pacific. Burgeoning new defense plants drew other millions to places like Hanford, Washington, and Oak Ridge, Tennessee, where great atomic energy installations were constructed, and to the aircraft factories of California and other states. As in earlier periods, the trend was from east to west, from south to north, and from countryside to the cities. The population of California increased by more than 50 percent in the 1940s, that of other far western states almost as much.

During the war, marriage and birth rates rose steeply. A kind of backlog existed because many people had been forced to put off marrying and having children for financial reasons during the Great Depression. Now wartime prosperity put an end to that problem at the same time that large numbers of young couples were feeling the need to put down roots when the husbands were going off to risk death in distant lands. The population of the United States had increased by only 3 million during the depression decade of the 1930s; during the next *five* years it rose by 6.5 million.

Minorities in Time of War: Blacks, Hispanics, and Indians

The war affected black Americans in many ways. Several factors operated to improve their lot. One was their own growing tendency to demand fair treatment. Another was the reaction of Americans to Hitler's murder of millions of Jews, an outgrowth of his doctrine of "Aryan" superiority. These barbarities compelled millions of white citizens to re-examine their views about race. If the nation expected blacks to risk their lives for the common good, how could it continue to treat them as second-class citizens? Black leaders pointed out the inconsistency between fighting for democracy abroad and ignoring it at home. "We want democracy in Alabama," the NAACP announced, and this argument too had some effect on white thinking.

Blacks in the armed forces were treated more fairly than they had been in World War I. They were enlisted for the first time in the air force and the marines, and they were given more responsible positions in the army and navy. The army commissioned its first black general. Some 600 black pilots won their wings. Altogether about a million served, about half of them overseas. The extensive and honorable performance of these units could not be ignored by the white majority. However, segregation in the armed services was maintained, and black soldiers were often provided with inferior recreational facilities and otherwise mistreated in and around army camps, especially those in the South. In 1943 William Hastie, the former New Dealer who

was serving as an adviser on racial matters to Secretary of War Stimson, resigned in protest because of the "reactionary policies and discriminatory practices of the Army and Air Force in matters affecting Negroes."

Economic realities operated significantly to the advantage of black civilians. More of them had been unemployed in proportion to their numbers than any other group; now the labor shortage brought employment for all. More than 5 million blacks moved from rural areas to cities between 1940 and 1945 in search of work. At least a million of these found defense jobs in the North and on the West Coast. The black population of Los Angeles, San Francisco, Denver, Buffalo, Milwaukee, and half a dozen other important cities more than doubled in that brief period. The migrants were mostly forced to live in dreadful urban ghettos, but their very concentration (and the fact that outside the South blacks could vote freely) made them important politically.

These gains failed to satisfy black leaders. The NAACP, which increased its membership from 50,000 in 1940 to almost 405,000 in 1946, adopted a more militant stance than in World War I. Discrimination in defense plants seemed far less tolerable than it had in 1917 and 1918. A. Philip Ran-

Though assigned to segregated units, black servicemen were not limited to the infantry or enlisted ranks. Here are five graduates of the Advanced Flying School, Tuskegee, Alabama, just before receiving their commissions in 1942 as second lieutenants in the Army Air Corps.

dolph, president of the Brotherhood of Sleeping Car Porters, organized a march of blacks on Washington in 1941 to demand equal opportunity for black workers. Fearing possible violence and the wrath of southern congressmen, Roosevelt tried to persuade Randolph to call off the march. "It would make the country look bad" and "help the Germans," he claimed. But Randolph persisted, and Roosevelt finally agreed to issue an order prohibiting discrimination in plants with defense contracts. He also set up the Fair Employment Practices Committee to see that the order was carried out. Executive Order 8802 was poorly enforced, but it opened up better jobs to some workers and led many employers to change their hiring practices.

Prejudice and mistreatment did not cease. In areas around defense plants, white resentment of the black "invasion" mounted. By 1943 50,000 new black residents had crowded into Detroit. A wave of strikes disrupted production at U.S. Rubber and several former automobile plants where white workers laid down their tools to protest the hiring of blacks. In June a race riot marked by looting and bloody fighting broke out. It went on for three days, and by the time federal troops finally restored order, 25 blacks and 9 whites had been killed. Other race riots erupted in New York and many other cities.

In Los Angeles the attacks were on Mexican-born "zoot suiters," gangs whose "uniforms" were broad-brimmed fedoras, long coats, and pegged trousers. Wartime employment needs resulted in a reversal of the depression policy of forcing Mexicans out of the Southwest, and many thousands flocked north in search of work. Most had to accept menial jobs, but work was plentiful and they, as well as resident Spanish-speaking Americans, experienced rising living standards.

Some of the young Hispanics in the Los Angeles region formed gangs. They had money in their pockets and their behavior (like their costume) was not always as circumspect as local residents would have preferred. A grand jury undertook an investigation, and the Los Angeles City Council even debated banning the wearing of zoot suits. In 1943 rioting broke out when sailors on shore leave, apparently resenting these prosperous-appearing foreign civilians, began roaming the area attacking anyone they could find wearing a zoot suit.

There were at least understandable reasons why white city dwellers resented the black and Hispanic

The zoot-suit fashion favored by Mexican gang members originated in urban black neighborhoods and became a national fad during the war. The zoot suiter here, photographed in 1943, lacks the requisite wide-brimmed fedora, and so reveals his slicked hairstyle—also part of the uniform.

newcomers, although these did not justify the way the whites acted. But the mindless revulsion and flagrant contempt of so many and the willingness of white leaders to tolerate such behavior at a time when national unity was so necessary were particularly frustrating. For example, blood plasma from blacks and whites was kept separately even though the two "varieties" were indistinguishable and the process of storing plasma had been devised by a black doctor, Charles Drew.

Blacks became increasingly embittered. Roy Wilkins, head of the NAACP, put it this way in 1942: "No Negro leader with a constituency can face his members today and ask full support for the war in the light of the atmosphere the government has created." Many black newspaper editors were so critical of the administration that conservatives demanded that they be indicted for sedition.

Roosevelt would have none of that, but the militants annoyed him; he felt that they should hold their demands in abeyance until the war had been won. Apparently he failed to realize the depth of black anger, and in this he was no different from the majority of whites. A revolution was in the making, yet in 1942 a poll revealed that a solid majority of whites still believed that black Americans were satisfied with their place in society. The riots of 1943 undoubtedly disabused some of them of this illusion.

Concern about national unity did lead to a reaction against the New Deal policy of encouraging Indians to preserve their ancient cultures and develop self-governing communities. There was even talk of going back to the allotment system and trying to "assimilate" Indians into the larger society. John Collier resigned as commissioner of Indian affairs in disgust in 1945.

In fact, the war encouraged assimilation in several ways. More than 24,000 Indians served in the armed forces, an experience that brought them in contact with new people, new places, and new ideas. Many thousands more left the reservations to work in defense industries in cities all over the country.

The Treatment of German-, Italian-, and Japanese-Americans

However, while World War II affected the American people far more drastically than World War I had, it produced much less intolerance and fewer examples of the repression of individual freedom of opinion. People seemed able to distinguish between Italian fascism and Italian-Americans and between the government of Nazi Germany and Americans of German descent in a way that had escaped their parents. The fact that few Italian-Americans

Identification tags hung from the collars of the Mochida children as they posed with their parents for photographer Dorothea Lange. The date was May 8, 1942, and the family was awaiting transportation to a detention camp from their home in Hayward, California.

admired Mussolini and that nearly all German-Americans were vigorously anti-Nazi helps explain this. So does the fact that both groups were well organized and prepared to use their considerable political power if necessary to protect themselves against abuse.

But the underlying public attitude was more important. Americans went to war in 1941 without illusions and without enthusiasm, determined to win but expecting only to preserve what they had. They therefore found it easier to tolerate dissent, to view the dangers they faced realistically, and to concentrate on the real foreign enemy without venting their feelings on domestic scapegoats. The nation's 100,000 conscientious objectors met with little hostility.

The one flagrant example of intolerance was the relocation of the West Coast Japanese in internment camps in Wyoming, Arizona, and other interior states. About 110,000 Americans of Japanese ancestry, the majority of them native-born U.S. citizens, were rounded up and sent off against their will. Not one was accused of sabotage or being an enemy agent.

The Japanese were properly indignant but also baffled, in some cases hurt more than angry. "We didn't feel Japanese. We felt American," one woman, the mother of three small children, recalled many years later. "When I think back to the internment, I want to call it a concentration camp, but it wasn't." A fisherman remembered that besides his nets and all his other equipment, he had to leave behind a "brand-new 1941 Plymouth." "We hadn't done anything wrong. We obeyed the laws," he told an interviewer. "I lost everything." Then he added, almost plaintively, "But I don't blame anyone. It was a war."

The government's excuse was fear that some of the Japanese *might* be disloyal. In this connection it must not be forgotten that the Japanese had attacked Pearl Harbor without warning, without even threatening war unless certain demands were met, something even the Nazis had not done before they marched into Poland. Nevertheless, racial prejudice (the "yellow peril") and frustration at not being able to strike a quick blow at Japan in retaliation had much to do with the callous decision of the government to force people into camps without specific evidence that any of them posed a danger to American security. The Supreme Court upheld the re-location order in *Korematsu* v. *United States* (1944), but in *Ex parte Endo* it forbade the internment of loyal Japanese-American citizens. Unfortunately, the latter decision was not handed down until December 1944.

Women's Contribution to the War Effort

With economic activity on the rise and millions of men going off to war, a sudden need for women workers developed. The trends of the 1920s—more women workers and more of them married—accelerated. By 1944 fully 6.5 million additional women had entered the work force, and at the peak of war production in 1945, more than 19 million women were employed. Additional thousands were serving in the armed forces: 100,000 in the Women's Auxiliary Army Corps (WACS), others in navy, marine and air corps auxiliaries.

At first there was considerable resistance to what was happening. About one husband in three objected in principle to his wife taking a job. Many employers in so-called heavy industry and in other fields traditionally dominated by men doubted that women could handle such tasks.

Unions frequently made the same point, usually without much evidence. A Seattle official of the International Brotherhood of Boilermakers and Iron Shipbuilders said of women job applicants: "They don't understand. . . . If one of these girls pressed the trigger on the yard rivet guns, she'd be going one way and the rivet the other." This was perhaps reasonable, though many women were soon doing "men's work" in the shipyards. But the Seattle taxi-cab union objected to women drivers on the ground that "drivers are forced to do things and go places that would be embarrassing for a woman to do."

These male attitudes lost force in the face of the escalating demand for labor. That employers usually did not have to pay women as much as men made them attractive, as did the fact that they were not subject to the draft. A breakthrough occurred when the big Detroit automobile manufacturers agreed to employ women on their wartime production lines. Soon women were working not only as riveters and cab drivers but also as welders, machine tool operators, and in dozens of other occupations formerly the exclusive domain of men.

Women welders beveling armor plate on tank bodies, photographed in 1943 by Margaret Bourke-White of Life.

Women took wartime jobs for many reasons other than the obvious economic ones. Patriotism, of course, was important, but so were the excitement of entering an entirely new world, the desire for independence, even loneliness. "It's thrilling work, and exciting, and something women have never done before," one woman reported. She was talking about driving a taxi.

Black women workers had a particularly difficult time, employers often hesitating to hire them because they were black, black men looking down on them because they were women. But the need for willing hands was infinite. Sybil Lewis of Sapula, Oklahoma, went to Los Angeles and found a job as a waitress in a black restaurant. Then she responded to a notice of a training program at Lockheed Aircraft, took the course, and became a riveter making airplane gas tanks. When an unfriendly foreman gave her a less attractive assignment, she moved on to Douglas Aircraft. By 1943 she was working as a welder in a shipyard.

Few wartime jobs were easy, and for women there were special burdens, not the least of which was the prejudice of many of the men they worked with. For married women there was housework to

do after a long day. One War Manpower Commission bureaucrat figured out that Detroit defense plants were losing 100,000 woman-hours a month because of employees taking a day off to do the family laundry. Although the government made some effort to provide day-care facilities, there were never enough; this was one reason why relatively few women with small children entered the labor market during the war.

The war also affected the lives of women who did not take jobs. Families by the hundreds of thousands pulled up stakes and moved to the centers of war production, such as Detroit and southern California. Housing was always in short supply in these areas, and while the men went off to the familiar surroundings of yard and factory, their wives had to cope with cramped quarters, ration books, the absence of friends and relatives, the problems encountered by their children in strange schools and playgrounds, in some situations even with outdoor toilets. With so many people living among strangers and in unstable circumstances, it is not surprising that crime, juvenile delinquency, and prostitution increased, as indeed they did in other parts of the country too.

Newlywed wives of soldiers and sailors (known generally as "war brides") often followed their husbands to training camps, where life could be as difficult as it was around defense plants. Those who did not faced other problems—adjusting to being married without having had much experience of marriage, loneliness, worry. Whatever their own behavior, war brides quickly learned that society applied a double standard to infidelity, especially when it involved a man presumably risking his life in some far-off land. There was a general relaxation of sexual inhibitions, part of a decades-long trend accelerated by the war. So many hasty marriages, followed by long periods of separation, also brought a rise in divorces from about 170 per 1,000 marriages in 1941 to 310 per 1,000 in 1945.

Of course, "ordinary" housewives also had to deal with shortages, ration books, and other inconveniences during the war. In addition, most took on other duties and bore other burdens, such as tending "victory gardens" and preserving their harvests, using crowded public transportation when there was no gas for the car, mending and patching old clothes when new ones were unavailable, participating in salvage drives, and doing volunteer work for hospitals, the Red Cross, or various civil defense and servicemen's centers.

Allied Strategy: Europe First

Only days after Pearl Harbor, Prime Minister Churchill and his military chiefs met in Washington with Roosevelt and his advisers. In every quarter of the globe, disaster threatened. The Japanese were gobbling up the Far East. Hitler's armies, checked outside Leningrad and Moscow, were preparing for a massive attack in the direction of Stalingrad, on the Volga River. German divisions under General Erwin Rommel were beginning a drive across North Africa toward the Suez Canal. U-boats were taking a heavy toll in the North Atlantic. British and American leaders believed that eventually they could muster enough force to smash their enemies, but whether or not the troops already in action could hold out until this force arrived was an open question.

The decision of the strategists was to concentrate first against the Germans. Japan's conquests were in remote and, from the Allied point of view, relatively unimportant regions. If Russia surrendered, Hitler might well be able to invade Great Britain, thus making his position in Europe impregnable by depriving the United States of a base for a counterattack.

But how to strike at Hitler? American leaders wanted a second front in France, at least by 1943, and the Russians, with their backs to the wall and bearing the full weight of the German war machine, heartily agreed. Churchill, however, was more concerned with protecting Britain's overseas possessions than with easing the pressure on the Soviet Union. He advocated instead air bombardment of German industry combined with an attempt to drive the Germans out of North Africa, and his argument carried the day.

During the summer of 1942 Allied planes began to bomb German cities. In a crescendo through 1943 and 1944, British and American bombers pulverized the centers of Nazi might. Though air attacks did not destroy the German armies' capacity to fight, they hampered war production, tangled communications, and brought the war home to the German people in awesome fashion. Humanitarians deplored the heavy loss of life among the civilian population, but the response of the realists was that Hitler had begun indiscriminate bombing, and victory depended on smashing the German war machine.

In November 1942 an Allied army commanded by General Dwight D. Eisenhower struck at French North Africa. After the fall of France, the Nazis had set up a puppet regime in the parts of France not occupied by their troops, with headquarters at Vichy in central France. This collaborationist Vichy government controlled French North Africa. But the North African commandant, Admiral Jean Darlan, promptly switched sides when Eisenhower's forces landed. After a brief show of resistance, the French surrendered.

The Allies were willing to do business with Darlan despite his record as a collaborationist. This angered General Charles de Gaulle, who had organized a government in exile immediately after the collapse of France and who considered himself the true representative of the French people. Many Americans agreed with de Gaulle, but the arrangement with Darlan paid large dividends. Eisenhower was able to press forward quickly against the Germans. In February 1943 at Kasserine Pass in the

WORLD WAR II, EUROPEAN THEATER

desert south of Tunis, American tanks met Rommel's Afrika Korps. The battle ended in a standoff, but with British troops closing in from their Egyptian bases to the east, the Germans were soon trapped and crushed. In May, after Rommel had been recalled to Germany, his army surrendered.

In July 1943, while air attacks on Germany continued and the Russians slowly pushed the Germans

One of Life *photographer Robert Capa's first "pictures of victory"—American troops entering the Sicilian town of Monreale on their way up the Italian peninsula in 1943.*

back from the gates of Stalingrad, the Allies invaded Sicily from Africa. In September they advanced to the Italian mainland. Mussolini had already fallen from power, and his successor, Marshal Pietro Badoglio, surrendered. However, the German troops in Italy threw up an almost impregnable defense across the rugged Italian peninsula. The Anglo-American army inched forward, paying heavily for every advance. Monte Cassino, halfway between Naples and Rome, did not fall until May 1944, Rome not until June, and months of hard fighting still remained before the country was cleared of Germans. The Italian campaign was an Allied disappointment even though it weakened the enemy.

Germany Overwhelmed

By the time the Allies had taken Rome, the mighty army needed to invade France had been collected in England under Eisenhower's command. On D

day, June 6, 1944, the assault forces stormed ashore at five points along the coast of Normandy, supported by a great armada and thousands of planes and paratroops. Against fierce but ill-coordinated German resistance, they established a beachhead; within a few weeks a million troops were on French soil.

Thereafter victory was assured, though nearly a year of hard fighting lay ahead. In August the American Third Army under General George S. Patton, an eccentric but brilliant field commander, erupted southward into Brittany and then veered east toward Paris. Another Allied army invaded France from the Mediterranean in mid-August and advanced rapidly north. Free French troops were given the honor of liberating Paris on August 25. Belgium was cleared by British and Canadian units a few days later. By mid-September the Allies were fighting on the edge of Germany itself.

The front now stretched from the Netherlands along the borders of Belgium, Luxembourg, and

France all the way to Switzerland. If the Allies had mounted a massive assault at any one point, as the British commander, Field Marshal Bernard Montgomery, urged, the struggle might have been brought to a quick conclusion. While the two armies were roughly equal in size, the Allies had complete control of the air and 20 times as many tanks as the foe. The pressure of the advancing Russians on the eastern front made it difficult for the Germans to reinforce their troops in the west. But General Ei-

senhower believed a concentrated attack too risky. He prepared instead for a general advance.

While he was regrouping, the Germans on December 16 launched a counterattack, planned by Hitler himself, against the Allied center in the Ardennes Forest. The Germans hoped to break through to the Belgian port of Antwerp, thereby splitting the Allied armies in two. The plan was foolhardy and therefore unexpected, and it almost succeeded. The Germans drove a salient ("the

Once into Germany, the Third Army advanced so quickly in the spring of 1945 that it came upon military installations almost without warning. The photograph here is of General Dwight D. Eisenhower inspecting the condition of the concentration camp at Gotha, Germany, where slain inmates had been left unburied by their fleeing captors.

bulge") about 50 miles into Belgium. But once the element of surprise had been overcome, their chance of breaking through to the sea was lost. Eisenhower concentrated first on preventing them from broadening the break in his lines and then on blunting the point of their advance. By late January 1945 the old line had been reestablished.

The Battle of the Bulge cost the United States 77,000 casualties and delayed Eisenhower's offensive, but it exhausted the Germans' last reserves. The Allies then pressed forward to the Rhine, winning a bridgehead on the far bank of the river on March 7. Thereafter, another German city fell almost daily. With the Russians racing westward against crumbling resistance, the end could not be long delayed.

As the Americans drove swiftly forward they began to overrun Nazi concentration camps where millions of Jews had been murdered. Word of this Nazi holocaust in which no less than 6 million people were slaughtered had reached the United States much earlier. At first the news had been dismissed as propaganda, then discounted as grossly exaggerated. Hitler was known to hate Jews and to have persecuted them, but that he could order the murder of millions of innocent people, even children, seemed beyond belief. By 1943, however, the truth could not be denied.

Little could be done about those already in the camps, but there were thousands of refugees in occupied Europe who might have been spirited to safety. President Roosevelt declined to make the effort; he even refused to bomb the Auschwitz death camp in Poland or the rail lines used to bring victims to its gas chambers on the grounds that the destruction of German soldiers and military equipment took precedence over any other objective. Thus when American journalists entered the camps with the advancing troops, saw the heaps of still unburied corpses, and talked with the emaciated survivors, their reports caused a storm of protest.

Why Roosevelt acted as he did has never been satisfactorily explained. In any case, it was far too late to save more than a handful. In April, American and Russian forces made contact at the Elbe River. A few days later, with Russian shells reducing his capital to rubble, Hitler, by then probably insane, took his own life in his Berlin air raid shelter. On May 8 Germany surrendered.

The Naval War in the Pacific

Defeating Germany first had not meant abandoning the Pacific region entirely to the Japanese. While armies were being trained and material accumulated for the European struggle, much of the available American strength was diverted to maintaining vital communications in the Far East and preventing further Japanese expansion.

The navy's aircraft carriers had escaped destruction at Pearl Harbor, a stroke of immense good fortune, because without most tacticians realizing it, the airplane had revolutionized naval warfare. Commanders discovered that carrier-based planes were far more effective against warships than the heaviest naval artillery because of their greater range and more concentrated firepower. Battleships made excellent gun platforms from which to pound shore installations and support land operations, but against other vessels aircraft were of prime importance.

This truth was demonstrated in May 1942 in the Battle of the Coral Sea. Having captured an empire in a few months without the loss of any warship larger than a destroyer, the Japanese believed the war already won. This led them to overextend themselves.

The Coral Sea lies northeast of Australia and south of New Guinea and the Solomon Islands. Mastery of these waters would cut Australia off from Hawaii and thus from American aid. Admiral Isoroku Yamamoto had dispatched a large fleet of troopships screened by many warships to attack Port Moresby, on the southern New Guinea coast. On May 7 and 8 planes from the American carriers *Lexington* and *Yorktown* struck the convoy's screen, sinking a small carrier and damaging a large one. Superficially, the battle seemed a victory for the Japanese, for their planes mortally wounded the *Lexington* and sank two other ships, but the transports had been forced to turn back—Port Moresby was saved. Although large numbers of cruisers and destroyers took part in the action, none came within sight or gun range of an enemy ship. All the destruction was wrought by carrier aircraft.

Encouraged by the Coral Sea "victory," Yamamoto decided to force the American fleet into a showdown battle by assaulting Midway Island, west of Hawaii. His armada never reached its destination.

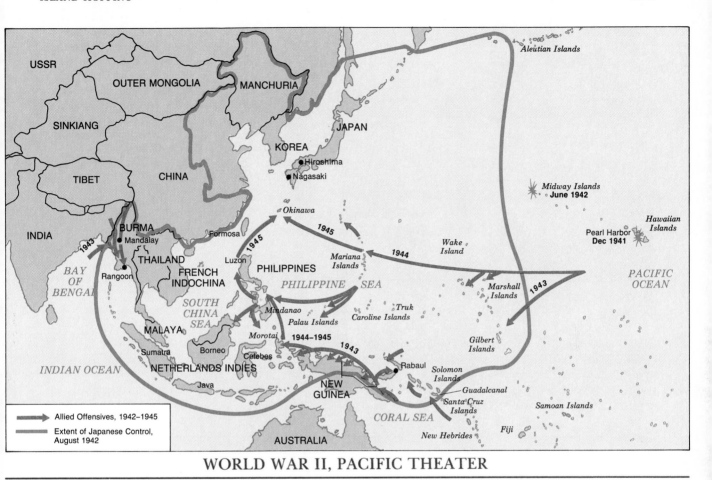

WORLD WAR II, PACIFIC THEATER

Between June 4 and 7 control of the central Pacific was decided entirely by air power. American dive bombers sent four large carriers to the bottom. About 300 Japanese planes were destroyed. The United States lost only the *Yorktown* and a destroyer. Thereafter the initiative in the Pacific war shifted to the Americans, but victory came slowly and at painful cost.

American land forces were under the command of Douglas MacArthur, a brilliant but egocentric general whose judgment was sometimes distorted by his intense concern for his own reputation. MacArthur was in command of American troops in the Philippine Islands when the Japanese struck in December 1941. After his heroic but hopeless defense of Manila and the Bataan peninsula, President Roosevelt had him evacuated by PT boat to escape capture.

Thereafter MacArthur was obsessed with the idea of personally leading an American army back to the Philippines. Although many strategists believed that the islands should be bypassed in the drive on the Japanese homeland, in the end MacArthur convinced the Joint Chiefs of Staff, who determined strategy. Two separate drives were undertaken, one from New Guinea toward the Philippines under MacArthur, the other through the central Pacific toward Tokyo under Admiral Chester W. Nimitz.

Island Hopping

Before commencing this two-pronged advance, the Americans had to eject the Japanese from the Solomon Islands in order to protect Australia from a

The often hand-to-hand combat required to dislodge the Japanese from entrenched positions on Pacific islands such as Bougainville, pictured here, prompted American military strategists to predict that a successful invasion of Japan itself would take 2 years and 2 million American lives.

flank attack. Beginning in August 1942, a series of land, sea, and air battles raged around Guadalcanal Island in this archipelago. Once again American air power was decisive, though the bravery and skill of the ground forces that actually won the island must not be underemphasized. American pilots, better trained and with tougher planes, had a relatively easier task. They inflicted losses five to six times heavier on the enemy than they sustained themselves. Japanese air power disintegrated progressively during the long battle, and this in turn helped the fleet to take a heavy toll of the Japanese navy. By February 1943 Guadalcanal had been secured.

In the autumn of 1943 the American drives toward Japan and the Philippines got under way at last. In the central Pacific campaign the Guadalcanal action was repeated on a smaller but equally bloody scale from Tarawa in the Gilbert Islands to Kwajalein and Eniwetok in the Marshalls. The Japanese soldiers on these islands fought like the Spartans at

Thermopylae for every foot of ground. They had to be blasted and burned from tunnels and concrete pillboxes with hand grenades, flamethrowers, and dynamite. They almost never surrendered. But Admiral Nimitz's forces were in every case victorious. By midsummer of 1944 this arm of the American advance had taken Saipan and Guam in the Marianas. Now land-based bombers were within range of Tokyo.

Meanwhile, MacArthur was leapfrogging along the New Guinea coast toward the Philippines. In October 1944 he made good his promise to return to the islands, landing on Leyte, south of Luzon. Two great naval clashes in Philippine waters, the Battle of the Philippine Sea (June 1944) and the Battle for Leyte Gulf (October 1944), completed the destruction of Japan's sea power and reduced its air force to a band of fanatical suicide pilots called *kamikazes*, who tried to crash bomb-laden planes against American warships and airstrips. The *ka-*

mikazes caused much damage but could not turn the tide. In February 1945 MacArthur liberated Manila.

The end was now inevitable. B-29 Superfortress bombers from the Marianas rained high explosives and firebombs on Japan. The islands of Iwo Jima and Okinawa, only a few hundred miles from Tokyo, fell to the Americans in March and June 1945. But such was the tenacity of the Japanese soldiers that it seemed possible that it would take another year of fighting and a million more American casualties to subdue the main Japanese islands.

"The Shatterer of Worlds"

At this point came the most controversial decision of the entire war, and it was made by a newcomer on the world scene. In November 1944 Roosevelt had been elected to a fourth term, easily defeating Thomas E. Dewey. Instead of renominating Henry A. Wallace for vice-president, whom conservatives considered too radical, the Democratic convention had nominated Senator Harry S Truman of Missouri, a reliable party man well liked by professional politicians. Suddenly, in April 1945, President Roosevelt died of a cerebral hemorrhage. Thus it was Truman, a man painfully conscious of his limita-

tions yet equally aware of the power and responsibility of his office, who had to decide what to do when a mere three months later American scientists placed in his hands a new and awful weapon, the atomic bomb.

After Roosevelt had responded to Albert Einstein's warning in 1939, government-sponsored atomic research had proceeded rapidly, especially after the establishment of the so-called Manhattan Project in May 1943. The manufacture of the element plutonium at Hanford, Washington, and of uranium 235 at Oak Ridge, Tennessee, continued along with the design and construction of a transportable atomic bomb at Los Alamos, New Mexico, under the direction of J. Robert Oppenheimer. Almost $2 billion was spent before a successful bomb was exploded at Alamogordo, in the New Mexican desert, on July 16, 1945. As that first mushroom cloud formed over the desert, Oppenheimer recalled the prophetic words of the *Bhagavad Gita*: "I am become death, the shatterer of worlds."

Should a bomb with the destructive force of 20,000 tons of TNT be employed against Japan? By striking a major city, its dreadful power could be demonstrated convincingly, yet doing so would bring death to tens of thousands of Japanese civilians. Many of the scientists who had made the bomb

Hiroshima's Museum of Science and Industry was reduced to a skeleton in the atomic bomb blast. City officials decided to preserve the wreckage as a memorial.

now argued against its use. Others suggested alerting the Japanese and then staging a demonstration explosion at sea, but that idea was discarded because of concern that the bomb might fail to explode. Even General Eisenhower and General MacArthur had reservations about the need to use the weapon.

Truman was torn between his awareness that the bomb was "the most terrible thing ever discovered" and his hope that using it "would bring the war to an end." The bomb might cause a revolution in Japan, might lead the emperor to intervene, might even persuade the military to give up. Considering the hundreds of thousands of Americans who would surely die in any conventional invasion of Japan and influenced by a desire to end the Pacific war before the Soviet Union could intervene effectively and thus claim a role in the peacemaking, the president chose to go ahead.

The moral soundness of Truman's decision has been debated ever since. There is no doubt that hatred of the Japanese had something to do with the decision. What is often forgotten by those who deplore it is the fact that even though the immediate result was the death of many thousands of innocent Japanese civilians, far more Japanese would have died—many more than the Americans who would have perished—if Japan had been invaded.

In any case, on August 6 the Superfortress *Enola Gay* dropped an atomic bomb on Hiroshima, killing about 78,000 persons (including 20 American prisoners of war) and injuring nearly 100,000 more out of a population of 344,000. Over 96 percent of the buildings in the city were destroyed or damaged. Three days later, while the stunned Japanese still hesitated, a second atomic bomb, the only other one that had so far been assembled, blasted Nagasaki. This second drop was far less defensible morally, but it had the desired result. On August 15 Japan surrendered.

Thus ended the greatest war in history. Its cost was beyond calculation. No accurate count could be made even of the dead; we know only that the total was in the neighborhood of 20 million. As in World War I, American casualties—291,000 killed in battle and 671,000 wounded—were smaller than those of the other major belligerents. About 7.5 million Russians died in the war, 3.5 million Germans, 1.2 million Japanese, and 2.2 million Chinese; Britain and France, despite much smaller populations, suffered losses almost as large as the United States'. And far

more than in World War I, American resources, human and material, had made victory possible.

No one could account the war a benefit to humanity, but in the late summer of 1945 the future looked bright. Fascism had been annihilated. Successful wartime diplomatic dealings among Roosevelt, Churchill, and Joseph Stalin, the Soviet dictator, encouraged the hope that the communists were prepared to cooperate in rebuilding Europe. In the United States isolationism had disappeared; the message of Wendell Willkie's best-selling *One World*, written after a globe-circling tour made by the 1940 Republican presidential candidate at the behest of President Roosevelt in 1942, appeared to have been absorbed by the majority of the people.

Out of the death and destruction had come technological developments that seemed to herald a better world as well as a peaceful one. Enormous advances in the design of airplanes and the development of radar (which some authorities think was more important than any weapons system in winning the war) were about to revolutionize travel and the transportation of goods. Improvements in surgery and other medical advances gave promise of saving millions of lives, and the development of penicillin and other antibiotics, which had greatly reduced the death rate among troops, would perhaps banish all infectious disease.

Above all, there was the power of the atom. The force that seared Hiroshima and Nagasaki could be harnessed to serve peaceful needs, the scientists promised, with results that might free humanity forever from poverty and toil. The period of reconstruction would be prolonged, but with all the great powers adhering to the new United Nations charter, drafted at San Francisco in June 1945, international cooperation could be counted on to ease the burdens of the victims of war and help the poor and underdeveloped parts of the world toward economic and political independence. Such at least was the hope of millions in the victorious summer of 1945.

Wartime Diplomacy

That hope was not to be realized, in large part because of a conflict that developed between the Soviet Union and the western allies. During the course of World War II every instrument of mass persuasion in the country had been directed at convincing the people that the Russians were fighting America's battle as well as their own. Even before Pearl Harbor, former Ambassador Joseph E. Davies wrote in his best-selling *Mission to Moscow* (1941) that the communist leaders were "a group of able, strong men" with "honest convictions and integrity of purpose" who were "devoted to the cause of peace for both ideological and practical reasons." Communism was based "on the same principle of the 'brotherhood of man' which Jesus preached." Stalin possessed great dignity and charm, combined with much wisdom and strength of character, Davies said. "His brown eye is exceedingly kind and gentle. A child would like to sit in his lap and a dog would sidle up to him." In another book published in 1941 the journalist Walter Duranty described Stalin (who had ruthlessly executed hundreds of his former comrades) as "remarkably long-suffering in his treatment of various oppositions."

During the war Americans with as different points of view as General Douglas MacArthur and Vice-President Henry A. Wallace took strongly pro-Soviet positions, and American newspapers and magazines published many laudatory articles about Russia. *Life* reported that Russians "think like Americans." In 1943 *Time* named Stalin its "Man of the Year." The film *Mission to Moscow*, a whitewash of the dreadful Moscow treason trials of the 1930s based on Ambassador Davies's book, portrayed Stalin as a wise, grandfatherly type, puffing comfortably on an old pipe. In *One World* (1943), Wendell Willkie wrote glowingly of the Russian people, their "effective society," and their simple, warmhearted leader. When he suggested jokingly to Stalin that if he continued to make progress in improving the education of his people he might educate himself out of a job, the dictator "threw his head back and laughed and laughed," Willkie recorded. "Mr. Willkie, you know I grew up a Georgian peasant. I am unschooled in pretty talk. All I can say is I like you very much."

These views of the character of Joseph Stalin were naive, to say the least, but the identity of interests of the United States and the Soviet Union was very real during the war. Russian military leaders conferred regularly with their British and American counterparts and fulfilled their obligations scrupulously.

The Soviets repeatedly expressed a willingness to cooperate with the Allies in dealing with postwar problems. Russia was in January 1942 one of the 26 signers of the Declaration of the United Nations, in which the Allies promised to eschew territorial aggrandizement after the war, to respect the right of all peoples to determine their own form of government, to work for freer trade and international economic cooperation, and to force the disarmament of the aggressor nations.*

In May 1943 the Soviet Union dissolved the Comintern, its official agency for the promulgation of world revolution. The following October, during a conference in Moscow with Secretary of State Cordell Hull and British Foreign Minister Anthony Eden, Soviet Foreign Minister V. M. Molotov joined in setting up the European Advisory Commission to divide Germany into occupation zones after the war. At a conference held in Teheran, Iran, that December, Roosevelt, Churchill, and Stalin discussed plans for a new league of nations. When Roosevelt described the kind of world organization he envisaged, the Russian dictator offered a number of constructive suggestions.

Between August and October 1944, Allied representatives met at Dumbarton Oaks, outside Washington, D.C. The chief Russian delegate, Andrei A. Gromyko, opposed limiting the use of the veto by the great powers on the future United Nations Security Council, but he did not take a deliberately obstructionist position. At another meeting, held at Yalta in the Crimean region of the Soviet Union in February 1945, Stalin joined Roosevelt and Churchill in the call for a conference to be held in April at San Francisco to draft a charter for the United Nations. "We argued freely and frankly across the table," Roosevelt reported later. "But at the end, on every point, unanimous agreement was reached. I may say we achieved a unity of thought and a way of getting along together." Privately Roosevelt characterized Stalin as "a very interesting man" whose rough exterior clothed an "old-fashioned elegant European manner." He referred to him almost affectionately as "that old buzzard" and on one occasion called him "Uncle Joe" to his face. At Yalta, Stalin gave Roosevelt a portrait photograph, with a long Cyrillic inscription in his small, tight hand.

---

* These were the principles first laid down in the so-called Atlantic Charter, drafted by Roosevelt and Churchill at a meeting on the U.S.S. *Augusta* off Newfoundland in August 1941.

While the powers argued at length over the form of the UN charter at the 50-nation San Francisco Conference, they conducted the debates in an atmosphere of optimism and international amity. Each UN member received a seat in the General Assembly, a body designed for discussion rather than action. The locus of authority in the new organization resided in the Security Council, "the castle of the great powers." This consisted of five permanent members (the United States, the Soviet Union, Great Britain, France, and China) and six others elected for two-year terms.

The Council was charged with responsibility for maintaining world peace, but any great power could block UN action whenever it wished to do so. The United States insisted on this veto power as strongly as the Soviet Union did. In effect the charter paid lip service to the Wilsonian ideal of a powerful international police force, but it incorporated the limitations that Henry Cabot Lodge had proposed in his 1919 reservation to Article 10 of the League Covenant, which relieved the United States from the obligation of enforcing collective security without the approval of Congress.

The Cold War Under Way

Long before the war in Europe ended, however, the Allies had clashed over important policy matters. Since later world tensions developed from decisions made at this time, an understanding of the disagreements is essential for evaluating several decades of history. Unfortunately, complete understanding is not yet possible, if it ever will be, which explains why the subject remains controversial.

Much depends on one's view of the postwar Soviet system. If the Soviet government under Stalin was bent on world domination, events of the so-called Cold War fall readily into one pattern of interpretation. If Russia, having bravely and at enormous cost endured an unprovoked assault by the Nazis, was seeking only to protect itself against the possibility of another invasion, these events are best explained differently. Because the United States has opened nearly all its diplomatic records, we know a great deal about how American foreign policy was formulated and about the mixed motives and mistaken judgments of American leaders. This helps explain why many scholars have been critical of

American policy and the "cold warriors" who made and directed it. The Soviet Union, in stark contrast, has excluded historians from its archives, and consequently we know little about the motivations and inner workings of Soviet policy. Was Russia "committed to overturning the international system and to endless expansion in pursuit of world dominance?" Daniel Yergin asks in *Shattered Peace*. Only access to Soviet records can provide an answer to this vitally important question.

The Soviets resented the British-American delay in opening up a second front. They were fighting for survival against the full power of the German armies; any invasion, even an unsuccessful one, would have relieved some of the pressure. Roosevelt and Churchill would not move until they were ready, and Stalin had to accept their decision. At the same time, Stalin never concealed his determination to protect his country against future attack by extending its western frontier after the war. He warned the Allies repeatedly that he would not tolerate any anti-Soviet government along Russia's western boundary.

Most Allied leaders, including Roosevelt, admitted privately during the war that the Soviet Union would annex territory and possess preponderant power in eastern Europe after the defeat of Germany, but they never said this publicly. They believed that free governments could somehow be created in countries like Poland and Bulgaria that the Soviets would trust enough to leave to their own devices. "The Poles," Winston Churchill said early in 1945, "will have their future in their own hands, with the single limitation that they must honestly follow . . . a policy friendly to Russia. This is surely reasonable."

However reasonable, Churchill's statement was impractical. The Polish question was a terribly difficult one. The war, after all, had been triggered by the German attack on Poland; the British in particular felt a moral obligation to restore that nation to its prewar independence. During the war a Polish government in exile was set up in London, and its leaders were determined—especially after the discovery in 1943 of the murder of some 5,000 Polish officers several years earlier at Katyn, in Russia, presumably by the Soviet secret police—to make no concessions to Soviet territorial demands. Public opinion in Poland (and indeed in all the states along Russia's western frontier) was not so much anti-

Soviet as anti-Russian. Yet the Soviet Union's legitimate interests (to say nothing of its power in the area) could not be ignored.

Yalta and Potsdam

At the Yalta Conference, Roosevelt and Churchill agreed to Soviet annexation of large sections of eastern Poland. In return they demanded that free elections be held in Poland itself. "I want this election to be . . . beyond question," Roosevelt told Stalin. "It should be like Caesar's wife." In a feeble attempt at a joke he added: "I did not know her but they said she was pure." Stalin agreed, almost certainly without intending to keep his promise. The elec-

tions were never held; Poland was run by a pro-Soviet puppet regime.

Stalin apparently could not understand why his allies were so concerned about the fate of a small country remote from their strategic spheres. That they professed to be concerned seemed to him an indication that they had some secret, devious purpose. He could see no difference (and "revisionist" American historians agree with him) between the Soviet Union's dominating Poland and maintaining a government there that did not reflect the wishes of a majority of the Polish people and the United States' dominating many Latin American nations and supporting unpopular regimes within them. Roosevelt, however, was worried about the political effects that Soviet control of Poland might have in

Churchill, Roosevelt, and Stalin photographed at the week-long Yalta conference in February 1945. By April 1945, Roosevelt was dead.

the United States. Polish-Americans would be furious if the United States allowed the Russians to control their homeland.

Had Roosevelt described the difficulties to the Poles and the rest of the American people more frankly, their reaction might have been less angry. In any case, when he realized that Stalin was going to act as he pleased, Roosevelt was irate. "We can't do business with Stalin," he said shortly before his death in April 1945. "He has broken every one of the promises he made at Yalta." In July 1945, following the surrender of Germany, the new president, Harry Truman, met with Stalin and Churchill at Potsdam, outside Berlin.* They agreed to try the Nazi leaders as war criminals, made plans for exacting reparations from Germany, and confirmed the division of the country into four zones to be occupied separately by American, Russian, British, and French troops. Berlin, deep in the Soviet zone, had itself been split into four sectors. Stalin rejected all arguments that he loosen his hold on eastern Europe, and Truman (who received news of the successful testing of the atomic bomb while at Potsdam) made no concessions, but he was impressed by Stalin. The dictator was "smart as hell," he wrote in his diary. "Stalin was an SOB," the plainspoken president explained to some officers while returning to the United States from Potsdam on the cruiser *Augusta*. Then he added: "Of course he thinks I'm one too."

On both sides suspicions were mounting, positions hardening. Yet all the advantages seemed to be with the United States. Was this not, as Henry Luce, the publisher of *Time* had declared, the "American century," an era when American power and American ideals would shape the course of events the world over? Besides its army, navy, and air force and its immense industrial potential, alone among the nations the United States possessed the atomic bomb. When Stalin's actions made it clear that he intended to control eastern Europe and to exert influence elsewhere in the world, most Americans first reacted somewhat in the manner of a mastiff being worried by a yapping terrier: Their resentment was tempered by amazement. It took time for them to realize that the war had caused a fundamental change in international politics. The

United States might be the strongest country in the world, but the western European nations, victor and vanquished alike, were reduced to the status of second-class powers. The Soviet Union, by contrast, had regained the influence it had held under the czars and lost as a result of World War I and the Communist Revolution.

Milestones

1941 Roosevelt creates Fair Employment practices Committee (FEPC)
Japanese attack Pearl Harbor
1942 West Coast Japanese ordered to relocation camps
Fall of the Philippines
Battle of the Coral Sea
Battle of Midway
American troops invade North Africa
1943 Manhattan Project to make atomic bomb
Race riots in Detroit and Los Angeles
Invasion of Italy
Teheran Conference
1944 Allied invasion of Normandy, France
Liberation of Paris
Battle of the Bulge
1945 Yalta Conference
San Francisco Conference to draft UN Charter
Germany surrenders (V-E Day)
Capture of Okinawa
Atomic bomb tested at Alamogordo, New Mexico
Potsdam Conference
Atomic bombs dropped on Hiroshima and Nagasaki, Japan
Japan surrenders (V-J Day)

---

* Clement R. Attlee replaced Churchill during the conference after his Labour party won the British elections.

SUPPLEMENTARY READING

Titles marked with an asterisk have been published in paperback.

On prewar American-Japanese relations, see Akira Iriye, **After Imperialism** (1965), and on Pearl Harbor, G. W. Prange, **At Dawn We Slept** (1981), and Roberta Wohlstetter, **Pearl Harbor: Warning and Decision*** (1962). C. C. Tansill, **Back Door to War** (1952), and C. A. Beard, **President Roosevelt and the Coming of the War** (1948), are interesting interpretations by isolationists, while L. C. Gardner, **Economic Aspects of New Deal Diplomacy*** (1971), is a critical scholarly analysis. Iriye's **Power and Culture: The Japanese-American War** (1981) looks at the war in the Pacific from both sides.

The home front is discussed in Richard Polenberg, **War and Society*** (1972), A. M. Winkler, **Home Front U.S.A.** (1988), and David Brinkley, **Washington Goes to War** (1988). H. M. Harris et al. (eds.), **The Homefront** (1984), contains a sampling of reminiscences by people in all walks of life. Social trends are covered in Steven Mintz and Susan Kellogg, **Domestic Revolutions*** (1988). The effect of the war on blacks is discussed in Ulysses Lee, **The Employment of Negro Troops** (1966), N. A. Wynn, **The Afro-American and the Second World War** (1976), D. J. Capeci, Jr., **Race Relations in Wartime Detroit** (1984), and A. R. Buchanan, **Black Americans in World War II** (1977). On the relocation of the Japanese, see Roger Daniels, **Concentration Camps USA: Japanese Americans and World War II** (1971), and Peter Irons, **Justice at War** (1984). The effects of the war on women are described in Karen Anderson, **Wartime Women** (1981), and S. M. Hartmann, **The Home Front and Beyond** (1982).

A. R. Buchanan, **The United States in World War II** (1964), provides an excellent overall survey of the military side of the conflict. S. E. Morison, **The Two-Ocean War*** (1963), deals with the naval side of the war. See also Stephen Ambrose, **Eisenhower** (1983), and D. S. Wyman, **The Abandonment of the Jews** (1984).

Wartime diplomacy is discussed in J. L. Gaddis, **The United States and the Origins of the Cold War*** (1972), Gar Alperovitz, **Atomic Diplomacy*** (1965), Martin Sherwin, **A World Destroyed** (1975), and Gaddis Smith, **American Diplomacy During the Second World War*** (1965).

The American Century

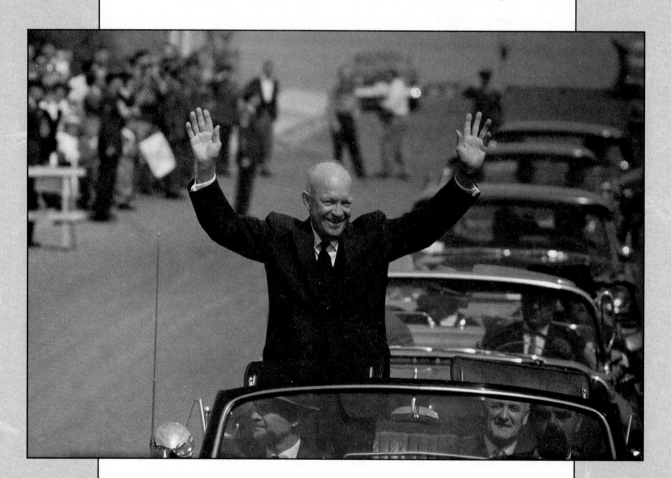

In the councils of government, we must guard against the acquisition of unwarranted influence, whether sought or unsought, by the military-industrial complex. The potential for the disastrous rise of misplaced power exists and will persist.

PRESIDENT DWIGHT D. EISENHOWER, *1961*

I n late 1945 most Americans were probably more concerned with what was happening at home than with foreign developments, and no one was more aware of this than Harry Truman. When he received the news of Roosevelt's death, he claimed that he felt as though "the moon, the stars, and all the planets" had suddenly fallen on him. Although he could not have been quite as surprised as he indicated (Roosevelt was known to have been in extremely poor health), he was acutely conscious of his own limitations.

Truman was born in Missouri in 1884. After service with a World War I artillery unit, he opened a men's clothing store in Kansas City. The store failed in the postwar depression. Truman then became a minor cog in the political machine of Democratic boss Tom Pendergast. In 1934 he was elected to the United States Senate, where he proved to be a loyal but obscure New Dealer. He first attracted national attention during World War II when his "watchdog" committee on defense spending, working with devotion and efficiency, saved the government immense sums. This led to his nomination and election as vice-president.

As president, Truman sought to carry on in the Roosevelt tradition. Curiously, he was at the same time humble and cocky, idealistic and cold-bloodedly political. He adopted liberal objectives only to pursue them sometimes by rash, even repressive means. Too often he insulted opponents instead of convincing or conciliating them. Complications tended to confuse him, in which case he either dug in his heels or struck out blindly, usually with unfortunate results. On balance, however, he was a strong and in many ways a successful chief executive.

The Postwar Economy

Nearly all the postwar leaders were worried by the possibility of a serious postwar depression, and nearly all accepted the necessity of employing federal authority to stabilize the economy and speed national development. The Great Depression and the successful application of the theories of John Maynard Keynes during the war had convinced Democrats and Republicans alike that it was possible to prevent sharp swings in the business cycle and therefore to do away with serious unemployment by monetary and fiscal manipulation. "The agents of government must . . . put a brake at certain points where boom forces develop . . . and support purchasing power when it becomes unduly depressed," the newly created Council of Economic Advisers reported.

When World War II ended, nearly everyone wanted to demobilize the armed forces, remove wartime controls, and reduce taxes. Yet everyone also hoped to prevent any sudden economic dislocation, to check inflation, and to make sure that goods in short supply were fairly distributed. Neither the politicians nor the public was able to reconcile these conflicting objectives. No group seemed willing to limit its own demands in the general interest. Labor wanted price controls retained but wage controls lifted; industrialists wished to raise prices and to keep the lid on wages. Farmers wanted subsidies but opposed price controls and the extension of social security benefits to agricultural workers.

In this difficult situation President Truman failed to win either the confidence of the people or the support of Congress. On the one hand, he proposed a comprehensive program of new legislation that included a public housing scheme, aid to education, medical insurance, civil rights guarantees, a higher minimum wage, broader social security coverage, additional conservation and public power projects patterned after TVA, increased aid to agriculture, and the retention of anti-inflationary controls. On the other hand, he ended rationing and other controls and signed a bill cutting taxes by some $6 billion. Whenever opposition to his plans developed, he vacillated between compromise and inflexibility.

Yet the country weathered the reconversion period with remarkable ease. The pent-up demand for homes, automobiles, clothing, washing machines, and countless other products, backed by the war-enforced savings of millions of people, kept factories operating at capacity. Economists had feared that the flood of millions of veterans into the job market would cause serious unemployment. But when the veterans returned (more than 60,000 of them accompanied by foreign brides), few found themselves unoccupied for long. Because of the boom, the demand for labor was large and growing. In addition, the government made an unprecedented educational opportunity available to veterans. Instead of a general bonus, which would have stimulated consumption and inflation, in 1944 Congress passed the GI Bill of Rights, which made subsidies available to veterans so that they could continue their education, learn new trades, or start new businesses. Nearly 8 million veterans took advantage of the education and training grants, greatly to their long-term advantage, and thus to the country's.

Cutting taxes and removing price controls did cause a period of rapid inflation. Food prices rose more than 25 percent between 1945 and 1947, which led to demands for higher wages and a wave of strikes (nearly 5,000 in 1946 alone). Inflation and labor unrest helped the Republicans win control of both houses of Congress in 1946 for the first time since the 1920s. High on the Republican agenda was the passage of a new labor relations act. Labor leaders tended to support the Democrats, for they remembered gratefully the Wagner Act and other help given them by the Roosevelt administration during the labor-management struggles of the 1930s. In 1943 the CIO had created a political action committee to mobilize the labor vote.

But the strikes of 1946 had alienated many citizens because they delayed the satisfaction of the demand for consumer goods. They even led President Truman, normally sympathetic to organized labor, to seize the coal mines, threaten to draft railroad workers, and ask Congress for other special powers to prevent national tie-ups.

This was the climate when in June 1947 the new Congress passed the Taft-Hartley Act over President Truman's veto. The measure outlawed both the closed shop (a provision written into many labor contracts requiring new workers to join the union before they could be employed) and secondary boycotts and strikes called as a result of disputes between unions over the right to represent workers. Most important, it authorized the president to seek court injunctions to prevent strikes that in his opinion endangered the national interest. The injunctions would hold for 80 days—a "cooling-off" period during which a presidential fact-finding board could investigate and make recommendations. If the dispute remained unresolved after 80 days, the president was to recommend "appropriate action" to Congress.

The Taft-Hartley Act made the task of unionizing unorganized industries more difficult, but it did not seriously hamper existing unions. Though it outlawed the closed shop, it permitted union shop contracts, which forced new workers to join the union after accepting employment.

Postwar Society: The Baby Boomers

The trend toward early marriage and larger families begun during the war continued and indeed accelerated when the conflict ended. In one year, 1946, more than 10 percent of all the single females in the country over the age of 14 got married. The birthrate had been under 20 per 1,000 population in the 1930s. It exceeded 25 in most years between 1946 and 1956.

Most servicemen had idealized the joys of domesticity while abroad, and they and their wives and sweethearts were eager to concentrate on "making a home and raising a family" now that the war had

Returning veterans and their growing families needed homes; wartime earnings and veterans' mortgages made possible their financing; developers were ready to build them. One result was the construction of hundreds of thousands of single-family homes laid out in massive tracts.

ended. People sought security after the strains and dangers of the war years, but they faced the future hopefully, encouraged by the booming economy and the sudden profusion of consumer goods. This satisfaction with the marital state was reflected in a slackening in the divorce rate. At the same time, perhaps because of the omnipresent signs of material progress and the confusion produced by rapid change, people tended to be conformists, looking over their shoulders, so to speak, rather than tackling life head on.

The period was marked by "a reaffirmation of domesticity," Elaine Tyler May writes in *Homeward Bound: American Families in the Cold War Era*. "Childlessness was considered deviant, selfish, and pitiable. . . . Nearly everyone believed that family togetherness, focused on children, was the mark of a successful and wholesome personal life." In 1955 a University of Michigan psychologist completed a study of 300 middle-class couples conducted over two decades. A large percentage of the women queried were college graduates. Some had apparently gone to college primarily to find a mate with a good future, but others had cheerfully sacrificed plans

for a professional career because "the right man" had come along. Of these, most had few regrets. "Marriage has opened up far more avenues of interest than I ever would have had without it," one reported.

Encouraged by magazines like the *Ladies' Home Journal* and *Woman's Home Companion*, which were full of articles on aspects of the subject, and by films that described the trials and triumphs of family life, many college-educated women made a "career" of home management and child development, claiming that this gave them satisfactions unavailable in the business and professional worlds.

The men of this generation also professed to have found fulfillment in family life. They tended to stress such things as the satisfactions gained by taking on the responsibilties that marriage and fatherhood entailed; they mentioned "the incentive to succeed" and the "motivation for intensive effort" produced by such responsibilties. For many men, however, these responsibilities provided a refuge from the competitive corporate world where they earned their living. The need to subordinate one's personal interests, even one's taste in clothes, to the requirements of "the organization," described in William Whyte's *Organization Man* (1956) and in novels like Sloan Wilson's *Man in the Gray Flannel Suit* (1955), caused strains that could best be relieved in the warmth and security of one's family. Wives were also directly affected by this pressure, since an executive's spouse was also expected to conform to corporate standards.

Blue-collar workers and clerical employees were not subjected to these pressures, but studies reveal that they did not differ in their attitudes toward marriage and child rearing. "The vast changes . . . are pervasive," two demographers concluded. "Social and economic variables . . . such as race, ethnic status, education and residence, do not indicate differences with respect to trends in fertility."

Government policies buttressed the inclinations of the people. Income tax deductions encouraged taxpayers to have children and to borrow money to purchase houses and furniture. Having a large family became a kind of national objective. "I'd like six kids," one husband reported. "It just seems like a minimum production goal." Life was family-centered, and family life was child-centered. Doctor Benjamin Spock's *Baby and Child Care* (1946), bible of the postwar generation, which sold well over 20 million copies in 20-odd years, was not as "permissive" as has often been suggested. Spock insisted that raising children called for professional skills. Responding blindly to children's desires was wrong. But he certainly emphasized the importance of loving care. "Children raised in loving families want to learn, want to conform, want to grow up," he explained.

The Containment Policy

While ordinary people seemed to concentrate almost compulsively on their personal affairs, foreign policy issues continued to vex the Truman presidency. Repeatedly, Stalin made it clear that he had no intention even of consulting with western leaders about his domination of eastern Europe, and he seemed intent on extending his power deep into war-devastated central Europe. The Soviet Union also controlled Outer Mongolia, parts of Manchuria, and northern Korea, and it had annexed the Kurile Islands and regained the southern half of Sakhalin Island from Japan. It was fomenting trouble in Iran. By January 1946 Truman had decided to stop "babying" the Russians. "Only one language do they understand," he noted in a memorandum. "How many divisions have you?"

American and Russian attitudes stood in sharp confrontation when the control of atomic energy came up for discussion in the UN. Everyone recognized the threat to human survival posed by the atomic bomb. In November 1945 the United States suggested allowing the UN to supervise all nuclear energy production, and the General Assembly promptly created the Atomic Energy Commission to study the question. In June 1946 Commissioner Bernard Baruch offered a plan for the eventual outlawing of atomic weapons. A system would be set up under which UN inspectors could operate without restriction anywhere in the world to make sure that no country was making bombs clandestinely. When, at an unspecified date, the system had been established, the United States would destroy its stockpile of bombs.

Most Americans thought the Baruch plan magnanimous and some considered it positively foolhardy; the Soviets simply rejected it. They would neither permit UN inspectors in the Soviet Union nor surrender their veto power over Security Council actions dealing with atomic energy. They demanded that the United States destroy its bombs at once.

"What struck most observers," the historian John Lewis Gaddis has written, "was the utter imperviousness of Stalin's regime to the gestures of restraint and goodwill that emanated from the West." Unwilling under the circumstances either to trust the Russians or to surrender what they considered their "winning weapon," the American leaders refused to agree. The resulting stalemate increased international tension.

Postwar cooperation had failed. By early 1946 a new policy was emerging. Many minds contributed to its development, but the key ideas were provided by George F. Kennan, a scholarly Foreign Service officer. Kennan had been stationed for five years in Russia and was a close student of Soviet history. He believed that the Soviet leaders saw the world as divided into socialist and capitalist camps separated by irreconcilable differences. Nothing the United States might do, however conciliatory, would reduce Soviet hostility, Kennan claimed. The nation should therefore accept this hostility as a fact of life and either resist Russian aggression firmly wherever it appeared or wait for time to bring about some change in Soviet policy.

Kennan's second alternative seemed both irresponsible and dangerous, whereas "getting tough with Russia" would find wide popular support. According to polls, a substantial majority considered American policy "too soft." During 1946 the Truman administration gradually adopted a tougher stance. The decisive policy shift came early in 1947 as a result of a crisis in Greece. Local Greek communists, waging a guerrilla war against the monarchy, were receiving aid from communist Yugoslavia and Bulgaria. Great Britain was assisting the monarchists but could no longer afford this drain on its resources. In February 1947 the British informed President Truman that they would have to cut off further aid to Greece.

The news came as a shock to American policy makers because the British predicament forced them to confront the fact that their European allies had not been able to rebuild their war-weakened economies. Russia's "Iron Curtain" (a phrase invented by Winston Churchill) seemed about to ring down on another nation. That the Greek government was reactionary appeared to them less im-

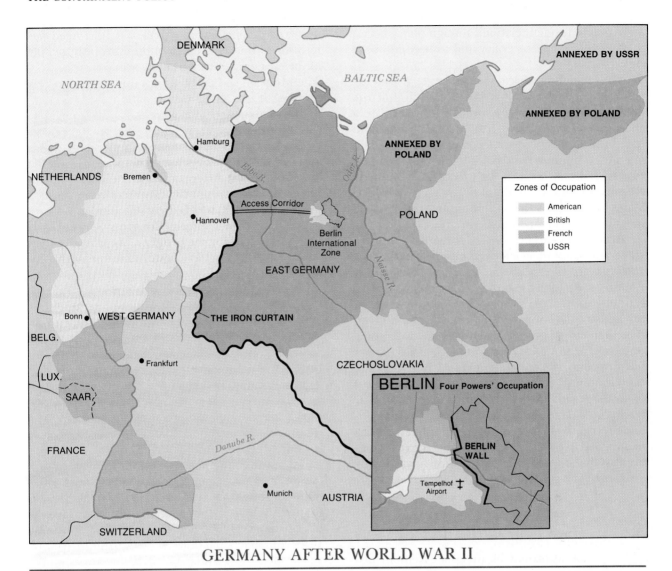

GERMANY AFTER WORLD WAR II

West Germany was created out of the merged French, British, and U.S. zones in 1947, as was West Berlin. The Russian zone became East Germany. The Berlin Wall was built later, in 1961, to keep an estimated 700 people a day from fleeing from East to West Germany.

portant than that it was threatened by communist forces. Truman therefore asked Congress to approve what became known as the Truman Doctrine. If Greece or Turkey fell to the communists, he said, all the Middle East might be lost. To prevent this "unspeakable tragedy," he asked for $400 million for military and economic aid for Greece and Turkey. "It must be the policy of the United States to support free peoples who are resisting attempted

subjugation by armed minorities or by outside pressures," he said.

By exaggerating the consequences of inaction and by justifying his request on ideological grounds, Truman attained his objective. But by not limiting his request to the specific problem posed by the situation in Greece, Truman caused considerable concern in many countries. And once official sanction was given to the communism-versus-democracy approach to foreign relations, foreign policy began to dominate domestic policy and to become more rigid.

The communist threat loomed large. With western Europe, in the words of Winston Churchill (the great phrasemaker of the era), "a rubble-heap, a charnel house, a breeding-ground of pestilence and hate," the entire continent seemed in danger of falling into communist hands without the Soviet Union raising a finger to speed the process. For humane reasons as well as for political advantage, the United States felt obliged to help these nations regain some measure of economic stability.

How might this be done? George Kennan provided an answer in an anonymous article in the July 1947 issue of *Foreign Affairs*, "The Sources of Soviet Conduct." Russian diplomacy, he wrote, moves inexorably along a prescribed path, "like a persistent toy automobile wound up and headed in a given direction, stopping only when it meets with some unmoveable force." A policy of "longterm, patient but firm and vigilant containment" based on the "application of counter-force" was the best means of dealing with Soviet pressures. The Cold War might be "a duel of infinite duration," Kennan admitted. It could be won if, without bluster, America maintained its own strength and convinced the communists that it would resist aggression firmly in any quarter of the globe.

The Marshall Plan

Although he approved its purpose, Kennan disagreed with the psychology of the Truman Doctrine, which seemed to him essentially defensive as well as vulnerable to criticism by anti-imperialists. He proposed a broad program to finance European economic recovery, the aid to be offered even to Russia if the Soviets would contribute some of their own resources to the cause. The Europeans themselves should work out the details, America providing the money, materials, and technical advice.

George C. Marshall, army chief of staff during World War II and now secretary of state, formally suggested this program, which became known as the Marshall Plan, in a Harvard commencement speech on June 5, 1947. "Hunger, poverty, desperation, and chaos" were the real enemies of freedom and democracy, Marshall said. The need was to restore "the confidence of the European people in the economic future of their own countries. . . . The program should be a joint one, agreed to by a number, if not all European nations."

The European powers seized eagerly upon Marshall's suggestion. They set up the 16-nation Committee for European Economic Cooperation, which soon submitted plans calling for up to $22.4 billion in American aid. After protracted debate, much influenced by a communist coup in Czechoslovakia in February 1948, which drew still another country behind the Iron Curtain, Congress appropriated over $13 billion for the program. Results exceeded all expectations. By 1951 western Europe was booming.

Whether the policy makers realized it or not, containment and the Marshall Plan were America's response to the power vacuum created in Europe by the debilitating effects of the war. Just as the Soviet Union extended its influence over the eastern half of the continent, the United States extended its influence in the west. Both powers were driven by insecurity—worry that the other was seeking world domination. A more accurate description of the situation would note that ignorance more than insecurity explains their worries.

In any case, the Marshall Plan formed the basis for western European economic recovery and political cooperation. In March 1948 Great Britain, France, Belgium, the Netherlands, and Luxembourg signed an alliance aimed at social, cultural, and economic collaboration. The western nations abandoned their understandable but counterproductive policy of crushing Germany economically. They instituted currency reforms in their zones and announced plans for creating a single West German republic with a large degree of autonomy.

These decisions further alarmed the Russians. In June they retaliated by closing off surface access to Berlin from the west. For a time it seemed that the Allies must either fight their way into the city or abandon it to the communists. Unwilling to adopt either alternative, Truman decided to fly supplies through the air corridors leading to the capital from Frankfurt, Hanover, and Hamburg. American C-47 and C-54 transports shuttled back and forth in weather fair and foul, carrying enough food, fuel, and other goods necessary to maintain more than 2 million West Berliners. The Berlin Airlift put the

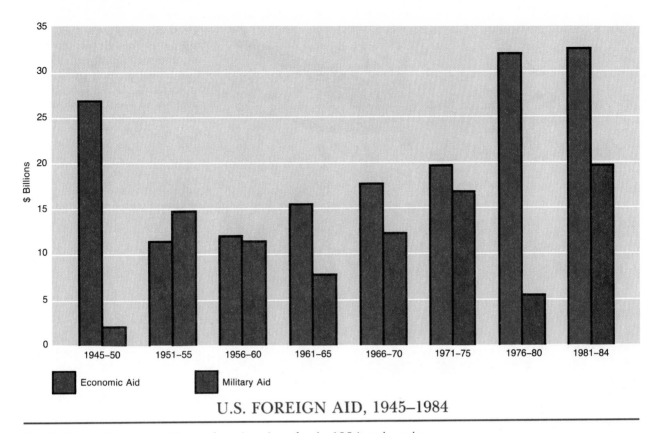

U.S. FOREIGN AID, 1945–1984

In 1945 the dollar was worth over four times its value in 1984, so in unin-flated dollars U.S. foreign aid has lessened over the years, especially during the decade 1971–1980. Even so, the total amount of U.S. foreign assistance from 1945 to 1984 was more than $280 billion.

Soviets in an uncomfortable position; if they were determined to keep supplies from West Berlin, they would have to begin the fighting. They were not prepared to do so. In May 1949 they lifted the blockade.

Containment, some of its advocates argued, required the development of a powerful military force. In May 1948 Republican Senator Arthur H. Vandenberg of Michigan, a prewar leader of the isolationists who had been converted to internationalism largely by President Roosevelt's solicitous attention to his views, introduced a resolution stating the "determination" of the United States "to exercise the right of individual or collective self-defense . . . should any armed attack occur affecting its national security." The Senate approved this resolution by a vote of 64 to 4, proof that iso-

lationism had ceased to be an important force in American politics.

Dealing with Japan and China

Containment worked well in Europe, at least in the short run; in the Far East, where the United States lacked powerful allies, it was both more expensive and less effective. V-J Day found the Far East a shambles. Much of Japan was a smoking ruin. In China chaos reigned; nationalists under Chiang Kai-shek dominated the south, communists under Mao Tse-tung controlled the northern countryside, and Japanese troops still held most northern cities.

President Truman acted decisively and effectively with regard to Japan, unsurely and with un-

American cargo plane flying in supplies to West Berlin, after Soviet authorities in the surrounding East Germany closed off road and rail access to the city. The airlift remained in operation for nearly a year until the blockade was lifted in May 1949.

fortunate results where China was concerned. Even before the Japanese surrendered, he had decided not to allow the Soviet Union any significant role in the occupation of Japan. The four-power Allied Control Council was established, but American troops commanded by General MacArthur governed the country.

MacArthur displayed exactly the proper combination of imperiousness, tact, and intelligence needed to accomplish his purposes. The Japanese, revealing the same remarkable adaptability that had made possible their swift westernization in the second half of the 19th century, accepted political and social changes that involved universal suffrage and parliamentary government, the encouragement of labor unions, the breakup of large estates and big industrial combines, and the de-emphasis of the importance of the emperor. Japan lost its far-flung island empire and all claim to Korea and the Chinese mainland. Japan emerged economically strong, politically stable, and firmly allied with the United States.

The difficulties in China were probably insurmountable. Few Americans appreciated the latent power of the Chinese communists. When the war ended, Truman tried to bring Chiang's nationalists and Mao's communists together. He sent General Marshall to China to seek a settlement, but neither Chiang nor Mao would make significant concessions. Mao was convinced—correctly, as time soon proved—that he could win all of China by force, while Chiang, presiding over a corrupt and incompetent regime, grossly exaggerated his popularity among the Chinese people. In January 1947 Truman recalled Marshall and named him secretary of state. Soon thereafter civil war erupted in China.

The Election of 1948

In the spring of 1948 President Truman's fortunes were at low ebb. Public opinion polls suggested that a majority of the people considered him incompetent or worse. The Republicans seemed sure to win the 1948 presidential election, especially if Truman was the Democratic candidate. Governor Dewey, who again won the Republican nomination, ran confidently, even complacently, certain that he would carry the country with ease.

Truman's position seemed hopeless because he had alienated both southern conservatives and northern liberals. The southerners were particularly distressed because in 1946 the president had established the Committee on Civil Rights, which had recommended antilynching and anti-poll-tax legislation and the creation of a permanent Fair Employment Practices Commission. When, despite the objections of administration delegates, the Democratic convention adopted a strong civil rights plank, the southern delegates walked out. Southern conservatives then founded the States' Rights ('Dixiecrat') party and nominated J. Strom Thurmond of South Carolina for president.

As for the liberals, in 1947 a group of them had founded Americans for Democratic Action (ADA) and sought an alternative candidate for the 1948 election. A faction led by former vice-president Henry A. Wallace, which believed Truman's containment policy a threat to world peace, organized a new Progressive party and nominated Wallace. Most members of ADA, however, thought Wallace too pro-Soviet; in the end the organization supported Truman. Yet with two minor candidates sure to cut into the Democratic vote, the president's chances seemed minuscule.

Promising to "give 'em hell," Truman launched an aggressive "whistle-stop" campaign. Traveling by rail,* he made several hundred informal but hard-hitting speeches. He excoriated the "do-nothing" Republican Congress, which had rejected his program and passed the Taft-Hartley Act, and he warned labor, farmers, and consumers that if Dewey won, Republican "gluttons of privilege" would do away with all the gains of the New Deal years.

Millions were moved by his arguments and by his courageous fight against great odds. The success of the Berlin Airlift during the presidential campaign helped him considerably, as did disaffection among normally Republican middle western farmers. The Progressive party fell increasingly into the hands of communist sympathizers, driving away many liberals who might otherwise have supported Wallace. Dewey's smug, lackluster campaign failed to attract independents. The president was thus able to reinvigorate the New Deal coalition, and he won an amazing upset victory on election day. He col-

---

* The term *whistle stop* referred to rural stations where trains stopped only on signal.

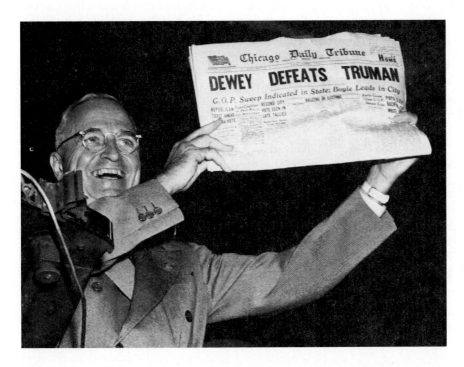

In 1948 the strongly Republican Chicago Daily Tribune guessed its post-election editions before all the returns were in. For Truman, it was the perfect climax to his hard-won victory.

lected 24.1 million votes to Dewey's 21.9 million, the two minor candidates being held to about 2.3 million. In the electoral college his margin was a thumping 303 to 189. In his speech conceding defeat, Dewey, a man not noted for wit, remarked ruefully: "Thought I heard the voice of the people. Must have been some other noise."

Truman's victory gave the ADA considerable influence over what the president called his Fair Deal program. ADA leaders took a middle-of-the-road approach, well described in a book by Arthur M. Schlesinger, Jr., *The Vital Center* (1949), which left room for individualism and social welfare, government regulation of the economy, and the encouragement of private enterprise. The approach fitted well with Cold War conditions, which favored both massive military output and continued expansion of the supply of civilian goods. Economic growth would solve all problems, social as well as material. Through growth, the poor could be helped without taking from the rich. The way to check inflation, for example, was not by freezing prices, profits, or wages but by expanding production.

However, relatively little of Truman's Fair Deal was enacted into law. Congress approved a federal housing program and measures increasing the minimum wage and social security benefits, but these were merely extensions of New Deal legislation.

Containing Communism Abroad

During Truman's second term the confrontation between the United States and the Soviet Union, and more broadly between what was seen as "democracy" and "communism," dominated the headlines and occupied a major part of the attention of the president and most other government officials. To strengthen ties with the European democracies, in April 1949 the North Atlantic Treaty was signed in Washington. The United States, Great Britain, France, Italy, Belgium, the Netherlands, Luxembourg, Denmark, Norway, Portugal, Iceland, and Canada* agreed "that an armed attack against one or more of them in Europe or North America shall be considered an attack against them all" and that in the event of such an attack, each would take

---

* In 1952 Greece and Turkey joined the alliance, and in 1954 West Germany was admitted.

"individually and in concert with the other Parties, such action as it deems necessary, including the use of armed force." No more entangling alliance could be imagined, yet the Senate ratified this treaty by a vote of 82 to 13. The pact established the North Atlantic Treaty Organization (NATO). Disturbed by the news, released in September 1949, that the Soviet Union had produced an atomic bomb, Congress appropriated $1.5 billion to arm NATO. In 1951 General Eisenhower was recalled to active duty and placed in command of NATO forces.

The success of containment was not without its price; every move evoked a Russian response. The Marshall Plan led to the seizure of Czechoslovakia; the buildup of West Germany led to the Berlin blockade; the creation of NATO led to the eastern European military alliance known as the Warsaw Pact. Both sides contributed by their actions and their continuing suspicions to the heightening of Cold War tensions.

In Asia the effort to contain communism exploded into war. By the end of 1949 Mao Tse-tung's communist armies had administered a crushing defeat to the nationalists. The remnants of Chiang Kai-shek's forces fled to the island of Formosa, now called Taiwan. The "loss" of China to communism strengthened right-wing opponents of internationalism in the Republican party. They and other critics charged that Truman had not backed the nationalists strongly enough and that he had stupidly underestimated Mao's dedication to the cause of world revolution. Despite superficial plausibility, neither charge made much sense. American opinion would not have supported military intervention, and such intervention would unquestionably have alienated the Chinese people. That any American action could have changed the outcome in China is unlikely. The United States probably gave the nationalists too much aid rather than too little.

The attacks of his critics aroused Truman's combativeness and led him into serious miscalculations elsewhere in Asia. After the war the province of Korea was taken from Japan and divided at 38° north latitude into the Democratic People's Republic, backed by the Soviet Union, and the Republic of Korea, backed by the United States and the UN. Both powers withdrew their troops from the peninsula, the Russians leaving behind a well-armed local force while the Republic of Korea's army was small and ill trained.

Hot War in Korea

American strategists, while seeking to "contain" communism in the Far East, had decided that military involvement on the Asiatic mainland was impracticable. America's first line of defense was to be its island bases in Japan, Taiwan, and the Philippines. In January 1950 Dean Acheson, who had succeeded Marshall as secretary of state, deliberately excluded Korea from what he described as the "defensive perimeter" of the United States in Asia. "We cannot scatter our shots equally all over the world," Acheson explained to the Senate Foreign Relations Committee. It was up to the South Koreans, backed by the UN, to protect themselves. This the Koreans were unable to do; when North Korean armored divisions struck suddenly across the 38th parallel in June 1950, they quickly routed the defenders.

At this point President Truman exhibited his finest qualities: decisiveness and courage. Whatever the actual importance of South Korea to the United States, if the blatant North Korean attack were not resisted, more serious aggressions seemed sure to follow. With the backing of the UN Security Council (but without asking Congress to declare war), he sent American planes into battle.* Ground troops soon followed.

Nominally the Korean War was a struggle between the invaders and the United Nations. General MacArthur, placed in command, flew the blue UN flag over his headquarters, and 16 nations supplied troops for his army. However, more than 90 percent of the forces employed were American. At first the North Koreans pushed them back rapidly, but by the beginning of September a front was stabilized around the port of Pusan, at the southern tip of Korea. Then MacArthur executed a brilliant amphibious flanking maneuver, striking at the west coast city of Inchon, about 50 miles south of the 38th parallel. Outflanked, the North Koreans retreated in disorder. By October the battlefront had moved north of the old boundary.

General MacArthur now proposed the conquest of North Korea, the bombing of "privileged sanctuaries" on the Chinese side of the Korean border,

THE KOREAN WAR, 1950–1953

and the redeployment of Chinese Nationalist troops on the mainland. Less sanguine military officials balked at taking on China but urged occupying North Korea to protect the future security of the south. Most of Truman's civilian advisers, led by George Kennan, opposed any advance beyond the 38th parallel, fearing intervention not only by the Red Chinese but by the Russians as well. "When we start walking inland from the tip of Korea, we have about a 10,000 mile walk if we keep going," Kennan pointed out. "We are going to have to stop somewhere."

Faced with conflicting advice, Truman authorized MacArthur to advance as far as the Yalu River,

---

* Russia, which could have vetoed this action, was at the moment boycotting the Security Council because the UN had refused to give the Mao Tse-tung regime China's seat on that body.

the boundary between North Korea and China, but to avoid war with China or the Soviet Union at all cost. It was a momentous and unfortunate decision, an example of how power, once unleashed, so often gets out of hand. As the advance progressed, ominous rumblings came from north of the Yalu. Foreign Minister Chou En-lai warned that the Chinese would not "supinely tolerate seeing their neighbors being savagely invaded by imperialists." Chinese "volunteers" began to turn up among the captives taken by UN units.

Alarmed, Truman flew to Wake Island, in the Pacific, to confer with MacArthur, but the general assured him that the Chinese would not dare to intervene. If they did, MacArthur added, his army would crush them easily; the war would be over by Christmas.

Seldom has a general miscalculated so badly. On November 26 a total of 33 Chinese divisions suddenly smashed through the center of MacArthur's line. Overnight a triumphant advance became a disorganized retreat. MacArthur now spoke of the "bottomless well of Chinese manpower" and justified his earlier confidence by claiming, not without reason, that he was fighting "an entirely new war."

The UN army rallied south of the 38th parallel, and by the spring of 1951 the front had been stabilized. MacArthur then urged that he be permitted to bomb Chinese installations north of the Yalu. He also suggested a naval blockade of the coast of China and the use of Chinese Nationalist troops in Korea. When Truman rejected these proposals on the grounds that they would lead to a third world war, MacArthur, who tended to ignore the larger polit-

Photographer David Douglas Duncan was with the First Marine Division in Korea when it was virtually isolated by the sudden Red Chinese offensive in November 1950. Conducting in frigid weather what the military historian S. L. A. Marshall called "the greatest fighting withdrawal of modern history," the marines broke out to safety.

ical aspects of the conflict, attempted to rouse Congress and the public against the president by criticizing administration policy openly. Truman ordered him to be silent, and when the general persisted, the president removed him from command.

At first the Korean "police action" had been popular in the United States, but as the months passed and the casualties mounted, many citizens became disillusioned and angry. The war had brought into the open a basic political (or better, psychological) disadvantage of the containment policy: Its object was not victory but balance; it involved apparently unending tension without the satisfying release of an action completed. To Americans accustomed to triumph and fond of oversimplifying complex questions, containment seemed, as its costs in blood and dollars mounted, a monumentally frustrating policy.

But in time the fundamental correctness of Truman's policy and his decision to remove MacArthur became apparent. Military men backed the president almost unanimously. General Omar N. Bradley, chairman of the Joint Chiefs of Staff, said that a showdown with the Chinese "would involve us in the wrong war, at the wrong place, at the wrong time and with the wrong enemy." In June 1951 the communists agreed to discuss an armistice in Korea, and though the negotiations dragged on, with interruptions, for two years while thousands more died along the static battlefront, both MacArthur and talk of bombing China subsided.

The Communist Issue at Home

The frustrating Korean War highlighted the paradox that at the pinnacle of its power, the influence of the United States in world affairs was declining. Its monopoly of nuclear weapons had been lost. China had passed into the communist orbit. Elsewhere in Asia and throughout Africa, new nations, formerly colonial possessions of the western powers, were adopting a neutralist position in the Cold War. Despite the billions poured into armaments and foreign aid, the safety and even the survival of the country seemed far from assured.

Internal as well as external dangers loomed. Alarming examples of communist espionage in Canada, in Great Britain, and in the United States itself convinced many citizens that clever conspirators were everywhere at work undermining American security. Both the Republicans and conservative Democratic critics of Truman's domestic policies were charging that he was "soft" on communists.

There were never more than 100,000 communists in the United States, and party membership plummeted after the start of the Cold War. However, the possibility that a handful of spies could do enormous damage fueled a kind of panic that could be used for partisan purposes. In 1947, hoping to defuse the communists-in-government issue by being more zealous in pursuit of spies than his critics, Truman established the Loyalty Review Board to check up on government employees. The program made even sympathy for a long list of vaguely defined "totalitarian" or "subversive" organizations grounds for dismissal. Persons so charged were not allowed to cross-examine their accusers. During the following ten years about 2,700 government workers were discharged, only a relative handful of them for legitimate reasons. A much larger number resigned.

In 1948 Whittaker Chambers, an editor of *Time* who had formerly been a communist, charged that Alger Hiss, president of the Carnegie Endowment for International Peace and a former State Department official, had been a communist in the 1930s. Hiss denied the charge and sued Chambers for libel. Chambers then produced microfilms purporting to show that Hiss had copied classified documents for dispatch to Moscow. Hiss could not be indicted for espionage because of the statute of limitations; instead he was charged with perjury. His first trial resulted in a hung jury, his second, ending in January 1950, in conviction and a five-year jail term.

The Hiss case fed the fears of those who believed in the existence of a powerful communist underground in the United States. The disclosure in February 1950 that a respected British scientist, Klaus Fuchs, had betrayed atomic secrets to the Russians heightened these fears, as did the arrest and conviction of his American associate, Harry Gold, and two other American traitors, Julius and Ethel Rosenberg, on the same charge.

Although they were obviously not major spies and the information they revealed was not impor-

The lean, well-dressed diplomat Alger Hiss (right) being asked to identify the frumpy, ex-communist spy Whittaker Chambers (left) by the chief counsel of the House Un-American Activities Committee hearings in 1948. Hiss denied knowing Chambers; Chambers insisted that he had been a colleague in treason.

tant, the Rosenbergs were executed, to the consternation of many liberals in the United States and elsewhere. However, information gathered by other spies had speeded the Soviet development of nuclear weapons. This fact encouraged some Republicans to press the communists-in-government issue hard.

McCarthyism

On February 9, 1950, an obscure senator, Joseph R. McCarthy of Wisconsin, casually introduced this theme in a speech before the Women's Republican Club of Wheeling, West Virginia: "The reason we find ourselves in a position of impotency," he stated, "is not because our only powerful potential enemy has sent men to invade our shores, but rather because of the traitorous actions of those who have been treated so well by this nation." The State Department, he added, was "infested" with communists. "I have here in my hand a list of 205—a list of names that were known to the Secretary of State as

being members of the Communist Party and who nevertheless are still working and shaping . . . policy."*

McCarthy had no shred of evidence to back up these statements, as a Senate committee headed by the conservative Democrat Millard Tydings of Maryland soon demonstrated. He never exposed a single spy or secret American communist. One reporter quipped that McCarthy could not tell Karl Marx from Groucho. But thousands of people were too eager to believe him to listen to reason. Within a few weeks he was the most talked-about person in Congress. Inhibited neither by scruples nor by logic, he lashed out in every direction, attacking international experts like Professor Owen Lattimore of Johns Hopkins and diplomats such as John S. Service and John Carter Vincent, who were already under attack for having courageously pointed out

---

* McCarthy was speaking from rough notes, and no one made an accurate record of his words. The exact number mentioned has long been in dispute. On other occasions he said there were 57 and 81 "card-carrying communists" in the State Department.

the deficiencies of the Chiang Kai-shek regime during the Chinese civil war.

When McCarthy's victims indignantly denied his charges, he distracted the public with still more sensational accusations directed at other innocents. Even General Marshall, whose patriotism was beyond question, was subject to McCarthy's abuse. The general, he said, was "steeped in falsehood," part of a "conspiracy so immense and an infamy so black as to dwarf any previous venture in the history of man."

McCarthy was totally unscrupulous. The "big lie" was his most effective weapon; the enormity of his charges and the status of his targets convinced thousands that there must be *some* truth to what he was saying. Nevertheless, his crude tactics would have failed if the public had not been so worried about communism. The worries were caused by the reality of Soviet military power, the attack on Korea, the loss of the nuclear monopoly, and the stories about spies. Having been plunged again into the tensions of international conflicts so soon after World War II, when they had expected to relax and enjoy life, heightened the concern of many citizens and added an irrational element to their fears.

In the 1950 election campaign McCarthy "invaded" Maryland to campaign against Senator Tydings, who was running for reelection. Tydings was defeated, and two years later William Benton of Connecticut, who had introduced a resolution calling for McCarthy's expulsion from the Senate, also failed reelection after McCarthy campaigned against him. Both would probably have lost in any case for reasons unrelated to the communism issue, but thereafter fainthearted congressmen who detested McCarthy dared not incur his wrath. Large numbers of Republicans found the temptation to take advantage of his voter appeal irresistible.

Dwight D. Eisenhower

As the 1952 presidential election approached, Truman's popularity was again at a low ebb. Senator McCarthy attacked him relentlessly for his handling of the Korean conflict and his "mistreatment" of General MacArthur. In choosing their candidate, the Republicans passed over the twice-defeated Dewey and their most prominent leader, Senator Robert A. Taft of Ohio, an outspoken conservative, and nominated General Dwight D. Eisenhower.

Eisenhower's popularity did not grow merely out of his achievements in World War II. Although a West Pointer (class of 1915), he struck most persons as anything but warlike. After the bristly, combative Truman, his genial tolerance and evident desire to avoid controversy proved widely appealing. Eisenhower's reluctance to seek political office reminded the country of George Washington, while his seeming ignorance of current political issues was no more a handicap to his campaign than the similar ignorance of Jackson and Grant in their times. People "liked Ike" because of his personality—he radiated warmth and sincerity—and because his management of the Allied armies promised that he would be equally competent as head of the complex federal government. His promise during the campaign to go to Korea if elected to try to bring the war to an end was a political masterstroke.

The Democrats nominated Governor Adlai E. Stevenson of Illinois, whose grandfather had been vice-president under Grover Cleveland. Stevenson's unpretentiousness was appealing, and his witty, urbane speeches captivated intellectuals. In retrospect, however, it is clear that he had not the remotest chance of defeating the popular Eisenhower. Disillusionment with the Korean War and a widespread belief that the Democrats had been too long in power were added handicaps. His foes turned his strongest assets against him, denouncing his humor as frivolity, characterizing his appreciation of the complexities of life as self-doubt, and tagging his intellectual followers "eggheads," an appellation that effectively caricatured the balding, slope-shouldered, somewhat endomorphic candidate. "The eggheads are for Stevenson," one Republican pointed out, "but how many eggheads are there?" There were far too few to carry the country, as the election revealed. The result was a Republican landslide: Eisenhower received almost 34 million votes to Stevenson's 27 million, and in the electoral college his margin was 442 to 89.

In office, Eisenhower was the antithesis of Truman. The Republicans had charged the Democratic administration with being wasteful and extravagant. Eisenhower planned to run his administration on sound business principles and to eschew increases in the activities of the federal government. He spoke scornfully of "creeping socialism," called for more local control of government affairs, and promised to reduce federal spending in order to balance the budget and cut taxes. He believed that by battling with Congress and pressure groups over the details of legislation, his immediate predecessors had sacrificed part of their status as chief representative of the American people. Like Washington, he tried to avoid being caught up in narrow partisan conflicts. Like Washington, he was not always able to do so.

Having successfully managed the complexities of military administration, Eisenhower used the same kind of staff system as president. He gave his Cabinet officers more responsibility than many other presidents because he did not like to devote time and energy to administrative routine. This did not mean that he was lazy or politically naive. He knew that if he left too many small decisions to others, they would soon be controlling, if not actually making, the large decisions as well.

Although conservative, Eisenhower was neither a reactionary nor a fool. He hoped to balance the federal budget and lower taxes, but he was unwilling to do away with existing social and economic legislation or to cut back on military expenditures. Some economists claimed that he reacted too slowly in dealing with business recessions and that he showed insufficient concern for speeding the rate of national economic growth. Yet he adopted an almost Keynesian approach to economic problems; that is, he tried to check downturns in the business cycle by stimulating the economy. In his memoir *Mandate for Change* (1963) he wrote of resorting to "preventative action to arrest the downturn (of 1954) before it might become severe" and of being ready to use "any and all weapons in the federal arsenal, including changes in monetary and credit policy, modifications of the tax structure, and a speed-up in the construction of . . . public works" to accomplish this end.

Eisenhower approved the extension of social security to an additional 10 million persons; created the Department of Health, Education, and Welfare and the St. Lawrence Seaway project; and in 1955 came out for federal support of schools and a highway construction act that eventually produced a 40,000-mile network of superhighways covering every state in the Union.

Eisenhower's somewhat doctrinaire belief in decentralization and private enterprise reduced the effectiveness of his social welfare measures, but on balance, he proved to be an excellent politician. He knew how to be flexible without compromising his basic values. His "conservatism" became first "dynamic conservatism" and then "progressive moderation." He summarized his attitude by saying that he was liberal in dealing with individuals but conservative "when talking about . . . the individual's pocketbook." He hoped to strengthen the moderate faction of his party, but despite his extraordinary popularity, he did not succeed in persuading many right-wing Republicans that this was a good idea.

The Eisenhower-Dulles Foreign Policy

After the 1952 election Eisenhower kept his pledge to go to Korea. His trip produced no immediate result, but the truce talks, suspended before the election, were resumed. In July 1953, perhaps influenced by a hint that the United States might use "tactical" atomic bombs in Korea, the communists agreed to an armistice. Korea remained divided. Containment had proved extremely expensive; the United States had suffered more that 135,000 casualties, including 33,000 dead. Yet aggression had been confronted and fought to a standstill.

The American people, troubled and uncertain, counted on Eisenhower to find a way to employ the nation's immense strength constructively. The new president shared the general feeling that a change of tactics in foreign affairs was needed. He counted on Congress and his secretary of state to solve the practical problems.

Given this attitude, his choice of John Foster Dulles as secretary of state seemed inspired. Dulles's experience in diplomacy dated to 1907, when he had served as secretary to the Chinese delegation at the Second Hague Conference.* Later he had a small place among the army of experts advising Wilson at the Versailles Conference. More recently he had been a representative of the United States in the UN General Assembly. "With my understanding of the intricate relationships between the peoples of the world and your sensitiveness to the

---

* The delegation was headed by Dulles's grandfather, John W. Foster, who had been secretary of state under Benjamin Harrison. An uncle, Robert Lansing, had been Woodrow Wilson's secretary of state during the First World War.

Dulles during a 1956 press conference at which he rejected suggestions by Russia and India that the United States suspend further hydrogen bomb tests. His stance and gesture project his "hard line" approach.

political considerations involved," he told Eisenhower, "we will make the most successful team in history."

Dulles combined amazing energy and strong moral convictions—"there is no way to solve the great perplexing international problems except by bringing to bear on them the force of Christianity," he insisted. His objectives were magnificent; his strategy was grandiose. Instead of waiting for the communist powers to make a move and then "containing" them, the United States should put more emphasis on nuclear bombs and less on conventional weapons. Such a "New Look" would prevent the United States from being caught up in "local" conflicts like the Korean war and both save money and inspire international respect. Potential enemies would know that "massive retaliation" would be the fate of any aggressor. With the communists im-

mobilized by this threat, positive measures aimed at "liberating" eastern Europe and "unleashing" Chiang Kai-shek against the Chinese mainland would follow. Dulles professed great faith in NATO, but he believed that if America's allies lacked the courage to follow its lead, the nation would have to undertake an "agonizing reappraisal" of its commitments to them.

Thus Dulles envisioned a policy broader, more economical, and more aggressive than Truman's. By concentrating on nuclear deterrents and avoiding "brushfire" wars in remote regions, the country could increase its security and dramatically reduce the cost of defense.

Despite his determination, energy, and high ideals, Dulles failed to make the United States a more effective force in world affairs. Most of Dulles's other schemes were quite unrealistic. "Unleashing" Chiang Kai-shek against the Chinese communists would have been like matching a Pekingese against a tiger. "Liberating" Russia's European satellites would have involved a third world war. When East German workers rioted in June 1953 and again when the Hungarians revolted in 1956, no help was forthcoming from America. Above all, massive retaliation made little sense when the Soviet Union possessed nuclear weapons as powerful as those of the United States. In November 1952 America had won the race to make a hydrogen bomb, but the Russians duplicated this feat the following August. Thereafter the only threat behind massive retaliation was the threat of human extinction. Actually, the awesome force of hydrogen bombs, the smallest of which dwarfed the bomb dropped on Hiroshima, provided both powers with a true deterrent. Willy nilly, nuclear power had established itself as a formidable force for world peace.

McCarthy Self-destructs

Dulles's saber-rattling tactics were badly timed as well as impractical. While he was planning to avert future Koreas, the Soviet Union was shifting its approach. Stalin died in March 1953, and after a period of internal conflict within the Kremlin, Nikita Khrushchev emerged as the new master of Russia. Despite his blunderbuss style, Khrushchev set out to obtain his objectives by indirection. He appealed to the antiwestern prejudices of countries just emerging from the yoke of colonialism, offering them economic aid and pointing to Soviet achievements in science and technology, such as the launching of *Sputnik,* the first satellite (1957), as proof that communism would soon "bury" the capitalist system without troubling to destroy it by force. The Soviet Union was the friend of all peace-loving nations, he insisted.

Khrushchev was a master hypocrite, yet he was a realist too. While Dulles, product of a system that made a virtue of compromise and tolerance, insisted that the world must choose between American good and Russian evil, Khrushchev, trained to believe in the incompatibility of communism and capitalism, began to talk of "peaceful coexistence."

Dulles failed to win the confidence of America's allies or even that of the State Department. Senator McCarthy moderated his attacks on the Department not a jot when it came under the control of his own party. In 1953 its overseas information program received his special attention. He denounced Voice of America broadcasters for quoting the works of "controversial" authors and sent Roy M. Cohn, youthful special counsel of his Committee on Governmental Operations, on a mission to Europe to ferret out subversives in the United States Information Service.

Dulles did not come to the defense of his people. Instead he seemed determined to out-McCarthy McCarthy in his zeal to get rid of "undesirables" of all sorts. He sanctioned the discharge of nearly 500 State Department employees, not one of whom was proved to have engaged in subversive activities. People were let go merely because they were suspected of being homosexuals, the argument being that they might be blackmailed into giving state secrets to the communists. By making such "concessions" to McCarthy, Dulles hoped to end attacks on the administration's foreign policy. The tactic failed; its only result was to undermine the morale of Foreign Service officers.

But McCarthy finally overreached himself. Early in 1954 he turned his guns on the army. After a series of charges and countercharges, he accused army officials of trying to blackmail his committee and announced a broad investigation. The resulting Army-McCarthy hearings, televised across the country, proved the senator's undoing. For weeks his dark scowl, his blind combativeness, and his disregard for every human value stood exposed for

Senator Joseph McCarthy conferring with his aide, Roy M. Cohn, during the 1954 televised hearings into alleged communist infiltration of the army. McCarthy's bullying tactics and evidence that he had tried to secure preferred treatment from the army for another aide cost him most of the popular support and political clout his outspoken anti-communism had earlier won him.

millions to see. When the hearings ended in June 1954 after some million words of testimony, his spell had been broken.

The Senate, with President Eisenhower quietly applying pressure behind the scene, at last moved to censure him in December 1954. This reproof completed the destruction of his influence. Although he continued to issue statements and wild charges, the country no longer listened. In 1957 he died of cirrhosis of the liver.

Asian Policy After Korea

While the final truce talks were taking place in Korea, new trouble was erupting far to the south in French Indochina. Since December 1946 nationalist rebels led by the communist Ho Chi Minh had been harassing the French in Vietnam, one of three puppet kingdoms (the others were Laos and Cambodia) fashioned by France in Indochina after the defeat of the Japanese in World War II. When Communist China recognized the rebels, who were known as the Vietminh, and began supplying them with arms, President Truman, applying the containment policy, countered with economic and military assistance to the French. When Eisenhower succeeded to the presidency, he continued and expanded this assistance.

Early in 1954 Ho Chi Minh's troops trapped and beseiged a French army in the remote stronghold of Dien Bien Phu. Facing the loss of 20,000 soldiers, France asked the United States to commit its air force to the battle. Eisenhower, after long deliberation, refused. Although the likelihood of communist control of Vietnam worried him, his desire to avoid any taint of imperialism was reinforced by his military judgment. The idea of using American air strikes, he believed, was "just silly." The communists were "secreted all around in the jungle. How are we, in a few air strikes, to defeat them?"

In May the French garrison at Dien Bien Phu surrendered, and in July, while the United States watched from the sidelines, France, Great Britain, Russia, and China signed an agreement at Geneva dividing Vietnam along the 17th parallel. France withdrew from the area. The northern sector became the Democratic Republic of Vietnam, controlled by Ho Chi Minh; the southern sector remained in the hands of the emperor, Bao Dai. An election to settle the future of all Vietnam was scheduled for 1956.

When it seemed likely that the communists would win that election, Ngo Dinh Diem, a conservative anticommunist, overthrew Bao Dai and became president of South Vietnam. The United States supplied his government liberally with aid. The planned election was never held, and Vietnam remained divided into two nations.

Dulles responded to the diplomatic setback in Vietnam by establishing the Southeast Asia Treaty Organization (SEATO) in September 1954, but only three Asian nations—the Philippine Republic, Thailand, and Pakistan—joined this alliance.* At the same time, the unleashed Chiang Kai-shek was engaging in a meaningless artillery duel with the Chinese communists from the tiny nationalist-held islands of Quemoy and Matsu, which lay in the shadow of the mainland. When it was suggested that the United States join in the fight, Eisenhower refused on the ground, sensible but inconsistent

---

* The other signatories were Great Britain, France, the United States, Australia, and New Zealand.

with Dulles's rhetoric, that intervention might set off an atomic war.

The Middle East Cauldron

Within a year the world teetered once again on the brink of war, this time in the Middle East. American policy in that region, aside from the ubiquitous problem of restraining Russian expansion, was influenced by the huge oil resources of Iran, Iraq, Kuwait, and Saudi Arabia—about 60 percent of the world's known reserves—and by the conflict between the new Jewish state of Israel (formerly the British mandate of Palestine) and its Arab neighbors. Although he tried to woo the Arabs, President Truman had consistently placed support for Israel before other considerations in the Middle East.

Angered by the creation of Israel, the surrounding Arab nations tried to destroy the country. (The Israeli question had the same impact on Arab emotions that the "bloody shirt" had had on Republicans after the Civil War.) Though badly outnumbered, the Israelis were better organized and better armed than the Arabs and drove them off with relative ease. With them departed nearly a million Palestinian Arabs, thereby creating a desperate refugee problem in nearby countries. Truman's support of Israel and the millions of dollars contributed to the new state by American Jews caused much Arab resentment of the United States.

Dulles and Eisenhower tried to redress the balance by de-emphasizing American support of Israel. In 1952 a revolution in Egypt had overthrown the dissolute King Farouk. Colonel Gamal Abdel Nasser emerged as the strongman of Egypt. The United States was prepared to lend Nasser money to build a huge dam on the Nile at Aswan. The dam was to be the key to an Egyptian irrigation program and a vast source of electric power. However, the Eisenhower administration would not sell Egypt arms. The communists would. For this reason Nasser drifted toward the communist orbit. In May 1956 he established diplomatic relations with Red China.

When Eisenhower then decided not to finance the Aswan Dam, Nasser responded by nationalizing the Suez Canal. This move galvanized the British and French. Influenced by Dulles's argument that Egypt could be made an ally by cajolery, the British had acceded in 1954 to Nasser's demand that they evacuate their military base at Suez. Now their traditional "lifeline" to the Orient was at Egypt's mercy. In conjunction with the French, and without consulting the United States, the British decided to take back the canal by force. The Israelis, alarmed by repeated Arab hit-and-run raids along their borders, also attacked Egypt.

Events moved swiftly. Israeli armored columns crushed the Egyptian army in the Sinai peninsula in a matter of days. France and Britain occupied Port Said, at the northern end of the canal. Nasser blocked the canal by sinking ships in the channel. In the UN the Soviet Union and the United States introduced resolutions calling for a cease-fire. Both were vetoed by Britain and France.

Then Khrushchev threatened to send "volunteers" to Egypt and launch atomic missiles against France and Great Britain if they did not withdraw. Eisenhower also demanded that the invaders pull out of Egypt. In London large crowds demonstrated against their own government. On November 6, only nine days after the first Israeli units invaded Egypt, British prime minister Anthony Eden, haggard and shaken, announced a cease-fire. Israel withdrew its troops. The crisis subsided as rapidly as it had arisen.

The United States had adhered to its principles and won a measure of respect in the Arab countries. But at what cost! Its major allies had been humiliated. Their ill-timed attack had enabled Russia to recover much of the prestige lost as a result of its brutal suppression of a Hungarian revolt which had broken out a week before the Suez fiasco. Eden and French premier Guy Mollet were claiming with considerable plausibility that Dulles's futile attempt to win Arab friendship without abandoning Israel had placed them in a dilemma and that the secretary had behaved dishonorably or at least disingenuously in handling the Egyptian problem.

The bad feeling within the western alliance soon passed. When Russia seemed likely to profit from its "defense" of Egypt in the crisis, the president in January 1957 announced the Eisenhower Doctrine, which stated that the United States was "prepared to use armed force" anywhere in the Middle East against "aggression from any country controlled by international communism." In practice, the Eisenhower Doctrine amounted to little more than a restatement of the containment policy.

Eisenhower and the Russians

In Europe the Eisenhower and Dulles policies differed little from those of Truman. When Eisenhower announced his plan to rely more heavily on nuclear deterrents, the Europeans drew back in alarm, believing that in any atomic showdown they were sure to be destroyed. Khrushchev's talk of peaceful coexistence found receptive ears, especially in France.

Eisenhower therefore yielded to European pressures for a diplomatic summit conference with the Russians. In July 1955 Eisenhower, Prime Minister Eden, and a new French premier, Edgar Faure, had met at Geneva with Khrushchev and his then co-leader, Nikolai Bulganin, to discuss disarmament and the reunification of West and East Germany. The meeting produced no specific agreement, but with the Russians beaming cheerfully for the cameramen and talking of peaceful coexistence and with Eisenhower pouring martinis and projecting his famous charm, observers noted a softening of tensions that was dubbed the "spirit of Geneva."

In 1956 Eisenhower was reelected, defeating Adlai Stevenson even more decisively than he had in 1952. Despite their evident satisfaction with their leader, however, the mood of the American people was sober. Hopes of pushing back the Soviet Union with clever stratagems and moral fervor were fading. America's first successful earth satellite, launched in January 1958, brought cold comfort, for it was much smaller than the earth-circling Russian *Sputniks*.

In 1957 Dulles underwent surgery for abdominal cancer, and in April 1959 he had to resign. The next month he was dead. Eisenhower had never avoided making decisions in the foreign policy area, but now he personally took over much of the actual conduct of diplomacy. The key to his approach was restraint; he exercised commendable caution in every crisis. Like U. S. Grant, he was a soldier who hated war. From Korea through the crises over Indochina, Hungary, and Suez, he avoided risky new commitments. His behavior, like his temperament, contrasted sharply with that of the aggressive, oratorically perfervid Dulles.

Amid the tension that followed the Suez crisis, the belief persisted in many quarters that the spirit of Geneva could be revived if only a new summit meeting could be arranged. World opinion was insistent that the great powers stop making and testing nuclear weapons, for every test explosion was contaminating the atmosphere with radioactive debris that threatened the future of all life. Unresolved controversies, especially the argument over divided Germany, might erupt at any moment into a globe-shattering war.

Neither the United States nor the Soviet Union dared ignore these dangers; each therefore adopted a more accommodating attitude. In the summer of 1959 Vice-President Richard M. Nixon visited the Soviet Union and his opposite number, Vice Premier Anastas I. Mikoyan, toured the United States. Although Nixon's visit was marred by a heated argument with Khrushchev about the virtues of their respective systems, conducted before a gaping crowd in the kitchen of a model American home that had been set up at a Moscow fair, the results of the exchanges raised hopes that a summit conference would prove profitable.

In September, Khrushchev came to America. His cross-country tour had its full share of comic contretemps—when denied permission to visit Disneyland because authorities feared they could not protect him properly on the grounds, the heavy-handed Khrushchev accused the United States, only half humorously, of concealing rocket launching pads there. But the general effect of his visit seemed salutary. At the end of his stay, he and President Eisenhower agreed to convene a new four-power summit conference.

The meeting never took place. On May 1, 1960, high over Sverdlovsk, an industrial center deep in the Soviet Union, an American U-2 reconnaissance plane was shot down by antiaircraft fire. The pilot of the plane, Francis Gary Powers, survived the crash, and he confessed to being a spy. His cameras contained aerial photographs of Soviet military installations. When Eisenhower assumed full responsibility for the mission, Khrushchev accused the United States of "piratical" and "cowardly" acts of aggression. The summit conference was canceled.

Latin America Aroused

Events in Latin America compounded Eisenhower's difficulties. During World War II the United States, needing Latin American raw materials, had sup-

Vice-President Richard M. Nixon and Soviet leader Nikita Khrushchev engaged in their "kitchen debate" over the future of capitalism at a Moscow trade fair in 1959. Though this encounter did little to advance U.S.-Soviet relations, it established Nixon's credentials as a tough negotiator.

plied its southern neighbors liberally with economic aid. In the period following victory, an era of amity and prosperity seemed assured. A hemispheric mutual defense pact was signed at Rio de Janeiro in September 1947, and the following year the Organization of American States came into being. In the OAS, decisions were reached by a two-thirds vote; the United States had neither a veto nor any special position.

But as the Cold War progressed, the United States neglected Latin American questions. Economic problems plagued the region, and in most nations reactionary governments reigned. Radical Latin Americans accused the United States of supporting cliques of wealthy tyrants, while conservatives blamed lack of sufficient American economic aid for the plight of the poor.

Eisenhower, eager to improve relations, stepped up economic assistance. Resistance to communism nonetheless continued to receive first priority. In 1954 the government of Jacobo Arbenz Guzman in Guatemala began to import Soviet weapons. The United States promptly dispatched arms to the neighboring state of Honduras. Within a month an army led by an exiled Guatemalan officer marched into the country from Honduras and overthrew Arbenz. Elsewhere in Latin America, Eisenhower, as Truman had before him, continued to support regimes that were kept in power by the local military.

The depth of Latin American resentment of the United States became clear in the spring of 1958, when Vice-President Nixon made what was supposed to be a goodwill tour of South America. Everywhere he was met with hostility. In Lima, Peru, he was mobbed; in Caracas, Venezuela, students kicked his shiny Cadillac and pelted him with eggs and stones. He had to abandon the remainder of his trip. For the first time the American people gained some inkling of Latin American feelings and the social and economic troubles that lay behind them.

That there was no easy solution to Latin American problems was demonstrated by events in Cuba. In 1959 a revolutionary movement headed by Fidel Castro overthrew Fulgencio Batista, one of the most noxious of the Latin American dictators. Eisenhower recognized the Castro government at once, but the Cuban leader soon began to criticize the United States in highly colored speeches. He confiscated American property without providing adequate compensation, suppressed civil liberties, and entered into close relations with the Soviet Union. After he negotiated a trade agreement with the Soviet Union in February 1960, which enabled the Russians to obtain Cuban sugar at bargain rates, the United States retaliated by prohibiting the importation of Cuban sugar into America.

Khrushchev then announced that if the United

Fidel Castro and his military advisers in the mountains of Cuba in 1957. His guerrilla assaults on the corrupt regime of Fulgencio Batista and identification of his cause with social justice won Castro the acclaim of many throughout Latin America and some support among Americans.

States intervened in Cuba, he would defend the country with atomic weapons. "The Monroe Doctrine has outlived its time," Khrushchev warned. Shortly before the end of his second term, Eisenhower broke off diplomatic relations with Cuba.

The Politics of Civil Rights

During Eisenhower's presidency a major change occurred in the legal status of American blacks. Eisenhower had relatively little to do with this change, which was part of a broad shift in attitudes toward the rights of minorities in democracies. After 1945 the question of racial equality took on special importance because of the ideological competition with communism. Evidence of color prejudice in the United States damaged the nation's image, particularly in Asia and Africa, where the United States and the Soviet Union were competing for influence. An awareness of foreign criticism of American racial attitudes, along with resentment that almost a century after the Emancipation Proclamation they were still second-class citizens, produced a growing militancy among American blacks. At the same time, fears of communist subversion in the United States led to the repression of the rights of many whites, culminating in the excesses of McCarthyism. Both these aspects of the civil rights question divided Americans along liberal and conservative lines.

As we have seen, the World War II record of the federal government on civil rights was mixed. As early as 1940, in the Smith Act, Congress made it illegal to advocate or teach the overthrow of the government by force or to belong to an organization with this objective. A dead letter during the era of Soviet-American cooperation, the law was used in the Truman era to jail the leaders of the American Communist party. The Supreme Court upheld its constitutionality in *Dennis et al.* v. *United States* (1951), in effect modifying the "clear and present danger" test established in the Schenck case of 1919 (see page 692).

In 1950 Congress passed the McCarran Internal Security Act, which made it unlawful "to combine, conspire or agree with any other person to perform any act that would substantially contribute to the establishment . . . of a totalitarian dictatorship." The law required every "Communist-front organization" to register with the attorney general. Members of front organizations were barred from defense work and from traveling abroad. Aliens who had even been members of any "totalitarian party" were denied admission to the United States, a foolish provision that prevented many anticommunists behind the Iron Curtain from fleeing to America; even a person who had belonged to a communist youth organization was kept out by its terms.

As for blacks, besides setting up the Committee on Civil Rights and beginning to desegregate the armed forces, Truman sought to establish a permanent fair employment practices commission, but Congress did not enact the necessary legislation. Under Eisenhower, while the McCarthy hysteria reached its peak and declined, the government compiled a spotty record on civil rights. The search for subversive federal employees continued.

The most glaring instance of the administration's catering to anticommunist extremists was the refusal to grant security clearance to J. Robert Oppenheimer, one of the fathers of the atomic bomb, on the grounds that he had associated with communists and communist sympathizers. The reasoning was based on the preposterous supposition that Oppenheimer could be denied access to discoveries that he already knew about because he had helped to make them.

On the positive side, Eisenhower completed the integration of the armed forces and appointed a civil rights commission. But he was temperamentally incapable of a frontal assault on the racial problem. This was accomplished by the Supreme Court, which interjected itself into the civil rights controversy in dramatic fashion in 1954.

Under pressure of litigation sponsored by the National Association for the Advancement of Colored People, the Court had been gradually undermining the "separate but equal" principle laid down in *Plessy* v. *Ferguson* in 1896. First it ruled that in graduate education, segregated facilities must be truly equal. In 1938 it ordered a black admitted to the University of Missouri law school because no law school for blacks existed in the state. This decision gradually forced some southern states to admit blacks to advanced programs. "You can't build a cyclotron for one student," the president of the University of Oklahoma confessed when the Court, in 1948, ordered Oklahoma to provide equal facilities. Two years later, when Texas actually attempted to fit out a separate law school for a single black applicant, the Court ruled that truly equal education could not be provided under such circumstances.

In 1953 President Eisenhower appointed California's Governor Earl Warren Chief Justice of the United States.* Convinced that the Court must take the offensive in the cause of civil rights, Warren succeeded in welding his associates into a unit on the question.

In 1954 an NAACP-sponsored case, *Brown v. Board of Education of Topeka,* came up for decision. The NAACP lawyer, Thurgood Marshall, challenging the "separate but equal" doctrine, submitted a mass of sociological evidence to show that the mere fact of segregation made equal education impossible and did serious psychological damage to both black children and white. Speaking for a unanimous Court, Warren reversed the Plessy decision. "In the field of public education, the doctrine of 'separate but equal' has no place," he declared. "Separate educational facilities are inherently unequal." The next year the Court ordered the states to proceed "with all deliberate speed" in integrating their schools.

Despite these decisions, few districts in the southern and border states seriously tried to integrate their schools. Two months after the ruling, white citizens' councils dedicated to all-out opposition had sprung up throughout the South. When the school board of Clinton, Tennessee, integrated the local high school in September 1956, a mob organized by a northern fanatic rioted in protest, shouting, "Kill the niggers!" and destroying the property of blacks. The school was kept open with the help of the National Guard until segregationists blew up the building with dynamite. In Virginia the governor announced a plan for "massive resistance" to integration that denied state aid to local school systems that wished to desegregate. When the University of Alabama admitted a single black woman in 1956, riots broke out. University officials forced the student to withdraw and then expelled her when she complained more forcefully than they deemed proper.

President Eisenhower thought equality for blacks could not be obtained by government edict. "I am convinced that the Supreme Court decision set back progress in the South at least fifteen years,"

he remarked to one of his advisers. "The fellow who tries to tell me you can do these things by force is just plain nuts." However, in 1957 events compelled him to act. When the school board of Little Rock, Arkansas, opened Central High School to a handful of black students, the governor of the state, Orval M. Faubus, called out the National Guard to prevent them from attending. Unruly crowds taunted the students and their parents.

Eisenhower could not ignore the direct flouting of federal authority. After the mayor of Little Rock sent him a telegram saying, in part, "SITUATION IS OUT OF CONTROL AND POLICE CANNOT DISPERSE THE MOB" he dispatched 1,000 paratroopers to Little Rock and summoned 10,000 National Guardsmen to federal duty. The black students then began to attend class. A token force of soldiers was stationed at Central High for the entire school year to protect them.

Extremist resistance strengthened the determination of blacks and many northern whites to make the South comply with the desegregation decision. Besides pressing cases in the federal courts, leaders of the movement organized a voter registration drive among southern blacks. As a result, the administration introduced what became the Civil Rights Act of 1957. It authorized the attorney general to obtain injunctions to stop election officials from interfering with blacks seeking to register and vote. The law also established a civil rights commission with broad investigatory powers and a civil rights division in the Department of Justice. Enforcing this Civil Rights Act was another matter. A later study of a typical county in Alabama revealed that between 1957 and 1960 more than 700 blacks with high school diplomas were rejected as unqualified by white election officials when they sought to register.

The Supreme Court under Chief Justice Warren did not limit itself to protecting the rights of black people. Its decision in *Yates* v. *United States* (1957) reinstated the "clear and present danger" principle that had been undermined in the Dennis case upholding the Smith Act ban on merely "advocating" the overthrow of the government by force. The rights of persons accused of crimes were enlarged in *Gideon* v. *Wainright* (1963), providing free legal counsel for indigent defendants, *Escobedo* v. *Illinois* (1964), requiring the police to inform accused persons of their right to remain silent, and *Miranda* v. *Arizona* (1966), giving the accused the right to have

---

* Eisenhower first offered the post to John Foster Dulles, but he declined on the grounds that he was too old to start a new career.

Angry jeers from whites rain down on Elizabeth Eckford, one of the first black students to arrive for registration at Little Rock's Central High School in 1957. State troops turned black students away from the school until President Eisenhower overruled the state decision and called in the National Guard to enforce integration.

a lawyer present while being questioned by the authorities.

In *Baker* v. *Carr* (1962), *Lucas* v. *Colorado* (1964), and other decisions, the Court put an end to unequal representation in state and local legislative bodies, thus establishing the principle known as "one man, one vote." In a much different area, the Court in *Griswold* v. *Connecticut* (1965) struck down a Connecticut statute banning the use of contraceptives on the ground that it violated individuals' right of privacy.

The Election of 1960

As the end of his second term approached, Eisenhower somewhat reluctantly endorsed Vice-President Nixon as the Republican candidate to succeed him. Richard Nixon had skyrocketed to national prominence by exploiting the public fear of communist subversion. "Traitors in the high councils

of our government," he charged in 1950, "have made sure that the deck is stacked on the Soviet side of the diplomatic tables." In 1947 he was an obscure young congressman from California; in 1950 he won a seat in the Senate; two years later Eisenhower chose him as his running mate.

Whether Nixon believed what he was saying at this period of his career is not easily discovered; with his "instinct for omnidirectional placation," he seemed wedded to the theory that politicians should slavishly represent their constituents' opinions rather than hold to their own views. Frequently he appeared to count noses before deciding what he thought. He projected an image of almost frantic earnestness, yet he pursued a flexible course more suggestive of calculation than sincerity.

Reporters generally had a low opinion of Nixon, and independent voters seldom found him attractive. He was always controversial, distrusted by liberals even when he supported liberal measures. But his defense of American values in his confrontation with Khrushchev at the Moscow Fair had won him much praise.

The Democrats nominated Senator John Fitzgerald Kennedy of Massachusetts, with his chief rival at the convention, Lyndon Johnson of Texas, the Senate majority leader, as his running mate. Kennedy was the son of Joseph P. Kennedy, a wealthy businessman and promoter who had served as ambassador to Great Britain under Franklin Roosevelt. As a PT boat commander in World War II, John Kennedy was severely injured in action. In 1946 he was elected to Congress. Besides wealth, intelligence, good looks, and charm, Kennedy had the advantage of his war record and his Irish-Catholic ancestry, the latter a particularly valuable asset in heavily Catholic Massachusetts. After three terms in the House, he moved on to the Senate in 1952 by defeating Henry Cabot Lodge, Jr. (Lodge's grandfather, Wilson's inveterate foe, had beaten Kennedy's maternal grandfather and namesake for the Senate in 1916.)

After his landslide reelection in 1958, only Kennedy's religion seemed to limit his political future. No Catholic had ever been elected president, and the defeat of Alfred E. Smith in 1928 had convinced most students of politics (including Smith) that none ever would be elected. Nevertheless, influenced by Kennedy's victories in the Wisconsin and West Virginia primaries, the latter establishing him as an effective campaigner in a predominantly Protestant region, the Democratic convention nominated him.

Kennedy had not been a particularly liberal congressman. He was friendly with Richard Nixon and admitted frankly that he liked Senator Joseph McCarthy and thought that "he may have something" in his campaign against supposed communists in government. However, as a presidential candidate, he sought to appear more forward-looking. He stressed his youth and "vigor" (a favorite word) and promised to open a "new frontier" for the country. Nixon ran on the Eisenhower record, which he promised to extend in liberal directions.

A series of televised debates between the candidates, observed by some 70 million viewers, helped Kennedy by enabling him to demonstrate his maturity and mastery of the issues. Although both candidates laudably avoided it, the religious issue was important. His Catholicism helped Kennedy in eastern urban areas but hurt him in many farm districts and throughout the West. Kennedy's victory, 303 to 219 in the electoral college, was paper-thin in the popular vote, 34,227,000 to 34,109,000.

Although Kennedy was rich, white, and a member of the upper crust by any definition, his was a victory of minority groups (Jews, blacks, and blue-collar "ethnics" as well as Catholics gave him overwhelming support) over the "traditional" white Protestant majority, which went as heavily for Nixon as it had four years earlier for Eisenhower.

Kennedy's New Frontier

Kennedy made a striking and popular president. He projected an image of originality and imaginativeness combined with moderation and good sense. He appointed two Republicans to his Cabinet. He further flouted convention by making his younger brother Robert F. Kennedy attorney general. (When critics objected to this appointment, the president responded with a quip, saying that he had "always thought it was a good thing for a young attorney to get some government experience before going out into private practice.")

Kennedy had a genuinely inquiring mind. He kept up with dozens of magazines and newspapers and consumed books of all sorts voraciously. He invited leading scientists, artists, writers, and musicians to the White House. On one occasion when he had invited a number of Nobel Prize winners to the White House, he called the group "the most extraordinary collection of talent . . . that has ever been gathered together at the White House with the possible exception of when Thomas Jefferson dined alone." This was typical political bunkum, but just as Jefferson had sought to teach Americans to value the individual regardless of status, Kennedy seemed intent on teaching the country to respect its most talented minds.

Kennedy was determined to change the direction in which the nation was moving. He hoped to revitalize the economy and extend the influence of the United States abroad. His inaugural address was a call for commitment: "Ask not what your country can do for you," he said. "Ask what you can do for your country." But he was neither a Woodrow Wilson nor a Franklin Roosevelt when it came to bending Congress to his will. Perhaps he was too amiable, too diffident and conciliatory in his approach. A coalition of Republicans and conservative southern Democrats resisted his plans for federal aid to ed-

Vice-President Richard M. Nixon and Senator John F. Kennedy during one of the three televised debates of the 1960 presidential campaign. An effective debater from his college days, Nixon had welcomed the opportunity to take on the less experienced junior senator from Massachusetts before 70,000,000 viewers. It was a mistake.

ucation, for urban renewal, for a higher minimum wage, for medical care for the aged.

The president reacted mildly, almost ruefully, when opponents in Congress blocked proposals that in his view were reasonable and moderate. He seemed to doubt at times that the cumbersome machinery of the federal government could be made to work. Even to some of his warmest supporters he sometimes appeared strangely paralyzed, unwilling either to exert strong pressure on Congress or to appeal to public opinion. Pundits talked of a "deadlock of democracy" in which party discipline had crumbled and positive legislative action had become next to impossible.

During the presidential campaign Kennedy had promised "to get the country moving again." The relatively slow growth of the economy in the Eisenhower years had troubled some economists. Three recessions occurred between 1953 and 1961, each marked by increases in unemployment. Moreover, in the later years of Eisenhower's presidency the rate of inflation began to rise.

During the recessions the Eisenhower administration reacted in the orthodox Keynesian man-

ner, cutting taxes, easing credit, and expanding public works programs. However, liberal economists argued that it was not employing the Keynesian medicine in large enough doses. At first Kennedy rejected proposals for increasing government spending in order to stimulate consumer spending. But in January 1963 the economist Walter Heller persuaded him to try a different approach. If personal and corporate income taxes were lowered, Heller argued, the public would have more money to spend on consumer goods and corporations could invest in new facilities for producing these goods. Federal expenditures need not be cut because the increase in economic activity would raise private and corporate incomes so much that tax revenues would rise even as the tax rate was falling.

Although the prospect of lower taxes was tempting, Kennedy's call for reductions of $13.5 billion ran into strong opposition. Republicans and conservative Democrats thought the reasoning behind the scheme too complex and theoretical to be practicable. It went nowhere.

The Cuban Crises

Kennedy's curious lack of determined leadership also marred his management of foreign affairs, particularly during his first year in office. He hoped to reverse the Truman-Eisenhower policy of backing reactionary regimes merely because they were anticommunist. Recognizing that American economic aid could accomplish little in Latin America unless accompanied by internal reforms, he organized the Alliance for Progress, which committed the Latin Americans to land reform and economic development projects with the assistance of the United States. At the first sign of pro-Soviet activity in any Latin American country, however, he tended to overreact. Critics have described his behavior toward Latin America as a mixture of "overambitious idealism" and "pointless obsessiveness" about security.

His most serious blunder involved Cuba. Anti-Castro exiles were eager to organize an invasion of their homeland, reasoning that the Cuban masses would rise up against Castro as soon as "democratic" forces provided a standard they could rally to. Under Eisenhower the Central Intelligence Agency had begun training some 2,000 of these men in Central America.

Kennedy was of two minds about this plan. Secretary of State Dean Rusk and a few of his other advisers opposed it, as did J. William Fulbright, the chairman of the Senate Foreign Relations Committee, who said, "The Castro regime is a thorn in the flesh but it is not a dagger in the heart." But after much soul-searching, Kennedy authorized the attack. The exiles were given American weapons, but no planes or warships were committed to the secret operation.

The invaders struck on April 17, 1961, landing at the Bay of Pigs, on Cuba's southern coast. But the Cuban people failed to support them, and they were soon pinned down and forced to surrender. Since America's involvement could not be disguised, the affair exposed the country to all the criticism that a straightforward assault would have produced, without accomplishing the overthrow of Castro. Worse, it made Kennedy appear impulsive as well as unprincipled. Castro soon acknowledged that he was a Marxist and tightened his connections with the Soviet Union. For his part, Kennedy imposed an economic blockade on Cuba, and he appears to have gone along with a CIA attempt to assassinate Castro.

In June, Kennedy met with Premier Khrushchev in Vienna. During their discussions he evidently failed to convince the Russian that he would resist pressure with determination. In August, Khrushchev abruptly closed the border between East and West Berlin and erected an ugly wall of concrete blocks and barbed wire across the city to stop the exodus of dissident East Germans. When Kennedy did not order American forces in Berlin to tear down the wall, the Soviet leader found further reason to believe he could pursue aggressive tactics with impunity. Resuming the testing of nuclear weapons, he exploded a series of gigantic hydrogen bombs, one with a power 3,000 times that of the bomb that had devastated Hiroshima.

When the Russians resumed nuclear testing, Kennedy followed suit. He expanded the American space program,* vowing that an American would

land on the moon within ten years, and called on Congress for a large increase in military spending. At the same time, he pressed forward along more constructive lines by establishing the Agency for International Development to administer American economic aid throughout the world and the Peace Corps, an organization that effectively mobilized American idealism and technical skills to help developing nations.

These actions had no observable effect on the Russians. In 1962 Khrushchev devised the boldest and most reckless challenge of the Cold War—he moved military equipment and thousands of Soviet technicians into Cuba. American intelligence reports revealed that in addition to planes and conventional weapons, guided missiles were being imported and launching pads were being constructed on Cuban soil. U-2 reconnaissance planes photographed these sites, and by mid-October, Kennedy had proof that the missile sites were approaching completion.

The president faced a dreadful decision. When he confronted Soviet Foreign Minister Andrei Gromyko, Gromyko insisted that only "defensive" (antiaircraft) missiles were being installed. But even if this were true, allowing the construction of missile sites so close to the United States was politically unacceptable, especially after the Bay of Pigs fiasco.

Kennedy decided that he must take strong action. On October 22 he went before the nation on television. The Soviet buildup was "a deliberately provocative and unjustified change in the status quo," he said. The navy would stop and search all vessels headed for Cuba and turn back any containing "offensive" weapons. Kennedy called on Khrushchev to dismantle the missile bases and remove from the island all weapons capable of striking the United States. Any Cuban-based nuclear attack would result, he warned, in "a full retaliatory response upon the Soviet Union."

For days, while the world held its breath, work on the missile bases continued. Then Khrushchev backed down. He withdrew the missiles and cut back his military establishment in Cuba to modest proportions. Kennedy then lifted the blockade.

Critics have argued that Kennedy overreacted to the Soviet missiles. There was no evidence that the Russians were planning an attack, and in any case they already had missiles in Siberia capable of striking American targets. The Cuban missiles

---

* Russian superiority in space was gradually reduced. In April 1961 the cosmonaut Yuri Gagarin orbited the earth; in August another Russian circled the globe 17 times. The first American to orbit the earth, John Glenn, made his voyage in February 1962. In 1965 the United States kept a two-man Gemini craft in orbit two weeks, effecting a rendezvous between it and a second Gemini.

U.S. United Nations Ambassador Adlai Stevenson (seated right) in the U.N. Security Council displaying aerial photographs of missile installations in Cuba in the midst of the Cuban Missile Crisis in October 1962. Until this moment, the Soviet delegate, Valerian Zorin (seated, third from left), had denied the existence of Soviet missiles in the western hemisphere. He could do so no longer.

might be seen as a deterrent against a possible attack on the Soviet Union by United States missiles in Europe, and by demanding their withdrawal, Kennedy risked triggering a nuclear holocaust as much as Khrushchev. Yet he probably had no choice once the existence of the sites was known to the public. (In some respects this is the most frightening aspect of the crisis.)

For better or worse, Kennedy's firmness in the missile crisis repaired the damage done his reputation by the Bay of Pigs affair. It also led to a lessening of Soviet-American tensions. Khrushchev agreed to the installation of a telephone "hot line" between the White House and the Kremlin so that in any future crisis the leaders of the two nations could be in instant communication. Although the arms race continued unabated, in 1963 nearly 100 nations, including all the major powers except France and China, signed a treaty banning the testing of nuclear weapons in the atmosphere.

Tragedy in Dallas

Although his domestic policies were making little progress in Congress and the economy remained in rather poor shape, Kennedy retained his hold on public opinion. In the fall of 1963 most observers believed he would easily win a second term. Then,

while visiting Dallas, Texas, on November 22, he was shot in the head by an assassin, Lee Harvey Oswald, and died almost instantly.

This senseless murder shocked the world and precipitated an extraordinary series of events. Oswald had fired on the president with a rifle from an upper story of a warehouse. No one saw him pull the trigger. He was apprehended largely because, in his demented state, he killed a policeman later in the day in another part of the city. He denied his guilt, but a mass of evidence connected him with the crime. Before he could be brought to trial, however, he was himself murdered by one Jack Ruby, the owner of a Dallas nightclub, while being transferred, in the full view of television cameras, from one place of detention to another.

This amazing incident, together with the fact that Oswald had defected to Russia in 1959 and then returned to the United States, convinced many people that some nefarious conspiracy lay at the root of the tragedy. Oswald, the argument ran, was a pawn, his murder designed to keep him from exposing the masterminds who had engineered the assassination. An investigation by a special commission headed by Chief Justice Earl Warren came to the conclusion that Oswald acted alone, yet doubts persisted in many minds.

Kennedy's election had seemed to mark the beginning of a new era in American history. Instead,

Jacqueline Kennedy and Robert F. Kennedy returning from the Arlington Cemetery on November 26, 1963, following the burial of President John F. Kennedy. Not since Lincoln's funeral had there been such an intense display of public grief over the loss of a political leader.

his assassination marked the end of an old one. Whatever their strengths and weaknesses, the three postwar presidents had achieved, at minimum, the respect of nearly everyone. There were critics who felt that the job was too big for Truman, others who considered Eisenhower a political amateur and Kennedy too much a showman. But as was true of most of their predecessors, their honesty and patriotism seemed beyond question. This was not to be said of their immediate successors.

Milestones

1944	GI Bill of Rights		UN counterattack in Korea driven back by Red Chinese army
1945	Roosevelt dies; Truman becomes president	**1953**	New Look foreign policy
1946	Benjamin Spock, *Baby and Child Care*		Korean War armistice
	Baruch plan for control of atomic energy	**1954**	Army-McCarthy hearings
1947	Taft-Hartley Act		Siege of Dien Bien Phu; French withdraw from Vietnam
	Truman Doctrine		Supreme Court orders school desegregation (*Brown* v. *Board of Education*)
	"X" (George Kennan), "Sources of Soviet Conduct"		
	Marshall Plan proposed	**1956**	Suez crisis
	Loyalty Review Board	**1957**	National Guard used to desegregate Little Rock high school
1948–			
1949	Berlin Airlift		Civil Rights Commission
1949	North Atlantic Treaty Organization (NATO) established	**1960**	U-2 affair
			United States breaks diplomatic relations with Cuba
1950	North Korea invades South Korea	**1961**	Bay of Pigs affair
	Alger Hiss convicted of perjury	**1962**	Cuban Missile Crisis
	Senator McCarthy charges that the State Department is riddled with communists	**1963**	President Kennedy assassinated

SUPPLEMENTARY READING

Titles marked with an asterisk have been published in paperback.

A good summary of the Cold War is T. G. Paterson, ***On Every Front: The Making of the Cold War*** (1979), which makes an effort to explain Soviet motives and tactics objectively. See also two books by J. L. Gaddis, **Strategies of Containment** (1982) and **The Long Peace** (1987). More critical of American policy are Walter La Feber, **America, Russia, and the Cold War*** (1968), and Daniel Yergin, **Shattered Peace** (1977). Harry Truman's **Memoirs*** (1955–1956) contain much useful information.

Postwar domestic politics is treated in W. L. O'Neill, **Riding High*** (1986), and two works by A. L. Hamby, **The Imperial Years** (1976) and **Beyond the New Deal: Harry S Truman and American Liberalism*** (1973). Interpretive works useful for understanding the period include A. M. Schlesinger, Jr., **The Vital Center*** (1949), R. E. Neustadt, **Presidential Power*** (1960), and J. M. Burns, **The Deadlock of Democracy*** (1963).

Biographical material on postwar political leaders is voluminous. On Truman, see D. R. McCoy, **The Presidency of Harry S Truman** (1984), and R. J. Donovan, **Conflict and Crisis** (1977). S. E. Ambrose's two-volume biography **Eisenhower** (1983–1984) is the fullest scholarly treatment of Dwight Eisenhower.

Among many analyses and evaluations of American foreign policy, G. F. Kennan's writings stand out, both as primary sources and as interpretations. See his **Memoirs*** (1969, 1972), **Realities of American Foreign Policy*** (1954), and **Russia and the West under Lenin and Stalin*** (1961).

On Truman's foreign policy, see Donovan's **Conflict and Crisis** and M. J. Hogan, **The Marshall Plan** (1987). W. P. Davison, **The Berlin Blockade** (1958), is also useful.

On the Korean War, consult Clay Blair, **Forgotten War: America in Korea** (1988).

McCarthyism and the Hiss case are covered in David Caute, **The Great Fear** (1978), Allen Weinstein, **Perjury: The Hiss-Chambers Case** (1978), and Robert Griffith, **The Politics of Fear*** (1970).

Economic trends are considered in Herbert Stein, **The Fiscal Revolution in America*** (1969). On labor, consult Philip Taft, **Organized Labor in American History** (1964), E. L. Dayton, **Walter Reuther** (1958), and R. H. Zieger, **John L. Lewis** (1988). On agriculture, see A. J. Matusow, **Farm Policies and Politics in the Truman Years*** (1970).

Eisenhower's own view of his presidency can be found in D. D. Eisenhower, **Mandate for Change*** (1963) and **Waging Peace** (1965). Herbert Parmet, **Eisenhower and the American Crusades** (1972), is a balanced account of his two administrations. See also C. C. Alexander, **Holding the Line: The Eisenhower Era** (1975). Dulles's views are discussed in M. A. Gun, **John Foster Dulles** (1972). The diplomacy of the Eisenhower era is also discussed in R. A. Divine, **Eisenhower and the Cold War*** (1981). For postwar constitutional issues, see P. L. Murphy, **The Constitution in Crisis Times*** (1972). Richard Kluger, **Simple Justice*** (1976), is an excellent account of *Brown* v. *Board of Education.*

On Kennedy, consult H. S. Parmet, **Jack: The Struggles of John F. Kennedy** (1980) and **JKF: The Presidency of John F. Kennedy** (1983), together a fair-minded account. A. M. Schlesinger, Jr., **A Thousand Days*** (1965), and Theodore Sorensen, **Kennedy*** (1965), are rich in eyewitness detail but extremely pro-Kennedy.

The Best of Times, the Worst of Times

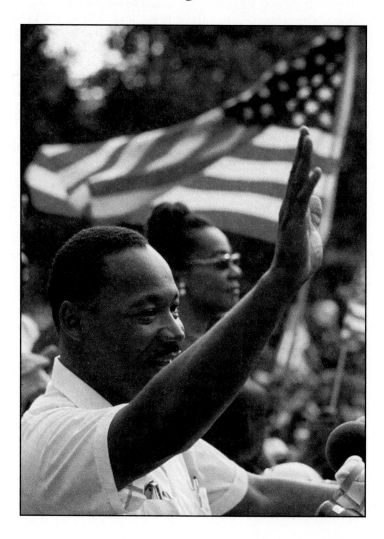

The obstruction of justice thing is a [expletive deleted] hard thing to prove in court.

PRESIDENT RICHARD M. NIXON, *April 16, 1973*

Lyndon Baines Johnson

John F. Kennedy's death made Lyndon B. Johnson president. The two had never been close. When Kennedy offered Johnson the vice-presidency at the 1960 Democratic convention, he had expected him to refuse. (When Johnson accepted, the chagrined Kennedy said to his brother Robert: "Don't worry Bobby, nothing's going to happen to me.") From 1949 until his election as vice-president Johnson had been a senator and, for most of that time, Senate Democratic leader. Early on he had displayed what one adviser called an extraordinary "capacity for manipulation and seduction." He could be both heavy-handed and subtle, and also devious, domineering, persistent, and obliging. Many people swore by him; few had the fortitude to swear at him. Above all he knew what to do with political power. "Some men," he said, "want power so they can strut around to 'Hail to the Chief.' . . . I wanted it to use it."

On taking office as president, Johnson benefited from the sympathy of the world and from the shame felt by many who had opposed Kennedy's proposals for political or selfish reasons. Sensing the public mood, he took advantage of it by pushing hard for Kennedy's programs. Early in his career he had voted against a bill making lynching a federal crime

A shot of President Johnson using his hands to emphasize a point while speaking to reporters conveys the talkative, intense, persuasive nature of the man.

and had opposed bills outlawing state poll taxes and establishing a federal fair employment practices commission. But after he became important in national affairs, he consistently championed racial equality. "Civil rightsers are going to have to wear sneakers to keep up with me," he now boasted.

Bills that had long been buried in committee sailed through Congress. Early in 1964 Kennedy's tax cut was passed, and the resulting economic stimulus caused a boom of major dimensions. A few months later, an expanded version of another Kennedy measure became law, the Civil Rights Act of 1964.

"We Shall Overcome"

Kennedy's original approach to the race question had been exceedingly cautious. He did not integrate the National Guard, for example, because he was afraid that if he did, southern Guard units would withdraw. His lack of full commitment dismayed many who were concerned about the persistence of racial discrimination in the country. But seemingly without plan, a grass-roots drive for equal treatment had sprung up among southern blacks themselves.

It began during the Eisenhower administration in the tightly segregated city of Montgomery, Alabama. On the evening of Friday, December 1, 1955, Rosa Parks boarded a bus on her way home from her job as a seamstress at the Montgomery Fair department store. She dutifully took a seat toward the rear as law and custom required. After white workers and shoppers had filled the forward section the driver ordered her to give up her place. Parks, who was also secretary of the Montgomery NAACP chapter, refused. She had decided, she later recalled, that "I would have to know once and for all what rights I had as a human being and a citizen."

Rosa Parks was arrested. Over the weekend, leaders of the blacks of Montgomery organized a boycott. "Don't ride the bus . . . Monday," their mimeographed notice ran. "If you work, take a cab, or share a ride, or walk." Monday dawned bitter cold, but the boycott was a total success. The black people of Montgomery, writes Taylor Branch in his stirring account of the boycott in *Parting the Waters*, "were turning the City Bus Lines into a ghost fleet."

Most Montgomery blacks could not afford to miss even one day's wages, so the protracted struggle to get to work was difficult to maintain. Black-owned taxis reduced their rates sharply, and when the city declared this illegal, car pools were quickly organized. But few blacks owned cars—nearly everyone who did volunteered, but there were never more than 350 available to carry more than about 10,000 people back and forth to their jobs every day. Nevertheless, the boycott went on.

Late in February the Montgomery authorities obtained indictments of 115 leaders of the boycott, but this move backfired because it focused national attention on the situation. A young clergyman, Martin Luther King, Jr., a gifted speaker who was emerging as the leader of the boycott, became an overnight celebrity; money poured in from all over the country to support the movement. Finally, after more than a year, the Supreme Court ruled that the segregation law was unconstitutional. Montgomery had to desegregate its public transportation system.

This success had encouraged blacks elsewhere in the South to band together against the caste system. A new organization, the Southern Christian Leadership Conference, headed by King, moved to the forefront of the civil rights movement. Other organizations joined the struggle, notably the Congress of Racial Equality (CORE), which had been founded in 1942.

In February 1960 four black students in Greensboro, North Carolina, sat down at a lunch counter in a Woolworth five-and-ten and refused to leave when they were denied service. Their "sit-in" sparked a national movement; students in dozens of other southern towns and cities copied the Greensboro blacks' example. By the end of 1961 over 70,000 persons had participated in sit-ins. Still another new organization, the Student Nonviolent Coordinating Committee (SNCC), was founded by black college students to provide a focus for the sit-in movement and conduct voter registration drives in the South, actions that more than any other aroused the fury of southern segregationists.

In May 1961 black and white foes of segregation organized a "freedom ride" to test the effectiveness of federal regulations prohibiting discrimination in interstate transportation. Boarding buses in Washington, they traveled across the South, heading for New Orleans. In Alabama they ran into bad trouble. At Anniston racists set fire to their bus, and in Birmingham they were assaulted by a mob. But violence did not stop the freedom riders. Other groups descended on the South, many deliberately seeking arrest in order to test local segregation ordinances in the courts. Repeatedly these actions resulted in the breaking down of racial barriers.

Integrationists like Martin Luther King, Jr., attracted an enormous following, but some blacks, contemptuous of white prejudices, were urging their fellows to reject "American" society and all it stood for. Black nationalism became a potent force. Elijah Muhammad, leader of the Black Muslim movement, disliked whites so intensely that he demanded that a part of the United States be set aside for the exclusive use of blacks. He urged his followers to be industrious, thrifty, and abstemious— and to view all whites with suspicion and hatred.

"This white government has ruled us and given us plenty hell, but the time has arrived that you taste a little of your own hell," Elijah Muhammad said. "There are many of my poor black ignorant brothers

Calling for black separatism, Malcolm X told an interviewer in 1964, "The Negro [must] develop his character and his culture in accord with his own nature."

. . . preaching the ignorant and lying stuff that you should love your enemy. What fool can love his enemy?" Another important Black Muslim, Malcolm X, put it this way in a 1960 speech: "For the white man to ask the black man if he hates him is just like the rapist asking the raped, or the wolf asking the sheep, 'Do you hate me?' " "If someone puts a hand on you," he advised blacks on another occasion, "send him to the cemetery."

Pushed by all these developments, President Kennedy reluctantly began to change his policy. But while the administration gave lip service to desegregation and encouraged activists' efforts to register black voters in the South, when confrontations arose, the president hesitated, arguing that it was up to state officials to enforce the law.

Ordinary black southerners (even schoolchildren) became increasingly impatient. In the face of brutal repression by local police, many adopted King's tactic of nonviolent protest. After leading a series of demonstrations in Birmingham, Alabama,

in 1963, King was thrown in jail. When local white clergymen, presumably sympathetic to the blacks' objectives, nonetheless urged them to cease their "untimely" protests, which, they claimed, "incite hatred and violence," King wrote his now-famous "Letter from Birmingham Jail," which contained this moving explanation of why he and his followers were unwilling to wait any longer for justice.

> When you have seen hate-filled policemen curse, kick, brutalize and even kill your black brothers and sisters with impunity; when you see the vast majority of your twenty million Negro brothers smothering in an airtight cage of poverty in the midst of an affluent society; when you suddenly find your tongue twisted and your speech stammering as you seek to explain to your six-year-old daughter why she can't go to the public amusement park that has just been advertised on television . . . when you take a cross-country drive and find it necessary to sleep night after night in the uncomfortable corners of your automobile because no motel will accept you; when you are humiliated day in and day out by nagging signs reading "white" and "colored": when your first name becomes "nigger" and your middle name becomes "boy" . . . then you will understand why we find it so difficult to wait.

The brutal repression of the Birmingham demonstrations brought a flood of recruits and money to the protesters' cause. Finally Kennedy gave his support to a comprehensive new civil rights bill that made racial discrimination in hotels, restaurants, and other places of public accommodation illegal and gave the attorney general the power to bring suits on behalf of individuals in order to speed up the lagging school desegregation movement. The measure also authorized agencies of the federal government to withhold federal funds from state-administered programs that failed to treat people of all races equally.

When this bill ran into stiff opposition in Congress, blacks organized a demonstration in Washington, attended by 200,000 people. At this gathering, King delivered his "I Have a Dream" address, looking forward to a time when racial prejudice no longer existed and people of all religions and colors could join hands and say, "Free at last! Free at last!"

Kennedy had sympathized with the purpose of the Washington gathering but feared it would make passage of the civil rights bill more difficult rather than easier. As in other areas, he was not a forceful advocate of his own proposals.

The Great Society

As finally passed, the Civil Rights Act outlawed discrimination by employers against blacks and also against women. It broke down the last legal barriers to black voting in the southern states and outlawed formal racial segregation of all sorts. Johnson's success in steering this and other Kennedy measures through Congress convinced him that he could be a reformer in the tradition of Franklin Roosevelt. He declared war on poverty and set out to create a "great society" in which poverty no longer existed.

During the New Deal, Franklin Roosevelt was accused of exaggeration when he said that one-third of the nation was "ill-housed, ill-clad, ill-nourished." In fact Roosevelt had underestimated the extent of poverty when he made that statement in 1937. Wartime economic growth reduced the percentage of poor people in the country substantially, but in 1960 between 20 and 25 percent of all American families—about 40 million persons—were living below the poverty line, a government standard of minimum subsistence based on income and family size.

That so many millions could be poor in a reputedly affluent society was deplorable but not difficult to explain. In any community a certain number of persons cannot support themselves because of physical incapacity, low intelligence, or psychological difficulties. There were also in the United States entire regions, the best known being the Appalachian area, that had been bypassed by economic development and no longer provided their inhabitants with adequate economic opportunities.

Moreover, prosperity and advancing technology had changed the definition of poverty. Things like telephones, radios, and electric refrigerators, unknown to the most affluent Americans of the 1860s, were necessities a century later. But as living standards rose, so did job requirements. A strong back and a willingness to work no longer guaranteed that the possessor could earn a decent living. Technology was changing the labor market. Educated workers with special skills and good verbal abilities could easily find well-paid jobs. Persons who had no special skills or were poorly educated could often find nothing.

Certain less obvious influences were at work too. Poverty tends to be more prevalent among the old and the young than among those in the prime of life; in the postwar decades these two groups were growing more rapidly than any other. Social security payments amounted to less than the elderly needed to maintain themselves decently, and some of the poorest workers, such as agricultural laborers, were not covered by the system at all. Unemployment was twice as high among youths in their late teens as in the nation as a whole and far higher among young blacks than among young whites.

As the middle class moved to the suburbs, poverty became, in the words of Michael Harrington, whose book *The Other America* (1962) did much to call attention to the problem, "less visible" to the well-meaning citizens whose energies had to be mobilized if it was to be eradicated. Many poor people were becoming alienated from society. In earlier times most of the poor were recent immigrants, believers in the American dream of rags to riches, strivers who accepted their low status as temporary. The modern poor, many studies indicated, tended to lack motivation; they felt trapped by their condition and gave up.

Poverty exacted a heavy price, both from its victims and from society. Statistics reflected the relationship between low income and bad health. Only about 4 percent of people from middle-income families were chronically ill, whereas more than 16 percent of poor families were so afflicted. Mental illness varied inversely with income, as did alcoholism, drug addiction, and crime.

Johnson's war on poverty had two objectives: to give poor people the opportunity to improve themselves and to provide them with direct assistance of various kinds. The first took the form of the Economic Opportunity Act of 1964. This law created a melange of programs, among them the Job Corps, similar to the New Deal Civilian Conservation Corps, a community action program to finance local efforts; an educational program for small children; a work-study program for college students; and a system for training the unskilled unemployed and for lending money to small businesses in poor areas. The Economic Opportunity Act combined the progressive concept of the welfare state with the conservative idea of individual responsibility. The government would support the weak and disadvantaged by giving them a fair chance to make it on their own.

Buttressed by this and other legislative triumphs, Johnson sought election as president in his own right in 1964. He achieved this ambition in unparalleled fashion. His championing of civil rights won him the almost unanimous support of blacks; his economy drive attracted the well-to-do and the business interests; his war on poverty held the allegiance of labor and other elements traditionally Democratic. His southern antecedents counterbalanced his liberalism on the race question in the eyes of many white southerners.

The Republicans played into his hands by nominating a conservative, Senator Barry M. Goldwater of Arizona. A large majority of the voters found Goldwater out of date on economic questions and dangerously aggressive on foreign affairs. During the campaign Democrats told a joke that went something like this:

(Goldwater is president. An aide rushes into his office.)

AIDE: Mr. President, the Russians have just launched an all-out nuclear attack on us. Their missiles will strike in fifteen minutes. What shall we do?
GOLDWATER: Have all the wagons form a circle.

In November, Johnson won a sweeping victory, collecting over 61 percent of the popular vote and carrying all the country except Goldwater's Arizona and five states in the Deep South. Quickly he pressed ahead with his Great Society program. In January 1965 he proposed a compulsory hospital insurance system for all persons over the age of 65, known as Medicare. As amended by Congress, the Medicare Act combined hospital insurance for retired people (funded by social security taxes) with a voluntary plan to cover doctors' bills (paid for in part by the government). The law also provided for grants to the states to help pay the medical expenses of poor people below the retirement age of 65. This part of the system was called Medicaid.

Next Congress passed the Elementary and Secondary Education Act. This measure supplied federal funds to school districts, the money to be devoted to improving the education of poor children. The theory was that children from city slums and impoverished rural areas tended to be "educationally deprived" and thus in need of extra help. The act was especially close to President Johnson's heart, having taught school in a Mexican-American district after graduating from college. To focus attention on it (and for obvious political purposes), he went back to his Texas birthplace to sign it, delivering a homily on education as the steppingstone to fame

A class for Spanish-speaking children of migrant workers in Salinas, California, funded by the federally supported Head Start Program. Launched in 1964 at President Johnson's urging, it was one of the most successful "Great Society" initiatives.

and fortune. Related to the Education Act was a program for poor preschool children, known as Head Start. This program was designed to prepare the children for elementary school. It also contributed incidentally to improving the health of the children by providing medical examinations and good meals.

Other laws passed at Johnson's urging in 1965 and 1966 dealt with support for the arts and for scientific research, highway safety, crime control, slum clearance, clean air, and the preservation of historic sites. Of particular significance was the Immigration Act of 1965, which did away with the national-origin system of admitting newcomers. Instead, 290,000 persons a year were to be admitted, priorities being based on such grounds as skill and the need for political asylum. The law also placed a limit of 120,000 persons a year on immigration from countries in the Western Hemisphere. Previously, immigration from these countries had been unrestricted.

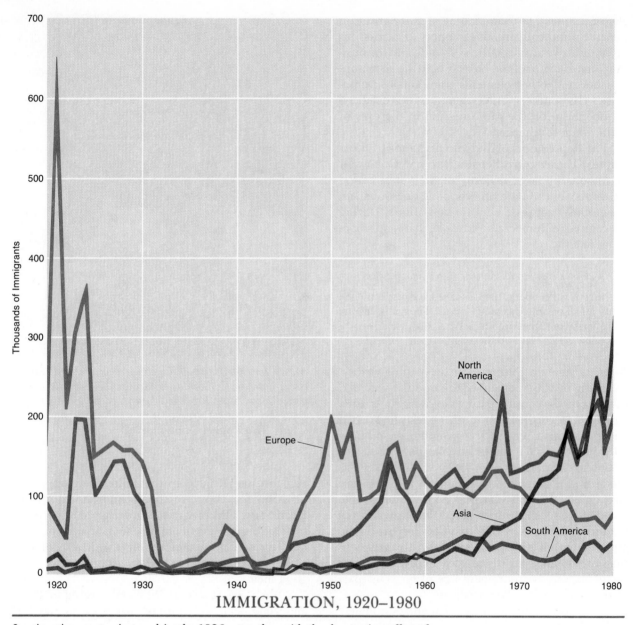

IMMIGRATION, 1920–1980

Immigration quotas imposed in the 1920s, together with the dampening effect of the depression years and World War II, meant that up to 1980, immigration had still not reached its pre–World War I levels, in spite of the post-1960 influx from Asia and North America. Canada, Mexico, Central America, and the West Indies are included in the North American category.

The Great Society program was one of the most remarkable outpourings of important legislation in American history. The results, however, were mixed. Head Start and a related program to help students in secondary schools prepare for college were unqualified successes. But the 1965 Education Act proved a disappointment. Too many local school districts found ways of using the federal money to cover their ordinary expenses, and the sums actually devoted to programs for the poor failed to improve most students' performances significantly. Medicare and Medicaid certainly provided good medical treatment for millions of people, but since the patients no longer paid most of the bills, doctors, hospitals, and drug companies were able to raise fees and prices without fear of losing business. Medical costs escalated far more rapidly than the rate of inflation.

The Job Corps, which was designed to help poor people get better-paying jobs by providing them with vocational training, was an almost total failure. The cost of the training was high, relatively few trainees completed the courses, and of those who did, few found jobs in which they could make use of their new skills. On balance, the achievements of the Great Society were far short of what President Johnson had promised.

The War in Vietnam

In the fall of 1967 President Lyndon Johnson seemed to have every intention of running for a second full term. Whether he would be reelected was not clear, but that any Democrat could prevent this shrewd and powerful politician from being nominated seemed out of the question. Nevertheless, within a few months opposition to him had become so bitter that he withdrew as a candidate. The cause of this opposition was his handling of a conflict on the other side of the world—the war in Vietnam.

When Vietnam was divided following the defeat of the French in 1954, a handful of American military "advisers" were sent there to train a South Vietnamese army. As time passed, more American aid and "advice" were dispatched in a futile effort to establish a stable government. Pro-communist forces, now called the Vietcong, soon controlled large sections of the country, some almost within sight of the capital city of Saigon.

Gradually the Vietcong, drawing supplies from North Vietnam and indirectly from China and the Soviet Union, increased in strength. In response, more American money and more military advisers were sent to bolster Ngo Dinh Diem's regime. By the end of 1961 there were 3,200 American military men in the country; by the time Kennedy was assassinated, the American military presence had risen to more than 16,000 and 120 American soldiers had been killed.

Shortly before Kennedy's death, a group of South Vietnamese generals overthrew Diem and killed him. The following summer, after announcing that North Vietnamese gunboats had fired on American destroyers in the Gulf of Tonkin, President Johnson demanded, and in an air of crisis obtained, an authorization from Congress to "repel any armed attack against the forces of the United States and to prevent further aggression."

With this blank check, and buttressed by his sweeping defeat of Goldwater in the 1964 presidential election, Johnson sent more troops to South Vietnam and authorized air attacks against targets in both South and North Vietnam.

At first the American ground troops were supposed to be merely teachers and advisers of the South Vietnamese army. Then they were said to be there to defend air bases, with the understanding that they would return fire if they were attacked. Next came word that the troops were being used to assist South Vietnamese units when they came under enemy fire. In fact the Americans were soon attacking the enemy directly, mounting search-and-destroy missions aimed at clearing the foe from villages and entire sections of the country.

Johnson's escalation of the American commitment occurred piecemeal and apparently without plan. At the end of 1965 some 184,000 Americans were in the field; a year later, 385,000; after another year, 485,000. By the middle of 1968 the number exceeded 538,000. Each increase was met by corresponding increases from the other side. Russia and China sent no combat troops but stepped up their aid, and thousands of North Vietnamese regulars filtered across the 17th parallel to join the Vietcong insurgents. As the scope of the action broadened, the number of American casualties rose. The United States was engaged in a full-scale war, one that Congress never declared.

Hawks and Doves

From the beginning, the war divided the American people sharply. Defenders of the president's policy, called *hawks,* emphasized the nation's moral responsibility to resist aggression and what President Eisenhower had called the domino theory. The domino theory was based on an analogy with the western powers' failure to resist Hitler before 1939. It predicted that if the communists were allowed to "take over" Vietnam, they would soon take its neighbors, then their neighbors, and so on until all Asia had been conquered. The United States was not an aggressor in Vietnam, the hawks insisted, and they

SOUTHEAST ASIA, 1954–1975

stressed Johnson's oft-expressed willingness to negotiate a general withdrawal of "foreign" forces from the country, which the communists repeatedly rejected.

American opponents of the war, called *doves*, argued that the struggle between the South Vietnamese government and the Vietcong was a civil war in which Americans should not meddle. They stressed the repressive character of the South Vietnamese government as proof that the war was not a contest between democracy and communism. They objected to the massive aerial bombings (more explosives were dropped on Vietnam between 1964 and 1968 than on Germany and Japan combined

in World War II); to the use of napalm and other chemicals such as the defoliants that were sprayed on forests and crops, which wreaked havoc among noncombatants; and to the killing of civilians by American troops. In his capacity as chairman of the Foreign Relations Committee, Senator Fulbright had introduced the Gulf of Tonkin Resolution in 1964. By 1967 he was calling the war "unnecessary and immoral," American participation in it a "false and dangerous dream of an imperial destiny."

The doves discounted the domino theory, pointing both to the growing communist split into Chinese and Russian camps and to the traditional hostility of all Vietnamese to the Chinese, which they claimed made Chinese expansion into Southeast Asia unlikely. And they deplored the heavy loss of American lives—over 40,000 dead by 1970. The cost of the war, which came to exceed $20 billion a year, was still another reason the doves opposed it. In large part because so many people objected to the war, Johnson refused to ask Congress to raise taxes to pay for it. The deficit forced the government to borrow huge sums, which caused interest rates to soar, adding to the upward pressure on prices.

Although Johnson's financial policies were shortsighted, if not outrightly irresponsible, and although his statements about the war were often lacking in candor, he and his advisers believed that they were defending freedom and democracy. "If I got out of Vietnam," the President said, "I'd be doing exactly what Chamberlain did in World War II. I'd be giving a big fat reward for aggression."

What became increasingly clear as time passed and the costs mounted was that military victory was impossible. Yet American leaders were extraordinarily slow to grasp this fact. Repeatedly they advised the president that one more escalation (so many more soldiers, so many more air raids) would break the enemy's will to resist. The smug arrogance bred by America's brief postwar monopoly of nuclear weapons persisted in some quarters long after the monopoly had been lost.

Kennedy's decision to authorize the Bay of Pigs invasion was an example of this, but as late as 1965 McGeorge Bundy, President Johnson's special assistant for national security affairs, apparently told an interviewer (he later claimed to have been misunderstood) that "the United States was the locomotive at the head of mankind, and the rest of the world the caboose." And like the proverbial donkey plodding after the carrot on the stick, Johnson repeatedly followed the advice of hawks like Bundy.

For a long time, as opinion polls demonstrated, a majority of the American people believed he was correct. Patriotism and pride, along with the costly lessons of 1931–1939 and a stubborn refusal to admit that a mistake had been made, held them to this course.

The Election of 1968

Gradually the doves increased in number. Even some of the president's hawkish advisers were turning against the war. As they did, Johnson became

almost paranoid. Critics, he said privately, were "out to get me." But as late as the fall of 1967, opposition remained disorganized. It was especially vehement on college campuses, some students objecting because they thought the United States had no business intervening in the Vietnam conflict, others because they feared being drafted, still others because so many students were obtaining educational deferments while young men who were unable to attend college were being conscripted. Then, in November 1967, Senator Eugene McCarthy of Minnesota, low-key, rather introspective, never a leading figure in the upper house, announced that he was a candidate for the 1968 Democratic presidential nomination. Opposition to the war was his issue.

Preventing Johnson from being renominated seemed on the surface impossible. Aside from the difficulty of defeating a "reigning" president, there were the domestic achievements of Johnson's Great Society program: the health insurance program for retired people, greatly expanded federal funding of education and public housing, to say nothing of the Civil Rights Act. Even Senator McCarthy took his chances of being nominated so lightly that he did not trouble to set up a real organization. He entered the campaign only to "alleviate . . . this sense of political helplessness." Someone, he decided, must step forward to put the Vietnam question before the voters.

Suddenly, early in 1968, on the heels of the latest announcement by the American military that the communists were about to crack, North Vietnam and Vietcong forces launched a general offensive to correspond with their Lunar New Year (Tet). Striking 39 of the 44 provincial capitals, many other towns and cities, and every American base, they caused chaos throughout South Vietnam. They held Hue, the old capital of the country, for weeks. To root them out of Saigon the Americans had to level large sections of the city. Elsewhere the destruction was total, an irony highlighted by the remark of an American officer after the recapture of the village of Ben Tre: "It became necessary to destroy the town to save it."

The Tet offensive was essentially a series of raids; the communists did not expect to hold the cities indefinitely, and they did not. Their losses were enormous. Nevertheless, the psychological impact in South Vietnam and in the United States made Tet a clear victory for the North. American

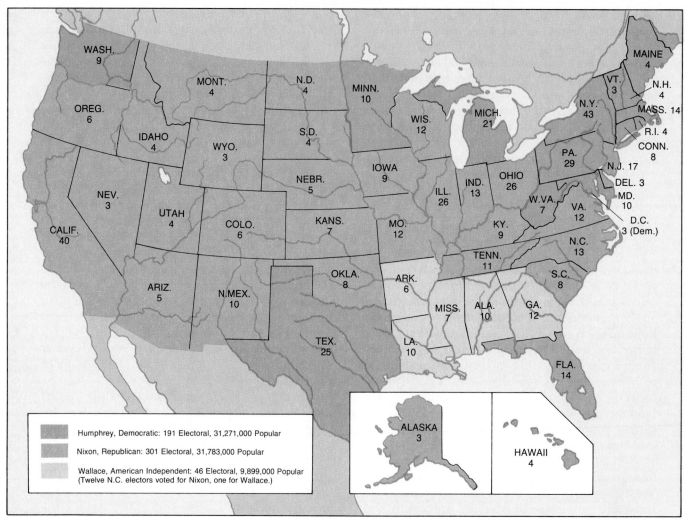

Humphrey, Democratic: 191 Electoral, 31,271,000 Popular

Nixon, Republican: 301 Electoral, 31,783,000 Popular

Wallace, American Independent: 46 Electoral, 9,899,000 Popular
(Twelve N.C. electors voted for Nixon, one for Wallace.)

THE ELECTION OF 1968

pollsters reported an enormous shift of public opinion against further escalation of the fighting. When the commander of American forces, General William C. Westmoreland, described Tet as a communist defeat and when it came out that the administration was considering sending an additional 206,000 American troops to South Vietnam, McCarthy, campaigning before the first primary in New Hampshire, suddenly became a formidable figure. Thousands of students and other volunteers flocked to the state to ring doorbells in his behalf. On election day he polled 42 percent of the Democratic vote.

The political situation was monumentally con-

fused. Before the primary, former attorney general Robert F. Kennedy, brother of the slain president, had refused either to seek the Democratic nomination or to support McCarthy, though he disliked Johnson intensely and was opposed to his policy in Vietnam. McCarthy's strong showing caused Kennedy to change his mind. Had he done so earlier, McCarthy might have withdrawn in his favor, for Kennedy had powerful political and popular support. After New Hampshire, McCarthy understandably decided to remain in the contest.

Compounding this confusion, President Johnson suddenly withdrew from the race. Vice-President Hubert H. Humphrey then announced his candidacy, though not until it was too late for him to enter the primaries. Kennedy carried the primaries in Indiana and Nebraska. McCarthy won in Wisconsin and Oregon. In the climactic contest in California, Kennedy won by a small margin. However, immediately after his victory speech at a Los Angeles hotel, he was assassinated by Sirhan Sirhan, a young Arab nationalist who had been incensed by Kennedy's support of Israel. In effect, Kennedy's death assured the nomination of Humphrey; most professional politicians distrusted McCarthy, who seemed a diffident and aloof politician.

The contest for the Republican nomination was far less dramatic, though its outcome, the nomination of Richard M. Nixon, would have been hard to predict a few years earlier. After losing to Kennedy in 1960, he ran unsuccessfully for governor of California in 1962, then moved to New York City and joined a prominent law firm. But he remained active in Republican affairs, making countless speeches and attending political meetings throughout the country. In 1964 he campaigned hard for Goldwater. When no other Republican developed extensive support as the 1968 election approached, Nixon entered the race, swept the primaries, and won an easy first-ballot victory at the Republican convention.

Nixon then astounded the country and dismayed liberals by choosing Governor Spiro T. Agnew of Maryland as his running mate. Agnew was a political unknown. ("Spiro who?" jokesters asked.) He had been elected governor by defeating a segregationist Democrat, but after the rioting in Baltimore following the murder of Martin Luther King, Jr., he had criticized Maryland blacks for not restraining the militants. Nixon chose him primarily to attract southern votes.

Placating the South seemed necessary because Governor George C. Wallace of Alabama was making a determined bid to win enough electoral votes for his American Independent party to prevent any candidate's obtaining a majority. Wallace was flagrantly antiblack and anti-intellectual. (College professors were among his favorite targets. In attacking them he used such worn images as "ivory tower folks with pointed heads" and, more inventive, people without "sense enough to park a bicycle straight.") He seemed sure to attract substantial southern and conservative support. He denounced federal "meddling," the "coddling" of criminals, and the forced

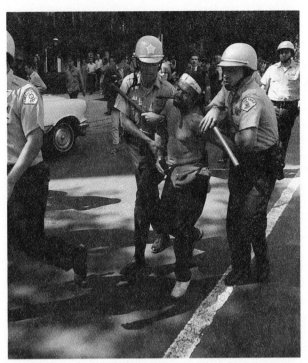

A protester at the Democratic convention in July 1968, being led away by Chicago policemen. Unruly opposition to the process by which Democrats settled on Hubert H. Humphrey as the party's nominee for the presidency, and the heavy-handed response of Mayor Richard Daley to these protests, persuaded many voters that the fate of the republic would be safer in Republican hands.

desegregation of schools. Nixon's choice of Agnew appeared to be an effort to appeal to the groups that Wallace attracted.

This Republican strategy heightened the tension surrounding the Democratic convention, which met in Chicago in late August. Humphrey delegates controlled the convention. The vice-president had a solid liberal record on domestic issues, but he had supported Johnson's Vietnam policy with equal solidity. Voters who could not stomach the Nixon-Agnew ticket and who opposed the war faced a difficult choice. Several thousand activists representing a dozen groups, advocating tactics ranging from orderly demonstrations to civil disobedience to indiscriminate violence, descended on Chicago to put pressure on the delegates to repudiate the Johnson Vietnam policy.

In the tense atmosphere that resulted, the party

hierarchy overreacted. The mayor of Chicago, Richard J. Daley, whose ability to influence election results had been demonstrated often, ringed the convention hall with policemen to protect it from disruption. This was a reasonable precaution in itself. Inside the building the delegates nominated Humphrey and adopted a war plank satisfactory to Johnson. Outside, however, provoked by the abusive language and violent behavior of radical demonstrators, the police tore into the protesters, in Norman Mailer's graphic phrase "like a chain saw cutting into wood," while millions watched on television in fascinated horror.

At first the mayhem in Chicago seemed to benefit Nixon by strengthening the convictions of many voters that the tougher treatment of criminals and dissenters that he and Agnew were calling for was necessary. Those who were critical of the Chicago police tended to blame Humphrey, whom Mayor Daley supported.

Nixon campaigned at a deliberate, dignified pace. He made relatively few public appearances, relying instead on carefully arranged television interviews and taped commercials prepared by an advertising agency. He stressed firm enforcement of the law and his desire "to bring us together." As to Vietnam, he would "end the war and win the peace," by just what means he did not say. Agnew, in his blunt, coarse way, assaulted Humphrey, the Democrats, and left-wing dissident groups. (Critics who remembered Nixon's own political style in the era of Joseph McCarthy called Agnew "Nixon's Nixon.")

The Democratic campaign was badly organized. Humphrey was subjected to merciless heckling from antiwar audiences. He seemed far behind in the early stages. Shortly before election day, President Johnson helped him greatly by suspending air attacks on North Vietnam, and in the long run the Republican strategy helped too. Black voters and the urban poor had no practical choice but to vote Democratic. Gradually Humphrey gained ground, and on election day the popular vote was close: Nixon slightly less than 31.8 million, Humphrey nearly 31.3 million. Nixon's electoral college margin, however, was substantial—301 to 191. The remaining 46 electoral votes went to Wallace, whose 9.9 million votes came to 13.5 percent of the total. Despite Nixon's triumph, the Democrats retained control of both houses of Congress.

Nixon as President

When he took office in January 1969, Richard Nixon projected an image of calm and deliberate statesmanship; he introduced no startling changes, proposed no important new legislation. The major economic problem he faced, inflation, was primarily a result of the heavy military expenditures and easy-money policies of the Johnson administration. Nixon cut federal spending and balanced the 1969 budget, while the Federal Reserve Board forced up interest rates in order to slow the expansion of the money supply. The object was to reduce the rate of economic growth without causing heavy unemployment or precipitating a recession (the word *depression* had apparently passed out of the vocabulary of economists). Even its supporters admitted that this policy would check inflation only slowly, and when prices continued to rise, there was mounting uneasiness. Labor unions demanded large wage increases. The problem was complicated by mounting deficits in the United States' balance of trade with foreign nations, the product of an overvaluation of the dollar that encouraged Americans to buy foreign goods.

In 1970 Congress passed a law giving the president power to regulate prices and wages. Nixon had opposed this legislation, but in the summer of 1971 he decided to use it. First he announced a 90-day price and wage freeze (Phase I) and placed a 10 percent surcharge on imports. Then he set up a pay board and a price commission with authority to limit wage and price increases when the freeze ended (Phase II). These controls did not check inflation completely—and they angered union leaders, who felt that labor was being shortchanged—but they did slow the upward spiral. A 7.9 percent devaluation of the dollar in December 1971 helped the economy by making American products more competitive in foreign markets.

In handling other domestic issues, the president was less firm, sometimes even confused. He advocated a bold plan for a minimum income for poor families, which alarmed his conservative supporters and got nowhere in Congress. Hoping to strengthen the Republican position in that body, he adopted a so-called southern strategy of seeking the support of southern conservative Democrats. He checked further federal efforts to force school desegregation on reluctant local districts, and he set out to add what he called "strict constructionists" to the Supreme Court, which he believed had swung too far to the left in such areas as race relations and the rights of persons accused of committing crimes.

When Chief Justice Earl Warren retired in June 1969, Nixon was eager to divert the Court from the strong civil rights positions that it had taken during the Warren years. To replace Warren he chose a conservative, Warren E. Burger. The Senate ratified the appointment of Burger, but when Nixon sought to fill the seat of Justice Abe Fortas, who had resigned under fire after it came out that he had accepted fees from questionable sources while on the bench, with another conservative, Judge Clement F. Haynsworth, Jr., of South Carolina, the Senate rejected him on political grounds. The angry president then submitted the name of Judge G. Harrold Carswell of Florida. He also was turned down because of his alleged racist attitudes and his mediocre record on the bench.

In the face of a mass of evidence, Nixon refused to believe that the nominations were rejected for the reasons stated; he declared that "no southern conservative" could run the "liberal" Senate gauntlet successfully, and to prevent the Senate from proving him wrong he nominated a liberal, Harry A. Blackmun of Minnesota. Blackmun won the unanimous approval of the Senate. Although the Burger Court was less liberal than the Warren Court, it was far from being as conservative as Nixon apparently wanted. In 1972 it declared that the death penalty, as currently used, was a cruel and unusual punishment and thus in violation of the Eighth Amendment, and in 1973 it struck down state antiabortion legislation.

"Vietnamizing" the War

Whatever his difficulties on the domestic front, Nixon considered the solution of the Vietnam problem his chief task. When the war in Southeast Asia first burst upon American consciousness in 1954, he had favored military intervention in keeping with the containment policy. As controversy over American policy developed, he had supported most of the actions of Presidents Kennedy and Johnson. During the 1968 campaign he played down the Vietnam issue. Though he insisted he would end the war on "honorable" terms if elected, he suggested nothing very different from what Johnson was doing.

In office, Nixon proposed a phased withdrawal of all non–South Vietnamese troops, to be followed by an internationally supervised election in South Vietnam. The North Vietnamese rejected this scheme and insisted that the United States withdraw its forces unconditionally. Their intransigence left the president in a difficult position. Probably the majority of Americans considered his proposal eminently fair. With equal certainty, a majority was unwilling to increase the scale of the fighting to compel the communists to accept it, and as the war dragged on, costs in lives and money rising, the desire to extricate American troops from the conflict intensified. However, large numbers of Americans would not face up to the consequences of gratifying this desire: ending the war on the communists' terms. Nixon could not compel the foe to negotiate meaningfully, yet every passing day added to the strength of antiwar sentiment, which, as it expressed itself in ever more emphatic terms, in turn led to deeper divisions in the country.

The president responded to the dilemma by trying to build up the South Vietnamese armed forces so that American troops could pull out without the communists overrunning South Vietnam. He shipped so many planes to the Vietnamese that they came to have the fourth largest air force in the world. The trouble with this strategy of "Vietnamization" was that for 15 years the United States had been trying without success to make the South Vietnamese capable of defending themselves. For complicated reasons—the incompetence, corruption, and reactionary character of the Saigon regime probably being the most important—South Vietnamese troops had seldom displayed much enthusiasm for the tough jungle fighting at which the North Vietnamese and the Vietcong excelled. Nevertheless, efforts at Vietnamization were stepped up, and in June 1969 Nixon announced that he would soon reduce the number of American soldiers in Vietnam by 25,000. In September he promised that an additional 35,000 men would be withdrawn.

These steps did not quiet American protesters. On October 15 a national antiwar demonstration, Vietnam Moratorium Day, organized by students, produced an unprecedented outpouring all over the country. This massive display produced one of Vice-

President Agnew's most notorious blasts of adjectival invective: He said that the moratorium was an example of "national masochism" led by "an effete corps of impudent snobs who characterize themselves as intellectuals." A few days later he called on the country to "separate" radical students from society "with no more regret than we should feel over discarding rotten apples from a barrel," which at least had a quality of terseness that most of Agnew's pronouncements lacked.

A second Moratorium Day brought a crowd estimated at 250,000 to Washington to march past the White House. The president was unmoved. He could not be influenced by protests, he insisted, and during one of the Washington demonstrations he passed the time watching a football game on television. On November 3 he defended his policy in a televised speech. He stressed the sincerity of his peace efforts, the unreasonableness of the communists, the responsibility of the United States to protect the South Vietnamese people from communist reprisals and to honor its international commitments. He announced that he planned to remove all American ground forces from Vietnam. The next day, reporting a flood of telegrams and calls supporting his position, he declared that a "silent majority" of the American people approved his course.

For a season, events appeared to vindicate Nixon's position. A gradual slowing of military activity in Vietnam had reduced American casualties to what those who did not find the war morally unbearable considered "tolerable" levels. Troop withdrawals continued in an orderly fashion. A new lottery system for drafting men for military duty eliminated some of the inequities in the selective service law.

But the war continued. Early in 1970 revelations that in 1968 an American unit had massacred civilians, including dozens of women and children, in a Vietnamese hamlet known as My Lai, revived the controversy over the purposes of the war and its corrosive effects on those who were fighting it. The American people, it seemed, were being torn apart by the war: one from another according to each one's interpretation of events, many within themselves as they tried to balance the war's horrors against their pride, their dislike of communism, and their unwillingness to turn their backs on their elected leader.

Not even Nixon's most implacable enemy could find reason to think that he wished the war to go on. Its human, economic, and social costs could only vex his days and threaten his future reputation. When he reduced the level of the fighting, the communists merely waited for further reductions. When he raised it, many of his own people denounced him. If he pulled out of Vietnam entirely, other Americans would be outraged.

Perhaps his error lay in his unwillingness to admit his own uncertainty, something the greatest presidents—one thinks immediately of Lincoln and Franklin Roosevelt—were never afraid to do. Facing a dilemma, he tried to convince the world that he was firmly in control of events, with the result that at times he seemed more like a high school valedictorian declaiming sententiously about the meaning of life than the mature statesman he so desperately wished to be. Thus he heightened the tensions he sought to relax—in America, in Vietnam, and elsewhere.

Even after the necessarily high-casualty "search and destroy" offensive strategy favored by President Johnson's military advisers gave way in 1969 to a more cautious use of American infantry units by President Nixon's commanders, combat deaths continued as "Vietnamization" proceeded.

The Cambodian "Incursion"

Late in April 1970 Nixon announced that Vietnamization was proceeding more rapidly than he had

An Ohio National Guard skirmish line of gas-masked troops advances up a hill on the campus of Kent State University, May 4, 1970. A moment later the guardsmen turned and fired on student antiwar demonstrators, killing four.

hoped, that communist power was weakening, that within a year another 150,000 American soldiers would be extracted from Vietnam. A week later he announced that military intelligence had indicated that the enemy was consolidating its "sanctuaries" in neutral Cambodia and that he was therefore dispatching thousands of American troops to destroy these bases.* He was in fact escalating the war. He even resumed the bombing of targets in North Vietnam. "You've got to electrify people with bold decisions," he told the Joint Chiefs of Staff. "Let's go blow the hell out of them."

To foes of the war, Nixon's decision seemed so appallingly unwise that some of them began to fear that he had become mentally unbalanced. The contradictions between his confident statements about Vietnamization and his alarmist description of powerful enemy forces poised like a dagger 30-odd miles from Saigon did not seem the product of a reasoning mind. His failure to consult congressional leaders or many of his advisers before drastically altering his policy, the critics claimed, was unconstitutional and irresponsible. His insensitive response to the avalanche of criticism that descended on him further disturbed observers.

Students took the lead in opposing the invasion

of Cambodia. Young people had been prominent in the opposition to the war from early in the conflict. Some objected to war in principle. Many more believed that this particular war was wrong because it was being fought against a small country on the other side of the globe where America's vital interests did not seem to be threatened. As the war dragged on and casualties mounted, student opposition to the draft became intense.

Nixon's shocking announcement triggered many campus demonstrations. One college where feeling ran high was Kent State University in Ohio. For several days students there clashed with local police; they broke windows and caused other damage to property. When the governor of Ohio called out the National Guard, angry students pelted the soldiers with stones. During a noontime protest on May 4 the Guardsmen, who were poorly trained in crowd control, suddenly opened fire. Four students were killed, two of them women who were merely passing by on their way to class.

While the nation reeled from this shock, two black students at Jackson State University were killed by Mississippi state policemen. A wave of student strikes followed, closing down hundreds of colleges, including many that had seen no previous unrest. Moderate students by the tens of thousands had joined with the radicals.

The almost unanimous condemnation of the invasion and of the way it had been planned shook

---

* American planes had been bombing Cambodia for some time, but this fact was not known to the public (or to Congress) until 1973.

Nixon hard. He backtracked, pulling American ground troops out of Cambodia quickly. But he did not change his Vietnam policy, and in fact the Cambodian uproar apparently stiffened his determination. As American ground troops were withdrawn, he stepped up air attacks. The balance of forces remained in uneasy equilibrium through 1971. But late in March 1972 the North Vietnamese again mounted a series of assaults throughout South Vietnam. The president responded with heavier bombing, and he ordered the approaches to Haiphong and other northern ports sown with mines to cut off the communists' supplies.

Détente

But in the midst of these aggressive actions, Nixon and his principal foreign policy adviser, Henry Kissinger, devised a bold and ingenious diplomatic offensive. Abandoning a lifetime of treating communism as a single worldwide conspiracy aimed at destroying capitalism, he was persuaded by Kissinger to deal with Russia and China as separate powers. If each dealt separately with the United States, they would have to deal differently one with the other as well.

First Nixon sent Kissinger secretly to China and the Soviet Union to prepare the way for summit meetings with the communist leaders. Both the Chinese and the Russians agreed to the meetings. Then, in February 1972, Nixon and Kissinger, accompanied by a small army of reporters and television crews, flew to Beijing. After much dining, sightseeing, posing for photographers, and consultation with Chinese officials, Nixon agreed to support the admission of China to the United Nations and to develop economic and cultural exchanges with the Chinese. Although these results appeared small, Nixon's visit, ending more than 20 years of adamant

President and Mrs. Nixon dining with Chinese Communist officials in Beijing in February 1972. Even Nixon's harshest critics conceded that his initiative in reopening U.S.-China relations was a diplomatic master stroke.

American refusal to accept the reality of the Chinese revolution, marked a dramatic reversal; as such it was hailed in the United States and elsewhere in the world.

In May, Nixon and Kissinger flew to Moscow. This trip also produced striking results. The mere fact that it took place while war still raged in Vietnam was remarkable. More important, however, the meeting resulted in the first Strategic Arms Limitation Treaty (SALT). The two powers agreed to stop making nuclear ballistic missiles and to reduce the number of antiballistic missiles in their arsenals to 200. Nixon also agreed to permit large sales of American grain to the Russians.

Nixon and Kissinger called the new policy *détente*, a French term meaning "relaxation of tensions." Détente lowered the cost of containment for the United States because it meant being more accommodating, which would reduce conflict, and making it easier to play one communist power off against the other. SALT did not end the production of atomic weapons, but such was the worldwide fear of a nuclear holocaust that any check on American and Russian arms production was regarded as encouraging. That both China and the Soviet Union had been willing to work for improved relations with the United States before America withdrew from Vietnam was also significant.

This fact, plus the failure of their offensive to overwhelm South Vietnam, led the North Vietnamese to make diplomatic concessions in the interest of getting the United States out of the war. Kissinger began negotiating seriously with their representatives in Paris in the summer of 1972. By October the draft of a settlement had been hammered out that provided for a cease-fire, the return of American prisoners of war, and the withdrawal of United States forces from Vietnam. Shortly before the presidential election, Kissinger announced that peace was "at hand."

Nixon Triumphant

A few days later President Nixon was reelected, defeating the Democratic candidate, Senator George McGovern of South Dakota, in a landslide—521 electoral votes to 17. McGovern carried only Massachusetts and the District of Columbia.

McGovern's campaign had been hampered by divisions within the Democratic party and by his tendency to advance poorly thought-out proposals, such as his scheme for funneling money directly to the poor, and his rather bumbling oratorical style. What was probably his worst blunder came after the discovery that the vice-presidential candidate he had chosen, Senator Thomas Eagleton of Missouri, had in the past undergone electroshock treatments following serious psychological difficulties. After some backing and filling, which left many voters with the impression that he was indecisive, McGovern forced Eagleton to withdraw. Sargent Shriver, former head of the Peace Corps, took Eagleton's place on the ticket.

The Eagleton affair hurt McGovern badly. Nevertheless, Nixon understandably interpreted his convincing triumph as an indication that the people approved of everything for which he stood. He had won over hundreds of thousands of voters who had supported Democrats in earlier elections. The "solid South" was again solid, but this time solidly Republican. Nixon's southern strategy of reducing the pressure for school desegregation and otherwise restricting federal efforts in behalf of blacks had a powerful attraction to northern blue-collar workers as well. They, and many people smarting from the repeated setbacks the country had experienced in Vietnam and resentful of what they considered the unpatriotic tactics of the doves, also approved of Nixon's refusal to pull out of Vietnam.

Suddenly Nixon loomed as one of the most powerful and successful presidents in American history. His bold attack on inflation, his tough-minded handling of the foreign trade question, even his harsh Vietnamese policy suggested decisiveness and self-confidence, qualities he had often seemed to lack. His willingness, despite his long history as a militant cold warrior, to negotiate with the communist nations in order to arrive at a détente that would lessen world tensions indicated a new flexibility and reasonableness. His landslide victory appeared to demonstrate that a large majority of the people approved of his way of tackling the major problems of the times.

His first reaction was to try to extract more favorable terms from the Vietnamese communists. Announcing that they were not bargaining in good faith over the remaining details of the peace treaty, he resumed the bombing of North Vietnam in December 1972, this time sending the mighty B-52s directly over Hanoi and other cities. The destructiveness of the attacks was great, but their effect-

	Electoral Vote		Electoral Vote		Electoral Vote

Popular Vote

Nixon, R.	31,783,783 (43.4%)
Humphrey, D.	31,271,839 (42.7%)
Wallace, I.	9,899,557 (13.5%)

Popular Vote

| Nixon, R. | 45,767,218 (60.6%) |
| McGovern, D. | 28,357,668 (37.5%) |

Popular Vote

| Ford, R. | 39,145,520 (48.4%) |
| Carter, D. | 40,828,657 (50.6%) |

ELECTION OF 1968   ELECTION OF 1972   ELECTION OF 1976
REPUBLICAN ADVANCE CHECKED

iveness as a means of forcing concessions from the North Vietnamese was at best debatable, and they led for the first time to the loss of large numbers of the big strategic bombers.

Nevertheless, both sides had much to gain from ending the war. In January 1973 a settlement was finally reached. The North Vietnamese retained control of large sections of the South, and they agreed to release American prisoners of war within 60 days. When this was accomplished, the last American troops were pulled out of Vietnam. More than 57,000 Americans had died in the long war, and over 300,000 more had been wounded. The cost had reached a staggering $150 billion.

Whatever the price, the war was over for the United States, and Nixon took the credit for having ended it. He immediately turned to domestic issues, determined, he made clear, to change the direction in which the nation had been moving for decades. He sought on the one hand to strengthen the power of the presidency vis-à-vis Congress and on the other to decentralize administration by encouraging state and local management of government programs. He announced that he intended to reduce the interference of the federal government in the affairs of individuals. People should be more self-reliant, he said, and he denounced what he called "per-

missiveness." Overconcern for the interests of blacks and other minorities must end. Criminals should be punished "without pity." No person or group should be coddled by the state.

These aims brought Nixon into conflict with liberal congressmen of both parties, with the leaders of minority groups, and with people concerned about the increasing power of the executive. The conflict came to a head over the president's anti-inflation policy. After his second inauguration he ended Phase II price and wage controls and substituted Phase III, which depended on voluntary "restraints" (except in the areas of food, health care, and construction). This approach did not work. Prices soared in the most rapid inflation since the Korean War. In an effort to check the rise, Nixon set a rigid limit on federal expenditures; to keep within the limit, he cut back or abolished a large number of social welfare programs, and he reduced federal grants in support of science and education. He even impounded (refused to spend) funds already appropriated by Congress for purposes he disapproved.

Impoundment created a furor on Capitol Hill, and when Congress failed to override his vetoes of bills challenging his policy, it appeared that Nixon was in total command. The White House staff, headed by H. R. Haldeman ("the Prussian") and John Ehrlichman, dominated the Washington bureaucracy like princes of the blood or oriental viziers and dealt with legislators as though they were lackeys or eunuchs. When asked to account for their actions, they took refuge behind the shield of "executive privilege," the doctrine, never before applied so broadly, that discussions and communications within the executive branch were confidential and therefore immune from congressional scrutiny. Critics began to grumble about a new "imperial presidency." No one seemed capable of checking Nixon at any point.

The Watergate Break-in

On March 19, 1973, James McCord, a former FBI agent accused of burglary, wrote a letter to the judge presiding at his trial. His act precipitated a series of disclosures that disrupted and then destroyed the Nixon administration.

McCord had been employed during the 1972 presidential campaign as a security officer of the Committee to Re-elect the President (CREEP). At about 1 A.M. on June 17, 1972, he and four other men had broken into Democratic party headquarters at the Watergate, an apartment house and office building complex in Washington. The burglars were members of an unofficial surveillance group known as "the plumbers." Nixon had formed this group in 1971 after the so-called Pentagon Papers, a secret report on government policy in Vietnam, had been leaked to the press. The plumbers had been caught rifling files and installing electronic eavesdropping devices.

Two other Republican campaign officials were soon implicated in the affair. Their arrest aroused suspicions that the Republican party was behind the break-in. Nixon denied this. "I can say categorically," he announced on June 22, "that no one on the White House staff, no one in this Administration presently employed, was involved in this very bizarre incident." Most people evidently took the president at his word, and the affair did not materially affect the election. When brought to trial early in 1973, most of the defendants pleaded guilty.

McCord, who did not, was convicted by the jury. Before Judge John J. Sirica imposed sentences on the culprits, however, McCord wrote his letter. High Republican officials had known about the burglary in advance and had persuaded most of the defendants to keep their connection secret, McCord claimed. Perjury had been committed during the trial.

The truth of McCord's charges swiftly became apparent. The head of CREEP, Jeb Stuart Magruder, and President Nixon's lawyer, John W. Dean III, admitted their involvement. Dean claimed in testimony before a special Senate Watergate investigation committee headed by Sam Ervin, Jr., of North Carolina, that Nixon had participated in efforts to cover up the affair. Among the disclosures that emerged over the following months were these:

That the acting director of the FBI, L. Patrick Gray, had destroyed documents related to the case.

That large sums of money had been paid the burglars at the instigation of the White House to ensure their silence.

That agents of the Nixon administration had burglarized the office of a psychiatrist, seeking evidence against one of his patients, Daniel Ellsberg, who had been charged with leaking the Pentagon papers to *The New York Times*. (This disclosure led to the immediate dismissal of the charges against Ellsberg by the presiding judge.)

That the CIA had, perhaps unwittingly, supplied equipment used in this burglary.

That CREEP officials had attempted to disrupt the campaigns of leading Democratic candidates during the 1972 primaries in a number of illegal ways.

That a number of corporations had made large contributions to the Nixon reelection campaign in violation of federal law.

That E. Howard Hunt, one of the Watergate criminals, had earlier forged State Department documents in an effort to make it appear that President Kennedy had been implicated in the assassination of President Ngo Dinh Diem of South Vietnam.

That the Nixon administration had placed wiretaps on the telephones of some of its own officials as well as on those of reporters critical of its policies without first obtaining authorization from the courts.

These revelations led to the discharge of John Dean and to the resignations of most of Nixon's closest advisers, including Haldeman, Ehrlichman, and Attorney General Richard Kleindienst. They also raised the question of the president's personal connection with the scandals. This he steadfastly denied. He insisted that he would investigate the Watergate affair thoroughly and see that the guilty were punished. He refused, however, to allow investigators to examine White House documents, again on grounds of executive privilege, which he continued to assert in very broad terms.

In the teeth of Nixon's denials, John Dean, testifying under oath before the Ervin committee, stated flatly and in circumstantial detail that the president had been closely involved in the Watergate cover-up. (Before testifying, Dean consulted with the conservative Senator Barry Goldwater. When he explained what he was going to say, Goldwater replied: "Hell, I'm not surprised. That goddamn Nixon has been lying all of his life.") Dean had been a persuasive witness, but—unlike Goldwater—many people were reluctant to believe that a president could lie so cold-bloodedly to the entire country. Therefore, when it came out during later hearings of the Ervin committee that the president had systematically made secret tape recordings of White House conversations and telephone calls, the disclosure caused a sensation. It seemed obvious that these tapes would settle the question of Nixon's involvement once and for all. Again he refused to allow access to the evidence.

One result of the scandals and of Nixon's attitude was a precipitous decline in his standing in public opinion polls. Calls for his resignation, even for impeachment, began to be heard. Yielding to pressure, he agreed to the appointment of an "independent" special prosecutor to investigate the Watergate affair, and he promised the appointee, Professor Archibald Cox of the Harvard Law School, full cooperation.

Cox swiftly aroused the president's ire by seeking access to White House records, including the tapes. When Nixon refused to turn over the tapes, Cox obtained a subpoena from Judge Sirica ordering the president to do so. The administration appealed and lost in the appellate court. Then, while the case was headed for the Supreme Court, Nixon ordered the new attorney general, Elliot Richardson, to dismiss Cox. Both Richardson, who had promised the Senate during his confirmation hearings that the special prosecutor would have a free hand, and his chief assistant, William Ruckelshaus, resigned rather than do so. The solicitor general, Robert H. Bork, third-ranking officer of the Justice Department, carried out Nixon's order.

Garry Trudeau and his politically biting cartoon strip Doonesbury *enlivened the Vietnam and Watergate years.* Doonesbury *became the first cartoon strip to win a Pulitzer Prize. (Ron Ziegler was President Nixon's press secretary.)*

These events, which occurred on Saturday, October 20, were promptly dubbed the Saturday Night Massacre. They caused an outburst of public indignation. Congress was bombarded by thousands of letters and telegrams demanding the president's impeachment. The House Judiciary Committee, headed by Peter W. Rodino, Jr., of New Jersey, began an investigation to see if enough evidence for impeachment existed.

Once again Nixon backed down. He agreed to turn over the tapes to Judge Sirica with the understanding that relevant materials could be presented to the grand jury investigating the Watergate affair, but that nothing would be revealed to the public. He then named a new special prosecutor, Leon Jaworski, and promised him access to whatever White House documents he needed. However, it soon came out that some of the tapes were missing and that an important section of another had been deliberately erased.

More Troubles

The nation had never before experienced such a series of morale-shattering crises. While the seemingly unending complications of Watergate were unfolding during 1973, a number of unrelated disasters struck. First, pushed by a shortage of grains resulting from massive Russian purchases authorized by the administration as part of its détente with the Soviet Union, food prices shot up; for example, wheat went from $1.45 a bushel to over $5.00. Nixon imposed another price freeze, which led to shortages, and when the freeze was lifted, prices resumed their steep ascent.

Then Vice-President Agnew (defender of law and order, foe of permissiveness) was accused of income tax fraud and of having accepted bribes while county executive of Baltimore and governor of Maryland. After vehemently denying all the charges for two months, Agnew, to escape a jail term, admitted in October that he had been guilty of tax evasion and resigned as vice-president. He was fined $10,000 and placed on three years' probation, and the Justice Department published a 40,000-word description of his wrongdoings.

Under the new Twenty-fifth Amendment, President Nixon nominated Gerald R. Ford of Michigan as vice-president, and he was confirmed by Congress. Ford had served continuously in Congress since 1949, as minority leader since 1964. His positions on public issues were close to Nixon's; he was an internationalist in foreign affairs and both a conservative and a convinced Republican partisan on domestic issues.

Not long after the Agnew fiasco, Nixon, responding to charges that he had paid almost no income taxes during his presidency, published his 1969–1972 returns. They showed that he had paid only about $1,600 in two years during which his income had exceeded half a million dollars. Although Nixon claimed that his returns were perfectly legal—he had taken huge deductions for the

gift of some of his vice-presidential papers to the National Archives—the legality of his deductions, to say nothing of their propriety, was questionable. Combined with charges that millions of dollars of public funds had been spent on improvements for his private residences in California and Florida, the tax issue further eroded his reputation, so much so that he felt obliged, during a televised press conference, to assure the audience: "I am not a crook."

The Oil Crisis

Still another disaster followed as a result of the new war that broke out in October 1973 between Israel and the Arab states. The fighting, though bloody, was brief and inconclusive; a truce was soon arranged under the auspices of the United States and the Soviet Union. But in an effort to force western nations to compel Israel to withdraw from lands held since the Six-Day War of 1967, the Arabs cut off oil shipments to the United States, Japan, and most of western Europe. A worldwide energy crisis ensued.

The immediate shortage resulting from the Arab oil boycott was ended by the patient diplomacy of Henry Kissinger, whom Nixon had made secretary of state at the beginning of his second administration. After weeks of negotiating in the spring of 1974, first with Egypt and Israel, then with Syria and Israel, he obtained a tentative agreement, which involved Israel's withdrawal from some of the territory it had occupied in the 1967 war. The Arab nations then lifted the boycott.

A revolution had taken place. From the middle of the 19th century until after World War II, the United States had produced far more oil than it could use. However, the phenomenal expansion of oil consumption that occurred after the war soon absorbed the surplus. By the late 1960s American car owners were driving more than a trillion miles a year. Petroleum was being used to manufacture nylon and other synthetic fibers as well as paints, insecticides, fertilizers, and many plastic products. Oil and natural gas became the principal fuels for home heating. Natural gas in particular was used increasingly in factories and electric utility plants, because it was less polluting than coal and most other fuels. The Clean Air Act of 1965 speeded the process of conversion from coal to gas by countless

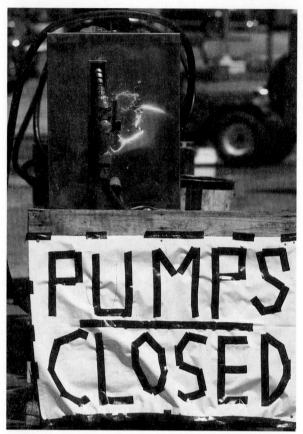

Gas stations all over the country began running out of gas in 1973; the shortage worsened through the winter and into 1974.

industrial consumers. Because of these developments, at the outbreak of the 1973 Arab-Israeli war the United States was importing one-third of its oil.

In 1960 the principal oil exporters—Venezuela, Saudi Arabia, Kuwait, Iraq, and Iran—had formed a cartel, the Organization of Petroleum Exporting Countries. For many years OPEC had been unable to control the world price of oil, which, on the eve of the 1973 war, was about $3.00 a barrel. The success of the Arab oil boycott served to unite the members of OPEC, and when the boycott was lifted, they boldly announced that the price was going up to $11.65 a barrel.

The announcement caused consternation throughout the industrial world. Soaring prices for oil meant soaring prices for everything made from petroleum or with petroleum-powered machinery. In the United States gasoline prices doubled over-

night, and the trend of all prices rose at a rate of more than 10 percent a year. This double-digit inflation, which afflicted nearly all the countries of the world, added considerably to President Nixon's woes.

The Judgment: "Expletive Deleted"

Meanwhile, special prosecutor Jaworski continued his investigation of the Watergate scandals, and the House Judiciary Committee pursued its study of the impeachment question. In March 1974 a grand jury indicted Haldeman, Ehrlichman, former attorney general John Mitchell, who had been head of CREEP at the time of the break-in, and four other White House aides for conspiring to block the Watergate investigation. The jurors also named Nixon an "unindicted co-conspirator," Jaworski having informed them that their power to indict a president was constitutionally questionable. Judge Sirica thereupon turned over the jury's evidence against Nixon to the Judiciary Committee. Then both the Internal Revenue Service and a joint congressional committee, having separately audited the president's income tax returns, announced that most of his deductions had been unjustified. The IRS assessed him nearly half a million dollars in taxes and interest, which he agreed to pay.

In an effort to check the mounting criticism, Nixon late in April released edited transcripts of the tapes he had turned over to the court the previous November. If he had expected the material to convince the public that he had been ignorant of the attempt to cover up the administration's connection with Watergate, he was sadly mistaken. In addition to much incriminating evidence, the transcripts provided a fascinating and to most persons shocking view of how he conducted himself in private. His repeated use of foul language, so out of keeping with his public image, offended millions. The phrase "expletive deleted," inserted in place of words considered too vulgar for publication in family newspapers, became a catchphrase overnight. Nixon appeared to be ignorant of the simplest legal principles. In conversations he seemed confused, indecisive, and devoid of concern for the public interest. The publication of the transcripts led even some of his strongest supporters to demand that he resign. And once the Judiciary Committee obtained the actual tapes, it became clear that the White House transcripts were in crucial respects inaccurate. Much material prejudicial to the president's case had been suppressed.

Yet impeaching a president seemed so drastic a step that many people felt that more direct proof of Nixon's involvement in the cover-up was necessary. Nixon insisted that all the relevant information was contained in these tapes; he adamantly refused to turn over others to the special prosecutor or the Judiciary Committee.

With the defendants in the Watergate case demanding access to tapes that they claimed would prove their innocence, Jaworski was compelled either to obtain them or to risk having the charges dismissed on the ground that the government was withholding evidence. He therefore subpoenaed 64 additional tapes. Nixon, through his lawyer James St. Clair, refused to obey the subpoena. Swiftly the case of *United States* v. *Richard M. Nixon* went to the Supreme Court.

In the summer of 1974 the Watergate drama reached its climax. The Judiciary Committee, following months of study of the evidence behind closed doors, decided to conduct its deliberations in open session. While millions watched on television, 38 members of the House of Representatives debated the charges. The discussions revealed both the thoroughness of the investigation and the soul-searching efforts of the representatives to render an impartial judgment. Three articles of impeachment were adopted. They charged the president with obstructing justice, misusing the powers of his office, and failing to obey the committee's subpoenas. On the first two, many of the Republicans on the committee joined with the Democrats in voting aye, a clear indication that the full House would vote to impeach.

On the eve of the debates, the Supreme Court had ruled unanimously that the president must turn over the 64 subpoenaed tapes to the special prosecutor. Executive privilege had its place, the Court stated, but no person, not even a president, could "withhold evidence that is demonstrably relevant in a criminal trial." For reasons that soon became obvious, Nixon seriously considered defying the Court. Only when convinced that to do so would make his impeachment and conviction certain—and would compel his lawyer, St. Clair, to withdraw from the case—did he agree to comply.

He would not, however, resign. Even if the

President Nixon, with his daughter Tricia at his side, announcing his resignation on August 8, 1974. His subsequent remarks to his staff, rambling, often incoherent and self-pitying, revealed a broken man.

House impeached him, he was counting on his ability to hold the support of at least 34 senators (one-third plus one of the full Senate) to escape conviction. But events were passing beyond his control. The 64 subpoenaed tapes had to be transcribed and analyzed; following the Supreme Court decision, Judge Sirica pointedly ordered St. Clair to prepare his material promptly.

Incredibly, up to this time, St. Clair had not listened to the tapes; Nixon had assured him that they contained no relevant evidence and had refused to allow him to judge the accuracy of this statement for himself. Now St. Clair had to listen, and when he did, Nixon's fate was sealed. Three recorded conversations between the president and H. R. Haldeman on June 23, 1972 (less than a week after the break-in and only one day after Nixon had assured the nation that no one in the White House had been involved in the affair), proved conclusively that Nixon had tried to obstruct justice by engaging the CIA in an effort to persuade the FBI not to follow up leads in the case on the spurious basis that national security was involved.

The president's defenders had all along insisted not so much that he was innocent as that solid proof of his guilt had not been demonstrated. Where, in the metaphor of the moment, was the "smoking

DEPRESSION, PROSPERITY, AND INFLATION, 1921–1985

Here is the third of three price graphs. The price scale on the left axis applies to the blue line; it shows wholesale prices as they have varied around the long-term trend line of 100. Prices were much below normal during the Great Depression of the 1930s and were held down by price controls during World War II, but since then they have skyrocketed, especially during OPEC oil cartel petroleum price hikes in the 1970s. On the right axis scale is the price of a gallon of gas; the green curve reflects OPEC's inflationary influence.

gun"? they asked. That weapon had now been found, and it bore the unmistakable fingerprints of President Richard M. Nixon.

Exactly what happened in the White House after St. Clair listened to the Nixon-Haldeman conversations is not yet known. The president's chief advisers pressed him to release the material at once and admit that he had erred in holding it back. This he did on August 5; that in so doing he specifically admitted that he had withheld information from his

lawyer suggests that St. Clair, whose professional reputation was at stake, had played a major role. When they read the new transcripts, all the Republican members of the Judiciary Committee who had voted against the impeachment articles reversed themselves. Understandably, they felt betrayed; they had accepted the president's assurances that all the evidence was in, and they had gone on record before millions of eyes in his defense. The last remnants of Nixon's congressional support

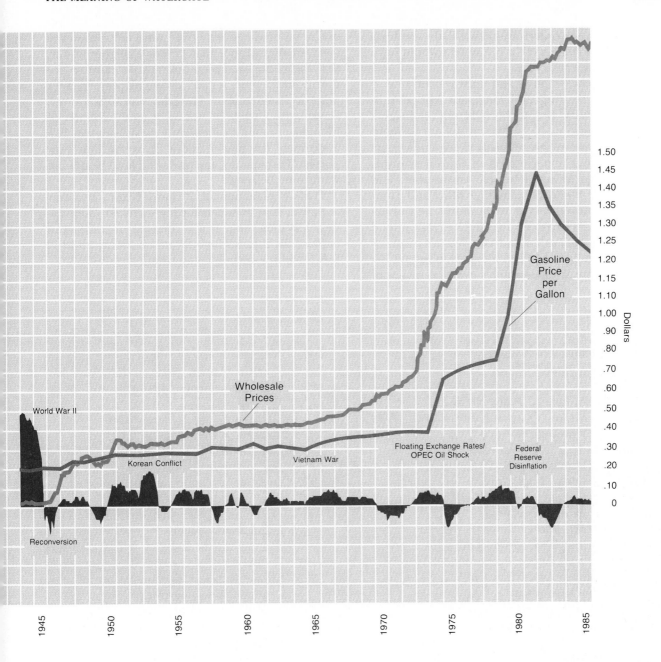

World War II

Reconversion

Korean Conflict

Wholesale
Prices

Vietnam War

Floating Exchange Rates/
OPEC Oil Shock

Federal
Reserve
Disinflation

Gasoline
Price
per
Gallon

Dollars

1.50
1.45
1.40
1.35
1.30
1.25
1.20
1.15
1.10
1.00
.90
.80
.70
.60
.50
.40
.30
.20
.10
0

1945 1950 1955 1960 1965 1970 1975 1980 1985

crumbled. Republican leaders told him categorically that the House would impeach him and that no more than a handful of senators would vote to acquit him.

The Meaning of Watergate

On August 8 Nixon announced his resignation. "Dear Mr. Secretary," his terse official letter to the secretary of state ran, "I hereby resign the Office of President of the United States. Sincerely, Richard Nixon." The resignation took effect at noon on August 9, when Gerald Ford was sworn in as president.

The meaning of "Watergate" became immediately the subject of much speculation. Whether Nixon's crude efforts to dominate Congress, to crush or inhibit dissent, and to subvert the electoral process would have permanently altered the American political system had they succeeded is beyond knowing. However, the orderly way in which these efforts were checked suggests that the system would have survived in any case.

Nixon's own drama is and must remain one of the most fascinating and enigmatic episodes in American history. Despite his fall from the heights because of personal flaws, his was not a tragedy in the Greek sense. When he finally yielded power, he seemed without remorse or even awareness of his transgressions. Although he enjoyed the pomp and circumstance attendant on his high office and trumpeted his achievements to all the world, he was devoid of the classic hero's pride. Did he really intend to smash all opposition and rule like a tyrant, or was he driven by lack of confidence in himself? His stubborn aggressiveness and his overblown view of

executive privilege may have reflected a need for constant reassurance that he was a mighty leader, that the nation accepted his right to exercise authority. One element in his downfall, preserved for posterity in videotapes of his television appearances, was that even while he was assuring the country of his innocence most vehemently, he did not look like a victim of the machinations of overzealous supporters. Perhaps at some profound level he did not want to be believed.

This explanation of Richard Nixon, however tentative, is at least comforting—it makes him appear less menacing. If it is correct, Americans can deplore the injuries he inflicted on society and still feel for him a certain compassion.

Milestones

1942	Congress of Racial Equality (CORE) founded
1955–	
1956	Montgomery, Alabama, bus boycott
1956	Southern Christian Leadership Conference founded
1960	Student Nonviolent Coordinating Committee (SNCC) founded
1961	Freedom Riders "invade" the South
1963	President Ngo Dihn Diem of South Vietnam assassinated
	Martin Luther King, Jr., "Letter from Birmingham Jail"
1964	Gulf of Tonkin Resolution leads to escalation of Vietnam War
	Civil Rights Act
	Economic Opportunity Act
1965	Immigration Act ends national origins system
	Medicare Act
	Elementary and Secondary Education Act
	Clean Air Act
1968	Communist Tet offensive in South Vietnam
	American troop strength in Vietnam reaches 538,000
	Lyndon Johnson withdraws as presidential candidate
1969	Nixon announces "Vietnamization" of the war
1970	Nixon announces "incursion" in Cambodia
	Demonstrating antiwar students killed at Kent State and Jackson State universities
1971	Nixon freezes prices
1972	Break-in at Democratic headquarters in Washington, D.C.
	Nixon and Kissinger visit China and the Soviet Union
	Strategic Arms Limitation Treaty (SALT)
1973	House Judiciary Committee begins impeachment hearings
	Vice-President Spiro Agnew resigns
	Last American troops withdraw from South Vietnam
	Nixon fires special prosecutor Archibald Cox (Saturday Night Massacre)
1973–	
1974	Arab oil boycott
1974	Supreme Court orders release of Nixon's White House tapes
	Nixon resigns; Gerald R. Ford becomes president

SUPPLEMENTARY READING

Titles marked with an asterisk have been published in paperback.

On Lyndon Johnson and the Johnson era, see J. F. Heath, **Decade of Disillusionment** (1980), and A. J. Matusow, **The Uraveling of America*** (1984). W. M. O'Neill, **Coming Apart: An Informal History of the 1960s*** (1971), and Geoffrey Hodgson, **America in Our Time** (1976), deal more broadly with the period. E. F. Goldman, **The Tragedy of Lyndon Johnson*** (1969), Doris Kearns, **Lyndon Johnson and the American Dream*** (1976), George Reedy, **Lyndon Johnson** (1982), and R. N. Goodwin, **Remembering America** (1988), are valuable memoirs.

To trace civil rights developments, consult Taylor Branch, **Parting the Waters*** (1988), David Garrow, **Bearing the Cross** (1981), Richard Kluger, **Simple Justice** (1975), Martin L. King, Jr., **Stride Toward Freedom*** (1958), and Malcolm X, **Autobiography** (1966).

On the election of 1968, T. H. White, **The Making of the President, 1968*** (1969), is lively and entertaining, while Joe McGinniss, **The Selling of the President, 1968*** (1969), is a fascinating account of the Republican advertising and television campaign. The best biography of Nixon is Stephen Ambrose, **Nixon** (1987–1989). Garry Wills, **Nixon Agonistes*** (1970), is a thoughtful though unfriendly analysis. See also R. S. Litwak, **Détente and the Nixon Doctrine** (1984), William Safire, **Before the Fall** (1975), and Rowland Evans, Jr., and R. D. Novak, **Nixon in the White House*** (1971). White's **Making of the President, 1972*** (1973) and **Breach of Faith: The Fall of Richard Nixon** (1975) are useful if not entirely satisfying.

The literature on the war in Vietnam is enormous. Stanley Karnow, **Vietnam: A History** (1983), is a straightforward narrative account, but see also A. J. Rotter, **The Path to Vietnam** (1987), Melvin Small, **Johnson, Nixon, and the Doves** (1988), Neil Sheehan, **A Bright and Shining Lie** (1988), Günter Lewy, **America in Vietnam*** (1980), Frances FitzGerald, **Fire in the Lake*** (1972), and David Halberstam, **The Best and the Brightest*** (1972); this last contains a mass of detail on the evolution of American policy, based on extensive interviews. William Shawcross, **Side-Show: Kissinger, Nixon, and the Destruction of Cambodia*** (1979), is extremely critical, and Norman Mailer, **The Armies of the Night*** (1968), is a vivid account of an antiwar demonstration in Washington.

R. S. Litwak, **Détente and the Nixon Doctrine** (1984), is a useful study of U.S.-Russian relations in the Nixon era, and Henry Kissinger's memoirs, **White House Years** (1979) and **Years of Upheaval** (1982), are important though, like most such works, self-serving.

A convenient summary of the almost infinite complexities of the Watergate affair is *New York Times* (ed.), **The End of a Presidency*** (1974), but see also Carl Bernstein and Robert Woodward, **All the President's Men*** (1974) and **Final Days*** (1976), J. W. Dean, **Blind Ambition*** (1976), and Leon Jaworski, **The Right and the Power*** (1976).

Society in Flux,
1945–1980

There's a time when the operation of the machine becomes so odious, makes you so sick at heart, that you can't take part. . . . You've got to indicate to the people that run it, the people who own it, that unless you're free, the machine will be prevented from working at all.

MARIO SAVIO, *student, University of California, 1964*

I'm not saying that women leaders would eliminate violence. We are not more moral than men; we are only uncorrupted by power so far.

GLORIA STEINEM, *1970*

Despite Lyndon Johnson's extravagant style and his landslide defeat of Barry Goldwater in the 1964 presidential election, the tone of his inaugural address in January 1965 was uncharacteristically restrained. The nation was "prosperous, great, and mighty," he said, but "we have no promise from God that our greatness will endure." He was obviously thinking of the enormous changes that were occurring in the country. He spoke of "this fragile existence," and he warned the people that they lived "in a world where change and growth seem to tower beyond the control, and even the judgment of men."

A Dynamic Society

The population was expanding rapidly. During the depressed 1930s it had increased by 9 million; in the 1950s it rose by more than 28 million, in the 1960s by another 24 million, and in the 1970s by 24 million more. Population experts observed startling shifts within this expanding mass. The westward movement had by no means ended with the closing of the frontier in the 1890s. One indication of this was the admission of Hawaii and Alaska to the Union in 1959. More significant was the growth of the Sunbelt—Florida and the states of the Southwest. California added more than 5 million to its population between 1950 and 1960, and in 1963 it passed New York to become the most populous state in the Union. Nevada and Arizona were expanding at an even more rapid rate.

The climate of the Southwest was particularly attractive to older people, especially after the perfection of mass-produced room air conditioners, and the population growth reflected the prosperity that enabled pensioners and other retired persons to settle there. At the same time, the area attracted millions of young workers, for it became the center of the aircraft and electronics industries and the government's atomic energy and space programs. These industries displayed the best side of modern capitalism: high wages, comfortable working conditions, complex and efficient machinery, and the marriage of scientific technology and commercial utility.

Advances in transportation and communication added to geographic mobility. In the postwar decades the automobile entered its golden age. In the booming 1920s, when the car became an instrument of mass transportation, about 31 million autos were produced by American factories. During the 1950s some 58 million rolled off the assembly lines; during the 1960s fully 77 million. Gasoline use increased accordingly. The more mobile population drove farther in more reliable and more comfortable vehicles over smoother and less congested highways. And the new cars were heavier and more powerful than their predecessors. Gasoline consumption first reached 15 billion gallons in 1931; it soared to 35 billion gallons in 1950 and to 92 billion in 1970. A new business, the motel industry (the word, *motel*, typically American, was a combination of *motor* and *hotel*), developed to service the millions of tourists and businessmen who burned all this fuel on their travels.

The development of the interstate highway system, begun under Eisenhower in 1956, was a major cause of increased mobility. The new roads did far more than facilitate long-distance travel; they accelerated the shift of population to the suburbs and the consequent decline of inner-city districts.

Despite the speeds that cars maintained on them, the new highways were much safer than the old roads. The traffic death rate per mile driven fell steadily, almost entirely because of the interstates.

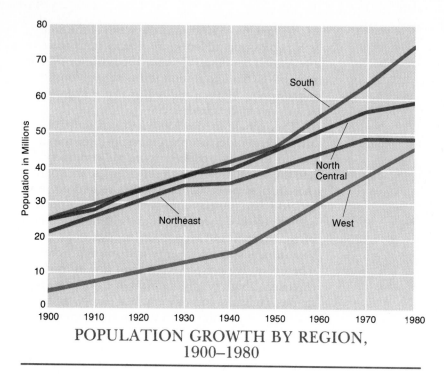

POPULATION GROWTH BY REGION,
1900–1980

The total population of the United States in 1980 was 226.5 million. During the decade 1971–1980, the West was the fastest growing region, the Northeast the slowest. The South had been the largest region since the 1950s, but it also grew 20 percent during the 1970s, owing to migration to the Sunbelt. The North Central region increased only 4 percent in this same period.

However, the environmental impact of the system was frequently severe. Elevated roads cut ugly swaths through cities, and the cars they carried released tons of noxious exhaust fumes into urban air. Hillsides were gashed, marshes filled in, forests felled, all in the name of speed and efficiency.

Although commercial air travel had existed in the 1930s and had profited from wartime technical advances in military aircraft, it truly came of age when the first jetliner—the Boeing 707, built in Seattle, Washington—went into service in 1958. Almost immediately jets came to dominate long-distance travel, to the detriment of railroad and steamship passenger service.

Television

Another important postwar change was the advent of television as a means of mass communication. Throughout the 1950s the public bought TV receivers at a rate of 6 to 7 million annually; by 1961 there were 55 million in operation, receiving the transmissions of 530 stations. During the 1960s the National Aeronautics and Space Agency (NASA)

began launching satellites capable of transmitting television pictures to earth, and the American Telephone and Telegraph Company orbited private commercial satellites that could relay television programs from one continent to another.

Television combined the immediacy of radio with the visual impact of films, and it displayed most of the strengths and weaknesses of both in exaggerated form. It swiftly became indispensable to the political system, both for its coverage of public events and as a vehicle for political advertising. Its handling of the events following President Kennedy's assassination, of national conventions and inaugurations, and of other news developments made history come alive for tens of millions. It brought sports events before the viewer vividly, attracting enormous audiences and producing so much money in advertising revenue that the economics of professional sports was revolutionized. Team franchises were bought and sold for tens of millions, and star players commanded salaries in the hundreds of thousands, eventually in the millions.

Some excellent drama was presented, especially on the National Educational Television network,

Astronaut Edwin Aldrin on the moon, July 1969. Reflected in his helmet visor are flight commander Neil Armstrong, who took this picture, and part of their spacecraft. Television enabled some 600 million people to see the historic event.

along with many filmed documentaries. "Sesame Street," a children's program presented on the educational network, won international recognition for its entertainment value and for its success in motivating underprivileged children. Commercial television indirectly improved the level of radio broadcasting by siphoning off much of the mass audience; more radio time was devoted to serious discussion programs and to classical music, especially after the introduction of frequency modulation (FM) transmissions.

The entertainment offered by most television stations was generally abominable; Newton Minow of the FCC called it a "vast wasteland." The lion's share of television time was devoted to uninspired and vulgar serials, routine variety shows, giveaway and quiz programs designed to reveal and revel in the ignorance of the average citizen, and reruns of old movies cut to fit rigid time periods and repeatedly interrupted at climactic points by "commercials." Most sets had poor accoustic qualities, which made them inferior instruments for listening to music. Serious discussion programs were too often relegated to inconvenient times, and there were not enough of them. Yet children found television fascinating, remaining transfixed before the screen when—their elders said—they should have been out of doors or curled up with a book.

Still another dubious virtue of television was its capacity for influencing the opinions and feelings of viewers. The insistent and strident claims of advertisers punctuated every program with monotonous regularity. Politicians discovered that no other device or method approached television as a means of reaching large numbers of voters with an illusion of intimacy. Since television time was expensive, only candidates who possessed or had access to huge sums could afford to use the medium—a dangerous state of affairs in a democracy. In time Congress clamped a lid on campaign expenditures, but this action did not necessarily reduce the amounts spent on television, with its capacity to reach so many people.*

"A Nation of Sheep"

Another postwar change was the marked broadening of the middle class. In 1947 only 5.7 million American families had what might be considered middle-class incomes—enough to provide something for leisure, entertainment, and cultural activities as well as for life's necessities. By the early 1960s more than 12 million families, about a third of the population, had such incomes. As they prospered, middle-class Americans became more culturally homogeneous and broader-gauged in their interests.

The percentage of immigrants in the population declined steadily; by the mid-1960s over 95 percent of all Americans were native-born. This trend contributed to social and cultural uniformity. So did the rising incomes of industrial workers and the changing character of their labor. By 1962 about 90 percent of all industrial workers enjoyed such fringe benefits as paid vacations and medical insurance at least partly financed by their employers, and nearly 70 percent participated in pension plans. The growth of pension funds made the union officials who managed them powers in the financial world. The merger in 1955 of the two great labor federations, the AFL and the CIO, added to the prestige of all union labor as well as to the power of the new organization.

As blue-collar workers invaded the middle class by the tens of thousands, they moved to suburbs previously reserved for junior executives, shopkeepers, and the like. They shed their work clothes for business suits. They took up golf. In sum, they adopted values and attitudes commensurate with their new status—which helps explain the growing conservatism of labor unions. During the Great Depression, when they were underdogs of sorts, the

---

* The government now provides substantial public funds to major candidates in presidential elections.

unions fought for social justice. In the 1960s many union workers seemed more interested in preserving their gains against the ravages of inflation and taxation than they were in social reform.

Religion in Changing Times

Sociologists and other commentators on contemporary affairs found in the expansion of the middle class another explanation of the tendency of the country to glorify the conformist. They attributed to this expansion the blurring of party lines in politics, the national obsession with moderation and consensus, the complacency of so many Americans, and their tendency, for example, to be at once more interested in churchgoing than with the philosophic aspects of religion.

Organized religion traditionally deals with eternal values, but it is always influenced by social, cultural, and economic developments. Never has this been more true in America than in the decades after World War II. All the major faiths, despite their differences, were affected. Immediately after the war the prosperity and buoyant optimism of the period led to an expansion of religious activity. The Catholic church alone built over 1,000 new schools and more than 100 hospitals along with countless new churches. By 1950 the Southern Baptists had enrolled nearly 300,000 new members and built some 500 churches for them to worship in, and the historian Arthur Hertzberg estimates that between 1945 and 1965, Jews spent at least $1 billion building 1,000 synagogues, "the largest building boom in the history of American Jews."

But while most faiths prospered materially, the faithful tended to accept the world as it was. In *Catholic, Protestant, Jew* (1955), Will Herberg argued that in America, religious toleration had become routine. President Eisenhower lent authority to this argument when he said: "Our government makes no sense unless it is founded on a deeply felt religious faith—and I don't care what it is." According to a Gallup poll taken shortly after the war, nearly everyone in America believed in God. However, another poll revealed that many people were woefully ignorant of religious history and doctrine. Large numbers of Christians, for example, were unable to tell pollsters the name of any of the four Gospels. Professor Herberg reports that groups at typical suburban synagogues "were much more likely to discuss current events, or busy themselves with bowling, than to study the Bible."

Church and state were by law and the Constitution separate institutions, yet acts of Congress and state legislatures frequently had indirect effects on every aspect of organized religion. New Deal welfare legislation took on a large part of a burden previously borne by church groups. The expansion of higher education resulting from the G.I. Bill introduced millions of young adults to new ideas and appeared to make people somewhat more tolerant of the beliefs of others, religious beliefs included. However, studies showed that better-educated people tended to be less involved in the formal aspects of organized religion, and some became interested in "exotic" nonwestern faiths, such as Zen Buddhism. Both these trends seemed alarming to the leaders of the established religious groups, in part because they reflected an "education gap" separating religious liberals from religious conservatives.

Unlike prewar critics who had attacked "rugged individualism," many post–New Deal social critics, alarmed by the conformity of the 1950s, urged people to be more individualistic. In *The Lonely Crowd* (1950), David Riesman drew a distinction between old-fashioned "inner-directed" people and new "other-directed" conformists who were group-centered, materialistic, and generally accommodating rather than tough and uncompromising. William Whyte's best-seller *The Organization Man* (1956) and Sloan Wilson's novel *The Man in the Gray Flannel Suit* (1955) dealt with the same phenomenon. These writers did not concern themselves directly with religion, but they were reacting to problems that also affected thoughtful religious leaders. One prominent divine complained of "the drive toward a shallow and implicitly compulsory common creed," a "religion-in-general, superficial and syncretistic, destructive of the profounder elements of faith."

The civil rights movement is another illustration of a political and social issue that had important religious implications. Many militant blacks (Malcolm X was an example) were attracted to Islam by its lack of racial bias. Among those in the public eye who became Muslims were the heavyweight champion boxer Cassius Clay, who changed his name to Mohammed Ali, and Lew Alcindor, the basketball star, who became Kareem Abdul Jabbar. All the "conventional" churches played significant roles in the fight for racial justice that erupted after the Supreme Court outlawed segregation. The enormous outpouring produced by Martin Luther King, Jr.'s March on Washington in 1963 was swelled by many clergymen, and their example put pressure on both church hierarchies and ordinary members to become civil rights activists. Shocking photographs of police dogs being used to "subdue" demonstrating Catholic nuns on another occasion converted uncounted thousands to the struggle. The controversy over America's role in the Vietnam War had similar effects.

All the social changes of the period had religious ramifications. Feminists objected to male domination of most Christian churches and called for the ordination of female ministers and priests; some religious leaders supported the feminists, but conservatives rejected their ideas out of hand. Every aspect of the sexual revolution (see pp. 901ff), from the practice of couples living together openly outside marriage to the tolerance of homosexuality and pornography to the legalization of abortion, caused shock waves in the religious community.

Scientific and technological developments also affected both religious values and the way people worshiped. Darwin's theory of evolution had had social effects as well as directly religious ones in the 19th and early 20th centuries, and these were to some extent still unresolved. Many religious groups still believed in the biblical explanation of Creation and sought to have "Creation theory" taught in the schools.

On another level, the prestige of secular science gave it a kind of religious aspect disturbing to some church leaders. Medical advances that some people marveled at, such as in vitro fertilization of human eggs, organ transplants, and the development of machines capable of keeping terminally ill people alive indefinitely, seemed to others "against nature" and indeed sacrilegious. More generally, the public was divided about the ultimate value of scientific progress. Controversies over the use of atomic energy in peace and war and over the conservation of natural resources all had religious aspects.

Radio and television had more direct effects on organized religion. The "Radio Priest" of the New Deal era, Father Charles Coughlin, was the prototype of a new kind of clergyman that flourished in the postwar period. The airwaves enabled rhetorically skilled preachers to reach millions with

California minister Robert Schuller, here televising his "Hour of Power" program from his church in Garden Grove, was one of many "televangelists" who created devoted and financially sustaining congregations through their nationally broadcast television ministries. His particular appeal is suggested in the title of one of his books: Positive Prayer for Power-Filled Living.

emotionally charged messages on religious topics and also on political and social questions. The most successful in the postwar years were the leaders of evangelical protestant sects, and by the 1960s they had mastered television. Whereas most postwar revivalists, the most famous being Billy Graham, stressed interdenominational cooperation, in the 1970s a more militant, fundamentalist type emerged. These TV preachers tended to found churches and educational institutions of their own and to use radio and television to raise money to support them, but they were extremely conservative both in their religious and in their political, social, and moral views. This brought them into conflict with many other developments of the period.

Literature and Art

For a time after World War II the nation seemed on the verge of a literary outburst comparable to the one that followed World War I. A number of excellent novels based on the military experiences of young writers appeared, the most notable being *The Naked and the Dead* (1948) by Norman Mailer and *From Here to Eternity* (1951) by James Jones. Unfortunately, a new renaissance did not develop. The most talented younger writers rejected materialist values but preferred to bewail their fate rather than rebel against it. Jack Kerouac, founder of the "beat" (for *beatific*) school, reveled in the chaotic description of violence, perversion, and madness. At the other extreme, J. D. Salinger, perhaps the most popular writer of the 1950s and the particular favorite of college students—*The Catcher in the Rye* (1951) sold nearly 2 million copies in hardcover and paperback editions—was an impeccable stylist, witty, contemptuous of all pretense; but he too wrote about people entirely wrapped up in themselves.

In *Catch-22* (1955), the book that replaced *The Catcher in the Rye* in the hearts of college students, Joseph Heller produced a war novel that was farcical and an indignant denunciation of the stupidity and waste of warfare. In *The Victim* (1947), *The Adventures of Augie March* (1953), and many other novels, Saul Bellow described characters possessed of their full share of eccentricities and weaknesses without losing sight of the positive side of modern life. Bellow won many literary awards, including a Nobel Prize.

All these novelists and a number of others whose books were of lesser quality were widely read. Year after year sales of books increased, despite much talk about how television and other diversions were undermining the public's interest in reading. Sales of paperbacks, first introduced in the United States in 1939 by Pocket Books, reached enormous proportions. By 1965 about 25,000 titles were in print, and sales were approaching 1 million copies a day.

Cheapness and portability only partly accounted for the popularity of paperbacks. Readers could purchase them in drugstores, bus terminals, and supermarkets as well as in bookstores. Teachers, delighted to find out-of-print volumes easily available, assigned hundreds of them in their classes. And there was a psychological factor at work, the paperback became fashionable. People who rarely bought hardcover books purchased weighty volumes of literary criticism, translations of the works of obscure foreign novelists, specialized historical monographs, and difficult philosophical treatises now that they were available in paper covers.

The expansion of the book market, like so many

other changes, was not an unalloyed benefit even for writers. It remained difficult for unknown authors to earn a decent living. Publishers tended to concentrate their interest and their money on authors already popular and on books aimed at a mass audience. Even among successful writers of unquestioned ability, the temptations involved in large advances and in book club contracts and movie rights diverted many from making the best use of their talents.

American painters were affected by the same forces that influenced writers. In the past the greatest American artists had been shaped by European influences. This situation changed dramatically after World War II with the emergence of abstract expressionism, or action painting. This "New York school" was led by Jackson Pollock (1912–1956), who composed huge abstract designs by laying his canvas on the floor of his studio and drizzling paint on it directly from tube or pot in a wild tangle of color.

The abstract expressionists were utterly subjective in their approach to art. "The source of my painting is the Unconscious," Pollock explained. "I am not much aware of what is taking place; it is only after that I see what I have done." Pollock tried to produce not the representation of a landscape but, as the critic Harold Rosenberg put it, "an inner landscape that is part of himself."

Untutored observers found the abstract expressionists crude, chaotic, devoid of interest. The swirling, dripping chaos of the followers of Pollock, the vaguely defined planes of color favored by Mark Rothko and his disciples, and the sharp spatial confrontations composed by the painters Franz Kline, Robert Motherwell, and Adolph Gottlieb required too much verbal explanation to communicate their meaning to the average observer. Viewed in its social context, however, abstract expressionism, like so much of modern literature, reflected the estrangement of the artist from the world of the atomic bomb and the computer, a revolt against contemporary mass culture with its unthinking acceptance of novelty for its own sake.

The experimental spirit released by the abstract expressionists led to op (for *optical*) art, which employed the physical impact of pure complementary colors to produce dynamic optical effects. Even within the rigid limitations of severely formal designs composed of concentric circles, stripes,

Jackson Pollock's "drip" paintings rejected all traditional techniques and representational subjects, resulting in a purely abstract expression. The title of this large 1950 canvas—it is about 17 by 9 feet—is Autumn Rhythm.

squares, and rectangles, such paintings appeared to be constantly in motion, almost alive.

Op was devoid of social connotations; another variant, pop art, playfully yet often with acid incisiveness satirized many aspects of American culture: its vapidity, its crudeness, its violence. The painters Jasper Johns, Roy Lichtenstein, and Andy Warhol created portraits of mundane objects such as flags, comic strips, soup cans, and packing cases. Op and pop art reflected the mechanized aspects of life; the painters made use of technology in their work—for example, they enhanced the shock of vibrating complementary colors by using fluorescent paints. Some artists imitated newspaper photograph techniques by fashioning their images of sharply defined dots of color. Others borrowed from contemporary commercial art, employing spray guns, stencils, and masking tape to produce flat, hard-edged effects. The line between op and pop was frequently crossed, as in Robert Indiana's *Love,* which was reproduced and imitated on posters, Christmas cards, book jackets, buttons, rings, and even a postage stamp.

Color and shape as ends in themselves, stark and often on a heroic scale, typified the new styles. Color-field painters covered vast planes with flat, sometimes subtly shaded hues. Frank Stella, one of the most universally admired of the younger artists, composed complicated bands and curves of color on enormous, eccentrically shaped canvases. To an unprecedented degree, the artist's hand—the combination of patience and skill that had characterized traditional art—was removed from painting.

The pace of change in artistic fashion was dizzying—far more rapid than changes in literature. Aware that their generation was leading European artists instead of following them gave both artists and art lovers a sense of participating in events of historic importance.

As with literature, the effects of such success were not all healthy. Successful artists became national personalities, a few of them enormously rich. For these, each new work was exposed to the glare of publicity, sometimes with unfortunate results. Too much attention, like too much money, could be distracting, even corrupting, especially for young artists who needed time and obscurity to develop their talents. "Schools" rose and fell in rapid order,

Along with Andy Warhol, Roy Lichtenstein is recognized as a master of pop art.

it seemed, at the whim of one or another influential critic or dealer. Being different was more highly valued than aesthetic quality or technical skill. No matter how outlandish, the newest thing attracted respectful attention. The idea of the avant-garde as a revolt of creative minds against the philistinism of the middle class no longer had meaning, despite the fact that the existence of an expanding middle class made the commercial success of modern art possible.

Two Dilemmas

The many changes of the era help to explain why President Johnson expressed so much uncertainty in his inaugural address. Looking at American society more broadly, two dilemmas seem to have confronted people in the 1960s. One was that progress was often self-defeating. Reforms and innovations instituted with the best of motives often made things worse rather than better. Instances of this dilemma, large and small, are so numerous as to defy summary. DDT, a powerful chemical developed to kill insects that were spreading disease and destroying valuable food crops, proved to have lethal effects on birds and fish—and perhaps indirectly on human beings. Goods manufactured to make life fuller and happier (automobiles, detergents, electric power) produced waste products that disfigured the land and polluted air and water. Cities built in order to bring culture and comfort to millions became pestholes of crime, poverty, and depravity.

Change occurred so fast that experience (the recollection of how things had been) tended to become less useful and sometimes even counterproductive as a guide for dealing with current problems. Foreign policies designed to prevent wars, devised on the basis of knowledge of the causes of past wars, led, because the circumstances were different, to new wars. Parents who sought to transmit to their children the accumulated wisdom of their years found their advice rejected, often with good reason, because that wisdom had little application to the problems their children had to face.

The second dilemma was that modern industrial society placed an enormous premium on social cooperation, at the same time undermining the individual citizen's sense of being essential to the proper functioning of society. The economy was as complicated as a fine watch; a breakdown in any one sector had ramifications that spread swiftly to other sectors. Yet specialization had progressed so far that individual workers had little sense of the importance of their personal contributions and thus felt little responsibility for the smooth functioning of the whole. Effective democratic government required that all voters be knowledgeable and concerned, but few could feel that their individual voices had any effect on elections or public policies. The exhaust fumes of millions of automobiles poisoned the air, but it was difficult to expect the single motorist to accept the inconvenience of leaving the car in the garage when such restraint would have no measurable effect on pollution overall. "One person just can't feel that she's doing anything," a frustrated teenager wrote. "I can use soap instead of detergent . . . but what good do I feel I'm doing when there are people next door having a party with plastic spoons and paper plates?"

People tried to deal with this dilemma by joining groups; then the groups became so large that members felt as incapable of influencing them as they did of influencing the larger society. The groups were so numerous and had so many conflicting objectives that instead of making citizens more socially minded, they often made them more self-centered. The organization—union, club, party, pressure group—was a potent force in society. Yet few organizations were really concerned with the common interest, though logic required that the common interest be regarded if individuals or groups were to achieve their special interests.

These dilemmas produced a paradox. The United States was the most powerful nation in the world, its people the best educated, the richest, and probably the most energetic. American society was technologically advanced and dynamic; American traditional values were idealistic, humane, democratic. Yet the nation seemed incapable of mobilizing its resources intelligently to confront the most obvious challenges, its citizens unable to achieve much personal happiness or identification with their fellows, the society helpless in trying to live up to its most universally accepted ideals.

In part the paradox was a product of the strengths of the society and the individuals who made it up. The populace as a whole was more sophisticated. People were more aware of their immediate interests, less willing to suspend judgment and follow leaders or to look on others as better qualified to decide what they should do. They belonged to the "me generation"; they knew that they lived in a society and that their lives were profoundly affected by that society, but they had trouble feeling that they were part of a society.

President Johnson recognized the problem. He hoped to solve it by establishing a "consensus" and building his Great Society. No real consensus emerged; American society remained fragmented, its members divided against one another and often among themselves. Awareness of the complexities and contradictions of life and human institutions was a mark of increasing maturity but also a source of uncertainty and insecurity.

The Costs of Prosperity

The vexing character of modern conditions could be seen in every aspect of life. The economy, after decades of hectic expansion, accelerated still more rapidly. The gross national product approached a trillion dollars, but inflation was becoming increasingly serious. Workers were under constant pressure to demand raises—which only served to drive prices still higher. Socially the effect was devastating; it became impossible to expect workers to see inflation as a social problem and to restrain their personal demands. Putting their individual interests before those of the whole, they were prepared to disrupt the economy regardless of social cost. Even public employees traditionally committed to a no-strike policy because they worked for the entire community—teachers, garbage collectors, firefighters, the police—succumbed to this selfish, if understandable, way of looking at life.

Economic expansion resulted in large measure from technological advances, and these too proved to be mixed blessings. As we have seen, World War II needs stimulated the development of materials such as plastics, nylon, and synthetic rubber and such electronic devices as radar and television. After the war these products came into their own. Plastics invaded field after field—automobile parts, building materials, adhesives, packaging materials.

In 1951 scientists began to manufacture electricity from nuclear fuels; in 1954 the first atomic-powered ship, the submarine *Nautilus*, was launched. Although the peaceful use of atomic energy remained small compared to other sources of power, its implications were immense. Equally significant was the invention of the electronic computer, which revolutionized the collection and storage of records, solved mathematical problems beyond the scope of the most brilliant human minds, and speeded the work of bank tellers, librarians, billing clerks, statisticians—and income tax collectors.

Computers lay at the heart of industrial automation, for they could control the integration and adjustment of the most complex machines. In automobile factories they made it possible to produce entire engine blocks automatically. In steel mills molten metal could be poured into molds, cooled, rolled, and cut into slabs without the intervention of a human hand, the computers locating defects and adjusting the machinery to correct them far more accurately than the most skilled steelworker, and in a matter of seconds. Taken in conjunction with a new oxygen smelting process six or eight times faster than the open-hearth method, computer-controlled continuous casting promised to have an impact on steelmaking as great as that of the Bessemer process in the 1870s.

The material benefits of technology commonly had what the microbiologist René Dubos described as "disastrous secondary effects, many of which are probably unpredictable." The consumption of petroleum necessary to produce power soared and began to outstrip supplies, threatening shortages that would disrupt the entire economy. The burning of this fuel released immeasurable tons of smoke and other polluting gases into the atmosphere, endangering the health of millions. "Life is enriched by one million automobiles," Dubos noted, "but can be made into a nightmare by one hundred million."

The vast outpouring of flimsy plastic products and the increased use of paper, metal foil, and other disposable packaging materials seemed about to bury the country beneath mountains of trash. The commercial use of nuclear energy also caused problems. Scientists insisted that the danger from radiation was insignificant, but the possibility of accidents could not be eliminated entirely, and the safe disposal of radioactive wastes became increasingly difficult.

Even an apparently ideal form of scientific advance, the use of commercial fertilizers to boost food output, had unfortunate side effects. Phosphates

As environmental issues became more prominent, shots like this view of raw sewage being dumped into the Niagara River appeared more often in the popular press. This photo was taken by Alfred Eisenstaedt for Life *in 1968.*

washed from farmlands into streams sometimes upset the ecological balance and turned the streams into malodorous death traps for aquatic life. Above all, technology increased the capacity of the earth to support people. As population increased, production and consumption increased, exhausting supplies of raw materials and speeding the pollution of air and water resources. Where would the process end? Viewed from a world perspective, it was obvious that the population explosion must be checked or it would check itself by pestilence, war, starvation, or some combination of these scourges. Yet how to check it?

New Racial Turmoil

President Johnson and most of those who supported his policies expected that the 1964 Civil Rights Act, the Economic Opportunity Act, Medicare and Medicaid, and the other elements in the War on Poverty would produce an era of racial peace and genuine social harmony—the Great Society that everyone wanted. The change that occurred in the thinking of the black radical Malcolm X seemed a straw in the wind. In 1964 Malcolm left the Black Muslims and founded his own Organization of Afro-American Unity. While continuing to stress black self-help and the militant defense of black rights, he now saw the fight for racial equality as part of a larger struggle for all human rights. "What we do . . . helps all people everywhere who are fighting against oppression," he said. Yet as in so many other aspects of modern life, progress itself created new difficulties. Early in 1965 Black Muslim fanatics, furious at his defection, assassinated Malcolm X while he was making a speech in favor of racial harmony.

The assassination was an act of vengeance, not of social protest. More significant was the fact that official white recognition of past injustices was making blacks more insistent that all discrimination be ended. The very process of righting past wrongs gave them the strength to fight more vigorously. Black militancy, building steadily during World War II and thereafter, had long been ignored by the white majority; in the mid-1960s it burst forth so powerfully that the most smug and obtuse white citizens had to accept its existence.

Even Martin Luther King, Jr., the standard-bearer of nonviolent resistance, became more demanding. A few weeks after Malcolm's death, King led a march from Selma, Alabama, to Montgomery as part of a campaign to force Alabama authorities to allow blacks to register to vote. His marchers were brutally assaulted by state policemen who wielded clubs and tossed canisters of tear gas. Liberal opinion was shocked as never before. Thousands of people descended on Selma to demonstrate their support for the black cause.

The Student Nonviolent Coordinating Committee, which had been born out of the struggle for racial integration, had become by late 1964 a radical organization openly scornful of integration and interracial cooperation. Many student reformers had been radicalized by the threats and open violence they had experienced while trying to register rural blacks and organize schools for black children in the South and by the slowness of the Kennedy administration to work all-out for racial justice. The slogan of the radicals was "Black Power," an expression that was given national currency by Stokely Carmichael, chairman of SNCC. Carmichael, West Indian by birth, had grown up in Harlem. In the early 1960s he had worked ceaselessly for black rights in the South, and as a result he had spent considerable time in southern jails. By 1964, though still willing to work with black moderates such as King, he was adamantly opposed to cooperating with white civil rights activists of any stripe. "The time for white involvement in the fight for equality has ended," Carmichael announced in 1966. "If we are to proceed toward true liberation, we must set ourselves off from white people." Since whites "cannot relate to the black experience," the movement "should be black-staffed, black-controlled, and black-financed."

"Integration is a subterfuge for the maintenance of white supremacy," Carmichael said on another occasion. Blacks should have their own schools, their own businesses, their own political parties, their own (African) culture.

Black Power caught on swiftly among militants. This troubled white liberals because people like Carmichael refused "to discriminate between degrees of inequity" among whites. Liberals feared that Black Power would antagonize white conservatives. They argued that since blacks made up only about 11 percent of the population, any attempt to obtain racial justice through the use of naked power was sure to fail.

Meanwhile, black anger erupted in a series of destructive urban riots. The most important occurred in Watts, a ghetto of Los Angeles, in August 1965. A trivial incident—police officers halted a motorist who seemed to be drunk and attempted to give him a sobriety test—brought thousands into the streets. The neighborhood almost literally exploded: For six days Watts was swept by fire, looting, and bloody fighting between local residents and 15,000 National Guardsmen, called up to assist the police. Order was restored only after 34 persons had been killed, more than 850 wounded, and 3,100 arrested. Property damage in Watts came to nearly $200 million.

The following summer saw similar outbursts in New York, Chicago, and other cities. In 1967 further riots broke out. In Newark, New Jersey, 25 were killed in a July outburst that lasted four days. In Detroit a few days later, what may have been the worst race riot since the Civil War erupted. The death toll in Detroit came to 43, and looting and arson assumed anarchic proportions. Then, in April 1968, the revered Martin Luther King, Jr., was murdered in Memphis, Tennessee, by a white man, James Earl Ray.* Blacks in more than 100 cities swiftly unleashed their anger in paroxysms of burning and looting. White opinion was shocked and profoundly depressed. King's death appeared to destroy the hope that his doctrine of pacific appeal to reason and right could solve the racial problem.

Public fear and puzzlement led to many investigations of the causes of the riots, the most important being that of the commission headed by Governor Otto Kerner of Illinois, which President Johnson appointed following King's murder. The conclusions of most of the studies were complex but fairly clear. Race riots had a long history in the United States, but the outbursts of the 1960s were different. Earlier troubles usually began with attacks by whites that led to black counterattacks. Riots of the Watts type were begun by blacks. Although much white-owned property was destroyed, the fighting was mostly between blacks and law enforcement officers trying to control them. White citizens tended to avoid the centers of trouble, and blacks seldom ranged outside their own neighborhoods.

---

* Ray fled to England but was apprehended, extradited, convicted, and sentenced to 99 years in prison.

The rioters were expressing frustration and despair; their resentment was directed more at the social system than at individuals. As the Kerner commission put it, the basic cause was an attitude of mind, the "white racism" that deprived blacks of access to good jobs, crowded them into slums, and, for the young in particular, eroded all hope of escape from such misery. Ghettos bred crime and depravity—as slums always have—and the complacent refusal of whites adequately to invest money and energy in helping ghetto residents, or even to acknowledge that the black poor deserved help, made the modern slum unbearable. While the ghettos expanded, middle-class whites tended more and more to flee to the suburbs or to call on the police "to maintain law and order," a euphemism for cracking down hard on deviant black behavior no matter how obvious the connection between that behavior and the slum environment.

The victims of racism employed violence not so much to force change as to obtain psychic release; it was a way of getting rid of what they could not stomach, a kind of vomiting. Thus the concentration of the riots in the ghettos themselves, the smashing, Samson-like, of the source of degradation even when this meant self-destruction. When fires broke out in black districts, the firefighters who tried to extinguish them were often showered with bottles and bricks and sometimes shot at, while above the roar of the flames and the hiss of steam rose the apocalyptic chant, "Burn, baby, burn!"

The most frightening aspect of the riots was their tendency to polarize society along racial lines. Advocates of Black Power became more determined to separate themselves from white influence; they exasperated white supporters of school desegregation by demanding schools of their own. Extremists formed the Black Panther party and collected weapons to resist the police. "Shoot, don't loot," the radical H. Rap Brown advised all who would listen. The Panthers demanded public compensation for injustices done to blacks in the past, pointing out that following World War II, West Germany had made payments to Jews to make up for Hitler's persecutions. In 1968 they nominated Eldridge Cleaver for president. Although Cleaver was a convict on parole, he was an articulate and intelligent man whose autobiographical *Soul on Ice,* written in prison, had attracted much praise.

Middle-class city residents often resented what

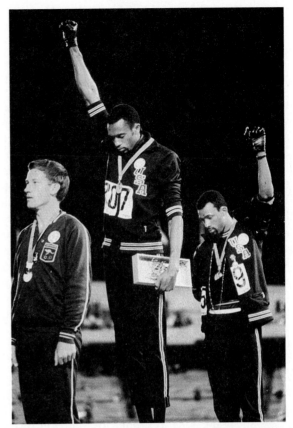

1968 Olympic gold and silver medal winners, T. Smith and J. Carlos, making the gloved salute of "black power" during the televised award ceremonies and the playing of the national anthem in Mexico City. Both athletes were removed from the team, but not before making their point.

seemed the favoritism of the federal government and state and local administrations, which sought through so-called affirmative action to provide blacks with new economic opportunities and social benefits. Efforts to desegregate ghetto schools by busing children out of their local neighborhoods was a particularly bitter cause of conflict.

These developments caused a powerful white backlash. Persons already subjected to the pressures caused by inflation, specialization, and rapid change that were undermining social solidarity and worried by the sharp rise in urban crime rates and welfare costs found black radicalism infuriating. In the face of the greatest national effort in history to aid them, blacks, they said, were displaying not merely ingratitude but contempt.

The Unmeltable Ethnics

The struggles of blacks for equality went hand in hand with those of Mexican-Americans, principally in the Southwest. After World War I, thousands of Mexicans flocked into the region. They could do so legally because the restrictive immigration legislation of the 1920s did not apply to Western Hemisphere nations. When the Great Depression struck, Mexican-Americans were the first to suffer—about half a million were either deported or persuaded to return to Mexico in the 1930s. But during World War II and again between 1948 and 1965, federal legislation encouraged the importation of *braceros* (temporary farm workers), and many other Mexicans entered the country illegally. The latter were known as *mojados,* or "wetbacks," because they often slipped across the border by swimming the Rio Grande. Many of these Mexicans, and other Spanish-speaking people, including the thousands from the territory of Puerto Rico who could immigrate to the mainland legally in unlimited numbers, settled in the great cities, where low-paying but usually steady work was available. They lived in slums called *barrios,* as segregated, crowded, and crime ridden as the black ghettos.

Spanish-speaking residents of the Southwest, and to a lesser degree those in the big eastern cities, were for a time largely apolitical; they tended to accept their fate with resignation, to mind their own business, to make little trouble. But in the early 1960s a new spirit of resistance arose. Leaders of the new movement called themselves Chicanos. The Chicanos demanded better schools for their children and easier access to higher education. They urged their fellows to take pride in their traditions and culture, to demand their rights, to organize themselves politically. As with the blacks, the dominant middle-class majority adjusted itself to Chicano demands grudgingly and very slowly.

One Chicano nationalist group, Alianza ("the alliance"), led by Reies Lopez Tijerina, tried to secede from New Mexico, an act that brought it into confrontation with the army and ended with Tijerina in prison. Another, the Crusade for Justice, headed by Rodolfo "Corky" Gonzales, a professional boxer, poet, and politician, focused on achieving social reforms and setting up political action groups. Its slogan, *"Venceremos,"* was Spanish for Martin Luther King's pledge: We shall overcome.

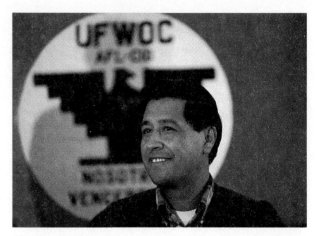

The Mexican-American founder of the National Farm Workers Association and later head of the United Farm Workers Organizing Committee, César Chávez successfully organized migrant workers throughout California in the early 1960s and later a nationwide boycott against California grape producers.

The Chicano leader with the widest influence was César Chávez, who concentrated on what was superficially a more limited goal—organizing migrant farm workers into unions. Chávez grew up in migrant camps in California; he had no schooling beyond the seventh grade. After serving in the navy during World War II, he went to work for the Community Service Organization, a group seeking to raise the political consciousness of the poor and to develop self-help programs for them. Chávez became general director of the CSO but resigned in 1962 because he felt that it was not devoting enough attention to the plight of migrant workers. He then founded the National Farm Workers' Association, later known as the United Farm Workers' Organizing Committee.

In 1965 the grape pickers in his union in Delano, California, struck for higher wages and union recognition. Chávez, seeing in the strike an opportunity to attack the very structure of the migrant labor system, turned it into a nationwide crusade. Avoiding violence, he enlisted the support of church leaders; he organized sit-ins, a march on the state capital, and then a national consumer boycott of grapes. He demonstrated convincingly that migrant workers could be unionized and that the demands of minorities for equal treatment did not necessarily lead to separatism and class or racial antagonism.

Nevertheless, racial controversies continued.

The struggles of black people for equal treatment in the 1950s and 1960s radicalized many Indians. These militants referred to themselves as Native Americans, not Indians. They used the term "Red Power" as the blacks spoke of Black Power and referred to more conservative colleagues as "Uncle Tomahawks." The National Indian Youth Council and later the American Indian Movement (AIM) demanded the return of lands taken illegally from their ancestors. They called for self-determination and a concerted effort to revive tribal cultures, even the use of peyote, a mind-altering controlled substance, in religious ceremonies,* and they organized a pan-Indian movement to advance the cause. Paradoxically, this policy brought them into conflict with traditionalist Indians devoted to local autonomy. (At least 40 Indian languages are still spoken.)

Some AIM leaders sought total separation from the United States; they envisaged setting up states within states such as the Cherokees had established in Georgia in Jacksonian days. In 1973 radicals occupied the town of Wounded Knee, South Dakota (site of one of the most disgraceful massacres of Indians in the 19th century), and held it at gunpoint for weeks. While traditionalists resisted the militants, liberal white opinion proved to be generally sympathetic. In 1975 Congress passed the Indian Self-determination Act, which gave individual tribes much greater control over such matters as education, welfare programs, and law enforcement.

Militant ethnic pride characterized the behavior of other racial minorities and of many white Americans too. Blacks donned dashikis and other African garments and wore their hair in natural "Afro" styles. Italian-Americans, Polish-Americans, and descendants of other "new immigrant" groups eagerly studied their histories in order to preserve their cultures and where necessary revive dying traditions. The American melting pot, some historians now argued, had not amalgamated the immigrant strains as completely as had been thought. Ethnic diversity became for some an end to be desired, despite the possibility that differences might as easily inspire conflict as harmonious adjustment.

For white ethnics, the concern for origins was in part nostalgic and romantic. As the number of,

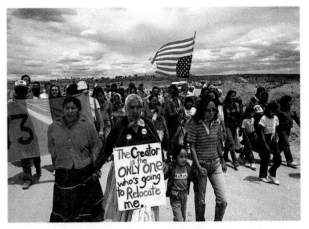

Navajo Indians protesting the federal government's intervention in an intertribal land dispute in Arizona. Disputes between Native Americans and government agencies occurred not only in the Southwest but in Maine and on Cape Cod as well.

say, Greek-Americans who had ever seen Greece declined, the appeal of Greek culture and the sense that some Greek-Americans had of belonging to a distinct cultural group increased. For blacks, whose particular origins were obscured by the catastrophe of slavery, awareness of their distinctiveness was more important. Racial pride was a reflection of the new black militancy and the progress that blacks had made in the postwar period. A black man sat on the Supreme Court (Thurgood Marshall, tactician of the fight for school desegregation). President Johnson had named the first black to a Cabinet post (Robert Weaver, secretary of housing and urban development). The first black since reconstruction (Edward W. Brooke of Massachusetts) was elected to the United States Senate in 1966. A number of large cities, including Atlanta, Georgia, elected black mayors.

The color line was broken in major league baseball in 1947, and soon all professional sports were open to black athletes. Whereas the reign of black heavyweight boxing champion Jack Johnson (1908–1915) had inspired an open search for a "white hope" to depose him, and whereas the next black champion, Joe Louis (1937–1949), was accepted by whites because he "knew his place" and was "well behaved," it was possible for champion Muhammad Ali to be a hero to both white and black boxing fans despite his often bizarre behavior, his militant ad-

---

* The California Supreme Court upheld the right to use peyote in this way in *People* v. *Woody* (1964).

vocacy of racial equality, and his adoption of the Muslim religion.

Their achievements and advances aside, black Americans had found real self-awareness. The attitude of mind that ran from the lonely Denmark Vesey to Frederick Douglass and to W. E. B. Du Bois had become the black consensus.

Rethinking Public Education

Young people were in the forefront in both the fight for the rights of blacks and the women's liberation movement. In a time of uncertainty and discontent, full of conflict and dilemma, youth was affected more strongly than the older generations, and it reacted more forcefully. No institution escaped its criticisms, not even the vaunted educational system, which, youth discovered, poorly suited its needs. This was still another paradox of modern life, for American public education was probably the best (it was certainly the most comprehensive) in the world.

After World War I, under the impact of Freudian psychology, the emphasis in elementary education shifted from using the schools as instruments of social change, as John Dewey had recommended, to using them to promote the emotional development of the students. "Child-centered" educators played down academic achievement in favor of "adjustment." It probably stimulated the students' imaginations and may possibly have improved their psychological well-being, but observers soon noted that the system produced poor work habits and fuzzy thinking and fostered plain ignorance. Although "educationists" insisted that they were not abandoning traditional academic subjects, they surely de-emphasized them. "We've built a sort of halo around reading, writing, and arithmetic," one school principal charged.

The demands of society for rigorous intellectual achievement made this distortion of progressive education increasingly less satisfactory. Following World War II, critics began a concerted assault on the system. The leader of the attack was James B. Conant, former president of Harvard. His book *The American High School Today* (1959) sold nearly half a million copies, and his later studies of teacher education and the special problems of urban schools also attracted wide attention.

Conant flayed the schools for their failure to teach English grammar and composition effectively, for neglecting foreign languages, and for ignoring the needs of both the brightest and the slowest of their students. He insisted that teachers' colleges should place subject matter above educational methodology in their curricula.

The success of the Soviet Union in launching the first artificial satellite, *Sputnik,* in 1957 increased the influence of critics like Conant because it dealt a healthy blow to American overconfidence. To match the Russian achievement, the United States needed thousands of engineers and scientists, and the schools were not turning out enough graduates prepared to study science and engineering at the college level. Suddenly the schools were under enormous pressure, for with more and more young people desiring to go to college, the colleges were raising their admission standards. The traditionalists thus gained the initiative, and academic subjects enjoyed revived prestige. The National Defense Education Act of 1958 supplied a powerful stimulus by allocating funds for upgrading work in the sciences, foreign languages, and other subjects and for expanding guidance services and experimenting with television and other new teaching devices.

Concern for improving the training of the children of disadvantaged minority groups (Mexican-Americans, Puerto Ricans, Indians, blacks) pulled the system in a different direction. Many of these children lived in horrible slums, often in broken homes. They lacked the incentives and training that middle-class children received in the family. Many did poorly in school, in part because they were poorly motivated, in part because the system was poorly adapted to their needs. But catering to the needs of such children threatened to undermine the standards being set for other children. In the cities, where blacks and other minorities were becoming steadily more numerous, many schools failed to serve adequately either the disadvantaged or those fairly well off. Added to the strains imposed by racial conflicts, the effect was to create the most serious crisis American public education had ever faced.

The post-*Sputnik* stress on academic achievement profoundly affected higher education too. Prestige institutions such as Harvard, Yale, Columbia, Stanford, and a dozen other colleges and universities, able to pick and choose among floods of

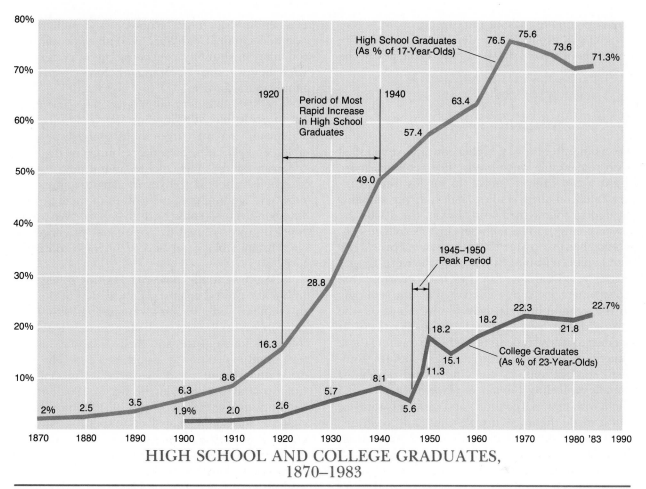

HIGH SCHOOL AND COLLEGE GRADUATES,
1870–1983

Lyndon Johnson's Elementary and Secondary Education Act, passed in 1965, was a landmark in the century-long expansion of high school education and directly influenced college education in the United States. The most rapid increase in high school graduates occurred between 1920 and 1940, but the number of graduates as a percentage of all people age 17 was greatest in 1967. The peak period for college graduates, 1945 to 1950, reflects the GI Bill after World War II.

applicants, became training centers for the intellectual elite. The federal and state governments, together with private philanthropic institutions such as the Carnegie Corporation and the Ford Foundation, poured millions of dollars into dormitory and classroom construction, teacher education, and scholarship funds. At the graduate level, the federal government's research and development program, administered by the National Science Foundation, provided billions of dollars for laboratories, equipment, professors' salaries, and student scholarships.

At the same time, population growth and the demands of society for specialized intellectual skills caused American colleges to burst at the seams. Enrollment had risen rapidly after the war, mostly because of the G.I. Bill; by 1950 there were 2.6 million students in American colleges and universities. Yet 20 years later the total had risen to 8.6 million, a decade after that to about 12 million. To bridge the gap between high school and college, two-year junior colleges proliferated. Almost unknown before 1920, there were 1,300-odd junior colleges in the 1980s.

Students in Revolt

For a time after the war, higher education expanded with remarkable smoothness. The veterans, more mature and eager to make up for lost time, concentrated on their studies, and younger students tended to follow their lead. But in the 1960s the mood changed. The members of this college generation had grown up during the postwar prosperity and had been trained by teachers who were, by and large, New Deal liberals. They had been told that government was supposed to regulate the economy in the general interest, help the weak against the strong, and protect the liberties of all its citizens. It seemed to many students not to be performing these functions. Modern industrial society with its "soulless" corporations, its computers, and its almost equally unfeeling human bureaucracies provided them with material comforts and social advantages, but it made them feel insignificant and powerless. Their advantages also made them feel guilty when they thought about the millions of Americans who did not have them. The existence of poverty in a country as rich as the United States seemed intolerable, race prejudice both stupid and evil. Yet the government seemed incapable of attacking these disgraceful conditions head on. Still worse in their eyes, the response of their elders to McCarthyism appeared contemptible—craven cowardice of the worst sort—and dangerous. In the age of the atom, rabid anticommunism might end in nuclear war.

All these influences were encapsulated in a manifesto put forth by a small group of students at a meeting of Students for a Democratic Society (SDS) held at Port Huron, Michigan, in 1962. "We are the people of this generation . . . looking uncomfortably to the world we inherit," their Port Huron Statement began. Their main concerns were racial bigotry, the atomic bomb, and the "disturbing paradoxes" associated with these concerns. How to reconcile the contradictions between the idea that "all men are created equal" with "the facts of Negro life in the South and the big cities of the North" and between the declared peaceful intentions of the government and its huge "economic and military investments in the Cold War." Too many people and too many institutions, concentrating on preserving what they own and can command, "have closed their minds to the future."

The SDS statement outlined a somewhat vague list of goals, including ending the "political party stalemate," making corporations "publicly responsible," and allocating national resources on the basis of "social needs." The chief technique advanced to accomplish these objectives was "participatory democracy," getting people involved in small groups where individuals could have an impact. "We would replace power rooted in possession, privilege, or circumstance by power and uniqueness rooted in love."

SDS grew rapidly, powered by rising college enrollments, protest against the escalation of the war in Vietnam, and a seemingly unending list of local campus issues. Radical students generally had little tolerance for injustice, and their dissatisfaction often found expression in public protests. The first great student outburst convulsed the University of California at Berkeley in the fall of 1964. Angry students, many veterans of the 1964 fight for black rights in the South, staged sit-down strikes in university buildings to protest the prohibition of political canvassing on the campus. What came to be known as the Free Speech movement disrupted the institution over a period of weeks. Hundreds were arrested, the state legislature threatened reprisals, the faculty became involved in the controversy, and the crisis led to the resignation of the president of the University of California, Clark Kerr.

On campus after campus in the late 1960s SDS organized sit-ins and employed other disruptive tactics. Frequently professors and administrators played into the radicals' hands, being so offended by their methods and manners that they refused to recognize the legitimacy of some of their demands.

At Columbia in 1968, SDS and black students occupied university buildings and refused to leave unless a series of "nonnegotiable" demands (concerning such matters as the university's involvement in secret military research and its relations with minority groups living in the Columbia neighborhood) were met. When, after long delays, President Grayson Kirk called in the police to clear the buildings, a riot broke out in which dozens of students, some of them innocent bystanders, were clubbed and

Student sit-ins kept professors and staff from gaining access to their offices on many campuses. A typical incident was photographed at a "liberated building" on the Columbia University campus in April 1968.

beaten. General student revulsion at the use of the police led to Kirk's resignation and the enactment of many university reforms.

Equally significant in altering the student mood was the frustration that so many of them felt with traditional aspects of college life. Regulations that students had formerly merely grumbled about evoked determined, even violent opposition. Dissidents denounced rules that restricted their personal lives, such as prohibitions on the use of alcohol and the banning of members of the opposite sex from dormitories. They complained that required courses inhibited their intellectual development. They demanded a share in the government of their

institutions, long the private preserve of administrators and professors.

Beyond their specific complaints, the radicals refused to put up with anything they considered wrong. The knotty social problems that made their elders gravitate toward moderation led these students to become intransigent absolutists. The line between right and wrong became as sharply defined as the edge of a ruler. Racial prejudice was evil: It must be eradicated. War in a nuclear age was insane: Armies must be disbanded. Poverty amid plenty was an abomination: End poverty now. To the counsel that evil can be eliminated only gradually, that misguided persons must be persuaded to mend their ways, that compromise was the path to true progress, they responded with scorn. Extremists among them, observing the flaws in American civilization, adopted a nihilistic position—the only way to deal with a "rotten" society was to destroy it; reform was impossible, constructive compromise corrupting.

Critics found the radical students infantile, old-fashioned, and authoritarian—infantile because they refused to tolerate frustration or delay, old-fashioned because their absolutist ideas had been exploded by several generations of philosophers and scientists, and authoritarian because they rejected majority rule. As time passed, SDS was plagued by factional disputes. Radical women in the movement, for example, claimed that it was run by male chauvinists; women who sought some say in policy matters, one of them has written, were met with "indifference, ridicule, and anger."

By the end of the 1960s SDS had lost much of its influence with the general student body. Nevertheless, it had succeeded in focusing attention on genuine social and political weaknesses both on the campuses and in the larger world.

Black students influenced the academic world in a variety of ways. Almost without exception, the colleges tried to increase black enrollments by their use of scholarship funds and by lowering academic entrance requirements when necessary to compensate for the poor preparation many black students had received in the schools. This did not mean that the black students were satisfied with college life. Most were not. They tended to keep to themselves and usually had little to do with the somewhat elitist SDS. But they demanded more control over all aspects of their education than white's typically did. They wanted black studies programs taught and administered by blacks. Achievement of these goals was difficult because of the shortage of black teachers and because professors—including most black professors—considered student control of appointments and curricula unwise and in violation of the principles of academic freedom. Nevertheless, the general academic response to black demands was accommodating; if "confrontations" occurred, they were usually resolved by negotiation. Unlike white radical students, blacks tended to confine their demands to matters directly related to local conditions. Although generalization is difficult, probably the majority of academics drew a distinction between black radicals, whose actions they found understandable even when they could not in conscience

approve of them, and white radicals, most of whom they thought self-indulgent or emotionally disturbed.

The Counterculture

Some young people, known generally as hippies, were so unattracted by the modern world that they retreated from it, finding refuge in communes, drugs, and mystical religions, often wandering aimlessly from place to place. During the 1960s and 1970s groups of them could be found in every big city in the United States and Europe. Some hippies, like the poet Allen Ginsberg, one of their "elder statesmen," and the novelist Ken Kesey, were genuinely creative people. Ginsberg's dark, desperate masterpiece, *Howl*, written in 1955, is perhaps the most widely read poem of the postwar era, certainly a work of major literary significance. *Howl* begins: "I saw the best minds of my generation destroyed by madness, starving hysterical naked," and goes on to describe the wanderings and searchings of these "angelheaded hipsters," a "lost battalion of platonic conversationalists . . . seeking jazz or sex or soup" in Houston, "whoring in Colorado," and "investigating the F.B.I. in beards and shorts" in California, all the while denouncing "the narcotic tobacco haze of Capitalism." *Howl* ends with Ginsberg's indignant, almost frantic assault on that "sphinx of cement and aluminum" the fire god Moloch, the devourer of children.

Others, however, such as the Youth International Party members ("Yippies") Abbie Hoffman and Jerry Rubin, are best described as professional iconoclasts. (In 1968 the group went through the motions of nominating a pig named Pigassus for president.) And most hippies were simply unwilling to confront the two dilemmas of contemporary existence described above (see p. 889).

The hippies developed a "counterculture" so directly opposite to the way of life of their parents' generation as to suggest to critics that they were still dominated by the culture they rejected. They wore old blue jeans and (it seemed) any nondescript garments they happened to find at hand. Male hippies wore their hair long and grew beards. Females avoided makeup, bras, and other devices more conventional women used to make themselves attractive to men. Both sexes rejected the old Protestant ethic; being part of the hippie world meant not caring about money, material goods, or power over other people. Love was more important than money or influence, feelings more significant than thought, natural things superior to anything manufactured.

Most hippies resembled the radicals in their political and social opinions. They were disgusted by the dishonesty and sordid antics of many politicians, horrified by the brutality of Vietnam, appalled by racism, contemptuous of the smugness they encountered in the colleges and universities. They believed in conservation, freedom of expression, tolerance, and peace.

But they rejected activism, being almost totally apolitical. Theirs was a world of folk songs and blaring acid rock music, of "be ins," casual sex, and drugs. Their slogan, "Make love, not war," was a general pacifist pronouncement, not a specific crit-

Woodstock, New York, August 1969, where half a million people gathered in open and mostly muddy fields for three days of "Peace and Music." Both, despite bad weather and no facilities, prevailed for the most part.

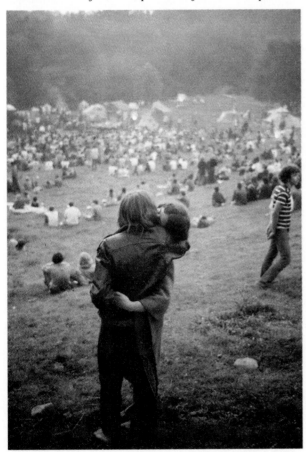

icism of events in Vietnam, although Vietnam surely had a great deal to do with their underlying pessimism. Indeed, passivity was with them a philosophy, almost a principle. At rock concerts they listened where earlier generations had danced. Hallucinogenic drugs heightened users' "experiences" while they were in fact in a stupor; witness the LSD user's proviso "Tune in, turn on, drop out." Another hippie motto, "Do your own thing," can only work in social situations if no one does anything. Hippie communes were a far cry from the busy centers of social experimentation of the pre–Civil War Age of Reform.

Charles Reich, a professor at Yale, praised the hippie view of the world in *The Greening of America* (1970), dignifying it with the title, "Consciousness III." Reich's Consciousness I was the do-it-yourself, laissez faire approach to life—having "more faith in winning than in love," while Consciousness II was the psychology of "liberal intellectuals" and "members of the Communist Party, U.S.A." and the Kennedys—marked by faith in institutional solutions to problems. Reich taught a course called "Individualism in America." One semester he had over 500 students, not one of whom failed. According to the *Yale Course Guide,* published by students, Professor Reich "thinks kids are neat and what can be bad about someone telling you how the system and the older generation have warped and destroyed things for us?"

The Sexual Revolution

Young people made the most striking contribution to the revolution that took place in the late 1960s in public attitudes toward sexual relationships. Here change came with startling swiftness. Almost overnight, it seemed in retrospect, conventional ideas about premarital sex, contraception and abortion, homosexuality, pornography, and a host of related matters were openly challenged. Probably the behavior of the majority of Americans did not alter radically. But the majority's beliefs and practices were no longer automatically acknowledged as the only valid ones. It became possible for individuals to espouse different values and to behave differently with at least relative impunity. Actions that in one decade would have led to social ostracism or even to imprisonment were in the next decade accepted almost as a matter of course.

Surely among the most startling changes to occur in the 1970s and 1980s has been the willingness of homosexuals to make public their sexual preferences in the course of demanding for themselves full legal standing.

The causes of this revolution were complex and interrelated; one change led to others. More efficient methods of birth control and antibiotics that cured venereal disease removed the two principal practical arguments against sex outside marriage; with these barriers down, many people found their moral attitudes changing. Almost concurrently, Alfred C. Kinsey's *Sexual Behavior in the Human Male* (1948), which was based on thousands of confidential interviews with persons from nearly every walk of life, revealed that where sex was concerned, large numbers of Americans did not practice what they preached. Premarital sex, marital infidelity, homosexuality, and various forms of perversion were, Kinsey's figures showed, far more common than most persons had suspected.

Sexual Behavior in the Human Male shocked many people, and Kinsey's research methods were criticized by some experts. When he published *Sexual Behavior in the Human Female* in 1958, a book that demonstrated that the sexual practices of women were as varied as those of men, he was subjected to a storm of abuse and deprived of the foundation support that had financed his research.

Nevertheless, Kinsey has aptly been called "the Marx of the sexual revolution." Once it became possible to look at sex in primarily physical terms and to accept the idea that one's own urges might not be as uncommon as one had been led to believe, it became much more difficult to object to any sexual activity practiced in private by consenting adults.

Homosexuals, for example, began openly to admit their feelings and to demand that the heterosexual society cease harassing and discriminating against them.

That the sexual revolution in its many aspects served useful functions was beyond dispute. Reducing irrational fears and inhibitions was liberating for many persons of both sexes, and it tended to help young people form permanent associations on the basis of deeper feelings than their sexual drives. Women surely profited from the new freedom, just as a greater sharing of family duties by husbands and fathers opened men's lives to many new satisfactions.

But like other changes, the revolution produced new problems, and some of its results were at best ambiguous. For young people, sexual freedom could be very unsettling; sometimes it generated social pressures that propelled them into relationships they were not yet prepared to handle, with grave psychological results. Equally perplexing was the rise in the number of illegitimate births. Easy cures did not eliminate venereal disease; on the contrary, the relaxation of sexual taboos produced what public health officials called a veritable epidemic of gonorrhea, a frightening increase in the incidence of syphilis, and the emergence of a deadly new disease, acquired immune deficiency syndrome (AIDS).

Exercising the right to advocate and practice previously forbidden activities involved subjecting people who found those activities offensive—still a large proportion of the population—to embarrassment and even acute emotional distress. Some people believed pornography to be ethically wrong, and most feminists considered it degrading to women. Abortion raised difficult legal and moral questions. Such questions exacerbated already serious social conflicts.

Women's Liberation

Sexual freedom also contributed to the revival of the women's rights movement. For one thing, freedom involved a more drastic revolution for women than for men. Effective methods of contraception obviously affected women more directly than men, and the new attitudes heightened women's awareness of the way the old sexual standards and patterns of family living had restricted their entire existence. In fact the two movements interacted in innumerable ways, some clear, others obscure. Concern for better job opportunities and for equal pay for equal work, for example, fed the demand for day-care centers for children.

Still another cause of the new drive for women's rights was concern for improving the treatment of minorities. Participation in and the mere observation of the civil rights movement encouraged American women, as it frequently had in earlier times, to speak out more forcefully for their own rights. Just as white people had callously demeaned and dominated black people until forced to desist by the victims of their prejudice, so, feminists argued, they were being demeaned and dominated by a male-oriented society and must fight back.

During the immediate postwar period, the women's movement had been relatively quiescent. However, pressures were mounting because social and economic conditions were changing. When the war ended, women who had taken jobs because of the labor shortage were expected and in many cases compelled to surrender them to veterans and return to their traditional roles as housewives and mothers. Some did, as the sharp increase in marriage and birth rates in the late 1940s and early 1950s indicates. In 1940 about 15 percent of American women in their early thirties were unmarried, in 1965 only 5 percent. Many, however, did not meekly return to the home, and many of those who did contin-

Betty Friedan, author of The Feminine Mystique, *spearheaded women's rights demonstrations like the National Women's Strike in August 1970. The strike called on women to boycott four consumer products whose advertising the protesters considered insulting to women.*

ued to hold down jobs in order to help pay for their veteran-husbands' war-interrupted educations. Other women went to work to counterbalance the onslaughts of inflation, still others (some married, some not) simply because they enjoyed the money and the independence that jobs made possible. Between 1940 and 1960 the proportion of women workers doubled, and thereafter it increased still more rapidly. The rise was particularly swift among married women, and the difficulties faced by anyone trying to work while having to perform household duties increased the resentment of these workers.

Married or single, more numerous or not, women workers still faced job discrimination of many kinds. In nearly every occupation they were paid less than men who did the same work. Many interesting jobs that they were capable of holding were either closed to them entirely or doled out on the basis of some illogical and often unwritten quota system. In challenging occupations where they could find employment, they were rarely given a chance to rise to positions of leadership. Many women objected to this state of affairs even in the 1950s; in the 1960s their protest erupted into an organized and vociferous demand for change.

One of the leaders of the new women's movement was Betty Friedan. In *The Feminine Mystique* (1963), Friedan argued that advertisers, popular magazines, and other opinion-shaping forces were undermining the capacity of women to use their intelligence and their talents creatively by a pervasive and not very subtle form of brainwashing designed to convince them of the virtues of domesticity. This Friedan deplored. She argued that without understanding why, thousands of women living supposedly happy lives were experiencing vague but persistent feelings of anger and discomfort. "The only way for a woman . . . to know herself as a person is by creative work of her own," she wrote. A "problem that had no name" was stifling women's potential.

The Feminine Mystique was what later came to be known as "consciousness raising" for thousands of women. Over a million copies were quickly sold. Back in 1922 a committee of physicians and social scientists had queried 1,000 middle-class women about their personal lives. To the question "Is your married life a happy one?" only 116 had answered no. But after her book came out, Friedan was deluged by hundreds of letters from women who had thought their feelings of unease and depression despite their "happy" family life to be both unique to themselves and unreasonable. Many now determined to expand their horizons by taking jobs or resuming their education.

Friedan had assumed that if able women acted with determination, employers would recognize their abilities and stop discriminating against them. This did not happen. In 1966 she and other feminists founded the National Organization for Women. Copying the tactics of black activists, NOW called for equal employment opportunities and equal pay as civil rights. "The time has come for a new movement toward true equality for all women in America and toward a fully equal partnership of the sexes," the leaders announced. "The silken cur-

tain of prejudice and discrimination against women" in government, industry, the professions, religion, education, "and every other field of importance" must be drawn back. In 1967 NOW came out for an equal rights amendment to the Constitution, for changes in the divorce laws, and for the legalization of abortion, the right of "control of one's body."

By 1967, however, many younger feminists were arguing that NOW was not radical enough. They deplored its hierarchical structure, its lobbying activities, its stress on attracting celebrities, its imitation of conventional pressure-group tactics. Equality of the two sexes smacked of "separate but equal" to these women, and indeed, many of them had been first radicalized by the struggle against racial segregation.

Typical was Kate Millett, whose *Sexual Politics* (1970) became a best-seller. Millett called for a "sexual revolution" to do away with "traditional inhibitions and taboos." She denounced male supremacy, which she described as "the institution of patriarchy," and drew a distinction between the immutable biological differences between men and women, and gender, how men and women relate to one another socially and culturally, which are learned ways of behaving and thus capable of change. For example, Millett said that people must stop thinking of words like *violent* and *efficiency* as male characteristics and *passive* and *tenderness* as female.

The radicals gathered in small consciousness-raising groups to discuss questions as varied as the need for government child-care centers, how best to denounce the annual Miss America contests, and lesbianism. They held conferences and seminars and published magazines, the most widely known being *Ms.*, edited by Gloria Steinem. Academics among them organized women's studies programs at dozens of colleges. One course on women's health led to a handbook, *Our Bodies, Ourselves* (1973), which went through many editions.

Some radical feminists advocated raising children in communal centers and doing away with marriage as a legal institution. "The family unit is a decadent, energy-absorbing, destructive, wasteful institution," one prominent feminist declared. Others described marriage as "legalized rape." Some rejected heterosexuality as a matter of principle.

The militants attacked all aspects of the standard

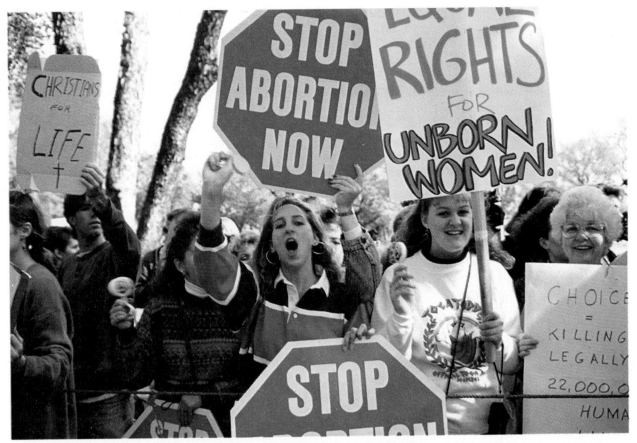

An anti-abortion or, as its adherents preferred, a "Right to Life" rally opposing the 1973 Supreme Court ruling upholding the right of a woman to terminate a pregnancy. Defenders of abortion, or of "Freedom of Choice," have been no less willing to take to the barricades when they sense a possible change in federal policy on this highly charged issue.

image of the female sex. Avoiding the error of the Progressive Era reformers who had fought for the vote by stressing differences between the sexes (the supposed purity and high moral character of women), they insisted on total equality. Clichés such as "the fair sex" and "the weaker sex" made them see red. They insisted that the separation of "Help Wanted—Male" and "Help Wanted—Female" classified ads in newspapers violated the Civil Rights Act of 1964, and they demanded that men bear as much of the burden of caring for their children, cooking, and housework as women traditionally did. They took courses in self-defense in order to be able to protect themselves from muggers, rapists, and casual mashers. They denounced the use of masculine words like *chairman* (favoring *chairperson*) and

of such terms as *mankind* and *men* to designate people in general.* They substituted *Ms.* for both *Miss* and *Mrs.* on the grounds that the language drew no such distinction between unmarried and married men.

The most radical of the feminists went beyond denouncing "male supremacy." As Todd Gitlin puts it in *The Sixties: Years of Hope, Days of Rage,* they attacked "not just capitalism, but men." In *The Dialect of Sex* (1970), Shulamith Firestone suggested

---

* The difficulty here was that this form of discrimination was built into the structure of the language. Even the word *woman* derives from the Anglo-Saxon *wif-mann,* "wife of a man." Efforts to avoid the use of masculine words in general references led to such awkward expressions as *his/her* and *(s)he.*

that childbearing (not merely child rearing) should be the responsibility of society, not of individuals, arguing that new technology made this possible.

At the other extreme, many women rejected the position even of moderate feminists like Betty Friedan. Conservatives rallied behind Phillis Schlafly to campaign against the equal rights amendment. After the Supreme Court declared in *Roe* v. *Wade* (1973) that women had a constitutional right to have an abortion during the early stages of pregnancy, a vigorous right-to-life movement dedicated to over-

turning the decision sprang up. But few people escaped being affected by the women's movement. The presence of women in new roles—as television commentators, airline pilots, police officers—did not prove that a large-scale shift in employment patterns had taken place. Yet even the most unregenerate male seemed to recognize that the balance of power and influence between the sexes had been altered. Clearly, the sexual revolution was not about to end, the direction of change in relationships not to be turned back.

Milestones

1948	Alfred C. Kinsey, *Sexual Behavior in the Human Male*		accused of crimes (*Gideon* v. *Wainright*)
1950	David Riesman, *The Lonely Crowd*	**1964**	Free Speech movement at University of California
1954	Launching of U.S.S. *Nautilus*, first atomic-powered ship	**1965**	Malcolm X murdered
1955	Allen Ginsberg, "Howl" AFL and CIO merge		César Chávez organizes boycott to support grape pickers
1956	William Whyte, *The Organization Man*	**1965–1967**	Riots in ghettos
		1966	National Organization for Women (NOW) founded
1957	Russians launch first *Sputnik* Supreme Court reinstates "clear and present danger" standard in First Amendment cases (*Yates* v. *United States*)	**1968**	Student strike at Columbia University broken by police Martin Luther King, Jr., assassinated
1958	National Defense Education Act	**1969**	American astronauts land on the moon
1962	Students for a Democratic Society's Port Huron Statement	**1970**	Kate Millett, *Sexual Politics*
		1973	Supreme Court guarantees right to abortion in early stages of pregnancy (*Roe* v. *Wade*)
1963	Betty Friedan, *The Feminine Mystique* Supreme Court guarantees free legal counsel for indigents	**1975**	Indian Self-determination Act

SUPPLEMENTARY READING

Titles marked with an asterisk have been published in paperback.

J. F. Heath, **Decade of Disillusionment: The Kennedy-Johnson Years** (1980), and A. J. Matusow, **The Unraveling of America*** (1984), contain material related to this chapter, as do W. M. O'Neill, **Coming Apart: An Informal History of the 1960s*** (1971), and Godfrey Hodgson,

America in Our Time (1976). Todd Gitlin, **The Sixties: Years of Hope, Days of Rage** (1987) is an "insider's" account.

Population trends are described in C. Taeuber and I. B. Taeuber, **The Changing Population of the United**

States (1958), the movement to the suburbs in K. T. Jackson, **Crabgrass Frontier*** (1985). On television, see David Marc, **Demographic Vistas: Television in American Culture** (1984), Barbara Matusow, **The Evening Stars** (1988), and G. A. Steiner, **The People Look at Television** (1963). Daniel Hoffman (ed.), **Harvard Guide to Contemporary American Writing** (1979), contains convenient discussions of postwar literature. Morris Dickstein, **Gates of Eden: American Culture in the Sixties** (1977), is part history, part literary criticism, part memoir. Modern art is discussed in Barbara Rose, **American Art Since 1900*** (1967).

For the causes and character of the poverty and urban problems that led Johnson to devise his Great Society program, see Michael Harrington, **The Other America*** (1962), and Oscar Lewis, **La Vida: A Puerto Rican Family in the Culture of Poverty*** (1966).

On the black radicals, see Malcolm X, **Autobiography*** (1966), Stokely Carmichael and C. V. Hamilton, **Black Power*** (1967), and Eldridge Cleaver, **Soul on Ice*** (1967). Other important books on race relations include Taylor Branch, **Parting the Waters** (1988), on the career of Martin Luther King Jr.; Clayborne Carson, **In Struggle: SNCC and the Black Awakening of the 1960s** (1981); and August Meier and Elliott Rudwick, **CORE: A Study in the Civil Rights Movement*** (1973). M. S. Meier and Feliciano Rivera, **The Chicanos*** (1972), provides a sympathetic discussion of the problems and aspirations of Mexican-Americans, but see also Joan London and Henry Anderson, **So Shall Ye Reap: The Story of César Chávez and the Farm Workers Movement** (1970), A. F. Corwin, **Immigrants—and Immigrants** (1978), and J. R. Garcia, **Operation Wetback** (1980). The revived interest in ethnicity is discussed in Michael Novak, **The Rise of the Unmeltable Ethnics** (1972), and Thomas Sowell, **Ethnic America** (1981).

Educational trends are discussed in Martin Mayer, **The Schools*** (1961), J. B. Conant, **The American High School Today*** (1959), and Robert Coles, **Children of Crisis*** (1967). On militancy among college students, see Kenneth Kenniston, **Young Radicals** (1968), S. M. Lipset and P. G. Altbach (eds.), **Students in Revolt** (1969), Roger Kahn, **The Battle of Morningside Heights** (1970), and Kirkpatrick Sale, **SDS** (1973). James Miller reprints the SDS Port Huron Statement in **"Democracy in the Streets"** (1987). See also Irwin Unger, **The Movement: A History of the American New Left** (1974), and Theodore Roszak, **The Making of a Counter-Culture** (1969).

The literature on the women's movement is voluminous and difficult to evaluate. In addition to W. H. Chafe, **The American Woman*** (1972) and **Women and Equality*** (1977), see Betty Friedan, **The Feminine Mystique*** (1963), Jo Freeman, **The Politics of Women's Liberation** (1975), S. M. Rothman, **Woman's Proper Place** (1978), and Sara Evans and H. C. Boyte, **Free Spaces** (1986).

For postwar religious trends, see Robert Wuthnow, **The Restructuring of American Religion** (1988), Arthur Hertzberg, **The Jews in America** (1989), and Will Herberg, **Catholic, Protestant, Jew** (1955).

America's Changing Environment

Travelers in the American West were overawed by the majestic beauty of places like Yosemite, in California. The above scene was painted by German-born artist Albert Bierstadt in 1865 shortly after Yosemite became a state park.

By the late 1800s, conservation had become a political issue. President Theodore Roosevelt and the naturalist John Muir, shown left riding through a redwood forest in California in 1903, represented two approaches to the question. Roosevelt favored controlled exploitation of the land in ways that would replenish natural resources. "The preservation of our forests," he declared, "is an imperative business necessity." Muir's contrary insistence on conservation as an end in itself finally led to a falling out between the two men. Above, a modern protester objects to the commercialization of Yellowstone National Park.

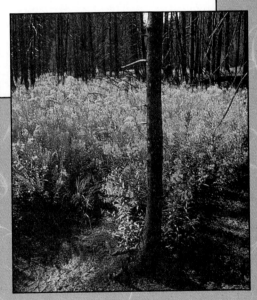

In the summer of 1988, a mammoth forest fire raged through more than half of Yellowstone National Park's 2.2 million acres (*left*). Ironically, the fire was the indirect result of a new environmental consciousness. For decades rangers sought to snuff out fires, whether caused by careless campers or by lightning, as quickly as possible. In the 1970s, officials decided to let naturally occurring fires burn. But the long accumulation of brush and decaying wood made the forest a tinderbox and the 1988 conflagration resulted. Nevertheless, the forest quickly began to recover. With spring, wildflowers daubed the charred landscape with pink and yellow, soon to be followed by shrubs and seedlings (*below*).

The untamed beauty of the "new" continent enchanted European settlers. "The country," William Penn stated with Quaker understatement in 1683, "in its soil, air, water, seasons, and produce . . . is not to be despised." But the seemingly limitless resources of America encouraged wasteful exploitation. Farmers were notoriously prodigal, manufacturers and miners even more so.

In the Progressive Era, however, the federal government and the states began to protect the environment, mainly by putting forests and other lands in parks and reserves. But only in the 1960s did a strong environmental protection movement appear. Rachel Carson's *Silent Spring* (1962) explained how pesticides such as DDT endangered wildlife. After the massive Earth Day rallies of 1970, environmentalists focused on the threats to health posed by food additives, carcinogenic pollutants, and toxic wastes.

Pollution accompanied settlement everywhere in the West. In his prototypical Western novel, The Virginian (1903), Owen Wister describes this scene in Wyoming: "We passed the ramparts of Medicine Bow—thick heaps and fringes of tin cans, and shelving mounds of bottles cast out of the saloons." The photograph above shows Pike's Peak, Colorado, in the 1890s. By the 1960s, places like the automobile graveyard at right marred the beauty of the landscape.

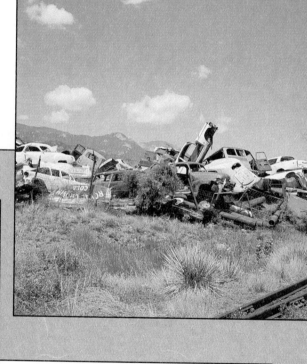

Today, disposal of solid waste is a pressing problem in many communities. New York City's only working landfill, which receives 25,000 tons of garbage per day and will soon be the highest point on the East Coast south of Maine, is not unique. The one at left, in Portland, Oregon is also running out of room.

Concern about dependence on foreign energy resulted in the exploitation of the oil resources of Alaska despite fears of the impact of development on the fragile Arctic environment. In March 1989, the worst fears of the environmentalists were realized when an Exxon tanker ran aground near the oil port of Valdez (shown at center in 1940), spilling 11 million gallons of crude oil into Prince William Sound. The spill, the biggest in American history, killed thousands of birds and sea animals. At left, workers assist in the much-criticized clean-up effort; top right, a rescued sea otter recuperates.

New technologies are helping to make waste products and other alternative sources of energy cost effective. Above a crane feeds garbage into the furnace of a steam turbine in Bridgeport, Connecticut. The turbine, which burns 2500 tons of waste daily, supplies electricity to towns in Fairfield County. At right, solar panels power a public telephone in Mystic, Connecticut.

In northern California, 300 wind turbines have turned a former cattle ranch into a hillside "wind farm." The electricity produced by the windmills is sold to Pacific Gas and Electric, saving approximately 60,000 barrels of oil per year.

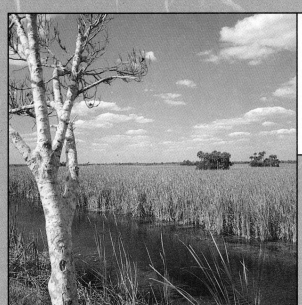

Florida's Everglades was once among the richest natural habitats in the United States (above). Wetland habitats are critical to many species but rapid development in south Florida has diverted water from the region, causing the sawgrass and Mangrove swamp to shrink dramatically. At left, a view of the Everglades from the Tamiami Trail.

Many current environmental issues—global warming, acid rain, and ozone depletion—demand transnational solutions. Pollutants from factories in the Middle West have caused acid rain along the East Coast of both the United States and Canada. Over time acid rain can kill marine life and even trees. The photograph at right shows acid rain damage on Mt. Mitchell in North Carolina.

Our Times

Shucks, I don't think [Jerry Ford] can chew gum and walk at the same time. . . . He's a nice fellow, but he spent too much time playing football without a helmet.

LYNDON B. JOHNSON

Call me Jimmy.

PRESIDENT JAMES EARL CARTER, *1977*

[Reagan] has contributed a spirit of good will and grace to the Presidency and American life generally.

SENATOR EDWARD M. KENNEDY, *1986*

America is never wholly herself unless she is engaged in high moral principle. We as a people have such a purpose today. It is to make kinder the face of the nation and gentler the face of the world.

PRESIDENT GEORGE BUSH, *1989*

T he country greeted the accession of Gerald Ford to the presidency with a collective sigh of relief. Most observers considered Ford unimaginative, certainly not brilliant. But he was hardworking and—most important under the circumstances—his record was untouched by scandal. Although he was an almost automaton-like Republican partisan, nearly all the Democrats in Congress liked him. He was Nixon's opposite as a person, gregarious and open, and he stated repeatedly that he took a dim view of Nixon's high-handed way of dealing with Congress. He insisted that the president and Congress must work together in the nation's interest. Being a most ordinary person, earnest but limited, Ford appeared unlikely to venture beyond conventional limits or to act rashly. This was what nearly everyone wanted of the president in the wake of Nixon.

Ford as President

Ford, who unlike any earlier vice-president had been appointed rather than elected to that post, obviously desired to live up to public expectations. Yet he was soon embroiled in controversy and subject to considerable criticism, not all of it partisan. At the outset he roused widespread resentment by pardoning Nixon for whatever crimes he had committed in office, even any, if such existed, that had not yet come to light. Not many Americans wanted to see the ex-president lodged in jail, but pardoning him seemed both illogical and incomprehensible when he had admitted no guilt and had not yet been officially charged with any crime. (Nixon's instant acceptance of the pardon while claiming to have done no wrong was also illogical, but not incomprehensible.)

Ugly rumors of a "corrupt bargain" arranged before Nixon resigned, similar to that supposedly made by John Quincy Adams and Henry Clay in the 1820s, were soon circulating, for the pardon seemed grossly unfair. Why should Nixon go scot-free when his chief underlings, Mitchell, Haldeman, and Erlichman, were being brought to trial for their part in the Watergate scandal? (All three were eventually convicted and jailed.)

Ford displayed inconsistency and apparent incompetence in managing the economy. He announced that inflation was the major problem and asked patriotic citizens to signify their willingness to fight it by wearing WIN buttons (Whip Inflation Now). Almost immediately the economy entered a precipitous slump. Production fell and the unemployment rate rose above 9 percent. The president was forced to ask for tax cuts and other measures aimed at stimulating business activity. While pressing for these measures, he continued to fulminate against spending money on social programs designed to help the urban poor. The economic problems were difficult and Ford was handicapped by the fact that the Democrats had solid control of Congress, but his performance was at best inept.

That Ford would never act rashly proved to be an incorrect assumption. In the spring of 1975 North Vietnamese forces increased their attacks in South Vietnam. Dispirited, short of guns and ammunition, and incompetently led, the South Vietnamese armies fell back, then fled headlong, then dissolved. As the communists advanced, tens of

"My fellow Americans, our long national nightmare is over," Gerald Ford announced as he succeeded Richard Nixon in August 1974. Ford's candor and humility reassured a public wearied by the "dirty tricks" and "executive privilege" of the Watergate years.

thousands of South Vietnamese asked for asylum in the United States, and about 140,000 were successfully evacuated. Thousands more were callously abandoned, although their earlier collaboration with the Americans made their situation in a communist-controlled Vietnam precarious. Ford had always taken a hawkish position on the Vietnam War. As the military situation deteriorated, he urged Congress to pour more arms into the South to stem the North Vietnamese advance. The legislators flatly refused to do so, and late in April Saigon fell. The long Vietnam War was finally over.

Two weeks earlier local communists of a particularly radical persuasion had overturned the pro-American regime in Cambodia. On May 12 Cambodian naval forces seized the American merchant ship *Mayaguez* in the Gulf of Siam. President Ford, apparently frustrated by his inability to prevent the communists from taking over South Vietnam and Cambodia, reacted to the seizure without fully investigating the situation or allowing the new regime time to respond to his perfectly proper demand that the *Mayaguez* and its crew be freed. He ordered marine units to attack Tang Island, where the captured vessel had been taken. The assault succeeded in that the Cambodians released the *Mayaguez* and its crew of 39, but 38 marines died in the operation. Since the Cambodians had released the ship before the marines struck, Ford's reflexive response was probably unnecessary, although it was popular with a majority of Americans.

After some hesitation Ford decided to seek the Republican presidential nomination in 1976. He was opposed by ex-governor Ronald Reagan of California, a movie actor turned politician who was the darling of the Republican right wing. Reagan's campaign was well organized and well financed. He was an excellent speaker, where Ford proved somewhat bumbling on the stump. The contest was close, both candidates winning important primaries and gathering substantial blocs of delegates in non-primary states. At the convention in August, Ford obtained a slim majority. That he did not win easily, possessed as he was of the advantage of incumbency, made his chances of election in November appear slim.

In the meantime the Democrats had chosen James Earl Carter, a former governor of Georgia, as their candidate. Carter's rise from almost total obscurity was even more spectacular than that of George McGovern in the 1972 campaign and was made possible by the same forces: television, the democratization of the delegate-selection process, and the absence of a dominant leader among the Democrats.

Carter had been a naval officer and a substantial peanut farmer and warehouse owner before entering politics. He was elected governor of Georgia in 1970. While governor he won something of a reputation as a southern public official who treated black citizens fairly. (He hung a portrait of Martin Luther King, Jr., in his office.) Carter's political style was informal—he preferred to be called Jimmy.

During the campaign for delegates he turned his inexperience in national politics to advantage, emphasizing his lack of connection with the Washington establishment rather than apologizing for it. He repeatedly called attention to his integrity and deep religious faith. "I'll never lie to you," he promised voters, a pledge that no candidate would have bothered to make before Nixon's disgrace.

Carter entered nearly all the Democratic primaries and campaigned hard in non-primary states. Running against many different candidates, he won few decisive victories, but he accumulated delegates steadily and went to the convention in New York City in July with a solid majority.

When the final contest began, Carter had a large lead. Most of it soon evaporated. Reagan supporters among the Republicans swung behind Ford, and the prestige of the presidency was another asset. Both candidates were vague with respect to issues, a situation that hurt Carter particularly because he had made so much of honesty and straight talk. Ford stressed the need to control inflation, Carter high unemployment. Three televised debates between the candidates attracted huge audiences without generating a trend toward either candidate.

As election day approached, pollsters predicted an extremely close contest, and they were right: Carter won, 297 electoral votes to 241, having carried most of the South, including Texas, and a few large industrial states. A key element in his victory was the fact that he got an overwhelming majority of the black vote (partly on his record in Georgia, partly because Ford had been unsympathetic toward the demands of the urban poor). He also ran well in districts dominated by labor union members and throughout the South. The public's wish to punish the party of Richard Nixon was probably a further reason for his victory.

The Carter Presidency

Carter shone brightly in comparison with Nixon, and he seemed more forward-looking and imaginative than Ford. He tried to give a tone of democratic simplicity and moral fervor to his administration. After delivering his inaugural address, he walked with his wife Rosalynn and their small daughter Amy in the parade from the Capitol to the White House instead of riding in a limousine.

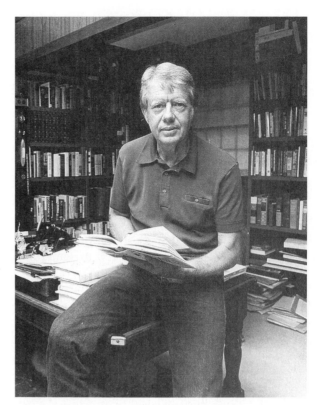

Jimmy Carter's informality was the perfect emblem of a post-Watergate reaction against the "imperial presidency." Yet, despite his image, Carter insisted on making many decisions—even minor ones—himself. This habit made it easy for voters to hold him personally responsible for failures.

He enrolled Amy, a fourth grader, in a largely black Washington public school. For his first talk on television he wore a sweater instead of a coat and tie, an advertisement for both his informality and the need to conserve energy by turning down thermostats. Soon after taking office he held a "call-in"; for two hours he answered questions phoned in by people from all over the country.

Carter's actual administration of his office did not go nearly so well. He put so many Georgians in important posts that his administration took on a most parochial character. Six of seven top White House aides came from his home state, as did his attorney general, the director of the Office of Management and Budget, the ambassador to the United Nations, and many lesser officials. Most of these people, like their boss, had little or no experience in national affairs. The administration developed a reputation for submitting complicated proposals to Congress with great fanfare and then failing to follow them up. Whatever matter Carter was considering at the moment seemed to absorb him totally—other urgent matters were allowed to drift.

This tendency frequently caused him to shift policies sharply when he returned to matters he had put aside. One journalist counted seven distinct changes of approach in Carter's economic policy in three years. While running for office he had emphasized the need to restrain inflation, but early in 1977 he came out for a $50 income tax rebate for individuals that would almost surely have caused prices to rise. When that idea ran into stiff congressional resistance, Carter turned to something else. And so it went.

In the face of so much frustration it was perhaps only human that Carter tended to blame others for his troubles. In a heralded television speech he described a national malaise that had sapped the people's energies and undermined civic pride. Although there was some truth in this observation, the effect was to make the president seem both ineffective and petulant.

Cold War or Détente?

In foreign affairs Carter announced that he intended to deal with all nations in a fair and humane way, putting defense of "basic human rights" before all other concerns. He cut off aid to Chile and Argentina because of human rights violations, but said little about what was going on in a long list of other repressive nations. He also negotiated treaties with Panama that provided for the gradual transfer of the isthmian canal to that nation and guaranteed its neutrality; in 1978, after long debate, the Senate ratified the treaties.

The president also intended to carry forward the Nixon-Kissinger policy of détente. He ended official American recognition of Taiwan, and in January 1979 the first exchange of ambassadors with the People's Republic of China took place. Maintaining good relations with the Soviet Union was more difficult, partly because while Secretary of State Cyrus Vance supported détente, Carter's national security adviser, Zbigniew Brzezinski, was strongly anti-Russian. (In his memoirs Vance complained of Brzezinski's "visceral anti-Sovietism," and another critic writes of his "rigid, simplified, Sovi-

Egypt's president Anwar Sadat, Jimmy Carter, and Israeli prime minister Menachem Begin clasp hands after the signing of the Camp David Agreement in 1978. Carter's active role in the peace negotiations showed his hands-on approach to the presidency.

etcentric view of the world.") Carter fluctuated between the two approaches yet seemed blissfully unaware of his ambivalence. He could complain about Soviet human rights violations and the need to strengthen NATO one day, and praise the idea of a new arms limitation agreement the next. The Russians certainly treated dissidents harshly, but they considered the president's frequent sermons on the subject politically motivated and out of keeping with his talk about détente.

In 1979 another Strategic Arms Limitation Treaty (SALT II) was signed with the Soviet Union, but the following winter the Soviet Union sent troops into Afghanistan in order to overthrow a government of which it disapproved. Carter denounced the invasion and warned the Russians that he would use force if they invaded any of the countries bordering the Persian Gulf. He stopped shipments of American grain and technologically advanced products, such as computers, to the Soviet Union, and he withdrew the SALT treaty, which he had sent to the Senate for ratification. He also refused to allow American athletes to compete in the Olympic games, which were held in the summer of 1980 in Moscow, and he began a new arms buildup.

Carter's one striking diplomatic achievement was the so-called Camp David Agreement with Israel and Egypt. Avoiding war in the Middle East was crucial because war in that part of the world was likely to result in the cutting off of oil supplies from the Arab nations. In September 1978 the president of Egypt, Anwar Sadat, and Prime Minister Menachem Begin of Israel came to the United States at Carter's invitation to negotiate a peace treaty ending the state of war that had existed between their two countries for many years. For two weeks they conferred at Camp David, the presidential retreat outside the capital, and Carter's mediation had much to do with their successful negotiations. In the treaty Israel promised to withdraw from territory captured from Egypt during the "six-day" war of 1967. Egypt in turn recognized Israel as a nation, the first Arab country to do so.

A Time of Troubles

Carter had promised to fight inflation by reducing government spending and balancing the budget, and to stimulate the economy by cutting taxes, policies that sounded (and in fact were) very much like those of Nixon and Ford. He advanced an admirable if complicated plan for conserving energy and reducing the dependence of the United States on OPEC oil. It involved raising the tax on gasoline and imposing a new tax on "gas guzzlers," cars that got relatively few miles per gallon. But in typical fashion he did not press for these measures, and he waffled on the important question of deregulating the price of American crude oil until late in his term.

For reasons that were not entirely Carter's fault, national self-confidence was at a low ebb. The crises of the Cold War had subsided and the hot war in Vietnam was over, but the United States had lost a considerable portion of its international prestige. To a degree this was unavoidable. The very success of American policies after World War II had something to do with the decline of American influence in the world. The Marshall Plan, for example, enabled the nations of western Europe to rebuild their economies; thereafter they were less dependent on outside aid, and in the course of pursuing their own interests they sometimes adopted policies that did not seem to be in the best interests of the United States. Under American occupation, Japan rebuilt its shattered economy. By the 1960s and 1970s it had become one of the world's leading manufacturing nations, its exporters providing fierce competition in markets previously dominated by Americans.

Similarly, to the extent that American aid to underdeveloped countries had improved their economies, they were more likely to act independently and not necessarily in ways that benefited the United States. On the other hand, when American aid was ineffective or used to bolster unpopular local regimes, American prestige also suffered. And the failure of the United States to achieve its objectives in the Vietnam War had a debilitating effect on its influence abroad long after the war ended.

At home the decay of the inner sections of the great cities was a continuing cause of concern. The older cities seemed almost beyond repair. Carter visited the South Bronx section of New York City in 1977. He was shocked to see block after block of rubble and rows of empty, fire-blackened buildings. He pledged that the federal government would clean up and rebuild this wasteland, but when his term ended that part of the South Bronx and similar parts of many cities remained barren ruins.

Crime rates were high in the inner cities, public transportation dilapidated and expensive, other city services undermanned and inefficient, the schools crowded, students' performances poor. Blacks, Hispanics, and other minorities made up a large percentage of the population in decaying urban areas. That they had to live in such surroundings made a mockery of the commitment of the civil rights legislation of the 1960s and Lyndon Johnson's Great Society program to treat all people equally and improve the lives of the poor.

Double-digit Inflation

The most disturbing problem that vexed the nation in the Carter years was soaring inflation. Prices had been rising for an unprecedentedly long period and in recent years at an unprecedentedly rapid pace. In 1971 an inflation rate of 5 percent had so alarmed President Nixon that he had imposed a price freeze. In 1979 a 5 percent rate would have seemed almost deflationary—the actual rate was nearly 13 percent.

Double-digit inflation had a devastating effect on the poor, the retired, and others who were living on fixed incomes. However, the squeeze that price increases put on these unfortunates was only part of the damage done. Inflation discouraged people from making long-term investments, and as time passed and the rate of inflation increased, it caused many to stop saving entirely. People began to anticipate inflation. They bought goods they did not really need, and without much regard for cost, on the assumption that whatever today's price, tomorrow's would be higher still. This behavior increased demand and thereby pushed prices up still more. Put differently, when the interest paid by savings banks was lower than the inflation rate, it seemed foolish to save money.

At another level, a kind of "flight from money" began. Well-to-do individuals transferred their assets from cash to durable goods such as land and houses, gold, works of art, jewelry, rare postage stamps, and other "collectibles." Interest rates rose rapidly as lenders demanded higher returns to compensate for expected future inflation.

Congress raised the minimum wage to help low-paid workers cope with inflation. It pegged social security payments to the cost of living index in an effort to protect retirees. Thereafter, when prices rose social security payments went up automatically. The poor and the pensioners got some immediate relief, but the laws made balancing the federal budget more difficult and the increased spending power of the recipients caused further upward pressure on prices. Inflation seemed to be feeding upon itself, and the price spiral seemed unstoppable.

The federal government made matters worse in several ways. People's wages and salaries rose in response to inflation, but their taxes went up more rapidly because large dollar incomes put them in higher tax brackets. This "bracket creep" caused resentment and frustration among middle-class families. There were "taxpayer revolts" as many people turned against long-accepted but expensive government programs for aiding the poor. Inflation also increased the government's need for money. Year after year it spent more than it received in taxes. By thus unbalancing the budget it pumped billions of dollars into the economy, and by borrowing to meet the deficits and pushing up interest rates, it increased the costs of all businesses that had to borrow.

The Carter Recession

In this situation Carter was more a bystander than a leader; he had little to suggest that was different from the policies of Nixon and Ford. In 1978 he proposed voluntary wage and price guidelines in another effort to slow inflation. Unions and manufacturers responded fairly well, but the guidelines did not apply to the prices that were going up most rapidly: oil, houses, and food. Finally, Carter named a conservative banker, Paul A. Volcker, as chairman of the Federal Reserve Board. Volcker belonged to the conservative monetarist school of economics, which taught that the way to check inflation was to limit the growth of the money supply. Under his direction the Board adopted a tight-money policy, which caused already high interest rates to soar.

High interest rates hurt all borrowers, but they were especially damaging to the automobile and housing industries because most car and home buyers borrow a large portion of the purchase price. American car manufacturers were already experiencing hard times because of the competition of

The Iranian crisis produced striking visual images that appeared worldwide in the press and on TV. These militants burned the American flag a few days after they seized the American Embassy.

Japanese and European automobiles, which gave better gasoline mileage and were seemingly better built than most American vehicles. Tens of thousands of automobile workers, among the highest paid workers in American industry, were out of work. Soaring mortgage rates had a similar effect on the sale of homes. The housing slump meant unemployment for thousands of carpenters, brick-layers, and other construction workers and bankruptcy for many builders. Double-digit interest rates also hurt small businesses seeking to expand. Savings and loan institutions were especially hard hit because they were saddled with countless mortgages made when rates were as low as four and five percent. Now they had to pay much more than that to hold deposits and offer even higher rates to attract new money.

The Iranian Crisis: Origins

By the autumn of 1979 Carter's standing in public opinion polls was extremely low—barely one respondent in four approved of his handling of the office. He had failed to provide the fresh point of view and the firm leadership that he had promised in the 1976 campaign. His chances of being elected to a second term seemed dim.

At this point a dramatic upheaval in the Middle East revived his prospects. On November 4, 1979, about 400 armed Muslim militants broke into the American Embassy compound in Teheran, Iran, and took everyone within the walls captive. The seizure came as a surprise, but it had roots that ran far back in Iranian history. During World War II Great Britain, Russia, and later the United States occupied Iran and forced its pro-German shah into exile, replacing him with his 22-year-old son, Muhammad Reza Pahlavi. Quarreling between Russia and the western allies over influence in Iran was one of the first of the many Cold War clashes; it resulted in Russian withdrawal in 1946. In the early 1950s when liberal and nationalist elements in Iran led by premier Muhammad Mossadegh sought to reduce the power of the Anglo-Iranian Oil Company, American mediators engineered a compromise that increased the price Iran received for its petroleum.

Mossadegh was a liberal by Iranian standards but by western standards somewhat eccentric. He carried out much public business from his bed, went about in pink pajamas, broke into tears at the slightest provocation. In 1953 a CIA coup (Operation Ajax), presumably designed to prevent the nationalization of Iranian petroleum resources and the abolition of the monarchy, resulted in his overthrow. (When the plan for Operation Ajax was shown to Secretary of State Dulles, he said with relish: "So this is how we get rid of that madman Mossadegh!")

As historian James A. Bill explains, the fall of Mossadegh "bought twenty-five more years for the Pahlavi dynasty and enabled the international oil industry to export at favorable terms 24 billion barrels of oil during this period." It turned most Iranians against the United States and shah Reza Pahlavi, however, and that led to the shah's purchase of enormous amounts of American arms. "He'll buy anything that flies," one American official explained.

In 1972 President Nixon gave the shah permission to buy any nonnuclear weapon in the American arsenal and the shah, whose oil-based wealth was almost unlimited, proceeded to load up on sophisticated F-14 and F-15 fighters and other arms. Over the years he spent billions and Iran became the most powerful military force in the region. While running for president Jimmy Carter had criticized Nixon's arms sales to Iran, but in office, in typical fashion, he reversed himself, even selling the shah F-16 fighters and several expensive AWACs, observation planes equipped with ultra-sophisticated radar.

Although Iran was an enthusiastic member of the OPEC cartel, the shah was for obvious reasons a firm friend of the United States. Iran seemed, as President Carter said in 1977, "an island of stability" in the troubled Middle East. The appearance of stability was deceptive because of the shah's unpopularity. He suppressed liberal opponents brutally. At the same time, his attempts to introduce western ideas and technology in Iran caused economic disruption and angered conservatives. Muslim religious leaders were particularly offended by such "radical" policies as the shah's tentative efforts to improve the position of women in Iranian society. Because his American-supplied army and his American-trained secret police kept the shah in power, his opponents hated the United States almost as much as they hated their autocratic ruler.

Throughout 1977 riots and demonstrations convulsed Iran. When soldiers fired on protesters, the bloodshed caused more unrest; that unrest caused more bloodshed. Over 10,000 civilians were killed, many times that number wounded. In 1978 the whole country seemed to rise against the shah. Finally, in January 1979, he was forced to flee. A revolutionary government headed by a revered religious leader, the Ayatollah Ruhollah Khomeini, who had recently returned to Iran in triumph after a long exile in France, assumed power.

Khomeini denounced the United States, the "Great Satan" whose support of the shah, he said, had caused the Iranian people untold suffering. When President Carter allowed the shah, who had been living in Mexico, to come to the United States for medical treatment, the Iranian revolutionaries were convinced that an attempt would be made to restore him to his throne. The seizure of the Teheran embassy resulted.

The Iranian Crisis: Carter's Dilemma

The militants announced that the captive Americans would be held as hostages until the United States returned the shah to Iran for trial as a traitor. They also demanded that the shah's vast wealth be confiscated and surrendered to the Iranian government. Of course President Carter rejected these demands. (He had no choice in the matter; deporting the shah, who had entered the United States legally, and confiscating his property were not possible under American law.) Instead he froze Iranian assets in the United States and banned trade with Iran until the hostages were freed.

Carter wanted to rescue the hostages, but there seemed to be no way to do so. Even going to war would surely result in their execution—and the deaths of others as well. He gave some consideration to blockading Iranian ports in order to force their release, but that could have no immediate effect and it might alarm the Arab states and lead to another cutoff of Middle Eastern oil. And there was always the danger of Soviet intervention.

The American public and most foreign observers approved of the president's restraint. If he made any mistake, it was a consequence of his habit of focusing on one matter at a time. This exaggerated the importance of the hostage issue. Some critics believed that Carter was playing into the hands of the Iranians by calling attention to the fact that they could hold the mighty United States at bay.

A stalemate developed. The Iranians released the women and black captives, but the others, more than 50 in number, were subjected to countless indignities and in some cases were physically abused.

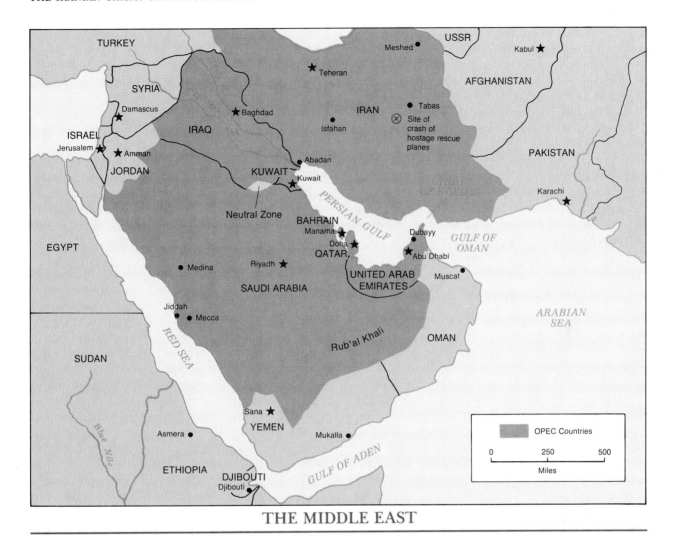

THE MIDDLE EAST

Months passed. Even after the shah, who was terminally ill with cancer, left the United States for Panama, the Iranians remained adamant.

The crisis produced a remarkable emotional response in the United States. For the first time since the Vietnam War the entire country agreed on something. One result of this was a revival of Carter's political fortunes. Before the attack on the Teheran embassy, Senator Edward M. Kennedy of Massachusetts, youngest brother of John F. Kennedy, had decided to run against Carter in the Democratic presidential primaries. He seemed a likely winner until the seizure of the hostages, but that event caused the public to rally around the president. Carter took clever political advantage of the

national concern. He refused to campaign in the primaries, insisting (without good reason) that the crisis made his constant presence in Washington essential.

Nevertheless the hostages languished in Iran. An intense debate raged within the administration about whether or not to attempt to rescue them, Brzezinski urging Carter "to lance the boil," Secretary Vance advising patience. In April 1980 Carter finally ordered a team of marine commandos flown into Iran in Sea Stallion helicopters in a desperate attempt to free them. The raid was a fiasco. Several helicopters broke down. While the others were gathered at a desert rendezvous south of Teheran, Carter called off the attempt. In the confusion of a night departure there was a crash and eight commandos were killed. The Iranians made political capital of the incident, gleefully displaying on television the wrecked aircraft and captured American equipment.

Unlike Carter's earlier actions, the raid was widely criticized. (Even before it began Secretary of State Cyrus Vance had quietly resigned on the ground that it was almost sure to result in many casualties and that if it succeeded the Iranians would only seize other Americans in the country.) And so the stalemate continued. In July 1980 the shah, who had moved from Panama to Egypt, died. It made no difference to the Iranians.

The Election of 1980

Despite the failure of the raid, Carter beat Kennedy decisively in the most important primaries without stirring from the White House. He had more than enough delegates at the Democratic convention to win nomination on the first ballot. His Republican opponent in the campaign that followed was Ronald Reagan, the former governor of California who had almost defeated Gerald Ford for the nomination in 1976. At 69, Reagan was the oldest person ever nominated for president by a major party. However, his age was not a serious handicap in the campaign; he was physically trim and vigorous and seemed no older than most other prominent politicians.

Reagan had grown up a New Deal Democrat, but during and immediately after World War II he became disillusioned with liberalism. He denounced government inefficiency and high taxation. As president of the Screen Actors' Guild he attacked the influence of communists in the movie industry. After his movie career ended (he always insisted that he had not been typed as "the nice guy who didn't get the girl"), Reagan did publicity for General Electric until 1960, then worked for various conservative causes. He campaigned for Barry Goldwater during the 1964 presidential contest. Two years later he was elected governor of California.

Reagan was a controversial governor, in part because, despite his professed conservatism and his emphasis on economy, government spending in California increased dramatically during his term. Despite or perhaps because of this shift, he was easily reelected in 1970.

The 1980 presidential campaign ranks among the most curious in American history. One of Reagan's opponents at the Republican convention, Congressman John Anderson of Illinois, refused to accept defeat and ran for president as an independent. He did so, he announced, because he thought both Carter and Reagan had little genuine popular support.

Indeed, many citizens appeared unable to decide whom to vote for. Of those who expressed a preference, many did so without enthusiasm. Anderson's problem was that he too inspired relatively little enthusiasm among voters. "None of the above" seemed the true desire of many citizens as they contemplated the list of candidates.

Both Carter and Reagan spent much time explaining why the other was unsuited to be president. Carter defended his record, though without much conviction. Reagan denounced criminals, drug addicts, and all varieties of immorality, and spoke in support of patriotism, religion, family life, and other "old-fashioned" virtues, which won him the enthusiastic backing of fundamentalist religious sects and other conservative groups. He also promised to transfer some functions of the federal government to the states, reduce spending and cut taxes, insisting at the same time that the budget could be balanced and inflation sharply reduced.

Reagan's tendency to depend on popular magazine articles, half-remembered conversations, and other informal sources for his economic "facts" reflected a mental imprecision that alarmed his critics, but his sunny disposition and his "laid-back" style compared favorably with Carter's personality. The president seemed tight-lipped and tense even when flashing his habitual toothy smile. A television debate between Carter and Reagan pointed up their personal differences, but Reagan's question to the audience, "Are you better off now than you were four years ago?" had more effect on the election than any policy he said he would pursue.

Because so many people said they were undecided, the contest seemed close—"too close to call," most experts said on election eve. It did not turn out that way. The voting was light, but those who cast ballots gave Reagan over 43 million votes to Carter's 35 million and Anderson's 5.6 million. Dissatisfaction with the Carter administration seems to have determined the result. The Republicans also gained control of the Senate and cut deeply into the Democratic majority in the House of Representatives.

Carter devoted his last weeks in office to the continuing hostage crisis. War had broken out between Iran and Iraq in September. The additional strain on an Iranian economy already shattered by revolution raised hopes that Ayatollah Khomeini would release the captive Americans. Iran needed both the assets Carter had frozen and spare parts for its American-made planes and tanks. With Algeria acting as intermediary, American and Iranian diplomats worked out an agreement. Reagan avoided involvement in the negotiations, but to put pressure on the Iranians he announced that he opposed paying "ransom" for "people who have been kidnapped by barbarians." Perhaps fearing that the new president might take some drastic action, Iran at last agreed to release the hostages in return for its assets in the United States. After 444 days in captivity, the 52 hostages were set free on January 20, the day Reagan was inaugurated.

Ronald Reagan rode to the White House in part on promises of reining in the federal government. "It's not my intention to do away with government," Reagan declared in his 1981 inaugural address. "It's rather to make it work—work with us, not over us; to stand by our side, not ride on our back."

Reagan as President

Despite his amiable, unaggressive style, Reagan acted rapidly and with determination once in office. He hoped to change the direction in which the country was moving by turning many functions of the federal government over to the states and relying more on individual initiative; the marketplace, not bureaucratic regulations, should govern most economic decisions. At the same time, Reagan called for greatly increased military expenditures. He believed that the Soviet Union had taken advantage of the relaxation of international tensions associated with détente to gain military superiority over the United States.

Cutting taxes was his first priority. He asked Congress to lower income taxes by 30 percent over three years and he demanded steep reductions in federal spending, focused chiefly on social services such as student loans and welfare payments and food stamps that went to poor people. He promised that despite these cuts he would maintain a "safety net" under the poor to protect them from real deprivation, and he insisted that in the long run they and everyone else would benefit from his program.

Reagan's tax policy was based on what was known as "supply-side economics." He claimed that since the tax cut would leave people with more money, they would invest in productive ways rather than spend the excess on consumer goods, and that the new investment would result in increased production, more jobs, prosperity, and therefore more income for the government despite the lower tax rates. There was a superficial similarity between this argument and the reasoning behind the successful tax cut proposed by President Kennedy in 1963 and engineered by President Johnson in 1964. However, the danger of inflation was much greater in 1981. Many congressmen hesitated, but the mandate of Reagan's big election victory was hard to resist.

In August 1981 Reagan displayed his determination in convincing fashion when the nation's air traffic controllers went on strike despite the fact that they were forbidden by law to do so. Reagan ordered them to return to work. Most of the controllers, feeling that their demands were just and that the airlines could not operate without them, refused to obey this order. Reagan therefore discharged all 11,400 of them and began a crash program to train replacements. Even after the strike collapsed, the president refused to rehire the strikers. The air traffic controllers' union was destroyed.

An event unrelated to economic policy added greatly to the president's popularity. On March 30, while leaving a Washington hotel, he was shot in the chest by one John W. Hinckley, Jr.* Although he was seriously wounded, Reagan reacted coolly and with his usual self-deprecating style. When he was wheeled into the operating room for emergency surgery, he told the team of doctors before going under the anesthetic that he hoped they were all Republicans. Later he complained of his bad luck— he had been wearing a brand new suit and now it was ruined. It was hard to oppose such bravery and good humor. That he made a swift and total recovery despite his age further increased the admiration of the country.

Helped by the votes of conservative Democrats, Reagan won congressional approval of a Budget Reconciliation Act that reduced government expenditures on domestic programs by $39 billion. But Congress resisted reducing the politically popular "entitlement" programs, such as Social Security and Medicare, which accounted for about half of the budget. Congress also enacted most of the tax cuts the president had asked for, lowering individual income taxes by 25 percent over three years. Since the percentage was the same for everyone, high-income taxpayers received a disproportionately large share of the savings. Business taxes were liberalized, and capital gains, gift, and inheritance levies were reduced. To further encourage investment, the law authorized anyone with earned income to invest up to $2,000 per year in an individual retirement account (IRA). This money, and the interest or dividends it earned, would not be taxed until the individual retired.

Reagan also eliminated many government regulations affecting businesses. Long and complicated antitrust suits against International Business Machines and American Telephone and Telegraph, two of the largest corporations in the country, were dropped.

"Reaganomics," as administration policy was called, was certainly not a new theory. Carter had also advocated tax cuts, reduced federal spending, and the tight money policy adopted by Chairman

Paul Volcker of the Federal Reserve Board. During his term the airlines were freed from control by the Civil Aeronautics Board. But Reagan's supply-side economics was old-fashioned to the point of being antique. It differed little from the policy conservative economists had favored in the Great Depression, which critics had derided as the "trickle-down" theory. As the economist James Tobin said in 1981, "old doctrines and policies, new forty years ago," were to be replaced by "new doctrines and policies, old forty years ago."

Tobin and most other economists did not think that Reaganomics would work. By December 1982 the economy was in a full-scale recession. More than 10 percent of the work force was unemployed. The combination of lower tax rates, soaring military expenditures without a corresponding reduction in domestic spending, and a slumping economy was further unbalancing the budget. In 1983 the federal deficit topped $195 billion, up from $59 billion only three years earlier, and it continued to expand thereafter. Month after month the Treasury was forced to borrow billions and its needs kept interest rates high.

Only the fact that inflation was slowing brightened the gloomy picture. Several causes contributed to this much-desired result. High unemployment and the economic slowdown gradually reduced consumer demand for goods and services. People began to worry about the future, and that weakened the inflationary psychology that had led them to spend in anticipation of further price increases. Most significant were the declining prices of gasoline and other petroleum products. Conservation and increased production by non-OPEC countries such as Mexico, Norway, and Great Britain gradually turned chronic shortages into an oil glut. The oil "shocks" of 1973 and 1979 had caused other prices to soar; the glut caused them to fall, though much less abruptly. All in all, the rate of inflation fell from more than 12 percent to less than 4 percent by 1984. When inflation moderated, the Federal Reserve Board relaxed its tight money policy. Interest rates then declined somewhat, making it easier to finance the purchase of homes and automobiles. The new lower tax rates left people with more spendable income for all kinds of purchases. Business began to pick up. Unemployment, while still high, fell below 8 percent in 1984.

But the recovery did not lead to much new busi-

---

* Two security officers and Reagan's press secretary were also wounded by Hinckley.

ness investment. People seemed to be spending their additional income on consumer goods. Together with the federal deficits caused by the large increase in military expenditures, this spending also prevented interest rates from going down as far as economists had hoped they would when inflation slackened.

Many of Reagan's advisers urged him to reduce the military budget and seek some kind of tax increase in order to bring the government's income more in line with its outlays. However, the president insisted that the military buildup was necessary because of the threat to world peace posed by the Soviet Union. He called Russia an "evil empire" and pursued a hard-line anticommunist foreign policy nearly everywhere. With the reluctant support of the governments of the western democracies, where many citizens feared Soviet retaliation against their countries, he installed new nuclear cruise missiles in Europe. Claiming that in Central America the communists were supplying arms to the left-wing Sandinista government of Nicaragua and encouraging communist rebels in El Salvador, he sought to undermine the Nicaraguan regime and bolster the conservative government of El Salvador. He also used American troops to overthrow a Cuban-backed regime on the tiny Caribbean island of Grenada.

In 1982 the continuing turmoil in the Middle East plunged the Reagan administration into a new crisis. Israel had invaded Lebanon to destroy PLO units that were staging raids on northern Israeli settlements from bases there. Israeli troops easily overran much of the country, but in the process the Lebanese government disintegrated and fighting broke out among Lebanese Christians and various Muslim sects. In an effort to end the bloodshed, Reagan agreed to send American troops to serve as part of an international peacekeeping force. Essentially their role was to act as a buffer between the occupying Israelis and the contending Lebanese units in and around Beirut. Before long, however, Israel pulled its troops back to southern Lebanon. Then the peacekeeping units came under fire from the different Lebanese factions. Soon the Americans were reduced to maintaining control of the Beirut airport, where they were under almost constant shelling.

At this point it would probably have been wise to withdraw, but Reagan believed that American prestige was at stake. Tragedy resulted in October 1983 when a fanatical Muslim crashed a truck loaded with explosives into a building at the airport housing American marines. The building collapsed, killing 239 marines. Early the next year, prestige or no, Reagan removed the entire American peacekeeping force from Lebanon.

Four More Years

Being a sitting president with an extraordinarily high standing in public opinion polls, Reagan was nominated for a second term at the 1984 Republican convention without opposition. The leading Democratic candidate was Walter Mondale of Minnesota, who had been vice-president under Carter. He was opposed in the primaries by half a dozen others, but only Senator Gary Hart of Colorado and the Reverend Jesse Jackson, a black civil rights activist, developed much support in the primaries. Hart aimed his campaign chiefly at younger voters; he claimed to offer "new ideas," and he accused Mondale of catering to "special-interest groups" such as organized labor. Jackson had little chance of winning, but being an excellent speaker as well as the first black to make a serious run for the presidential nomination of a major party, he roused the enthusiasm of millions of blacks. Tens of thousands of them responded to his appeal that they register and vote in the coming election.

The contest was fairly close between Mondale and Hart, but by the time of the Democratic convention, Mondale had a majority of the delegates. He was nominated on the first ballot. He then electrified the country by choosing Representative Geraldine Ferraro of New York as his running mate. Being an Italian-American and a Catholic, Ferraro was expected to appeal to conservative Democrats who had supported Reagan in 1980, but Mondale undoubtedly chose her chiefly because she was a woman—Democrats expected that she would win the votes of many Republican women and that her selection would counter the claims that Mondale was unimaginative and overly cautious.

Reagan began the campaign with several important advantages. He was especially popular among religious fundamentalists and other social conservatives and these groups were increasingly vocal. President Nixon had spoken of them as a "silent majority." By 1980 the kind of people he was

Walter Mondale and Geraldine Ferraro held a press conference in Minnesota shortly after the Democratic nominating convention in July of 1984.

referring to were no longer silent. Fundamentalist TV preachers were almost all fervent Reaganites and the most successful of them were collecting tens of millions of dollars annually in contributions from viewers. One of these, the Reverend Jerry Falwell, founded Moral Majority in 1979 and set out to create a new political movement. "Americans are sick and tired of the way the amoral liberals are trying to corrupt our nation," Falwell announced in 1979.

During the first Reagan administration Moral Majority had become a powerful political force. Falwell was against drugs, the "coddling" of criminals, homosexuality, communism, and abortion, all things that Reagan also disliked. While not openly antiblack, he disapproved of forced busing and a number of other government policies designed to help blacks and other minorities. Of course, Walter Mondale was also against many of the things that Falwell and his followers denounced, but Reagan was against them all. In addition, Reagan was in favor of government aid to private schools run by church groups, something dear to the hearts of Moral Majority types despite the constitutional principle of separation of church and state.

But Moral Majority, despite its name, was far from being an actual majority. Reagan's support was much more broadly based. Thousands of working people and an enormous percentage of white southerners, types that had been solidly Democratic during the New Deal and beyond, now voted Republican. Many younger northern Democrats who had voted in the primaries for Hart voted for Reagan in the general election. The president's personality was another important plus—voters continued to admire his informal yet firm style, and his stress on patriotism and other "old-fashioned" virtues. He was a confirmed optimist, telling the voters over and over that things were getting better and that four more years of Republican leadership would make them better still.

The tendency of voters to support a sitting president when the economy was on the rise was still another advantage. Inflation eased, unemployment fell to a bit over 7 percent, investment finally picked up, and inflation remained low. Interest rates were moving down slowly but steadily.

From the start Mondale emphasized the difficulties that he saw ahead for the nation. The president's economic policies, he said, hurt the poor, women, and minorities. Mondale also tried to focus attention on the huge increase in the federal deficit that Reagan's policies had produced, and he accused the president of misleading the public by saying that he would not raise taxes if reelected.

These were conventional campaign tactics. But Mondale, in a daring move, announced in his acceptance speech at the Democratic convention that he would raise taxes if elected. This promise, most unusual for a person running for office, was another attempt to counter his reputation for political caution.

Most polls showed Reagan far in the lead when the campaign began, and this remained true throughout the contest. Optimism and opportunity were his catchwords. Mondale, he said, "sees America wringing her hands. We see America using her hands. He sees America divided by envy. . . . We see an America inspired and uniting for opportunity."

This tactic proved effective. Nothing Mondale or Ferraro did or said affected the president's popularity. Bad news, even his own mistakes, had so little effect on his standing that people began to call him "the Teflon president." On election day he got nearly 60 percent of the popular vote and lost only in Minnesota, Mondale's home state, and in the District of Columbia. His electoral college margin was overwhelming, 523 to 13.

Of all the elements in the New Deal coalition, only the blacks, who voted solidly for Mondale, remained loyal, and their unity may have had something to do with the shift of so many white Democrats to Reagan. The Democratic strategy of nominating a woman for vice-president was a fail-ure; far more women voted for Reagan than for the Mondale-Ferraro ticket. Reagan's triumph, like the two landslide victories of Dwight Eisenhower in the 1950s, was a personal one. The Republicans made only minor gains in the House of Representatives and actually lost two seats in the Senate.

"The Reagan Revolution"

Reagan's agenda for his second term closely resembled that of his first. In foreign affairs, he ran into continuing congressional resistance to his requests for military support for his anticommunist crusade. His anti-Soviet policies, and particularly his belligerent rhetoric, attracted no better than lukewarm support among all but the most fervent American anticommunists. This was particularly true after Mikhail S. Gorbachev became the Russian premier in March 1985. Gorbachev seemed far more moderate and flexible than his predecessors. (He was certainly more concerned about public opinion in the western democracies, which he cultivated assiduously.) He began to encourage political debate and criticism in the Soviet Union—the policy known as *glasnost*—and sought to stimulate the stagnant Russian economy by decentralizing administration and rewarding individual enterprise (*perestroika*).

Gorbachev also announced that he would continue to honor the unratified SALT II agreement,

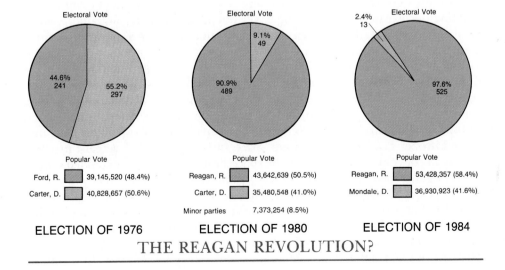

ELECTION OF 1976

Popular Vote

Ford, R.   39,145,520 (48.4%)
Carter, D.   40,828,657 (50.6%)

ELECTION OF 1980

Popular Vote

Reagan, R.   43,642,639 (50.5%)
Carter, D.   35,480,548 (41.0%)
Minor parties   7,373,254 (8.5%)

ELECTION OF 1984

Popular Vote

Reagan, R.   53,428,357 (58.4%)
Mondale, D.   36,930,923 (41.6%)

THE REAGAN REVOLUTION?

The arms cuts made at the 1988 Moscow summit showed how Ronald Reagan's ideas about the "evil empire" had changed. Yet Reagan was surprised to find that Mikhail Gorbachev believed "the communist propaganda he's grown up hearing about our country"— above all, that business dominates the government.

whereas Reagan, arguing that the Russians had not respected the limits laid down in the pact, seemed bent on pushing ahead with the expansion and modernization of America's nuclear arsenal. He sought funds to develop an elaborate computer-controlled strategic defense initiative, popularly known as "Star Wars," that would supposedly be capable of destroying enemy missiles in outer space where they could do no damage. Despite his insistence that Star Wars would be a defensive system, the Russians objected to it vociferously.

When he realized that the Russians were eager to come to some agreement limiting nuclear weapons, the president gradually abandoned his talk about Russia being an "evil empire." In October 1986 he met with Mikhail Gorbachev in Iceland in search of an agreement on arms control. This "summit" got nowhere, partly because Reagan was determined to push Star Wars and partly because he apparently did not understand the implications of nuclear disarmament for western Europe. The Europeans, fearing Soviet superiority in conventional weapons, were horrified by the thought of *total* nuclear disarmament. The Iceland setback, however, proved to be temporary and in 1988 at a second summit, Reagan and Gorbachev signed a treaty eliminating medium-range nuclear missiles.

Reagan nevertheless persisted in pressing for the

Star Wars defense-in-space system. After NASA's spectacular Apollo program, which sent six expeditions to the moon between 1969 and 1972, the space agency's prestige was beyond measurement. Its Skylab orbiting space station program (1973–1974) was equally successful. Next, shortly after the beginning of Reagan's first term, the manned space shuttle Columbia, launched by rocket power, was able, after orbiting for several days, to return to earth intact, gliding on its stubby, swept-back wings to an appointed landing strip. Columbia and other shuttles were soon transporting satellites into space for the government and private companies, and its astronauts were conducting military and scientific experiments of great importance.

Congress, however, boggled at the enormous estimated cost of Star Wars, which some feared would mount into the trillions of dollars. Costs aside, the idea of relying for national defense on the complex technology involved in controlling machines in outer space suffered a further setback in 1986, when the space shuttle Challenger exploded shortly after takeoff, killing its seven-member crew. This disaster put a stop to the program until the cause had been discovered and complex engineering changes made. Finally, in 1989 the shuttles began to fly again.

The president was more successful in winning

public support for his get-tough-with-terrorists policy. In October 1985, four Arabs seized control of the Italian cruise ship *Achille Lauro* in the eastern Mediterranean. After killing an elderly Jewish-American tourist and tossing his body into the sea, they surrendered to Egyptian authorities on condition that they be provided with safe passage to Libya on an Egyptian airliner.

The terrorist chose Libya because the president of that nation, Muammar al-Qaddafi, was a bitter enemy of Israel and the United States and an open supporter of terrorist activities. To stop them, Reagan ordered Navy F-14 jets to intercept the airliner. The jets forced the Egyptian pilot to land in Italy instead of Libya and the terrorists were taken into custody.

Then, after a Libyan-planned bombing of a West German club frequented by American servicemen, Reagan launched an air strike against Libyan bases from airfields in Great Britain. This attack alarmed Europeans, but in America the public responded enthusiastically. The president's popularity reached an all-time high.

Reagan's basic domestic objectives—to reduce the scope of federal activity, particularly in the social welfare area, to lower income taxes, and to increase the strength of the armed forces—did not change in his second term. Despite the tax cuts already made, congressional leaders of both parties agreed to the Income Tax Act of 1986, which reduced the top levy on personal incomes from 50 percent to 28 percent and the tax on corporate profits from 46 percent to 34 percent. "When I think of coming here with the tax rate at 70 percent and ending my first term under 30 percent, it's amazing," one delighted Republican senator told reporters.

Liberal members of Congress, remembering how the voters had reacted to Mondale's talk about *increasing* taxes, had found it politically difficult to oppose the measure. But the existing tax system was extremely complicated and full of "loopholes" benefiting particular interest. The new law did away with most of the tax shelters and special credits that corporations and well-to-do individuals had used to reduce their tax bills. The law also relieved six million low-income people from paying any federal income tax at all.

The objective of the law was a system that required people with similar incomes to pay roughly equal taxes. But it also undermined the principle of progressive taxation, the practice, dating back to the first income tax enacted after the adoption of the Sixteenth Amendment in 1913, of requiring high-income people to pay a larger *percentage* of their income than those with smaller incomes. The new law set only two rates: 15 percent on taxable incomes below $29,750 for families, and 28 percent on incomes above this limit. A family with a taxable income of $30,000 would pay at the same rate as one with $300 million, should any such exist.

In this and other ways, the government, in the words of economist Peter Passell, "ceased acting as a buffer against the vicissitudes of capitalism." Whatever the overall effect on the nation's economy (which continued to expand throughout Reagan's presidency) the new tax system did not prevent the gap between rich and poor from widening. At the end of his second term the standard of living of the

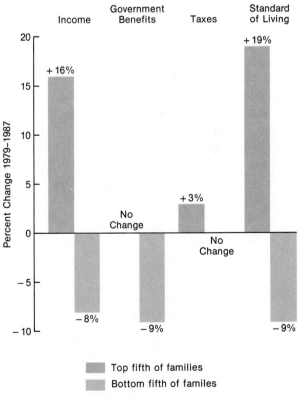

Top fifth of families
Bottom fifth of families

CHANGING LIVING STANDARDS
1979–1987

poorest fifth of the population (40 million people) was 9 percent lower than it had been in 1979, while that of the wealthiest fifth had risen about 20 percent.

Reagan advanced another of his objectives more gradually, but with effects likely to be long-lasting. This was his appointment of conservatives to federal judgeships. During his first year in office he appointed Sandra Day O'Connor to the Supreme Court. Justice O'Connor was the first woman ever appointed to the Court, but she was also conservative on most constitutional questions. When Chief Justice Warren C. Burger resigned in 1986 Reagan replaced him with Associate Justice William H. Rehnquist, probably the most conservative member of the Supreme Court, and he filled the vacancy with Antonin Scalia, an even more conservative judge. After the resignation of Associate Justice Lewis F. Powell in 1987, the President nominated Robert Bork, the man who, while Nixon's Solicitor General, had discharged the Watergate special prosecutor, Archibald Cox. Bork was both conservative and rigidly doctrinaire. After protracted hearings, the Senate refused to confirm him and eventually the appointment went to a less controversial but by no means liberal judge, David Kennedy. By 1988 Reagan had appointed well over half of the members sitting on the federal bench.

Change and Uncertainty

If the "Reagan Revolution" seemed to have triumphed, powerful forces were at work that no individual or party could effectively control. For one thing, the makeup of the American people, always in a state of flux, was changing at a rate approaching that of the early 1900s when the "new" immigration was at its peak. In the 1970s, after the Immigration Act of 1965 had put an end to the national origins concept, more than 4 million immigrants entered the country; the vast majority of these newcomers came from Asia and Latin America. This trend continued; of the 601,000 who arrived in 1986, nearly 500,000 were from these regions. In addition, uncounted thousands entered the country illegally, most crossing the long, sparsely settled border with Mexico.

Some of the immigrants were refugees fleeing from repressive regimes in Vietnam, Cuba, Haiti, and Central America, and nearly all were poor. Most were hardworking and law-abiding, but some became public charges and others lawbreakers. Most tended, like their predecessors, to crowd together in ethnic neighborhoods. Spanish could be heard more often than English in sections of Los Angeles, New York, Miami, and many other cities.

No strong demand for immigration restrictions

The most recent wave of immigrants has changed the face of America's cities just as earlier ethnic groups did. Street scenes from Union City, New Jersey, and Berkeley, California, reveal strong Hispanic—in this case Cuban—and Vietnamese influences (facing page).

developed, perhaps because so many Americans were themselves the children of immigrants. However, conservatives found it appalling that so many people could enter the country illegally and even Americans sympathetic to the "undocumented aliens" agreed that control was desirable. Finally, in 1986, Congress passed a law offering amnesty to illegal immigrants with long residency in the country and penalizing employers who hired illegal immigrants in the future. Many persons legalized their status under the new law, but the influx of illegal immigrants continued. Problems developed because some employers refused to hire anyone with a foreign accent on the ground that they might be "illegals" bearing false papers.

There were other trends that deeply disturbed thousands of Americans. The postwar population explosion and the subsequent decline in the birth rate made pressure on the social security system inevitable when the "baby boomers" reached retirement age in the early 21st century. More immediately, the traditional family consisting of a husband and wife and their children, the man a "breadwinner," the woman a "housewife and mother," seemed in danger of ceasing to be the norm. An ever-larger number of families were headed by single parents, in most cases by women. A disproportionate number of these families were black, and many were poor. Between 1979 and 1987, the number of single-parent families living

below the poverty line increased by 46 percent.

Year after year more than 1.1 million marriages ended in divorce. The tendency of couples to live together without getting married continued, helping to explain why the number of illegitimate births rose steadily. So did the number of abortions—from 763,000 in 1974 after abortion was legalized to an average of 1.3 million a year in the 1980s.

The Reagan administration devoted much effort to reducing the amount of crime in the country, but despite the fact that the number of persons confined in prisons reached an all-time high, little progress was made. A campaign against illegal drugs resulted in many arrests, but the drugs remained widely available. Cocaine became available in a cheap, smokable, and especially addictive form called "crack," causing a problem of epidemic proportions.

The drug problem was part of a larger and still more threatening one, the spread of a deadly new disease, acquired immune deficiency syndrome (AIDS). AIDS was caused by a virus that destroyed the body's immune system, exposing the victim to a host of deadly diseases. It was uniformly fatal. Since it was transmitted by the exchange of bodily fluids, intravenous drug users (who frequently shared needles) and homosexuals were its chief victims. But since it was a venereal disease, the possibility of its spreading through the general population was a constant danger.

Other massive social and economic changes that were difficult to control were also occurring. One was the continuing shift of employment opportunities from the production of goods to the production of services—from raising wheat and manufacturing steel to advertising, banking, and recordkeeping. This meant a shift from blue- to white-collar work, which called for more better-educated workers than were currently available and increasing joblessness for the unskilled. Union membership had been falling since long before Reagan became president, but by 1985 it was down to about 19 percent of the work force, in large part because white-collar workers were difficult to organize. Furthermore, by producing goods in Asia and Latin America where labor costs were low, "multinational" manufacturing companies could avoid tariff barriers and often make larger profits than would be possible in the United States, but with harmful effects on American workers.

The Merger Movement

Another worrisome trend was the merger movement, which saw often unrelated companies swallowing up one another in unprecedented fashion. The movement began under President Carter, but Reagan's abandonment of strict enforcement of the antitrust laws encouraged the trend. The merger movement was also encouraged by the federal tax structure; corporations had to pay taxes on stock dividends, which were treated as distributed profits. But the interest paid on corporate bonds was a business expense and thus a tax deduction. In 1989 Time Inc. borrowed $13.9 billion to purchase Warner Communications, thus forming one of the world's largest publishing concerns. This combination would never have been permitted by earlier administrations and would have been financially unprofitable if Time were forced to raise the money by issuing new stock.

Piratical corporate "raiders" raised cash by issuing high-interest bonds secured by the assets of the company purchased. A shrewd broker, Michael Milkin of the firm of Drexel Burnham Lambert, emerged as the "king" of this "junk bond" business by convincing banks, corporations, and well-heeled investors that the extremely high interest paid by these bonds compensated for the risks involved.

The system made it possible for a small company or even a single entrepreneur to buy a giant corporation. In 1985 Ronald Perelman, an aggressive entrepreneur who had recently obtained control of Pantry Pride, a supermarket chain with a net worth of about $145 million, managed to take over the cosmetics and health-care firm of Revlon, the net worth of which exceeded $1 billion. One deal often led to another. In 1985 the R. J. Reynolds Tobacco Company purchased the food conglomerate Nabisco for $4.9 billion. Three years later this new giant, RJR Nabisco, was itself taken over by Kohlberg, Kravis, Roberts and Company for $24.9 billion.

Still another economic trend that defied national control was the fluctuating price of petroleum. The falling price of oil during Reagan's presidency eased inflationary pressures and helped speed recovery in the United States, but cheaper oil dealt a devastating blow to the economy of the Southwest, a region where support of Reagan's policies was particularly strong. Lower oil prices also forced oil-producing countries in and out of OPEC to cut back on their imports of manufactured goods. Mexico was particularly hard hit. The situation there was so serious that Mexico could not even pay the interest on its debts without obtaining further loans.

Many American banks suffered heavy losses when domestic and foreign oil-related loans went sour. But oil could also go up in price for reasons unrelated to events that any single nation could control, in which case it would have adverse effects on the economy.

A similar situation developed in the nation's agricultural heartland. In the 1970s, a time of rising agricultural prices, farmers borrowed heavily to expand output. With the price of land and farm products soaring, it seemed safe to do so. In 1985 about half the farmers in the country were in debt and interest payments on their debts came to $21 billion.

By that time inflation had slowed to a crawl because of the tight money policy, and world agricultural prices were falling. Between 1982 and 1986 the value of American wheat exports fell from $8 billion to between $3 and $4 billion. For many debt-ridden farmers, this meant bankruptcy. More generally, the popularity of the Reagan tax reductions and the president's refusal to consider any change in course on this subject meant that the federal government continued to run at a huge deficit; the shortfall rose from $179 billion in 1985 to more than $220 billion in 1986.

The Iran-contra Arms Deal

All these matters were partly beyond human control, or at least beyond what seemed practicable under the American political system. Overall, they diminished the effectiveness of the Reagan administration, but they did not seriously undermine it. That was the result of two self-inflicted wounds involving American policy in Central America and the Middle East.

The Central American problem resulted from a revolution in Nicaragua, where in 1979 leftist rebels had overthrown the dictatorial regime of Anastasio Somoza. Because the victorious "Sandinista" government turned out to be Marxist oriented (and supported by both Cuba and the Soviet Union) President Reagan was determined to force it from power. He backed anti-Sandinista elements in Nicaragua known as the "contras" (*contra* is Spanish for against) and in 1981 persuaded Congress to provide these "freedom fighters" with arms.

However, the contras made little progress and many Americans feared that aiding them would lead, as it had in Vietnam, to the use of American troops in the fighting. In October 1984, in the Boland Amendment, Congress banned further military aid to the rebels. The president then sought to persuade other countries and private American

Oliver North's poise and earnestness while testifying before a congressional committee investigating the Iran-contra affair prompted an outpouring of sympathy from the American people. Thousands sent telegrams and letters of support, and many included money to help "Ollie" cover the cost of his defense.

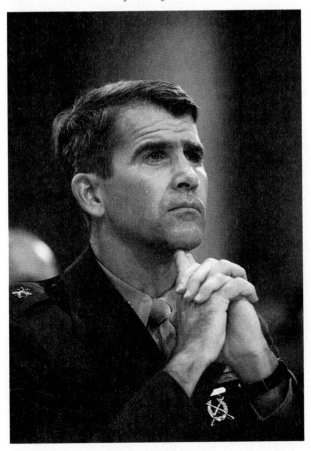

groups to help the contras (as he put it) to keep "body and soul together."

In the Middle East, a bloody war had been raging between Iran and Iraq since 1980. The chief interest of the United States in the conflict was to make sure that it did not cause the flow of Middle Eastern oil to the West to be cut off. But public opinion in the country was particularly hostile toward the Iranians. Memories of the hostage crisis of the Carter years did not fade, and Iran was widely believed to be responsible for the fact that a number of Americans were being held hostage by terrorists in Lebanon. Reagan was known to oppose any bargaining with terrorists. Nevertheless, he was eager to find some way to free the captive Americans. During 1985 he made the fateful decision to allow the indirect shipment of arms to Iran by way of Israel, his hope being that this would result in the hostages being released. When this did not happen, he went further, and in January 1986 he authorized the secret sale of American weapons directly to the Iranians.

The arms sale was arranged by Marine Colonel Oliver North, an aide of Reagan's national security adviser, Admiral John Poindexter. North was already in charge of the administration's effort to supply the Nicaraguan contras indirectly. With Poindexter's knowledge, he used $12 million of the profit from the Iranian sales to provide weapons for the contras, in plain violation of the congressional ban on such aid. North prepared a memorandum describing the transaction for Poindexter to show Reagan, but Poindexter testified under oath that he did not do so, in order, he claimed, to spare the president possible embarrassment.

News of the sales to Iran and of the use of the profits to supply the contras came to light in November 1986 and of course caused a sensation. Poindexter resigned, Colonel North was fired from his job with the security council, a special prosecutor, Lawrence E. Walsh, was appointed to investigate the affair, and both a presidential committee and a joint congressional committee began investigations. Reagan insisted that he knew nothing about the aid to the contras, but according to polls, a majority of the people did not believe him, and critics pointed out that if he was telling the truth it meant that he had not been able to control his own administration.

In May 1989 North was found guilty of destroying government documents in order to mislead Congress and obstruct its work; the following April Poindexter was convicted of five felonies, including conspiracy and lying to Congress, and was sentenced to six months in jail. Although he remained personally popular, President Reagan's influence with Congress and his reputation as a political leader plummeted. Critical comments by reporters ranged from "disengaged" and "gravely uninformed" to "out to lunch." Even earlier the Democratic elder statesman Clark Clifford described him as an "amiable dunce," and Martin Anderson, Reagan's chief economic adviser, admitted that the president "made decisions like an ancient king or a Turkish pasha, passively letting his subjects serve him."

The Election of 1988

The decline of Reagan's influence was also related to his status as a "lame duck" president entering the last year of his tenure. In both the major political parties, attention turned to the choice of presidential candidates.

After a shaky start, Reagan's vice-president, George Bush, ran away with the Republican primaries and won the nomination easily. The Democratic race was more complicated by far. So many candidates entered the field that the average citizen found it hard to tell them apart. Wits began to call the Democratic hopefuls "the seven dwarfs," referring to both their lack of distinguishing qualities and their lack of distinction.

Gradually, however, the field shrank and the race settled down to a contest between Governor Michael S. Dukakis of Massachusetts and the black leader Jesse Jackson. Jackson took consistently more liberal positions than any of the other candidates. He proposed to reduce military spending sharply and invest the savings in improving education, health care, and other social services. As in his earlier campaign, Jackson had the nearly unanimous support of blacks, but he also attracted a larger percentage of white Democrats than in 1984.

Dukakis stressed his record as an efficient manager—the Massachusetts economy was booming. Unlike the charismatic Jackson, who was an extraordinarily effective speaker, Dukakis was low-key, and an uninspired orator. But his campaign was well organized and well financed. Without overwhelming the opposition, he accumulated delegates steadily and by the end of the primary season he had a solid majority.

The chief remaining uncertainty involved the selection of Dukakis's running mate. Jackson professed to want the post, but Dukakis selected a con-

In the 1988 campaign, Michael Dukakis blasted the Republicans for favoring the rich, but avoided identifying himself as a liberal. "If anyone tells you that the American dream belongs only to the privileged few and not to all of us," Dukakis declared, "you tell them that the Reagan era is over."

servative senator, Lloyd Bentsen of Texas. When Jackson, swallowing his disappointment, gave the ticket his support in a rousing speech, the convention became a Democratic love feast.

The resulting campaign was another matter. In his capacity as vice-president, Bush had been accused by critics of being a "wimp"—a weak, bloodless kind of person who slavishly accepted every Reagan policy. As candidate for president, he set out to destroy this impression and he did so without rejecting the conservative Reagan philosophy. He attacked Dukakis savagely, charging him with coddling criminals because of a Massachusetts law granting furloughs to prisoners serving life sentences for murder. Dukakis had vetoed a Massachusetts bill compelling students to recite the pledge of allegiance because he believed it violated the constitutional guarantee of free speech. Brushing aside the constitutional issue, Bush denounced the veto repeatedly, claiming that it was a sign of Dukakis's poor judgment, if not of his lack of patriotism.

Dukakis conducted a curiously lifeless campaign. He stressed "competence," his supposed leadership qualities and his administrative abilities, but he avoided speaking out strongly for the liberal social policies that every Democratic presidential candidate since Franklin Roosevelt had supported. Consequently he found himself more often than not on the defensive against Bush's emotionally charged attacks.

On the other hand, Bush's choice of Senator Dan Quayle of Indiana as his running mate proved embarrassing to the Republicans. Although Quayle was an ardent supporter of military preparedness, it came out that he had avoided the Vietnam draft by enrolling in the Indiana National Guard, and the charge that he had used the influence of his wealthy family to get in the Guard was hard to refute. More seriously, he proved rather slow-witted in political debate, and it was difficult for Bush to explain why he had selected him.

As the campaign progressed, neither presidential candidate aroused much enthusiasm among voters, but polls indicated that Bush was gradually pulling away from his Democratic opponent. On election day he won handily, garnering 54 percent of the vote and carrying the Electoral College, 426 electoral votes to Dukakis's 112.

The End of the Cold War

Once in office, President Bush softened his tough tone, saying in his inaugural address that he hoped to "make kinder the face of the nation and gentler the face of the world." He also displayed a more traditional command of the workings of government and the details of current events than his predecessor, which was reassuring to persons put off by Reagan's lack of interest in the details of government. At the same time he pleased right-wing "Reagan loyalists" by his opposition to abortion and gun control, and by calling for a constitutional amendment prohibiting the burning of the American flag. His standing in the polls soared from high to astronomic.

One important reason for this was the flood of good news from abroad. The reforms instituted in the Soviet Union by Gorbachev led to demands for similar liberalization by the peoples of all of the Soviet Union's East European satellites, and Gorbachev responded by announcing that the Soviet Union would not use force to keep communist governments in power in these nations. Swiftly the peoples of Poland, Hungary, Czechoslovakia, Bulgaria, Romania, and East Germany did away with the repressive regimes that had ruled them throughout the postwar era and moved toward more democratic forms of government. Except in Romania, where the dictator Nicolae Ceausescu was seized, tried, and summarily executed by revolutionary leaders, all of these fundamental changes were carried out peacefully and in an orderly manner.

Almost overnight the international political climate changed. Soviet-style communism had been discredited. The Warsaw Pact was no longer a significant force in European international politics, and without it a Soviet attack anywhere on the continent was almost unthinkable. The cold war was over at last.

With pro-democratic forces in power in East Germany, demand for reunification with West Germany quickly emerged. The infamous Berlin Wall was torn down, talks were begun that seemed certain to lead to unification. This development alarmed the Russians, many Poles, and also all members of NATO, because an enlarged Germany would, on its own, approach superpower status. But given the new spirit of national self-determination, German unification seemed unavoidable.

The United States had nothing to do with the East European upheavals, but President Bush profited from them immensely. In truth, he handled the rapidly changing situation well, expressing moral support for new governments (and in the case of some, providing modest amounts of financial assistance), but refraining from trying to embarrass the Russians. His policy won the support of leaders in both the Republican and Democratic parties.

More controversial was the president's decision to send troops into Panama to overthrow General Manuel Noriega, who had refused to yield power even when his figurehead presidential candidate was defeated in a national election. Noriega was under indictment in the United States for drug trafficking, and after temporarily seeking refuge in the Vatican embassy in Panama, he surrendered to the American forces and was taken to the United States to stand trial.

At a summit meeting in Washington in June 1990 Bush and Gorbachev signed agreements reducing American and Russian stockpiles of long-range nuclear missiles by 30 percent and eliminating chemical weapons. They also announced plans for further cuts in weaponry, and President Bush agreed to the relaxation of barriers against trade with the Soviet Union, a measure designed to help the limping Russian economy.

Bush thus accomplished the objective of the invasion. However, Latin Americans were alarmed by

Most Americans supported George Bush's decision to invade Panama in order to overthrow and arrest General Manuel Noriega. Yet the Panama invasion left unanswered questions—about the total number of civilians killed, and about Noriega's long tenure as an employee of the CIA.

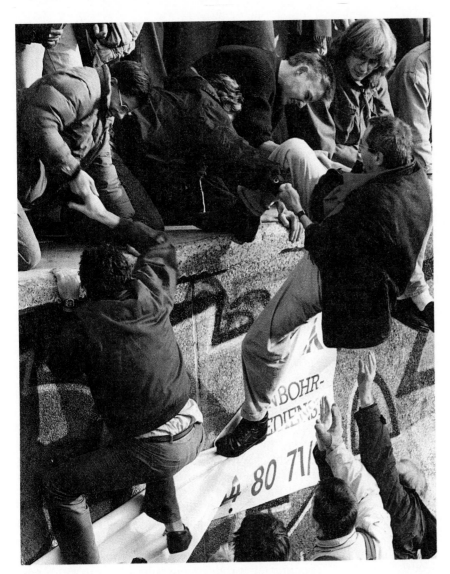

The opening, and then destruction, of the Berlin Wall drove home the astonishing changes taking place in Eastern Europe in 1989. When the euphoria passed, however, the United States faced new uncertainties about the status of a reunited Germany and the role of NATO—and America—in Europe.

the way the United States had used force in the region; the fact that far more Panamanian civilians than armed supporters of Noriega were killed and wounded in the affair also led to much criticism. The president's popularity, however, was not affected.

The president also benefited from the ending of the conflict between the Sandinistas and the contras in Nicaragua although, as in Eastern Europe, he did not contribute much to its solution. For the first time in that small nation's history, a free presidential election was held. The result was a victory for middle-of-the-road democratic forces. In April 1990 the new president, Violeta Chamorro, took office without incident.

Domestic Problems and Possibilities

Bush's approach to domestic issues was also politically effective, but it aroused a great deal of criticism even among Republicans. In general, he substituted words for action, urged voluntarism rather than new legislation in dealing with problems. During the presidential campaign he made a politically popular promise not to raise taxes if elected and in office he recommitted himself to that objective; in fact he proposed reducing the tax on capital gains, a measure that would increase revenues briefly but cost the government billions in the long run. No one enjoys paying taxes; the difficulty was that the national debt was huge and rapidly increasing. Dealing with it by reducing nonmilitary expenditures was extremely difficult, and what was known as the "peace dividend" expected to result from the relaxation of international tensions was slow in materializing.

Moreover, unforeseen needs for *more* expenditures were constantly arising. Nearly everyone favored extending aid to Poland and other Eastern European countries struggling to revive their stagnant economies. The invasion of Panama had been expensive and the cost of repairing the damage and helping the new government get on its feet was also substantial.

Larger still were the sums needed to bail out the invalid savings and loan industry. The combination of Reagan-inspired bank deregulation, inflation, and rising interest rates had led many savings and loan institutions to lend money recklessly. A large number invested huge sums in risky "junk" bonds that paid high interest rates and in questionable real estate ventures. In booming states such as Texas, Florida, and California such policies led to disaster when the economy cooled. In some cases the bankers had been little better than thieves, but their depositors were innocent victims and in any case their deposits were insured. The government (meaning the general public) had to make good, and the price was enormous. Shortly after his inauguration Bush estimated the cost at $30 billion. Within months estimates had risen to $130 billion and some economists predicted that, with interest charges, the cost might reach $500 billion.

Logic would suggest that if the tax burden had been roughly proportional to the needs of society when President Bush was elected, these unplanned but legitimate expenses justified and indeed required a tax increase. But Bush refused to be influenced by such logic and the Democrats were unwilling to press for new revenues unless he would agree. One indirect result of the no-new-taxes policy was to strain the resources of state governments, which had to assume burdens previously borne by Washington.

Another result was the tendency of the Bush administration to settle for half measures even when addressing matters the president considered important. Bush professed to be concerned about Jap-

anese domination of the electronics industry, yet he cut back support of research on high-definition television, semiconductors, and similar projects. He called himself the "education president" and he recognized the government's obligation to tackle the drug problem, to protect the environment, and to support efforts to discover a cure for AIDS. In all of these matters, however, critics (not all of them Democrats) believed the sums budgeted by the administration were too small.

The Imponderable Future

If historians can locate suitable records and other sources about a past event, they are able to explain, or at least make plausible guesses about, what it was and why it happened at that time, no matter how remote. Historians are also probably better than most other people at explaining how things got to be the way they are at any present moment. This is because events have causes and results, and these are things that historians are trained to study and understand. But historians are no better than anyone else at predicting the future. Results, quite obviously, come after the events that cause them; it takes time for them to unfold, which means that "at present," even the most hardworking and intelligent historians do not know anything important about what the future will bring.

Another way of putting this is to point out that in the modern world just about everything that happens is in some way related to everything else that is going on. There are far too many things happening (all producing results of some kind) for anyone to sort out which of them is going to have what effect on events that will happen tomorrow, let alone next year or in the 21st century. "Then" (whether tomorrow or next year or the 21st century) historians will be able to study those particular events that interest them and puzzle out their chief causes—but not "now."

Yet "now" is where we happen to be, and thus this book, so full of events and their causes and results, must end inconclusively. No one knows what will happen next. But of course not knowing what will happen next is one of the main reasons life is so interesting.

Milestones

1974 President Ford issues blanket pardon to Richard Nixon

1975 End of the war in Vietnam

1978 Camp David Agreement between Israel and Egypt

Paul A. Volcker named chairman of Federal Reserve Board

1979 Sandinistas overthrow Somoza government in Nicaragua

The Reverend Jerry Falwell founds Moral Majority

American interest rates exceed 10 percent

United States recognizes People's Republic of China

Shah forced to flee Iran; Ayatollah Khomeini rules nation

Radical students seize U.S. Embassy in Iran and hold occupants as hostages

1980 Commando raid designed to free hostages in Iran aborted

1981 American hostages in Iran released

Reagan appoints Sandra Day O'Connor to Supreme Court

Tax Reform Act lowers rates and eliminates loopholes

1984 Boland Amendment bans military aid to Nicaraguan contras

1985 Mikhail Gorbachev becomes premier of Soviet Union

President Reagan proposes Strategic Defense Initiative ("Star Wars") plan

1986 American "retaliatory" air raid on Libya

Reagan-Gorbachev summit meeting in Iceland

Immigration Act grants amnesty to long-term illegal aliens

Secret Iran-contra arms deal exposed

1987 Senate rejects nomination of Robert Bork to Supreme Court

1988 American-Soviet treaty bans medium-range missiles

1989 Gorbachev allows Eastern European nations to establish independent democratic governments

Oliver North convicted of destroying documents and obstructing Congress

1990 John Poindexter convicted of conspiracy and lying to Congress

SUPPLEMENTARY READING

Authoritative works on recent history are hard to find. On Gerald Ford, see Clark Mollenhoff, **The Man Who Pardoned Nixon** (1976), Richard Reeves, **A Ford, Not a Lincoln** (1975), and Ford's autobiography, **A Time to Heal** (1979). Betty Ford's frank autobiography **The Times of My Life** (1978) is a cut above most such memoirs.

For the Carter years see Betty Glad, **Jimmy Carter in Search of the Great White House** (1980), which is critical of Carter's style and actions. Zbigniew Brzezinski, **Power and Principle** (1983), discusses the foreign policy of the administration, while James A. Bill, **The Eagle and the Lion** (1988), and Michael Ledeen and William Lewis, **Debacle** (1981), cover the Iranian hostage crisis.

Books dealing with Reagan and his administration include Hedrick Smith, **Reagan, the Man, the President** (1980), Robert Dallek, **Ronald Reagan: The Politics of Symbolism** (1984), and Rowland Evans and Robert No-

vak, **The Reagan Revolution** (1981). D. A. Stockman, **The Triumph of Politics** (1986), contains a frank discussion of administration fiscal policies. Of the memoirs by insiders, Martin Anderson, **Revolution** (1988), is favorable to Reagan and D. T. Regan, **For the Record** (1988), is critical. Peggy Noonan, **What I Saw at the Revolution** (1990), is both insightful and amusing. For the Reagan foreign policy, see J. J. Girkpatrick, **Dictatorships and Double Standards** (1982), and Strobe Talbott, **The Russians and Reagan** (1984). W. S. Cohen and G. J. Mitchell, **Men of Zeal** (1988), describes the congressional Iran-contra hearings.

Contrasting views of recent conservative trends are provided by Alan Crawford, **Thunder on the Right** (1980), and Richard Viguerie, **The New Right** (1981). See also John Kater, **Christians on the Right** (1982).

The Declaration of Independence

When in the Course of human events, it becomes necessary for one people to dissolve the political bands which have connected them with another, and to assume among the Powers of the earth, the separate and equal station to which the Laws of Nature and of Nature's God entitle them, a decent respect to the opinions of mankind requires that they should declare the causes which impel them to the separation.

We hold these truths to be self-evident, that all men are created equal, that they are endowed by their Creator with certain unalienable Rights, that among these are Life, Liberty and the pursuit of Happiness. That to secure these rights, Governments are instituted among Men, deriving their just powers from the consent of the governed, That whenever any Form of Government becomes destructive of these ends, it is the Right of the People to alter or to abolish it, and to institute new Government, laying its foundation on such principles and organizing its powers in such form, as to them shall seem most likely to effect their Safety and Happiness. Prudence, indeed, will dictate that Governments long established should not be changed for light and transient causes; and accordingly all experience hath shown, that mankind are more disposed to suffer, while evils are sufferable, than to right themselves by abolishing the forms to which they are accustomed. But when a long train of abuses and usurpations, pursuing invariably the same Object evinces a design to reduce them under absolute Despotism, it is their right, it is their duty, to throw off such Government, and to provide new Guards for their future security.—Such has been the patient sufferance of these Colonies; and such is now the necessity which constrains them to alter their former Systems of Government. The history of the present King of Great Britain is a history of repeated injuries and usurpations, all having in direct object the establishment of an absolute Tyranny over these States. To prove this, let Facts be submitted to a candid world.

He has refused his Assent to Laws, the most wholesome and necessary for the public good.

He has forbidden his Governors to pass Laws of immediate and pressing importance, unless suspended in their operation till his Assent should be obtained; and when so suspended, he has utterly neglected to attend to them.

He has refused to pass other Laws for the accommodation of large districts of people, unless those people would relinquish the right of Representation in the Legislature, a right inestimable to them and formidable to tyrants only.

He has called together legislative bodies at places unusual, uncomfortable, and distant from the depository of their Public Records, for the sole purpose of fatiguing them into compliance with his measures.

He has dissolved Representative Houses repeatedly, for opposing with manly firmness his invasions on the rights of the people.

He has refused for a long time, after such dissolutions, to cause others to be elected; whereby the Legislative Powers, incapable of Annihilation, have returned to the People at large for their exercise; the State remaining in the mean time exposed to all the dangers of invasion from without, and convulsions within.

He has endeavoured to prevent the population of these States; for that purpose obstructing the Laws of Naturalization of Foreigners; refusing to pass others to encourage their migration hither, and raising the conditions of new Appropriations of Lands.

He has obstructed the Administration of Justice, by refusing his Assent to Laws for establishing Judiciary Powers.

He has made Judges dependent on his Will alone, for the tenure of their offices, and the amount and payment of their salaries.

He has erected a multitude of New Offices, and sent hither swarms of Officers to harass our People, and eat out their substance.

He has kept among us, in times of peace, Standing Armies without the Consent of our legislature.

He has affected to render the Military independent of and superior to the Civil Power.

He has combined with others to subject us to a jurisdiction foreign to our constitution, and unacknowledged by our laws; giving his Assent to their acts of pretended legislation:

For quartering large bodies of armed troops among us:

For protecting them, by a mock Trial, from Punishment for any Murders which they should commit on the Inhabitants of these States:

For cutting off our Trade with all parts of the world:

For imposing taxes on us without our Consent:

For depriving us in many cases, of the benefits of Trial by Jury:

For transporting us beyond Seas to be tried for pretended offences:

For abolishing the free System of English Laws in a neighbouring Province, establishing therein an Arbitrary government, and enlarging its Boundaries so as to render it at once an example and fit instrument for introducing the same absolute rule into these Colonies:

For taking away our Charters, abolishing our most valuable Laws, and altering fundamentally the Forms of our Governments:

For suspending our own Legislature, and declaring themselves invested with Power to legislate for us in all cases whatsoever.

He has abdicated Government here, by declaring us out of his Protection and waging War against us.

He has plundered our seas, ravaged our Coasts, burnt our towns, and destroyed the lives of our people.

He is at this time transporting large armies of foreign mercenaries to compleat the works of death, desolation and tyranny, already begun with circumstances of Cruelty & perfidy scarcely paralleled in the most barbarous ages, and totally unworthy the Head of a civilized nation.

He has constrained our fellow Citizens taken Captive on the high Seas to bear Arms against their Country, to become the executioners of their friends and Brethren, or to fall themselves by their Hands.

He has excited domestic insurrections amongst us, and has endeavoured to bring on the inhabitants of our frontiers, the merciless Indian Savages, whose known rule of warfare, is an undistinguished destruction of all ages, sexes and conditions.

In every stage of these Oppressions We have Petitioned for Redress in the most humble terms: Our repeated Petitions have been answered only by repeated injury. A Prince, whose character is thus marked by every act which may define a Tyrant, is unfit to be the ruler of a free People.

Nor have We been wanting in attention to our British brethren. We have warned them from time to time of attempts by their legislature to extend an unwarrantable jurisdiction over us. We have reminded them of the circumstances of our emigration and settlement here. We have appealed to their native justice and magnanimity, and we have conjured them by the ties of our common kindred to disavow these usurpations, which, would inevitably interrupt our connections and correspondence. They too have been deaf to the voice of justice and of consanguinity. We must, therefore, acquiesce in the necessity, which denounces our Separation, and hold them, as we hold the rest of mankind, Enemies in War, in Peace Friends.

We, therefore, the Representatives of the united States of America, in General Congress, Assembled, appealing to the Supreme Judge of the world for the rectitude of our intentions, do, in the Name, and by Authority of the good People of these Colonies, solemnly publish and declare, That these United Colonies are, and of Right ought to be Free and Independent States; that they are Absolved from all Allegiance to the British Crown, and that all political connection between them and the State of Great Britain, is and ought to be totally dissolved; and that as Free and Independent States, they have full Power to levy War, conclude Peace, contract Alliances, establish Commerce, and to do all other Acts and Things which Independent States may of right do. And for the support of this Declaration, with a firm reliance on the Protection of Divine Providence, we mutually pledge to each other our Lives, our Fortunes and our sacred Honor.

John Hancock,

Josiah Bartlett, Wm Whipple, Saml Adams, John Adams, Robt Treat Paine, Elbridge Gerry, Steph. Hopkins, William Ellery, Roger Sherman, Samel Huntington, Wm Williams, Oliver Wolcott, Matthew Thornton, Wm Floyd, Phil Livingston, Frans Lewis, Lewis Morris, Richd Stockton, Jno Witherspoon, Fras Hopkinson, John Hart, Abra Clark, Robt Morris, Benjamin Rush, Benja Franklin, John Morton, Geo Clymer, Jas Smith, Geo. Taylor, James Wilson, Geo. Ross, Caesar Rodney, Geo Read, Thos M:Kean, Samuel Chase, Wm Paca, Thos Stone, Charles Carroll of Carrollton, George Wythe, Richard Henry Lee, Th. Jefferson, Benja Harrison, Thos Nelson, Jr., Francis Lightfoot Lee, Carter Braxton, Wm Hooper, Joseph Hewes, John Penn, Edward Rutledge, Thos Heyward, Junr., Thomas Lynch, Junor., Arthur Middleton, Button Gwinnett, Lyman Hall, Geo Walton.

The Constitution of the United States

We the people of the United States, in Order to form a more perfect Union, establish Justice, insure domestic Tranquility, provide for the common defence, promote the general Welfare, and secure the Blessings of Liberty to ourselves and our Posterity, do ordain and establish this CONSTITUTION for the United States of America.

ARTICLE I

Section 1. All legislative Powers herein granted shall be vested in a Congress of the United States, which shall consist of a Senate and House of Representatives.

Section 2. The House of Representatives shall be composed of Members chosen every second Year by the People of the several States, and the Electors in each State shall have the Qualifications requisite for Electors of the most numerous Branch of the State Legislature.

No Person shall be a Representative who shall not have attained to the Age of twenty-five Years, and been seven Years a Citizen of the United States, and who shall not, when elected, be an Inhabitant of that State in which he shall be chosen.

Representatives and direct Taxes shall be apportioned among the several States which may be included within this Union, according to their respective Numbers, which shall be determined by adding to the whole Number of free Persons, including those bound to Service for a Term of Years, and excluding Indians not taxed, three fifths of all other Persons. The actual Enumeration shall be made within three Years after the first Meeting of the Congress of the United States, and within every subsequent Term of ten Years, in such Manner as they shall by Law direct. The Number of Representatives shall not exceed one for every thirty Thousand, but each State shall have at Least one Representative; and until such enumeration shall be made, the State of New Hampshire shall be entitled to chuse three, Massachusetts eight, Rhode-Island and Providence Plantations one, Connecticut five, New-York six, New Jersey four, Pennsylvania eight, Delaware one, Maryland six, Virginia ten, North Carolina five, South Carolina five, and Georgia three.

When vacancies happen in the Representation from any State, the Executive Authority thereof shall issue Writs of Election to fill such Vacancies.

The House of Representatives shall chuse their Speaker and other Officers; and shall have the sole Power of Impeachment.

Section 3. The Senate of the United States shall be composed of two Senators from each State, chosen by the Legislature thereof, for six Years; and each Senator shall have one Vote.

Immediately after they shall be assembled in Consequence of the first Election, they shall be divided as equally as may be into three Classes. The Seats of the Senators of the first Class shall be vacated at the Expiration of the second Year, of the second Class at the Expiration of the fourth Year, and of the third Class at the Expiration of the sixth Year, so that one-third may be chosen every second Year; and if Vacancies happen by Resignation, or otherwise, during the Recess of the Legislature of any State, the Executive thereof may make temporary Appointments until the next Meeting of the Legislature, which shall then fill such Vacancies.

No Person shall be a Senator who shall not have attained to the Age of thirty Years, and been nine Years a Citizen of the United States, and who shall not, when elected, be an Inhabitant of that State in which he shall be chosen.

The Vice President of the United States shall be President of the Senate, but shall have no vote, unless they be equally divided.

The Senate shall chuse their other Officers, and also a President pro tempore, in the absence of the Vice President, or when he shall exercise the Office of the President of the United States.

The Senate shall have the sole Power to try all Impeachments. When sitting for that purpose, they shall be on Oath or Affirmation. When the President of the United States is tried, the Chief Justice shall preside: And no person shall be convicted without the Concurrence of two thirds of the Members present.

Judgment in Cases of Impeachment shall not extend further than to removal from Office, and disqualification to hold and enjoy any Office of honor, Trust, or Profit under the United States: but the Party convicted shall nevertheless be liable and subject to Indictment, Trial, Judgment, and Punishment, according to Law.

Section 4. The Times, Places and Manner of holding

Elections for Senators and Representatives, shall be prescribed in each state by the Legislature thereof; but the Congress may at any time by Law make or alter such Regulations, except as to the Places of Chusing Senators.

The Congress shall assemble at least once in every Year, and such Meeting shall be on the first Monday in December, unless they shall by Law appoint a different Day.

Section 5. Each House shall be the Judge of the Elections, Returns and Qualifications of its own Members, and a Majority of each shall constitute a Quorum to do Business; but a smaller number may adjourn from day to day, and may be authorized to compel the Attendance of absent Members, in such Manner, and under such Penalties, as each House may provide.

Each House may determine the Rules of its Proceedings, punish its Members for disorderly Behavior, and, with the Concurrence of two thirds, expel a Member.

Each House shall keep a Journal of its Proceedings, and from time to time publish the same, excepting such Parts as may in their Judgment require Secrecy; and the Yeas and Nays of the Members of either House on any question shall, at the Desire of one fifth of those Present, be entered on the Journal.

Neither House, during the Session of Congress, shall, without the Consent of the other, adjourn for more than three days, nor to any other Place than that in which the two Houses shall be sitting.

Section 6. The Senators and Representatives shall receive a Compensation for their Services, to be ascertained by Law, and paid out of the Treasury of the United States. They shall in all Cases, except Treason, Felony, and Breach of the Peace, be privileged from arrest during their Attendance at the Session of their respective Houses, and in going to and returning from the same; and for any Speech or Debate in either House, they shall not be questioned in any other Place.

No Senator or Representative shall, during the Time for which he was elected, be appointed to any civil Office under the Authority of the United States, which shall have been created, or the Emoluments whereof shall have been increased, during such time; and no Person holding any Office under the United States shall be a Member of either House during his continuance in Office.

Section 7. All Bills for raising Revenue shall originate in the House of Representatives; but the Senate may propose or concur with Amendments as on other bills.

Every Bill which shall have passed the House of Representatives and the Senate, shall, before it become a Law, be presented to the President of the United States; If he approve he shall sign it, but if not he shall return it, with his Objections, to that House in which it shall have originated, who shall enter the Objections at large on their Journal, and proceed to reconsider it. If after such Reconsideration two thirds of that House shall agree to pass the bill, it shall be sent, together with the objections, to the other House, by which it shall likewise be reconsidered, and if approved by two thirds of that House, it shall become a Law. But in all such Cases the Votes of both Houses shall be determined by Yeas and Nays, and the Names of the Persons voting for and against the Bill shall be entered on the Journal of each House respectively. If any Bill shall not be returned by the President within ten Days (Sundays excepted) after it shall have been presented to him, the Same shall be a Law, in like Manner as if he had signed it, unless the Congress by their Adjournment prevent its Return, in which Case it shall not be a Law.

Every Order, Resolution, or Vote to which the Concurrence of the Senate and House of Representatives may be necessary (except on a question of Adjournment) shall be presented to the President of the United States; and before the Same shall take Effect, shall be approved by him, or being disapproved by him, shall be repassed by two thirds of the Senate and House of Representatives, according to the Rules and Limitations prescribed in the Case of a Bill.

Section 8. The Congress shall have Power To lay and collect Taxes, Duties, Imposts and Excises, to pay the Debts and provide for the common Defence and general Welfare of the United States; but all Duties, Imposts and Excises shall be uniform throughout the United States;

To borrow money on the credit of the United States;

To regulate Commerce with foreign Nations, and among the several States, and with the Indian Tribes;

To establish an uniform Rule of Naturalization, and uniform Laws on the subject of Bankruptcies throughout the United States;

To coin Money, regulate the Value thereof, and of foreign Coin, and fix the Standard of Weights and Measures;

To provide for the Punishment of counterfeiting the Securities and current Coin of the United States;

To establish Post Offices and post Roads;

To promote the Progress of Science and useful Arts, by securing for limited Times to Authors and Inventors the exclusive Right to their respective Writings and Discoveries;

To constitute Tribunals inferior to the Supreme Court;

To define and punish Piracies and Felonies committed on the high Seas, and Offences against the Law of Nations;

To declare War, grant Letters of Marque and Reprisal, and make Rules concerning Captures on Land and Water;

To raise and support Armies, but no Appropriation of Money to that Use shall be for a longer Term than two Years;

To provide and maintain a Navy;

To make Rules for the Government and Regulation of the land and naval forces;

To provide for calling forth the Militia to execute the Laws of the Union, suppress Insurrections and repel Invasions;

To provide for organizing, arming, and disciplining the Militia, and for governing such Part of them as may be employed in the Service of the United States, reserving to the States respectively, the Appointment of the Officers, and the Authority of training the Militia according to the discipline prescribed by Congress;

To exercise exclusive Legislation in all Cases whatsoever, over such District (not exceeding ten Miles square) as may, by Cession of particular States, and the acceptance of Congress, become the Seat of Government of the United States, and to exercise like Authority over all Places purchased by the Consent of the Legislature of the State in which the Same shall be, for the Erection of Forts, Magazines, Arsenals, dock-Yards, and other needful Buildings;—And

To make all Laws which shall be necessary and proper for carrying into Execution the foregoing Powers, and all other Powers vested by this Constitution in the government of the United States, or in any Department or Officer thereof.

Section 9. The Migration or Importation of such Persons as any of the States now existing shall think proper to admit, shall not be prohibited by the Congress prior to the Year one thousand eight hundred and eight, but a tax or duty may be imposed on such Importation, not exceeding ten dollars for each Person.

The privilege of the Writ of Habeas Corpus shall not be suspended, unless when in Cases of Rebellion or Invasion the public Safety may require it.

No Bill of Attainder or ex post facto Law shall be passed.

No capitation, or other direct, Tax shall be laid unless in Proportion to the Census or Enumeration herein before directed to be taken.

No Tax or Duty shall be laid on Articles exported from any State.

No Preference shall be given by any Regulation of Revenue to the Ports of one State over those of another: nor shall Vessels bound to, or from, one State, be obliged to enter, clear, or pay Duties in another.

No Money shall be drawn from the Treasury, but in Consequence of Appropriations made by Law; and a regular Statement and Account of the Receipts and Expenditures of all public Money shall be published from time to time.

No Title of Nobility shall be granted by the United States: And no Person holding any Office of Profit or Trust under them, shall, without the Consent of the Congress, accept of any present, Emolument, Office, or Title, of any kind whatever, from any King, Prince, or foreign State.

Section 10. No State shall enter into any Treaty, Alliance, or Confederation; grant Letters of Marque and Reprisal; coin Money; emit Bills of Credit; make any Thing but gold and silver Coin a Tender in Payment of Debts; pass any Bill of Attainder, ex post facto Law, or Law impairing the Obligation of Contracts, or grant any Title of Nobility.

No State shall, without the Consent of the Congress, lay any Imposts or Duties on Imports or Exports, except what may be absolutely necessary for executing its inspection Laws: and the net Produce of all Duties and Imposts, laid by any State on Imports or Exports, shall be for the Use of the Treasury of the United States; and all such Laws shall be subject to the Revision and Control of the Congress.

No State shall, without the Consent of Congress, lay any duty of Tonnage, keep Troops, or Ships of War in time of Peace, enter into any Agreement or Compact with another State, or with a foreign Power, or engage in War, unless actually invaded, or in such imminent Danger as will not admit of delay.

ARTICLE II

Section 1. The executive Power shall be vested in a President of the United States of America. He shall hold his Office during the Term of four years, and, together with the Vice President, chosen for the same Term, be elected, as follows:

Each State shall appoint, in such Manner as the Legislature thereof may direct, a Number of Electors, equal to the whole Number of Senators and Representatives to which the State may be entitled in the Congress; but no Senator or Representative, or Person holding an Office of Trust or Profit under the United States, shall be appointed an Elector.

The Electors shall meet in their respective States, and vote by Ballot for two persons, of whom one at least shall not be an Inhabitant of the same State with themselves. And they shall make a List of all the Persons voted for, and of the Number of Votes for each; which List they shall sign and certify, and transmit sealed to the Seat of the Government of the United States, directed to the President of the Senate. The President of the Senate shall, in the Presence of the Senate and House of Representatives, open all the Certificates, and the Votes shall then be counted. The Person having the greatest Number of Votes shall be the President, if such Number be a Majority of the whole Number of Electors appointed; and if there be more than one who have such Majority, and have an equal Number of Votes, then the House of Representatives shall immediately chuse by Ballot one of them for President; and if no Person have a Majority, then from the five highest on the List the said House shall in like Manner chuse the President. But in chusing the President, the votes shall be taken by States, the Representation from each State having one Vote; a quorum for this Purpose shall consist of a Member or Members from two-thirds of the States, and a Majority of all the States shall be necessary to a Choice. In every Case, after the Choice of the President, the Person having the greatest Number of Votes of the Electors shall be the Vice President. But if there should remain two or more who have equal votes, the Senate shall chuse from them by Ballot the Vice President.

The Congress may determine the time of chusing the Electors, and the Day on which they shall give their Votes; which Day shall be the same throughout the United States.

No person except a natural-born Citizen, or a Citizen of the United States, at the time of the Adoption of this Constitution, shall be eligible to the Office of President; neither shall any Person be eligible to that Office who shall not have attained to the Age of thirty-five years, and been fourteen Years a Resident within the United States.

In Case of the Removal of the President from Office, or of his Death, Resignation, or Inability to discharge the Powers and Duties of the said Office, the same shall devolve on the Vice President, and the Congress may by Law provide for the Case of Removal, Death, Resignation, or Inability, both of the President and Vice President, declaring what Officer shall then act as President, and such Officer shall act accordingly, until the disability be removed, or a President shall be elected.

The President shall, at stated Times, receive for his Services a Compensation, which shall neither be increased nor diminished during the Period for which he shall have been elected, and he shall not receive within that Period any other Emolument from the United States, or any of them.

Before he enter on the execution of his Office, he shall take the following Oath or Affirmation:—"I do solemnly swear (or affirm) that I will faithfully execute the Office of President of the United States, and will, to the best of my Ability, preserve, protect, and defend the Constitution of the United States."

Section 2. The President shall be Commander in Chief of the Army and Navy of the United States, and of the Militia of the several States, when called into the actual Service of the United States; he may require the Opinion, in writing, of the principal Officer in each of the executive Departments, upon any subject relating to the Duties of their respective Offices, and he shall have Power to Grant Reprieves and Pardons for Offences against the United States, except in Cases of Impeachment.

He shall have Power, by and with the Advice and Consent of the Senate, to make Treaties, provided two thirds of the Senators present concur; and he shall nominate, and by and with the Advice and Consent of the Senate, shall appoint Ambassadors, other public Ministers and Consuls, Judges of the supreme Court, and all other Officers of the United States, whose Appointments are not herein otherwise provided for, and which shall be established by Law: but the Congress may by Law vest the Appointment of such inferior Officers, as they think proper, in the President alone, in the Courts of Law, or in the Heads of Departments.

The President shall have Power to fill up all Vacancies that may happen during the Recess of the Senate, by granting Commissions which shall expire at the End of their next Session.

Section 3. He shall from time to time give to the Congress Information of the State of the Union, and recommend to their Consideration such Measures as he shall judge necessary and expedient; he may, on extraordinary occasions, convene both Houses, or either of them, and in Case of Disagreement between them, with respect to the Time of Adjournment, he may adjourn them to such Time as he shall think proper; he shall receive Ambassadors and other public Ministers; he shall take Care that the Laws be faithfully executed, and shall Commission all the Officers of the United States.

Section 4. The President, Vice President and all civil Officers of the United States, shall be removed from Office on Impeachment for, and Conviction of, Treason, Bribery, or other high Crimes and Misdemeanors.

ARTICLE III

Section 1. The judicial Power of the United States, shall be vested in one supreme Court, and in such inferior Courts as the Congress may from time to time ordain and establish. The Judges, both of the supreme and inferior Courts, shall hold their Offices during good Behaviour, and shall, at stated Times, receive for their Services, a Compensation, which shall not be diminished during their Continuance in Office.

Section 2. The judicial Power shall extend to all Cases, in Law and Equity, arising under this Constitution, the Laws of the United States, and treaties made, or which shall be made, under their Authority;—to all Cases affecting ambassadors, other public ministers and consuls;—to all cases of admiralty and maritime Jurisdiction;—to Controversies to which the United States shall be a Party;—to Controversies between two or more States;—between a State and Citizens of another State;—between

Citizens of different States,—between Citizens of the same State claiming Lands under Grants of different States, and between a State, or the Citizens thereof, and foreign States, Citizens or Subjects.

In all Cases affecting Ambassadors, other public Ministers and Consuls, and those in which a State shall be Party, the supreme Court shall have original Jurisdiction. In all the other Cases before mentioned, the supreme Court shall have appellate Jurisdiction, both as to Law and Fact, with such Exceptions, and under such Regulations as the Congress shall make.

The trial of all Crimes, except in Cases of Impeachment, shall be by Jury; and such Trial shall be held in the State where the said Crimes shall have been committed; but when not committed within any State, the Trial shall be at such Place or Places as the Congress may by Law have directed.

Section 3. Treason against the United States, shall consist only in levying War against them, or in adhering to their Enemies, giving them Aid and Comfort. No Person shall be convicted of Treason unless on the testimony of two Witnesses to the same overt Act, or on Confession in open Court.

The Congress shall have power to declare the Punishment of Treason, but no Attainder of Treason shall work Corruption of Blood, or Forfeiture except during the Life of the Person attained.

ARTICLE IV

Section 1. Full Faith and Credit shall be given in each State to the public Acts, Records, and judicial Proceedings of every other State. And the Congress may by general Laws prescribe the Manner in which such Acts, Records and Proceedings shall be proved, and the Effect thereof.

Section 2. The Citizens of each State shall be entitled to all Privileges and Immunities of Citizens in the several States.

A Person charged in any State with Treason, Felony, or other Crime, who shall flee from Justice, and be found in another State, shall on demand of the executive Authority of the State from which he fled, be delivered up, to be removed to the State having Jurisdiction of the crime.

No Person held to Service or Labour in one State, under the Laws thereof, escaping into another, shall, in Consequence of any Law or Regulation therein, be discharged from such Service or Labour, but shall be delivered up on Claim of the Party to whom such Service or Labour may be due.

Section 3. New States may be admitted by the Congress into this Union; but no new State shall be formed or erected within the Jurisdiction of any other State; nor any State be formed by the Junction of two or more States, or parts of States, without the Consent of the Legislatures of the States concerned as well as of the Congress.

The Congress shall have Power to dispose of and make all needful Rules and Regulations respecting the Territory or other Property belonging to the United States; and nothing in this Constitution shall be so construed as to Prejudice any Claims of the United States, or of any particular State.

Section 4. The United States shall guarantee to every State in this Union a Republican Form of Government, and shall protect each of them against Invasion; and on Application of the Legislature, or the Executive (when the Legislature cannot be convened) against domestic Violence.

ARTICLE V

The Congress, whenever two-thirds of both Houses shall deem it necessary, shall propose Amendments to this Constitution, or, on the Application of the Legislatures of two-thirds of the several States, shall call a Convention for proposing Amendments, which, in either Case, shall be valid to all Intents and Purposes, as part of this Constitution, when ratified by the Legislatures of three-fourths of the several States, or by Conventions in three-fourths thereof, as the one or the other Mode of Ratification may be proposed by the Congress; Provided that no Amendment which may be made prior to the Year One thousand eight hundred and eight shall in any Manner affect the first and fourth Clauses in the Ninth Section of the first Article; and that no State, without its Consent, shall be deprived of its equal Suffrage in the Senate.

ARTICLE VI

All Debts contracted and Engagements entered into, before the Adoption of this Constitution, shall be as valid against the United States under this Constitution, as under the Confederation.

This Constitution, and the Laws of the United States which shall be made in Pursuance thereof; and all Treaties made, or which shall be made, under the Authority of the United States, shall be the supreme Law of the Land; and the Judges in every State shall be bound thereby, any Thing in the Constitution or Laws of any State to the Contrary notwithstanding.

The Senators and Representatives before mentioned, and the Members of the several State Legislatures, and all executive and judicial Officers, both of the United States and of the several States, shall be bound by Oath or Affirmation to support this Constitution; but no religious Test shall ever be required as a qualification to any Office or public Trust under the United States.

ARTICLE VII

The Ratification of the Conventions of nine States shall be sufficient for the Establishment of this Constitution between the States so ratifying the same.

Done in Convention by the Unanimous Consent of the States present the Seventeenth Day of September in the Year of our Lord one thousand seven hundred and Eighty seven, and of the Independence of the United States of America the Twelfth. In Witness whereof We have hereunto subscribed our Names.

Go. Washington, *President and deputy from Virginia; Attest* William Jackson, *Secretary; Delaware:* Geo. Read,* Gunning Bedford, Jr., John Dickinson, Richard Bassett, Jaco. Broom; *Maryland:* James McHenry, Daniel of St. Thomas' Jenifer, Danl. Carroll; *Virginia:* John Blair, James Madison, Jr.; *North Carolina:* Wm. Blount, Richd. Dobbs Spaight, Hu Williamson; *South Carolina:* J. Rutledge, Charles Cotesworth Pinckney, Charles Pinckney, Pierce Butler; *Georgia:* William Few, Abr. Baldwin; *New Hampshire:* John Langdon, Nicholas Gilman; *Massachusetts:* Nathaniel Gorham, Rufus King; *Connecticut:* Wm. Saml. Johnson, Roger Sherman;* *New York:* Alexander Hamilton; *New Jersey:* Wil. Livingston, David Brearley, Wm. Paterson, Jona. Dayton; *Pennsylvania:* B. Franklin,* Thomas Mifflin, Robt. Morris,* Geo. Clymer,* Thos. FitzSimons, Jared Ingersoll, James Wilson, Gouv. Morris.

Articles in Addition to, and Amendment of, the Constitution of the United States of America, Proposed by Congress, and Ratified by the Legislatures of the Several States, Pursuant to the Fifth Article of the Original Constitution.

AMENDMENT I [1791]

Congress shall make no law respecting an establishment of religion, or prohibiting the free exercise thereof; or abridging the freedom of speech, or of the press; or the right of the people peaceably to assemble, and to petition the Government for a redress of grievances.

AMENDMENT II [1791]

A well regulated Militia, being necessary to the security of a free State, the right of the people to keep and bear Arms shall not be infringed.

AMENDMENT III [1791]

No Soldier shall, in time of peace, be quartered in any house, without the consent of the Owner, nor in time of war, but in a manner to be prescribed by law.

* Also signed the Declaration of Independence

AMENDMENT IV [1791]

The right of the people to be secure in their persons, houses, papers, and effects, against unreasonable searches and seizures, shall not be violated, and no Warrants shall issue, but upon probable cause, supported by Oath or affirmation, and particularly describing the place to be searched, and the persons or things to be seized.

AMENDMENT V [1791]

No person shall be held to answer for a capital or otherwise infamous crime, unless on a presentment or indictment of a Grand Jury, except in cases arising in the land or naval forces, or in the Militia, when in actual service in time of War or public danger; nor shall any person be subject for the same offence to be twice put in jeopardy of life or limb; nor shall be compelled in any criminal case to be a witness against himself, nor be deprived of life, liberty, or property, without due process of law; nor shall private property be taken for public use, without just compensation.

AMENDMENT VI [1791]

In all criminal prosecutions, the accused shall enjoy the right to a speedy and public trial, by an impartial jury of the State and district wherein the crime shall have been committed, which district shall have been previously ascertained by law, and to be informed of the nature and cause of the accusation; to be confronted with the winesses against him; to have compulsory process for obtaining witnesses in his favor, and to have the Assistance of Counsel for his defence.

AMENDMENT VII [1791]

In suits at common law, where the value in controversy shall exceed twenty dollars, the right of trial by jury shall be preserved, and no fact tried by a jury, shall be otherwise reexamined in any Court of the United States, than according to the rules of the common law.

AMENDMENT VIII [1791]

Excessive bail shall not be required, nor excessive fines imposed, nor cruel and unusual punishments inflicted.

AMENDMENT IX [1791]

The enumeration in the Constitution, of certain rights, shall not be construed to deny or disparage others retained by the people.

AMENDMENT X [1791]

The powers not delegated to the United States by the Constitution, nor prohibited by it to the States, are reserved to the States respectively, or to the people.

AMENDMENT XI [1798]

The Judicial power of the United States shall not be construed to extend to any suit in law or equity, commenced or prosecuted against one of the United States by Citizens of another State, or by Citizens or Subjects of any Foreign State.

AMENDMENT XII [1804]

The Electors shall meet in their respective States and vote by ballot for President and Vice-President, one of whom, at least, shall not be an inhabitant of the same State with themselves; they shall name in their ballots the person voted for as President, and in distinct ballots the person voted for as Vice-President, and they shall make distinct lists of all persons voted for as President, and of all persons voted for as Vice-President, and of the number of votes for each, which lists they shall sign and certify, and transmit sealed to the seat of the government of the United States, directed to the President of the Senate;—The President of the Senate shall, in the presence of the Senate and House of Representatives, open all the certificates and the votes shall then be counted;—The person having the greatest number of votes for President, shall be the President, if such number be a majority of the whole number of Electors appointed; and if no person have such majority, then from the persons having the highest numbers not exceeding three on the list of those voted for as President, the House of Representatives shall choose immediately, by ballot, the President. But in choosing the President, the votes shall be taken by states, the representation from each state having one vote; a quorum for this purpose shall consist of a member or members from two-thirds of the states, and a majority of all the states shall be necessary to a choice. And if the House of Representatives shall not choose a President whenever the right of choice shall devolve upon them, before the fourth day of March next following, then the Vice-President shall act as President, as in the case of the death or other constitutional disability of the President.—The person having the greatest number of votes as Vice-President, shall be the Vice-President, if such number be a majority of the whole number of Electors appointed, and if no person have a majority, then from the two highest numbers on the list, the Senate shall choose the Vice-President; a quorum for the purpose shall consist of two-thirds of the whole number of Senators, and a majority of the whole number shall be necessary to a choice. But no person constitutionally ineligible to the office of President shall be eligible to that of Vice-President of the United States.

AMENDMENT XIII [1865]

Section 1. Neither slavery nor involuntary servitude, except as a punishment for crime whereof the party shall have been duly convicted, shall exist within the United States, or any place subject to their jurisdiction.

Section 2. Congress shall have power to enforce this article by appropriate legislation.

AMENDMENT XIV [1868]

Section 1. All persons born or naturalized in the United States, and subject to the jurisdiction thereof, are citizens of the United States and of the State wherein they reside. No State shall make or enforce any law which shall abridge the privileges or immunities of citizens of the United States; nor shall any State deprive any person of life, liberty, or property, without due process of law; nor deny to any person within its jurisdiction the equal protection of the laws.

Section 2. Representatives shall be apportioned among the several States according to their respective numbers, counting the whole number of persons in each State, excluding Indians not taxed. But when the right to vote at any election for the choice of electors for President and Vice-President of the United States, Representatives in Congress, the Executive and Judicial officers of a State, or the members of the Legislature thereof, is denied to any of the male inhabitants of such State, being twenty-one years of age, and citizens of the United States, or in any way abridged, except for participation in rebellion, or other crime, the basis of representation therein shall be reduced in the proportion which the number of such male citizens shall bear to the whole number of male citizens twenty-one years of age in such State.

Section 3. No person shall be a Senator or Representative in Congress, or elector of President and Vice-President, or hold any office, civil or military, under the United States, or under any State, who, having previously taken an oath, as a member of Congress, or as an officer of the United States, or as a member of any State legislature, or as an executive or judicial officer of any State, to support the Constitution of the United States, shall have engaged in insurrection or rebellion against the same, or given aid or comfort to the enemies thereof. But Congress may by a vote of two-thirds of each House, remove such disability.

Section 4. The validity of the public debt of the United States, authorized by law, including debts incurred for payment of pensions and bounties for services in suppressing insurrection or rebellion, shall not be questioned. But neither the United States nor any State shall assume or pay any debt or obligation incurred in aid of insurrection or rebellion against the United States, or any claim for the loss or emancipation of any slave; but all such debts, obligations, and claims shall be held illegal and void.

Section 5. The Congress shall have the power to enforce, by appropriate legislation, the provisions of this article.

AMENDMENT XV [1870]

Section 1. The right of citizens of the United States to vote shall not be denied or abridged by the United States or by any State on account of race, color, or previous condition of servitude—

Section 2. The Congress shall have power to enforce this article by appropriate legislation.

AMENDMENT XVI [1913]

The Congress shall have power to lay and collect taxes on incomes, from whatever source derived, without apportionment among the several States, and without regard to any census or enumeration.

AMENDMENT XVII [1913]

The Senate of the United States shall be composed of two Senators from each State, elected by the people thereof, for six years; and each Senator shall have one vote. The electors in each State shall have the qualifications requisite for electors of the most numerous branch of the State legislatures.

When vacancies happen in the representation of any State in the Senate, the executive authority of such State shall issue writs of election to fill such vacancies: *Provided,* That the legislature of any State may empower the executive thereof to make temporary appointments until the people fill the vacancies by election as the legislature may direct.

This amendment shall not be so construed as to affect the election or term of any Senator chosen before it becomes valid as part of the Constitution.

AMENDMENT XVIII [1919]

Section 1. After one year from the ratification of this article the manufacture, sale, or transportation of intoxicating liquors within, the importation thereof into, or the exportation thereof from the United States and all territory subject to the jurisdiction thereof for beverage purposes is hereby prohibited.

Section 2. The Congress and the several States shall have concurrent power to enforce this article by appropriate legislation.

Section 3. This article shall be inoperative unless it shall have been ratified as an amendment to the Constitution by the legislatures of the several States, as provided in the Constitution, within seven years from the date of the submission hereof to the States by the Congress.

AMENDMENT XIX [1920]

The right of citizens of the United States to vote shall not be denied or abridged by the United States or by any State on account of sex.

Congress shall have power to enforce this article by appropriate legislation.

AMENDMENT XX [1933]

Section 1. The terms of the President and Vice-President shall end at noon on the 20th day of January, and the terms of Senators and Representatives at noon on the 3d day of January, of the years in which such terms would have ended if this article had not been ratified; and the terms of their successors shall then begin.

Section 2. The Congress shall assemble at least once in every year, and such meeting shall begin at noon on the 3d day of January, unless they shall by law appoint a different day.

Section 3. If, at the time fixed for the beginning of the term of the President, the President elect shall have died, the Vice-President elect shall become President. If a President shall not have been chosen before the time fixed for the beginning of his term, or if the President elect shall have failed to qualify, then the Vice-President elect shall act as President until a President shall have qualified; and the Congress may by law provide for the case wherein neither a President elect nor a Vice-President elect shall have qualified, declaring who shall then act as President, or the manner in which one who is to act shall be selected, and such person shall act accordingly until a President or Vice-President shall have qualified.

Section 4. The Congress may by law provide for the case of the death of any of the persons from whom the House of Representatives may choose a President whenever the right of choice shall have devolved upon them, and for the case of the death of any of the persons from whom the Senate may choose a Vice-President whenever the right of choice shall have devolved upon them.

Section 5. Sections 1 and 2 shall take effect on the 15th day of October following the ratification of this article.

Section 6. This article shall be inoperative unless it

shall have been ratified as an amendment to the Constitution by the legislatures of three-fourths of the several States within seven years from the date of its submission.

AMENDMENT XXI [1933]

Section 1. The eighteenth article of amendment to the Constitution of the United States is hereby repealed.

Section 2. The transportation or importation into any State, Territory, or possession of the United States for delivery or use therein of intoxicating liquors, in violation of the laws thereof, is hereby prohibited.

Section 3. This article shall be inoperative unless it shall have been ratified as an amendment to the Constitution by conventions in the several States, as provided in the Constitution, within seven years from the date of the submission hereof to the States by the Congress.

AMENDMENT XXII [1951]

No person shall be elected to the office of the President more than twice, and no person who has held the office of President, or acted as President, for more than two years of a term to which some other person was elected President shall be elected to the office of the President more than once.

But this Article shall not apply to any person holding the office of President when this Article was proposed by the Congress, and shall not prevent any person who may be holding the office of President, or acting as President, during the term within which this Article becomes operative from holding the office of President or acting as President during the remainder of such term.

AMENDMENT XXIII [1961]

Section 1. The District constituting the seat of Government of the United States shall appoint in such manner as the Congress may direct:

A number of electors of President and Vice President equal to the whole number of Senators and Representatives in Congress to which the District would be entitled if it were a State, but in no event more than the least populous State; they shall be in addition to those appointed by the States, but they shall be considered, for the purposes of the election of President and Vice President, to be electors appointed by a State; and they shall meet in the District and perform such duties as provided by the twelfth article of amendment.

Section 2. The Congress shall have power to enforce this article by appropriate legislation.

AMENDMENT XXIV [1964]

Section 1. The right of citizens of the United States to vote in any primary or other election for President or Vice President, for electors for President or Vice President, or for Senator or Representative in Congress, shall not be denied or abridged by the United States or any State by reason of failure to pay any poll tax or other tax.

Section 2. The Congress shall have the power to enforce this article by appropriate legislation.

AMENDMENT XXV [1967]

Section 1. In case of the removal of the President from office or his death or resignation, the Vice President shall become President.

Section 2. Whenever there is a vacancy in the office of the Vice President, the President shall nominate a Vice President who shall take the office upon confirmation by a majority vote of both houses of Congress.

Section 3. Whenever the President transmits to the President pro tempore of the Senate and the Speaker of the House of Representatives his written declaration that he is unable to discharge the powers and duties of his office, and until he transmits to them a written declaration to the contrary, such powers and duties shall be discharged by the Vice President as Acting President.

Section 4. Whenever the Vice President and a majority of either the principal officers of the executive departments, or of such other body as Congress may by law provide, transmit to the President pro tempore of the Senate and the Speaker of the House of Representatives their written declaration that the President is unable to discharge the powers and duties of his office, the Vice President shall immediately assume the powers and duties of the office as Acting President.

Thereafter, when the President transmits to the President pro tempore of the Senate and the Speaker of the House of Representatives his written declaration that no inability exists, he shall resume the powers and duties of his office unless the Vice President and a majority of either the principal officers of the executive departments, or of such other body as Congress may by law provide, transmit within four days to the President pro tempore of the Senate and the Speaker of the House of Representatives their written declaration that the President is unable to discharge the powers and duties of his office. Thereupon Congress shall decide the issue, assembling within 48 hours for that purpose if not in session. If the Congress, within 21 days after receipt of the latter written declaration, or, if Congress is not in session, within 21 days after Congress is required to assemble, determines by two-thirds vote of both houses that the President is unable to discharge the powers and duties of his office, the Vice President shall continue to discharge the same as Acting President; otherwise, the President shall resume the powers and duties of his office.

AMENDMENT XXVI [1971]

Section 1. The right of citizens of the United States, who are 18 years of age or older, to vote shall not be denied or abridged by the United States or any state on account of age.

Section 2. The Congress shall have the power to enforce this article by appropriate legislation.

Presidential Elections, 1789–1988

Year	Candidates	Party	Popular Vote*	Electoral Vote**
1789	**George Washington**			69
	John Adams			34
	Others			35
1792	**George Washington**			132
	John Adams			77
	George Clinton			50
	Others			5
1796	**John Adams**	Federalist		71
	Thomas Jefferson	Democratic Republican		68
	Thomas Pinckney	Federalist		59
	Aaron Burr	Democratic Republican		30
	Others			48
1800	**Thomas Jefferson**	Democratic Republican		73
	Aaron Burr	Democratic Republican		73
	John Adams	Federalist		65
	Charles C. Pinckney	Federalist		64
1804	**Thomas Jefferson**	Democratic Republican		162
	Charles C. Pinckney	Federalist		14
1808	**James Madison**	Democratic Republican		122
	Charles C. Pinckney	Federalist		47
	George Clinton	Independent Republican		6
1812	**James Madison**	Democratic Republican		128
	DeWitt Clinton	Federalist		89
1816	**James Monroe**	Democratic Republican		183
	Rufus King	Federalist		34
1820	**James Monroe**	Democratic Republican		231
	John Quincy Adams	Independent Republican		1
1824	**John Quincy Adams**	Democratic Republican	108,704 (30.5%)	84
	Andrew Jackson	Democratic Republican	153,544 (43.1%)	99
	Henry Clay	Democratic Republican	47,136 (13.2%)	37
	William H. Crawford	Democratic Republican	46,618 (13.1%)	41
1828	**Andrew Jackson**	Democratic	647,231 (56.0%)	178
	John Quincy Adams	National Republican	509,097 (44.0%)	83

* Because only the leading candidates are listed, popular vote percentages do not always total 100.
** The elections of 1800 and 1824, in which no candidate received an electoral vote majority, were decided in the House of Representatives.

Year	Candidates	Party	Popular Vote*	Electoral Vote**
1832	**Andrew Jackson**	Democratic	687,502 (55.0%)	219
	Henry Clay	National Republican	530,189 (42.4%)	49
	William Wirt	Anti-Masonic	33,108 (2.6%)	7
	John Floyd	National Republican		11
1836	**Martin Van Buren**	Democratic	761,549 (50.9%)	170
	William H. Harrison	Whig	549,567 (36.7%)	73
	Hugh L. White	Whig	145,396 (9.7%)	26
	Daniel Webster	Whig	41,287 (2.7%)	14
1840	**William H. Harrison** (**John Tyler,** 1841)	Whig	1,275,017 (53.1%)	234
	Martin Van Buren	Democratic	1,128,702 (46.9%)	60
1844	**James K. Polk**	Democratic	1,337,243 (49.6%)	170
	Henry Clay	Whig	1,299,068 (48.1%)	105
	James G. Birney	Liberty	62,300 (2.3%)	
1848	**Zachary Taylor** (**Millard Fillmore,** 1850)	Whig	1,360,101 (47.4%)	163
	Lewis Cass	Democratic	1,220,544 (42.5%)	127
	Martin Van Buren	Free Soil	291,263 (10.1%)	
1852	**Franklin Pierce**	Democratic	1,601,474 (50.9%)	254
	Winfield Scott	Whig	1,386,578 (44.1%)	42
1856	**James Buchanan**	Democratic	1,838,169 (45.4%)	174
	John C. Frémont	Republican	1,335,264 (33.0%)	114
	Millard Fillmore	American	874,534 (21.6%)	8
1860	**Abraham Lincoln**	Republican	1,865,593 (39.8%)	180
	Stephen A. Douglas	Democratic	1,382,713 (29.5%)	12
	John C. Breckinridge	Democratic	848,356 (18.1%)	72
	John Bell	Constitutional Union	592,906 (12.6%)	39
1864	**Abraham Lincoln** (**Andrew Johnson,** 1865)	Republican	2,206,938 (55.0%)	212
	George B. McClellan	Democratic	1,803,787 (45.0%)	21
1868	**Ulysses S. Grant**	Republican	3,013,421 (52.7%)	214
	Horatio Seymour	Democratic	2,706,829 (47.3%)	80
1872	**Ulysses S. Grant**	Republican	3,596,745 (55.6%)	286
	Horace Greeley	Democratic	2,843,446 (43.9%)	66
1876	**Rutherford B. Hayes**	Republican	4,036,572 (48.0%)	185
	Samuel J. Tilden	Democratic	4,284,020 (51.0%)	184
1880	**James A. Garfield** (**Chester A. Arthur,** 1881)	Republican	4,449,053 (48.3%)	214
	Winfield S. Hancock	Democratic	4,442,035 (48.2%)	155
	James B. Weaver	Greenback Labor	308,578 (3.4%)	
1884	**Grover Cleveland**	Democratic	4,874,986 (48.5%)	219
	James G. Blaine	Republican	4,851,981 (48.2%)	182
	Benjamin F. Butler	Greenback Labor	175,370 (1.8%)	

Year	Candidates	Party	Popular Vote*	Electoral Vote**
1888	**Benjamin Harrison**	Republican	5,444,337 (47.8%)	233
	Grover Cleveland	Democratic	5,540,050 (48.6%)	168
1892	**Grover Cleveland**	Democratic	5,554,414 (46.0%)	277
	Benjamin Harrison	Republican	5,190,802 (43.0%)	145
	James B. Weaver	People's	1,027,329 (8.5%)	22
1896	**William McKinley**	Republican	7,035,638 (50.8%)	271
	William Jennings Bryan	Democratic; Populist	6,467,946 (46.7%)	176
1900	**William McKinley** (**Theodore Roosevelt,** 1901)	Republican	7,219,530 (51.7%)	292
	William Jennings Bryan	Democratic; Populist	6,356,734 (45.5%)	155
1904	**Theodore Roosevelt**	Republican	7,628,834 (56.4%)	336
	Alton B. Parker	Democratic	5,084,401 (37.6%)	140
	Eugene V. Debs	Socialist	402,460 (3.0%)	
1908	**William H. Taft**	Republican	7,679,006 (51.6%)	321
	William Jennings Bryan	Democratic	6,409,106 (43.1%)	162
	Eugene V. Debs	Socialist	420,820 (2.8%)	
1912	**Woodrow Wilson**	Democratic	6,286,820 (41.8%)	435
	Theodore Roosevelt	Progressive	4,126,020 (27.4%)	88
	William H. Taft	Republican	3,483,922 (23.2%)	8
	Eugene V. Debs	Socialist	897,011 (6.0%)	
1916	**Woodrow Wilson**	Democratic	9,129,606 (49.3%)	277
	Charles E. Hughes	Republican	8,538,221 (46.1%)	254
1920	**Warren G. Harding** (**Calvin Coolidge,** 1923)	Republican	16,152,200 (61.0%)	404
	James M. Cox	Democratic	9,147,353 (34.6%)	127
	Eugene V. Debs	Socialist	919,799 (3.5%)	
1924	**Calvin Coolidge**	Republican	15,725,016 (54.1%)	382
	John W. Davis	Democratic	8,385,586 (28.8%)	136
	Robert M. La Follette	Progressive	4,822,856 (16.6%)	13
1928	**Herbert C. Hoover**	Republican	21,392,190 (58.2%)	444
	Alfred E. Smith	Democratic	15,016,443 (40.8%)	87
1932	**Franklin D. Roosevelt**	Democratic	22,809,638 (57.3%)	472
	Herbert C. Hoover	Republican	15,758,901 (39.6%)	59
	Norman Thomas	Socialist	881,951 (2.2%)	
1936	**Franklin D. Roosevelt**	Democratic	27,751,612 (60.7%)	523
	Alfred M. Landon	Republican	16,681,913 (36.4%)	8
	William Lemke	Union	891,858 (1.9%)	
1940	**Franklin D. Roosevelt**	Democratic	27,243,466 (54.7%)	449
	Wendell L. Willkie	Republican	22,304,755 (44.8%)	82
1944	**Franklin D. Roosevelt** (**Harry S Truman,** 1945)	Democratic	25,602,505 (52.8%)	432
	Thomas E. Dewey	Republican	22,006,278 (44.5%)	99

Year	Candidates	Party	Popular Vote*	Electoral Vote**
1948	**Harry S Truman**	Democratic	24,105,812 (49.5%)	303
	Thomas E. Dewey	Republican	21,970,065 (45.1%)	189
	J. Strom Thurmond	States' Rights	1,169,063 (2.4%)	39
	Henry A. Wallace	Progressive	1,157,172 (2.4%)	
1952	**Dwight D. Eisenhower**	Republican	33,936,234 (55.2%)	442
	Adlai E. Stevenson	Democratic	27,314,992 (44.5%)	89
1956	**Dwight D. Eisenhower**	Republican	35,590,472 (57.4%)	457
	Adlai E. Stevenson	Democratic	26,022,752 (42.0%)	73
1960	**John F. Kennedy** **(Lyndon B. Johnson,** 1963)	Democratic	34,227,096 (49.9%)	303
	Richard M. Nixon	Republican	34,108,546 (49.6%)	219
1964	**Lyndon B. Johnson**	Democratic	43,126,233 (61.1%)	486
	Barry M. Goldwater	Republican	27,174,989 (38.5%)	52
1968	**Richard M. Nixon**	Republican	31,783,783 (43.4%)	301
	Hubert H. Humphrey	Democratic	31,271,839 (42.7%)	191
	George C. Wallace	Amer. Independent	9,899,557 (13.5%)	46
1972	**Richard M. Nixon** **(Gerald R. Ford,** 1974)	Republican	45,767,218 (60.6%)	520
	George S. McGovern	Democratic	28,357,668 (37.5%)	17
1976	**Jimmy Carter**	Democratic	40,828,657 (50.6%)	297
	Gerald R. Ford	Republican	39,145,520 (48.4%)	240
1980	**Ronald Reagan**	Republican	43,899,248 (51%)	489
	Jimmy Carter	Democratic	36,481,435 (41%)	49
	John B. Anderson	Independent	5,719,437 (6%)	
1984	**Ronald Reagan**	Republican	54,455,075 (59%)	525
	Walter F. Mondale	Democratic	37,577,185 (41%)	13
1988	**George Bush**	Republican	48,881,221 (54%)	426
	Michael Dukakis	Democratic	41,805,422 (46%)	111

Vice-Presidents and Cabinet Members, by Administration

Washington, 1789–1797

Vice-President	John Adams	1789–1797
Secretary of State	Thomas Jefferson	1789–1793
	Edmund Randolph	1794–1795
	Timothy Pickering	1795–1797
Secretary of War	Henry Knox	1789–1794
	Timothy Pickering	1795–1796
	James McHenry	1796–1797
Secretary of Treasury	Alexander Hamilton	1789–1795
	Oliver Wolcott, Jr.	1795–1797
Postmaster General	Samuel Osgood	1789–1791
	Timothy Pickering	1791–1794
	Joseph Habersham	1795–1797
Attorney General	Edmund Randolph	1789–1793
	William Bradford	1794–1795
	Charles Lee	1795–1797

John Adams, 1797–1801

Vice-President	Thomas Jefferson	1797–1801
Secretary of State	Timothy Pickering	1797–1800
	John Marshall	1800–1801
Secretary of War	James McHenry	1797–1800
	Samuel Dexter	1800–1801
Secretary of Treasury	Oliver Wolcott, Jr.	1797–1800
	Samuel Dexter	1800–1801
Postmaster General	Joseph Habersham	1797–1801
Attorney General	Charles Lee	1797–1801
Secretary of Navy	Benjamin Stoddert	1798–1801

Jefferson, 1801–1809

Vice-President	Aaron Burr	1801–1805
	George Clinton	1805–1809
Secretary of State	James Madison	1801–1809
Secretary of War	Henry Dearborn	1801–1809
Secretary of Treasury	Samuel Dexter	1801
	Albert Gallatin	1801–1809
Postmaster General	Joseph Habersham	1801
	Gideon Granger	1801–1809
Attorney General	Levi Lincoln	1801–1805
	Robert Smith	1805
	John C. Breckinridge	1805–1806
	Caesar A. Rodney	1807–1809
Secretary of Navy	Robert Smith	1801–1809

Madison, 1809–1817

Vice-President	George Clinton	1809–1813
	Elbridge Gerry	1813–1817
Secretary of State	Robert Smith	1809–1811
	James Monroe	1811–1817
Secretary of War	William Eustis	1809–1812
	John Armstrong	1813–1814
	James Monroe	1814–1815
	William H. Crawford	1815–1817
Secretary of Treasury	Albert Gallatin	1809–1813
	George W. Campbell	1814
	Alexander J. Dallas	1814–1816
	William H. Crawford	1816–1817
Postmaster General	Gideon Granger	1809–1814
	Return J. Meigs, Jr.	1814–1817
Attorney General	Caesar A. Rodney	1809–1811
	William Pinkney	1811–1814
	Richard Rush	1814–1817
Secretary of Navy	Paul Hamilton	1809–1813
	William Jones	1813–1814
	Benjamin W. Crowninshield	1814–1817

Monroe, 1817–1825

Vice-President	Daniel D. Tompkins	1817–1825
Secretary of State	John Quincy Adams	1817–1825
Secretary of War	George Graham	1817
	John C. Calhoun	1817–1825
Secretary of Treasury	William H. Crawford	1817–1825

Monroe, 1817–1825 (continued)

Postmaster General	Return J. Meigs, Jr.	1817–1823
	John McLean	1823–1825
Attorney General	Richard Rush	1817
	William Wirt	1817–1825
Secretary of Navy	Benjamin W. Crowninshield	1817–1818
	Smith Thompson	1818–1823
	Samuel L. Southard	1823–1825

John Quincy Adams, 1825–1829

Vice-President	John C. Calhoun	1825–1829
Secretary of State	Henry Clay	1825–1829
Secretary of War	James Barbour	1825–1828
	Peter B. Porter	1828–1829
Secretary of Treasury	Richard Rush	1825–1829
Postmaster General	John McLean	1825–1829
Attorney General	William Wirt	1825–1829
Secretary of Navy	Samuel L. Southard	1825–1829

Jackson, 1829–1837

Vice-President	John C. Calhoun	1829–1832
	Martin Van Buren	1833–1837
Secretary of State	Martin Van Buren	1829–1831
	Edward Livingston	1831–1833
	Louis McLane	1833–1834
	John Forsyth	1834–1837
Secretary of War	John H. Eaton	1829–1831
	Lewis Cass	1831–1837
	Benjamin Butler	1837
Secretary of Treasury	Samuel D. Ingham	1829–1831
	Louis McLane	1831–1833
	William J. Duane	1833
	Roger B. Taney	1833–1834
	Levi Woodbury	1834–1837
Postmaster General	William T. Barry	1829–1835
	Amos Kendall	1835–1837
Attorney General	John M. Berrien	1829–1831
	Roger B. Taney	1831–1833
	Benjamin F. Butler	1833–1837
Secretary of Navy	John Branch	1829–1831
	Levi Woodbury	1831–1834
	Mahlon Dickerson	1834–1837

Van Buren, 1837–1841

Vice-President	Richard M. Johnson	1837–1841
Secretary of State	John Forsyth	1837–1841
Secretary of War	Joel R. Poinsett	1837–1841
Secretary of Treasury	Levi Woodbury	1837–1841
Postmaster General	Amos Kendall	1837–1840
	John M. Niles	1840–1841
Attorney General	Benjamin F. Butler	1837–1838
	Felix Grundy	1838–1840
	Henry D. Gilpin	1840–1841
Secretary of Navy	Mahlon Dickerson	1837–1838
	James K. Paulding	1838–1841

William Harrison, 1841

Vice-President	John Tyler	1841
Secretary of State	Daniel Webster	1841
Secretary of War	John Bell	1841
Secretary of Treasury	Thomas Ewing	1841
Postmaster General	Francis Granger	1841
Attorney General	John J. Crittenden	1841
Secretary of Navy	George E. Badger	1841

Tyler, 1841–1845

Vice-President	None	
Secretary of State	Daniel Webster	1841–1843
	Hugh S. Legaré	1843
	Abel P. Upshur	1843–1844
	John C. Calhoun	1844–1845
Secretary of War	John Bell	1841
	John C. Spencer	1841–1843
	John M. Porter	1843–1844
	William Wilkins	1844–1845
Secretary of Treasury	Thomas Ewing	1841
	Walter Forward	1841–1843
	John C. Spencer	1843–1844
	George M. Bibb	1844–1845
Postmaster General	Francis Granger	1841
	Charles A. Wickliffe	1841
Attorney General	John J. Crittenden	1841
	Hugh S. Legaré	1841–1843
	John Nelson	1843–1845

Secretary of Navy	George Badger	1841
	Abel P. Upshur	1841
	David Henshaw	1843–1844
	Thomas W. Gilmer	1844
	John Y. Mason	1844–1845

Polk, 1845–1849

Vice- President	George M. Dallas	1845–1849
Secretary of State	James Buchanan	1845–1849
Secretary of War	William L. Marcy	1845–1849
Secretary of Treasury	Robert J. Walker	1845–1849
Postmaster General	Cave Johnson	1845–1849
Attorney General	John Y. Mason	1845–1846
	Nathan Clifford	1846–1848
	Isaac Toucey	1848–1849
Secretary of Navy	George Bancroft	1845–1846
	John Y. Mason	1846–1849

Taylor, 1849–1850

Vice- President	Millard Fillmore	1849–1850
Secretary of State	John M. Clayton	1849–1850
Secretary of War	George W. Crawford	1849–1850
Secretary of Treasury	William M. Meredith	1849–1850
Postmaster General	Jacob Collamer	1849–1850
Attorney General	Reverdy Johnson	1849–1850
Secretary of Navy	William Preston	1849–1850
Secretary of Interior	Thomas Ewing	1849–1850

Fillmore, 1850–1853

Vice- President	None	
Secretary of State	Daniel Webster	1850–1852
	Edward Everett	1852–1853
Secretary of War	Charles M. Conrad	1850–1853
Secretary of Treasury	Thomas Corwin	1850–1853
Postmaster General	Nathan K. Hall	1850–1852
	Sam D. Hubbard	1852–1853

Attorney General	John J. Crittenden	1850–1853
Secretary of Navy	William A. Graham	1850–1852
	John P. Kennedy	1852–1853
Secretary of Interior	Thomas M. T. McKennan	1850
	Alexander H. H. Stuart	1850–1853

Pierce, 1853–1857

Vice- President	William R. King	1853
Secretary of State	William L. Marcy	1853–1857
Secretary of War	Jefferson Davis	1853–1857
Secretary of Treasury	James Guthrie	1853–1857
Postmaster General	James Campbell	1853–1857
Attorney General	Caleb Cushing	1853–1857
Secretary of Navy	James C. Dobbins	1853–1857
Secretary of Interior	Robert McClelland	1853–1857

Buchanan, 1857–1861

Vice- President	John C. Breckinridge	1857–1861
Secretary of State	Lewis Cass	1857–1860
	Jeremiah S. Black	1860–1861
Secretary of War	John B. Floyd	1857–1861
	Joseph Holt	1861
Secretary of Treasury	Howell Cobb	1857–1860
	Philip F. Thomas	1860–1861
	John A. Dix	1861
Postmaster General	Aaron V. Brown	1857–1859
	Joseph Holt	1859–1861
	Horatio King	1861
Attorney General	Jeremiah S. Black	1857–1860
	Edwin M. Stanton	1860–1861
Secretary of Navy	Isaac Toucey	1857–1861
Secretary of Interior	Jacob Thompson	1857–1861

Lincoln, 1861–1865

Vice- President	Hannibal Hamlin	1861–1865
	Andrew Johnson	1865
Secretary of State	William H. Seward	1861–1865

Lincoln, 1861–1865 (continued)

Secretary of War	Simon Cameron	1861–1862
	Edwin M. Stanton	1862–1865
Secretary of Treasury	Samuel P. Chase	1861–1864
	William P. Fessenden	1864–1865
	Hugh McCulloch	1865
Postmaster General	Horatio King	1861
	Montgomery Blair	1861–1864
	William Dennison	1864–1865
Attorney General	Edward Bates	1861–1864
	James Speed	1864–1865
Secretary of Navy	Gideon Welles	1861–1865
Secretary of Interior	Caleb B. Smith	1861–1863
	John P. Usher	1863–1865

Andrew Johnson, 1865–1869

Vice-President	None	
Secretary of State	William H. Seward	1865–1869
Secretary of War	Edwin M. Stanton	1865–1867
	Ulysses S. Grant	1867–1868
	John M. Schofield	1868–1869
Secretary of Treasury	Hugh McCulloch	1865–1869
Postmaster General	William Dennison	1865–1866
	Alexander W. Randall	1866–1869
Attorney General	James Speed	1865–1866
	Henry Stanbery	1866–1868
	William M. Evarts	1868–1869
Secretary of Navy	Gideon Welles	1865–1869
Secretary of Interior	John P. Usher	1865
	James Harlan	1865–1866
	Orville H. Browning	1866–1869

Grant, 1869–1877

Vice-President	Schuyler Colfax	1869–1873
	Henry Wilson	1873–1875
Secretary of State	Elihu B. Washburne	1869
	Hamilton Fish	1869–1877
Secretary of War	John A. Rawlins	1869
	William T. Sherman	1869
	William W. Belknap	1869–1876
	Alphonso Taft	1876
	James D. Cameron	1876–1877
Secretary of Treasury	George S. Boutwell	1869–1873
	William A. Richardson	1873–1874
	Benjamin H. Bristow	1874–1876
	Lot M. Morrill	1876–1877

Postmaster General	John A. J. Creswell	1869–1874
	James W. Marshall	1874
	Marshall Jewell	1874–1876
	James N. Tyner	1876–1877
Attorney General	Ebenezer R. Hoar	1869–1870
	Amos T. Ackerman	1870–1871
	G. H. Williams	1871–1875
	Edwards Pierrepont	1875–1876
	Alphonso Taft	1876–1877
Secretary of Navy	Adolph E. Borie	1869
	George Robeson	1869–1877
Secretary of Interior	Jacob D. Cox	1869–1870
	Columbus Delano	1870–1875
	Zachariah Chandler	1875–1877

Hayes, 1877–1881

Vice-President	William A. Wheeler	1877–1881
Secretary of State	William B. Evarts	1877–1881
Secretary of War	George W. McCrary	1877–1879
	Alexander Ramsey	1879–1881
Secretary of Treasury	John Sherman	1877–1881
Postmaster General	David M. Key	1877–1880
	Horace Maynard	1880–1881
Attorney General	Charles Devens	1877–1881
Secretary of Navy	Richard W. Thompson	1877–1880
	Nathan Goff, Jr.	1881
Secretary of Interior	Carl Schurz	1877–1881

Garfield, 1881

Vice-President	Chester A. Arthur	1881
Secretary of State	James G. Blaine	1881
Secretary of War	Robert T. Lincoln	1881
Secretary of Treasury	William Windom	1881
Postmaster General	Thomas L. James	1881
Attorney General	Wayne MacVeagh	1881
Secretary of Navy	William H. Hunt	1881
Secretary of Interior	Samuel J. Kirkwood	1881

Arthur, 1881–1885

Vice-President	None	
Secretary of State	Frederick T. Frelinghuysen	1881–1885
Secretary of War	Robert T. Lincoln	1881–1885
Secretary of Treasury	Charles J. Folger	1881–1884
	Walter Q. Gresham	1884
	Hugh McCulloch	1884–1885
Postmaster General	Timothy O. Howe	1881–1883
	Walter Q. Gresham	1883–1884
	Frank Hatton	1884–1885
Attorney General	Benjamin H. Brewster	1881–1885
Secretary of Navy	William H. Hunt	1881–1882
	William E. Chandler	1882–1885
Secretary of Interior	Samuel J. Kirkwood	1881–1882
	Henry M. Teller	1882–1885

Cleveland, 1885–1889

Vice-President	Thomas A. Hendricks	1885
Secretary of State	Thomas F. Bayard	1885–1889
Secretary of War	William C. Endicott	1885–1889
Secretary of Treasury	Daniel Manning	1885–1887
	Charles S. Fairchild	1887–1889
Postmaster General	William F. Vilas	1885–1888
	Don M. Dickinson	1888–1889
Attorney General	Augustus H. Garland	1885–1889
Secretary of Navy	William C. Whitney	1885–1889
Secretary of Interior	Lucius Q. C. Lamar	1885–1888
	William F. Vilas	1888–1889
Secretary of Agriculture	Norman J. Colman	1889

Benjamin Harrison, 1889–1893

Vice-President	Levi P. Morton	1889–1893
Secretary of State	James G. Blaine	1889–1892
	John W. Foster	1892–1893
Secretary of War	Redfield Proctor	1889–1891
	Stephen B. Elkins	1891–1893
Secretary of Treasury	William Windom	1889–1891
	Charles Foster	1891–1893
Postmaster General	John Wanamaker	1889–1893
Attorney General	William H. H. Miller	1889–1891
Secretary of Navy	Benjamin F. Tracy	1889–1893
Secretary of Interior	John W. Noble	1889–1893
Secretary of Agriculture	Jeremiah M. Rusk	1889–1893

Cleveland, 1893–1897

Vice-President	Adlai E. Stevenson	1893–1897
Secretary of State	Walter Q. Gresham	1893–1895
	Richard Olney	1895–1897
Secretary of War	Daniel S. Lamont	1893–1897
Secretary of Treasury	John G. Carlisle	1893–1897
Postmaster General	Wilson S. Bissell	1893–1895
	William L. Wilson	1895–1897
Attorney General	Richard Olney	1893–1895
	Judson Harmon	1895–1897
Secretary of Navy	Hilary A. Herbert	1893–1897
Secretary of Interior	Hoke Smith	1893–1896
	David R. Francis	1896–1897
Secretary of Agriculture	Julius Sterling Morton	1893–1897

McKinley, 1897–1901

Vice-President	Garret Hobart	1897–1899
	Theodore Roosevelt	1901
Secretary of State	John Sherman	1897–1898
	William R. Day	1898
	John M. Hay	1898–1901
Secretary of War	Russell A. Alger	1897–1899
	Elihu Root	1899–1901
Secretary of Treasury	Lyman J. Gage	1897–1901
Postmaster General	James A. Gary	1897–1898
	Charles E. Smith	1898–1901
Attorney General	Joseph McKenna	1897–1898
	John W. Griggs	1898–1901
	Philander C. Knox	1901
Secretary of Navy	John D. Long	1897–1901
Secretary of Interior	Cornelius N. Bliss	1897–1899
	Ethan A. Hitchcock	1899–1901
Secretary of Agriculture	James Wilson	1897–1901

Theodore Roosevelt, 1901–1909

Vice-President	Charles Warren Fairbanks	1905–1909
Secretary of State	John M. Hay	1901–1905
	Elihu Root	1905–1909
	Robert Bacon	1909
Secretary of War	Elihu Root	1901–1904
	William Howard Taft	1904–1908
	Luke E. Wright	1908–1909
Secretary of Treasury	Lyman J. Gage	1901–1902
	Leslie M. Shaw	1902–1907
	George B. Cortelyou	1907–1909
Postmaster General	Charles Emory Smith	1901–1902
	Henry C. Payne	1902–1904
	Robert J. Wynne	1904–1905
	George B. Cortelyou	1905–1907
	George von L. Meyer	1907–1909
Attorney General	Philander C. Knox	1901–1904
	William H. Moody	1904–1906
	Charles J. Bonaparte	1906–1909
Secretary of Navy	John D. Long	1901–1902
	William H. Moody	1902–1904
	Paul Morton	1904–1905
	Charles J. Bonaparte	1905–1906
	Victor H. Metcalf	1906–1908
	Truman H. Newberry	1908–1909
Secretary of Interior	Ethan A. Hitchcock	1901–1907
	James R. Garfield	1907–1909
Secretary of Agriculture	James Wilson	1901–1909
Secretary of Labor and Commerce	George B. Cortelyou	1903–1904
	Victor H. Metcalf	1904–1906
	Oscar S. Straus	1906–1909

Taft, 1909–1913

Vice-President	James S. Sherman	1909–1912
Secretary of State	Philander C. Knox	1909–1913
Secretary of War	Jacob M. Dickinson	1909–1911
	Henry L. Stimson	1911–1913
Secretary of Treasury	Franklin MacVeagh	1909–1913
Postmaster General	Frank H. Hitchcock	1909–1913
Attorney General	George W. Wickersham	1909–1913
Secretary of Navy	George von L. Meyer	1909–1913
Secretary of Interior	Richard A. Ballinger	1909–1911
	Walter Lowrie Fisher	1911–1913
Secretary of Agriculture	James Wilson	1909–1913
Secretary of Labor and Commerce	Oscar S. Straus	1909
	Charles Nagel	1909–1913

Wilson, 1913–1921

Vice-President	Thomas R. Marshall	1913–1921
Secretary of State	William Jennings Bryan	1913–1915
	Robert Lansing	1915–1920
	Bainbridge Colby	1920–1921
Secretary of War	Lindley M. Garrison	1913–1916
	Newton D. Baker	1916–1921
Secretary of Treasury	William Gilbert McAdoo	1913–1918
	Carter Glass	1918–1920
	David F. Houston	1920–1921
Postmaster General	Albert Sidney Burleson	1913–1921
Attorney General	James Clark McReynolds	1913–1914
	Thomas Watt Gregory	1914–1919
	A. Mitchell Palmer	1919–1921
Secretary of Navy	Josephus Daniels	1913–1921
Secretary of Interior	Franklin Knight Lane	1913–1920
	John Barton Payne	1920–1921
Secretary of Agriculture	David F. Houston	1913–1920
	Edwin T. Meredith	1920–1921
Secretary of Commerce	William C. Redfield	1913–1919
Secretary of Labor	William Bauchop Wilson	1913–1921

Harding, 1921–1923

Vice-President	Calvin Coolidge	1921–1923
Secretary of State	Charles Evans Hughes	1921–1923
Secretary of War	John W. Weeks	1921–1923
Secretary of Treasury	Andrew W. Mellon	1921–1923
Postmaster General	Will H. Hays	1921–1922
	Hubert Work	1922–1923
	Harry S. New	1923
Attorney General	Harry M. Daugherty	1921–1923
Secretary of Navy	Edwin Denby	1921–1923
Secretary of Interior	Albert B. Fall	1921–1923
	Hubert Work	1923
Secretary of Agriculture	Henry C. Wallace	1921–1923
Secretary of Commerce	Herbert C. Hoover	1921–1923
Secretary of Labor	James J. Davis	1921–1923

Coolidge, 1923–1929

Vice-President	Charles G. Dawes	1925–1929
Secretary of State	Charles Evans Hughes	1923–1925
	Frank B. Kellogg	1925–1929
Secretary of War	John W. Weeks	1923–1925
	Dwight F. Davis	1925–1929
Secretary of Treasury	Andrew W. Mellon	1923–1929
Postmaster General	Harry S. New	1923–1929
Attorney General	Harry M. Daugherty	1923–1924
	Harlan Fiske Stone	1924–1925
	John G. Sargent	1925–1929
Secretary of Navy	Edwin Derby	1923–1924
	Curtis D. Wilbur	1924–1929
Secretary of Interior	Hubert Work	1923–1928
	Roy O. West	1928–1929
Secretary of Agriculture	Henry C. Wallace	1923–1924
	Howard M. Gore	1924–1925
	William M. Jardine	1925–1929
Secretary of Commerce	Herbert C. Hoover	1923–1928
	William F. Whiting	1928–1929
Secretary of Labor	James J. Davis	1923–1929

Hoover, 1929–1933

Vice-President	Charles Curtis	1929–1933
Secretary of State	Henry L. Stimson	1929–1933
Secretary of War	James W. Good	1929
	Patrick J. Hurley	1929–1933
Secretary of Treasury	Andrew W. Mellon	1929–1932
	Ogden L. Mills	1932–1933
Postmaster General	Walter F. Brown	1929–1933
Attorney General	William D. Mitchell	1929–1933
Secretary of Navy	Charles F. Adams	1929–1933
Secretary of Interior	Ray L. Wilbur	1929–1933
Secretary of Agriculture	Arthur M. Hyde	1929–1933
Secretary of Commerce	Robert P. Lamont	1929–1932
	Roy D. Chapin	1932–1933
Secretary of Labor	James J. Davis	1929–1930
	William N. Doak	1930–1933

Franklin D. Roosevelt, 1933–1945

Vice-President	John Nance Garner	1933–1941
	Henry A. Wallace	1941–1945
	Harry S Truman	1945
Secretary of State	Cordell Hull	1933–1944
	Edward R. Stettinius, Jr.	1944–1945
Secretary of War	George H. Dern	1933–1936
	Henry A. Woodring	1936–1940
	Henry L. Stimson	1940–1945
Secretary of Treasury	William H. Woodin	1933–1934
	Henry Morgenthau, Jr.	1934–1945
Postmaster General	James A. Farley	1933–1940
	Frank C. Walker	1940–1945
Attorney General	Homer S. Cummings	1933–1939
	Frank Murphy	1939–1940
	Robert H. Jackson	1940–1941
	Francis Biddle	1941–1945
Secretary of Navy	Claude A. Swanson	1933–1940
	Charles Edison	1940
	Frank Knox	1940–1944
	James V. Forrestal	1944–1945
Secretary of Interior	Harold L. Ickes	1933–1945
Secretary of Agriculture	Henry A. Wallace	1933–1940
	Claude R. Wickard	1940–1945
Secretary of Commerce	Daniel C. Roper	1933–1939
	Harry L. Hopkins	1939–1940
	Jesse H. Jones	1940–1945
	Henry A. Wallace	1945
Secretary of Labor	Frances Perkins	1933–1945

Truman, 1945–1953

Vice-President	Alben W. Barkley	1949–1953
Secretary of State	Edward R. Stettinius, Jr.	1945
	James F. Byrnes	1945–1947
	George C. Marshall	1947–1949
	Dean G. Acheson	1949–1953
Secretary of War	Robert P. Patterson	1945–1947
	Kenneth C. Royall	1947
Secretary of Treasury	Fred M. Vinson	1945–1946
	John W. Snyder	1946–1953
Postmaster General	Frank C. Walker	1945
	Robert E. Hannegan	1945–1947
	Jesse M. Donaldson	1947–1953
Attorney General	Tom C. Clark	1945–1949
	J. Howard McGrath	1949–1952
	James P. McGranery	1952–1953
Secretary of Navy	James V. Forrestal	1945–1947
Secretary of Interior	Harold L. Ickes	1945–1946
	Julius A. Krug	1946–1949
	Oscar L. Chapman	1949–1953

Truman, 1945–1953 (continued)

Secretary of Agriculture	Clinton P. Anderson	1945–1948
	Charles F. Brannan	1948–1953
Secretary of Commerce	Henry A. Wallace	1945–1946
	W. Averell Harriman	1946–1948
	Charles W. Sawyer	1948–1953
Secretary of Labor	Lewis B. Schwellenbach	1945–1948
	Maurice J. Tobin	1948–1953
Secretary of Defense	James V. Forrestal	1947–1949
	Louis A. Johnson	1949–1950
	George C. Marshall	1950–1951
	Robert A. Lovett	1951–1953

Eisenhower, 1953–1961

Vice-President	Richard M. Nixon	1953–1961
Secretary of State	John Foster Dulles	1953–1959
	Christian A. Herter	1959–1961
Secretary of Treasury	George M. Humphrey	1953–1957
	Robert B. Anderson	1957–1961
Postmaster General	Arthur E. Summerfield	1953–1961
Attorney General	Herbert Brownell, Jr.	1953–1958
	William P. Rogers	1958–1961
Secretary of Interior	Douglas McKay	1953–1956
	Fred A. Seaton	1956–1961
Secretary of Agriculture	Ezra Taft Benson	1953–1961
Secretary of Commerce	Sinclair Weeks	1953–1958
	Lewis L. Strauss	1958–1959
	Frederick H. Mueller	1959–1961
Secretary of Labor	Martin P. Durkin	1953
	James P. Mitchell	1953–1961
Secretary of Defense	Charles E. Wilson	1953–1957
	Neil H. McElroy	1957–1959
	Thomas S. Gates, Jr.	1959–1961
Secretary of Health, Education, and Welfare	Oveta Culp Hobby	1953–1955
	Marion B. Folsom	1955–1958
	Arthur S. Flemming	1958–1961

Kennedy, 1961–1963

Vice-President	Lyndon B. Johnson	1961–1963
Secretary of State	Dean Rusk	1961–1963
Secretary of Treasury	C. Douglas Dillon	1961–1963
Postmaster General	J. Edward Day	1961–1963
	John A. Gronouski	1963
Attorney General	Robert F. Kennedy	1961–1963
Secretary of Interior	Stewart L. Udall	1961–1963
Secretary of Agriculture	Orville L. Freeman	1961–1963
Secretary of Commerce	Luther H. Hodges	1961–1963
Secretary of Labor	Arthur J. Goldberg	1961–1962
	W. Willard Wirtz	1962–1963
Secretary of Defense	Robert S. McNamara	1961–1963
Secretary of Health, Education, and Welfare	Abraham A. Ribicoff	1961–1962
	Anthony J. Celebrezze	1962–1963

Lyndon Johnson, 1963–1969

Vice-President	Hubert H. Humphrey	1965–1969
Secretary of State	Dean Rusk	1963–1969
Secretary of Treasury	C. Douglas Dillon	1963–1965
	Henry H. Fowler	1965–1969
Postmaster General	John A. Gronouski	1963–1965
	Lawrence F. O'Brien	1965–1968
	Marvin Watson	1968–1969
Attorney General	Robert F. Kennedy	1963–1964
	Nicholas Katzenbach	1965–1966
	Ramsey Clark	1967–1969
Secretary of Interior	Stewart L. Udall	1963–1969
Secretary of Agriculture	Orville L. Freeman	1963–1969
Secretary of Commerce	Luther H. Hodges	1963–1964
	John T. Connor	1964–1967
	Alexander B. Trowbridge	1967–1968
	Cyrus R. Smith	1968–1969
Secretary of Labor	W. Willard Wirtz	1963–1969
Secretary of Defense	Robert F. McNamara	1963–1968
	Clark Clifford	1968–1969
Secretary of Health, Education, and Welfare	Anthony J. Celebrezze	1963–1965
	John W. Gardner	1965–1968
	Wilbur J. Cohen	1968–1969
Secretary of Housing and Urban Development	Robert C. Weaver	1966–1969
	Robert C. Wood	1969
Secretary of Transportation	Alan S. Boyd	1967–1969

Nixon, 1969–1974

Vice-President	Spiro T. Agnew	1969–1973
	Gerald R. Ford	1973–1974
Secretary of State	William P. Rogers	1969–1973
	Henry A. Kissinger	1973–1974
Secretary of Treasury	David M. Kennedy	1969–1970
	John B. Connally	1971–1972
	George P. Shultz	1972–1974
	William E. Simon	1974
Postmaster General	Winton M. Blount	1969–1971
Attorney General	John N. Mitchell	1969–1972
	Richard G. Kleindienst	1972–1973
	Elliot L. Richardson	1973
	William B. Saxbe	1973–1974
Secretary of Interior	Walter J. Hickel	1969–1970
	Rogers Morton	1971–1974
Secretary of Agriculture	Clifford M. Hardin	1969–1971
	Earl L. Butz	1971–1974
Secretary of Commerce	Maurice H. Stans	1969–1972
	Peter G. Peterson	1972–1973
	Frederick B. Dent	1973–1974
Secretary of Labor	George P. Shultz	1969–1970
	James D. Hodgson	1970–1973
	Peter J. Brennan	1973–1974
Secretary of Defense	Melvin R. Laird	1969–1973
	Elliot L. Richardson	1973
	James R. Schlesinger	1973–1974
Secretary of Health, Education, and Welfare	Robert H. Finch	1969–1970
	Elliot L. Richardson	1970–1973
	Caspar W. Weinberger	1973–1974
Secretary of Housing and Urban Development	George W. Romney	1969–1973
	James T. Lynn	1973–1974
Secretary of Transportation	John A. Volpe	1969–1973
	Claude S. Brinegar	1973–1974

Ford, 1974–1977

Vice-President	Nelson A. Rockefeller	1974–1977
Secretary of State	Henry A. Kissinger	1974–1977
Secretary of Treasury	William E. Simon	1974–1977
Attorney General	William B. Saxbe	1974–1975
	Edward H. Levi	1975–1977
Secretary of Interior	Rogers C. B. Morton	1974–1975
	Stanley K. Hathaway	1975
	Thomas S. Kleppe	1975–1977
Secretary of Agriculture	Earl L. Butz	1974–1976
	John A. Knebel	1976–1977

Secretary of Commerce	Frederick B. Dent	1974–1975
	Rogers C. B. Morton	1975–1976
	Elliot L. Richardson	1976–1977
Secretary of Labor	Peter J. Brennan	1974–1975
	John T. Dunlop	1975–1976
	W. J. Usery, Jr.	1976–1977
Secretary of Defense	James R. Schlesinger	1974–1975
	Donald H. Rumsfeld	1975–1977
Secretary of Health, Education, and Welfare	Caspar W. Weinberger	1974–1975
	F. David Mathews	1975–1977
Secretary of Housing and Urban Development	James T. Lynn	1974–1975
	Carla Anderson Hills	1975–1977
Secretary of Transportation	Claude S. Brinegar	1974–1975
	William T. Coleman, Jr.	1974–1977

Carter, 1977–1981

Vice-President	Walter F. Mondale	1977–1981
Secretary of State	Cyrus R. Vance	1977–1980
	Edmund S. Muskie	1980–1981
Secretary of Treasury	W. Michael Blumenthal	1977–1979
	G. William Miller	1979–1981
Attorney General	Griffin B. Bell	1977–1979
	Benjamin R. Civiletti	1979–1981
Secretary of Interior	Cecil D. Andrus	1977–1981
Secretary of Agriculture	Robert Bergland	1977–1981
Secretary of Commerce	Juanita M. Kreps	1977–1979
	Philip M. Klutznick	1979–1981
Secretary of Labor	F. Ray Marshall	1977–1981
Secretary of Defense	Harold Brown	1977–1981
Secretary of Health, Education, and Welfare	Joseph A. Califano, Jr.	1977–1979
	Patricia Roberts Harris	1979
Secretary of Health and Human Services	Patricia Roberts Harris	1979–1981
Secretary of Housing and Urban Development	Patricia Roberts Harris	1977–1979
	Moon Landrieu	1979–1981
Secretary of Transportation	Brock Adams	1977–1979
	Neil E. Goldschmidt	1979–1981
Secretary of Energy	James R. Schlesinger, Jr.	1977–1979
	Charles W. Duncan, Jr.	1979–1981
Secretary of Education	Shirley M. Hufstedler	1979–1981

Reagan, 1981–1989

Vice-President	George Bush	1981–1989
Secretary of State	Alexander M. Haig, Jr. George P. Shultz	1981–1982 1982–1989
Secretary of Treasury	Donald T. Regan James A. Baker, III Nicholas F. Brady	1981–1985 1985–1988 1988–1989
Attorney General	William French Smith Edwin A. Meese, III Richard Thornburgh	1981–1985 1985–1988 1988–1989
Secretary of Interior	James C. Watt William P. Clarke, Jr. Donald P. Hodel	1981–1983 1983–1985 1985–1989
Secretary of Agriculture	John R. Block Richard Lyng	1981–1986 1986–1989
Secretary of Commerce	Malcolm Baldrige C. William Verity, Jr.	1981–1987 1987–1989
Secretary of Labor	Raymond J. Donovan William E. Brock Ann D. McLaughlin	1981–1985 1985–1987 1987–1989
Secretary of Defense	Caspar W. Weinberger Frank C. Carlucci	1981–1987 1987–1989
Secretary of Health and Human Services	Richard S. Schweiker Margaret M. Heckler Otis R. Bowen	1981–1983 1983–1985 1985–1989
Secretary of Housing and Urban Development	Samuel R. Pierce, Jr.	1981–1989
Secretary of Transportation	Andrew L. Lewis, Jr. Elizabeth Hanford Dole James H. Burnley	1981–1983 1983–1987 1987–1989
Secretary of Energy	James B. Edwards Donald P. Hodel John S. Herrington	1981–1982 1982–1985 1985–1989
Secretary of Education	Terrel H. Bell William J. Bennett Lauro F. Cavazos	1981–1985 1985–1988 1988–1989

Bush, 1989–

Vice-President	Dan Quayle	1989–
Secretary of State	James A. Baker	1989–
Secretary of Treasury	Nicholas F. Brady	1989–
Attorney General	Richard Thornburgh	1989–
Secretary of Interior	Manuel Lujan, Jr.	1989–
Secretary of Agriculture	Clayton K. Yeutter	1989–
Secretary of Commerce	Robert A. Mosbacher	1989–
Secretary of Labor	Elizabeth Hanford Dole	1989–
Secretary of Defense	Richard Cheney	1989–
Secretary of Health and Human Services	Louis Sullivan	1989–
Secretary of Housing and Urban Development	Jack Kemp	1989–
Secretary of Transportation	Samuel K. Skinner	1989–
Secretary of Energy	James D. Watkins	1989
Secretary of Education	Lauro F. Cavazos	1989–
Secretary of Veterans Affairs	Edward J. Derwinski	1989–

Justices of the Supreme Court

Chief Justices in italics.

	Term of Service	Years of Service		Term of Service	Years of Service
John Jay	1789–1795	5	Ward Hunt	1873–1882	9
John Rutledge	1789–1791	1	*Morrison R. Waite*	1874–1888	14
William Cushing	1789–1810	20	John M. Harlan	1877–1911	34
James Wilson	1789–1798	8	William B. Woods	1880–1887	7
John Blair	1789–1796	6	Stanley Matthews	1881–1889	7
Robert H. Harrison	1789–1790	—	Horace Gray	1882–1902	20
James Iredell	1790–1799	9	Samuel Blatchford	1882–1893	11
Thomas Johnson	1791–1793	1	Lucius Q. C. Lamar	1888–1893	5
William Paterson	1793–1806	13	*Melville W. Fuller*	1888–1910	21
*John Rutledge**	1795	—	David J. Brewer	1890–1910	20
Samuel Chase	1796–1811	15	Henry B. Brown	1890–1906	16
Oliver Ellsworth	1796–1800	4	George Shiras, Jr.	1892–1903	10
Bushrod Washington	1798–1829	31	Howell E. Jackson	1893–1895	2
Alfred Moore	1799–1804	4	Edward D. White	1894–1910	16
John Marshall	1801–1835	34	Rufus W. Peckham	1895–1909	14
William Johnson	1804–1834	30	Joseph McKenna	1898–1925	26
H. Brockholst Livingston	1806–1823	16	Oliver W. Holmes, Jr.	1902–1932	30
Thomas Todd	1807–1826	18	William R. Day	1903–1922	19
Joseph Story	1811–1845	33	William H. Moody	1906–1910	3
Gabriel Duval	1811–1835	24	Horace H. Lurton	1910–1914	4
Smith Thompson	1823–1843	20	Charles E. Hughes	1910–1916	5
Robert Trimble	1826–1828	2	Willis Van Devanter	1911–1937	26
John McLean	1829–1861	32	Joseph R. Lamar	1911–1916	5
Henry Baldwin	1830–1844	14	*Edward D. White*	1910–1921	11
James M. Wayne	1835–1867	32	Mahlon Pitney	1912–1922	10
Roger B. Taney	1836–1864	28	James C. McReynolds	1914–1941	26
Philip P. Barbour	1836–1841	4	Louis D. Brandeis	1916–1939	22
John Catron	1837–1865	28	John H. Clarke	1916–1922	6
John McKinley	1837–1852	15	*William H. Taft*	1921–1930	8
Peter V. Daniel	1841–1860	19	George Sutherland	1922–1938	15
Samuel Nelson	1845–1872	27	Pierce Butler	1922–1939	16
Levi Woodbury	1845–1851	5	Edward T. Sanford	1923–1930	7
Robert C. Grier	1846–1870	23	Harlan F. Stone	1925–1941	16
Benjamin R. Curtis	1851–1857	6	*Charles E. Hughes*	1930–1941	11
John A. Campbell	1853–1861	8	Owen J. Roberts	1930–1945	15
Nathan Clifford	1858–1881	23	Benjamin N. Cardozo	1932–1938	6
Noah H. Swayne	1862–1881	18	Hugo L. Black	1937–1971	34
Samuel F. Miller	1862–1890	28	Stanley F. Reed	1938–1957	19
David Davis	1862–1877	14	Felix Frankfurter	1939–1962	23
Stephen J. Field	1863–1897	34	William O. Douglas	1939–1975	36
Salmon P. Chase	1864–1873	8	Frank Murphy	1940–1949	9
William Strong	1870–1880	10	*Harlan F. Stone*	1941–1946	5
Joseph P. Bradley	1870–1892	22	James F. Byrnes	1941–1942	1
			Robert H. Jackson	1941–1954	13
			Wiley B. Rutledge	1943–1949	6

* Never confirmed as Chief Justice.

	Term of Service	Years of Service
Harold H. Burton	1945–1958	13
Fred M. Vinson	1946–1953	7
Tom C. Clark	1949–1967	18
Sherman Minton	1949–1956	7
Earl Warren	1953–1969	16
John Marshall Harlan	1955–1971	16
William J. Brennan, Jr.	1956–	—
Charles E. Whittaker	1957–1962	5
Potter Stewart	1958–1981	23
Byron R. White	1962–	—
Arthur J. Goldberg	1962–1965	3
Abe Fortas	1965–1969	4
Thurgood Marshall	1967–	—
Warren E. Burger	1969–1986	18
Harry A. Blackmun	1970–	—
Lewis F. Powell, Jr.	1971–1987	15
*William H. Rehnquist***	1971–	—
John P. Stevens III	1975–	—
Sandra Day O'Connor	1981–	—
Antonin Scalia	1986–	—
Anthony M. Kennedy	1988–	—

** Chief Justice from 1986 on.

Territorial Expansion

Louisiana Purchase	1803
Florida	1819
Texas	1845
Oregon	1846
Mexican Cession	1848
Gadsden Purchase	1853
Alaska	1867
Hawaii	1898
Philippines	1898–1946
Puerto Rico	1899
Guam	1899
American Samoa	1900
Canal Zone	1904
U.S. Virgin Islands	1917
Pacific Islands Trust Territory	1947

Population, 1790–1980

1790	3,929,214
1800	5,308,483
1810	7,239,881
1820	9,638,453
1830	12,866,020
1840	17,069,453
1850	23,191,876
1860	31,443,321
1870	39,818,449
1880	50,155,783
1890	62,947,714
1900	75,994,575
1910	91,972,266
1920	105,710,620
1930	122,775,046
1940	131,669,275
1950	151,325,798
1960	179,323,175
1970	204,765,770
1980	226,504,825

Picture Credits

Chapter-opening Illustrations

Chapter 1 Bonaventura Peeters, *Dutch-Men-of-War in the West Indies*, 1648: Wadsworth Atheneum, Hartford.

Chapter 2 Johann Adam Eyer, Fraktur: Drawing of Soldiers and Ladies, 1800: Henry Francis duPont Wintertheur, Delaware.

Chapter 3 Redcoats and Union Jacks: Free Library of Philadelphia.

Chapter 4 M.M. Stanford, "Washington at Princeton, 1850": New York State Historical Association, Cooperstown, N.Y.

Chapter 5 L.M. Cooke, *Salute to General Washington in New York:* National Gallery, Washington, D.C.; Gift of Edgar William and Bernice Chrysler Garbisch.

Chapter 6 Thomas Chambers, *The Hudson Valley Sunset:* The National Gallery of Art, Washington D.C.; Gift of Edgar William and Bernice Chrysler Garbisch.

Chapter 7 Collection of Davenport West, Jr.: New York Public Library, Picture Collection.

Chapter 8 James Bard, *America.* ca. 1850: Smithsonian Institution, Van Alstyne Collection.

Chapter 9 Birch, *Conestoga Wagons:* Shelbourne Museum, Shelbourne, Vt.

Chapter 10 Kimmel, *Election Day at the State House:* Historical Society of Pennsylvania.

Chapter 11 John Jenny, *The House and Ship of David Alling:* The Newark Museum.

Chapter 12 Anonymous. *The Drawing Class,* c. 1820: The Art Institute of Chicago; Gift of Emily Crane Chadbourne.

Chapter 13 Albert Bierstadt, *The Oregon Trail,* 1869: The Butler Institute of American Art, Youngstown, Ohio.

Chapter 14 Anonymous. "The Suspension Bridge," 1855: Museum of Fine Arts, Boston.

Chapter 15 Bingham, *Order No. 11:* Historical Society of Missouri.

Chapter 16 "Battle of Atlanta": Atlanta Cyclorama.

Chapter 17 Edgar Degas, *New Orleans Cotton Merchants:* Art Resource Center, N.Y.

Chapter 18 Arthur F. Tait, *Life of the Hunter:* Super-Stock.

Chapter 19 S.B. Shiley, *Teeming Ingots at the Bessamer Shop,* 1895: Bethlehem Steel Corporation, Bethlehem Pa.

Chapter 20 Theodore Groll, *Washington Street, Indianapolis at Dusk,* 1892–1895: © 1990, Indianapolis Museum of Art, Gift of a Couple of Old Hoosiers.

Chapter 21 Poster, *Harper's/February:* Joseph Martin/Scala/Art Resource.

Chapter 22 H. Schuldt, *The Traffic Halt,* 1878: The Rhode Island School of Design.

Chapter 23 Naval demonstration near Havana, 1898: The Free Library of Philadelphia, Joseph Martin/Scala/Art Resource.

Chapter 24 Maurice Prendergast, *Central Park, 1901,* 1901: Collection of Whitney Museum of Art.

Chapter 25 World War I poster: SuperStock.

Chapter 26 *Rhapsody in Blue,* Advertising poster for Steinway pianos, 1928: Courtesy of Steinway & Sons.

Chapter 27 John Sloan, *Sixth Avenue Elevated At Third Street,* 1928: Collection of Whitney Museum of American Art.

Chapter 28 Isaac Soyer, *Employment Agency,* 1937: Collection of the Whitney Museum of American Art.

Chapter 29 Pearl Harbor: SuperStock.

Chapter 30 President Dwight D. Eisenhower: Wayne Miller/Magnum Photos.

Chapter 31 Martin Luther King, Jr.: Flip Schule/Black Star.

Chapter 32 Woodstock Weekend, August 1969: Bill Pierce/Sygma.

Chapter 33 President George Bush, Vice-President Dan Quayle, their wives, at inaugural festivities, January 1989: Tom Sobolik/Black Star.

Portfolios (Listed by Page Number)

Portfolio One: **62** Van Bergen farm, Hudson Valley: New York State Historical Association, Cooperstown. John White "Pomeiooc": Trustees of the British Museum. **64** Greenway: South Carolina Historical Society. Thomas Coram, *View of Mulberry (House and Street)*: Carolina Art Association/Gibbes Art Gallery. New England Salt-box house: Richard Candee. **65** Quaker marriage contract with Richard Penn's stamp: Historical Society of Pennsylvania. Anon., Baby in Red High Chair: Abby Aldrich Rockefeller Folk Art Center, Williamsburg. **66** Anon., *The Cheney Family:* National Gallery of Art, Smithsonian Institution; gift of Edgar William and Bernice Chrysler Garbisch. **67** Payne Limner, *Alexander Spotswood Payne and His Brother, John Dandridge Payne, and The Nurse,* 1790–1800: Virginia Museum of Fine Arts; gift of Miss Dorothy Payne.

Portfolio Two: **190** Portrait by Gilbert Stuart, 1805: National Portrait Gallery/Thomas Jefferson Memorial Foundation. **191** Bust by Jean Antoine Houdin: New-York Historical Society. Photo of Monticello exterior: © 1982

Langdon Clay. **192** Monticello drawing room with harpsichord and music stand: © 1982 Langdon Clay. **193** View from bed with telescope and surveying equipment: © 1982 Langdon Clay. Monticello entry hall with buffalo head and bones: © 1982 Langdon Clay. **194** Close-up of polygraph and revolving chair © 1982 Langdon Clay. **195** Daguerreotype of Isaac Jefferson by John Plumbe, ca. 1845: University of Virginia Library. Slave-owning document: Massachusetts Historical Society/University of Virginia Library.

Portfolio Three: **306** Thomas Coke Ruckle, *Fairview Inn or Three Mile House on Old Frederick Road,* 1829: Collection of The Maryland Historical Society, Baltimore. **307** *The Emigrants,* early nineteenth century: The Granger Collection. Advertisement, 1837: The Carnegie Library of Pittsburgh. **308** *Harper's Ferry, Virginia,* 1860–1863: I. N. Phelps Stokes Collection, Miriam & Ira D. Wallach Division of Art, Prints and Photographs, The New York Public Library, Astor, Lenox and Tilden Foundations. Pavel Petrovich Svinin, *A Ferry Scene on the Susquehanna at Wright's Ferry, near Havre de Grace:* The Metropolitan Museum of Art, Rogers Fund, 1942. **309** Anonymous, *Rafting Downstream,* c. 1840–1850: Indiana University Art Museum, Bloomington, Indiana. *Our City* (St. Louis), 1859: Missouri Historical Society. **310** Edward K. Thomas, *Ft. Snelling,* c. 1850: Minnesota Historical Society. Samuel Coleman, *Emigrant Train Fording Medicine Bow Creek,* n.d.: The Shearson Lehman Hutton Collection. **311** C. C. A. Christensen, *Handcart Company:* Courtesy of The Church of Jesus Christ of Latter Day Saints. Artist unknown, *Telegraph Hill, San Francisco,* late 1840s: Wells Fargo Bank, San Francisco.

Portfolio Four: **472** "Freedom to Slaves," 1863: Library Company of Philadelphia. **473** Edwin White, *Thoughts of Liberia,* ca. 1830–1840: New York Historical Society. George Fuller, "Cotton Press and Gin, Feb. 2, 1858": Private Collection. Five generations of a South Carolina slave family, photo by T. H. O'Sullivan, 1862: Library of Congress. **474** "Meeting in the African Church, Cincinnati, Ohio," *Frank Leslie's Illustrated Newspaper,* April 30, 1853: Library of Congress. Thomas Rice playing "Jump Jim Crow" on the Bowery, 1833: Museum of the City of New York. **475** Edwin Taylor, *American Slave Market,* 1852: Chicago Historical Society. Bill of sale for Ned: The Old Slave Mart Museum, Charleston, S.C. **476** Winslow Homer, *A View from the Old Mistress,* 1876: National Museum of American Art, Smithsonian Institution. **477** Sharecropper cabin with slaughtered hogs: Library of Congress. W. L. Sheppard, "Workers Stripping Tobacco in Danville, Va.," *Harper's Weekly,* Jan. 29, 1887: Virginia State Library.

Portfolio Five: **562** Charles W. Witham, "Grand View of Baxter Street": Theatre and Music Collection, Museum of the City of New York. **563** Lewis Hine, Italian mother and child, Ellis Island: New York Public Library. Ellis Island—stethoscope examination: Brown Brothers. **564** Orchard Street looking south from Hester Street, 1898:

The Byron Collection, Museum of the City of New York. Lewis Hine, communal faucet in tenement: International Museum of Photography at George Eastman House. Mulberry Bend, ca. 1890; **565** Lewis Hine, labor agency on lower West Side, New York City, 1910: New York Public Library. Immigrant family sewing garments in tenement: Culver Pictures. Italian district of Manhattan's Lower East Side, photo by Langill & Darling: Museum of the City of New York. **566** Levi Strauss ad, 1870s: Levi Strauss & Co. **567** Jacob Riis: The Granger Collection. Emma Goldman: Brown Brothers. Nikola Tesla: The Bettmann Archive. Felix Frankfurter: UPI/Bettmann Newsphotos. Sidney Hillman: The Granger Collection. Irving Berlin: The Bettmann Archive.

Portfolio Six: **672** "Look! The Boss Has a Woman to Write His Letters": National Archives and Record Service. **673** Visiting nurse on Henry Street rooftop: Visiting Nurse Service of New York. Lewis Hine, *Carolina Cotton Mill,* 1908: George Eastman House. Black domestic servant: Valentine Museum, Richmond, Virginia. **674** Triangle Shirtwaist Co. fire: Brown Brothers. Women's Trade Union League demonstration: Brown Brothers. **675** YWCA war effort poster: The Granger Collection. Cooking class, Vassar College, ca. 1918: Brown Brothers. **676** Woman streetcar conductors, 1918: Brown Brothers. Women polishing cars, Northern Pacific Railroad: Brown Brothers. Women welding bombs, munitions factory, ca. 1917: The Granger Collection. **677** Reginald Marsh, *Subway, 14th St.,* 1930: Private collection, New York; photo by Ronald L. C. Kienhuis.

Portfolio Seven: **736** Edward Hopper, *Early Sunday Morning,* 1930: Whitney Museum of American Art. John Marin, *Sun Spots,* 1920: The Metropolitan Museum of Art; Alfred Stieglitz Collection. **737** Georgia O'Keeffe, *Cow Skull: Red, White, and Blue,* 1931: The Metropolitan Museum of Art; Alfred Stieglitz Collection. Thomas Hart Benton, *Romance,* 1931–1932: Archer M. Huntington Art Gallery, The University of Texas at Austin; lent by James and Mari Michener. **738** Reginald Marsh, *Twenty Cent Movie,* 1936: Whitney Museum of American Art. Ben Shahn, *Willis Avenue Bridge,* 1940: Collection, The Museum of Modern Art, New York; gift of Lincoln Kirstein. Mark Rothko, *Number 10,* 1950: Collection, The Museum of Modern Art, New York; gift of Philip Johnson. **739** Robert Motherwell, *Elegy to the Spanish Republic 108,* 1965–1967: Collection, The Museum of Modern Art, New York; Charles Mergentine Fund. Willem de Kooning, *Woman and Bicycle,* 1952–1953: Whitney Museum of American Art. **740** Jasper Johns, *Target With Four Faces,* 1955: Collection, The Museum of Modern Art, New York; gift of Mr. and Mrs. Robert C. Scull, Josef Albers, *Homage to the Square: Apparition,* 1959: Solomon R. Guggenheim Museum. **741** Andrew Wyeth, *Albert's Son,* 1959: National Gallery, Oslo, Norway; photo by J. Lathion.

Portfolio Eight: **908** Albert Bierstadt, *Yosemite Landscape:* SuperStock. President Theodore Roosevelt with John Muir and others in Yosemite National Park, May 1903: Magnum Photos. Earth First Protest in Yellowstone National Park, 1989: Gamma-Liaison/Neal Palumbo. **909** Forest fires in Yellowstone: Gamma-Liaison/B. Willcox. Trees felled by forest fires in Yellowstone: Photo Researchers/William Munoz. Yellowstone in bloom: Gamma-Liaison/B. Willcox. **910** Pike's Peak in the Rocky Mountains, 1891: Culver Pictures. Automobile graveyard near Pike's Peak: Photo Researchers/Maurice and Sally Landre. Ever mounting solid waste in landfills in Portland, Oregon: Photo Researchers/David Weintraub. **911** Workers clean up after oil spill in Valdez, 1989: Sygma/J. L. Atlan. Valdez, Alaska on Prince William sound, 1940: Culver Pictures. Sea otter rescued after oil spill recuperates at salmon hatchery, 1989: Sygma/J. L. Atlan. **912** Recycled waste used to produce electricity for Fairfield County, Connecticut: Photo Researchers/Hank Morgan/Science Source. Solar-powered telephone: Photo Researchers/Eunice Harris. Windmills, as alternate sources of energy to electricity, provide power to Altamont, California: Photo Researchers/Lowell ' Georgia. **913** Nineteenth-century view of Florida Everglades: Culver Pictures. Pollution and other environmental problems threaten the Everglades: Photo Researchers/Max Hunn. Effects of acid rain on North Carolina forest: Stock, Boston/Judy Canty.

American Lives (Listed by Page Number)

Benjamin Franklin and John Adams: **69** Detail from *A Westerly View of the Colledges in Cambridge, New England.* Engraving by Paul Revere, 1767: Courtesy American Antiquarian Society.

George Washington: **105** Detail from *A View of Mount Vernon,* c. 1790 or later: American National Gallery of Art, Washington; Gift of Edgar William and Bernice Chrysler Garbisch.

Three Families in the Post-Civil War South: **446** Detail from *Village Post Office,* Thomas Waterman Wood, 1873, Oil on Canvas: New York State Historical Association, Cooperstown. **447** *The Homestead:* Courtesy Bethune Cookman College, Daytona Beach, Florida.

The Steltzles and the Smiths: **534** Lower East Side: Culver Pictures. **535** Swimming in the East River: Brown Brothers. Fulton Fish Market in the 1880s: Brown Brothers.

The Johnson Family of Nebraska: **588** Settlers entering Nebraska: The Bettmann Archive. **589** Family farm in northern Nebraska: The Nebraska Historical Society. Country school: The Bettmann Archive.

Emma Goldman: **638** Emma Goldman in the 1890s: Culver Pictures. **639** Emma Goldman and Alexander Berkman: The Bettmann Archive.

Clement Vann Rogers and George William Norris: **506** Clement Vann Rogers: Oklahoma Historical Society. **507** Beaver City, late nineteenth century: Nebraska State Historical Society.

Text (Listed by Page Number)

Chapter 1: **2** Theodor de Bry, engraving of Columbus departing from Palos, 1590: New York Public Library, Rare Book Collection. **4** Bettmann Archive. **9** Aztec picture writing, in *Codex Porfirio Diaz:* Tozzer Library, Harvard University. **10** John White, Indians "sitting at meat": Courtesy of the Trustees of the British Museum. **13** Sir Francis Drake: Virginia Historical Society. **15** Early map of Virginia: Hariot: *Virginia* (Dover Publications, Inc.). **17** New York Public Library, Picture Collection. **20** New England primer: American Antiquarian Society. **24** Charles Town, South Carolina: Colonial Williamsburg Society. **26** Mary Evans Picture Library/Photo Researchers, Inc. **27** "'t' Fort nieuw Amsterdam op de Manhattans," ca. 1626–1628 (pub. 1651): Museum of the City of New York.

Chapter 2: **34** Indenture agreement, April 29, 1718: Historical Society of Pennsylvania. **37** Announcement of sale of slaves, Charleston, S.C., May 6, 1763: Library of Congress. **39** William Berkeley: Virginia State Library and Archives. **41** Aquatint idealized view of slave life, from J. Ferrario, *Les Costumes des Peuples. . . .* Milan, 1827: Library Company of Philadelphia. **42** Benjamin Latrobe, *Rippon Lodge:* Maryland Historical Society. **44** G. von Redeker, "A View of Salem," 1787: Moravian Archive. **47** The Mason Children: *David, Joanna, and Abigail,* attributed to the Freake-Gibbs Painter, 1670: The Fine Arts Museums of San Francisco; gift of Mr. and Mrs. John D. Rockefeller III. **51** A Full and Plain Evidence Concerning Witches and Apparitions, London, 1726: Granger Collection. **53** Title page of Eliot's Indian Bible: Bettmann Archive. **60** Carington Bowles, "An East Perspective View of the City of Philadelphia," 1731–1736: New York Public Library, Stokes Collection.

Chapter 3: **72** John Watson, *Governor Lewis Morris:* Brooklyn Museum. **74** Engraving of sugar refining, from P. Pomet, *A Compleat History of Drugs. . . .* London, 1712: Library Company of Philadelphia. Phyllis Wheatley, "An Elegiac Poem, on the Death of . . . George Whitefield," Boston, 1770: Library Company of Philadelphia. **81** David Martin, portrait of Benjamin Franklin, 1767: The White House Historical Association: photo by National Geographic Society. **82** David Rittenhouse, orrery, 1950s restoration: Princeton University Observatory. **84** Detail of illustration of Sir William Johnson's Indian Testimonial, wood engraving c. 1770: New-York Historical Society. **87** Thomas Davies, watercolor of seizure of Louisbourg, 1758: Royal Artillery Museum, London. **94** J. W. Barber, wood engraving of New Hampshire stamp master in effigy, from Interesting Events in the History of the U.S., 1829: Metropolitan Museum of Art; bequest of Charles Allen Munn. **95** Cockpit Hill factory, Derby: ceramic teapot, "Stamp Act Repeal'd," ca. 1766: Essex Institute, Salem, Mass. **97** John Singeton Copely, portrait of Samuel Adams, ca. 1771: Museum of Fine Arts, Boston. **98** Paul Revere, engraving of Boston Massacre: American Antiquarian Society. **100** Society of

Smith: Brown Bros. **298** Daguerreotype of Dorothea Linde Dix: The Granger Collection. **300** Daguerreotype of William Lloyd Garrison by Southworth and Hawes: The Metropolitan Museum of Art; gift of I. N. Phelps Stokes, Edward S. Hawes, Alice Mary Hawes, Marion Augusta Hawes, 1937. **300** Portrait of Frederick Douglass by Ritchie: New York Historical Society. **302** Daguerreotype of Elizabeth Cady Stanton and her daughter Harriet, 1856: Library of Congress.

Chapter 12: **314** Thomas Cole, *Falls of Kaaterskill,* 1826: New York State Historical Association, Cooperstown, N.Y. **316** William Furness, portrait of Ralph Waldo Emerson: The Pennsylvania Academy of Fine Arts; gift of Horace Howard Furness. **317** Thoreau: New York Public Library, Picture Collection. **318** Samuel S. Osgood, portrait of Edgar Allan Poe, ca. 1845: New York Historical Society. **319** Charles Osgood, portrait of Nathaniel Hawthorne, 1840: Essex Institute, Salem, Mass. **320** Daguerreotype of Walt Whitman: National Archives and Record Service. **322** Smithsonian Institution: Comstock. **323** William Sidney Mount, *Eel Spearing at Setauket,* 1845: New York Historical Association, Cooperstown, N.Y. Hiram Powers, *The Greek Slave,* 1847: The Newark Museum; gift of Franklin Murphy Jr., 1926. Photograph © The Newark Museum. **325** Henry Inman, *The Dismissal of School on an October Afternoon,* 1845: Museum of Fine Arts, Boston. **326** Anonymous, "A Lecture by James Pollard Espy, Meteorologist, at Clinton Hall . . . ," ca. 1841: Museum of the City of New York. **328** John C. Wild. *Fourth Street Cincinnati:* Cincinnati Historical Society. **330** "American Journal of Science and Arts": Beinecke Rare Book and Manuscript Library, Yale University.

Chapter 13: **336** Daguerreotype of John Tyler, ca. 1850: Chicago Historical Society. **337** Texas insurgents taking Ft. San Antonio: Texas State Archives. **338** Davy Crockett's Death-Battle of the Alamo from *Davy Crockett's Almanack,* 1837: Library of Congress. **340** Oregon trail: Denver Public Library, Western History Dept. **343** Polk cartoon: Bettmann Archive. **344** Currier & Ives, "The Battle of Resaca de la Palma, May 9, 1846": Museum of the City of New York. **348** Daguerreotype of General John E. Wood and Staff, Saltillo, Mexico, 1846: Yale University, Beinecke Library. **351** J. Goldsborough Bruff, "Seeing the Elephant No. 1" and "Seeing the Elephant No. 5," ca. 1850: Yale University, Beinecke Library. **353** Southworth and Hawes, daguerreotype of Henry Clay, ca. 1845–1850: The Metropolitan Museum of Art; gift of I. N. Phelps Stokes, Edward S. Hawes, Alice Mary Hawes, Marion Augusta Hawes, 1937. Southworth and Hawes daguerreotype of Daniel Webster, 1851: The Metropolitan Museum of Art; gift of I. N. Phelps Stokes, Edward S. Hawes, Alice Mary Hawes, Marion Augusta Hawes.

Chapter 14: **361** Fraz Holzlhuber, "Rice Fields in the State of Arkansas," 1856–1860, and "Sugar Harves in Louisiana and Texas," 1856–1860: Glenbow Foundation, Calgary, Alberta. **363** Plantation in the American South; colored engraving, nineteenth century: The Granger Collection. **366** "Deck of the Bark *Wildfire,*" in *Harper's Weekly,* June 2, 1860: Library of Congress. **367** B. H. Latrobe, "Preparations for the enjoyment of a fine Sunday among the Blacks": Maryland Historical Society. **370** Frontispiece, Carstensen and Gildemeister, *New York Crystal Palace* (New York 1854): New-York Historical Society. **375** New Bedford Whaling Museum, New Bedford, Mass. **377** Steamer *Princess* at mail line packet landing for Vicksburg, Natchez, and New Orleans, ca. 1850–1860: Courtesy the Historic New Orleans Collection. **379** Advertisement, Illinois Central Railroad: The Newberry Library, Chicago. **381** McCormick Plant: from Mayer and Wade, *Growth of a Metropolis:* University of Chicago, 1969.

Chapter 15: **388** Poster, Uncle Tom's Cabin: The Granger Collection. **389** Cartoon: Library of Congress. **390** Gesson Ogata, "First Landing at Kurihama, July 14, 1853": United States Naval Academy Museum. **391** Daguerreotype of Stephen A. Douglas, ca. 1860: Library of Congress. **393** Albert J. Fountain, Jr., *The Signing of the Gadsden Purchase,* 1929: Courtesy of Mary Veitch Alexander, Gadsden Museum, Mesilla, N.M. **395** Poster, Kidnapping Again: The Boston Public Library. **396** Battle of Hickory Point: Kansas Historical Society. **398** "Southern Chivalry-Argument versus Clubs," 1856: Library Company of Philadelphia. **399** G. P. A. Healey, portrait of James Buchanan, 1859: Smithsonian Institution, National Portrait Gallery. **402** Alexander Hesler, daguerreotype of Abraham Lincoln, June 3, 1860: Chicago Historical Society. Daguerreotype of Lincoln, April 10, 1865: Library of Congress. **404** Lincoln-Douglas Debate Poster: Illinois State Historical Society. **406** Thomas Hovenden, *The Last Moments of John Brown,* 1884: The Metropolitan Museum of Art; gift of Mr. and Mrs. Carle Stoeckel, 1987.

Chapter 16: **418** John Robertson, portrait of Jefferson Davis, 1863: Museum of the Confederacy, Richmond, Va. **420** Anonymous, "Panic on the Road between Bull Run and Centerville," 1861: Museum of the Fine Arts, Boston. **421** David G. Blythe, Lincoln versus the Copperheads: Museum of Fine Arts, Boston. **426** H. R. Wand, *McClellan's Return From Richmond:* Library of Congress. **427** Julian Vannerson, photo of Robert E. Lee, 1863: Library of Congress. **429** Adalbert Johann Volck, "Lincoln Writing the Emancipation Proclamation": Museum of Fine Arts, Boston; M and M Karolik Collection. David Gilmore Blythe, "Abraham Lincoln Writing the Emancipation Proclamation," 1863: Museum of Art, Carnegie Institute; gift of Mr. & Mrs. John F. Walton. **432** 22nd U.S. Colored Troops, Petersburg, June 1864: West Point Museum, New York. **435** M. Brady, U.S. Grant, Washington, D.C., 1862: Chicago Historical Society. **438** Elizabeth Blackwell: Bettmann Archive. **439** Grant at Cold Harbor: Library of Congress. **442** From "Death in the Trenches," Time-Life, 1986. **443** Library of Congress.

Chapter 17: **450** Matthew Brady, daguerreotype of Andrew Johnson: Library of Congress. **451** Matthew

Brady, daguerreotype of Thaddeus Stevens: Library of Congress. **453** Freedman's Bureau: Library Company of Philadelphia. **455** The Bettmann Archive. **457** Cartoon: American Antiquarian Society, Worcester, Mass. **458** The First Colored Senators and Representatives in the 41st and 42nd Congress of the United States, 1842. Lithograph by Currier & Ives: Granger Collection. **460** "Primary School for Freedman, in Charge of Mrs. Green," *Harper's Weekly,* June 23, 1866: New-York Historical Society. **462** Black sharecroppers: Culver Pictures. **465** Carpetbaggers being hanged, *Tuscaloosa Independent Monitor,* September 1, 1868: Alabama Dept. of Archives and History, Montgomery. **467** Nast cartoon: *Harper's Weekly,* August 24, 1872.

Chapter 18: **481** Joseph Keppler, "None but Millionaires Need Apply," *Puck,* March 12, 1890: New-York Historical Society. **482** Louis Dalrymple, "Getting Troublesome Again," 1896: The Granger Collection. **484** Frances Benjamin Johnston, students working on construction, ca. 1900–1905: Library of Congress; courtesy of National Park Service, Tuskegee Institute National Historical Site; photo by John Scott. **487** Immigrant construction crew laying tracks along west slope of the Cascades in 1885; The Bettmann Archive. **488** Kills Two, "An Indian Horse Dance": Yale University Library, Coe Collection. **490** Comanche, the only survivor on the Army's side at the Battle of Little Big Horn: The Bettmann Archive. **492** Geronimo and Natiche with their sons, preparing to surrender to Gen. Crook: National Archives and Record Service. **493** Nat Love, a cowboy in the Dakotas in the 1880s: The Bettmann Archive. **494** Illustration by T. L. Dawes, "Mining in the Comstock," 1872: Bancroft Library, University of California. **496** 30-horse combines, wheat harvest, Stockton, California, 1907: Oregon Historical Society. **497** J. K. Hillers, railroad bridge near Santa Fe, New Mexico: National Archives and Record Service. **499** Old map of Atlantic & Pacific Railroad: National Archives and Record Service. **503** S. D. Butcher, masked Nebraska ranchers cutting fence, 1885: Nebraska State Historical Society, S. D. Butcher Collection.

Chapter 19: **512** Circular inviting settlers to come to Iowa and Nebraska, 1873: The Bettmann Archive. **513** Strip mining, Mesabi Range, 1899: Minnesota Historical Society. **515** Thomas A. Edison with wax-cylinder phonograph, 1888: Edison National Historic Site, National Park Service, U.S. Dept. of the Interior. **517** Edward Steichen, photo of J. P. Morgan, 1906: Museum of Modern Art; gift of A. Conger Goodyear. **518** Theobald Chartran, portrait of Andrew Carnegie, 1895: Museum of Art, Carnegie Institute, Pittsburgh; gift of Mr. Henry Clay Frick. **519** Cartoon of John D. Rockefeller, *Puck,* March 6, 1901: New-York Historical Society. **521** The glove counter in Rike's Department Store, Dayton, Ohio, 1893: The Bettmann Archive. **526** Thomas Nast cartoon ridiculing the willingness of the U.S. Senate to do the bidding of the railroad lobbyists in 1888: New York Public Library.

Chapter 20: **539** Student nurses in New York City in 1899. Library of Congress. **541** Minnesota farming family in front of house, 1895: The Bettmann Archive. **543** An 1890s public school classroom: The Bettmann Archive. **547** Frank Beard cartoon about unrestricted immigration, 1885: The Granger Collection. **550** Jacob Riis, "Bandit's Roost, Lower East Side": New York, *Sun.* **551** Herald Square, New York City, 1900: The New York Historical Society. **553** Design for Chicago's 1893 World Fair by Daniel H. Burham. John Ross Key, *Administration, Mining and Electrical Buildings from Wooded Islands, World's Columbian Exposition,* 1894: Chicago Historical Society. **555** Thomas Eakins' *Baseball Players Practicing,* 1875: Museum of Art, Rhode Island School of Design; Jesse Metcalf and Walter H. Kimball Funds. **557** Henry Ward Beecher, widely admired minister in the second half of the nineteenth century: The Bettmann Archive. **559** Portrait of Jane Addams by Alice Kellog Tyler, 1896: Chicago Historical Society.

Chapter 21: **570** John Singer Sargent, portrait of Joseph Pulitzer, 1905: Courtesy of Joseph Pulitzer, Jr. **571** William Randolph Hearst in 1906: The Bettmann Archive. **574** Smith College students setting out on geology field trip, ca. 1880–1890: Smith College Archives. **577** John Dewey, progressive educator: Brown Brothers. **578** Oliver Wendell Holmes, Associate Supreme Court Justice, 1902: Brown Brothers. **580** Mark Twain in his easy chair, ca. 1905 in Hartford, Conn.: The Bettmann Archive. Frederick Waddy, caricature of Mark Twain, 1872: The Granger Collection. **583** Thomas Eakins, Marey wheel photo of an unidentified model, 1884: Philadelphia Museum of Art; gift of Charles Bregler. **584** Thomas Eakins, *The Swimming Hole,* 1883: Permanent Collection, The Fort Worth Art Museum; photo by David Wharton. **585** Mary Cassatt, *Mother and Child:* Metropolitan Museum of Art; George A. Hearn, 1909. **586** Henry and William James, ca. 1900: The Bettmann Archive.

Chapter 22: **593** Thomas Nast, "Let Us Pray," *Harper's Weekly,* September 23, 1887: Library of Congress. **595** Currier & Ives, "Farmer Garfield Cutting a Swath to the White House," 1880: The Granger Collection. **597** Anders Zorn, portrait of Grover Cleveland: National Portrait Gallery, Smithsonian Institution. **599** F. M. Howarth, "Put Your Application in The Slot and Get An Office," 1889: The Bettmann Archive. **600** Bernhard Gillan, "Phryne Before the Chicago Tribunal," *Puck,* 1884: Culver Pictures. **601** Guthrie, Oklahoma, May 1889: University of Oklahoma Library, Western History Collection. **603** Mary Elizbeth Lease: Culver Pictures. **604** Jeremiah "Sockless Jerry" Simpson, a Populist and a flamboyant campaigner, speaking at a political debate, 1892: The Kansas State Historical Society, Topeka. **607** William Jennings Bryan: The Granger Collection. **608** Louis Dalrymple, "Making-Up for a New Role," *Judge:* The Bettmann Archive.

Chapter 23: **618** Admiral Alfred Thayer Mahan, 1904: The Bettmann Archive. **622** Louis Dalrymple, "Some

Time in the Future," 1895: The Granger Collection. **624** Highly decorated female recruiting officer during Spanish-American War, 1898: The Bettmann Archive. **626** "His Foresight," *Puck*, 1901: Culver Pictures. **628** Emilio Aguinaldo and his son: The Bettmann Archive. **633** Rendering of a multinational assault upon Chinese militants, the Boxers, 1900: Library of Congress. **634** Panama Canal under construction: The Bettmann Archive.

Chapter 24: **643** Ida Tarbell: UPI/Bettmann Newsphotos. *McClure's* Magazine Cover, 1903: Culver Pictures. **645** George Luks's "The Miner," 1924, from the "ashcan" school of American painting: SuperStock. **646** William Balfour-Ker, *From the Depths*, in John Ames Mitchell, *The Silent War*, 1906, New York Public Library, Astor, Lenox and Tilden Foundations. **648** Robert La Follette, Cumberland, Wisconsin, 1897: State Historical Society of Wisconsin. **651** Suffrage Parade, New York, May 6, 1911: Culver Pictures. **654** President Theodore Roosevelt: Brown Brothers. **655** Theodore Roosevelt in the lions' den: Culver Pictures. **657** Coal miners' strike, Shenandoah, Pa. **659** "Best" tonic advertisement, ca. 1890–1900: The Granger Collection. **660** William Howard Taft playing golf: Culver Pictures. **662** Cartoon caricaturing Presidents Theodore Roosevelt and William H. Taft: The Bettmann Archive. **665** Woodrow Wilson at 1906 Princton graduation with Andrew Carnegie: Brown Brothers. **668** Winold Reiss, portrait of W. E. B. DuBois, ca. 1925: National Portrait Gallery, Smithsonian Institution.

Chapter 25: **680** Francisco "Pancho" Villa, upon his capture by the Mexican Army in 1920: Brown Brothers. **681** Anti-war protesters in 1916: The Bettmann Archive. **684** Warning poster to transatlantic passengers by German embassy, New York *Times*, 1915: Brown Brothers. **686** Wilson 1916 Campaign van: UPI/Bettmann Newsphotos. **687** *"U-Boote Heraus!"* poster, ca. 1914, encouraging German submarine crews: The Granger Collection. **690** Rival Horse Meat & Sausages, Inc., 1917: National Archives and Record Service. **691** Removing statue of Germania, April 1, 1918: New York Historical Society. **693** Young women in their "victory" garden during World War I: UPI/Bettmann Newsphotos. **696** American infantrymen under shell fire in France during World War I: The Bettmann Archive. **700** "Big Four," Hotel Crillon, Paris, December 1918: The Granger Collection. **701** President and Mrs. Woodrow Wilson during the Versailles Peace Conference, 1919: Culver Pictures. **702** "Overweighted," *Punch*, March 26, 1919: Punch Publications, Ltd. **704** William Gropper cartoon: *The Liberator*, February 1920.

Chapter 26: **710** Immigrants entering the United States through New York City's Ellis Island: The Bettmann Archive. **712** Illustration by John Held, Jr., which appeared on the cover of *McClure's* Magazine in the 1920s: Culver Pictures. **714** Young saleswoman at work in ready-to-wear store in the 1920s: Brown Brothers. **716** Charlie Chaplin in *One A.M.*: Museum of Modern Art/

Film Stills Archive, New York. **718** Gertrude Ederle, 1926, greased for swim across the English Channel. UPI/Bettmann Newsphotos. **719** John Steuart Curry, *Baptism in Kansas*, 1928: Whitney Museum of American Art, purchase acq. no. 31.159. **722** Ben Shahn, *Prohibition Alley*: Museum of the City of New York. **723** Ku Klux Klan initiation ceremony, ca. 1920–1925: Kansas State Historical Society. **724** Sacco and Vanzetti arriving at court, April 1927: Brown Brothers. **726** F. Scott Fitzgerald: Brown Brothers. Ernest Hemingway: John F. Kennedy Library. **729** Jacob Lawrence, *The Migration of the Negro* (Panel 1), 1940–1941: The Phillips Collection. **731** Henry Ford: Courtesy of Ford Motor Company. **733** Charles A. Lindbergh, two years before his solo flight across the Atlantic: Culver Pictures.

Chapter 27: **744** President Warren G. Harding throwing first ball: Culver Pictures. **746** *Life*, cover, March 6, 1924: Culver Pictures. **747** Cartoon satirizing President Calvin Coolidge: Culver Pictures. **749** Members of the Women's International League for Peace and Freedom, ca. 1918: Library of Congress. **751** "They Shall Pay!" Los Angeles *Times* cartoon reprinted in *The Outlook*, January 1923: Library of Congress. **753** President Herbert Hoover during 1928 presidential campaign: The Bettmann Archive. **755** James Rosenberg, "Oct. 29 *Dies Irae*": Philadelphia Museum of Art, Lola Downin Peck Fund. **758** Children begging for money beside signs blaming Hoover for problems of the Depression: Art Resource. **759** Bonus Marchers demonstrating in front of the Capitol Building, July 5, 1932: The Bettmann Archive. **760** Bread line: National Archives and Record Service. **762** Franklin D. Roosevelt and John N. Garner campaigning, 1932: UPI/Bettmann Newsphotos.

Chapter 28: **766** Franklin D. Roosevelt and admirers, Warm Springs, Ga., 1933: UPI/Bettmann Newsphotos. **771** WPA workers widening streets in government work program in 1935: The Bettmann Archive. **773** John Steinbeck: Magnum Photos/Erich Hartmann. William Faulkner: Black Star/Bern Keating. **774** Huey Long: The Bettmann Archive. **775** Father Charles Coughlin, Detroit: UPI/Bettmann Newsphotos. **780** "No Boost for the Administration Make-Up Department," New York *Tribune*, 1937: Culver Pictures. **781** Sit-down strikers: Wide World Photos. **783** Cartoon, Uncle Sam and federal agencies: © 1935, 1963 Conde-Nast Publications, Inc. *Vanity Fair*, July 1935. New York Public Library, Lenox and Tilden Foundations. **784** Francis Perkins visiting steel plant: Brown Brothers. **786** Arthur Rothstein, photo of evicted sharecroppers, Missouri, 1939: Library of Congress. **788** Eleanor and Franklin D. Roosevelt with their son, Franklin, Jr. at the family home in Hyde Park, New York: UPI/Bettmann Newsphotos. **790** Students and faculty at the University of Chicago demonstrate for peace in 1937: Wide World Photos. **791** American volunteers for the Lincoln Brigade, which fought on the side of the Loyalists in the Spanish Civil War: Magnum Photos/Robert Capa. **792** German poster, 1938: The Granger Collection. **793** Wendall Wilkie, Republican candidate for the presidency, 1940: UPI/Bettmann Newsphotos.

Chapter 29: **801** Black graduates of the Advanced Flying School, 1942: Culver Pictures. **802** Zoot suiter, 1943: UPI/Bettmann Newsphotos. **803** Dorothea Lange, Mochida family, Hayward, California, May 8, 1942: National Archives and Record Servcice. **805** Margeret Bourke-White, "Women in Steel": Life Magazine, © 1943 *Time* Inc. **808** Victorious American troops entering Sicilian town, 1943: Magnum Photos/Robert Capa. **809** Scene from "The True Glory," General Dwight D. Eisenhower's film report as he inspects the horrific conditions in a German concentration camp: Culver Pictures. **812** American soldiers in hand-to-hand combat with the Japanese on the Pacific island of Bourgainville, 1944: Black Star. **813** Ruins of Hiroshima's Museum of Science and Industry: UPI/Bettmann Newphotos. **817** Churchill, Roosevelt, and Stalin at Yalta, February 1945: The Granger Collection.

Chapter 30: **823** Post-war communities of single-family homes developed to house returning veterans and their families: Magnum Photos/Elliott Erwitt. **828** The Berlin Airlift: The Bettmann Archive. **829** Truman with Chicago *Daily Tribune* headline, November 1948: UPI/Bettmann Newsphotos. **832** David Douglas Duncan, 1st Marine Division, November 1950: © David Douglas Duncan, *Life*. **834** Alger Hiss being asked to identify Whittaker Chambers at Congressional hearings in 1948: UPI/Bettmann Newsphotos. **837** John Foster Dulles, 1956: UPI/Bettmann Newsphotos. **838** Senator Joseph McCarthy conferring with aide Roy M. Cohn during televised Congressional hearings, 1954: UPI/Bettmann Newsphotos. **841** Vice-president Richard M. Nixon debates Nikita Khrushchev over the future of capitalism, 1959: Magnum Photos/Elliott Erwitt. **842** Fidel Castro and his military advisers at secret base in Cuba, 1957: UPI/Bettmann Archive. **845** Little Rock Central High School, September 4, 1957: UPI/Bettmann Archive. **847** Vice-president Richard M. Nixon and Senator John F. Kennedy debating in presidential campaign, 1960: UPI/Bettmann Newsphotos. **849** Aerial photographs of Soviet missiles in Cuba being displayed to the U.N. Security Council, 1962: UPI/Bettmann Newsphotos. **850** Jacqueline and Robert F. Kennedy returning from burial ceremony of President John F. Kennedy, 1963: Magnum Photos/Eliott Erwitt.

Chapter 31: **853** Lyndon B. Johnson, July 6, 1966: UPI/Bettmann Newsphotos. **855** Malcolm X, May 10, 1963: UPI/Bettmann Newsphotos. **857** Head Start class for children of migrant workers, Salinas, California: Monkmeyer Press Photo Service/Paul Conklin. **863** Protester at Democratic Convention, Chicago, 1968, being led away by police: Woodfin Camp & Associates/Rick Windsor. **866** American combat troops in Vietnam, 1967: Gamma-Liaison: Gilles Caron. **867** Troops charging just before Kent State shootings, May 1970: UPI/Bettmann Newsphotos. **868** President and Mrs. Richard M. Nixon during initial visit to China, February, 1972: Magnum Photos. **872** Gary Trudeau, Watergate cartoon: Copyright 1973 by G. P. Trudeau. Reprinted with permission of Universal Press Syndicate. All rights reserved. **874** Gasoline shortage, 1973–1974: © Sepp Seitz 1983/Woodfin Camp & Associates. **875** President Richard M. Nixon with daughter Tricia announcing his resignation, August 8, 1974: Black Star/Fred Ward.

Chapter 32: **883** Edwin Aldrin walking on the moon, July 1969: UPI/Bettmann Newsphotos. **886** California minister Robert Schuller televising his Sunday morning service: Gamma-Liaison/Tom Zimberoff. **887** Jackson Pollack *Autumn Rhythm,* 1950: Metropolitan Museum of Art, Gerald A. Hearn Fund. **888** Roy Lichtenstein, *Masterpiece,* 1962: Photo courtesy Leo Castelli Gallery, New York. **891** Alfred Eisenstadt, sewage in Niagara River, 1968; *Life* Magazine, © Time Inc. **893** T. Smith and J. Carlos, Olympic medal winners in 1968, making "black power salute": UPI/Bettmann Newsphotos. **894** Cesar Chavez: Black Star/Bob Fitch. **895** Navajo Indians protesting federal government's intervention in intertribal land dispute: Black Star/Monty Roessell. **899** Student sit-in demonstration, Columbia University, April 1968: UPI/Bettmann Newsphotos. **901** Half a million people gathered for "Peace and Music" at Woodstock, New York, August 1969: Magnum Photos/Elliot Landy. **902** Gay rights march, Washington, D.C.: Sygma/J. L. Atlan. **903** Betty Friedan, August 25, 1970: UPI/Bettmann Newsphotos. **905** Anti-abortion rally: Sygma/P. F. Gero.

Chapter 33: **916** President Gerald Ford: UPI/Bettmann Newsphotos. **917** President Jimmy Carter in his office in Plains, Georgia, July 1976: Sygma/Hawkins. **918** Carter, Sadat, and Begin at Camp David, 1978: Black Star: Dennis Brack. **921** Iranians burning U.S. flag, October 11, 1979: Gamma-Liaison/Mingam. **925** President Ronald Reagan: Sygma: J. L. Atlan. **928** Walter Mondale and Geraldine Ferraro, Minnesota, July 1984: Sygma/Tannenbaum. **930** President Ronald Reagan and Mikhail Gorbachev at Moscow Summit, 1988: Woodfin Camp & Associates/Larry Downing. **932** Cuban neighberhood, Union City, N.J.: Chuck Fishman. **933** Vietnamese billiard hall, Calif., 1985: Photoreporters/P. F. Bentley. **935** Colonel Oliver North at Iran-Contra congressional hearings, 1987: Black Star/Dennis Brack. **936** Michael Dukakis, Democratic candidate for President in the 1988 campaign: *Time*/Steve Liss. **938** U.S. soldiers sent to invade Panama, December 1989: Black Star/Christopher Mossris. **939** Ecstatic West Berliners climb atop Berlin Wall, November 1989: UPI/Bettmann Newsphotos.

Index

Note: Italicized page numbers refer to maps and graphs.

THE UNITED STATES IN THE WORLD